SWANSEA
TOWN/CITY F.C.

*The First Comprehensive
Player A–Y*

Colin Jones

CYHOEDDWYR
DINEFWR
PUBLISHERS

Copyright © Colin Jones

Published in 2005 by
Cyhoeddwyr Dinefwr Publishers
Rawlings Road, Llandybie
Carmarthenshire, SA18 3YD

A CIP catalogue record for this book is
available from the British Library.

ISBN 1 902638 75 1
9 781902 638751

Printed and bound in Wales by
Dinefwr Press Ltd.
Rawlings Road, Llandybie
Carmarthenshire, SA18 3YD

Contents

Foreword
by Professor David Farmer
(President of Swansea City Football Club)

A brief examination of this book will make it clear to the reader that the quality and quantity of information contained within its covers can only have resulted from many, many hours of painstaking research in national, as well as local archives. The sheer volume of information included in this welcome volume is remarkable and it is evident that all players who have appeared are included, whether they were listed on relatively few occasions, or like stalwarts such as Wilf Milne and Herbie Williams, who wore our colours so often. The result is a comprehensive, well written, produced and well presented reference book. It is a volume which will grace any bookshelf, but one which will not gather dust, rather it will be read and re-read on many occasions.

In setting out to compile the first comprehensive A to Y of Swansea Town/City, the author will have had to solve many problems. One of these relates to men who played only a handful of games for the club, which, not surprising since, when a man plays in the first team for several seasons, the probability is that there will be a great deal of information about him in the archives. Conversely, in all probability, the man who played very few games in one season will have had very little, if anything in his file. In addition, when the individual has a name which is common in this part of the world, such as Davies or Jones, the problems are even greater. As a result, the author would have been obliged to use his network of football contacts, search out relatives of the man concerned, and write, e-mail, or telephone people who had played with the individual or knew him. Only someone who is a dedicated fan of his club would have undertaken such a task. Colin Jones is to be congratulated on so doing and thanked by all of us who support the Swans.

It is interesting to note that, in recent years, the club has received something like 20 or 30 requests from people who have been researching their family trees. With the growth in interest in this hobby, it will not be surprising to find that the number of enquiries which we receive will increase. Often the enquirer wants to confirm whether his or her father/uncle/brother/cousin or whoever, played for the Swans. It has been an ongoing task to answer these questions; with the advent of Colin Jones's book we shall be able to respond far more quickly with assurance of the accuracy of the content.

Among the men listed in this book are those who are legends in the club's history. At a dinner in a marquee at the Vetch Field to bid fair well to the old lady, one of these players told me that the entry which Colin Jones had written about him contained information about which he had forgotten. Others were delighted to receive their entry as a momento of their time at the Vetch Field, and one or two were said to have been so touched by the gesture that their eyes welled-up and handkerchiefs were hurriedly placed to cover their embarrassment. In this coming season the Swans will be adding men to their squad who will start their Swansea career in our new stadium. Hopefully, when the new boys read of the men who preceded them, it may help them to understand something about the ethos of the club.

Henry Ford had a less than subtle criticism of history. He is reported to have said that 'All History is bunk'. The book which Colin Jones has produced flies in the face of this nonsense. For example, players are attracted to join particular clubs because of their heritage, e.g. Manchester United, Liverpool or Arsenal. Those who decide on Swansea City will do so, not only because we have a wonderful new stadium, or what we are going to pay them, but also because of the quality of the players on our books, as well as our recent form. All that is short term history, the longer term relates to how the club had performed over the medium and longer term and which famous names have turned-out for them. Simply to list players like Ivor Allchurch, Mel Charles, Cliff Jones, John Toshack, Alan Curtis, Roy Paul as well as today's stars, will help put the club's potential into context.

This book will be enjoyed. It is one which will help solve disputes about the past, one which will provide quiz masters with many ideas, and one which will add to the knowledge of all who read it. I wish Colin Jones and his publishers the success which they deserve for bringing this book to the market.

Introduction
& Acknowledgements

Assisting Professor David Farmer with team line-ups in a spreadsheet format for his book printed in 2000, *The Swans, Town & City*, I had already began the process of collating information/statistics on Swans' players who had made appearances for the club since the first League game against Portsmouth on the 28th August 1920, and also the players who made appearances during the Southern League era starting on the 7th September 1912 to the end of the 1919/20 season. By May 2005, 713 players had made Football League appearances for the Swans, with a further 55 making Southern League appearances.

The Town/City of Swansea has for a long time been recognised by football lovers in the United Kingdom as a major 'producer' of footballing talent, not only for the Wales National team, but also for the Football League and Welsh Leagues. Numerous books, autobiographies have reached the bookshelves on the star players, but no book had been published profiling the 'bread and butter' players. So, the task began, collating as much information as possible through the various sources listed below, and by Christmas 2004, I had seriously wondered whether or not my vocation in life should have been in the Police Force, such was the amount of research undertaken in tracking down players, via families, fans, work colleagues, newspaper advertisements and obituaries.

During the early 1920's, Welsh Cup team line-ups usually consisted of reserve team players at the Vetch Field, and hence, line-ups were sometimes impossible to ascertain. Therefore, the deciding factor regarding entries into the book revolved around players' appearances in the Southern League and Football League (whether as a substitute, or starting a game), and then statistics from the following competitions were also included.

- (a) League, Football League games
- (b) P/Offs, Play Off matches
- (c) FAC, Football Association Challenge Cup
- (d) FLC, Football League Cup(also under the titles, Milk Cup, Littlewoods Challenge Cup, Rumbelows League Cup, Coca Cola Cup, Worthington Cup and the Carling Cup.
- (e) WC, Football Association of Wales Challenge Cup
- (f) FRT, SVT, LDAF, AGT, AWS, LDV, Football League Associate Members Cup, (also under the titles Freight Rover Trophy, Sherpa Van Trophy,

Leyland Daf Cup, Autoglass Trophy, Auto Windscreens Shield, and the LDV Vans Trophy).

(g) ECWC, European Cup Winners Cup

(h) FAWP, Welsh Invitation, Premier Cup, FAW Premier Cup

Also included where known are honours gained in War-time Cup competitions, West Wales Senior Cup Finals, Scottish and Irish Football, and Non-League statistics.

Emphasis was placed on including as much information on individual players as possible, not only with the Swans, but during the entire player's career; Full Name, Date and Place of Birth, Death, Height, Weight, Swans' debut, their Full Swans' Career Statistics, all the senior clubs the player signed for during his career, transfer details and dates, and also Honours the player attained during his career. Information was also obtained on a large percentage of players' early education, schools attended, area they grew up in, and also their junior career. Following retirement as a player, information was also sought on managerial/coaching career, and also player's employment details on leaving football. Unfortunately, there were a number of players from the Southern League era whose Christian names have been extremely difficult to obtain, let alone their birthplace, height & weight and career details. Browsing through the local newspaper, the *Daily Post*, I found it was quite normal for information and match reports during the club's early years, to mention players by their surname, with just the established players referred to by their full name.

As a member of the Association of Football Statisticians for a number of years, I was able to contact, and talk to many statisticians/historians who were able to give me valuable information on players who had made appearances for their club as well as the Swans, and also, contact details of former players, who were able to give me their career details either in an interview over the phone, e-mail, or by questionnaire.

Jim Creasy in particular provided an enormous amount of facts regarding players' statistics prior to WW2, and his assistance was very much appreciated. With almost 600 photographs included in the book, I would also like to give a special mention to David Evans and Gareth Vincent at the *South Wales Evening Post* for allowing me the use of photographs from their library.

Once the project was underway, friends and supporters were made aware of my search for information on players and family members, and match days at the Vetch Field became a focal point where the game itself became a side issue, such was the interest generated by supporters who were eager to give me the smallest of contact details on players. I would think that of the surviving players from the fifties to present day, I was able to contact at least 95% of them, either interview over the phone, or send them a questionnaire enquiring about their professional and personal career details. To all these fans who gave me these contacts, many thanks. I would also like to thank Professor David Farmer for all the help and support he has given me in the project, whether it was by cross referencing his overall knowledge of the club and it's players, or to suggestions regarding the eventual publication of the book.

Also, many thanks to the following for their help in making my task that little bit easier; Brian Lile, Gareth M. Davies & Peter Jones – Wrexham; all the Staff at the Reference Library in Swansea; Jim Creasy, Grimsby Town Historian; Dave Wherry, *The Football Who's Who* (July 1935) edited by Frank Johnston; The AFS Reports; Mario Risoli at the *Western Mail*; Richard Shepherd; Leigh Edwards; Barry J. Hugman; Roy Gourley; Peter Stead; Huw Bowen; Peter Owen; Ceri Stennett; Ron Walton; Peter Raath (South African Football Historian/Author); Dr. A. K. Hignell – Glamorgan County Cricket Club; Gilbert Upton – Tranmere Rovers; Ray Goble – *Manchester City – The Complete Record 1887-1987*; Mark Elliott – *The Definitive Aldershot FC*; Mike Jackman & Garth Dykes – *Accrington Stanley – A Complete Record, 1894-1962*; Gareth Dykes – *Oldham Athletic, a complete record 1899-1988*; Ian Ross & Gordon Smailes – Everton; Tony Matthews – West Bromwich Albion; Brian Knight – *Plymouth Argyle – the complete record 1903-1989*; Mike Peterson – *Tiger's Tales*; Roy Morris – Haverfordwest County; Wally Popham, Gerald Smith – St. Josephs FC; John Evans – Cwmfelin Social Club; Bob Waygood – West Wales Football Association; Des Shanklin – Football Association of Wales; Roy Griffiths, Chris Berrison, Gwyn Rees; *Albion A-Z: A Who's Who of Brighton & Hove Albion F.C.* by Tim Carder and Roger Harris; Mike Purkiss – Crystal Palace; Geoff Allman – Walsall; Michael Slater – Wolverhampton Wanderers; Frank Coumbe – Brentford; David Downs – Reading; Dave Smith – Leicester City; Frank Grande – Northampton Town; Stuart Basson – Chesterfield; Andrew Frazier – Kidderminster Harriers; Wade Martin – Stoke City; Gerald Mortimer – Derby County; Audrey Adams, Trefor Jones – Watford; Bill Cook – Worcester City; Gordon Macey – QPR; Tony Woodburn – Preston North End; David Batters – York City; John Maguire – Manchester United; Andrew Kirkham – Sheffield United; John Brodie – Sheffield Wednesday; Brian Attmore and Graham Nurse – *100 Greats Cambridge United*; *Lancashire Daily Post Yearbook*; Bob Cain – Fulham; Paul Clayton – Charlton Athletic; Phil Sumbler – Jackarmy website; Dave Edwards – *Rhondda Leader*; Tom Hedley – Blyth Spartans; David Price – Swansea RFC; Paul Cullen – Bury; Ray Driscoll – Chelsea; Frank Tweddle – Darlington; Paul Joannou – Newcastle United; Mike Jay – Bristol Rovers; Robert W. Reid – Partick Thistle; David Steele – Carlisle United; Fred Ollier – Arsenal; Frank Holt – Aston Villa; Paul Hiscock – Leyton Orient; *South Wales Football Annual 1949/50, 1950/51*; A. K. Ambrosen – Newport County; David Howgate – Southport; Dave Goody – Southend United; Phil Sweet, David Watkins, Mike Donovan – Merthyr Tydfil; Gary Chalk – Southampton; Brian Walder – Minehead FC; Harold Finch – Crewe Alexandra; Roger Harrison – Blackpool; Alan Harding – Swindon Town; Gordon Small – Hartlepool United; Paul Godfrey – Cheltenham Town; Dave Woods – Bristol City; Brian Moore – Yeovil Town; Ian Nannestad – Lincoln City; Phil Sherwin – Port Vale; Wallace Chadwick – Burnley; John Litster – Raith Rovers; Richard Prime – Hereford United; Richard Owen – Portsmouth; Tom Allen – Workington FC; Terry Frost – Bradford City; Huw Cooze – Visions Creative.

If I have left anybody out please accept my sincere apologies. Last, but not least, I would like to give my sincere thanks to my wife Glynis and daughter Bethan for giving me enormous support through long, arduous hours of research for the project.

Photographs supplied by kind permission of the *South Wales Evening Post*.

A

1. ABBOTT, PETER Ashley

Birthplace: Rotherham, 1/10/1953
Ht: 6ft-1ins, **Wt:** 11st-12lbs
Swans debut: v. Stockport County (h), 17/2/1974

Swansea City Career Statistics			
Season	League	FLC	WC
1973/74	14+1/2gls		
1974/75	20+3/1gls	1/1gls	1
1975/76	0+3		
Total	34+7/3gls	1/1gls	1

Career:
Manchester United (ass. schoolboy in 30/12/1969, apprentice in 20/7/1970, professional in 19/10/1970)
Swansea City (loan in 15/2/1974, signed in 15/3/1974)
Hartford Bi-Centennials, USA (between May 1976 and August 1976) Total apps 10/1gls
Crewe Alexandra (signed in August 1976) lge 27+4/8 gls, FAC 1, FLC 2
Southend United (signed in July 1977) lge 26+1/4 gls, FLC 2

Former Manchester United apprentice who initially signed for United as an associate schoolboy at the age of fourteen, and who arrived at the Vetch Field on an initial loan basis from Old Trafford in February 1974, after Swans manager Harry Gregg had spotted him playing in a practice match. The former Rotherham and Yorkshire Schoolboy had left school with good 'O' level results, but had no hesitation in joining United as an apprentice, despite offers from eight other clubs. His first Central League game saw him line up at the age of sixteen alongside Nobby Stiles, Ian Ure and Paddy Crerand, and although a professional at Old Trafford for four years he failed to make a first team appearance for United, being confined to

the club's reserve teams and playing in Lancashire Cup competitions. He was also Wilf McGuinness's first professional signing after he had taken over from Sir Matt Busby as manager at Old Trafford. After making his first appearance for the Swans, in his second full match he scored two goals in a 2-0 home win over high flying Reading, which prompted the club to make the move permanent a month later. An old fashioned style centre forward, one could never fault him for effort, but coming into a side which struggled for quality, he was unable to find the net consistently, scoring just the one more goal. During his first close season at the Vetch Field he was unfortunate to suffer a bout of glandular fever after a holiday in the Scilly Isles, which saw him make a late entry into his first full season with the Swans. After he was released by the Swans, in May 1976, he had a short spell in American Football with Hartford Bi-Centennials, and on his return to the UK was signed a second time by Harry Gregg, this time for Crewe Alexandra. After just one season at Crewe he joined Southend United on a free transfer in July 1977, remaining at Roots Hall until mid-way through the 1979/80 season when he drifted out of the game.

2. AGBOOLA, REUBEN Omajola Folasanje

Birthplace: Camden, 30/5/1962
Ht: 5ft-9ins, **Wt:** 12st-7lbs
Swans debut: v. Cardiff City (h), FAC–1, 16/11/1991

Swansea City Career Statistics					
Season	League	FLC	FAC	AGT	WC
1991/92	20+1		3	1	1
1992/93	6+1	2			
Totals	26+2	2	3	1	1

Career:
Southampton (apprentice in July 1978, professional in April 1980) lge 89+1 apps
Sunderland (£150,000 signed in 1/1/1985) lge129+11
Charlton Athletic (loan in 30/10/1986) lge 1
Port Vale (loan in 21/11/1990) lge 9
Swansea City (signed in 8/11/1991)
Woking (signed in August 1993) Conf 6
Gosport Borough (signed in November 1994)

Honours: Nigeria–1, Third Division Champions–1988

Educated at Cheshunt Grammar school, Reuben joined the 'Saints' as an apprentice in July 1978, making his league debut at Old Trafford on the 29th November 1980, playing in the next two league matches, making a total of six league games by the end of the season. The start of the 1982/83 season saw Reuben command a regular place in the 'Saints' starting line-up making thirty-seven league appearances that season. Joining Sunderland for £150,000 in January 1985, he was an influential figure in the club's Third Division Championship success of season 1987/88. Following loan transfers to Charlton Athletic and Port Vale, the experienced left sided full back and central defender with First and Second Division experience was signed by manager Frank Burrows on the 8th November 1990, and played primarily for the Swans as a left full back. Reuben had a baptism of fire with the Swans, making his debut in a local derby game with rivals Cardiff City in a first round tie of the FA Cup, and three days later playing against the same opposition at the Vetch Field in an Auto Glass Trophy cup tie preliminary round. He captained the side on a number of occasions, and towards the end of his first season at the Vetch Field was capped by Nigeria in the African Nations Cup competition against Benin in April 1991. Despite starting the 1992/93 season in the first team, the excellent partnership of Mark Harris and Keith Walker at central defence, plus Des Lyttle and Stephen Jenkins at full backs saw him make only occasional appearances as cover through injury or suspension. At the end of the season he was given a free transfer, returned to the Southampton area where he became involved in the Sporting View Bar at Southampton Sports Club, also making appearances for Vauxhall Conference side Woking, and later with Wessex League team Gosport Borough.

3. AGNEW, PAUL

Birthplace: Lisburn, County Antrim (N/Ireland), 15/8/1965
Ht: 5ft-9ins, **Wt:** 10st-12lbs
Swans debut: v. Macclesfield Town (a), 13/9/1997

Swansea City Career Statistics		
Season	*League*	*FAWP*
1997/98	7	1+1
Total	7	1+1

Career:
Cliftonville (signed in 1981)
Grimsby Town (£4,000 signed in 15/2/1984) lge 219+22/3gls, FLC 17, FAC 23+1, Others 12+2
WBA (£65,000 signed in 23/2/1995) lge 38+1/1gls, FLC 1, FAC 0+1
Ilkeston Town (signed in July 1997)
Swansea City (non-contract signed in 12/9/1997)
Wisbech Town (signed in December 1997)

Honours: NI Sch–4, Yth–11, U-23–1, Northern Intermediate League Champions–1984

Experienced Northern Ireland left sided full back who had been released at the end of the 1996/97 season at the Hawthorns by West Bromwich Albion, arrived at the Vetch Field on a non-contract basis in early September 1997. Graduating from St. Patrick's Secondary Modern School and Lisburn Youth, he made his debut in senior football in Northern Ireland at Cliftonville, had trials with Coventry City and Manchester United, also signing associate schoolboy forms for Bolton Wanderers. Capped at schoolboy level, he had been spotted by Grimsby manager Chris Nicholl at a Northern Ireland youth squad session at Lilleshall, and invited him to Blundell Park. Joining Grimsby Town in November 1983 on an initial trial basis, he later signed as a professional in February 1984, skippered the Irish Youth side during the season, and was also a member of the Mariners reserve side that won the Northern Intermediate League Championship that season. On the 7th May 1984 he made his Football League debut at Oldham Athletic, with his initial transfer fee of £4,000 rising eventually to £15,000. It took him until the 1986/87 season before he established himself as first choice in the left full back position, scoring his first league goal the following season at York City. Not a noted goalscorer during his career, he scored just two more goals for Grimsby Town during his eleven year career at Blundell Park. The vastly experienced left sided full back failed to play for his country at Full level, but in April 1993 was included in the national squad that played in Seville against Spain in a World Cup qualifying game, missing out on a place on the substitute's bench because of a cracked rib. He did however play for his country in Danny Blanchflower's Benefit Match at White Hart Lane in May 1990. Two weeks after the benefit match he played for his country at U-23 level against Eire. In February 1995 he followed his ex-Mariners boss Alan Buckley to West Bromwich Albion, and had a spell as captain before his career was halted by injury problems. Given a free transfer by Albion in July 1997, he initially linked up with former Grimsby Town player Keith Alexander at Ilkeston, but after arriving at the Vetch Field, following the sacking of manager Jan Molby in early October 1997, he left the Vetch Field playing staff after making just seven league appearances. In December 1997 he linked up with former Grimsby team mate Gary Childs at Wisbech Town, remaining at the club until 1999. Living in Sutton Coldfield, in 2001 he was working for a CCTV company as well as coaching part time, and playing occasionally for the West Bromwich Albion Veterans team.

4. ALLAN, Alexander (SANDY) Begg

Birthplace: Forfar, 29/10/1947
Ht: 5ft-11ins, **Wt:** 11st-9lbs
Swans debut: v. Blackburn Rovers (a), 17/3/1973

Swansea City Career Statistics	
Season	*League*
1972/73	6+1/1gls

Career:
Rhyl (signed in 1966)
Cardiff City (£12,500 signed in March 1967) lge 8/1gls,
   ECWC 2/3gls
Bristol Rovers (£12,500 signed in 15/3/1970) lge 51+7/18gls
Swansea City (loan in 9/3/1973)
Cape Town City (£5,000 signed in 4/3/1973)

Centre forward or inside forward who had a flair for
goalscoring at non-league level, possessing good positional
sense, coupled with determination in the penalty area. The
former Clackmannan schoolboy had earlier in his career been an
amateur with Barnsley (1963) and Doncaster Rovers (1964),
prior to signing for North Wales side Rhyl in 1966. After scoring
thirty-three goals for the club, he attracted the attention of
Cardiff City, but after signing found regular appearances in the
starting line-up at Ninian Park limited because of the form of
Toshack and Clark. The highlight of his time at Ninian Park was
probably the hat-trick of headed goals he scored against
Mjondalen in a European Cup Winners Cup tie in October 1969.
Joining Rovers in March 1970, the young Scot impressed in his
debut game against promotion rivals Orient, finishing the
season with four goals. He was signed by Swans manager Harry
Gregg on loan in March 1973 in an effort to bolster the side's
poor scoring record as they battled to avoid relegation to the
Fourth Division. Unfortunately, he scored just the one goal for
the Swans against Halifax Town at the Vetch Field. Returning to
Eastville after his loan period, he was given the opportunity to
play in South Africa at the end of the season, joining Cape Town
City where he enjoyed a great deal of success. He had a spell
back in the U.K. in the late 1970's, and was player manager of
Harrogate Railway Athletic in the Yorkshire League for three
years, gaining promotion from the Second Division, while
working for Polypipe in Harrogate. He returned to South Africa,
continuing his playing career, and setting up a business
manufacturing high class sash windows.

5. ALLCHURCH, IVOR John M.B.E.

Birthplace: Swansea, 16/10/1929. **Died:** Swansea, 10/5/1997
Ht: 5ft-10ins, **Wt:** 11st-8lbs
Swans debut: v. West Ham United (a), 26/12/1949

Career:
Swansea Town (signed in 10/5/1947)
Newcastle United (£28,000 signed in 7/10/1958) lge 143/46gls,
   FLC 3/1gls, FAC 8/4gls
Cardiff City (£15,000 signed in August 1962) lge 103/39gls,
   ECWC 2
Swansea Town (£6,500 signed in 30/7/1965)
Worcester City (signed in July 1968) lge 60/16goals

Honours: Wales Sch, Full–68, Welsh Cup Winner–1950, 1964,
1965, 1966, Welsh League Representative XI, West Wales Senior
Cup Winner–1955, 1956

Swansea Town Career Statistics					
Season	*League*	*FLC*	*FAC*	*WC*	*ECWC*
1949/50	18/3gls		2/1gls	3/2gls	
1950/51	42/8gls		1	1/1gls	
1951/52	41/11gls		3/3gls		
1952/53	41/15gls		1	1	
1953/54	40/18gls		3/2gls		
1954/55	36/19gls		4/1gls	3/2gls	
1955/56	37/15gls		1	3/3gls	
1956/57	30/13gls		1/1gls	4/2gls	
1957/58	32/16gls		1		
1958/59	10/6gls				
1965/66	34/12gls	1/1gls	1	7/3gls	
1966/67	44/11gls	4/2gls	3	1	2
1967/68	38+2/17gls	1/1gls	4/1gls	2/2gls	
Total	443+2/164gls	6/4gls	25/9gls	25/15gls	2

Former Swans skipper Joe Sykes, youth team trainer and scout
under Haydn Green was attending a game at Cwm Level, when
he noticed a blonde youngster preparing to go onto the pitch in
an U-18 game, after previously playing in an U-16 match. It did
not take long for Sykes to notice the outstanding skills of the
young blonde substitute, and after asking his name, was
convinced he had unearthed a gem of rare quality. Obtaining an
agreement from Ivor's father that he would sign for the Swans
after leaving school at the age of fifteen, on leaving Plasmarl
school, Ivor went to work in the office at Baldwins Foundry,
who made bomb castings, and on Tuesdays and Thursdays
trained with the Swans. As an amateur many scouts tried to
persuade him to sign for other clubs, but he said that he and his
father had given their word to the Swans that he would sign for
them. At the age of 18 he served in the Army, ostensibly as a
gunner, based at Oswestry, where he represented his Unit, his
Corps, Western Command, and the Army, in addition to
guesting for Shrewsbury Town, and Wellington Town (now
Telford United). In January 1949, whilst serving in the Army he
played in a Welsh Cup tie for Shrewsbury Town at Newport
against Lovells Athletic. Capped for Wales 68 times, when there
were far fewer internationals played compared to modern day,
he was universally known as the 'Golden Boy', and was sold to
Newcastle United for £28,000, plus Reg Davies, and was
probably the greatest footballer to play for the Swans. At the end
of season 1952/53 he was included in the Welsh International
Touring party that played games in France and Yugoslavia.
A beautiful balanced athlete who looked languid in his play, he
possessed deceptive pace, and was a lovely ball player with
great vision. He had an eye for goal but also distributed the ball
exceptionally well. Universally admired, he was first capped at
twenty, and went on to play in 26 consecutive games for Wales,
whilst on the Swans books. Gaining his first cap against
England in 1951, he also held the goal scoring record for Wales
for a number of years. In 1955 and 1956 he played in consecutive
West Wales Senior Cup Final wins over Llanelly. He rejoined the

Swans, signed by manager Glyn Davies for £6,500 in July 1965, a couple of months short of his 36th birthday. His first season back saw Ivor, Keith Todd and Jimmy McLaughlin score an incredible 48 goals between them, unfortunately the Swans defence was just as generous, struggling to keep a clean sheet through the season, keeping only eight clean sheets. Ivor sampled European Football in his second season back at the Vetch Field, playing against Slavia Sofia. Top goalscorer for the Swans in his last season with 17 league goals, plus 4 in the cup competitions, in all probability, Ivor would have signed for another season, but sadly, in seeking economies, the Vetch Field management at the time asked him to take a twenty per cent reduction in his wages. Given the service he had given the club throughout his career, a penny pinching decision resulted in the club losing a most gifted player, regular goalscorer, as well as leaving the man himself a little disgruntled. Approaching his 38th birthday he was a member of the Swan's side that was to be so unlucky against the mighty Arsenal in an FA Cup tie at the Vetch Field which drew a record 32,786 attendance. Ivor was an extremely elegant and skilful inside forward with mesmerising ball control, surging pace and a fierce shot. He was also a very modest, self effacing person whose personality seemed at odds with that of a star professional footballer, even in the less demanding days of the 1950's and 1960's. He made his last international appearance for Wales against Chile in May 1966 in Santiago, a couple of months short of his 36th birthday, and his seventh cap on his return to the Vetch Field to play for the Swans in the Third Division. At the time of his retirement he held the Welsh record for both caps and goals, gaining the first of his 68 caps in November 1950 in a 4-2 defeat by England, and twelve months later he scored the first of his 23 international goals when scoring the only goal of the match against Scotland at Hampden Park. One of Ivor's finest international performances came when Wales beat the Rest of the United Kingdom XI, 3-2 at Ninian Park in December 1951. In May 1951 he played for a Welsh League Representative side at the Vetch Field against their Irish League counterparts. Joining Newcastle United for £28,000 in October 1958, he became a favourite in the North East, contributing to many goals, either by scoring himself or supplying chances for others. His time at St. James Park co-incided with a period of decline for United and he was unable to prevent the club from dropping into the Second Division in 1961. In August 1962 he returned to Wales to join Cardiff City for £15,000, winning two Welsh Cup Winners medals, to add to the two he won with the Swans, plus two runners up medals with the Swans during his career. In the 1964/65 Welsh Cup Final against Wrexham, Ivor scored two goals in the 3-0 victory. He was appointed MBE in 1966 for his services to football and will be remembered for his gentlemanly behaviour, on and off the field. The legendary 'Golden Boy' of football, Ivor scored a club record 164 goals in 445 League games during two spells at Swansea before moving to Worcester City in July 1968. He took over as player manager of Haverfordwest County in May 1969, later finishing his playing career with Pontardawe Athletic, retiring in April 1980. He subsequently worked as a storeman until he retired, playing golf at Langland Bay Golf Club until his death in July 1997.

6. ALLCHURCH, Leonard (LEN)

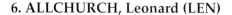

Birthplace: Swansea, 12/9/1933
Ht: 5ft-6ins, **Wt:** 10st-6lbs
Swans debut: v. Pembroke Borough (h), WC-5, 10/2/1951

Career:
Swansea Town (amateur in November 1949, professional in October 1950)
Sheffield United (£14,000 signed in 15/3/1961) lge 123/32gls
Stockport County (signed in September 1965) lge 131/16gls
Swansea Town (signed in July 1969)
Haverfordwest County (signed in close season 1971)

Swansea Town/City Career Statistics				
Season	League	FLC	FAC	WC
1950/51	2			
1951/52	1			
1952/53	1			
1953/54	17			
1954/55	38/7gls		4/1gls	3
1955/56	40/4gls		1	4/2gls
1956/57	37/6gls		1	6/1gls
1957/58	40/11gls		1	2/2gls
1958/59	42/9gls		1	2
1959/60	34/9gls		3	1/1gls
1960/61	24/3gls	1	3/1gls	
1969/70	44+1/7gls	2	3	3
1970/71	26/4gls	2+1/1gls	4/1gls	2/1gls
Total	346+1/60gls	4+1/1gls	21/3gls	23/7gls

Honours: Wales Sch, Full–11, Great Britain Army Cadets, Fourth Division Champions–1967, British Army Representative XI, West Wales Senior Cup Winner–1955, 1956, 1957, 1960

Former Swansea Schoolboys, and Welsh Schoolboy cap, Len also played for the Great Britain Army Cadets at the Vetch Field against Northern Ireland in mid-January 1950. In May 1952, Private Len Allchurch was included in a British Army Representative XI that played two games in France later in the month. Capped 7 times for Wales while with the Swans, his first cap was against Northern Ireland in 1955. Despite his short stature, earlier in his career he had skippered the Swansea Schoolboys side, and even at a young age had a deceptive body swerve and splendid ball control, likened at the time to a miniature edition of Stanley Matthews. A 'crafty' winger, Len could beat his man on either flank, and provide precision crosses to his team mates. Stockily built, he withstood the battering from old fashioned full backs, through guile and balance, with his 'baby' face hiding a mental toughness, which sustained him throughout his long career. The scorer of many fine goals from narrow angles, like his brother Ivor, Lennie was a modest and extremely likeable man. He made his first team debut in a fifth round Welsh Cup tie against Pembroke Borough on the 10th February 1951, scoring in a 5-0 win, one of many occasions when he would play alongside his brother Ivor. He made his league debut almost two and a half months later against Grimsby Town at the Vetch Field in a 1-3 defeat, retaining his place for the next match, the last of the season against Leeds United at Elland Road. Very much a squad player over the next three seasons, he made the breakthrough in season 1954/55, becoming an influential player in the Swans first team line-up. That season would also see him score his first league goal for the Swans, against Port Vale in a 7-1 home win, and by the end of the season he would score 7 league goals. Played in consecutive West Wales Senior Cup Final successes in 1955, 1956

1957, and also in 1960. Not noted as a goalscorer, his best return for goalscoring came during season 1957/58 when he returned 11 league goals, plus 2 in the Welsh Cup competition. In March 1961 he was given the opportunity to join Sheffield United for £14,000, and within a few games had helped the club gain promotion to the First Division as runners up to Ipswich Town. After four seasons in the First Division, he joined Fourth Division Stockport County, contributing to the club's 1967 Championship success, and also being voted Player of the Year by County supporters. He returned to the Vetch Field in July 1969, signed by a club who had yet to appoint a manager following the resignation of Billy Lucas the previous March, and with caretaker boss Walter Robbins running the team until the end of the season. With a new manager in Roy Bentley in place, Len's return to the Vetch Field saw the Swans gain promotion, with Len being an inspirational figure on the right flank, providing quality crosses for Gwyther and Williams, who between them scored thirty league goals during the season. The following season, the last before he announced his retirement, he showed, that even at the age of 38 he could still provide some sparkle, and quality from the flanks. In two consecutive seasons during his first period at the Vetch Field, Len played in both Welsh Cup Final defeats by Cardiff City in 1956, and Wrexham twelve months later. He left the Vetch Field in May 1971, finished his playing career with Haverfordwest County, and concentrated on his business interests in the Swansea area.

7. ALLON, Joseph (JOE) Ball

Birthplace: Gateshead, 12/11/1966
Ht: 5ft-11ins, **Wt**: 11st-2lbs
Swans debut: v. Stockport County (a), 15/8/1987

Swansea City Career Statistics					
Season	League	FLC	FAC	FRT	WC
1987/88	26+6/12gls	2	2	2	2/1gls
1988/89	1+1				
Total	27+7/12gls	2	2	2	2/1gls

Career:
Newcastle United (from trainee in 16/11/1984) lge 9/2, FLC 1
Swansea City (signed in 6/8/1987)
Hartlepool United (£10,000 signed in 29/11/1988) 112/48gls, FLC 5/2gls, FAC 6+1/5gls, Others 7/2gls
Chelsea (£300,000 signed in 14/8/1991) lge 3+11/2gls, FLC 0+2, Others 1+1/1gls
Port Vale (loan in 27/2/1992) lge 2+4
Brentford (£275,000 signed in 19/11/1992) lge 38+7/19gls, FLC 2, FAC 2/2gls, Others 7/7gls
Southend United (loan in 16/9/1993) lge 2+1
Port Vale (signed in 24/3/1994) lge 13+10/9gls, FLC 0+1, FAC 2/1gls

Lincoln City (£42,500 signed in 17/7/1995) lge 3+1, FLC 1
Hartlepool United (£42,500 signed in 13/10/1995) lge 52+4/19gls, FLC 3/2gls, FAC 1, Others 3/1gls

Honours: England Yth, FAYC 1985

There haven't been many players at the Vetch Field who have come close to creating a goal scoring record in their first season with the Swans, but Gateshead born striker Joe Allon almost equalled Ivor Allchurch's consecutive goal scoring record of nine from nine games during his only full season with the Swans. Signed on a free transfer from Newcastle United in August 1987 by manager Terry Yorath, after making his Swans debut as a substitute for Tommy Hutchison against Stockport County, Joe scored in seven consecutive matches for the Swans, starting with a goal in a 2-1 home win over Wrexham on 10th October 1987, to a one goal contribution in a 2-1 home league defeat by Wolverhampton Wanderers on 3rd November. A member of United's successful youth side which beat Watford to win the FA Youth Cup at the end of the 1984/85 season, playing alongside the legendary Paul Gascoigne, Joe also scored what was arguably the goal of the season for the Swans, with an acrobatic scissors kick in the New Year's Day clash with local rivals Cardiff City at the Vetch Field. Despite ending his first season as second top goalscorer with eleven league goals, and promotion via the Play Offs to the Third Division, Joe missed the start of the 1988/89 season with knee problems, and in October was surprisingly allowed to join Hartlepool for £10,000. The knee problems would slowly get worse, and would ultimately force his early retirement from the game. Before his retirement however, Joe made history at Hartlepool by equalling the highest amount of goals scored in a season, and in August 1991 Chelsea paid the club £300,000 for his transfer. Apart from his career with the Swans and Hartlepool, Joe enjoyed a good goal scoring reputation with Brentford between November 1992 and March 1994. Prior to his joining Port Vale in March 1994, he scored thirteen goals from just 21 league appearances for the 'Bees', a record which would see him top the club's goalscoring charts at the end of the season, despite his having joined Port Vale six weeks before the season's end. Following his return to 'Pool' in October 1995, his two full seasons at the club also saw him top the goalscorers chart on both occasions, despite periods on the sidelines through knee injuries. Injuries, which also included a fractured knee cap, would ultimately force his retirement from the game. His last game for 'Pool', was when he came on as a substitute against Macclesfield Town on 30th August 1997, and before the end of the season, the continual deterioration with his knees had forced him to retire from the professional game. Since retiring from the game, Joe has no involvement with football on a full time basis at present, confining himself to the golf course, and media work with the Century Radio Station, functions and presentations. During the football season however, he works at St. James's Park, entertaining guests in United's hospitality suites on matchdays, working alongside former United favourite Bobby Moncur.

8. ALSOP, JULIAN Mark

Birthplace: Nuneaton, 28/5/1973
Ht: 6ft-4ins, **Wt:** 13st-9lbs
Swans debut: v. Scunthorpe United (a), 24/1/1998

Swansea City Career Statistics						
Season	League	FLC	FAC	AWS	FAWC	P/Offs
1997/98	12/3gls				2/2gls	
1998/99	37+4/10gls	2	4+1/1gls	2	3/1gls	2
1999/2000	29+8/3gls	2+2	2	1	2/3gls	
Total	78+12/16gls	4+2	6+1/1gls	3	7/6gls	2

Career:
Tamworth
Halesowen Town (£2,300 signed in July 1996)
Bristol Rovers (£15,000 signed in 14/2/1997) lge 20+13/4gls,
    FLC 2/1gls, FAC 1/1gls, Others 2
Swansea City (loan in 20/1/1998, £30,000 signed in 12/3/1998)
Cheltenham Town (signed in 3/7/2000) lge 99+18/35gls,
    FLC 4+1, FAC 8+2/6gls, Others 6+1/3gls
Oxford United (signed in 14/6/2003) lge 29+5/5gls, FLC 1,
    FAC 1
Northampton Town (signed in 22/10/2004) lge 1+6/1gls,
    FAC 0+1, Others 2/1gls
Forest Green Rovers (signed in 23/12/2004) Conf 2/1gls
Tamworth (signed in July 2005)

Honours: Third Division Champions–2000

Signed by Rovers manager Ian Holloway from non-league
Halesowen Town, Julian made his league debut as a substitute
for Peter Beadle in a 3-2 home win over Luton Town in February
1997, scoring his first league goal in the next game against
Burnley, and making regular appearances for Rovers until the
end of the season. His second season with Rovers saw him
competing with Barry Hayles, Peter Beadle and Jamie Cureton
for the two main striker places, and despite starting the new
season in the Rovers line-up, lost his place, and in January 1998
was signed by Swans manager Alan Cork on an initial loan
basis, which was made permanent within weeks of the striker
returning to Rovers for a fee in the region of £30,000. Starting his
career on the non-league circuit at Nuneaton Town, he made
further appearances for VS Rugby and Racing Club Warwick
prior to signing for Tamworth. Scoring 44 goals from 88
appearances in all competitions for Tamworth, including a hat-
trick in just two minutes in a Dr. Martens League match against
Armitage in the 1994/95 season, 'Jules' also had a trial spell
with Doncaster Rovers in September 1995. Despite his relative
inexperience at league level, he had just over 12 months
experience with Rovers following his upgrade from non-league
football with Halesowen Town in February 1997, the giant
striker, out of the old fashioned style of centre forwards became
an instant hit with the Swans fans with his no-nonsense
aggressive style of play. A handful for the modern type of
defender, especially when the Swans played teams in a higher
grade of football in cup ties, he suffered with a lack of quality of
crosses from the flanks, a fact evident when after leaving the
Swans and joining Cheltenham Town, he scored 20 league goals
during the club's promotion campaign from the Third Division.
Ideal for the physical style of lower division football, he scored
his first league goal for the Swans in his second match on loan,
in a 4-0 win over Darlington. His first full season for the Swans,
season 1998/99 saw him return 11 league and cup goals for the
Swans, but during the Championship season the following year
returned just 3 league goals. On the 26th October 1999, he scored
a hat-trick for the Swans in a 7-0 win over Cwmbran Town in
the Welsh Premier Cup Competition, although this competition
was not recognised as a first team fixture for statistics purposes.
The hat –trick also proved to be the quickest ever by a Swans
player, three goals in four minutes, beating Darren Perrett's

effort against Rhyl in a Welsh Cup tie in December 1994.
Following the Swans Championship winning season of
1999/2000 he failed to agree a contract at the Vetch Field, joining
Cheltenham Town on a free transfer. On transfer deadline day,
March 2000, the Swans had reportedly turned down a six figure
offer from Rushden & Diamonds for the player. In both his
seasons with Cheltenham, Julian finished top goalscorer, with
twenty league goals scored in his first, and a goal in the Play Off
Final success against Rushden & Diamonds, and ten in his
second season. 'Jules' joined Oxford United in June 2003, and
despite a good first half to the season, a number of suspensions
during the second half of the season saw him miss a number of
matches, and with a change of management late in the season,
the club failed to get in a place in the end of season Third
Division Play Off places. In mid-October 2004 his contract was
cancelled at the Kassam Stadium after a disciplinary hearing
following an incident during training at the club the previous
week, shortly after he joined Northampton Town. Two days
before Xmas 2004 he signed a contract until the end of the
season at Conference side Forest Green Rovers, linking up with
former Swans team mates Stuart Roberts and Richie Appleby.
In mid-January 2005 a Football League disciplinary hearing
suspended Alsop until the 31st May 2005 following the training
ground incident earlier in the season whilst he was on the
playing staff at Oxford United. Training to be an Accountant, in
July 2005 he signed for Conference side Tamworth.

9. AMPADU, Patrick KWAME (PADDY)

Birthplace: Bradford, 20/12/1970
Ht: 5ft-10ins, **Wt**: 11st-10lbs
Swans debut as substitute: v. Barnet (h), 18/2/1994

Swansea City Career Statistics

Season	League	FLC	FAC	AGT	WC	P/Offs	FAWC
1993/94	11+2			2	1+1		
1994/95	36+8/6gls	3+1	3/1gls	2	5/1gls		
1995/96	40+3/2gls	2/1gls		3			
1996/97	25+4/4gls	1	2	1		3	
1997/98	17+2	2	0+1				3+1
Total	129+19/	8+1/1gls	5+1/1gls	8	6+1/1gls	3	3+1
	12gls						

Career:
Arsenal (from trainee in 19/11/1988) lge 0+2
Plymouth Argyle (loan in 31/10/1990) lge 6/1gls, Others 1
WBA (£50,000 signed in 24/6/1991) lge 27+22/4gls, FLC 6+1,
    FAC 1, Others 5/1gls
Swansea City (£15,000 signed in 16/2/1994)
Leyton Orient (signed in 30/7/1998) lge 69+3/1gls, FLC 8,
    FAC 4+1/1gls, Others 1
Exeter City (signed in 18/7/2000) lge 80+15, FLC 2+1/1gls,
    FAC 4+1, Others 1, Conf 49+10/1gls
Newport County (signed in July 2005)

Honours: Rep of Ire Yth, U–21–4, AMC 1994, Football Combination Champions–1990, West Wales Senior Cup Winner–1994

'Paddy' started his career as a trainee with Arsenal, making his First Division debut as substitute for Kevin Campbell at Derby County in a 3-1 win for the Gunners in March 1990. Seven days later he made his Highbury debut, again as substitute for the same player, in 1-0 win over Everton. He played his early football with Sherrards United (Dublin) and Belvedere FC (Dublin), making appearances at youth and U–21 level for the Republic of Ireland whilst at Highbury, by virtue of his parentage qualification, with his first U–21 cap coming in October 1990 against Turkey. Following a loan transfer at Plymouth Argyle, he joined West Bromwich Albion for £50,000 in June 1991, making twenty-one league appearances under manager Bobby Gould. With Ossie Ardiles replacing Gould in May 1992, 'Paddy' struggled to make the WBA first team line-up, not making the club's Play Off success at the end of the season against Port Vale, also beating the Swans in the semi-final stages. An astute £15,000 signing by Swans manager Frank Burrows in February 1994, 'Paddy' displayed a lot of aggression and skill on the Swans left side of midfield. Indeed his first four games for the Swans saw him accumulate bookings in each game. A clever passer, and accurate deadball kicker, 'Paddy' became an influential member of the Swans midfield alongside Cornforth, Penney and Pascoe. Within seven weeks of his joining the Swans, he became a member of the first Swans' side to play at Wembley, when he was selected to play in the AutoGlass Trophy Final against Huddersfield Town, and also against Ammanford Town in the West Wales Senior Cup Final. At the end of the 1996/97 season under Jan Molby he was to return to Wembley for the Third Division Play Off Final against Northampton Town. Twelve months later, he became the first Swans' player to leave the Vetch Field under the new 'Bosman' ruling, signing on a free transfer for Leyton Orient. After joining Leyton Orient he became a regular in their side during the 1998/99 season, but missed out on a trip to Wembley at the end of the season for the Third Division Play Off Final following an injury sustained a couple of weeks earlier. The same season, the Swans lost out to Scunthorpe United in the semi-final stage of the Third Division Play Off Finals, a team that went on to beat Orient in the Final. Joining Exeter City in July 2000, he linked up for a second time in midfield with former Swans skipper John Cornforth, but by the end of season 2002/03, was unable to prevent the club from relegation to the Conference. The 2003/04 season in the Conference saw 'Paddy' make regular appearances for the 'Grecians', and the following season the experienced campaigner played an important role when his side took the mighty Manchester United to a replay in the FA Cup competition. In July 2005 he linked up with former Swans and Exeter team mate John Cornforth at Newport County.

10. ANDERSON, IJAH Massai

Birthplace: Hackney, 30/12/1975
Ht: 5ft-8ins, **Wt**: 10st-6lbs
Swans debut: v. Bury (h), 27/11/2004

Swansea City Career Statistics			
Season	League	FAC	FAWC
2004/05	8+5	1+1	3/1gls
Total	8+5	1+1	3/1gls

Career:
Southend United (from trainee at Tottenham Hotspur signed in 2/8/1994)
Brentford (signed in 31/7/1995) lge 196+6/4gls, FLC 19/1gls, FAC 5+3, Others 12+1

Wycombe Wanderers (loan in 27/11/2002) lge 5
Bristol Rovers (signed in 7/2/2003) lge 51+2, FLC 1, Others 1
Swansea City (signed in 24/11/2004)

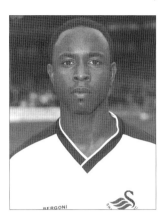

Honours: Third Division Champions–1999, FAW Cup Winner–2005

Signed an initial monthly contract at the Vetch Field on the 24th November 2004, after he had been released the previous month at Bristol Rovers, and had also had trials with Oldham Athletic and Peterborough United prior to arriving at the Vetch Field. With an offer of a contract in Irish Football, at the end of his second monthly contract he signed a new contract to stay at the Vetch Field for a further eighteen months. Initially a junior at White Hart Lane, the left sided attacking midfielder joined Southend United as a YTS trainee, failed to break into the first team at Roots Hall, and after being released in May 1995, joined Brentford. Ijah made his league debut in the opening match of the 1995/96 season at York City, and by the end of the season had taken over from the departed Martin Grainger at left full back. An ever present the following season, by the time the 'Bees' had claimed the Third Division Championship in 1999, Ijah had become an influential member of the club's defence. Failing to make the club's starting line-up for the LDV Final at the Millennium Stadium Cardiff in 2001, twelve months later he played in the Second Division Play Off Final defeat by Stoke City. Following a loan spell at Wycombe Wanderers, Ijah was released by Brentford after making over two hundred league appearances in February 2003, joining Bristol Rovers. He made his Swans debut at the Vetch Field at left full back against Bury, in a side that was minus five first team regulars missing through either injury or suspension. His experience and versatility was evident through the season as he alternated between either a left full back position, or on the left side of midfield. Whilst with Bristol Rovers he became the first player for the club to be sent off in both fixtures against the same team in one season, against Macclesfield Town in season 2003/04. Played in all three FAW Cup games including the defeat of Wrexham in the Final.

11. ANDREW, Matthew (MATT)

Birthplace: Johnstone, 5/1/1922
Ht: 5ft-11ins, **Wt**: 11st-10lbs
Swans debut v. Leyton Orient (a), 16/9/1948

Career:
Bristol City (amateur, professional in October 1947) lge 0
Swansea Town (trial in 23/7/1948, professional in August 1948)
Workington (£750 in June 1951) lge 22

Honours: London Combination Cup Winner–1950, West Wales Senior Cup Winner–1949, 1950, Welsh League First Division Champions–1951

Swansea Town Career Statistics	
Season	*League*
1948/49	1
1949/50	2
1950/51	1
Total	4

After being released by Bristol City he was invited to the Vetch Field for a trial in late July 1948, playing in the public trial matches, later signing a contract. A solid type of player, he played nearly all of his football with the Swans at reserve team level in his three years at the Vetch Field, a strong tackler, but lacked the pace required for first team duty. First season with the Swans he covered at right full back for Jim Feeney, but his appearances in the second and third season were as cover for Paul, Weston and Lucas at half back. At the end of his first season at the Vetch Field he played in the Swans side that beat Llanelly to win the West Wales Senior Cup, and twelve months later was included in the Swans side that beat Haverfordwest in the same final. In May 1950 he was a member of the Swans reserve side that won at Southend United to win the London Combination Cup Final. A reserve team player at Ashton Gate with Bristol City, he had been recommended to City by Don Clark, the former City centre forward who had been stationed in the R.A.F. at Weston-Super-Mare with Andrews. He joined City initially as an amateur, later signing professional forms for the club. A big, strong defender, he had impressed Swans officials playing for City in Football Combination games between the two clubs the previous season. During season 1950/51 he made appearances in the Swans' Welsh League side that won the First Division Championship. Transferred to newly elected Third Division North side Workington for £750 in June 1951, he was included in the club's first Football League game at the start of the 1951/52 season, but after making twenty-two league appearances he drifted out of the game, eventually returning to Scotland.

12. ANDREWS, KERI Anthony

Birthplace: Swansea, 28/4/1968
Ht: 5ft-9ins, **Wt:** 10st-11lbs
Swans debut: v. Shrewsbury Town (h), WC S/F, First Leg, 2/4/1985

Swansea City Career Statistics					
Season	*League*	*FLC*	*FAC*	*FRT*	*WC*
1984/85	1				2
1985/86	1	0+1			
1986/87	14+3/2gls	3/1gls	2+1	2	1
1987/88	16+6/1gls	0+1	0+1	1	1
Total	32+9/3gls	3+2/1gls	2+2	3	4

Career:
Swansea City (signed from YTS in July 1986)
Newport County (signed in July 1988) 33+8/3gls
Merthyr Tydfil (signed in summer of 1989)

Honours: Macbar Cup Winner–1987, West Wales Senior Cup Winner–1987

Former Cefn Hengoed schoolboy midfielder who played for Swansea schoolboys side, and who joined the Swans as a YTS trainee in 1984. He fractured his arm while playing for the Wales youth side against Ireland, a game in which he scored two goals during season 1985/86, during a time when he would have played more first team games for the Swans. Equally adept at playing in a defensive, midfield, or attacking left wing role, he failed to establish himself in the first team line-up in any one position during his playing career with the Swans. Included by manager Colin Appleton as non playing substitute in the Swans' Milk Cup First Round, Second Leg tie at Walsall, at the age of 16 years and 5 months, Keri was eventually given his first team debut by manager John Bond against Shrewsbury Town in a Welsh Cup semi-final, first leg at the Vetch Field, three weeks short of his seventeenth birthday, just short of celebrating his first year as a YTS trainee. In May 1987 he was included in the Swans reserve side that beat Plymouth Argyle to win the Macbar Cup Final, and was also in the Swans squad that beat Briton Ferry Athletic in the West Wales Senior Cup Final. He was released at the end of season 1987/88 joining Newport County in the Vauxhall Conference, during a season which saw County fail to fulfil their fixtures because of worsening financial problems at the football club, and ultimately fold. He then signed for Merthyr Tydfil prior to the start of season 1989/90 after they had been promoted to the Conference, but did not make any league appearances. He then played for a number of Welsh League clubs, ending his playing career in the Swansea Senior League with Port Tennant Colts, and is currently working in the Energy Advice Centre in Swansea.

13. ANSTISS, Henry Augustus (HARRY)

Birthplace: Chiswick, 22/8/1899. **Died:** Isleworth, Middlesex, 9/3/1964
Ht: 5ft-9½ins, **Wt:** 11st-7lbs
Swans debut: v. Leeds United (h) 29/8/1931

Swansea Town Career Statistics			
Season	*League*	*FAC*	*WC*
1931/32	22/6gls	1	5/1gls
1932/33	6		
Total	28/6gls	1	5/1gls

Career:
Hammersmith Athletic
Brentford (amateur in August 1920, professional in November 1920) lge 42/19gls, FAC 2

Millwall (£650 signed in May 1922) lge 19/3gls
Watford (£150 signed in June 1923) lge 18/5gls
Rochdale (signed in June 1924) lge 72/39gls
Sheffield Wednesday (£100 signed in July 1926) lge 12/5gls
Port Vale (player exchange in February 1927) lge 109/36gls,
    FAC 8/4gls
Swansea Town (signed in 23/5/1931)
Crewe Alexandra (signed in 3/7/1933) lge 30/7gls
Gillingham (signed in July 1934) lge 33/6gls
Tunbridge Wells Rangers (signed in September 1935)
Cray Wanderers (signed in January 1937)

Honours: Third Division North Champions–1930, Welsh Cup
Winner–1932

Earlier in his career he took part in an international schoolboy
trial, but was found to be nine days too old to play for his
country. Prior to joining the Swans Harry played in the Third
Division South for Brentford, Millwall and Watford, but did not
feature in any game against the Swans. He initially signed for
Brentford as an amateur from Hammersmith Athletic in August
1920 before signing professional three months later. As well as
playing in the Third Division North with Rochdale, Harry also
made league appearances for Sheffield Wednesday in the First
Division, and for Port Vale in the Second Division before signing
for the Swans. Joining Vale in exchange for Alf Strange, he
scored on his debut at Notts. County, and went on to make
thirty-six appearances in the side that won the 1929/30 Third
Division North Championship, scoring fourteen goals, and the
following season made regular appearances in the side that
reached 5th in the Second Division, the club's highest ever
position in the League. A survivor of the Battle of Jutland, the
much travelled inside forward, who operated on either right, or
left sided positions, joined the Swans in May 1931, in a transfer
deal which saw Swans player Easton go in the opposite
direction, plus a cash adjustment. His first season at the Vetch
Field saw Harry score six league goals, with his first goal being
at Leeds United in December 1931, and his second in the next
league game at the Vetch Field against Manchester United. At
the end of the season Harry featured in the Swans Welsh Cup
Final defeat of Wrexham. He struggled to make the same impact
during his second season at the Vetch Field, and in May 1933
joined Crewe Alexandra. After playing his last league match
with Gillingham he joined non-league side Tunbridge Wells in
September 1935, before finishing his career with Cray
Wanderers in January 1937.

14. APPLEBY, Richard (RICHIE) Dean

Birthplace: Middlesbrough, 18/9/1975
Ht: 5ft-8ins, **Wt:** 11st-4lbs
Swans debut: v. Rochdale (h), 17/8/1996

	Swansea City Career Statistics					
Season	League	FLC	FAC	AWS/LDV	FAWC	P/Offs
1996/97	8+3/1gls	2				1
1997/98	33+2/3gls	1+1	1/1gls		4	
1998/99	36+3/3gls		2+1/1gls	1/1gls	2+1/1gls	0+2
1999/2000	10+10/4gls	1+2	2	1+1	4/3gls	
2000/01	0+5				1	
2001/02	3+7	0+1		0+1		
Total	90+30/11gls	4+4	5+1/2 gls	2+2/1gls	11+1/4gls	1+2

Career:
Newcastle United (from trainee in 12/8/1993), Others 2
Ipswich Town (signed in 12/12/1995) lge 0+3, Others 1
Swansea City (signed in 16/8/1996)
Kidderminster Harriers (loan in 9/11/2001, signed in
    12/12/2001) lge 18+1/4gls, FAC 1
Hull City (signed in 7/6/2003) lge 6, FLC 1
Kidderminster Harriers (signed in 1/8/2004) lge 6+3, FLC 0+1
Forest Green Rovers (signed in 16/10/2004) Conf 4+3

Honours: England Yth

The younger brother of Darlington, Barnsley and Oldham
Athletic defender Matt Appleby, Richie gained international
recognition for England at youth level when he was a trainee
with Newcastle United, and during his period at St. James's
Park with United made two first team appearances alongside
his brother in the 1992/93 Anglo Italian Cup competition
against Bari, and Cesena. A skilful winger/midfielder, he failed
to make any further first team appearances with United, and
joined Ipswich Town in December 1995, making his League
debut as substitute for Mowbray at Portman Road against
Barnsley, also featuring in the next league march as substitute.
Apart from one other substitute appearance later in the season
his only start for Ipswich came in the Anglo Italian Cup
competition the same season. Released on a free transfer at the
end of the season, he was signed by Swans manager Jan Molby,
making his first league start in the opening fixture of the
1996/97 season at the Vetch Field against Rochdale. His
appearances for the Swans during the early part of his career
came at right wing back, but throughout his Swans career he
suffered a persistent hamstring problem, limiting him from
making a bigger impact with the Swans. Offered a free transfer
by the Swans at the end of the 2000/2001 season, he had a
week's trial with John Beck at Cambridge United towards the
end of June 2001, but a virus prevented him making an
impression at the Abbey Stadium, returning to the Vetch Field
for the pre-season fitness build up. After a number of
appearances from the substitute's bench, and a period on the
sidelines with a hamstring problem he was given the
opportunity to re-unite with Jan Molby at Kidderminster
Harriers on an initial loan transfer. By the end of his second
month on loan, and following an agreement with his contract he
joined the Harriers on a permanent basis. Made a good
impression as an attacking midfielder at Aggborough with the
Harriers, and after Molby had joined Hull City towards the end
of the 2001/2002 season, he was re-united for a third time with
the Dane, joining the Tigers in July 2002. Capable of playing in a
wide, or central midfield position, Richie also had an eye for
goal, scoring many spectacular goals for the Swans, and scoring
two goals in a game on two occasions, at Macclesfield and
against Rochdale at the Vetch Field. A fiery character, although
not a dirty player, he had the misfortune to be sent off on three
occasions during the 1997/98 season, twice in consecutive
games, and a third red card a month later. Further injury
problems during his time with Hull City saw Richie negotiate
an early cancellation of his contract with the club in early
December 2003, and during the 2004 close season he linked up
with Jan Molby for the fourth time during his career, signing on
a non-contract basis. With no offer of a full contract from
Harriers, despite being regularly included in the first team, in

October 2004 he was offered, and signed a contract with Nationwide Conference side Forest Green Rovers.

15. ARMAND, John Edward (JACK)

Birthplace: Sabathu, India, 11/8/1902. **Died**: Grimsby, AMJ, 1974
Ht: 5ft-8ins, **Wt**: 11st-0lbs
Swans debut: v. Stoke City (h) 7/9/1929

Swansea Town Career Statistics			
Season	League	FAC	WC
1929/30	25/7gls		
1930/31	29/3gls	1	2
Total	54/10gls	1	2

Career:
Army Football
Newport County (amateur)
West Stanley (signed in July 1922)
Leeds United (signed in November 1922) lge 74/23gls
Swansea Town (£500 in 2/5/1929)
Ashton National (signed in 10/6/1931)
Newport County (£300 in 6/8/1932) lge 3/1gls
Scarborough (signed in October 1933)
Denaby United (signed in January 1934)

Honours: British Army XI, Welsh League Representative XI

John 'Snowy' Armand gained representative honours whilst serving in the Army with the British Army XI against France in Belgium, and when stationed at Newport Barracks had a trial period with Newport County's reserve team. When the Brigade was removed from Newport, he went with them, and was later bought out of the Army by Leeds United, serving them for five seasons prior to joining the Swans. Whilst at Elland Road he was involved in two promotions with the club, winning the Second Division Championship in 1924, and Second Division Runners Up in 1928. The Championship season saw him make just seven league appearances, scoring two goals, whilst in the season they finished Runners Up to Manchester City he made just two league appearances, scoring two goals. Regularly included in the Leeds United first team between 1924 and 1927, his best season was during 1925/26 when he returned nine goals from seventeen league appearances. Signed by Swans manager James Hunter Thomson in May 1929, he made his debut at inside right replacing Harry Deacon, retaining his place for most of the season in either inside forward position, or at centre forward. He scored his first goal for the Swans in his fifth game, in a 5-0 win over Bradford City at the Vetch Field, and by the end of the season had scored a further six league goals. Opening the 1930/31 season at inside left against Cardiff City,

he was used on regular occasions throughout the season, but was unable to improve on his goalscoring. In May 1930 he scored two goals in a 6-1 win for a Welsh League Representative side against the Irish Free State at the Vetch Field. Listed at £500 at the end of the 1930/31 season, after a period in non-league football with Ashton National (Gas Company), where he scored forty-eight goals, he returned to South Wales to join Third Division South side Newport County for £300 in August 1932. He struggled to make an impact at Somerton Park, and after just three league appearances joined non-league Scarborough, later, making appearances for Denaby United.

16. ASPINALL, WARREN

Birthplace: Wigan, 13/9/1967
Ht: 5ft-9ins, **Wt**: 10st-06lbs
Swans debut: v. Rotherham United (a) 16/10/1993

Swansea City Career Statistics			
Season	League	AGT	WC
1993/94	5	1	1
Total	5	1	1

Career:
Wigan Athletic (from apprentice in 31/8/1985) lge 21+12/10gls
    FLC 1, FAC 2+3/2gls, Others 1+5/2gls
Everton (£150,000 in 4/2/1986) lge 0+7, FLC 0+1, Others 0+2
Wigan Athletic (loan in 6/2/1986) lge 18/12gls, Others 2/2gls
Aston Villa (£300,000 in 19/2/1987) lge 40+4/14gls, FLC 4/2gls,
    FAC 1+1
Portsmouth (£315,000 in 26/8/1988) lge 97+35/21gls,
    FLC 8+3/3gls, FAC 4+5/2gls, Others 6+1/2gls
Bournemouth (loan in 27/8/1993) lge 4+2/1gls
Swansea City (loan in 14/10/1993)
Bournemouth (£20,000 in 31/12/1993) lge 26+1/8gls, FLC 4,
    FAC 1, Others 1
Carlisle United (signed in 8/3/1995) lge 99+8/12gls,
    FLC 8/3gls, FAC 6, Others 10+1/1gls
Brentford (£50,000 in 21/11/1997) lge 41+2/5gls, FLC 8/3,
    FAC 1+1, Others 2
Colchester United (signed in 9/2/1999) lge 22/5gls, FLC 2
Brighton (signed in 24/9/1999) lge 19+13/3gls, FAC 3, Others 2

Honours: England Yth, AMC 1985, 1997, Third Division Champions–1999

An experienced professional who started his playing career as a striker, creating a good impression as a consistent goalscorer, but by the time of his arrival at the Vetch Field on a loan basis, had reverted to an advanced midfield role. Warren made his debut in the Football League for Wigan during the 1984/85 season, and within eighteen months had landed himself a transfer to

First Division side Everton. The 1985/86 season which was his first full season in the Football League, saw him create a good understanding with Mike Newell at Wigan, but by the beginning of February he had been transferred to Everton. Four days later however, with Wigan Athletic in contention for a promotion place to the Second Division, he was loaned back to the Springfield Park side. At the end of the season, despite topping the goalscoring charts with 21 goals for Wigan, his side failed in their promotion bid by just the one point from Derby County in the third promotion place. Returning to Goodison Park he made his first team debut for Everton a couple of days after Wigan had finished their league campaign as a substitute against West Ham United. The following season, after failing to make a league start with Everton he was transferred to Second Division side Aston Villa, and within eighteen months had forged a strong partnership with Gary Thompson, with both strikers ending the season on eleven goals apiece to take the Midlands side back to the First Division. Shortly after the start of the 1988/89 season he was transferred to Second Division side Portsmouth for another six figure transfer fee, ending the season as second top goalscorer with eleven league goals. With injury problems during his second season at Fratton Park preventing from making an impact, midway through the 1990/891 season he was switched to a midfield role by manager Frank Burrows. It was Burrows who was to bring him to the Vetch Field in October 1993, as the club tried to build on their previous season's unsuccessful Play Off disappointment. An extremely skilful player on the ball, despite appearing to be overweight, he received a red card playing for the Swans at Stockport County in his fourth game for the Swans, a game which would also see the Swans skipper John Cornforth earn himself a red card. Returning to Fratton Park he was transferred to Bournemouth on a permanent transfer before the end of the season. An England Youth international during his days with Wigan Athletic, further honours came to him during his career with Wigan when he made a substitute appearance at Wembley in the 1984/85 Freight Rover Trophy Final, beating Brentford. At the end of the 1996/97 season he was to be successful for a second time in the same competition, re-named the AWS playing for Carlisle United against Colchester United, winning on penalties. During Brentford's Championship winning season of 1998/99 he made a significant impression for the 'Bees' during the first half of the season, despite joining Colchester United before the Championship had been claimed. During his career he proved to be a reliable taker of penalties, with his first league goal being from the spot in only his fifth league game. After joining Brighton & Hove Albion in September 1999 on a month to month contract, Warren suffered an ankle injury that was to bring his professional career to a close.

17. ATKINSON, PAUL Graham

Birthplace: Otley, Yorks, 14/8/1961
Ht: 5ft-10ins, **Wt:** 11st-5lbs
Swans debut: v. Cardiff City (a) 26/12/1986

Swansea City Career Statistics	
Season	League
1986/87	18/3gls
Total	18/3gls

Career:
Oldham Athletic (apprentice in August 1977, professional in August 1979) lge 139+4/11gls, FLC 9+1/1gls, FAC 4
Watford (£175,000 signed in July 1983) lge 8+3, FAC 0+2
Oldham Athletic (£30,000 signed in August 1985) lge 29+4/1gls, FLC 2, FAC 1
Swansea City (loan in December 1986)
Bolton Wanderers (loan in February 1987) lge 2+1
Swansea City (loan in March 1987)
Burnley (signed in July 1988 to May 1990) 18+4/1gls, FLC 3, FAC 6
Northwich Victoria (signed in March 1991) Conf 6+3
RWS Binchoise, Belgium (signed in July 1991)
Altrincham (signed in August 1993)
Frickley Athletic
Farsley Celtic (signed by November 1994)

Signed as an apprentice at Boundary Park with Oldham Athletic in August 1977, signing professional forms in August 1979. Capped at youth level by England, he was involved in Oldham's six-a-side winning youth team at Wembley just prior to the 1978 Charity Shield Final. Paul started his career as a left winger making 38 league appearances in the Second Division during his first season as a professional during the 1979/80 season. Reverted to an attacking midfielder in later years, he was involved in a £175,000 transfer fee to First Division Watford in July 1983, but suffered a serious leg injury which prevented him from making a greater impact at a higher level in the game. Earlier in his career at Oldham, Liverpool had offered a fee in the region of £300,000 for his signature. With just eleven First Division appearances following his transfer, he was used as a substitute in the 1984 FA Cup Final at Wembley against Everton, replacing Neil Price, a player who twelve months later was brought to the Vetch Field by manager John Bond. The following season injuries prevented him from making any appearances at Vicarage Road, and by August 1985 had returned to Oldham. He was signed by Swan's manager Terry Yorath in December 1986, making his debut at Ninian Park against Cardiff City on Boxing Day. Returning to Oldham after six league appearances for the Swans, he then went to Bolton Wanderers shortly after returning to Oldham, but just prior to the transfer deadline returned to the Vetch Field for a second loan spell until the end of the season. Impressed a number of supporters at the Vetch Field, showing plenty of pace, and guile to the midfield area. At one stage towards the end of the season it was thought that the transfer would have been made permanent, but instead returned to Boundary Park. After one more season at Boundary Park he was released in July 1988, joining Burnley, where he remained until May 1990. He later signed for Vauxhall Conference side Northwich Victoria, and in July 1991 joined Belgian side RWS Binchoise, and on his return to the U.K. made non-league appearances for Altrincham, Frickley Athletic and Farsley Celtic.

18. ATTLEY, BRIAN Robert

Birthplace: Cardiff, 27/8/1955
Ht: 5ft-9ins, **Wt:** 9st-12lbs
Swans debut: v. Exeter City (a), 24/2/1979

Career:
Cardiff City (signed in August 1973) lge 73+6/1gls, FLC 1+1, FAC 5, ECWC 3
Swansea City (£20,000 signed in February 1979)

Derby County (£25,000 signed in 5/2/1982) lge 54+1/1gls,
    FLC 4, FAC 2
Oxford United (loan in March 1983) lge 5
Gresley Rovers (signed in July 1984)
Stapenhill (signed in March 1986)

Swansea City Career Statistics

Season	League	FLC	FAC	WC	ECWC
1978/79	19+1/1gls			1	
1979/80	30+3/3gls	4		4	
1980/81	32/2gls	1	1	5/2gls	
1981/82	2+2	0+1		0+1/1gls	1
Total	83+6/6gls	5+1	1	10+1/3gls	1

Former apprentice at Ninian Park with Cardiff City, who played
in either full back positions, but struggled to command a regular
place ahead of Phil Dwyer and Freddie Pethard. His 'Bluebirds'
debut came as substitute for Gil Reece at Ninian Park in a 1-0
defeat by Bristol City on the 14th September 1974. He
experienced European Cup Winners Cup football with Cardiff
City, as they regularly represented Wales in the competition
during the 1970's, and played in both legs of the 1974/75 Welsh
Cup Final against Wrexham, losing on aggregate 5-2. He was
included in the Bluebirds side that defeated Spurs in the third
round of the FA Cup at Ninian Park during season 1976/77,
going on to lose to Everton in the fifth round. Making his Swans
debut as substitute for Robbie James at Exeter City on 26th
February 1979, Brian proved to be a bargain £20,000 signing,
with his electric turn of pace enabling him to take on the
opposition from either his right back role, or at a more advanced
position on the right side of midfield, providing numerous
goalscoring opportunities for his team mates. Although not the
strongest in the tackle, he always gave 100% commitment
during the game. After the Swans had gained First Division
status, he failed to hold down a regular place in the starting line-
up, and joined Derby County for a fee in the region of £25,000 in
February 1983. A consistent performer during the first eighteen
months with County, he had a five game loan spell with Oxford
United in March 1983, but after being unable to command a
regular place the following season, was released, joining non-
league side Gresley Rovers in July 1984, later making
appearances for Stapenhill almost two years later. Returning to
South Wales he later settled in Rhoose, near Barry, working as a
floor tiler.

19. AUSTIN, KEVIN Levi

Birthplace: Hackney, 12/2/1973
Ht: 6ft-0ins, **Wt:** 14st-0lbs
Swans debut: v. Rochdale (a), 10/8/2004

Career:
Leyton Wingate (signed in 1991)

Saffron Walden (signed in 1/8/1992)
Leyton Orient (signed in 19/8/1993) lge 101+8/3gls,
    FLC 4/1gls, FAC 6, Others 7
Lincoln City (£30,000 signed in 31/7/1996) lge 128+1/2gls,
    FLC 9, FAC 6, Others 4
Barnsley (signed in 5/7/1999) lge 3, FLC 2+1
Brentford (loan in 27/10/2000) lge 3
Cambridge United (signed in 1/8/2001) lge 4+2, Others 1
Bristol Rovers (signed in 1/7/2002) lge 52+4, FAC 4+1
Swansea City (signed in 18/6/2004)

Honours: Trinidad & Tobago–1, FAW Cup Winner–2005

Swansea City Career Statistics

Season	League	FLC	FAC	LDV	FAWC
2004/05	41+1	1	5	2	1+1
Total	41+1	1	5	2	1+1

Experienced defender brought to the Vetch Field by Swans
manager Kenny Jackett in the 2004 close season, and showed his
versatility after a couple of games by his impressive
performances at either left full back, or in central defence.
He attended the Edward Readhead School in Walthamstow
when he was younger, joined Leyton Orient as a schoolboy, and
at 18 years of age played football in the USA in Arizona.
Returning to the UK in 1991 he played for Diadora Division One
side Leyton Wingate, joined Diadora Division Two side Saffron
Walden Town in August 1992, signing professional forms for
Leyton Orient twelve months later. Given his league debut at
Brentford on the 14th September 1993 at left full back instead of
the experienced Terry Howard, he played a further twelve
league matches, and came back into the Orient starting line-up
for the last seventeen league matches of the season, either at full
back, or in central defence. For the next couple of seasons, either
with Orient or at Lincoln City he featured regularly, missing few
games. After joining First Division side Barnsley prior to the
1999/2000 season, within weeks of being included in the
starting line-up he was sidelined with a ruptured Achilles
Tendon, suffering the same injury on the other foot the
following season. In between however he had been selected at
International level for Trinidad & Tobago, playing against
Panama in a World Cup Qualifying game in November 2000.
Released by Barnsley, and after failing to secure a permanent
contract with Cambridge United, he joined Bristol Rovers at the
start of the 2002/03 season, featuring regularly in a Rovers side
battling to avoid relegation to the Conference. By the end of the
season Kevin missed just four league games in the Swans side
that gained automatic promotion in third place in the Second
Division behind Scunthorpe United and Yeovil Town, and also
played in the FAW Cup Final win over Wrexham.

B

1. BAKER, MARK

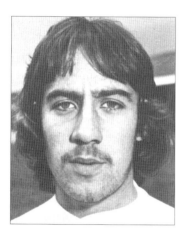

Birthplace: Swansea, 26/4/1961
Ht: 5ft-9ins, **Wt**: 11st-4lbs
Swans debut: v. Chesterfield (a), 7/10/1978

Swansea City Career Statistics		
Season	League	FLC
1978/79	2+3/2gls	
1979/80	1+5	0+2
Totals	3+8/2gls	0+2

Career:
Ragged School
Swansea City (signed professional in September 1978)
Merthyr Tydfil (signed in season 1980/81)

Honours: Wales U-21-2

Former Manselton, Dynevor and Swansea schoolboy striker who played for Swansea Senior League side Waun Wen at 16 years of age, and who signed professional at the start of the 1978/79 season straight from Ragged School, of the Swansea Senior League, becoming John Toshack's first signing. After making his league debut as substitute for Kevin Moore at Chesterfield in October 1978, his next appearance for the Swans, and his first start, he scored two goals in an exciting 3-2 home win over Mansfield Town. Unfortunately for him, with the Swans continuing to gain success, and no reserve team to gain experience he was released from his contract in October 1980, returning to Ragged School, before signing for Merthyr Tydfil. During his time at the Vetch Field he gained two caps for the Wales U-21 side against Norway, home and away. Since then Mark has played in the Welsh League for Haverfordwest County, Llanelli (twice), Maesteg, Port Talbot, Morriston, and returned to the Swansea Senior League to make appearances for Ragged School and Swansea Boys Club. After leaving the professional football scene, Mark has been employed in the Post Office, and in season 2004/05 was still turning out for Morriston Town's Welsh League side.

2. BALA'C, PETA John

Birthplace: Exeter, 9/12/1953
Ht: 5ft-10ins, **Wt**: 11st-11lbs
Swans debut: v. Stockport County (a), 13/10/1973

Swansea City Career Statistics		
Season	League	FAC
1973/74	4	1
Total	7	1

Career:
Plymouth Argyle (from apprentice in December 1971) lge 40
Hereford United (loan in August 1973) lge 2
Swansea City (loan in September 1973)
Durban City, S.A (signed in 1974)
Lusitano, S.A. (signed in 1977)
Sacramento Gold, USA (signed in 1979)
Kaizer Chiefs, S.A. (signed in 1980)

Young 19-year-old keeper who was signed on loan shortly after the start of the season replacing Welsh International Tony Millington. During his four league game loan transfer, he kept three clean sheets with the Swans winning three out of four matches he played in. Earlier in the season he had previously had a loan spell with Hereford United before arriving at the Vetch Field. At Argyle he had struggled for a couple of seasons to gain a regular place in the first team starting line-up because of the consistency of the veteran Jim Furnell. Brought up in Exeter, his father a Yugoslav, he attended Ladysmith Boys School, played for the school side along with former England international Trevor Francis, also playing for the East Devon County team. Whilst at Home Park with Argyle he attended an England U-19 training camp in Bisham Abbey along with Len Bond, Paul Cooper, Mervyn Day and Graham Moseley. After two years as a professional with Argyle, at the age of 21 he took up the opportunity of playing in South Africa with Durban City, three years later joined Lusitano, before having the opportunity to play in the United States with Sacramento Gold. Included in the Sacramento side that won the Championship that season were five players who had played alongside him in the Lusitano team. Returning to play for Lusitano after just twelve months in the USA, before he had made an appearance for the club, he was transferred to Kaizer Chiefs. During his career in South Africa, he won League and Cup honours with Lusitano in 1977 and

1978, also a finalist for the 'Footballer of the Year' Award whilst at the club, and with Kaizer Chiefs won League and Cup Honours between 1980 and 1985, also in 1984 being runner up in the Goalkeeper of the Year Award. During his career in South Africa he became the only sportsman to play in a White, Black and Asian Cup Final. Involved with coaching in private schools during his period in South Africa, along with Willie Castle he started a football coaching centre which continues to this day. He returned to the UK in the late 1980's working as a representative in 1985, and has since been involved in the bar/restaurant trade, opening a business in Chester named 'Amakhozi', the nickname of South African team Kaizer Chiefs. He continues to play football and cricket in the local leagues in the Chester area for Bourton Hall Nomads, and is planning to go back to South Africa to play for the Kaizer Chiefs Veterans side in an Exhibition match against Orlando Pirates.

3. BAMFORD, Thomas (TOMMY)

Birthplace: Aberavon, Port Talbot, 2/9/1905. **Died:** Wrexham 14/12/1967
Ht: 5ft-9ins, **Wt**: 11st-11lbs
Swans debut: v. Manchester City (a), 27/8/1938

Swansea Town Career Statistics			
Season	League	FAC	WC
1938/39	36/14gls	1	3/1gls
Total	36/14gls	1	3/1gls

Career:
Cardiff Docks
Cardiff Wednesday
Bridgend Town
Wrexham (signed in 4/4/1929) lge 204/174gls
Manchester United (signed in 17/10/1934) lge 98/53gls
Swansea Town (signed in 3/6/1938)
Wrexham (WW2 guest, May 1940) 17apps/8gls
Hartlepool United (WW2 guest 1943/44) 13apps/6gls

Honours: Wales Full–5, Welsh Cup Winner–1931, Second Division Championship Winner–1936, Northern Command XI

Aberavon born centre forward Tommy Bamford, played his early football in the Aberavon and Port Talbot area with Dock Stars and Aberavon Quins, later in the Cardiff and Bridgend area before signing for Wrexham, after turning to the north of the Principality in search of work. Launching his league career at the late age of 23, Tommy scored six goals in just seven league games at the end of the 1928/29 season. In a couple of years he had earned himself a call up to the International team, playing against Scotland at Hampden Park in a 1-1 draw in October

1930, scoring Wales's goal. In 1931 he played for Wrexham in their 7-0 Welsh Cup Final win over Shrewsbury Town, and during the remainder of his career received four runners up medals from Welsh Cup Finals, in 1932, 1933 (with Wrexham), 1938 & 1940 (with the Swans). Following a spell at Manchester United, where he gained a Second Division Championship medal in 1936, he returned to his native South Wales to sign for the Swans in June 1938. During his only Football League season at the Vetch Field Bamford returned 14 league goals, including scoring two goals in a game on three occasions, and arriving at the Vetch Field at the age of 33. At one stage of the 1938/39 season he scored 6 goals in a four match league spell. The start of the season the Swans played a replay of the 1937/38 Welsh Cup Final, carried over from the end of the previous season against Shrewsbury Town, losing 1-2. For a number of seasons the Swans had struggled in the bottom half of the Second Division, finding goalscoring a great difficulty. With only fifty goals being scored during the season, the Swans had narrowly avoided relegation, not for the first time. Starting the 1939/40 season with the Swans, he scored three goals from the first three league matches, before the competition was brought to a close because of the start of the war. He continued to play for the Swans until the end of the season in a re-organized regional football competition, the South West Regional League/Cup, appearing at the end of the season in the Welsh Cup Final defeat by Wellington. During the War period he played as a guest for Wrexham and Hartlepool United, represented Northern Command, before settling back in Wrexham after the war, and working in a local steelworks, prior to his death in Wrexham in December 1967.

4. BARBER, JOHN Nathaniel

Birthplace: Tamworth, 19/10/1929. **Died:** Lichfield, September 2002
Ht: 5ft-6ins, **Wt**: 10st-6lbs
Swans debut: v. Doncaster Rovers (h), 2/9/1950

Swansea Town Career Statistics	
Season	League
1950/51	4
Total	4

Career:
Arsenal (signed as amateur in 2/3/1946)
Swansea Town (signed in August 1950)
Walsall (signed in July 1951) lge 6
Hereford United (signed in July 1952)

Honours: Welsh League First Division Champions–1951

Signed amateur forms for Arsenal in early March 1946, and between January 1948 to November 1949 did his National Service in the Army. He failed to make a senior appearance for the 'Gunners', but during season 1945/46 played in one junior friendly match, season 1947/48 one reserve team friendly, and in season 1949/50 played one match in the Eastern Counties League. Released in early May 1950, he arrived at the Vetch Field on an extended trial basis, linking up with the players as they returned for pre-season training, and was included in the Swans' first Public Trial game at the Vetch Field on Saturday 12th August 1950. An Outside Left, he found his first team opportunities limited at the Vetch Field with the signing of Cyril Beech, but did play in four consecutive league games for the Swans, as cover for the injured Beech during the 1950/51 season, winning one, and losing in three games. He proved himself to be a lively raider on the flank, possessing good crossing ability. During the season he made a number of appearances in the Swans' Welsh League side that won the First Division Championship. He was released at the end of the season, joining Walsall in July 1951, staying at Fellows Park for the remainder of the 1951/52 season. Despite making just six league appearances, the determined winger, playing mostly on the right wing for the 'Saddlers', made his Walsall debut in a 1-1 draw at Swindon on the 9th February 1952. With the club finishing bottom of the Third Division South, and having to apply for re-election to the Football League, 'Felix' as he was nicknamed by the club's supporters was released. In July 1952 he joined Hereford United.

5. BARBER. KEITH

Birthplace: Luton, 21/9/1947
Ht: 5ft-11ins, **Wt**: 11st-6lbs
Swans debut: v. Swindon Town (a) 16/8/1977

Swansea City Career Statistics				
Season	League	FLC	FAC	WC
1977/78	42	1	5	2
Total	42	1	5	2

Career:
Dunstable Town
Luton Town (signed in April 1971) lge 142
Swansea City (signed in July 1977)
Cardiff City (signed in 7/9/1978) lge 2
Bridgend Town (signed in September 1978)

At the start of his professional career, Keith Barber had been a member of the Luton Town side that gained promotion to the First Division at the end of the 1973-74 season. He had earlier in his career shown impressive form with non-league side Dunstable Town prior to signing a professional contract with his hometown club Luton. A goalkeeper with experience in the First and Second Divisions during his playing career, his last match for Luton saw him being stretchered off at Notts. County on September 1976. At the end of the season with Luton failing in their promotion bid by just four points, and his number one jersey being taken by former Spurs goalkeeper Milija Aleksic, Keith was allowed to join the Swans on a free transfer in July 1977, after a total of 142 league appearances for the 'Hatters.' Signed by Swans manager Harry Griffiths, he impressed the Swans supporters during the season with his consistency, which was rewarded with promotion at the end of the season from the Fourth Division. Stephen Potter had opened the season wearing the number one jersey in a League Cup tie against Swindon Town, but when the league games commenced, Barber lined up in the goalkeeper jersey for the Swans. During the season he missed just 4 league games through injury, kept eighteen clean

sheets, distinguishing himself as a brave, agile, shot stopper as the Swans gained promotion from the Fourth Division in the last game of the season. Following the club's promotion to the Third Division, manager John Toshack surprised a number of fans by paying a record transfer fee for Crewe Alexandra's goalkeeper Geoff Crudgington at the start of the season, a move which was to signal the end of his stay at the Vetch Field with the Swans. Following 2 loan appearances for Cardiff City in September 1978, the last, a 7-1 hammering at his previous club Luton Town, Keith joined Southern League Premier Division strugglers Bridgend Town for a couple of games, before returning to the Luton area. Following a period as a pub landlord, Keith, was employed at Newmarket Racecourse.

6. BARNHOUSE, DAVID John

Birthplace: Swansea, 19/3/1975
Ht: 5ft-9ins, **Wt:** 11st-9lbs
Swans debut: v. Hull City (a), 2/5/1992

Swansea City Career Statistics					
Season	League	FLC	FAC	AGT	WC
1991/92	0+1				
1992/93					
1993/94	2+1			1	0+1
1994/95	4		1		1
1995/96	12+3	2	1		3
Total	18+5	2	2	1	4+1

Career:
Swansea City (from trainee in 8/7/1993)
Merthyr Tydfil (signed in August 1996)
Carmarthen Town (signed during season 1996/97)
Haverfordwest County (signed in close season 2004)

Honours: Wales Sch, Yth, U–21–3, Wales Semi-Professional XI, West Wales Senior Cup Winner–1995

Made his Swans debut as substitute for Shaun Chapple at Hull City in May 1992, in the last league game of the season whilst still a first year trainee, six weeks passed his 17th birthday. Earlier he had attended Dillwyn Llewellyn Comprehensive school, played for the school team, and Swansea schoolboys, gaining Welsh caps at U-15 and U-16 levels. Joined the Swans as a YTS trainee on leaving school, and whilst at the Vetch Field represented Wales at U-21 level on three occasions, his first cap against Moldova in 1995, and two further appearances against Moldova and San Marino the following season. Season 1993/94 was his first season as a professional, making his second league appearance for the Swans at Cambridge United in September 1993, losing 0-2, replacing the injured Keith Walker. He made a couple of appearances later in the season, and towards the end of the season made a substitute appearance against Cardiff City in a Welsh Cup semi-final first leg tie at the Vetch Field which the Bluebirds won 2-1. Season 1994/95 saw David make four consecutive league appearances, also appearing against Middlesbrough in the third round of the FA Cup at the Vetch Field. At the end of the season he was included in the Swans side that beat Morriston Town in the West Wales Senior Cup Final. Starting season 1995/96 at right full back instead of Mark Clode, he made regular appearances for the Swans up to the midway point of the season, including playing in the humiliating 7-0 hammering at Craven Cottage against Fulham in the first round of the FA Cup competition. During his Swans career he usually played at right full back, but was also used in central defence, and, despite being not tall, possessed good spring to win aerial challenges. He was released in May 1996, joining Merthyr Tydfil, but after a short spell at Penydarren Park, signed for Carmarthen Town, where he forged a tremendous central defensive partnership with the experienced Neil O'Brien. At Richmond Park with Carmarthen Town he gained honours for the Welsh Semi-Professional representative side against England. Towards the end of season 1998/99, he played in the Welsh Cup Final defeat by Inter Cardiff on penalties. In the 2004 close season he joined fellow League of Wales side Haverfordwest County, playing in the UEFA Cup First Round tie against Iceland side FH Hafnarfjordur.

7. BARNWELL-Edinboro, JAMIE

Birthplace: Hull, 26/12/1975
Ht: 5ft-10ins, **Wt:** 11st-6lbs
Swans debut: v. Burnley (h), 16/12/1995

Swansea City Career Statistics	
Season	*League*
1995/96	2+2
Total	2+2

Career:
Coventry City (from YTS in 1/7/1994) PL 0+1
Swansea City (loan in 15/12/1995)
Wigan Athletic (loan in 2/2/1996) lge 2+8/1gls
Cambridge United (signed in 29/3/1996) lge 53+10/12gls, FLC 2, FAC 2+1/1gls, Others 0+2
Doncaster Rovers (signed in season 1998/99) Conf 6+4/1gls
Scarborough (signed in close season 2001/02) Conf 2+2
Hall Road Rangers (signed in season 2001/02)

Honours: Conference League Cup Winner–1999

Brought up in Hull, Jamie attended Amy Johnson High School, played for all the different age sides in school, Hull Schoolboys, Humberside, and also had trials for the England Schoolboys team prior to arriving at Highfield Road with Coventry City on a two year YTS training on leaving school in 1992. The young second year professional during season 1995/96 made league appearances for four different clubs. In September 1995 he made his league debut for Coventry City in the Premiership, replacing Paul Cook from the substitute bench against Middlesbrough. He was signed by Swans manager Bobby Smith in December 1995 on a month loan transfer, making his debut in a 4-2 home defeat by Burnley in mid-December 1995. Returning to Coventry City after his loan period with the Swans, he joined Wigan Athletic on loan in February 1996, and later in the season joined Cambridge United in a permanent transfer, making his United debut against Rochdale, and scoring in a 2-1 home win. The following season he was a regular inclusion for United, making 40 appearances, and midway through the season scored

four goals in a six match spell for the club. The 1997/98 season was a frustrating one for him, as he struggled to make inroads into the United side, and at the end of the season he was released. In his short time at the Vetch Field he showed a lot of promise, was very pacy, and willing, and showed his ability to get to the by-line by setting up a goal for another debutant, Glyn Hurst. By the time he left the Vetch Field, Smith had resigned his position, with his assistant Jimmy Rimmer taking on the role of caretaker manager. Joining Vauxhall Conference side Doncaster Rovers in season 1998/99, Jamie played in the successful Rovers side that won the League Cup at the end of the season, but at the end of the season had spells with Stevenage, Goole and Scarborough before he signed for Northern Counties League side Hall Road Rangers in season 2001/02. In season 2003/04 Jamie became player manager with Rangers, but resigned at the end of the season, staying with the club as a player. By the start of the 2004/05 season he returned to Hall Road Rangers as player coach, and had been expected to sign for North Ferriby, but after playing in a couple of pre-season matches opted instead to rejoin Hall Road. The last twelve months has seen Jamie become a Residential Social Worker working with Children in Care in Hull.

8. BARTLEY, Daniel (DANNY) Robert

Birthplace: Paulton, 3/10/1947
Ht: 5ft-8ins, **Wt:** 10st-10lbs
Swans debut: v. Chester (h), 25/8/1973

Swansea City Career Statistics				
Season	*League*	*FLC*	*FAC*	*WC*
1973/74	17	2		
1974/75	14			
1975/76	31+2/1gls	2		2
1976/77	45/1gls	6/1gls	1	2
1977/78	43/4gls	2	5	2
1978/79	40+2/2gls	5	2+1	1
1979/80	4	3		
Total	194+4/8gls	20/1gls	8+1	7

Career:
Bristol City (from apprentice in October 1964) lge 92+8/7gls
Swansea City (£12,000 package with Dave Bruton on 3/7/1973)
Hereford United (signed in 12/3/1980) lge 112+2/6gls, FLC 5/1gls, FAC 2

Honours: England Yth, West Wales Senior Cup Winner–1975

Played as a left winger in the North East Somerset Schools team, joining Bristol City straight from school, and eventually graduated to the City first team showing his ability to take on opposing full backs, and deliver accurate crosses for his team mates. A fast elusive winger, who could play on either flank, he was converted to left full back towards the end of the 1974/75 season by Swans manager Harry Griffiths, who during his playing career had made the same change. He was signed by Swans manager Harry Gregg in a joint £12,000 package with Dave Bruton in July 1973 following the Swans relegation to the Fourth Division, and also seeing Danny drop down two divisions from playing his football with Bristol City in the Second Division. He took some time before he settled down to the rigours of Fourth Division football, struggling initially to make his mark with the Swans. His second season with the Swans saw Danny make just one league appearance in November, before returning to the side at left back at the end of February following Harry Griffiths taking over the managerial role. In May 1975 he was included in the Swans side that beat Briton Ferry Athletic to win the West Wales Senior Cup. With Griffiths operating a more adventurous approach to the game, Danny started the 1975/76 season at left full back, switching occasionally to a left wing role, a move which brought him his first goal for the Swans in March 29th against Stockport County at the Vetch Field in a 5-0 victory. He had always been capable of delivering telling crosses from the flanks, but in his new role, Danny had more time to utilise his talent to get to the by-line from a deeper position. With the Swans developing into a free scoring unit, his accurate crosses became one of the main outlets for young strikers like Curtis, Charles and James to exploit from the left flank. This was carried on when Toshack arrived at the club in a player manager role, which saw the club overcome the disappointment of missing out on promotion during the 1976/77 season, to finally earn themselves a promotion place in 1978 following a last match win over Halifax Town at the Vetch Field. That season saw Danny record 4 league goals, which included two in one match at Aldershot in a 2-2 draw. Retaining his placed the following season in the Third Division, he was once again a vital component in the side that earned themselves a second successive promotion place, returning the club to the Second Division for the first time since 1965. Despite playing in the opening league matches in the Second Division, he lost his place to Chris Marustik initially, then summer signing Dave Rushbury. He joined Fourth Division Hereford United on a free transfer in 12th March 1980, and was a regular inclusion over the next three seasons until he was released in May 1983, when United finished the season bottom of the Fourth Division.

In season 1980/81 he played in both legs against the Swans in the Welsh Cup Final, losing 2-1 on aggregate. That same season United had been knocked out of the FA Cup by non-league side Enfield, the second occasion Danny had suffered the fate of being beaten in the FA Cup competition by a non-league side. In November 1976 he had been a member of the Swans side that were beaten at the Vetch Field by Minehead in the first round of the FA Cup competition. After leaving Edgar Street, he played for Trowbridge, Forest Green Rovers, Maesteg, Port Talbot, Bridgend and Llanelli, also acting as caretaker manager at Stebonheath Park with Llanelli between October 1996 to November 1996, and he is still residing in Swansea, working for a leading finance company. His son Kevin went on to become a trainee with Cardiff City, and after failing to make a league appearance has had a lengthy career in the League of Wales with Port Talbot Town.

9. BARWOOD, Daniel (DANNY) David

Birthplace: Caerphilly, 25/2/1981
Ht: 5ft-9ins, **Wt**: 11st-0lbs
Swans debut: v. Hull City (h), 17/1/1998

Career:
Swansea City (trainee in 1999)
Merthyr (signed by November 2000)

Swansea City Career Statistics		
Season	League	FAW
1997/98	1+2/1gls	1+1
1998/99		0+1
1999/2000		3/1gls
2000/2001		1/1gls
Total	1+2/1gls	5+2/2gls

Honours: Wales Sch, Yth

An exceptionally talented schoolboy who possessed electrifying pace, and strength on the ball, and who played for the Welsh Schoolboys side prior to signing for the Swans as a trainee. He was given his debut by Swans manager Alan Cork almost a month before his seventeenth birthday as substitute for Steve Watkin at the Vetch Field against Hull City on the 17th January 1998 whilst still a trainee. A further substitute appearance a few weeks later against Exeter City at the Vetch Field, was followed at the end of March by him making his first start for the Swans against Chester City at the Vetch Field, with Danny opening the Swans scoring in the fourteenth minute, with the Swans going on to win 2-0. He failed to make any further appearances in the Swans first team, apart from outings in the FAW Cup competition. In March 1998 he was called up for the Wales U-18 squad to play in the Paolo Valenta Tournament in Italy. Following his release from the Swans, he joined Dr. Martens side Merthyr Tydfil on the 10th November 2000, following a trial spell with Cardiff City. He failed to make any appearances for Merthyr, and decided to switch codes, and play rugby after failing to agree a contract with Merthyr Tydfil, following his father Adrian Barwood into Rugby Union, and who also played Rugby League with Cardiff and Bridgend in the 1980's.

10. BASHAM, MICHAEL

Birthplace: Barking, 27/9/1973
Ht: 6ft-2ins, **Wt:** 12st-8lbs
Swans debut: v. Burnley (a), 15/4/1994

Swansea City Career Statistics				
Season	League	FAC	AGT	WC
1993/94	5		1	
1994/95	13	5	5	2
1995/96	9+2/1	1	0+2	
Total	27+2/1gls	6	6+2	2

Career:
West Ham United (from trainee in 3/7/1992)

Colchester United (loan in 18/11/1993) lge 1
Swansea City (signed in 24/3/1994)
Peterborough United (signed in 19/12/1995) lge 17+2/1gls,
    FLC 1, FAC 0+1
Barnet (signed in 5/8/1997) lge 74+1/2gls, FLC 2, FAC 0+1,
    Others 7+1
York City (signed in 14/3/2001) lge 32+4/3gls, FLC 1, FAC 4,
    Others 0+1
Chelmsford City (signed in February 2003)

Honours: England Sch, Yth, AMC–1994, West Wales Senior Cup
Winner–1995

Signed by manager Frank Burrows as cover in central defence
on transfer deadline day, March 24th 1994 on an initial loan until
the end of the season from West Ham United. He had failed to
make an appearance for the 'Hammers', and the former England
schoolboy, and youth defender's only first team experience had
been on loan to Colchester United in November 1993, making
his league debut against Walsall. Following two league
appearances for the Swans, Mike was included in the side that
played in the Final of the AutoGlass Trophy at Wembley. With
an injury to Keith Walker weeks before sidelining him for the
final, and doubts over the fitness of John Ford, Burrows had
brought in Basham as cover, despite the youngster's
inexperience. At the end of the season he signed a permanent
contract with the Swans, but his first full season at the Vetch
Field, saw him miss the opening fixtures through a thigh injury,
although he did enjoy an exciting FA Cup run later, with a win
over Middlesbrough before losing to Newcastle United in the
fourth round, and a close defeat by Birmingham City in the
semi-final of the AWS cup competition. In May 1995 he made a
substitute's appearance in the West Wales Senior Cup Final win
over Morriston Town. Midway through his second full season at
the Vetch Field, he was allowed to join Peterborough United on
an initial trial basis after failing to settle in the city. His last game
for the Swans had been in the 7-0 demolition by Fulham in the
first round of the FA Cup competition. An elegant player in the
heart of the defence, possessing a strong ability to bring the ball
out from defence, he was a good reader of the game, and also
possessed accurate passing skills. He scored just the one goal for
the Swans, in the opening fixture of the 1995/96 season at
Bristol Rovers. After suffering relegation at the end of season
1996/97 with Peterborough United he joined Barnet where he
enjoyed two Third Division Play Off semi-final appearances
during his four seasons at Underhill. He joined York City in
March 2001, but then returned south to sign for Chelmsford City
in February 2003, linking up later with Ryman League side
Thurrock in July 2003.

11. BEAN, MARCUS Tristam

Birthplace: Hammersmith, 2/11/1984
Ht: 5ft-11ins, **Wt:** 11st-6lbs
Swans debut: v. Grimsby Town (h), 19/2/2005

Swansea City Career Statistics		
Season	League	FAWC
2004/05	6+2	1
Total	6+2	1

Career:
Queens Park Rangers (from trainee in 2002) lge 40+18/2gls, FLC
    1+1, FAC 2, Others 3+1
Swansea City (loan in 16/2/2005)

Arrived at the Vetch Field at the same time as team mate Kevin
McLeod on a three month loan transfer, with the possibility of
the transfer being made permanent at the end of the season.
A former scholar at Loftus Road with Queens Park Rangers, he
had been attached to the club's junior sides since the age of
eleven. He made his league debut during season 2002/03 as a
substitute for Richard Langley in a 4-1 defeat at Wycombe
Wanderers on the 26th August 2002, and unfortunately for him,
he was one of four players who received a red card in the game,
two from each side. His first start came two games later in a 4-0
win at Mansfield Town. He did not feature in the 2003 Second
Division Play Off Final defeat by Cardiff City at the Millenium
Stadium, but within twelve months had made thirty-one league
appearances in the Rangers midfield that finished runners up to
Plymouth Argyle, gaining automatic promotion from the
Nationwide Second Division. After making his debut for the
Swans at the Vetch Field against Grimsby Town, he was a
regular inclusion in the starting line-up prior to being recalled to
Loftus Road in April owing to an injury crisis in the Rangers
playing staff.

12. BEAUCHAMP, Joseph (JOEY) Daniel

Birthplace: Oxford, 13/3/1971
Ht: 5ft-10ins, **Wt:** 11st-10lbs
Swans debut: v. Wigan Athletic (a), 1/11/1991

Swansea City Career Statistics		
Season	League	AGT
1991/92	5/2gls	1
Total	5/2gls	1

Career:
Oxford United (trainee from 16/5/1989) lge 117+7/20gls, FLC
    6+1/2gls, FAC 8/3gls, Others 5+1

Swansea City (loan signed in 30/10/1991)
West Ham United (£1,000,000 signed in 22/6/1994)
Swindon Town (£850,000 signed in 18/8/1994) lge 39+6/3gls, FLC 7+2/1gls, FAC 2, Others 4
Oxford United (£75,000 signed in 4/10/1995) lge 203+35/43gls, FLC 22+2/8gls, FAC 12+3/1gls, Others 2+4

Loan transfer signing by Swans manager Frank Burrows on the 30th October 1991 from Oxford United, the pacy, wide midfielder scored his first goal for the Swans in only his second game for the Swans against Leyton Orient at the Vetch Field in a 2-2 draw. Two games later he played in an incredible match at Bradford City which saw Beauchamp score one of the Swans six goals in a 6-4 away win at Valley Parade, with John Williams netting a hat-trick. A player who possessed an electric turn of pace, during his career he proved to be capable of scoring spectacular goals, especially from long range. Earlier in his career it appeared that he would go on to make a big impression in the Premiership with West Ham United following a £1M transfer in June 1994, but without starting a game for the 'Hammers' felt he was unable to adapt to life in the City, and quickly moved back to his Oxford roots, joining Swindon Town for a fee of £850,000, which involved central defender Adrian Whitbread moving in the opposite direction. He struggled to make an impression in a Swindon Town side that had lost it's Premiership status, and was in freefall down the divisions. After just fourteen months at the County Ground with Swindon Town, he returned to his first club Oxford United for a fee of £75,000, and in his first season with Oxford United, the club finished runners up behind Swindon Town in the Second Division. Top goalscorer for United in season 1997/98 with 13 league goals, plus 6 in the Coca Cola Cup competitions, in which they reached they reached the fourth round was followed by relegation in 1999, and a second relegation, two years later in 2001 to the Third Division. Joined Ryman Second Division side Abingdon in December 2003 after an operation on his toe, scoring fifteen goals from twelve games to steer the club away from the relegation zone, playing alongside his brother Luke. The 2003/04 season saw Joey link up with former Oxford team mate Paul Powell at GLS Hellenic Premier Division side Didcot Town.

13. BEECH, CYRIL

Birthplace: Tamworth, 12/3/1925. **Died:** Merthyr, 4/5/2001
Ht: 5ft-10ins, **Wt:** 11st-8lbs
Swans debut: v. Sheffield United (h), 1/9/1949

Career:
Merthyr Tydfil
Swansea Town (£6,000 signed in 6/8/1949)
Worcester City (signed in August 1954)
Newport County (signed in July 1955) lge 39/8gls
Hereford United (signed in March 1957) Total Aps 103/41gls

Merthyr Tydfil (signed in August 1960)
Brecon Corinthians (signed in late August 1960)
Brierley Hill

Swansea Town Career Statistics			
Season	League	FAC	WC
1949/50	37/10gls	2	2/2gls
1950/51	33/3gls		1
1951/52	9/3gls		1
1952/53	34/9gls		2/1gls
1953/54	23/4gls	3/2gls	
Total	136/29gls	5/2gls	6/3gls

Honours: Welsh Cup Winner–1950

Staffordshire born left winger who made his first league appearance for the Swans just four league games into the 1949/50 season, shortly after signing for the Swans, and scoring on his debut against Sheffield United, the only goal of the game. He was brought up in the Tamworth area of Wedlecote, played for the Wedlecote Central and Tamworth School sides prior to moving to Merthyr Tydfil. By the end of his first season, the outside left had topped the Swans goalscoring charts with 10 league goals, also playing alongside his brother Gilbert in the Welsh Cup Final against Wrexham in April 1950, which the Swans won 4-1, with Cyril scoring one of the goals. Known as 'Tulyar' after the famous racehorse of his era because of his pace and bravery, Cyril was a hard working player with a blistering shot. He played for the Swans predominately on the left wing, also at times on the right, and at centre forward. Released at the end of season 1953/54, Cyril joined Southern League side Worcester City in July 1954, then was re-united with former Swans skipper Billy Lucas at Newport County twelve months later. With Worcester he scored 18 goals from 43 appearances. Adding another eight goals in 39 league matches for County, he then joined Hereford United in Spring 1956, becoming one of the principal members of the side at Edgar Street which saw the club firmly established in non-league circles under the player managership of Joe Wade. One of his goals for Hereford came in an early Hereford FA Cup giantkilling, a remarkable 6-1 demolition of QPR. In August 1960 he rejoined Merthyr, but a few weeks later, along with his brother Gilbert signed for Welsh League side Brecon Corinthians. By March 1961 he had left Brecon and signed for West Midlands side Brierley Hill. After ending his playing career, as well as being a coach driver, he spent many productive years scouting for Coventry City and Luton Town, and was responsible for producing Welsh internationals John Hartson, Mark Pembridge, Ceri Hughes, Jason Rees, Cardiff born brothers Kurt and Lee Nogan, remaining in Merthyr until his death in Merthyr in May 2001.

14. BEECH, GILBERT

Birthplace: Tamworth, 9/1/1922
Ht: 5ft-10ins, **Wt:** 11st-6lbs
Swans debut: v. Southampton (a), 14/1/1950

Career:
Merthyr Tydfil
Swansea Town (£5,000 signed in 10/11/1949)
Merthyr Tydfil (signed in July 1958)
Hereford United (signed in close season 1959) Sth Lge 19, Cup 4
Brecon Corinthians (signed in September 1960)

Honours: Welsh Cup Winner–1949, 1950, Southern League Champions–1948, Southern League Cup Winner–1948, Southern League Representative XI–1947/48, Football Combination Second Division Champions–1955

Swansea Town Career Statistics			
Season	League	FAC	WC
1949/50	9		3/2gls
1950/51	42		1
1951/52	42	3	1
1952/53	18/1gls		
1953/54	11		
1954/55			1/1gls
1955/56	18/2gls		1
1956/57	5		1
1957/58	12		
Total	157/3gls	3	8/3gls

A member of the Merthyr Tydfil team that won the Southern League Championship in season 1947/48, and when they beat the Swans in the Welsh Cup Final at the end of season 1948/49, Gilbert initially joined the Swans as an inside forward, but was then successfully converted to a left full back, turning out to be a thoughtful defender, who had good ball distribution. He also made representative appearances for the Southern League XI during the 1947/48 season. In April 1949 he scored one of Merthyr's five goals that beat Colchester United in the final of the Southern League Cup, held over from the previous season. Brought up in Wedlecote near Tamworth, Gilbert played for both Wedlecote Central and Tamworth School sides, and after leaving school took an apprenticeship as a sheet metal worker in the Singer car factory in Birmingham, later working in the Rover car plant. Playing for his works football teams he had trials with both Coventry City and Walsall before a bad injury saw him sidelined for a spell, with his family later moving to live in Merthyr Tydfil. His potential was spotted by Merthyr manager Albert Lindon, and prior to his signing for the Swans, West Ham United and West Bromwich Albion had both been interested in signing him. His first season at the Vetch Field saw him line up with his brother in the Welsh Cup Final success over Wrexham in April 1950. He scored his first goal for the Swans during a 2-1 home defeat by Southampton in October 1952, and during season 1954/55 made regular appearances in the reserve side that won the Football Combination Second Division Championship. The older brother of Cyril Beech, the long-serving left-back contested a first-team slot with Dai Thomas, prior to re-joining Merthyr Tydfil in July 1958. In February 1958 it was thought he would go to Newport County as part of the transfer involving Pat Terry to the Vetch Field. But at the time Gilbert had a grocery business in Mount Pleasant, Swansea and was undecided about the move to County. He was subsequently reunited with his brother at Southern League rivals Hereford United prior to the start of the 1959/60 season, having the unenviable task of trying to follow his manager, former Arsenal captain Joe Wade in Hereford's left back position. He also led the Hereford United forward line in one cup tie at Headington, but after just one season at Edgar Street was released by United, and in September 1960 linked up with his brother Cyril at

Brecon Corinthians, remaining at the club until March 1961. After leaving the Vetch Field Gilbert continued with his grocery business in Swansea up to his retirement, and for a period was also involved with scouting duties for Luton Town.

15. BEER, ALAN Desmond

Birthplace: Swansea, 11/3/1950
Ht: 5ft-7ins, **Wt**: 10st-7lbs
Swans debut: v. Reading (h), 27/3/1971

Swansea City Career Statistics			
Season	League	FAC	WC
1970/71	4+3/2gls		
1971/72	5+2/1gls	1	1
Total	9+5/3gls	1	1

Career:
West End
Swansea City (signed in February 1971)
Weymouth (signed in August 1972)
Exeter City (£8,000 signed in November 1974) lge 114/52gls

Honours: Wales Amateur–4, Southern League Cup Winner–1973

Alan started training with the Swans at the age of 18 after earlier playing in the Swansea Senior League with Tower United, United (Superheaters), and West End. Predominantly a left winger, he signed for the Swans as a part-time professional while he continued his craft apprenticeship, gaining Amateur Honours for Wales against Holland (twice), Scotland and Ireland in a competition on the Continent, and signing full time professional forms on completion of his apprenticeship. A very useful player to have around in the penalty box, with his eye for half chances, he played in a high scoring Swans Football Combination reserve side coached by Roy Saunders that regularly attracted four figure attendances to the Vetch Field. Just prior to his 21st birthday, he signed professional forms with the Swans, and was given his first team debut by manager Roy Bentley later in the season against Reading as substitute for Clive Slattery. After two further appearances from the substitute bench, Alan made his first start at the Vetch Field against Bristol Rovers, scoring the Swans goal in a 3-1 defeat. Used mainly on the left wing, Alan possessed an electric turn of speed, coupled with explosive shooting ability when cutting in from the flanks. After showing a lot of promise during his early games in the Swans Football League side, he suffered a number of ankle problems which limited his first team opportunities, and at the end of his first full season as a professional, along with a number of other young professionals, because of financial restraints was given a free transfer. Alan joined Southern League Premier Division side Weymouth prior to the start of the

1972/73 season, and at the end of his first season with the club, he topped the club's goalscoring charts with thirty-six goals, with Weymouth winning the Southern League Cup competition, beating Hillingdon in the Final. After scoring over 20 goals during his second season, an £8,000 transfer fee saw him return to the Football League to sign for Exeter City in November 1974. Scoring the equalizing goal on his debut against Rochdale, Alan scored nine goals from twenty-seven league games during his first season back in professional football, and over the next two seasons was top goalscorer for the Devon club in each season, scoring twenty goals, and twenty-one goals respectively, and also finishing in 1977 as runners up in the Fourth Division. Despite starting season 1977/78 brightly with two goals from three league games, tragedy struck Alan when he twisted his knee playing against Shrewsbury Town. In what was to be his last game for the 'Grecians' as the club had agreed an £80,000 transfer to Leicester City after the game, despite treatment, he had to retire from the professional game, with his contract as a player being terminated in September 1978. He continued his association at St. James' Park by becoming first team coach to manager Brian Godfrey, and after a successful three year coaching spell at St. James Park, including the 1980/81 season when the Grecians lost narrowly to Spurs in the FA Cup quarter final, he returned to Swansea. Apart from a brief spell as assistant to former Swans team mate Wyndham Evans at Pembroke Borough in 1985, Alan's work commitments with Bassetts Honda Group in the Enterprise Zone in Swansea prevented him from coaching on a regular basis, and his only involvement in football has seen him watching his young son play for the West End junior sides.

16. BEKKER, JAN Franciscus

Birthplace: Cardiff, 24/12/1951
Ht: 5ft-6ins **Wt**: 10st-6lbs
Swans debut: v. Chester (a), 22/2/1975

Swansea City Career Statistics			
Season	League	FLC	FAC
1974/75	12+1/3gls		
1975/76	4+3/1gls	2/1gls	1
Total	16+4/4gls	2/1gls	1

Career:
Cardiff Corries
Everwarm (Bridgend Town)
Swansea City (signed in February 1975)
Everwarm (Bridgend Town) (signed in August 1976)
Tondu Robins

Honours: Wales Amateur, Welsh League Premier Division Champions–1973, West Wales Senior Cup Winner–1975

The son of a former Dutch airforce mechanic who came to Britain after the occupation, Jan was born in Cardiff, and made his mark in school football, playing for Llanishen High School as a winger, then moved to play for Roath Rangers in the Cardiff Combination. He then played for a number of sides, always as a striker and scoring consistently. Joining Welsh League side Cardiff Corries at the age of 19, his goalscoring brought him to that attention of Bridgend Town (Everwarm), and after signing for Bridgend Town, his first season with the club saw them win the Welsh League Premier Division Title, with Jan scoring thirty-one goals. During his first spell with Bridgend Town Jan made an appearance for the Wales Amateur side against England. However, a dispute with the club towards the end of the season saw Jan join Southern League First Division North side, Barry Town. Struggling to come to terms with the travelling involved with Southern League football, Jan continued to score goals on a regular basis, and after settling his differences with Bridgend Town, rejoined the club. Just over twelve months later, Swans manager Harry Griffiths approached him with a view to sign for the Swans. At the time it was not an easy decision for Jan to leave his job as a motor mechanic, but after signing on an initial amateur basis, after a bright start, signed for the Swans as a full time professional. Part of the arrangement for Jan to sign for the Swans was that the Swans played at Bridgend in a friendly, so that the club would benefit from the deal financially. Making his league debut at Chester in February 1975, his first goal was scored three games later against Lincoln City at the Vetch Field, and by the end of his first season in the professional game had scored a further two goals. In May 1975 he was included in the Swans side that beat Briton Ferry Athletic to win the West Wales Senior Cup. His first full season with the Swans saw Jan compete with new signing Geoff Bray for one of the striker positions, and despite starting the season from the substitute bench, struggled to make an impact, especially when a muscle tear kept him sidelined for a number of weeks, and would eventually prevent him from continuing as a professional footballer. He returned to Bridgend Town after his release from the Vetch Field, later having a successful time with Welsh League side Tondu Robins as player manager, and then as manager of Garw Athletic, taking both sides to promotion. Since leaving the professional game Jan has been employed in European Traffic Management for a company in Bridgend.

17. BELL, GORDON

Birthplace: Sunderland, 9/1/1906. **Died**: Sunderland, AMJ, 1979
Ht: 5ft-8ins, **Wt**: 10st-8lbs
Swans debut: v. Barnsley (a), 1/9/1930

Swansea Town Career Statistics		
Season	League	FAC
1930/31	19/6gls	1
Total	19/6gls	1

Career:
Newcastle United Swifts
Chilton Colliery
Sunderland (signed in June 1922)
Darlington (signed in June 1922)
Durham City (signed in September 1925)
Carlisle United (signed in August 1927)
Leeds United (signed in June 1928) lge 0
Wrexham (signed in 21/11/1929) lge 24/7gls
Swansea Town (£100 signed in 23/6/1930)
Carlisle United (signed in April 1931) lge 1
Consett (signed in January 1934)

Honours: England Sch–4

Showed plenty of promise as a Sunderland Schoolboy, representing England on four occasions in 1920, including one game against Wales at Mid-Rhondda in April 1920, and on leaving school joined Newcastle United, playing for their junior side, the Swifts. After failing to make an appearance at Newcastle, he returned home to play for Chilton Colliery. Following an unproductive time with Sunderland, he joined Third Division side Darlington, then signed for Carlisle United, helping the side to gain election to the Football League. Just prior to Carlisle United's first league game he joined Leeds United, and after just one season at Elland Road signed for Wrexham. He made a good impression at the Racecourse from the outside left position, providing a lot of the ammunition for top goalscorer Tommy Bamford, before he was surprisingly involved in a transfer to the Swans. Signed for the Swans for a fee of £100 on the 23rd June 1930 from Wrexham, he missed the first game of the season, but from then on he secured a regular place on the left wing, until midway through the season when he lost his place to new signing DJ (Jinky) Lewis, despite operating on a number of occasions on the right flank. He was released on a free transfer, returning north to rejoin Carlisle United in April 1931. Earlier in his career he had played for Carlisle United prior to the club gaining their league status, and on his return he made just one league appearance before signing for non-league side Consett.

18. BELLAMY, Herbert (BERT)

Birthplace: Kettering, 7/4/1896. **Died:** Grimsby, 16/11/1978
Ht: 5ft-10½ins, **Wt:** 11st-9lbs
Swans debut: v. Luton Town (h), 25/8/1923

Swansea Town Career Statistics			
Season	League	FAC	WC
1923/24	36/1gls	4	
1924/25	42/1gls	2	2
1925/26	12		1
Total	90/2gls	6	3

Career:
Kettering White Cross
Army Football
Kettering Town (signed in 1919)
Watford (signed in May 1921) lge 36/2gls
Swansea Town (signed in 16/6/1923)
Brentford (signed in April 1926) lge 33, FAC 6
Wellingborough (signed as player manager in June 1927)

Former Kettering and Watford half back who was on the Swans books until he signed for Brentford in 20/4/1926. Started the 1923/24 season as the Swans right half back, played a couple of matches at left half, becoming a regular throughout the season. His only goal for the Swans during his first season was against Brentford in a 2-2 draw in April 1924. He remained an automatic choice during his second season at the Vetch Field, scoring just the one more goal for the Swans against Millwall at the Vetch Field in February 1925, again in a 2-2 draw game. Despite starting the 1925/26 season he missed quite a lot of games through the season, returning to the first team in mid-April, and missed out at the end of the season Welsh Cup Final against Ebbw Vale, despite playing in the fifth round against Wrexham. He was allowed to sign for Third Division South team Brentford in April 1926. When Brentford's F.A. Cup tie at Oldham was abandoned, the party booked into a hotel to await the re-arranged game the following Monday. With the hotel bar being placed 'out of bounds', Bellamy was caught having a drink, and was dropped for the game the next day. Initially with Kettering White Cross before the First World War, he developed his game

in Army football, signing for Kettering after being demobbed. After playing his last league game with Brentford he joined non-league side Wellingborough as player manager in June 1927, before returning to a player role with the United Counties Bus Company, Irthlingborough as a permit player in February 1928, and finally with Kidderminster Harriers in August 1928. By 1934 he had spent a number of years coaching in Finland with Helsingfors, and in 1936 was involved with coaching and training a second class team in the Hague, along with a number of ex-professionals from the English game who after retiring had progressed to coaching in Holland.

19. BELLIS, Alfred (ALF)

Birthplace: Ellesmere Port, 8/10/1920
Ht: 5ft-6ins, **Wt:** 9st-0lbs
Swans debut: v. Luton Town (a), 18/8/1951

Swansea Town Career Statistics			
Season	League	FAC	WC
1951/52	37/11gls	3/1gls	
1952/53	4		1
Total	41/11gls	3/1gls	1

Career:
Shell Juniors
Burnells Iron Works
Port Vale (signed in March 1938) lge 84/18gls, FAC 14/3gls
Bury (signed in January 1948) lge 95/18gls
Swansea Town (signed in August 1951)
Chesterfield (£550 signed in August 1953) lge 13/3gls
Rhyl Athletic (signed in close season 1954)

Graduated to the Football League with Port Vale from non-league sides Shell Juniors and Burnells Iron Works before the Second World War, also playing for Vale after the war, before transferring to Second Division side Bury in an exchange deal involving Walter Keeley. During the war years he made guest appearances for Rochdale (1940/41), Manchester United (1940/41), Manchester City (1942/43), Lincoln City (1943/44), Notts County (1944/45), and Ellesmere Port Town, and was top goalscorer for Vale during season 1944/45. He made sixty war-time appearances, scoring twenty-five goals for Vale. Making his Football League debut with Third Division South side Port Vale, following a transfer to Second Division side Bury in January 1948, he scored on his debut in a 4-1 win over Rochdale, made regular appearances for the club, and scored against the Swans at the Vetch Field in a 1-1 draw in April 1951, a couple of months before he joined the Swans. A busy winger, hard working, with an eye for goal, he started his first season at the Vetch Field at outside left, and was practically an automatic inclusion apart from the last four league matches, during a season which saw the winger finish joint runner up in the goalscoring charts with eleven league goals. After missing the start of his second season at the Vetch Field, he struggled throughout to make an impression, losing his place on the left flank to Cyril Beech. In August 1953 he was sold to Third Division North side Chesterfield for £550, in 2 instalments of £275 each. Joining Rhyl Athletic in the 1954 close season, he later made non-league appearances for North Wales sides Colwyn Bay and Penmaenmawr.

20. BELLOTTI, DEREK Christopher

Birthplace: East Ham, 25/12/1946
Ht: 6ft-1ins, **Wt:** 13st-0lbs
Swans debut: v. Darlington (a), 17/8/1974

Swansea City Career Statistics

Season	League	FLC	FAC
1974/75	19	1	2
Total	19	1	2

Career:
QPR (from apprentice in 1963)
Bedford Town (signed in August 1964)
Gillingham (signed in July 1966) lge 35
Southend United (loan in October 1970) lge 3
Charlton Athletic (£5,000 signed in October 1970) lge 14
Fulham (loan in October 1971)
Southend United (signed in December 1971) lge 74
Swansea City (£3,000 signed in May 1974)
Maidstone United (signed in July 1975)

Goalkeeper who started his career as an apprentice professional with Queens Park Rangers, and after being released signed for non-league side Bedford Town. He returned to the league with Gillingham in July 1966, and contested the number one jersey at the Priestfield Stadium with the experienced John Simpson. Earlier in his career he had played for his school in Walthamstow, making appearances for the County and London schoolboys sides. Derek played against the Swans in a 1-1 home draw in September 1966, but did not make the return trip to the Vetch Field. Following a loan spell at Southend United in early October 1970, by the end of the same month he had joined Second Division Charlton Athletic on a permanent basis. Fourteen months later however he had returned to Roots Hall to join Southend United on a permanent basis, after struggling to command a place in the Charlton Athletic starting line-up. His first full season with United saw the club finish runners up to Grimsby Town in 1972 and gain promotion. He was signed by Swans manager Harry Gregg during the club's second season in

Division Four, and was first choice goalkeeper from the start of the season following the release of experienced keeper Tony Millington in the summer of 1974. In what turned out to be a season of struggle, and with Gregg resigning midway through the term, Bellotti gave way to a young Steve Potter, on loan from Manchester City, as the club failed in their struggle to move away from the bottom four places of the league. He was released at the end of the season by the Swans, joining non-league side Maidstone United, had a short period with Margate before moving to the West Country as a sales representative in the print industry. He has since started his own business, Kingfisher Print & Design in Dartington, Devon, where he continued to play part-time with St. Blazey, Torquay United (September 1981), Falmouth Town (1982), Bideford Town (1983), Newquay, Torrington (1988), and Ilfracombe Town (November 1977). Over the years his company have printed matchday programmes for Exeter City and Torquay United. His son Ross, also followed him as a professional goalkeeper, and after making his debut for Exeter City became the club's youngest keeper at the time of his debut.

21. BENNETT, EDWARD Thomas

Birthplace: Barton Regis, Bristol, 10/8/1904
Ht: 5ft-8ins, **Wt:** 11st-10lbs
Swans debut: v. Watford (h), 24/3/1923

Swansea Town Career Statistics

Season	League	WC
1922/23	7	1
1923/24	1	
1924/25	3	2
Total	11	3

Career:
Bristol City
Swansea Town (signed in 30/3/1923)
Wrexham (signed in 6/5/1925) lge 37, FAC 1,WC 3
Manchester City (signed in 4/5/1926) lge 19
Norwich City (signed in 10/5/1931) lge 11

Honours: Division Two Champions–1928, West Wales Senior Cup Winner–1923, 1925

Spotted by Bristol City in local football, he failed to make any league appearances for the 'Robins', and was signed by Swans manager Joe Bradshaw in March 1923. He was primarily utilised as a reserve full back, covering for either Morley, or Milne in either full back position. He enjoyed his most productive time in the Swans first team shortly after arriving at the Vetch Field, missing just two league games from the last nine of the season. With further competition from Langford, his next two seasons at the Vetch Field saw the defender make just a handful of league appearances, but after signing for Wrexham in May 1925, he had his most successful period in the game, where he became a regular in either full back position at the Racecourse, also gaining a runners up medal in the North Wales Coast FA Challenge Cup Final in 1926. In November 1923 he was included in the Swans reserve side that beat Pembroke Dock to win the West Wales Senior Cup Final, and also in January 1925 when they beat Llanelly in the same final. At the end of his first season with Wrexham, his form must have impressed the scouts watching him, as he signed for Second Division Manchester City in May1926. Making his debut for City at Port Vale in October 1926, he had a run of 12 games in the first team before returning to the reserve side. Season 1927/28 saw him make five appearances in the City side that won the Second Division Championship. Making just two appearances in City's First

Division line-up, and becoming a little disenchanted with his lack of opportunities, he signed for Third Division South side Norwich City. In two seasons at Carrow Road he made just eleven league appearances, and returned to Bristol where he became a licensee, and then worked for the local council.

22. BERESFORD, DAVID

Birthplace: Middleton, 11/11/1976
Ht: 5ft-5ins, **Wt:** 11st-4lbs
Swans debut: v. Shrewsbury Town (h), 12/8/1995

Swansea City Career Statistics	
Season	League
1995/96	4+2
Total	4+2

Career:
Oldham Athletic (associate schoolboy in January 1991, from
   trainee in 22/7/1994) P/lge 32+32/2gls, FLC 3+3, FAC 0+1,
   Others 3
Swansea City (loan in 11/8/1995)
Huddersfield Town (£350,000 on 27/3/1997) lge 24+11/3gls,
   FLC 2+3, FAC 1+1
Preston North End (loan in 17/12/1999) lge 1+3, FAC 0+1,
   Others 1
Port Vale (loan in 15/9/2000) lge 4
Hull City (signed in 4/7/2001) lge 33+8/1gls, FLC 2, FAC 1,
   Others 3
Plymouth Argyle (signed in 23/7/2002) lge 6+10, Others 2
Macclesfield Town (loan in 2/10/2003) lge 5, Others 0+1
Tranmere Rovers (signed in 4/11/2003) lge 21+24/4gls,
   FLC 1+1, FAC 6, Others 0+2

Honours: England Sch, Yth

Signed by manager Frank Burrows on a loan transfer shortly before the start of the 1995/96 season, he made his debut as a substitute for Jonathan Coates against Shrewsbury Town at the Vetch Field in the opening match of the 1995/96 season. Signed associate schoolboy with Oldham Athletic from Bluecoat School, going on to become a trainee at Boundary Park, gaining honours at youth level for England to add to his schoolboy honours. An extremely quick, tricky, right sided midfielder, Burrows had been looking for a player to deliver pace and quality crosses from the flanks. He had his best spell with Athletic during season 1996/97, making 33 league appearances, before being transferred to Huddersfield Town in March 1997 for a fee of £300,000, plus midfielder Paul Reid joining Oldham Athletic, and by the end of the season Oldham were relegated to Division Two, with Huddersfield Town managing to stay in Division

One. During season 1998/99 with Huddersfield Town, he was impressive during the club's exciting FA Cup run, which saw them reach the 5th round, but in later seasons injury problems prevented him from progressing, even during a loan spell at Preston North End in December 1999. Possessing plenty of tricks on the ball, following another loan spell, this time with Port Vale shortly after the start of the 1999/2000 season, after returning to Huddersfield, he was given a free transfer, signing for Hull City in July 2001, where he enjoyed his most injury free season for a long time, missing just four league games through the season. Twelve months later he signed for Plymouth Argyle, but he found his opportunities mainly restricted to the substitute bench. After a loan spell with Third Division Macclesfield Town in October 2003, he was re-united with manager Brian Little at Tranmere Rovers a month later, and was a non-playing substitute for Rovers when they beat the Swans in the 5th Round of the FA Cup competition, also starting in the 6th Round replay defeat by Millwall. Scored in the League One Play Off semi-final defeat by Hartlepool United in May 2005.

23. BERESFORD, Joseph (JOE)

Birthplace: Chesterfield, 26/2/1906. **Died:** Birmingham,
   22/2/1978
Ht: 5ft-5ins, **Wt:** 11st-2 lbs
Swans debut: v. Southampton (a), 25/12/1937

Swansea Town Career Statistics			
Season	League	FAC	WC
1937/38	13/1gls	1	3/2gls
Total	13/1gls	1	3/2gls

Career:
Mexborough
Mansfield Town (signed in May 1926)
Aston Villa (£750 signed in May 1927) lge 224/66gls
Preston North End (signed in September 1935) lge 76/10gls
Swansea Town (signed in 21/12/1937)
Stourbridge (signed in May 1938)

Honours: England Full–1, English League Rep XI–1, Midland League Championship–1926, Welsh League XI

Prior to signing for Mansfield Town in their pre-Football League days from non-league side Mexborough Athletic, Joe had earlier played for Bentley Toll Bar School, Askeln Road Workingmens Club and Bentley Colliery. Failing to make an appearance for the 'Stags', Joe did however in the one season at Field Mill be a member of the club's reserve sides that was a Midland Combination Cup Winner, Notts. F.A. Senior Cup Winner, Notts. Benevolent Bowl Winner, and a Mansfield Hospital Charity Cup

Winner in 1927. The season previous to joining Mansfield he won the Midland League Championship with Mexborough. A short, stocky, tenacious inside forward, he became a hero at Villa Park with the supporters who appreciated his wholehearted approach, and high workrate. Making his Villa debut against Liverpool at Anfield, two days later he scored three goals in his first home game, with Villa beating Portsmouth 7-2. During his period at Villa Park, the club were runners up in the First Division on two occasions, in 1931, and in 1933. In 1931 he played for an English League Representative side against the Irish League, and on the 16th May 1934 made his only appearance for the Full England side, in Prague, in a 2-1 defeat by Czechoslovakia. Joining Preston North End in 1935, he appeared in the FA Cup Final defeat by Sunderland in 1937, and in December 1937, along with Joseph Vernon, and with George Lowrie moving in the opposite direction, he signed for the Swans. Already a seasoned campaigner with Aston Villa and Preston North End before he arrived at the Vetch Field, he remained on the Swans books until the end of the season, when he was released, joining non-league side Stourbridge Swifts. After making his debut for the Swans at Southampton, he played in the next eleven league games, mainly at inside right, but managed just one more game before the end of the season. His only league goal for the Swans came in a 1-1 draw at the Vetch Field against Sheffield Wednesday in January 1938. On the 23rd April 1938 he played for the Welsh League XI in Brussels against Diables Rouges along with team mates John and Harris. At the end of the season he played in the Welsh Cup Final drawn game with Shrewsbury Town. After returning to the Midlands to play for Stourbridge Swifts, he linked up with former Villa team mates Sam Bowen and Alec Talbot in the Birmingham and District League, and opened a fish and chip shop in Kingstanding, Birmingham up to the time of his death in 1978. During the Second World War, in season 1943/44 he made guest appearances for Hartlepool.

24. BEVAN, PAUL Philip

Birthplace: Shrewsbury, 20/10/1952
Ht: 5ft-11ins, **Wt:** 10st-9lbs
Swans debut: v. Chester (h), 25/8/1973

Swansea City Career Statistics				
Season	League	FLC	FAC	WC
1973/74	39+2/3gls	2	1	1
1974/75	38+1/2gls	1	2	3
Total	77+3/5gls	3	3	4

Career:
Shrewsbury Town (from apprentice in October 1970) lge 66+5/1gls
Swansea City (£5,000 signed in 21/8/1973)
Crewe Alexandra (signed in July 1975) lge 170+2/7gls

Worcester City (loan in March 1980)
Worcester City (signed in September 1980)
Newtown

Signed by Swans manager Harry Gregg for £5,000 prior to the start of the 1973/74 season, after previously playing under Gregg when he was manager of Shrewsbury Town. A workmanlike figure in midfield, he was a regular inclusion under Gregg for the two seasons he spent at the Vetch Field, and, after Gregg had left the Vetch Field in January 1975 to join Crewe Alexandra, he teamed up with him for a third time. The season prior to signing for the Swans, Bevan had missed just four league games for the 'Shrews' in the Third Division, making his Football League debut at Halifax Town as substitute for Roberts on the 3rd October 1970. Besides being a workmanlike figure in midfield, he was also a more than capable defender, occupying the right full back position on a number of occasions during his playing career, and arrived at the Vetch Field with the Swans facing up to life back in the Fourth Division. His second season with the Swans was probably, at the time, the lowest in the club's history, with the club finishing the season third from the bottom of the league, and having to apply for re-election to the Football League in the close season. Not a regular on the goalscoring charts, one goal he scored that does stand out for him during his time with the Swans was against Workington, when he drove home from outside the penalty area to score the only goal of the game. Born in Shrewsbury, Paul attended Coleham Infants and Meole Brace Schools, played for Shrewsbury and Shropshire Schoolboys prior to joining his hometown side as an apprentice, and in 1967 had a week's trial at Stoke City. He remained in the Football League with Crewe Alexandra until March 1980, making almost two hundred league and cup appearances. During his last two seasons at Gresty Road, the club survived two re-election campaigns to the Football League, finishing each season in the bottom two positions. Joining non-league Worcester City on loan in March 1980, after being recalled to Gresty Road in May 1980, he had his contract cancelled, rejoining Worcester on a permanent basis in September 1980. Making fifty-six appearances for City, he sustained a broken leg in January 1981, had a season and a half with Mid-Wales side Newtown before finishing his playing career in the Shrewsbury Sunday League. Since leaving the full time game Paul has worked in a Creamery in Minsterley, outside Shrewsbury.

25. BEYNON, BEN

Birthplace: Swansea, 14/3/1894. **Died:** Swansea, 21/5/1969
Ht: 5ft-8ins, **Wt:** 11st-7lbs
Swans debut: v. Pontypridd (h), 28/11/1914, Sth. Lge

Career:
Swansea Town (trial by 23/10/1914, signed by 28/11/1914)
Swansea Rugby Club (returned to Rugby after the war in 1918)

Swansea Town (signed in 11/2/1919 from Swansea RFC)
Oldham Rugby League Club (signed in 10/5/1922)
Swansea Town (signed part-time in 9/8/1926)
Mid-Rhondda (signed in May 1927)

Swansea Town Career Statistics		
Season	*League*	*FAC*
1920/21	12/9gls	1
1921/22	13/2gls	
Total	25/11gls	1

Honours: Wales Rugby International

The former steel worker originally signed for the Swans during their Southern League days, impressed during a Welsh League game against Mardy on the 23rd October 1914 when he scored two goals, and made his Southern League debut at the Vetch Field against Pontypridd on the 28th November 1914, signing as an amateur (at this time rugby games were cancelled because of the war). Previously he had played football for Waun Wen, captained their side, but in 1912 switched to playing rugby for Manselton. The slick-moving, two-footed half-back caught the attention of the All Whites who were desperately searching for an outside-half, and from Manselton he stepped into the Swansea Athletic XV, played three games for them before – at the age of 19 – he was thrown into the deep end against Newport, who came to St Helen's with an unbeaten record, with nine internationals in their side. In what was a brilliant debut, Beynon scoring the first try, as Swansea went on to pull off a sensational 17-3 win. A few months later he joined the Swans as the only amateur on the staff. In January 1915, with the Swans playing in the Second Division of the Southern League they were drawn to play the mighty Blackburn Rovers of the First Division, and Football League Champions the previous season. Beynon the only amateur on the field, scored the only goal of the game. When rugby was resumed after the war, he rejoined Swansea Rugby Club, played as an outside half, gaining international honours for Wales against England and Scotland. Taking up the Swans' offer of £6 a week and allowing him to keep his job as a tin-plate worker, he unfortunately signed too soon, as it cost him his Welsh rugby cap as well as his Swansea cap and blazer. He scored a hat-trick in the opening Welsh League game on the Thursday and scored another two in a 3-1 win over QPR the following Saturday. A knee injury ruined his chances of playing for Wales – he was picked for a Welsh trial at Wrexham – and at one time threatened to end his career altogether. He had rejoined the Swans on the 11th February 1919, playing 15 games for the Swans in the Southern League First Division, remaining on the Swans books for the club's first two seasons in the Football League. He missed out on the first couple of Football League matches the Swans played, but during his Football League debut at the Vetch Field against Norwich City, scored a hat-trick in a 5-2 win for the Swans. That initial season in the Football League saw Beynon finish as runners up in the goalscoring charts with nine league goals. In October 1920, along with Robson and Ogley, he was suspended for a month for an alleged serious breach of training discipline. Featuring in just thirteen league games the following season, he was released by the Swans, and after taking up the offer of a trial with Oldham Rugby League Club, scored a try and was signed for £325. His knee held out and he played for Oldham for four years, scoring two tries in their 1925 Cup Final win over Hull Kingston Rovers at Leeds. After returning to Wales, rejoined the Swans in August 1926 and played one more season at the Vetch as a part-timer, also working as a Tin Worker. Twelve months later he joined Welsh League side Mid-Rhondda, later played for a local works team for a further six years until he was 39, but in later years he admitted that rugby, not football was his first love.

26. BIGGS, Alfred (ALFIE) George

Birthplace: Bristol, 8/2/1936
Ht: 6ft-0ins **Wt:** 11st-8lbs
Swans debut: v. Doncaster Rovers (a), 6/11/1968

Swansea Town Career Statistics			
Season	*League*	*FAC*	*WC*
1968/69	16/4gls	4/1gls	3+1
Total	16/4gls	4/1gls	3+1

Career:
Bristol Rovers (signed from juniors in February 1953)
   lge 214/77gls
Preston North End (£18,000 signed in 17/7/1961) lge 49/22gls
Bristol Rovers (£12,000 signed in 5/10/1962) lge 210/101gls
Walsall (£10,000 signed in 16/3/1968) lge 23+1/9gls
Swansea Town (signed in 31/10/1968)
Taunton Town (signed in July 1969)

Experienced, old fashioned style centre forward who was signed by Swans manager Billy Lucas in a part exchange deal, which saw Swans midfielder Jimmy McMorran going to Walsall, with Biggs arriving at the Vetch Field, plus a cash adjustment to Walsall. Difficult to knock off the ball, and strong in aerial challenges, he had earlier made a name for himself with hometown club Bristol Rovers, scoring 178 goals from 424 league appearances, in two separate spells at Eastville. A former Connaught Road School, Bristol Boys and Eagle House Youth club player who originally signed for Rovers as a junior in 1952, signing professional in February 1953, he made his league debut on the 6th February 1954 against Lincoln City. Early in his career he was in the Royal Army Ordnance and represented Southern Command against Weymouth in April 1955, returning to play for Rovers on weekdays whilst stationed in Wiltshire. During this period, the Swans regularly played Rovers in the Second Division, with Biggs regularly appearing on the goalsheet for Rovers. Transferred to Preston North End for £18,000 in July 1961, he averaged almost a goal every two games, topped the club's goalscoring charts, before returning to Eastville for a record transfer fee of £15,000, and to a Rovers side that was now in the Third Division. During the 1963/64 season he created another club record when scoring 37 goals in league and cup matches for the Rovers. An extremely popular player with the Rovers supporters, well built, extremely effective in and around the penalty box, he had returned to Rovers in October 1962 in an attempt to help his former club win back its Second Division status. However, after failing to get Rovers back into the Second Division, despite him scoring over 100 league goals, in March 1968 he joined Walsall. His stay at Fellows Park with the 'Saddlers' however lasted just a couple of months, with Swans manager Billy Lucas adding his experience to the Swans forward line. Alfie had to wait until his fourth league game for the Swans before registering his first league goal, in a 1-0 home win over Exeter City. During the season his experience in the Swans forward line saw the club reach the third round of the FA Cup, and although he only played up to the quarter final stage, the Swans eventually reached the final of the Welsh Cup, before losing out to Cardiff City. He left the Vetch Field in July 1969 to join his former Rovers team mate Doug Hillard at Taunton Town, and has since worked as a car salesman, postman, baker and a business parcel delivery service, besides working on the maintenance staff at Eastville. In 2004 he moved to live in Devon.

27. BIRD, Francis JOHN

Birthplace: Cardiff, 21/11/1940
Ht: 5ft-8½ins, **Wt**: 11st-8½lbs
Swans debut: v. Brentford (h), 5/9/1967

Swansea Town Career Statistics		
Season	League	FAC
1967/68	8	1
Total	8	1

Career:
Newport County (from juniors in November 1957) lge 276/3gls
Swansea Town (signed in 19/7/1967)
Hereford United (signed in close season 1968)
  Total Apps 185/21gls
Merthyr Tydfil (signed in 1971)

Honours: Wales Sch

Experienced left sided full back who had made almost 300 appearances for Newport County in the Fourth Division prior to joining the Swans prior to the start of the 1967/68 season. Brought up in the Splott area of Cardiff, he attended Greenway Juniors and Caer Castell Schools prior to joining the groundstaff at Somerton Park with Newport County. Representing Wales at U-11, 13, 14 and 15 age groups, within two months of joining the County groundstaff he became the youngest player to make his league debut for County when he was selected to play against Northampton Town. During his period with County he was also selected as a reserve for the Wales U-23 side against Scotland. Brought to the Vetch Field by his former manager at County, Billy Lucas, he unfortunately found himself in competition with Vic Gomersall for the left full back position, with his first team outings limited. He was released in May 1968 after just one season at the Vetch Field, linking up with John Charles at Hereford United along with Roy Evans and Brian Purcell. A popular and efficient full back at Edgar Street, making almost two hundred appearances, most of his goals were scored from the penalty spot for the Bulls, and at the end of the 1970/71 season he joined Merthyr Tydfil. He later played for Welsh

League side Caerau, before finishing his playing career as player manager of Pontyclun. In the summer months, John played Baseball for the St. Albans club in Cardiff for a number of years. The last seven years he has been working for Amey (formerly British Rail) on track laying.

28. BIRD, Anthony (TONY)

Birthplace: Cardiff, 1/9/1974
Ht: 5ft-10ins, **Wt**: 12st-8lbs
Swans debut: v. Brighton (h), 9/8/1997

Swansea City Career Statistics						
Season	League	FLC	FAC	AWS	P/Offs	FAWC
1997/98	35+7/ 14gls	2	1	1		4/2gls
1998/99	8+20/3gls	0+1	1+1	1+1/2gls	1+1/1gls	4+1/2gls
1999/2000	8+8/1gls	3+1/ 1gls		0+1		4+1/5gls
Total	51+35/ 18gls	5+2/ 1gls	2+1	2+2/2gls	1+1/1gls	12+2/9gls

Career:
Cardiff City (from trainee in 4/8/1993) lge 44+3/13gls,
  FLC 8/2gls, FAC 4+1/1gls, Others 12+4/3gls
Barry Town (signed in January 1996)
Swansea City (£40,000 signed in 8/8/1997)
Merthyr Tydfil (loan in 3/12/1999)
Kidderminster Harriers (signed in 14/7/2000) lge 30+21/3gls,
  FLC 3/2gls, FAC 2+1/1gls, Others 2+1/1gls
St. Patricks (signed in August 2002)
Drogheda United (signed in 30/7/2004)

Honours: Wales Yth, U-21–6, Third Division Champions–1993, 2000, League of Wales Champions–1996, 1997, Gilbert League Cup–1996, 1997, Welsh Cup Winner–1997

A former trainee at Ninian Park with Cardiff City who made his league debut as a substitute for Cohen Griffiths at Walsall in August 1992 whilst still a trainee, and by the end of the season had gained a Third Division Championship medal. The following season he gained European experience with the Bluebirds, scoring twice in the away defeat by Belgium side Standard Liege. Despite missing out on the Welsh Cup Final success, the following season he made an appearance as substitute for Gary Thompson in the defeat by Barry Town. Capped at youth level, in October 1993 he made his first appearance at U-21 level for Wales in Cyprus. With the Bluebirds making their third consecutive appearance in a Welsh Cup Final, Tony made his first start in the 2-1 defeat by the North Wales club. Starting the 1995/96 season with Cardiff City, he had his contract cancelled in January 1996, joining League of Wales side Barry Town. By the end of the season he featured in his third consecutive Welsh Cup Final, although Barry lost out on penalties to Llansantffraid. With Barry Town becoming the first League of Wales side to have gone full time professional, over the next couple of seasons the club would sweep the honours board, also compete in Europe with distinction. The next two seasons Barry Town won both the League of Wales Championships, and the Gilbert League Cup in both seasons. The 1996/97 season also saw Barry Town win the Welsh Cup Final against Cwmbran Town, with Bird featuring in his fourth consecutive final, and also become the first League of Wales side to reach the first round of the UEFA Cup Competition, when after beating Dinaburg 2-1 on aggregate in the Preliminary Round, beat BVSC on away goals, before losing to Scottish side Aberdeen. The 1997/98 season saw Bird make appearances for Barry Town against Dynamo Kiev in the Champions League in late July, and after being signed by Swans manager Jan Molby on an initial loan basis, along with team mate Dave O'Gorman, to enable both players to make their debut twenty-four hours later in the opening fixture of the season against Brighton, both transfers were made permanent for a combined fee of £60,000. Opening his goalscoring account in his debut game for the Swans, by the end of the season, Bird finished top goalscorer on his return to League action with fourteen league goals. By the time he had started his second season with the Swans, not only Molby had been sacked, but Micky Adams and his replacement Alan Cork had both left the Vetch Field managerial position, with John Hollins becoming Bird's fourth manager at the Vetch Field in twelve months. Not making the same impact during his second season, he nevertheless helped the Swans reach the Third Division Play Offs at the end of the season, and the following season make sixteen league appearances during the club's Third Division Championship success. Midway through the 1999/2000 season he also made some loan appearances for Merthyr Tydfil, scoring on his debut for the club against Atherstone United. Released by the Swans in May 2000, he was re-united with Jan Molby at newly promoted Kidderminster Harriers, making a substitute appearance in the club's first ever Football League match. Spending two seasons with the Harriers, after his release in May 2002 he went to play in Ireland with St. Patricks. His first season saw Tony play virtually all the season on the left wing, but after a change of management, he was moved to a more central striker role where he finished his second term as top goalscorer for the Saints with fifteen goals, firmly establishing himself as the 'Birdman of Inchicore'. In July 2004 he signed for Eircom Premier League side Drogheda United, and in July 2005 he had offers to join Carmarthen Town and Forest Green Rovers.

29. BLACK, JOHN

Birthplace: Blackburn, 4/11/1945
Ht: 5ft-10ins, **Wt:** 12st-6lbs
Swans debut: v. Cardiff City (a), WC SF, 10/3/1965

Swansea Town Career Statistics			
Season	League	FLC	WC
1964/65	8		1
1965/66	7	1	
Total	15	1	1

Career:
Arsenal (from juniors in February 1963)
Swansea Town (signed in 22/12/1964)
Worcester City (signed in 25/11/1965) Total apps 87
Ammanford Town (signed in June 1967)

Honours: Wales Sch–5, International Youth Tournament Winner–1964, Football Combination Champions–1963, West Wales Senior Cup Winner–1965

After four seasons at Highbury, John Black was given the opportunity to join the Swans, a month after his nineteenth birthday, in December 1964 after failing to break into the 'Gunners' first team. Born in Blackburn, John came to live in Swansea at an early age, living initially in Fforestfach, prior to moving to Gendros, and attending Gendros and Cwmbwrla Junior School, and then Penlan Multilateral. Representing Swansea Schoolboys in football and cricket, John gained five Schoolboy caps for Wales against England (twice), Scotland and Northern Ireland, with his only victory against Southern Ireland. Arriving at Highbury as an apprentice on leaving school, he signed professional on his seventeenth birthday, and in 1963 gained a Football Combination Championship medal. As a youth team player he played for London Youth against Paris Youth, and also gained selection for the England Youth team that won the 1964 International Youth Tournament in Holland, in a squad featuring the likes of John Hollins, John Sissons, Howard Kendall and Harry Redknapp. A couple of months after joining the Swans, he was given his first team debut at Somerton Park against Cardiff City in the semi-final of the Welsh Cup, with his league debut coming a few weeks later against Preston North End at the Vetch Field. Replacing Irishman Ronnie Briggs, he retained his place for the next league game at Newcastle United, and after missing the next league match, was brought back into the side, playing in the last six league games of the season, but was unable to prevent the Swans from relegation to the Third Division. In May 1965 he was included in the Swans side that beat Llanelli in the Wet Wales Senior Cup Final. Despite starting the 1965/66 season as first choice goalkeeper, a poor run of results which saw the Swans win just one out of the first seven league games, and also a home defeat by Aston Villa in the League Cup First Round, saw him lose his place to close season signing George Heyes. A promising young goalkeeper, who lost confidence in a Swans side that had started the new season in the Third Division poorly, and had he played in a side that was more successful, might have had a longer career in the professional game. Joining non-league Worcester City in November 1965 on an initial loan transfer, he signed permanently at the end of the season, playing a further season with City, making a total of eighty-seven appearances. Despite being voted 'Player of the Year', a dispute over his contract saw him join Welsh League side Ammanford Town in the 1967 close season, staying at Rice Road for two seasons before he returned to the London area, joining the Metropolitan Police Force. After a five year period playing divisional football with the Metropolitan Police, John transferred to the police force in Swansea, working in CID until his retirement in 1999, and although not involving himself with football, played cricket for North End in the Central League, and for AWCO in the South Wales & Monmouthshire League. John currently works part-time for a Solicitor in Swansea.

30. BLACK, WILLIAM F.

Birthplace: Linlithgow, 1905
Ht: 5ft-8ins, **Wt**: 11st-0lbs
Swans debut: v. Chelsea (a), 25/8/1928

Swansea Town Career Statistics		
Season	League	WC
1928/29	11/1gls	1
Total	11/1gls	1

Career:
Heart of Midlothian (signed professional in June 1926)
Hamilton Academical (loan in season 1927/28)
Swansea Town (£425 signed in 11/5/1928)
Forfar (signed in close season 1929)
Bo'ness (signed in October 1929)
Greenock Morton (signed in April 1930)
East Stirlingshire (signed in June 1931)
Dundee United (signed in September 1938)

A tricky inside forward who started the 1928/29 season in the inside left position, but lost his place to Ken Gunn. Signed by Swans manager Hunter Thomson, he had a good start to his Swans career, but was told that he was surplus to requirements and left to join Forfar in the 1929 close season. His early career in Scottish football had seen him sign professional with Heart of Midlothian, and make loan appearances for Hamilton Academical during season 1927/28, prior to joining the Swans. After Forfar he made further Scottish appearances for Bo'ness, Greenock Morton, East Stirlingshire, Dundee United, and in January 1942 made War Time appearances for Gateshead.

31. BLACKBURN, DEREK John

Birthplace: Wakefield, 5/7/1931
Ht: 6ft-0ins, **Wt**: 12st-10lbs
Swans debut: v. Hereford United (h), WC–5, 7/2/1957

Swansea Town Career Statistics		
Season	League	WC
1956/57		1
1957/58	2	
Total	2	1

Career:
Burnley (signed in June 1953)
Chesterfield (signed in June 1954)
Ossett Town
Swansea Town (trial in December 1956, £1,500 signed professional in 2/1/1957)
Yeovil Town (signed in 10/7/1958) Total apps 159/15gls

Honours: Southern League Cup Winner–1961

A former semi-professional defender with Burnley and Chesterfield, who failed to make any league appearances prior to arriving at the Vetch Field on an initial trial period, playing for the Combination side at the Vetch Field against Plymouth Argyle on the 15th December 1956. The strongly built, Yorkshire League player from Ossett Town, had been recommended by chief scout Tom Kiley after returning from a scouting trip in the North of England, and been invited to the Vetch Field on a two week trial. Kiley said of him at the time as being a really promising player in the Reg Weston mould. The central defender first came to prominence playing for Yorkshire & District Schoolboys, joining Ossett Town at the age of seventeen, with whom he was a part-time player. His progress in non-league football had alerted a number of clubs, but at the time he was not interested in giving up his job as a miner, preferring to stay as a part-time player, but, after the interest shown by the Swans, decided to take up the club's offer of a trial, and later a professional contract. Making his first team debut for the Swans in a friendly game at the Vetch Field against German First Division side Essen in late January 1957, he made his first class debut in a Welsh Cup, Fifth Round tie at the Vetch Field against Hereford United on the 7th February 1957, but had to wait until the following season to make his debut for the Swans in the Football League, replacing Dudley Peake in the home defeat by Blackburn Rovers. Making just one more league appearance later in the season, the second half of the season, following the signing of Ray Daniel his first team opportunities were limited further, and he was released at the end of the season. Joining Yeovil Town for the 1958/59 season, he played for five seasons at Huish, with season 1960/61 finishing third in the Premier Division of the Southern League, and beating Chelmsford in the replayed final of the Southern League Cup competition. That 1960/61 season saw him play in fifty-two league and cup appearances for Yeovil. The following season when the club finished in fourth place in the league he played forty-nine league and cup appearances. In later years he returned north and took up employment as a catering officer with Barnsley Council.

32. BLAIR, HUGH

Birthplace: Belfast, 21/5/1906
Ht: 5ft-7ins, **Wt**: 10st-7lbs
Swans debut v. West Ham United (h), 27/8/1932

Swansea Town Career Statistics			
Season	League	FAC	WC
1932/33	40/9gls	1	2/1gls
1933/34	14		1
1934/35	8/2gls	2	
Total	62/11gls	3	3/1gls

Career:
Queen's Island (signed in 1927)
Portadown (signed in 20/8/1927)
Nantwich Town
Manchester City (signed in November 1931)
Swansea Town (signed in 3/8/1932)
Millwall (signed in July 1935) 6/1gls

Honours: Northern Ireland Full–3, Irish League XI

Formerly with Ivy Swifts and Ballyclare Comrades prior to signing for Queen's Island in 1927, and later in the same year joining Portadown. He also played Inter League Representative games for the Irish League against Scotland, Wales, and the Free State. At the end of the 1926/27 season he gained an Irish League Runners Up Medal with Queen's Island. He gained his first cap for Northern Ireland with Portadown in 1931 against Scotland, also making a further appearance whilst with Portadown against Scotland in 1932, also capped once after signing for the Swans, against Scotland in 1934. A tricky right winger, tenacious, he provided numerous opportunities for Tudor Martin from the right flank during his first season at the Vetch Field, in a season that saw him miss just two league games. He also scored his share of goals for the Swans, with nine being scored in his first season at the Vetch Field. Despite starting his second season as first choice, he lost his place at outside right following the return of Willie Davies to the Vetch Field, and although he was switched to inside left for the last couple of games in the season, his only appearances during his third season with the Swans came from outside right as a replacement for Davies. In April 1935 he joined Third Division South side Millwall, but by the end of the season had left full time football, later becoming a teacher in Liverpool.

33. BODAK, PETER John

Birthplace: Birmingham, 12/8/1961
Ht: 5ft-8ins, **Wt:** 9st-10lbs
Swans debut v. Leyton Orient (a), 26/3/1988

Swansea City Career Statistics					
Season	*League*	*FAC*	*WC*	*FRT*	*P/Offs*
1987/88	9				3
1988/89	16+6/4gls	0+2	2/2gls	0+1	
Total	25+6/4gls	0+2	2/2gls	0+1	3

Career:
Coventry City (from apprentice in May 1979) lge 30+2/5gls
Manchester United (signed in August 1982)
Manchester City (signed in December 1982) lge 12+2/1gls
Royal Antwerp, Belgium (signed end of season 1982/83)
Seiko, Hong Kong (signed in season 1983/84)
Crewe Alexandra (signed in December 1986) lge 49+4/7gls
Swansea City (signed in 25/3/1988)
Happy Valley (Hong Kong)
Walsall (signed in August 1990) lge 3+1/1gls

Honours: Hong Kong First Division Champions–1984, Senior Cup Winner–1984

Started his playing career as an apprentice at Highfield Road with Coventry City, making his league debut in the First (Premiership) Division against Crystal Palace on the 6th September 1980, in a 3-1 home win. The following game at Wolves, he scored the only goal of the game netting his first goal for the club. He remained a regular inclusion in City's side that season as a pacy right winger, also possessing good crossing ability. After a short spell with Manchester United, he joined Manchester City in December 1982 on a contract until the end of the season, but with the club being relegated along with the Swans to the Second Division, he was released, and in the 1982 close season went to play for Royal Antwerp, Belgium. The 1983/84 season saw him enjoy success in Hong Kong with Seiko, winning the First Division Championship and the Senior and Puma Cup competitions. Returning to the UK, he signed for Crewe Alexandra in December 1986, with his first game for the club as substitute against Preston North End on Boxing Day 1986. By the end of the season he had been a regular inclusion in the Alexandra starting line-up, alongside David Platt, Gary Blissett and Geoff Thomas, scoring seven goals, including his first league hat trick at Molyneux against Wolverhampton Wanderers. He was signed by Swans manager Terry Yorath on the 24th March 1988 as a transfer deadline day replacement for Colin Pascoe who had joined Sunderland on the same day. He featured in the Fourth Division Play Off semi-final games against Rotherham United, and in the first leg against Torquay United in the Final, but not in second leg in Torquay. He netted four goals the following season for the Swans in the Third Division, but missed out in the end of season Welsh Cup Final against Kidderminster Harriers. He was released in May 1989, returning to Hong Kong to sign for Happy Valley, before returning to the Football League to sign non-contract forms with Walsall in August 1990. With the club coming to terms with a new ground, and two successive relegation seasons, he made his debut as substitute for Peter Skipper in the goal less draw against Hereford United on the 22nd September 1990. Ten days later he scored in a 3-0 win over Scunthorpe United, but after a month on the playing staff was released by the club, later playing for non-league side Atherstone United.

34. BOERSMA, Philip (PHIL)

Birthplace: Liverpool, 24/9/1949
Ht: 5ft-10ins, **Wt:** 11st-7lbs
Swans debut v. Rotherham United (h), 12/9/1978

Career:
Liverpool (signed amateur in 1966, professional in 24/9/1966) lge 73+9/17gls

Wrexham (loan in March 1970) lge 4+3
Middlesbrough (£72,000 signed in 4/12/1975) lge 41+6/3gls
Luton Town (£35,000 signed in 5/8/1977) lge 35+1/8gls
Swansea City (£35,000 signed in 9/9/1978)

Swansea City Career Statistics				
Season	*League*	*FLC*	*FAC*	*WC*
1978/79	15+3/1gls	1	1	1+1
Total	15+3/1gls	1	1	1+1

Honours: First Division Champions–1973,
UEFA Cup Winner–1973, Charity Shield Winner–1974

Signed by former Liverpool team mate John Toshack for a record signing of £35,000 on the 9th September 1978 from Luton Town, Phil Boersma's short playing career with the Swans lasted until 14th April 1979 at the County Ground, Swindon, where, after sustaining a compound fracture of the right ankle during a tense promotion tussle with the home side, he was forced to retire from first team football five months short of his 30th birthday. A natural athlete, who possessed a lot of pace, the attacking midfielder's signing for the Swans was yet another addition to the Vetch Field playing staff from Anfield, following the earlier signings of Alan Waddle, Tommy Smith and Ian Callaghan at the start of the 1978/79 season. Previously an amateur at Anfield, signing professional forms after completing his apprenticeship, he made his Liverpool debut at West Bromwich Albion on the 27th September 1969, and made a total of 82 league appearances for Liverpool, winning a Championship medal, and a UEFA Cup Medal during the 1972/73 season, and also playing in the Charity Shield at Wembley the following August. Joining Middlesbrough in December 1975, he was then transferred to Luton Town in August 1977, and after being second top goalscorer with 8 league goals during the 1977/78 season, joined the Swans 13 months later. Following his injury, he was sidelined for most of the 1979/80 season, but was able to make a number of appearances in the club's Welsh League side as his fitness levels improved. By the start of the 1980/81 season however, he had realised that despite taking a full part in pre-season training, and reaching a high standard in his overall fitness levels, he had to make a difficult decision and call it a day as a professional footballer. Given a coaching role at the Vetch Field by John Toshack, following the retirement of Terry Medwin, Phil was appointed assistant manager to Toshack, later taking on the role of physiotherapist at the Vetch Field, replacing Lew Clayton who had returned to Middlesbrough. Following Toshack's resignation at the end of October 1983, by the time the former Liverpool striker had returned to the Vetch Field almost two months later, Boersma, along with Livermore had left the Vetch Field. In July 1985 he joined Lincoln City as assistant to John Pickering, staying until December 1985 when he was sacked along with Pickering, and, at the start of the 1986/87 season he was appointed physiotherapist at Doncaster Rovers under

player manager David Cusack. At approximately the same time as his appointment at Doncaster Rovers, his former team mate at Middlesbrough, Graeme Souness had taken over at Glasgow Rangers in a player manager capacity, and before the end of the season Boersma had also taken the journey north to link up with the club initially as physiotherapist, but then later utilised as a coach. That association North of the Border would see both parties continue to work together all over the world in club football at Liverpool, Galatasaray, Southampton, Benfica, and Blackburn Rovers, where he took over the reserve team manager's role in May 2003. Early September 2004 saw Phil follow Graeme Souness to Newcastle United as a member of his coaching team.

35. BOOTH, LLEWELLYN

Birthplace: Merthyr, 28/2/1912. **Died:** Swansea, July 1984
Swans debut: v. Fulham (a), 1/12/1934

Swansea Town Career Statistics	
Season	*League*
1934/35	1
Total	1

Career:
Merthyr Town
Swansea Town (trial in August 1934, professional in September 1934)
Bangor City (signed in August 1935)
Bristol City (£300 signed in November 1936) lge 65/22gls

Honours: West Wales Senior Cup Winner–1934

Former Merthyr Town inside forward who had an extended trial period at the Vetch Field, playing in the public trial games in August 1934. In October 1934 he was included in the Swans side that beat Llanelly to win the West Wales Senior Cup. A hard working inside forward in the Swans reserve sides, his only first team appearance came in December 1934, replacing Bussey at inside forward. He was released at the end of the season joining North Wales side Bangor City, then returned to the Football League to join Third Division South side Bristol City. Making guest appearances during WW2 for Bristol Rovers during season 1939/40, he retired from playing in close season 1946.

36. BOOTH, Robert (BOBBY)

Birthplace: West Hartlepool, 20/12/1890
Ht: 5ft-9ins, **Wt:** 12st-0lbs
Swans debut: v. Luton Town (h), 25/8/1923

Swansea Town Career Statistics		
Season	*League*	*WC*
1923/24	35/3gls	2
1924/25	1	
Total	36/3gls	2

Career:
Blackpool
Spennymoor United
Blackpool (signed in May 1912) lge 96/5gls
Birmingham (signed in May 1920) lge 8/1gls
Southend United (signed in July 1922) lge 28/1gls

Swansea Town (£175 signed in 27/6/1923)
Merthyr (signed on loan from Swans 6/3/1925) lge 15/1gls
New Brighton (signed in 1925) lge 12/1gls
Skelmersdale United
Peasley Cross Athletic (signed in August 1928)

Left half back, capable of playing anywhere in the half back line, and who had earlier in his career come to prominence as a member of the famous middle line at Blackpool some years earlier, composed of Booth, Wilson and Carney. Wilson later became England's International centre half and captain. After transferring to Birmingham in 1920 he played alongside Roulson, Deacon and Thompson, now at the Vetch Field. The season prior to joining the Swans saw him play in both games for Southend United against the Swans, and his consistent form attracted the attention of manager Bradshaw as early as the close season of 1920, when instead of signing Booth, Bradshaw signed Holdsworth from Preston North End. Booth made his Swans debut in the opening match of the 1923/24 season against Luton Town at the Vetch Field at left half back, playing in every game up until early January 1924. His second season saw him make just the one league start, and in March 1925 joined Merthyr Town on a loan transfer, before making a permanent switch to Third Division North side New Brighton in 1925. Made WW1 appearances for Workington.

37. BOSTON, HENRY James

Birthplace: Nantwich, 20/10/1899. **Died:** Nantwich, 2/6/1973
Ht: 5ft-5½ins, **Wt:** 10st-5lbs
Swans debut: v. Leeds United (h), 29/8/1931

Swansea Town Career Statistics		
Season	League	WC
1931/32	19	2
Total	19	2

Career:
Nantwich Town (signed in December 1922)
Bolton Wanderers (£200 signed in November 1923) lge 39/3gls
WBA (£550 signed in June 1929) lge 27/6gls
Swansea Town (signed in May 1931)
Nantwich Town (signed in 2/8/1933)

Outside Right who played in the first sixteen league games of season 1931/32, but who later made just three more league appearances that season. Earlier in his career he had made his league debut with First Division side Bolton Wanderers, and after signing for West Bromwich Albion in June 1929, made appearances in the club's 1930/31 Division Two promotion campaign when they finished as runners up. An adventurous footballer, he had joined Albion basically as cover for Tommy Glidden, having his best spell towards the end of the 1929/30

season, and the beginning of the following one when Glidden was switched to inside right. He failed to make any appearances during his second season at the Vetch Field, and in early August 1933 returned to non-league side Nantwich Town. Prior to signing for Bolton Wanderers in January 1924 he had joined Nantwich Town from Shavington Town, also playing for Ravensmoor & Wistanton Schools. During his playing career he had a reputation as a well built, fast, and resourceful player, and after his retirement became a tailor's cutter in Nantwich.

38. BOUND, Matthew (MATT) Terence

Birthplace: Melksham, 9/11/1972
Ht: 6ft-2ins, **Wt:** 14st-0lbs
Swans debut v. Chester (a), 26/11/1997

Swansea City Career Statistics						
Season	League	FLC	FAC	AWS	P/Offs	FAWC
1997/98	28			1/1gls		2
1998/99	45/2gls	2	5	2	2/1gls	4
1999/2000	43/2gls	4/1gls	2	2		
2000/01	39+1/3gls	2/1gls	1	0+1		8
2001/02	18/2gls		2	1		
Total	173+1/9gls	8/2gls	10	6+1/1gls	2/1gls	14

Career:
Southampton (from trainee signed in 3/5/1991) PL/lge 2+3
Hull City (loan in 27/8/1993) lge 7/1gls
Stockport County (£100,000 signed in 27/10/1994) lge 44/5gls, FLC 1, FAC 3/1gls, Others 3/1gls
Lincoln City (loan in 11/9/1995) lge 3+1, Others 1
Swansea City (£55,000 signed in 21/11/1997)
Oxford United (initial loan in 21/12/2001) lge 88+4/2gls, FLC 5, FAC 4, Others 2
Weymouth (signed in July 2004) Conf Sth 30+1/2gls, FAT 1+1/1gls, CC 1

Honours: Third Division Champions–2000,
PFA Third Division XI

A £55,000 signing from Stockport County on the 21st November 1997, the strong left sided central defender forged a good partnership with Jason Smith at the heart of the Swans defence, during a time when the Swans reached the Third Division Play Offs, beat Premiership opposition in the FA Cup, and also winning the Third Division Championship in 2000. Rugged, uncompromising central defender, he had made his league debut as substitute for Kevin Moore with Southampton against Oldham Athletic on the 25th April 1992 in the First Division, with the remainder of his league appearances for the 'Saints' coming in the following two seasons in the Premier League.

Following a loan transfer with Hull City at the start of the 1993/94 season, he made the permanent switch to Second Division Stockport County in October 1994 for £100,000. Failing to command a regular place in the County starting line-up, after another loan transfer, this time to Lincoln City in September 1995, he was signed by Swans manager Alan Cork. Used in a three man defence by Cork, Bound immediately added height and strength to the Swans rearguard, and also started to make a name for himself with his strong left footed free kicks from around the penalty area. A change of management at the Vetch Field brought success to the club, and following the Third Division Championship success of 2000, Bound was included in the PFA Third Division team of the season. His form that season had also seen Bound placed on the Welsh squad standby list in September 2000 for the games against Norway and Poland, by virtue of his Welsh grandparentage. Unfortunately the club could not build on that success, and within twelve months had suffered relegation, and off the field problems lurching the club from one crisis to another. In October 2001 he was one of fifteen players on the Swans staff who were either sacked, or offered massive pay cuts by the club's new chairman, and within a couple of weeks had started a loan transfer at Oxford United, and a week into his second month, the transfer was made permanent after contractual problems had been sorted out. During the season his form for Oxford United was one of the factors that saw the club compete for a promotion place through the season. With a change of management at the Kassam Stadium, he was released at the end of the season, and in mid-July signed for player manager Steve Claridge at Conference South side Weymouth.

39. BOWEN, JASON Peter

Birthplace: Merthyr, 24/8/1972
Ht: 5ft-6ins, **Wt:** 9st-10lbs
Swans debut: v. Exeter City (h), 26/2/1990

Swansea City Career Statistics					
Season	League	FLC	FAC	AGT	WC
1990/91	1+2				
1991/92	5+6		3	1+1	0+1
1992/93	23+15/10gls		2+2/2gls	0+1	2
1993/94	39+2/11gls	3/2gls	2	6/1gls	7/3gls
1994/95	25+6/5gls	3+1	2	3+1/4gls	3+1/1gls
Total	93+31/26gls	6+1/2gls	9+2/2gls	10+3/5gls	12+2/4gls

Career:
Swansea City (trainee signed in 1/7/1990)

Birmingham City (£350,000 signed in 24/7/1995)
   lge 35+13/7gls, FLC 4+6/2gls, FAC 1+4, Others 2/2gls
Southampton (loan in 2/9/1997) PL 1+2
Reading (£200,000 signed in 24/12/1997) lge 12+3/1gls,
   FLC 1+1, FAC 5
Cardiff City (signed in 12/1/1999) lge 105+29/34gls,
   FLC 6/2gls, FAC 15+2, Others 2+2/1gls
Newport County (signed in July 2004) Total Apps 48/15gls

Honours: Wales Sch, Yth, U-21–5, 'B'–1, Full–2, AMC 1994, West Wales Senior Cup Winner–1990, 1991

Jason started his football at Goytre School Merthyr and signed as a YTS trainee at the Vetch Field, signing professional with the Swans on the 8th January 1992. In May 1990 and in 1991 he had been a member of the Swans side that beat Llanelli to win consecutive West Wales Senior Cup Finals. A prolific goalscorer at youth level, during season 1989/90, between himself and Marc Coates the frontrunners scored over 100 goals between them. That season saw him appear in the Welsh Youth Cup Final defeat by Cardiff City, as well as gaining youth honours for Wales to go with his schoolboy honours. After being included on a couple of occasions as a non-playing substitute during season 1989/90, Jason was finally given his debut by manager Terry Yorath at the Vetch Field against Exeter City in February 1990. The following season, this time with Frank Burrows as manager, Jason made eleven league appearances, and although yet to score his first goal was showing enough promise to impress the supporters. Jason started the 1992/93 season as substitute in the opening game of the season, and by May had scored ten league goals, which featured 7 goals in a four match spell, including his first league hat-trick, against Chester City at the Vetch Field in March 1993. Injury prevented him from playing in the end of season Play Off games against West Bromwich Albion. That season saw him gain the first of five U-21 caps for Wales, all gained with the Swans, scoring in a 4-1 win over Cyprus. Jason toped the goalscoring charts for the 1993/94 season with eleven league goals, also playing at Wembley when the Swans defeated Huddersfield Town in the Autoglass Trophy Cup Final. The end of the season saw Jason gain his first Full cap for Wales, playing in the 2-1 away win against Estonia. Although capable of playing as a central striker, Jason was at his best in either a wide right side role, or playing just behind the two front runners, where his tricky ball play and pace were more effective. In July 1995 he signed for Birmingham City in a tribunal fixed fee of £350,000, making a big impact in his first season with the 'Blues' reaching the semi-final stages of the Coca Cola Cup competition. A change of management at St. Andrews saw Jason join Premiership side Southampton on loan in September 1997, making his debut against Coventry City, and two further Premiership games. A £200,000 transfer to Reading in December 1997 saw the club relegated to the Second Division at the end of the season, but in January 1999 he had been re-united with Frank Burrows, this time at Ninian Park with Cardiff City. His first season saw the club gain promotion from the Third Division in third position, but after topping the goalscoring charts the following season with twelve league goals, the club suffered relegation back to the Third Division. However, over the next three seasons the 'Bluebirds' had not only returned to the Second Division at the first attempt, but by the end of season 2002/03 had gained promotion to the First Division. Injury problems prevented Jason from making an impact in the Bluebirds First Division side, and on the 6th April 2004 he had his contract cancelled with the club by mutual consent, leaving Ninian Park. In late July Jason signed a contract with non-league side Newport County, and later had an involvement running a Brazilian style soccer school with coaches at Eveswell United FC. At the end of his first season at County he had finished top goalscorer with fifteen league and cup goals.

40. BOYD, WALTER

Birthplace: Jamaica, 1/1/1972
Ht: 5ft-11ins, **Wt**: 11st-10lbs
Swans debut v. Rotherham United (h), 12/10/1999

Swansea City Career Statistics					
Season	League	FLC	FAC	AWS	FAWC
1999/2000	21+6/7gls		1+1	1	1/1gls
2000/01	14+3/3gls	2		1	5+1
Total	35+9/10gls	2	1+1	2	6+1/1gls

Career:
Arnett Gardens (Jamaica)
Colorado Foxes (USA)
Swansea City (signed in 8/10/1999)
Arnett Gardens (signed for season 2001/02)

Honours: Jamaica Full, Third Division Champions–2000

Walter 'The Pearl' Boyd was an extremely gifted yet
controversial player, who emerged as the third all time leading
goal-scorer in Jamaica's soccer history. A player with an
abundance of skill, capable of shooting with either foot, he was
one of the finest players Jamaica has produced in years. 'Blacka'
as he's also called, was a tough competitor whose off the field
antics always appeared to get him in trouble with the then team
manager of the national side, Rene Simoes. Despite being one of
the frontrunners in the Jamaica forward line in their early World
Cup qualifying games for France 1998, he was dropped from the
squad for the second round, and almost never made the trip to
France. During the World Cup, he made three substitute
appearances in the 1998 Finals against Croatia, Argentina and
Japan. He left Jamaican side Arnett Gardens to play for the
Colorado Foxes of the USA A-League, but was signed by
manager John Hollins on the 11th October 1999 on a free
transfer, making an electrifying start to his Football League
career by scoring both goals in a 2-0 home win over Rotherham
United. However, six weeks later he was sent off in a record
breaking 57 seconds after coming on the field as substitute for
Jonathan Coates against Darlington. Struggling at times to come
to terms with the rigorous demands of Third Division football,
by the end of the season he had scored seven league goals, and
was joint top scorer with Nick Cusack and Steve Watkin, and
also a Third Division Championship medal. At the end of the
season he won a recall to the Jamaican national side for friendly
matches against Cuba and Barbados. His second season at the
Vetch Field was interrupted through injury problems, and it was
only towards the end of the season, with relegation almost
assured that he returned to action, scoring two goals in one
game against Wycombe Wanderers. Released in May 2001, it
was thought after leaving the Vetch Field that he was going to
play in Korea, but he eventually returned to his former club
Arnett Gardens, also regaining his place in the national side.

41. BOYLE, Terrence (TERRY) David John

Birthplace: Llanelli, 29/10/1958
Ht: 5ft-10ins, **Wt:** 12st-12lbs
Swans debut v. Huddersfield Town (a), 19/8/1989

Swansea City Career Statistics					
Season	League	FLC	FAC	WC	ECWC
1989/90	27/1gls	2	2	1	2
Total	27/1gls	2	2	1	2

Career:
Tottenham Hotspur (apprentice signed in 1/11/1975) lge 0
Crystal Palace (signed in 17/1/1978) lge 24+2/1gls
Wimbledon (loan in 2/10/1981) lge 5/1gls
Bristol City (signed in 29/10/1981) lge 36/1gls
Newport County (signed in 12/11/1982) lge 165+1/11gls
Cardiff City (£22,000 signed in 19/8/1986) lge 126+2/7gls
Swansea City (£11,000 signed in 18/8/1989)
Merthyr Tydfil (£5,000 in August 1990) Conf 120+1/3gls

Honours: Wales Sch, Yth, U-21–1, Full–2, Wales Semi-
Professional XI, Welsh Cup Winner–1988, 1994, Welsh League
First Division Champions–1994, West Wales Senior Cup
Winner–1990

Brought up in the rugby stronghold of Llanelli, the former
Morfa Primary School and Llanelli Grammar Schoolboy
captained the Welsh Schoolboys U-15 side, and played for
juniors clubs Llanelli YMCA and Trostre Road Colts prior to
signing for Spurs. He captained the Llanelli Schoolboy side for
three years, became the first Llanelli schoolboy to be capped at
U-15 level for Wales, also playing in amateur and professional
youth trials whilst still a schoolboy. By December 1974 he had
already made several youth team appearances for Spurs, and
two of his Llanelli Schoolboy team mates, Glan Letheran and
Byron Stevenson would also go on to make a career in the
professional game. Joining Crystal Palace in January 1978, he
made his league debut against Oldham Athletic on the 1st April
1978. The following season he failed to make an appearance in
Terry Venables's side that won the Second Division
Championship, and later to be dubbed 'the team of the century',
but did make five First Division appearances the following
season, plus playing against the Swans in the twice replayed FA
Cup tie. Following a loan spell with Wimbledon, he joined Third
Division side Bristol City in October 1981, but in just over
twelve months following relegation, he was signed by Colin
Addison for Newport County. An almost ever present in
County's free scoring side, he then joined Cardiff City for a fee
of £22,000 in August 1986, and by the end of season 1987/88 had
recorded a Welsh Cup Final win over Wrexham, and finished
runners up to Wolverhampton Wanderers in the Fourth
Division. Not the biggest of defenders in central defence,

Terry was a rugged defender who won his share of aerial battles, and was mobile around the field. In August 1989 he joined the Swans for a fee of £11,000, and re-united with his former Palace colleague, Ian Evans, who had taken over as manager of the Swans. A regular inclusion in the first two thirds of the season, but after Terry Yorath had returned as manager at the Vetch Field, he struggled to feature in the line-up, and at the end of the season was allowed to sign for Conference side Merthyr Tydfil for £5,000. One of his last games for the Swans came against Llanelli in the West Wales Senior Cup Final in May 1990. Following spells with Inter Cardiff, Merthyr Tydfil (second time) and Cinderford Town as player coach, he joined Barry Town as manager just prior to the start of the 1993/94 season. Twelve months later he celebrated by winning the Welsh League First Division Championship, and beating Cardiff City in the Final of the Welsh Cup at the National Stadium in Cardiff. After a period as manager of Ebbw Vale, a player with Carmarthen Town, he then joined Bangor City as assistant manager following his appointment as Football Development Officer in Gwynedd, jointly funded by the FAW Trust and Gwynedd Council. Prior to moving to North Wales, Terry had worked for Plumb Centre, and also at Channel View Leisure Centre in Cardiff. In June 2004 he was named assistant to Caernarfon Town boss Wayne Phillips, enabling the former Wrexham midfielder to use his experience in a playing capacity, with the benefit of Boyle's experience being utilised from the touchline. The former Welsh international, has a UEFA 'A' licence, and has also managed the Welsh women's side.

42. BRACEY, LEE Michael Ian

Birthplace: Barking, 11/9/1968
Ht: 6ft-1ins, **Wt**: 12st-8lbs
Swans debut: v. Cardiff City (a), LWC–1, 30/8/1988

Swansea City Career Statistics						
Season	League	FLC	FAC	FRT/LDV	WC	ECWC
1988/89	30	2	3	2	7	
1989/90	31	2	4	1		2
1990/91	35	2	4	5	4	
1991/92	3	2				
Total	99	8	11	8	11	2

Career:
West Ham United (from trainee in 6/7/1987)
Swansea City (signed in 27/8/1988)
Halifax Town (£47,500 signed in 17/10/1991) lge 73, FLC 2, FAC 1, Others 2
Bury (£20,000 signed in 23/8/1993) lge 65+2, FLC 4, FAC 2, Others 1
Ipswich Town (£40,000 signed in 5/8/1997) lge 0

Hull City (signed in 5/7/1999) lge 19+1, FLC 6, FAC 3, Others 1
Ossett Town (signed in August 2001)
Chorley Town (signed in November 2002)
Mossley (signed in August 2004) Total Apps 24

Honours: Welsh Cup Winner–1989, West Wales Senior Cup Winner–1991

Goalkeeper Lee Bracey proved to be quite a popular signing with the Swans supporters considering that he had no first team experience prior to arriving at the Vetch Field shortly after the start of the 1988/89 season on a free transfer from West Ham United. A trainee at Upton Park, Lee's opportunities had been limited to the occasional reserve team game with the 'Hammers', but after watching the Swans give a convincing performance at Gillingham in the opening match of the season, he was offered the opportunity by Swans manager Terry Yorath to play in a Littlewoods Cup tie at Ninian Park just three days later. Although he was attached to West Ham United, Lee had been training with Colchester United leading up to the start of the season, and following a conversation with Mark Walton, the U's goalkeeper and son of Swans youth team manager Ron Walton he was recommended to Yorath. With the enforced retirement of Michael Hughes towards the end of the previous season, Yorath had signed the talented Welsh U-21 keeper Rhys Wilmot from Arsenal, but part of the loan transfer arrangement was that he would not be utilised in any cup matches. At the end of his first full season in the Football League, Lee was a member of the Swans side that beat non-league Kidderminster Harriers 5-0 in the Final of the Welsh Cup, and the following season played in both legs for the Swans in the European Cup Winners Cup competition against Greek side Panathinaikos. In May 1991 he was included in the Swans side that beat Llanelli to win the West Wales Senior Cup. In three years with the Swans, perhaps his performance against Liverpool at the Vetch Field stood out, although the replay remains a game he will want to forget. With new manager Frank Burrows signing Roger Freestone, and also the experienced Mark Kendall on the playing staff, Lee went to Halifax Town on an initial loan transfer during the early part of the 1991/92 season, with the transfer eventually being made permanent for a fee of £47,500 before the month was over. Joining Bury in August 1993, four years later he joined Ipswich Town, where he failed to make any first team appearances, acting as cover for the up and coming Richard Wright. Lee finished his league career at Hull City, before signing for non-league Ossett Town in August 2001. Lee was persuaded to join Unibond League First Division side Ossett Town by former Bury team-mate Peter Swan, despite an offer from newly promoted Conference side Stalybridge Celtic. At this stage in his career Lee had also started the process of applying to join the police force. His first season with Ossett Town saw the club fail to earn themselves promotion to the Premier Division because their ground was not up to the required standard. Joining Chorley Town in November 2002, by the start of the 2004/05 season he had signed for Unibond First Division side Mossley.

43. BRAIN, Joseph (JOE)

Birthplace: Ebbw Vale, 28/1/1910. **Died**: Norwich, 15/3/1981
Ht: 5ft-11ins, **Wt**: 11st-0lbs
Swans debut v. Hull City (h), 10/11/1934

Swansea Town Career Statistics			
Season	League	FAC	WC
1934/35	8/3gls		1
1935/36	20/13gls	1	1
1936/37	21/10gls	2	2
Total	49/26gls	3	4

Career:
Ebbw Vale (signed in 1926)
Sunderland (signed in March 1930) lge 0
Norwich City (signed in May 1931) lge 13/5gls
Barrow (signed in August 1932) lge 29/17gls
Preston North End (£300 signed in April 1933) lge 7/2gls
Swansea Town (£100 signed in 1/7/1934)
Bristol City (£300 signed in 1/6/1937) lge 32/9gls, FAC 3/1gls,
   Div 3 Cup 5/4gls, WC 1

Centre forward who failed to make any appearances for his first club Sunderland, making his league debut for Third Division South side Norwich City. Earlier in his career he had been a product of the Ebbw Vale Schoolboy side, and played for Ebbw Vale's Southern League and Welsh League sides at the age of sixteen, prior to signing for Sunderland. Twelve months later he joined Third Division North side Barrow, scoring over a goal every two games which brought him to the attention of Second Division side Preston North End. His only season at Deepdale saw Joe struggle to gain a regular place in the starting line-up which at the end of the season saw them gain promotion by finishing runners up to Grimsby Town, with Joe scoring two goals from seven league appearances, including one goal in a three nil defeat of the Swans at Preston in November 1933. Joining the Swans for a £100 transfer fee in July 1934, he did not have the best of starts at the Vetch Field, making just 8 league apps, scoring 3 goals in his first season. However, during the next two seasons he was top goalscorer in both seasons with 13 and 10 league goals respectively, despite missing the start of each season through injuries. Stocky, quick, a talented leader of the forward line, his ratio of a goal every other game speaks for itself. Primarily a centre forward, he also played in either inside forward position during his time at the Vetch Field. He was transferred to Bristol City in June 1937 for £300, and by the end of his first season at Ashton Gate scored nine goals to help the club finish in runners up place in the Third Division South. He made one appearance for Bristol City during season 1937/38 in the Welsh Cup competition. The *Lancashire Daily Post Yearbook* had earlier described him as a thrustfull go getting type of player who could shoot with both feet and has the quickness to turn openings into goals. Playing for Bristol City until November 1939, he also made WW2 guest appearances for Norwich City (1939/40), Bristol City (1941/42) and Watford (1943/44).

44. BRAY, Geoffrey (GEOFF) Charles

Birthplace: Rochester, 30/5/1951
Ht: 5ft-8ins, **Wt:** 11st-13lbs
Swans debut v. Tranmere Rovers (h), 16/8/1975

Career:
Gillingham (signed on groundstaff in July 1966)
Oxford United (signed in July 1971) lge 22+11/6gls

Swansea City (signed in July 1975)
Torquay United (signed in November 1976) lge 7/2gls
Dartford (signed in July 1977)

Swansea City Career Statistics				
Season	*League*	*FLC*	*FAC*	*WC*
1975/76	40+3/19gls		1	3/2gls
1976/77	3	2/1gls		
Total	43+3/19gls	2/1gls	1	3/2gls

Brought up in the Gillingham area, Geoff attended Barnsole Infants, and Upbury Manor Secondary School, played for Medway District, and Kent County, and also Twydall Colts prior to joining the groundstaff at the Priestfield Stadium on leaving school. Released by Gillingham, he signed his first professional contract with Oxford United, but had to wait a full season before he was given his first team opportunity, making his league debut at Huddersfield Town on the 9th September 1972 as a substitute for Clayton, and midway through the season had a spell where he scored three goals in three league matches. Struggling to make regular appearances in United's Second Division line-up, he was released in May 1975, and was snapped up by Swans manager Harry Griffiths. Geoff only really had one full season with the Swans, but after arriving at the Vetch Filed was top goalscorer for season 1975//76 with 19 league goals, the highest league goals scored in a season by a Swans player since season 1964/65 when Keith Todd scored 20 league goals. The emergence of a young Jeremy Charles the following season however was probably the main reason for the striker being allowed to sign for fellow Fourth Division side Torquay United in November 1976, despite Bray playing in the first 5 league and cup games, and scoring two goals. Scoring two goals in his third game for United, he was unable to consolidate his place in the United starting line-up, and in May 1977 was released. Returning to the South East, he signed for Southern League Premier Division side Dartford for season 1977/78, finishing the season as top goalscorer with the club with twenty league and cup goals. After just one season with Dartford he retired from football, going into the motor trade. Since then he has since obtained the dealership for both Vauxhall and Mitsubishi in the Southend area, with garages in Southend and Rayleigh.

45. BRAYSON, PAUL

Birthplace: Newcastle, 16/9/1977
Ht: 5ft-7ins, **Wt:** 10st-10lbs
Swans debut: v. Cambridge United (h), 31/1/1997

Career:
Newcastle United (from trainee in 1/8/1995) FLC 1+1
Swansea City (loan in 30/1/1997)

Reading (£100,000 signed in 26/3/1998) lge 15+26/1gls,
    FLC 0+2, FAC 1+1, Others 2
Cardiff City (signed in 16/3/2000) lge 48+36/19gls, FLC 2,
    FAC 3+4/1gls, Others 1
Cheltenham Town (signed in 7/8/2002) lge 34+17/8gls,
    FLC 0+1, FAC 3+1/2gls, Others 2/2gls
Northwich Victoria (signed in August 2004) Conf 21+4/13gls
Gateshead (loan in 16/3/2005)

Swansea City Career Statistics	
Season	League
1996/97	11/5gls
Total	11/5gls

Honours: England Yth

A prolific goalscorer at reserve and youth team level, he made
his only start for Newcastle United in the Coca Cola Cup 2nd
round, 2nd leg against Bristol City in October 1995. Signed on a
loan transfer by Swans manager Jan Molby in January 1997, he
scored on his debut for the Swans at the Vetch Field against
Cambridge United, and played a large part in the club reaching
the Third Division Play Offs, although he had returned to
Newcastle United by the time the Swans played at Wembley in
the Final against Northampton Town. He was unable to break
into the United side on his return, and in March 1998 joined
First Division side Reading for £100,000, but within a couple of
weeks the club had failed to avoid relegation to the Second
Division. Struggling to hold down a regular place at Reading,
he was then allowed to join Cardiff City on a free transfer in
March 2000, but within a couple of weeks the Bluebirds had
been relegated to the Third Division. The next season however,
he ended up with 15 league goals, as the Bluebirds regained
their Second Division status at the first attempt under manager
Alan Cork, by finishing as runners up in the Third Division
behind Brighton & Hove Albion. Despite his short stature, he
was capable of playing up front, or in a wide capacity, with his
pace and quick thinking a feature of his play. At youth team
level with Newcastle United he had international youth honours
with England. He failed to feature in the Bluebirds Play Off
defeat in his second full season at Ninian Park, and in August
2002 signed for newly promoted Cheltenham Town on a free
transfer. His first season at Whaddon Road saw Paul display
good form, but as the season progressed, and the club struggled,
he was unable to make an impact. Released in May 2004,
after making appearances for York City in pre-season friendlies
he signed for Conference side Northwich Victoria, later in the
season returning to the North East for a loan spell with
Gateshead.

46. BRAZIL, DEREK Michael

Birthplace: Dublin, 14/12/1968
Ht: 6ft-0ins, **Wt**: 12st-6lbs
Swans debut: v. Preston North End (h), 14/9/1991

Swansea City Career Statistics				
Season	League	FLC	AGT	WC
1991/92	12/1gls	2	2	1
Total	12/1gls	2	2	1

Career:
Rivermount BC
Manchester United (signed in 12/3/1986) lge 0+2
Oldham Athletic (loan in 20/11/1990) lge 1, Others 1
Swansea City (loan in 12/9/1991)
Cardiff City (£85,000 signed in 26/8/1992) lge 109+6/1gls, FLC
    8, FAC 9, Others 13+3/1gls
AFC Newport (signed in August 1996)

Honours: Rep of Ireland Sch, Yth, U-21–7, U-23–2, 'B', Third
Division Champions–1993, Welsh Cup Winner–1993, 1999

Defender Derek Brazil gained schoolboy and youth honours for
the Republic of Ireland prior to joining Manchester United from
Rivermount Boys Club in March 1986, after earlier making
appearances for Belvedere FC, later making an appearance for
the Republic's 'B' side against England in March 1990 in Cork,
and also against Northern Ireland. He attended St. Kevins
School and Patrician College in Dublin prior to signing for
Manchester United in 1986. He made his First Division debut
against Everton as substitute for Mick Duxbury on the 10th May
1989, and apart from one other substitute appearance for
United, made a couple of appearances for Oldham Athletic
during a loan spell prior to being signed by Swans manager
Frank Burrows on loan in September 1991. After two months on
loan he returned to Old Trafford, with the Swans unable to
afford the transfer fee to make his transfer permanent. In August
1989 he joined Cardiff City for £85,000, and by the time he was
released in May 1996 had played a large part in the Bluebirds
Third Division Championship success of season 1992/93, also a
member of the Bluebirds Welsh Cup Final team the same season.
Derek also played in the 1995 Welsh Cup Final defeat by
Wrexham. After being released by the Bluebirds, he played in
one friendly game for Merthyr Tydfil, then linked up with AFC
Newport, where he was also Football in the Community Officer.
He had a successful period with Cardiff based side Inter
Cabletel, gaining his second Welsh Cup Final winning medal in
1999 when they beat Carmarthen Town on penalties, and also
playing in European games the following season. He also
played for the club the following season in the UEFA Cup
competition, losing over two legs to Gorica. A knee problem
which saw him have two operations saw him finish his playing

career at League of Wales side Haverfordwest, and for a five year period worked as Football in the Community Officer at Cardiff City at Ninian Park. Since leaving Ninian Park Derek has been involved in coaching with the International Soccer Development, linked to the Coerver coaching method, working in schools in the Cardiff and Newport area. Season 2003/04 has seen him involved as player manager of his local pub side, Sporting Cwrt Rawlin, in the Taff Ely & Rhymney Alliance League.

47. BRIDDON, Samuel (SAM)

Birthplace: Alfreton, 26/7/1915. **Died:** Mansfield, AMJ, 1975
Ht: 6ft-0ins, **Wt:** 11st-2lbs
Swans debut: v. WBA (h), 31/8/1946

Swansea Town Career Statistics	
Season	League
1946/47	18
Total	18

Career:
Port Vale (signed in 1934) lge 0
Stanton Hill
Devessall FC
Port Vale (amateur in February 1933)
Brentford (signed in August 1935) lge 6
Swindon Town (signed in July 1939) lge 0
Swansea Town (signed in 11/7/1939)

Former Port Vale wing half who after failing to make a league appearance with Vale, returned to the Football League after playing non-league for Stanton Hill and Devessall FC, re-joining Port Vale as an amateur between February 1933 to May 1934. Prior to joining Brentford, in February 1935 he had a trial with Scunthorpe United. He managed just six league appearances in four seasons at Griffin Park, and after a transfer to Swindon Town, where he again failed to feature in their league side, was signed by Swans manager Haydn Green in July 1939. He played in all three league games at the start of the 1939/40 season before war broke out, prior to the Football League being suspended. He remained with the Swans, playing for the rest of the season in the Regional South West organised football, also playing war time football as a guest with Bolton Wanderers (1942/43) and West Ham United (August 1944). When the Football League was resumed after the war, he played in the opening couple of matches, and returned to play in the last fourteen league games of the season. Described as a thoughtful full back, with good skills and vision, he unfortunately lost six seasons of his career because of the Second World War. After retiring as a player he became a miner.

48. BRIGGS, William Ronald (RONNIE)

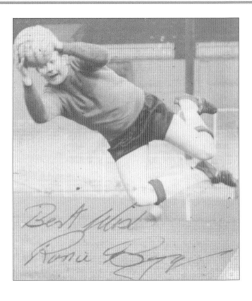

Birthplace: Belfast, 29/3/1943
Ht: 6ft-2ins, **Wt:** 12st-12lbs
Swans debut v. Rotherham United (h), 25/8/1964

Swansea Town Career Statistics				
Season	League	FLC	FAC	WC
1964/65	27	4	4	2
Total	27	4	4	2

Career:
Manchester United (from juniors in March 1960) lge 9
Swansea Town (signed in May 1964)
Bristol Rovers (signed in 25/5/1965) lge 35
Minehead (loan in December 1966) Sth Lge 4
Frome Town (signed in 22/7/1968)
Glastonbury (signed in 10/6/1969)
Taunton Town (signed in 1971)

Honours: Northern Ireland Sch–3, U-23-2, Full–2

Northern Ireland international goalkeeper who joined the Swans on a free transfer from Manchester United in May 1964, and who earlier in his career had represented his country at Schoolboy, U-23 and Full level. He gained his first full cap against Wales in Cardiff, replacing Harry Gregg on the 11th April 1962, and his second full cap came when he was with the Swans, playing against Holland in March 1965, this time replacing Pat Jennings. He also gained his U-23 caps with United and the Swans, and initially joined the United groundstaff in July 1958, signing professional in March 1960. His first team opportunities were limited at Old Trafford, with Gregg and Gaskell before him, but he did make his league debut at the age of seventeen, when with both keepers injured, he made his first start against Leicester City in January 1961, unfortunately conceding six goals. A week later he did better, conceding just the one goal in a 1-1 FA Cup draw at Hillsbrough against Sheffield Wednesday. The replay unfortunately saw Biggs concede seven goals in a 7-2 defeat, and with his confidence shattered, United signed amateur international Mike Pinner, giving Briggs a chance to recover in the club's reserve side. A good solid goalkeeper, he was understudy to Noel Dwyer at the start of the 1964/65 season, but after making his debut against Rotherham United became the Swans number one choice for most of the season, also playing in all the cup games, bar the Welsh Cup semi-final against Cardiff City. Despite reaching the fifth round of the FA Cup competition, form in the league however saw the club lose it's Second Division status at the end of the season. Released at the end of the season, he signed for Bristol Rovers after impressing on the club's end of season tour of Eire, playing against Bohemians and Dundalk. He made his Rovers debut on the 1st November 1965 against Shrewsbury Town, struggled to command a regular place in the starting line-up, and following a mid-season loan spell in December 1966 at non-league Minehead was released, and drifted into non-league football with Frome Town, Glastonbury and Taunton Town. A hand injury suffered playing for Rovers eventually forced his retirement from the game, and since then has been employed as a security guard, and is currently employed by Reliance Security and living in Frenchay, Bristol.

49. BRITTON, LEON

Birthplace: Wimbledon, 16/9/1982
Ht: 5ft-5ins, **Wt**: 9st-10lbs
Swans debut: v. Exeter City (a), 14/12/2002

Swansea City Career Statistics					
Season	League	FLC	FAC	LDV	FAWP
2002/03	25				1
2003/04	41/3gls	1	5		0+1
2004/05	16+14/1gls	1	2+1	0+1	2+1
Total	82+14/4gls	2	7+1	0+1	3+2

Career:
West Ham United (from trainee in 21/9/1999)
Swansea City (loan in 2/12/2002)

Honours: England U-15, U-16, U-18, FA Academy U-19 Championship–2000, FAW Cup Winner–2005

Went to Raynes Park High School until the age of 14, and then attended the Football League Academy at Lilleshall for two years up to the age of 16 whilst attached to Arsenal. During this time he missed almost six months through injury, and at the age of 16, West Ham United paid Arsenal £400,000 for him to start as a trainee at Upton Park. He has represented England at U-16 and at U-18 level, and also played for the England U-15 side in a Nordic Tournament. His only honours with West Ham United have been with the U-19 Academy side which won their championship during the 1999/2000 season, beating Arsenal in the final after penalties. Leon came to the Vetch Field on an initial one week trial basis in December 2002, before deciding to sign for a month on loan. However, on New Year's Day 2003 his loan transfer was extended until the end of the season. By the end of the season he had become an integral part of the Swans midfield, securing its Third Division status in the last league game of the season. He made a terrific impression with the Swans fans, despite playing his first six games for the Swans

with six straight defeats. Despite his small stature, Leon proved to be a real handful, coping exceptionally well with the physical part of Third Division football. Although he returned to Upton Park at the end of the season, and had a year left on his contract, he was given a free transfer, enabling him to make the switch to the Vetch Field permanent on a two year contract. One of the clauses in his release by the Hammers was a sell on clause should he move on from the Vetch Field in the future for a transfer fee. His second season at the Vetch Field saw Leon continue to excite the fans with his surging midfield runs, also finding the net on a couple of occasions. Season 2004/05 saw him struggle to make an impression, especially in a wide, right sided midfield role, although he did play in the last game victory at Bury which sealed promotion, and the FAW Cup Final win over Wrexham.

50. BRODIE, STEPHEN Eric

Birthplace: Sunderland, 14/1/1973
Ht: 5ft-7ins, **Wt**: 10st-8lbs
Swans debut: v. York City (a), 20/11/2001

Swansea City Career Statistics			
Season	League	FAC	FAWC
2001/02	21+5/2gls	1	1+1
Total	21+5/2gls	1	1+1

Career:
Sunderland (Ass. Schoolboy in May 1987, trainee in July 1989, professional in 1/7/1991) lge 1+11
Doncaster Rovers (loan in 31/8/1995) lge 5/1gls
Scarborough (signed in 20/12/1996) lge 109+2/27gls, FLC 4, FAC 3, Others 2+1
Swansea City (signed in 15/11/2001)
Chester City (signed in July 2002) Conf 3+3
Nuneaton Borough (loan in 2002/03) Conf 11/4gls
Forest Green (loan in season 2003/04) Conf 7/3gls
Droylsden (loan in December 2003) Total Apps 23+2/7gls
Leigh R.M.I. (loan in 10/2/2004) Conf 12+2/4gls
Droylsden (signed in close season 2004) Total Apps 48+1/6gls

Honours: West Wales Senior Cup Winner–2002

The former Scarborough midfielder was re-united with his former manager Colin Addison following his signing for the Swans in mid November. Showed up well when utilised in an attacking central midfield role, but played most of his games in a right sided midfield position. Possessing a good awareness on the ball, Steve was also a hard worker in midfield. With Scarborough in financial difficulties, his contract was taken over by the Swans until the end of the season. Six days previously

Scarborough had turned down a Swans offer of £7,500 for the player, to enable him to play in a televised FA Cup tie at the Vetch against QPR. In his previous three seasons at Scarborough, Brodie had been top goalscorer on each occasion. Starting his career as a trainee with Sunderland at Roker Park, he made his league debut as substitute for Gary Owers at Notts. County on the 28th August 1993, making his first start in the last league game of the next season against WBA. Unable to command a regular place in Sunderland's first team line-up, following a loan spell with Doncaster Rovers he joined Scarborough on a free transfer in December 1996. The 1997/98 season saw Scarborough lose to Torquay United in the Third Division Play Off semi-finals, and twelve months later the club were relegated to the Conference. Following Nick Cusack taking over the managerial reins at the Vetch Field, Steve was released in May 2002, signing a two year contract with Conference side Chester City, but midway through his first season at the Deva Stadium was loaned to Nuneaton Borough in a deal which saw Mark Quayle join Chester. One of his last matches for the Swans was in the West Wales Senior Cup Final win over Hakin United. Season 2003/04 saw Steve continue to struggle to make an impact at Chester, and during the season he had loan appearances with Forest Green Rovers and Droylsden before signing for Leigh R.M.I. on an initial loan basis in February 2004. Opening his goalscoring account with four goals in five games, he was released by Chester City, joining Leigh R.M.I. on a permanent basis. Prior to the start of the 2004/05 season he signed for Droylsden.

51. BROOKES, GILBERT Henry

Birthplace: Churchill, Kidderminster, 2/4/1895.
Died: Kidderminster, 22/2/1952
Ht: 6ft-1ins, **Wt:** 12st-0lbs
Swans debut v. Luton Town (h), 25/8/1923

Swansea Town Career Statistics			
Season	League	FAC	WC
1923/24	37	4	3
Total	37	4	3

Career:
Kidderminster Harriers
Shrewsbury Town (signed in February 1922)
Stoke City (£300 in May 1922) lge 14
Swansea Town (signed in 16/6/1923)
Luton Town (signed in 22/5/1924) lge 42
Merthyr Town (signed in May 1925) lge 38
Kidderminster Harriers (signed in close season 1926)

Honours: Worcestershire Senior Cup Winner–1921

A former non-league player with Kidderminster Harriers and Shrewsbury Town prior to joining First Division side Stoke City in May 1922, making his league debut during Stoke's unsuccessful fight to stay in the First Division. The previous season to joining the Swans he had made fourteen appearances for Stoke. Joining the Swans in June 1923, after making his league debut against Luton Town, he missed just five league games through the season, also playing in all the cup ties the Swans played in. Joining Luton Town the following season, he played in both league games against the Swans for the 'Hatters'. He then returned to South Wales to sign for Third Division South side Merthyr Town before rejoining Kidderminster Harriers in the 1926 close season. During his first stint with Harriers he played in the side that won the Worcestershire Senior Cup in season 1920/21. After he retired from playing he was landlord of The Sportsman Inn in Kidderminster up to the time of his death.

52. BROWN, GRAHAM Cummings

Birthplace: Matlock, 21/3/1944
Ht: 5ft-11ins, **Wt:** 12st-0lbs
Swans debut v. Exeter City (h), 6/11/1976

Swansea City Career Statistics		
Season	League	FAC
1976/77	4	1
Total	4	1

Career:
Crawley Town
Millwall (amateur signed in July 1964, professional in December 1964)
Crawley Town
Brighton & Hove Albion (signed in February 1966)
Crawley Town
Watford (signed in August 1968)
Mansfield Town (signed in August 1969) lge 142
Doncaster Rovers (signed in July 1974) lge 53
Portland Timbers, USA (signed in close season 1975)
Swansea City (signed in 18/9/1976)
Southport (signed in December 1976)
Portland Timbers, USA (signed in close season 1977)
York City (signed in August 1977) lge 69
Rotherham United (signed in February 1980) lge 31
Mansfield Town (signed non-contract January 1982) lge 1

Honours: Notts. FA County Cup Winner–1971-72

Initially with Millwall as an amateur, prior to signing as a professional in December 1964, he had a spell as an outfield player with Crawley Town, and also with Brighton and Watford, before following Ray Keeley to Mansfield Town in August 1969. He featured in their 1969/70 FA Cup run and displaced Welsh international Dave Hollins at Field Mill, but after the arrival of Rod Arnold was allowed to join Doncaster Rovers on a free transfer in July 1974. In 1971 and 1972 he was a member of the Mansfield side that won the Notts. FA County Cup. He took up the offer of joining American side Portland Timbers in 1975, helping the club to reach the NASL Soccer Bowl Final, before returning to the UK to sign on a non-contract basis for the Swans. An experienced goalkeeper, Swans manager Harry Griffiths, with little or no money at his disposal, was slowly rebuilding the Swans side, and at the time of Brown arriving at the Vetch Field, young Stephen Potter and the inexperienced Dutchman Nico Schroder were contesting the goalkeeper jersey. He made his debut against Exeter City at the Vetch Field in November 1976, the first of four consecutive league appearances, before returning to the United States to rejoin Portland Timbers. By August 1977 he had returned to the UK, via Southport, signing for York City, contesting a first team place with Joe Neenan, prior to joining Rotherham United in February 1980. He featured strongly in Rotherham's 1980/81 season, making 31 league games, before rejoining Mansfield Town on a non-contract basis in January 1982. He later became a scout for Aberdeen, subsequently becoming a salesman, and has also been involved as a scout and part-time goalkeeper coach for Rotherham United in the late 1990's.

53. BROWN, LINTON James

Birthplace: Hull, 12/4/1968
Ht: 5ft-9ins, **Wt:** 11st-0lbs
Swans debut v. Brentford (a), 23/3/1996

Swansea City Career Statistics						
Season	League	FLC	FAC	AWS	P/Offs	FAWC
1995/96	3+1					
1996/97	13+9/3gls	1+1	1	1	0+2	
1997/98	0+2					3
Total	16+12/3gls	1+1	1	1	0+2	3

Career:
Bridlington (semi-professional in February 1966)
North Ferriby United (signed in August 1991)
Guiseley (signed in July 1992)
Halifax Town (non-contract signed in December 1992) lge 3
Hull City (signed in January 1993) lge 111+10/23gls
Swansea City (signed in 22/3/1996)
Scarborough (loan in 28/8/1997) lge 4/1gls
Emley Town (signed in 26/3/1998)
Gainsborough Trinity (signed in August 1998)

Linton Brown was a popular figure at Hull City with the supporters, as it was their fund raising efforts which enabled the club, during troubled times to pay for his signature. Manager at the time, Terry Dolan had made Brown one of the club's first signings during the campaign 'put a Tiger in your team', signing the striker from non-league Guiseley, after he had a short trial spell with Halifax Town. The money raised from donations from the club's supporters went to pay for Brown's wages during his first season at the club. His electric turn of pace saw him forge a good understanding with Dean Windass, scoring 23 goals from 121 league games for the 'Tigers'. Joining the Swans in March 1996 for £60,000, he was unable to produce consistent performances for the Swans, under Jan Molby, or Alan Cork, with groin and hamstring injuries being the main problem, and was limited to a substitute appearance for the Swans in the Wembley Third Division Play Off Final against Northampton Town in May 1997. Shortly after the start of the 1997/98 season he joined Scarborough on loan, scoring on his debut in a 3-3 draw at Lincoln City in August 1997. Made available for transfer after returning to the Vetch Field, on the 26th March 1998 he had fifteen months of his contract paid up, enabling him to join Unibond Premier League side Emley on transfer deadline day.

Earlier in the season, Emley had narrowly lost at Upton Park to West Ham United in the third round of the FA Cup competition. In August 1998 he joined non-league Gainsborough Trinity, linking up with a number of former Hull City players. He later played in East Riding Junior Football in July 1999. He has recently retired from playing, and is living in Beverly, and working in his father's business in Bridlington.

54. BROWN, Thomas (TOM) Hugh

Birthplace: Liverpool, 8/5/1930
Ht: 5ft-10ins, **Wt:** 12st-2lbs
Swans debut v. Rotherham United (a), 3/5/1956

Swansea Town Career Statistics			
Season	League	FAC	WC
1955/56	1		1
1956/57	26	5	1
1957/58	26	1	1
1958/59	15		
Total	68	6	3

Career:
South Liverpool
Doncaster Rovers (signed in February 1951) lge 86/1gls
Llanelly Town (signed in 9/7/1954)
Swansea Town (£7,500 signed in 29/11/1955)

Honours: England Yth, West Wales Senior Cup Winner–1956

Former non-league defender with South Liverpool who during his three and a half years with Doncaster Rovers in the Second Division played on numerous occasions against the Swans, prior to signing for Southern League side Llanelly, after being on the transfer list at Rovers. Capped at Youth level for England against the Netherlands in 1948, he joined the Swans in late November 1955 for a £7,500 transfer fee, which was paid to Doncaster Rovers, who had held his Football League registration following the defender's move to Stebonheath Park. Transfer listed by Rovers, during the 1953/54 season he played in both games for Rovers against the Swans, and at the time of his arriving at the Vetch Field, both Liverpool and Walsall were interested in signing him. He made his Swans debut at Rotherham United in the last league game of the season, and during his period at the Vetch Field alternated between right back, and wing half back, also playing at left half back. In April 1956 he returned to Stebonheath Park to play in the Swans side that beat Llanelly in the final of the West Wales Senior Cup. A strong, keen tackler, and good in the air, following the arrival of Roy Saunders in March 1959, he lost his place, and in March 1959 had been placed on the transfer list. In late April 1959 he appealed to the Football League to reduce the £4,000 transfer fee the Swans had placed on him, but after the season had ended left the Vetch Field playing staff.

55. BROWN, William (BILLY) Young

Birthplace: Dysart, 23/2/1889. **Died:** Walton-on-Thames, 1/4/1963
Ht: 5ft-10ins, **Wt:** 12st-0lbs
Swans debut v. Exeter City (a), 20/9/1919, Sth. Lge

Swansea Town Career Statistics			
Season	League	FAC	WC
1920/21	35/6gls	3/1gls	
1921/22	30/10gls	5	1
Total	65/16gls	8/1gls	1

Career:
QPR (amateur)
Chelsea (signed in close season 1910) lge 10/2gls
Bristol City (signed in November 1913) lge 62/23gls
Swansea Town (signed in 5/9/1919)
Northampton Town (signed in June 1922) lge 2
Sittingbourne (signed in August 1923)

'Billy' Young Brown attended Kirkcaldy High School where he played rugby, later played football for St. Columba's Church, The Heathen, Post Office Savings Department XI, Raith Rovers, Civil Service League XI, and made one guest appearance in WW1 for QPR, at a time when he was recovering from an injury suffered in the Great War. He played for the Swans during the club's last season in the Southern League, finishing top goalscorer with ten goals, but failed to make the Swans starting line-up for the club's first match in the Football League at Portsmouth in August 1920. His first couple of league games for the Swans saw him playing at inside left, centre half and inside right, before settling into the inside left position. Transfer listed by Bristol City at £350, with no agreement between the Football League and the Southern League at the time over transfers, he was able to join the Swans without a transfer fee being paid. Earlier in his career he had made league appearances for Chelsea in the First and Second Divisions. He made his debut for Chelsea at Leeds City on the 9th September 1911 in a 0-0 draw. The Scottish inside forward had been a regular goalscorer in the Chelsea London Combination side, but failed to establish himself in the first team, making three league appearances in his first season, and six league appearances during his second season at Stamford Bridge. His second season with the Swans saw him finish as second top goalscorer with ten league goals, which included a hat-trick in the 8-1 win over Bristol Rovers in April 1922. Jimmy Collins also scored a hat trick in same game.

He left at the end of season 1921/22 to join Portsmouth, but before the start of the 1922/23 season had joined Northampton Town where he was utilised mainly as cover, but when called into action was found to be too slow, failing even to make appearances in the club's reserve side. A nasty leg injury had kept him sidelined for most of his time with the 'Cobblers', and it was only in February 1923 that he was able to return to full training. He left the County Ground at the end of the season, signing for non-league side Sittingbourne in August 1923. In January 1928 he played for a Britannic House, London side at Penyrally, Skewen against the National Oil Refineries team (later BP Llandarcy).

56. BRUCE, Walter

Birthplace: Sunderland 15/5/1912. **Died:** Sunderland, August 1984
Ht: 5ft-9ins, **Wt:** 11st-4lbs
Swans debut: v. Manchester City (a), 27/8/1938

Swansea Town Career Statistics		
Season	League	WC
1938/39	13/1gls	1
Total	13/1gls	1

Career:
Southport (trial in February 1932)
Southampton (trial in March 1932)
Workington (signed in August 1932)
Bradford City (signed in 29/7/1933) lge 76/17gls, FAC 3
Swansea Town (£200 signed in 22/7/1938)
West Ham United (£250 signed in 20/5/1939) lge 0

He began his career with Southwick St. Columba's and Silkworth Colliery, had trials with Southport and Southampton in February, March 1932, returning to Silkworth Colliery, prior to signing for North Eastern League side Workington in August 1932, scoring a hat-trick for the side against Bedlington United in an Eastern League County Cup tie in 1933. Joining Bradford City in July 1933, he made his Football League debut at Turf Moor against Burnley in the Second Division on the 17th March 1934, and for three seasons became a regular inclusion in the City side. His first senior goals for the club came the following season when he scored two goals in the game against Hull City in April 1935, and he was a member of the side that suffered relegation to the Third Division North at the end of the 1936/37 season. The former inside forward scored Bradford City's consolation goal in an 8-1 defeat at the Vetch Field in season 1935/36. After being signed by manager Neil Harris in July 1938, he made his debut in the opening fixture of the 1938/39 season at Maine Road against Manchester City, scoring his first goal two games later against Millwall. He also played at outside right, inside right, and at centre forward during his only season with the Swans, before being sold to West Ham United in May 1939 for £250. In March 1939 he scored all five goals in a Swans' reserve team victory over Troedyrhiw. During WW2 he made guest appearances for Halifax Town in season 1939/40.

57. BRUTON, David (DAVE) Edward

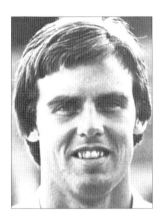

Birthplace: Dursley, 31/10/1952
Ht: 6ft-2ins, **Wt:** 14st-0lbs
Swans debut v. Chester (h), 25/8/1973

Swansea City Career Statistics

Season	League	FLC	FAC	WC
1973/74	45/6gls	2	1	1
1974/75	42+1/5gls	1	2	4/1gls
1975/76	37+3/5gls	2/1gls	1	2/1gls
1976/77	26+2	6	1	
1977/78	28/3gls			2
1978/79	7+1	4		
Total	185+7/19gls	15/1gls	5	9/2gls

Career:
Bristol City (from apprentice in July 1971) lge 16+1
Swansea City (£12,000 joint signing with Danny Bartley in 3/8/1973)
Newport County (loan in 25/2/1977) lge 6/1gls
Newport County (£15,000 in 13/10/1978) lge 79+3/9gls, ECWC 4/1gls
Gloucester City (signed in close season 1981)

Honours: West Wales Senior Cup Winner–1975

Former apprentice at Ashton Gate with Bristol City, he made his league debut as a replacement for the experienced Dickie Rooks at Sunderland on the 27th November 1971, making a further ten league appearances that season in the Second Division.
After making a further six league appearances the following season, along with winger Danny Bartley, both players were signed by manager Harry Gregg in a package worth £12,000. A composed central defender, he also proved to be a reliable penalty taker during his period with the Swans, regularly converting from the penalty spot. A 4-2 home win over Rotherham United in January 1974 saw him score twice from the penalty spot. His first season at the Vetch Field saw him voted 'Player of the Year'. In May 1975 he was included in the Swans side that beat Briton Ferry Athletic in the West Wales Senior Cup Final. It was only after Harry Griffiths had taken over as manager that his accomplished qualities in defence were noticeable, with the Swans playing attractive, open football, and Bruton forming a good partnership with Paul Harris initially, and then with Eddie May. After missing out on promotion by

one point at the end of season 1976/77, the following season the Swans gained promotion, finishing in third place behind Watford and Southend United. Despite starting the new season in the Swans line-up in the Third Division, after a couple of games he lost his place to Nigel Stevenson, and in February made loan appearances for Newport County. In October 1988 the transfer was made permanent for a fee of £15,000, and by the end of season, County had gained promotion from the Fourth Division and also won the Welsh Cup Final, although Dave did not feature in the final against Shrewsbury Town. The following season, County lost narrowly in the quarter final stage of the European Cup Winners Cup competition to Carl Zeiss Jena, the eventual losing finalist. Released at the end of the season he joined Gloucester City, then made further non-league appearances for Forest Green Rovers, Trowbridge, Pontllanfraith, Caerleon, Cwmbran, Wotton Rovers. Currently living in Thornbury, Dave is an area manager for Provident Finance Company.

58. BUDD, KEVIN John

Birthplace: Hillingdon, 20/3/1962
Ht: 5ft-9ins, **Wt:** 11st-4lbs
Swans debut v. Bristol City (h), 23/11/1985

Swansea City Career Statistics

Season	League
1985/86	1
Total	1

Career:
Bournemouth (apprentice)
Norwich City (signed in October 1979) lge 0
Manchester City (signed in February 1981) lge 0
Hillingdon Borough
Swansea City (signed non-contract in November 1985)

A former pupil at Eveling Comprehensive School in West London, after leaving school Kevin started his playing career as an apprentice at Dean Court with Bournemouth, failed to make a first team appearance, later followed his coach at Dean Court John Benson, to Norwich City and then to Manchester City. In all teams he joined, John Bond had been the manager, and his arrival at the Vetch Field on an initial trial basis saw him link up for the fourth time with Bond. In early November 1985 he had contacted John Bond with a view to training with the Swans, at the time having no job, and was prepared to pay his own way, in the hope of establishing himself back in the professional game. After a number of impressive performances in the Swans' Football Combination side, he was given his league debut at the Vetch Field against Bristol City, stepping out of reserve team football when the Swans had a number of first team players sidelined through injury. Playing at right full back, he was replaced by sixteen-year-old Andrew Melville after seventy minutes after he had chipped a bone in his ankle, an injury which saw him in plaster for several weeks. By the time he had returned to fitness, John Bond had been sacked by the Official Receiver, and the Swans were faced with a battle for survival off the field, and no finances available to increase the playing staff. He failed to make any further appearances, drifted into non-league football with Hillingdon Borough, but the injury he sustained in his debut Football League game at the Vetch Field was to ultimately force his retirement from the game at all levels. Kevin has since been involved with coaching children in the Hillingdon area, as well as developing his own business interests in West London.

59. BURGESS, William Arthur Ronald (RON)

Birthplace: Ebbw Vale, 9/4/1917 **Died**: Swansea, 14/2/2005
Ht: 5ft-9ins, **Wt**: 11st-10lbs
Swans debut v. West Ham United (h), 21/8/1954

Swansea Town Career Statistics			
Season	League	FAC	WC
1954/55	38/1gls	4	2/1gls
1955/56	8	1	1
Total	46/1gls	5	3/1gls

Career:
Cwm Villa
Cardiff City (signed in 1935) lge 0
Tottenham Hotspur (signed in May 1936) lge 297/14gls
Northfleet (amateur in April 1937, professional in May 1938)
Swansea Town (signed in 7/8/1954)

Honours: Wales Full–32, WW2 War-Time–10, Great Britain v. Rest of Europe (1947), Football League Rep. XI, Second Division Champions–1950, First Division Champions–1951, West Wales Senior Cup Winner–1955

Brought up on the slag heaps of South Wales with local side Cwm Villa before signing for Second Division side Tottenham Hotspur in May 1936, he was loaned out to the club's nursery side in Kent, Northfleet, where many of the club's stars of the double Championship success started their career. After making his league debut, he went on to captain the Spurs side managed by Arthur Rowley to consecutive Championships in the Second and First Division in 1950 and 1951, and also runners up in the First Division in 1952. Dark haired before prematurely going bald and aggressive, he inspired by example, became an automatic choice for Wales after gaining his first international cap against Scotland on the 19th October 1946, in the Home International Championships, playing also that season against England and Northern Ireland. During the Second World War

he made ten appearances for Wales from 1940 to 1946, and made guest appearances for Brighton & Hove Albion (December 1941), Nottingham Forest (January 1941), Millwall (April 1944), Notts. County (season 1942/43), and Reading (season 1943/44). He represented the Football League on the 12th March 1947 against the Scottish League in Hampden Park, also playing for a Great Britain XI against the Rest of Europe in season 1946/47, to celebrate the home nations rejoining FIFA. He gained all of his Welsh international caps whilst at White Hart Lane with Spurs, his last cap on the 9th May 1954 against Austria, joining the Swans later in August. In April 1949 he was included in an F.A.W. Touring party that played international matches against Portugal, Belgium and Switzerland at the end of the season. Brought to the Vetch Field by manager Billy McCandless as player coach, he later was appointed assistant to McCandless. A classy wing half but abrasive, he led by example, and although many supporters felt he was past his best when he came to the Vetch Field, he gave his all, sometimes playing at centre half. His contemporaries at Spurs said that he never played poorly, displaying consistency as well as genius. Making his Swans debut in the opening league fixture of the 1954/55 season against a West Ham United side that featured John Bond, Noel Cantwell, Malcolm Allison and Dave Sexton, he inspired the Swans to 5-2 win, and at the end of the season finishing in tenth place in the Second Division. In May 1955 he played in the Swans side that beat Llanelly to win the West Wales Senior Cup. Prior to the start of his second season at the Vetch Field, the club was stunned when the death of Bill McCandless was announced, with Burgess taking over as player manager. Following the death of McCandless in the close season, the directors decided not to appoint a manager to replace him, and instead gave Burgess the title of 'team manager', also establishing a 3 man selection committee of Ivor Allchurch, Burgess and Joe Sykes. Despite a fine start to the season, the second half proved to be disappointing, with an injury to key pivot, Tom Kiley, who was not replaced adequately.
New players were brought to the club, but with no real quality, with players like Cliff Jones, Terry Medwin all being transferred. In June 1958, Trevor Morris arrived at the Vetch Field as general manager, in what could be seen as a man to delegate the running of the club. By the end of August 1958 however, Burgess had resigned, saying he was not prepared to accept the post of assistant manager. Faced with lack of funds during his term in office as manager, he did not make the transition to manager, but inspired his men whilst on the field to play constructive football. Joining the Watford coaching staff later in 1958, he was appointed manager in March 1959, led the club to promotion, by finishing in fourth place in the Fourth Division in his first full season at Vicarage Road. He was replaced by Bill McGarry as manager in May 1963, appointed manager at Hendon later in the month, and in the 1965 close season joined the coaching staff at First Division Fulham. He later had managerial appointments at Bedford Town and Harrow Borough. The former Swans' player manager returned to live in Swansea, and died on the 14th February 2005 after a long illness.

60. BURNS, Christopher (CHRIS)

Birthplace: Manchester, 9/11/1967
Ht: 6ft-0ins, **Wt**: 14st-0lbs
Swans debut v. York City (h), 18/12/1993

Swansea City Career Statistics			
Season	League	FAC	AGT
1993/94	4		1/1gls
1994/95	3+2	0+1	
Total	7+2	0+1	1/1gls

Career:
Cheltenham Town, Conf 67+13/5gls
Portsmouth (£25,000 signed in 15/3/1991) lge 78+12/9gls,
   FLC 7+2/2gls, FAC 7, Others 9+1/1gls
Swansea City (loan in 17/12/1993)
Bournemouth (loan in 11/3/1994) lge 13+1/1gls
Swansea City (non-contract in 25/11/1994)
Northampton Town (signed in 13/1/1995) lge 62+4/9gls,
   FLC 3/1gls, FAC 2, Others 3/1gls
Gloucester City (signed in October 1996)
Forest Green Rovers (signed in May 1999) Conf 65/5gls
Gloucester City (signed in June 2001)

Honours: Southern League XI–1998, 1999

Chris Burns started his career with junior sides Brockworth and
Sharpness, prior to signing for Conference side Cheltenham
Town. He was signed by Frank Burrows during his period as
manager of Portsmouth in March 1991, making his league debut
in the opening fixture of season 1991/92 at Blackburn Rovers.
By the end of the season, the attack minded midfielder had not
only played in every league game for 'Pompey', but also
finished the season as second in the goalscoring charts with
eight league goals. That same season the club were also
involved in an exciting FA Cup run which saw them lose out in
the replay on penalties to Liverpool. The following season
Portsmouth reached the first Division Play Off semi-final, losing
to Leicester City, with Chris making an appearance in the first
leg of the semi-final as substitute. A change of management at
Fratton Park saw Burns struggle to make an impression in the
first team line-up, and he linked up with Burrows a second time
in December 1993, on a loan transfer to the Swans as cover for
the injured Colin Pascoe. After returning to Portsmouth, he
made loan appearances for Bournemouth later in the season, but
in November 1994 he returned to the Vetch Field for a second
stint after he had been released by Portsmouth and was
available on a free transfer. However, after his trial period, he
was not offered a contract, and joined Northampton Town on an
initial trial basis which then led to a permanent contract,
becoming one of manager Ian Atkin's first signings. A strong,
tackling midfielder, he will probably be best remembered by
Swans fans for his goal scored at the Vetch Field against Port
Vale in the AutoGlass Trophy Southern Quarter final, a season
which the Swans went on to win the cup against Huddersfield
at Wembley. The previous season, Vale had won the competition
at Wembley, and were a prominent force in the Second Division
at the time. The cost of travelling from his West Country home
was the reason he quit full time professional football at the age
of 28, shortly after the start of the 1996/97 season, returning to
play for Leroy Rosenior's Gloucester City, despite overtures
from Cheltenham Town for his signature. Getting himself
involved with coaching the club's youth team, Burns at that
early stage in his coaching career showed great management
promise, which would lead him to returning to the club in June
2001 as player manager. During this period with City, Burns was
selected for the Southern league XI in seasons 1997/98, and
1998/99. Burns had left City for Forest Green in May 1999 after a
financial falling-out, but after returning to the club, as player

manager, his impact at the club saw him recognised with the
DML Western Manager of the Month Award for January 2003.
which resulted in him signing a five year contract, and taking
City to the edge of promotion in season 2003/04. At Forest
Green Rovers, Burns had been included in the side that lost to
Canvey Island at Villa Park in the 2001 FA Umbro Trophy Cup
Final.

61. BURNS, Francis (FRANKIE) Joseph

Birthplace: Workington, 11/11/1924. **Died:** Southend,
   April 1987
Ht: 5ft-7½ins, **Wt:** 12st-0lbs
Swans debut v. WBA (h), 31/8/1946

Swansea Town Career Statistics			
Season	League	FAC	WC
1946/47	25/5gls	2	1
1947/48	42/2gls	1	1
1948/49	42	2/1gls	4/1gls
1949/50	41	2/1gls	4/1gls
1950/51	18/1gls		1
1951/52	3		
Total	171/8gls	7/2gls	11/2gls

Career:
Wolverhampton Wanderers (amateur)
Swansea Town (signed in August 1944)
Southend United (signed in July 1952) lge 89/14gls, FAC 4
Crewe Alexandra (signed in November 1956) lge 30/7gls

Honours: Third Division South Champions–1949, London
Combination Cup Winner–1947

An amateur earlier in his career with Wolverhampton
Wanderers, Frankie Burns originally signed for the Swans in
August 1944, played War Time Regional Football for the Swans,
before signing professional in July 1946. Frank was in the Army
at Neath during the War, when he started to play for the Swans
and sometimes would stay with Terry Medwin in his house
inside Swansea Prison, where Medwin's father was a Prison
Warder. In June 1947 he was a member of the Swans reserve side
that beat Arsenal at White Hart Lane to win the London
Combination Cup. A tenacious tackler with good positional
sense, he was a key member of the 1948/49 Third Division
South Championship winning team. A terrier of a wing half, he
possessed excellent fitness levels, and was a perfect foil for Roy
Paul. Unorthodox, but fearless at left half, he was a clever ball
player who was an accurate passer of the ball, and who was just
as effective at inside forward. In July 1952 he signed for Third

Division South team Southend United, staying at Roots Hall until November 1956 when he joined Third Division North side Crewe Alexandra. After retiring as a player Frank returned to live in Southend.

62. BURROWS, PAUL Samuel

Birthplace: Swansea, 2/10/1967
Ht: 5ft-8ins, **Wt**: 10st-4lbs
Swans debut v. Wolverhampton Wanderers (a), 14/9/1985

Swansea City Career Statistics		
Season	League	FAC
1985/86	1+2	1/1gls
Total	1+2	1/1gls

Career:
Swansea City (from apprentice signed in October 1985)
Haverfordwest (signed in close season 1987)
Barry Town (signed in close season 1990)

Honours: Wales Yth

Former St. Thomas, Cefn Hengoed schoolboy and Swansea schoolboy striker who joined the Swans as an apprentice after leaving school, signing professional in October 1985. Included during the early part of season by manager John Bond as substitute, Paul made his league debut for the Swans at Wolverhampton Wanderers as substitute for Chris Marustik. He made his first start in December 1985 in the First Round of the FA Cup competition at the Vetch Field against Bristol Rovers, scoring in a 2-1 defeat, making his first league start seven days later, again at the Vetch Field against York City. During his second season as a professional, Paul struggled to figure under Swans manager Terry Yorath, and in May 1987 he was released, joining Haverfordwest, the first of a number of spells at the West Wales club. Joining Beazer Homes League, Midland Division side Barry Town in the 1990 close season, he enjoyed two successful seasons at the club, including playing against the Swans in both legs of the semi-final of the Welsh Cup. After two successful seasons, and after overcoming an injury, he joined Cardiff based side Inter Cabletel, finishing runners up in the league in his first season, and the following season playing in the UEFA Cup competition. After a spell with Briton Ferry and Carmarthen Town, he returned to Haverfordwest, eventually retiring from the game after off the field financial problems at the club saw all of the players having their contracts cancelled in favour of playing a side made up of local talent. After a couple of seasons of no involvement in football, Paul took an active role as manager of one of the young age group sides with Llangyfelach Colts in 2003, overseeing the

progress of his young son, Sammy. His first job after leaving the Vetch Field as a professional footballer was in the Swansea Guildhall as a rent collector, and he has since worked himself into the position of Housing Manager with the Local Authority in the city. By the summer of 2005 he was also involved with coaching at the Swans' Development Centre.

63. BUSSEY, WALTER

Birthplace: Chesterfield, 6/12/1904. **Died**: Exeter, Jan 1982
Ht: 5ft-10ins, **Wt**: 11st-6lbs
Swans debut v. Notts. County (h), 25/8/1934

Swansea Town Career Statistics			
Season	League	FAC	WC
1934/35	37/7gls	2/1gls	3/2gls
1935/36	32/11gls		2/1gls
1936/37	3		
Total	72/18gls	2/1gls	5/3gls

Career:
Aughton Common Celtic
Dinnington Main Athletic
Anston Athletic
Denaby United (signed in close season 1924)
Stoke City (signed amateur in March 1925, £250 professional in November 1925) lge 197/49gls
Blackpool (£1,050 in September 1933) lge 25/8gls
Swansea Town (signed in 3/8/1934)
Exeter City (signed in December 1936) lge 75/16gls

Honours: Third Division North Champions–1927

Walter Bussey played non-league football with a number of clubs before he signed for Stoke City in March 1924, initially as an amateur, before signing professional in November 1925. He made his league debut for Stoke City during season 1925/26, playing against the Swans in a 1-1 home draw during a season which saw the club relegated to the Third Division North. Twelve months later Stoke had won the Third Division North Championship and re-instated themselves back in the Second Division. Over the next six seasons Bussey scored for Stoke City in matches against the Swans in almost every season, scoring two goals in a 5-0 defeat of the Swans in season 1930/31. Joining Second Division Blackpool in September 1933 for £1,050, he continued his goalscoring exploits against the Swans, scoring in a 2-2 draw in February 1934. He spent just one season at Bloomfield Road, signing for the Swans in August 1934, making his debut in the opening league fixture of season 1934/35 at the Vetch Field against Notts. County. The next league game, again at the Vetch Field he opened his goalscoring account for the Swans in a 5-1 win over Oldham Athletic. Fair haired, slight, later in the season he scored against his old club, Stoke City in an FA Cup tie at the Vetch Field which the Swans won 4-1. His best season for the Swans as a goalscorer was the 1935/36 season, when he returned 11 league goals, 4 in one game against Bradford City in an 8-1 victory for the Swans. Even though that day he was opposed by former England centre half Sam Cowan who had been signed by Bradford City from Manchester City. He joined Third Division South side Exeter City in January 1936 making seventy-five league appearances before retiring as a player, and was appointed assistant trainer at the club in May 1946.

64. BYE, LESLIE

Birthplace: Blackwood, Mon, 30/6/1913. **Died:** Blackwood, 11/3/1970
Ht: 5ft-7ins, **Wt:** 10st-7lbs
Swans debut v. Bristol City (a), WC–6, 3/3/1937

Swansea Town Career Statistics		
Season	League	WC
1936/37		2
1937/38	2	
1938/39	1	
Total	3	2

Career:
Swansea Town (amateur in season 1935/36, signed in July 1936)
Dartford (signed in August 1939)
Lovells Athletic (signed by season 1942/3)

Initially arrived at the Vetch Field as a winger, played most of his earlier reserve team games for the Swans on the flank, but made his league debut at half back in a Welsh Cup, Sixth Round match at Bristol City, retaining his place for the semi-final tie at Newport County, in what was predominately a reserve team put out by the Swans. During season 1935/36 he had played a number of matches as an amateur for the Swans' Football Combination and Welsh League sides, signing as a professional in July 1936. He had to wait until the following season before he was given his first Football League game, at left half back against Bury at the Vetch Field, also playing in the next game at Burnley, before giving way to the returning Joe Lloyd. The 1938/39 season saw him make just the one league appearance, this time as a replacement for Imrie at Norwich City early in the season. Released by the Swans in April 1939, he later joined non-league side Dartford in August 1939, making guest appearances later for Lovells Athletic during WW2. Towards the end of the 1942/43 season he played for Lovells Athletic in a Regional League West Cup Final defeat by the Swans. In March 1949 he lined up for Lovells Athletic in a Welsh League match against the Swans.

65. BYRNE, SHAUN Ryan

Birthplace: Chesham, 21/1/1981
Ht: 5ft-9ins, **Wt:** 11st-12lbs
Swans debut: v. Torquay United (h), 7/2/2004

Swansea City Career Statistics		
Season	League	FAC
2003/04	9	1
Total	9	1

Career
West Ham United (from trainee in 2/7/1999) PL 0+2, FLC 0+1
Bristol Rovers (loan in 7/1/2000) lge 1+1, Others 2
Swansea City (loan in 29/1/2004)
Dublin City (signed in 19/8/2004)
Chesham United (signed in January 2005)

Honours: Republic of Ireland Yth, U-21–10, European Youth Champions–1998

Signed by manager Brian Flynn on loan on 29th January 2004, following two other previous West Ham United signings, Leon Britton and Izzy Iriekpen to the Vetch Field. Injury problems had limited the former Republic of Ireland Youth and U-21 international's progress over the previous two seasons at Upton Park. In 1998 he captained the Republic of Ireland Youth side that won the European Youth Championships in Scotland playing alongside John O'Shea, Andy Reid and Liam Miller, and had been attached to the 'Hammers' from the age of eight. He made his debut for the 'Hammers' at left back as substitute for Keller at Newcastle United during the 1999/2000 season, joining Second Division side Bristol Rovers a couple of days later. A pacy defender who likes to get forward, he scored a decisive penalty for Rovers, in a penalty shootout at Northampton Town in the AWS competition, also captaining the Republic of Ireland U-18 side during the same season. Capable of playing in either full back position, as well as in midfield, he was included in West Ham United's FA Youth Cup winning squad of season 1998/99, but an injury suffered during the season saw him sidelined for almost twelve months. He returned to Upton Park towards the end of his second month on loan at the Vetch Field, and following the sacking of manager Brian Flynn, he turned down an offer from the Swans of a permanent contract at the Vetch Field. Released by the 'Hammers' at the end of the season, in late July 2004 he made a surprise second half appearance for the Swans at a pre-season friendly game at Hereford United, but in mid-August 2004, along with former West Ham United player Keith Rowland, signed for Eircom League side Dublin City. In January 2005 he joined Ryman League side Chesham United.

C

1. CALDWELL, Thomas (TOMMY) Somerville

Birthplace: Camlachie, Glasgow 30/1/1909
Ht: 5ft-10½ins, **Wt:** 11st-5lbs
Swans debut: v. Wolverhampton Wanderers (h), 30/3/1929

Swansea Town Career Statistics			
Season	League	FAC	WC
1928/29	3		
1929/30	4		1
1930/31			
1931/32	1		
1932/33	2		
1933/34	1		1
1934/35	1		2
1935/36	4		2
1936/37	39	4	
Total	55	4	6

Career:
Newmains Juniors
Swansea Town (trial in 5/4/1928, professional in late April 1928)

Honours: West Wales Senior Cup Winner–1930, 1934

Arrived initially on trial at the Vetch Field in early April 1928 with team mate Alexandra from Scottish Junior side Newmains Juniors, playing in a reserve game against Luton Town a couple of days later. He signed professional at the end of the month, and initially struggled to make an impression during the early part of his Vetch Field career, because of the consistency of Wilf Milne at left full back, restricting him mainly to playing in the reserve team at the Vetch Field. In May 1929 he was included in the Swans' reserve team that were beaten 4-2 by Cardiff City at

Llanelly in the Final of the South Wales & Monmouthshire Cup Final. It was also with the Swans' reserve side that he gained West Wales Senior Cup honours, beating Newport County in October 1930, and Llanelly in October 1934. In May 1932 he was listed by the Swans, but as he proved to be a good, reliable deputy for Milne, he was kept on the playing staff. Milne's last season at the Vetch Field, saw Caldwell start the season at outside left, then played for most of the season at left back. He left the Vetch Field in June 1938, his career at an end following an injury in a practice game. At the club's AGM in June 1938 it was stated that prior to his injury he had been rated the best left full back in the division. Something of a joker, Tommy earned the following comment from his manager, 'Has developed into a first class player, but does not take his task seriously.'

2. CALLAGHAN, IAN Robert, M.B.E.

Birthplace: Liverpool, 10/4/1942
Ht: 5ft-7ins, **Wt:** 11st-11lbs
Swans debut: v. Tranmere Rovers (h), 16/9/1978

Swansea City Career Statistics				
Season	League	FLC	FAC	WC
1978/79	40	1	4	2
1979/80	36/1gls	3	3	2
Total	76/1gls	4	7	4

Career:
Liverpool (from groundstaff in 1957, professional in March 1960)
   lge 637+3/50gls
Fort Lauderdale (USA)
Swansea City (signed in 15/9/1978)

Cork Hibernians
Soudifjord (Norway)
Crewe Alexandra (signed in October 1981) lge 15

Honours: England U-23–4, Full–4, English Football League XI, Second Division Champions–1962, First Division Champions–1964, 1966, 1973, 1976, 1977, FA Cup Winner–1965, 1974, European Cup Winner–1977, UEFA Cup Winner–1973, 1976, European Super Cup Winner–1977, Charity Shield–1964, 1965 (both shared), 1966, 1974, Football Writers Player of the Year–1974

Signed from the club's juniors in March 1960 as a professional, former Liverpool schoolboy footballer, Ian Callaghan is not only Liverpool's record holder for first team appearances at Anfield, but he is the only player to play in the Second Division, and right through to the club's first European Cup triumph in Rome in 1977. Replacing his boyhood idol Billy Liddell for his league debut against Bristol Rover in the Second Division on the 16th April 1960, he was at the club as a junior when Bill Shankly arrived in 1959 and still playing when the legendary Scot left in 1974. Starting his career as a raiding right winger, he then impressed in a central midfield role during the Bob Paisley era, and was a member of the club's first European Cup success at the age of 35. A gentleman of the game, he was booked only once in a remarkable career which brought him a cascade of medals and an MBE. He gained his first England U-23 cap against Germany in 1963, later playing twice against Yugoslavia, and Rumania all in same year. His first full cap for England was in Helsinki on the 26th June 1966, and his last against Luxembourg in 1978. His club form was such that at the age of 35, he gained a recall to the England team for the game against Switzerland on the 2nd September 1977, after an absence of 11 years, and was included in England's World Cup winning squad of 1966, although he did not feature. Besides the Second Division Championship medal gained in 1962, First Division Championship medals in 1964, 1966, 1973, 1976, 1977, FA Cup Winners medal in 1965 and 1974, F.A. Cup Finalist in 1971, European Cup Winners Medal in 1977, UEFA Cup Winner in1973, 1976, European Super Cup Winner in 1977, Charity Shield in 1964, 1965 (both shared), 1966 and 1974, Ian Callaghan was also voted Player of the Year for season 1973/74 by the Football Writers Association. Ian Callaghan also gained First Division Runners Up medals in 1969, 1974, 1975 and 1978, Football League Cup Finalist in 1978, and was recognised in the New Year's Honours List with an MBE for his services to Football. Signing for the Swans on the 15th September 1978 after a spell in USA with Fort Lauderdale Strikers, (he had joined the exodus of British players to the United States, along with Tommy Smith), making his debut at the Vetch Field against Tranmere Rovers twenty-four hours later alongside his former Anfield team mate Tommy Smith. He played a major part in the Swans promotion winning side, full of running, still going strong, and despite doing most of his training at Anfield, and travelling to Swansea on Thursdays for home games, he maintained the same zest for the game which he had graced for so long. Playing a major role in the Swans promotion success from the Third Division, 'Cally' played a prominent part in establishing the Swans back in the Second Division, scoring his only goal whilst with the Swans, against Charlton Athletic in December 1979. In January 1981 he was released by John Toshack, joining Irish side Cork Hibernians, then playing for Norwegian side Soudifjord, before returning to the Football League to play for Crewe Alexandra in October 1981, before announcing his retirement from the game at the end of the season. Since retiring, one of his involvements has been in media work.

3. CAMPBELL, Alexander Ferguson (SANDY)

Birthplace: Dalmuir, Clydebank 24/1/1897. **Died:** Blackpool, 25/4/1975
Ht: 5ft-9ins, **Wt:** 11st-0lbs
Swans debut: v. Merthyr (h), 26/8/1922

Swansea Town Career Statistics	
Season	*League*
1922/23	7/2
Total	7/2

Career:
Old Kilpatrick
Glasgow Ashfield
Oldham Athletic (signed in June 1920, professional in August 1920) lge 41/8gls
Swansea Town (£70 signed in June 1922)
Oldham Athletic (signed in 16/5/1923) lge 4/2

Honours: B.E.F. XI, West Wales Senior Cup Winner–1923

Played for junior sides Old Kilpatrick and Glasgow Ashfield before making guest appearances for Queens Park during the First World War in close season 1919, joining Oldham Athletic, initially as an amateur in June 1920, before turning professional in August 1920. He had been spotted by Oldham while playing football for B.E.F.XI v. French XI in Paris in 1918. He scored on his debut for Oldham Athletic in the First Division, and after two seasons with the club signed for the Swans in August 1922. Despite being on the small side, he was solidly built and was a tricky player. Signing for the Swans in June 1922 from First Division side Oldham Athletic, after just seven league appearances he returned to Boundary Park to rejoin Oldham Athletic, who had been relegated to the Second Division. At inside left he had found his position in the Swans line-up limited following the signing of Len Thompson. Scored his two goals for the Swans in the game at Reading in August 1922, in what was his second match for the Swans. In May 1923 he was included in the Swans reserve side that beat Llanelly to win the West Wales Senior Cup. His release by the Swans in May 1923 was surprising as he was rated one of the cleverest and most natural footballers' at the Vetch Field at the time, also very versatile, capable of playing in either inside forward position, wing half, and at full back. After returning to Oldham Athletic, he was forced to retire from the game after injury in May 1924, and was later on the committee of Oldham Rugby League Club, but in 1929 made appearances for Mossley.

4. CANNING, Leslie Daniel (DANNY)

Birthplace: Penrhiwceiber, 21/2/1926
Ht: 5ft-11ins, **Wt:** 12st-4lbs
Swans debut: v. Notts. County (h), 22/1/1949

Swansea Town Career Statistics		
Season	*League*	*WC*
1948/49	18	2
1949/50	23	3
1950/51	6	
Total	47	5

Career:
Abercynon Athletic
Cardiff City (signed in 1944) lge 80

Swansea Town (£3,000 signed in 6/1/1949)
Nottingham Forest (£2,000 signed in July 1951) lge 5
Yarmouth (signed in close season 1952)
Newport County (signed in August 1955) lge 0
Abergavenny

Honours: Wales ATC–2, Third Division South Champions–1947, 1949

Danny Canning joined the Cardiff City playing staff at the age of eighteen in 1944, after earlier making appearances for the Wales Air Training Corps against England and Scotland. He made rapid progress at Ninian Park, playing a big part in the club's Championship success of season 1946/47, and made regular appearances in the 'Bluebirds' first team line-up prior to his arriving at the Vetch Field in January 1949. In September 1944 he made a couple of appearances for Aberaman in South West Regional Football, and the following season made regular appearances for Cardiff City, also in Regional Football. Brought up in Penrhiwceiber, Danny attended Penrhiwceiber Junior and Abercynon Central Schools (Ysgol Ganol), and with limited opportunities for playing football, started an apprenticeship as a fitter and turner at Penrhiwceiber Colliery after leaving school. His senior playing career started in the Pontypridd League with Abercynon Athletic, prior to his signing for Cardiff City. After arriving at the Vetch Field he initially contested the number one jersey with Jack Parry, but midway through the 1950/51 season, a certain John King made his entry, and by the end of the season both Canning and Parry would leave the Vetch Field. Canning and Parry alternated in the Swans' goal during the 1948/49 Third Division South Championship winning season, with Canning playing in the last eighteen league games of the season. A tall, athletic goalkeeper, Canning had the physical advantage over the shorter Parry, but lacked consistency, although on his day however he was a superb keeper. At the end of his first season at the Vetch Field Canning also played in the 2-0 Welsh Cup Final defeat by Merthyr at Ninian Park, Cardiff in May 1949. Although he started the 1950/51 season as first choice, Canning lost his placed initially to Parry, but after Johnny King had made his mark, shortly after the end of the season, Canning was sold to Nottingham Forest for £2,000. Making just five league appearances for Forest, his last in January 1952, he was transfer listed in June 1952 by Forest for £2,000, but then signed for non-league side Yarmouth before returning to the Football League to sign for Newport County in August 1955. By now, injury problems prevented him from making an impact at Somerton Park, and after being released played a couple of games for Abergavenny before retiring from the game. On returning to South Wales he returned to his former trade as a fitter and turner at Penrhiwceiber Colliery, and after a couple of years later worked for Cardiff Lathe Tools, BOAC, and AB Electronics, gaining promotion to a management role up to his retirement. Now living in Kilgetty, Pembrokeshire, Danny has recently been recovering from major surgery.

5. CARR, James Edward Charles (JIMMY)

Birthplace: Maryhill, 18/12/1893. **Died:** Harrow, 26/6/1980
Ht: 5ft-7½ins, **Wt:** 10st-5lbs
Swans debut: v. Grimsby Town (a), 30/8/1926

Swansea Town Career Statistics		
Season	League	WC
1926/27	7/1gls	1
Total	7/1gls	1

Career:
Watford Orient (signed in close season 1912)
Pinner
Watford (signed as amateur in February 1913, professional in August 1913)
West Ham United (signed in May 1914)
Reading (signed in close season 1919) lge 116/8gls
Southampton (£25 signed in June 1923) lge 86/10gls
Swansea Town (signed in May 1926)
Southall (signed in July 1927)
QPR (signed in October 1927)

Honours: West Wales Senior Cup Winner–1927

A founder member of Watford Orient, he signed professional with Watford before signing for West Ham United, and in the summer of 1919 joined Reading. During WW1 he made guest appearances for Portsmouth and Kilmarnock whilst a private in the Army. At Elm Park he formed an exciting left wing partnership with Len Andrews, and after Andrews had left for Southampton, he took over the number eleven shirt, missing just ten games in the club's first three seasons in the League. After arriving at the Dell in June 1923 he resumed his partnership with his former Reading team mate Andrews in the 'Saints' line-up, and in 1925 he helped the 'Saints' reach the semi-finals of the F.A. Cup competition. He joined the Swans in August 1926, but found his opportunities in the Swans first team limited owing to the form of D. S. Nicholas, the regular left winger. In April 1927 he was included in a Swans reserve side that beat Bridgend Town in the West Wales Senior Cup Final. His only goal for the Swans was scored in his last game, against Darlington in May 1927, and shortly after he was released. Approaching his mid-thirties he then took the unusual step of placing an advert in the sporting paper, The Athletic News, offering his services in exchange for a business, which later saw him for a brief spell become the proprietor of The Red Lion Hotel at Southall, Middlesex. Joining non-league side Southall, he later signed for QPR, but failed to make a league appearance for the club. At the age of 61, Jimmy represented England at Bowls in the 1954 Empire Games in Vancouver.

6. CARVER, David (DAVE) Francis

Birthplace: Wickersley, 16/4/1944
Ht: 6ft-1ins, **Wt:** 11st-10lbs
Swans debut: v. Brentford (h), 26/1/1973

Swansea City Career Statistics	
Season	League
1972/73	3
Total	3

Career:
Rotherham United (from apprentice in January 1962) lge 82

Cardiff City (£11,000 signed in January 1966) lge 210+1/1 gls,
ECWC 13
Swansea City (loan in 17/1/1973)
Hereford United (signed in 24/8/1973) lge 14
Doncaster Rovers (loan in 9/3/1974) lge 29+1
Retford Town (signed in close season 1974)

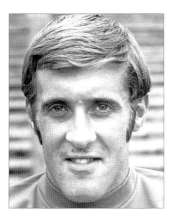

Honours: Welsh Cup Winner–1968, 1969, 1970, 1971

Experienced right full back who made just three league
appearances on loan to the Swans starting on the 17th January
1973. One of Swans' manager Harry Gregg's first signings, the
three matches he played for the Swans brought two victories,
returning to Ninian Park at the end of his month loan. He
attended Wickersley Secondary Modern earlier in his career,
played for his school side, and also Rother Valley Schoolboys
prior to joining Rotherham United as an apprentice on leaving
school. One of his earliest first team matches for United was at
the Vetch Field against the Swans in April 1962 in the Second
Division, prior to joining Cardiff City in January 1966 for a fee of
£11,000. An automatic choice in the 'Bluebirds' side that
regularly contested the final of the Welsh Cup, he also gained
European experience on a regular basis following the club's
success in the Welsh Cup, including the semi-final against
Hamburg in the 1967/68 season. He played in four consecutive
Welsh Cup Final victories, and in 1972 played in the final when
the 'Bluebirds' were beaten by Wrexham. He returned to Cardiff
City after his loan spell, and after failing to make any further
appearances for the 'Bluebirds' joined Hereford United in
August 1973. Promoted from the Fourth Division the previous
season, he started the season in United's Third Division line-up,
but after losing his place, had a loan spell at Doncaster Rovers
towards the end of the season. In the 1974 close season he joined
Midland League side Retford Town, retiring from the game
twelve months later. Up until his retirement three years ago,
Dave had been a licensee for twenty-four years in Norwich and
Cambridge, and is currently living in Winterton-on-Sea.

7. CASEY, RYAN Peter

Birthplace: Coventry, 3/1/1979
Ht: 6ft-1ins, **Wt:** 11st-2lbs
Swans debut: v. Leyton Orient (a), 1/10/1996

Swansea City Career Statistics					
Season	League	FLC	FAC	FAWP	AWS/LDAF
1996/97	3+7				
1997/98	2+4			2+3	1
1998/99	5+5/1gls	1+1		3+1/1gls	
1999/2000	0+11		0+1	4+1	1
2000/01	3+6/1gls		0+1	2	0+1
2001/02	6+10			1+1	
Total	19+43/2gls	1+1	0+2	12+6/1gls	2+1

Career:
Swansea City (from trainee in 7/5/1997)
Merthyr Tydfil (loan in September 2001)
St. Patricks, Ireland (signed in August 2002)
Cork City
Galway United (signed in 4/2/2004)

Honours: Republic of Ireland U-18, U-21

Ryan made his league debut for the Swans as a second half
substitute whilst still a trainee at Leyton Orient for Richie
Appleby, a player who earlier in the game had came on as a
substitute for Lee Jenkins. During his career, injuries at critical
moments in the season prevented him from establishing himself
in the first team starting line-up, and had a big part to play in
him failing to attain the level of consistency required. Also a lack
of reserve team opportunities at the Vetch Field also played it's
part. During the Swans season of 2000/01 in Division Two, he
suffered a depressed fracture of the tibia and ruptured medial
ligaments, and during season 2001/02 a knee injury, fractured
skull, and a broken bone in his ankle in the penultimate league
match of the season at Hartlepool. In September 2001 he had a
loan spell at Merthyr Tydfil, and after his return was regularly
included in the Swans matchday squad, having his best run in the
first team, showing signs when selected of consolidating his
position as first choice on the left side of midfield with his
ability to deliver quality crosses from the left flank. Represented
the Republic of Ireland at U-18 and U-21 level earlier in his
career, and scored on his debut for the Republic of Ireland U-18
side in October 1997 against Northern Ireland. In April 1999
Ryan was a member of the Republic U-21 squad that competed
in the World U-21 Championships in Nigeria, where they lost in
the second round to the hosts, with Ryan failing to make an
appearance in the tournament. His first Swans league goal was
scored at Cambridge United on the 15th August 1998. Primarily
a left sided winger, Ryan on occasions also played at left full
back. After he was released by manager Nick Cusack, following
his rehabilitation at the Vetch Field, he returned to Ireland on a
trial basis with St. Patricks, linking up with former Swans player
Tony Bird. Making further appearances for Cork City, Ryan
signed for Eircom Division One side Galway United in February
2004.

8. CASH, BRIAN Dominick

Birthplace: Dublin, 24/11/1982
Ht: 5ft-9ins, **Wt:** 12st-0lbs
Swans debut: v. Southend United (h), 19/10/2002

Swansea City Career Statistics		
Season	League	AWS
2002/03	5	1
Total	5	1

Career:
Nottingham Forest (from trainee in 15/12/1999) lge 0+7, FLC 0+1
Swansea City (loan in 18/10/2002)
Rochdale (loan in 20/8/2004) lge 6, FLC 1
Bristol Rovers (non-contract signed in 24/12/2004) lge 0+1
Heart of Midlothian (trial in January 2005)
Derry City (signed in 14/2/2005)

Honours: Republic of Ireland Yth, U-21–3

Signed by manager Brian Flynn on a month's loan in October 2002, the right sided wide midfielder possessed a good turn of pace, and made a good impression during the early part of his loan period with the Swans. Finding opportunities difficult to come by with Forest since making his league debut as a substitute for Andy Reid at Stockport County on the 2nd February 2002, he was unable to come to terms with the more physical side of Third Division football, and after returning to Forest played mainly in the reserve team apart from a substitute appearance in the last game of the season. The Irish winger returned to Nottingham Forest after boss Paul Hart confirmed that he didn't want Cash to play in the FA Cup tie with the Swans, although at the time it appeared that there remained a possibility that he might have been retained for a second month. Gained youth and U-21 honours for the Republic of Ireland whilst with Forest. Shortly after the start of the 2004/05 season he joined Rochdale on loan, making appearances in the League, and in the League Cup Competition. After returning to Forest, in late October he was a non-playing substitute in Forest's League Cup win over Doncaster Rovers, with Forest being spared a League Cup ko after apologising to the Football League for their mistake in including the player in the squad. In early November he was released by Forest, signed for Bristol Rovers in late December, making just one substitute appearance for the club on a non-contract basis against Northampton Town. After a further trial period, this time in Scotland with Heart of Midlothian, Brian returned to Irish football to sign for Derry City on Valentines Day.

9. CATLOW, THOMAS

Swans debut: v. Southampton (h), 16/10/1920

Swansea Town Career Statistics	
Season	League
1920/21	1
Total	1

Career:
Southend United
Barry AFC (signed in September 1913)
Swansea Town (trial in September 1920, signed in September 1920)
Mid-Rhondda (signed in October 1920)
Rochdale (signed in October 1921) lge 1

Previously a Southern League defender with Southend United, he was one of three Southend United players, Steel (goalkeeper) and McNaught (inside forward) who signed for Barry AFC prior to the club's first season in the Southern League. Appointed vice-captain to Jim Wightman, he missed the club's first game against Mid-Rhondda on the 6th September 1913, but made his debut for 'The Linnets' in the defeat by the Swans a week later, becoming a regular inclusion for the remainder of the season. He arrived at the Vetch Field on a trial basis shortly after the start of the club's first season in the Football League and made a good impression playing for the Swans' reserve side in Western League matches. Replacing Holdsworth for his debut at centre half in a one all draw at the Vetch Field against Southampton, it was felt at the time that he was not the type of centre half the club were looking for, and within a couple of weeks had joined Western League side Mid-Rhondda. He returned to the Football League with Third Division North side Rochdale in October 1921, but again, made just the one league appearance for the club, against Stockport County on the 22nd October 1921 before being released.

10. CHALMERS, PAUL

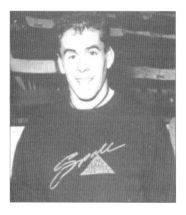

Birthplace: Glasgow, 31/10/1963
Ht: 5ft-10ins, **Wt:** 10st-3lbs
Swans debut: v. Blackpool (h), 2/12/1989

Swansea City Career Statistics					
Season	League	FLC	FAC	WC	L/DAF
1989/90	13+3/4gls		3/2gls		2
1990/91	12+9/2gls			1+2/3gls	
1991/92	14+7/7gls	0+1			
Total	39+19/13gls	0+1	3/2gls	1+2/3gls	2

Career:
Glasgow Celtic (signed 'S' form in 1979, professional in October 1980) lge 0+4/1gls
Bradford City (loan in January 1986) lge 2
St. Mirren (signed before start of season 1986/87) lge 77+24/23gls, SLC 3/1gls, SFC 4+2/3gls
Swansea City (£124,000 signed in 23/11/1989)
Dunfermline Athletic (signed in August 1992) lge 23+9/9gls, SFC 1/1gls
Hamilton Academicals (signed in July 1993) lge 33+11/7gls, SLC 3, SFC 1

Ayr United (signed in September 1993) lge 5/1gls
East Fife (signed in February 1994) lge 6+2/4gls

Honours: Scotland Yth, Welsh Cup Winner–1991, West Wales
Senior Cup Winner–1991

Paul Chalmers commenced his football career with St. Helen's
Primary School, and Turnbull High School Glasgow, played for
Eastercraigs Amateurs before signing 'S' forms with Glasgow
Celtic in 1979, following his father who played for Celtic when
they won the European Cup in 1967 against Inter Milan. In five
seasons as a professional with Celtic he failed to make a start for
Glasgow Celtic, but in his debut as substitute scored in the 4-0
win over Morton on the 19th February 1985. After gaining
honours with the Scottish Youth side, he made a further three
substitute appearances for Celtic, a short spell with Bradford
City, before joining St. Mirren at the start of the 1986/87 season
after a trial period with Nottingham Forest in August 1986.
His first season with St. Mirren saw him score three goals in
consecutive cup games, but missed the semi-final and final of
the Scottish Cup through injury, with his club beating Dundee in
the final 1-0. Finishing the next two seasons as top goalscorer for
St. Mirren, he was signed by Swans manager Ian Evans in
October 1989 for £124,000, in a total deal of £300,000, which also
included Keith Walker and John Hughes. His first goals for the
Swans came when he scored two goals against Peterborough
United in an FA Cup tie in December 1989, a week after he had
signed. He scored a hat trick against Fulham on the 10th
February 1990, and also scored another hat-trick for the Swans
against Llanelli in a Welsh Cup tie third round in 30/10/1990 at
the Vetch Field. At the end of the season he made a substitute
appearance, replacing Andy Watson for the Swans in the Welsh
Cup Final win over Wrexham in the National Stadium in
Cardiff. Paul possessed a good eye for goalscoring
opportunities, but always appeared to struggle to maintain the
fitness levels required for regular selection. Returning north of
the border to sign for Dunfermline Athletic in August 1992, he
made further Scottish League appearances for Hamilton
Academical, Ayr United and East Fife. During season 1995/96
which was his last season in Scottish professional football, he
started with Hamilton, then went to Ayr United in September
1995, then joined East Fife in February 1994.

11. CHAPMAN, LEE Roy

Birthplace: Lincoln, 5/12/1959
Ht: 6ft-2ins, **Wt:** 13st-0lbs
Swans debut: v. Bradford City (a), 30/3/1996

Swansea City Career Statistics	
Season	League
1995/96	7/4gls
Total	7/4gls

Career:
Stafford Rangers
Stoke City (from juniors in 22/6/1978) lge 95+4/34gls,
    FLC 5/3gls, FAC 3/1gls
Plymouth Argyle (loan in 5/12/1978) lge 3+1
Arsenal (£500,000 in 25/8/1982) lge 15+8/4gls, FLC 0+2,
    FAC 0+1, Others 2/2gls
Sunderland (£200,000 in 29/12/1983) lge 14+1/3gls, FAC 2/1gls
Sheffield Wednesday (£100,000 in 24/8/1984) lge 147+2/63gls,
    FLC 17/6gls, FAC 17+1/10gls, Others 2+1
Niort, France (£350,000 in 1/6/1988)
Nottingham Forest (£350,000 in 17/10/1988) lge 48/15gls,
    FLC 12/6gls, FAC 5/3gls, Others 6/3gls
Leeds United (£400,000 in 11/1/1990) lge 133+4/62gls,
    FLC 15/10gls, FAC 11/4gls, Others 10/4gls
Portsmouth (£250,000) in 11/8/1993) lge 5/2gls, Others 1
West Ham United (£250,000 in 16/9/1993) lge 33+7/7gls,
    FLC 4+1/2gls, FAC 6/2gls
Southend United (loan in 11/1/1995) lge 1/1gls
Ipswich Town (£70,000 in 19/1/1995) lge 11+11/1gls, FLC 1,
    Others 2
Leeds United (loan in 11/1/1996) lge 2
Swansea City (signed in 28/3/1996)

Honours: England U-21–1, B–1, FLC 1989, FMC 1989, Second
Division Champions–1990, First Division Champions–1992

Son of former Aston Villa, Lincoln City, Mansfield Town, Port
Vale player Roy Chapman, his only England U-21 cap was
against the Republic of Ireland in 1981, when playing for Stoke
City, also gaining representation for the England 'B' side. A
former Stoke Schoolboy front runner, Lee started with Stafford
Rangers prior to starting his professional career with Stoke City,
he was top goalscorer for the club in 1980/81 and 1981/82, and
later in his career ended top goalscorer for Sheffield Wednesday
in seasons 1986/87 and 1987/88, and for Leeds United in
seasons 1990/91, 1991/92 and 1992/93. At Nottingham Forest
he was a member of the side that won both the Simod Cup, and
the League Cup in the same season (1988/89). With Leeds
United he gained a Second Division Championship medal in
1990, and two seasons later was a member of the side that won
the First Division Championship. He was signed by Swans
manager Jan Molby on transfer deadline day, 28th March 1996
on a contract until the end of the season, and at that stage the
Swans still had a slight chance of avoiding relegation. Despite
scoring on his debut at Bradford City, and scoring three further
goals, he was unable to prevent the Swans from relegation to the
Third Division, and at the end of the season retired from the
professional game. Married to television actress Leslie Ash
(Men Behaving Badly), following his retirement from football,
Lee concentrated on his business interests which included a
night club and restaurant in London.

12. CHAPPELL, Leslie (LES) Alan

Birthplace: Nottingham, 6/2/1947
Ht: 5ft-8ins, **Wt:** 10st-5lbs
Swans debut: v. Newport County (h), FLC 1-1, 14/8/1976

Swansea City Career Statistics				
Season	League	FLC	FAC	WC
1976/77	39+1/5gls	4/1gls		2
1977/78	26+1	1	1	1
Total	65+2/5gls	5/1gls	1	3

Career:
Rotherham United (from groundstaff in April 1963, signing as
    professional in February 1965) lge 106+2/37gls

Blackburn Rovers (£20,000 signed in May 1968) lge 7
Reading (signed in July 1969) lge 193+8/78gls
Doncaster Rovers (signed in 19/12/1974) lge 57+1/10gls
Swansea City (signed in July 1976)

A schoolboy footballer with Southgrove Secondary Modern School and Rotherham Boys, Les joined the groundstaff at Millmoor on leaving school, making his league debut in 1965 at the age of seventeen in the Second Division, and who went on to make over one hundred league appearances, before signing for Blackburn Rovers in May 1968 in an exchange transfer deal involving Alan Gilliver, plus £20,000. After an unhappy spell at Ewood Park, where at one time he considered giving up football, he was persuaded to join Reading by manager Jack Mansell in July 1969. His first season at Elm Park saw Les become an important part of Reading's free scoring forward line, scoring twenty-four league goals, which included a nine-minute hat-trick against Barnsley, which was completed with a spectacular diving header, that has been regarded as one of Elm Park's greatest goals. During season 1973/74 he was the league's top scorer at Easter, but an ankle injury kept him sidelined for the remainder of the season. His twenty-eight league and cup goals that season included a club record equalling four league hat-tricks. Following a spell with Doncaster Rovers, the midfielder was signed by Swans manager Harry Griffiths to add some experience to his team. Making his Swans debut against Newport County in League Cup First Round, First Leg at the Vetch Field, he scored the Swans first goal in a 4-1 victory. He started in the return leg at Somerton Park, but was then sidelined until the end of September. Les played a prominent part in the Swans Fourth Division campaign that season, missing out on promotion in the last couple of games of the season. The following season he again featured regularly, with the Swans this time gaining promotion, in what was to be the start of the most historic era in the club's history. He was appointed player manager of the club's reserve side at the start of the 1978/79 season in the Welsh League, also taking on the youth team coaching position. After coaches Phil Boersma and Doug Livermore had left the Vetch Field in 1983, following the return of Toshack as manager in December 1983, he was appointed his assistant, and within a couple of months took over as caretaker manager of the Swans in March 1984, following the sacking of Toshack. With the Swans virtually relegated to the Third Division, he was unable to halt the club's slide, and with the Football League placing an embargo on the club preventing him from signing players, most of the youngsters he had been grooming in the club's reserve team were given their first team opportunities. With the appointment of Colin Appleton as manager in May 1984, Les had a period as his assistant up to December 1984, when, following the sacking of Appleton, he again reverted to a short spell as caretaker until John Bond was appointed the new manager. Within days of Bond's appointment however, Les left the Vetch Field, later taking up an appointment as manager of non-league side Farnborough Town in October 1984. Appointed manager of Basingstoke Town in July 1985, twelve months later he returned to the Football League as assistant manager at Torquay United

to Stuart Morgan. After a season at Plainmoor, he joined John Mahoney at Newport County in the Vauxhall Conference, just prior to the club ceasing to trade. For the last seven to eight seasons Les has been the South West Area Representative for Premiership side Southampton, and also has a commercial cleaning business in Torquay.

13. CHAPPLE, SHAUN Ronald

Birthplace: Swansea, 14/2/1973
Ht: 5ft-11ins, **Wt:** 12st-3lbs
Swans debut: v. Welling (h), FAC–1, 17/11/1990

Swans City Career Statistics								
Season	League	FLC	FAC	WC	AGT/ AWS	P/Offs	ECWC	FAWP
1990/91			0+1					
1991/92	17+4/ 2gls	0+1/ 1gls	2	2/ 2gls	2		0+1	
1992/93	4		1+1		1			
1993/94	19+10/ 3gls	2	2	2	1/ 1gls			
1994/95	4+5/ 2gls		2+1	2	2+1			
1995/96	15+7/ 2gls	1	1					
1996/97	10+7	1+1			1	0+1		
1997/98	3+1							2/ 1gls
Total	72+34/ 9gls	4+2/ 1gls	8+3	6/ 2gls	7+1/ 1gls	0+1	0+1	2/ 1gls

Career:
Swansea City (from YTS in 15/7/1991)
Barry Town (loan during season 1994/95)
Merthyr Tydfil (signed in 29/10/1997)
Forest Green Rovers (£5,000 signed in December 1998) Conf 7+8
Carmarthen Town (signed during 1999/00 season)

Honours: Wales Sch, Yth, Wales U-21–8, 'B', West Wales Senior Cup Winner–1991, 1994, 1995

Former Cefn Hengoed, Swansea Schoolboy and Welsh Schoolboy international midfielder, who had trials with Nottingham Forest prior to joining the Swans as a YTS trainee on leaving school, signing professional in July 1991. He made his Swans debut as substitute for Paul Raynor against Welling United, three months short of his seventeenth birthday in the first round of the FA Cup on the 17th November 1990, with his first league appearance coming in September 1991 against Fulham. Following appearances for the Welsh Youth side, he made his first appearance for the Welsh U-21 side in May 1992, in a 3-2 win over Rumania, later making an appearance for the Welsh 'B' side. In May 1991 he was included in the Swans side that beat Llanelli to win the West Wales Senior Cup, in 1994 when the Swans beat Ammanford Town in the same competition, also making a substitute appearance twelve months later against Morriston Town. A good competitor in midfield, not possessing a great deal of pace, he was unable to step up a level to command a regular position in the Swans starting line-up, although at the time he was competing against John Cornforth for a central midfield position, and became very much a squad player. When Jan Molby was manager of the Swans, he thought that Shaun was the best passer of a ball at the club, and but for a number of injury problems at a time when he had started to establish himself in the Swans first team, his career in the professional game could have been extended. When the Swans reached the Third Division Play Off Final at Wembley in season 1996/97 against Northampton Town, Shaun was a non-playing substitute. During his career with the Swans he had loan spells with non-league sides Barry Town in season 1994/95, and with Merthyr Tydfil in October 1997. Always capable of getting himself on the scoresheet for the Swans, in a West Wales Senior Cup semi-final tie against Pembroke Borough in March 1995, he scored five goals in a 16-0 victory. In December 1998 Shaun joined Conference side Forest Green Rovers for £5,000, later in the 1999/2000 season joining League of Wales side Carmarthen Town, where he combined his football with working for the Post Office in Swansea.

14. CHARLES, JEREMY Melvyn

Birthplace: Swansea, 26/9/1959
Ht: 6ft-1ins, **Wt:** 12st-0lbs
Swans debut: v. Newport County (h), FLC 1–1, 14/8/1976

Swansea City Career Statistics					
Season	League	FLC	FAC	WC	ECWC
1976/77	36+5/23gls	5+1/3gls	1	2	
1977/78	27+6/3gls	1+1/1gls	2+1/1gls	2	
1978/79	36+4/12gls	3/1gls	3/2gls	1+1/1gls	
1979/80	39+1/5gls	4	4	4/3gls	
1980/81	37+1/5gls	1/1gls	1	6/2gls	
1981/82	9+4/2gls	1		2	1/1gls
1982/83	30+2/2gls	4	1	6	5/4gls
1983/84	10	1			2
Total	224+23/52gls	20+2/6gls	12+1/3gls	23+1/6gls	8/5gls

Career:
Swansea City (signed as apprentice in July 1976, professional in January 1977)
QPR (£100,000 signed in 28/11/1983) lge 10+2/5gls, FAC 1
Oxford United (£100,000 signed in 7/2/1985) lge 41+5/13gls, FLC 6/2gls

Honours: Wales Sch, Yth–3, U–21–2, Full–19, FLC Winner–1986, Welsh Cup Winner–1981, 1983

Son of former Swans legend Mel Charles, former Dynevor and Swansea schoolboy, Jeremy made his Swans debut as a substitute for Robbie James in a League Cup First Round, First Leg at the Vetch Field against Newport County making a sensational start, scoring two goals in a 4-1 win, six weeks short of his 17th birthday whilst still an apprentice at the Vetch Field. As a fifteen-year-old whilst still in school, he played a season for Bishopston in the First Division of the Swansea Senior League. During his first season with the Swans he scored 2 goals in consecutive league games against Brentford and Newport County, and later in season scored two goals in a game on three more occasions, against Aldershot, Newport County and Hartlepool United. Starting off as a frontline striker, where he was able to use his large frame, and strength in the air to an advantage, he scored twenty-three league goals in season 1976/77, but later in his career he was to follow his father, and be capable of playing in either a midfield, or defensive role. A member of the Swans side that gained consecutive promotions in 1978 and 1979, Jeremy scored the third Swans goal at Preston North End which clinched promotion to the First Division in May 1981, and also scored the first Swans goal in the First Division, against Leeds United in the opening league fixture of the 1981/82 season. During his period at the Vetch Field Jeremy played in two Welsh Cup Final wins, against Hereford United in 1981, and against Wrexham in 1983. Capped at schoolboy and youth level, Jeremy made his first appearance at U-21 level for Wales against England in 1979, making his debut for the Full Welsh team against Czechoslovakia at Ninian Park, Cardiff in November 1980. He was capped on twelve occasions whilst with the Swans, twice with QPR, and five times whilst with Oxford United. Following relegation to the Second Division in 1983, and with financial problems off the field increasing, the Swans were forced to offload players, with Jeremy being sold to QPR in November 1983 for a modest £100,000. Fifteen months later he moved to Oxford United for a similar transfer fee, and in April 1986 Jeremy scored United's third goal at Wembley in a 3-0 Milk Cup win over QPR. At the end of the 1985/86 season he finished runner up to John Aldridge at United, scoring nine league goals. Despite starting the 1986/87 season in United's first team, he missed most of the season through injury, and midway through the following season was forced to retire from the professional game, taking up a position in the youth development and centre of excellence department at Oxford United. Following the Silver Shield takeover at the Vetch Field in August 1997, Llanelli born Malcolm Elias, who was involved with the youth development department at Oxford United, who Charles had worked under, was appointed Director of Youth Development at the Vetch Field in March 1988, with Charles returning to the Vetch Field a month later as his assistant. In late February 2000, with Elias announcing he was leaving the Vetch Field, Jeremy was appointed Director of Youth Development until the end of the season, before leaving the Vetch Field to take up a similar appointment with Elias at Southampton. Since leaving the Saints in 2003, Jeremy has been involved in the Coerver Method of Football coaching in schools in the Oxford area, also assisting his brother-in-law in his electrical installation business.

15. CHARLES, Melvyn

Birthplace: Swansea, 14/5/1935
Ht: 6ft-1ins, **Wt:** 14st-0lbs
Swans debut: v. Sheffield United (a), 20/12/1952

Swansea Town Career Statistics

Season	League	FAC	WC
1952/53	20	1	2
1953/54	31/10gls	2	
1954/55	38/11gls	4	2/3gls
1955/56	34/8gls	1	4/1gls
1956/57	39/13gls	1	6/1gls
1957/58	40/10gls	1/1gls	2
1958/59	31/14gls	1/1gls	2
Total	233/66gls	11/2gls	18/5gls

Career:
Swansea Town (from juniors, professional in 17/5/1952)
Arsenal (£42,750 signed in 26/3/1959) lge 60/26gls
Cardiff City (£27,000 signed in February 1962) lge 81/24gls,
  ECWC 1
Portmadoc (signed in season 1965/66)
Port Vale (signed in February 1967) lge 7
Haverfordwest County

Honours: Wales U-23–1, Full–31, Welsh Cup Winner–1964,
British Army XI, English Schools Shield Winner–1950,
West Wales Senior Cup Winner–1956, 1957

Brought up in the Cwmdu area of Swansea, the former
Manselton Senior Schoolboy was the younger brother of the
legendary John Charles, played in the Swansea Boys side that
beat Manchester Boys in the English Schools Shield Final,
Second Leg in May 1950, and made his debut for the Swans at
centre half at Bramall Lane against Sheffield United on the 20th
December 1952, remaining in the Swans side, apart from two
games, until the end of the season, either at centre half, or
occasionally at right full back. Before the end of the season Mel
had come up against his brother playing for Leeds United, with
the Swans winning 3-2 at the Vetch Field. Earlier in his career
Mel had signed amateur forms for Leeds United. One of the
most versatile players in the game, at full back, half back or as a
forward, he could always be relied upon to give a good account
of himself. Very much attack minded, Mel figured prominently
in the Swans goalscoring charts, scoring his first hat-trick
against Llanelly in a Welsh Cup tie in January 1955, scoring four
goals against Blackburn Rovers in the opening fixture of the
1956/57 season. In April 1956 and in May 1957 he played in
successful West Wales Senior Cup Finals against Llanelly and
Haverfordwest. In April 1958 he scored a hat-trick against Stoke

City, and during season 1958/59 scored hat-tricks against both
Middlesbrough (November 1958), and Sheffield Wednesday
(December 1958). Mel made his first appearance for Wales on
the 20th April 1955 in Belfast against Northern Ireland at right
half, with his brother John scoring a hat-trick in a 3-2 win for
Wales. Making a further twenty appearances for Wales whilst
with the Swans, he also made six with Arsenal, and four with
Cardiff City. Whilst with the 'Bluebirds' Mel scored four goals
for Wales at Ninian Park against Northern Ireland on the 11th
April 1962. Like his brother John, Mel was extremely versatile,
but was probably most effective at wing half where he appeared
to produce more consistent all round performances. The long
time target of bigger clubs, Mel eventually signed for Arsenal
for £42,750 in late March 1959, with Arsenal player Peter Davies
joining the Swans as part of the package, and David Dodson
joining the Swans in the close season. Unfortunately, he never
settled in the big city, and after three years joined Cardiff City in
1962 for £27,000. Mel won a Welsh Cup Winner's medal whilst
with Cardiff City in 1964, following the 2-0 win over Bangor
City, also making appearances in the European Cup Winners
Cup competition. At the Vetch Field he had been unlucky with
the Swans in appearing in two Welsh Cup Final defeats by
Cardiff City and Wrexham. He started off well at Ninian Park,
but after suffering a number of injuries was released at the end
of season 1965/66, joining North Wales side Portmadoc, coming
up against the Swans in a Welsh Cup tie in February 1966. In
February 1967, after scoring four goals for a Port Vale reserve
side against Bromsgrove he was given a contract by the club's
manager Sir Stanley Matthews until the end of the season. A big,
combative player, he suffered from his versatility, probably most
effective as an attacking wing half, fast and strong, with fine ball
control, possessing also a fierce shot in either foot.
After appearances for Oswestry Town, he returned to Swansea,
became involved in various businesses in Swansea, and finished
his senior career in the Welsh League with Haverfordwest
County, also turning out for Swansea Senior League side
Cwmfelin in the early 1970's.

16. CHEDGZOY, SIDNEY

Birthplace: Ellesmere Port, 17/2/1912. **Died:** Liverpool,
  17/1/1983
Ht: 5ft-9½ins, **Wt:** 11st-4lbs
Swans debut: v. Manchester City (a), 27/8/1938

Swansea Town Career Statistics

Season	League	FAC	WC
1938/39	18/2gls	1	1
Total	18/2gls	1	1

Career:
Orwell Wednesday Wavertree (signed in January 1928)
Burscough Rangers (trial in August 1929)
New Brighton (amateur in February 1928)
Everton (signed in April 1929) lge 0
Burnley (signed in May 1933) lge 5/1
Millwall (signed in May 1934) lge 3
Runcorn (signed in May 1935)
Halifax Town (trial in May 1936) lge 0
Runcorn (signed in September 1936)
Sheffield Wednesday (signed in May 1937) lge 4
Runcorn (signed in October 1937)
Swansea Town (signed in May 1938)

The son of former Everton and England International footballer
Samuel Chedgzoy, Sidney, a former Liverpool Schoolboy
footballer, graduated from non-league football with Orwell
Wednesday Wavertree and New Brighton to sign for First

Division side Everton in April 1929, but after failing to make a first team appearance joined Second Division side Burnley thirteen months later. Making league appearances for both Burnley and Millwall, he then played non-league with Runcorn before a trial period with Halifax Town in May 1936, later returning to Runcorn. He then had a spell with Sheffield Wednesday, returned to Runcorn, then joined the Swans in July 1938. He played initially for the Swans at outside right, but also played at right half towards the end of the season. He scored his first goal for the Swans in a 1-1 draw at Millwall in January 1939. A strong, fast, outside right who possessed a powerful shot, he remained at the Vetch Field until May 1938, and during WW2 he made guest appearances for New Brighton (January 1940), Cardiff City (1942/43), Tranmere Rovers (1942/43), and also Aberaman.

17. CHEETHAM, John (JACKIE)

Birthplace: Wishaw, 25/3/1904. **Died:** Manchester, 16/10/1987
Ht: 5ft-10ins, **Wt:** 11st-6lbs
Swans debut: v. West Bromwich Albion (h), 2/2/1929

Swansea Town Career Statistics	
Season	League
1928/29	15/9gls
1929/30	10/2gls
Total	25/11gls

Career:
Broxburn United
Brighton & Hove Albion (signed in October 1925) lge 8
West Ham United (trial in 1926) lge 0
Eccles United
Hurst (signed in August 1928)
Swansea Town (£250 signed in January 1929)
Connah's Quay & Shotton (signed in August 1930)
Ashton National (trial in November 1930)
Hyde United (signed in December 1930)
Accrington Stanley (signed in May 1933) lge 39/15gls
Stalybridge Celtic (signed in September 1934)
Witton Albion (signed in June 1936)
Linotype (signed in August 1938)

A relatively in-experienced centre forward who scored on his Swans debut against West Bromwich Albion in February 1929 at the Vetch Field in a 6-1 win, without any of the opposing players touching the ball. Resulting from a superb piece of McPherson strategy, Jackie scored direct from the kick off, with the first Albion player to touch the ball being the goalkeeper when he picked the ball out from the back of the net. He scored three goals in the next two league fixtures, and by the end of the season had scored nine goals from fifteen league appearances, just three goals behind the top goalscorer Deacon. Earlier in his career he had travelled south to join Brighton & Hove Albion in October 1925 from Scottish Second Division side Broxburn United, initially as a trialist, before signing professional two months later with the reputation of a highly promising inside-forward. However, he failed to live up to expectations at the Goldstone Ground, with all his first-team appearances coming in the latter part of the 1925–26 season, playing for the reserve team for the whole of the following campaign. Placed on the free-transfer list at the end of 1926–27, Jack had an unsuccessful trial with West Ham United before dropping into non-League football with Eccles Borough and Hurst, but he returned to the League fold in January 1929 signing for manager James Hunter Thomson, for a fee in the region of £250. In August 1930 he returned to non-league football to sign firstly for Connah's Quay, then Ashton National (Gas Company) and Hyde United.

In just over two seasons in the Cheshire League with Hyde United, Jack was reputed to have scored 160 goals, and was rewarded with a move to Accrington Stanley in the Third Division (North) in May 1933. He was leading scorer for Stanley in 1933–34 with fifteen goals in 39 League games, but was released at the end of the season and had a couple of years with Stalybridge Celtic before ending his career with a spell at Witton Albion, and finally with Linotype in August 1938.

18. CHINAGLIA, GIORGIO

Birthplace: Carrara, Italy, 24/1/1947
Ht: 6ft-1ins, **Wt:** 11st-12lbs
Swans debut: v. Rotherham United (a), FLC-3, 14/10/1964

Swansea Town Career Statistics		
Season	League	FLC
1964/65	1	1
1965/66	3+1/1gls	
Total	4+1/1gls	1

Career:
Swansea Town (from apprentice in April 1965)
Lazio (signed in 1969)
New York Cosmos (signed in 1976)

Honours: Italy Full–14, NASL Champions–1977, 1978, 1980, 1982, West Wales Senior Cup Winner–1965

Son of a Cardiff Italian restauranteur, a big, bustling type of centre forward with good pace, who would go on to make his mark in not only Italian club football, but on the international stage with Italy, as well as playing a pioneering part in reviving football in the United States with Beckenbauer and Pele. He did not develop as expected at the Vetch Field with the Swans, and was released, briefly going back to Cardiff, but then starting again back in Italy. Making his Swans first team debut whilst still an apprentice, he replaced Brian Evans in a League Cup Third Round tie at Rotherham United early in season 1964/65, making one further league start that season, at the Vetch Field against Portsmouth in February 1964. Signing professional in April 1965 he featured in the early games of season 1965/66, scoring in the second game of the season at Bournemouth. In May 1965 he scored in the 3-0 win over Llanelli in the West Wales Senior Cup Final. Given a free transfer in 1966, because the coaching staff considered him too lazy and disliked his attitude, Chinaglia returned to his native Italy to rebuild his ailing career, playing in lower league football with Massese and Internapoli before joining Lazio in 1969. He soon became the idol of the Lazio fans, finishing Serie A top goalscorer in 1974 with 24 goals, helping Lazio to their first league title, and also playing two games for Italy in the 1974 World Cup Finals. Giorgio Chinaglia had an eight year career from 1976 to 1983 with the New York Cosmos, after playing seven seasons with Lazio in the Italian Serie A. He was second to Archie Stark as being the most prolific goal scorer in the history of the North American Soccer League, scoring a total of 193 goals in 213 matches, and 50 goals in 43 play off games. In the 1980 playoffs he scored 18 goals in 7 games, including a remarkable 7 in one game against Tulsa. As well as winning the NASL Championship in 1977, 1978, 1980 and 1982, he scored 24 or more goals in 6 straight seasons, with his best season in 1980 when he scored 32 goals from 32 matches. He was a First Team NASL ALL STAR in 1976, 1978, 1979, 1980, 1981 and 1982, and the League's Most Valuable Player in 1981. In 2000 he was Inducted into the U.S. National Soccer Hall of Fame. After retiring in 1983, Chinaglia purchased a majority interest in the Cosmos, but within a year the league folded and Chinaglia returned to Italy. At one time he served as the director of sports for both a television station and a newspaper in Rome, and has been an influential figure as President of Italian club Lazio.

19. CHIVERS, GARY Paul Stephen

Birthplace: Stockwell, 15/5/1960
Ht: 5ft-11ins, **Wt:** 11st-5lbs
Swans debut: v. Brighton (h), 10/9/1983

Swansea City Career Statistics	
Season	League
1983/84	10
Total	10

Career:
Chelsea (apprentice in July 1976, signed professional in 7/8/1978) lge 128+5/4gls, FLC 8, FAC 8
Swansea City (signed in 1/8/1983)
QPR (signed in 15/2/1984) lge 58+2, FLC 6, FAC 2, Others 1
Watford (signed in 10/9/1987) lge 14, FLC 1, FAC 4
Brighton & Hove Albion (£40,000 in 18/3/1988) lge 215+2/14gls, FLC 12, FAC 12, Others 11/2gls
Lyn, Norway (signed after being released in May 1993)
Bournemouth (Non–contract in 1/11/1993) lge 29+2/2gls, FAC 4, Others 1+2

Honours: London Sch

Born a Chelsea supporter in South London, he represented the London Schools and graduated through an apprenticeship with his favourite club to sign professional forms at the age of eighteen in August 1978. Within nine months of becoming a professional he made his league debut against Middlesbrough

on the 21st April 1979, retaining his place and playing in the final four league games of the season, which saw Chelsea relegated to the Second Division. Making over one hundred league appearances in the Chelsea first team over the next four seasons, he was released in May 1983, and was signed by Swans manager John Toshack in August 1983 on a free transfer. He arrived at the Vetch Field following relegation from the First Division, and after a poor start to the season, and off the field money problems, within two months of the season starting, the club was offloading as many of it's high earners for next to nothing, with young professionals and reserves being placed in the club's league side. He followed Jeremy Charles to QPR and despite having to wait until November 1984 before he made his league debut for the club made regular appearances in the Rangers first team, before transferring to First Division Watford in September 1987. A defender who was capable of playing in any defensive position, right, or left side, a change of manager at Vicarage Road resulted in a transfer request after just fourteen League games. Brought to the Goldstone in 1988 to deputise for the injured Kevan Brown, Gary Chivers rapidly became an indispensable member of the Albion team. The new acquisition performed admirably as the club finished runners-up in Division Three, and after an indifferent spell the following season, the versatile Londoner soon won the fans over with his reliable and consistent displays, going on to skipper the side on many occasions. Particularly good at reading a game and snuffing out danger before it arose, Gary started a match at Millwall in September 1991 in goal following a pre-match injury to Perry Digweed, keeping a clean sheet for eight minutes until he was replaced by Mark Beeney. Granted a testimonial in August 1992 in lieu of a signing-on fee after just over four years at the Goldstone, Gary was released in May 1993, largely in an attempt to reduce the wage bill, and spent the summer in Oslo with the Norwegian League club Lyn, but he returned to England to join AFC Bournemouth in November 1993, making his home debut in the 'Cherries' F.A. Cup win over the Albion. In August 1994 he appeared to be on the point of joining Scarborough as player-coach, but after the club had dismissed manager Steve Wicks, Gary went back to Bournemouth. In January 1995 he returned to Sussex with the ambitious Hastings-based County League club Stamco (while also running Chelsea's under-13 team), and took over as Worthing player-manager in September 1996, but he left Woodside Road after just three months following a dispute with the board. Gary then became a chauffeur with ambitions to become a London taxi-driver.

20. CLARKE, Patrick KEVIN Noel

Birthplace: Santry, 3/12/1921
Ht: 6ft-0ins, **Wt:** 12st-8lbs
Swans debut: v. Millwall (a), 12/3/1949

Career:
Drumcondra
Swansea Town (signed in November 1948)

Honours: League of Ireland, Republic of Ireland–2, London Combination Cup Winner–1950, Welsh League First Division Champions–1951

Swansea Town Career Statistics	
Season	League
1948/49	1
1949/50	1
1950/51	3
1951/52	5
Total	10

An Eire cap and League of Ireland Representative XI player who gained two caps for the Republic of Ireland in 1948 whilst with Drumcondra against Portugal and Spain. Signed by manager Billy McCandless in November 1948, he was on the Swans books until the end of season 1951/52. A classy type of footballer, Kevin did not adjust to English league football and played most of his Swans games in the reserves. He arrived at the Vetch Field at a time when the club had a strong Irish contingent. Playing at right full back, wing half, or at centre half, he struggled to oust either Elwell, Keane, O'Driscoll, Weston or Paul from the Swans first team line-up. In May 1950 he was a member of the Swans reserve side that won at Southend United to win the London Combination Cup Final. Twelve months later he made appearances during the season for the Welsh League side that won the First Division Championship. In May 1952 he was placed on the open to transfer list by the Swans, later returning to Ireland.

21. CLODE, MARK James

Birthplace: Plymouth, 24/2/1973
Ht: 5ft-10ins, **Wt:** 10st-10lbs
Swans debut: v. York City (a), 14/8/1993

Swansea City Career Statistics						
Season	League	FLC	FAC	WC	AGT/AWS	FAWP
1993/94	26+2/1gls	2	2	5+1	4	
1994/95	33/1gls	4	1	3	2	
1995/96	25+5	0+2			1	
1996/97	16+2/1gls	1	2		0+2	
1997/98	7+1		1		1	1
1998/99	2				1	
Total	109+10/3gls	7+2	6	8+1	9+2	1

Career:
Plymouth Argyle (from trainee in 30/3/1991) lge 0

Swansea City (signed in July 1993)
Bath City (signed in July 1999)
Clevedon Town (signed in July 2001)

Honours: AutoGlass Trophy Winner–1994

A surprise signing by manager Frank Burrows, the former midfielder had been released by Plymouth Argyle after failing to make an appearance in Argyle's first team, and for the start of the 1993/94 season he had been included in the Swans first team at right full back for the opening game of the season at York City. By the end of the season he had switched to a left sided full back position, playing at Wembley in the AutoGlass Trophy Final success over Huddersfield Town. Mark also scored his first goal during his first season at the Vetch Field, in a 2-0 home win over Exeter City. Possessing good skill on the ball, a tigerish tackler, at times he looked a far better player than his lack of experience showed, and could quite easily have played in a higher standard of the game. Remaining a regular first team member over the next three seasons, during the 1996/97 season, a hamstring injury, plus a broken ankle in reserve team outing, as well as undergoing surgery on a chronic shin problem the following season limited his first team opportunities. That season also saw him undergo an operation for the removal of his appendix. With Michael Howard taking over at left full back, Mark was released at the end of season 1998/99, signing for non-league Bath City in the close season. In July 2001 he signed for Clevedon Town, where he finished his playing career, and working for a bakery in Bath.

22. COATES, JONATHAN Simon

Birthplace: Swansea, 27/6/1975
Ht: 5ft-8ins, **Wt:** 10st-4lbs
Swans debut: v. Fulham (a), 27/11/1993

Swansea City Career Statistics						
Season	League	FLC	FAC	FAWP	AWS/LDV	P/Offs
1993/94	0+4/1gls					
1994/95	0+5					
1995/96	7+11	1+1	1		2	
1996/97	38+2/3gls	1	2		2	3
1997/98	41+2/7gls	2/1gls	1	3	0+1	
1998/99	30+3	1	3	3	1+1	2
1999/00	41+1/6gls	3+1	1	1	0+1	
2000/01	16+3/1gls	1		5/2gls		
2001/02	44+1/5gls	1	2	3/1gls	1/1gls	
2002/03	2+1					
2003/04	13+13	0+1	1+3	2	1	
Total	232+46/23gls	10+3/1gls	11+3	17/3gls	7+3/1gls	5

Career:
Swansea City (from trainee in 8/7/1993)
Cheltenham Town (signed in 18/10/2002) Others 1
Woking (signed in 15/11/2002) Conf 14+2/1gls
Swansea City (signed in 27/3/2003)
Newport County (signed in August 2004)
Aberystwyth Town (signed in January 2005)

Honours: Wales Yth, U-21–5, 'B', Third Division
Champions–2000, West Wales Senior Cup Winner–1995, 2002

Surprisingly released at the end of season 2001/02 by manager
Nick Cusack, after pre-season training with Swindon Town and
Oxford United, he broke his forearm in a friendly with Oxford
United sidelining him until after the start of the season. Earlier,
in May 1995 he was included in a Swans reserve side that beat
Morriston Town in the West Wales Senior Cup Final, and almost
seven years later was included in the Swans side that beat
Hakin United in the final of the same competition. When he
returned to fitness, he trained at the Vetch Field with the Swans,
hoping to impress the new Swans manager Brian Flynn, but
with no offer of a contract, signed non-contract with
Cheltenham Town, playing in an LDV cup tie for the club, but
with no firm contract offered to him, eventually signed until the
end of the season with Conference side Woking. A left sided
winger initially, then midfielder, occasionally left full back, who
many people thought never fulfilled his potential with the
Swans, having the ability to beat his opponent with ease, strike a
lovely left cross, and capable of scoring spectacular goals from
outside the penalty area. The younger brother of former Swans
trainee Marc Coates, the former Morriston Schoolboy made his
first team debut at Fulham as a substitute for Darren Perrett on
the 27th November 1993, and scored his first goal for the Swans
at Bristol Rovers in his third league appearance. He had to wait
until August 1995 before he made his first start for the Swans in
the opening league fixture against Shrewsbury Town, and at one
stage during the season it was thought that he could have been
given a free transfer, as the club were reeling from one
managerial crisis to another. His elder brother Marc had also
been a trainee at the Vetch Field but did not make a first team
appearance, despite a couple of times being named as a
substitute. Marc went on to make a name for himself as a
goalscorer in non-league football with Merthyr and Macclesfield
Town, playing at Wembley in FA Trophy final for Macclesfield.
The 1996/97 season under Jan Molby saw Jonathan start to
establish himself as an integral part of the Swans midfield, and
by now had been capped at U-21 level for Wales, and at the end
of the season was included in the Swans team that lost to
Northampton Town in the Third Division Play Off Final at
Wembley. Two seasons later Jonathan played against Scunthorpe
United in the Third Division Play Off semi-final, and also
during the season made an appearance for the Wales 'B' side
that beat Northern Ireland in Wrexham. The following season
under John Hollins he missed just four league games during the
club's Third Division Championship success, also scoring six
league goals. Not noted for his strength in the tackle, Jonathan
nevertheless covered a lot of ground in attack, or in defence,
getting in many last ditch tackles in his own area, and scored a
couple of remarkable goals from outside the penalty area. In
May 2003 he signed a one year contract with the Swans, but
despite figuring regularly in the first team squad in midfield, or
at left full back towards the end of the season was given a free
transfer by new manager Kenny Jackett, linking up with non-
league side Newport County on a part-time basis, and working
in the building industry in Swansea. A regular member of the
County side during the first half of the 2004/05 season, in early
January 2005 he was released from the playing staff because of
financial cutbacks at the club, joining Welsh Premiership side
Aberystwyth Town.

23. COBB, GARY Edward

Birthplace: Luton, 6/8/1968
Ht: 5ft-8ins, **Wt:** 11st-5lbs
Swans debut: v. Huddersfield Town (a), 19/8/1989

Swansea City Career Statistics			
Season	League	FLC	ECWC
1989/90	5	2	1
Total	5	2	1

Career:
Luton Town (from apprentice in 5/8/1986) lge 6+3
Northampton Town (loan in 13/10/1988) lge 1
Swansea City (loan in 14/8/1989)
Fulham (signed in August 1990) lge 8+14, FLC 0+1, FAC 2,
Others 2
Chesham United (signed in September 1992)
Aylesbury Town (signed in close season 1995)
St. Albans City (signed in July 1996)
Chertsey Town
Old Dunstablians (signed in September 1999)
Bedford Town (signed in November 1999)
Berkhamstead (signed by October 2000)

Honours: Diadora Premier Division Champions–1993

Former apprentice at Kenilworth Road with Luton Town who
made his debut as a replacement for Brian Stein against
Charlton Athletic on the 2nd May 1987 in the First Division, also
playing in the next league game against Oxford United. The
following season he made his first start for the 'Hatters' early in
the season against West Ham United and Chelsea, and made a
further five first team appearances later in the season.
Making one loan appearance for Northampton Town in October
1988, he was signed by Swans manager Ian Evans just prior to
the start of the 1989/90 season, making his debut in the opening
league fixture against Huddersfield Town. A midfielder who
liked to go forward, Gary also played in the Littlewoods Cup
games against Exeter City, and also for the Swans in the
European Cup Winners Cup tie in Greece against Panathinaikos,
before returning to Kenilworth Road. Returning to Kenilworth
Road, he failed to make any further appearances for the
'Hatters' and at the end of season 1989/90 was released by
Luton Town. In October 1990 he joined Third Division side
Fulham, making his debut at the beginning of October against
Birmingham City. He was released at the end of the 1991/92
season joining non-league Chesham United in September 1992,
helping the club by the end of the season to win the Diadora
Premier Division Championship. Further non-league
appearances were made for Aylesbury Town, St. Albans City,
Chertsey Town, Old Dunstablians, Bedford Town and

Berkhamstead. During the 2000/01 season he played in a number of matches for Berkhamstead, but did not play in the FA Vase Final defeat by Taunton Town at Villa Park. Whilst with St. Albans City, Gary was on the staff of Chelsea's Football in the Community Scheme.

24. COLE, DAVID Andrew

Birthplace: Barnsley, 28/9/1962
Ht: 6ft-3ins, **Wt:** 12st-4lbs
Swans debut: v. Brentford (a), 22/9/1984

Swansea City Career Statistics			
Season	League	FAC	WC
1984/85	7+1	2	2/2gls
Total	7+1	2	2/2gls

Career:
Sunderland (signed in 10/10/1983) lge 0
Swansea City (signed in 21/9/1984)
Swindon Town (signed in 18/2/1985) lge 69/3gls, FLC 6, FAC 2, Others 2
Torquay United (signed in 28/11/1986) lge 107+3/6gls
Rochdale (signed in July 1989) lge 73+11/7gls
Exeter City (signed in August 1991) lge 0+2
Merthyr Tydfil (signed in season 1992/93) Conf 11+1

Honours: Fourth Division Champions–1986

Raw, inexperienced central defender who was signed by Swans manager Colin Appleton on a non-contract basis after being released by Sunderland, and after having trials with Crewe Alexandra and Scottish side St. Mirren. Tall, and slight in build, he made his debut at Brentford in late September 1984, and had to wait almost two months before his next league appearance against Reading, but had also made appearances in the FA Cup replay defeat at Bognor Regis, and saved the Swans by scoring the equalizer at the Vetch Field against Spencer Works in a Welsh Cup tie. He also scored in the 5-0 replay win at Spencer Works. Following the appointment of John Bond as manager, he was released after playing against Lincoln City in early January 1985. Joining Fourth Division Swindon Town, after making his debut he remained in the side until the end of the season, and the following term, missed just two matches as the 'Robins' won the Championship of the Fourth Division, and also reached the Fourth Round of the Milk Cup. Signed by Torquay United midway through the 1986/87 season, he played in twenty-three consecutive game helping the 'Gulls' to narrowly avoid relegation to the Vauxhall Conference. The following season he came up against the Swans in the Fourth Division Play Off Final, playing in both legs. Missing few matches following a transfer to Rochdale in July 1989, he enjoyed an exciting FA Cup run in his first season, losing 1-0 to eventual finalists Crystal Palace. After a move to Exeter City in August 1991, he had his contract cancelled midway through the 1991/92 season, made Vauxhall Conference appearances for Merthyr Tydfil during the 1992/93 season, prior to ending his playing career with Newport AFC and Cinderford.

25. COLEMAN, Christopher (CHRIS)

Birthplace: Swansea, 10/6/1970
Ht: 6ft-2ins, **Wt:** 14st-6lbs
Swans debut: v. Stockport County (a), 18/8/1987

Swansea City Career Statistics							
Season	League	FLC	FAC	WC	FRT/L.DAF	ECWC	P/Offs
1987/88	29+1	2	2	1	2		4
1988/89	43	2	3/	6/	1		
			1gls	1gls			
1989/90	46/2gls	2	4	1	2	2	
1990/91	41	2	4	7/1gls	4		
Total	159+1/2gls	8	13/1gls	15/2 gls	9	2	4

Career:
Manchester City (signed Ass. Schoolboy in November 1984, YTS in 1986)
Swansea City (trainee in March 1987, signed professional in September 1987)
Crystal Palace (£275,000 signed in 19/7/1991) PL/lge 143+11/13gls, FLC 24+2/2gls, FAC 8/1gls, Others 2
Blackburn Rovers (£2,800,000 signed in 16/12/1995) PL 27+1, FLC 2, FAC 2
Fulham (£1,900,000 signed in 1/12/1997) lge 136/8gls, FLC 13/2gls, FAC 11/1gls, Others 3

Honours: Wales Sch–4, Yth, U-21–3, Full–32, Welsh Cup Winner–1989, 1991, First Division Champions–1994, 2001, Second Division Champions–1999, Fourth Division Play Offs–1988

Former Townhill, Bishop Vaughan and Swansea Schoolboys defender who left his home city to join Manchester City as a YTS trainee in the summer of 1986, but returned home after failing to settle in Manchester, with the Swans agreeing to take over his apprenticeship. Terry Phelan was the Swans left full back that season, and after he left in the summer of 1987 to sign for Wimbledon, Chris was given the opportunity by manager Terry Yorath to start the 1987/88 season as first choice left full back. Playing in front of him on the left side of midfield was Tommy Hutchison, and like Phelan the previous season, the canny Scotsman encouraged the young defender, nurturing him through his first seasons in the professional game. By the end of his first season, Coleman had made thirty-five league appearances, and also played in the end of season successful Play Off Final win over Torquay United. Gaining international honours as a schoolboy, he played for the Wales youth side after joining the Swans, and on the 19th May 1990 he made his debut at U-21 level, scoring in the 2-0 defeat of Poland, the first of three U-21 appearances for his country whilst at the Vetch Field.

For the Welsh U-21 side he often played in central defence, unlike his left full back position with the Swans at the time, but in years to come he would settle into central defence, maturing into a classy, international quality central defender. His second season in the Swans first team saw him play in the Welsh Cup Final defeat of non-league Kidderminster Harriers, and his last match for the Swans in May 1991 he would play in his second Welsh Cup Final success, this time over Wrexham at the National Stadium in Cardiff. After playing in his first Welsh Cup Final, Chris sampled European Cup Winners Cup football the following season when the Swans drew Greek side Panathinaikos, but on the other side of the coin was a member of the Swans team that played in the 8-0 record defeat at Anfield against Liverpool in an FA Cup replay in January 1990. At the end of his last season with the Swans, in April 1991 he was voted by his fellow professionals as top choice in his position in the Third Division of the Barclays League. Joining First Division side Crystal Palace for £275,000 in July 1991, primarily as a left full back, at Selhurst Park he often played in a central defensive role, and also as a central striker, where his strength in the air was utilised to great effect. His sale to Palace, decided by a transfer tribunal, was to bring the Swans a further £800,000 from a sell on clause when the defender signed for Blackburn Rovers for £2.8 M in December 1995, from which the Swans were obliged to pay Manchester City £200,000, from a clause inserted when Coleman joined the Swans from the Maine Road club. At Selhurst Park, despite suffering relegation in his second season, he also played in the semi-final of the Coca Cola Cup competition, and at the end of season 1993/94 gained himself a First Division Championship medal. The following season he played in his second semi-final for the club, against Manchester City in the FA Cup. With Palace he also gained the first of his thirty-two international caps for Wales, when he was selected to play against Austria in Vienna on the 29th April 1992. Making his international debut as a substitute for Young, Chris scored the Welsh equalizer in a creditable 1-1 draw. Making regular appearances in the Rovers Premiership line-up, Chris was then signed by Kevin Keegan for Fulham for £1.9M in December 1987, becoming the club's most expensive signing, and by the end of the season had played in his club's semi-final defeat in the Second Division Play Offs against Grimsby Town. The following season they were crowned Champions of the Second Division, and within two season s had reached the Premiership by winning the First Division Championship. Unfortunately for Chris, after playing in the first twenty-five league matches he suffered a car crash which eventually forced his retirement from the game. Despite appearances in the Fulham's reserve side in his attempt at a comeback, his last game was as a substitute for Wales in Cardiff against Germany. Requiring a series of operations on his badly damaged leg, he was still on crutches when he received the First Division Championship Trophy at the final home game of the season, and his form had been such during the first half of the season that he had been named in the PFA Divisional awards for the fourth successive season. On the 2nd October 2002, club captain Coleman was forced to announce his retirement from the professional game following the injuries he sustained in the car crash. He retained his links with Fulham, joining manager Jean Tigana's coaching staff later in October, working alongside first team coaches and academy coaches. During the last month of the 2002/03 season he took over as caretaker manager after Tigana had left Fulham, steering the club away from the relegation zone, and within twelve months, following his appointment as manager of Fulham on a permanent basis, had not only guided the club to almost qualifying for a Champions League place, but also showed himself to be a manager of the modern era with great vision and enthusiasm.

26. COLLINS, James (JIMMY) D.C.M.

Birthplace: Dundee, **Died:** Chester
Ht: 5ft-10ins, **Wt:** 12st-0lbs
Swans debut: v. Luton Town (a), 30/8/1919, Sth. Lge

Swansea Town Career Statistics			
Season	League	FAC	WC
1920/21	36/1gls	3	
1921/22	39/4gls	7	2
1922/23	8		
1923/24	39/2gls	4	2
1924/25	21		
1925/26	38	7	3
1926/27	22/1gls	5	1
1927/28	21		1
1928/29	36	2	
1929/30	15	1	
Total	275/8gls	29	9

Career:
Lochee Harp
Llandrindod Wells Red Cross FC
Swansea Town (signed in 30/8/1919)

Honours: Third Division South Champions–1925, Welsh League Representative XI, West Wales Senior Cup Winner–1923, 1925

Played football at Pembroke Dock whilst in the Army, and was discovered by the Swans playing for Red Cross at Llandrindod, signing for the Swans in August 1919. He became the first player to sign as a professional for the Swans after the First World War, and was a member of the Swans Southern League team that started season 1919/20 in the First Division of the Southern League. In 1919 he was decorated by the King, receiving the Albert Medal and Gold Medal. A War Office statement said, "he put his foot on a Mills Bomb and saved many lives." In April 1920 he played for a Welsh League Representative side against Welsh League Champions, Mid-Rhondda, and in late-September 1921 he made a second appearance for a Welsh League XI, this time against a Southern League XI at Aberdare. In March 1925 he was included in a Welsh League Representative side that played the Irish Free State in Dublin and in Cork. Making his league debut for the Swans in the second league game of the 1920/21 season at the Vetch Field against Watford, he played almost all of his career with the Swans as a wing half and centre half, but during the 1921/22 season, following injuries to regular forwards Edmundson and Beynon, played the last five league games of the season as centre forward, or inside right. Against Bristol Rovers he scored a hat trick in an 8-1 win. In May 1923, and in January 1925 he was included in the Swans reserve side that beat Llanelly to win the West Wales Senior Cup. He made twenty-one league appearances during the Swans Third Division South Championship success in season 1924/25, and the following season played in all the rounds of the FA Cup, when the Swans reached the semi-finals. The 1925/26 season also saw him play in the Welsh Cup Final defeat by Ebbw Vale. After being transfer listed by the Swans in December 1929, his last game for the Swans came in January 1930 against Wolverhampton Wanderers, and on the 17th March 1933 he set sail for South Africa to take up a coaching appointment with the Transvaal Football Association, coaching in schools and colleges in Witwatersrand, with his headquarters being in Johannesburg. On his return to the United Kingdom he became trainer at Millwall in late 1931, coach and assistant trainer at Chester in November 1933, returned to South Africa in March 1934 as a coach with the Southern Transvaal Association, returning to Chester as trainer in May 1936. In 1943 he joined the Army for the second time, going to France in 1944. He sustained a bad accident to his leg whilst in Holland, spending a lot of time in hospital, undergoing treatment after three operations. After the war, after failing to get back into football he joined the N.A.A.F.I. Staff civilian section, volunteering for Palestine, and working in Haifa. By April 1949 he had returned to the U.K. and rejoined his old club Chester, where he was involved in looking after the club's younger players.

27. COLLINS, Terence (TERRY) James

Birthplace: Penrhiwceiber, 8/1/1943
Ht: 5ft-7ins, **Wt:** 10st-7lbs
Swans debut: v. Aldershot (h), 13/4/1968

Swansea Town Career Statistics	
Season	League
1967/68	1
Total	1

Career:
Barry Town (signed in close season 1961)
Hereford United (signed in close season 1964)
Haverfordwest County (signed in close season 1966)
Ton Pentre (signed during season 1966/67)
Swansea Town (signed in 17/3/1967)
Haverfordwest County (signed in close season 1968)
Merthyr Tydfil (signed in close season 1970)
Abercynon Athletic (signed in close season 1973)

Honours: South Wales Senior Cup Winner–1961, Southern League First Division Champions–1965

Terry Collins attended Old Ladies R.C. School in Mountain Ash, played no football at school, but was spotted by a Swans scout playing for Penrhiwceiber Colts U-18 side, and invited to join the ground staff at the Vetch Field on leaving school. He was released two years later, joined Southern League side Barry Town, and his first game for the club came in a held over from the previous season South Wales Senior Cup Final against Ton Pentre. During the four seasons he spent at Jenner Park, he played in some exciting F.A. Cup ties, one notably against Queens Park Rangers. Joining non-league Hereford United, he made appearances in the United side that won the Southern League First Division Championship in season 1964/65 under manager Alf Sherwood. Returning to the Welsh League to join Haverfordwest County in 1966, following a short spell with Ton Pentre, he returned to the Vetch Field, signed by manager Billy Lucas as a professional in March 1967. He played just one league game for the Swans, in a 1-0 home win over Aldershot. An inside forward, or midfielder, he was primarily a reserve

team player with the Swans, and was released in May 1968, rejoining Haverfordwest County, managed by Ivor Allchurch. After three seasons at Bridge Meadow, he signed for Southern League Premier side Merthyr Tydfil, and shortly after John Charles had been appointed manager dropped down to the Welsh League with Abercynon Athletic, eventually taking over as manager. During his ten year period as manager he led the club from the basement of the Second Division of the Welsh League, to the First Division Championship in season 1982/3, and some exciting Welsh Cup games, notably against Hereford United, Shrewsbury Town and the Swans at the Vetch Field, which turned out to be one of Doug Livermore's last games in charge of the Swans on a caretaker basis. Up to his retirement Terry worked for thirty years with the Local Authority.

28. COMLEY, Leonard (LEN) George

Birthplace: Swansea, 25/1/1922
Ht: 5ft-7ins, **Wt:** 11st-6lbs
Swans debut: v. West Bromwich Albion (h), 31/8/1946

Swansea Town Career Statistics			
Season	League	FAC	WC
1946/47	6/1gls		
1947/48	22/6gls	1	1
Total	28/7	1	1

Career:
Swansea Town (from juniors in 11/5/1946)
Milford United (signed in 27/8/1948)
Newport County (signed in October 1948) lge 76/29gls
Scunthorpe United (£850 signed in March 1951) lge 12/5gls

Honours: London Combination Cup Winner–1947, Wales Fire Service XI–2, Welsh League Division Two Champions–1955, Regional League Cup Winner–1943

Local product who joined the Swans from the club's junior side, and played for the Swans during war time organised football. When the Swans had to play their games at St. Helen's during the war, Len scored the goal that beat Reading in the first game at the ground. Towards the end of the 1942/43 season he played in a Regional League West Cup Final win over two legs against Lovells Athletic. He also made appearances for Aberaman (1944/45) during the war years. Brought up in the Hafod area of the city, Len attended Hafod School before starting work at the RTB Cwmfelin Press Works on leaving school at the age of fourteen, prior to joining the Swans on the groundstaff in 1946. A lively forward with a good touch, he was a versatile player, capable of playing in all forward positions. During the war he made appearances for the Wales Fire Service side against

Scotland and England. Making his Swans debut in the opening fixture of the 1946/47 season at outside left against West Bromwich Albion, he also played at outside right and inside left during the season for the Swans, and at the end of the season scored the winning goal for the Swans Reserve side against Arsenal in the Football Combination Cup Final. He opened his goal scoring account for the Swans in a 6-1 defeat by Bradford Park Avenue at the Vetch Field in September 1946, and in the following season enjoyed a longer run in the first team, returning six goals from twenty-two league appearances. After a dispute with the club, he joined Welsh League side Milford United in August 1948, but within a couple of months returned to Football League action with Third Division South side Newport County. Rarely missing a game for County, his first season at Somerton Park saw the club reach the last sixteen of the F.A. Cup competition before being beaten in extra time by Portsmouth, the eventual winners. In March 1951 he joined newly elected to the Football League side Scunthorpe United, returning to Swansea at the end of the season to return to work at the RTB Cwmfelin Press Works, and also finish his playing career at newly elected Welsh League side Carmarthen Town, where former Swans player Len Emmanuel was player manager, winning the Championship of the Second Division of the Welsh League in 1955. Len also had a season with Llanelly in the Southern League, the season after Jock Stein had returned to Scotland. For some years after leaving Carmarthen Town he was involved as trainer to his works side in the Swansea Senior League, also captaining Hafod Cricket Club for several years in the summer months.

29. CONNOLLY, KARL Andrew

Birthplace: Prescot, 9/2/1970
Ht: 5ft-10ins, **Wt:** 11st-2lbs
Swans debut: v. Bury (h), 9/8/2003

Swansea City Career Statistics				
Season	League	FLC	FAC	FAWP
2003/04	4+6/1gls	1/1gls	1	1/1gls
Total	4+6/1gls	1/1gls	1	1/1gls

Career:
Napoli (Warrington Sunday League)
Wrexham (signed in 8/5/1991) lge 337+21/88gls, FLC 22/4gls, FAC 37+1/16gls, Others 32+1/6gls
QPR (signed in 31/5/2000) lge 53+19/12gls, FLC 2, FAC 4+2, Others 2
Swansea City (signed in July 2003)
Prescot Cables (signed in June 2004)

Honours: Welsh Cup Winner–1995, Welsh Invitation Cup Winner–1998, Welsh Premier Cup Winner–1999

Spotted by a Wrexham scout playing for Warrington Sunday League side Napoli, Karl signed professional for Wrexham after an initial trial period, and a spell on non-contract terms. Making his debut in the opening game of the 1991/92 season against Hereford United, he finished the season as joint top goalscorer with Steve Watkin with eight league goals, and in every season from then on was consistently among the club's top goalscorers. Rejected by Tranmere Rovers as a schoolboy, Karl drifted into local football in the St. Helens Combination, prior to signing for Napoli, in the Warrington Sunday League. Capable of playing at centre forward, or in a wide. Left sided midfield position, he scored sixteen league goals in his second season at the Racecourse, helping the club to claim runners up place to Cardiff City in the Third Division. In May 1995 he gained a Welsh Cup Winners medal with Wrexham when they defeated Cardiff City 2-1 at the National Stadium in Cardiff. A member of the Wrexham side that defeated Arsenal in the FA Cup in season 1992/93, he was also in the side that reached the fifth round of the FA Cup in season 1996/97, and at the end of the 1995/96 season he was selected by his fellow professionals for the PFA Second Division team. Karl signed for First Division side QPR in May 2000, and produced consistent performances until he sustained a leg injury, ironically against his former club, Wrexham in February 2002, which sidelined him until the rest of the season. Despite starting season 2002/03 in the first team, within a couple of months Karl had suffered a foot problem which prevented him from regaining his place in the first team, and also miss the end of season Play Off Final against Cardiff City. He was re-united with his former manager Brian Flynn at the Vetch Field in the 2003 close season, and after an initial trial period to prove his fitness in pre-season training, he signed a one year contract. Scored his first goal for the Swans in the Carling Cup first round tie at Bristol City, but was carried off later in the game with a calf injury. In his first comeback match, at the Vetch Field against Huddersfield Town, after coming on as substitute, he suffered a fractured ankle which kept him out of action until the New Year. The second half of his only season with the Swans saw him continue to have injury problems which prevented him from making a bigger impact, and at the end of the season was released by new manager Kenny Jackett. Linking up with his former Wrexham team-mate Barrie Jones at Prescot Cables in the 2004 close season, in May 2005 Karl scored in the 3-1 Unibond Premier League Play Off semi-final defeat by Workington.

30. CONNOR, John (JACK)

Birthplace: Garngad, 7/9/1911. **Died:** Glasgow, 28/5/1994
Ht: 5ft-7ins, **Wt:** 10st-9lbs
Swans debut: v. West Ham United (a), 8/10/1938

Career:
Celtic
Airdrieonians (loan in November 1932)

Airdrieonians (signed in June 1934)
Albion Rovers (loan in March 1935)
Plymouth Argyle (£4,000 signed in May 1936) lge 44/19gls
Swansea Town (£500 in 2/7/1938)
Queen of the South (£100 in 28/6/1939)
Alloa Athletic (signed in June 1946)
St. Johnstone (signed in November 1946)

Swansea Town Career Statistics	
Season	*League*
1938/39	12/1gls
Total	12/1gls

A former Scottish League player with Glasgow Celtic, Airdrieonians and Albion Rovers, prior to arriving at Home Park to sign for Plymouth Argyle for the 1936/37 season in the Second Division. He attended St.Roch's School earlier in his career, played for St. Roch's, Boys Brigade, St. Roch's Juniors in 1930, had a trial with Celtic in August 1931, signing professional in June 1932. Initially on loan with Airdrie, after signing a permanent contract he joined Albion Rovers on loan, then travelled south to sign for Argyle. He scored two goals on his Football League debut for Plymouth Argyle in September 1936, and was the leading goalscorer in the Argyle team that season. In his two seasons at Home Park, he played three times against the Swans, and on the 18th September 1937 scored Argyle's second goal in a 2-2 draw at Home Park. A consistent goalscorer with Argyle, he joined the Swans for a £500 transfer fee in July 1938, making his Swans debut at West Ham United in October 1938, in a 5-2 defeat. Played at centre forward in his first game for the Swans, he made the remainder of his appearances either at inside left, or at outside left, competing with Olsen and Millington for a first team place through the season. In June 1939 he returned north of the border to sign for Queen of the South for £100. During WW2 he made guest appearances for Airdrie (July 1940), Third Lanark (October 1940), Dundee United (March 1944), and Raith Rovers (September 1944). When organised football was resumed after the war, he made further Scottish League appearances for Alloa Athletic and St. Johnstone, then signed for British Railways Works XI in 1948. Returning to St. Roch's he was appointed match secretary in April 1948, manager from April to December 1948, and by 1955 was coach with Metro Vickers. From 1949 to 1959 he was involved with the Glasgow Celtic Old Crocks team.

31. CONNOR, PAUL

Birthplace: Bishop Auckland, 12/1/1979
Ht: 6ft-1ins, **Wt:** 11st-5lbs
Swans debut: v. Southend United (a), 13/3/2004

Career:
Middlesbrough (from trainee in 4/7/1996)

Gateshead (loan in 1/8/1997) Conf 5/3gls
Hartlepool United (loan in 6/2/1998) lge 4+1
Stoke City (signed in 25/3/1999) lge 18+18/7gls, FLC 3+3/3gls, FAC 0+1, Others 2+3
Cambridge United (loan in 9/11/2000) lge 12+1/5gls, FAC 1
Rochdale (£150,000 signed in 9/3/2001) lge 76+18/29gls, FLC 3, FAC 8+1/3gls, Others 0+2
Swansea City (£35,000 signed 12/3/2004)

Swansea City Career Statistics				
Season	*League*	*FAC*	*LDV*	*FAWC*
2003/04	11/5gls			1
2004/05	34+6/10gls	5/3gls	1	1+1
Total	45+6/15gls	5/3gls	1	2+1

Honours: FAW Cup Winner–2005

Former Middlesbrough trainee who failed to make his league debut for Middlesbrough, but after a successful loan period with Conference side Gateshead, made his league debut the same season on loan with Hartlepool United against Darlington on the 7th February 1998. He joined Stoke City on an initial loan spell in March 1999, with the move being made permanent at the end of the season. In his third game for Stoke, he scored his first league goal in the last game of the season against Walsall. Starting the 1999/2000 season in the Stoke City line-up, he scored five goals from twenty-six league appearances, and in April 2000 was a non-playing substitute in the Northern Final Second Leg against Rochdale, but failed to make the squad for the Final at Wembley against Bristol City in the Auto Windscreens Shield Final. In the 2000 end of season Division Two Play Off Semi-Final against Gillingham, he made appearances from the bench in both games. During the 2000/01 season as well as making league appearances for Stoke, Paul had a loan spell with Cambridge United, scoring two goals against Wrexham, and one against the Swans in the next game, before signing for Rochdale for a club record transfer fee of £150,000. Playing in the last fourteen league games of the season, he finished as top goalscorer with ten league goals, including a hat-trick against Carlisle United, almost securing the club a place in the Third Division Play Offs. The following season, Rochdale were successful in reaching the Play Offs, despite Paul missing most of the season through injury, but returning to action as substitute in the second leg of the semi-final defeat by Rushden & Diamonds. Returning twelve league goals for season 2002/03, Paul was signed by manager Brian Flynn in March 2004 for £35,000, the first transfer fee the Swans had paid for a player since signing Tommy Mutton in September 1999. In his home debut he scored two goals in a 4-2 defeat of Scunthorpe United, and in the short time he has been at the Vetch Field has already demonstrated his good positional sense, strength in the air, and possessing a good shot with both feet. Season 2004/05 saw him strike up a fine understanding with Lee Trundle netting ten league goals during the club's promotion success, also playing in the FAW Cup Final over Wrexham.

32. CONNOR, Terence (TERRY) Fitzroy

Birthplace: Leeds, 9/11/1962
Ht: 5ft-9ins, **Wt:** 11st-8lbs
Swans debut: v. Leyton Orient (a), 25/8/1990

Career:
Leeds United (from apprentice in 13/11/1979) lge 83+13/19gls, FLC 4+2/1gls, FAC 6/2gls
Brighton & Hove Albion (Player exchange in 25/3/1983) lge 153+3/51gls, FLC 7/4gls, FAC 10+1/3gls

Portsmouth (£200,000 signed in 1/7/1987) lge 42+6/14gls,
  FLC 5/1gls, FAC 3+1/1gls
Swansea City (£150,000 signed in 14/8/1990)
Bristol City (£197,000 signed in 21/9/1991) lge 11+5/1gls
Swansea City (loan in 20/11/1992)
Yeovil Town (signed in 1993/94 season) Conf 14

Swansea City Career Statistics						
Season	League	FLC	FAC	WC	LDV	ECWC
1990/91	33/5gls	2	4/2gls	6/3gls	5	
1991/92	6/1gls	2				1
1992/93	3					
Total	42/6gls	4	4/2gls	6/3gls	5	1

Honours: England Yth, U-21–1, Welsh Cup Winner–1991

Terry lived in Chapeltown and went to Foxwood School, and
played for Leeds City Schoolboys prior to signing for Leeds
United as an apprentice. An outstanding prospect as a
youngster, he had the best possible debut, going on as a 17-year-
old substitute for Paul Madeley, and scoring the only goal of the
game against West Brom. Despite making regular appearances
in United's first team over the next three seasons, Terry was
transferred to Brighton & Hove Albion in a straight swap for the
more experienced Andy Ritchie. It did not take long for Connor
to become a popular figure at Brighton, regaining the form that
had won him an England Youth cap, gaining his only
appearance for the England U-21 side against Yugoslavia in
1987. Relegated with the Swans from the First Division in 1983,
over the next four seasons he became top goalscorer in three out
of four seasons, with the fourth finishing joint top with Dean
Saunders in season 1985/86, which also saw the 'Seagulls' reach
the sixth round of the FA Cup competition. Following relegation
to the Third Division in 1987, Terry was transferred to
Portsmouth for £200,000, but during three seasons at Fratton
Park struggled with injuries, and in August 1990 was signed by
Swans manager Terry Yorath for £200,000. Making his Swans
debut in the opening league fixture of the season, it took him
until November before he registered his first goal, in the FA Cup
tie against Walsall, then scoring two goals in December at the
Vetch Field in a 2-0 win over Birmingham City. In May 1991,
Terry played in the Swans side that beat Wrexham in the Welsh
Cup Final at the National Stadium in Cardiff. Shortly after the
start of his second season at the Vetch Field, and after he had
played for the Swans against Monaco at the Vetch Field in an
European Cup Winners Cup tie, he was transferred to Second
Division side Bristol City for £197,000. After eleven league
appearances, two as substitute, Terry suffered an injury,
sidelining him for the remainder of the season, and ultimately
force him to retire as a player. He did return to the Vetch Field
on loan in November 1992 as part of his attempt to regain match
fitness, but at the end of season 1992/93 was released by City,
joining Conference side Yeovil Town the following season.

Involving himself in coaching he became Bristol Rovers' reserve
manager and has since worked under John Ward at Bristol City
and in season 2003/04 was first team coach with
Wolverhampton Wanderers.

33. CONWAY, Michael (MICKY) Denis

Birthplace: Sheffield, 11/3/1956
Ht: 5ft-7ins, **Wt:** 10st-3lbs
Swans debut: v. Crewe Alexandra (h), 3/1/1976

Swansea City Career Statistics				
Season	League	FLC	FAC	WC
1975/76	20/1gls			2
1976/77	23+2/8gls	2	0+2	2
1977/78	13+3/2gls	0+1	2	1+1
Total	56+5/11gls	2+1	2+2	5+1

Career:
Brighton (from apprentice in March 1974) lge 1+1/1gls
Swansea City (£3,000 signed in 24/12/1975)

Born in Sheffield, near the Sheffield Wednesday ground, his
family moved to Brighton when he was young, and as a
schoolboy his pace on the wing as a schoolboy was noticed, and
brought to the attention of manager Pat Saward, when he
played for Westdene against Albion's U-18 side in the Sussex
Sunday Minor Cup Final of 1972. Micky signed as an apprentice
at the age of sixteen the following September, not taking long to
make his mark in the London Midweek league, and then the
club's Football Combination side. With Albion facing relegation
to the Third Division, Micky made his league debut against
Nottingham Forest on the 28th April 1973, scoring Albion's
second goal with a right foot volley into the corner of the net,
and at the age of seventeen years and forty-eight days, became
the club's youngest ever player in a peacetime game.
In September 1973 the young winger was included in England's
youth squad and signed as a professional twelve months later.
Following a change of management at the Goldstone Ground,
he made just the one more appearance, as a substitute against
Chesterfield, before being signed by Swans manager Harry
Griffiths on an initial loan basis, which was later made
permanent for £3,000. He had earlier been spotted by Griffiths
playing for Albion in an exhibition match in the Rhondda, a
gutsy character, who Griffiths recognised immediately as a
player who if channelled along the right lines could serve the
Swans with rich rewards. Making his Swans debut in a 4-0 win
at the Vetch Field over Crewe Alexandra in January 1976, his
pace and sparkling control on the left wing, contributed
significantly to the team's brand of exciting football, with Micky
being affectionately nicknamed 'Billy Whiz', giving the Swans
fans something by tradition they had always enjoyed watching,
attacking football of enterprise and ingenuity. His career came to

a halt however following a car crash, and although he regained his place in the Swans side, could not reproduce the form that had excited supporters, and after the Swans had gained promotion from the Fourth Division at the end of season 1977/78, Micky was given a free transfer by manager John Toshack, and retired from the professional game. After Albion had taken their newly promoted First Division side to the Vetch Field for his testimonial in May 1979, Micky subsequently returned to the Brighton area and turned out for his old club Westdene. In the early 1990s he was believed to be a mature student at college in London.

34. COOK, Andrew (ANDY) Charles

Birthplace: Romsey, 10/8/1969
Ht: 5ft-9ins, **Wt:** 12st-0lbs
Swans debut: v. York City (a), 14/8/1993

Swansea City Career Statistics					
Season	League	FLC	FAC	WC	AGT/AWS
1993/94	23+4	2	2	3	6+1/2gls
1994/95	1			1	
1995/96	30+3		1		2
Total	54+7	2	3	4	8+1/2gls

Career:
Southampton (trainee in July 1985, signed professional in 6/7/1987) lge 11+5/1gls, FLC 4, FAC 1, Others 1
Exeter City (£50,000 signed in 13/9/1991) lge 70/1gls, FLC 2, FAC 7/1gls, Others 6/1gls
Swansea City (£125,000 signed in 23/7/1993)
Portsmouth (£35,000 signed in 20/12/1996) lge 7+2
Millwall (£50,000 signed in 8/1/1998) lge 4+1
Salisbury City (signed in season 1999/2000)

Former apprentice at the Dell with Southampton who made his league debut in the opening fixture of season 1987/88 at Old Trafford against Manchester United at left full back, playing in the next First Division game against Norwich City, before being replaced by new signing Derek Statham. Born in Romsey, Andy attended Halterworth Primary, and Mount Batten Secondary Modern Schools, gained honours with Southampton Schoolboys, Hampshire County, and the South of England Schoolboy sides prior to arriving at the Dell as an apprentice. Whilst with the 'Saints' he had a call up to the England U-20 side to play in Brazil but was unable to get a visa in time. Making occasional appearances in the 'Saints' First Division side over the next two seasons, he was then signed by Alan Ball at Exeter City for £50,000, making consistent appearances in his two seasons for the 'Grecians'. The 1992/93 season saw Cook impress with his attacking full back displays on the left flank in

the league, and also in the an AutoGlass Trophy cup tie against the Swans, which saw the 'Grecians' lose out in the Southern Area Final to eventual winners Port Vale. Twelve months later however after signing for the Swans, a week after he had helped the Swans reach Wembley for the AutoGlass Trophy Final against Huddersfield Town, he suffered a broken leg at Hartlepool, which kept him on the sidelines for twelve months, and miss the final. His second season at the Vetch Field saw Andy recover from his broken leg, but only make one appearance in the league, plus a Welsh Cup tie against Cardiff City. The 1995/96 season saw Andy make thirty-three league appearances, but off the field, management problems and a failed take over of the club saw the Swans lurch from one crisis to another, with eventual relegation to the Third Division. A disagreement over contract talks in the close season, and with a new left full back signed for the new season, saw Andy walk out on the club in July 1996. He eventually returned to the game in December 1996, joining Portsmouth for £35,000, then later signing for Millwall in January 1998 for £50,000. A hamstring injury in his second game for Millwall saw him struggle to make an impression for the Lions, and after being restricted to games in the club's reserve team, had his contract cancelled during the 1999/2000 season. Joining non-league side Salisbury City midway through the 1999/2000, Andy has continued to play for the club, and is currently assistant to manager Nick Holmes, as well as being the Football in the Community Officer for the football club.

35. COOK, ARTHUR Frederick

Birthplace: Stafford, AMJ 1889. **Died:** Doxey, Stafford, 7/2/1930
Ht: 5ft-8ins, **Wt:** 10st-10lbs
Swans debut: v. Merthyr (h), 26/8/1922

Swansea Town Career Statistics		
Season	League	WC
1922/23	17	2
Total	17	2

Career:
Old Wesleyans
Stafford Rangers (signed in September 1906)
Wrexham (signed in August 1910)
West Bromwich Albion (signed in May 1911) lge 55
Swansea Town (signed in June 1922)
Whitchurch (signed in August 1923)

Experienced right full back who had been Joseph Pennington's 'partner' in defence at First Division side West Bromwich Albion earlier in his career. At the end of his first season with Albion he had replaced the injured Joe Smith at right full back in the 1912 F.A. Cup Final extra time 1-0 defeat by Barnsley. Starting his playing career at Cannock Road Council School in Stafford, he went on to play for Old Wesleyans before signing for Stafford Rangers, and then progressing to Wrexham in August 1910. Joined the Swans prior to the start of the 1922/23 season, he started the season at right full back, before losing his place to Ernie Morley. Although he regained his place later in the season, he was released at the end of the season joining Cheshire League side Whitchurch, retiring in May 1925. Easy-going and a fluent full-back, he proved to be a difficult defender to pass, possessing boundless enthusiasm. He died in tragic circumstances, falling to his death whilst sleepwalking from the bedroom window above his licensed premises, The Doxey Arms in Stafford, in February 1930. He was only 39.

36. CORBISIERO, ANTONIO Giovanni

Birthplace: Exmouth, 17/11/1984
Ht: 5ft-8ins, **Wt:** 11st-4lbs
Swans debut: v. Mansfield Town (h), 30/8/2003

Swansea City Career Statistics		
Season	League	FAWC
2003/04	1+4	0+1
2004/05		1
Total	1+4	1+1

Career:
Swansea City (scholar from summer of 2001)
Newport County (loan in 3/12/2004) Conf Sth 3/1gls
Newport County (loan in 31/3/2005) Conf Sth 5

Honours: Welsh Youth Cup Winner–2003, West Wales Senior Cup Winner–2003

A schoolboy player with Hugh Faringdon School, Reading, Antonio also played representative football for Berkshire. At an early age he attended QPR and Crystal Palace Centre of Excellence, also played a few games for Reading's Academy side before impressing during a trial period at the Vetch Field, which led to him signing a three year scholarship prior to the start of the 2001/02 season. In his first pre-season with the Swans he showed his ability, scoring a hat-trick playing for a Swans reserve side against Welsh League team Ammanford Town. A driving, influential midfielder, with a lot of energy, he skippered the Swans youth team to the 2003 Welsh Youth Cup Final success over Llanelli at Stebonheath Park in his second season as a scholar, also playing in the West Wales Senior Cup win over Carmarthen Town. With a number of first team players on the injured list, he made his league debut for the Swans at the Vetch Field against Mansfield Town, going on the field as a substitute for Andy Robinson. Making his second substitute appearance in the next league game against Yeovil Town, Antonio continued to be included in the first team squad for the remainder of the season, and he was eventually given his first start, at the Vetch Field in April 2004 against promotion frontrunners Hull City. Towards the end of the season he was offered a professional contract, signing as a full time professional in the summer of 2004. In early December 2004 he joined Conference South side Newport County on loan with a view to improving his development in the game, and in late March 2005 returned to County for a second loan spell. He was told by Swans' manager Kenny Jackett in late April 2005 that he would not be offered a new contract at the Vetch Field, and after suffering an injury during a game for Newport, his season came to an early close. After failing to earn himself a contract at Conference side Hereford United, he returned to Newport County, scoring in a pre-season friendly at Bodmin Town in late July 2005.

37. CORKINGDALE, William Joseph (BILLY)

Birthplace: Langley Green West Bromwich, 19/5/1901.
Died: Ampthill, Beds, 3/8/1972
Ht: 5ft-10ins, **Wt:** 10st-5lbs
Swans debut: v. Norwich City (h), 22/12/1923

Swansea Town Career Statistics		
Season	League	WC
1923/24	10	2
1924/25	2	1
1925/26	6/2gls	2
Total	18/2gls	5

Career:
Wellington Town (signed in close season 1922)
Swansea Town (£250 signed in 21/11/1923)
Clapton Orient (signed in 5/6/1926) lge 96/17gls, FAC 6/1gls
Millwall (signed in May 1929) lge 40/4gls
Luton Town (£250 signed in 26/8/1932) lge 1
Shrewsbury Town (signed in July 1934)

Honours: West Wales Senior Cup Winner–1926

Outside left signed from leading non-league side at the time, Wellington Town, and who replaced Joe Spottiswoode for his league debut. Bandy legged, nicknamed 'Corky', Joe continued for the remainder of the season to battle for the outside left position with Spottiswoode, but also made appearances on the right flank against Wrexham in Welsh Cup ties. Attended Woodville Road School early in his career, then made appearances for Worcester City and Stourbridge prior to signing for Wellington Town. During his second season at the Vetch Field, 'Corky' struggled to make an impression in a Swans side that would win the Third Division South Championship, making just two league appearances. His only other appearance was in a Welsh Cup semi-final defeat by Wrexham. His third season at the Vetch Field saw him this time compete with Nicholas and Ernie Edwards for the left wing berth, but after making just six league appearances, he was allowed to join Clapton Orient at the end of the season. In April 1926 he was included in the Swans reserve side that beat Merthyr Town to win the West Wales Senior Cup. During the season however he did get his name on the scoresheet for the Swans with two league goals. His three seasons with Clapton Orient saw him play regularly against the Swans, scoring a penalty for Orient in a 2-1 defeat in season 1928/29, also playing against the Swans in season 1929/30 after he had signed for Millwall. He signed for Luton Town in late August 1932, later developing business interests in the town. In January 1934 he finished his playing career in non-league football with Shrewsbury Town.

38. CORNFORTH, JOHN Michael

Birthplace: Whitley Bay, 7/10/1967
Ht: 6ft-1ins, **Wt:** 13st-12lbs
Swans debut: v. Stockport County (a), 17/8/1991

Swansea City Career Statistics						
Season	League	FLC	FAC	WC	AGT/AWS	P/Offs
1991/92	17	2				
1992/93	44/5gls	2	5/1gls	1	3	2
1993/94	37+1/6gls	4	1	6/1gls	7	
1994/95	32+1/3gls	4	5	3/1gls	4	
1995/96	17/2gls	2				
Total	147+2/16gls	14	11/1gls	10/2gls	14	2

Career:
Sunderland (from apprentice in 11/10/1985) lge 21+11/2gls
Doncaster Rovers (loan in 6/11/1986) lge 6+1/3gls, Others 2
Shrewsbury Town (loan in 23/11/1989) lge 3, Others 2
Lincoln City (loan in 11/1/1990) lge 9/1gls
Swansea City (£50,000 signed in 2/8/1991)
Birmingham City (£350,000 signed in 26/3/1996) lge 8
Wycombe Wanderers (£50,000 signed in 5/12/1996)
  lge 35+12/6gls, FLC 6, FAC 2/2gls, Others 0+2
Peterborough United (loan in 13/2/1998) lge 3+1
Cardiff City (signed in 6/8/1999) lge 6+4/1gls, FLC 1+2
Scunthorpe United (signed in 4/11/1999) lge 2+2/1gls, Others 1
Exeter City (signed in 18/2/2000) lge 23+1/2gls

Honours: Wales Full–2, Third Division Champions–1988,
AutoGlass Trophy Winner–1994, West Wales Senior Cup
Winner–1994

Educated at Monkseaton High School Whitley Bay, he played
for Northumberland Schoolboys prior to joining Sunderland as
an apprentice, making his league debut in the last game of the
1984/85 season against Ipswich Town, with Sunderland already
relegated to the Second Division. He had to wait until the
1988/89 season to make his first start, against Wigan Athletic,
during a season which saw 'Corny' make twelve league
appearances in the club's Third Division Championship success.
He continued to make regular appearances in Sunderland's first
team, also making loan appearances for Doncaster Rovers
(November 1986), Shrewsbury Town (November 1989), and
Lincoln City (January 1990), prior to being signed by Swans
manager Frank Burrows for £50,000 in August 1991.
Overcoming a dreadful start to his Vetch Field career, which saw
him sidelined with a broken leg after just three league
appearances, 'Corny' turned out to be one of the most popular
skippers of the Swans since the Toshack era, captaining the side
to honours at Wembley in the AutoGlass Trophy Cup Final
against Huddersfield Town, and also against Ammanford Town
in the 1994 West Wales Senior Cup Final, also gaining two Welsh
caps whilst at the Vetch Field. He gained his two Welsh
international caps, by virtue of a grandparent born in the
Principality, his first as substitute for Jones in Sofia against
Bulgaria in 29th March 1995, and his second, starting against
Georgia on the 7th June 1995. A thoughtful midfielder, with
good passing and vision, after recovering from his broken leg,
he guided the Swans to the 1992/93 Second Division Play Off
semi-finals, losing narrowly to West Bromwich Albion, and after
the AutoGlass success, led the Swans to an exciting FA Cup run
in season 1994/95, when after beating Middlesbrough at
Ayresome Park, lost 3-0 at Newcastle United in the fourth
round. With the Swans struggling to avoid relegation towards
the end of the 1995/96 season, and with a new manager in Jan
Molby at the helm, 'Corny' was transferred to Birmingham City
in March 1996 for £350,000. Struggling to find his form at
St. Andrews with Birmingham City, nine months later he was
transferred to Wycombe Wanderers, but suffered a hamstring
and Achilles tendon injury which prevented him from
establishing himself. After a loan spell with Peterborough

United he was released in May 1999, and returned to the Vetch
Field, joining in pre-season training with a view to be offered a
contract. With manager John Hollins not offering him a contract,
'Corny' linked up for a second time with Frank Burrows, this
time at Ninian Park with Cardiff City. Released in November
1999, he joined Scunthorpe United, before finishing his playing
career with Exeter City. Involved on the coaching side with the
'Grecians', 'Corny' took over as manager at Exeter City in
October 2001, steering the club to a mid table position during
his first season in charge. In November 2002 despite bringing in
a number of new players, he was sacked as boss, being replaced
by Neil McNab. During season 2003/04 he was involved in
scouting for Sheffield Wednesday, and on the 28th September
2004 he was appointed manager of Nationwide South side
Newport County.

39. COTTEY, Philip Anthony (TONY)

Birthplace: Swansea, 2/6/1966
Ht: 5ft-5ins, **Wt:** 9st-7lbs
Swans debut: v. York City (h), 1/9/1984

Swansea City Career Statistics		
Season	League	WC
1984/85	2+1	1
Total	2+1	1

Career:
Swansea City (from apprentice in June 1984)
Merthyr Tydfil (signed in season 1985/86)

Honours: Wales Yth–3

Former Bishopston Comprehensive and Swansea Schoolboy
midfielder who signed as an apprentice with the Swans in 1982,
playing in the Swans Youth Team Championship Winning side
of 1982/83. Signing as a professional prior to the start of the
1984/85 season, making his league debut at the Vetch Field
against York City in September 1984, the diminutive midfielder
made just two more league appearances, one as substitute, as
well as a Welsh Cup appearance against Spencer Works, and at
the end of the season was released by manager John Bond.
Brought up in the Three Crosses and Gowerton area of the
Gower Peninsula, Tony came through the Swansea Schoolboys
sides and also played for the Swans Cygnets Development sides
prior to arriving as an apprentice at the Vetch Field. A talented
cricketer from a very early age, he made his debut for
Glamorgan Second Eleven at the age of fifteen. During his
apprenticeship he captained the Wales U-18 side in European
Youth Championship games against Scotland, also playing
against Northern Ireland in a friendly. Slightly disillusioned
with football after his release by manager John Bond, Tony spent

the summer of 1985 with the Glamorgan Second Eleven, and just before the end of the cricket season accepted the offer of a professional contract by the County, despite the offer of a three month trial with Birmingham City. From that moment on, cricket became his priority as far as his career was concerned, with football secondary. Playing semi-professionally for Merthyr Tydfil during season 1985/86, over the years Tony has made occasional appearances for Ammanford Town, Pembroke Borough and Llanelli, only because of his close relationship with people at the clubs, namely Anthony Rees, and Wyndham Evans. Another factor also preventing him from making more appearances during the winter months in football, is that for the first four years of his career as a professional cricketer, he travelled the world coaching, and did not kick a ball apart from in charity games. Establishing himself as a fine fielder, and top order batsman, Tony became part of the Glamorgan County Cricket Club success story, winning the Championship and Sunday League competitions, and after joining Sussex in 2003 won further honours in the game, gaining a County Championship Medal. Also involved as a coach and professional with Gowerton Cricket Club during his career, Tony is looking to get more involved in the coaching side of the game when he eventually retires as a player. He was released from the playing staff at Sussex at the end of the 2004 season.

40. COTTON, Terence (TERRY)

Birthplace: Liverpool, 25/1/1946
Ht: 6ft-1ins, **Wt:** 11st-7lbs
Swans debut: v. Wrexham (h), WC–6 Replay, 26/2/1969

Swansea Town/City Career Statistics			
Season	*League*	*FLC*	*WC*
1968/69	4		1/1gls
1969/70	1		
1970/71	7/1gls	2	1
Total	12/1gls	2	2/1gls

Career:
Llanelli
Ammanford Town (signed in 1966)
Swansea City (signed in June 1968)
Yeovil Town (signed in July 1971)
Salisbury (signed in July 1977)
Yeovil Town (signed in July 1978)
Taunton Town (signed in season 1979/80)

Honours: Wales Amateur–4

Liverpool born, Terry's family moved to Swansea when he was three, and after attending Penlan Multilateral School, started his

playing career with Swansea based side Ragged School, then stepped up to Welsh League football firstly with Llanelli, then joined Ammanford Town, managed at the time by former Swans player Roy Saunders. A prolific goalscorer at Welsh League level, he made four appearances for the Wales Amateur team, despite being born in England, the first during the 1967/68 season against Ireland. Signed for the Swans initially as a part-timer, but was then offered full professional terms by manager Billy Lucas in July 1968. The previous season he had signed Combination forms for the Swans, also playing for Ammanford Town in the Welsh League. Good in the air, very strong, and an aggressive type of centre forward, Terry made his Swans debut against Wrexham in a Welsh Cup sixth round replay at the Vetch Field replacing Alfie Biggs, scoring the winning goal in a 2-1 win for the Swans. He made his league debut in the Swans next game against Bradford Park Avenue, also playing in the next two league matches for the Swans without adding his name to the scoresheet. Terry made just one league appearance during the Swans Fourth Division promotion winning season of 1969/70, but scored his first league goal in the second match of the Swans Third Division campaign in a 4-1 defeat at Fulham in August 1970. Released by manager Roy Bentley at the end of the 1971/72 season, Terry had an offer to join former Swans player Peter Davies in South Africa, but decided to join Southern League Premier Division side Yeovil Town, and finished the club's leading goalscorer in his first season with twenty-one league goals. A consistent goalscorer throughout his first spell at Yeovil Town, in 1976 and 1977 he helped the club reach consecutive Southern League Cup Finals, losing both on aggregate to Wimbledon and Dartford respectively. He joined Southern League First Division South team Salisbury in July 1977, helping the club finish in third place in the division in his first season, before returning to Yeovil Town twelve months later as player/commercial manager. His first season back at Yeovil saw Terry play in his third Southern League Cup Final, and was again on the losing side, losing 1-0 on aggregate to Bath City. With the formation of the Alliance Premier League for season 1979/80, Terry made a couple of appearances for Yeovil Town before transferring to Taunton Town of the Southern League Midland Division. By the time he had played his last game for Yeovil, Terry had made a total 415 appearances, scoring 83 goals. In latter years with Yeovil, Terry had reverted to an accomplished centre half, and had also been assistant manager to both Graham Roberts and Steve Thompson. After Taunton Town, Terry also had a three year period as player manager of Bridport Town. Since returning to Yeovil, Terry has worked in numerous roles on matchdays, from manning the bars, to operating the turnstiles, and his current role sees him involved with hospitality. Away from the club, Terry is an Accounts Manager with Honeywell, while his wife Jean, is Yeovil Town Football Club Company Secretary.

41. COUGHLIN, DENIS Michael

Birthplace: Houghton-le-Spring, Tyne & Wear, 26/11/1937
Ht: 5ft-9ins, **Wt:** 13st-0lbs
Swans debut: v. Oldham Athletic (h), 29/8/1966

Swansea Town Career Statistics				
Season	*League*	*FLC*	*FAC*	*WC*
1966/67	33/9gls	1	3	1
1967/68	6+1/1gls	1		
Total	39+1/10gls	2	3	1

Career:
Durham City
Barnsley (signed in October 1957)
Yeovil Town (signed in 1959) Total apps 114/70gls
Bournemouth (£2,500 signed in April 1963) lge 86+2/41gls
Swansea Town (signed in August 1966)
Exeter City (loan in March 1968) lge 13/2gls
Chelmsford City (signed in July 1968)

Honours: Southern League Champions–1963, Southern League
Cup Winner–1961, England NABC XI

Attended Houghton St. Michael's RC School from 1949 to 1952,
playing for the school team. Whilst in school he also played for
the Lambton & Heaton District Team, and the Durham County
Football Association in December 1952. Selected to play for
England NABC against Germany at Ayresome Park in season
1956/57, after starting his senior career with non-league side
Durham City, Denis joined Barnsley as a part-timer in
November 1957, whilst working in his trade as a plumber, but
after failing to make any league appearances, signed for non-
league side Yeovil Town in 1959 whilst doing his National
Service. Up to the time he signed for Bournemouth in March
1963, Denis scored had 70 goals for Yeovil Town, also winning
the Southern League in season 1962/63, and scoring against
Chelmsford in the 1961 Southern League Cup Final. The
1961/62 season saw Denis score thirty-four league and cup
goals for Yeovil, and the following season scored twenty-eight
league and cup goals, including creating a scoring record for
Yeovil by scoring in eight consecutive games. Averaging almost
a goal every other game for the 'Cherries' in the Third Division,
Denis was lured to the Vetch Field in June 1966 by Swans
manager Glyn Davies, himself a former manager at Yeovil
Town. In what turned out to be a disastrous season for the
Swans, with relegation to the Fourth Division for the first time,
Denis scored nine league goals in a high scoring Swans outfit,
which unfortunately conceded more goals than they scored.
Midway through his first season at the Vetch Field, Denis
returned five goals from six league games. With only three
seasons since the Swans had reached the FA Cup semi-final,
Denis played in the Swans side during the 1966/67season that
lost for the first time against non-league opposition in the FA
Cup competition, when they were beaten by Nuneaton Borough
in January 1967. Despite starting his second season in the Swans
line-up, within a couple of months he had lost his place, and in
March 1968 had joined Exeter City on loan. Denis later signed
for Southern League side Chelmsford City, before finishing his
playing career with Kings Lynn, Bedford Town and South
Shields in 1972. After retiring as a player he returned to his trade
as a plumber, working on the oil rigs on the Tyne, up to his
retirement in November 2002.

42. COUGHLIN, RUSSELL James

Birthplace: Swansea, 15/2/1960
Ht: 5ft-8ins, **Wt:** 11st-12lbs
Swans debut: v. Fulham (h), 20/10/1990

Career:
Manchester City (apprentice in July 1976, professional in
3/3/1978)
Blackburn Rovers (£40,000 signed in 26/3/1979) lge 22+2,
FLC 1+1

Carlisle United (£20,000 signed in 30/10/1980) lge
114+16/13gls, FLC 5+1/1gls, FAC 12
Plymouth Argyle (£20,000 signed in 25/7/1984) lge
128+3/18gls, FLC 8/2gls, FAC 8/1gls, Others 5/1gls
Blackpool (£75,000 signed in 11/12/1987) lge 100+2/8gls, FLC
9/1gls, FAC 13, Others 10/1gls
Shrewsbury Town (loan in 11/9/1990) lge 4+1/1gls, FLC 1
Swansea City (£30,000 signed in 17/10/1990)
Exeter City (P/Exchange with John Hodge on 12/7/1993) lge
64+4, FLC 5, FAC 5, Others 4
Torquay United (signed in 13/10/1995) lge 22+3, FAC 3, Others 1
Dorchester Town
Gretna

Swansea City Career Statistics							
Season	*League*	*FLC*	*FAC*	*WC*	*LDC/AGT*	*ECWC*	*P/Offs*
1990/91	29		2	4	5		
1991/92	32+1/1gls	2+1	3	3		2	
1992/93	38+1/1gls	2	3/1gls	1	1+1		2
Total	99+2/2gls	4+1	8/1gls	8	6+1	2	2

Honours: Wales Sch, Yth, Welsh Cup Winner–1991

Former schoolboy footballer with St. Josephs, Bishop Vaughan,
and Swansea Schoolboys, capped at Schoolboy and youth level
by Wales, who joined Manchester City on leaving school as an
apprentice at the age of fifteen years old, signing professional on
his eighteenth birthday. He failed to make a league appearance
at Maine Road with City, but after joining Blackburn Rovers in
March 1979 for £40,000, made his league debut two days later
against Cambridge United, missing just two league games up to
the end of his first season at Ewood Park, which unfortunately
saw the club relegated to the Third Division. Despite starting the
1980/81 season in the Rovers first team line-up, Russell was
transferred to Carlisle United in October 1980 for £20,000, going
on to make over 100 league appearances for the Cumbrians, and
making thirty-seven league appearances during season 1981/82
when they gained promotion as runners up to Burnley in the
Third Division. He returned to the Third Division July 1984,
joining Plymouth Argyle for £20,000, and in only his second
season at Home Park gained a second runners up medal in the
Third Division, gaining promotion behind Champions Reading.
A player who always enjoyed a battle, a footballing midfielder,
always in the thick of the action, he retained a remarkable level
of consistency, rarely missing games through injury. Following a
£75,000 transfer to Blackpool in December 1987, and a loan spell
with Shrewsbury Town, he was signed by Swans manager Terry
Yorath in October 1990 for £30,000. At the end of his first season
back in his home city, Russell was a member of the Swans side
that beat Wrexham at the National Stadium in Cardiff to win the
Welsh Cup Final. What was surprising in view of the fact that
Russell was a consistent goalscorer from midfield was that it
took him until November 1991 to register his first goal for the
Swans. His third season at the Vetch Field saw Russell play a
major role in the club reaching the Second Division Play Off

semi-finals, losing by the odd goal on aggregate to West Bromwich Albion. In July 1993 he was included in a part exchange transfer deal with Exeter City winger John Hodge, plus a fee of £20,000 when he joined Exeter City. Two seasons of struggle at St. James Park saw the club relegated in 1994, and at the end of the 194/95 season found themselves at the bottom of the Third Division. Joining Torquay United in October 1995, at the end of the season he was given a free transfer, signing for Dr. Martens side Dorchester Town, before returning north to Cumbria to finish his playing career with Gretna, and take up a position as a postman in Carlisle.

43. CRAIG, ARNOTT

Birthplace: Motherwell
Ht: 5ft-10ins, **Wt:** 12st-0lbs
Swans debut: v. Blackpool (a), 21/12/1929

Swansea Town Career Statistics	
Season	*League*
1929/30	1
1930/31	2
Total	3

Career:
Wishaw
Motherwell (signed in June 1926)
Swansea Town (£450 in May 1929)
Glentoran (£150 in 20/8/1932) 55/5gls
Bangor (signed in 18/8/1934)
Waterford Celtic

Honours: West Wales Senior Cup Winner–1930, Irish Cup Winner–1933

Reserve team player at the Vetch Field who made his only appearance during the 1929/30 season at centre half against Blackpool, and who was unable to command a regular place in the Swans side because of the form of Joe Sykes initially, and then Harry Hanford. In October 1930 he was included in the Swans reserve side that beat Newport County in the West Wales Senior Cup Final. He made two consecutive appearances in his second season, and in August 1932, signed for Irish side Glentoran for £150. During his two years in Irish Football he was a member of the Glentoran side that won the Irish Cup in 1933, and Gold Cup Runners Up the following season. He made further appearances in Irish football with Bangor (August 1934), Waterford Celtic, Coleraine and Newry (May 1935)

44. CRAIG, Thomas (TOMMY) Brooks

Birthplace: Penilee, Glasgow, 21/11/1950
Ht: 5ft-7½ins, **Wt:** 11st-7lbs
Swans debut: v. Bournemouth (h), FLC 1–1, 11/8/1979

Swansea City Career Statistics				
Season	*League*	*FLC*	*FAC*	*WC*
1979/80	33/6gls	4/1gls	5	3/1gls
1980/81	14+5/3gls	1		7/1gls
Total	47+5/9gls	5/1gls	5	10/2gls

Career:
Aberdeen (signed in 1966)
Sheffield Wednesday (£100,000 signed in May 1969) lge
    210+4/38gls

Newcastle United (£110,000 signed in December 1974)
    lge 122+2/22gls, FLC 11/2gls, FAC 13/3gls
Aston Villa (£275,000 signed in January 1978) lge 27/2gls
Swansea City (£150,000 signed in 10/7/1979)
Carlisle United (signed in 11/3/1982) lge 92+6/10gls
Hibernian (£6,000 signed in 25/10/1984) SL 10+1

Honours: Scotland Sch–3, Yth–12, U–21–1, U–23–9, Full–1, Welsh Cup Winner–1981

Started his playing career with Avon Villa Juveniles and Drumchapel Amateurs, a Glasgow junior club in 1965, the former Glasgow Schoolboy was then signed by Aberdeen, originally as a groundsman's boy, making his league debut for Aberdeen against Stirling Albion at Pittodrie in December 1967, and within 2 years had smashed the record for the youngest teenager to be signed for a fee of £100,000 when he joined Sheffield Wednesday in May 1969, making his Football League debut at Hillsbrough against Tottenham Hotspur a couple of days later. Capped at schoolboy and youth level, the midfielder gained his first U-23 cap whilst with Sheffield Wednesday in 1974 against England, the following season playing three more times for the U-23 side against Wales, Rumania and Sweden. Relegated after his first season at Hillsbrough, Tommy made over two hundred league appearances in a struggling Wednesday side, and midway through season 1974/75 joined Newcastle United, a couple of months before Wednesday had suffered relegation to the Third Division. Establishing himself in the United midfield, Tommy played in the 1975/76 Football League Cup Final defeat by Manchester City. He gained his only Full cap for Scotland whilst with United, appearing against Switzerland in Hampden Park, Glasgow on the 7th April 1976 in a 1-0 win. Midway through the 1977/78 season Tommy joined Aston Villa for £275,000, and two years later arrived at the Vetch Field for a club record transfer fee of £150,000. In what was the first season for the Swans back in the Second Division, manager John Toshack had gone for a midfielder who would add experience to a basically young Swans outfit, who had played most of their football in the lower leagues. Scoring six league goals from midfield in his first season at the Vetch Field, Tommy also played his part in the club's exciting FA Cup run to the fifth round, also losing to Shrewsbury Town in the semi-final of the Welsh Cup. Although Tommy struggled to make the Swans line-up during the first half of season 1980/81, he was to put his name in the record books the second half, scoring the second goal at Preston which ensured the Swans promotion to the First Division, also being a member of the side that beat Hereford United over two legs to win the Welsh Cup the same season. Tommy failed to feature in the Swans First Division side, and in March 1982 he joined Carlisle United on a free transfer, becoming player/assistant manager to Bob Stokoe. He finished his playing career in Scotland with Hibernian, following his move north of the border in late October 1984. Since retiring as a player, Tommy has been involved as a coach and assistant manager at Hibernian, assistant manager at Celtic, Aberdeen, the Scotland U-21 side, and during the 2004/05 season was coaching at Newcastle United.

45. CRAPPER, Joseph (JOE)

Birthplace: Wortley, Sheffield 3/3/1899. **Died:** Sheffield, 4/2/1989
Ht: 5ft-7ins, **Wt:** 11st-0lbs
Swans debut: v. Exeter City (h), 22/3/1924

Swansea Town Career Statistics		
Season	League	WC
1923/24	3	1
Total	3	1

Career:
Notts. County (amateur signed in April 1922) lge 2
Huddersfield Town (signed in November 1922) lge 0
Swansea Town (signed in July 1923)

Honours: West Wales Senior Cup Winner–1923

Outside left who started his playing career with Sheffield junior side Swallownest FC, made his Football League debut with Notts. County in the Second Division, and after failing to make an appearance for Huddersfield Town, arrived at the Vetch Field in July 1923. His three league appearances for the Swans came in consecutive league games towards the end of the season, and throughout his only season at the Vetch Field he was usually third choice for the outside left position behind Spottiswoode and Corkingdale. In November 1923 he was included in the Swans reserve side that beat Pembroke Dock to win the West Wales Senior Cup. He also made an appearance for the Swans in a Welsh Cup replay with Wrexham on the right wing, but in May 1924 he was given a free transfer by the Swans.

46. CRAVEN, Joseph (JOE) Gerrard

Birthplace: Preston, 28/12/1903. **Died:** Chorley, JAS 1972
Ht: 5ft-11ins, **Wt:** 11st-12lbs
Swans debut: v. Leeds United (h), 29/8/1931

Swansea Town Career Statistics			
Season	League	FAC	WC
1931/32	36	1	3
1932/33	4		
1933/34	9		
Total	49	1	3

Career:
St. Augustines FC, Preston
Croston
Stockport County (signed as amateur in 9/12/1922, professional in February 1923) lge 5

Preston North End (signed in 30/10/1925) lge 65/1gls, FAC 2
Swansea Town (signed in June 1931)
Port Vale (signed in 15/6/1934) lge 11
Newport County (signed in 22/6/1935) lge 28
Accrington Stanley (signed in 16/6/1936) lge 57
Leyland Motors (signed August 1938)

Honours: Welsh Cup Winner–1932

Formerly with junior sides Frenchwood Villa, Preston YMCA, St. Augustines and Croston prior to signing for Second Division side Stockport County in December 1922 as an amateur, before turning professional in February 1923. He signed for Second Division Preston North End in October 1925, and over the space of almost six seasons made sixty five league appearances up to his signing for the Swans in July 1931, also touring North America with Preston in 1929. His only league goal during his playing career came in his debut match for Preston on 2nd January 1926 against Wolves. With Hanford sidelined for almost the entire 1931/32 season, his replacement Craven missed just six league games, and also played in the Welsh Cup Final win over Wrexham at the end of the season, which needed to go to a replay. Over the next two seasons, with Hanford occupying the centre half berth, Craven found games hard to come by, and in June 1934 he joined Port Vale. The next three seasons saw him make appearances for Vale, Newport County and Accrington Stanley, before playing non-league for Leyland Motors. His father played for Nelson F.C.

47. CROTTY, COLIN

Birthplace: Aberfan, 12/2/1951
Ht: 5ft-10ins, **Wt:** 12st-7lbs
Swans debut: v. York City (a), 2/5/1969

Swansea Town Career Statistics	
Season	League
1968/69	1+1/1gls
Total	1+1/1gls

Career:
Swansea Town (from juniors in August 1968)
Barry Town (signed in close season 1969)
Merthyr Tydfil (signed in close season 1970)

Honours: Wales Sch–3, Boys Club of Wales–2, Wales Yth–1

Born in Aberfan, Colin attended Pantglas School, Quakers Yard Grammar School, and Afan Taff Comprehensive school prior to signing a one year groundstaff deal at the Vetch Field with the Swans. Capped on three occasions for the Wales schoolboy side against England, Scotland and Northern Ireland, Colin also made two appearances for the Boys Club of Wales side whilst playing for Troedyrhiw Boys Club. After joining the Swans he went on to make an appearance in the Welsh Youth side against Scotland. Scoring on his debut for the Swans at York City in a 2-0 win on the 2nd May 1969, he also made a substitute appearance in the next league game against Exeter City at the Vetch Field, replacing Denley Morgan. A consistent goalscorer in the reserve team at the Vetch Field, he was released at the end of the season, joining Barry Town, but after just one season at Jenner Park, joined Merthyr Tydfil. At the age of twenty-eight, Colin finished his playing career with Hills Plymouth, and has since become an accomplished cricketer and bowls player, working as a production operator with Hoovers in Merthyr.

48. CROWE, Edward (TED) Wilfred

Birthplace: Stourport-on-Seven, 27/11/1911. **Died:** Stourport, 5/3/1982
Ht: 6ft-0ins, **Wt:** 12st-3lbs
Swans debut: v. Bury (h), 20/3/1937

Swansea Town Career Statistics	
Season	League
1936/37	1
Total	1

Career:
Stourport Swifts
WBA (signed in June 1930) lge 15
Swansea Town (£375 signed in 18/5/1936)
Aldershot (signed in October 1937) lge 19

Honours: England Junior International, Central League Champions–1933, 1934, 1935, Worcestershire F.A.

Goalkeeper who had made his Football League debut with First Division side West Bromwich Albion in 1933 after signing for the club from non-league Stourport Swifts, initially as an amateur in June 1930, before signing professional in October the same year. Playing for Stourport Council School, he had played for the Worcestershire County Boys team prior to signing for Stourport Swifts. In 1928 he had toured the USA with the Worcestershire F.A. XI, and in May 1928 had a trial period with Wolverhampton Wanderers. A very useful goalkeeper, signed as cover for Harold Pearson and George Ashmore, Ted Crowe made his League debut for Albion against Blackburn Rovers at home in January 1934. An England Junior international in 1931, he was restricted to just 16 first team outings during his time at The Hawthorns, but did gain three Central League

championship medals in successive seasons (1932-35). He made just one league appearances for the Swans in 2-0 win over Bury, with the regular keeper Stan Moore returning for the next league game. During the first half of his debut he suffered a knee injury, which restricted him severely for all of the second half, keeping him out of contention for a number of weeks. Two games later veteran full back Wilf Milne was forced to make two appearances in goal in consecutive away league games. Moore returned from injury to claim his goalkeeper jersey for the remainder of the season, with Ted leaving the Vetch Field to sign for Third Division South team Aldershot in May 1937, joining Wilden FC two years later, retiring in May 1942.

49. CRUDGINGTON, Geoffrey (GEOFF)

Birthplace: Wolverhampton, 14/2/1952
Ht: 6ft-0ins, **Wt:** 12st-6lbs
Swans debut: v. Colchester United (a), 19/8/1978

Swansea City Career Statistics				
Season	League	FLC	FAC	WC
1978/79	46	5	4	2
1979/80	6	4		
Total	52	9	4	2

Career:
Wolverhampton Wanderers Juniors
Aston Villa (signed in September 1969) lge 4
Bradford City (loan in March 1971) lge 1
Crewe Alexandra (signed in March 1972) lge 250
Swansea City (£30,000 signed in 31/7/1978)
Plymouth Argyle (£45,000 signed in 3/10/1979) lge 326

Honours: England Sch–3

Born in Wolverhampton, Geoff joined his hometown club as a junior after being capped at schoolboy level for England and represented South East Staffordshire Boys, but later joined Aston Villa in September 1969, a couple of months short of his seventeenth birthday. Very much in the pecking order behind Jimmy Cumbes, John Findlay and Tommy Hughes, Crudgington had a loan spell with Bradford City in March 1971, and following his return to Villa Park, after making five first team appearances, joined Fourth Division Crewe Alexandra in March 1972. Over the next five seasons he established himself in the Alexandra side making 250 league appearances. During the 1977/78 season when the Swans under John Toshack were making a bold attempt to escape from the Fourth Division, Crudgington had an outstanding game for Crewe against the Swans, and it was probably that performance that persuaded

Toshack to sign the goalkeeper for £30,000, a club record at the time for the Swans for a goalkeeper. What surprised the Swans fans more than anything was that in Keith Barber, the club already had a goalkeeper who had impressed many a supporter the previous term. Even more surprisingly, two months after being an ever present in a Swans side which had recorded their second consecutive promotion, and rated as the club's first choice keeper, Toshack broke the club record fee for a keeper a second time, paying Chesterfield £45,000 for Welsh U-23 keeper Glan Letheran, with Crudgington joining Plymouth Argyle within a couple of days for £45,000. At Argyle he established himself as the club's number one keeper up until his retirement in 1987, making 326 league appearances, achieving promotion as Third Division Runners Up in season 1985/6, and reaching the FA Cup Semi-Finals in 1984. Since retiring as a player, he has held the youth team manager's post, and is currently Football in the Community Officer at the club.

50. CRUMLEY, JAMES Brymer

Birthplace: Dundee, 17/7/1890. **Died:** Raynes Park, 19/4/1981
Ht: 5ft-9ins, **Wt:** 11st-0lbs
Swans debut: v. Plymouth Argyle (a), 27/12/1919, Sth. Lge

Swansea Town Career Statistics			
Season	League	FAC	WC
1920/21	12		
1921/22	14	2	1
1922/23	2		
Total	28	2	1

Career:
Dundee Hibernian (signed in September 1911)
USA (August 1912)
Dundee Hibernian
WW1
Swansea Town (£100 signed in 22/12/1919)
Bristol City (signed in 8/8/1923) lge 2
Darlington (signed in June 1924) lge 66, FAC 5
Bournemouth & Boscombe (signed in August 1926) lge 54

Honours: Southern League Representative XI, Third Division North Champions–1925, West Wales Senior Cup Winner–1923

Former Dundee Hibernian goalkeeper who kept goal for the Swans in the club's first ever Football League fixture at Portsmouth in August 1920. Went to the USA in August 1912, and after returning home rejoined Dundee Hibernian, enlisted in WW1, and after demobilisation joined the Swans. Played in the Southern League for the Swans following his arrival at the Vetch Field in December 1919, making twenty-two Southern League appearances. In April 1920 he played for a Southern

League Welsh Clubs XI at the Vetch Field against a Southern League English Clubs XI. A daring keeper, with wonderful anticipation, he did however have a habit of doing foolish things at times. After the first twelve league matches for the Swans, he was replaced by Jock Denoon, and despite returning for fourteen league games in season 1921/22, and two appearances in season 1922/23, was released by the Swans, joining Bristol City in August 1923. In May 1923 he played in a Swans reserve side that beat Llanelly to win the West Wales Senior Cup. He later signed for Darlington, and was an ever present in the club's 1924/25 Third Division (North) Championship winning side, conceding just thirty-three goals. He later returned south to sign for Bournemouth in 1925, playing until the 1928/29 season. His brother Bob also played for Dundee.

51. CULLEN, Anthony (TONY) Scott

Birthplace: Gateshead, 30/9/1969
Ht: 5ft-6ins, **Wt:** 11st-7lbs
Swans debut: v. Burnley (a), 15/8/1992

Swansea City Career Statistics					
Season	League	FLC	FAC	WC	P/Offs
1992/93	20+7/3gls	2	2/1gls	1	2
Total	20+7/3gls	2	2/1gls	1	2

Career:
Newcastle United (YTS)
Sunderland (signed in 12/9/1988) lge 11+18
Carlisle United (loan in 13/12/1989) lge 2/1gls
Rotherham United (loan in 29/1/1991) lge 3/1gls
Bury (loan in 31/10/1991) lge 4
Swansea City (signed in August 1992)
Gateshead (signed in August 1993) Conf 2

Former trainee with Newcastle United who joined Sunderland in September 1988, making his league debut in a 3-0 defeat by Walsall in February 1989 as substitute for Reuben Agboola. He had earlier attended Coalgate Junior and Highfield Comprehensive Schools, played for Gateshead Boys prior to signing for United as a YTS trainee. The next five league games saw him make appearances in Sunderland's league side, either starting or from the substitute bench. He started season 1990/91 as first choice on the right side of midfield for Sunderland, but played no part in the end of season Play Offs. Following loan spells with Carlisle United, Rotherham United and Bury, he was released by Sunderland at the end of season 1991/92, arriving at the Vetch Field on an initial trial spell at the start of the 1992-93 season, and within a couple of games was given a one year contract by the Swans. Short in stature, Tony possessed plenty of pace and control on the right flank, where he was capable of producing good quality crosses, resulting in a number of goalscoring opportunities for the Swans frontrunners. He scored his first goal for the Swans in a 1-1 draw at Stockport County in October 1992. He was not as influential in his play during the second half of his only season at the Vetch Field, but did play in both Second Division Play Off semi-final legs against West Bromwich Albion. He was released at the end of the season, returned to his native North East, joining Conference side Gateshead, but after making just two appearances, and trials with Doncaster Rovers and York City signed for Seaham Red Star. Unfortunately for him an ankle injury picked up playing for the Swans would see him have to give up the game at professional level. He finished his playing career with Northern League side Tow Law Town, later at Vaux Wearside League side Jarrow Roofing. For the last ten years Tony has worked at Sunderland and Washington Leisure Centres.

52. CUNLIFFE, Reginald (REG)

Birthplace: Wigan, 4/12/1920. **Died:** Fleetwood, August 2000
Ht: 5ft-11ins, **Wt:** 13st-0lbs
Swans debut: v. Manchester City (a), 19/10/1946

Swansea Town Career Statistics		
Season	*League*	*WC*
1946/47	1	1
1947/48	1	
Total	2	1

Career:
Garswood St. Andrew's
Wigan Athletic (signed in 25/9/1945)
Swansea Town (signed in 21/5/1946)
Wigan Athletic (signed in close season 1948)

Honours: RAF XI, London Combination Cup Winner–1947

On Manchester City's books prior to signing for non-league side Wigan Athletic, and had earlier played for the RAF against Munster. Joined the Swans originally as a forward, but made both his league appearances at full back. He made his league debut at left full back, with Fisher switching to the other flank, and in his second appearance for the Swans in September 1947 against Bristol Rovers, played at right full back instead of Jim Feeney. Reg had been watched by the Swans during the second half of season 1945/46, and at the time there was interest from Arsenal for his signature. In June 1947 he played at left full back in the Swans reserve side that beat Arsenal at White Hart Lane to win the London Combination Cup Final. He also had a spell with the Swans Combination side playing at centre forward. He rejoined Lancashire Combination side Wigan Athletic in the 1948 close season after being released by the Swans, but in January 1949 was granted a free transfer after struggling to command a regular place in the side.

53. CURTIS, ALAN Thomas

Birthplace: Pentre, Treorchy, 16/4/1954
Ht: 5ft-11ins, **Wt:** 12st-3lbs
Swans debut: v. Southend United (a), 25/8/1972

Career:
Swansea City (from juniors in July 1972)
Leeds United (£400,000 signed in 5/6/1979) lge 28/5gls
Swansea City (£175,000 signed in 14/12/1980)
Southampton (£75,000 signed in 31/11/1983) lge 43+7/5gls
Stoke City (loan in March 1986) lge 3
Cardiff City (signed in July 1986) lge 122+3/10gls
Swansea City (£8,000 signed in 6/10/1989)
Barry Town (signed in July 1990)
Haverfordwest County (signed in July 1991)

Swansea City Career Statistics						
Season	*League*	*FLC*	*FAC*	*WC*	*ECWC*	*L/Daf*
1972/73	13		1	1		
1973/74	36+2/4gls	1	1	1		
1974/75	35+2		2	3		
1975/76	41/9gls	1	1	3/1gls		
1976/77	46/14gls	6/2gls	2	2/3gls		
1977/78	39/32gls	2	5/2gls			
1978/79	34/12gls	4/3gls	3/5gls	2/3gls		
1980/81	16+4/6gls		1	3/2gls		
1981/82	40/10gls	2/1gls	1	7/3gls	2	
1982/83	17+4/4gls	3	1	2/1gls	3/2gls	
1983/84	9/1gls	1			2	
1989/90	21+5/3gls		4	1		0+1
Total	347+17/95gls	20/6gls	21/7gls	25/13gls	7/2gls	0+1

Honours: Wales Yth, U-21–1, U-23–1, Full 35, Welsh Cup Winner–1981, 1982, 1988, 1994, Welsh League First Division Champions–1994

Born in the Rhondda Valley, a highly talented nephew of former Wales star Roy Paul, who came straight from Porth County Grammar School, signing professional forms in the close season of 1972 for the Swans. The previous season had seen the young striker produce exciting performances in the Swans high scoring Football Combination side, leading to him being given his league debut by manager Roy Bentley at Southend United in August 1972. Although he had to wait until September 1973 to register his first goal for the Swans, at Torquay United, it was following the appointment of Harry Giffiths as manager that 'Curt's' career took off as a frontline striker. The attacking philosophy of Griffiths saw Curtis develop into an international frontrunner, coming to within three goals in season 1977/78 to breaking the long standing goalscoring record of 35 goals in one season scored by Cyril Pearce in 1931/32. The scorer of four hat-tricks for the Swans during his career, the first in January 1977 against Newport County in a Welsh Cup tie, followed by two in the 1977/78 Fourth Division promotion winning season, against Crewe Alexandra in November 1977, and Hartlepool United in April 1978, and a hat-trick in the FA Cup Second Round replay against non-league Woking. Capped at youth level for Wales, 'Curt' made his only Wales U-23 appearance against Scotland as a substitute in 1976, with his only U-21 cap coming in 1977 against England. At Full international level his first cap came on the 24th March 1976 at the Racecourse against England, with 'Curt' scoring in a 2-1 defeat. Within a month of promotion to the Second Division being secured at the end of the 1978/79 season, 'Curt' was involved in a record breaking transfer to Leeds United for £400,000. However, despite a good start to his Elland Road career, in which he scored two goals in his league debut against Bristol City, a knee ligament injury saw him sidelined, and with doubts over whether he would ever play again, within eighteen months he had returned to the Vetch Field to give impetus to a side that by the end of the season would claim promotion to the First Division, and win the Welsh Cup for the first time since 1966. Incidentally, his first game back for the Swans, saw him come off the substitute bench to score the only goal of the game from the penalty spot to beat Watford at the Vetch Field. Opening his First Division account for the Swans with a goal in the opening fixture against his former club, Leeds United, 'Curt', along with his team mates would be responsible for scoring some memorable goals that season, and be regularly featured on BBC TV's Match of the Day programme in their Goal of the Month Competition. Injuries in the second half of the club's second season in the top flight saw 'Curt' unable to give assistance to the Swans in their bid to avoid relegation, but with worsening financial problems off the field looming, he was one of the players who needed to be sacrificed midway through the 1983/84 season to keep the club's bankers happy. Injury problems at the Dell prevented him from making a greater impact with Southampton, and following a loan transfer with Stoke City, joined Cardiff City in July 1986 on a free transfer. His second season at Ninian Park saw the 'Bluebirds finish as runners up in the Fourth Division, and also beat Wrexham in the Welsh Cup Final, with 'Curt' scoring in front of the Vetch Field supporters. In October 1989 he returned to the Vetch Field for the third time, and finish his last season as a full time professional where he started his career in 1972. After leaving the Vetch Field in May 1990, 'Curt' had two spells with Barry Town, and in between played for Haverfordwest, Carmarthen Town, Morriston, and occasional games for Swansea Senior League side Mumbles Rangers. He skippered the 1990/91 Barry Town side when they lost narrowly to the Swans in the Welsh Cup semi-finals, with Barry Town at that time playing in the Beazer Homes League, Midland Division. The start of the 1991/92 season saw Alan return to the Vetch Field, this time as Football in the Community Officer, whilst still continuing playing non-league. With Barry Town returning to the Welsh League for the start of the 1993/94 season, by the end of the season the club had not only won the First Division Championship, but also beaten Cardiff City in the Welsh Cup Final, with 'Curt' scoring against his former club. His Football in the Community job at the Vetch Field took him up to the 1996/97 season when he took over as youth team manager of the Swans. From November 1997 he started to get involved with the Swans first team, joining John Hollins as his assistant in 1998, with the Third Division Championship being won in 2000. Along with Hollins, Alan left the Vetch Field in September 2001, to work for kit manufacturer Bergoni, and also commentate on Swans matches for Independent Radio Station Real Radio, but shortly before the end of the season, he had been appointed by the new Swans manager, Nick Cusack to be his assistant for the end of season FA Premier Cup Final against Cardiff City. A change of management shortly after the start of season 2002/03 saw Alan revert to First Team Coach under Brian Flynn, and in May 2003 he was appointed Head of Youth Development at the Vetch Field. Following the sacking of Flynn in March 2004, for a short time, 'Curt' was caretaker manager of the Swans before handing over to Kenny Jackett. In November 2004 following the appointment of John Toshack as manager of the Wales National team, 'Curt' was involved at U-21 level alongside former Swans' manager Brian Flynn. On the 18th May 2005 he was relieved of his postion as Head of Youth Development at the Vetch Field, later taking on an ambassadorial role with the Swans as the club geared itself to moving into a new 20,000 all seater stadium in Landore.

54. CUSACK, Nicholas (NICK) John

Birthplace: Maltby, 24/12/1965
Ht: 6ft-0ins, **Wt:** 12st-8lbs
Swans debut: v. Cardiff City (a), 2nd November 1997

Swansea City Career Statistics						
Season	League	FLC	FAC	LDV	FAWP	P/Offs
1997/98	32		1	1	2	
1998/99	42+1/1gls	2/1gls	5	1	4+1/1gls	2
1999/00	43/7gls	2	2/1gls			
2000/2001	30+10/2gls	1	1	0+1	6+1	
2001/02	33+2/2gls	0+1	2/2gls	1	2	
2002/03	4+1/1gls		1			
Total	184+14/13gls	5+1/1gls	12/3gls	3+1	14+2/1gls	2

Career:
Long Eaton United
Alvechurch
Leicester City (signed in 18/6/1987) lge 5+11/1gls, FAC 0+1, Others 1+1
Peterborough United (£40,000 in 29/7/1988) lge 44/10gls, FLC 4/1gls, FAC 4/1gls, Others 2
Motherwell (£100,000 in 2/8/1989) Slge 68+9/17gls, SLC 5/4gls, SC 3+1/2gls, Others 1+1/1gls
Darlington (£95,000 in 24/1/1992) lge 21/6gls
Oxford United (£95,000 in 16/7/1992) lge 48+13/10gls, FLC 3/2gls, FAC 4+2/1gls, Others 2+1
Wycombe Wanderers (loan in 24/3/1994) lge 2+2/1gls
Fulham (loan in 4/11/1994, £60,000 in January 1995) lge 109+7/14gls, FLC 6+4/1gls, FAC 7+1/1gls, Others 5+2/3gls
Swansea City (£50,000 in 30/10/1997)

Honours: Division Three Champions–2000, West Wales Senior Cup Winner–2002

Nick Cusack started his non-league career with Birmingham Polytechnic, Long Eaton United and Alvechurch prior to joining Leicester City as a centre forward. Despite not being a prolific marksman, he was a handful for defenders with his ability to bring his team mates into play, and create goalscoring opportunities. In August 1989 a £100,000 transfer fee took him to Scottish football with Motherwell, and in his first season was top goalscorer in the league with eleven goals. The following season (1990/91), Motherwell won the Scottish Cup, and although Cusack did not play, he did make a substitute appearance in the semi-final win over Celtic. Returning to the Football League with Darlington for a record fee of £95,000 in January 1992, he scored on his debut for the club at the Vetch Field in a 4-2 defeat. Relegated at the end of the season, a further transfer fee in the region of £95,000 was followed in July 1992 to Oxford United, and one of his first matches for his new club was against the Swans in the two legs of the Coca Cola Cup competition, which United won on aggregate. Later in the season Oxford returned to the Vetch Field for an FA Cup third round tie, in which Cusack scored United's equalising goal to take the game to a replay. After joining Fulham in November 1994 he alternated between a striker, midfield, and even a central defensive role for the club, enjoying success when Fulham gained promotion from the Third Division at the end of the 1996/97 season as runners-up to Wigan Athletic. His arrival at the Vetch Field for a fee in the region of £50,000 saw Cusack make almost all of his early appearances in a midfield role, where his ability to read the game, and his level of fitness saw him make an important contribution to the club's success in league and cup matches under manager John Hollins, captaining the side to the 1999/2000 Third Division Championship. Despite suffering relegation after one season in the Second Division, the 2001/02 season proved to be quite a remarkable season for the experienced midfielder, which culminated in him taking on a player coach role at the Vetch Field towards the end of the season on a twelve month contract, and including himself in the Swans side that beat Hakin United to win the West Wales Senior Cup in late April 2002.

Elected Chairman of the players section of the PFA in November 2001, Nick gained enormous respect from not only the players, but also the supporters at the way he handled events off the field at the Vetch Field that season as the club lurched from one crisis to another, the sacking of players, non-payment of wages, a compulsory winding up order, and even taking on a role as joint caretaker manager with Roger Freestone towards the end of the season. On the field Nick again showed his versatility, playing as a striker, midfield, and even in a central defensive role where the need demanded. He started season 2002/03 as player manager, bringing in 10 new players in the close season, still continuing with his Chairman of the PFA role. Unfortunately, despite a good start, a run of poor results saw him leave the Vetch Field after a midweek defeat at Boston United in mid-September, with his position taken over by Brian Flynn. He turned down Flynn's offer of a playing contract, retiring from the game to take up a full time position with the PFA.

55. CUTLER, NEIL Anthony

Birthplace: Birmingham, 3/9/1976
Ht: 6ft-1ins, **Wt:** 12st-0lbs
Swans debut: v. Wrexham (h), 1/3/2003

Swansea City Career Statistics	
Season	*League*
2002/03	13
Total	13

Career:
West Bromwich Albion (from trainee in 7/9/1993)
Chester City (loan in 27/3/1996) lge 1
Crewe Alexandra (signed in 30/7/1996)
Chester City (loan in 30/8/1996) lge 5
Chester City (signed in 8/7/1998) lge 23, FLC 1, FAC 1, Others 1
Aston Villa (signed in 30/11/1999) PL 0+1
Oxford United (loan in 15/12/2000) lge 11
Stoke City (signed in 24/7/2001) lge 65+4, FLC 3, FAC 6+1, Others 3
Swansea City (loan in 28/2/2003)
Stockport County (signed in 4/6/2004) lge 22, FLC 1. FAC 1+1, Others 2
Rotherham United (signed in 4/8/2005)

Honours: England Sch, Yth, Second Division Play Off Winner–2002

Former England Schoolboy and Youth goalkeeper who prior to joining Chester City on loan March 1996 had a brief spell at non-league Tamworth. A former trainee with West Bromwich Albion, Neil made his league debut for Chester at Torquay on the 20th April 1996 in a 1-1 draw. After signing for Crewe Alexandra in July 1996 as cover for Mark Gayle, he joined non-league Leek Town later in the season to gain experience, and after failing to make an appearance for Alexandra joined Chester City in July 1998 on a permanent basis. Despite struggling to hold a regular place in the Chester side, his potential was noticed when Aston Villa took him on loan in November 1999 as cover for their keepers, with Cutler pressed into service as substitute for David James in a Premiership match at Middlesbrough. A further loan spell with Oxford United in season 2000/01 saw him released on a free transfer by Chester, with Neil signing for Second Division side Stoke City. Again signed as cover for Gavin Ward, Neil made the most appearances in one season in his short career, making thirty-six appearances in Stoke's promotion challenge, which saw the 'Potters' gain promotion by beating Brentford in the Play Off Final at Cardiff. The following season however saw a change of management at the Britannia Stadium, with Neil sidelined once more. Despite starting his first season as first choice keeper for the first time in his career, Neil was replaced by Steve Banks halfway through the season, leading the way for him to join the Swans on an initial month loan to replace the suspended Roger Freestone at the Vetch Field. Keeping a clean sheet in his debut game for the Swans against Wrexham, he stayed for the remainder of the season, making a significant contribution in the club's successful fight against relegation to the Conference. Producing many memorable saves, he proved to be a crucial signing by manager Flynn, returning to Stoke City at the end of the season with a year left on his contract. His place at the Britannia Stadium was in jeopardy again for season 2003/04 when Stoke City brought in ex-Dutch international Ed De Goey from Chelsea prior to the start of the season. Despite showing impressive form when called into action through the 2003/04 season, and the offer of a new contract on the table, he was about to join the Swans, when a better offer from Stockport County tempted him to sign for the Coca Cola League One side. During the season he played against the Swans in an FA Cup tie, but by May his County side had been relegated to Coca Cola League Two, and he had been placed on the transfer list. In early August 2005 he joined Rotherham United.

D

1. DACKINS, HAYDN Vernon

Birthplace: Pontypridd, 10/7/1912. **Died:** Catonia, Sicily, 2/8/1943
Ht: 5ft-8ins, **Wt:** 10st-4lbs
Swans debut: v. Chester (a), WC–6, 7/2/1934

Swansea Town Career Statistics		
Season	*League*	*WC*
1933/34		1
1934/35	2	1
Total	2	2

Career:
Swansea Town (amateur in season 1932/33, professional in 9/8/1933)
Port Vale (signed in July 1935) lge 9/1gls
Northwich Victoria (signed in July 1936)
Macclesfield Town (signed in October 1937)
Hurst (signed in December 1938)

Honours: West Wales Senior Cup Winner–1934

Formerly on the groundstaff at the Vetch Field, played as an amateur during season 1932/33, before joining the professional ranks in August 1933. He made his Swans debut in a Welsh Cup, sixth round tie at Chester in February 1934 at outside left, but had to wait until January 1935 before he made his debut in the Football League for the Swans. Replacing Lowry at outside left, he made just one more appearance before the end of the season in the league, also making an appearance in the Welsh Cup semi-final tie against Chester at Wrexham. In October 1934 he was a member of the Swans side that beat Llanelly at Stebonheath Park to win the West Wales Senior Cup. Joining Second Division side Port Vale in the 1935 close season,

he played against the Swans at Port Vale in November 1935, but at the end of his first season with Vale signed for non-league side Northwich, making further non-league appearances for Macclesfield Town. A school teacher who gained a BSC at Bristol University, he was killed in action in the Second World War in August 1943 at Catonia, Sicily with the 6th Battalion Royal Inniskillen Fusiliers.

2. DALLING, NIGEL Aubrey

Birthplace: Swansea, 20/2/1959
Ht: 5ft-6ins, **Wt:** 9st-0lbs
Swans debut: v. Southport (h), 6/12/1974

Swansea City Career Statistics		
Season	*League*	*FLC*
1974/75	0+3	
1975/76	1	1
1976/77		
1977/78	1+3	
Total	2+6	1

Career:
Swansea City (from apprentice in February 1977)
Bridgend Town (signed in January 1978)

Honours: Welsh League First Division Champions–1976, British Post Office Cup Winner

Former Cefn Hengoed and Swansea Schoolboy winger Nigel Dalling schoolboy Nigel Dalling became the youngest player to make an appearance in the Football League for the Swans on the 6th December 1974 when he came on as substitute for Tony

Screen against Southport at the Vetch Field at the age of 15 years and 289 days old. Signed by manager Roy Bentley whilst still in school he linked up with his Cefn Hengoed teacher Walter Quick at the Vetch Field, a coach who was highly respected in the Swansea area for his involvement in schools, local and professional football. Given his league debut by Harry Gregg he also played under Harry Griffiths and Roy Saunders at the Vetch Field, and left a week before John Toshack was appointed manager of the club. Initially disappointed that he had been unable to make an impression in the professional game, especially with the success Toshack was to have, but since then has made a career outside the game, which, on looking back he might not have had if he stayed in football. He made his first start for the Swans in a League Cup tie at Torquay United during the 1975/76 season, making his first league start a few weeks later against Cambridge United at the Vetch Field. During the season he made regular appearances in the reserve side that won the Welsh League First Division Championship. After leaving the Swans, he worked for five years at Unit Superheaters in the Strand area of the city, and after being made redundant when the factory suddenly shut down, then worked for the local authority at Dillwyn Llewellyn School before joining the Post Office as a postman. He has since worked himself up to a managerial position, and after being in charge of the Mail Centre for ten months, now works in the Gorseinon Branch. A right winger during his playing career, small in stature he did not go on to make an impression in league football but stayed on the non-league scene up until 2000 with Swansea Senior League side Port Tennant Colts. At international level his only opportunity to gain representative honours for Wales came when he was selected for the Welsh Youth squad but an injury in training tearing ligaments in his ankle forced him to withdraw from the squad. After leaving the Swans he signed for Southern League side Bridgend Town in January 1978 staying until the end of the season. The following season he linked up with former Swans midfielder Willie Screen at Ammanford Town with former Swans players Tony Screen and Paul Fury also in the squad. He then had a spell at Llanelli with Wyndham Evans, a manager he spoke very highly about with his enthusiastic approach to the game. A successful period with Afan Lido which saw the club challenging for the championship, playing alongside Cyril Hartson and former Cardiff City winger Nigel Rees was ended when he left the club after a dispute over wages. He then linked up with Swansea Senior League side Ragged School, then signed for Port Tennant Colts. Since his retirement he has no involvement with football apart from watching on television. Since starting with the Post Office he has also played for the postal side in a team, which at one stage included eleven ex-professionals in their side, winning the British Post Office Cup on three occasions.

3. DANIEL, William Raymond (RAY)

Birthplace: Swansea, 2/11/1928. **Died:** Clevedon, Avon, 7/11/1997
Ht: 6ft-0ins, **Wt:** 12st-9lbs
Swans debut: v. Leyton Orient (h), 8/3/1958

Swansea Town Career Statistics

Season	League	WC
1957/58	10/1gls	
1958/59	30/4gls	2/1gls
1959/60	4/2gls	
Total	44/7gls	2/1gls

Career:
Swansea Town (amateur during season 1944/45)
Arsenal (amateur signed in 19/8/1946, professional October 1946) lge 87/5gls, FAC 12
Sunderland (£27,500 signed in June 1953) lge 136/6gls, FAC 17/1gls
Cardiff City (signed in October 1957) lge 6
Swansea Town (£3,000 signed in 6/3/1958)
Hereford United (signed in July 1960, player/manager) Total Apps 314/65gls

Honours: Wales Full–21, First Division Champions–1953, Football Combination Champions–1952, Southern League First Division Champions–1965

Ray Daniel was brought up in the Plasmarl district of Swansea, played for Plasmarl Youth Club, skippered the Swansea Schoolboys team, and played for the Swans as an amateur in wartime football at the age of fifteen in November 1944 at Bristol City at full back. With his brother Bobby on the groundstaff at Arsenal before the war, at the end of the war Ray himself joined Arsenal whilst still an amateur in August 1946, turning professional a couple of months later. His brother Bobby unfortunately lost his life serving in the RAF during the war when on a bombing raid. The previous season he had been a prominent figure in the Swans' Welsh League side. National Service restricted his opportunities in the 'Gunners' first team, but after his demobilisation he finally made his league debut, against Charlton Athletic in the last match of the 1948/49 season as a replacement for Leslie Compton, who was making his first appearance of the cricket season for Middlesex. At the end of the season he was included in the club's playing squad that toured Brazil. Making only a handful of appearances over the next couple of seasons, he gained his first Welsh cap whilst playing for the 'Gunners' reserve side, playing at centre half against England on the 15th November 1950 at Roker Park in Sunderland. He finally secured a regular place in the Arsenal side at the start of the 1951/52 season, and at the end of the season won an FA Cup runners up medal playing with a broken arm encased in plaster for the Gunners in a 1-0 defeat against Newcastle United, also winning a Football Combination Championship Medal. The following season he won a First Division Championship Medal missing only one game all season, and at this stage in his career was a regular in the Welsh international side. A big, strong defender, and confident on the ball, he was very much an unorthodox centre half for his time, preferring to play the ball out of defence, rather than clearing his lines with a big kick. In June 1953 after asking for a transfer, he joined Sunderland for £27,500, who at the time were the big spenders in the Football League, and what was a record transfer fee for a centre half. Attempting to buy a team to win major honours, Daniel was among seven Sunderland players later suspended for illegal payments. He moved to Cardiff City in October 1957 but after only six league matches he joined the Swans in March 1958. Making his Swans debut at the Vetch Field against Leyton Orient in March 1958 at centre half, over the next two seasons he often played at full back, and at centre forward. Linking up with his old Arsenal team-mate Joe Wade at Hereford at the start of the 1960 season, although primarily a centre-half during his league career, Daniel led the attack during his first season at Edgar Street with great success, scoring 32 goals in 39 appearances in the Southern League. After Wade left the club at the end of the following season, Daniel had a somewhat traumatic time in charge himself, spending 15 months at the helm before being replaced by Bob Dennison. Under Dennison, he successfully continued his playing career for a few more seasons before retiring at the end of the 1966-7 season. During that last season, he had again linked up with old Welsh international team-mate John Charles. At the end of season 1964/65 United won the Southern League First Division Championship, setting a new points record of 72 in doing so. After retiring from the game he ran a pub (The Ivorites, in Swansea's High Street), then became area manager for Courvoisier Brandy and later a sub-postmaster until 1989 in Cockett, Swansea.

4. D'AURIA, DAVID Alan

Birthplace: Swansea, 26/3/1970
Ht: 5ft-10ins, **Wt:** 12st-6lbs
Swans debut: v. Hartlepool United (h), 31/8/1987

Swansea City Career Statistics

Season	League	FLC	FAC	FRT	WC	ECWC
1987/88	0+4					
1988/89	9+5/2gls	0+1		0+1	1+1	
1989/90	6+1	2				1
1990/91	12+8/4gls	0+1	1+1	3	2+3	
Total	27+18/6gls	2+2	1+1	3+1	3+4	1

Career:
Swansea City (from trainee in July 1988)
Merthyr Tydfil (signed in July 1991) Conf apps, 70+7/7gls
Barry Town (signed in August 1993)
Scarborough (signed in 22/8/1994) lge 49+3/8gls,
    FLC 3+2/1gls, FAC 4+1, Others 2
Scunthorpe United (£40,000 in 6/12/1995) lge 103+4/18gls,
    FLC 6, FAC 7/1gls, Others 4+1
Hull City (signed in 16/7/1998) lge 52+2/4gls, FLC 5+2, FAC 5,
    Others 2/1gls
Chesterfield (£50,000 in 25/11/1999) lge 18+7/1gls,
    FAC 3+1/1gls, Others 3+1/1gls
Newport County (signed in August 2002)
Llanelli (signed in November 2002)

Honours: Wales Yth, Welsh Cup Winner–1994, Welsh League First Division Champions–1994, West Wales Senior Cup Winner–1990, 1991, Macbar Cup Winner–1987

Landore born, Pentrehafod and Swansea schoolboys midfielder who joined the Swans as a YTS trainee on leaving school, signing professional in July 1988, and who had already made his league debut, replacing Phil Williams from the substitute bench in August 1987 against Hartlepool United whilst still a trainee. In May 1987, whilst still a trainee he played in the Swans reserve side that beat Plymouth Argyle in the Macbar Cup Final. Capped at Welsh Youth level, making his first appearance at Dundee against Scotland in February 1987 in a European Qualifying match, he made a further three substitute appearances for the Swans during the season. A hard working midfielder, he developed into a competent central midfielder, with high fitness levels, good tackling abilities, and an eye for goalscoring opportunities. In his first season as a professional he scored in consecutive league games for the Swans, with both games finishing in 1-0 victories. Season 1989/90 saw 'Dai' start in the first leg of the European Cup Winners Cup tie in Athens against Panathinaikos. In May 1990 and in 1991 he was included in the Swans squad that beat Llanelli in consecutive West Wales Senior Cup Finals. Despite having his best season with regard first team appearances, he was released at the end of season 1990/91, joining Conference side Merthyr Tydfil, where he scored five goals from midfield in his first season, helping the club to finish in fourth place in the Conference. With Barry Town dropping out of the Beazer Homes Midland Division at the end of season 1992/93, and entering the Welsh League First Division, 'Dai' and a number of former Swans players made appearances for Barry during a season in which they won the First Division Championship, and also beat Cardiff City at the National Stadium in Cardiff to win the Welsh Cup Final, with 'Dai' scoring one of the goals. Included in the Barry team in the final were former Swans players Terry Boyle, Alan Curtis, Phil Williams and Paul Wimbleton. Dai returned to the Football League with Scarborough in August 1994, where his consistency in midfield saw him return seven goals from midfield in his first season, resulting in a £40,000 transfer to Scunthorpe United midway through his second season with Scarborough. His vision and creativity in midfield, and eye for goal saw him score ten league goals during season 1997/98, with the 'Iron' just missing out on a Play Off place. After signing for Hull City in July 1998, and making the most appearances in one season of forty-two league games, he was sold to Chesterfield in November 1999 for £50,000. Unfortunately for 'Dai', during his time at Saltergate he suffered with a back problem, before being sidelined with a foot, and ankle injury, which severely limited his appearances for the club. He was released at the end of season 2001/02, and in late August 2002 joined Dr. Martens Premier Division side Newport County. By November however, he had moved further west to sign for League of Wales club Llanelli, and at the start of the 2003/04 season joined CC Sports Welsh League side Skewen Athletic. Prior to returning to live in the Swansea area he had undertaken a Plumbing Training programme, and has since set up his own business in the Swansea area. In the 2005 close season he was appointed assistant manager to Andrew Dyer at Neath Athletic following the merger of Skewen Athletic and Neath AFC.

5. DAVEY, SIMON

Birthplace: Swansea, 1/10/1970
Ht: 5ft-10ins, **Wt:** 12st-2lbs
Swans debut: v. Torquay United (h), 7/4/1987

Swansea City Career Statistics

Season	League	FLC	FAC	LDV	WC	ECWC
1986/87	0+1					
1987/88	4				0+1	
1988/89	3					
1989/90	16+2/2gls		1/1gls		1	
1990/91	11+7/2gls		0+2	0+2	2	
1991/92	3+2	1+1				2
Total	37+12/4gls	1+1	1+2/1gls	0+2	3+1	2

Career:
Swansea City (from trainee in July 1989)
Carlisle United (signed in 5/8/1992) lge 105/18gls,
    FLC 10/1gls, FAC 7/2gls, Others 2+3
Preston North End (£125,000 signed in 22/2/1995)
    lge 97+9/21gls, FLC 4/1gls, FAC 2+1, Others 9
Darlington (loan in 1/9/1997) lge 10+1

Honours: Wales Yth, Third Division Champions–1995, 1996,
Welsh Cup Winner–1991, West Wales Senior Cup Winner–1990,
1991

At the age of sixteen and a half years of age, Simon became one
of the youngest players to make his debut in the league for the
Swans, after he was taken out of the fifth form at Olchfa School
as a sixteen-year-old by manager Terry Yorath, hardly having
enough time to change out of his school uniform to make an
appearance in a midweek game against Torquay United, as a
second half substitute for Steve Kean. Over the next two seasons
as a trainee at the Vetch Field he was involved on a regular basis
with the first team squad, and after starting his first year as a
professional in the 1989/90 season, scored his first goals for the
Swans. His first season also saw him sample the atmosphere of
European competition when he was selected for both legs of the
games against Greek side Panathinaikos as a substitute,
although he failed to make an appearance from the bench in
both legs The following season saw the return of Terry Yorath as
manager, he was a regular inclusion in the Swans' first team
squad, scoring 2 goals in a 3-2 away win at Rotherham United,
and also playing in both legs of the Welsh Cup semi-final
against Barry Town, but having to be content with a non playing
substitute role in the Final against Wrexham. In May 1990 and in
1991 he was included in the Swans side that beat Llanelli in
consecutive seasons to win the West Wales Senior Cup.
Although he played in both legs of the European Cup Winners
Cup match against Arsene Wenger's Monaco, his back injury
prevented him from making an impression in Frank Burrows'
first team squad, and he was released at the end of the season,
with grave doubts surrounding his future as a professional
footballer. Many football observers suspected that when Simon
Davey was released from the Vetch Field playing staff by
manager Frank Burrows in July 1992, his professional playing
career would be at an end. A back injury sustained working
with medicine balls on the training ground had put his career in
the professional game at risk. However, within a couple of
months of being offered a contract at Carlisle United he had
been appointed captain, and continued to play a major part in
the club's success over the next three seasons, and fortunately
for him, suffering very limited trouble from his back problem.
Carlisle United manager Aidan McCaffery gave Simon the
opportunity of re-establishing himself in the professional game
when he offered him a contract for the 1992/93 season, and
within two months he had been appointed captain at Carlisle
United. Making thirty-eight league appearances in his first
season, his second at Brunton Park saw Simon finish second top
goalscorer, and also reach the Third Division Play Off semi-
finals before losing to Wycombe Wanderers. A 'box to box'

midfielder with a good goalscoring record, he made twenty-five
league appearances during season 1994/95 when Carlisle
United won the Third Division Championship, but missed out
on the celebrations after being transferred to Preston North End
in February for £125,000. However, by the end of the season
Simon had played in his second consecutive Third Division Play
Off semi-final, this time losing out to Bury. He was appointed
skipper shortly after joining North End, and scored his first goal
for Preston in his second match for the club, in a game against
Doncaster Rovers which also featured a certain David Beckham
making his debut for the club on loan from Manchester United.
Despite the disappointment of losing in the Play Off semi-final,
his first full season at Deepdale saw Simon claim his second
Third Division Championship Medal. Establishing himself as a
strong tackler in midfield, and a dead ball specialist who
supplied his quota of goals during the season, he suffered a
recurrence of the back problem during season 1997/98 which
earlier in his career had questioned his continuing as a
professional, and which was to ultimately force his retirement
from the game at the age of 28. Since then he taken on the role of
youth team manager at Deepdale, and hopes to progress
eventually into a managerial role, via the reserve team, and then
the first team.

6. DAVIDS, NEIL Graham

Birthplace: Bingley, 22/9/1955
Ht: 6ft-0¾ins, **Wt:** 13st-9lbs
Swans debut: v. Huddersfield Town (a), 21/8/1977

Swansea City Career Statistics			
Season	League	FLC	FAC
1977/78	9	2	2
Total	9	2	2

Career:
LeedsUnited (from apprentice in August 1973) lge 0
Norwich City (signed in 11/4/1975) lge 2
Northampton Town (loan in 4/9/1975) lge 9
Stockport County (loan in 29/1/1976) lge 5/1gls
Swansea City (signed in July 1977)
Wigan Athletic (signed in July 1978) lge 66+2/1gls, FLC 5+2,
    FAC 5
Bromsgrove Rovers (signed in July 1981)

Honours: England Yth

Former Leeds United apprentice, who gained youth honours for
England during his period at Elland Road, and after failing to
make a league appearance for United, joined Norwich City in
April 1975, and in September the same year after joining

Northampton Town on loan, made his league debut against Bradford City, playing in a further eight league matches for the 'Cobblers.' Returning to Carrow Road, he made his league debut for the 'Canaries' in March 1976 in the local derby game with Ipswich Town as a replacement for Duncan Forbes, also playing in the next league match against Sheffield United. Following a further loan move to Stockport County in January 1976, he was offered a contract by Swans manager Harry Griffith, arriving at the Vetch Field in July 1977. Starting in a midfield holding role, within a couple of games he had reverted to a central defensive position alongside veteran Eddie May. Losing out on promotion by one point the previous season, expectations were high at the Vetch Field for a good season, but after a poor start to the 1977/78 season, Neil's place in the Swans line-up was in jeopardy, with numerous combinations being made in defence, and in midfield. After missing just one out of the first nine league games, Neil made just one more league appearance during the season, as well as appearances in the League and FA Cup competitions. Not a particularly speedy defender, it was probably a wrong combination between himself and the veteran May in central defence, with Bruton getting the nod because of his skill on the ball, and the ability to get on the score sheet regularly. With promotion gained at the end of the season, Neil was released on a free transfer, joining newly elected Football League club Wigan Athletic. Elected to the Football League at the expense of Southport, Neil played in the club's first ever league game, at Hereford United on the 19th August 1978, but struggled throughout the season to make regular appearances for his new club. His second season at Springfield Park saw Neil miss just five league appearances, combining well with Colin Methven in central defence, with Wigan finishing in sixth place, and also reaching the Fourth Round of the FA Cup competition. The 1980/81 season saw him play in the first fifteen league games, but after suffering a twice broken leg, was forced to retire from the professional game, making no further appearances for Athletic, and in July 1981 he signed for non-league side Bromsgrove Rovers. Living in Cleveleys, he has since built up a chain of jewellers shops on the Fylde coast which he sold in 1988, and now has a large portfolio of investment properties in Preston.

7. DAVIES, ALAN

Birthplace: Manchester 5/12/1961. **Died:** Horton, Nr. Swansea, 5/2/1992
Ht: 5ft-8ins, **Wt:** 11st-4lbs
Swans debut: v. Stockport County (a), 18/8/1987

Career:
Manchester United (Ass. Schoolboy in September 1977, from apprentice in July 1978) lge 6+1
Newcastle United (signed in 29/7/1985) lge 20+1/1gls, FLC 2+1
Charlton Athletic (loan in 20/3/1986) lge 1

Carlisle United (loan in 29/11/1986) lge 4/1gls
Swansea City (signed in 6/8/1987)
Bradford City (£130,000 on 29/6/1989) lge 24+2/1gls
Swansea City (player exchange signed in 21/8/1990)

Swansea City Career Statistics							
Season	League	FLC	FAC	FRT	ECWC	WC	P/Offs
1987/88	42/3gls	2	2	2		2	4/1gls
1988/89	42/5gls	2	3	2		7	
1990/91	35/3gls	2	4	5/1gls		5/2gls	
1991/92	6+2/1gls	2		1+1	2		
Total	125+2/12gls	8	9	10+1/1gls	2	14/2gls	4/1gls

Honours: Wales Yth, U-21–6, Full–13, FA Cup Winner–1983

Son of a policeman from North Wales, Alan Davies played for North Manchester High School and Mancunian Juniors, signing initially as an associate schoolboy for United in September 1977, signing professional in 1978, but only made six league appearances for the club plus one as substitute, although he was a member of the United team that won the 1983 FA Cup Final against Brighton & Hove Albion at Wembley. Within a week of the Cup Final success, he gained his first cap for Wales, playing against Northern Ireland in Belfast in the Home International Championship, with his second international appearance coming the following month at Ninian Park against Brazil. Capped at youth level, in October 1982 he made his first U-21 appearance for Wales against France. Overcoming an injury sustained in pre-season training in August 1983, Alan joined Newcastle United in July 1985, and in two seasons made just twenty-one league appearances, plus loan appearances at Charlton Athletic and Carlisle United. In August 1987, along with striker Joe Allon, both players were signed by Swans manager Terry Yorath from Newcastle United, with Alan becoming an influential member of the Swans midfield that went on to gain promotion via the Play Offs, missing just four league games. Possessing excellent ball skills in midfield, and a high workrate, he was a cut above the average lower division midfielders, and was able to take the step up to international football in his stride. When Terry Yorath left the Vetch Field to take over at Bradford City he signed Davies a second time in June 1989, but within fourteen months, both Yorath and Davies had returned to the Vetch Field, with Davies involved in a swap deal which saw Swans legend Robbie James going to Bradford City in exchange. Throughout his playing career, injuries at various times had prevented Alan from realising his true potential as a player, and midway through his second season back at the Vetch Field a tragic incident shocked the football world, when he was found dead in his fume filled car at Horton, near Swansea on the day when his club were due to play their Welsh rivals Cardiff City in the quarter finals of the Welsh Cup. The match was postponed as a mark of respect.

8. DAVIES, Alexander (ALEX) John

Birthplace: Swansea, 2/11/1982
Ht: 6ft-1ins, **Wt:** 13st-0lbs
Swans debut: v. Bury (a), 3/3/2001

Swansea City Career Statistics	
Season	League
2001/02	0+1
Total	0+1

Career:
Swansea City (from trainee in May 2001)

Port Talbot (signed in 25/7/2001)
Rushden & Diamonds (signed in September 2001)
Port Talbot
Pontardawe Town
Garden Village (signed in March 2002)
Carmarthen Town (signed in March 2002)
Llanelli (signed in August 2002)

Honours: Wales U-16, U-18

Former Bishop Vaughan, Swansea Schoolboy and West Glamorgan goalkeeper Alex Davies, was initially on the books with Millwall prior to joining the Swans as a trainee in 1999, and was also a keen rugby player at school, representing West Glamorgan. In his last year at school, when available, he also played on Saturdays for Swansea Senior League side Wern Athletic. Capped at U-16 level by Wales against the Faroe Islands in a European Championship match, he was also included in the U-18 squad that played in Slovakia in November 2000. Playing mainly in the Swans youth team at the Vetch Field, Alex, a second year trainee at the time, was called in to the first team for the away match at Bury in March 2001, when reserve keeper Jason Jones replaced the suspended Freestone, to take over the substitute keeper's role. During the game, Jones received a red card, which not only gave Alex his league debut, but also saw him face a penalty before he had touched the ball. Incredibly, the young keeper saved the penalty, but with the referee awarding a retake, Bury scored. He made a good impression during the remainder of the second half pulling off some good saves, but for the remainder of the season had to be content with matches in the Swans youth team. He was offered a month to month professional contract in May 2001 by manager John Hollins, but shortly after pre-season training had commenced was released, signing initially for League of Wales side Port Talbot, before being offered a three month contract with Rushden & Diamonds in September 2001. Returning from Rushden, he rejoined Port Talbot midway through season 2001/02, later linking up with Welsh League side Pontardawe Town before signing for Garden Village, also in the Welsh League. After just a couple of games for Garden Village, Alex signed League of Wales forms with Carmarthen Town. At the start of season 2002/03 he signed for Llanelli, managed by former Swans winger Leighton James, playing for most of the season, even after a change of management at Stebonheath Park. Season 2003/04 saw Alex step down to play for St. Josephs in the Swansea Senior League First Division.

9. DAVIES, William David (DAI)

Birthplace: Ammanford, 1/4/1948
Ht: 6ft-1ins, **Wt:** 13st-4lbs
Swans debut: v. Chesterfield (a), 22/4/1970

Career:
Ammanford Town
Swansea Town (signed in July 1969)

Everton (£20,000 signed in 14/12/1970) lge 82
Swansea City (loan in February 1974)
Wrexham (£8,000 signed in 22/9/1977) lge 144
Swansea City (£45,000 signed in 13/7/1981)
Tranmere Rovers (signed in June 1983) lge 42
Bangor City (signed in August 1985)
Wrexham (signed in November 1985)

Swansea Town/City Career Statistics					
Season	League	FLC	FAC	WC	ECWC
1969/70	1				
1970/71	8		2		
1973/74	6				
1981/82	41	2	1	7	2
1982/83	30	4	1	3	5
Total	86	6	4	10	7

Honours: Wales Sch, U-23–4, Full–52, Third Division Champions–1978, Welsh Cup Winner–1978, 1982, 1986, Wales Amateur Cup Winner–1969, PFA Third Division XI–1978

A late convert to football, Dai played rugby at his school, Amman Valley Grammar School, but he did play for Ammanford Town under former Swans player Roy Saunders, and it was Saunders who recommended Dai to the Swans manager Roy Bentley. During the time Dai played for Ammanford Town, he made one appearance for Swansea Senior League side St. Josephs, in an end of season relegation battle against Port Tennant Stars. After leaving school Dai went to Cardiff College of Education to qualify as a PE Teacher, during which time he picked up a Wales Amateur Cup Winners medal in 1969 with the college team. He returned to Swansea in July 1969 and signed professional forms before going on to make his debut in the last match of the 1969/790 season when the Swans played the champions Chesterfield away, with promotion already assured for the Swans. Making a further eight league appearances the following season, just before Christmas time he was transferred to First Division side Everton for a £20,000 fee. Prior to being transferred, he represented Wales at U-23 level against England at Wrexham. A further £15,000 came the Swans way after he had completed thirty league appearances. Finding himself understudy to both Andy Rankin and Gordon West, he made his Everton debut in March 1971 in a 2-1 defeat at Newcastle United. After another league outing he spent almost three years in the reserves, returning to the Vetch Field for a loan spell under Harry Gregg. Season 1974/75 saw him established at Goodison Park as first choice keeper for Everton. Regular First Division appearances also saw him given his first full cap for Wales, in Budapest against Hungary on the 16th April 1975. Following the signing of George Wood by Everton, Dai was allowed to join Wrexham in September 1977, and by the end of his first season at the Racecourse had helped his club to win the Third Division Championship, and also beat Bangor City in the Final of the Welsh Cup. Signed by his international team mate

Arfon Griffiths, Dai developed into a commanding keeper, with superb organizational skills at club, and at international level. Following the Swans promotion to the First Division, he returned to the Vetch Field in July 1981 for a tribunal fixed transfer fee of £45,000. His return to the Vetch Field was not taken kindly by a number of supporters who felt that Dave Stewart, who had played a large part in the club's promotion should have been given his opportunity in the First Division. Nevertheless, Dai overcame the sceptical supporters to play his part in a tremendous season for the Swans in the First Division, and also win his second Welsh Cup Medal, when the Swans beat Cardiff City. Before the end of his second season at the Vetch Field, with financial problems off the field mounting, he was allowed to leave on a free transfer, joining Tranmere Rovers in June 1983. Missing just four league games at Prenton Park, Dai retired from the game at the end of season 1983/84, to start a Welsh Book, and Craft Shop in Mold. Answering an SOS to assist Bangor City in the club's European Cup Winners Cup games with Athletico Madrid, it was not long after that Wrexham manager Dixie McNeill asked him to appear for Wrexham in Welsh Cup matches, and at the end of the season Dai had won his third Welsh Cup Winners medal. His final season for Wrexham saw him utilised as substitute keeper for Wrexham in European games, also playing one game for the club in the Welsh Cup. A proud Welsh-speaking Welshman he was the recipient of a rare honour in August 1978 when he became the first Welsh footballer to be admitted to the Gorsedd Circle of Bards at the National Eisteddfod in Cardiff. He works frequently for BBC Wales and Radio Cymru as well as appearing regularly on GÔL (a Welsh language football programme), and as a TV pundit his views are always interesting to listen to, and he is not afraid of voicing his opinions on football topics. A qualified teacher, he has often done supply work, but he now runs a natural healing centre in Llangollen.

10. DAVIES, DAVID John

Birthplace: Port Talbot, 21/5/1952
Ht: 6ft-0ins, **Wt:** 12st-2lbs
Swans debut: v. Barnsley (h), 27/10/1973

Swans City Career Statistics				
Season	League	FLC	FAC	WC
1973/74	24		1	1
1974/75	3+1	1	2	1
Total	27+1	1	3	2

Career:
Swansea City (signed in July 1973)
Afan Lido (signed in close season 1975)
Maesteg Park

Honours: Wales Yth–3

Former Glanafan schoolboy who joined the Swans after leaving school as an amateur, while starting his apprenticeship as a fitter and turner at BSC Port Talbot. He played all of his early football with Yellow Stars BC, Baglan BC and Margam Boys Club prior to arriving at the Vetch Field. Dai made three appearances for the Wales Youth side early in his career against England, Scotland and Northern Ireland. Graduating through the Swans Football Combination, Welsh League and Swansea Senior League sides, the centre half was included in the Swans squad during season 1971/72 after some impressive displays in the Football Combination team whilst still an amateur, and was included as substitute in April 1972 against Halifax Town, but was not called into action. He made his league debut whilst still working in BSC in October 1973 at the Vetch Field against Barnsley, replacing the injured John Moore. Making twenty-two consecutive league appearances, the young central defender formed a good partnership with Dave Bruton, which saw the Swans move from the lower end of the league table into the top ten placings of the Fourth Division. His second season as a professional saw his first team opportunities limited, with loan players being utilised in a bid to improve the club's position in the league table. Towards the end of his career at the Vetch Field, Dai had reverted to playing as a part-time professional, having gone back to BSC to his trade as a fitter. He was released in May 1975, linking up with Afan Lido, also playing for Maesteg Park and Port Talbot Athletic prior to his retirement at the age of thirty-eight. Since returning to BSC Port Talbot, Dai was involved as a trainer in the Apprentice Training School, and prior to his retirement had spent twenty-three years as a lecturer in Port Talbot College, also involving himself as a coach with the Afan Nedd schoolboys side for ten years. His son Darren was an apprentice at White Hart Lane with Tottenham Hotspur, and after a spell with Barry Town and Scottish side Greenock Morton has signed for Forest Green Rovers for the 2004/05 season.

11. DAVIES, DAVID Lamb

Birthplace: Pontypridd, 11/7/1956
Ht: 6ft-0ins, **Wt:** 13st-5lbs
Swans debut: v. Bournemouth (a), 21/4/1973

Swansea City Career Statistics	
Season	League
1972/73	0+1
Total	0+1

Career:
Swansea City (from apprentice in July 1974)
Crewe Alexandra (signed in March 1975) lge 196+13/26gls

Former apprentice at the Vetch Field who was handed his league debut as substitute for Geoff Thomas in the last away game of the 1972/73 season at Bournemouth, with the Swans already relegated to the Fourth Division. Given his league debut by manager Harry Gregg, whilst still an apprentice, and three months short of his 17th birthday, David failed to make any further appearances for the Swans, and in March 1975 joined Crewe Alexandra, re-uniting with former Swans manager Harry Gregg, who had been installed as manager at Gresty Road after resigning his position at the Vetch Field. He made his league debut for Alexandra on the 12th April 1975 against the Swans in a 2-2 home draw, playing in the remaining three league fixtures of the season. Over the next six seasons the midfielder would make a good impression with Crewe, appearing in over two hundred league matches, and score consistently from midfield. He was released in May 1981, went to work in the Post Office in the Crewe area, and played occasionally for the Post Office side.

12. DAVIES, Edward George Gladstone (GLEN)

Birthplace: Swansea, 30/6/1950
Ht: 5ft-9ins, **Wt:** 10st-4½lbs
Swans debut: v. Aston Villa (h), 29/8/1970

Swansea City Career Statistics				
Season	League	FLC	FAC	WC
1970/71	7			
1971/72	35/7gls	1	5/1gls	1
1972/73	28+1	2	1	2
1973/74	16+2/5gls		1	
1974/75	27+1		1	3
1975/76	26+2/1gls	2	1	1+1
Total	139+6/13gls	5	9/1gls	7+1

Career:
Swansea City (from juniors, professional in close season 1970)
Everwarm (signed in May 1976)

Honours: Wales YMCA, West Wales Senior Cup Winner–1975

Born and raised in the Sandfields area of Swansea, Glen and his two brothers Alan and Kevin all made their mark with league clubs. Alan joined the Swans playing staff at the same time as Glen, failed to make a league appearance for the Swans, but made a name for himself on the Welsh League circuit for a number of years, while Kevin was an apprentice at Cardiff City, although he failed to make an appearance for the 'Bluebirds' first team. Glen attended St Helens School, where he played rugby, and Oxford Street school, where he played football. He left school in 1965, joining Atlas Sprinklers as an apprentice

draughtsman, and had a trial with Leeds United at the age of 16, played for the Wales YMCA side, then had a six month spell with Bristol City. He signed for Cardiff City at the age of 17 as an amateur, then a year later signed for the Swans, again as an amateur. Continuing his five year apprenticeship, he was a part-timer with the Swans, and played in the club's Football Combination side that came close to winning the Championship in the late 1960's and early 1970's. Signing professional for the Swans at the age of twenty, he made his league debut at the Vetch Field against Aston Villa in August 1970, and played in six more league games during the season. Opening his goal scoring account for the Swans in the first league game of the 1971/72 season at Bradford City, at the end of the season he had scored eight league and cup goals, and impressed many with his pace, and aerial ability. In May 1975 he scored two goals in the West Wales Senior Cup Final win over Briton Ferry Athletic. He remained on the Swans playing staff until the end of the 1975/76 season, and by this time had reverted to either a centre half, or full back. Glennie went to work in the Post Office after leaving the Vetch Field, signing also for Southern League side Everwarm (Bridgend Town), before making appearances for Welsh League sides Afan Lido, Maesteg, Milford United and Llanelli. A cartilage injury at Llanelli saw him sidelined for a period, but he then rejoined Swansea Senior League side Ragged School, a team he had played for at the age of 12. After a couple of seasons with West End, he returned as player manager with Ragged School, and started to take his coaching badges in the mid-1990's. During his time with Ragged School and West End, all the honours available in the Swansea League at the time were usually shared between either of these two sides. Concentrating on the coaching side of football with the FAW Development Centre, he then returned to the Vetch Field to join the coaching staff in the club's Centre of Excellence.

13. DAVIES, GLYN

Birthplace: Swansea, 31/5/1932
Ht: 5ft-9ins, **Wt:** 10st-8lbs
Swans debut: v. Charlton Athletic (a), 18/8/1962

Swansea Town Career Statistics	
Season	League
1962/63	18/1gls
Total	18/1gls

Career:
Derby County (amateur in May 1949, professional in July 1949)
  lge 200/5gls, FLC 4, FAC 9
Swansea Town (signed in July 1962)

Yeovil Town (signed in May 1963) Total apps 22/5gls
Pembroke Borough (signed in December 1966)

Honours: Wales Sch, Third Division North Champions–1957, Southern League Premier Division Champions–1964

Former Swansea Schoolboy and Welsh Schoolboy international, who earlier in his career was in the same class in school as John Charles, and who signed as an amateur for Derby County in May 1949 at the age of 17, signing professional two months later. A product of Gendros Youth Club he had earlier in his playing career captained the Swansea Schoolboys side, and had attended Cwmbwrla and Manselton Schools. Despite having to wait four years before he made his league debut for County, during his period at the Baseball Ground, Glyn was renowned for his unquestionable commitment and tackling ability. He made his league debut in a 5-2 defeat at Millmoor against Rotherham United in the First Division with the 'Rams' having already resigned themselves to relegation. Playing either at left half, or at left full back, Glyn played in the last fifteen league matches of season 1956/57, when the 'Rams' regained their Second Division status, winning the Championship. Not noted for his goalscoring, with just five league goals during his career, however, two of them were scored against the Swans in December 1958, and in April 1960, in a 3-1 win at the Vetch Field. Season 1957/58 saw Glyn firmly established in the 'Rams' line-up, making 37 appearances that season, varying his position between left half, and left back with the occasional appearance at right back or right half. That season also saw him take over the captaincy at Derby, and under his leadership they finished the term in 7th place. Failing to agree a new contract at the Baseball Ground, he returned to his hometown, signing for the Swans in July 1962. Despite starting season 1962/63 in the opening fixture against Charlton Athletic, a persistent knee injury saw his appearances limited to just eighteen league games, and in May 1963 he signed for non-league side Yeovil Town, initially as a player, but then taking over from Basil Hayward as manager. At the end of his first season with Yeovil, the club won the Southern League Premier Division Championship. His second season with Yeovil saw the club finish in fourth place, and in July 1965 he returned a second time to the Vetch Field, this time as manager, succeeding Trevor Morris. With the Swans having been relegated a couple of months prior to his appointment, his first season back at the Vetch Field saw the Swans adopt a somewhat cavalier approach to the game, scoring 81 goals in the league, but concede 96, the highest since the 1957/8 season. Other success that season came in winning the Welsh Cup and putting the club back in European competition. With dwindling support at the turnstiles, and increasing pressure from the club's bankers to reduce the overdraft, Davies had no money to spend on players, relying on free transfers. Despite what seemed to be on paper an adequate playing staff at the club, a dismal start to the 1966/7 season in which only one game was won from the first 14 in the league, Davies was sacked as manager of the football club with the Swans bottom of the league. In December 1966 he returned to football, playing for the remainder of the season with Welsh League side Pembroke Borough in a player coaching capacity. He went into business at the end of the season, later had a twelve month association with Oswestry Town, before retiring completely from the game, apart from playing in Charity games, and Sunday football with Swansea Civil Service, featuring regularly alongside former Swans players Harry Griffiths and Roy Saunders. Glyn worked for a number of years for a Sheffield based company as Sales Director, and currently he is semi-retired.

14. DAVIES, Glyndwr (GLYN)

Birthplace: Aberaman, 1/10/1908. **Died:** Carmarthen, 6/11/1997
Ht: 5ft-7ins, **Wt:** 10st-8lbs
Swans debut: v. Cardiff City (a), 5/10/1929

Swansea Town Career Statistics	
Season	League
1929/30	1
1930/31	2
Total	3

Career
Swansea Town (signed in May 1926)
Bristol University
Swansea Town
Corinthians (signed in August 1931)
Brentford (signed in 1932) lge 0
Corinthians (signed in season 1932/33)
Norwich City (signed in June 1933) lge 3

Honours: Wales Sch, Wales Junior, Wales Amateur–11, Universities Athletic Board XI, F.A. XI, A.F.A. XI, Isthmian League XI

Attended Aberdare County School and Ystalyfera Grammar School from 1920 to 1928, initially joining the Swans as an amateur in May 1926, prior to going to Bristol University where he gained a BSc in the summer of 1930. During the 1927/28 season he made the first of eleven appearances for the Wales Amateur side against England. Whilst at University he regularly made the journey back to play for the Swans reserve sides on weekends, and in October 1929 he made his first team debut at outside left, replacing Thomas, with Hole switching to the right wing, in the derby game at Ninian Park against Cardiff City, also playing for the Wales Amateur side in Glasgow against Scotland on the 8th February 1930. Returning to the Vetch Field in August 1930, he again impressed in pre-season trial games with his speed, and ability on the ball, and although it was hoped that he would settle in the Swans line-up now that he was free of his scholastic duties, he made just two appearances during the season, both in November. In February 1931 he played for the Wales Amateur side against Scotland at the Vetch Field, also against England in the same season. He joined Corinthians in August 1931 later made appearances for an F.A. XI, A.F.A. XI, and an Isthmian League XI, to add to the honours he had gained whilst at Bristol University with the Universities Athletic Board XI. The outside left had in his school days been capped for Wales as a Schoolboy in 1923, and at Junior level two years later. Returning to the Football League to sign for Brentford in 1932, after failing to make an appearance returned to the amateur scene with Corinthians, making an appearance for the Wales Amateur side in Torquay against England in January 1933, before joining Third Division South side Norwich City, making a couple of appearances in the side that won the Championship by the end of the season. In the 1933/34 season he became housemaster, senior science master and coach at Kimbolton School in Huntingdon, then, after returning to South Wales spent 25 years as senior physics master at Ystalyfera Grammar School. He later remained on the Board of Governors at Pontardawe Comprehensive School until he was 81 years of age.

15. DAVIES, Wilfred GORDON

Birthplace: Swansea, 31/7/1915. **Died:** Swansea, February 1992
Swans debut: v. Bury (a), 8/2/1936

Swansea Town Career Statistics		
Season	League	WC
1935/36	1	
1936/37	3	2
1937/38	3	1
1938/39	20	2
1946/47	22	1
Total	49	6

Career:
Swansea Town (signed in 4/11/1933)
Barry Town (signed in close season 1947)
Llanelly (signed in 7/8/1948)
Haverfordwest (signed in close season 1950)
Pembroke Borough (signed in January 1951)

Honours: London Combination Cup Winner–1947, West Wales Senior Cup Winner–1934

Young full back who made his league debut against Bury in February 1936 as a replacement for Syd Lawrence, and who struggled up until the start of season 1938/39 before establishing himself in the Swans starting line-up. Earlier, in October 1934 he had played in the Swans side that beat Llanelly to win the West Wales Senior Cup. Signing for the Swans in November 1933, one of his first games was in the club's 'A' side that lost to Ammanford Corinthians in a Welsh League Cup tie. Capable of playing in either full back positions, he lost a large part of his professional career because of the War. He was captain of the Swans side that started season 1939/40, and can also claim to be one off few Swans players who played wartime football with the Swans, and also continued their league career at the Vetch Field when the Football League was resumed after the war. In June 1947 he skippered the Swans reserve side that beat Arsenal at White Hart Lane to win the London Combination Cup Final. He joined Barry Town after being released at the end of the 1946/47 season, joined Llanelly twelve months later, then in later seasons made appearances for Pembrokeshire sides Haverfordwest and Pembroke Borough. Captained Barry Town, Llanelly and Haverfordwest whilst with the clubs. A month after signing for Pembroke Borough, he played against the Swans in Welsh Cup tie.

16. DAVIES, IAN Claude

Birthplace: Bristol, 29/3/1957
Ht: 5ft-8ins, **Wt:** 10st-8lbs
Swans debut: v. Notts. County (a), 30/11/1985

Swansea City Career Statistics				
Season	League	FAC	WC	FRT
1985/86	11	1	1	2
Total	11	1	1	2

Career:
Norwich City (apprentice in July 1973, professional in April 1975) lge 29+3/2gls
Detroit Express, USA (loan in 29/3/1978 to August 1978)
Newcastle United (£175,000 signed in 26/6/1979) lge 74+1/3gls, FLC 6/1gls, FAC 1
Manchester City (signed in 1/8/1982) lge 7
Bury (loan in November 1982) lge 14
Brentford (loan in November 1983) lge 2
Cambridge United (loan in 3/2/1984) lge 5
Carlisle United (signed in 17/5/1984) lge 4
Exeter City (signed in December 1984) lge 5
Bath City (signed in close season 1985)
Yeovil Town
Bury Town
Diss Town
Bristol Rovers (non-contract signed in 8/8/1985) lge 13+1/1gls
Swansea City (non-contract signed in 21/11/1985)
Gloucester City (signed in November 1987)

Honours: Wales U-21–1

Previously with Bristol Junior sides Fisons Sports and Cleveland Juniors, Ian was signed as an apprentice in July 1973, and made his league debut for Norwich City at Carrow Road as substitute in the last game of the 1973/74 season at Leicester City, a month after his seventeenth birthday, becoming the 'Canaries' youngest ever debutant at the time. He had to wait until the 1976/77 season before making his next league appearance, but after switching to an attacking left full back role, made twenty-seven league appearances during season 1978/79, which saw him transferred to Newcastle United for £175,000. At Carrow Road, he also made a substitute appearance for the Welsh U-21 side against Scotland. Making regular appearances in Newcastle's Second Division side over the next three seasons, he joined Manchester City in August 1982, but after struggling to establish himself at Maine Road, made loan appearances for Bury, Brentford and Cambridge United, before signing on a free transfer for Carlisle United in August 1984. Moving on to Exeter City in Exeter in December 1984, prior to signing non-contract with Bristol Rovers in August 1985 made non-league appearances for Bath City, Yeovil Town, Bury Town and Diss Town. Ian missed just four league games for Rovers prior to arriving at the Vetch Field to sign for the Swans, re-uniting with manager John Bond for the third time. Making his debut at Notts. County, Ian played in the next ten league games before suffering a broken leg at Doncaster Rovers, which left him out of action for the remainder of the season, and brought a halt to his professional career. An attacking, left sided midfielder, he later made a brief comeback with non-league Gloucester City in November 1987. An accomplished cricketer, he was on Somerset's books before deciding to make a career in football.

17. DAVIES, JACK

Birthplace: Chorley, 1902
Ht: 6ft-0½ins, **Wt:** 12st-0lbs
Swans debut: v. Barnsley (h), 1/9/1928

Swansea Town Career Statistics	
Season	*League*
1928/29	5
Total	5

Career:
Horwich R.M.I.
Bury (signed as amateur in May 1923, professional in 1925) lge 5
Swansea Town (£400 signed in 27/5/1927)
Horwich R.M.I. (signed in season 1929/30)
Wigan Athletic (signed in December 1932)
Horwich R.M.I. (signed in February 1935)

Joined First Division Bury from non-league side Horwich R.M.I. in 1925, and after making just five league appearances for the 'Shakers' signed for the Swans in May 1927 for £400, following the Swans manager James Hunter Thomson to the Vetch Field, who had in February 1927 resigned as manager of Bury. He failed to make any first team appearance during his first season at the Vetch Field, because of the form of Alex Ferguson, with his league debut for the Swans coming in September 1928 at the Vetch Field against Barnsley as a replacement for Ferguson. He played in the next four league games, failed to keep a clean sheet, conceding fifteen goals, before Ferguson returned to the first team. Returning to Horwich R.M.I., he then had a spell with non-league Wigan Athletic, before returning to Horwich R.M.I. in February 1935.

18. DAVIES, JAMIE

Birthplace: Swansea, 12/2/1980
Ht: 6ft-0ins, **Wt:** 11st-9lbs
Swans debut: v. Carlisle United (h), 13/2/1999

Swansea City Career Statistics		
Season	*League*	*FAWC*
1998/99	0+1	0+2
Total	0+1	0+2

Career:
Pontardawe Youth
Swansea City (from trainee in 16/7/1998)
Bangor City (loan in September 1999)
Llanelli (loan in November 1999)
Llanelli (signed in August 2001)
Garden Village (signed in March 2002)
Carmarthen Town (signed in March 2002)

Striker who impressed with the Pontardawe Town youth side, and after showing good form in a trial in April 1997 with the Swans, was given a one year YTS contract at the Vetch Field. He signed a one year professional contract in January 1999, and a month later made his only league appearance, as a substitute for Aidan Newhouse at the Vetch Field against Carlisle United. Season 1999/2000 saw Jamie make loan appearances for Bangor City in September 1999, and Llanelli in November 1999, scoring on his debut against Connah's Quay Nomads, and after a

second loan spell at Stebonheath Park in February 2000, he was released at the end of the season by Swans manager John Hollins. He subsequently signed for the Reds on a permanent basis for the 2000-1 season, but was badly injured in a Welsh Cup match at Cardiff Corinthians that season and had little opportunity afterwards, and made a total of 16 League of Wales appearances (plus 5 more as substitute) for Llanelli during the 1999-2001 period. He left the Reds in 2001, signing for recently elected Welsh League side Garden Village, and in season 2002/03 made appearances for Pontardawe Town. Working on the Gower Peninsula as a postman, Jamie started season 2004/05 back with Welsh League side Garden Village.

19. DAVIES, David LYN

Birthplace: Skewen, Neath, 29/9/1947
Ht: 6ft-0ins, **Wt:** 11st-2lbs
Swans debut: v. Notts. County (a), 27/9/1972

Swansea City Career Statistics	
Season	*League*
1972/73	3
Total	3

Career:
Cardiff City (from apprentice in October 1965) lge 16
Hereford United (signed in season 1968/69) Total Apps 49
Llanelli (signed in October 1969)
Swansea City (signed in July 1972)
BP Llandarcy (signed in August 1973)

Honours: Wales Sch, U-23–1, Welsh League Premier Division Champions–1971

Former apprentice goalkeeper with Cardiff City at Ninian Park, making sixteen league appearances, also gaining Welsh U-23 honours against England during the 1966/67 season. Earlier in his career the former Neath Schoolboy keeper had played for the Wales Schoolboys side against Scotland in May 1963. A former team-mate of Hereford's player-manager John Charles at Cardiff City, the goalkeeper was one of the Gentle Giant's first signings for his first full season in charge of the 'Bulls' and Davies went on to play in 34 of the 42 Southern League matches during season 1968/69, later returning to South Wales to sign for Welsh League side Llanelli in late October 1969. At the end of season 1970/71, the 'Reds' won the Premier Division Championship of the Welsh League, and his consistency through the season alerted Swans' manager Roy Bentley, who signed the keeper in July 1972 as understudy to Welsh International Tony Millington. After making his Swans debut at Notts. County in September 1972, he played in the next game against Bristol Rovers, before Millington was restored in goal. In early November Bentley was replaced by Harry Gregg, with Davies making just one more appearance for the Swans, in the last league game of the season against Charlton Athletic. With the Swans failing to avoid relegation to the Fourth Division, Davies was released, later taking up employment at BP Baglan Bay as a general auxiliary, later as a rigger, and also signing for Welsh League side BP Llandarcy. A couple of years later he joined the police force, later becoming a traffic policeman in South West Wales, retiring from football. Throughout his football career, Lyn had also been a keen cricketer in the summer months, playing regularly in the semi-professional South Wales and Monmouthshire League for Skewen.

20. DAVIES, MARK

Birthplace: Swansea, 9/8/1972
Ht: 5ft-11ins, **Wt:** 11st-8lbs
Swans debut: v. Monaco (h), ECWC 1-1, 17/9/1991

Swansea City Career Statistics

Season	League	ECWC
1991/92	1	2
Total	1	2

Career:
Swansea City (from trainee in July 1991)
Merthyr Tyfil (signed in August 1992) Conf 86+5/2gls
Llanelli (signed in season 1995/96)

Honours: South Wales Boys U-15, U-19, West Wales Senior Cup Winner–1991

Educated at Penyrheol Comprehensive School, Gorseinon, Mark joined the Swans as an apprentice, prior to signing a one year professional contract in July 1991. In May 1991 he was included in the Swans squad that beat Llanelli to win the West Wales Senior Cup. Mark made his Swans debut in a First Round, First Leg European Cup Winners Cup game at the Vetch Field against Monaco, managed by Arsene Wenger, also playing in the return leg which the Swans lost 8-0. That season EUFA had restricted the number of non-Welsh players to just four for qualification to play in European ties, which saw the Swans having to field Welsh born players in the competition. Capable of playing in either central defence, or at full back, he made his League debut later in the season at the Vetch Field against Huddersfield Town at right full back, replacing Stephen Jenkins. Released by manager Frank Burrows at the end of the season, he joined Merthyr Tydfil, enjoying three good seasons in the Vauxhall Conference, before he was advised to give up the game because of a medical condition. He later resumed his career at Llanelli in

the 1995/96 season, but after just one season at Stebonheath Park, following a serious head injury suffered during a game he was forced to retire from playing.

21. DAVIES, PETER

Birthplace: Dafen, Llanelli, 8/3/1936
Ht: 5ft-10ins, **Wt:** 10st-8lbs
Swans debut: v. Brighton & Hove Albion (h), 11/4/1959

Swansea Town Career Statistics

Season	League	FLC	FAC	WC
1958/59	2			
1959/60	2			
1960/61	27/2gls	1	2	5
1961/62	30	1		3
1962/63	36/1gls	1	1	3
1963/64	21	2		1
1964/65	16/2gls			1
Total	134/5gls	5	3	13

Career:
Dafen FC
Llanelli (signed amateur for season 1956/57, professional for season 1957/58)
Arsenal (£5,000 signed in 8/11/1957) lge 0
Swansea Town (signed in March 1959)
Brighton & Hove Albion (signed in July 1965) lge 6
Merthyr Tydfil (signed in January 1966)
Germiston Callies, South Africa (signed in 1966)
Ammanford (signed in close season 1968)

Honours: Welsh Cup Winner–1961, London FA Challenge Cup Winner–1958, Metropolitan League Champions–1959, West Wales Senior Cup Winner–1961, 1965

Brought up in Dafen, a village near the rugby stronghold of Llanelly, Peter attended Dafen Junior School, and Stebonheath Secondary School, which overlooked Stebonheath Park, home of Llanelly, and was influenced from an early age by Llanelly's player manager Jock Stein. Starting his playing career with local club Dafen in the Carmarthenshire League, Peter joined Llanelly as an amateur during the club's last season in the Southern League, signing professional twelve months later, and within a couple of months of his signing professional he was sold to Arsenal for £5,000 at the age of twenty-one. He failed to make a league appearance for the 'Gunners', but was a regular in the club's reserve team, and was also included in the first team that beat West Ham United in season 1957/58 to win the London F.A. Challenge Cup, and the following season becoming

Champions of the Metropolitan League. Within a couple of weeks of the season finishing however, he had returned to South Wales as part of the record breaking transfer of Mel Charles to Arsenal in March 1959. Despite his lack of experience after arriving at the Vetch Field, he proved to be a useful wing half, who was capable of using the ball well. He made his league debut with the Swans in a 4-2 home win over Brighton & Hove Albion in April 1959, playing also in the next league fixture against Cardiff City. Starting season 1959/60 in the Swans first team line-up, he suffered an injury in his second game which sidelined him until October 1960, when he regained his place at right half, missing few games through to the end of the season, and also playing in the end of season Welsh Cup Final success over Bangor City. He failed to make an appearance in the Swans European Cup Winners Cup ties in East Germany against Motor Jena, but over the next two seasons played in successive Welsh Cup semi-final defeats to Wrexham and Newport County. During the club's exciting FA Cup exploits in season 1963/64, despite featuring in the Swans line-up for the first half of the season, he lost his place at right half to Mike Johnson, with Brian Purcell brought in at centre half, failing to make any FA Cup appearances. In May 1965 he returned to Stebonheath Park, playing in a Swans side that beat Llanelli to win the West Wales Senior Cup. Following another Welsh Cup semi-final defeat in season 1964/65 by Cardiff City, and relegation to the Third Division, Peter joined Third Division side Brighton & Hove Albion in July 1965 but after arriving at the Goldstone Ground on a free transfer, he again failed to make his mark, making just six league appearances. Peter returned to South Wales after just seven months in January 1966, played a couple of games to maintain his fitness for Harry Griffiths at Merthyr Tydfil, before joining Durban side Germiston Callies in South Africa. Recovering from a twice broken leg he returned to the UK after two years, played a further season with Ammanford Town before retiring. Since returning to Swansea from South Africa, up to his retirement Peter has been involved in the licensed trade in the city as landlord of the Criterion (now Eli Jenkins), the Prince of Wales, and the Bay View on the Mumbles Road. During his period as landlord of the Criterion, Swansea Senior League side Unit Superheaters had their base in the public house.

22. DAVIES, Ellis Reginald (REG)

Birthplace: Cymmer, Port Talbot, 27/5/1929
Ht: 5ft-8ins, **Wt:** 11st-0lbs
Swans debut: v. Bristol City (a), 11/10/1958

Career:
Cwm Athletic
Southampton (amateur)
Southend United (signed in July 1949) lge 41/18gls
Newcastle United (£9,000 signed in April 1951) lge 157/49gls, FAC 13/1gls
Swansea Town (player + cash exchange signed in October 1958)

Carlisle United (£4,000 signed in June 1962) lge 65/13gls
Merthyr Tydfil (signed in July 1964)
King's Lynn (player manager in 1965)

Swansea Town Career Statistics					
Season	League	FLC	FAC	ECWC	WC
1958/59	31/11gls		1		1
1959/60	27/5gls		2		1/1gls
1960/61	24/9gls		3/1gls		4/1gls
1961/62	29/4gls	1/1gls		2	2
Total	111/29gls	1/1gls	6/1gls	2	8/2gls

Honours: Wales Full–6, Welsh Cup Winner–1961, West Wales Senior Cup Winner–1960, 1961

After leaving school Reg toured theatres throughout Great Britain with Steffan's Silver Singsters as a boy soprano. Beginning his football career with local side Cwm Athletic, after doing his National Service in the Army, he joined Southampton as an amateur. He then signed for Third Division South side Southend United in July 1949, playing two seasons at Roots Hall, before being transferred to First Division Newcastle United in April 1951. Averaging almost a goal every three league games at St. James' Park, he was twelfth man for the 1952 FA Cup Final, and was unlucky to miss the 1955 FA Cup Final against Manchester City through tonsillitis. He made all his six international appearances for Wales during his period with the club, his first cap coming on the 18th October 1952 against Scotland. Five of his appearances were in the Annual Home International Championships, with his last appearance for Wales against East Germany in a World Cup qualifying match. Despite his slight build, during his playing career he proved himself to be a scheming inside forward with first class distribution, had good ball control, and a good goal scoring reputation, also possessing a good burst of speed over short distances. In October 1958 he returned to his native South Wales to join the Swans in a transfer deal which saw Ivor Allchurch sign for Newcastle United. It took Reg four games before he registered his first goal for the Swans, but by the end of the season had scored eleven league goals including a hat-trick against Derby County. In May 1960 he scored one of the Swans goals in the West Wales Senior Cup Final win over Llanelly, also scoring two goals twelve months later in the same cup final, this time against Haverfordwest. Scorer of the third Swans goal in the 1961 Welsh Cup Final win over Bangor City, Reg played in both European Cup Winners Cup games against East German side Motor Jena the following season, the first Welsh club side to play in a European competition. Reg joined Third Division Carlisle United in June 1962, and despite suffering relegation in his first season, the club bounced back twelve months later in runners up place in the Fourth Division, with Reg scoring ten goals, and scoring his hundreth goal in a 6-0 win at Hartlepool. Returning to South Wales a second time, he linked up with Merthyr Tydfil, then joined Kings Lynn as player manager before emigrating to Australia in 1971, settling in Perth where Reg continued to play and coach up until the age of 55 with Bayswater United and Ascot F.C. At the age of forty-seven he represented Western Australia against New Zealand, Aberdeen and Hertha Berlin. An article in the *South Wales Evening Post* in February 2003 mentioned how Reg was re-united with the Welsh shirt he wore against East Germany in 1958 when it was presented to him during a concert he had attended in Perth given by the Morriston Orpheus Choir. Reg had earlier given the shirt to the Sunnybank Workingman's Club in Clydach, but for a number of years had wanted to give the shirt to his daughter Caroline, a football fanatic. When Reg's brother John heard about the impending Australia tour by the choir, he contacted the club who agreed to give him the shirt, resulting in Reg being presented with the shirt during the choir's concert in Perth. During his period at the Vetch Field, Reg played cricket during the summer for Clydach CC.

23. DAVIES, Ronald (RONNIE) George

Birthplace: Swansea, 13/11/1935
Ht: 5ft-10½ins, **Wt:** 12st-2lbs
Swans debut: v. Stoke City (h), 7/2/1958

Swansea Town Career Statistics		
Season	League	WC
1958/59	2	1
Total	2	1

Career:
Tower United
Swansea Town (signed in May 1958)
Plymouth Argyle (£2,000 signed in 5/6/1959)
Haverfordwest County (signed in close season 1960)

Brought up in the Mayhill district of Swansea, Ronnie attended Townhill School prior to going to work for Bernard Hastie and the local corporation. Gaining no schoolboy honours, he did his National Service in the Army in Germany and Brecon, and after being demobbed played in the local Swansea League with Tower United. Joining the Swans in May 1958, he made two consecutive league appearances as deputy for Mal Kennedy, but failed to make any further league appearances during his time at the Vetch Field. He was released by the Swans at the end of the season, joined Plymouth Argyle, but failed to break into the Argyle first team, returning to Swansea after just twelve months at Home Park. Linking up with Welsh League side Haverfordwest County prior to the start of the 1960/61 season, he played for a number of years with the West Wales club before finishing his Welsh League career with Ton Pentre and Llanelli in the late 1960's. Working as a postman in Swansea before his retirement, Ronnie played a number of games for Swansea Senior League side West End before retiring through knee problems.

24. DAVIES, Thomas (TOM) E.

Birthplace: Briton Ferry, JAS 1912
Ht: 6ft-0ins, **Wt:** 12st-6lbs
Swans debut: v. Bradford Park Avenue (h), 4/11/1933

Swansea Town Career Statistics		
Season	League	WC
1933/34	3	1
1934/35	5	1
Total	8	2

Career:
Swansea Town (trial in August 1932, professional in 29/8/1932)
Torquay United (signed in May 1935) lge 5
Bangor Town (signed in July 1936)

Briton Ferry born, Tom 'Dasher' Davies, a full back from the Garthmor Football Club in Neath, and previously with Briton Ferry Athletic, was invited to play in the Swans' Public Trial matches in August 1932, and after showing good form in both trial matches, was signed as a professional in late August 1932. However, he had to wait until his second season at the Vetch Field before making his league debut, at right full back, instead of Syd Lawrence. Making two more league appearances, and one in the Welsh Cup at Chester, he made five league appearances the following season, all as a replacement for Syd

Lawrence, also playing in the Welsh Cup semi-final defeat by Chester, before being released to join Third Division South side Torquay United in the close season. A right full back, standing six feet tall, he started playing for the Swans at the age of nineteen, and was signed by manager Brown at Torquay United in the 1935 close season. After just the one season at Plainmoor with United, he joined Bangor Town as a professional, who at the time were playing in the Birmingham League.

25. DAVIES, William (WILLIE)

Birthplace: Troedyrhiwfach, Bargoed, 6/12/1900.
Died: Llandeilo 6/8/1953
Ht: 5ft-7ins, **Wt:** 10st-7lbs
Swans debut: v. Plymouth Argyle (h), 14/1/1922

Swansea Town Career Statistics			
Season	League	FAC	WC
1921/22	13/2gls	1	1
1922/23	3/1gls		
1923/24	27/1gls	4	
1933/34	33/6gls	4/2gls	
1934/35	32/7gls		3
1935/36	21/5gls		
Total	129/22gls	9/2gls	4

Career:
Troedyrhiwfach
Rhymney
Swansea Amateurs (signed in close season 1920/21)
Swansea Town (signed in 10/5/1921)
Cardiff City (£3,000 in 7/6/1924) lge 85/17gls
Notts. County (signed in 1927) lge 71/9gls
Tottenham Hotspur (£3,000 signed in February 1930)
   lge 109/19gls
Bargoed
Swansea Town (signed in September 1933)
Llanelli (signed in April 1936 as player coach)

Honours: Wales Full–17, West Wales Senior Cup Winner–1923

Formerly with his home town side Troedyrhiwfach and Rhymney, Willie joined Swansea Amateurs prior to the start of the 1920/21 season, and by May 1921 had signed professional forms for the Swans. That season with the Amateurs had seen him score fifty-nine goals, appearing at centre forward, drawing good reviews from Swans' manager Bradshaw as a player in the making, and well worth watching in the future. Signed initially for a ten shillings and sixpence donation to Rhymney, later paying a £25 gift to the club, he started his career at the Vetch Field at centre forward, before switching to outside right, going on to make regular appearances for Wales at international level, and also play in an FA Cup Final for Cardiff City. Willie scored on his league debut for the Swans at the Vetch Field against Plymouth Argyle, and was the type of player who liked to beat his man, had good ball control, and was extremely quick over 10 yards. At the end of his first season at the Vetch Field he contracted TB, resulting in him missing almost the entire 1922/23 season, returning to play in just three league games that season. At the end of the season he played in the Swans reserve side that beat Llanelly to win the West Wales Senior Cup. The second half of the 1923/24 season saw Willie make his first international appearance for Wales, against Scotland on the 16th February 1924 at Ninian Park, Cardiff, scoring the first goal in a 2-0 win for Wales. He also scored in the next international against England, made a further appearance against Ireland, before being transferred to First Division Cardiff City for £3,000. Making his 'Bluebirds' debut at Birmingham on the

13th September 1924, by the end of his first season at Ninian Park, the club had firmly established themselves in the First Division. Making an appearance in the losing FA Cup Final against Sheffield United, he failed to feature in the 1926/27 success over Arsenal. Willie gained a further eight international caps whilst with Cardiff City, gaining a further six with Notts. County whilst playing in the Second Division. In January 1925, Willie was the recipient of a specially designed Championship Gold Medal, a gift from the Football Association of Wales in recognition of playing for his country during the previous season when they won the International Championship, beating England, Scotland and Ireland. Joining Notts. County prior to the start of the 1927/28 season, he then joined Second Division Tottenham Hotspur in 1929, before returning for his second spell at the Vetch Field, signing in September 1933. Over the next three seasons Willie would be consistent in front of goal, in October 1934 scoring four goals in two games against Newcastle United and Burnley. In April 1936 he joined Llanelly as player coach, retiring from the game in 1938, with his final season for the Reds as Team captain. He was a school caretaker in Pontardulais up to his retirement, prior to his death in August 1953.

26. DAVIS, Joseph (JOE)

Birthplace: Bristol, 24/8/1938
Ht: 5ft-9ins, **Wt:** 11st-6lbs
Swans debut: v. Brighton & Hove Albion (h), 11/3/1967

Swansea Town Career Statistics			
Season	League	FAC	WC
1966/67	4		
1967/68	32	4	2/1gls
Total	36	4	2/1gls

Career:
Soundwell
Bristol Rovers (from juniors in March 1956) lge 210+1/4gls
Swansea Town (£1,000 signed in 10/3/1967)

Long serving Bristol Rovers defender who regularly made league appearances against the Swans for Rovers in the Second and Third Divisions prior to his being signed by Manager Billy Lucas in March 1967. Playing initially at left full back, he eventually partnered Brian Purcell in central defence before sustaining an injury against Aldershot in mid-April 1968, which would see him miss the remainder of the season, and ultimately retire from the game. In February he featured in the Swans team that narrowly lost 1-0 to Arsenal in a FA Cup Fourth Round tie at the Vetch Field which recorded a record gate of 32,796. Earlier in his career at Eastville with Bristol Rovers he captained the

side in the mid-sixties, making his league debut against Luton Town on the 25th February 1961, almost five years after signing for the club from Soundwell. Not noted for his goalscoring prowess during his career, all of his four goals for Rovers were from the penalty spot, and he became the first substitute used by Rovers when introduced in the game against Walsall in October 1965. He returned to Eastville when his career was ended through a knee injury, working for a number of years as youth coach, scout, and helping to develop the young talent at the club. Involved as a committee member of the Rovers ex-players club he later worked as a sales manager for the *Bristol Evening Post* newspaper.

27. DEACON, Henry (HARRY)

Birthplace: Darnall, Sheffield 25/4/1900. **Died:** Rotherham, 5/1/1946
Ht: 5ft-8ins, **Wt:** 11st-0lbs
Swans debut: v. Merthyr (h), 26/8/1922

Swansea Town Career Statistics			
Season	League	FAC	WC
1922/23	41/15gls	2	3/1gls
1923/24	32/16gls	4/1gls	3
1924/25	39/15gls	2/1gls	3/1gls
1925/26	37/9gls	7/3gls	3
1926/27	42/7gls	5/3gls	
1927/28	37/8gls	1	1
1928/29	37/12gls	2/1gls	1
1929/30	34/2gls	1	1
1930/31	20/2gls		2
Total	319/86gls	24/9gls	17/2gls

Career:
Hallam
Sheffield Wednesday (signed as amateur in 1919) lge 0
Birmingham (signed in May 1920) lge 2
Swansea Town (signed in 28/7/1922)
Crewe Alexandra (£250 signed in August 1931) lge 118/47gls
Southport (signed in June 1934) lge 9/2gls
Accrington Stanley (signed in December 1934) lge 25/11gls
Rotherham United (signed in June 1935 to May 1936) lge 6

Honours: England Junior International, Third Division South Champions–1924, Welsh League XI, West Wales Senior Cup Winner–1930

Formerly with junior side Hallam, before signing for First Division side Sheffield Wednesday, where after failing to make a first team appearance, signed for First Division Birmingham in

1921. After making his league debut with the 'Blues' he joined the Swans in July 1922 for a substantial transfer fee, missing just one league game in his first season at the Vetch Field. The previous season he gained a Junior International Cap with England. Finishing the season with fifteen league goals, his second season with the Swans saw him finish top goalscorer with sixteen league goals, including two goals in a game on three occasions. The Third Division South Championship winning season of 1924/25 saw Deacon again go into double figures with goals scored, with his first hat-trick recorded, at the Vetch Field against Brentford in a 7-0 win in November 1924. Missing few matches during his period with the Swans, Deacon was also a prominent figure during season 1925/26 when the Swans reached the semi-final of the FA Cup. An extremely popular player with the fans at the Vetch Field, he possessed good dribbling skills, also scoring a number of goals direct from free kicks for the Swans. A month after losing to Bolton Wanderers in the FA Cup semi-final, Deacon played in the Swans side that lost 3-0 to Ebbw Vale in the Welsh Cup Final. Season 1928/29 saw the Swans open with a 4-0 defeat by Chelsea, but in the next match at home to Blackpool, Deacon scored four goals in a 5-5 draw. Towards the end of his career with the Swans, Deacon switched to a right half back position, rarely playing in his usual inside forward role. In October 1930 he was included in the Swans reserve side that beat Newport County in the West Wales Senior Cup Final, and later in the season, in May, played for a Welsh League XI against the Irish League. Twelve months previously he had made an earlier appearance for the Welsh League Representative side against the Irish Free State at the Vetch Field. Signing for Third Division North side Crewe Alexandra for £250 in May 1931, he made over one hundred league appearances, averaging almost a goal every two league games, before signing for Southport in 1934. Between 1934 and 1935 he made league appearances for Accrington Stanley and Rotherham United before retiring from the professional game to concentrate on his business interests in Rotherham. On the 26th March 1928, Scottish side Hearts became the first Scottish side to play at the Vetch Field in his Benefit game, with the Swans winning 3-2 with goals from Deacon, Fowler and Lewis, producing an attendance of 9,265. During WW1 he was a guest player for Abergele. During the period when he played for the Swans, he was also an accomplished musician, playing second fiddle in the Swansea Philharmonic.

28. DENNISON, Robert (ROBBIE)

Birthplace: Banbridge (NI), 30/4/1963
Ht: 5ft-7ins, **Wt:** 12st-0lbs
Swans debut: v. Bradford City (h), 7/10/1995

Career:
Glenavon
West Bromwich Albion (£40,000 signed in 13/9/1985) lge
    9+7/1gls, FLC 1, FAC 2, Others 1

Wolverhampton Wanderers (£20,000 signed in 13/3/1987)
    lge 264+29/40gls, FLC 12+4/3gls, FAC 16+2/2gls,
    Others 24+2/4gls
Swansea City (loan in 5/10/1995)
Hednesford Town (signed in July 1997) Conf 33/4gls
Hereford United (signed in December 1998) Conf 19/1gls

Swansea City Career Statistics		
Season	League	AWS
1995/96	9	2
Total	9	2

Honours: Northern Ireland Yth, 'B', Full–18, AMC 1988, Fourth Division Champions–1988, Third Division Champions–1989

Experienced left sided winger, midfielder who had a two month loan spell at the Vetch Field, also covered at left full back on occasions for the Swans, before returning to Molineux after his loan had ended. He started his playing career with Gilford & Craigavon Schools (Banbridge), Sunnypark FC and Gilford FC prior to joining Glenavon initially as an amateur in August 1978, before signing professional in April 1980. Starring for Glenavon where he scored 52 goals in 184 appearances prior to arriving at the Hawthorns for £40,000 making his debut twenty-fours hours later against Newcastle United on the 13th September 1985. Producing some excellent displays at times, he was transferred across the Black Country to Molineux (after Robert Hopkins had established himself as Albion's wide-man) where he teamed up with his former colleagues Steve Bull and Andy Thompson and soon to be joined by Ally Robertson. In ten years at Molineux, he helped the club to successive Championships in the Fourth and Third Divisions in 1988 and 1989 respectively. In 1988 he also played at Wembley with Wolves when they beat Burnley to win the Sherpa Van Trophy, scoring the second goal. Consistently among the goalscorers during the seasons, he was also a good supplier of ammunition for the likes of Steve Bull and Andy Mutch in the Wolves frontline for many seasons. Capped at youth and 'B' level for Northern Ireland, Robbie made his first appearance at Full level for his country when he was capped against France in Belfast on the 27th April 1988. During season 1996/97 the veteran winger was recalled to the international side playing against Italy as substitute. That same season also saw him score his 50th goal for Wolves, prior to being released in May 1997. Receiving a testimonial after eleven years service with Wolves, he joined Conference side Hednesford Town in July 1997, but was then re-united with former Wolves manager Graham Turner at Hereford United in December 1998. During season 2000/01 he signed for Warley Borough, joining Warley Rangers twelve months later as coach. Dennison now works in the sports trophy business.

29. DENOON, John (JOCK)

Birthplace: Inverness, 10/4/1890
Ht: 6ft-0ins, **Wt:** 12st-10lbs
Swans debut: v. Luton Town (a), 30/8/1919, Sth. Lge

Career:
Inverness Thistle
Chelsea (signed in March 1910) lge 0
Norwich City (signed in 12/5/1916) lge 0
Swansea Town (£75 signed in June 1919)
Mid-Rhondda (signed in May 1927)
New Tredegar (signed in October 1927)

Honours: Third Division South Champions–1925, Welsh League Representative XI, West Wales Senior Cup Winner–1923, 1927

Swansea Town Career Statistics			
Season	League	FAC	WC
1920/21	29	3	
1921/22	26	5	1
1922/23	40	2	3
1923/24	5		
1924/25	28	2	3
1925/26	27	7	
1926/27	18	5	
Total	173	24	7

Former Inverness Thistle goalkeeper who was a policeman prior to signing as a professional, and who joined Second Division Chelsea in 1910, failed to make a first team appearance, signing for Southern League side Norwich City in May 1916. A WW1 guest player for Chelsea in October 1915, and with QPR, prior to signing for Inverness Thistle he had played for Tockgolm FC and Nelson FC (Inverness). With Nelson he was a Junior Cup and Shield Winner. Signing for the Swans for a fee of £75 in June 1919, he played in goal during the club's last season in the Southern League, and made his League debut against QPR at the Vetch Field in October 1920. In April 1920 he played for a Welsh League Representative side against the Welsh League Champions, Mid-Rhondda. A beanpole of a goalkeeper, towards the end of his career with the Swans, he was sent off, and on one occasion he was suspended by the Swans for fisticuffs and insubordination. Nevertheless he was a consistent goalkeeper, who remained first choice for the Swans up to the 1923/24 season, before losing his place to Brookes, and for the next three seasons contested the keeper's jersey with Robson. In November 1923 he was included in a Swans reserve side that beat Pembroke Dock to win the West Wales Senior Cup, and four years later when they beat Bridgend Town in the final. During the 1924/25 Third Division South Championship winning season, he took over in goal from Robson after the first seven games of the season, playing in twenty-eight league games. He also played in the Welsh Cup semi-final defeat by Wrexham later in the same season. The following season he was included in the Swans side that lost 3-0 to Bolton Wanderers in the FA Cup semi-final, but failed to make the Welsh Cup Final line-up at the end of the season against Ebbw Vale. Originally released in May 1924, 'Jock' remained at the Vetch Field until May 1927, when he signed for Mid-Rhondda, finishing his playing career with New Tredegar. In April 1930 he was involved with coaching cricket with Ynystawe Cricket Club. By 1934 he was assistant groundsman and scout with QPR, and in August 1936 was appointed trainer at Tunbridge Wells Rangers after previously being assistant trainer at Rangers and at Fulham. Following the collapse of Tunbridge Wells Rangers, season 1946/47 saw Jock take over as manager of Hastings & St. Leonards, a Corinthian League Club, also working as a Sports Supervisor for the Hastings Youth Organizations. In May 1948 he was appointed manager of newly formed Tonbridge Football Club.

30. DEVULGT, LEIGH Stewart

Birthplace: Swansea, 17/3/1981
Ht: 5ft-9ins, **Wt:** 11st-1lbs
Swans debut: v. Leyton Orient (a), 26/12/1999

Swansea City Career Statistics			
Season	League	LDV	FAWP
1999/2000	0+2	1	4+2
2000/01	6+1	2	5+3
2001/02	7+3	1	1
2002/03	3+1		
Total	16+7	4	10+5

Career:
Swansea City (from trainee in 5/7/1999)
Merthyr (loan in 25/10/2001)
Llanelli (loan in February 2002)
Llanelli (loan in December 2002)
Carmarthen Town (signed in January 2003)
Port Talbot Town (signed in October 2004)

Honours: Wales Yth, U-21–2

Former Swansea schoolboy defender who arrived at the Vetch Field as a trainee in the summer of 1997, prior to signing as a professional in July 1999. Capable of playing in either full back position, who was able to go forward with the ball, he also made appearances in central defence earlier in his career. An extremely fit player, he lacked consistency in a position that troubled the Swans during his period at the Vetch Field. After making his league debut at Leyton Orient in December 1999, he had to wait until season 2001/02 before he was regularly included in the Swans starting line-up. Capped at youth level for Wales, he gained his first Welsh U-21 cap in August 2001 as a substitute for Price against Armenia, making his first U-21 start against Belarus in October 2001. In late October 2001 he suffered a broken foot playing in an F.A. Trophy Cup tie during a loan spell with Merthyr Tydfil, and after returning to fitness joined League of Wales side Llanelli in February 2002 for match practice. Making a few first team appearances for the Swans during the latter stages of the 2001/02 season, Leigh then suffered with a knee ligament and cartilage injury, sustained during a Wales U-21 training squad get together. The start of season 2002/03 saw Leigh unable to make inroads into the Swans starting line-up, and following a change of management at the Vetch Field, played a couple of games under the new manager, Brian Flynn, before having his contract paid up in mid-December 2002, joining League of Wales side Carmarthen Town in January 2003. In October he joined Port Talbot Town.

31. DEWSBURY, JOHN

Birthplace: Swansea, 16/2/1932
Ht: 5ft-6ins, **Wt:** 10st-9lbs
Swans debut: v. Everton (h), 4/10/1952

Swansea Town Career Statistics		
Season	*League*	*WC*
1952/53	9	2
Total	9	2

Career:
Swansea Town (from juniors in 4/4/1950)
Newport County (signed in August 1955) lge 2
Milford United (signed in close season 1956)

Honours: West Wales Senior Cup Winner–1954

John Dewsbury was born in Port Tennant, went to Danygraig School, and then Dynevor school before going to work for Hancocks Brewery in Wind Street as an office boy after leaving school, although at the time his parents had a newsagents business in Port Tennant Road. He captained the first school team at Dynevor after the war, playing full back behind big John Charles, and despite no representative honours during his school days, was lucky enough to be selected for the final twenty-two in one of their trials. Prior to joining the Swans youth side at the age of seventeen years old he played for Danygraig and St. Thomas youth sides. During the Second World War he was called up, and joined the RAF, went to Hereford on a course, and stayed there for 18 months, primarily because of his football ability, and then moved on to St. Athan. Returning to Swansea after the war, he graduated through the Welsh League and Combination sides at the Vetch Field, then signed as a professional in April 1950. He made his league debut at the Vetch Field in front of 22,954 against Everton in a 2-2 draw, coming up against the legendary Irish left winger Tommy Eglington. In the previous match, the high scoring left winger had scored five goals for Everton, and he must have thought he would be led a merry dance on his debut. However, after replacing Steve Leavy in the Swans line-up for his debut, he retained his place for a further eight league games before Leavy was switched to right full back to accommodate Arthur Morgan in the left full back position. The second half of the season saw Dewsbury make two further first team appearances for the Swans, both in Welsh Cup ties, in January against Kidderminster Harriers at the Vetch Field, and in early March at the Vetch Field in the semi-final against Rhyl. Was a member of the Swans side that beat Llanelly in May 1954 to win the West Wales Senior Cup. With strong competition for the right full back position at the Vetch Field from Steve Leavy, Rory Keane and Dai Thomas, England International Arthur Willis was

signed by manager Ronnie Burgess from Tottenham Hotspur shortly after the start of the 1954/55 season, and in August 1955 joined Newport County, who had as their player manager, former Swans' wing half Billy Lucas. Making just two league appearances for County, he then joined Welsh League side Milford United, and two seasons later retired from the game. Since leaving the West Wales side he has had no involvement in the game on the coaching or managerial side, and initially went into business with his parents. Then, after they sold their newsagents business, went to work for Corona pop as wages clerk, and then in sales. He later worked for Lyons cakes as a salesman before retiring in 1991.

32. DODDS, Thomas (Tommy) Black

Birthplace: Hebburn-on-Tyne, 20/12/1918. **Died:** South Shields, April 1999
Ht: 5ft-9ins
Swans debut: v. Bradford Park Avenue, 18/1/1947

Swansea Town Career Statistics		
Season	*League*	*FAC*
1946/47	8/1gls	1
1947/48	3/1gls	
Total	11/2gls	1

Career:
Hebburn St. Cuthberts
North Shields
Aston Villa (signed in January 1939) lge 1
Swansea Town (signed in 11/1/1947)
North Shields (signed in close season 1948)
Barry Town (signed in 25/1/1949)
Hereford United (signed in August 1950)

Signed for the Swans as part of the Trevor Ford deal from Aston Villa. Formerly with junior side Hebburn St. Cuthberts prior to joining North Shields, he joined First Division side Aston Villa in January 1939, played in Midland Mid-Week League, and Birmingham Combination matches prior to the outbreak of WW2. For a time Tommy worked in the shipyards until he joined the Royal Navy in which he served during the war. He was demobilised in time for the start of the 1946/47 season, but played in just one league game for Villa, wearing the number ten shirt in the club's first game when Football League was resumed, on the 31st August 1946 in a 1-0 home defeat by Middlesbrough in front of 50,000 spectators. His debut came after impressing in pre-season trial and practice games. He was described as a strong, virile forward who possessed a powerful shot, and after arriving at the Vetch Field, made his debut a week later at inside right at Bradford Park Avenue. By the end of the season he had also made appearances for the Swans at inside left, and at centre forward. His only goal scored for the Swans came in his second game, in a 5-1 defeat of Newport County at the Vetch Field. Deemed to be not quick, and strong enough for league football, he also suffered from being compared to Trevor Ford. A newspaper report said that he had returned to join North Shields in August 1948, mentioning that in his first game for the club in the North Eastern League he suffered a fractured cheekbone. He returned to South Wales in late January 1949 to sign for Southern League side Barry Town, and after a spell with Hereford United settled back in South Shields.

33. DODSON, DAVID Alfred

Birthplace: Gravesend, 20/1/1940
Ht: 5ft-8ins, **Wt:** 10st-6lbs
Swans debut: v. Lincoln City (h), 22/8/1959

Swansea Town Career Statistics		
Season	League	FLC
1959/60	19/7gls	
1960/61	8/3gls	1
Total	27/10gls	1

Career:
Fleet Minors (Gravesend)
Arsenal (signed amateur in 25/5/1955, professional in 18/11/1957)
Swansea Town (signed in 6/7/1959)
Portsmouth (£4,000 signed in December 1961) lge 53/15gls
Aldershot (signed in January 1965) lge 59/12gls
Hereford United (signed in August 1967)

Honours: England Yth–8, South East Counties Champions–1956, South East Counties League Cup Winner–1956, Will Mather Cup Winner–1956, Metropolitan League Champions–1959, Third Division Champions–1962, West Wales Senior Cup Winner–1960, Football Combination Second Division Champions–1961

Former Kent Schoolboy and England Schoolboy trialist who joined the 'Gunners as an amateur from Gravesend side Fleet Minors in May 1955, signing professional in November 1957. A consistent goalscorer in the 'Gunners' reserve side, despite failing to a make a first team appearance, gained honours at Highbury, winning the Will Mather Cup, South East Counties League Championship, and the South East Counties League Cup in 1956, runner up in the 1958 Southern Junior Floodlight Cup competition, and winning the Metropolitan League

Championship in 1959. He also played for the England Youth side in seasons 1955/56 and 1956/57. Signed by Swans manager Trevor Morris, he arrived at the Vetch Field in early July 1959, and made his league debut in the opening game of the 1959/60 season at the Vetch Field against Lincoln City, scoring his first league goal four games later in a 2-1 home defeat by Sunderland. In May 1960 he scored one of the Swans goals in the West Wales Senior Cup Final win over Llanelly. However, by the end of his first season in league football, the inexperienced outside left, or centre forward, had scored seven league goals from nineteen league appearances, including a goal in four consecutive league games at the end of the season. Season 1960/61 saw him make regular appearances in the reserve side that won the Combination Second Division Championship. Despite starting his second season in the opening league fixtures, and scoring two goals in the second league game against Huddersfield Town, he struggled to command a regular place, and in December 1961 was transferred to Portsmouth for £4,000. By the end of the season he had made appearances in 'Pompey's' successful Third Division Championship winning side. In January 1965 he signed for Fourth Division side Aldershot, later joining Hereford United in August 1967, and making further non-league appearances for Guildford City, Andover, Fleet Town (where he was trainer), whilst living in Barnstaple.

34. DONNELLY, PETER

Birthplace: Kingston upon Hull, 22/9/1936
Ht: 5ft-11ins, **Wt:** 11st-5lbs
Swans debut: v. Liverpool (a), 25/11/1961

Swansea Town Career Statistics			
Season	League	FAC	WC
1961/62	16/3gls	1	3/2gls
Total	16/3gls	1	3/2gls

Career:
Doncaster Rovers (juniors in 1953, professional in March 1954) lge 6/1gls
Scunthorpe United (signed in July 1958) lge 39/19gls, FAC 2
Cardiff City (signed in June 1960) lge 31/8gls, FLC 1/1gls, WC 4/2gls
Swansea Town (£6,500 signed in October 1961)
Brighton & Hove Albion (£7,000 signed in July 1962) lge 56/13gls, FLC 2, FAC 1
Bradford City (£500 signed in 16/3/1965) lge 13/5gls
Margate (signed in July 1963)

Honours: Midland League Representative XI, West Wales Senior Cup Winner–1962

Peter attended Welton High School, representing Hull and Yorkshire Schoolboys, and was a former junior at Doncaster Rovers who later made a good goal scoring impression with Scunthorpe United, averaging almost a goal every two league games for the 'Iron'. He also made an appearance for a Midland League Representative XI against Peterborough United. Something of an all-round sportsman, Peter Donnelly was an excellent club-cricketer, and became the Army's light-heavy and heavyweight boxing champion during his National Service. He embarked on a Football League career at the age of seventeen in March 1954 when he signed professional forms for Doncaster Rovers, scored on his debut on the 17th April 1954 at the age of seventeen years and 229 days old, in the Second Division against Birmingham City. His two years in the Army doing his National Service limited his appearances for Rovers, but he did make appearances in the side that suffered relegation at the end of the 1957/58 season. Joining Scunthorpe United in July 1958, the Hull-born forward met with greater success in Lincolnshire, scoring nineteen goals in 39 Second Division outings, including two goals on his debut on the 30th March 1959 against Lincoln City. He was leading goalscorer with fifteen goals for the 1959/60 season, and in June 1960 he joined First Division Cardiff City in exchange for Joe Bonson, going on to hit the net eight times in 31 League games before a £5,000 move to Swansea Town in October 1961. He had to wait a couple of games to score his first league goal for the 'Bluebirds' but he did score in the club's inaugural match in the Football League Cup, against Middlesbrough in October 1960. During the 1959/60 season he scored against the Swans in both league fixtures, and after signing for newly promoted First Division side Cardiff City in June 1960, played against the Swans in both Welsh Cup semi-final matches that season. Making his Swans debut at Anfield against Liverpool in November 1961 at inside left, he scored his first goal in his third game for the Swans in a 3-0 home win over Brighton & Hove Albion, scoring a further two goals by the end of the season. A bustling type of inside forward, he appeared to not fit into the style of play at the Vetch Field, and was sold to Brighton & Hove Albion for £7,000 in July 1962. In May 1962 he scored one of the Swans goals in the West Wales Senior Cup win over Llanelly. Signed by Albion manager George Curtis, Peter was bought to bolster relegated Albion's attack for their first campaign back in the Third Division, but the campaign proved a complete disaster for the club, suffering relegation, with Donnelly topping the goalscorers with 11 goals out of a modest total of 58. Strong and experienced, he appeared in three forward positions and missed just one League game all season, but lost his place the following term after damaging a knee early on. The start of the 1964–65 season saw him in dispute with the club over financial terms, and he had just three first-team outings before joining Bradford City for a £500 fee in March 1965, scoring after eighty-three minutes in his debut game at Newport County. Three weeks later he wreaked revenge on his former club by scoring twice in a 4–1 defeat of Albion at Valley Parade, temporarily denting Brighton's promotion hopes. On leaving City after just thirteen League appearances he played for Margate in the Southern League for several seasons, and later appeared with Canterbury City.

35. DONOVAN, Francis (FRANK) James

Birthplace: Pembroke, 26/2/1919
Died: Pembroke, 17/4/2003
Ht: 5ft-6ins, **Wt:** 10st-0lbs
Swans debut: v. Birmingham City (h), 19/8/1950

Swansea Town Career Statistics	
Season	League
1950/51	15/2gls
Total	15/2gls

Career:
Milford United
Haverfordwest
Pembroke Borough
Swansea Town (signed in 13/5/1950)
Pembroke Borough (signed in close season 1951)

Honours: Wales Amateur–8, Great Britain Olympic XI, Welsh League First Division Champions–1954, Welsh League Challenge Cup Winner–1954

Former Welsh Amateur International outside right with Pembroke Borough who arrived at the Vetch Field in late July 1950 for pre-season training, played in the opening fixtures of the 1950/51 season, but lost his place to the returning Jack O'Driscoll. Both of the goals he scored for the Swans came in consecutive league games against Barnsley and Chesterfield at the Vetch Field. He was released at the end of his first season, returning to Pembroke Borough. The Swans had been chasing Frank for a number of years, and had originally attempted to sign him in October 1948, only for Donovan's club to put in a protest. Cardiff City had also been interested at the time in signing the player. A Coronation School, Pembroke Dock product he first played with Pembroke Dock Stars, later Milford United and Haverfordwest in the First Division of the Welsh League. Frank skippered the Pembroke Borough side that had gained promotion at the end of season 1947/48. His outstanding form had seen him capped for the Wales Amateur side against England in January 1948 and 1949, and against England and Scotland in 1950, also being included in the 1948 Great Britain Olympic squad managed by Sir Matt Busby, playing in all the games through to the semi-finals, with all the games being played at Wembley. In season 1946/47 he had been included in the final trial for the Welsh Amateur side at Barry, but was left out of the trial at the last minute. He also played for the Wales Amateur side that entertained the Indian Olympic side at the Vetch Field on the 26th August 1948. His selection for the Great Britain Olympic squad was recognised in Pembroke Dock by a public presentation of a clock organised by the supporters club. A crafty, clever winger, he possessed a powerful shot in either foot, who came into league football at the late age of thirty-one, but too late to make an impact, and could not match the pace of the professional game. After he had returned to Pembroke Borough, by the end of the 1953/54 season, Borough had won the Welsh League First Division Championship, and also the Welsh League Challenge Cup Final, beating Aberystwyth at Llanelly, with Frank scoring one of the goals in a 2-1 victory. When he retired as a player, he had managerial experience with both Pembroke Borough and Milford United. A legendary figure in Pembrokeshire football, he played almost thirty years in the Welsh League, and in later years he received an award from the Welsh FA for his service to amateur football. An electrician at Pembroke Docks before and after he played as a professional with the Swans, he also had a sports outfitters shop in Pembroke Dock, was heavily involved with coaching youngsters at Pennar Robins, Pembroke and Monkton Swifts, also playing in Charity games up to a couple of years before his death. Along with his daughter Wendy, Frank also bred Pedigree Horses.

36. DRAPER, CRAIG James Edwin

Birthplace: Swansea, 4/12/1982
Ht: 5ft-10ins, **Wt:** 9st-7lbs
Swans debut: v. Rochdale (h), 9/10/2001

Career:
Swansea City (from trainee in 4/7/2001)
Llanelli (loan in April 2002)
Llanelli (signed in close season 2002/3)
Winch Wen (signed in season 2002/3)
Garden Village (signed in close season 2004/5)

Swansea City Career Statistics		
Season	League	FAWP
2000/01		0+2
2001/02	0+2	0+1
Total	0+2	0+3

Honours: West Wales Senior Cup Winner–2002

Former Cefn Hengoed and Swansea Schoolboy midfielder who joined the Swans as a trainee in the summer of 1999, signing as a professional in July 2001. He was given his league debut as a last second substitution for Lee Jenkins at the Vetch Field in October 2001 against Rochdale. Apart from a second appearance from the substitute bench in the last game of the season against Torquay United, his only other first team appearance came again from the substitute bench at Somerton Park in January 2002 in the FAW Premier Cup competition against Newport County. The previous season the midfielder had made two substitute appearances in the competition against Merthyr in the semi-final, and against Wrexham in the Final. Highly rated at the Vetch Field with his awareness in midfield, Craig struggled to last the pace over ninety minutes in a higher grade of football. In a bid to increase his stamina level to cope with the demand required for league football, midway through the 2001/2002 season, a joint sponsorship venture with the owner of a Spanish restaurant in the city, saw Craig and Richard Duffy given free pasta meals in an effort to improve their diet. In late April 2002 he was included in the Swans side that beat Hakin United in the West Wales Senior Cup Final. He joined League of Wales side Llanelli on loan in April 2002, and after being released by the Swans, initially joined the Reds on a permanent basis at the start of the 2002/03 season, who were managed at the time by former Swans First Team coach Peter Nicholas. However, within a couple of weeks of the start of the new season he left Stebonheath Park to sign for his local club Winch Wen, in the Swansea Senior League. During the season he unfortunately suffered a serious knee injury which required surgery, leaving him sidelined for a long period. The start of the 2004/05 pre-season saw Craig make appearances for Welsh League side Garden Village, but after a couple of appearances he returned to his former club, Winch Wen.

37. DRAPER, DEREK

Birthplace: Swansea, 11/5/1943
Ht: 5ft-8ins, **Wt:** 11st-0lbs
Swans debut: v. Newcastle United (h), 16/3/1963

Career:
Swansea Town (from juniors, professional in 11/5/1962)
Derby County (£5,000 signed in April 1966) lge 8/1gls, FLC 1
Bradford Park Avenue (signed in September 1967) lge 60+3/9gls
Chester City (signed in January 1969) lge 316+6/54gls

Swansea Town Career Statistics				
Season	League	FLC	FAC	WC
1962/63	4/1gls			2
1963/64	31/4gls	2/1gls	7/2gls	2
1964/65	23/5gls	3/1gls	2	
1965/66	3			
Total	61/10gls	5/2gls	9/2gls	4

Honours: Wales Yth, U-23–1, Welsh League First Division Champions–1963, West Wales Senior Cup Winner–1965

On the groundstaff at the Vetch Field prior to signing as a professional in May 1962, 'Didi' as he was nicknamed was a classy player who was thought to have a great future in the game, but did not quite fulfil his early promise. One of his earliest jobs during his early days on the Swans groundstaff was to clean Ivor Allchurch's boots, and watching the magical style of play from one of the greatest post war footballers in training, or on the playing field rubbed off on Draper as he eventually graduated to the Swans first team after impressive performances in the reserves, and being capped by Wales at Youth level. He made regular appearances in the reserve side that won the Welsh League First Division Championship in 1963. His first team debut was made against Newcastle United at the Vetch Field on March 16th, 1963, with 'Didi' scoring the only goal of the game. By the end of his first season in the game, he had made a further three league appearances, and played twice in Welsh Cup matches. Brought up in the Greenhill area of Swansea, he attended Hafod School prior to joining the groundstaff at the Vetch Field. Derek had been nicknamed 'Didi' by the Swans fans as they warmed to his attacking and adventurous style of play from the inside forward position. Twelve months later, in what was his first full season in the Football League he was involved in the Swans march to the FA Cup semi finals, scoring two goals in a third round replay win over Sheffield United. His growing maturity in the Swans Second Division side was recognised during the 1964/65 season when he was selected to play for Wales at U-23 level against England, despite playing in a Swans side destined for relegation to the Third Division. In May 1965 he was included in the Swans side that beat Llanelli to win the West Wales Senior Cup. With Ivor Allchurch returning to the Vetch Field at the start of the 1965/66 season, Derek's opportunity to play with the man whose boots he had cleaned vanished early in the season as he was sidelined with injury, after he had made just three league appearances. On regaining his fitness he was unable to force his way back into the Swans side and just prior to transfer deadline day was offered the opportunity to join Derby County for £5,000. After just twelve months at the Baseball Ground he was transferred to Bradford Park Avenue, after making just eight league appearances for the 'Rams.' Eighteen months later, despite being a regular in the Park Avenue line-up, he joined Chester City in January 1969, and left a club who would later lose it's Football League status. In eight and a half seasons at Chester, up until his retirement from football in 1978 he made a total of 331 league appearances for Chester, scoring 55 goals, and retired 77 league appearances short of the club's record held by Ray Gill. A highly respected player in lower division football his memories from a long stay at Sealand Road as it was then, include a promotion winning season in 1974/75 from the Fourth Division, and reaching the League Cup semi-finals in the same season losing to Aston Villa over two legs, 5-4 on aggregate. In season 1972/73, Derek ended the season as top goalscorer for the club with sixteen league and cup goals. He worked for a number of years after his retirement in the commercial department at Sealand Road, then took a job as a milkman with Express Dairies, and for the last seven years has been working for the Post Office in Chester.

38. DUFFY, RICHARD Michael

Birthplace: Swansea, 30/8/1985
Ht: 5ft-10ins, **Wt:** 10st-4lbs
Swans debut: v. Macclesfield Town (a), FAC-2, 8/12/2002

Swansea City Career Statistics			
Season	League	FAC	LDV
2001/02		0+1	
2003/04	16+2/1gls	3	1
Total	16+2/1gls	3+1	1

Career:
Swansea City (from trainee in August 2002)
Portsmouth (£175,000 signed in 23/1/2004) PL 0+1
Burnley (loan in 23/9/2004) lge 3+4/1gls, FLC 2
Coventry City (loan in 26/1/2005) lge 14, FAC 1
Coventry City (loan in 7/6/2005)

Honours: Wales Yth, U-21–6, Welsh Youth Cup Winner–2003, West Wales Senior Cup Winner–2003

First year scholar Richard Duffy joined a unique set of Swans players during the second half of the FA Cup tie at Macclesfield in December 2002 when he made his Swans first team debut as a second half substitute, at the tender age of 16 years and 99 days, becoming the third youngest in the history of the Swans. Also having a week on trial with Nottingham Forest in December 2001, at the time of his debut he had been placed in the shop window with a view of raising money by Swans chairman Tony Petty, but within a couple of weeks had suffered a stress fracture in his back which kept him out of the game for almost twelve months. His talent had been recognised at a very early stage by the Swans, with a professional contract being offered to the defender on his seventeenth birthday prior to his signing as a scholar. The Brynhyfryd born defender who attended Pentrehafod Comprehensive prior to starting his scholarship at

the Vetch Field, had been involved with the Swans for four years prior to signing as a scholar, with Richard beating his elder brother Robert, who was a striker with Rushden & Diamonds to making his debut at first team level. An assured defender with the youth team, he has good pace, and ball distribution, and was more than capable of playing first team football in midfield. Season 2002/03 had seen Richard involved with the Swans youth team who won the Merit League Championship, the Welsh Youth Cup Final against Llanelli, and also beating Carmarthen Town in the West Wales Senior Cup Final. In August 2003 he made an impressive introduction to first team football at the Vetch Field against Mansfield Town, retaining his place at right full back, prior to his transfer to Premiership side Portsmouth in the January transfer window. By the time of his transfer, Richard had scored his first league goal, against Macclesfield Town at the Vetch Field in mid-September, and also received two red cards. With no official transfer figure being quoted in the press regarding his transfer to Portsmouth, Swans chairman Huw Jenkins stated that agreement had been made between the two clubs, and although no figure was actually made public, it was though that a fee of around £175,000, plus more for appearances, and a sell on clause had been agreed between the two clubs. On the 1st May 2004, Richard made his Premiership debut, as a replacement for Linvoy Primus in Pompey's home game with Fulham. In mid-August 2004 he made his first appearance for the Wales U-21 side in a friendly game in Latvia, followed later in the season with appearances against England, Poland, Germany and Austria (2) in the European U-21 Championship. Towards the end of September 2004 he started a loan spell at Coca Cola Championship side Burnley, and in late January 2005 started a three month loan spell at Championship side Coventry City, making his 'Sky Blues' debut in the FA Cup Fourth Round game against Newcastle United. In early June 2005 he returned to Coventry City on a season long loan transfer from Pompey.

39. DURKAN, KIERON John

Birthplace: Chester, 1/12/1973
Ht: 5ft-11ins, **Wt:** 12st-10lbs
Swans debut: v. Bury (h), 14/1/2003

Swansea City Career Statistics				
Season	League	FLC	FAC	LDV
2002/03	4+2			
2003/04	11+4/1gls	1	2/1gls	1
Total	15+6/1gls	1	2/1gls	1

Career:
Wrexham (from trainee in 16/7/1992) lge 43+7/3gls, FLC 3+1, FAC 4+2/2 gls, Others 15/1gls
Stockport County (£95,000 in 16/2/1996) lge 52+12/4gls, FLC 10+1, FAC 4/3gls, Others 4+2

Macclesfield Town (£15,000 in 25/3/1998) lge 92+11/13gls,
    FLC 4+3, FAC 2+3, Others 1+1
York City (loan in 5/10/2000) lge 7
Rochdale (signed in 4/7/2001) lge 16+14/1gls, FLC 2, FAC 3,
    Others 1
Swansea City (signed in 9/1/2002)

Honours: Republic of Ireland U-21–3, Welsh Cup Winner–1995,
Welsh Youth Cup Winner–1991, 1992

Kieron began playing schools football in Runcorn with Weston
Point, and after joining St. Michael's in Widnes was invited to
train with Crewe Alexandra at the age of twelve. Approached by
Wrexham's youth development officer Mike Buxton, he then
represented his school team, Heath in Runcorn, before playing
for Halton and Cheshire schoolboys, winning the Cheshire Cup
with Halton. Signing YTS with Wrexham when he left school, he
progressed through the club's youth teams, collecting a Welsh
Youth Cup Winners medal in 1991 with a 1-0 win over the
Swans. He made his Wrexham league debut in September 1991
against Mansfield Town at Field Mill as a second half substitute
for Micky Thomas. The following season he gained his second
Welsh Youth Cup Final Winners medal when Wrexham beat
Cardiff City 2-1. The 1994/95 season saw Kieron make his mark
in the Wrexham side, also wining caps at U-21 level for the
Republic of Ireland against England and Austria (scored in the
3-0 win), and also playing in the Wrexham side that beat Cardiff
City to win the Welsh Cup. A fine crosser of the ball, he never
possessed the pace to become a top class player, but after falling
out of favour at the Racecourse following the arrival of Craig
Skinner, he was sold to Stockport County for £95,000 in
February 1996, and played a large part in the club's successful
1996/97 season when they finished runners up to Bury in the
Second Division, and also reached the semi-finals of the Coca
Cola Cup competition. Despite starting the new season in
County's First Division line-up, by March 1998 he had lost his
place, and joined Macclesfield Town, helping the 'Silkmen' gain
promotion from the Third Division. After a loan spell at York
City, he joined Rochdale in July 2001, later signing for the Swans
on a free transfer in January 2002, re-uniting for a second time
with Brian Flynn. Kieron suffered with numerous injury
problems during his first season with the Swans, and in May
2003 was offered a new contract by Flynn subject to him proving
his fitness in pre-season training. Included regularly in the first
team squad during the first half of the season, he scored his first
goal for the Swans at the Vetch Field against Mansfield Town,
and a couple of weeks later scored a goal against Rushden &
Diamonds with a lob from thirty-five yards over the keeper's
head. He had his contract paid up by the Swans on the 27th
February 2004, asking to leave on personal reasons, to be near
his family, who still lived in Manchester. After leaving the
Swans he was prevented from signing for Conference side
Halifax Town, and returning to England because of the closing
of the transfer window, but was a regular at the Shay training
sessions. He was expected to sign for Halifax Town in the 2004
close season, but has instead decided to go part-time and join
Runcorn FC Halton, taking up also a job offer outside the game.
Also making appearances for Leek Town in the 2004/05 season,
in July 2005 he signed for Newi Cefn Druids.

40. DURNAN, JOHN

Birthplace: Campbeltown, 10/11/1894
Ht: 5ft-9ins, **Wt:** 11st-7lbs
Swans debut: v. Luton Town (a), 30/8/1919, Sth. Lge

Swansea Town Career Statistics			
Season	League	FAC	WC
1920/21	12		1
1921/22	12	1	
Total	24	1	1

Career:
Campbeltown Academical
Plymouth Argyle (signed in 1914)
Partick Thistle
Dumbarton
Swansea Town (signed in 30/8/1919)
Llandrindod Wells (signed in close season 1923)
Northampton Town (trial in 13/11/1924)

Former Southern League player with Plymouth Argyle who
arrived at Home Park after making WW1 guest appearances for
Scottish Football League sides Partick Thistle and Dumbarton.
He had earlier played for hometown side Campbeltown
Academical in the Renfrewshire Cup Final in 1914. During
season 1916/17 he made twenty-five appearances for Partick
Thistle, nearly all of them at right half, with just two
appearances at centre half. Signing for the Swans in August
1919, in the club's last season in the Southern League, the wing
half made his Football League debut in September 1920 at the
Vetch Field against Norwich City. Playing at right half back in
the next league fixture, he had to wait until the end of the
season before adding to his first team appearances for the
Swans. He started season 1921/22 in the Swans first team line-
up, but lost his place to Williams, and by the end of the season
had made a handful of appearances at either left half back, or at
centre half. In the 1923 close season he joined Llandrindod Wells
as coach and professional, staying there until November 1924
when he took up the offer of a month's trial with at the time
Third Division South leaders Northampton Town.

41. DWYER, NOEL Michael

Birthplace: Dublin 23/4/1934. **Died:** Wolverhampton,
    6/12/1992
Ht: 5ft-11ins, **Wt:** 12st-10lbs
Swans debut: v. Sunderland (a), 20/8/1960

Swansea Town Career Statistics					
Season	League	FLC	FAC	WC	ECWC
1960/61	27			4	
1961/62	31	2	1	2	2
1962/63	39	1	2	2	
1963/64	36	2	7	1	
1964/65	7				
Total	140	5	10	9	2

Career:
Ormeau, Dublin
Wolverhampton Wanderers (signed in August 1953) lge 5
West Ham United (signed in December 1958) lge 36
Swansea Town (£3,500 signed in August 1960)

Plymouth Argyle (£7,500 signed in January 1965) lge 26
Charlton Athletic (signed in December 1965) lge 6

Honours: Republic of Ireland 'B', Full–14, Welsh Cup Winner–1961, Central League Champions–1958, West Wales Senior Cup Winner–1961

A great favourite at the Vetch Field who will always be remembered for his fantastic performance at Anfield against Liverpool in the 1964 FA Cup quarter final. An athletic goalkeeper, something of a showman, brilliant on his day, he was quick off his line and good with crosses, despite his relative lack of height. Joining top First Division side Wolverhampton Wanderers from Irish side Ormeau in August 1953, he managed just five First Division appearances for Wanderers during a period when they won the First Division Championship on three occasions during his period at Molineux. At Molineux he also gained a Central League Championship medal in season 1957/58, also making a 'B' appearance for his country. Staying in the First Division, Noel joined West Ham United in December 1959, and eighteen months later arrived at the Vetch Field for a fee in the region of £3,500. At Upton Park he had made his first international appearance for the Republic of Ireland at Full level, against Sweden in 1960. During his period with the Swans, Noel made a further ten international appearances for the Republic of Ireland. Arriving at the Vetch Field, Noel competed with the fan's favourite, Johnny King, an almost legendary figure for the Swans since making his league debut in December 1950. In his first season at the Vetch Field he helped the Swans finish in a healthy top ten position in the Second Division, also playing in the end of the season Welsh Cup Final win over Bangor City, which saw Noel play in both European Cup Winners Cup ties the following season against East German side Motor Jena, and also in the West Wales Senior Cup Final win over Haverfordwest. The next three seasons saw the Swans struggle in the Second Division, but following successive Welsh Cup Semi-Final defeats to Wrexham and Newport County respectively, the Swans third semi-final this time was in the F.A. Cup at Villa Park against Preston North End. Noel's performance in the quarter final at Anfield against Liverpool will long be remembered for the numerous breathtaking saves he made. His inspirational form that day included a penalty save late in the game from full back Ronnie Moran, with Dwyer continually thwarting the home side's efforts to get the equalizer. Continually pelted with coins from the Liverpool supporters, in the dressing room after the game, Noel counted out 3 shillings and nine pence, equivalent to around twenty pence in modern day coinage. In January 1965 he was sold to Plymouth Argyle for £7,500, and less than twelve months later, returned to London to sign for Charlton Athletic but at the end of the 1956/66 season retired on medical advice after a cartilage operation. He settled in Wolverhampton after leaving the Vetch Field, became a Publican in several licenced premises in the town up to his death in December 1992.

E

1. EASTHAM, GEORGE Richard

Birthplace: Blackpool, 13/9/1914. **Died:** South Africa, January 2000
Ht: 5ft-8ins, **Wt:** 10st-3lbs
Swans debut: v. Bournemouth (a), 23/8/1947

Swansea Town Career Statistics	
Season	*League*
1947/48	15
Total	15

Career:
Bolton Wanderers (signed amateur in May 1932, professional in August 1932) lge 114/16gls
Brentford (£4,000 signed in May 1937) lge 49/1gls
Blackpool (£5,000 signed in November 1938) lge 44/9gls
Swansea Town (signed in 13/8/1947)
Rochdale (signed in 2/6/1948) lge 2
Lincoln City (signed in January 1949) lge 27/1gls

Honours: England–1, F.A. XI–2

Capable of playing in either inside forward position as well as at outside right, George Eastham started his playing career with Blackpool junior sides Central Juniors, Cambridge Road Juniors and South Shore Wednesday, prior to signing as a junior with Bolton Wanderers in August 1932. His elder brother Henry made league appearances for Liverpool, Tranmere Rovers and Accrington Stanley. He made a goalscoring league debut against his hometown club Blackpool in April 1933 at the age of 19, and at the time it was said that the club had received a bid of £10,000 for the youngster. Despite suffering relegation in his first season, by the time the club had regained their First Division status, Eastham had become a regular in the side. The same season that Wanderers had regained their First Division status, they also reached the semi-final stages of the F.A. Cup competition, and within a couple of weeks, George had gained his one and only cap for England, playing against Holland on the 18th May 1935. Joining First Division Brentford in June 1937 for £4,000, his first season at Griffin Park saw the club finish in the top ten in the league, and also reach the quarter-final stage of the F.A. Cup competition. In November 1938 he moved to his home town club Blackpool, staying at Bloomfield Road until the outbreak of the Second Word War. His Army service limited his football during the war years, making war-time appearances for Blackpool, but also making guest appearances for Birmingham (1940/41), Bolton (1940/1, 1941/42), Brentford (1940/41), York City (1940/41), Mansfield Town (1941/42), Millwall (February 1942) and QPR (1941/42), and also having a spell in South Africa, a country where he would later make his home. The first season after the war he played at First Division Blackpool, but then signed for the Swans in August 1947, who had just been relegated to the Third Division South. Making regular appearances during the first half of the season for the Swans at inside left, he then joined Third Division North side Rochdale in June 1948, later signing for Lincoln City in January 1949. By signing for Second Division Lincoln City he became the only player since the Football League was resumed to have played football in all four divisions. Finishing his career in England with non-league side Hyde United (September 1950), he then took over as player manager with Northern Ireland side Ards in September 1953, where he was able to introduce his son George to the professional game, taking over as manager in October 1958. Not only did both father and son represent their country during their careers, but both played together in a first class game when they lined up to play against Distillery in a Gold Cup game. Returning to the UK to join Accrington Stanley as manager in 1958, within a season he was back in Ireland as manager of Distillery (June 1959), taking the club to the League Championship in 1963. Rejoining Ards in late 1964, he stayed at the club until March 1970, and following a spell coaching/scouting with Stoke City, took over as manager of South African side Hellenic F.C. in late 1971. In 1972 he returned to Ireland to take over as manager of Glentoran, and in a successful eighteen month period took the club into the European Cup Winners Cup competition, before returning to South Africa where he retired from the game, worked in a bakery, and lived for over twenty years prior to his death in 2000.

2. EASTON, William (BILLY)

Birthplace: Newcastle, 10/3/1904. **Died:** County Cleveland, OND, 1960
Ht: 5ft-9ins, **Wt:** 11st-5lbs
Swans debut: v. Barnsley (h), 1/2/1930

Swansea Town Career Statistics			
Season	League	FAC	WC
1929/30	16/1gls		1/2gls
1930/31	40/17gls	1/1gls	2
Total	56/18gls	1/1gls	3/2gls

Career:
Blyth Spartans (signed in January 1923)
Rotherham County (£150 signed in May 1923) lge 6/1gls
Montreal Maroons, Canada (by April 1925)
Everton (£200 signed in March 1927) lge 15/3gls
Swansea Town (£750 signed in January 1930)
Port Vale (signed in 27/5/1931) lge 25/6gls
Aldershot (signed in June 1933) lge 5
Workington (signed in August/October 1934)
Walkers Celtic (signed in season 1934/35)
North Shields (signed in close season 1936)
Walker Celtic (signed in close season 1938)

Honours: Welsh League Representative XI

Inside forward who started his career with Blyth Catholic Young Mens' Society and Eston, prior to having a trial with West Stanley in the 1922 close season. Joining Blyth Spartans in January 1923, he later signed for Rotherham County in May 1923, made his league debut for them, also touring with the club to Canada. He later had a spell in Canada playing for Montreal Maroons, and after returning to the UK, joined Everton in March 1927. Making fifteen league appearances for Everton's First Division side, he was signed by Swans manager James Hunter Thomson for £850 in January 1930, making his debut in a 2-0 home defeat by Barnsley. He remained in the Swans side for the rest of the season at either inside left, or at inside right, and during his first full season at the Vetch Field, missed just two league games during the 1930/31 season, also finishing as joint top goalscorer with Ronnie Williams on seventeen league goals. Very much the penalty taker for the Swans that season, with four successes, also scoring a hat-trick against Bury at the Vetch Field in September 1930 in a 5-2 win. In May 1930 he was one of eight Swans players who were selected to play for a Welsh League Representative side at the Vetch Field against the Irish Free State. The 1930/31 season also saw him score two goals in a game on three occasions. He was transferred to Port Vale in May 1931 in a part exchange deal which saw Anstiss arrive at the Vetch Field. Twelve months later he joined Aldershot, later finishing his playing career with non-league sides Workington (August to October 1934), Walker Celtic (1934/35), North Shields (close season 1936), and finally returning to Walker Celtic in close season 1938.

3. EDMUNDSON, JOHN

Birthplace: Tarleton, JFM, 1895
Ht: 5ft-10½ins, **Wt:** 12st-4lbs
Swans debut: v. Portsmouth (a), 28/8/1920

Career:
Leyland
Leeds City (signed in April 1914) lge 11/6gls
Sheffield Wednesday (£750 signed in October 1914) lge 14/2gls

Swansea Town (£500 signed in 10/6/1920)
Exeter City (£150 signed in 20/9/1923) lge 6/1gls

Swansea Town Career Statistics			
Season	League	FAC	WC
1920/21	32/20gls	3/4gls	
1921/22	24/11gls	7/3gls	2/1gls
1922/23	4/2gls		
Total	60/33gls	10/7gls	2/1gls

John Edmundson could probably be classed as the first Swans top goalscorer following his 20 league goals for the Swans in their first season in the Football League. A centre forward, his appearances and goalscoring record prior to arriving at the Vetch Field did not mark him out as an outstanding goalscorer, but after playing for the Swans in the club's first league match in the Football League, finished top goalscorer, scoring two goals in a game on five occasions. Arriving at the Vetch Field in a £500 transfer from First Division side Sheffield Wednesday, before the First World War he had made his Football League debut with Leeds City, after signing from Leyland, and joined Wednesday at a time when Leeds had been suspended. The Swans second season in the Football League also saw him top the goalscoring chart with eleven league goals, plus another four in cup games. He struggled to hold on to his place for the 1922/23 season following the signing of Billy Smith, and in September 1923 he joined fellow Third Division South side Exeter City for £150, but after just six league appearances was forced to retire with a leg injury after sustaining an injury against Norwich City. He returned north and for a period was working at Leyland Motor Works in Lancashire, often going to watch the Swans when they played in the county. During WW1 he made guest appearances for Preston North End.

4. EDWARDS, Christian (CHRIS) Nicholas Howells

Birthplace: Caerphilly, 23/11/1975
Ht: 6ft-2ins, **Wt:** 12st-8lbs
Swans debut: v. Rhyl (h) WC-4, 7/12/1994

Swansea City Career Statistics						
Season	League	FLC	FAC	WC	AWS	P/Offs
1994/95	9			1+1		
1995/96	36+2/2gls	2	1		3	
1996/97	36	1	2		2	3
1997/98	32/2gls	2	1			
Total	113+2/4gls	5	4	1+1	5	3

Career:
Swansea City (from trainee in 20/7/1994)
Nottingham Forest (£175,000 signed in 26/3/1998)
   P/lge 44+10/3gls, FLC 1, FAC 1
Bristol City (loan in 11/12/1998) lge 3
Oxford United (loan in 24/2/2000) lge 5/1gls
Crystal Palace (loan in 16/11/2001) lge 9
Tranmere Rovers (loan in 17/9/2002) lge 12, FLC 1, FAC 2,
   Others 2
Oxford United (loan in 17/1/2003) lge 5+1
Bristol Rovers (signed in 3/7/2003) lge 79+5/2gls, FLC 3, FAC 3,
   Others 5

Honours: Wales Sch, Yth, U-21–7, 'B'–2, Full–1, West Wales
Senior Cup Winner–1995

A big no nonsense style of central defender, strong in the air,
quick on the ground, also possessing the ability to score goals at
set pieces. Usually a right sided central defender, Christian also
played at right full back earlier in his career with the Swans.
Involved with the Swans development centre whilst at school in
Caerphilly, the former Wales schoolboy international joined the
Swans as a trainee on leaving school, made youth appearances
for Wales, signing professional in July 1994. Making his Swans
debut in a Welsh Cup tie against Rhyl, he made his league debut
at Stockport County in February 1995, as a replacement for Dave
Penney, with John Ford switching to midfield. In May 1995 he
played in the West Wales Senior Cup Final win over Morriston
Town. For the next three seasons Christian became a central
figure in the Swans centre of defence, gaining Wales U-21
honours against Germany on the 10th October 1995, and making
a substitute appearance in a Full international in a friendly in
Lugano against Switzerland on the 24th March 1996. In March
1998 he played for the Welsh 'B' side against Scotland in Clyde,
and within a couple of days had signed for Premiership bound
side Nottingham Forest for £175,000. A few weeks earlier he had
enjoyed a successful trial spell at Forest. Making twelve
Premiership appearances for Forest during season 1998/99, as
well as a loan spell with Bristol City, he failed to make any
appearances during season 1999/2000, apart from a loan spell
with Oxford United. Christian finally established himself in the
Forest defence during season 2000/01 making thirty-six league
appearances, but apart from loan appearances with Crystal
Palace, Tranmere Rovers and Oxford United in January 2003
remained in the background with Forest prior to his full transfer
to Bristol Rovers in July 2003. Seasons 2003/04 and 2004/05 saw
him make a good impression in a Rovers side struggling to
make any headway in the league, earning himself numerous
Man of the Match performances, especially when facing the
Swans.

5. EDWARDS, Clifford (CLIFF)

Birthplace: Carmarthen, 4/12/1928
Ht: 5ft-10ins, **Wt:** 11st-4lbs
Swans debut: v. Huddersfield Town (a), 25/12/1952

Swansea Town Career Statistics

Season	League	WC
1952/53	1	
1953/54		1
Total	1	1

Career:
Loughor Rovers
Grovesend Welfare
Swansea Town (signed in October 1951)
Llanelly (signed in 2/6/1954)
Caerau Athletic (signed in September 1956)

Honours: West Wales Senior Cup Winner–1954

A goalkeeper who signed for the Swans after impressing in a
Charity Match, playing for Loughor Rovers against the Swans.
Attended Gorseinon Elementary School as a young boy, signing
for his local club Loughor Rovers before graduating to Welsh
League football with Grovesend Welfare. Signing for the Swans,
initially as an amateur in October 1951, he was understudy to
Johnny King, and following the signing of Gwyn Groves, shared
the reserve team position with Groves. The 1952/53 season saw
King and Groves share goalkeeping duties in the Swans' first
team, but on 25th December 1952, Cliff received his first team
call up for a league fixture at Huddersfield Town, in what was
to be his only league appearance for the Swans. His only other
first team appearance came during the following season in a
Welsh Cup tie at Newport County. He was released by the
Swans in May 1954, joining Southern League side Llanelly, and
taking employment in Gorseinon's 3M's factory. After two
seasons at Stebonheath Park with the Reds, he joined Welsh
League side Caerau Athletic in early September 1956, the only
professional in the club's playing squad. A glandular illness saw
Cliff forced to retire from the game. During his career with the
Swans, Cliff won a West Wales Senior Cup Medal, beating
Llanelly in the Final in May 1954, and after joining the 'Reds'
gained a second West Wales Senior Cup Medal, this time beating
the Swans in the Final.

6. EDWARDS, EVAN JENKIN

Birthplace: Bedlinog, 14/12/1896. **Died:** 1958
Ht: 5ft-7½ins, **Wt:** 11st-0lbs
Swans debut: v. Sheffield Wednesday (a), 10/10/1925

Swansea Town Career Statistics

Season	League	WC
1925/26	11/1gls	1
Total	11/1gls	1

Career:
Bedlinog
Merthyr Town (amateur in 1919, professional in July 1920)
   lge 80/10gls
Wolverhampton Wanderers (signed in 12/5/1923) lge 70/3gls
Mid-Rhondda United (signed in July 1925)
Swansea Town (£175 signed in 8/10/1925)
Northampton Town (signed in 23/7/1926) lge 10/2gls
Halifax Town (signed in September 1927) lge 0
Ebbw Vale
Darlington (signed in August 1928) lge 25/3gls, FAC 3
Clapton Orient (signed in September 1929) lge 4

Honours: Wales Amateur–1, Third Division North
Champions–1924

Starting his career with hometown side Bedlinog, he made his name initially as an amateur with Merthyr Town prior to the club entering the Football League in 1920, becoming a consistent goalscorer with both Merthyr and later with Wolverhampton Wanderers. Earlier he had made an appearance for the Welsh Amateur team against England during the 1919/20 season whilst at Penydarren Park with Merthyr. With Wolves he made appearances during their Third Division North Championship season of 1923/24. Although signed from Welsh League side Mid-Rhondda, Wolves had an interest in the player, with the Swans paying Wolves £275 for his transfer in 8/10/1925. A comment made by the Swans manager Joe Bradshaw at the time was, 'Like all good sprinters, he thinks more of his ankles than football at present.' A speedy outside left, the former Merthyr Town winger was unable to oust his former Merthyr team mate Nicholas from a regular left wing position at the Vetch Field. He made his Swans debut two days after signing, and although he played in 8 consecutive league matches, when Nicholas was available he remained on the sidelines. Edwards signed for Third Division South side Northampton Town in July 1926, one of several left wingers tried during the season, but although starting as first choice, once he had lost his place was unable to regain his place in the side. The following season after a transfer to Third Division North Halifax Town, failed to make an appearance, returning to South Wales before the end of the season to sign for Welsh League side Ebbw Vale. He returned to League action for the 1928/29 season, signing for Third Division North side Darlington, but after playing in the first twenty league games, the outside left only played five more games before he left the club to finish his professional career with Clapton Orient. His appearances for Orient all came in the 1929/30 season, and he remained at the club for a further two seasons, often assisting with coaching duties.

7. EDWARDS, GEORGE

Birthplace: Treherbert, 2/12/1920
Ht: 5ft-8ins, **Wt:** 11st-0lbs
Swans debut: v. Tranmere Rovers (h), 10/4/1939

Swansea Town Career Statistics	
Season	League
1938/39	2
Total	2

Career:
Swansea Town (signed as amateur in May 1938)
Birmingham City (signed in July 1944) lge 84/9gls
Cardiff City (£12,000 signed in December 1948) lge 196/36gls

Honours: Wales Amateur–1, Full–12, Football League South Champions–1946, Second Division Champions–1948

Moving from Treherbert to Pembrokeshire at the age of six, George Edwards attended Stepaside Junior and Narberth Grammar Schools, played for Pembrokeshire side Kilgetty, and had a trial at the Vetch Field just days before the start of the 1936/37 season, at the age of fifteen, making regular reserve team appearances prior to his starting in Swansea University in September 1938. Capped at Amateur level for Wales at Cheltenham against England in January 1939, also playing for the University and the Swans reserve teams, he made his league debut whilst still an amateur at outside left in April 1939 against Tranmere Rovers, playing in the next match a few days later against Plymouth Argyle at the Vetch Field. Following the outbreak of the Second World War, and competitive football suspended, Edwards played a couple of seasons with the Swans in Regional South West Football prior to his joining the RAF in 1941. A talented cricketer, during his time at RAF Wellsbourne, playing at inside forward for the RAF, he was spotted by Coventry City manager Harry Storer, and made guest appearances for City in season 1943/44. A good provider from the left flank, possessing a supreme left foot, in July 1944 he joined Birmingham City, making appearances in the 1945/46 Football League South Championship success, and when the Football League was resumed after the war, the club's Second Division Championship success in season 1947/48, also gaining his first full international cap for Wales against Scotland in Wrexham on the 19th October 1946. George made a further five international appearances whilst at St. Andrews with City before returning to South Wales to sign for Cardiff City in December 1948 for £12,000. In April 1949 he was included in an F.A.W. Touring party that played international matches against Portugal, Belgium and Switzerland at the end of the season. He had continued his education whilst at St. Andrews, gained his M.A. at Birmingham University, with his main thesis writing on the Pembrokeshire Coal Field. He later taught Geography at Saltley Grammar School. After returning to South Wales to sign for Cardiff City, he made almost two hundred league appearances for the 'Bluebirds' on the left wing, with the occasional game at left half back as cover. George was an influential figure in the 'Bluebirds' promotion to the First Division in season 1951/52, as well as gaining a further six international caps for Wales, and after his retirement in 1955, he went to work for the Mobil Oil Company, attaining the position of Regional Manager for Wales and the West Country. In May 1957 he became a Director of Cardiff City, serving the club for twenty-five years, wrote articles for the Empire News and also had an involvement with the BBC during the company's formative years covering Football in Wales. George later became involved with the Sports Council of Wales, set up by the Labour Party in 1965, later becoming vice-chairman.

8. ELWELL, Terence (TERRY) Thomas

Birthplace: Newport, 13/4/1926. **Died:** Newport, 21/8/2004
Ht: 5ft-11ins, **Wt:** 12st-9lbs
Swans debut: v. Millwall (a), 12/3/1949

Swansea Town Career Statistics

Season	League	FAC	WC
1948/49	11		2
1949/50	28		3
1950/51	9	1	1
1951/52	14	2	1
Total	62	3	7

Career:
Newport County (amateur)
Barry Town
Swansea Town (signed in August 1948)
Swindon Town (£1,250 signed in July 1952) lge 61, FAC 2
Lovells Athletic (signed in 9/7/1954)
Abergavenny Thursday (signed in 1958)

Honours: Third Division South Champions–1949, Welsh Cup Winner 1950

A product of Newport Junior football, and previously an amateur in Newport County's reserve side during season 1945/46, he then joined Southern League side Barry Town, prior to arriving at the Vetch Field in August 1948. A steady full back, who could operate in either full back positions, Terry was a good tackler, and always tried to use the ball out from defence. Deputised for Rory Keane at left full back for his debut, but made the remainder of his appearances that season at right full back instead of Jim Feeney as the Swans won the Championship of the Third Division South. At the end of the season he played in the Welsh Cup Final defeat by Merthyr at Ninian Park. The 1949/50 season saw him have his best run in the first team, making twenty-eight league appearances, and this time win a Welsh Cup Winners medal when the Swans beat Wrexham 4-1. Despite starting both the 1950/51 & 1951/52 seasons in the opening matches of both seasons, he failed to command a regular place in either season, and in July 1952 was sold to Swindon Town for £1,250. He left Swindon Town in the 1954 close season, joining Southern League side Lovells Athletic, and in 1958 joined Welsh League side Abergavenny, remaining a player at the club into the 1960's.

9. EMMANUEL, John GARY

Birthplace: Swansea, 1/2/1954
Ht: 5ft-9ins, **Wt:** 11st-0lbs
Swans debut: v. Blackpool (a), 31/8/1985

Career:
Birmingham City (from apprentice in July 1971) lge 61+10/6gls
Bristol Rovers (loan in December 1978, £50,000 in 29/1/1979) lge 59+6/2gls
Swindon Town (signed in July 1981) lge 109+2/8gls
Newport County (signed in July 1984) lge 12
Bristol City (non-contract signed in August 1985) lge 2
Swansea City (signed in August 1985)
Merthyr Tydfil (signed in July 1988)
Ton Pentre (signed in December 1988)

Swansea City Career Statistics

Season	League	FLC	FAC	WC	FRT
1985/86	38+2/3gls		2	4/1gls	4
1986/87	44/2gls	4	5		2/1gls
1987/88	22+5		2	1	2
Total	104+7/5gls	4	9	5/1gls	8/1gls

Honours: Wales U-23–1, West Wales Senior Cup Winner–1987

Gary Emmanuel followed in the footsteps of his father Len, and uncle Tom in wearing the white shirt of the Swans, but only after making over 250 league appearances for Birmingham City, Bristol Rovers, Swindon Town, Newport County and Bristol City, unlike his family who started their professional playing career at the Vetch Field with the Swans. A former Dynevor and Swansea schoolboy player, he left school to join Birmingham City as an apprentice in 1971, and made his league debut in the old First Division at Stoke City on the 11th January 1975, scoring his first goal in his next outing for the Blues. In 1975 Gary made an appearance for the Welsh U-23 side against Scotland. Not noted for his goalscoring prowess from midfield, one of the goals he scored during his career, at Filbert Street against Leicester City during the 1976/77 season, was featured on BBC TV's Match of the Day, Goal of the Month competition. Midway through his fifth season as a professional at St. Andrews he was involved in a record breaking transfer fee of £50,000, when he was signed by Bristol Rovers manager Bobby Campbell, initially on loan, dropping down to the Second Division. During his three seasons at Eastville he played against the Swans in consecutive seasons in the Second Division, enjoying a 4-1 Boxing Day victory in 1979/80, with Republic of Ireland international Miah Dennehy scoring a hat-trick, and the following season scoring at the Vetch Field for the Rovers in a 2-1 defeat. In the 1981 close season, before he was able to kick a ball in the Third Division for Rovers, he was involved in a player exchange transfer, which saw him join Swindon Town, with Brian Williams moving in the opposite direction. Joining Newport County in July 1984 under manager Colin Addison, twelve months later, Gary joined a select band of players when he signed for Bristol City in August 1985 on a non-contract basis. Two weeks later, and after just two league games for City, he joined the Swans after being offered a permanent contract by manager John Bond. With Bristol City recovering from serious financial problems, little did he know that within three months the Swans would go bust, and manager John Bond would be sacked by the Official Receiver! Despite relegation at the end of his first season at the Vetch Field, eventually, with a new management team of Terry Yorath, and the experienced Tommy Hutchison working minor miracles on the playing side, the fortunes of the club on the field turned, with promotion via the Play Off's achieved at the end of the 1987/88 season, a season which was to prove to be Gary's last in the Football League. In May 1987 he was included in the Swans side that beat Briton Ferry Athletic to win the West Wales Senior Cup. It was to be another back problem which would eventually affect his movement on the pitch, and eventually force his retirement from the professional game. Following a short period at Penydarren Park with Merthyr, and one season with Ton Pentre, Gary had his first taste in a managerial role when he took over from Wyndham Evans at Llanelli on a caretaker basis between March 1991 to June 1991 for six months. With Llanelli he followed in his uncle Tom's footsteps by captaining the Reds, and also his father Len who was a great favourite at Stebonheath Park. A further two seasons with Haverfordwest as player manager saw him eventually sever all active ties with football, in either a managerial or coaching capacity. Working in the Post Office for a number of years, Gary has on occasions been involved as a scout for Preston North End, checking out players whenever they appear at the Vetch Field against the Swans.

10. EMMANUEL, David Leonard (LEN)

Birthplace: Treboeth, Swansea, 3/9/1917
Ht: 5ft-10ins, **Wt:** 11st-10lbs
Swans debut: v. Nottingham Forest (a), 2/10/1937

Swansea Town Career Statistics		
Season	League	WC
1937/38	25/1gls	3/3gls
1938/39	20	2
1946/47	4	
Total	49/1gls	5/3gls

Career:
Swansea Town (signed in April 1936)
Newport County (signed in May 1947) lge 33/7gls
Kidderminster Harriers (signed in July 1948) lge 79/5gls
Llanelly (signed in 17/6/1950) Total Apps 171/16gls
Carmarthen Town (signed in 20/7/1954)

Honours: Wales Sch, Regional League Cup Winner–1943, West Wales Senior Cup Winner–1952

Brought up in the Treboeth area of Swansea, Len played for the Welsh Schoolboy side, prior to joining the Swans from local football in May 1936. He made his league debut in October 1937 as a replacement for Cyril Pearce, playing in the same team as his brother Tom at Nottingham Forest, with Len scoring for the Swans in a 2-1 defeat. He retained his place for the next league fixture, but following the return of Pearce, reverted to a left half back role, also playing a couple of games during his first season in the league at left full back. His elder brother Tom, was regularly used in the left full back position, but when he was released and signed for Southampton shortly after the start of the 1938/39 season, Len commanded a regular place in the Swans starting line-up for the second half of the season. At the end of his first season at the Vetch Field he played in the Welsh Cup final against Shrewsbury Town which ended in a 2-2 draw, with the replay carried over until the next season, but did not feature in the replay. He played occasionally in war-time football with the Swans, and towards the end of the 1942/43 season scored in the second leg of the Regional League West Cup Final win over Lovells Athletic at the Vetch Field. He also made guest appearances for Luton Town (1939/40), Swindon

Town (1939/40), Bristol City (1940/41), Wolverhampton Wanderers (1942/43) and Walsall (December 1942), and when the Football League was resumed made occasional appearances in the Swans line-up for season 1946/47. In March 1947, shortly before the end of the season he joined Newport County, who unfortunately were unable to avoid relegation from the Second Division. Prior to the start of the 1948/49 season he joined Southern League side Kidderminster Harriers, staying there for two seasons, before returning to South West Wales to join Llanelly who had been successful in their application to rejoin the Southern League. Len made his debut for the Harriers on the 21st August 1948 at home to Chingford in the Southern League. In May 1952 he was included in the Llanelly side that beat the Swans to win the West Wales Senior Cup. On the 20th July 1954 he was appointed player manager of Carmarthen Town, recently elected to the Welsh League Second Division. One of the finest clubmen to play for the Reds, he was regarded extremely highly at Stebonheath Park, being an automatic choice for all four seasons. Winning the Welsh League Second Division Championship whilst at Richmond Park, he remained at the club until the early 1960's, working also as a wharehouse manager for the Co-op in Swansea up until his retirement. In later years he has been hospitalised with Alzheimers Disease.

11. EMMANUEL, Thomas (TOM) D.

Birthplace: Treboeth, Swansea, 1/8/1915. **Died:** December 1997
Ht: 5ft-10ins, **Wt:** 11st-8lbs
Swans debut: v. Newcastle United (a), 11/4/1936

Swansea Town Career Statistics			
Season	League	FAC	WC
1935/36	3		
1936/37	4		2
1937/38	38/1gls	1	3
1938/39	1		
Total	46/1gls	1	5

Career:
ICI Works FC
Swansea Town (signed in 31/8/1935)
Southampton (£2,200 signed in 21/9/1938) lge 36
Milford United (signed in August 1946)
Llanelly (signed in September 1946)

Honours: West Wales Senior Cup Winner–1948, West Wales Transport XI

Elder brother of Len Emmanuel, Tom signed for the Swans initially in 1935 from local football side ICI Works team, where he had been spotted by manager Neil Harris. Tom deputised for veteran left full back Wilf Milne when he made his debut at

Newcastle United in April 1936, missed the following two league games, but returned to play in the remaining two league games of season 1935/36 at left full back. Despite starting the 1936/37 season at left full back, he lost his place to Tommy Caldwell, making just one more appearance in April 1937. The 1937/38 season saw Tom make the left full back position his own missing just four league games, and scoring his only league goal, in a 1-0 win over Bury at the Vetch Field. At the end of the season he also played alongside his brother in the Welsh Cup Final draw with Shrewsbury Town, with the replay held over until the next season. By the time of the replayed cup final, he had joined Second Division Southampton, and during season 1938/39 played in both league fixtures against the Swans. Everton had also expressed an interest in signing him, and the fee Southampton paid the Swans was the club's highest at the time for a full back. During the war he made guest appearances for Swindon Town (1939/40) and Wrexham (August 1940). He resumed his career with Southampton after the war, but after failing to add to his first team appearances at the Dell, and being placed on the transfer list at £1,000, returned to South Wales to sign for Welsh League side Milford United initially, signing for Llanelly a month later in September 1946, and was appointed captain at Stebonheath Park from 1946 to 1948, playing in the 'Reds' side that beat Briton Ferry Athletic in May 1948 to win the West Wales Senior Cup. Tom worked as an Inspector on the buses with South Wales Transport up until his retirement, prior to his death in December 1997. In March 1950 he captained a West Wales Transport XI at the Vetch Field against a South Wales Police XI, captained by former Swans player Reuben Simons.

12. EVANS, BRIAN Clifford

Birthplace: Brynmawr, 2/12/1942. **Died:** Swansea 26/2/2003
Ht: 5ft-7½ins, **Wt:** 9st-12½lbs
Swans debut: v. Derby County (h), 3/9/1963

Swansea Town/City Career Statistics					
Season	League	FLC	FAC	WC	ECWC
1963/64	29/4gls	1	6/1gls	1	
1964/65	30/3gls	3	4	3/2gls	
1965/66	29/7gls		1	6	
1966/67	42/10gls	4/1gls	3/1gls	1	2
1967/68	36/3gls	1	4/1gls	2	
1968/69	42/4gls	4/1gls	4	8/1gls	
1969/70	43+1/8gls	2	3/1gls	4/4gls	
1970/71	33+1/7gls	2	3/3gls	1/2gls	
1971/72	37/5gls	1	2		
1972/73	31+1/6gls	2	1	2	
Total	352+3/57gls	20/2gls	31/7gls	28/9gls	2

Career:
Abergavenny Thursdays
Swansea Town (£750 signed in July 1963)
Hereford United (£7,000 signed in 24/8/1973) lge 44+4/9gls
Bath City (signed in August 1975)
Llanelli (signed in August 1976)

Honours: Wales U-23–2, Full–7, Welsh Cup Winner 1966, Welsh League Premier Division Champions–1977, 1978, West Wales Senior Cup Winner–1965

Born in Brynmawr, Brian Evans played rugby and soccer for Crickhowell Juniors before joining Abergavenny Thursdays as a part-time professional at the age of 17, and even at that early age it was obvious that a player of his class would not remain in the Welsh League for very long, with his dazzling wing displays attracting scouts from many league clubs. After being signed by Swans manager Trevor Morris for £750 in July 1963, he made his league debut two months later against Derby County, going on to become an integral member of not only the Swans side that reached the 1963/64 FA Cup semi-finals, but also a major influence in the 1969/70 Fourth Division Promotion winning team under Roy Bentley. It took him just six league games to register his first league goal, scoring also in his next league outing. By the end of his first season in the Football League he had helped the Swans reach the semi-finals of the FA Cup competition, with injury unfortunately forcing him to miss the game against Preston North End at Villa Park. In May 1965 he was included in the Swans side that beat Llanelli to win the West Wales Senior Cup. Awarded two U-23 caps for Wales early in his Vetch Field career against England and Scotland, he made his first appearance for Wales at Full level on the 13th October 1972 at the Vetch Field against Finland, retaining his place for the next international game against Czechoslovakia. A tricky winger, capable of causing havoc to defences on either flank, he was not only an accurate crosser of the ball, but had an eye for goalscoring opportunities, as his 57 goals for the Swans will testify. Disappointment at the end of season 1965/66 with relegation to the Third Division, Brian played in the end of season Welsh Cup Final win over Chester, playing in both European Cup Winners Cup ties against Slavia Sofia the following season. That season saw Brian reach double figures for goals scored for the first time, scoring twelve league and cup goals. Despite some disappointing seasons at the Vetch Field after the European venture, Brian continued to provide much needed flair from the flanks, played in the 1969 Welsh Cup Final defeat by Cardiff City, and in season 1969/70 the combination of Evans and the veteran Lennie Allchurch on either flank, supplied enough ammunition for the Swans strikeforce of Williams and Gwyther to secure the club's promotion to the Third Division. By the time of the end of the 1972/73 season, with the Swans back in the Fourth Division, financial problems saw the club obliged to unload a number of players, with Evans joining newly promoted Third Division side Hereford United for £7,000. At Edgar Street, Brian made his seventh and final appearance for Wales against Poland in 1974 in front of 120,000 fans at Chorzow, becoming United's first Football League player to play in an international. Signed by Colin Addison, his first season at Edgar Street saw Brian score on his debut against Grimsby Town, and also finish top goalscorer in the league with eight goals. Following a change of management at United, at the end of his second season he was released, joining Southern League Premier Division side Bath City on a free transfer in 1975. Twelve months later he joined Welsh League side Llanelli, winning the League Championship, then finishing his playing career with Haverfordwest and Pontardawe Athletic. He retired from football in 1977, continued to live in Killay employed in his own painting and decorating business. The father of current Swans' Physiotherapist Richard Evans, 60 year-old Brian passed away at the city's Singleton Hospital on the 26th February 2003 after a short battle with cancer.

13. EVANS, James Henry (JIMMY)

Birthplace: Rhyl, 29/12/1894. **Died:** Rhuddlan, 25/4/1975
Ht: 5ft-7ins, **Wt:** 11st-10lbs
Swans debut: v. Middlesbrough (h), 12/9/1925

Swansea Town Career Statistics	
Season	*League*
1925/26	7
Total	7

Career:
Rhyl
Ton Pentre
Southend United (signed in August 1919) lge 99/14gls, FAC 7/1gls
Burnley (signed in April 1923) lge 20
Swansea Town (£400 signed in July 1925)
Rhyl (signed in October 1926)

Honours: Wales Full–4

Experienced Welsh International left full back who commanded a £400 transfer fee when he joined the Swans in September 1925 from Burnley, after scoring 14 goals from 96 league matches for Southend United between 1920 and 1922. He made his debut instead of Langford at left full back, played the next five league matches, but was then not utilised following the return of Wilf Milne. Signed by Joe Bradshaw for the Swans new season in the Second Division, following their Championship success the previous term, Bradshaw later said of the player that he was not that impressed, commenting, 'Has put on a lot of weight since commencing training, and in the opinion of our trainer, will continue to do so.' Formerly with North Wales side Rhyl, after joining Southend United from Welsh League side Ton Pentre, he made his first appearance for Wales at left back against Scotland in Wrexham on the 4th February 1922, playing in the next two internationals that season against England and Ireland. After almost one hundred league appearances for Southend he joined First Division Burnley in 1922. Jimmy still holds the record at Roots Hall with Southend United as the only full back to finish a season as top goalscorer. During the dismal 1921/22 season he scored ten league goals, all penalties, with his nearest challenger scoring four. He was de-registered by the Swans in July 1925, returning to play for Rhyl. He later became trainer, and also worked in the club's social club. In 1931 he played for Kinmel Bay United. He was a nephew of former Manchester United player Harry Stafford.

14. EVANS, KEITH

Birthplace: Trealaw, 15/9/1953
Ht: 5ft-9ins, **Wt:** 11st-7lbs
Swans debut: v. Bury (a), 1/5/1971

Swansea City Career Statistics		
Season	*League*	*FAC*
1970/71	2	
1971/72	8	2
1972/73	2	1
Total	12	3

Career:
Swansea City (from apprentice in July 1971)

Ton Pentre (signed in close season 1973)
Ferndale (signed in close season 1975)

Honours: Wales Yth–1

Born in the Rhondda Valley, Keith Evans attended Trealaw Secondary Modern School, and after twelve months in college doing a painting and decorating course, signed for the Swans as an apprentice professional. Keith made one appearance for the Welsh Youth side at home against the Republic of Ireland, with the return leg being cancelled because of the problems in the country. Signing professional in July 1971, Keith made his debut at the end of season 1970/71 at Bury along with a number of promising youngsters from the club's Football Combination side who were also given their first team opportunity. Following an injury to Herbie Williams midway through the 1971/72 season Keith was given a four game spell in central defence in the Swans Third Division side alongside the experienced Alan Williams. Although short for a centre half, he did possess the ability to win ball in aerial challenges, and was particularly quick on the ground. At the end of the season he returned to the first team, playing in the last four league games of the season, linking up this time with Geoff Thomas in central defence. The following season, he made just two league appearances, also playing in the Swans side that were beaten by non-league Margate in the First Round of the FA Cup competition. Following a change of management he was released at the end of the season by Harry Gregg, and joined Welsh League side Ton Pentre. For the remainder of his playing career he switched between Ton Pentre and Ferndale, before taking over as player manager at Ferndale. At the end of season 1989/90 he led Ferndale into the Abacus Welsh League National Division, finishing runners up to Sully in the Premier League. Since leaving the professional game. Keith has returned to his painting and decorating trade, and is currently self employed in the Rhondda area.

15. EVANS, Kenneth (KEN) Phillip

Birthplace: Swansea, 17/7/1931. **Died:** Swansea, 27/5/2000
Swans debut: v. Leeds United (a), 22/1/1955

Swansea Town Career Statistics			
Season	*League*	*FAC*	*WC*
1954/55	7	3	2
1955/56	1		
1956/57	6		
Total	14	3	2

Career:
Swansea Town (part-time in June 1950, professional in 26/10/1954)
Walsall (signed in August 1957) lge 2

Yeovil Town (signed in close season 1958)
Pembroke Borough (signed in August 1960)

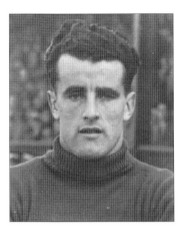

Honours: Football Combination Second Division
Champions–1955

A product of local football signed from Swansea League team,
South Wales Builders, Ken served an apprenticeship in the
Building Trade on leaving school, worked on the construction of
the new Townhill Council Estate and signed part-time for the
Swans in June 1950, signing professional forms in October 1954
after completing his National Service in the Army. He had
created a good impression in London Combination matches for
the Swans, and made his league debut a few months later in
January 1955. Not a particularly tall goalkeeper, he was however
extremely athletic. Very much a reserve team goalkeeper at the
Vetch Field, he made regular appearances in the Swans' reserve
side that won the Football Combination Second Division
Championship in 1955. When he did eventually make his Swans
debut, it was at a time however, when the team was more
renowned for their goalscoring, rather than their defending,
with many games high scoring affairs for a number of seasons.
Also, after signing for the Swans he had to contend with
competition from Canning, King, Parry and Groves for the
number one jersey. After making his league debut against Leeds
United in January 1955, apart from two league games he
remained as the Swans first choice keeper until early April,
when Johnny King returned to action. With just one league
appearance the following season, the last league game against
Rotherham United, the 1956/57 season saw Evans make six
league appearances, again as cover for King. His first
appearance of the season ironically came at Millmoor against
Rotherham United, with Johnny King being pressed into action
as a centre forward. In August 1957 he left the Vetch Field to
sign for Third Division South side Walsall, making his debut in a
2-1 home defeat by QPR on the 26th October, and playing in a
second 2-1 defeat, this time at Exeter City on the 2nd November
1957. The arrival of big John Savage a few weeks later meant
that he was unlikely to make any further appearances, and Ken
was released at the end of the season. Signing for non-league
side Yeovil Town in the 1958 close season, he was re-united with
former Swans' team mate, keeper Dai Jones, contesting the
number one jersey for the two seasons he played at Huish. His
first season with the club saw him make twenty-three
appearances. Returning to the Swansea area after being released
in May 1960, he joined forces with Pembroke Borough by the
start of season 1960, and finished his playing career in the
Swansea Senior League alongside Mel Charles for Cwmfelin in
the early 1970's.

16. EVANS, KEVIN Aherne

Birthplace: Carmarthen, 16/12/1980
Ht: 6ft-2ins, **Wt:** 12st-10lbs
Swans debut: v. Lincoln City (h), 4/2/2000

Swansea City Career Statistics		
Season	League	FAWP
1999/2000	1+1	1
Total	1+1	1

Career:
Leeds United (from trainee in 13/1/1998)
Swansea City (loan in 17/1/2000)
Cardiff City (signed in 31/8/2000) lge 24+6/3gls, FLC 1,
    FAC 3/2gls, Others 0+1
Merthyr Tydfil (signed in September 2002) Total Apps 87/13gls
Newport County (signed in June 2004)
Carmarthen Town (signed in November 2004)

Honours: Wales Yth, U-21–4, Wales Semi-Professional XI,
Dr. Martens Western Division Champions–2003

Former Carmarthen schoolboy who joined Leeds United as a
trainee from school, was signed on a month's loan by Swans
manager John Hollins from Premiership side Leeds United on
the 17th January 2000, making his debut the following night in a
Welsh Premier Cup tie at Inter Cardiff alongside veteran Keith
Walker. With injury and suspension doubts regarding the Swans
regular central defensive partners Jason Smith and Matthew
Bound, he made his league debut as substitute for Smith against
Lincoln City, making his full debut a few days later at
Cheltenham Town. He impressed in a central defensive role, but
returned to Leeds United before the end of his second month on
loan. Released by United, he was signed by Bobby Gould for
Cardiff City in August 2000 on a free transfer, and after
switching to a midfield role in pre-season matches, made thirty
league appearances, scoring three goals, during the club's
promotion campaign, when they finished runners up to
Brighton & Hove Albion in the Third Division. He failed to
make an appearance in Cardiff's Division Two side the
following season, and was released by the club shortly after the
start of the 2002/03 season, joining Dr Martens side Merthyr
Tydfil. At Elland Road he had made his first appearance for the
Welsh U-21 side in Italy as substitute for Earnshaw on the 4th
June 1999, and four days later, starting against Denmark, scored
in a 2-1 defeat. He made two further U-21 appearances whilst on
the staff at Ninian Park, Cardiff. A successful period at
Penydarren Park, with Merthyr winning the Western Division
Championship at the end of the season, and gaining promotion
to the Premier Division of the Dr. Martens League, saw interest
in him by Nationwide League Second Division side Cheltenham
Town boss Bobby Gould who wanted to take him on trial.

Unfortunately for Kevin, with the new rules by the governing body FIFA stating that he would require international clearance and a transfer from Merthyr before he could play in a competitive game for Cheltenham Town, he was unable to take up the trial offer. In May 2003 he was a member of the Welsh Semi-Professional squad that played in the end of season Home International competition in West Wales against England, Scotland, Northern Ireland. He continued to be a consistent performer for Merthyr Tydfil in season 2003/04. In June 2004 he joined Dr. Martens rivals Newport County, but in early November was released by the club, and a few weeks later joined Carmarthen Town.

17. EVANS, Michael (MICKY)

Birthplace: West Bromwich, 3/8/1946
Ht: 6ft-0ins, **Wt:** 12st-6lbs
Swans debut: v. Shrewsbury Town (h), 26/12/1972

Swansea City Career Statistics				
Season	*League*	*FLC*	*FAC*	*WC*
1972/73	18/1gls			
1973/74	39/2gls	2	1	1
1974/75	35/3gls		2	4
Total	92/6gls	2	3	5

Career:
Vono Sports Club
Walsall (signed in May 1964) lge 229+2/7gls
Swansea City (signed in December 1972)
Crewe Alexandra (signed in July 1975) lge 62/4gls
Worcester City (signed in August 1977)

A West Bromwich youngster who joined Third Division Walsall initially as an amateur from local Midlands junior side Vono Sports in 1963, turning professional in May 1964. Strong, fearless, and an uncompromising left sided full back, he made his league debut in a 4-2 home defeat by Hull City on the 17th December 1965, going on to make 263 league and cup appearances for the 'Saddlers' prior to his being signed by Manager Harry Gregg on an initial loan basis on the 24th December 1972, with the transfer being made permanent on the 2nd January 1973. Making his Swans debut in a 2-0 home defeat on Boxing Day 1972 against Shrewsbury Town, he remained in the Swans side until the end of the season, barring missing matches through suspensions. A rugged left full back, difficult to knock off the ball, and capable of scoring his share of goals, Micky also had a reputation as a physical player, who collected his share of bookings and red cards during his period at the Vetch Field. With Harry Gregg resigning his position at the Vetch Field in January 1975, at the end of season 1974/75 when

Micky was released by the Swans, he linked up a second time with Gregg at Crewe Alexandra two months later. In eighteen months at Gresty Road, Micky missed few matches, and during a 3-0 defeat at the Vetch Field in January 1977 he suffered an injury, forcing him out for the remainder of the season, and being released in May 1977 by the club. Signing for Worcester City in August 1977, he later played for Stourbridge, Stafford Rangers, Halesowen Town and Rushall Olympic, also playing for the Midland All Stars team in Charity games. In 1992 he won an Over 35's medal playing for the West Bromwich Albion over 35's side. In recent years Micky has been involved with a number of Midland clubs as a scout.

18. EVANS, Philip (PHIL)

Birthplace: Swansea, 14/5/1957
Ht: 6ft-0½ins, **Wt:** 12st-0lbs
Swans debut: v. Stockport County (a), 28/11/1975

Swansea City Career Statistics		
Season	*League*	*WC*
1975/76	10	1
Total	10	1

Career:
Swansea City (signed in August 1975)
Bridgend Town (signed prior to start of season 1976/77)
Merthyr Tydfil (signed prior to start of season 1987/88)
    Conf 50+11, ECWC 2

Honours: Wales Semi-Pro International, Boys Club of Wales, Sth Lge Midland Division Champions–1980, Sth Lge Title Winner–1980, Sth Lge. Midland Div Champions–1988, Beazer Homes Lge Premier Div Champions–1989

Young central defender who played for the Swans as an amateur whilst working as an engineer with British Telecom in Swansea. During his last year in school, at the age of fifteen he played in the Swans Football Combination side, and signed part-time professional forms for the Swans at the age of seventeen. Educated at Cwmglas School and then Dynevor he played in various Swansea Schoolboys sides with Robbie James and Steve Thomas, and when playing for Brynmill Colts gained representation for the Boys Club of Wales. In season 1970/71 he played in the Schoolboys side that won the Welsh Shield. He made his league debut, replacing Dave Bruton in central defence at Stockport County in November 1975, played in the next seven league matches, but was then not utilised until the end of the season, when Bruton was selected as a striker, with Evans playing in defence. Preferring to continue his career with British Telecom, he left the Vetch Field at the end of the season joining

Welsh League side Afan Lido, and then linked up for the first time with manager Lyn Jones at Bridgend Town, then followed him to Merthyr Tydfil, prior to start of season 1987/88. At Bridgend Town the club won the Southern League Midland Division Championship in season 1980, winning the Southern League Title in the Play Off against Dorchester Town. After joining Merthyr, he was also involved when the club won the Southern League Midland Division Championship in 1988, and the following year when the club won the Championship of the Premier Division. He captained the Wales Semi-Professional side during his career, and although he did not play for Merthyr in their Welsh Cup Final success over Newport County in 1987, he did play in both legs of European Cup Winners Cup ties against Italian side Atalanta, winning 2-1 at Penydarren Park, but losing out 2-0 in return leg in Italy. After one season in the Southern League with Barry Town, he was re-united with Lyn Jones at Inter Cardiff, finishing runners up in the League of Wales on two occasions, also making further appearances in European Football in the EUFA Cup. Returning to play and coach alongside Lyn Jones at Merthyr Tydfil, he finished his playing career at Penydarren Park, with one of his last appearances for the club in the semi-final of the Welsh Cup competition against Wrexham. Progressing his career with British Telecom, over the last ten years he has been working in the South of England and London as a Senior Manager with the company.

19. EVANS, Royston (ROY) Sidney

Birthplace: Southgate, Swansea, 5/7/1943. **Died:** Bedwellty, 20/1/1969
Ht: 5ft-7¾ ins, **Wt:** 10st-6¼ lbs
Swans debut: v. Grimsby Town (h), 17/11/1962

	Swansea Town Career Statistics				
Season	*League*	*FLC*	*FAC*	*WC*	*ECWC*
1962/63	24		2	3	
1963/64	40/2gls	2	7/1gls	2	
1964/65	22	1		2	
1965/66	42+1/4gls	1	1	8	
1966/67	45/1gls	4	3	1	2
1967/68	39+1	1	4	2	
Total	212+2/7gls	9	17/1gls	18	2

Career:
Swansea Town (signed in 25/7/1960)
Hereford United (signed in July 1968)

Honours: Wales U-23–4, Full–1, Welsh Cup Winner–1966, Football Combination Second Division Champions–1961, Welsh League First Division Champions–1962, West Wales Senior Cup Winner–1965

Originally signed for the Swans as a winger in July 1960, but converted to right full back, although on occasions he did play at left full back. By May 1961 he had made regular appearances in the Swans reserve side that won the Football Combination Second Division title, and twelve months later made appearances in the reserve side that won the Welsh League First Division Championship for the first time in eleven years. After just eight league appearances he gained his first Wales U-23 cap against England, playing further games at U-23 level against Northern Ireland, England and Scotland, and within two seasons had gained a full cap against Northern Ireland in 1964 at the Vetch Field. A classy player, dapper, dedicated and determined, having the inclination to move forward at every opportunity, he was of the breed of footballers who hated to lose. He had moulded his play on the style made popular by Blackpool and England full back Jimmy Armfield and he liked nothing better than to take part in an overlap and attack down the right flank. Given his opportunity in the Swans side in place of Alan Sanders against Grimsby Town in November 1962, Roy kept his place for the remainder of the season. Recognised as a reliable penalty taker, all his goals for the Swans came from the spot, bar one. After playing in the FA Cup semi-final defeat against Preston North End, he suffered the other side of the coin as part of the Swans side beaten by non-league side Nuneaton Borough in the F.A. Cup competition in season 1966/67. That season also saw him play in both legs for the Swans in European competition against Slavia Sofia. Another high spot during his career with the Swans was in the game against Arsenal in the F.A. Cup which attracted a record attendance to the Vetch Field of 32,796, on a day when they were desperately unlucky not to have beaten the First Division side. In May 1965 he was included in the Swans side that beat Llanelli to win the West Wales Senior Cup. Released at the end of season 1967/68, along with centre half Brian Purcell joined Southern League side Hereford United, managed at the time by John Charles. Tragically, both players were killed in a car crash on a fog bound Heads of the Valleys road near Ebbw Vale, on their way to play for Hereford in a Cup match at Nuneaton in January 1969. Roy had recently given up his job as a representative with Serck Radiators with a view to getting back into the professional game, and was also due to tour USA and Canada with a John Charles select side at the end of the season.

20. EVANS, Stephen (STEVE)

Birthplace: Caerphilly, 25/9/1980
Ht: 6ft-1ins, **Wt:** 11st-6lbs
Swans debut: v. Torquay United (a), 10/11/2001

Career:
Crystal Palace (from trainee in 31/10/1998) lge 0+6, FLC 0+1

Swansea City (loan in 9/11/2001)
Brentford (signed in 27/3/2002) lge 34+14/5gls, FLC 1+1,
    FAC 3+2, Others 4
Woking (signed in early August 2004) Conf 19+1/5gls

Swansea City Career Statistics		
Season	League	FAC
2001/02	4	2
Total	4	2

Honours: Wales Yth, U-21–2

Caerphilly born defender who joined Crystal Palace straight
from school as a trainee after previously being a schoolboy at
Ninian Park with Cardiff City, making his league debut for
Palace against Birmingham City on the 6th February 1999 as
substitute for Leon McKenzie. He made a further three
substitute appearances during the season, and for next two
seasons, was limited to just two substitute appearances for
Palace in the league. His first start in the league came during a
loan spell with the Swans in November 2001 during a 2-1 win at
Plainmoor, against Torquay United. An attacking left wing back,
Stephen made two appearances for Wales at U-21 level, his first
against Belarus on the 1st September 2000, and his second in
March 2000 against Armenia. Out of action for a long spell with
a serious knee injury, Steve possesses good ball skills, and the
ability to deliver telling crosses from the flanks, especially when
overlapping. He returned to Crystal Palace after a successful
month loan because of a new manager being appointed at
Selhurst Park. In late March 2002 he joined Second Division
Brentford on an initial loan basis, with the transfer being made
permanent shortly after, but failed to make an appearance in the
'Bees' side in their successful challenge for a Second Division
Play Off place. Making his first start as substitute for Brentford
in mid-September at Ninian Park against Cardiff City, in only
his fifth game for the 'Bees' scored two goals in a 5-0 home win
over Blackpool a few weeks later, scoring his third goal in the
last game of the season against Peterborough United. In May
2004 he was released by Brentford, and by early August had
signed a one year contract with Conference side Woking.

21. EVANS, TERRY

Birthplace: Pontypridd, 8/1/1976
Ht: 5ft-7ins, **Wt:** 11st-8lbs
Swans debut: v. Rushden & Diamonds (h), 3/11/2001

Career:
Cardiff City (from trainee in 8/7/1994) lge 12+2, FLC 2+1,
    FAC 1, Others 2+2
Barry Town (signd in February 1996) Ch Lge 10, UEFA 3+1/1gls

Swansea City (signed in 30/10/2001)
Newport County (signed in May 2003)
Grange Quins (signed in August 2004)

Swansea City Career Statistics				
Season	League	FLC	FAC	FAWP
2001/02	16		2	1
2002/03	25+2	1	1	1
Total	41+2	1	3	2

Honours: Wales U-21–4, Wales Semi-Professional XI, League of
Wales Champions–1996, 1997, 1998, 1999, 2001, League Cup
Winner–1997, 1998, 1999, 2000, Welsh Cup Winner–1997, 2001

Former Pontypridd schoolboy who joined Cardiff City as an
apprentice, making his league debut in his first season as a
professional at Bristol Rovers on the 23rd January 1994. The last
month of the season saw him adding to his first team
appearances for what was at the time a struggling 'Bluebirds'
outfit in the bottom half of the Second Division. Starting the
following season as first choice at right back for the 'Bluebirds',
disappointment came at the end of the season with relegation to
the Third Division. Overcoming a foot injury at the start of the
1995/96 season, he joined Barry Town midway through the
season on an initial loan basis, and with still a year left on his
contract with the 'Bluebirds', he eventually joined Barry on a
full time basis. Terry soon developed a reputation at Barry as a
solid full back who loved getting forward at every opportunity,
with the 'Dragons' going from strength to strength as a full time
professional outfit in the League of Wales. Terry played for the
Welsh semi-professional side during his time with the
'Dragons', adding to the four Welsh U-21 caps he gained whilst
at Ninian Park, the first as a substitute against Bulgaria in
December 1994. By the time Terry had returned to the Football
League when he signed for the Swans in late October 2001, he
had gained League of Wales Championship honours in 1996,
1997, 1998, 1999 and 2001, League Cup Winners in 1997, 1998,
1999 and 2000, Welsh Cup Winners in 1997 and 2001, also
playing in European competition, in either the Champions
League or in the EUFA Cup in six consecutive seasons. In 1997
there was an offer to return to the League with Tranmere
Rovers, but Barry manager Gary Barnett had let Tony Bird and
Dave O'Gorman join the Swans, and felt that the money they
would receive for Evans was not worth the club letting him go.
Regular European competition with the Dragons saw Evans find
the net against BVSC, also play against Dynamo Kiev, Aberdeen
and Porto. On his return to the Football League with the Swans
he linked up with his former Barry Town manager Peter
Nicholas, who was working alongside Colin Addison at the
Vetch Field, and proved to be an useful acquisition with his
ability to play in either a right back role, or on a wide, right
sided wing back position, where he was able to deliver good
crosses from the flanks when pushing forward. Unfortunately
for Terry, after making sixteen consecutive league appearances,
he was carried off at Leyton Orient with a double fracture of the
jaw following a challenge from an Orient midfielder.
He returned to action at the start of the 2002/03 season with
Nick Cusack as manager, playing in an unfamiliar central
defensive role with a three man defence. Switched to his normal
full back position following a change of management, he then
picked up a thigh strain at Oxford which sidelined him for a few
weeks, then had toe and knee injuries which limited his first
team opportunities. At the end of the season he was released by
manager Brian Flynn, and within a couple of weeks had linked
up for a third time with Peter Nicholas, this time at Dr. Martens
Premier Division side Newport County. The move to Newport
in the summer was accompanied by the chance to put his
accountancy training into practice with club sponsors Acorn
securing him employment at the Welsh Assembly, where he
continued to study and gain professional status within the
profession. In June 2004 he was released from the playing staff

at Newport County, later joining Welsh League Division One side Grange Quins in August 2004, making his debut for the club against Barry Town. Finished runners up to Ton Pentre at the end of the season, gaining promotion to the Welsh Premier League.

22. EVANS, William B. (BILLY)

Birthplace: Llanidloes, 1895
Ht: 5ft-10ins, **Wt:** 12st-0lbs
Swans debut: v. Portsmouth (a), 28/8/1920

Swansea Town Career Statistics		
Season	League	WC
1920/21	1	1
Total	1	1

Career:
Everton (signed in June 1919) lge 2
Llanelly (loan during season 1919/20)
Swansea Town (signed in 6/5/1920)
Southend United (signed in June 1921) lge 65, FAC 4
QPR (signed in August 1924) lge 17

Signed by manager Joe Bradshaw in May 1920 from First Division side Everton, making his debut for the Swans in their first ever Football League game in August 1920. Unfortunately, the 3-0 defeat at Portsmouth was to be his only league appearance for the Swans, replaced firstly by Ogley, then by Wilf Milne in the left full back position. Later in the season he did play in a Welsh Cup tie, in what was the club's reserve side, as there was a league fixture on the same day, in a 1-0 defeat at Mid-Rhondda in January 1921. Early in season 1919/20 he had a loan spell with Llanelly, and within weeks of returning to Goodison Park, made an appearance for Everton against Newcastle United in late January 1920. He joined fellow Third Division South team Southend United in June 1921 where he was to play on a more regular basis in the Football League, playing in either full back position, also playing in both games against the Swans over the next two seasons. He later signed for fellow Third Division South side QPR in 1924.

23. EVANS, WYNDHAM Edgar

Birthplace: Llanelli, 19/3/1951
Ht: 5ft-9ins, **Wt:** 12st-0lbs
Swans debut: v. Bristol Rovers (h), 10/4/1971

Swansea City Career Statistics				
Season	League	FLC	FAC	WC
1970/71	2+1			
1971/72	24+1	1	1+1	
1972/73	38/5gls		1	2
1973/74	37+2/2gls	0+2	1	1
1974/75	42/7gls	1	0+1/1gls	4
1975/76	43	2	1	3
1976/77	43	4	1	2
1977/78	46/3gls	2	4	2
1978/79	35	5	3	1
1979/80	16			
1980/81	13			5
1981/82	1			
1982/83	6	1		
1983/84	17			
1984/85	18+2	2	1	1
Total	383+6/15gls	18	13/1gls	21

Career:
Swansea City (signed in February 1971)
Llanelli (signed in August 1983)
Swansea City (signed in December 1983)
Pembroke Borough (signed in August 1985)
Llanelli (signed in August 1986)

Honours: Welsh Cup Winner–1981, West Wales Senior Cup Winner–1975

Former Llanelli Grammer School and Llanelli schoolboys defender Wyndham Evans, earlier in his career played as an amateur with Carmarthenshire League side Llanelli Steel, prior to signing as an amateur for Stoke City, making appearances for the club in their Central League side, whilst starting an apprenticeship in Llanelli as a toolmaker. A member of the Swans Football Combination side during the last years of his toolmaker apprenticeship, he turned professional with the Swans in February 1971, making his league debut as substitute for Geoff Thomas at the Vetch Field against Bristol Rovers in April 1971. A totally committed player throughout his playing career, he started as a central defender, was moved up front to lead the attack by manager Harry Gregg, but finally settled at right full back, where he often worked himself into overlap situations. He was offered a professional contract at the Vetch Field by Swans boss Roy Bentley in February 1971, along with fellow Llanelli youngster Denley Morgan. Between 1971 and 1985, Wyndham sampled the highs and lows in the game, from the re-election season of 1974/75, to making his First (Premier) Division debut at White Hart Lane against Tottenham Hotspur in May 1981, a member of the 1981 Welsh Cup Winning side when the Swans beat Hereford United, and also being involved in European Cup Winners Cup ties. His appearance at White Hart Lane saw Wyndham carried off in the second half, and he had to wait until the end of October the following season before he would make his home debut for the Swans in the top flight of football, against Southampton. In February 1974 he was a reserve for the Wales U-23 side that played in Aberdeen, and in May 1975 was included in the Swans side that beat Briton Ferry Athletic to win the West Wales Senior Cup. Given a free transfer by the Swans, he joined Llanelli as player manager and following Toshack's re-appointment as manager at the Vetch Field, Wyndham returned to the club in a player coach capacity seven months later. During his career at the Vetch Field, Wyndham, along with Nigel Stevenson, Alan Curtis, Robbie James and Jeremy Charles created history by playing for the club in every division from the Fourth to the First. Released by the Swans a second time in May 1985, Wyndham took over the role of player manager at Pembroke Borough, and twelve months later was appointed manager at Carmarthen Town, during a period which saw the club eventually earn themselves promotion to the League of Wales. Returning to Stebonheath Park in 1999, firstly as Development Manager, and then as General Manager, Wyndham took over the reins again at the club in a joint capacity with Martin Evans in February 1998 following the tragic death of the club's player manager, and fellow Swans team-mate Robbie James. By the start of the 1998/99 season he had become assistant to Leighton James, but at the end of the 1999/2000 season left the club after the controversial sacking of James as manager. Employed with a double glazing company in Llanelli, Wyndham had a break from football for a couple of years before he was re-united with former Swans star Leighton James, when he took over at Llanelli for a second time midway through the 2002/03 season.

His nephew Stuart Roberts came through the ranks at the Vetch Field.

F

1. FABIANO, NICOLAS

Birthplace: Paris, 8/2/1981
Ht: 5ft-9ins, **Wt:** 11st-7lbs
Swans debut: v. Millwall (h), 12/2/2001

Swansea City Career Statistics		
Season	League	FAWP
2000/01	12+4/1gls	3
Total	12+4/1gls	3

Career:
Paris St. Germain (signed in 1999)
Swansea City (loan in 6/2/2001)
Istres (signed in 2001) lge apps 6
Aberdeen (signed in 29/8/2002) SPL 8+4, SLC 1, SC 0+2
Racing Club, Paris (signed for season 2004/05)

Honours: France Yth, U-18, 20, 21

Right sided midfielder who joined the Swans on loan from Paris St. Germain along with striker Mattias Verschave on the 6th February 2001. During his period at the Vetch Field with the Swans he played for the French U-21 side against Finland. A member of the French squad that won the European U-18 Youth Championship in Iceland, after moving into the U-20 squad was included in both the Toulon Tournament and the FIFA World Youth Championship in Argentina. An extremely talented midfielder, tricky on the ball, and fiery in the tackle, he scored his only goal for the Swans in a 2-1 defeat at Northampton Town. He made his Swans debut against Millwall, as a second half substitute for Michael Keegan, having played four days earlier in the Swans side that beat Connah's Quay Nomads in a Welsh Premier Cup game, played at Stebonheath Park, Llanelli. In the semi-final, second leg of the competition

against Merthyr Tydfil at the Vetch Field he was sent off for a reckless challenge. Returning to Paris St. Germain in May 2001, he then had a spell with French National Division side Istres, and after illness had prevented him attending a trial with Scottish side Aberdeen, he eventually returned to Scotland, impressed in trial games, and was given a contract for the 2002/03 season. Making appearances for the 'Dons' in the Scottish Premier League and in domestic cup matches, he was released in May 2003 returning to France, and prior to the start of season 2004/05 had signed for French National Division side Racing Club of Paris.

2. FEENEY, James (JIM) McBurney

Birthplace: Belfast, 23/6/1921. **Died:** Ireland, 1985
Ht: 5ft-9½ins, **Wt:** 11st-4lbs
Swans debut: v. Chesterfield (a), 14/12/1946

Swansea Town Career Statistics			
Season	League	FAC	WC
1946/47	24	2	1
1947/48	26		
1948/49	26	2	2
1949/50	12	1	1
Total	88	5	4

Career:
Crusaders
Linfield (signed in 14/11/1941) Apps 201/4gls
Swansea Town (signed in 11/12/1946)
Ipswich Town (signed in 2/3/1950) lge 214

Honours: Ireland Full–2, Irish League Rep XI–5, Irish League Champions–1943, 1945, 1946, Irish Cup Winner–1942, 1945,

1946, Gold Cup Winner–1943, 1945, County Antrim Shield Winner–1942, Third Division South Champions–1949, 1954

Northern Ireland full back who after starting his career with Crusaders, joined Linfield, gaining his first cap at left full back for Ireland on the 27th November 1946 against Scotland at Hampden Park in a 0-0 draw. During a distinguished career in the Irish League with Linfield, apart from the Championship and Cup Medals he won, he was also a member of the Linfield side that were Runners Up in the Irish League in 1942 and 1944, Irish Cup Runner Up in 1944, Gold Cup Runner Up in 1946, and a County Antrim Shield Runner Up in 1943 and 1945. He also made five Inter-League appearances during his career in Irish football with Linfield. After signing for the Swans in December 1946 he made his second appearance for his country in a 9-2 defeat against England on the 6th November 1949, this time at right full back at Maine Road, Manchester. He proved to be a sound defender and cool under pressure during his career with the Swans. A classy player, he rarely wasted a ball, possessed excellent positional sense, quick in the interception, and a perfect foil for Rory Keane on the other flank. Making his debut for the Swans at left full back with Fisher switching to centre half, he later moved to right full back before the end of the season. Making twenty-six league appearances during the club's Championship winning season of 1948/49, he missed the Welsh Cup Final later in the season against Merthyr Tydfil through injury. In March 1950 he was transferred to Third Division South side Ipswich Town, along with centre forward Sam McCrory. He would prove to be a stalwart defender for the East Anglian team, making over two hundred league appearances, and playing a part in the club's 1953/54 Third Division South Championship success, gaining his second Championship medal, during a season which saw him miss just two league games. The following season he played in both Second Division games against the Swans and retired in April 1956. In 1976 Jim's son Warren played for Northern Ireland against Israel, and on the 27th March 2002, his grandson Warren, a striker with Bournemouth made his first appearance for his country against Leichtenstein, the only time three generations have played for Ireland. Following his retirement from the game, Jim spent a number of years in Canada, before returning to Belfast where he died in 1985.

3. FERGUSON, Alexander (ALEX) Stirling Brown

Birthplace: Lochore, 5/8/1903. **Died:** Swansea, OND, 1974
Ht: 6ft-3ins, **Wt:** 13st-7lbs
Swans debut: v. Nottingham Forest (h), 10/3/1927

Career:
Vale of Clyde
Wigan Borough (signed in November 1924) lge 1
Gillingham (signed in June 1925) lge 67
Swansea Town (£750 signed in February 1927)
Middlesbrough (signed in 1936) lge 0
Bury (signed in June 1936) lge 63
Newport County (signed in June 1938) lge 44
Bristol City (signed in May 1946) lge 32
Swindon Town (signed in September 1947) lge 7
Milford United (signed by January 1949)

Swansea Town Career Statistics			
Season	League	FAC	WC
1926/27	14		1
1927/28	42	1	2
1928/29	37	2	1
1929/30	42	1	2
1930/31	39	1	1
1931/32	42	1	7
1932/33	34	1	
1933/34	16		1
1934/35	12		
1935/36	2		
Total	280	7	15

Honours: Scotland Junior International, Third Division South Champions–1939, Welsh Cup Winner–1932, West Wales Senior Cup Winner–1934, Welsh League Representative XI

Goalkeeper who after starting his playing career north of the border with Vale of Clyde, gained honours at Junior level for Scotland, came south to join Third Division North side Wigan Borough, before signing for Third Division South side Gillingham in 1925. Joining the Swans in March 1927, replacing Denoon for his debut, he was an ever present during seasons 1927/28, 1929/30 and 1931/31, and also set a consecutive appearance record for a Swans goalkeeper with 108 league appearances between September 1928 to February 1931, which would last until the 1990's before being broken by Roger Freestone. One of three brothers who were goalkeepers, two of which played in the Football League, James was with Notts. County. Alex played against his brother James in April 1927 at the Vetch Field in December 1927, and in both league matches during the 1928/29 season. A brave goalkeeper in the days when the centre forward was able to charge the keeper, he became an institution at the Vetch Field seeing off the challenge to his place from a number of keepers brought in by manager Thomson. Consistent, never flashy, unsmiling, Alex always looked menacing, possessed fine anticipation, and could kick a massive length. He was one of eight Swans players who played for a Welsh League Representative side at the Vetch Field in May 1930 against the Irish Free State. Playing all his games for the Swans in the Second Division, in May 1932 Alex played in the Swans side that beat Wrexham to win the Welsh Cup Final. In October 1934 he played in the Swans side that beat Llanelly to win the West Wales Senior Cup. Losing his place to Stan Moore for the 1935/36 season, Alex joined First Division Middlesbrough prior to the end of the season, and after failing to make appearances joined Bury for the 1936/37 season. Alex returned to South Wales to join Newport County prior to the start of the 1938/39 season, making a large contribution to the team winning the Third Division South Championship at the end of the season. During his time with Newport County, in the war years when the Football League was suspended, Ferguson along with a number of other Newport County players signed for Lovells Athletic, who played in the Regional South West League, also with Grimsby Town (1941/42) and Bristol City (1944/45). Towards the end of the 1942/43 season he played for Lovells Athletic in a Regional League West Cup Final defeat by the Swans. When the Football League was resumed after the war, Alex joined Bristol City in 1946, and the following year signed for Swindon Town, playing in a Football Combination fixture against the Swans in January 1948. By January 1949 he was still actively involved as a player with Welsh League side Milford United. His son Stuart played rugby for Swansea RFC, and later for Leigh RFLC.

4. FIELDWICK, LEE Peter

Birthplace: Croydon, 6/9/1982
Ht: 5ft-11ins, **Wt:** 12st-2lbs
Swans debut: v. Huddersfield Town (a), 27/3/2004

Swansea City Career Statistics	
Season	League
2003/04	4+1
Total	4+1

Career:
Brentford (from trainee in 4/7/2001) lge 10+2
Swansea City (loan in 25/3/2004)
Lewes (signed in August 2004) Conf Sth 15+3

Signed for the Swans as cover on transfer deadline day in March 2004, making his debut as substitute for Stuart Roberts at Huddersfield Town a couple of days later. He made his first start for the Swans in the next game at the Vetch Field against Carlisle United, also playing in the next three league matches before being told by manager Kenny Jackett that he would not be offered a contract for the new season ahead. A few days earlier he had been told by Brentford's new manager Martin Allen that he was being released at the end of the season. A former trainee at Griffin Park with the 'Bees', he made his league debut on the 22nd February at Luton as a replacement in defence for Marshall. Playing in the next two league games, he made further appearances later in the season for Brentford. Glandular fever in the summer of 2002 put him out of action for the best part of six months. Just prior to the start of the 2004/05 season he signed for Conference South side Lewes.

5. FIRTH, JACK

Birthplace: Doncaster, 8/8/1907. **Died:** Doncaster, 8/12/1987
Ht: 5ft-9ins, **Wt:** 11st-0lbs
Swans debut: v. Bury (a), 26/8/1933

Career:
Brodsworth Main Colliery
Doncaster Rovers (signed in March 1926) lge 0
Birmingham (signed in 1927) lge 93/7gls
Swansea Town (£350 signed in 9/8/1933)

Bury (£200 signed in 25/5/1936) lge 7/4gls
Brodsworth Main Colliery

Swansea Town Career Statistics			
Season	League	FAC	WC
1933/34	34/10gls	4	
1934/35	36/4gls	2	3/2gls
1935/36	32/2gls	1	1
Total	102/16gls	7	4/2gls

Joined Third Division North side Doncaster Rovers from non-league side Brodsworth Main Colliery in 1926, failed to make a league appearance, joining First Division Birmingham in 1927. He had earlier played for Woodlands School, Woodlands Primitives before having his first spell with Doncaster Rovers. In six seasons at St. Andrews with Birmingham he made almost a hundred league appearance, but did not make the team's FA Cup Final line-up in season 1930/31 against West Bromwich Albion. Joining the Swans in July 1933 for £350, the inside forward finished his first season at the Vetch Field runner up as goal scorer with ten league goals. During his second and third seasons at the Vetch Field he reverted to a mainly right half back. In May 1933 he was sold to Second Division Bury for £200, featuring in the Bury side that lost 2-0 at the Vetch Field in March 1937. He later returned to play for Brodsworth Main Colliery.

6. FISHER, CHARLES Kitchener (KITCH)

Birthplace: Pontypridd, 4/1/1915. **Died:** Tynewydd, Treherbert 14/3/1986
Swans debut: v. West Bromwich Albion (h), 31/8/1946

Swansea Town Career Statistics			
Season	League	FAC	WC
1946/47	39	2	
1947/48	26	1	1
Total	65	3	1

Career:
Ton Pentre (signed in 1933)
Lovells Athletic (signed in 1936)
Swansea Town (signed in August 1939)
Lovells Athletic (signed in close season 1949)

Honours: Wales Amateur International–2, Regional League Cup Winner–1943

Played for Penyrenglyn School, Treherbert, at the age of 11 years old, and in the same school side four youngsters would go on to earn Welsh International representations. 'Kitch' at soccer, Ossie Jones, Dai James and Richie Evans at Rugby. At the age of fifteen he played for Tynewydd USA, Upper St. Alban in Treherbert, and from the age of eighteen played Welsh League for Ton Pentre, signing for Lovells Athletic at the age of 21, also working in their factory. Capped twice for the Wales Amateur international side, his first in 1933 against England at Aberystwyth, and his second in Brussels. Showing plenty of vigour and determination in the Swans' public trial matches, shortly after signing in August 1939, when the Football League was suspended because of the Second World War, played South West Regional football with the Swans, also working in the pits in the Treherbert area. At the time, people employed in the mines were exempt from call up, and 'Kitch' captained the Swans for two seasons during this period. Towards the end of the 1942/43 season he played in a Regional League West Cup Final win over two legs against Lovells Athletic, and played for the Swans in the 'Victory' season at the end of the war, prior to the Football League being restarted. When the Football League restarted he was a regular in the first team line-up, making his debut in the opening fixture of the campaign at left full back against West Bromwich Albion at the Vetch Field, and missing just three league games during the season in which he often played at centre half, and at right full back. Despite relegation to the Third Division South, he started season 1947/48 at left full back, switched to right full back, but then lost his place to new signing to Rory Keane, with Feeney switching full back positions. An imposing figure in defence, red headed, he was a brave, strong competitor on the field. In the 1949 close season he returned to Lovells Athletic, skippering the side, before retiring from the game, returning to the coal mines, where he took his Fireman's Certificate in Fernhill Tower Colliery, working there up until his retirement. In 1986 he died at home in Tynewydd, Treherbert, Rhondda.

7. FISHER, Philip (PHIL) John

Birthplace: Ammanford, 10/1/1958
Ht: 5ft-9ins, **Wt:** 10st-10lbs
Swans debut: v. Newport County (h), 17/3/1985

Swansea City Career Statistics		
Season	League	FRT
1984/85	2	1
Total	2	1

Career:
Ammanford Town
Bridgend Town

Exeter City (£6,000 signed in February 1981) lge 9+2/1gls
Merthyr Tydfil (signed in season 1982/83)
Swansea City (signed in March 1985)
Merthyr Tydfil (signed in May 1985)
Barry Town (signed in August 1985)
Ammanford Town (signed in July 1988)

Honours: Wales Semi-Pro International, Southern League Midland Division Champions–1980, Abacus Welsh League National Division Champions–1986, 1987

Looking back on his career in the professional game, Phil Fisher's claim to fame arose when he was told he was being released from the Swansea City playing staff by manager John Bond on the same day as Dean Saunders was given the same information by the manager. Saunders went on to make a name for himself on the international scene, whilst Fisher, who had already made semi-professional appearances for Wales against England, made a name for himself on the non-league football scene. Brought up in the rugby stronghold of Amman Valley, Phil's only football opportunity came with Llanelli Schoolboys whilst at school, and then with Welsh League side Ammanford Town on weekends after leaving school, whilst he continued his apprenticeship as a plasterer. For the couple of seasons he played for the town he grew up in, they were one of the most formidable sides in the Welsh League at the time, and were unlucky not to win the League Championship during his early years at Rice Road. Playing on the right flank, and with former Swans player Ioan Rees on the left flank, at centre forward a young Paul Bannon would create such an impression that he would eventually grace the football league with Carlisle United and Bristol Rovers. After just one season with his hometown side, he joined Bridgend Town, who at the time had just entered the Southern League. A successful period with the mid-Glamorgan based outfit saw Phil gain runners up honours during their first season, and in 1979/80 win the Championship of the Midland Division, and beat Dorchester United in the Play Off Final to win the Southern League Title. In January 1981 his consistent form on the right flank for Bridgend Town warranted Football League side Exeter City pay £6,000 for his transfer, and give him the opportunity to become a full time professional. That season, unfortunately for Phil, he was unable to join in the club's FA Cup exploits, which led to a sixth round defeat by Tottenham Hotspur, as he had played in a previous qualifying round for Bridgend Town earlier in the season. His first team opportunity came towards the end of the season, and after making his league debut against Chester at St. James Park in 29th April 1981, drawing 2-2, he played in the last two league fixtures of the season. His first full season with Exeter saw Phil given his opportunity shortly after the start of the season in the Second Leg of the Football League Cup First Round against Cardiff City. Trailing 2-1 from the First Leg at Ninian Park, Phil scored the second goal to bring the scores level, and laid on the cross for Joe Cooke to score the winner. Playing in the next two league games, which saw the club lose to Swindon Town and Bristol Rovers, he was replaced in the City first team by Peter Rogers. Returning to first team action midway through the season, he scored his only league goal for City in a 2-1 defeat at Southend United, and at the end of the season with the club slipping to eighteenth position in the Third Division was given a free transfer. By the start of the 1982/83 season, Phil had returned to his trade as a plasterer, and signed for Southern League side Merthyr Tydfil, managed at the time by Fred Davies. In what proved to be a successful period with the club, including recognition at semi-professional level for Wales against England, following Davies being appointed assistant to John Bond at the Vetch Field, on Davies's recommendation he signed for the Swans on non-contract terms. In what were dismal days at the Vetch Field, and the Swans being unable to sign players on full contracts because of restrictions imposed on the club by the Football League, Phil was given his second opportunity in the Football League when John Bond gave him his debut in the Welsh 'Derby' game at the Vetch Field with Newport County. Following a further appearance in the Freight Rover Trophy competition, plus a second league outing for the Swans, Phil was allowed to rejoin Merthyr Tydfil in May 1985, enabling him to play in the First leg of the South Wales Senior Cup against Barry Town. By August 1985 he rejoined Barry Town, returning to the Abacus Welsh League National Division, where in three seasons he gained two Championship medals, and a runners up medal. Returning to his hometown club Ammanford Town, he also made Welsh League appearances for Llanelli, Haverfordwest and Ton Pentre, before dropping down a level to play in the Neath & District League with local side Cwmamman. Season 2002/03 saw the club admitted to the Welsh League following the club's success in local leagues, with Phil being re-united with his former manager from Bridgend Town Lyn Jones, who was appointed Director of Football at the club, with a brief to assist the club acclimatise to the higher level of competition in the Welsh League. Throughout Phil's footballing career, during the period of inactivity in the summer he has continued to play cricket at a high level with his local side Ammanford Town in the South Wales Leagues, winning a lot of honours in the game. Season 2003/04 saw Phil return to his old club Ammanford Town, making appearances for the club in the Welsh League, still going strong on the wing at the age of 46.

8. FISKEN, GARY

Birthplace: Watford, 27/10/1981
Ht: 6ft-0ins, **Wt:** 12st-7lbs
Swans debut: v. Rochdale (a), 10/8/2004

Swansea City Career Statistics				
Season	League	FLC	FAC	FAWC
2004/05	1+4	0+1	0+1	1
Total	1+4	0+1	0+1	1

Career:
Watford (from trainee in 8/2/2000) lge 15+7/1gls, FLC 3+2, FAC 1
Swansea City (signed in 22/6/2004)
Cambridge City (loan in 31/3/2005)

Working his way up through the club's Academy, the former trainee at Vicarage Road made his Watford debut in the Nationwide First Division at Manchester City as substitute for Tommy Smith in a 3-0 defeat in the opening game of season 2001/02, making his first start four games later at home to Wimbledon, making a total of seventeen appearances for Watford during the season. He scored his first league goal with a spectacular long range lob at Walsall in late December 2001. Gary attended Tannerswood and Parmiters Schools, and played for Watford & District and Hertfordshire Schoolboys, also having trials with the England squad at Lilleshall. He also played for Sunday League sides Evergreen (Watford League), and Western Rangers (Middlesex League). The start of season 2002/03 saw him undergo knee surgery in the summer, had a long battle to regain fitness including two operations, finally returning to action in March 2003, showing the commitment to earn himself a new contract. A hard working and creative midfielder, he linked up with Swans manager Kenny Jackett for a second time, joining the Swans in late June 2004 on a two year contract. He made his Swans' debut as a second half substitute for Andy Robinson in the second game of the season at Rochdale, but had to wait until the end of November before making his first start. Struggling to break into the Swans' first team, he joined non-league side Cambridge City in late March 2005, scoring on his debut against Weymouth, helping the club reach the Nationwide South Play Off Final.

9. FITZGERALD, SCOTT

Birthplace: Hillingdon, 18/11/1979
Ht: 5ft-11ins, **Wt:** 11st-6lbs
Swans debut: v. Luton Town (h), LDV-1, 28/9/2004

Swansea City Career Statistics		
Season	League	LDV
2004/05	0+3	1
Total	0+3	1

Career:
Northwood
Watford (signed in 5/3/2003) 29+26/11gls, FLC 0+3/1gls, FAC 0+1
Swansea City (loan in 28/9/2004)
Leyton Orient (loan in 13/1/2005) lge 1
Brentford (loan in 4/3/2005) lge 2+2/2gls
Brentford (signed in 24/3/2005) lge 5+3/2gls, Others 1

The former Sales Representative with Fujitsu in Watford signed for the 'Hornets' on a free transfer from Ryman League side Northwood in March 2003, after proving himself to be a consistent goalscorer at non-league level, scoring twenty-six goals prior to his arrival at Vicarage Road. He made the step up into full time football, making his Football League as substitute for Michael Chopra at Vicarage Road against Derby County on the 21st April 2003, and in the final game of the season scored his first league goal in what was his first league start, against Sheffield United. Season 2003/04 saw him miss just two league games, although he made sixteen appearances from the subs bench, also finishing as the 'Hornets' top goalscorer with eleven league and cup goals. Signed by Swans' manager Kenny Jackett on a month's loan, he made his debut same day in an LDV Cup tie at the Vetch Field against First Division Luton Town. He failed to start a league game for the Swans, making three appearances from the substitute's bench before returning to Vicarage Road. In January 2005 he had a loan spell with Second Division side Leyton Orient, and in early March 2005 started a loan spell with First Division Brentford, with the move being made permanent towards the end of the month. Played in the end of season Play Off semi-final defeat by Sheffield Wednesday.

10. FOLEY, William (WILL)

Birthplace: Bellshill, 25/6/1960
Ht: 5ft-10ins, **Wt:** 11st-7lbs
Swans debut: v. Cardiff City (a), FRT–1, 28/1/1986

Swansea City Career Statistics			
Season	League	WC	FRT
1985/86	4+1/2gls	1/1gls	1+1
Total	4+1/2gls	1/1gls	1+1

Career:
York City (trial in August 1985)
Frickley Athletic (signed in November 1985)
Swansea City (non-contract signed in January 1986)
Cardiff City (non-contract signed in March 1986) lge 5+2/1gls
Newport County (signed for season 1988/89) Conf 7+3/1gls
Point Chevalier, New Zealand
Hereford United
Worcester City (signed in October 1990)
AFC Newport (signed in December 1990)
Brecon Corries

After writing to the Vetch Field requesting a trial, Will Foley played in a Football Combination match against Chelsea, and a couple of days later was signed on a non-contract basis, making his Swans debut as substitute for defender Paul Price in a First Round Freight Rover Trophy Cup tie at Ninian Park against Cardiff City. With his family coming to live in Newport in 1962, Will played for his school team, St. Josephs Senior High School, local side Fields Park before graduating to Merthyr Tydfil, Pontllanfraith, Newport YMCA, Barry Town before having a trial with York City. Prior to returning to South Wales he had also made non-league appearances for Frickley Athletic, joining the club in November 1985 from York City, scored a hat-trick on his debut in a 5-1 home win against Boston United. He then scored 2 more in his second game in a 4-0 win against Telford United in the Bob Lord Trophy. He went on to score 4 more times for Frickley before leaving to return to Swansea after he started a new job in the area. A couple of days after playing in the Freight Rover Cup tie, he made his league debut for the Swans, again from the substitute bench, this time for Nigel Stevenson in a 4-1 defeat at Rotherham United. He started the next league game for the Swans in a midweek 0-0 draw at Doncaster Rovers, and the following Saturday starred for the Swans, scoring two goals in a 3-1 home defeat of Bolton Wanderers. Signed on a non-contract basis by the Swans, who at the time were being managed by veteran midfielder Tommy Hutchison on a player/manager caretaker basis, after the Official Receiver had sacked John Bond just before Christmas, Foley, despite scoring against non-league Kidderminster Harriers at the Vetch Field in a Welsh Cup tie was looking for a permanent contract, and with no offer forthcoming, left the Vetch Field. Within a month of playing his last game for the Swans in February 22nd, he had joined Cardiff City on a non-contract basis, making his league debut as substitute against Bolton Wanderers, but at the end of season 1985/86 was released from the Ninian Park squad. Following Newport County's relegation to the GM Vauxhall Conference at the end of the 1987/88 season, he returned to the South Wales area playing seven Conference games for the side, before financial problems worsened and the club had to fold before the end of the season. He then played in New Zealand for Point Chevalier before returning to sign for Hereford United where he failed to make a league appearance. Joining Worcester City in October 1990, he was released by the club two months later for financial reasons, signing for AFC Newport, later playing for Welsh League side Brecon Corries.

11. FORBES, ADRIAN Emmanuel

Birthplace: Ealing, 23/1/1979
Ht: 5ft-8ins, **Wt:** 11st-4lbs
Swans debut: v. Northampton Town (h), 7/8/2004

Swansea City Career Statistics					
Season	League	FLC	FAC	LDV	FAWC
2004/05	36+4/7gls	1	5	2	2
Total	36+4/7gls	1	5	2	2

Career:
Norwich City (from trainee in 21/1/1997) lge 66+46/8gls, FLC 1+4, FAC 2+2
Luton Town (£60,000 in 16/7/2001) lge 39+33/14gls, FLC 1, FAC 5/6gls, Others 0+1
Swansea City (signed in 24/6/2004)

Honours: England Yth, FAW Cup Winner–2005

Former Middlesex Schoolboy footballer who joined Norwich City from school as a trainee, making his league debut as a substitute for Daryl Sutch at Carrow Road against Wolverhampton Wanderers on the 31st August 1996, with his first start coming in early November 1996 against Charlton Athletic. By the end of his first season he had made ten league appearances and played against Leicester City in the FA Cup Fourth Round. That season saw him also make two appearances for the England U-18 side that played Portugal. Still relatively inexperienced, the 1997/98 season saw him start on twenty-eight occasions, score his first goals, in an away win at Birmingham City, and also gain selection for a Nationwide U-21 side against their Italian counterparts, only to withdraw from the squad because of injury. Joining Third Division Luton Town in July 2001, he made forty league appearances, twenty-five from the substitute bench during the season when the 'Hatters' finished runners up to Plymouth Argyle. After finishing second top goalscorer with nine league goals during the 2004/05 season, he joined the Swans on a free transfer, making his debut in the opening league fixture of the season at the Vetch Field against Northampton Town. A hard working player when utilised in a wide midfield role, he is also more than capable of playing in a central striking position as his goals during the previous season testify. He opened his goal scoring account for the Swans against Mansfield Town, scoring also in the next two league games before a knee injury saw him sidelined for a number of matches. His goals in the last two league games of the season saw the club claim an automatic promotion place from Division Two, and after promotion had been secured played in the FAW Cup Final win over Wrexham.

12. FORD, Jonathan (JON) Steven

Birthplace: Birmingham, 12/4/1968
Ht: 6ft-1ins, **Wt:** 12st-3lbs
Swans debut: v. Bolton Wanderers (h), 24/8/1991

Swansea City Career Statistics

Season	League	FLC	FAC	WC	AGT/AWS	P/Offs
1991/92	42+2	2	2	3	1	
1992/93	36+7/3gls	2	1+3	1	3	0+2
1993/94	21+6/1gls	3+1	0+2	3+1	3+2	
1994/95	46/3gls	4	5/2gls	3	4	
Total	145+15/7gls	11+1	8+5/2gls	10+1	11+2	0+2

Career:
Cradley Town
Swansea City (£5,000 signed in 19/8/1991)
Bradford City (£210,000 signed in 26/7/1995) lge 18+1, FLC 4, FAC 2, Others 1
Gillingham (£15,000 signed in 16/8/1996) lge 2+2, FLC 3, FAC 0+1, Others 1
Barnet (£25,000 signed in 21/2/1997) lge 47/2gls, FLC 6, FAC 2, Others 1
Kidderminster Harriers (signed in February 1999) Conf 16/4gls
Telford United (signed in season 1999/2000) Conf 29+2/3gls
Halesowen Town

Honours: AutoGlass Trophy Winner–1994, West Wales Senior Cup Winner–1994

Jon Ford started his playing career with Redhill School Birmingham, and then signed as a 16-year-old for Halesowen Town, spending three years on their staff before joining Bromsgrove. Two years later he left to join Cradley Town, and then twelve months later he attracted the interest of Swans manager Frank Burrows, who signed Ford and striker John Williams in a joint package worth £10,000 just days before the start of the 1991/92 season. He signed for the Swans as very much an utility player, where he was able to feature in either full back position, in central defence, as well as a number of games in a midfield role. Making his league debut as substitute for his former Cradley Town team mate John Williams at the Vetch Field against Bolton Wanderers in the first home game of the season, by the end of the season he missed just one league game, playing in either full back position, as well as in midfield. His second season again saw him feature strongly in the Swans line-up, not looking out of place for a player of his inexperience, as the Swans reached the semi-final stage of the AutoGlass Trophy competition, and were beaten in the Second Division Play Off semi-finals by West Bromwich Albion. In April 1994 he made a substitute appearance at Wembley in the AutoGlass Trophy Final against Huddersfield Town, replacing Mark Clode at full back, played in the Welsh Cup semi-final defeat by Cardiff City over two legs, and was also included in the side that beat Ammanford Town in the West Wales Senior Cup Final. Not known for his goalscoring achievements on the field, he did score a memorable goal at the Vetch Field in January 1995 against Middlesbrough in the FA Cup Third Round, a twenty-five yarder from outside the penalty area. An ever present that season, he also scored three league goals. He signed for Second Division Bradford City in July 1995 for a fee of £210,000 settled at a League Tribunal, with his former club Cradley Town receiving approximately £52,000 from a sell on clause agreed when he joined the Swans in 1991. His first season at Valley Parade saw him fail to make an appearance for the club in the successful Play Off success, and within twelve months had joined Gillingham. Less than six months later he signed for Third Division Barnet, missing out a second time on making appearances in the end of season Play Off semi-final against Colchester United in 1998. Jon signed for Vauxhall Conference side Kidderminster Harriers in February1999, played a further season in the Conference with Telford United, before returning to his former club Halesowen Town in 2000. After a short period with Evesham Town, along with Gary Hackett, Jon became joint manager of Bromsgrove Rovers during season 2002/03, and after taking the club to third place in the Dr. Martens Western Division, both were controversially sacked at the end of the season. Within a week the managerial pair were snapped up by Midland Alliance champions Stourbridge. Unfortunately for Stourbridge they were denied promotion to the Dr. Martens League because their ground was not up to the required standard. During season 2003/04 Jon was still involved as a player with Stourbridge.

13. FORD, TREVOR

Birthplace: Swansea, 1/10/1923. **Died:** Swansea, 29/5/2003
Ht: 5ft-11ins, **Wt:** 13st-4lbs
Swans debut: v. West Bromwich Albion (h), 31/8/1946

Swansea Town Career Statistics	
Season	League
1946/47	16/9gls
Total	16/9gls

Career:
Swansea Town (signed in May 1942, professional in December 1944)
Aston Villa (£9,500 signed in 11/1/1947) lge 121/59gls, FAC 8/1gls
Sunderland (£29,500 signed in October 1950) lge 108/67gls
Cardiff City (£29,500 signed in December 1953) lge 96/39gls
PSV Eindhoven (£5,000 signed in March 1957)
Newport County (£1,000 signed in July 1960) lge 8/3gls
Romford (signed in 15/3/1961)

Honours: Wales Full–38, Welsh Cup Winner–1956, Regional League Cup Winner–1943

From the Townhill district of Swansea, Trevor Ford, a former Powys Avenue, Townhill Senior, and Swansea Schoolboy, at the age of fifteen, along with Leslie Davies played in a trial match at Cardiff for an Arsenal side. The son of the under manager of the Tower Cinema and a well known referee in the town, Trevor was the youngest playing member to represent Swansea Schoolboys, playing for them at the age of ten and a half years old, playing regularly for them for four years. Playing for Townhill Seniors, for three seasons they had won three successive League Championships, and in 1937 he represented Wales in Cricket. On leaving school, he started working initially at the Mannesman Steel works in Landore, played for Tower United, prior to joining the Swans. Signed in 1942 on the groundstaff initially, as a left full back, but after being conscripted during the Second World War, whilst serving in the Army he was switched to centre forward. Towards the end of the 1942/43 season he played in a Regional League West Cup Final win over two legs against Lovells Athletic, scoring two goals in the away leg at Rexville, also making guest appearances for Clapton Orient during season 1943/44. He returned to his hometown immediately after the end of the war and was part of the Swansea Town side that took part in the 1945/46 'Victory League' season. Consisting of clubs who had been in the First or Second Division at the outbreak of the war, the 'Victory League' was regionalised with the Swans playing in the Southern area alongside Arsenal, Spurs and West Ham. Ford made his debut on the opening day against West Bromwich Albion, and although he was unknown to the majority of the Vetch crowd at

kick-off, he was the name on everybody's lips at the final whistle after scoring on his debut. The goals kept coming for Trevor, including a hat-trick in a famous 5-4 win over Aston Villa, obviously making an impression on the Villa management. In all, he scored 40 times in that memorable post-war season. When the Football League resumed after the war, with the Swans in the Second Division, Ford continued his fine form in front of goal, netting nine goals in sixteen league appearances before signing for Aston Villa in January 1947 for £9,500, plus Tommy Dodds from Villa joining the Swans. He made his international debut for Wales whilst at the Vetch Field against Scotland at Wrexham on the 19th October 1946, scoring the second goal in a 3-1 win. Earlier in 1946 he played for Wales against Ireland in a war-time international, with no caps being awarded. In April 1949 he was included in an F.A.W. Touring party that played international matches against Portugal, Belgium and Switzerland at the end of the season. Cementing his reputation as a brave, fast, and powerful centre forward, with a trick or two up his sleeve, he took to First Division football with Villa, topping the goalscoring charts in three successive seasons, and also at International football like a duck to water, and his 59 goals in 121 matches for Villa prompted Sunderland to spend £29,500 to take him to Roker Park in 1950 where he netted 67 times in just 108 matches. Further moves followed to Cardiff City, PSV Eindhoven and Newport County before he finished his career in non-league football at Romford. Playing for PSV Eindhoven, his club finished runners up in the Dutch First Division in 1958. Whilst at Ninian Park with Cardiff City, Trevor played in the 1955/56 Welsh Cup Final defeat of the Swans. Trevor's legendary status was confirmed by the Football League at the Millennium when he was named in their list of the 100 greatest Football League players of the 20th century, one of four Swansea born players in the list, the others being from the same era, John Charles, Cliff Jones and Ivor Allchurch. After bringing out his book, *I Lead the Attack*, Ford's justification for publicizing his case was that wage restraint and individual bargaining in football constituted a massive hypocrisy which dominated the domestic game at the time. Ford felt compelled to be honest, but he was determined to tell the truth. His initial signing for Sunderland ended with him being fined £100 for allegedly demanding more than the specified £10 signing on fee. The full revelations of the under the counter methods being revealed led to an unprecedented fine for Sunderland, 'The Bank of England Football Club' as it was known at the time, and to the suspension of several players and directors, including Ford himself who by now was playing for Cardiff City. In the 1955 close season he was in dispute with Cardiff City over terms offered to him, and in mid-August 1955, instead of playing in a pre-season trial game for the 'Bluebirds', flew to Jersey to fulfil a long standing promise to play in a friendly game for Channel Island side Grouville against Brighton & Hove Albion, a game organised to open the Jersey club's new pitch. A few days later he played for a Jersey Saturday Football League XI against the same opponents. After his re-instatement Ford was again suspended for not substantiating his claims. His reaction was to head for Holland where he signed for PSV Eindhoven. With supporters knowing very little about continental football at this time, it was never the less regarded as an exile in the wilderness. Unfortunately he was to miss the Welsh attempt at the 1958 World Cup Finals, and his nation's greatest moment of soccer glory. A sad ending to a great career in international football. In the motor trade for many years after his retirement as a player, Trevor died in Swansea in May 2003.

14. FOREMAN, JOHN Joseph

Birthplace: Tanfield, Co. Durham OND, 1914
Ht: 5ft-9ins, **Wt:** 11st-12lbs
Swans debut: v. Luton Town (h), 11/12/1937

Career:
Tanfield Lea Institute

West Stanley
Crook Town (signed in April 1933)
Sunderland (signed in May 1933) lge 2
West Ham United (signed in September 1934) lge 49/7gls
Bury (signed in March 1937) lge 4/1gls
Swansea Town (signed in 10/12/1937)
Workington (signed in May 1938)
Hartlepool United (signed in 1939) lge 3

Swansea Town Career Statistics

Season	League	FAC
1937/38	14/2gls	1
Total	14/2gls	1

John Foreman was a schoolboy player with County Durham when younger, also a capable cricket and tennis player, and joined Sunderland in 1932 from junior side Tanfield Lea Institute. After a short period at West Stanley and Crook Town he signed for Sunderland in May 1933, making his First Division debut for the club, and after just one more appearance signed for West Ham United in September 1934, established himself in the club's Second Division line-up before moving to Bury. During season 1936/37 he made appearances for both West Ham United and Bury against the Swans. Signed by Swans manager Neil Harris in December 1937 for £290, he made his debut against Luton Town at the Vetch Field, replacing Lewis at outside right. He had a spell on the sidelines when Lewis returned to action, but after regaining his place on the right wing towards the end of the season scored in consecutive league games against Tottenham Hotspur and Sheffield United in March 1938. At the end of the season he joined non-league side Workington, before returning to league action with Third Division North side Hartlepool United twelve months later. Scoring two goals for Hartlepool in a 6-1 win over Darlington in the Football League Jubilee Fund game, he left the club at the start of WW2 and relocated to Crewe, making guest appearances for the club during season 1939/40.

15. FOSTER, Thomas (TOM) Curtis

Birthplace: Easington, 30/6/1908. **Died:** Congleton, OND, 1982
Ht: 5ft-9ins, **Wt:** 11st-4lbs
Swans debut: v. Coventry City (h), 7/9/1936

Swansea Town Career Statistics

Season	League	FAC	WC
1936/37	14/3gls	1	2
Total	14/3gls	1	2

Career:
Reading (signed in December 1933) lge 1
Clapton Orient (signed in June 1934) lge 19/11gls
Swansea Town (signed in May 1936)
Crewe Alexandra (signed in June 1937) lge 62/27gls

A renowned sprinter in his early days, Tom Foster played for Leasingthorne Council School, Page Bank Rovers, Crook Town and Stanley United prior to signing for Reading in December 1933, making his only league appearance for the club when he was selected to play at centre forward in a home game against Newport County in January 1934, failing to get on the scoresheet in a 4-0 win. It was only after joining Clapton Orient the following season that he was to make regular appearances, as well as get his name on the scoresheet, topping the O's reserve team goalscoring charts during season 1934/35 with thirty-four goals, also scoring on his league debut for the club in October 1934 against Crystal Palace. That season also saw him score a total of ten goals from thirteen first team appearances, including a hat-trick against Brighton & Hove Albion. Arriving at the Vetch Field in September 1936, he made his debut at inside right at the Vetch Field against Coventry City, replacing Lewis, and scoring two goals on his debut in a 2-0 win. The second half of the season saw him struggle to make appearances for the Swans, and in April 1937 he joined Third Division North side Crewe Alexandra where he averaged almost a goal in every two games he played for the club.

16. FOWLER, John (JACK)

Birthplace: Cardiff, 3/12/1898. **Died:** Swansea, 26/2/1975
Ht: 5ft-11ins, **Wt:** 12st-2lbs
Swans debut: v. Southend United (h), 1/3/1924

Career:
Mardy (signed in 1919)
Plymouth Argyle (signed in May 1921) lge 37/25gls

Swansea Town (£1,280 signed in February 1924)
Clapton Orient (signed in June 1930) lge 75/15gls

Swansea Town Career Statistics			
Season	League	FAC	WC
1923/24	14/6gls		
1924/25	42/28gls	2	2
1925/26	32/28gls	7/7gls	
1926/27	39/19gls	5/3gls	1
1927/28	28/15gls	1	1
1928/29	11/6gls	1	1
1929/30	1		
Total	167/102gls	16/10gls	5

Honours: Wales Full–6, Third Division South Champions–1925, Welsh Section of Southern League Representative XI

Jack Fowler lied about his age and saw late service in the First World War as a member of the Royal Naval Air Service. He started his career with Rhondda side Mardy, following Moses Russell from Mardy to Plymouth Argyle. Many Argyle supporters thought he did not get a fair opportunity at Home Park, but still scored 25 goals from 37 league apps, and in April 1923 scored two goals against the Swans. Impressing Swans manager Joe Bradshaw, he arrived at the Vetch Field for a record transfer fee at the time of £1,280, which was to stand until 1938 when the Swans paid Newcastle United £1,500 for Bill Imrie. Scoring on his league debut for the Swans, by the end of the season he had registered his first hat-trick for the Swans in a 4-0 home win over Brentford. The Third Division South Championship winning season of 1924/25 saw Fowler score five goals in a 6-1 win over Charlton Athletic, and his second hat-trick, this time against Luton Town, from a season that saw him finish with twenty-eight goals from forty-two appearances. A change in the offside law the following season saw him score a further 28 goals in the Second Division during the 1925/26 season, from just 32 league appearances. Further hat-tricks were scored against Darlington, Preston North End and Southampton, whilst in the exciting FA Cup run which took them to the semi-finals, Fowler scored four goals against Stoke City in a 6-3 win at the Vetch Field. No doubt his presence was missed at the end of the season in the Welsh Cup Final defeat by Ebbw Vale. Powerfully built, aggressive, and determined, the menacing front runner was regarded as somebody who put himself about. Not necessarily a bulldozer type of player, but very quick, constructive, and extremely clever. Fowler made his international debut for Wales at the Vetch Field against England on the 28th February 1925, and thirteen months later opened his goalscoring account at international level with two goals against England at Selhurst Park in March 1926. The 1926/27 season saw Fowler return nineteen goals for the Swans, including a hat-trick against Barnsley, followed by another hat-trick in season 1927/28 against Wolverhampton Wanderers, in a 6-0 Vetch Field win. In early May 1929 he scored both goals for the Swans in their 4-2 defeat by Cardiff City in the Final of the South Wales & Monmouthshire Cup Final at Llanelly. By the time he joined Clapton Orient in June 1930, Fowler had lost his place in the Swans line-up, firstly to Lewis, Cheetham, and then to Ronnie Williams. Immediately given the role of captain, he started his career in London's East End in typical fashion, scoring five goals, which included a hat trick against Coventry City, in his first five games, also scoring the first goal at the club's new Lea Bridge Ground, on the 4th September 1930 against Newport County, before reverting to a centre half role. Orient had a reputation at the time of not paying it's players, and Fowler would often distribute his wages amongst the players in the team. He still remained popular in Swansea after leaving to sign for Orient, often organizing boxing matches on stage during benefit concerts. He retired from football through a succession of injuries in 1932, returning to Swansea to become a licensee, an

enthusiastic small scale entrepreneur who moved easily in theatrical circles, often performing on stage telling jokes and reading his own monologues, but who was often dogged by bad luck. A landlord at the Rhyddings Public House for 35 years, he lost interest in the Swans as he got older, and became more interested in rugby, cricket and horse racing up to his death in February 1975.

17. FRANCIS, Gerald (GERRY) Charles James

Birthplace: Chiswick, 6/12/1951
Ht: 5ft-10ins, **Wt:** 12st-2lbs
Swans debut: v. Walsall (h), 20/10/1984

Swansea City Career Statistics	
Season	League
1984/85	3
Total	3

Career:
QPR (signed from apprentice in June 1969) lge 290+5/53gls
Crystal Palace (£465,000 signed in 3/7/1979) lge 59/7gls
QPR (£150,000 signed in 25/2/1981) lge 17/4gls
Coventry City (£150,000 signed in 13/2/1982) lge 50/2gls
Exeter City (signed in 20/7/1983) lge 28/3gls
Cardiff City (signed in 4/9/1984) lge 7
Swansea City (signed in 18/10/1984)
Portsmouth (non-contract signed in late November 1984) lge 3
Wimbledon (signed in August 1985)
Bristol Rovers (non-contract signed in 1/9/1985) lge 33

Honours: England U-23–6, Full–12

Gerry Francis played Sunday League Football in Chiswick prior to signing as an apprentice at Loftus Road with Queens Park Rangers, had a lengthy career in top flight football as an attacking midfielder, and after gaining U-23 honours with England, made his debut at full level against Czechoslovakia on the 30th October 1974 at Wembley, captaining his country on eight occasions. Ten seasons at Loftus Road with QPR, saw the club finish runners-up to Burnley in the old Second Division in season 1972/73, runners-up to Liverpool in the old First Division in season 1975/76, and the following season lose in the semi-finals of the League Cup to Aston Villa. In season 1979/80 he played against the Swans at the Vetch Field for Crystal Palace in the Third Round of the FA Cup competition, but did not feature in the replays due to injury. In later years he sampled management as player boss at Exeter City in 1983, then played on a non-contract basis for Cardiff City, Swans, Portsmouth, coached alongside Dave Bassett at Wimbledon (1986), Bristol Rovers, before taking over from Bobby Gould as boss at Rovers in July 1987, and putting £20,000 of his own money into the club. Winning the Third Division Championship in 1990, and losing in the Final of the Leyland Daf Cup the same season, he was then appointed boss at QPR a year later in June 1991. Consolidating the club's position in the First Division, then what became known as the Premiership with top ten placings in the first two seasons of the Premiership, he was then appointed boss at White Hart Lane with Spurs in November 1994. After 3 seasons at White Hart Lane, he resigned his position in November 1997, ten months later returning to his old club QPR as boss in October 1998. Joining Bristol Rovers in July 2001 from Ian Holloway, who had made the reverse journey to take over at QPR as player manager in February 2001, he lasted less than half a season at Rovers with Gary Thompson being unable to prevent the club from slipping into the Third Division. Personal problems at the time saw him not only leave his managerial post with Rovers in December 2001, but also his position as a Director of the club. During his non-contract period at the Vetch Field, the Swans had serious financial problems, and season 1983/84 would see the club record the most players used in the league for one season, as manager Colin Appleton attempted to turn the club around with trialists and non-contract players, with the club having a transfer embargo still in place by the Football League. After making his debut at the Vetch Field in a 2-1 defeat by Walsall, Francis was injured in the next game at Hull City, and after returning for the away match at Doncaster Rovers joined Portsmouth in late November 1985 before joining the coaching staff of Wimbledon. After leaving football he was later involved in the PR and Media side of the Musical, 125th Street, in London's West End.

18. FREEMAN, ALBERT (Paddy)

Birthplace: Preston, 21/10/1899
Ht: 5ft-9ins, **Wt:** 11st-8lbs
Swans debut: v. Hull City (a), 31/8/1929

Swansea Town Career Statistics		
Season	League	FAC
1929/30	23	1
Total	23	1

Career:
Leyland
Burnley (signed in March 1923) lge 78/19gls, FAC 4
Swansea Town (£500 signed in May 1929)
Chorley (signed in June 1930)

Signed by manager James Thomson for £500 from Burnley in May 1929, Albert Freeman made his Swans debut at inside left in the opening fixture of the 1929/30 season against Hull City. After his next appearance he missed a couple of games, and when he returned to action played either at right, or at left half back. Towards the end of the season he reverted to his customary inside forward position, but in August 1930 was released, returning to Lancashire to sign for non-league side Chorley. Starting his playing career with Leyland, Freeman joined First Division Burnley in 1922, making all his first team appearances for the club in the First Division prior to his arrival at the Vetch Field. He scored on his second appearance for Burnley in a 2-0 home win over Sunderland, and remained at Turf Moor for six years until arriving at the Vetch Field. Season 1927/28 was his only season as a regular in the Burnley line-up when he partnered George Beel, who scored a record thirty-five league goals during the season. He was retained for a second season at Chorley for season 1931/32.

19. FREEMAN, CLIVE Richard

Birthplace: Leeds, 12/9/1962
Ht: 5ft-8½ins, **Wt:** 12st-7lbs
Swans debut: v. Bradford City (a), 22/9/1990

Swansea City Career Statistics			
Season	League	WC	AGT
1990/91	2		
1991/92	8+4	1	1
Total	10+4	1	1

Career:
Farsley Celtic
Doncaster Rovers (signed in 1987)
Farsley Celtic
Bridlington Town
Swansea City (£5,000 signed in August 1990)
Carlisle United (loan in January 1992) lge 4
Altrincham (signed prior to start of season 1992/93)
　Conf 26+6/8gls
Doncaster Rovers (signed in August 1993) lge 23+2/2gls

Honours: West Wales Senior Cup Winner–1991

A former Leeds Schoolboy who joined Third Division Doncaster Rovers at the start of season 1987/88 from non-league Farsley Celtic, but did not make any appearances in the first team. He returned to Celtic, where he switched from an outside left to left full back. During season 1989/90 Freeman and Terry Yorath were team mates for Beechwood Santos in the Jubilee Premier Division of the Leeds Sunday Combination. Yorath had been sacked midway through the 89/90 season, but Freeman was involved with Bridlington in the FA Vase competition, and in the Northern Counties East League. His appearances in the Sunday games were limited towards the end of the season at his club progressed in both cup and league competitions. When Yorath took over at the Vetch Field a second time in March 1990 he contacted Freeman, who was working in the 'ACCENT' menswear clothes shop in Leeds with the offer of a contract with the Swans. Freeman opted to take what he thought at the time was probably his last chance of playing in the Football League, and although a relatively late entry to league football, signed for the Swans in July 1990 from non-league side Bridlington for £5,000, a couple of months short of his 28th birthday. A successful season the previous year saw him play for Bridlington against Yeading in the FA Vase Final at Wembley, which went to a replay at Elland Road, before losing 1-0, playing in both matches at left full back. At a younger age he gained Boys County caps with Leeds and Yorkshire, and prior to signing for the Swans worked as a clothes shop manager and sales representative. An ankle injury in pre-season training with the Swans saw him miss a number of pre-season friendly matches, with his league debut being delayed until after the season had started, at Bradford City in late September 1990. His only other appearance that season came in the next game against Tranmere Rovers at the Vetch Field. With Frank Burrows replacing Yorath in March 1991, Clive's second season at the Vetch Field saw him make most of his appearances for the Swans during the second half of the season, after returning from a loan spell at Carlisle United, and again after he had missed the start of the season through injury. Released in May 1992, he then joined Conference side Altrincham for pre-season trials which led to him signing terms just prior to the start of the season, and being appointed captain. Despite finishing the season as top goalscorer with eight league goals in the Vauxhall Conference, and scoring a goal in the FA Cup defeat of league side Chester that won BBC TV's Goal of the Month competition on Match of the Day, he was unwilling to conform with the defensive duties allotted him at the club, preferring to play in midfield, which resulted in him leaving after just one season to sign for Doncaster Rovers. He later played for Emley and Bradford Park Avenue, before signing for UniBond Division One side Guiseley, where he was player/assistant manager during the 2004/05 season, and working as a sales representative for security accessory company Keypac.

20. FREESTONE, ROGER

Birthplace: Caerleon, 19/8/1968
Ht: 6ft-3ins, **Wt:** 14st-6lbs
Swans debut: v. Notts. County (h), 30/9/1989

Swansea City Career Statistics

Season	League	FLC	FAC	WC	LDAF/ AGT/AWS	P/Offs	FAWP
1989/90	14			1	1		
1991/92	42	2	3	3	2		
1992/93	46	2	5	1	3	2	
1993/94	46	4	2	6	8		
1994/95	44+1/1gls	4	5	5	4		
1995/96	45/2gls	2	1		3		
1996/97	45	2	2		2	3	
1997/98	43	2	1		1		3
1998/99	38	2	5		2	2	4
1999/00	46	4	2		2		
2000/01	43	2	1		3		5
2001/02	43	1	2		1		3
2002/03	33	1	1		1		1
2003/04	35+2		5				1
Total	563+3/3gls	28	35	16	33	7	17

Career:
Newport County (from youth trainee in 2/4/1986) lge 13
Chelsea (loan in 10/3/1987, £95,000 in April 1987) lge 42, FLC 2, FAC 3, Others 6
Swansea City (loan in 29/9/1989)
Hereford United (loan in 9/3/1990) lge 8
Swansea City (£45,000 signed in 5/9/1991)
Newport County (signed in June 2004)

Honours: Wales Sch, Yth, Full–1, Second Division Champions–1989, Third Division Champions–2000, AutoGlass Trophy Winner–1994, West Wales Senior Cup Winner–1994

Earlier in season 2002/03 Swans keeper Roger Freestone became only the third player in the club's history to pass the milestone of 500 league appearances, when he played against Bournemouth at the Vetch Field. In his long career at the Club, Freestone had always been a popular figure and had smashed many records, including an incredible 179 consecutive league appearances. His reliability and fitness was further illustrated by the fact that between 1991 and 1997 he missed just three league games for the club. Capped for Wales at schoolboy and youth levels, Freestone was earmarked for a great future in the game from the very beginning, signing for his hometown club Newport County, and making his league debut at Port Vale on the 27th December 1986. The Gwent side were in severe financial difficulties at the time, and the young Freestone was thrown in at the deep end, handed his first team debut as an 18-year-old. Some eye-catching performances saw him on the move to Chelsea just 13 games into his career, as County were forced to cash in on their only saleable asset. With the club losing money, there were desperate times at Somerton Park, but the £95,000 they received for Roger did not save the club from eventually having to fold. The young Freestone was seen as a long term prospect at Stamford Bridge, with Blues boss John Hollins happy to give his new signing the occasional game where needed. However, with Roger struggling to settle in West London, he did play enough games during season 1988/89 to receive a Second Division Championship medal, but after Chelsea had signed Dave Beasant, Roger failed to make any more appearances, and in the autumn of 1989 arrived at the Vetch Field on an initial month's loan. Making sixteen league and cup appearances for the Swans, he returned to Stamford Bridge, and after another loan stint, this time with Hereford United eventually returned to the Vetch Field for £45,000, some £100,000 less than what the Swans had offered two years previously! Since returning to the Vetch Field on a permanent basis, Freestone has inevitably experienced many highs and lows, but winning the Third Division Championship in 2000 was without doubt the high spot in his career at the Vetch Field. Setting so many new records during the Championship winning season, conceding only 30 goals and keeping 22 clean sheets was a great achievement and rounding the season off with a Welsh cap against Brazil at the Millenium Stadium in Cardiff made it perfect. Another high spot in 'Dodger's 'career came on Sunday 24th April 1994 when the Swans played at Wembley Stadium for the first time ever against Huddersfield Town in the AutoGlass Trophy. With the game having to be decided on penalties, it was an afternoon that saw Roger carve his name into the Vetch history books forever, saving the last penalty to take the cup home to South West Wales. In May 1995 he was included in the Swans side that beat Ammanford Town to win the West Wales Senior Cup. Roger has been involved in three Play-Off campaigns during his time at the club, in 1992-93 when the Swans played West Bromwich Albion in the Second Division Play Off semi-final, losing narrowly in the second leg at the Hawthorns. The second time was when the Swans lost to Northampton Town in the Third Division Play Off Final at Wembley in what turned out to be the last kick of the game. The third time was against Scunthorpe United in the Third Division Play Off semi-final, losing again in almost the last few minutes of the game. Besides being an ever present in three seasons for the Swans, Roger also holds the club record for ppearances during a season with Mark Harris, making 66 league and cup appearances during season

1993/94. He can also claim to be the only goalkeeper to have scored a goal for the Swans following his penalty successes during season 1994/95 at Oxford, and the following season when he scored penalties against both Shrewsbury Town and Chesterfield at the Vetch Field. During the bleak, uncertain days during the 2001/02 season when controversial chairman Tony Petty sacked most of the playing staff, Roger was one of the players the chairman tried to offload, turning down the advances of QPR on two occasions. By the end of the season however, along with Nick Cusack, 'Dodger' took on the role of joint caretaker manager. With injury forcing 'Dodger' onto the sidelines for the last couple of weeks of the season, there was no stranger sight in football seeing Roger bellowing out instructions from the technical area in front of the dugout. Overcoming a string of injury problems over the last couple of seasons, including disc and ligament damage in his back which threatened his career, Roger returned to action displacing close season signing Brian Murphy shortly after the start of the 2003/04 season to make thirty-five league starts, plus two more from the substitute bench. Shortly after the last game of the season Roger was given a free transfer by manager Kenny Jackett, and in early June 2004 rejoined his first club, Newport County on a part-time basis, which included a role as goalkeeper coach. Just prior to the start of the 2004/05 season, Roger embarked on a new career as a trainee financial advisor with Ethical Finance, a company based in Cardiff Bay, but after a couple of months left the company to become a delivery driver for DHL in the Risca/Newport area. An ankle injury saw him sidelined in October and by the end of November he announced his retirement from the game, severing all contact with the game apart from watching his son play at weekends.

21. FRENCH, NIGEL Peter

Birthplace: Swansea, 24/3/1968
Ht: 5ft-9ins, **Wt:** 9st-13lbs
Swans debut: v. Wigan Athletic (h), 17/8/1985

Season	League	FLC	FAC	WC	FRT
Season	League	FLC	FAC	WC	FRT
1985/86	11+3/1gls	1	0+1	1/1gls	2/1gls
1986/87	2+10/2gls	0+2	1	0+1	0+1
Total	13+13/3gls	1+2	1+1	1+1/1gls	2+1/1gls

Swansea City Career Statistics

Career:
Swansea City (signed from YTS in March 1986)
Merthyr Tydfil (signed prior to start of season 1987/88)
    Conf 1+2
Haverfordwest County (signed after start of season 1989/90)

Honours: Wales Sch, Yth, Wales Semi-Pro International, Beazer Homes Midland Division Champions–1988, Beazer Homes

Premier Division Champions–1989, Abacus Welsh League National Division Champions–1990

One of three youngsters (Keri Andrews and Paul Burrows) from the East Side of the City who joined the club as YTS trainees from Cefn Hengoed School in 1984. A midfield player with his school team, Swansea Schoolboys U-11, U-13 sides and U-15 side, he was also capped for the Welsh U-15 side prior to leaving school. He made his debut for the Swans whilst a second year trainee at the age of 17 years and five months old against Wigan Athletic in the opening game of season 1985/86, going on as a substitute for Colin Pascoe. Three days later he made his first start for the Swans at Ninian Park against Cardiff City in the Milk Cup, First Round, First Leg, again as a replacement for Pascoe. He had to wait until late October to make his first league start, scoring the Swans goal in a 5-1 defeat at Gillingham. During his first season as a professional he struggled to make the starting line-up under Terry Yorath, with ten of his twelve first team appearances in the league coming from the bench, despite scoring the winning goal against Aldershot after replacing Sean McCarthy. He was released in May 1987, joining Beazer Homes Midland Division side Merthyr Tydfil, and a period which was to be his most successful in the game. His first season saw Merthyr win the Championship of the Midland Division, and the following season the Championship of the Premier Division, and promotion to the Conference. With the club winning the Welsh Cup in 1987, Nigel's first season at Penydarren Park saw him play in both legs against Italian side Atalanta, winning the first leg at Penydarren Park, before losing 2-0 in Italy. He was also capped for the Wales Semi-Professional side against England during his first season with Merthyr. Nigel made 3 league appearances, two as substitute for Merthyr in the GM Vauxhall Conference during season 1989/90, and after a period on the sidelines with glandular fever joined Haverfordwest County in the Abacus Welsh League National Division, winning the Championship later in the season. After making appearances for Aberystwyth and a spell back at Haverfordwest, he joined Barry Town for the start of the 1993/94 season, but halfway through the season returned to Haverfordwest. At the end of the season, Barry had not only won the Welsh League First Division Championship, but had also won the Welsh Cup. He finished his playing career with Swansea Senior League side Port Tennant Colts, working for the Royal Mail, and for the last five years has been a postman seconded to NTL in Llansamlet.

22. FURY, PAUL

Birthplace: Swansea, 16/3/1955
Ht: 5ft-9lbs, **Wt:** 11st-4lbs
Swans debut: v. Blackburn Rovers (h), 4/4/1972

Career:
Swansea City (signed from apprentice in 1972/73)

Cork Celtic (signed in close season 1973)
Bridgend Town (signed in 1974)

Swansea City Career Statistics	
Season	League
1971/72	9
1972/73	2
Total	11

Honours: Wales Sch–1, Yth–4

Former Swans Schoolboys defender who joined the Swans as an apprentice from school, and who made his league debut whilst still an apprentice at the Vetch Field against Blackburn Rovers in April 1972, replacing Wyndham Evans at right full back, a couple of weeks after his seventeenth birthday.
Offered professional terms by manager Roy Bentley for the 1972/73 season, his only league outings that season came early in the season at right full back. However, with a change of management midway through the season, he was released in May 1973 on a free transfer. The former Dynevor schoolboy, and Swansea schoolboy defender was capped at schoolboy level for Wales against the Republic of Ireland, making a further four international appearances for the Welsh Youth side, against France (2), and Scotland (2) when he was an apprentice. He initially signed for the Swans in 1968 on the same day that he was playing for his school side, in a game in which he broke his leg! Released by the Swans at the end of the 1972/73 season, for the majority of the following season he played in Ireland with Cork Celtic, before returning to the UK to sign for Bridgend Town, later making appearances for Welsh League sides Haverfordwest County, Llanelli and Ammanford Town. With his brother John on the books of Leeds United as a youngster, Paul's daughter Sarah has also made her mark on the British squash circuit, whilst nephew Warren has recently signed a contract with London Wasps rugby team.

G

1. GALE, DARREN

Birthplace: Port Talbot, 25/10/1963
Ht: 5ft-10½ins, **Wt**: 12st-3lbs
Swans debut: v. Aston Villa (a), 21/5/1982

Swansea City Career Statistics						
Season	*League*	*FLC*	*FAC*	*WC*	*ECWC*	*FRT*
1981/82	0+1					
1982/83	10+5/3gls		1/1gls	4/2gls	1/2gls	
1983/84	16+4/3gls	2/1gls	1	2/2gls	0+2	
1984/85	0+1			1		1
Total	26+11/6gls	2/1gls	2/1gls	7/4gls	1+2/2gls	1

Career:
Swansea City (from apprentice in October 1980)
Exeter City (signed in September 1985) lge 19+1/5gls

Honours: Wales Sch, Yth, U-21–2, Welsh Cup Winner–1983

Former Afan Nedd schoolboy who had a week's trial with Manchester City prior to signing as an apprentice with the Swans in 1980. Capped at schoolboy level, he also made appearances for the Welsh Youth side earlier in his career with the Swans, with his first U-21 appearance coming against Bulgaria on the 26th April 1983 at Bangor. His second appearance coming on the 15th November 1983 as a substitute for Hughes in Norway. Darren made his Swans debut as substitute for the injured Colin Irwin in the last First Division game of season 1981/82 at Villa Park, after earlier in the season being included as a non-playing substitute in Welsh Cup games. With financial problems behind the scenes at the Vetch Field, Darren became a regular inclusion during the second half of season 1982/83 as experienced professionals were offloaded in a bid to reduce the club's monthly wage bill, and youngsters from the club's reserve and youth teams were given their league opportunities. Darren scored his debut First Division goal at the Vetch Field against Notts. County in a 2-0 win in January 1983, scoring a further two goals before the end of the season.

A consistent goalscorer at youth, and reserve team level, he was a speedy, rugged centre forward, difficult to knock off the ball, and brave in challenges. His braveness was to ultimately force his retirement from the game in later years, as he never fully recovered from a collision with the Bristol Rovers goalkeeper during a Football Combination match at the Vetch Field. As a goalscorer his record for the Swans saw him score in league, League Cup, FA Cup, Welsh Cup, and ECWC games for the Swans. At the end of season 1982/83 he played in both legs of the Welsh Cup Final against Wrexham, scoring the Swans first goal in the first leg at Wrexham. Struggling to recapture his fitness levels after his broken leg, he was released by the Swans in May 1985, joining Exeter City on an initial trial basis, linking up with former Swans manager Colin Appleton. Making regular appearances for Exeter during the first half of the season, scoring two goals in one match against Preston in November 1985, and finishing with five goals from eighteen league appearances. During his second season at St. James Park he started the season, but received an injury in his second game at Crewe Alexandra in September, failing to make any further appearances for the 'Grecians', having his contract cancelled halfway through the season. He stayed in the Exeter area for a number of years, but later returned to his home town and worked for a spell in BSC Port Talbot.

2. GARDNER, PAUL Anthony

Birthplace: Southport, 22/9/1957
Ht: 5ft-9½ins, **Wt:** 12st-0lbs
Swans debut: v. Orient (h), 6/10/1984

Swansea City Career Statistics	
Season	League
1984/85	4
Total	4

Career:
Blackpool (from apprentice in September 1975) lge 149+3/1gls
Bury (signed in August 1982) lge 90
Swansea City (signed non-contract in 3/10/1984)
Preston North End (signed non-contract)
Wigan Athletic (signed non-contract in January 1985) lge 5
Chorley
Leyland Motors

Former apprentice at Bloomfield Road with Blackpool who after making his league debut on the 25th September 1976 against Chelsea in the Second Division became a regular member of the club's first team squad at right full back. Suffering two relegations during his time at Bloomfield Road, he joined Fourth Division Bury in August 1982, missing two league games in two seasons before leaving the club. Signed by Swans manager Colin Appleton on non-contract terms during a season when the club broke their record for players making appearances in the Swans first team, he made just four consecutive league appearances before being released, joining Preston North End, then Wigan Athletic, both as non-contract. Following his release by Wigan Athletic, he has since become a fireman and played non-League football for Chorley and Leyland Motors.

3. GARNETT, SHAUN Maurice

Birthplace: Wallasey, 22/11/1969
Ht: 6ft-2ins, **Wt:** 13st-4lbs
Swans debut: v. Brentford (h), 12/3/1996

Swansea City Career Statistics		
Season	League	FLC
1995/96	9	
1996/97	6	2
Total	15	2

Career:
Tranmere Rovers (associate schoolboy, trainee, signed professional in June 1988) lge 110+2/5gls, FLC 13/1gls, FAC 4, Others 15+2
Chester City (loan in 1/10/1992) lge 9
Preston North End (loan in 11/12/1992) lge 10/2gls, Others 1
Wigan Athletic (loan in 26/2/1993) lge 13/1gls

Swansea City (£150,000 signed in 11/3/1996)
Oldham Athletic (£150,000 signed in 18/9/1996) lge 189+8/9gls, FLC 7, FAC 12, Others 4
Halifax Town (loan in 9/9/2002) Conf 29/1gls
Halifax Town (signed in 31/5/2003) Conf 11
Morecambe (signed in 1/11/2003) Conf 23

Honours: Leyland Daf Cup Winner–1990

An experienced central defender who became Jan Molby's first signing after he had taken over as manager in mid-February, arriving at the Vetch Field for £150,000 in March 1996. Unfortunately, his experience was unable to prevent the Swans at the end of the season from slipping back into the Third Division. A poor start to the 1996/97 campaign, which saw both Keith Walker and Christian Edwards injured, or unavailable, saw Shaun unable to settle in Swansea, and he was sold to Oldham Athletic for the same fee as his transfer to the Vetch Field. Despite a poor start by the Swans that season, by Christmas time the side had settled down, and figured in the end of season Play Off Final against Northampton Town. A former associate schoolboy and trainee at Prenton Park with Tranmere Rovers, earlier in his career he was a member of the Rovers side in the late 1980's and early 1990's that made regular visits to Wembley Stadium for end of season Play Offs and Cup Finals. Shaun was a member of the 1989/90 Rovers side that beat Bristol Rovers in the Leyland Daf Cup Final 2-1, and in the same season, his second visit to Wembley he played in the Rovers side that lost to Notts. County in the Division Two Play Off Final, after playing just five league games for Rovers from a midfield role. At the end of the following season, Rovers beat Bolton Wanderers in the Division Two Play Off Final 1-0 in which he was a member, but missed out the same season when they lost to Birmingham City in the Leyland Daf Cup Final. Establishing himself in a central defensive role with Rovers in the First Division, the 1993/94 season saw the club lose out on penalties to Aston Villa in the Coca Cola Cup semi-final. Included in the side that beat Villa in the first leg 3-1, Shaun did not figure in the second leg defeat by Villa. In the 1992/93 season Shaun made league appearances for Chester City, Preston North End and Wigan Athletic on a loan basis. After making almost two hundred league appearances for Oldham Athletic, he was released at the end of the 2002/03 season, joining Conference side Halifax Town, after previously playing on loan for the club the previous season. After just eleven Conference appearances he signed for fellow Conference side Morecombe, staying until the end of the season before being released in May 2004. Signing a contract with Harrogate Town in the 2004 close season, before playing a game for the club, he returned to Prenton Park with Tranmere Rovers in late July in a youth team manager/coaching capacity, assisting youth and reserve team manager John McMahon.

4. GIBBINS, ROGER Graeme

Birthplace: Enfield, 6/9/1955
Ht: 5ft-10ins, **Wt:** 11st-9lbs
Swans debut: v. Lincoln City (h), 11/10/1985

Swansea City Career Statistics				
Season	League	FAC	WC	FRT
1985/86	35/6gls	2	4/1gls	4
Total	35/6gls	2	4/1gls	4

Career:
Tottenham Hotspur (from apprentice in 1/12/1972)
Oxford United (signed in 1/8/1975) lge 16+3/2gls
Norwich City (signed in 1/6/1976) lge 47+1/12gls

New England Teamen (USA, March 1978)
Cambridge United (signed in 27/9/1979) lge 97+3/12gls
Cardiff City (signed in 1/8/1982) lge 135+4/17gls
Swansea City (p/exchange in 10/10/1985)
Newport County (signed in 22/8/1986) lge 79/8gls
Torquay United (£5,000 signed in 25/3/1988) lge 32+1/5gls
Newport County (£10,000 signed in January 1989) Conf 1
Cardiff City (signed in 23/3/1989) lge 132+10/7gls

Honours: England Sch, FAYC–1974, Third Division
Champions–1993, Welsh Cup Winner–1992

Former Enfield Schoolboy, Middlesex, London and England
Schoolboy international Roger Gibbins joined Tottenham
Hotspur as an apprentice, playing in the Spurs youth side that
beat Huddersfield Town to win the FA Youth Cup in 1974.
A professional for two seasons at White Hart Lane, after failing
to break into the Spurs league side joined Oxford United in
August 1975, making his league debut during the 1975/76
season. Joining the Swans in a part exchange deal in October
1985, which saw midfielder Chris Marustik go in the opposite
direction to Ninian Park, earlier in the season he had played for
the Bluebirds in both legs of the Milk Cup against the Swans.
Capable of playing in either a midfield, or a striker role, by the
end of his only season at the Vetch Field he was top goalscorer
with six league goals, with the Swans off the field lurching from
one crisis to another. Midway through the season, manager John
Bond had been sacked by the Official Receiver, gates to the club
locked, relegation to the Fourth Division decided a long time
before the end of the season, and numerous visits to the High
Court. Released along with experienced professionals Jimmy
Rimmer, Alan Waddle, Colin Sullivan and Paul Price, Roger
signed for Newport County in August 1986, completing the
triangle of appearances for Welsh clubs in the Football League.
He was to return to Somerton Park when County were in the
GM Vauxhall Conference in season 1988/89, playing just one
league game prior to the club folding through worsening
financial problems. Returning to Ninian Park in March 1989,
Roger played in the 1992 Welsh Cup Final victory over
Hednesford, and played his last league game at Scarborough in
April 1993, a month later the Bluebirds won the Fourth Division
Championship. He continued to play non-league at Merthyr
and at Cwmbran Town in the League of Wales, finishing his
playing career in 1997, at the age of 42, but still retaining a
coaching position with the Gwent based outfit. Roger also held
managerial positions at Weston-Super-Mare in 1998, and at
Merthyr Tydfil from April to December 1999. For a number of
years he has been employed by the PFA for the South and South
West Area as a Regional Merit Officer, with responsibilities in
the scholarship programme for youngsters attached to Football
League Clubs. With the amount of foreign players in the
modern day British game, Roger can look back earlier in his
career and reflect on the experience he had in the USA. In March
1978 he was offered a contract with New England Teamen, just
before he had completed his third consecutive season of league
action with Oxford United and Norwich City. At the age of 22,
Roger joined a number of players who had been tempted to try

their luck in the USA, at a time when the American game was
enjoying a high profile with the likes of Brazilian legend Pele,
German Franz Beckenbauer, and Dutch players Neeskens, and
Cruyff coming to the end of their playing career with New York
Cosmos, and playing regularly in front of 70,000 attendances.
The New England Teamen were managed by Irishman Noel
Cantwell, and former Manchester United forward Denis Violett,
and Roger felt it was too good an opportunity to miss after he
had been approached about playing in the USA. Other British
players who took up the offer at the same time included Keith
Weller, Gerry Daly, Mike Flanagan and Peter Simpson of
Arsenal. It had been reported that British based players such as
Peter Osgood, George Best, Rodney Marsh and Johnny Giles
had been offered in the region of £1,000 a game to cross the
Atlantic, such was the money being poured into the NASL to
make it a counter attraction to American Football and Baseball.
Like Roger, not all the players crossing the Atlantic were at the
end of their playing career, quite a number like Roger were still
learning their trade, such as Trevor Francis at Birmingham City.

5. GILES, DAVID Charles

Birthplace: Cardiff, 21/9/1956
Ht: 5ft-7ins, **Wt:** 10st-5lbs
Swans debut: v. Wrexham (a), 1/12/1979

Swansea City Career Statistics				
Season	League	FLC	FAC	WC
1979/80	25/8gls		5/4gls	4/1gls
1980/81	24+3/5gls	2	0+1	3
1981/82	0+2			
Total	49+5/8gls	2	5+1/4gls	7/1gls

Career:
Cardiff City (from apprentice in September 1974) lge 51/8gls,
    ECWC 1+1
Wrexham (£30,000 signed in 21/12/1978) lge 38/3gls, FLC 3,
    FAC 3, WC 4/1gls, ECWC 2
Swansea City (£70,000 signed in 28/11/1979)
Leyton Orient (loan in November 1981) lge 3/2gls
Crystal Palace (signed in March 1982) lge 83+5/6gls
Birmingham City (signed in August 1984) lge 0
Newport County (loan in 5/10/1984) lge 6
Newport County (signed in 6/11/1984) lge 22+4/1gls
Cardiff City (signed in September 1985) lge 50
Barry Town (signed in January 1987)
Merthyr Tydfil (signed in August 1988)
Newport County (signed in November 1988) Conf 3/2gls
Sully FC (signed in April 1989)
AFC Cardiff (signed in close season 1989)
Abergavenny Thursdays (signed in February 1990)

Stroud FC (signed in March 1991)
Barri (signed in 1992)
Inter Cardiff (signed in 1992)
Ebbw Vale (signed in 1993)
Barry Town (signed in 1995)

Honours: Wales Sch–3, Yth–5, U–21–3, Full–12, Welsh Cup Winner–1976, 1981, Abacus Welsh League National Division Champions–1987

Spotted by Cardiff City as a 10-year-old, the former Cardiff and Wales schoolboy player turned professional in 1974, making his first team debut in a Welsh Cup tie against Oswestry Town, with his league debut coming against Nottingham Forest on the 22nd February 1975, playing in the next two league games against Manchester United and Blackpool. He never really established himself at Ninian Park, but did play in some of the club's important matches, like the FA Cup ties against Spurs and Wrexham in the 1976/77 season, in which he scored City's opening goal, and in the club's European adventures. At the end of the 1975/76 season he played in the Bluebirds side that beat Hereford United to win the Welsh Cup Final, and later with the Swans he also played against Hereford United at the end of season 1980/81 in the second leg to win a second Welsh Cup Winners Medal. He also made appearances for the Wales Youth and U-21 side whilst at Ninian Park, with his first U-21 cap coming in 1977 against Scotland. His younger brother Paul also played for the Bluebirds. David left Ninian Park in December 1978 to join Wrexham for £30,000, making his debut along with Steve Fox in the home defeat by Preston North End on Boxing Day 1978. A hard working midfielder, he was well liked at the Racecourse, and it was a surprise that he left to join the Swans in November 1978 for £70,000. Making his debut for the Swans against Wrexham, although it took him seven league games to register his first goal for the Swans, against Cardiff City in January 1980, by the end of the season he had finished as top goalscorer in the league with eight goals. Later in the season a £400,000 offer from Crystal Palace was turned down, after he had starred against them in FA Cup ties. At the end of the season he gained his first Full cap for Wales, against England, also playing in the remaining Home International Championship matches against Scotland and Northern Ireland. His second season saw him start in the Swans line-up, but for the promotion deciding end of season game at Preston, David was a non-playing substitute. At one stage during David's playing career with the Swans there were seven Welsh Internationals, an England cap in Bob Latchford, two Yugoslav caps in Hadziabdic and Rajkovic, and two Scottish caps in Tommy Craig and Dave Stewart on the playing staff at the Vetch Field. Besides playing in two winning Welsh Cup Final sides, David also gained runners up medals in the competition with Cardiff City and Wrexham, and gained European match experience playing with Cardiff City and Wrexham, and was a non-playing substitute for the Swans against Lokomotiv Leipzig in September 1981. Following a loan transfer to Leyton Orient in November 1981, David was involved in a player exchange transfer in March 1982 which saw Welsh international Ian Walsh arrive at the Vetch Field with David going in the opposite direction to Crystal Palace. Within a couple of years he had returned to South Wales on an initial loan transfer to Newport County, before the transfer was made permanent in November 1984, returning to Ninian Park six months later. After making a further fifty league appearances for the Bluebirds, David signed for Abacus Welsh League National Division side Barry Town, helping them to win the Championship at the end of the season, before signing for Beazer Homes Premier Division side Merthyr Tydfil in August 1988. He returned to Newport County in November 1988 for a fee of £1,000, a few months before they were finally wound up in March 1989. David then played for a number of South Wales non league clubs, Sully, AFC Cardiff (where he was player manager), and Abergavenny Thursdays before returning to the Beazer League Midland Division to sign for Stroud. During season 1992/93 he appeared for Welsh Exiles side Barri in the Beazer Homes Midland Division, and League of

Wales side Ebbw Vale in 1993/94, taking over as their player manager in the close season of 1994. A year later he was appointed the joint manager of Barry Town with his brother Paul, and they led them to the League of Wales Championship, and to the Welsh Cup Final. However, at the end of the season the brothers were shocked to find out that they were surprisingly being relieved of their duties. He returned to Ebbw Vale where he became assistant to John Lewis, and the 1996/97 season saw them lead the Gwent club into Europe by qualifying for the Inter Toto Cup. He later rejoined Lewis in a similar position with Merthyr Tydfil for the 1998/99 season. Following a short period at Stebonheath Park with Llanelli, David joined local side Cardiff Civil Service who had just been promoted to the Welsh League. In what turned out to be a successful period for the club, David, mainly involved with coaching duties at the club, was quite happy to pay his £2 subs for the privilege of being involved at grass roots level. After stepping down from the full time game in 1987, David worked for Chubb Alarms after leaving Ninian Park, and in his own words, "set off more alarms, than what he sold!" Currently employed by Blood Screening Company, Johnson and Johnson, David has been engaged by Commercial Radio Station Real Radio over the last couple of seasons as a football analyst on matchdays, either at the Vetch Field, or at Ninian Park.

6. GILLIGAN, James (JIMMY) Martin

Birthplace: Hammersmith, 24/1/1964
Ht: 6ft-2ins, **Wt:** 11st-7lbs
Swans debut: v. Leyton Orient (a), 25/8/1990

Swans City Career Statistics						
Season	League	FLC	FAC	ECWC	WC	AGT
1990/91	36+1/16gls	2	4/2gls		5/4gls	3/2gls
1991/92	24+1/7gls	2/1gls	3/1gls	1	3	2
Total	60+2/23gls	4/1gls	7/3gls	1	8/4gls	5/2gls

Career:
Watford (signed schoolboy in April 1978, apprentice in July 1980, professional in 4/8/1981) lge 18+9/6gls
Lincoln City (loan in 7/10/1982) lge 0+3
Grimsby Town (£100,000 signed in 6/8/1985) lge 19+5/4gls
Swindon Town (£31,500 signed in 17/6/1986) lge 13+4/5gls
Newport County (loan in 5/2/1987) lge 4+1/1gls
Lincoln City (£35,000 signed in 26/3/1987) lge 11/1gls
Cardiff City (£17,500 signed in 22/7/1987) lge 99/35gls
Portsmouth (£215,000 in 3/10/1989) lge 24+8/5gls
Swansea City (£125,000 in 7/8/1990)
Boreham Wood (signed in March 1993)

Honours: England Yth–3, FAYC–1982, Welsh Cup Winner–1988

Signing for Watford as an apprentice from school, Jimmy Gilligan was part of a successful youth team at Vicarage Road, and had earlier in his career been a member of the club's youth side that won the F.A. Youth Cup, beating Manchester United 7-6 on aggregate in the final. His early school days were spent at Longmeadow Junior School, Barnwell Secondary School, playing for Longmeadow Athletic and Stevenage Boys.
He made his league debut for the 'Hornets' against Barnsley as substitute for Malcolm Poskett on the 3rd October 1981, his only appearance that season as Watford finished runners up in the Second Division. The following season, Jimmy scored two goals in a 2-0 home win over Manchester City, and in the 1983/84 season scored four goals for Watford in the First Division.
In October 1981 he was selected to play for England at U-18 level in a tournament in Yugoslavia, playing against Austria, Sweden and Hungary. He made loan appearances for Lincoln City in October 1982, but after struggling to make regular appearances in Watford's First (Premier) Division line up, he joined Grimsby Town in August 1985 for £100,000.
Within eighteen months, after appearances for Swindon Town and Newport County on loan, he had returned to Lincoln City on a permanent basis, with the club at the time in a seemingly healthy midway position in the Fourth Division. By the end of the season however, a defeat in the last league game of the season at the Vetch Field against the Swans saw the club drop into the Vauxhall Conference. Getting over the trauma of being part of a club that had lost it's league status, Gilligan was able to kick start his playing career with a move to Cardiff City. Signed by one of the most astute manager's in the professional game, Frank Burrows, he not only regained his confidence, and goal scoring touch in front of goal, but also followed Burrows to Portsmouth for a fee in the region of £215,000 two seasons later. He was signed by Terry Yorath at the Vetch Field in August 1990, and was re-united with Burrows six months later, when the Scotsman took over the managerial position at the Vetch Field. Top goalscorer for the Swans in his first season with 16 league goals, the first sign of a problem with his back came towards the end of his first season, when an injury forced him to miss the last seven league games of the season, and the Welsh Cup Final against Wrexham. Missing the first month of the 1991/92 season, and playing through the pain barrier on numerous occasions, he was forced into having to undergo surgery. Despite a period of rehabilitation, the problem never got any better, and before the start of the 1992/93 season he had been forced into calling it a day as far as his playing career was concerned, otherwise he could quite possibly have ended up in a wheelchair for the rest of his life. Supporters at the Vetch Field saw enough of the striker in the short time he was at the club to realise that for the first time since the days of Bob Latchford, they had at last somebody in the forward line who was capable of regularly getting on the score sheet. During one month in December 1991, he scored an incredible eight goals from four league matches. Highlights of his short career at the Vetch Field include goals against Tottenham Hotspur and Cardiff City in the Rumbelows, and FA Cup competitions respectively, and hat-tricks against Llanelli (Welsh Cup), and Wigan Athletic and Chester in the league. Following a period of rehabilitation, he joined Boreham Wood in March 1993, then played for Stamco FC (by November 1993), before taking over at Watford in September 1993 as Community Officer. Within two years he went from youth development officer to youth team coach at Vicarage Road, turning the club's centre of excellence into academy status. After three and a half years as youth coach, he joined Nottingham Forest as reserve team coach, at a time when David Platt was manager of the club. When Platt left the club to join the England backroom staff, he followed him, taking up a position on the coaching staff with a brief to look at countries who the England team were due to play. Following his appointment as regional coach with the PFA, his role with Platt was on a part-time basis, looking at teams in England's U-21 group, and full time with the PFA as a coach educator.
After joining the coaching staff of MK Dons (Wimbledon) in 2002, helping the club in their move from Selhurst Park to Milton Keynes, he graduated to assistant manager and on the

8th November 2004 he was placed in a caretaker manager role following the sacking of Stuart Murdoch. Following the appointment of Danny Wilson as the club's new manager, within a few days of Xmas 2004 Jimmy left the club.

7. GILLIGAN, MALCOLM

Birthplace: Cardiff, 11/10/1942
Ht: 5ft-7ins, **Wt:** 10st-3lbs
Swans debut: v. Portsmouth (h), 27/4/1963

Swansea Town Career Statistics	
Season	League
1962/63	3
Total	3

Career:
Swansea Town (signed groundstaff in 1959, professional in 11/5/1962)
Llanelly (loan by October 1961)
Bath City (signed in close season 1964)
Lovells Athletic (signed in close season 1965)

Honours: Wales Amateur–3, Yth, Welsh League Champions–1963, 1964, 1966, South Wales Senior Cup Winner–1970

Brought up in the Riverside area of Cardiff, Malcolm attended Kitchener Road school and Seven Road school prior to leaving school to work in a factory before joining the groundstaff at the Vetch Field in 1959. Playing youth club football with Mike Hayes, despite scoring three goals in a final trial game, he failed to make any appearances for Cardiff schoolboys. He soon followed Mike Hayes onto the groundstaff at the Vetch Field, and over the years both players would play in the same side for numerous teams throughout their playing career. Soon after joining the Swans groundstaff, Malcolm gained youth honours with Wales, and during a season loan spell at Stebonheath Park with Llanelly in 1961, made three Amateur appearances for Wales against England, Scotland and Northern Ireland. Malcolm made his league debut during his first season as a professional at outside right, playing in the next two league games, but failed to make an appearance during his second season as a professional. Unfortunately, during the time when Malcolm was trying to establish himself as a winger at the Vetch Field, there was too much competition from the likes of Barrie Jones, Graham Williams and Brian Evans for him to gain further first team experience at the Vetch Field, despite being a consistent goalscorer with the Swans' Welsh League reserve team during both seasons as a professional. At the end of season 1963/64 he was released, joining Bath City along with veteran goalkeeper

Johnny King. Twelve months later he linked up with Brayley Reynolds and Alan Wilkins at Lovells Athletic, winning the Welsh League Championship in his first season with the club. Two seasons later he had his first spell with Merthyr Tydfil, linking up former Swans players Reynolds, Hayes, Harris and Dil John. Following one season with Barry Town he returned to Penydarren Park, and played in the side that beat Cardiff City to win the 1969/70 South Wales Senior Cup Final. Malcolm also scored the winning goal for Merthyr when they beat Hereford United in the Welsh Cup competition. He left Merthyr after John Charles had taken over, playing one season with Ton Pentre, before finishing his playing career with Mike Hayes, who at the time was player manager of Welsh League Caerau. Mal trained as a carpenter after leaving the professional game, a trade he returned to after being released by the Swans, and continued to work for a number of years with the John Lang Construction Company.

8. GODDERIDGE, ALAN Edward

Birthplace: Tamworth, 23/5/1928
Swans debut: v. Bury (a), 11/4/1952

Swansea Town Career Statistics	
Season	League
1951/52	1
Total	1

Career:
Tamworth
Swansea Town (trial in August 1950, professional in October 1950)
Walsall (signed in July 1952) lge 3
Tamworth (signed in close season 1953)

Honours: Welsh League First Division Champions–1951

Arrived at the Vetch Field at the start of pre-season training on an extended trial basis from Midlands non-league side Tamworth, playing in the club's first Public Trial game at the Vetch Field on Saturday 12th August 1950. Primarily a reserve team player at the Vetch Field, by the end of his first season at the Vetch Field he had made appearances in the Welsh League side that won the First Division Championship. Signing a professional contract in October 1950, the left sided half back's only Swans appearance came towards the end of season 1951/52 at Bury, when he took the place of Frankie Burns. He was released at the end of the season, signing for Third Division South side Walsall. Making his Walsall debut in a 3-0 defeat at Millwall on the 23rd August 1952, the opening game of the season, his other two appearances for the 'Saddlers' came in 3-1 home defeat by Brighton, and later in the season in a 5-1 defeat at Bournemouth. Alan was the son of pre-war Leicester and Barnsley player Albert Godderidge, and after being released by Walsall in 1953 returned to play for Tamworth.

9. GOMERSALL, Victor (VIC)

Birthplace: Manchester, 17/6/1942
Ht: 5ft-9ins, **Wt:** 12st-7lbs
Swans debut: v. Bristol Rovers (a), 20/8/1966

Career:
Manchester City (from apprentice in July 1960) lge 39
Swansea Town (£5,000 signed in 18/8/1966)

Chelmsford City (signed in August 1971)
Llanelli (signed start of 1975/76 season)
Haverfordwest County
Pontardawe Athletic

Swansea Town/City Career Statistics					
Season	League	FLC	FAC	WC	ECWC
1966/67	39	3	1	1	2
1967/68	41/1gls		4	2	
1968/69	43/2gls	4	4	7	
1969/70	42/3gls	2	3	3	
1970/71	13	2	2	1	
Total	178/6gls	11	14	14	2

Honours: Southern League Champions–1972, Welsh League Premier Division Champions–1977, 1978, Welsh League First Division Champions–1980

From a young age Vic always wanted to be a footballer, and after graduating from Holland Street School at the age of 14 to play for Manchester Boys North Area, it was only after he moved to Miles Platt Secondary School that he was spotted playing for St. Phillips youth club side, run by his father. He was invited to a trial with Manchester City at the age of 15, and fortunately for Vic, he was one of only two boys from that trial who was asked to sign amateur forms for City. Signing as a groundstaff boy with City six months later, going on to clean the boots of his idol Bert Trautmann, he graduated through the ranks, and made his debut against Chelsea at left full back, and in the opposition camp, a certain Ron Harris was also making his league debut for Chelsea the same day. With opportunities in City's First Division side extremely rare, in 9 years at Maine Road he made just 39 league appearances. Despite signing a new contract with Joe Mercer, he felt he needed a new club and play football at the highest level on a regular basis every weekend. Initially wanting to stay locally, he looked at Stockport County where former City player Jimmy Meadows was manager, but after receiving no firm offers looked further afield. With interest from Plymouth Argyle and Bristol City coming to nothing, he was contacted one day by Swans manager Trevor Morris who arranged to meet him at Cardiff Railway Station. Since signing for the Swans, Vic enjoyed six good years at the Vetch Field, and despite relegation to the Third Division, there were some highlights during his career with the Swans, with matches against Arsenal, which drew a record attendance at the Vetch Field of 32,796, and Leeds United in the FA Cup competition, Slavia Sofia in the European Cup Winners Cup, and losing to Cardiff City in the Welsh Cup Final in 1969. Released by manager Roy Bentley in May 1971, he had offers to stay in the Football League with Southport, Colchester United, Exeter, Rochdale and Bury, with interest also from non-league sides Kettering Town and Chelmsford City. Signing for Chelmsford's manager Dave Bumstead, during those days the club was probably the biggest on the non-league circuit, winning the Southern League Championship during Vic's first season, but each season failing in their attempt to gain election to the Football League. After four years at Chelmsford, during an exhibition game in which Vic was playing at the Vetch Field, he was approached by Swans Chairman Malcolm Struel and was asked if he fancied a job in the club's Commercial Department, knowing full well that for a number of years, Vic had been involved with the Commercial Department at Chelmsford. Accepting the job offer, Vic later saw some incredible days at the Vetch Field, when the lottery ticket 'Moonraker' was to sell upwards of 45,000 tickets a week. He continued to play for Llanelli during this time, and also had an involvement with former Swans player Mel Nurse in a business venture in Penclawdd. Success on the field for the 'Reds', saw the club win two Welsh League Championships in a side that featured former Swans players Brian Evans, Dai Lawrence, Carl Slee, and Cyril Hartson. Deciding to join Haverfordwest County along with Brian Evans, and winning a further Welsh League Championship, Vic finished his playing career alongside the legendary Ivor Allchurch at Pontardawe Athletic, and his last season as a player saw the club just miss out on promotion. President of the Swansea Junior League for 25 years, he still has an involvement in coaching young kids, and for a number of years worked with Reds Chairman Bobby Jones at his Skoda Garage, but is currently full time commercial manager with the Reds in Stebonheath Park.

10. GOODFELLOW, MARC David

Birthplace: Swadlincote, 20/9/1981
Ht: 5ft-8ins, **Wt:** 10st-6lbs
Swans debut: v. Bury (h), 27/11/2004

Swansea City Career Statistics		
Season	League	FAC
2004/05	6/3gls	1+1/1gls
Total	6/3gls	1+1/1gls

Career:
Stoke City (signed from juniors in 29/1/1999) lge 17+37/6gls, FLC 3+3/2gls, FAC 1+6, Others 4/1gls
Bristol City (£50,000 signed in 9/1/2004) lge 8+12/4gls, Others 0+2/1gls
Port Vale (loan in 4/10/2004) lge 4
Swansea City (loan in 24/11/2004)
Colchester United (loan in 16/3/2005) lge 4+1/1gls
Swansea City (signed in 30/6/2005)

Former trainee at Stoke City who joined the Swans on loan in late November 2004 from Bristol City making his debut two days later at the Vetch Field against Bury. The left sided midfield/winger, did not have much opportunity in his debut to shine, but in later games showed his awareness in front of goal scoring four goals. Just as he was starting his second month on loan he was recalled by Bristol City following illness and injuries to a number of the first team squad at Ashton Gate, and with the Swans unwilling to pay the £65,000 transfer fee required by City to make the transfer permanent, he remained a Bristol City player. Mark made his league debut for Stoke City as substitute for Thordarson on the 23rd September 2000 in a 1-1 draw with Rotherham United, making a further six substitute appearances in the season. Three days prior to his league debut he had made a goal scoring appearance from the substitute's bench in a Worthington Cup, Second Round, First Leg 2-1 win over Charlton Athletic. A consistent goalscorer in the club's reserve and youth sides, he also possessed blistering pace, and was capable of playing as either a central striker, or in a left sided midfield role. He made his first league start in January 2002 in a 2-0 home win over Blackpool, also playing in the FA Cup defeat by non-league side Nuneaton Borough in the same season. Despite making a substitute appearance in the 2002 Second Division Play Off semi-final against Cardiff City, he failed to feature in the Play Off Final, but two years later made a substitute appearance for Bristol City in the Second Division Play Off Final defeat by Brighton & Hove Albion. After returning to Ashton Gate from his loan spell at the Vetch Field he regained his place in the Bristol City starting line-up, but after a couple of games was omitted from the team. In mid-March 2005 he joined Colchester United on loan, and just prior to returning to Ashton Gate for pre-season training, signed a full contract with the Swans. Scored the first goal for the Swans at the New Stadium in Landore in a pre-season friendly v. Fulham in 23/7/2005.

11. GOUGH, CLAUDE Francis

Birthplace: Rhayader, 17/10/1900. **Died:** Hillingdon, June 1990
Ht: 5ft-8ins, **Wt:** 10st-10lbs
Swans debut: v. Brentford (h), 28/4/1921

Swansea Town Career Statistics	
Season	League
1920/21	2/1gls
1922/23	10/3gls
Total	12/4gls

Career:
Llandrindod Wells
Swansea Town (signed amateur in October 1920)
Coventry City (signed in August 1921) lge 15/1gls
Swansea Town (£50 signed in July 1922)

Made his debut for the Swans initially at inside right during the Swans inaugural season in the Football League at the Vetch Field against Brentford, making his only other appearance two matches later, at the Vetch Field against Swindon Town, in which he scored the Swans goal in a 1-1 draw. Joined the Swans initially as an amateur from Llandrindod Wells in October 1920, but at the end of the season was not offered a contract by the Swans and released. He signed for Coventry City in the 1921 close season, but rejoined the Swans in July 1922 for £50. Missing the first three league games, he returned to the Swans first team, and in his sixth game scored a hat-trick in a 5-0 win over Swindon Town. In his tenth game for the Swans at Exeter City in late October 1922 he sustained a bad injury which resulted in him eventually having to retire from the game. In January 1923 he was placed in the hands of a specialist in Cardiff in the hope that he could return to fitness, with the injury proving to be of greater seriousness that at first thought. Signing a contract for the 1923/24 season, after starting training his knee was still giving him problems and after seeing specialist after specialist, returned to his home in Llandrindod Wells, receiving compensation of 35 shillings a week. After an operation in a Swansea Nursing Home in August 1924, his knee had still not responded to treatment and he received compensation until October 1929. When he was later seen by a doctor on behalf of the football club, he was given notice that his compensation was being reduced to five shillings a week. In April 1930 Claude Francis Gough was the applicant at Swansea County Court when he asked for an increase of compensation with regard to the injury he received whilst playing for the Swans against Exeter City on the 28th October 1922. He was later awarded compensation from the Football League Provident Fund of £698 and five shillings, equivalent to 399 weeks. On the 3rd January 1931 he was awarded a further £475 from the Football League Fund. In the tribunal Gough had said that he had tried and failed to get other employment, showing one application for a steward's position he had applied for in Barry.

12. GRAY, GEORGE Robert

Birthplace: South Hylton, Co. Durham 4/1/1894. **Died:** JFM 1972
Ht: 5ft-9ins, **Wt:** 11st-0lbs
Swans debut: v. Northampton Town (a), 25/9/1920

Swansea Town Career Statistics			
Season	League	FAC	WC
1920/21	32/1gls	3	
1921/22	7	4	2
Total	39/1gls	7	2

Career:
Gillingham (signed in July 1914)
Army Football
West Hartlepool
Swansea Town (signed in September 1920)
Bury (£250 signed in March1922) lge 0
Northampton Town (signed in May 1923) lge 11, FAC 1
Clydebank (signed in June 1925)
Yoker Athletic (signed in July 1925)
Rushden Town

Played his early football with New Riddick Colliery, Seaham Harbour before joining Gillingham in July 1914, played football in the Army during WW1, before joining West Hartlepool, and linking up with the Swans in September 1920. Signed prior to the start of season 1920/21 by manager Joe Bradshaw, the first season for the Swans in the Football League, he made his league debut in September against Northampton Town at right half back, and almost until the end of the season was an automatic choice for the Swans in either a right half, or left half back position. His only goal for the Swans came against Grimsby Town in November 1920, with the Swans winning 3-1. He left the Vetch Field for Second Division side Bury in March 1922, but after failing to make a league appearance joined Third Division South side Northampton Town in December 1923. Taking over the right half position with the 'Cobblers', following the introduction of George Needham he lost his place, leaving the club at the end of the season, joining Scottish side Clydebank. He later made appearances with Yoker Athletic (Scotland), and Rushden Town. He was appointed trainer at Barrow in August 1935, later joining Clydebank in the same capacity up to May 1939, later serving South Shields as trainer. In August 1946 the Daily Post mentioned that he was spongeman at Sunderland's Roker Park, and presided over the club's modern hospital room with up to date apparatus, justly proud of the diploma he had achieved for electric therapy etc. His brother Thomas Gray played for Bury in 1921.

13. GRAY, MARK Stuart

Birthplace: Tenby, Pembs, 24/11/1959
Ht: 5ft-9ins, **Wt:** 11st-3lbs
Swans debut: v. Stockport County (a), 22/10/1977

Swansea City Career Statistics	
Season	League
1977/78	1+1
Total	1+1

Career:
Swansea City (from apprentice in September 1977)
Fulham (signed in January 1978) lge 0
Orient (signed in February 1979) lge 1+1
Pembroke Borough
Spearwood Dalmatinac F.C. (Australia)

Honours: Wales Yth–2

Played for the Swans Youth team, and the Welsh League side whilst on schoolboy forms, signing as an apprentice at the Vetch Field on leaving school in July 1976. Impressive appearances in the Swans Welsh League side saw him finally given his league debut as substitute for Pat Lally at Stockport County in October 1977 after previously being a non-playing substitute for an earlier league game at Watford. Later in the season the midfielder made his only start for the Swans at Halifax Town in a 3-1 defeat. The former Tenby Junior School, and Greenhill Secondary Schoolboy had played junior football for Saundersfoot Sports and Pembroke Borough prior to arriving at the Vetch Field. Capped twice for the Wales Youth side against Iceland in a European Youth Competition, home and away, Mark scored in a 1-1 away draw. A consistent goalscorer in the Swans reserve team, from either an attacking midfield role, or as a striker, he left the Vetch Field in January 1978 to go to Fulham, but after failing to make a first team appearance at Craven Cottage signed for Orient in February 1979 as part of the £100,000 deal that took Peter Kitchen to Craven Cottage. Confined mainly to making appearances in the O's reserve side, he made his league debut for Orient as substitute for John Chiedozie against Fulham on the 22nd February 1979, making his only start for the club in late April at Burnley. At the end of the 1979/80 season he was released by Orient having made no further appearances for the club. At the time of his going to Brisbane Road, Orient were a formidable outfit in the old Second Division. After he was released by Orient, he returned to West Wales, played a season in the Welsh League with Pembroke Borough, and then spent three years in Australia playing for Western Australia State League side Spearwood Dalmatinac. A successful period in Western Australia saw Mark gain League Championship Honours twice, Cup Winner three times, including a Man of the Match Award in one Final, awarded Footballer of the Year in Western Australia, and also represent West Australia against Nottingham Forest, also touring India in the D.C.M. Cup. On his return to West Wales he was sidelined through injury for almost twelve months, and was offered the opportunity by Swans manager Terry Yorath of a trial back at the Vetch Field in 1987. Declining the offer, Mark became manager of Pembroke Borough, and later had an involvement with Pembrokeshire League sides Saundersfoot Sports and Narberth F.C. Mark worked in his family's Farm Feed Sales business initially after returning to West Wales, and has since ran a country pub/restaurant for seven years, an estate agent for five years, and at present is Area Sales Manager for James Williams/S.A. Brains Brewery in Narberth.

14. GREAVES, EDWARD

Birthplace: Mardy, 1901
Ht: 5ft-9ins, **Wt:** 11st-12lbs
Swans debut: v. Merthyr Town (a), 2/9/1922

Swansea Town Career Statistics	
Season	League
1922/23	1
Total	1

Career:
Porth
Swansea Town (signed in August 1922)
Swindon Town (signed in June 1923) lge 1
Bridgend Town (signed by September 1925)

Honours: West Wales Senior Cup Winner–1923

Signed from Welsh League side Porth in early August 1922, Edward made just the one league appearance at right half back against Swindon Town in September 1922, instead of Joe Roulson. He was unable to displace Roulson from the side as the season progressed, making no further appearances for the Swans. In May 1923 he was included in the Swans reserve side that beat Llanelly to win the West Wales Senior Cup. He was released at the end of the season, joining fellow Third Division South side Swindon Town, where he made just the one more league appearance. Returning to South Wales by September 1925 he was playing for Bridgend Town.

15. GREENE, Christopher (CHRIS)

Birthplace: Dublin: 1/12/1911. **Died:** Coventry 24/10/1975
Ht: 5ft-10ins, **Wt:** 11st-10lbs
Swans debut: v. Norwich City (h), 5/12/1936

Swansea Town Career Statistics			
Season	League	FAC	WC
1936/37	4	1	2
Total	4	1	2

Career:
Brideville
Shelbourne (signed in 1931)
Southport (signed in August 1933) lge 49/1gls

Wolverhampton Wanderers (£500 signed in November 1934) lge 7/2gls
Swansea Town (signed in September 1936)
Bury (signed in 11/12/1937) lge 0
Workington (signed in close season 1939)

Irish inside forward who was signed by Swans manager Neil Harris from First Division side Wolverhampton Wanderers in September 1936, making his Swans debut at inside right at the Vetch Field against Norwich City in December 1936, replacing Foster. An aggressive type of forward who had experience of playing at wing half, centre half, and also in the forward positions. All his other league and cup appearances for the Swans that season came at left half back, and he was released at the end of the season, joining Second Division Bury. Earlier in his career he had made his name in the Leinster League with Brideville, and was barely eighteen when he secured his place in the Shelbourne side. Prior to joining Southport, Everton had made a four figure offer for his transfer, but at the time, Greene was loath to leave a good job in Dublin. He was eventually persuaded to play in the Football League at Southport, by a manager, James Commins, who had previously been his manager at Shelbourne. Following a successful period with Third Division North side Southport, he joined Wolves the following season for an initial £500, plus a further £500. Known as 'Christy' he was believed to have been a German P.O.W later during WW2.

16. GREEN, Ronald (RONNIE) Clarence George

Birthplace: Frampton Cottrell, 12/3/1912. **Died:** Coalpit Heath, Bristol 16/10/1979
Ht: 5ft-9ins, **Wt:** 11st-0lbs
Swans debut: v. West Ham United (a), 30/8/1937

Swansea Town Career Statistics	
Season	League
1937/38	8/4gls
Total	8/4gls

Career:
Coalpit Heath
Bath City (signed in season 1930/31)
Bristol Rovers (signed in 3/6/1932) lge 22/2gls
Arsenal (signed in July 1933) lge 0
Notts. County (signed in February 1935) lge 35/5gls
Charlton Athletic (£500 signed in 29/7/1936) lge 3/2gls
Swansea Town (signed in 6/5/1937)
Coalpit Heath (signed in 1938)

Honours: London Combination Champions–1934

Ronald Green was a former non-league player with Coalpit Heath and Bath City prior to joining Bristol Rovers in 1932.

After making his league debut in December 1932 for Rovers against Aldershot, he helped the club to equal their best ever position of ninth in the Third Division South. Within twelve months, after making his league debut with Rovers he had signed for First Division Arsenal, but after failing to break into the 'Gunners' line-up joined Second Division Notts County a year later. At Highbury he helped the 'Gunners' to the London Combination Championship in 1934, finishing top goalscorer with twenty-two goals, averaging more than a goal every two games for the 'Gunners' reserve side. Despite relegation in his first season at Meadow Lane, two seasons later he joined Charlton Athletic for £500, making a couple of appearances in the side that finished runners up in the First Division. Twelve months later he was signed by Swans manager Neil Harris, making his debut in the second league game of the season at West Ham United, replacing Lowrie at inside right. His next game for the Swans saw him score in a 1-1 draw at Sheffield Wednesday. Making three appearances at outside right, towards the end of the season he also played at inside left for the Swans, scoring in both matches. Rated a talented inside forward, who until an injury forced his retirement from the game, was classed by manager Neil Harris as the best player at the Vetch Field since Ivor Jones, Len Thompson and Ivor Brown. He rejoined Coalpit Heath in 1938, later becoming a director at the club in June 1946. A keen cricketer, he represented Frenchay CC, and worked as a newsagent in Bristol.

17. GREGG, Matthew (MATT) Stephen

Birthplace: Cheltenham, 30/11/1978
Ht: 5ft-11ins, **Wt:** 12st-0lbs
Swans debut: v. Brentford (h), 16/2/1999

Swansea City Career Statistics		
Season	League	FAWP
1998/99	5	1
Total	5	1

Career:
Torquay United (from trainee in 4/7/1997) lge 32, FLC 5, FAC 1, Others 1
Crystal Palace (£400,000 signed in 24/10/1998) lge 7, FLC 2+1
Swansea City (loan in 12/2/1999)
Exeter City (loan in 14/9/2001) lge 2
Bray Wanderers (signed in October 2001)
Bohemians (signed in April 2003)

Started with Swindon Town as a schoolboy, but after failing to make the grade with Swindon, went to Torquay United after being spotted playing for his County in Devon. Taken on at Plainmoor by Torquay United, after just three months of starting his traineeship he was called up for his first team debut against Wigan Athletic on the 16th September 1995, instead of Ashley Bayes. He made one more appearance for the 'Gulls' the following season whilst still a trainee, before signing professional at the end of the season when he was eighteen. He started season 1997/98 as first choice keeper at Plainmoor, playing at Wembley for Torquay in the Third Division Play Off Final against Colchester United which they lost 1-0. Veteran Ken Veysey had taken over for the second half of the season in goal for the 'Gulls', but because of a suspension, it gave Matthew the opportunity to play at Wembley. In October 1998 he joined First Division side Crystal Palace for £400,000, and after occupying the reserve team goalkeeping position at Selhurst Park was signed on loan by Swans manager John Hollins on the 12th February 1999 following an injury crisis at the Vetch Field with both Roger Freestone and reserve Jason Jones injured, making his Swans debut at the Vetch Field against Brentford four days later. He returned to Selhurst Park after his loan spell with the

Swans, but had to wait almost eighteen months before he made his first team debut for Palace, against Fulham on 1st April 2000. Missing the next game, he then returned to first team duty, playing in the last five league games of the season. Following a loan spell with Third Division Exeter City in September 2001, he was released from his contract at Selhurst Park, and joined League of Ireland side Bray Wanderers. In three seasons with Palace he made just ten league and cup appearances for the 'Eagles.' In April 2003 he signed a two year contract with fellow League of Ireland Premier Division side Bohemians.

18. GREY, William BRIAN

Birthplace: Swansea, 7/9/1948
Ht: 5ft-6½ins, **Wt:** 10st-3lbs
Swans debut: v. Exeter City (h), 30/9/1967

Swansea Town/City Career Statistics			
Season	League	FLC	WC
1967/68	12+1/3gls		
1968/69	13+1/5gls		5+1
1969/70	2+1	1	
Total	27+3/8gls	1	5+1

Career:
Swansea Town (apprentice signed in 10/9/1966)
Yeovil Town (signed in July 1970) Total apps 90+5/33gls
Folkestone (signed in July 1972)
Merthyr Tydfil

Honours: Wales Sch, Southern League Premier Division Champions–1971

Local player brought up in the east side of Swansea, had a glittering schoolboy career with Swansea Schoolboys and Wales Schoolboys, and in one match for the Swansea schoolboys side scored three goals in three minutes. Taken on as an apprentice at the Vetch Field after leaving school, he was given a full professional contract shortly after the start of season 1966/67. He made his league debut at inside right against Exeter City in September 1967 replacing Denis Coughlin, retaining his place in the Swans line-up for the next eight league matches. During this spell in the first team he scored his first league goal, in a 5-2 win over Workington at the Vetch Field, and scoring in consecutive league games against Bradford City and Crewe Alexandra. The following season, after failing to make the starting line-up at the beginning of the season, from fourteen league appearances he scored five goals, also playing in both legs of the Welsh Cup Final defeat by Cardiff City. He struggled to make an impression with new manager Roy Bentley in season 1969/70, and following the club's successful promotion campaign was released, joining Southern League side Yeovil Town. His first season at Yeovil Town saw the club win the Premier Division Championship of the Southern League, with Brian playing a prominent part from either midfield or in attack, topping the goalscoring charts with twenty-three league and cup goals, and also playing in the side that beat Fourth Division side Bournemouth at Dean Court in the FA Cup second round, before losing to Arsenal at home in the next round. Brian scored a total of 33 goals in 95 games while at Huish, before signing for Southern League Premier Division side Folkestone in July 1972 with Ron Bayliss. Not a tall front runner, but he did possess exceptional pace. During season 1967/68 at the Vetch Field he was top goalscorer for the Swans' Football Combination side with eight goals, and also scored thirteen goals in the club's Welsh League side. After two seasons with Yeovil he joined fellow Southern League Premier Division side Folkestone, before returning to South Wales to sign for Merthyr Tydfil, and after retiring from the game, became a licensee in a number of public houses in Swansea, also working in the double glazing trade in the city.

19. GRIFFITHS, James Henry (HARRY)

Birthplace: Swansea, 4/1/1931. **Died:** Swansea, 25/4/1978
Ht: 5ft-7ins, **Wt:** 10st-10lbs
Swans debut: v. Chesterfield (h), 15/4/1950

Swansea Town Career Statistics

Season	League	FLC	FAC	WC	ECWC
1949/50	1				
1950/51					
1951/52					
1952/53	38/9gls		1	2	
1953/54	26/5gls		2	1	
1954/55	42/17gls		4/1gls	4/4gls	
1955/56	40/16gls		1/1gls	4/5gls	
1956/57	40/18gls		1	4	
1957/58	42/3gls		1	2	
1958/59	41/3gls		1	2	
1959/60	37/1gls		3	2	
1960/61	34	1	2	5	
1961/62	42	2	1	3	2
1962/63	30	1	2	3	
1963/64	8	1			
Total	421/72gls	5	19/2gls	32/9gls	2

Career:
Swansea Town (signed groundstaff, professional in June 1949)

New York Americans (loan in May 1961)
Merthyr Tydfil (signed in April 1964)

Honours: Wales Full–1, Welsh Cup Winner–1961, Welsh League Rep XI, West Wales Senior Cup Winner–1955, 1956, 1957, 1960, 1961, Welsh League First Division Champions–1964

A former Swansea schoolboy before joining the Swans groundstaff in July 1949, he made his league debut against Chesterfield in April 1950 at outside right, but had to wait until September 1952 before making his next Swans first team appearance. During his National Service he played football in the Army. One of Swansea's finest-ever servants, up to midway through the 1957/58 season he had played in all forward positions, possessing a terrific shot, and had the ability to fight for the ball. He made just one appearance for Wales, against Ireland in Belfast on the 15th April 1953 at outside left. In December 1957 he made his first appearance in a defensive role for the Swans, and for the remainder of his playing career was equally at home in either full back positions. Predominantly a winger, he also played at inside forward as well as centre forward before switching to a defensive role for the Swans. Initially switched to right full back as a replacement for Dai Thomas, when Thomas returned to action, Harry was switched to the other full back position. Given the importance of scoring goals as far as results are concerned, it was strange then, having scored 48 league goals in 3 seasons, he was moved to left full back. What a fantastic 'wing back' he would have made in today's modern football world. Harry scored his first hat-trick for the Swans in a Welsh Cup tie at Newtown in season 1955/56, in a 9-4 win for the Swans. The following season he scored a hat-trick in the league, against Doncaster Rovers in October 1956. The 1955/56 and 1956/57 seasons saw Harry play in two losing Welsh Cup Finals against Cardiff City and Wrexham respectively, but at the end of the 1960/61 season was included in the side that beat Bangor City to win the Welsh Cup, also competing in both legs of the European Cup Winners Cup against Motor Jena the following season. Played in West Wales Senior Cup Final successes in 1955, 1956, 1957, 1960 and 1961. Harry was released from the Vetch Field playing staff in April 1964 to join Merthyr Tydfil as player manager, but in April 1967 returned to the Vetch Field to serve the club as coach, chief scout, trainer, physiotherapist, manager, and assistant manager, up until his death at the Vetch Field hours before the home game with Scunthorpe United on the 25th April 1978. In early May 1961 he enjoyed a six week spell in the USA playing for New York Americans, taking part in a World Club Tournament. The manager of the side was former Wales international Alf Sherwood. A great hearted player, and personality, he gave 100% in every thing he did for the Swans, and rarely missed a match over a dozen seasons. Quick, with a good eye for an opening, he could beat a man on either foot. His tenacity and resolve saw him convert easily into the full back position, and one of his most memorable games (for him), was when the Swans played Stoke City in the FA Cup and he marked Stanley Matthews. Well liked by everyone, he had a room named after him at the Vetch Field, underneath the Centre Stand, and coupled with Joe Sykes, Harry was Swans' greatest servant. After the club had successfully been re-elected to the Football League at the end of the 1974/75 season, along with chairman Malcolm Struel, Harry began the task of rebuilding the football club in the true Swansea tradition, playing attractive football and scoring a lot of goals, and on two occasions prior to the arrival of John Toshack as manager, missed out on promotion. Reverting to Toshack's assistant, the football world was stunned when news came of Harry's death, following his collapse in the Vetch Field medicine room at the Vetch Field, just prior to the Scunthorpe United league game later that night. Possessing honesty, integrity, dedication and loyalty, Harry applied himself to whatever role was required of him by the football club.

20. GRIFFITHS, Jeffrey (JEFF) Kenneth

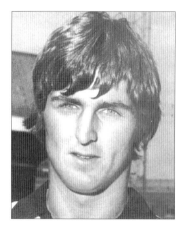

Birthplace: Swansea, 19/3/1957
Ht: 6ft-0ins, **Wt:** 11st-8lbs
Swans debut: v. Brentford (h), 26/4/1976

Swansea City Career Statistics			
Season	League	FAC	WC
1975/76	2		
1976/77	0+4		1
1977/78	5+3/1gls	2	
Total	7+7/1gls	2	1

Career:
Sketty Park Boys Club
Swansea City (initial non-contract, signed professional in April 1976)
Bridgend Town (signed in close season 1978)
Haverfordwest County (signed in close season 1979)

Honours: Boys Club of Wales–2, Welsh League First Division Champions–1980, Welsh League Premier Division Champions–1981

Brought up in the Sketty Park area of Swansea, Jeff went to Olchfa school, played occasionally at full back for Swansea schoolboys before joining Swansea Senior League side Sketty Park Boys Club. Capped twice for the Boys Club of Wales side against England and Scotland, after a couple of successful trials at the Vetch Field, he made his league debut towards the end of the 1975/76 season against Brentford at the Vetch Field.
The following season he gained a lot of experience with the Swans reserve team in the Welsh League, scoring, and creating a number of goals, and making four league appearances as substitute, plus starting in a Welsh Cup tie against Newport County. The 1977/78 season saw Jeff make his most appearances for the Swans, having a run of seven consecutive league outings, two as substitute, and scoring his only league goal, in a 2-1 win over Reading at the Vetch Field. The middle of that season also saw him make two appearances in the FA Cup competition against Leatherhead. He was released in May 1978, going on to sign for Southern League Premier Division side Bridgend Town, but after just one season joined Welsh League side Haverfordwest County. The next two seasons saw the club win the First Division Championship, followed by the Premier Division Championship. After a five year period in West Wales with Haverfordwest, Jeff then joined Morriston Town, the first of many spells with the Swansea based Welsh League club. Prior to his retirement a couple of years back, Jeff also made Welsh League appearances for Pontardawe, Milford United and Ammanford Town. For a brief period at the start of season 2003/04, Jeff was manager of Welsh League side Pontardawe, with his son Dale playing in defence, but stepped down to coach

the club's youth side after a poor run of results. He still plays in Charity matches on occasions, and for a number of years he has been involved in the taxi business in Swansea.

21. GROVES, Edward Gwynfryn (GWYN)

Birthplace: Aberfan, Merthyr Tydfil, 24/7/1930. **Died:** Merthyr, 24/3/1997
Ht: 6ft-0ins, **Wt:** 12st-6lbs
Swans debut: v. Luton Town (a), 10/9/1952

Swansea Town Career Statistics			
Season	League	FAC	WC
1952/53	23	1	3
1953/54	4		
Total	27	1	3

Career:
Brecon Corinthians
Troedyrhiw (signed in close season 1950)
Swansea Town (signed in 24/6/1952)
Hereford United (signed in close season 1954)

Honours: Wales Yth, Amateur–4

Attended Quakers Yard Grammar School, and earlier in his playing career had completed a physical training course at Exeter University, made reserve team appearances for Aston Villa, Bristol Rovers, Barry Town and Merthyr prior to establishing himself in the Welsh League initially with Brecon Corries, and then with Troedyrhiw. The former Physical Training Instructor at Gaiter College signed initially for the Swans as an amateur in June 1952 from Troedyrhiw, contesting the reserve team goalkeeper spot with Cliff Edwards. Capped at Youth level for Wales, whilst with Brecon Corinthians he gained his first cap for the Wales Amateur side in season 1949/50 against England and Scotland, and after signing for Troedyrhiw made an appearance for the Welsh Amateur side in January 1951 at Leicester against England, and also during the season against Scotland. He made his league debut at Luton Town in September 1952, deputising for Johnny King. Returning to the reserve team after his debut, he made a couple of appearances in the Swans first team, but on December 27th, returned to the first team, retaining his place for the remainder of the season. With Johnny King the number one choice at the club for the goalkeeper spot, his second season saw Groves make just four league appearances. Starting his second season (1953/54) in the Swans first team line-up, after the first two league games of the season, he alternated the number one jersey with King, only to play his last Swans game against Plymouth Argyle on 12th September 1953, with King remaining as first choice for the rest of the season. A well built, elegant goalkeeper he lost confidence and faded out of league football after a promising start, and in May 1954 was released by the Swans, linking up with non-league Hereford United, where he remained for over five seasons. He returned to the teaching profession after leaving the professional game, and was teaching at Afan Taff High School in Troedyrhiw up to his retirement. A useful cricketer in the summer months, Gwyn played in the South Wales & Monmouthshire League for Hills Plymouth for a number of seasons.

at the Vetch Field, by donating £375 to go towards a loan player's wages. He also offered to raise more money to help the trust even further by offering the trust, a percentage of the profits made for all customers in the SA1 to SA15 Postcode area who signed up for his company ENERGY SPY, an internet based utilities brokerage company. In late June 2004 an article in the *South Wales Evening Post* reported that the former Swans player had been jailed for eight months for a vicious assault arising out of a business venture, and that he would probably lose his job as manager in the sports retail field.

22. GUARD, Anthony (TONY) Francis

Birthplace: Swansea, 19/4/1964
Ht: 5ft-7ins, **Wt:** 9st-3lbs
Swans debut: v. Colchester United (a), MC 2-2, 25/10/1983

Swansea City Career Statistics			
Season	League	FLC	WC
1983/84	1	1	1
Total	1	1	1

Career:
Swansea City (from apprentice signed in April 1982)

Former Pentrehafod schoolboy, and Swansea schoolboy defender who signed as an apprentice with the Swans in October 1980. He was a second year professional at the start of the season when the Swans had been relegated to the Second Division, after two seasons in the First Division, and made his Swans debut in the Milk Cup competition, Second Round, Second Leg at Colchester United, losing 1-0. Deputising for the injured Paul Maddy, with Emlyn Hughes switching to midfield, Tony played at right full back. Four days later he made his Football League debut for the Swans at the Vetch Field, at right back against Blackburn Rovers. His only other Swans appearance was later in the season at Barry Town in a Welsh Cup, Fifth Round tie, drawing 1-1. The 1983/84 season proved to be one of financial hardship, and within two months of the start of the season, the club would have to offload it's better players in a bid to ease the monthly wage bill. As the season progressed, young professionals such as Tony Guard were given their opportunity in the first team ahead of schedule, as most of the experienced professionals had been offloaded. In May 1984 he was released from the playing staff at the Vetch Field as the club failed to avoid a second successive relegation. After being released by the Swans he played for a number of years in Australia (with former Swans players Huw Lake and Colin Irwin at Perth Azzurri), Singapore and Finland. Returning to his home city, in December 2002, he backed the Swansea City Supporters Trust Appeal for financing the wages of loan players

23. GUERET, WILLY

Birthplace: Saint Claude, Guadeloupe, 3/8/1973
Ht: 6ft-1ins, **Wt:** 13st-5lbs
Swans debut: v. Northampton Town (h), 7/8/2004

Swansea City Career Statistics					
Season	League	FLC	FAC	LDV	FAWC
2004/05	44	1	5	2	1
Total	44	1	5	2	1

Career:
Le Mans (signed in 1/8/1999)
Millwall (signed in 31/7/2000) lge 13+1, FAC 3, Others 2
Swansea City (trial initially in August 2004, signed in 6/8/2004)

Honours: France U-19, Second Division Champions–2001, FAW Cup Winner–2005

Released by Millwall at the end of season 2003/04, within weeks of being a non-playing substitute at the Millenium Stadium, Cardiff in the FA Cup Final defeat by Manchester United. Willy arrived at the Vetch Field in early August on an initial trial basis, and then secured himself a one year contract a week before the start of the season, taking over as first choice keeper from Brian Murphy in the opening league fixture of the 2004/05 season. Born in Guadeloupe, Willy arrived in Paris at the age of seven, played little schoolboy football, signed for Paris St. Germain initially, before moving on to Red Star Paris, and then to Second Division side Le Mans. He represented France at U-19 level, also playing in the semi-final stage of the French Cup with Le Mans during the 1999/2000 season. Joining Millwall in the 2000 close season, after making his league debut in a 3-0 home win over Bristol Rovers on the 3rd February 2001, he made a further ten consecutive league appearances as a replacement for Tony Warner, keeping a total of eight clean sheets. Over the next three seasons at the New Den he managed just three league appearances prior to his release in May 2004. His consistency in the Swans rearguard during his first season at the Vetch Field saw him sign a further two year extension to his contract in

January 2005, and, after claiming the last automatic promotion place following the away win at Bury, four days later Willy was included in the Swans side that beat Wrexham at the Vetch Field to win the FAW Cup.

24. GUNN, Kenneth (KEN)

Birthplace: Newmains, Lanarkshire, 9/4/1909.
Died: Northampton, 15/8/1991
Ht: 5ft-10ins, **Wt:** 11st-4lbs
Swans debut: v. Hull City (a), 6/4/1928

Swansea Town Career Statistics			
Season	League	FAC	WC
1927/28	8/3gls		
1928/29	24/8gls	1	
1929/30	18/9gls	1	
1930/31	7/2gls		
1931/32	34/14gls	1/1gls	5
1932/33	4		1
Total	95/36gls	3/1gls	6

Career:
Newmains FC (Glasgow Junior Side)
Swansea Town (£50 signed in 23/1/1928)
Port Vale (signed in 13/5/1933) lge 134/10gls, FAC 1
Northampton Town (signed in May 1937) lge 74/1gls, FAC 2, Others 1

Honours: Lanarkshire County XI, Welsh Cup Winner–1931, West Wales Senior Cup Winner–1930

Signed by Swans manager James Thomson, who during his time as manager at the Vetch Field brought a number of Scottish players to the club. A Scot he played for junior side Newmains FC, before transferring to the Swans for £50. He had earlier impressed the Swans manager playing for Lanarkshire in an Inter-County game, and after he had been able to get his release from his employment, signed professional for the Swans.
He played most of his games for the Swans at inside left, but during his last season at the club played at right half back. Despite not being an automatic inclusion in the Swans starting line-up, he proved to be a consistent goalscorer, as his 36 goals from 95 league games testify. Scored on his debut for the Swans at Hull City in April 1928, and he also scored two hat-tricks, against Preston North End (in March 1929), and against Burnley (in November 1934). In October 1930 he was included in the Swans reserve side that beat Newport County in the West Wales Senior Cup Final. He had his best season as a goalscorer during the 1931/32 season, scoring 14 league goals, with Cyril Pearce

scoring 35 league goals the same season. At the end of the 1931/32 season he played in the Swans Welsh Cup Final side against Rhyl, winning 2-0. He was transferred to Port Vale a week after the end of the 1932/33 season for a fee of £500, at the time the third highest transfer fee the Swans had received. A couple of days before he signed for Port Vale, another player from the Vetch Field, Bill Tabram had joined the club. Gunn was injured in the game against Burnley at the end of the season, and went to Scotland to recuperate before signing for Vale. However, he had to undergo a cartilage operation before making an appearance for Vale. Moving to Northampton Town in 1937, he captained the 'Cobblers' during the last season before WW2. He made a couple of guest appearances for the 'Cobblers' and Portsmouth (1944/45) during the war, and after the war retired from the professional game, later working as a coal merchant prior to his death in Northampton in August 1991.

25. GURNEY, Andrew (ANDY) Robert

Birthplace: Bristol, 25/1/1974
Ht: 5ft-10ins, **Wt:** 11st-6lbs
Swans debut: v. Yeovil Town (a), 4/9/2004

Swansea City Career Statistics			
Season	League	FAC	LDV
2004/05	25+3/1gls	4	1
Total	25+3/1gls	4	1

Career:
Bristol Rovers (from trainee in 10/7/1992) lge 100+8/9gls, FLC 7/1gls, FAC 5, Others 15
Torquay United (signed in 7/10/1997) lge 64/10gls, FLC 6, FAC 5/1gls, Others 3
Reading (£100,000 signed in 15/1/1999) lge 55+12/3gls, FLC 5, FAC 5+1, Others 5+1
Swindon Town (signed in 2/7/2001) lge 132/22gls, FLC 4/1gls, FAC 4/2gls, Others 4+1
Swansea City (signed in 1/9/2004)

Honours: FAW Cup Winner–2005

Attended Marlwood School, played for the Northavon Schools Representative side, Yate Town, Kingsmead and St. Vallier Youth prior to joining the Rovers as a trainee, and signing professional in July 1992. Former captain of the Rovers youth side, he made his league debut against a Reading side on the 2nd April 1994 on the verge of winning the Second Division Championship. He played for Rovers at Wembley in the 1995 Second Division Play Off Final defeat by Huddersfield Town, and also played in the Southern Final defeat by Shrewsbury Town over two legs in the

Auto Windscreen Shield in 1996. Capable of playing in either full back position, he has scored some excellent long range goals during his career, and despite missing a penalty for Swindon Town in season 2003/04 Second Division Play Off semi-final penalty shoot out at Brighton, has proved to be a reliable penalty taker in the past. In three seasons at the County Ground with Swindon, he missed just twelve league games. Joined the Swans on a three year contract, making his debut as a late first half substitute for Paul Connor at Yeovil Town in early September 2004. A tough tackling full back, he also had a number of games in midfield for the Swans, and his only goal was scored at the Vetch Field against Rochdale. Failing to make an appearance from the substitute's bench in the promotion clinching away win at Bury, four days later he also failed to make an appearance from the substitute's bench in the FAW Cup Final win over Wrexham.

26. GUTHRIE, PETER John

Birthplace: Newcastle, 10/10/1961
Ht: 6ft-1ins, **Wt:** 12st-13lbs
Swans debut: v. Cambridge United (a), 27/2/1988

Swansea City Career Statistics		
Season	League	P/Offs
1987/88	14	4
Total	14	4

Career:
Whickham
Blyth Spartans
Weymouth (signed for 1987/88 season) Conf 20
Tottenham Hotspur (£100,000 signed in 4/1/1988) lge 0
Swansea City (loan in 26/2/1988)
Charlton Athletic (loan in 23/12/1988) lge 0
Barnet (£60,000 signed in 1/8/1989) Conf 18
Bournemouth (£15,000 signed in 1/8/1990) lge 10
Sing Tao, Hong Kong (signed in 1991)
Happy Valley, Hong Kong (signed in 1994)
Bedlington Terriers (signed in 2001)

Honours: Fourth Division Play Off Winner–1988

An inexperienced goalkeeper at Football League level who did not become a full time professional until he was twenty-seven years of age, joining the Swans on loan from Tottenham Hotspur as cover for Mike Hughes, featuring in the 1987-88 Fourth Division Play Off Final triumph. The Swans had to obtain special dispensation from the Football League to play Guthrie in the Play Offs after he had already played for the Swans the maximum period on loan (three months), and the club did not have any other goalkeeper on the playing staff. He had earlier

signed for Tottenham Hotspur in January 1988 for a record transfer fee for a goalkeeper of £100,000 from non-league Weymouth. Returning to White Hart Lane after the Play Off success, he failed to make an appearance for Spurs, was released, joining Barnet in the Vauxhall Conference at the start of the 1989/90 season, sharing the goalkeeping duties there with Gary Phillips. He then returned to league action with Bournemouth for a fee of £15,000, but after he was unable to oust Vince Bartram from the goalkeeper's jersey at Bournemouth, he had his contract cancelled at Dean Court in 1991 to go and play in Hong Kong. Spending eleven years in Hong Kong with Sing Tao and Happy Valley, he won League Titles, Cup Finals and Senior Shields during his period in the Hong Kong League. Peter returned to the UK in 2001, joining Northern League side Bedlington Terriers, remaining at the club for one and a half years before retiring from the game. Brought up in Newcastle, he was educated at St. Mary Technical School in Long Benton, played for Newcastle Schoolboys as a centre forward in the same side as current Birmingham City manager Steve Bruce. After leaving school he worked for a Gaming Machine Company repairing video machines, joined Wearside League side Whickham, started his career with the club as a goalkeeper, and played in the 1983/84 FA Vase semi-final defeat by eventual winners Stansted. From Whickham he signed for Northern League side Blyth Spartans prior to signing for Weymouth. Peter has no connections at the present time with football apart from watching his son play in local football, and works for the Stagecoach Bus Company as a bus driver in Newcastle.

27. GWYTHER, David (DAI) Jeffrey Andrew

Birthplace: Birmingham, 6/12/1948
Ht: 5ft-11ins, **Wt:** 11st-10lbs
Swans debut: v. Brighton & Hove Albion (h), 28/5/1966

Swansea Town/City Career Statistics				
Season	League	FLC	FAC	WC
1965/66	1			
1966/67	1			
1967/68	5+1			0+1
1968/69	37/8gls	4/2gls	4/2gls	7
1969/70	45+1/15gls	2/2gls	3/5gls	4/2gls
1970/71	38/18gls	2/2gls	4/7gls	2/1gls
1971/72	46/9gls	1	6/2gls	1
1972/73	39+2/10gls	2	1	2
Total	212+4/60gls	11/6gls	18/16gls	16+1/3gls

Career:
Fairwood Rangers
South Gower

Swansea Town (signed as apprentice in July 1964, professional in 5/2/1967)

Halifax Town (£12,000 signed in 8/8/1973) lge 104/26gls

Rotherham United (signed in 17/2/1976) lge 162/45gls

Newport County (signed in 6/12/1979) lge 84+21/29gls, ECWC 6/2gls

Crewe Alexandra (signed in January 1982) lge 7/1gls

Port Talbot Athletic (signed in July 1984)

Newport County (non-contract signed in March 1985) lge 1+1

Honours: Wales U-23–2, Welsh Cup Winner–1980, Welsh F.A. XI, West Wales Senior Cup Winner–1966

Former Penclawdd schoolboy who played rugby for his school team in the morning, and at the age of thirteen played for Swansea Senior League side Fairwood Rangers in the afternoon. At fifteen years of age he signed for Swansea Senior League side South Gower, and on leaving school joined the Swans groundstaff as an apprentice, signing professional in early February 1967, after previously making his league debut whilst still an amateur at the Vetch Field in the last match of the 1965/66 season. In May 1966 he was included in the Swans reserve side that beat Llanelly to win the West Wales Senior Cup. He was top goalscorer in the Swans Football Combination side of 1967/68 with 8 league goals, and two in the cup, also scoring 8 goals for the Swans in the Welsh League team the same season. After signing a professional contract with the Swans he had to wait until season 1968/69 before establishing himself as a regular in the first team line-up, and getting himself on the scoresheet. He played in the losing Welsh Cup Final first leg against Cardiff City in season 1968/69, scoring his first league goal against Aldershot at the Vetch in the second game of the season. After he had established himself in the Swans first team line-up, he toured New Zealand with the Welsh FA in 1971, and also gained U-23 caps for Wales against England and

Scotland in 1972. A strong, physical hard running centre forward who was also underestimated on the skill level, he ended up top goalscorer for the Swans on four occasions prior to his £12,000 transfer to Halifax Town in 1973. In February 1976 he signed for Rotherham United and on one of the few occasions he returned to the Vetch Field to play against the Swans, he scored a hat trick for Rotherham United in a 4-4 draw in front of 17,035 fans. During season 1969/70, with the Swans gaining promotion to the Third Division he was joint top goalscorer with Herbie Williams, his strike partner with 15 league goals, and also in the season scored 4 goals in an FA Cup tie against Oxford City. The following season he showed his liking for goalscoring in the FA Cup competition by scoring hat-tricks in consecutive rounds against Telford and Rhyl. His only league hat-trick for the Swans came against Reading in the same season as his cup hat-tricks, in a 5-1 win at the Vetch Field. Joining Newport County in December 1979, at the end of the season he gained a Welsh Cup Winners medal when they beat Shrewsbury Town in the final. The following season, combining with Tommy Tynan, Gwyther finished top goalscorer with 15 league goals, also sampling European Cup Winners Cup action with County, playing in six games, scoring 2 goals, as the club lost in the quarter finals to Carl Zeiss Jena, the eventual losing finalist in the competition. Joining Crewe Alexandra in January 1982, after his release from Gresty Road in May 1983 he joined Port Talbot in the Welsh League, but returned to Football League with Newport County three quarters through the 1984/85 season on a non-contract basis, making just one league start, and one as substitute. Ironically, his last league game in his career came at the Vetch Field for Newport County when he came on as substitute for Tony Kellow in a 3-0 win for County on the 17th March 1985. For a number of years during his career as a professional, during the close season Dai worked in his painting and decorating business, and after finishing his playing career with Briton Ferry and Port Talbot has continued with his business, living in the Killay district of Swansea.

H

1. HAASZ, JOHN

Birthplace: Budapest, Hungary, 7/7/1934
Swans debut: v. Liverpool (a), 10/12/1966

Swansea Town Career Statistics	
Season	League
1960/61	1
Total	1

Career:
Gainsborough Trinity
Swansea Town (signed in September 1960)
Workington (signed in July 1961) lge 50/17gls
Cambridge United (signed in 1963)

Honours: Football Combination Second Division
Champions–1961

John left his native Hungary during the uprising in 1956, where he played in the First Division with the Air Force Team, settled in Doncaster, but was prevented from playing in British football by FIFA for three years, like Hungarian internationals Kocsis and Puskas. He had also played for Hungarian First Division side Legiero. At one stage after coming to England he worked in a travelling Circus, where he fought in the Boxing ring. Joining Gainsborough Trinity as an amateur, he was recommended to Swans manager Trevor Morris by their manager, arrived at the Vetch Field for the 1960 close season, played in the first public trial match at the Vetch Field, later playing in a number of games for the Swans reserves, gaining a reputation as a high scoring forward. Also included in the trial game was Trinity goalkeeper Mansel. By the end of his only season at the Vetch Field he had scored forty-one goals for the Swans reserve side, twenty-five in the Combination, and sixteen in the Welsh

League side, with the Combination side winning the Second Division Championship. Playing for Gainsborough Trinity in the Midland League he made twelve appearances, averaging two goals a match. He made his Swans debut at outside left on an icy pitch at Anfield against Liverpool, going down 4-0, made no further appearances, and was released at the end of the season, joining Fourth Division side Workington. Unfortunately for him he broke his leg playing in only his second game at Doncaster, but over two seasons made fifty appearances, scoring seventeen goals. Joining non-league side Cambridge United in 1963, in the month of September he scored two hat-tricks in seven days, scoring a total of forty-two goals that season. Very fast, and a good provider, his last goal for United came at Corby, a team he then joined, and he later made appearances for Scarborough. He later settled in Doncaster working as a tyre fitter.

2. HADZIABDIC, Dzemal (JIMMY)

Birthplace: Yugoslavia, 25/7/1953
Ht: 5ft-8¼ins, **Wt:** 10st-11lbs
Swans debut: v. Arsenal (a) , FLC 1–2, 2/9/1980

Swansea City Career Statistics					
Season	League	FLC	FAC	WC	ECWC
1980/81	38/1gls	1	1	3	
1981/82	25+1			7	2
1982/83	24+1	3	1	1	6
Total	87+2/1gls	4	2	11	8

Career:
Velez Mostar
Swansea City (signed in 9/8/1980)

Honours: Yugoslavia, Yth–10, Full–21, Welsh Cup Winner–1981, 1982

Dzemal Hadziabdic did not originally come to the UK to sign for the Swans, but was possibly going to sign for Crystal Palace. His agent Borko Krunic, a Yugoslav journalist told him about Swansea City, and although he had not heard of the Swans, told his agent that he would go for a couple of days to Swansea and talk to John Toshack. Toshack asked him to play in a friendly game at the Vetch Field, and despite telling the Swans manager that he had played more than 400 games for his club in Yugoslavia, represented his country, and had a heavy cold, he agreed to play the first forty-five minutes against Tottenham Hotspur. His performance in the first half had all the supporters admiring his style of play, and after doing almost a lap of honour after coming off the field, was cheered by the fans all the way to the players entrance. Dzemal knew then that he would be signing a contract for the Swans, even turning down a late offer from Norwich City manager John Bond. Capped on twenty-one occasions by Yugoslavia, he played for his country against Wales in both legs of the 1976 European Football Championships quarter finals, with the second leg played at Ninian Park in danger at one time of being abandoned when play was suspended by the East German referee after objects had been thrown onto the pitch. Besides Toshack in the Welsh team, other players who played in both legs, and who would be team mates in the Swans side a coupe of years later included Dai Davies, John Mahoney, Leighton Phillips, Alan Curtis and Leighton James. Within a couple of games the former Yugoslavian youth international would set up an understanding on the left flank for the Swans which would be a critical factor in the club's promotion success at the end of the season. Missing just four league games through the season, and scoring against his fellow countryman Borota in the Chelsea goal, and playing in the First Leg of the Welsh Cup Final against Hereford United, he continued to display consistency during the club's first season in the top flight, picking up a second Welsh Cup Final Winner's medal at the end of the season, playing in both legs of the Final against Cardiff City. The love affair with the club finally ended in March 1983 after a game with Southampton, when after being named substitute, he had a row with Toshack, never made another appearance for the Swans, returning to his native Yugoslavia in May 1983 to coach. His coaching career back home was interrupted by the civil war in Yugoslavia, which split the country, and from which his family was forced to flee. A benefit match was held in his honour at the Vetch Field in 1992, a couple of months after the Hadziabdic family had returned from the now Bosnia-Herzegovina. He returned from his home in Mostar in Bosnia in 1992, and briefly helped in the Development Officer role with Alan Curtis before heading to the Middle East to take up a coaching role with league outfit Al-Ithead Sports, winning numerous cups and leagues with the club before taking on the national post at a caretaker level at the latter stages of qualifying for the World Cup Finals in France 1998. Without a point before Jimmy took the reins, Qatar narrowly failed to qualify, losing to Saudi Arabia in the final game. Taking the job on a full time basis, he arranged high profile fixtures with Bosnia, Nigeria and even invited the Welsh team, who only just pipped the Persian Gulf side 1-0.
After spending a short time as manager of Qatar national side, he went on to coach at club level with some success, and in March 2003 was coach of club side AL Vacra in Qatar with his family still retaining their home in Swansea.

3. HAINES, John (JACK) Thomas William

Birthplace: Wickhamford, Worcs, 24/4/1920. **Died:** Evesham, Worcs, 13/3/1987
Ht: 5ft-9ins, **Wt:** 10st-9lbs
Swans debut: v. West Bromwich Albion (h), 31/8/1946

Swansea Town Career Statistics	
Season	League
1946/47	30/6gls
Total	30/6gls

Career:
Evesham Town (signed in 1934)
Cheltenham Town
Liverpool (signed in November 1937) lge 0
Swansea Town (signed in June 1939)
Leicester City (£10,000 signed in June 1947) lge 12/3gls, FAC 3/1gls
West Bromwich Albion (signed in March 1948) lge 59/23gls
Bradford Park Avenue (£10,000 signed in December 1949) lge 136/34gls
Rochdale (£2,000 signed in October 1953) lge 60/16gls
Chester City (signed in July 1955) lge 47/8gls
Wellington Town (signed in close season 1957)
Kidderminster Harriers (signed in close season 1958)
Evesham Town (signed in October 1958)

Honours: England–1

Jack Haines originally signed for the Swans in the last Football League season before the outbreak of the Second World War, arriving at the Vetch Field in June 1939 from Liverpool. Did not play in the opening games of the 1939/40 season, but after the league was suspended played regularly for the Swans in the Regional South West League, also making guest appearances for Worcester City (1939/40, 16 goals from15 appearances), Bradford Park Avenue, Doncaster, Lincoln, Wrexham and Notts County. He was leading scorer for Lincoln City in season 1944-45 with 21 goals, and also played for the Air Command and RAF teams during WW2. Football mad as a youngster with Badsey Council & Evesham Grammar Schools, he played for Evesham Town and Cheltenham Town, before joining Liverpool as a trialist in 1938. Re-joining the Swans playing staff after the war, after making his league debut for the Swans in the opening game against West Bromwich Albion at inside left, scoring the Swans first goal, he continued to make regular appearances throughout the season, finishing with nine league goals, and runner-up to Norman Lockhart in the goalscoring charts. Through the season he also played at left half, centre forward, and even at outside left for the Swans. A neat inside forward, good ball skills and distribution in the Frankie Squires mould, he also possessed a deceptive body swerve, reminiscent of Lachlan McPherson. Joining Second Division Leicester City in June 1947, he made his debut for City at Leeds United in late August 1947. He played in a number of positions for City, but before the end of the season he joined Second Division West Bromwich Albion in part exchange for Peter McKennan, gaining a runners up medal the following season, as the side gained promotion to the First Division. Used exclusively in the forward line at the Hawthorns, on the 1st December 1948 he made his one and only appearance for England, at Highbury in a 6-0 win over Switzerland in which he scored two goals. Joining Second Division Bradford Park Avenue in December 1949, he was unable to prevent the club from suffering relegation to the Third Division North, and after four seasons was signed by Rochdale manager Harry Catterick for a record transfer fee of £2,000, before finishing his league career at Chester in July 1955. Joining Wellington Town in the 1957 close season, he later joined Kidderminster Harriers, before signing for Evesham Town in October 1958, retiring in season 1959/60. He returned to his Wickhamford birthplace after retirement, working for a local engineering company, prior to his death in March 1987.

4. HALE, Joseph Richard (DIXIE)

Birthplace: Waterford, 29/5/1935
Ht: 5ft-7ins, **Wt:** 11st-0lbs
Swans debut: v. Cardiff City (a), 7/11/1959

Swansea Town Career Statistics			
Season	League	FAC	WC
1959/60	19/1gls	2	
1960/61	15/2gls	1	1
Total	34/3gls	3	1

Career:
Waterford
Shamrock Rovers
Cork Hibernians
Swansea Town (trial on 17/8/1959, signed in October 1959)
Barrow (signed in 8/7/1961) lge 118/16gls
Workington (signed in August 1964) lge 131/10gls
Watford (£3,500 signed in July 1967) lge 95+3/7gls, FLC 6, FAC 8+1/3gls
Kings Lynn (signed in September 1970)
Wealdstone (signed in close season 1971)
Pembroke Borough
Pontardawe Athletic (player manager in season 1981/82)
Milford United

Honours: Ireland Sch, League of Ireland, Third Division Champions–1969, West Wales Senior Cup Winner–1960, Football Combination Second Division Champions–1961

Represented the League of Ireland during his earlier years in Irish football with Waterford, Shamrock Rovers and Cork Hibernians before being signed by Swans manager Trevor Morris in mid-August 1959 on an initial month trial basis. A couple of days previously he had made a good impression playing in a pre-season friendly for Cork Hibernians against the Swans. Given a further month's trial, he later signed professional forms for the Swans. Dixie attended Mount Sign and Del-a-Sel Schools, and played for the Irish Schoolboys at Goodison Park against England in season 1950/51, with Duncan Edwards included in the England side. For Waterford he played alongside his three brothers, of whom Alfie became a Full international. Making his league debut at Ninian Park against Cardiff City in November 1959 at left half back, replacing Roy Saunders, he made regular appearances through to the end of the season in either half back position, scoring his first league goal in the return fixture with the Bluebirds later in the season at the Vetch Field. In May 1960 he played in the Swans side that beat Llanelly to win the West Wales Senior Cup. Starting the 1960/61 season at left half back, he was replaced by Malcolm Kennedy midway through the season, and after failing to make a further first team appearance joined Fourth Division side

Barrow in the close season for £3,000. During the Swans exciting F.A. Cup run to the semi-finals in the 1963/64 season, 'Dixie' was included in the Barrow line-up in the third round game at the Vetch Field. A neat wing half, good passer of the ball, he lacked that extra bit of pace for Second Division football, but made up for it by sound positional sense. His second season at the Vetch Field saw Dixie make regular appearances in the Swans reserve side that won the Combination Second Division Championship. After making over one hundred league appearances for Barrow, and after they had finished bottom of the Fourth Division in 1964, he joined Third Division Workington, and during seasons 1965/66 and 1966/67 played in some high scoring games against the Swans, scoring on two occasions. By the end of the 1967/68 season when Workington finished bottom of the league, he signed for Third Division Watford, winning a Championship medal with the 'Hornets' at the end of his second season at Vicarage Road. Joining Kings Lynn in September 1970, he linked up with former Swans winger Cliff Jones, and after making further non-league appearances with Wealdstone, and working for British Leyland, he returned to Swansea, signing for Pembroke Borough, and also taking up employment with the Ford Motor Company in the city, where he remained until his retirement in 1994. Dixie joined Pontardawe Athletic as player manager in the late seventies, alongside the legendary Ivor Allchurch, returned to Pembroke for a spell as manager before joining West Wales side Milford United as player manager, winning the West Wales Cup in season 1985/86, beating the Swans in the final. His Welsh League career, either as a player, player/manager, or as a manager, saw him have three spells with Pembroke Borough, two with Milford United, and two with Pontardawe Athletic. He finished his managerial career in the early 1990's in the Swansea Senior League with West End.

5. HANDLEY, Charles (CHARLIE) Harold James

Birthplace: Edmonton, 12/3/1899. **Died:** Edmonton, 21/1/1957
Ht: 5ft-7ins, **Wt:** 10st-12lbs
Swans debut: v. Hull City (a), 31/8/1929

Swansea Town Career Statistics		
Season	League	WC
1929/30	19/4gls	2
Total	19/4gls	2

Career:
Edmonton Juniors
Tottenham Hotspur (signed in April 1921) lge 120/26gls
Swansea Town (signed in 10/5/1929)
Sittingbourne (signed in October 1930)
Sheppey United (signed in February 1931)
Thames (£50 signed in October 1931) lge 29/3gls
Sittingbourne (signed in 1932)
Norwich City (signed in September 1932) lge 0
Berne, Switzerland (November 1932 to August 1934)

Joining First Division Tottenham Hotspur in 1921 from Edmonton Juniors, Charlie made most of his appearances for Spurs in the First Division, prior to signing for the Swans for £500 in May 1929. Unfortunately for Charlie, he was usually an understudy to the likes of Jimmy Dimmock, Jimmy Seed and Frank Osbourne during his career at White Hart Lane. The season before he arrived at the Vetch Field he did not make an appearance for Spurs in either league fixture against the Swans. It was said at the time of his joining the Swans that he was probably the most versatile forward to have played for Tottenham. Originally signed as an inside left, he had played in all forward positions for the club after arriving at White Hart Lane in April 1921. Making his Swans debut at outside left in the opening fixture of the 1929/30 season, he missed the next eight league games, but was then recalled to the side, replacing Davies at outside left, playing in the next ten league games, scoring his first goal for the Swans at the Vetch Field against Millwall in mid-November 1929. The second half of the season saw him compete with Deacon for the outside left position, but by the end of the season had added a further three league goals. He failed to make another appearance for the Swans and joined non-league sides Sittingbourne and Sheppey United, prior to signing for Third Division South side Thames for £50 in 1931. After Thames had withdrawn from the Football League in May 1932 he was given a free transfer, rejoining Kent League Division One side Sittingbourne. He later returned to the Football League to sign for Third Division South side Norwich City, but failed to make the league side. In November 1932 to August 1934 he played football in Switzerland with Berne.

6. HANFORD, Harold (HARRY)

Birthplace: Blaengwynfi 9/10/1908. **Died:** Melbourne, Australia 26/11/1995
Ht: 5ft-10ins, **Wt:** 10st-11lbs
Swans debut: v. Preston North End (a), 26/12/1927

Swansea Town Career Statistics			
Season	League	FAC	WC
1927/28	2		
1928/29	2		1
1929/30	9		2
1930/31	37	1	1
1931/32	6		4
1932/33	39	1	2
1933/34	39	4	
1934/35	42	2	1
1935/36	25	1	
Total	201	9	11

Career:
Blaengwynfi Juniors
Ton Pentre
Swansea Town (signed in August 1925, professional in 14/5/1926)
Sheffield Wednesday (signed in February 1936) lge 88/1gls
Swindon Town (signed in May 1939)
Exeter City (signed in May 1946) lge 36
Haverfordwest (signed in July 1947)

Honours: Wales Sch, Full–7, West Wales Senior Cup Winner–1927, Welsh League Representative XI

Harry Hanford signed for the Swans in August 1925 after playing for Ton Pentre and Blaengwynfi Juniors, playing initially in the club's 'A' team at the Vetch Field. A good passer of the ball, he was an incisive tackler, cool in defence, and was influenced a great deal by the legendary Joe Sykes alongside him in his early years at the Vetch Field. In April 1927 he was included in the reserve side that beat Bridgend Town to win the West Wales Senior Cup. Making his debut for the Swans at Preston North End on Boxing Day 1927, as a replacement for Collins at centre half, he also played in the return fixture against the club the following day at the Vetch Field. In May 1929 he was included in the Swans' reserve side that were beaten by Cardiff City at Llanelly in the South Wales & Monmouthshire Cup Final. He had to wait until the end of the 1929/30 season before he was able to become an automatic inclusion in the Swans starting line-up, starting the following season as first choice at centre half, also going on to captain the Swans side. In May 1930 he was included in a Welsh League Representative side that played the Irish Free State at the Vetch Field. Capped at schoolboy level, he made his first appearance for Wales in a full international in Belfast against Ireland on the 4th November 1933, making a further two appearances for Wales whilst at the Vetch Field. He was transferred to Sheffield Wednesday in exchange for £4,000 and Peter Leyland in February 1936, initially as deputy to Walter Millership, and after the club had been relegated to the Second Division in May 1937, he then secured a regular first team berth up to the war. During WW2 he returned to Swansea, served in the Police War Reserve and managed only 8 wartime games for the 'Owls', after having played 88 league matches for the club. He also played wartime football as a guest for the Swans, Swindon and Aberaman Athletic (1944/45 and 1945/46), and at the end of the war he was awarded a benefit by Wednesday, but he had already left for Exeter City. Playing just one season at St. James Park, he returned to West Wales to join Welsh League side Haverfordwest in late July 1947 before retiring a couple of seasons later. Taking up physiotherapy after his retirement as a player, he served both Northampton Town and Exeter City as club physiotherapist, also a period at Exeter City as trainer from 1954 to 1958. A qualified Physiotherapist and Chiropodist, he returned to Swansea in June 1958 to open up a practice. He later emigrated to Australia, worked for the MEB Power Station, remaining there until his death in Melbourne in November 1995, with his ashes brought back to Swansea and scattered onto the Vetch Field.

7. HANVEY, KEITH

Birthplace: Newton Heath, Manchester, 18/1/1952
Ht: 6ft-1ins, **Wt:** 13st-0lbs
Swans debut: v. Scunthorpe United (a), 12/8/1972

Career:
Manchester City (from juniors in August 1971) lge 0, Others 1

Swansea City (signed in 10/7/1972)
Rochdale (signed in July 1973) lge 121/10gls
Grimsby Town (£12,000 signed in February 1977) lge 54/2gls
Huddersfield Town (£14,000 signed in July 1978) lge 205/14gls
Rochdale (signed in July 1984) lge 15

Swansea City Career Statistics		
Season	League	FLC
1972/73	11	2
Total	11	2

Honours: Fourth Division Champions–1980

One of three youngsters signed by Swans manager Roy Bentley prior to the start of the 1972/73 season on a season loan from Manchester City. Tall, slight, an inexperienced centre half who made nearly all of his first team appearances for the Swans during the first half of the season. When Harry Gregg was appointed manager in November 1972 his only first team appearance under him came in March at Port Vale. He returned to Maine Road at the end of the season, joining Rochdale in July 1973 on a free transfer. Prior to signing for Manchester City in September 1970 he had attended Briscoe Lane Primary School, Brookdale Park Secondary School, playing for North Manchester Grammer School and Brookdale Juniors. His only first team appearance at Maine Road came in a Texaco Cup tie against Airdrie in 27/9/1971. He suffered relegation to the Fourth Division in his first season at Spotland, but after becoming a regular in the starting line-up, making over one hundred league appearances in four seasons, joined Third Division Grimsby Town in February 1977. Once again he suffered relegation at the end of his first season, but once he had signed for Huddersfield Town in July 1978, he gained success at the top of the division, winning the Fourth Division Championship in 1980, missing just seven league matches over the next three seasons in the Third Division with the 'Terriers'. Returning to Spotland in July 1984, after playing in the first nineteen league games he suffered a pelvic injury at the age of 33, which forced him to retire from playing. In late 1984/85 a benefit Match was organised by Rochdale when an All Stars XI played a Huddersfield side at Spotland. Since then he has been involved as Commercial Manager at Huddersfield Town (1986/90), Bradford City (1990-93), Leeds United East Stand Manager (1993-97), club Commercial Manager at Elland Road for a year from May 1997, and then serving as Sales Manager. He has also been a regular contributor to the football pages of the Yorkshire Post.

8. HARLEY, ALBERT George

Birthplace: Chester, 17/4/1940. **Died:** Chester, June 1993
Ht: 5ft-8ins, **Wt:** 10st-6lbs
Swans debut: v. Manchester City (h), 26/9/1964

Swansea Town Career Statistics				
Season	League	FLC	FAC	WC
1964/65	23	3	4	2
1965/66	2+1			
Total	25+1	3	4	2

Career:
Shrewsbury Town (signed from juniors in April 1957)
    lge 220/14gls
Swansea Town (£10,000 signed in September 1964)
Guildford City (signed in November 1965)
Crewe Alexandra (signed in July 1966) lge 22/4gls

Stockport County (signed in February 1967) lge 77+3/11gls
Chester City (signed in June 1969) lge 3/1gls

Honours: Fourth Division Champions–1967

Albert Harley had the reputation at Shrewsbury of being one of the outstanding wing halves in the Third Division, making over two hundred league appearances for the club prior to signing for the Swans in September 1964 for £10,000. A non-stop player with tremendous energy, he was a tough tackling wing half, who joined the Swans shortly after the start of a season that would see the club lose it's Second Division status and return to the Third Division. With a change of manager at the start of his first full season at the Vetch Field, despite making history by becoming the club's first ever substitute in the Football league when he replaced Derek Draper in the opening game of the 1965/66 season at Southend United, Harley rarely featured, resulting in him joining Southern League Premier Division side Guildford City in November 1965. He returned to the Football League in July 1966, joining Crewe Alexandra, but midway through the season joined Stockport County, winning a Fourth Division Championship medal a couple of months later. Joining Third Division Chester City in June 1969, he made just three league appearances before drifting into non-league football with Connah's Quay. He continued to live in the Chester area, suffered with multiple sclerosis in later years until his death in June 1993.

9. HARRIS, James (JAMIE) Christopher

Birthplace: Swansea, 28/6/1979
Ht: 6ft-2ins, **Wt:** 13st-7lbs
Swans debut: v. Reading (h), CCC 1-2, 26/8/1997

Swansea City Career Statistics			
Season	League	FLC	FAWP
1997/98	0+6	0+1	1+3
Total	0+6	0+1	1+3

Career:
Mumbles Rangers
Swansea City (signed in July 1997)
Haverfordwest (loan in March 1998)
Merthyr Tydfil (loan in August 1998)
Bohemians (signed in November 1998)
St. Patricks (signed in 2001)
Shelbourne (signed midway through 2003)

Honours: Boys Club of Wales, Eircom Premier Lge
Champions–2003, League Cup–2003

Jamie Harris was spotted by youth team coach Alan Curtis when he was involved with training Swansea Senior League side Mumbles Rangers, later recommending him to Swans' manager Jan Molby. His 'A' level studies prevented him signing for the Swans in season 1996/97, playing mainly with the reserves towards the end of the season, scoring his first goal for the club in a reserve game against against Swindon Town. Earlier in his career the striker had represented Swansea schoolboys and played for the Boys Club of Wales, whilst playing for Gorseinon Boys Club. After his trial period he was given a one year professional contract by Swans manager Jan Molby. A strong running central striker, he made his first team debut as substitute for defender Joao Moreira at the Vetch Field in the second leg of the Coca Cola Cup first round against Reading. Seven days later he made his league debut for the Swans, again as substitute at Barnet, this time for winger Dave Puttnam. He went on to make a further five substitute league appearances for the Swans that season, but his only start came in an FAW Cup competition at Bangor City. Had a month on loan with League of Wales side Haverfordwest in March 1998, but a knee injury the following month saw him having to undergo an operation in the close season. Signing a six month contract, shortly after the start of the 1998/99 season he joined Merthyr Tydfil on a month loan, but in early November 1998 he was given two weeks notice by the Swans of terminating his contract, joining Bohemians in the Eircom League. Jamie is the grandson of former Swans legend Rory Keane. By the time he had joined Eircom Premier Division side St. Patricks in 2001, Jamie had been a more than capable performer in defence as well as in attack, making a fine contribution towards the club winning the League Cup in the early part of the 2003 season, prior to his signing for Shelbourne midway through the 2003 season. At the end of the season Shelbourne won the Eircom Premier League Championship, and in early August 2004 Jamie was included in the squad that played against Croatia's Hajduk Split in the Champions League Second Qualifying Round, losing in the next round to Spanish side Deportivo La Coruna.

10. HARRIS, JOHN

Birthplace: Gorbals, Glasgow, 30/6/1917. **Died:** Sheffield, 15/7/1988
Ht: 5ft-9ins, **Wt:** 10st-9lbs
Swans debut: v. Bradford Park Avenue (a), 20/4/1935

Career:
Swindon Town (amateur signed in 1933) lge 0
Swansea Town (signed in 29/8/1934)
Tottenham Hotspur (signed in February 1939) lge 0
Wolverhampton Wanderers (signed in 9/5/1939) lge 0
Chelsea (£8,000 signed in August 1945) lge 326/14gls, FAC 38
Chester (player manager signed in July 1956) lge 27/1gls

Swansea Town Career Statistics			
Season	League	FAC	WC
1934/35	1		2
1935/36			
1936/37	15/2gls	3	
1937/38			3
1938/39	13/2gls	1	
Total	29/4gls	4	5

Honours: Scotland-War Time International–1, First Division Champions–1955, League South Cup Winner–1945, Welsh League XI, West Wales Senior Cup Winner–1934

Joined the Swans in late August 1934 from Swindon Town after impressing in trial matches, making his debut as a seventeen-year-old at Bradford Park Avenue at right half back instead of Warner, with his father Neil, at the time, the manager of the Swans. In October 1934 he was included in the Swans reserve side that beat Llanelly to win the West Wales Senior Cup. A composed, and competent player, he failed to make an appearance during season 1935/36, but the following season made fifteen appearances, also scoring his first league goals. His only appearances during season 1937/38 were in the Welsh Cup competition, playing against Shrewsbury Town in the final, with the replay having to be carried over until the following year. On the 23rd April 1938 he played for the Welsh League XI in Brussels against Diables Rouges along with team mates John and Beresford. He had a good run of appearances during season 1938/39, prior to being sold to Tottenham Hotspur in February 1939 for a substantial fee, plus Joe Meek joining the Swans. However, by the end of the season he had joined Wolverhampton Wanderers. Capped for Scotland in a war time international in 1945 against England, he made 114 war time guest appearances (league and cup) for Chelsea prior to the transfer being made permanent in August 1945 for £5,000. Apart from his appearances during war-time with Chelsea he also made guest appearances for Portsmouth (1939/40) and Southampton (1940/41). He made his Chelsea debut in an FA Cup third round match against Leicester City on the 5th January 1946. For most of his fourteen seasons he was a dominant figure on the field at either centre half, or later in his career at full back, also an influential captain. He had led the side to two war time finals at Wembley in 1944, losing to Charlton Athletic 3-1, and in 1945 when they beat Millwall 2-0. Renowned for his hard tackling and shrewd positional sense, but for his lack of inches he would have undoubtedly gained more international recognition for his country. During the 1954/55 First Division Championship winning season he made thirty-one league appearances, and ended his playing career with Chester, signing for the club in 1956 as player manager, managing the side in the Third Division North up to April 1959, when he took over as manager of Sheffield United, remaining in charge at Bramall Lane until July 1968 when he took over as General Manager. Arthur Rowley had replaced Harris as team manager in 1968, but after he had been relieved of his duties, Harris took over in August 1969 for a second time as manager, leading the club through to December 1973 as team manager, before he was replaced by Ken Furphy. After occupying a chief scout position at Bramall Lane, he became a coach at rivals Sheffield Wednesday in the late 1970's.

11. HARRIS, Leslie (LES)

Birthplace: Llanfaircaereinion, Powys, 1/11/1941
Ht: 5ft-8ins, **Wt:** 10st-7lbs
Swans debut: v. Lovells Athletic (a), WC-5, 1/2/1964

Career:
Aberystwyth University (signed in 1959)
Aberystwyth Town (signed in 1960)

Swansea Town (signed in August 1963)
Merthyr Tydfil (signed in season 1964/65)

Swansea Town Career Statistics		
Season	*League*	*WC*
1963/64	1	1
1964/65	3	
Total	4	1

Honours: Welsh Universities–2, British Universities–1962, Welsh League First Division Champions–1964

Les Harris was born in the Montgomeryshire village of Llanfaircaereinion after his family had been relocated from the Rhondda Valley after their house had been bombed during the war. Returning to the Rhondda after just six weeks, he lived for eighteen years in Cwmparc, attending Pentre Grammar School. With no organised football at the school, Les played for his school rugby team and Treorchy Boys Club prior to enrolling at Aberystwyth University on a Geography Degree Course. Apart from playing for the college football team, Les also played for the Welsh Universities against England and Ireland, and also in an eight country tournament in Belgium with the British University Representative team, coached by Malcolm Allison. During his second and third year at college, Les played Welsh League for Aberystwyth Town before being offered a two year professional contract by Swans manager Trevor Morris. At the same time Les also had an offer from top Belgium side Anderlecht to go on trial. Predominantly a left sided full back, who also operated on the left side of midfield, during his eighteen months at the Vetch Field played mainly in the club's reserve team in the Welsh League, winning the Championship at the end of his first season as a professional. Halfway through his second season at the Vetch Field he took the opportunity to join the Midland Bank on a graduate trainee programme, remaining with the company for twenty-nine years, until his retirement in November 1991 when he held the position of Senior Corporate Manager for South Wales. At the same time as leaving the Vetch Field, Les had offers off Malcolm Allison to join him at non-league Bath City, and also at Manchester City. Linking up with Harry Griffiths at Merthyr Tydfil after leaving the Swans, Les also had a period as player manager with Mid-Wales League side Knighton, later playing one season with Cinderford Town. Working himself up the corporate structure within the Midland Bank saw Les take up various management appointments in South Wales, giving him the opportunity to make appearances for Caerau, Ton Pentre, and in the Southern League with Barry Town. His senior football career came to a close after he suffered a broken ankle whilst playing rugby for Glamorgan Wanderers, but up to the age of fifty-seven Les still managed to play in a veterans competition in the Cardiff mid-week league. He has since had appointments with the Bank in Jersey (assistant manager), Oxted in Surrey (Tutor at the Management College), Cardiff (Branch Superintendant), Neath (Area Manager) and Bridgend (Area Manager) prior to his retirement.

12. HARRIS, MARK Andrew

Birthplace: Reading, 15/7/1963
Ht: 6ft-3ins, **Wt:** 13st-6lbs
Swans debut: v. Reading (h), 23/9/1989

Career:
Wokingham Town (signed in August 1986)
Crystal Palace (£25,000 signed in 29/2/1988) lge 0+2
Burnley (loan in 7/8/1989) lge 4, FLC 2
Swansea City (£12,000 signed in 22/9/1989)

Gillingham (£15,000 signed in 11/8/1995) lge 63+2/3gls, FLC 8, FAC 5+1, Others 0+1
Cardiff City (signed in 6/8/1997) lge 38/1gls, FLC 2, FAC 6
Kingstonian (signed in August 1998) Conf 103+3/6gls
Henley
Bromley

Swansea City Career Statistics							
Season	*League*	*FLC*	*FAC*	*WC*	*AWS/AGT*	*ECWC*	*P/Offs*
1989/90	41/2gls		4	1	2		
1990/91	41/1gls	2	4	6/2gls	5/1gls		
1991/92	44/3gls	4	3/1gls	3	2	2	
1992/93	42/5gls	2	5	1	3		2/1gls
1993/94	46/3gls	4	2	6	8/1gls		
1994/95	14	4		1	1		
Total	228/14gls	16	18/1gls	18/2gls	21/2gls	2	2/1gls

Honours: AutoGlass Trophy Winner–1994, West Wales Senior Cup Winner–1994, F.A. Trophy Winner–1999, 2000

Mark Harris was signed by Swans manager Ian Evans the day before he made his debut against his home town side Reading, in which Reading striker Trevor Senior scored a hat trick in a 6-1 win at the Vetch Field. Not put off by that defeat on his debut for the Swans, 'Chopper' would go on to make a huge impression in the centre of the Swans defence, forging a strong partnership with Keith Walker. Up to his achilles heel injury in October 1994, which was to sideline him for the remainder of the 1994/95 season, 'Chopper' would miss just 16 league games. During the 1993/94 season, along with goalkeeper Roger Freestone, he established a record with the Swans of playing 46 league games, plus 20 cup matches through the season. Highlights of his career at the Vetch Field include European Cup Winners Cup action against Monaco, although he was unable to make an appearance in the Welsh Cup Final against Wrexham at the end of the previous season, the 1993 Play Off semi-finals against West Bromwich Albion, and the 1994 AGT Final at Wembley against Huddersfield Town, which the Swans won on penalties. He was also included in the Swans side that beat Ammanford Town in May 1994 to win the West Wales Senior Cup. Starting his career with non-league side Wokingham, 'Chopper' joined Crystal Palace in February 1988 for a fee in the region of £25,000, making his league debut as substitute for Barber at Swindon Town on the 25th April 1989, making a further substitute appearance two games later. He started the 1989/90 season on loan at Turf Moor with Burnley, playing in the first four league games of the season before returning to Selhurst Park. Thirteen days later he signed for the Swans. An extremely consistent central defender, at the start of the 1995/96 season he was allowed to join Gillingham on an initial loan transfer, but before the end of the month the transfer was made permanent for a fee of £15,000. His first season with Gillingham saw him make 44 league appearances, gaining promotion from the Third Division, finishing the season in runners up position. Shortly after the start of the 1997/98 season he signed for Cardiff City, playing 38 league games, before he dropped down into non-league, firstly with Kingstonian, then made appearances for Henley and Bromley. At Kingstonian he played in consecutive FA Trophy Finals at Wembley, beating Forest Green Rovers in 1999, and Kettering Town in 2000. After making ninety appearances for Bromley, in May 2004 Mark retired from playing, was studying for his UEFA coaching badges, and working as a Sales Representative for a Tool Hire Company.

13. HARRIS, PAUL Edwin

Birthplace: Hackney, 19/5/1953
Ht: 5ft-10ins, **Wt:** 11st-4lbs
Swans debut: v. Torquay United (h), FLC 1-1, 9/8/1975

Swansea City Career Statistics				
Season	League	FLC	FAC	WC
1975/76	43/1gls	2	1	3
1976/77	4+2/1gls	2	1	
Total	47+2/2gls	4	2	3

Career:
Leyton Orient (from apprentice in July 1970) lge 96/4gls
Swansea City (signed in July 1975)
Bridgend Town (signed in August 1977)
Dartford (signed in 1978)

With the Swans having to seek re-election to the Football League at the end of the 1974/75 season, one of manager Harry Griffiths's priorities during the close season, once the club had been re-elected to the Football League was to sign an experienced central defender to tighten up a defence that had conceded 73 league goals the previous term. Leyton Orient's Paul Harris had been released by his club in May 1975, and after some persuasion from Griffiths, signed a two year deal with the Swans. Having made almost 100 league appearances for Leyton Orient, in the Second and Third Division, he had first caught the eye of scouts in the London area playing for Hackney Schoolboys, during a time when the East London side was one of the most outstanding in Britain, being part of a defence that had won the English Schools Shield. As a schoolboy Paul was a talented cricketer, and could quite possibly have made a name for himself on the county cricket circuit, as Middlesex were keen to sign him prior to his joining Orient as an apprentice. Orient were in the Third Division when he signed for them but before too long had gained promotion to the Second Division. Missing out on promotion to the First Division by one point in 1974, the following season, after a run of 13 league games from the start

of the season, Paul was released by Orient manager George Petchey. Dropping down to play for the Swans in the Fourth Division, Paul took some time to adjust to the more robust style of play in the Fourth Division, but after missing just three league games, by the end of the season the Swans defence had tightened up as a unit remarkably. His second season however, started badly, with a suspension at the start of the season, and a knee problem preventing him from carrying on his form of the previous term. During a season which saw him struggle to break up the partnership of Dave Bruton and Eddie May, he was confined to a player managerial role alongside Roy Saunders with the club's reserve team in the Welsh League, which at the time was made up mostly of youth team players. Prior to his being released at the end of the 1976/77 season, Paul had started a business in the motor trade in Swansea, and following his release by the Swans in May 1977, stayed on in the Swansea area, living in Cwmrhydyceirw. During the 1977/78 close season he was contacted by Bridgend Town manager Lyn Jones about playing for the club in the Southern League, and after some persuasion played a season for Bridgend during which the club gained promotion to the Southern League Premier Division by finishing in runners up position to Witney Town in the First Division North. Deciding to return to the London area in 1978, he continued in the motor trade, and also trained to be a black cab driver. An old friend of his, former Chelsea player, John Boyle approached him about playing for Dartford, and after signing a two year contract with the Southern League Premier Division Club, made his first appearance against, Bridgend Town. At the end of the season he had his contract paid up, and started training to become a Chiropodist. Since then he has been appointed Leyton Orient's Official Chiropodist, and on matchdays his involvement at the Matchroom Stadium involves the hospitality side of the club, dealing with sponsors, mascots and vice-presidents in the executive club.

14. HARRISON, Christopher (CHRIS) Colin

Birthplace: Launceston, 17/10/1956
Ht: 5ft-9ins, **Wt:** 11st-0lbs
Swans debut: v. Reading (a), 21/9/1985

Swansea City Career Statistics						
Season	League	FLC	FAC	WC	FRT	P/Offs
1985/86	34+2/5gls	2	2	4	4	
1986/87	46/7gls	4/3gls	5	1	2	
1987/88	34+1/2gls		0+1	1	0+1	4
Total	114+3/14gls	6/3gls	7+1	6	6+1	4

Career:
Plymouth Argyle (from apprentice in October 1974)
  lge 315+9/7gls

Swansea City (signed in September 1985)
Saltash United (signed in close season 1988)

Honours: Fourth Division Play Off Winner–1988, Great Mills League Champions–1989, West Wales Senior Cup Winner–1987

Experienced defender who was signed by Swans manager John Bond in September 1985 after being released by Plymouth Argyle. Educated at Callington Comprehensive School, Chris played for East Cornwall Schoolboys prior to joining Argyle as an apprentice at Home Park, giving the club great service since turning professional in 1974. Chris was a member of the Argyle side that lost in the semi-finals of the 1983/84 FA Cup to Watford 1-0 at Villa Park, and included in the Watford side was Neil Price, a player who also joined the Swans at the start of the 1985/86 season. As an apprentice Chris attended trials for the England Youth team at Lilleshall, but did not gain any caps. Starting his career as a midfielder, Chris made his league debut for Argyle in the last match of the 1975/76 season at Carlisle United at right full back. It took him a couple of seasons before he was regularly making appearances in the Argyle starting line-up, and by season 1979/80 had established himself a left full back for Argyle. Switching to a central defensive role, he missed just eleven league games for Argyle between the 1980/81 and 1983/84 seasons. After joining the Swans, he played primarily in central defence under John Bond, but after Terry Yorath had been installed as manager at the Vetch Field, Chris reverted to an attacking right full back role. Not noted as a prolific goalscorer during his days with Argyle, for the first couple of seasons at the Vetch Field, he became a consistent scorer for the Swans from the penalty spot, including 8 league and cup penalties during the 1986/87 season. In May 1987 he was included in the Swans side that beat Briton Ferry Athletic to win the West Wales Senior Cup. Despite missing a number of games during the 1987/88 season, he came back to play an influential part in the club's successful Play Off side that beat Torquay United over two legs at the end of the season, gaining promotion to the Third (Second) Division. He was released at the end of the season, returning to his native Cornwall, signing initially for two years as a player with Saltash United in the Western League, and for two more years as player manager. His first season at Saltash saw the club win the Great Mills League Championship, and as player manager the club were runners up one season, and also won the Cornwall Senior Cup. Since returning to Cornwall, Chris has started up his own driving school, become involved with coaching at Home Park with Plymouth Argyle School of Excellence, and for the last eight years has been a retained fireman.

15. HARROP, John (JACK)

Birthplace: Manchester, 25/6/1929. **Died:** Hemel Hempstead, Herts, 18/2/1977
Ht: 5ft-10ins, **Wt:** 11st-12lbs
Swans debut: v. Fulham (a), 11/4/1953

Swansea Town Career Statistics	
Season	*League*
1952/53	1
1953/54	9
Total	10

Career:
Charlton Athletic (signed in September 1949) lge 0
Swansea Town (signed in August 1952)
Watford (signed in July 1956) lge 111, FAC 6
Hastings United (signed in July 1960)
Tunbridge Wells (signed in close season 1961)

Honours: Football Combination Second Division Champions–1955

Former amateur with Charlton Athletic who was spotted at Bridgend by a Swans scout, playing for the Army R.E.M.E. team during his National Service, and offered a contract which he signed in August 1952. A terrier type of full back, whose best spell in the first team came midway through his second season (1953/54), when he played in eight consecutive league matches, mostly at left full back, two of which at right full back. He had made his Swans league debut towards the end of the 1952/53 season, deputising for Dai Thomas at left full back. Very much a reserve team defender at the Vetch Field, he made regular appearances in the Swans' reserve side that won the Football Combination Second Division Championship in 1955. Released by the Swans in July 1956, he joined Third Division South side Watford, where he went on to make over 100 league appearances, giving good service for the 'Hornets' from left full back. His last six league games for Watford all ended in defeats. Drifting into non-league football with Hastings United in July 1960, he signed for Tunbridge Wells the following season.
A keen cricketer during his playing career, he succeeded Frank Mitchell as cricket coach at Dulwich College, and in 1960 he was appointed captain of Watford Town Cricket Club.

16. HARTFIELD, Charles (CHARLIE) Joseph

Birthplace: Lambeth, 4/9/1971
Ht: 6ft-0ins, **Wt:** 13st-8lbs
Swans debut: v. Shrewsbury Town (a), 29/11/1997

Swansea City Career Statistics			
Season	*League*	*AWS*	*FAWP*
1997/98	22/2gls	1	1
Total	22/2gls	1	1

Career:
Aston Villa (associate schoolboy in July 1986, trainee in
    September 1987)
Arsenal (trainee in July 1988, professional in 20/9/1989)
Sheffield United (signed in 6/8/1991) lge 45+11/1gls, FLC 2+1,
    FAC 4+1, Others 1
Fulham (loan in 5/2/1997) lge 1+1
Swansea City (signed in 28/11/1997)
Lincoln City (loan in 17/9/1998 and in March 1999)) lge 3/1gls
Telford United (signed in October 1999) Conf 18+2/3gls
Sheffield FC
Caernarfon Town (signed in 2003)
Halifax Town (signed in 20/11/2002)
Ilkeston Town (signed in 2003)
Buxton (signed in November 2003)

Honours: England Yth

Released by Sheffield United during the summer of 1997, after
trials with Brentford, Southend United and Fulham, Charlie
signed for the Swans in November 1997 on a month to month
contract. A strong tackling midfielder, with an eye for goal, he
did score in consecutive games for the Swans, one of the goals
being a cheeky strike from a quickly taken free kick against
Notts. County. He later had a trial spell with Lincoln City in
August 1998, joining the club a month later on loan. After a
couple of games he damaged stomach muscles, returned to the
Vetch Field, and despite another brief trial with Lincoln City in
March 1998, no firm offer of a contract was given, and in June
1999 had the remaining 10 months of his contract paid up by the
Swans. An associate schoolboy with Aston Villa in July 1986, he
became a trainee in September 1987, but a year later served the
second year as a trainee at Highbury with Arsenal. Although he
failed to make a league appearance for the 'Gunners', he made
international appearance for England at youth level prior to
signing for Premiership side Sheffield United in August 1991.
He made his league debut for the 'Blades' at Crystal Palace on
the 31st August 1991, and the following season played in the
United side that beat Blackburn Rovers on penalties in the
quarter final of the F.A. Cup. Unfortunately he missed out on
playing rivals Sheffield Wednesday in the semi-final of the
competition a couple of weeks later through suspension. He
continued to make regular appearances in the 'Blades' midfield
until his release at the end of the 1996/97 season. After leaving
the Vetch Field, Charlie signed for Vauxhall Conference side
Telford United in the 1999/2000 season, then signed for
Northern Counties League side Sheffield F.C. Later, Charlie
made appearances for North Wales side Caernarfon Town in
2000, Conference side Halifax Town (November 2002), Ilkeston
Town (2003), and Buxton (Nov. 2003).

17. HARVEY, LEIGHTON

Birthplace: Neath, 27/8/1959
Ht: 5ft-8ins, **Wt:** 10st-7lbs
Swans debut: v. Darlington (a), 28/4/1976

Swansea City Career Statistics		
Season	League	WC
1975/76	0+1	
1976/77	1	1
Total	1+1	1

Career:
Swansea City (from apprentice in August 1976)

Honours: Welsh League First Division Champions–1976

Midfielder Leighton Harvey was still an apprentice at the Vetch
Field when he made his debut as substitute for Paul Harris in
the last game of the 1975/76 season at Darlington. During that
season he made a number of appearances in the club's reserve
side that won the Welsh League First Division Championship.
The following season, his first as a professional, he made his
first start for the Swans in a sixth round Welsh Cup tie at
Wrexham and, two weeks later played in a 4-2 Vetch Field win
over Aldershot. Earlier he had attended Llangewydd Primary
School (Bridgend), Catwg Primary School in Cadoxton, and
Neath Grammar Schoolboy, prior to starting his apprenticeship
at the Vetch Field, also playing for Neath Boys Club. He made
just one more league appearance during the 1976/77 season in a
home win over Aldershot, as well as an appearance in the Welsh
Cup competition at Wrexham, before being released by the
Swans at the end of the 1976/77 season. Having no further
involvement in any level of football, Leighton initially worked
as a gas pipe fitter, and after working as a photocopier
repairer, has since become a Paramedic with the Local Health
Authority.

18. HARWOOD, John (JACK)

Birthplace: Wandsworth, 1/2/1891. **Died:** Wandsworth, JAS,
    1956
Ht: 5ft-11ins, **Wt:** 12st-0lbs
Swans debut: v. Merthyr Town (h), 26/8/1922

Swansea Town Career Statistics			
Season	League	FAC	WC
1922/23	42/3gls	2	3
1923/24	3		1
Total	45/3gls	2	4

Career:
Tooting Town
Southend United (signed in 1911)
Chelsea (signed in May 1912) lge 4
Portsmouth (signed in March 1913) lge 41/2gls
Swansea Town (signed in May 1922)
Aberdare Athletic (signed in May 1924) lge 103/8gls
Barrow (signed in October 1927) lge 3
Royal Naval Volunteer Reserves (signed in December 1928)

Honours: Southern League Representative XI, West Wales
Senior Cup Winner–1923

Signed by Swans manager Joe Bradshaw in August 1922 prior to
the start of the season, Jack was an ever present at centre half
during his first season with the club, which co-incided with an
injury to regular stopper Jimmy Collins. When Collins returned
the following season, Harwood rarely featured, being released
to join Aberdare Athletic in May 1924. He scored three league
goals for the Swans in his first season, his first against Newport
County on Boxing Day 1922. Starting his career with non-league
sides Tooting Town and Southend United, Jack signed for
Chelsea in May 1912, and after making his league debut with
the club on the 4th January 1913 at Sheffield United in a 3-3
draw, made just three more appearances before signing for
Portsmouth a couple of months later. Becoming members of the
Football League the same season as the Swans, the opening
fixture of the 1920/21 newly formed Third Division on the 28th
August 1920 saw Portsmouth take on the Swans, with Jack
playing at centre half for Pompey. Also playing in the return
fixture at the Vetch Field a couple of weeks later, the following
season saw Jack make appearances for Pompey. In April 1920 he
had played at the Vetch Field for a Southern League English
Clubs XI against a Southern League Welsh Clubs XI. His form in

the centre of defence must have impressed Swans manager Joe Bradshaw, and by May 1922 he had been added to the playing staff at the Vetch Field. In November 1923 he was included in the Swans reserve side that beat Pembroke Dock to win the West Wales Senior Cup. Signing for Third Division South side Aberdare Athletic in May 1924, Jack made over one hundred league appearances for the club prior to signing for Third Division North side Barrow, after Aberdare Athletic had finished bottom of the Third Division South League table at the end of the 1926/27 season, and dropped out of the Football League. After just three league appearances for Barrow he signed up for the Royal Naval Volunteer Reserves, and in August 1930 had become second team trainer at Fulham, and by January 1933 was first team trainer at Craven Cottage. He later became trainer at Tooting & Mitcham from 1935 to 1943.

19. HAYES, MARTIN

Birthplace: Walthamstow, 21/3/1966
Ht: 5ft-10ins, **Wt:** 11st-11lbs
Swans debut: v. Fulham (h), 9/1/1993

Swansea City Career Statistics						
Season	League	FLC	FAC	WC	AGT/AWS	P/Offs
1992/93	8+7		2		1+1/1gls	2
1993/94	22/4gls	4	2	2	3	
1994/95	14+10/4gls	1+1	3+1	2+3/4gls	2+3/1gls	
Total	44+17/8gls	5+1	7+1	4+3/4gls	6+4/2gls	2

Career:
Arsenal (signed amateur in 1981, apprentice in June 1982, professional in 2/11/1983) lge 70+32/26gls, FLC 14+7/5gls, FAC 8+1/3gls, Others 0+2
Glasgow Celtic (£650,000 signed in 29/5/1990) SL 3+4, SLC 3
Wimbledon (loan in 22/2/1992) lge 1+1
Swansea City (signed in 6/1/1993)
Southend United (signed in 18/8/1995) Others 1
Dover Athletic (signed in 1995/6 season) Conf 14+1/2gls

Honours: England U-21–3, First Division Champions–1989, Football League Cup Winner–1987, Football Combination Champions–1984, 1990, Southern Junior Floodlight Cup Winner–1984, West Wales Senior Cup Winner–1995

Somewhat of a surprise signing by Swans manager Frank Burrows in January 1993 from Scottish side Glasgow Celtic. Represented Waltham Forest and Essex Schoolboys earlier in his career, he joined Arsenal as an amateur in 1981, prior to signing as an apprentice, and after graduating to the professional ranks, made his league debut on the 16th November 1985 at Highbury against Oxford United, making a further ten league

appearances, and scoring two goals in his first season in the Football League. The following season he ended top goalscorer with nineteen league goals, also playing in the Arsenal side that beat Liverpool at Wembley to win the Littlewoods Cup. On the 18th February 1987 he made his first appearance for the England U-21 side against Spain in Burgos, making his second appearance at that level in the next match against Turkey. He returned to Wembley twelve months later in the same competition, making a substitute appearance for Perry Groves in the defeat by Luton Town. During the early and latter part of his career at Highbury, Martin was a consistent goalscorer in the club's Football Combination and South East Counties sides, winning the Combination Championship in 1984 and 1990, and the Southern Junior Floodlight Cup in 1984. The 1988/89 season saw Martin make seventeen league appearances for the 'Gunners' as they won the First Division Championship. Struggling to hold down a regular place in the 'Gunners' starting line-up, Martin signed for Glasgow Celtic for £650,000 in July 1990, but a broken leg, and a loss of form saw him unable to reproduce his goalscoring touch in Scottish football. Following a short loan spell back in the First Division with Wimbledon, Martin was given the opportunity almost twelve months later of returning south on a permanent basis to sign for the Swans. Ten days after making his debut for the Swans, he scored the winning goal against Cardiff City in the first round of the Auto Glass Trophy Cup tie at Ninian Park in extra time. The following season, a hernia injury prevented him from making an appearance for the Swans in the final of the same competition at Wembley against Huddersfield Town. Never a prolific goalscorer for the Swans, he was used mainly as a link man from midfield, but he did score a hat-trick against Porthmadog in a Welsh Cup, fifth round tie at the Vetch Field in an 8-0 win in February 1995. In May 1995 he was included in the Swans side that beat Morriston Town in the West Wales Senior Cup Final. Released by the Swans during the 1995 close season, he played one game for Southend United in an Anglo Italian cup tie against Brescia, but was not offered a contract, and later joined Vauxhall Conference side Dover Athletic. He later played for Cliftonville, Crawley Town, Collier Row and Romford, ending season 1997/98 as top goalscorer. After a short period as manager of Romford FC, following a spell with Purfleet, he joined Bishops Stortford as player manager in November 1999, taking the club to a respectable fourth place in his first season. His second season saw the club secure promotion to the Ryman Premier League by finishing in second place behind Champions Ford United, finishing the 2003/04 season in the Premier League in a respectable 13th position. Martin combines his player manager role whilst working as a car salesman in Croydon.

20. HAYES, Michael (MIKE) Charles

Birthplace: Aberdare, 24/3/1944
Ht: 5ft-8ins, **Wt:** 11st-2lbs
Swans debut: v. Portsmouth (h), 27/4/1963

Swansea Town Career Statistics	
Season	League
1962/63	3
Total	3

Career:
Swansea Town (from juniors in June 1961)
Lovells Athletic (signed in close season 1965)
Barry Town (signed in close season 1967)
Merthyr Tydfil (signed in close season 1968)
Caerau

Honours: Wales Sch–3, Welsh League First Division Champions–1963, 1964, 1965, 1966

A right half who after making his league debut for the Swans at the Vetch Field against Portsmouth in April 1963, retained his place for the next two league matches. Educated at Court Road Infants, and then Radyr Secondary Modern in Cardiff, the former Cardiff schoolboy, played in three internationals for the Welsh schoolboys side against England, Scotland and Northern Ireland prior to leaving school. Having a number of temporary jobs on leaving school, he was then taken on the groundstaff at the Vetch Field by manager Trevor Morris in 1960, turning professional a year later. A regular member of the club's successful reserve side, following relegation to the Third Division, Mike was released by the Swans in May 1965, joining Welsh League side Lovells Athletic as a part-time professional, combining a job as a sales representative with the company as well. With the Swans reserve team playing in the Welsh League First Division, in three consecutive seasons they won the League Championship, and his first season with Lovells Athletic, saw him win a fourth consecutive League Championship. Having two good seasons with Lovells, it was only after the factory shut down, and the team disbanded, that Mike moved on to sign for Barry Town, spending one season at Jenner Park before joining Merthyr Tydfil. A couple of seasons later he finished his football career with Caerau Athletic, where as player manager he took the club from the Second Division to the Premier Division of the Welsh League, also making an appearance at the Vetch Field himself for the club against the Swans. Retiring from football at the age of thirty-six he has continued working as a sales representative, and is currently working for FDD International, supplying Pharmacies and Department Stores.

21. HEEPS, JAMES Andrew

Birthplace: Luton, 16/5/1971
Ht: 5ft-11¼ins, **Wt:** 11st-10lbs
Swans debut: v. Chester City (a), 26/1/1990

Swansea City Career Statistics	
Season	League
1989/90	1
Total	1

Career:
Luton Town
Swansea City (from trainee in July 1989)
Cheltenham Town (signed in season 1993/94)

Honours: West Wales Senior Cup Winner–1990

Previously on the books with Luton Town before joining the Swans as a second year YTS trainee in 1987, signing professional forms in 1989. He made his only league appearance for the

Swans against Chester at Sealand Road, but was also included as a substitute in both matches in the European Cup Winners Cup against Greek side Panathinaikos. He attended Cedars Comprehensive school, at Leighton Buzzard, and played for Bedfordshire County Schoolboys, signed schoolboy forms for Luton Town but dropped out of the soccer scene to work as a motor mechanic before joining the Swans. He made his debut for the Swans shortly after Roger Freestone had completed his loan spell from Chelsea, and had returned to Stamford Bridge. In May 1990 he was included in the Swans reserve side that beat Llanelli to win the West Wales Senior Cup. Competing with Lee Bracey, he went further down the pecking order at the Vetch Field following the permanent signing of Freestone in September 1991, before being released in July 1993. Signing for Dr. Martens side Cheltenham Town, he then made appearances for Leighton Town, Baldock Town before an upturn in fortunes took him to Vauxhall Conference challengers Bedford Town. Heeps has played in several FA representative games and won a number of Man of the Match Awards, whilst working as a HGV driver.

22. HEGGS, CARL Sydney

Birthplace: Leicester, 11/10/1970
Ht: 6ft-0ins, **Wt:** 11st-8lbs
Swans debut: v. Shrewsbury Town (h), 12/8/1995

Swansea City Career Statistics					
Season	League	FLC	FAC	AWS	P/Offs
1995/96	28+4/5gls	2	1	2	
1996/97	5+9/2gls		1		2+1/1gls
Total	33+13/7gls	2	2	2	2+1/1gls

Career:
Leicester United (signed in August 1988)
West Bromwich Albion (£25,000 signed in 22/8/1991)
    lge 13+2/7gls, FLC 2, FAC 0+1, Others 6+3/1gls
Bristol Rovers (loan in 27/1/1995) lge 2+3/1gls
Swansea City (£60,000 signed in 27/7/1995)
Northampton Town (£40,000 signed in 31/7/1997)
    lge 29+17/5gls, FLC 3+2/2gls, FAC 4+1/1gls, Others 3+1/4gls
Rushden & Diamonds (£65,000 in 23/10/1998) Conf 22+12/4gls
Chester City (loan in 10/3/2000) lge 11/2gls
Carlisle United (signed in 1/8/2000) lge 16+14/5gls, FLC 1,
    FAC 0+3, Others 1
Forest Green Rovers (signed in August 2001) Conf 28+2/10gls
Ilkeston Town (signed in November 2002)

Carl Heggs had a bright start to his Vetch Field career, scoring in his debut for the Swans in the opening league game of the season against Shrewsbury Town. Possessing good close skills, and having the ability for hard running, he was unfortunate to also suffer injuries during his two years with the Swans, a broken arm, and a broken ankle which seriously affected the number of appearances for the first team, plus having to put up with the upheaval at the club during his first season, which ended in relegation to the Third Division, and a humiliating 0-7 defeat by Fulham in the FA Cup First Round tie. During his second season he ended top goalscorer for the Swans in the Football Combination, scoring four goals in one game at Wimbledon. He played in the 1997 Third Division Play Off Final for the Swans against Northampton Town at Wembley, hitting the crossbar early in the game, only for the Swans to lose out to a last minute goal. In the close season he signed for Northampton Town for a fee of £40,000 decided by a transfer tribunal, and at the end of his first season with the 'Cobblers', played in his second consecutive Play Off Final at Wembley, losing 1-0 to Grimsby Town in the Second Division Play Off Final. Earlier in his career, after joining West Bromwich Albion from non-league side Leicester United, after graduating from Leicester City Boys Club, Carl had made his league debut on the 14th March 1992 at Bury, and the following season come on as substitute at the Vetch Field for the 'Baggies' in a Second Division Semi-final Play Off, first leg game. Midway through his second season with Northampton Town, Carl joined Vauxhall Conference side Rushden & Diamonds in a £65,000 transfer, but after the club had failed to secure promotion to the Football League, he joined Third Division side Chester City in March 2000 in a bid to help them avoid relegation to the Conference. In August 2000 he was re-united with his former boss Ian Atkins, this time at Carlisle United, and twelve months later signed for Vauxhall Conference side Forest Green Rovers, finishing the season as second top goalscorer with ten league goals. In November 2002 he joined Dr. Martens side Ilkeston Town as player/assistant manager, but after the departure of manager Charlie Bishop joined Ryman League Premier side Bedford Town in September 2003.

23. HENDRY, JOHN

Birthplace: Glasgow, 6/1/1970
Ht: 5ft-11ins, **Wt:** 10st-6lbs
Swans debut: v. Chester City (a), 8/10/1994

	Swansea City Career Statistics		
Season	League	WC	AWS
1994/95	8/2gls	1/2gls	3/3gls
Total	8/2gls	1/2gls	3/3gls

Career:
Hillington YC
Dundee (signed in July 1988)

Forfar Athletic (loan in 1/2/1990) SL 10/6gls
Tottenham Hotspur (£50,000 signed in 31/7/1990) lge 5+12/5gls
Charlton Athletic (loan in 27/2/1992) lge 1+4/1gls
Swansea City (loan in 7/10/1994)
Motherwell (signed in July 1995) SL 23+12/6gls, SC 0+1
Stirling Albion (signed in July 1998) SL 6+1/2gls

Honours: Scotland U-21–1

Scottish U-21 international striker who joined the Swans on loan from Tottenham Hotspur in October 1994, and scored his first Swans goal in his second league game, during his home debut at the Vetch Field against Oxford United in a 1-3 defeat. Three days later he scored two goals for the Swans at Torquay in an AWS cup tie. In the next home league match against Peterborough United he scored his second league goal for the Swans. Three days earlier he had scored two goals for the Swans against Taff Wells in a Welsh Cup tie. Despite scoring just two league goals during his short period at the Vetch Field, he did enough to convince the club's fans that he would be worthy of a permanent transfer. However, this did not materialize, and he returned to White Hart Lane. Joining Scottish Premier Division side Dundee from junior side Hillington YC, the former Paisley schoolboy made two substitute appearances for Dundee during the 1988/89 season, and in February 1990 joined Forfar Athletic on loan, scoring six goals from ten appearances. Despite his relative inexperience, he joined Tottenham Hotspur for £50,000 in July 1990, making his First Division debut at Norwich City on the 10th April 1991, scoring in a 2-1 defeat. He played a further three league games for Spurs during the season, and in the last game, scored the Spurs goal in a 1-1 draw with Manchester United. During his period at White Hart Lane he gained an U-21 cap for Scotland against Denmark on the 18th February 1992 as a substitute for Booth. Making the remainder of his appearances for Spurs from the substitute bench, he had a short loan spell with Charlton Athletic prior to his arriving at the Vetch Field. He returned to Scottish football in July 1995, signing for Scottish Premiership side Motherwell, and during three seasons at the club, injury prevented him from making a greater impact, moving on to Stirling Albion in July 1998.

24. HENNING, Robert (BOBBY) Iva

Birthplace: Glyncorrwg, 30/12/1931
Ht: 5ft-8½ins, **Wt:** 11st-0lbs
Swans debut: v. Barrow (a), FAC-3, 9/1/1954

Career:
Swansea Town (signed in 27/8/1947)
Oswestry Town (loan in season 1951/52)
Barry Town (signed in July 1957)
Caerau (signed in season 1958/59)
Carmarthen Town (signed in close season 1959)

Swansea Town Career Statistics			
Season	League	FAC	WC
1953/54		1	1
1954/55			
1955/56	9/1gls		
1956/57	1		
Total	10/1gls	1	1

Honours: Welsh League Second Division Champions–1960, West Wales Senior Cup Winner–1954

Brought up in the Afan Valley in Glyncorrwg, after moving to live in Swansea, Bobby attended Brynmill and Sketty Schools, made appearances for the Swansea Schoolboys side in 1944 to 1946, captaining the side in 1944/45 season from right full back. The following season, at centre forward he scored twenty-five goals, a record that still stands today. He played his early football with Manselton Youth Club, playing in season 1946/47 in the Swansea Youth League, playing mostly with players who had played with him in the schoolboys side in season 1945/46. He played for the Swansea League Team against Liverpool ex-Schoolboys, winning 3-1 at the Vetch Field. Season 1947/48 saw him join Sketty Baptist in the Senior Division of the Swansea League, finishing Champions. Bobby joined the Swans from school along with John Charles, Harry Griffiths, Terry Jones and Brian Sykes, all members of the Swansea Schoolboys side. A clever player who did not quite fulfil the huge potential he had as a boy, playing the majority of his football at the Vetch Field with the reserves. He joined the groundstaff at the Vetch Field, and signed professional in October 1949. Prior to making his debut for the Swans, Bobby spent a period on loan at Oswestry Town in the Birmingham District League, whilst doing his National Service. His first team debut came at Barrow in an FA Cup third round tie in January 1954, and he had to wait until late October before he made his league debut, against Hull City at the Vetch Field in a 4-1 victory. A month later he returned to first team duty, making five consecutive appearances in place of the injured Mel Charles at wing half. His only league goal for the Swans came against Bristol City during this five game run, and during his last season at the Vetch Field skippered the Swans reserve side. In May 1954 he was a member of the Swans side that beat Llanelly to win the West Wales Senior Cup. After he was released in July 1957, he joined Southern League side Barry Town, had a season in the Welsh League with Caerau in 1958, and in 1959 joined Carmarthen Town, captaining the side to the Welsh League Second Division Championship twelve months later. Between 1957 and 1978 Bobby owned a grocers and confectionery business in Brynmill, later worked in the Aluminium, Wire and Cable Company in Port Tennant, prior to his retirement.

25. HENSON, GEORGE Horace

Birthplace: Stoney Stratford, Bucks, 25/12/1911. **Died:** Stoney Stratford, Bucks, 25/4/1988
Ht: 5ft-11ins, **Wt:** 12st-7lbs
Swans debut: v. Aston Villa (h), 29/8/1936

Swansea Town Career Statistics		
Season	League	FAC
1936/37	23/5gls	1/2gls
Total	23/5gls	1/2gls

Career:
Stoney Stratford FC
Wolverton Town
Northampton Town (amateur in November 1932, professional in August 1933) lge 43/23gls, FAC 6/1gls, Others 3/4gls

Wolverhampton Wanderers (£1,700 signed in 7/11/1934) lge 6/1gls
Swansea Town (£850 signed in 7/5/1936)
Bradford Park Avenue (£400 signed in 12/6/1937) lge 60/33gls
Sheffield United (£3,000 signed in 10/3/1939) lge 13/6gls
Bedford Town (signed in season 1946/47)
Stoney Stratford FC (by 1949)

A consistent goalscorer earlier in his career with Northampton Town after signing from North Buckinghamshire League side Wolverton Town, averaging a goal every two games for the 'Cobblers', prompting First Division side Wolverhampton Wanderers to pay £1,700 for his transfer in November 1934. The former North Bucks schoolboy player struggled to make an impact with Wolves, joined the Swans for £850 in May 1936, scoring on his debut against Aston Villa during the opening match of season 1936/37, also scoring in his next league game at Coventry City. Vying with Joe Brain for the centre forward position through the season, he scored three more league goals, and also two goals in an F.A. Cup replay against York City. At the end of the season he was sold to Second Division side Bradford Park Avenue for £400, and in his first appearance against the Swans, scored the only goal of the game at the Vetch Field early in the season, and finishing his first season as top goalscorer. In March 1939 he was sold to Second Division Sheffield United for £3,000, scoring in his debut against the Swans in a 2-1 home defeat at Bramall Lane. By the end of the season however United had finished runners up to Blackburn Rovers, and promotion to the First Division, with Henson playing in ten matches, scoring twice in a vital 6-1 final day win over Tottenham Hotspur which meant United would finish the season one point ahead of rivals Wednesday. In the last game before the onset of the Second World War he scored against Leeds United, and although retained during the war period played only a few games. During WW2 he made guest appearances for Watford in season 1941/42. After the war he joined Bedford Town, later rejoining Bedfordshire League side Stoney Stratford by 1949, retiring in 1951.

26. HENSON, Philip (PHIL) Michael

Birthplace: Manchester, 30/3/1953
Ht: 5ft-10ins, **Wt:** 9st-12lbs
Swans debut: v. Scunthorpe United (a), 12/8/1972

Swansea City Career Statistics		
Season	League	FLC
1972/73	1	1+1
Total	1	1+1

Career:
Manchester City (from apprentice in July 1970) lge 12+4

Swansea City (signed in 19/7/1972)
Sheffield Wednesday (£50,000 signed in 7/2/1975) lge 65+8/9gls
Sparta Rotterdam
Stockport County (signed in September 1978) lge 65+2/13gls
Rotherham United (signed in 22/2/1980) lge 87+5/7gls

Honours: Third Division Champions–1981

One of three players who joined the Swans from Manchester City, in what was thought initially to be a season long loan transfer between the two clubs. Jeff Johnson and Keith Hanvey being the other two players. The previous season he had made his First Division debut for City as substitute for Colin Bell at Crystal Palace in January 1972. After making his league debut at Scunthorpe United for the Swans in the opening match of the 1972/73 season, and included in the starting line-up for the first round of the League Cup tie at the Vetch against Newport County, he missed the next league game, and played his last game for the Swans coming on as a substitute at Newport in the second leg for Tony Screen. A talented, attacking midfielder, who perhaps at his young age was too lightweight for the rough and tumble of Third Division football. Returning to Maine Road, his next City appearance came against neighbours United as substitute in the last match of the 1973/74 season. After starting the 1974/75 season in City's opening line-up a good run in the first team saw him become a regular for the first half of the season, but in February 1975 he was sold to Sheffield Wednesday for £50,000, playing in the club's fourteen league appearances at the end of the season, but failing to prevent the club from relegation the Third Division. In what turned out to be another season of struggle for Wednesday, finishing just one point above the last relegated club, Aldershot, Henson returned eight goals through the season from midfield. He failed to make an appearance during season 1977/78, and spent some time in Dutch football with Sparta Rotterdam, before having his contract cancelled in April 1978 by Sheffield Wednesday. Returning to the Football League to sign for Fourth Division Stockport County in September 1978, Phil scored consistently from midfield, but then joined Rotherham United in February 1980. His first full season saw him make thirty-four league appearances during the club's Championship success during season 1980/81 in the Third Division, and he remained at Millmoor as a player until the 1983/84 season when he had his contract cancelled. Since retiring as a player, Phil took up a coaching position at the club, was manager for a period between 1991 to 1994, and prior to the start of season 2004/05 had been Chief Executive at Millmoor for a number of years.

27. HEYES, GEORGE

Birthplace: Bolton, 16/11/1937
Ht: 5ft-10¾ins, **Wt:** 13st-2lbs
Swans debut: v. Bristol Rovers (h), 25/9/1965

Career:
Rochdale (signed from juniors in April 1956) lge 24

Leicester City (signed in July 1960) lge 25
Swansea Town (signed in September 1965)
Barrow (signed in July 1969) lge 26
Bedford Town (signed in August 1970)

Swansea Town Career Statistics					
Season	*League*	*FLC*	*FAC*	*WC*	*ECWC*
1965/66	39		1	8	
1966/67	37	4	3	1	2
1967/68	11				
1968/69	12	3			
Total	99	7	4	9	2

Honours: Welsh Cup Winner–1966

Goalkeeper George Heyes learned his trade as a telephone engineer prior to starting out on the road to become a professional goalkeeper with Rochdale in April 1956. In 1971 after stepping down from the rigours of shot stopping on a professional basis, he returned to work with BT as an engineer, and 12 years later became self employed in his own company. Now retired, his footballing involvement now revolves around scouting for Nottingham Forest in the Midlands area, after previous stints as goalkeeper scout for Blackburn Rovers, Aston Villa and Leicester City. England U-21 'keeper, Chris Kirkland, who signed for Liverpool for £9M from Coventry City is one of George's discoveries, spotted playing for Blaby-Wheatstone Boys Club, before joining Coventry as a trainee. The Boys Club was the same one that a certain Peter Shilton played for before he embarked on his goalkeeping career. Starting his league career with Rochdale in 1956, George made just 24 league appearances before signing for First Division side Leicester City in July 1960. Unfortunately for him, although he could have had no greater tutor, he became almost a permanent understudy to England goalkeeper Gordon Banks, making just 25 league appearances in just over 5 seasons before he was signed by Swans manager Glyn Davies in late September 1965. Another factor which could have given him a greater incentive to leave Filbert Street in search of regular league appearances was the emergence of Peter Shilton, who was an apprentice with Leicester at the time of Heyes's departure. The Swans had started the 1965/66 season with the inexperienced, former Arsenal apprentice John Black in goal, but with just the one win during the first seven league matches, George was recruited from Leicester City. Going on to play in the remaining 39 league matches, plus being a member of the victorious Welsh Cup winning side that beat Chester, and also playing in European Cup Winners Cup competition the following season against Slavia Sofia, George remained the number one choice for the keeper shirt until February 1967, when following a change in management, with Billy Lucas taking over from Glyn Davies, Dil John was signed from neighbours Cardiff City. Over the next two seasons, John remained first choice, with George limited to a further 23 league appearances, and at the end of the 1968/69 season was allowed to join Barrow on a free transfer, having made 99 league appearances for the Swans. After just the one season at Barrow, a further twelve months at Southern League side Bedford Town, George retired from professional football.

28. HILES, William Robert (BILLY)

Birthplace: Cardiff, 28/11/1901. **Died:** Newport, 24/7/1978
Ht: 5ft-5ins, **Wt:** 10st-5lbs
Swans debut: v. Manchester City (a), 29/8/1927

Swansea Town Career Statistics	
Season	League
1927/28	7/2gls
Total	7/2gls

Career:
Lovells Athletic
Newport County (signed in August 1924) lge 28/4gls
Swansea Town (signed in 10/5/1927)
Merthyr Town (signed in May 1928) lge 0
Lovells Athletic (signed in August 1928)
Evesham Town (signed in August 1931)
Lovells Athletic (by November 1933)

Honours: Wales Junior International–1, Welsh FA Tour XI–1927, Welsh League Representative XI

Former dockworker at Newport, who, after playing football and baseball for the Dock's teams started his professional football career with non-league side Lovells Athletic. Capable of playing on either flank, he joined Third Division South side Newport County in 1924, and three seasons later joined the Swans for a fee of £100. A couple of days previous to joining the Swans, he had impressed in a Benefit game for County's Jimmy Gittins, and within days of signing had joined the Swans end of season tour to Denmark. He made his league debut for the Swans, deputising for Dai Nicholas on the left wing at Manchester City, in the second match of the 1927/28 season, and scoring for the Swans from the penalty spot in a 7-4 defeat. He had to wait until early December for his next Swans appearance, again as a replacement for Nicholas, making six consecutive appearances, which included one more goal. At the end of the season he joined Third Division South team Merthyr Town, in a player exchange transfer involving Merthyr's Allan Livingstone, then returned to his first club Lovells Athletic for the start of the 1928/29 season. Signing for Evesham Town in August 1931, he had returned to Lovells Athletic during season 1933/34, playing at Stebonheath Park in November 1933 against Llanelly, continuing his employment in the Lovells Confectionery factory where he worked for thirty-four years. A former Welsh Junior

international during season 1924/25 against Ireland, in 1927 he was a member of a Welsh FA Touring party to Ireland, and earlier, in March 1925 he was included in a Welsh League side that played the Irish Free State in Dublin and Cork. On the 12th February 1932 he played for the Welsh League XI against the Irish Free State at Stebonheath Park, Llanelly, in a game which the Irish side won 4-2. In April 1938 in Brussels, at the age of thirty-seven he played for a Welsh League Representative side against their Belgian League counterparts (Diables Rouges).

29. HILL, Leonard (LEN) Winston

Birthplace: Caerleon, 14/4/1942
Ht: 5ft-8ins, **Wt:** 10st-6lbs
Swans debut: v. Port Vale (h), 15/8/1970

Swansea City Career Statistics		
Season	League	WC
1970/71	12/1gls	1
Total	12/1gls	1

Career:
Caerleon
Lovells Athletic (signed in September 1961)
Newport County (signed in November 1962) lge 267+2/52gls
Swansea City (£5,000 signed in July 1970)
Newport County (£2,500 signed in January 1972) lge 93+4/13gls
Barry Town (signed in September 1974)
Minehead Town (signed by November 1978) 18/1gls
Cinderford Town (signed in July 1979)

Honours: Wales Yth

Len Hill started his football career with local club Caerleon, joined Lovells Athletic in late September 1961, making his Welsh League debut on the last Saturday of September against Milford United, whilst serving his apprenticeship as an electrical engineer, later joining Newport County. At Somerton Park he gained Youth honours for Wales, signing as a full time professional in 1962 on completion of his apprenticeship. He stayed at Somerton Park for eight seasons scoring over fifty league goals before joining the Swans in July 1970 for £5,000. During his time with County he was a keen cricketer, and was a registered professional with Glamorgan County Cricket Club in the summer months, continuing his involvement with Glamorgan whilst on the playing staff at the Vetch Field. He had impressed Swans manager Roy Bentley the season the Swans gained promotion from the Fourth Division, while Hill was playing for County, with his attacking ability from midfield. With County struggling financially off the field, and two consecutive seasons of applying for re-election to the Football League, the experienced midfielder no doubt savoured the challenge of Third Division football. He started his first season at the Vetch Field, making his debut in the opening game of the 1970/71 season against Port Vale, but after playing against Fulham in the next league match, suffered an ankle injury playing in a Football Combination game at Chelsea which kept him on the sidelines for a couple of games. Returning to first team action, he scored his only goal for the Swans in a 3-0 win over Bury at the Vetch Field, during a run of games which saw him make nine consecutive league appearances. He failed to make any appearances during his second season, and in January 1972 rejoined County on a free transfer. Hill had been a key player with County, but although he was a skilful player on the ball, it was felt that he did not possess the pace for a higher grade of football in the Third Division. His first full season back at Somerton Park saw County almost gain promotion from the Fourth Division, losing out to fourth placed Aldershot on goal difference. After finishing season 1973/74 in mid-table he was released by County on a free transfer, joining Barry Town in September 1974, later in the 1978/79 season joining former County team mates Willie Brown and Ron Walker at Minehead Town, playing his first game for the club at Dover on the 11th November 1978. At the end of the season he left to join Midland Combination side Cinderford Town initially as a player, later taking on the role of player manager. In later years he was also President of the Football Club.

30. HILLS, Joseph John (JOE)

Birthplace: Plumstead, Kent, 14/10/1897. **Died:** Westbourne, Dorset, 21/6/1969
Ht: 5ft-11½ins, **Wt:** 12st-6lbs
Swans debut: v. South Shields (a), 6/11/1926

Swansea Town Career Statistics	
Season	League
1926/27	8
Total	8

Career:
Great Eastern Railway Works XI
Bexley Heath
Northfleet
Cardiff City (signed in September 1924) lge 14
Swansea Town (signed in May 1926)
Fulham (signed in 28/6/1927) lge 0

Goalkeeper signed from First Division side Cardiff City in November 1926, who after making his league debut at South Shields made a further seven league appearances, before being replaced by Owen Marlow, after conceding 12 goals in games at Middlesbrough and Oldham Athletic. With the signing of 'keeper Alex Ferguson in March 1927, the writing was on the wall as far as first team opportunities were concerned, and in June 1927 he signed for Fulham, remaining at Craven Cottage until the 1928 close season. During his career he was also a wicketkeeper for Glamorgan County Cricket Club, scored 3,500 runs, with a top score of 166. After retiring from playing cricket he became a first class umpire remaining on the first class list until 1956. Earlier in his career, prior to joining Cardiff City he had made appearances for Great Eastern Railway Works XI (Romford), BexleyHeath and Northfleet United. His step brother is Edwin Redvers Baden Herod, formerly of Charlton Athletic, Brentford and Tottenham Hotspur.

31. HILLS, JOHN David

Birthplace: St. Annes-on-Sea, 21/4/1978
Ht: 5ft-9ins, **Wt:** 11st-2lbs
Swans debut: v. Cambridge United (h), 31/1/1997

Swansea City Career Statistics		
Season	League	FAWP
1996/97	11	
1997/98	7	1/1gls
Total	18	1/1gls

Career:
Blackpool (signed from trainee in 27/10/1995) lge 0
Everton (£90,000 signed in 4/11/1995) PL 1+2
Swansea City (loan in 30/1/1997)
Swansea City (loan in 22/8/1997)
Blackpool (£75,000 in 16/1/1998) lge 141+16/16gls, FLC 5, FAC 12/2gls, Others 13+1/2gls
Gillingham (signed in 11/6/2003) lge 47+5/2gls, FLC 3/1gls, FAC 2
Sheffield Wednesday (signed in 28/6/2005)

Honours: LDV Vans Trophy Winner–2002

Exciting, attacking left wing back who first arrived on loan at the Vetch Field from Everton, and after two months at the Vetch Field, with the Swans in sight of a Play Off place, returned to Goodison Park. Shortly after the start of the next season he rejoined Jan Molby's side for a second loan transfer, scoring his only goal in an FAW Invitation Cup tie at Barry Town. His return to Everton after just one month was shortly followed with Molby being sacked as manager of the Swans. At an early age he caused a stir when he was transferred to Everton from Blackpool in November 1995 only a week after signing professional forms. He quickly made a name for himself at Goodison Park as one of the club's best athletes, joining the 1996/97 pre-season group, and being included on the substitute's bench on regular occasions, before making his first team debut against Wimbledon on the 26th December 1996, making a further substitute appearance, and his first start for Everton in the final two games of the 1996/97 season. After his second loan stint at the Vetch Field, midway through the season he rejoined his former club Blackpool on an initial loan transfer, with the move being made permanent a month later for £75,000. An attacking left sided wing back, he was equally reliable in midfield, gaining a reputation at Blackpool as a free kick specialist from almost anywhere around the penalty area. Besides his attacking instincts, his defensive play was also steady. Towards the end of the 2001/02 season he scored Blackpool's third goal against Cambridge United in the final of the LDV Vans Trophy Cup Final at the Millenium Stadium in Cardiff. Having made over one hundred and fifty league appearances for Blackpool, he joined Gillingham in June 2003 on a free transfer. In late June 2005 he returned north to sign for newly promoted Championship side Sheffield Wednesday.

32. HINDLEY, Robert (BOB) Andrew

Birthplace: Leigh, 17/3/1907
Ht: 6ft-0ins, **Wt:** 12st-0lbs
Swans debut: v. Stoke City (h), 7/3/1931

Swansea Town Career Statistics		
Season	*League*	*WC*
1930/31	3	1
Total	3	1

Career:
Southampton (signed in August 1927) lge 0
Mossley
Atherton
Swansea Town (£760 signed in June 1929)
Barrow (signed in July 1931) lge 37
Ramsgate Press Wanderers (signed in August 1933)
Folkestone Town (signed in September 1936)

Honours: West Wales Senior Cup Winner–1930

Former Southampton youth and reserve team goalkeeper who joined non-league Mossley and Atherton before signing for the Swans in May 1929 for £760. Signed by Swans manager James Hunter Thomson, during his first season at the Vetch Field he was mainly the reserve team keeper, and was an understudy to Alex Ferguson. In October 1930 he was included in a Swans reserve side that beat Newport County in the Final of the West Wales Senior Cup competition held over from the previous season. He eventually made his league debut at the Vetch Field against Stoke City in early March 1931, playing in the next two league games before Ferguson returned to action. After making his league debut against Stoke City he played in the next two league games, before Ferguson reclaimed his keeper's jersey after injury. At the end of the season he joined Third Division North side Barrow on a free transfer, before later making appearances for Kent League side Ramsgate Press Wanderers and Folkestone.

33. HODGE, JOHN

Birthplace: Skelmersdale, 1/4/1969
Ht: 5ft-7ins, **Wt:** 11st-12lbs
Swans debut: v. York City (a), 14/8/1993

Career:
Newquay (signed in 1989)
Falmouth Town (signed in July 1991)
Exeter City (signed in 12/9/1991) lge 57+8/10gls, FLC 3/1gls,
    FAC 2, Others 8+2/1gls
Swansea City (£20,000 signed in 14/7/1993)
Walsall (signed in 23/9/1996) lge 67+9/12gls, FLC 5,
    FAC 7+1/2gls, Others 5+2
Gillingham (signed in 10/7/1998) lge 8+41/1gls, FLC 4+1,
    FAC 3+2/1gls, Others 2+4
Northampton Town (£25,000 signed in 7/3/2000)
    lge 33+27/2gls, FLC 0+2, FAC 0+1, Others 0+2
Kidderminster Harriers (trial in 2003)

Swansea City Career Statistics					
Season	*League*	*FLC*	*FAC*	*WC*	*AGT/AWS*
1993/94	15+12/2gls	1+1		2	2+3
1994/95	38+5/7gls	3+1/1gls	5	4	5
1995/96	34+7/1gls	2/2gls	1		2+1
Total	87+24/10gls	6+2/3gls	6	6	9+4

Honours: AutoGlass Trophy Winner–1994, West Wales Senior Cup Winner–1994, Cornwall County Representative XI

Brought up in Skelmersdale, John attended Barnes Road Primary, Glenburn High School, was attached to Everton as a schoolboy for two years, also playing for Skelmersdale, West Lancashire and Lancashire Schoolboy teams. After leaving school he started on the YTS training scheme as an electrician, playing in the Liverpool Sunday League for Darby Arms FC, consistently winning League and Cup Honours over a three season period. At the age of eighteen he went to live in Newquay, Cornwall, working in his uncle's bakery and in a sports shop in the town. A successful period playing for Jewson South Western League side Newquay saw him win League and Cup Honours, gain selection for a Cornwall County Representative XI, winning an Inter-County competition in 1990, before joining Falmouth Town, and two months later joining the professional ranks at Exeter City. Signed by Swans manager Frank Burrows in July 1993 for a fee of £20,000, plus midfielder Russell Coughlin joining Exeter City as part of the transfer, he had earlier impressed manager Frank Burrows when the Swans had played the 'Grecians' in FA Cup and Auto Glass Trophy cup ties during the 1992/93 season. During his period at the Vetch Field he proved to be an extremely popular figure with the club's supporters, who appreciated his wing play, having the pace, skill, and ability to cross accurate balls to his team mates. His first season at the Vetch Field culminated in him playing at Wembley in the AutoGlass Trophy Final against Huddersfield Town, and in the following two seasons, after establishing himself as a vital component of the Swans line-up saw both glory and humiliation in the FA Cup competition, following success against Middlesbrough, and a good performance against Newcastle United, with humiliation at Fulham, losing 0-7. In May 1994 he was included in the Swans squad that beat Ammanford Town in the West Wales Senior Cup Final, and at the end of the season was voted 'Player of the Year' at the Vetch Field. During the 1996 close season, he was unable to agree terms over a new contract with the Swans, and in September 1996 he was allowed to join Walsall on a free transfer. Joining Gillingham in July 1998, he made a substitute appearance in the Second Division Play Off Final at Wembley, replacing Patterson, against Manchester City, but lost out 3-1, on penalties. By the end of season 1999/2000, with Gillingham this time gaining success over Wigan Athletic in the Play Off Final, he had joined Northampton Town, making eight league appearances for the 'Cobblers' as they secured the third automatic promotion place from the Third Division behind the Champions, Swansea City. Earlier in that season he had played a large part in Gillingham reaching the sixth round of the FA Cup competition. He made a sparkling debut for the 'Cobblers' against Leyton Orient by laying on both goals in a 2-1 victory, but despite thrilling the crowd with some dazzling runs failed to maintain the high standard, and at the end of the 2002/03 season was released by Northampton Town on a free transfer. After his second day on trial at Kidderminster Harriers he signed a monthly contract, but before he had played a game decided to retire from professional football. Since then he has operated a Grass Roots Soccer Coaching School in Herefordshire and Worcestershire, under a franchise arrangement with Arsenal FC from his home in Worcester. In February 2005 he will be returning to live in Cornwall, and as well as extending his coaching franchise in the county will be coming out of retirement to play for St. Blazey. During his career 'Hodgy' was very much the dressing room joker at all the clubs he played for.

34. HODGES, Leonard (LEN) Herbert

Birthplace: Bristol, 17/2/1920. **Died:** Bristol, 5/8/1959
Ht: 5ft-6ins, **Wt:** 10st-10lbs
Swans debut: v. Doncaster Rovers (h), 2/9/1950

Swansea Town Career Statistics	
Season	League
1950/51	3
Total	3

Career:
Army Football
Soundwell
Bristol Rovers (signed in 9/8/1946) lge 118/20gls
Swansea Town (signed in 28/7/1950)
Reading (£250 signed in 1/8/1951) lge 6/2gls
Chippenham Town (signed in 8/7/1953 to May 1954)

Honours: British SFA

A member of the Bristol Rovers playing staff since leaving school, Len made over one hundred league appearances for the 'Pirates' prior to signing for the Swans in August 1950, and had made regular appearances for Rovers against the Swans in Third Division South fixtures prior to his arriving at the Vetch Field. A slightly built inside forward, he had earlier served in the RAF during the War, and was twenty-six years of age before signing for Rovers. Prior to joining the professional ranks with Rovers in August 1946, he had played for Soundwell in the Bristol Western League, Kingswood Aero, and Portway. Stockily built, and exceptionally quick off the mark, he made his league debut for the Swans at inside right against Doncaster Rovers in early September 1950, played in the next two league fixtures, but failed to make another appearance for the Swans, and at the end of the season joined Third Division South side Reading for £250. Basically a reserve team player at the Vetch Field, he did not appear to fit in with the style of play at the Vetch Field. Despite making just six league appearances for Reading, he did play in the reserve side that won their division in the Football Combination in his first season at Elm Park. He was released at the end of the 1952/53 season joining Chippenham Town, linking up with former Rovers full back Jack Preece. Hodges lived in Kingswood prior to his death in August 1959.

35. HODGSON, DAVID James

Birthplace: Gateshead, 1/11/1960
Ht: 5ft-10ins, **Wt:** 11st-8lbs
Swans debut: v. Bradford City (h), 28/3/1992

Swansea City Career Statistics	
Season	League
1991/92	1+2
Total	1+2

Career:
Middlesbrough (apprentice in August 1976, professional in August 1978) lge 116+9/16gls
Liverpool (£450,000 signed in 11/8/1982) lge 21+7/4gls
Sunderland (£125,000 signed in 24/8/1984) lge 32+8/5gls
Norwich City (signed in 18/7/1986) lge 3+3/1gls
Middlesbrough (loan signing in 27/2/1987) lge 2
Jerez Club de Portivo, Spain
Sheffield Wednesday (signed in 2/8/1988) lge 6+5/1gls
Mazda, Japan (signed in July 1989)
Metz, France
Swansea City (non-contract signed in 26/3/1992)
Mainz, Germany (signed in August 1992)
Rochdale (signed in September 1992)

Honours: England U-21–6, First Division Champions–1983

Educated at Elgin Senior High School, David Hodgson played for his school team, Redheugh Boys' Club, had trials with Ipswich Town and Bolton Wanderers prior to joining Middlesbrough as an apprentice on leaving school. Making his league debut for Middlesbrough as a substitute for McAndrew at Nottingham Forest on the 23rd September 1978, he played in the next league game, again as substitute, and five games later made his first start for the club. Starting the 1978/79 season as first choice in the Boro attack, he remained first choice at the club until his transfer to Liverpool in August 1982. By the end of the season he had made twenty-three league appearances, scoring four goals as the Reds won the First Division Championship. His two seasons at Anfield saw him miss out on successive Milk Cup Final appearances, but he did play for the club in the quarter final stages of the 1982/83 European Cup ties against Widzew Lodz. After signing for Sunderland, he played in the 1985 Milk Cup defeat by Norwich City, signing for the Carrow Road side twelve months later. In his last season at Ayresome Park with Boro, he gained the first of his six U-21 caps for England, playing against Norway at Southampton in September 1980. During season 1980/81 he scored two goals for Middlesbrough at the Vetch Field against the Swans in a third round FA Cup tie, which Boro won 5-0. A talented striker, although not a prolific goalscorer during his career, he was a good leader of the line who unfortunately suffered a number of injury problems which prevented him from making a bigger impact in the game. Signing for Norwich City in July 1986, by the time he had his contract cancelled by Sheffield Wednesday during the 1989/90 season, he had played less than twenty league games. Prior to arriving at the Vetch Field at the age of 31, David had played in Spain for Jerez Club de Portivo, and had signed for the Swans on a non-contract basis to prove his fitness. It took a number of weeks before he was able to get his release from Metz, with the French club insisting initially on a transfer fee, who reluctantly then gave him clearance to play for the Swans. Making his debut as a substitute for Jason Bowen in a 2-2 home draw with Bradford City, David started the next league fixture at Preston North End, but made just the one more appearance for the Swans before being released. A trial period in Germany with Mainz was followed by a similar trial period at

Rochdale in September 1992, before returning to the north east to concentrate on his business interests. In May 1995, along with former Middlesbrough team mate Jim Platt he embarked on a managerial career, when he was named as Director of Coaching at Darlington, but left midway through his first season, which saw Darlington lose to Plymouth Argyle in the end of season Third Division Play Off Final. He returned as manager of Darlington in November 1996, and after two seasons of stability, the club lost for the second time in the Third Division Play Off Final at Wembley, this time, 1-0 to Peterborough United in May 2000. On 2nd August 2000 he quit the club after a row with the Chairman George Reynolds. In November 2003, with the club having moved into a new 27,000 all seater stadium he returned to the club for the third time as manager, and despite being successful in keeping the club in the Football League, he was unable to avoid the club being placed into Administration. By May 2005 he had steered the club to the verge of the Play Off places.

36. HOLDSWORTH, DEAN Christopher

Birthplace: Walthamstow, 8/11/1968
Ht: 5ft-11ins, **Wt:** 11st-13lbs
Swans debut: v. Gillingham (a), 27/8/1988

Swansea City Career Statistics	
Season	League
1988/89	4+1/1gls
Total	4+1/1gls

Career:
Watford (schoolboy in May 1984, apprentice in April 1985, professional in November 1986) lge 2+14/3gls, Others 0+4
Carlisle United (loan in 11/2/1988) lge 4/1gls
Port Vale (loan in 18/3/1988) lge 6/2gls
Swansea City (loan in 25/8/1988)
Brentford (loan in 13/10/1988) lge 2+5/1gls
Brentford (£125,000 signed in 29/9/1989) lge 106+4/53gls, FLC 7+1/6gls, FAC 6/7gls, Others 12+2/9gls
Wimbledon (£720,000 signed in 20/7/1992) PL 148+21/58gls, FLC 16+3/11gls, FAC 13+7/7gls
Bolton Wanderers (£3,500,000 signed in 3/10/1997) PL/lge 92+5/39gls, FLC 11+4/4gls, FAC 5+2/3gls, Others 5/3gls
Coventry City (loan in 28/11/2002) lge 6
Coventry City (signed in 1/1/2003) lge 7+4, FAC 3/1gls
Rushden & Diamonds (signed in 27/3/2003) lge 4+3/2gls
Wimbledon (signed in 24/7/2003) lge 14+14/3gls, FLC 0+1, FAC 2
Havant & Waterlooville (signed in August 2004) Conf Sth 40/24gls, FAC 1, FAT 4/4gls

Honours: England 'B', Third Division Champions–1992, First Division Play Off Winner–2001, Third Division Champions–2003

Young in-experienced striker who in a short time at the Vetch Field showed his ability, and who, within a couple of seasons would mark his mark in the First Division with Wimbledon. Signed by manager Terry Yorath shortly before the start of the 1988/89 season, he made his Swans' debut in the opening fixture of the season, coming on as substitute for Brian Wade, in a 3-2 away win at Gillingham. At the end of his month loan transfer, his last game against Wolverhampton Wanderers at the Vetch Field saw him score his only goal for the Swans, in a 2-5 defeat. During Brentford's Third Division Championship winning season of 1991/92 he was top goalscorer for the 'Bees', scoring 24 in the league, plus another 10 in cup competitions. At the end of that season he was transferred to First Division side Wimbledon, and for the next two seasons in the First Division would top the goalscoring charts for Wimbledon. Joining Watford as a schoolboy with his twin brother in May 1984, he signed professional in November 1986. Joining Premiership side Bolton Wanderers in October 1997, he was unable to stop the club from being relegated to the First Division in May 1998, but in the next three seasons, his goals would see Wanderers lose out in two Play Off Finals, before securing a place back in the Premiership, by beating Preston North End in the 2000/01 First Division Play Off Final. Dean joined First Division Coventry City on an initial loan in November 2002, with the transfer being made permanent the following January, but on transfer deadline day he joined Third Division pacesetters Rushden & Diamonds, scoring two goals for the club as they secured the Championship at the end of the season. In July 2003, Dean returned to Wimbledon, who by this time were battling to save themselves from freefalling down the divisions, and battling against their supporters opposition regarding relocating the club to Milton Keynes. Unable to save the club from relegation to the Second Division, Dean was released in May 2004, joining Conference South side Havant & Waterlooville on a two year contract, despite offers to remain in the Football League with Rushden and Leyton Orient. His aim is to get his coaching badges, and eventually he hopes it will lead him into management.

37. HOLDSWORTH, EDWARD

Birthplace: Halifax, JFM, 1888
Ht: 5ft-9ins, **Wt:** 11st-10lbs
Swans debut: v. Portsmouth (a), 28/8/1920

Swansea Town Career Statistics		
Season	League	FAC
1920/21	7	1
Total	7	1

Career:
South Working Lads
Southport Central (signed in May 1907)
Preston North End (signed in December 1907) lge 222/3gls, FAC 11
Swansea Town (signed in 22/5/1920)

Honours: Second Division Champions–1913

Centre half in the Swans side that played their first game in the Football League at Portsmouth on the 28th August 1920. Signed in late May 1920, after making over 200 league appearances for Preston North End, he reverted to right half back after the opening league fixture, then played just two more league games for the Swans at centre half later in the season. Competing with Collins for the centre half berth, and with McCallum for the right half position, at the end of the season he was released, joining Third Division North side Southport. At Preston, he played mostly in the First Division, but after relegation at the end of season 1911/12, the club bounced back immediately, winning the Second Division Championship twelve months later. Within twelve months however, Preston were back in the Second Division, but again, the club bounced back, this time finishing runners up to Derby County, and promotion from the Second Division. At Deepdale he captained the side for three seasons prior to WW1, and during the war he made guest appearances for Southport Central. On the 4th August 1922 an article in the *Evening Post* mentioned that Holdsworth, now identified with the Tenby Hotel in Walters Road, Swansea had signed professional forms for the Swans, and was willing to play for no remuneration or reward, and had already started training with the club. He made no further appearances for the Swans, and later became licensee of the Belle Vue Vaults public house. From *Lancashire Daily Post Yearbook 1913-14*: "Right half and captain. Did not after all take long to decide that he would stay with his old club. One of the most artistic wing halves in England. A devotee of pure science, he did not relish Second Division methods at all." From *Lancashire Daily Post Yearbook 1914-15*: ". . . probably the best right half in England when he settled down after being unfortunate at the start of last season. May yet receive the international cap which is fairly due to a cultured artist who is a model of deportment on the field. Has had little differences of opinion with the club in times past, but now 'orl is peas' as Artemus Ward says." From *Lancashire Daily Post Yearbook 1919-20*: ". . . may still be regarded as one of the cleverest wing halves in England, though no younger than he used to be. Is seen to best advantage in creative work, being a judicious schemer, who passes perfectly."

38. HOLE, ALAN Vincent

Birthplace: Swansea, 26/12/1930
Ht: 5ft-11½ins, **Wt:** 11st-0lbs
Swans debut: v. Bury (a), 19/9/1953

Swansea Town Career Statistics			
Season	League	FAC	WC
1953/54	21	3	1
Total	21	3	1

Career:
Swansea Town (signed in July 1951)
Kettering Town (signed in July 1954)
Llanelly (signed in May 1955)
Pembroke Borough (signed in close season 1957)

Brought up in the St. Helens, Sandfields area of Swansea, Alan Hole, along with his brothers Barrie and Colin, all played for the

Swans at one stage of their career. Colin unfortunately did not make a league appearance, unlike Barrie who went on to follow in his father's footsteps, Billy, and grace the international field with Wales. He attended St. David's Junior School prior to going to the Technical College, playing for local league side St. Augustines before serving two years in the RAF for his National Service. Stationed near Bolton he had trials with the Wanderers, but on returning to Swansea, signed professional for the Swans at the age of twenty-one. Alan made his Swans' debut at centre half, deputising for Tom Kiley at Bury in September 1953, making nineteen consecutive league appearances, and also playing in four cup ties. By the end of the season he had made a further two league appearances. Confined mainly to the reserve side, he was released in April 1954 joining Southern League side Kettering Town in July 1954 along with his brother Colin. Twelve months later he returned to South West Wales to sign for Welsh League side Llanelly, staying two seasons at Stebonheath Park before ending his career in 1961 with Pembroke Borough. Since leaving the professional game, he went into the family newsagency business in the Swansea area up to his retirement.

39. HOLE, Barrington (BARRIE) Gerard

Birthplace: Swansea, 16/9/1942
Ht: 5ft-11ins, **Wt:** 11st-4lbs
Swans debut: v. Port Vale (h), 15/8/1970

Swansea City Career Statistics				
Season	League	FLC	FAC	WC
1970/71	42/3gls	2/1gls	4/1gls	3
1971/72	36	1	5	1
Total	78/3gls	3/1gls	9/1gls	4

Career:
Cardiff City (from apprentice in September 1959) lge 211/16gls, ECWC 8
Blackburn Rovers (£40,000 signed in July 1966) lge 79/13gls
Aston Villa (£50,000 signed in September 1968) lge 47/6gls
Swansea City (£20,000 signed in July 1970)

Honours: Wales Sch, U-23-5, Full-30, Welsh Cup Winner-1964, 1965, Welsh League Challenge Cup Winner-1960

Played two seasons for Swansea schoolboys and even at that early age showed outstanding potential being awarded numerous schoolboy international caps. Joined Cardiff City groundstaff at the age of 15 years making his league debut two years later, signing professional just prior to making his league debut. At the end of his first season as a professional he won a Welsh League Challenge Cup medal with the 'Bluebirds'. He remained at Ninian Park with Cardiff for over five years, playing for two seasons with the club in the First Division, after which he was transferred to Blackburn Rovers. In 1964 and 1965 he played in consecutive Welsh Cup Final wins over Bangor City and Wrexham. With the 'Bluebirds' he made five appearances for the Welsh U-23 side, the first in 1961 against Scotland, and on the 3rd April 1963 he made his first Full appearance for Wales, in Belfast against Northern Ireland, gaining 26 consecutive Welsh international caps. His last international appearance for Wales came against Rumania in November 1970, whilst on the books as a Swans player. A tall, cultured wing half, or inside forward, Barrie was the son of a famous father Billy, who pre-war had represented Wales, and also played for the Swans. Barrie also had two elder brothers, Alan and Colin, who both played for the Swans. Playing just two seasons in the First Division with the 'Bluebirds', he spent the rest of his career prior to joining the Swans in the Second Division with Blackburn Rovers and Aston Villa, at a time when both clubs were striving to attain former glories. Following relegation to the Third Division for the Villa, Barrie signed for the Swans in July 1970, for what was at the time a record transfer fee of £20,000. He was signed by manager Roy Bentley to add a bit of class to a Swans side that had just achieved promotion from the Fourth Division, but after the club's first season in the Third Division when they finished a creditable eleventh position, they were unable too improve during his second season at the Vetch Field, and before the end of season 1971/72 he announced his retirement from the game to concentrate on his business interests in the city. Owning a newsagent business in the city for a number of years, he sold the business in early 2004. Barrie became a keen golfer after leaving football.

40. HOLE, William (BILLY) James

Birthplace: Swansea, 1/11/1897. **Died:** Swansea, 7/12/1983
Ht: 5ft-8ins, **Wt:** 10st-10lbs
Swans debut: v. Millwall (a), 18/10/1919, Sth. Lge

Swansea Town Career Statistics			
Season	League	FAC	WC
1920/21	40/2gls	3/1gls	
1921/22	38/4gls	6/2gls	
1922/23	41/15gls	2	3
1923/24	12/1gls		
1924/25	15/1gls		2
1925/26	36/2gls	7/1gls	3
1926/27	41/1gls	5/1gls	
1927/28	37/2gls	1/1gls	2
1928/29	28/4gls	2	
1929/30	32/4gls	1	1
1930/31	21		2
Total	341/36gls	27/6gls	13

Career:
Hillside (Swansea)
Swansea Town (signed amateur in April 1919, professional in August 1919)
Llanelly (signed in 13/6/1931)

Honours: Wales Full–9, Third Division South Champions–1925, West Wales Senior Cup Winner–1925, Welsh League Representative XI

Signed for the Swans in February 1919 from local Swansea League side Hillside as an amateur, played in friendly and Welsh League games, later signing as a professional in August 1919. After making appearances as an amateur for the Swans' reserve side during the 1918/19 season, he made his professional debut in a Southern League fixture at Millwall on the 18th October 1919, as a replacement for Fred Harris on the right wing, making his home debut seven days later against Brighton & Hove Albion, and becoming a regular inclusion on the right flank for the Swans during the second half of the season. When the Swans were admitted to the Football League Third Division in 1920, Billy played in the club's first ever league fixture, at Portsmouth on the 28th August 1920. He gained his first cap for Wales on the 9th April 1921 at the Vetch Field against Ireland, scoring the first goal in a 2-1 win for Wales, and also becoming the first Swansea born player to be capped for Wales whilst on the club's books. His international debut at the Vetch Field against Ireland saw Hole line up alongside his Swans team mate Ivor Jones on the right flank. His last international appearance for Wales again came at the Vetch Field, this time against England in November 1928. During his career he proved to be a silky, thoughtful right winger, very penetrative with good pace. Consistently on the score sheets for the Swans, he did however manage to score 15 league goals during season 1922/23, his best ever return. During the club's championship winning season of 1924/25, he missed the first half of the season, recovering from an injury that had sidelined him for most of the previous term. In January 1925 he was included in the Swans reserve side that beat Llanelly to win the West Wales Senior Cup, and played a prominent part also in the club's FA Cup run to the semi-finals the following season before losing out to Bolton Wanderers. The same season also saw Billy play in the Welsh Cup Final defeat by Ebbw Vale. In early May 1929 he was included in the Swans' side that were beaten by Cardiff City at Llanelly in the Final of the South Wales & Monmouthshire Cup Final, and twelve months later he was one of eight Swans players selected to play for a Welsh League Representative side at the Vetch Field against the Irish Free State. He remained on the Swans books until June 1931, when he joined his brother Jimmy at Llanelly, who at that time were playing in the Southern League, staying at Stebonheath Park until May 1932. The Swans had initially asked for a fee of £250 for his transfer to the Reds, which was later reduced to a free transfer. After making a couple of appearances at the start of the 1931/32 season, Billy suffered an injury which saw him sidelined until mid-February. Like his son Barrie, who retired from the game to concentrate on his business interests in the city, Billy had also been a prominent member of the business fraternity in Swansea with his newsagents and tobacconist business in Swansea before his death in 1983. As well as Barrie, both his other sons, Alan and Colin, played for the Swans.

41. HOLLAND, John (JACK)

Birthplace: Preston, 23/4/1901. **Died:** Preston, April 1979
Ht: 5ft-8ins, **Wt:** 10st-7lbs
Swans debut: v. Merthyr Town (h), 10/11/1923

Career:
Preston North End (signed amateur in December 1919, professional in June 1920) lge 6, FAC 2

Swansea Town (signed in 15/6/1923)
Wrexham (signed in 5/5/1925) lge 9/2gls
Crewe Alexandra (signed in 17/12/1925) lge 23/3gls
Newport County (signed in 21/6/1926) lge 10/2gls
Clapton Orient (signed in October 1927) lge 19/4gls
Carlisle United (signed in July 1929) lge 34/13gls
Barrow (signed in July1930) lge 8

Swansea Town Career Statistics			
Season	League	FAC	WC
1923/24	16/2gls	3	2/1gls
1924/25	5		1
Total	21/2gls	3	3/1gls

Honours: Welsh League Representative XI, West Wales Senior
Cup Winner–1923, 1925

Jack Holland joined his hometown side Preston initially on
amateur forms, before signing professional in 1920. Making just
six First Division appearances in three seasons as a professional
for Preston, he joined the Swans in June 1923, and during his
time at the Vetch Field was included in a Welsh League
Representative side that played the Irish Free State in Dublin
and in Cork in March 1925. Capable of playing as a right winger,
he spent most of his career as an inside forward, on either side
of the pitch, a direct front runner, with a fair amount of power as
a goalscorer. At the Vetch Field he was very much a reserve
team player, who made appearances in the first team when
injuries occurred to regulars Deacon, Thompson and
Spottiswoode. After making his debut for the Swans against
Merthyr Town in November 1923 as a replacement for Deacon,
his next league outing came in mid-January 1924, and for the
remainder of the season he missed just four league games,
operating at either outside right, or at inside forward. In mid-
April 1924 he scored in consecutive league games, and his only
other goal that season came in a Welsh Cup tie against Ebbw
Vale. Making just five league appearances during his second
season at the Vetch Field, in May 1925 he was released, joining
Third Division North side Wrexham. In November 1923 he
played for the Swans reserve side that beat Pembroke Dock in
the West Wales Senior Cup Final, and two years later picked up
his second medal in the competition when the Swans beat
Llanelly. Midway through his only season at the Racecourse, he
signed for Crewe Alexandra in December 1925. A consistent
member of the Alexandra side for the remainder of the season,
in June 1925 he returned to South Wales to sign for Third
Division South side Newport County. Scoring on his debut for
County against Plymouth Argyle in the opening game of the
1926/27 season, for the remainder of the season he was unable
to command a regular place in the starting line-up, and in
October 1927 signed for Second Division side Clapton Orient,
making his debut for the club in December 1927 in a 2-1 victory
over Leeds United. Spending two seasons in East London,
mainly in the O's reserve team, he returned north to join Third
Division North side Carlisle United in July 1929, and in his only
season at Brunton Park, had his most productive season during
his career, scoring thirteen goals from thirty-three league games.
After twelve months he signed for fellow Third Division North
side Barrow, where he finished his playing career in February
1932. During his period with Preston North End the *Lancashire
Evening Post* described him as, "a local lad who received his
football lessons along with Billy Mercer at the Roebuck Council
School, gaining many honours while a schoolboy under the
tutorship of his schoolmaster, former Preston defender Jack
Winchester. A courageous, and conscientious inside forward
who should develop effectively when he gains poundage,
and speed in the dribble." Originally placed on the transfer list
by North End at £500, but the League had given him a free
transfer.

42. HOLME, Philip (PHIL) Charles

Birthplace: Briton Ferry, 21/6/1947
Ht: 6ft-1ins, **Wt:** 13st-4lbs
Swans debut: v. Torquay United (h), 12/4/1971

Swansea City Career Statistics			
Season	League	FAC	WC
1970/71	3/1gls		
1971/72	16+4/4gls	4/1gls	1
Total	19+4/5gls	4/1gls	1

Career:
Bridgend Town
Swansea City (signed in March 1971)
Hull City (signed in July 1972) lge 29+9/11gls

Honours: Wales Amateur–8, Great Britain Olympic Squad

Former Briton Ferry Steelworks electrician who started his
career in professional football at the relatively late age of 23,
making a name for himself as a goal scorer for Bridgend Town
in the Welsh League, after earlier being on the books of Cardiff
City as an amateur. Capped at amateur level by Wales on eight
occasions, the first in season 1968/69 against Ireland and then
Scotland, Phil was also a member of the 1968 Great Britain
Olympic squad prior to joining the Swans. His other six caps
came in seasons 1969/70 against Holland, England and Ireland,
and in season 1970/71 against England, Scotland and Ireland.
Following some impressive reserve team games for the Swans,
he made his league debut against Torquay United at the Vetch
Field in April 1971, and, despite being on the losing side, scored
his first league goal two matches later against Halifax Town in
the last match of the season. Torquay United were to become a
side that was to bring him his greatest thrill in the game, when
he scored a hat-trick at Plainmoor for the Swans the following
season, on New Year's Day 1972, and being presented with the
matchball after the game. By his own admission he found full
time training very demanding and found himself very naïve to
the goings on in the professional game. Unfortunately for him,
and a number of young, promising professionals, cost cutting
measures at the Vetch Field saw him given a free transfer at the
end of the 1971/72 season, but unknown to him however, was
that Hull City had been monitoring his progress, and manager
Terry Neill had decided to offer him a contract. Neill had seen
enough potential in the striker to offer him a second chance and
by the end of his first season at Boothferry Park he had scored a
remarkable 11 goals from 32 league appearances. A serious
injury during a game against Carlisle United affecting the
cruciate and medial ligaments saw Phil make just six league
appearances during his second season with Hull, and ultimately
force him to retire from the full time game. Coaching
appointments with Hull City youth, reserve team and first team

saw Phil spend a happy six years with the club before returning home to South Wales. Within days of returning home he linked up with Welsh League club Afan Lido, and started a coaching career in South Wales which would see him create a good name for himself with the likes of Lido, Bridgend Town, Port Talbot, and Maesteg Park. At Maesteg Park they reached the semi-finals of the Welsh Cup under his guidance, before a controversial decision by the club's committee saw Maesteg switch their tie with Cardiff City to Ninian Park. He later linked up with former Cardiff goalkeeper George Wood at Inter Cardiff, whilst working as an electrician at the Ford Motor plant in Bridgend, and when Porthcawl entered the Welsh League was involved with coaching at the club.

43. HOLTHAM, DEAN Mark

Birthplace: Pontypridd, 30/9/1963
Ht: 5ft-8ins, **Wt:** 10st-5lbs
Swans debut: v. Portsmouth (h), 17/12/1983

Swansea City Career Statistics		
Season	League	WC
1983/84	6	3/1gls
Total	6	3/1gls

Career:
Cardiff City (from apprentice in September 1981) lge 0
Swansea City (signed in August 1982)
Yeovil Town (signed in July 1984)
Ebbw Vale (signed in August 1986)
Newport County (signed in September 1987) lge 4+2

Honours: Wales Sch, Yth

Dean Holtham went to Rhydyfelin school, played for Ynysybwl, then a team in Caerphilly called BTM, before joining Cardiff City at the age of 14, gaining international caps as a schoolboy, and at youth level during the period he was at Ninian Park. He failed to make the first team with the 'Bluebirds', and had his contract cancelled in April 1982, joining the Swans on a trial basis before the end of the season. Given a two year contract in the close season by John Toshack, he was primarily a reserve team left full back, before he was given his first team opportunity at the Vetch Field against Portsmouth in December 1983. With the Swans in a lot of financial problems, and players being offloaded in an attempt to satisfy the club's bankers, the season following relegation from the First Division was to prove to be quite traumatic, and by midway through the season, despite Toshack being re-instated as manager, the majority of players lining up for league duty were in most cases first, or

second year professionals. His only goal for the Swans came in a Welsh Cup Third Round tie against Abercynon, which the Swans won 5-2. At the end of the season he was released joining Gola League side Yeovil Town, before returning to South Wales to sign for Ebbw Vale. Dean returned to league action in September 1987 with Newport County, making his appearances during the first third of the season, and by May the club had been relegated to the Vauxhall Conference, and within nine months would cease to exist. Following appearances for Weston-super-Mare, Bath City and Merthyr Tydfil, Dean retired at the age of 25 to concentrate on an Old People's Home he had set up at the time with his wife. During his time as a youth player at Cardiff he had gained his coaching badges, and in later years used these qualifications to enter the Football in the Community programme. Dean is currently working as the Football in the Community Officer at Birmingham City, having been in the post for the last seven years.

44. HONOR, Christian (CHRIS) Robert

Birthplace: Bristol, 5/6/1968
Ht: 5ft-9ins, **Wt:** 10st-9lbs
Swans debut: v. Brentford (a), 26/1/1991

Swansea City Career Statistics		
Season	League	LDAF
1990/91	2	2
Total	2	2

Career:
Bristol City (from apprentice in June 1986) lge 44+16/1gls
Torquay United (loan in November 1986) lge 3
Hereford United (loan in December 1989) lge 2+1
Swansea City (loan in 22/1/1991)
Airdrie (£20,000 signed in 14/8/1991) SL 91+3/5gls, SLC 5, SC 12, Others 2+2
Cardiff City (loan in 3/2/1995) lge 10
Bath City (signed in September 1996) Conf 14+1/2gls
Forest Green Rovers (signed in 1998/99 season) Conf 42+1
Bath City (signed in season 2002/03) lge 13+10

Played for Nailsea School, and Bristol Schoolboys before joining Bristol City as an apprentice on leaving school in 1984. Prior to making his league debut for Bristol City in March 1987, he had made three league appearances during a loan spell at Torquay United the previous November. Prior to joining the Swans on loan, Chris had also made loan appearances for Hereford United. Making his Swans debut at Brentford in January 1991, during the time he was at the Vetch Field, all his games for the Swans were away from home, and came during one of the worst spells in the history of the club as far as results away from home were concerned. By mid-March Terry Yorath, who signed him on loan was sacked and replaced by Frank Burrows. All four games he played in, two league, and two in the Leyland Daf Cup competition were lost. Shortly after the start of the 1991/92 season he joined Scottish side Airdrieonians for £20,000, and during his first season at Broomfield Park saw the club lose out in the semi-final stage of the League Cup to Dunfermline Athletic, while in the Scottish Cup, Chris made an appearance in the final, only to lose to Glasgow Rangers 2-1. After three successful seasons with Airdrie, contract problems during the 1994/95 season saw him fail to make any appearances, until he joined Cardiff City on a loan transfer in February 1995. Since then he has played Conference football, firstly with Bath City and then Forest Green Rovers, before returning to play for Bath City in the Dr. Martens League. During his first season with Forest Green Rovers, he played in the FA Trophy Cup Final at Wembley against Kingstonian, losing 1-0. His first spell with Bath City saw Chris make fifteen Conference appearances between September 1996 and September 1997, scoring one goal, and when he rejoined the club during the 2002/03 season, made a further thirteen starts, and ten substitute appearances, before a knee injury three games from the end of the season ended his City career. He has not played for any other club since suffering that knee injury.

45. HOOPER, PERCY George William

Birthplace: Lambeth, 17/12/1914. **Died:** Kings Lynn 3/7/1997
Ht: 6ft-1ins, **Wt:** 13st-2lbs
Swans debut: v. Fulham (a), 15/3/1947

Swansea Town Career Statistics	
Season	League
1946/47	9
1947/48	3
Total	12

Career:
Cheddington Athletic
Islington Corinthians
Tottenham Hotspur (signed amateur in October 1933, professional in January 1935) lge 97, FAC 11
Northfleet United (loan in October 1933)
Swansea Town (signed in March 1947)
Chingford (signed in July 1948)
Kings Lynn (signed in 1949)

A goalkeeper who came through the ranks at Tottenham Hotspur, Percy first signed as an amateur in October 1933 after spells with Tufnell Park and Islington Corinthians. He spent part of 1933/34 with the Spurs nursery club Northfleet United and then progressed through the Spurs junior, 'A' and reserve teams. He signed as a professional for the club in January 1935, and by that time had grown to well over 6ft and weighed 12st 13lbs, ideal proportions for a goalkeeper at the time. In April 1935 he played the first of his 97 league matches for Spurs keeping a clean sheet against Blackburn Rovers in the First Division, retaining his place for the next two games, but making no further appearances in a Spurs side that were relegated at the end of the season. He played fairly regularly until the Second World War, and amongst his eleven FA Cup games was the 1938 Sixth Round clash with Sunderland before a White Hart Lane record crowd of 75,038. Unfortunately the team went down 1-0 and Percy's dream of a Cup Final faded. During the war he played wartime matches for Spurs and also guested for Arsenal (February 1942), Brighton (February 1944), Crystal Palace (1941/42) and Bath City. He stayed at White Hart Lane until March 1947, before being signed by Swans manager Haydn Green, replacing 'Tiger' Roberts in the Swans goal, playing in

nine consecutive league games. Parry and Roberts continued to contest the goalkeeper's jersey during his second season, limiting Percy to just three league appearances, all at the end of the season. He was unable to command the number one jersey on a regular basis, and like numerous footballers of his generation, lost six seasons of his career to the war. At the end of the 1947/48 season he was released, joining Southern League side Chingford, and after one season with the Southern League outfit, began a long association with Kings Lynn in 1949. In five years there as a player he made 186 appearances, including the 1951/52 FA Cup tie with Exeter City which saw a record crowd at a Kings Lynn home match of 13,000. On retiring from playing he took up an appointment as manager at Downham Town but after a few years he returned to Kings Lynn on their coaching staff. For an eight week spell in 1965 he was caretaker manager and stayed with the club in various capacities until 1974. A keen cricketer, he opened the batting for Ructon for several years. At one stage he ran a pub in Kings Lynn and he later worked for 23 years with the Eastern Electricity Board.

46. HOPKINS, GARETH Gersom

Birthplace: Pontlliw, Swansea, 12/4/1923
Ht: 5ft-6ins, **Wt:** 9st-7lbs
Swans debut: v. Watford (h), 28/8/1947

Swansea Town Career Statistics	
Season	League
1947/48	2
Total	2

Career:
Swansea Town (signed part-time professional in 14/8/1946)
Llanelly (signed in 7/8/1948)
Milford United (signed in close season 1949)

Honours: London Combination Cup Winner–1947

Born in the village of Pontlliw, outside Swansea, Gareth Hopkins was brought up in Gorsddu, near Penygroes, attended Amman Valley County School, played rugby in school, and made the occasional appearance for his village team, Gorsddu in the Carmarthenshire Football League. After leaving school he had a short spell working nightshift at the Blaen Hirwaun Colliery, but then went to work as an assistant wages clerk at the Pantyffynon Tin Works. He joined the RAF in April 1942, attended a wireless operator course in Blackpool, spent a year at RAF Compton Bassett, where he played for the team, and then became a High Speed Telegraphist prior to spending over three years in India. Regularly playing football in the Far East, he was selected for a Touring Services team in February 1946 captained by former England Amateur International Bob Hardisty that won 33 out of 35 games played, with Gareth scoring 26 goals. Also included in the services side were internationals Denis Compton, Ted Ditchburn and Ivor Powell. He returned to the Tin Works after the war in 1946, and after attending a trial game at the Vetch Field, was signed on part-time professional forms by manager Haydn Green. Capable of playing on either flank, he had to wait until the 1947/48 season before making his league debut at the Vetch Field against Watford in the second match of the season, replacing O'Driscoll on the right flank. Despite playing in the next game, also at the Vetch Field against Ipswich Town, he failed to make another first team appearance for the Swans, being unable to oust the likes of O'Driscoll, Comley, Scrine and Lockhart from first team duty. In June 1947 he was a member of the Swans reserve side that beat Arsenal at White Hart Lane to win the London Combination Cup.

He played in a trial match for Llanelly in mid-August 1948, later signing for the club, but in March 1949 had severed his connection with the Reds after failing to command a regular place in the starting line-up. By the start of the 1948/49 season he had linked up with former Swans player Billy Sneddon at Milford United, later making occasional appearances for Carmarthen Town (under Len Emmanuel), Caerau Athletic, and Port Talbot, where he finished his playing career. After retirement he remained at Victoria Road with Port Talbot, serving the club for over ten years as secretary. Since returning to his job after the war in the Tin Works, Gareth later worked at the Dynevor Works in Morriston before joining the Statistics Department at the Abbey Works in Port Talbot, spending over 30 years in the Accountancy Department up until his retirement in 1981.

47. HOUGH, DAVID John

Birthplace: Crewe, 20/2/1966
Ht: 5ft-11ins, **Wt:** 11st-6lbs
Swans debut: v. Barry Town (a),WC-5, 8/2/1984

Swansea City Career Statistics						
Season	League	FLC	FAC	WC	FRT/ LDAF	ECWC
1983/84	1+1			1		
1984/85	24+1/ 2gls	1+1	2	2/2gls	2	
1985/86	30+1/ 3gls		2	4	4	
1986/87	27+4/ 3gls	3/1 gls	2+1/ 1gls		2	
1987/88	14+6	2	1	1	2	
1988/89	30+10	2	3	5+1	2	
1989/90	32/1gls	2	1	1	1	2
1990/91	39+2	1	4	5+1	4	
1991/92	5	2				
Total	202+25/ 9gls	13+1/ 1gls	15+1/ 1gls	19+2/ 2gls	17	2

Career:
Swansea City (signed from apprentice in February 1984)
South Wales Police (signed in season 1991/92)
Barry Town

Honours: Wales Sch, Welsh Cup Winner–1991, 1994, Welsh League First Division Champions–1994, Macbar Cup Winner–1987, West Wales Senior Cup Winner–1987

Former Olchfa schoolboy and Wales schoolboy, who joined the Swans on schoolboy forms, signed as an apprentice in 1981, becoming a prominent member of the Swans youth championship side of 1982/83. He made his first team debut whilst still an apprentice at Barry Town in the Welsh Cup, fifth round tie in February 1984, making his league debut in the last home game of the season against Leeds United as a substitute for Jimmy Loveridge. Five days later he made his first start in the league in the last game of the season at Portsmouth, with the Swans already relegated to the Third Division. Capable of playing in any defensive role, at full back, or in central defence, he has also been used on occasions in midfield when needed. Quite a capable full back, always made himself available for overlaps, and could always be relied on to get his share of goals when pushed forward for set piece plays. Scored his first goal for the Swans at Gillingham in February 1985, in a 1-1 draw. In May 1987 he played in the Swans reserve side that beat Plymouth Argyle to win the Macbar Cup Final, and also in the West Wales Senior Cup Final defeat of Briton Ferry Athletic. He did not make the 1989 Welsh Cup Final side that defeated Kidderminster Harriers, despite playing in both legs of the semi-finals against Barry Town, however, he was a member of the Swans side that beat Wrexham in 1991 to win the Welsh Cup at the National Stadium in Cardiff. Three years later he returned to the National Stadium, this time with Barry Town to win the Welsh Cup for a second time, scoring the winning goal in the process. He also missed out on Fourth Division Play Off glory in 1988, missing the second half of the season through injury. Shortly after the start of the 1991/92 season, following a disagreement over a contract, he walked away from football, joining the police force, and played for the South Wales Police Force side in the Welsh League. After a couple of years he joined Barry Town in the Beazer Homes Midland Division, and when the club returned to the Welsh League, had success in 1994 winning the First Division Championship, and beating Cardiff City in the Welsh Cup Final at the National Stadium. He has since been promoted to sergeant, and is currently serving in the Child Protection Unit at Cockett Police Station in Swansea.

48. HOWARD, Michael (MIKE) Anthony

Birthplace: Birkenhead, 2/12/1978
Ht: 5ft-9ins, **Wt:** 11st-13lbs
Swans debut: v. Notts. County (a), 24/2/1998

Career:
Tranmere Rovers (from trainee in 9/7/1997) lge 0
Swansea City (signed in 6/2/1998)
Morecambe (signed in 28/7/2004) Conf 17+2

Honours: Third Division Champions–2000

Swansea City Career Statistics						
Season	League	FLC	FAC	AWS/LDV	P/Offs	FAWP
1997/98	2+1					1
1998/99	38+1/1gls	2	5	1	2	3
1999/2000	39+1	3	2			
2000/01	39+2	2	1	2		6
2001/02	42/1gls	1	1	1		3
2002/03	36+2	1	1	1		
2003/04	25		5	1		1
Total	221+7/2gls	9	15	6	2	14

Since being given a trial at the Vetch Field, left sided defender Michael Howard made the left-back slot his own in time, missing only a handful of games from the opening day of the 1998/99 season. The Birkenhead born player originally came to Swansea in February 1998 at the invitation of Alan Cork, earning himself a longer stay after impressing on trial. A gritty, dependable left sided full back who scored his first league goal in a 2-1 win at Carlisle United in September 1998, made the left full back position his own, displaying a consistency belying his inexperience, averaging over thirty-six league games in each of the six seasons he was involved at the Vetch Field. Attached to his boyhood heroes Liverpool from the age of nine upwards, his disappointment at not being offered an apprenticeship at Anfield on leaving school at the age of 16, was tempered when Tranmere Rovers opened the doors for him to start a career in professional football. One of only two trainees to be kept on after completing his apprenticeship, after struggling to command a game in the club's reserves, he was given the opportunity of a trial with the Swans. He did enough during the trial period to be offered a contract for the next season, but by the time he came back to the Vetch Field, Cork had been replaced as manager by John Hollins. His first full season at the Vetch Field saw him pit his wits against Premiership sides West Ham United and Derby County in F.A. Cup ties, and also play his part in the Swans reaching the End of Season Play Offs, only to lose to Scunthorpe United over two legs in the semi-final. The following season however, the Swans went one better by winning the Championship of the Third Division, with Howard making forty league appearances from left full back.

A disappointing season in the Second Division which resulted in relegation, was soon replaced by consecutive appearances in FAW Cup Finals against Wrexham and Cardiff City. Despite criticism from a minority of supporters over his style of play, whoever has been manager at the Vetch Field since Howard signed his first contract have always pencilled his name on the team sheet, as his average games each season show.

A troublesome groin/hernia problem over his last two seasons at the Vetch Field saw his season finish early in late March 2004, with him having to undergo a hernia operation at the end of the season. Unfortunately, new manager Kenny Jackett did not have the opportunity to see him in action, resulting in Howard being given a free transfer in May 2004. In late July 2004 he signed for Conference side Morecambe.

49. HOWARTH, Sydney (SYD)

Birthplace: Bristol, 28/6/1923. **Died:** Cardiff, 11/1/2004
Ht: 5ft-8½ins, **Wt:** 11st-4lbs
Swans debut: v. Southampton (a), 23/9/1950

Swansea Town Career Statistics			
Season	League	FAC	WC
1950/51	33/7gls	1	2/3gls
1951/52	7	2	
Total	40/7gls	3	2/3gls

Career:
Merthyr
Aston Villa (£6,500 signed in 16/6/1948) lge 8/2gls, FAC 1
Swansea Town (signed in September 1950)
Walsall (£750 signed in September 1952) lge 6
Merthyr Tydfil (signed in season 1953/54)

Honours: Southern League Champions–1948, 1954

Born in Bristol, Syd's family moved to Newport when he was just ten days old. Making his name at Penydarren Park with Merthyr Tydfil, he was a member of the Merthyr Tydfil side that won the Southern League Championship in season 1947/48, joining Aston Villa in June 1948 for £6,500, a record fee for a non-league player at the time. He was selected to play for Wales but prevented from joining the squad by his father (who was a former Bristol City player) because he was born in Bristol. Possessing a terrific right foot shot, at Villa Park he provided cover for George Edwards, Trevor Ford and Johnny Dixon, which limited his first team opportunities to just nine games during which he scored two goals. He made his Villa debut at Villa Park in the First Division against Charlton Athletic on the 23rd October 1948 in a 4-3 victory, playing at Stoke City the following week, and subsequently against Preston North End, Chelsea, Wolverhampton Wanderers, Blackpool, Sheffield United and Manchester United, all in the First Division. Syd's first goal was scored against Wolverhampton Wanders on Boxing Day, Monday 27 December 1948, in a 5-1 Villa victory before a crowd of 63, 769, with his other goal being scored in a 1-0 win against Sheffield United at Bramall Lane on the 26th February 1949. His only FA Cup appearance for Villa came in a 1-1 Third Round draw against Bolton Wanderers on the 8th January 1949. With limited first team opportunities at Villa Park, in September 1950 he returned to South Wales to sign for the Swans, and after replacing Stan Richards in the Swans forward line, finished the season joint top goalscorer with Ronnie Turnbull, with ten league and cup goals. The signing of Turnbull had seen Howarth switch from a centre forward role, to either an inside forward, or right wing position. His second season, with Frankie Scrine returning from injury, saw Howarth struggle to make the first team line-up, managing just seven league appearances, which included five consecutive appearances at outside right in place of the injured in O'Driscoll. With young Terry Medwin coming through to the first team at the end of the 1951/52 season, and starting the new term in the first team line-up, Howarth joined Third Division South side Walsall in October 1952 for £750, after failing to make an appearance. Bought by the Swans as a Trevor Ford type centre forward, his strike rate was deemed not good enough for Second Division football, and when Turnbull was brought to the Vetch Field he was made available for transfer. He made his Walsall debut in a midfield role in a 3-0 win over Reading on the 25th September 1952. Making just five more league appearances for the 'Saddlers', Syd returned to Merthyr Tydfil becoming an influential figure in the side's Southern League success in season 1953/54, when they were again crowned Champions. Syd was the son of pre-war Bury, Bristol City, Leeds and Bristol Rovers player Tommy Howarth. A regular at Penydarren Park as a spectator in his later years, he died in Cardiff's Heath Hospital in January 2004.

50. HOWELLS, Ronald (RON) Gilbert

Birthplace: Ponthenry, Carms, 12/1/1927
Ht: 5ft-11ins, **Wt:** 12st-0lbs
Swans debut: v. Walsall (h), 7/2/1948

Swansea Town Career Statistics	
Season	League
1947/48	9
Total	9

Career:
Swansea Town (trial in May 1946, amateur signed in 7/9/1946, professional in April 1948)
Barry Town (signed in August 1949)
Cardiff City (signed in 3/7/1950) lge 154
Worcester City (signed in August 1957)
Chester City (signed in September 1958) lge 80
Ton Pentre (signed in season 1960/61)

Honours: Wales Full–2, Welsh League First Division Champions–1961

Ron Howells joined the Swans in September 1946 from Ponthenry after impressing during a trial spell playing for the Swans' Welsh League side in May 1946 at the Vetch Field, and had initially played as an inside forward in Carmarthenshire League football. A collier from Ponthenry, he often worked a night shift prior to playing for the Swans on a Saturday. Swans manager Haydn Green and coach Joe Sykes had seen his potential as a goalkeeper, and after impressing in Welsh League matches was given his Combination debut against Watford early during the 1946/47 season. Unfortunately he suffered a fractured wrist, keeping him sidelined until Xmas Day. Following an impressive display against Plymouth Argyle reserve side in January 1948, the young 21-year-old amateur was given his first team opportunity a few weeks later, in February 1948 at the Vetch Field against Walsall in the Third Division South, drawing 1-1. He retained his place for the next seven league games, but following a 4-0 defeat at Crystal Palace, he lost his place to Percy Hooper for the next league game, but was then re-instated for one more league game before Hooper regained his first team position. That season saw the Swans use four different goalkeepers in the league. With Jack Parry and Danny Canning being the two most likely to claim the number one jersey in season 1948/49, Howells was content to play Combination and Welsh League football until joining Southern

League side Barry Town in August 1949. In July 1950 he returned to league football signing for Cardiff City, making sixteen league appearances in the 'Bluebirds' side that gained promotion to the First Division in 1952. He made his First Division debut with the 'Bluebirds' against Tottenham Hotspur on the 27th January 1951, and gained his first international cap at Ninian Park against England on the 10th October 1953, making his second appearance the following month against Scotland, both as replacements for Shortt. Making over one hundred and fifty league appearances for the 'Bluebirds', he was released in August 1957 joining non-league side Worcester City. He struggled to hold down a regular place in the Worcester side, making just one appearance, before returning to Football League action in September 1958 with Fourth Division side Chester. Despite playing in every game for Chester during season 1959/60, in May 1960 he was given a free transfer, and at one time during the close season, Llanelly were looking to offer him terms, as he was still living near to the town in Ponthenry. During the 1960/61 season he linked up with former Cardiff City team mate Ken Hollyman at Ton Pentre, and by the end of his first season at the club had made a significant contribution in the club winning the Championship of the Welsh League First Division, remaining at the club until 1969. When Barry Town were going through a difficult period in the mid-1960's he made a couple of appearances for the club. Employed as a painter and decorator, in March 1974 he applied for the role as Wales's first Full Time Football Manager despite having no formal coaching qualifications.

51. HOYLAND, Frederick (FRED)

Birthplace: Moorthorpe, 10/12/1897. **Died:** Lower Agbrigg, JAS, 1971
Ht: 5ft-6ins, **Wt:** 11st-0lbs
Swans debut: v. Newport County (a), 9/4/1921

Swansea Town Career Statistics			
Season	League	FAC	WC
1920/21	1		
1921/22	8	1	2
Total	9	1	2

Career:
Frickley Colliery
Swansea Town (£125 signed in 31/1/1921)
Bury (£75 signed in May 1922) lge 0
Glossop
Birmingham (signed in August 1923) lge 6
Brighton & Hove Albion (signed in May 1924) lge 5

Signed by manager Joe Bradshaw from Frickley Colliery in late January 1921, Fred Hoyland, a right winger was basically a reserve to Billy Hole during his time with the Swans. His first game for the Swans was against Pembroke Dock in a Welsh League game at the Vetch Field at outside right in early February 1921. On the other flank was Smith, a trialist from Brynmill Athletic. He made his debut as a replacement for the injured Hole in April 1921, during the club's first season in the Football League, but found limited opportunities again in his second season, making a further eight league, and three cup appearances. In May 1922 he was placed on the transfer list, and later joined Second Division Bury in May 1922 for a £75 fee in May 1922. Unfortunately, he wasn't a great success at Gigg Lane either and quickly drifted into non-League football for a brief spell with Glossop until joining Birmingham in August 1923. After playing in six First Division matches for the 'Blues' during 1923–24, Charlie Webb secured his services for the Albion in August 1924. Fred remained at the Goldstone for two seasons but, with Jack Nightingale occupying the outside-right berth to great effect, he had little chance of a run in the Third Division team and left the Football League circuit on his release in May 1926.

52. HUGHES, ALLAN Leslie

Birthplace: Swansea, 11/3/1951
Ht: 5ft-8ins, **Wt**: 11st-1lbs
Swans debut: v. Colchester United (a), 25/4/1969

Swansea Town Career Statistics	
Season	League
1968/69	1
Total	1

Career:
Swansea Town (signed from apprentice in March 1969)
Pembroke Borough (signed in August 1969)

Alan attended school in Dunvant, played for Swansea schoolboys, and joined the Swans as apprentice professional prior to start of season 1966/67, at the age of 15. After signing professional in March 1969, 'Ossie' made his first team debut at Colchester United at right full back instead of the experienced Vic Gomersall, with the Swans winning 1-0. Gaining no honours during his short time at the Vetch Field, he was released at the end of the season, signing for Welsh League side Pembroke Borough, playing a couple of seasons until he returned to play in the Swansea Senior League with Waunarlwydd. After leaving the Vetch Field as a professional, he initially went to work in the labour pool at BSC Trostre, but then joined British Telecom, where he is to the present day, working on payphones, phone repairs and maintenance. He played in the Swansea Senior League well into the 1990's with Waunarlwydd, North End and the Casuals, before finishing his playing career with Carmarthenshire League team Drefach.

53. HUGHES, BRIAN

Birthplace: Swansea, 22/11/1937
Ht: 5ft-10ins, **Wt**: 11st-4¼lbs
Swans debut: v. Grimsby Town (h), 29/11/1958

Career:
BP Llandarcy
Swansea Town (signed in July 1956)

Atlanta Chiefs, USA (signed in December 1966)
Swansea Town (signed in January 1969)
Atlanta Chiefs, USA (signed in May 1969)
Merthyr Tydfil (signed in August 1969)

Swansea Town Career Statistics					
Season	League	FLC	FAC	WC	ECWC
1958/59	23		1	1	
1959/60	33		3/1gls	2	
1960/61	25/2gls	1	1	1	
1961/62	4	1			2
1962/63	20	1	1		
1963/64	28/1gls	1	7	1	
1964/65	37/1gls	3	4	1	
1965/66	36	1	1	6	
1966/67	13/3gls	3	2		1
1968/69	12			3	
Total	231/7gls	11	20/1gls	15	3

Honours: Wales Sch, Yth, U-23–2, Welsh Cup Winner–1966, West Wales Senior Cup Winner–1960, 1965, 1966

Former Swansea schoolboy and Welsh schoolboy defender, who after signing for the Swans, also made appearances for Wales at Youth level. Replacing Alan Woods for his league debut at the Vetch Field against Grimsby Town in November 1958, he missed just two league matches for the rest of the season, playing at either right half back, or at right full back. A teenage discovery by Swans Director Laidlaw Murray, he joined the Swans from Neath League side BP Llandarcy, and in a short time was capped at Youth level by Wales, subsequently winning U-23 honours. A reserve for the Full International side on a number of occasions, there was little doubt that but for a succession of injuries which threatened to end his career, he would have gained Full International Honours for Wales. He started the 1959/60 season as first choice right full back, reverting also to either a right or left half back during the season where needed. In May 1960 he played in the Swans side that beat Llanelly to win the West Wales Senior Cup, and also in May 1965, and in August 1966. He made his first appearance for the Wales U-23 side in 1960 against Scotland, his second against England the following year. Exceptionally strong in the tackle and a tireless worker, he missed the 1961 Welsh Cup Final win over Bangor City through injury, but played in European football the next season against Motor Jena. Despite missing a number of Welsh Cup semi-finals over the years with the Swans, Brian skippered the Swans side in the 1965/66 Welsh Cup triumph over Chester, also playing in the following season's European cup tie against Slavia Sofia. With the Swans struggling to hold onto their Second Division status during the early part of the 1960's, their 1963/64 FA Cup run to the semi-finals did take their mind off the every day league battle, with Brian playing in all seven cup ties. Having accepted a two year contract, with an option for a further two years to play for North American League side

Atlanta Chiefs in early December, he played his last game for the Swans against Bristol Rovers on the 17th December 1966, sailing on the liner Iberia on the 17th January 1967. In the North American close season in August 1967, Brian had a period of two months coaching football in the Caribbean. He returned to the UK shortly before Christmas 1968, rejoining the Swans, who had retained his signature with the Football League, making his debut after the Swans had obtained International clearance in early January 1969 against Peterborough United. Making a dozen league appearances in either fullback position, as well as in central defence, Brian left the Swans just before the end of the season to return to the USA, and rejoin Atlanta Chiefs as a part-time professional, with a job already lined up for him on his return to the country. He returned to the UK in the 1969 close season, and after playing a couple of games for Merthyr Tydfil, on the 9th September 1969, after being released from his contract at Penydarren Park, left to take up a three month coaching appointment in schools in Jamaica.

54. HUGHES, EMLYN Walter O.B.E.

Birthplace: Barrow, 28/8/1947. **Died:** Sheffield, 9/11/2004
Ht: 5ft-10ins, **Wt:** 12st-6lbs
Swans debut: v. Huddersfield Town (a), 17/9/1983

Swansea City Career Statistics		
Season	League	FLC
1983/84	7	2
Total	7	2

Career:
Blackpool (from juniors in September 1964) lge 27+1
Liverpool (£65,000 signed in March 1967) lge 474/35gls
Wolverhampton Wanderers (£90,000 signed in 3/8/1979) lge 56+2/2gls
Rotherham United (signed in September 1981) lge 55+1/6gls
Hull City (signed in March 1983) lge 9
Mansfield Town (non-contract in August 1983)
Swansea City (signed in September 1983)

Honours: England U-23–8, Full–62, Football League XI, First Division Champions–1973, 1976, 1977, 1979, F.A. Cup Winner–1974, Football League Cup Winner–1980, European Cup Winner–1977, 1978, UEFA Cup Winner–1973, 1976

Recruited by John Toshack to give some experience to a young, faltering Swans side, the former team mate of Toshack at Liverpool was 36 years of age at the time he came to the Vetch Field, and although he had the appetite for the challenge, he unfortunately did not possess the legs to last the course. He arrived during a time when the Swans were trying to come to terms with relegation from the First Division, amid increasing debts off the field, and offloading the better quality players in an

effort to trim their monthly wage bill. Toshack was sacked in late October 1983, and Hughes left the Vetch Field 48 hours later, with six weeks left on his short term contract. An inspirational player during his earlier years, Emlyn, the son of a former Welsh Rugby Union player who had travelled north to play Rugby League for Barrow, captained both the Liverpool and England international sides during his playing career, and was also appointed skipper of the Swans side on his arrival. Signed as a 19-year-old by Bill Shankly from Blackpool for £65,000 in 1967 after a handful of first team appearances. His infectious enthusiasm, skill and endless drive combined to make him a player of impressive stature and also prompted Liverpool fans to give him the nickname 'Crazy Horse'. An inspirational figure for club and country, he crowned his energetic displays with some spectacular goals, including two in the Mersey derby win at Everton in March 1973. As a player with Liverpool he gained Division One Championship medals in 1973, 1976, 1977, 1979, FA Cup Winners medal in 1974, FA Cup Runners up medal in 1971, 1977, League Cup Winners medal 1980 (with Wolves), League Cup Runners up medal 1978, UEFA Cup Winners medal 1973, 1976, European Cup Winners medal in 1977,1978, Charity Shield Winners medal 1974, 1976 and 1977 (shared), and European Super Cup Winner medal in 1977. Emlyn had his first taste of management in July 1981 as player manager at Rotherham United, and despite some early success, following a season of relegation to the Third Division he left the club in March 1983, joining Hull City as a player, helping them to promotion from the Fourth Division in runners up position. The start of the 1983/84 season saw him training with Mansfield Town, but after playing in a friendly match he was not offered a contract, and left the club, later to link up with Toshack at the Vetch Field. His first U-23 cap for England came against Wales in 1968, and his first full cap was against the Netherlands on the 5th November 1969 in Amsterdam. His last international cap was in Glasgow against Scotland on the 24th May 1980, when he came on as substitute for Paul Mariner. Captaining the England side on 23 occasions, most of his caps were when he was with Liverpool, but three came with Wolves. Between 1969 and 1974 he played three times for the Football League Representative Team against the Scottish League Representative Team. Awarded an OBE for his services to sport in 1980, Emlyn went on to become a popular team captain opposite former England Rugby Union skipper Bill Beaumont on BBC TV's Question of Sport programme. At the end of the 1976/77 season, Emlyn was awarded the Football Writers Association Footballer of the Year Award, becoming the third Liverpool player in four seasons to receive the award, following Kevin Keegan and Ian Callaghan. In February 2004 Emlyn revealed that after collapsing during a charity match, he'd had surgery and radiotherapy in an attempt to shrink a brain tumour, but his condition deteriorated in the last couple of days prior to his death at home in Sheffield in November 2004.

55. HUGHES, JOHN

Birthplace: Edinburgh, 19/9/1964
Ht: 6ft-0ins, **Wt:** 13st-7lbs
Swans debut: v. Bristol Rovers (a), 25/11/1989

Swansea City Career Statistics			
Season	League	FAC	L/Daf
1989/90	16+6/4gls	2	2
Total	16+6/4gls	2	2

Career:
Berwick Rangers (signed in 1/8/1988) SL 41/14gls, SLC 2, SC 2/1gls

Swansea City (£70,000 signed in 23/11/1989)
Falkirk (£70,000 signed in 22/8/1990) SL 129+5/7gls, SLC 7, SC 7/1gls, Others 5/1gls
Glasgow Celtic (£750,000 signed in 7/8/1995) SL 31+1/2gls, SLC 5, SC 3
Hibernian (signed in 1/11/1996) SL 70+2/4gls, SLC 6, SC 5
Ayr United (signed in 31/5/2000) SL 48/2gls. SLC 5, SC 6, Others 3
Falkirk (signed in 4/6/2002) SL 76+2/5gls, SLC 4+1, SFC 5, Others 5

Honours: Scottish First Division Champions–1991, 1994, 1999, B+Q Cup Winner–1994

John Hughes was the least known and inexperienced of the three footballers who were presented to the Swans fans at a press gathering on the 24th November 1989 by manager Ian Evans. Previously a part-time professional with Berwick Rangers, the £70,000 signing was one third of a £300,000 package which included Paul Chalmers and Keith Walker. However, in the short period of time he was at the Vetch Field, Hughes had convinced quite a number of supporters that his willingness for hard work far outweighed his inexperience in the full time game. Despite his having settled in Swansea, living close to the Vetch Field, it was only his wife's homesickness which prevented him from staying in the area, and going on to create a far bigger impression with the home fans. In the six months he was at the Vetch Field he made just 22 league appearances for the Swans, scoring 4 goals, with the goal scored at Ninian Park against Cardiff City being the one most Swans will remember him by. A goal which almost virtually saw the Swans avoid relegation to the Fourth Division. Within a couple of weeks of his signing for the Swans he faced the mighty Liverpool at the Vetch Field in the FA Cup, hitting the post with one effort, and his overall performance suggesting the club had added a talented player to it's playing squad. Within six months of his returning to Scotland, and signing for Falkirk in a £70,000 deal, Hughes had reverted to a central defender, a role he often played at junior, and schoolboy football, and started a playing career which would see him play in the Scottish Premier League with Glasgow Celtic, Hibernian and Ayr United. Winning the First Division Championships on three occasions, twice with Falkirk in 1991 and 1994, and in 1999 with Hibernian, the B+Q Cup with Falkirk in 1994, his transfer fee to Celtic in 1995 was set at £750,000, and following a league tribunal, Falkirk were ordered to pay the Swans £70,000 in March 1996 as part of the sell on clause administered by the tribunal. With Falkirk desperately in need of cash, and in no position to pay the Swans their share of the transfer fee, former Scotland Youth and U-21 International Colin McDonald moved to the Vetch Field in exchange for the money owed. It was a move to his hometown City of Edinburgh to play for Hibernian which brought Hughes his most productive period in the game to date, with the club winning the Scottish First Division at the end of the 1998/99 season. Hughes played in the first 23 league matches, but following a knee injury, his next appearance came in the last match of the season against his old club Falkirk. During this period Hughes almost made his debut at International level, being regularly named in Scotland's International squad. Captaining Ayr United in both his seasons with the club, Hughes played in the CIS League Cup Final defeat by Rangers in 2002. During the 2002/03 close season Hughes returned to Falkirk, where he was initially interviewed for the manager's position, but later undertook a player coach role under manager Ian McCall. In late January 2003 he was appointed joint caretaker manager with team mate Owen Coyle following manager Ian McColl's move to Dundee United, and in May 2003 John was named manager of Falkirk. By May 2005 he had steered the club back into the Premiership after winning the Championship of the Scottish First Division.

56. HUGHES, MARK

Birthplace: Port Talbot, 3/2/1962
Ht: 6ft-0ins, **Wt:** 12st-8lbs
Swans debut: v. Millwall (a), 25/8/1984

Swansea City Career Statistics	
Season	League
1984/85	12
Total	12

Career:
Bristol Rovers (from apprentice in 1/2/1980) lge 73+1/3gls, FLC 1, FAC 9+1, Others 3/1gls
Torquay United (loan in 23/12/1982) lge 9/1gls, FAC 3/1gls
Swansea City (signed in 25/6/1984)
Bristol City (signed in 7/2/1985) lge 21+1, FLC 1, Others 3
Tranmere Rovers (£3,000 signed in 19/9/1985) lge 258+8/9gls, FLC 27/2gls, FAC 12+3, Others 36+1/1gls
Partick Thistle (trial in August 1993)
Shrewsbury Town (signed in 4/7/1994) lge 18+2, FAC 1, Others 1

Honours: Wales Sch, Yth, Third Division Play Off Winner–1991, Leyland Daf Cup Winner–1990

A solid central defender who became one of Colin Appleton's first signings at the Vetch Field after Mark had been released by Bristol Rovers. Mark had initially joined Rovers as an apprentice from school, where he had gained international honours for Wales. His brother Wayne was a striker with Cardiff City, whilst his cousin was former England captain Emlyn Hughes. He struggled to create an impression at the Vetch Field, initially starting in a midfield role, but with off the field financial problems at the club, results proved to be extremely difficult to achieve, especially when the club was only able to bring in non-contracted players, and trialists. New manager John Bond gave Hughes the opportunity of joining Bristol City in February 1985 on a free transfer, linking up with Terry Cooper a second time, with the manager giving him his league debut whilst boss of Bristol Rovers. Shortly after the start of the 1985/86 season however, he joined Fourth Division Tranmere Rovers for a fee in the region of £3,000. He settled into a sweeper role for Johnny King's Rovers side, and within three seasons would leave the Fourth Division in the runners up place, and the next two seasons would play at Wembley on no fewer than four occasions. A losing Third Division Play Off Finalist in 1990 to Notts. County, but beating Bristol Rovers in the Leyland Daf Cup Final, was followed twelve months later by beating Bolton Wanderers in the Third Division Play Off Final, and losing to Birmingham City in the Leyland Daf Cup Final. He was released at the end of the 1993/94 season after almost 350 league and cup appearances for Tranmere Rovers, and joined Shrewsbury Town. However, at the end of his first season he was forced to retire through injury.

57. HUGHES, Michael (MIKE) Richard

Birthplace: Bridgend, 19/8/1964
Ht: 5ft-10½ins, **Wt:** 11st-3lbs
Swans debut: v. Derby County (h), 31/12/1983

Swansea City Career Statistics

Season	League	FLC	FAC	WC	FRT
1983/84	21		1	5	
1984/85	13			3	2
1985/86	27	1	1	4	3
1986/87	46	4	5	1	3
1987/88	32	2	2	2	2
Total	139	7	9	15	10

Career:
Swansea City (signed from apprentice in August 1982)
Poole Town (signed in season 1995/96)

Honours: Wales Yth, West Wales Senior Cup Winner–1987

Brave goalkeeper whose career was cut short through a brain abnormality. He was led from the field during a pre-season friendly at the start of the 1987/88 season with concussion, and seven months later was forced to retire after taking specialist advice, playing his last game for the Swans at the Vetch Field against Stockport County on 19th February 1988. Prior to visiting the specialist he had been complaining of headaches, and dizzy spells. Signing professional forms at the start of the 1982/83 season, with the Swans in Division One, it was midway through the following season (1983/84) that he was given his

league opportunity by John Toshack, who had returned to manage the club for a second spell. Prior to the start of the season he was third in line for the first team goalkeeper's jersey, behind Jimmy Rimmer and Chris Sander. Rimmer was taken from the field injured in mid-November, an injury which would keep him out for the remainder of the season, and after Sander had made 4 league appearances, Hughes was given his opportunity at the Vetch Field against Derby County. Despite relegation to the Third Division, and Rimmer being reinstated as first choice at the start of the season, in January 1985 Swans manager John Bond gave young Hughes another opportunity in the Swans goalkeeper jersey. The experienced Rimmer was reinstated threequarters through the season, as the club successfully averted a third consecutive relegation. Financial problems had not abated off the field, and just prior to the club being wound up in the High Court, Hughes was given his third opportunity as the club's number one custodian, with the club hurtling towards the Fourth Division. A new manager in Terry Yorath at the start of the 1986/87 season saw Hughes become the only goalkeeper on the club's books, with young Mark Walton, just about to start his apprenticeship with the club changing his mind and signing for Luton Town. In May 1987 he was included in the Swans side that beat Briton Ferry Athletic to win the West Wales Senior Cup. With the Swans now playing a brand of attacking football under Yorath, promotion was a distinct possibility up to the time of Hughes's last match for the club, against Stockport County. Following the advice of his consultant, after retiring from football, Hughes started a new career in Insurance, as the Swans successfully gained promotion via the Play Offs at Torquay United. Since then, Hughes has moved away from the Swansea area, and made occasional appearances during Poole Town's last season in the Southern League before the club was wound up. He later became a Physical Training Instructor at Pentonville Prison.

58. HUMPHRIES, BRINLEY

Birthplace: Swansea, 26/12/1901. **Died:** Swansea, AMJ, 1972
Ht: 5ft-10ins, **Wt:** 10st-6lbs
Swans debut: v. Derby County (a), 3/10/1925

Swansea Town Career Statistics

Season	League	WC
1925/26	7/1gls	2
1926/27	4	
Total	11/1gls	2

Career:
Stepney FC
Swansea Town (amateur in season 1922/23, professional in 16/6/1923)
Swindon Town (£250 signed in June 1927) lge 55/2gls, FAC 8

Honours: Wales Junior International, Gwalia League Representative XI, West Wales Senior Cup Winner–1923, 1926

Signed as a professional from local league side Stepney in June 1923, he had earlier during the previous season spent a trial period at the Vetch Field, and had played reserve team football for two seasons before making his league debut as Joe Sykes's replacement at Derby County in October 1925. Initially he had joined the Swans as a centre forward, earning good reviews with his style of play, and was easily the most promising of all the young trialists who had been given their opportunities in the reserve team during season 1922/23. He was predominately a reserve team player during the early part of his career at the Vetch Field, and in November 1923 was included in the Swans reserve side that beat Pembroke Dock to win the West Wales

Senior Cup. He was also included in the reserve side that won the same competition, beating Merthyr Town in April 1926, scoring two goals. The majority of his first team outings for the Swans was as Sykes's replacement, although towards the end of season 1925/26 he did revert to his former position of centre forward instead of Harry Morris. He scored his only goal for the Swans at the Vetch Field against Portsmouth in March 1926.
In June 1927 he was sold to Third Division South side Swindon Town for a fee in the region of £250. Making regular appearances in the Swindon Town side during his three years at the County Ground, he retired from the professional game in the 1930 close season. In February 1926 he was included in the Wales Juniors side that played Ireland at Holyhead.
After returning to Swansea, a report in the local newspaper, the *Daily Post*, mentioned him playing in November 1930 for Fforestfach & District side Mynydd Newydd Colliery XI against Grovesend United. On the 26th January 1933 he played for a Gwalia League Representative side against a Bridgend & District XI in an Inter League game.

59. HUMPHRIES, William (WILLIE) McCauley

Birthplace: Belfast, 8/7/1936
Ht: 5ft-4½ins, **Wt:** 10st-1lbs
Swans debut: v. Middlesbrough (h), 20/3/1965

Swansea Town Career Statistics					
Season	League	FLC	FAC	WC	ECWC
1964/65	10/2gls				
1965/66	44/6gls	1	1	7/1gls	
1966/67	46/8gls	4	3/2gls	1	2
1967/68	43/6gls	1	4/2gls	2	
Total	143/22gls	6	8/4gls	10/1gls	2

Career:
Glentoran (amateur)
Ards (signed in season 1953/54)
Leeds United (signed in 24/9/1958) lge 25/2gls
Ards (signed in 1960)
Coventry City (signed in April 1962) lge 109/23gls
Swansea Town (£14,000 signed in 16/3/1965)
Ards (signed in close season 1968)

Honours: Northern Ireland Full–14, Irish League Rep XI–12, Third Division Champions–1964, Welsh Cup Winner–1966, Irish League Champions–1958, Irish Cup Winner–1969, 1974, Gold Cup Winner–1973, County Antrim Shield Winner–1972, Blaxnit Cup Winner–1974

Diminutive right winger who was signed by Swans manager Trevor Morris prior to transfer deadline day in March 1965 for

£14,000 from Coventry City, in a bid to add experience to a Swans side that was fighting to avoid relegation to the Third Division. However, despite winning three out of the last four league games, relegation was confirmed after the last game defeat at Coventry City. Willie did prove to be an excellent signing for the Swans, with his consistent displays on the right flank. A compact player, good ball control, fine crosser, he could beat his opponent, and had a good eye for goal. He was released in May 1968, returning to Ards, the team he had started his professional career with. Starting his career as an amateur with Glentoran, after joining Ards in 1953, he made appearances in the side that won the Irish Championship in season 1957/58, and was then given the opportunity of league football with First Division side Leeds United in September 1958. Returning to Ards midway through the 1959/60 season, at the end of the season he was a member of the side that lost in the final of the Irish Cup. He was given his second opportunity of league football in April 1962, this time with Third Division side Coventry City. Within a couple of seasons he had become a part of Jimmy Hills's Sky Blue revolution, playing in the side that won the Third Division Championship in 1964, only to join the Swans prior to the club gaining promotion to the First Division. Despite relegation to the Third Division with the Swans, Willie played in the 1966 Welsh Cup Final win over Chester, also playing in both European Cup Winners Cup matches against Slavia Sofia the following season. During his last season with the Swans he played in the FA Cup tie against Arsenal at the Vetch Field which drew a record attendance to the Vetch Field. Willie gained his first international cap whilst with Ards on the 11th April 1962 at Ninian Park against Wales. A further ten caps were gained with Coventry City, and whilst he was with the Swans he made two more international appearances, the last in Belfast against Albania in May 1965. During his career in Ireland he made a dozen appearances for the Irish League Representative side. Returning to Ards for a third spell after being released by the Swans in May 1968, he gained further success on the field, Irish League Runner-Up in 1973, Irish Cup Winner in 1969 and 1974, Gold Cup Winner in 1973, Gold Cup Runner-Up in 1974, County Antrim Shield Winner in 1972, County Antrim Shield Runner-Up in 1970, Blaxnit Cup Winner in 1974, and Carlsberg Cup Runner-Up in 1973 and 1974. From season 1970/71 to 1978 he became player manager of Ards, and he made a total of 578 appearances for the club, scoring 138 goals. He retired as a player in 1980, becoming manager until 1982.

60. HUNTLEY, KEITH Stanley Murray

Birthplace: Swansea, 12/2/1931. **Died:** Swansea, December 1995
Ht: 5ft-9ins, **Wt:** 10st-0lbs
Swans debut: v. Hull City (a), 26/8/1950

Career:
Swansea Town (amateur signed in 1948, professional in August 1951)
Milford United (signed in August 1954)

Swansea Town Career Statistics		
Season	League	WC
1950/51	2	1
Total	2	1

Honours: Wales Amateur–2, London Combination Cup Winner–1950, West Wales Senior Cup Winner–1950

Brought up in the Mount Pleasant district of Swansea, Keith attended Terrace Road School, Dynevor Grammar and Swansea College, and on leaving school started an apprenticeship as a Fitter and Turner at the IMI Works in Waunarlwydd, remaining there for forty years up to his retirement. Signed from local Swansea League side St. Judes in August 1950, the eighteen-year-old former Wales Amateur International left winger made two consecutive league appearances for the Swans as a replacement for the injured Cyril Beech shortly after the start of season 1950/51, making a further appearance in the Welsh Cup against Pembroke Borough in February 1951. In April 1950 he played for a Swansea Youth League XI against a Scottish Juvenile XI at the Vetch Field. In May 1950 he was a member of the Swans reserve side that won at Southend United to win the London Combination Cup Final, and also that month when the Swans beat Haverfordwest to win the West Wales Senior Cup Final. His first Welsh Amateur appearance came at the age of eighteen at Leicester against England on the 20th January 1951, later playing against Scotland, following his father Walter Huntley who had earlier played for the Welsh Amateur side against England in 1923 and in 1925. Possessing good pace and ball control, despite the promise shown as a youngster, he did not make the grade for Football League standards and was released from the playing staff at the Vetch Field. In August 1954 he joined Welsh League side Milford United, later going on to become vice-captain of the team, and also make more than two hundred appearances for the club before finishing his career in the Swansea League with Kilvey Athletic. A keen Bowls player in later years, he played for St. Thomas Bowling Club.

61. HURST, GLYNN

Birthplace: Barnsley, 17/1/1976
Ht: 5ft-10ins, **Wt:** 11st-10lbs
Swans debut: v. Burnley (h), 16/12/1995

Swansea City Career Statistics	
Season	League
1995/96	2/1gls
Total	2/1gls

Career:
Tottenham Hotspur (trainee)
South Africa
Barnsley (signed in 13/7/1994) lge 0+8, FLC 1
Swansea City (loan signed in 15/12/1995)
Mansfield Town (loan in 18/11/1996) lge 5+1, Others 0+1
Emley Town (signed in 27/3/1997)
Ayr United (£30,000 signed in 23/3/1998) SL 78/49gls,
    SLC 6/2gls, SC 10, Others 1+2
Stockport County (£150,000 signed in 16/2/2001) lge 22+4/4gls,
    FLC 0+1
Chesterfield (signed in 14/12/2001) lge 77+7/29gls, FLC 1,
    FAC 0+1
Notts. County (signed in June 2004) lge 36+5/14gls, FLC 2,
    FAC 2+1, Others 1/1gls

Honours: South Africa U-21–5

Inexperienced striker who was brought to the Vetch Field on a loan transfer by manager Bobby Smith in 15th December 1995. Scored on his debut for the Swans at the Vetch Field against Burnley, but with weather conditions cancelling games, made just one more appearance at Bristol City before returning to Barnsley. The former Spurs trainee was released by Barnsley in March 1997, dropping out of the league to play for non-league Emley Town, but after a thrilling FA Cup run, and a narrow defeat at West Ham United in the third round, was signed by Scottish side Ayr United for £30,000 in March 1998. He proved to be a consistent goalscorer in Scottish football, topping the Ayr United goalscoring charts in his first two seasons, and in his third was second top goalscorer as the side just failed to earn themselves promotion to the Premier Division in Scotland. He returned south to sign for Stockport County in February 2001 for a six figure transfer fee, later joining Chesterfield on a free transfer. Joining Chesterfield the day after Luke Beckett had gone to Stockport for £100,000 and although the Hurst deal is officially a completely separate deal and a free transfer (under Administration rules at the time the club was not allowed to pay transfer fees) most fans consider it to be a sort of "Hurst plus cash for Beckett" deal. When Hurst arrived it was said that he'd played for South Africa U-21's, but the player himself said that he was resident in South Africa for 10 years from the age of six, and won five U-21 caps while at Barnsley. At the end of season 2003/04, he finished top goalscorer with thirteen league goals with Chesterfield avoiding relegation to the Third Division by beating Luton Town in the last game of the season. In the 2004 close season he signed for Notts. County who had failed in their bid to escape from relegation to the Third Division.

62. HUTCHISON, Thomas (TOMMY)

Birthplace: Cardenden, 22/9/1947
Ht: 5ft-11ins, **Wt:** 11st-2lbs
Swans debut: v. Wigan Athletic (h), 17/8/1985

Swansea City Career Statistics

Season	League	FLC	FAC	WC	FRT/LDaf	ECWC	P/Offs
1985/86	38+3/ 3gls	4		2	3		
1986/87	40+1/ 1gls	3	5/ 2gls	1	3		
1987/88	6+1	1					4
1988/89	42+2/ 3gls	1+1	3/ 1gls	7/ 1gls	2		
1989/90	31+5/ 2gls	1	0+1	1	1+1	2	
1990/91	6+3			1			
Total	163+15/ 9gls	10+1	8+1/ 3gls	12/ 1gls	9+1	2	4

Career:
Dundonald Bluebell
Alloa Athletic
Blackpool (£7,000 signed in 1/2/1968) lge 163+2/10gls
Coventry City (£145,000 signed in 1/10/1972) lge 312+2/24gls
Manchester City (£47,000 signed in 23/10/1980) lge 44+2/4gls
Bulova, Hong Kong (loan in February 1982)
Burnley (signed in 16/8/1983) lge 92/4gls
Swansea City (signed in 22/7/1985)
Merthyr Tydfil (signed in March 1991) Conf. 56+17/2gls

Honours: Scotland U-23–1, Full–17, Welsh Cup Winner–1989, Fourth Division Play Off Winner–1988, West Wales Senior Cup Winner–1987, 1990

The 1981 Centenary FA Cup Final replay has become known as the 'Ricky Villa Cup Final' following the goal scoring exploits of the Argentinian international striker. In the first game however, Scotland international winger, Tommy Hutchison at the age of 33, took all the highlights from the first ninety minutes at Wembley, scoring two goals, one for each side! Opening the scoring for Manchester City, Hutchison had the misfortune to score an own goal, and force a replay. A subdued performance by the Argentinian striker Ricky Villa in the first game, was in complete contrast in the replay as the international striker weaved his magic to score two goals, and see Spurs win the replay 3-2. Five years later, two months short of his 38th birthday, Tommy became the oldest player to sign for the Swans, and by the time he left to join Merthyr Tydfil as player coach in March 1991 would create a record as the oldest player to play a league game for the club. Following his last match for the Swans against Southend United on 12th March 1991, at the age of 43 years and 171 days, Tommy's total league appearances stood at 863 from Alloa, Blackpool, Coventry City, Manchester City, Burnley and the Swans, and at the time placed him top of the all time record of appearances in British football. Since then Peter Shilton, Tony Ford and Graeme Armstrong have overtaken Tommy in the record books. Tommy had already made 685 league appearances prior to his being persuaded to join the Swans by his old boss at Burnley, John Bond. Little did he know that by the end of the year, after the Official Receiver had sacked Bond, within days following a reprieve by the High Court, Hutchison would be starting his managerial career with Ron Walton as his assistant at the Vetch Field. Capped by Scotland at U-23 level when with Blackpool against Wales in 1961, Tommy gained all his Full international caps whilst with Coventry City, the first on the 26th September 1974 against Czechoslovakia. Joining Second Division Blackpool in February 1968, Tommy gained a runners up medal following the club's promotion to the First Division in 1970, but after finding himself back in the Second Division twelve months later, signed for First Division Coventry City in October 1972. Making over three hundred league appearances for the Sky Blues, Tommy then joined Manchester City, and after a loan spell in Hong Kong in

February 1982, returned to the Football League to sign for Third Division Burnley. Two seasons later with Burnley relegated to the Fourth Division at the expense of the Swans home draw against Bristol City in the last game of the season, Tommy signed for the Swans. Throughout his career, Tommy had always been a difficult player to shake off the ball, and his fitness levels during his career with the Swans left many players fifteen years younger in the shade, even overcoming a broken leg at one stage during his time at the Vetch Field. An inspiration to a number of younger players at the club at one time or other, Tommy played mostly on the left side of midfield, and was instrumental in kick starting the career of left back Terry Phelan after he had been given a free transfer from Elland Road by Leeds United. Phelan would go on to make an impact, not only in the Premiership, but also gain international honours for the Republic of Ireland. Another youngster who was to step into the position vacated by Phelan, was young Chris Coleman. A first year apprentice with Manchester City, the Swansea born defender had failed to settle at Maine Road, and, after returning to Swansea, had continued his apprenticeship at the Vetch Field with the Swans. For the next couple of seasons he would be nursed along by the evergreen Hutchison on the left side of defence, gaining the tricks of the trade that would eventually see him grace the international stage with Wales, and be the subject of big money transfers to Crystal Palace, Blackburn Rovers and Fulham. Despite the financial problems during the early part of his Vetch Field career, Tommy returned from a spell on the sidelines with a broken leg to make his presence felt in the end of season Play Off Final success against Torquay United in 1988, scored in the Welsh Cup Final defeat of non-league Kidderminster Harriers twelve months later, also playing in both legs of the European Cup Winners Cup tie against Panathinaikos the following season. In May 1987 he played in the Swans side that beat Briton Ferry Athletic in the West Wales Senior Cup Final, and also in 1990 when the Swans beat Llanelli to win the same competition. Shortly after Frank Burrows had replaced Terry Yorath in the Swans managerial hot seat, Tommy left the Vetch Field after making 178 league appearances to join Merthyr as player/assistant manager. He continued to play in the Vauxhall Conference with Merthyr, finally hanging up his boots a couple of months passed his 46th birthday. Two and a half years later he retired from the game to take up a position as PFA Community officer in the Merthyr, Taff/Ely Area. After four years in that position he left the PFA to join up with the FAW of Wales at the Vale of Glamorgan as a coach in their Centres of Excellence and Development centre, a position which had been newly created, to work with all age groups of younger players. At the same time he also had a short spell as manager of the Welsh U-15 age group representative side. A couple of years ago he returned to the professional side of football to join Bristol City at Ashton Gate to work as a Community Officer.

63. HYLTON, LEON

Birthplace: Birmingham, 27/1/1983
Ht: 5ft-9ins, **Wt:** 11st-0lbs
Swans debut: v. Bournemouth (a), 11/2/2003

Swansea City Career Statistics

Season	League	FLC	FAC	FAWP
2002/03	7+1			
2003/04	10+1	1	0+1	2
Total	17+2	1	0+1	2

Career:
Aston Villa (from trainee in 23/2/2000)
Swansea City (loan in 6/2/2003)
Swansea City (signed in May 2003)

Honours: England Yth, U-20–8

Signed for the Swans on an initial month loan on the 6th February 2003, which was later extended until the end of the season, twenty-four hours after playing in the England U-20 side that beat Germany at the Madejski Stadium. Leon had earlier, in December 2002 impressed manager Brian Flynn in a behind closed doors friendly game at Villa's training ground against the Swans. Limited opportunities at Villa Park saw the left sided full back, or central defender join the Swans' squad as a non playing substitute in the side's first away win of the season at Macclesfield two days later after the Germany game. He impressed with his defensive capabilities at left full back, possessing good ball distribution, but an ankle injury sustained at Kidderminster saw him miss a number of games, before he was able to return for the last two games of the season. Given a free transfer by Villa in May after he had returned from France where he had been involved in the England U-20 side in the Toulon Tournament, he later signed a two year contract with the Swans. First choice at left full back at the start of the season at the Vetch Field, he later suffered a groin and ankle injury in September which limited his first team opportunities throughout the season. He made a few attempts at comebacks, but after playing in an FAW Premier Cup tie at Rhyl, suffered a hamstring problem which kept him out of action for the remainder of the season. Failing to regain full fitness, even after undergoing a hernia operation in the early part of season 2004/5, he had his contract paid up on the 14th January 2005 leaving the Vetch Field playing staff. He made his England U-17 debut against France in December 2000, making a further six appearances at that level during season 2001/02. During season 2002/03 he made eight appearances for the England U-20 team.

I

1. ILLINGWORTH, JOHN William

Birthplace: Castleford, 3/9/1904. **Died:** Weymouth, 4/9/1964
Ht: 5ft-7ins, **Wt:** 10st-11lbs
Swans debut: v. Bury (h), 5/10/1935

Swansea Town Career Statistics	
Season	League
1935/36	1
Total	1

Career:
Castleford Town
Tottenham Hotspur (signed in March 1927)
Northfleet (loan as professional in March 1927)
Tottenham Hotsur (signed in May 1929) lge 10
Swansea Town (signed in May 1935)
Barry Town (signed in May 1936)

Right full back who made his only Swans appearance as a replacement for the injured Syd Lawrence at the Vetch Field against Bury in October 1935, in a game which saw the Swans win 4-1, with Tudor Martin scoring all four goals. Illingworth had signed for the Swans in May 1935 from Tottenham Hotspur, after spending a period on loan with the club's nursery side Northfleet in 1927, and had made just ten league appearances for Spurs prior to his joining the Swans, also failing to make any appearances for Spurs in the Second Division against the Swans up to the season when they gained promotion to the First Division in 1933. In May 1936 he was released by the Swans, joining Barry Town.

2. IMRIE, William (BILL) Noble

Birthplace: Buckhaven, Fife, 4/3/1908. **Died:** Windygates, Fife 26/12/1944
Ht: 5ft-11ins, **Wt:** 12st-3lbs
Swans debut: v. Manchester City (a), 27/8/1938

Swansea Town Career Statistics		
Season	League	WC
1938/39	27/1gls	2/2gls
Total	27/1gls	2/2gls

Career:
Kirkcaldy Juniors
East Fife Juniors
Dunnikier Juniors
St. Johnstone (signed in May 1927)
Blackburn Rovers (£4,775 signed in September 1929) lge 165/23gls
Newcastle United (£6,500 signed in March 1934) lge 125/24gls, FAC 3
Swansea Town (£2,500 signed in 1/7/1938)
Swindon Town (£800 signed in July 1939) lge 2

Honours: Scotland Full–2

Former Scottish international wing half, centre half who was signed by the Swans for a record fee at the time of £2,500 from Newcastle United. Gained his first cap for Scotland whilst with St. Johnstone on the 26th May 1929 in Bergen against Norway, playing at right half in a 7-3 victory. A month later, prior to his signing for Blackburn Rovers he gained his second international cap, against Germany, scoring his country's goal in a 1-1 draw in Berlin. An experienced campaigner prior to his arrival at the Vetch Field at the age of 30, he was a long throw specialist, penalty taker, and a fast, accurate passer of the ball. Red headed, a good leader of the team, he was said at the time to 'run the show', but unfortunately results on the field did not match his reputation. Signing for the Swans in July 1938, he made his debut in the opening match of the 1938/39 season at left half back, and surprisingly left the Swans in July 1939 for £800 to Swindon Town. For most of his only season with the Swans he alternated between either half back positions, or at centre half. He scored just the one league goal for the Swans, in a 4-2 home defeat by Coventry City in December 1938. In September he scored for the Swans against Shrewsbury Town, in a Welsh Cup Final replay defeat held over from the previous season. His other goal also came in a Welsh Cup tie, this time against Cardiff City in February 1939, in a 4-1 defeat at the Vetch Field. Prior to signing for St. Johnstone in May 1927, Bill had made his name in junior football in Scotland with Kirkcaldy Juniors, East Fife Juniors, and Dunnikier Juniors. Making regular appearances in Rovers's First Division side, after joining Newcastle United in 1933, he was unable to prevent the club from suffering relegation to the Second Division in his first season with the club. Despite playing at a low point in United's history, he was still a popular personality with the club's supporters. Playing regularly against the Swans over the next four seasons in the Second Division, Imrie scored against the Swans in season 1934/35 and 1937/38. He made a handful of appearances for Swindon Town after leaving the Swans before the League was suspended because of the start of the Second World War. Later he had a butcher's business in Gateshead, but became a victim of the Second World War whilst serving in the RAF.

3. INGRAM, Gerald (GERRY)

Birthplace: Merthyr Tydfil, 28/1/1951
Ht: 5ft-8ins, **Wt:** 11st-4lbs
Swans debut: v. Fulham (a), 22/8/1970

Swansea City Career Statistics		
Season	League	FLC
1970/71	5+1	1
1971/72	13	
1972/73	18+1/1gls	2
Total	36+2/1gls	3

Career:
Swansea City (signed in August 1970)
Merthyr Tydfil (signed in August 1973)
Ton Pentre

Honours: Wales Sch–3

Gerry Ingram made his Swans debut as an amateur whilst still a student at Cardiff College of Education shortly after the start of

the 1970/71 season, signing a two year contract after he had completed his studies. A workmanlike midfielder, he also operated at left full back when needed. His last season at the Vetch Field saw him. start the season at left full back, before reverting to his normal midfield position. Educated at Quakers Yard Grammar School, he made three international appearances as a schoolboy for Wales in the Home International Championships against England, Scotland and Northern Ireland, and signed for Bristol City as a part-timer whilst studying for his 'A' levels. After starting a Physical Education degree at Cardiff College of Education, he also played for the Welsh Colleges, and after being enticed to the Vetch Field by the legendary Harry Griffiths, played initially in the club's reserve side before making his league debut whilst still an amateur. Instead of going into teaching, Gerry signed as a full time professional at the Vetch Field, but after a change of management, and relegation to the Fourth Division, Gerry was released, joining his hometown club, Merthyr Tydfil, managed by John Charles in August 1973. Despite a number of offers to stay in the game as a full time professional, Gerry decided to look at a career outside the full time game, and continue as a part-timer. Instead of going into the teaching profession, he entered the world of computers, combining a career in selling business computers and involving himself in IT, with playing for Merthyr (two spells) and Ton Pentre, finally finished his playing career as player manager with Treharris in the Welsh League in the mid-1980's. Currently, Gerry is still involved in the computer industry, working as Business Unit Executive with IBM, responsible for Europe, Middle East and Africa. His son Richard is a professional with Cardiff City.

4. IRIEKPEN, Ezomo (IZZY)

Birthplace: Upton Park, East London, 14/5/1982
Ht: 6ft-1ins, **Wt:** 12st-4lbs
Swans debut: v. Oxford United (a), 25/8/2003

Swansea City Career Statistics				
Season	League	FAC	LDV	FAWP
2003/04	33+1/1gls	5		
2004/05	29/2gls	2	0+1	2
Total	62+1/3gls	7	0+1	2

Career:
West Ham United (from trainee in 25/5/1999)
Leyton Orient (loan in 22/10/2002) lge 5/1gls, FAC 1, Others 2/1gls
Cambridge United (loan in 28/2/2003) lge 13/1gls
Swansea City (signed in 22/8/2003)

Honours: England Yth, FAYC 1999, FAW Cup Winner–2005

Released in May 2003 from West Ham United, after a two weeks trial period with the Swans at the Vetch Field, Izzy played in a friendly game against Neath FC, and in the first Combination game of the season at Bournemouth, afterwards signing a three month contract on 22nd August 2003 with the Swans. Nigerian background, born in the Upton Park area of East London, he went to Hartley Primary School, then went to Langdon Secondary school, where he played for his school, and also for the county. Signing for West Ham United at an early age, despite interest from Ipswich Town, he also could have followed his youth team manager to Arsenal, but decided against it, and stayed on at West Ham United. Had trials with England schoolboys, and was initially disappointed not to make an appearance. He first met Swans team mate Leon Britton at the age of 14, and when Izzy was 17 he signed his first 'Hammers' contract, also receiving at the time his first England call up for the U-18's side. At the age of sixteen, Izzy was a non-playing substitute for the 'Hammers' Premiership side at Old Trafford. He sustained an injury shortly after signing professional forms, which unfortunately sidelined him for a long time. Season 2002/03 was his first full season after the injury, and he made loan appearances for Leyton Orient and Cambridge United. Disappointed to have been released by West Ham United, he had an offer to sign permanently with Cambridge but decided not to take it, had trials with Oxford United in pre-season, prior to arriving at the Vetch Field. A central defender, preferably right side of defence, he can also play in a defensive midfield position. Towards the end of the 1998/99 season he captained the 'Hammers' Youth side in the FA Youth Cup Final against Coventry City, winning on aggregate 9-0. Following his trial period with the Swans, Izzy initially signed a three month contract, which was later increased to the end of the 2004/05 season. Izzy proved himself to be a good competitor in central defence for the Swans, having good aerial ability, also extremely quick when covering in defence. He scored his first goal for the Swans in the 1-0 away win at Cambridge United in March 2004, but during the second half of the season was forced to miss a number of matches through an ankle injury. Missing most of the first half of the 2004/05 season through ankle and knee injuries, when he was introduced to the first team in mid-December, he kept his place through to the end of the season as the Swans clinched an automatic promotion place and also beat Wrexham to win the FAW Cup.

5. IRWIN, COLIN Thomas

Birthplace: Liverpool, 9/2/1957
Ht: 6ft-1ins, **Wt:** 12st-13½lbs
Swans debut: v. Leeds United (h), 29/8/1981

Career:
Liverpool (from apprentice in December 1974) lge 26+3/3gls
Swansea City (£350,000 signed in 22/8/1981)
Perth Azzurri, Australia

A club record signing in August 1981 of £375,000 from Liverpool, who made a guest appearance on the Swans pre-season tour of Yugoslavia, played against Velez Mostar, and officially signed when the team returned to Swansea.
An influential central defender, he became Toshack's first non-

Swansea City Career Statistics					
Season	League	FLC	FAC	WC	ECWC
1981/82	37	2/1gls	1	4/1gls	
1982/83	8				3
1983/84	3			2	
Total	48	2/1gls	1	6/1gls	3

international six figure transfer signing when he completed his move from Anfield, and was handed the captaincy immediately on his arrival. During the club's inaugural season in the First Division his combination with Rajkovic in central defence was an integral feature of the Swans side that did not leave the top six places of the First Division throughout the season. Despite his lack of inexperience, he had been given his debut by Liverpool against West Bromwich Albion in August 1979 as a replacement for Alan Hansen, scoring his first goal for the club in the next match at Southampton in a 3-2 defeat. His second full season in the Liverpool line-up, saw him have a run of 14 consecutive league appearances in the second half of the season as a replacement for Phil Thompson, and in his last season at Anfield, he made an appearance in the League Cup Final against West Ham United which ended in a 1-1 draw, but did not take part in the replay. A couple of days prior to signing for the Swans, Liverpool had signed Brighton & Hove Albion defender Mark Lawrenson, to add more competition for first team places at Anfield. Playing the first seven league games of his second season at the Vetch Field, Irwin suffered an injury at Villa Park against Aston Villa that was to ultimately end his career as a professional footballer. The club's record signing snapped the patella tendon in his right knee, and even though he returned too play in the Swans' last First Division game before being relegated, his promising career in the game was over. He made a couple of appearances for the Swans in the Second Division, but after Colin Appleton had been appointed manager following the club's relegation to the Third Division, he had decided to call it a day as far as his playing career was concerned in the Football League, and went to Australia to join Perth Azzurri, linking up with former Swans team mates Huw Lake and Tony Guard. After returning to the U.K., he assisted former Liverpool team-mate Phil Neal at Bolton Wanderers on the coaching side for a short time, before returning to Perth, Western Australia, where he became distribution manager for a large wine and spirits wholesaler.

J

1. JACKSON, MICHAEL Douglas

Birthplace: Cheltenham, 26/3/1980
Ht: 5ft-7ins, **Wt:** 10st-10lbs
Swans debut: v. Southend United (h), 19/10/2002

Swansea City Career Statistics		
Season	League	AWS
2002/03	0+1	0+1
Total	0+1	0+1

Career:
Cheltenham Town (from trainee in 1/8/1997) lge 2+7, FLC 0+2, FAC 0+1, Others 1
Weston-super-Mare (loan in 2002)
Swansea City (signed in 1/7/2002)
Bath City (signed in 1/12/2002)
Cirencester Town (loan in December 2002)

Released by Cheltenham Town at the end of the 2001/02 season, he featured in a behind doors end of season trial game at the Vetch Field organised by manager Nick Cusack, and was offered a one year contract a few weeks later. Apart from being named as one of the substitutes during Cusack's reign as manager, his debut for the Swans came under Brian Flynn when he made an appearance at the Vetch Field as a substitute for Leigh Devulgt. Three days later, with the Swans squad decimated with injuries, he made a second substitute appearance, this time in the AWS cup tie at non-league Stevenage Borough when he replaced Damian Lacey. A midfielder capable of going from box to box, he reached a settlement over the remaining term of his contract in mid-November 2002, and left the Vetch Field, linking up with Dr. Martens side Bath City. A few weeks later he was loaned out to Western league side Cirencester Town in a bid to improve his fitness levels. One of a number of players at the time at the Vetch Field who, without no reserve team competition struggled to play in matches to keep in touch. Midway through the 2002/03 season he joined Weston Super Mare, helping them gain promotion as runner-up to Merthyr Tydfil in the Dr. Martens Western Division. In Christmas 2003 he returned to Cirencester Town.

2. JACKSON, Samuel (SAM)

Birthplace: Belfast, JAS, 1900
Ht: 5ft-7ins, **Wt:** 10st-10lbs
Swans debut: v. Millwall (h), 26/3/1921

Swansea Town Career Statistics		
Season	League	FAC
1920/21	5/1gls	
1921/22	1	1
Total	6/1gls	1

Career:
Barnville FC
Cliftonville
Belfast Distillery
Swansea Town (signed in 18/2/1921, professional in 12/5/1921)
Barnsley (signed in August 1922) lge 1
Portadown (signed in 30/9/1925)
Ards (signed in 20/8/1927)
Broadway United (signed in 5/3/1930)

Honours: Northern Ireland Amateur–1, Irish League Rep XI–2

Former Northern Ireland Amateur international left winger who was signed by manager Joe Bradshaw in February 1921 from Belfast Distillery, but did not attend the Vetch Field for training until a couple of weeks later. The outside left made a further three consecutive league appearances after making his Swans debut at the Vetch Field against Millwall in March 1921 as a replacement for Joe Spottiswoode. He scored his first goal for the Swans in his second league game, the first goal in a three nil win at Reading. In May 1921 his form in the club's reserve side had seen him sign professional forms at the Vetch Field. After making a further two league and cup appearances the following season, he was released by the Swans in May 1922, joining Second Division side Barnsley where he made just the one league appearance. His appearance for the Irish Amateur side came against France whilst with Cliftonville in 1921, and his first Irish League Representative appearance came prior to joining the Swans, against the Scottish League, with his second Representative appearance coming after he returned to play in Ireland with Portadown. He later made appearances in Irish Football with Ards and Broadway United, ending his playing career in 1931.

3. JAMES, ANTHONY Ralph

Birthplace: Swansea, 24/2/1960
Ht: 5ft-7ins, **Wt:** 9st-8lbs
Swans debut: v. Northampton Town (h), 3/12/1977

Swansea City Career Statistics				
Season	League	FLC	FAC	WC
1977/78	5+3/1gls		2	1
1978/79	1+1			
1979/80	0+1	0+1		
Total	6+5/1gls	0+1	2	1

Career:
Swansea City (signed from apprentice in December 1977)
Merthyr Tydfil (signed in January 1981)
Haverfordwest County (signed in close season 1983)

Honours: Wales Sch, Abacus Welsh League National Division Champions–1990

A cousin of the legendary Robbie James, Anthony signed professional for the Swans after completing his apprenticeship at the Vetch Field in November 1977, and had been attached to the Swans from the age of twelve. He made his first team debut as substitute for defender Neil Davids against Northampton Town at the Vetch Field in December 1977, also making the starting line-up for the Boxing Day 1977 home game against Torquay United. Later in the season, following the arrival of Toshack as manager, he scored his first goal for the Swans in a 3-0 away win at Southport. A confident, exciting winger, who could also play in midfield, he perhaps did not develop as quickly as what was first expected, although with the club gaining promotion season after season, and the continual influx of players, it was difficult to obtain a place in the Swans side under Toshack with his emphasis on experience as a vehicle to move up the divisions. Midway through season 1980/81 he was released from his contract signing for Merthyr Tydfil. Brought up in the Townhill district of Swansea, Anthony attended Powys Avenue, Townhill, and Bishop Gore Schools, played for Swansea Schoolboys, and was selected to play for a Welsh Schoolboys side in a friendly against Wrexham. A member of Cwm Albion Colts prior to leaving school, during most of the first year of his apprenticeship at the Vetch Field, because of limited reserve team opportunities with the Swans, along with Jeremy Charles he played almost a season for Swansea Senior League First Division side Bishopston FC. In the 1983 close season he signed for Haverfordwest County, regularly finishing in the top five places in the Abacus Welsh League National Division, eventually winning the Championship in season 1989/90. Anthony has since played for Clydach United, Morriston Town, Llanelli and BP Llandarcy, retiring as a player at the end of the 1997/98 season. Since leaving the professional game Anthony

has been involved in the Financial Services Sector, and is currently working for Cattles PLC in Personal and Corporate Finance. Earlier, during a period when he had been relocated with his company to Stevenage, he also made appearances for non-league side Baldock Town.

4. JAMES, David (DAI)

Birthplace: Swansea, 29/9/1917. **Died:** Swansea, 22/12/1981
Ht: 5ft-7ins, **Wt:** 10st-10lbs
Swans debut: v. Bristol City (a), 6/9/1947

Swansea Town Career Statistics	
Season	League
1947/48	12/7gls
Total	12/7gls

Career:
Derby County (trial in February 1933)
Leeds United (signed in September/November 1934) lge 0
Bradford City (signed in 22/5/1935) lge 5
Mossley (signed in July 1937)
Chelsea (signed in April 1938) lge 0
Swansea Town (signed in 13/5/1947)
Haverfordwest (signed in August 1948)

Honours: Wales Sch, London Combination Cup Winner–1947

'Dai' possessed a small stature for the type of centre forward of his day, but was a neat player, had good ball control, and knew the way to goal. Shortly after signing for the Swans, in June 1947 he was a member of the Swans reserve side that beat Arsenal at White Hart Lane to win the London Combination Cup. Despite scoring on his Swans debut at Bristol City in September 1947, and scoring seven goals during his first nine league matches, the manager at the time, Haydn Green, preferred a big targetman like Frank Rawcliffe, the player James replaced to make his debut. Towards the end of the season he returned to first team duty at inside forward. The former Pentrepoeth and Swansea Schoolboy had gained representative honours for Wales at Schoolboy level, had a trial with Derby County in February 1933 prior to signing for First Division side Leeds United from local football, but after failing to make any first team appearances, joined Second Division Bradford City. His Football League debut was made against the Swans on the 5th September 1936 when he replaced Travis in a 4-0 home win over the Swans. Making five league appearances during the club's relegation season of 1936/37, he then signed for non-league side Mossley, before returning to the Football League to sign for First Division Chelsea in April 1938. He failed to make the starting line-up at Stamford Bridge, and when the Football League was resumed after the war, joined his hometown team. During WW2 he made appearances for Chelsea, and the Swans during season 1939/40. Earlier in his career the former schoolboy from Morriston had played for the Midland Athletic Club in Morriston, prior to making appearances for the Swans 'A' team. He scored two goals for Midland Athletic to beat Gordon Villa in the club's first ever match in local league football. He had also been a cricketer of outstanding merit. Released by the Swans in May 1948, in late August he signed for Welsh League side Haverfordwest, captained the side until ill health forced him to retire in 1952. Following relegation to the Second Division of the Welsh League, in July 1954 he was appointed manager of the club.

5. JAMES, GEORGE

Ht: 5ft-7ins, **Wt:** 10st-10lbs
Swans debut: v. Fulham (h) 20/1/1934

Swansea Town Career Statistics	
Season	League
1933/34	4/1gls
Total	4/1gls

Career
Aberaman
Swansea Town (signed in 13/1/1934)
Aberaman (signed in close season 1934)

A centre forward who arrived at the Vetch Field along with team mate Jack Warner from Aberaman in January 1934 on a trial basis, scored in a reserve game at Lovells Athletic on his debut, and two days later made his league debut at the Vetch Field against Fulham as a replacement for the injured Tudor Martin. He made his second league appearance two games later in a 1-0 defeat at Southampton. Towards the end of March 1934 he made his third league appearance for the Swans, scoring his first league goal in a 2-1 home defeat by Preston North End, retaining his place for the next fixture at Lincoln City.
In May 1934 he was released by the Swans rejoining Welsh League side Aberaman. In September 1936 he scored a hat trick for Aberaman against the Swans in a Welsh League game.

6. JAMES, Walter GEORGE

Birthplace: Swansea, 15/6/1924
Ht: 5ft-11ins, **Wt:** 12st-4lbs
Swans debut: v. Luton Town (a), 4/2/1950

Swansea Town Career Statistics		
Season	League	FAC
1949/50	4	1
Total	4	1

Career:
Tawe United
Swansea Town (signed in August 1942)
Newport County (£1,500 signed in July 1950) lge 13/5gls
Milford United (signed in season 1952/53)
Caerau (signed in June 1954)

Honours: London Combination Cup Winner–1950, West Wales Senior Cup Winner–1949

Arriving at the Vetch Field in August 1942 from local Swansea League side Tawe United, he played South West Regional football for the Swans during the Second World War years, and initially joined the Swans playing staff as a centre forward, before being converted to a full back. He made his debut for the Swans as replacement for Jim Feeney at Luton Town in February 1950, and after Feeney had been transferred to Ipswich Town made a further three league appearances at right full back. He also played for the Swans against Arsenal in the Fourth Round of the FA Cup at Highbury, in which the Swans could count themselves unlucky to lose by the odd goal in three. In May 1950 he captained the Swans reserve side that won at Southend United to win the London Combination Cup Final. During WW2 when he was serving his country in the Far East he had built up quite a reputation as goalscoring centre forward. In May 1949 he was captain of the Swans side, scoring two penalties in the 5-1 over Llanelly in the West Wales Senior Cup Final at Stebonheath Park. Prior to his move to Newport County he had scored twenty-three goals for the Swans reserve side from the penalty spot. Mostly a reserve team player at the Vetch Field, he joined Third Division South side Newport County in July 1950, later signing for Welsh League team Milford United. Top goalscorer and captain at Milford United during season 1953/54, in June 1954 he signed for Welsh League side Caerau.

7. JAMES, LEIGHTON

Birthplace: Loughor, 16/2/1953
Ht: 5ft-9ins, **Wt:** 12st-6lbs
Swans debut: v. Charlton Athletic (a), 3/5/1980

Swansea City Career Statistics					
Season	League	FLC	FAC	WC	ELWC
1979/80	0+1/1gls				
1980/81	40/15gls	2/1gls		7/1gls	
1981/82	34+4/9gls	2/1gls	1	7/2gls	2
1982/83	14+5/2gls	2		1	3+2
Total	88+10/27gls	6/2gls	1	15/3gls	5+2

Career:
Burnley (apprentice in October 1968, professional in February 1970) lge 180+1/44gls
Derby County (£300,000 signed in 4/12/1975) lge 67+1/15gls
QPR (£180,000 signed in 27/10/1977) lge 27+1/4gls
Burnley (£165,000 signed in 9/9/1978) lge 76/9gls
Swansea City (£130,000 signed in 1/5/1980)
Sunderland (signed in 13/1/1983) lge 50+2/4gls
Bury (signed in August 1984) lge 46/5gls

Newport County (signed in 14/8/1985) lge 21+7/2gls
Burnley (signed in 21/8/1986) lge 75+4/13gls

Honours: Wales Sch–2, Yth–12, U-23–7, Full–54, Second Division Champions–1972, Welsh Cup Winner 1981, 1982, Anglo Scottish Cup Winner–1978

A former Gowerton, Penyrheol, Swansea Schoolboy and Wales Schoolboy international left winger who joined Burnley on leaving school, serving his apprenticeship at Turf Moor, and graduating to the club's first team for his league debut on the 21st November 1970 against Nottingham Forest in the First Division. He gained the first of seven U-23 caps for Wales against England in 1972, earning his call up to the full international side in Prague against Czechoslovakia in 1971. By the time he joined the Swans for £130,000 just prior to the last league game of the season at Charlton Athletic, he had gained a reputation as a consistent goalscorer from the flanks, and although temperamental, was a class act on his day. Prior to joining the Swans, Leighton had been involved in three six figure transfer deals after leaving Turf Moor for Derby County in December 1975, and in his first full season with Burnley scored ten league goals during the club's Second Division Championship success in 1972. His £300,000 transfer to Derby County in December 1975 created a new record for the club, and by the end of his first season at the Baseball Ground had finished top goalscorer. Following a further transfer to QPR in October 1977, within twelve months he had returned to Turf Moor, with the highlight of his second spell being involved in the two leg defeat of Oldham Athletic in the 1978 Anglo Scottish Cup Final. His Swans debut saw him go on as substitute for Alan Waddle, score the first goal at Charlton Athletic, and the following season become top goalscorer at the Vetch Field with fifteen league goals, as the Swans claimed their place in the First Division. His opening goal at Preston in the final game of the season would go down as one of the most crucial in the history of the club. During that epic season of 1980/81, he scored two hat-tricks in the league, both at the Vetch Field against Derby County, and Bolton Wanderers. Within days of clinching promotion, Leighton played in both legs of the Welsh Cup Final defeat of Hereford United. A successful season with the Swans in the First Division saw him return nine league goals, and also play in his second successive Welsh Cup Final for the Swans, this time against Cardiff City. Midway through the 1982/83 season, with results on the field disappointing, and financial matters coming to a head, he was given a free transfer by the Swans, after being available for transfer a couple of months earlier at £50,000, joining First Division Sunderland. After appearances for Bury and Newport County, he returned to Burnley for the third time prior to the start of the 1986/87 season, playing what he thought was his final games for the club. He was released at the end of the season, but returned to Turf Moor as youth team coach, finding himself back in the first team after a couple of games, and playing in defence. Towards the end of the 1987/88 season he made an entry at Wembley as substitute for McGrory in the Sherpa Van Trophy Final defeat by Wolverhampton Wanderers, and he played his final game for Burnley against Scarborough in May 1989, at the age of 36. At Newport County he had been involved in coaching and management, and continued when he had retired from playing, initially in England, where he was coach at Bradford City in February 1990, and for a short time as caretaker manager of Bradford City following the sacking of John Docherty. One of his games in charge saw the Swans beat City 6-4 at Valley Parade in November 1991. Linking up with Gainsborough Trinity as manager, he then became a coach at Haslingden FC, in the 1991 close season, Morecambe manager from January to June 1994, manager at Darwen and Netherfield, Ilkeston Town manager from 1995 to February 1996, and Accrington Stanley manager to February 1998. Returning home to South Wales, he took over as manager of Welsh League side Llanelli in July 1998. During a successful period with the Reds, including playing in one West Wales Senior Cup tie in season 1998/99, he was controversially sacked as manager at the end of the 1999/2000 season after he

had guided the club into the League of Wales. Combining his role as match analyst with commercial radio station Real Radio and coaching with local Welsh League side Garden Village, he returned to Stebonheath Park with Llanelli midway through the 2002/03 season, but with little financial assistance was unable to prevent the club from relegation to the Welsh League, and was later relieved of his position as manager at Stebonheath Park. He has since then continued his media work, involved himself with coaching, and in the summer of 2004 was appointed Director of the Academy at League of Wales side Port Talbot Town, a joint venture with local school, St. Josephs. A talented cricketer, earlier in his career whilst with Burnley, he made appearances for both Lowerhouse and Burnley in the Lancashire League.

8. JAMES, Robert (ROBBIE) Mark

Birthplace: Swansea 23/3/1957. **Died:** Llanelli 18/2/1998
Ht: 5ft-10ins, **Wt:** 13st-0lbs
Swans debut: v. Charlton Athletic (h), 28/4/1973

Swansea City Career Statistics							
Season	League	FLC	FAC	WC	FRT	ECWC	P/Offs
1972/73	1						
1973/74	28/2gls	1					
1974/75	41+1/8gls		1+1	4/1gls			
1975/76	44+1/8gls	1	1	3/1gls			
1976/77	46/16gls	5+1/2gls	1	2			
1977/78	41+1/16gls	2	5/1gls	1			
1978/79	43/15gls	5/4gls	4/2gls	2/4gls			
1979/80	29/6gls	2	5/1gls	2/1gls			
1980/81	30+5/8gls	2	0+1	6/3gls			
1981/82	42/14gls	1	1	8/5gls	2		
1982/83	40/9gls	4	1	7/3gls	5		
1987/88	19/3gls						4
1988/89	38+3/9gls	2	3	7/2gls	2		
1989/90	25+4/4gls	2	0+1		1	2/1gls	
Total	467+15/118gls	27+1/6gls	22+3/4gls	42/20gls	3	9/1gls	4

Career:
Swansea City (signed from apprentice in April 1974)
Stoke City (£160,000 signed in 20/7/1983) lge 48/6gls, FLC 7/1gls,
QPR (£100,000 signed in 23/10/1984) lge 78+9/5gls, FLC 9, FAC 5/1gls
Leicester City (£70,000 signed in 24/6/1987) lge 21+2, FLC 4, Others 1

Swansea City (£35,000 signed in 16/1/1988)
Bradford City (P/Exchange in 23/8/1990) lge 89/6gls,
   FLC 9/1gls, FAC 4, Others 6/1gls
Cardiff City (signed in 14/8/1992) lge 51/2gls, FLC 4/1gls,
   FAC 1, AGT 2, ECWC 2/1gls
Merthyr Tydfil (P/Manager in October 1993) Conf 16/3gls

Honours: Wales Sch, Yth–11, U-21–3, Full–47, Welsh Cup
Winner–1981, 1982, 1983, 1989, 1993, Fourth Division Play Off
Winner–1988, Third Division Champions–1993, West Wales
Senior Cup Winner–1975

Robbie James was a tremendously talented midfielder, or striker,
who gave the Swans great service from the Fourth to the First
Division, and in later years in the Third and Fourth Divisions,
possessing the pace to break on the right flank, a high workrate
in midfield, as well as an eye for goalscoring opportunities.
During the latter part of his career he also showed his defensive
qualities when switched to a full back role. After being given his
league debut by manager Harry Gregg in the last game of the
1972/73 season at the Vetch Field against Charlton Athletic on
the right wing, Robbie became the youngest player in the
Football League to reach 100, 200 and 300 matches, and gained
his first International cap against Malta on the 25th October 1978
at the Racecourse, Wrexham, after earlier being capped at youth
and U-21 level by Wales. During seasons 1973/74 and 1974/75
he played for the Wales youth team in a mini-World Cup
Tournament. In May 1975 he was included in the Swans side
that beat Briton Ferry Athletic in the West Wales Senior Cup
Final. Following the Swans relegation to the Second Division in
1983, he was sold to Stoke City for £160,000, and after further
moves to QPR and Leicester City, rejoined the Swans for £35,000
in January 1988, playing a leading role in the club's successful
promotion via the end of season Play Off matches against
Rotherham United and Torquay United. The following season
he gained his fourth Welsh Cup Winner's Medal with the Swans
following the win over non-league side Kidderminster Harriers.
His previous three winners medals had been gained against
Hereford United (1981), Cardiff City (1982), and Wrexham
(1983). Against Hereford United he scored in both legs of the
final, also scoring in the final against Kidderminster. During his
spell at Loftus Road with QPR, he played in the Milk Cup Final
losing side at Wembley against Oxford United, where he was up
against his former playing colleague at the Vetch Field, Jeremy
Charles. Following a disagreement with the Swans chairman, in
August 1990 he joined Bradford City in an exchange deal
involving the return to the Vetch Field of Welsh International
midfielder Alan Davies. Hardly missing a match for the next
three seasons, and playing mainly in a right back role, he also
picked up the Player of the Year Awards at both Bradford City,
and his last professional club, Cardiff City in each season. At
Ninian Park he gained a Third Division Championship medal in
1993, also gaining his fifth Welsh Cup Winner's Medal following
the win over Rhyl. Ironically, as a schoolboy playing for Bishop
Vaughan school in Swansea, after being selected to play for
Swansea Schoolboys he signed schoolboy forms for Cardiff City,
but after leaving school worked initially as an electrical
apprentice at Potters in Swansea, before Swansea City manager
Harry Gregg signed him on amateur terms. In November 1974
Arsenal recognised his talent and signed him on a month's loan
from the Vetch Field, but unfortunately, he returned home
within two days with homesickness, and without playing a
game for the Gunners. After a short spell as player manager at
Merthyr Tydfil in the Vauxhall Conference after leaving Ninian
Park, Robbie initially joined the Reds at Stebonheath Park,
Llanelli as a player at the start of the 1995-6 season in the League
of Wales, also, making appearances for Barry Town. At the end
of the season, Robbie joined Dr. Martens Southern Division side
Weston-super-Mare for the 1996-7 campaign, but was enticed
back to Stebonheath Park for the start of season 1997/98 as
player manager. At that time, the Reds were still in the top
division of the Welsh League, and were in the process of
recovering from the financial problems that had contributed so
much to their fall from the League of Wales, and the 1997/98

season was proving to be one of gradual re-building and
recruitment, with the team undoubtedly improving as a playing
force. On the field, Robbie made a number of appearances,
although his policy seemed to be to play emerging players in the
team where ever possible. Perhaps his biggest playing
contribution during this season was in central defence where he
was still a difficult player to get past. However, tragedy struck
on February 18th 1998, when Robbie, playing for Llanelli at
Stebonheath in a midweek Welsh League match against
Porthcawl Town, collapsed and died on the pitch at the age
of 40.

9. JENKINS, LEE David

Birthplace: Pontypool, 28/6/1979
Ht: 5ft-9ins, **Wt:** 11st-0lbs
Swans debut: v. Hereford United (h), 10/9/1996

	Swansea City Career Statistics				
Season	League	FLC	FAC	AWS/LDV	FAWP
1996/97	21+2/2gls		1	1	
1997/98	14+7			1	2+1
1998/99	6+6	0+1	0+1	2	7
1999/2000	7+9			2	6
2000/01	29+10	1	1	2	3
2001/02	14+1/1gls	1			
2002/03	26+6	1	1	1	1
2003/04	8+3			0+1	
Total	125+44/3gls	3+1	3+1	9+1	19+1

Career:
Swansea City (from trainee in 20/12/1996)
Kidderminster Harriers (signed in 12/12/2003) lge 36+3, FLC 1,
   FAC 0+1, Others 0+1
Redditch United (signed by 20/5/2005)

Honours: Wales Sch, Yth, U-21–9, Third Division
Champions–2000

Lee made his Swans debut whilst still a trainee alongside player
manager Jan Molby, in a 4-0 win over Hereford United, scoring
the Swans fourth goal. Some fine performances from the young
midfielder, saw him cement a regular place in the first team,
until he shattered his cheekbone in a clash of heads in an AWS
cup tie at the Vetch Field against Bristol City. That was to be the
first of many injuries that would hamper his progress over the
seasons. One of the most versatile of midfielders at the Vetch
Field, capable of playing in either a centre, or a left or right
sided midfield position, before reverting to either a right full
back, or right wing back role, and even at left full back. After his

debut goal against Hereford United, Lee scored his second league goal for the club a few weeks later in a 1-0 win at Scarborough. There was to be a break of five seasons before he scored his next goal, the first goal in a 2-0 win at Kidderminster. A Wales schoolboy international prior to signing for the Swans, Lee also made appearances for Wales at youth level prior to receiving his first U-21 cap, as a substitute for Lee Jarman on the 19th August 1976 in Turkey. His last two seasons at the Vetch Field saw Lee play predominantly as a right sided wing back, with occasional appearances in central midfield. Too versatile for his own good at times, Lee suffered a left knee medial ligament injury in October 2001, and after making a comeback encountered further problems which sidelined him for the remainder of the season. The 2002/03 season saw Lee become of the side's most consistent players, usually from a right wing back role as the Swans fought a successful battle to retain their league status. Signing a one year contract in June 2003, despite making a number of appearances during the first three months of the season, an ankle ligament injury saw him miss a number of matches, losing his place which he failed to regain. Shortly before the Christmas period, he signed an eighteen month contract, linking up a second time with Jan Molby, this time at Kidderminster Harriers. Following relegation to the Conference in May 2005, within a few weeks of being released by Harriers he signed for Conference North side Redditch United.

10. JENKINS, Stephen (STEVE) Robert

Birthplace: Merthyr, 16/7/1972
Ht: 5ft-10ins, **Wt:** 10st-10lbs
Swans debut: v. Cambridge United (a), 11/5/1991

Season	League	FLC	FAC	WC	AGT/ AWS	ECWC	P/Offs
Swansea City Career Statistics							
1990/91	0+1						
1991/92	31+3	4	1+1	2	2	2	
1992/93	29+4	0+1	5	0+1	3		2
1993/94	38+2/1gls	2		5+1	7		
1994/95	42	4	4	4	5		
1995/96	15	2		1	1		
Total	155+10/1gls	12+1	10+1	11+2	18	2	2

Career:
Swansea City (from trainee in 1/7/1990)
Huddersfield Town (£275,000 signed in 3/11/1995) lge 257+1/4gls, FLC 18, FAC 14, Others 5
Birmingham City (loan in 15/12/2000) lge 3, FLC 1

Cardiff City (signed in 5/2/2003) lge 4
Notts. County (signed in 7/8/2003) lge 17, FLC 3, FAC 2, Others 1
Peterborough United (signed in 5/1/2004) lge 11+3/1gls, Others 1
Swindon Town (loan in 29/10/2004) lge 4, FAC 1
Swindon Town (signed in 29/11/2004) lge 20, FAC 1/1gls

Honours: Wales Yth, U-21–2, Full–16, AutoGlass Trophy Winner–1994, West Wales Senior Cup Winner–1990, 1991, 1994

Given a full professional contract by Swans manager Terry Yorath in July 1990, the former Swans trainee was told midway through the 1990/91 season by manager Terry Yorath that he was going to be given a free transfer, without having made a first team appearance for the Swans. In late March 1991, Yorath was replaced as manager by Frank Burrows, and during the last league game of the season at Cambridge United, he was given his league debut as a midfielder. In May 1990 and 1991 he was included in the Swans side that beat Llanelli in consecutive West Wales Senior Cup Finals, and also in 1994 when the Swans beat Ammanford Town in the same final. Throughout his career up to this point he had always played as a midfielder for the Swans, but after being given a new contract for the 1991/92 season, he switched to a full back role, and within a couple of games had cemented a place in the Swans first team at either right, or left full back. His first full season saw him make European appearances against Monaco in both the home and away legs. Prior to joining the Swans as a trainee, Steve attended Vaynor and Penderyn Schools, and gained a Mid-Glamorgan soccer cap as a centre forward. From Georgetown Boys Club he signed for the Swans in mid 1988 as a YTS trainee, gaining his first youth cap for Wales during his first year as a trainee. He made his first appearance for Wales at U-21 level on the 13th October 1992 as a substitute for Hughes, and his first Full appearance for Wales came against Germany at Cardiff on the 11th October 1995 in a European Qualifying match. Within a couple of weeks the steady defender had joined Huddersfield Town for a tribunal fixed fee of £275,000, with the Swans looking to receive 25% of any future transfer involving the player. Unfortunately his move to Cardiff City in the second half of season 2002/03 was on an initial loan transfer with the move being made permanent on a free transfer because of Huddersfield Town having financial difficulties, and being unable to afford his wages. After establishing himself at full back in season 1991/92, Steve would create a good name for himself defensively in the Swans rearguard, playing against WBA in the 1993 end of season Play Offs, the 1994 AutoGlass Trophy winning side at Wembley, and in the 1994/95 season, reaching the fourth round of the FA Cup, the Southern Area semi-final stage of the AWS competition, and reaching the semi-final stage of the Welsh Cup. His move to Huddersfield Town saw him become a regular in their side as they just failed to get themselves into the Division One Play Off places, also lose to Wimbledon in the fifth round of the FA Cup. Following relegation to the Second Division in 2001, the following season they lost on aggregate to Brentford in the Division Two Play Off Semi-Finals, and his consistent form for the club saw him given the captaincy during his spell with the 'Terriers'. Financial problems off the pitch at the McAlpine Stadium during the 2002/03 season saw Steve join Cardiff City on a free transfer, and re-inforce the Bluebirds squad for the end of season Play Off matches, which saw the club regain their place in the First Division. Signing for Second Division side Notts. County in August 2003 on a monthly contract, midway through the season he joined Peterborough United on a free transfer, later signing for Swindon Town in October 2004 on an initial loan transfer with the move being made permanent a month later.

11. JENNINGS, WALTER

Birthplace: Grimsby, 20/10/1897. **Died:** Grimsby, 15/11/1970
Ht: 5ft-10ins, **Wt:** 10st-7lbs
Swans debut: v. Swindon Town (a), 7/5/1921

Swansea Town Career Statistics		
Season	League	WC
1920/21	1	1
1921/22	2	
Total	3	1

Career:
Welhome Old Boys
Grimsby Town (signed in July 1919) lge 2, FAC 1
Swansea Town (signed in September 1920)
Southend United (signed in 10/5/1922) lge 15
Barnsley (signed in September 1923)
Boston Town (signed in July 1924)
Blackpool (signed in May 1925) lge 4

Goalkeeper Walter Jennings made just three league appearances for the Swans, his debut coming in the last match of the 1920/21 season, replacing Crumley at Swindon Town, in a 0-0 draw, with his other two league appearances the following season when he was in contention with both Crumley and Denoon for a place in the Swans starting line-up. He was released in May 1922 to join fellow Third Division South side Southend United, played in both league games against the Swans during season 1922/23, but after playing in the first fourteen matches of the season was replaced in goal by Joe Hall following a 2-5 away defeat at Northampton Town, playing just one more game for the club later in the season. After a trial period with Barnsley in September 1923, Jennings later signed for Lincolnshire League side Boston Town in August 1924, only to return to the Football League to make appearances for Second Division side Blackpool in May 1925. Walter had earlier in his career joined his hometown club Grimsby Town at the age of 20, after impressing in a pre-season trial game. Playing for Wellhome School and Grimsby Boys as a schoolboy, after joining the Army in December 1916, he returned after the War to join Wellhome Old Boys in the Grimsby League for the 1918/19 season, before being offered a professional contract with the 'Mariners' in July 1919. He made his league career with Grimsby Town on the 1st January 1920 in a 1-0 defeat at home to Coventry City in the Second Division, with his other two appearances also being home defeats. His lack of physical presence was reported to be a handicap at senior level, mainly being a reserve team player with all his clubs.

12. JOHN, DENNIS Carl

Birthplace: Swansea, 27/1/1935
Ht: 5ft-9ins, **Wt:** 12st-0lbs
Swans debut: v. Brighton & Hove Albion (a), 22/11/1958

Swansea Town Career Statistics		
Season	League	WC
1958/59	4	2
Total	4	2

Career:
Plymouth Argyle (from juniors in February 1952) lge 3
Swansea Town (signed in August 1958)
Scunthorpe United (signed in 17/8/1959) lge 88

Millwall (signed in June 1962) lge 101+5/6gls
Highlands Park, Johannesburg S.A. (signed in 1966)
Corinthians, S.A. (signed in 1968)

Honours: Wales Sch, Devon & Cornwall Yth

Although born in Swansea, he stayed only a couple of months in the town before his family moved back to Mardy in the Rhondda. His early football was played for Ferndale Senior School, then for Ferndale District, and for the Welsh Schoolboys, playing with goalkeeper Johnny King, and Griff Phillpott who also signed for the Swans. Despite offers from Cardiff City, Chelsea, Fulham and Tottenham Hotspur to sign at the age of 15, he wanted to join the Swans, but with no offer forthcoming continued playing for Mardy youth side. He was invited for a trial to Plymouth Argyle with a number of youngsters from the youth team, and after playing just one half for the Argyle 'A' side, was taken off at half time and told that he was being offered a groundstaff position at Home Park, the club's first apprentice. At the age of 17 he signed his first professional contract, and stayed at Home Park until the age of 22, before Ronnie Burgess signed him for the Swans, initially on a two month trial basis. Captain of Argyle's reserve side, he captained the club's U-23 team at the age of 17, also captaining the Devon & Cornwall youth side. Signing for the Swans in August 1958, he made his Swans debut at right full back at Brighton instead of Dai Thomas, retained his place for the next game against Grimsby Town at the Vetch Field, and following the return of Thomas, had to wait another seven matches before playing in two more league game against Lincoln City and Sunderland respectively. In between these two matches, he made two appearances for the Swans at full back in the Welsh Cup against Newport County and Bangor City. He spent just the one season at the Vetch Field, and after playing against Scunthorpe United for the Swans, was signed by United manager Frank Soo. A hard tackling full back, and good on the ball, Denis had four seasons with United, just missing out on promotion to the First Division on goal average to Sunderland, and after Soo had left the club to take up a coaching appointment in Sweden, Dennis signed for Millwall, in a transfer deal involving Alan Anderson. Four seasons at the Den saw Denis play in almost every position, including one FA Cup tie against Fulham at left wing. With an offer to follow his Millwall manager Billy Gray to Watford, the opportunity came along for him to join Wally Barnes in South Africa, and play for top Johannesburg side Highlands Park FC. At the age of 31, the offer doubled his wages, included a lump sum, and also, was able to take his family out with him. During his time at Millwall, his singing career also took off, with the opportunity to make records with EMI. Deciding to take up the playing offer in South Africa, his singing career flourished, making records with Highveldt record company, and also singing for South Africa in the Olympiad of Song in Athens. Winning League and Cup honours with Highlands Park, he finished his playing career in South Africa with Corinthians, and then went to live in Australia, where he was a construction supervisor in Queensland, had an RCA recording contract during his 19 years in the country, gained his football coaching qualifications with the Australian Football Association in Sydney, before returning to live in his hometown Mardy. It was at Millwall that he first started coaching, when he was involved with Forest Hill School in London, a couple of days a week.

13. JOHN, Dilwyn (DIL)

Birthplace: Tonypandy, 3/6/1944
Ht: 5ft-10ins, **Wt:** 10st-6lbs
Swans debut: v. Colchester United (h), 27/3/1967

Career:
Cardiff City (juniors in 1959, professional in June 1961) lge 88, ECWC 4

Swansea Town (£2,000 signed in 16/3/1967)
Merthyr Tydfil (signed in July 1970)
Caerau Athletic

Swansea Town/City Career Statistics				
Season	League	FLC	FAC	WC
1966/67	9			
1967/68	35	1	4	2
1968/69	34	1	4	7
1969/70	2	1		
Total	80	3	8	9

Honours: Wales Amateur–3, U-23–1, Welsh League Challenge Cup Winner–1960, Welsh League First Division Champions–1977

Signed by manager Billy Lucas in March 1967 from Cardiff City, where he had earlier made eighty-seven league appearances in the Second Division after making his league debut in a 3-2 win at Stamford Bridge against Chelsea in season 1962/63. Born in Tonypandy, Dil moved to live in Cardiff at the age of seven and attended Radnor Road School, played for the school and Cardiff Schoolboys, and only a broken leg suffered before the Welsh Schoolboys trial prevented him from attaining International Schoolboy Honours. He initially started an apprenticeship as a bricklayer after leaving school, but after two years joined Cardiff City as a professional. His form was such as a youngster coming through the ranks at Ninian Park that he was expected to take over from Gary Sprake in the full Welsh side, and at the age of sixteen, in May 1960 he gained a Welsh League Challenge Cup medal playing for the 'Bluebirds', and in 1965 made an appearance for the Welsh U-23 side against Scotland. Replacing George Heyes in the Swans goal, he kept a clean sheet on his debut in a 1-0 win against Colchester United. Not particularly tall, and having a slight build for a goalkeeper, he did possess good agility and positional play, and safe ball handling. Contesting the goalkeeper's number one jersey with George Heyes during his first three season at the Vetch Field, following the signing of Tony Millington prior to the start of the 1969/70 season, his opportunities became limited. During the club's successful promotion winning season of 1969/70, he made just two league appearances, both early in the season. Highlight of his Swans career was being part of the side that took the mighty Arsenal so close in the FA Cup fourth round, which attracted a record attendance of 32,796 in February 1968, and the following season playing in the second leg of the Welsh Cup Final against his old club, Cardiff City. In mid-April 1969 he was called up as reserve for the Welsh international side that was playing East Germany in Dresden after Gary Sprake had withdrawn through injury, with Tony Millington having been called up earlier to replace Sprake. At the time he was out of favour at the Vetch Field, with George Heyes being the current holder of the number one jersey. He was released in May 1970, joining Southern League side Merthyr Tydfil, remaining at Penydarren

Park for almost three seasons, including a short spell as caretaker manager prior to the appointment of John Charles as manager of Merthyr Tydfil. Dil was involved as trainer to Cardiff local league side Whitchurch Hospital after leaving Merthyr, but he then linked up with former Swans' team mate Mike Hayes at Caerau Athletic, won the Welsh League Second Division Championship at the end of the 1976/77 season, playing as a centre forward. During his time at the Vetch Field, Dil made a number of appearances for the Swans' reserve side in this position. A keen snooker player from an early age, in 1972 he was a semi-finalist in the Welsh Championship, 1977 was Welsh Snooker Scene Trophy Runner-Up, 1985 Welsh Championship Runner-Up, and in 1985 the IBSF World Snooker Championship Runner-Up. As a schoolboy he represented Wales in Baseball, playing at senior level for the EverOpen Eye Club, and since taking up golf, has won the County Senior Championship, playing out of Llanishen Golf Club.
Since coming out of the full time professional game, Dil reverted to the building industry as a self employed building contractor, and has recently taken semi-retirement after undergoing heart surgery. During his playing career with the Swans, he became one of the few Swans' players who can claim to have played for the club when it was named Swansea Town, and then Swansea City.

14. JOHN, William Ronald (ROY)

Birthplace: Briton Ferry, 29/1/1911. **Died:** Port Talbot 12/7/1973
Ht: 5ft-11½ins, **Wt:** 11st-10lbs
Swans debut: v. Plymouth Argyle (h), 29/1/1938

Swansea Town Career Statistics			
Season	League	FAC	WC
1937/38	17		4
1938/39	23	1	1
Total	40	1	5

Career:
Briton Ferry Athletic
Swansea Town (signed in 1927)
Manchester United (trial in 1928) lge 0
Walsall (signed in 9/5/1928) lge 88
Stoke City (signed in April 1932) lge 71
Preston North End (signed in June 1934) lge 0
Sheffield United (£1,250 signed in 24/12/1934) lge 29
Manchester United (£600 signed in June 1936) lge 15
Newport County (signed in 16/3/1937) lge 10
Swansea Town (signed in 1/7/1937)

Honours: Wales Full–14, Second Division Champions–1933, Welsh League XI

Goalkeeper who initially joined the playing staff at the Vetch Field from local side Briton Ferry Athletic as a full back in 1927, who, after being released played for Cwmtillery United, and had trials with Middlesbrough (September 1927), Manchester United (1928), Cardiff City, Ebbw Vale, signed as an amateur with Newport County, and after joining Walsall was converted into a goalkeeper. Earlier in his career he had played for Neath Road Council School, Briton Ferry schoolboys, prior to signing for the senior Ferry side. The former Swans 'A' team player appeared in a Charity game for Walsall in early May 1928, and accepted professional terms with the club after the game. At the Vetch Field he had been restricted to 'A' team appearances, and occasional call ups to the reserve side. He made his Walsall debut at left full back in a 5-1 defeat at Fulham on the 6th October 1928, making a further three appearances that season. During the 1929/30 season he was tried out in goal for the reserves at Fellows Park, playing in goal for the first team towards the end of the season. He gained his first Welsh international cap whilst at Walsall, making his international debut against Ireland on the 22nd April 1931. In June 1931 the chairman of Briton Ferry Athletic FC presented him with a silver cigarette case, holder and matchbox on behalf of the club's members as a mark of esteem. Later in his career he would make international appearances for Wales with Stoke City, Preston North End, Sheffield United, and the Swans. According to Football League records he signed for Sheffield United on the 24th December, yet made his debut on the 22nd, missing just one game through until the end of the season. After three seasons with Walsall in the Third Division South, the keeper joined Second Division Stoke City in 1931, playing twice against the Swans during his club's Championship winning season of 1932/33. He failed to make an appearance following his move to Preston North End, and in December 1934 he joined Second Division Sheffield United, playing against the Swans in mid-January 1935 in a 1-1 draw at Bramall Lane. Further transfers saw him make appearances for Manchester United before returning to South Wales to sign for Third Division South side Newport County in mid-March 1937. Joining the Swans for a fee of £200 in July 1937 the keeper made two appearances for Wales during his time at the Vetch Field, against England in October 1938 at Cardiff, and in November 1938 in Edinburgh against Scotland, where he captained his country in a 3-2 defeat, and also played later in a war-time international game for Wales against England in 1940, although no caps were awarded. After arriving back at the Vetch Field, Roy had to wait until midway through the 1937/38 season before making his debut for the Swans, and despite starting the 1938/39 season as first choice, competed throughout the season with Moore for first team duty. On the 23rd April 1938 he played for a Welsh League XI in Brussels against Diables Rouges, along with team mates Harris and Beresford. When the Football League was suspended during season 1939/40, Roy played occasionally during the season in the Regional South West competition with the Swans, and also guested for Burnley (1941/42), Rochdale (1941/42), Blackburn Rovers (August 1942), Bolton Wanderers (October 1942), Southport (1942/43), Blackpool (October 1943) and Derby County (January 1944). A spritely goalkeeper, unorthodox for his day, the advent of the Second World War brought an end to his Football League career, although it was extended through making guest appearances for various clubs during the war period, and by March 1948 he had returned to his first club, Briton Ferry Athletic. In 1939 he became manager of a Swansea Public House, which was later destroyed by enemy action in 1941, and shortly after he was called up to the RAF. In July 1948 he entered business on his own account as licensee of the Royal Exchange Hotel in Aberavon, continuing for a number of years up until 1960. In the summer months he also played cricket for Briton Ferry Town CC.

15. JOHNROSE, Leonard (LENNY)

Birthplace: Preston, 29/11/1969
Ht: 5ft-10ins, **Wt:** 12st-6lbs
Swans debut: v. Lincoln City (h), 25/1/2003

Swansea City Career Statistics			
Season	League	FLC	FAC
2002/03	15/3gls		
2003/04	21+4	1	3
Total	36+4/3gls	1	3

Career:
Blackburn Rovers (ass. schoolboy in January 1984, trainee in July 1986, professional in 16/6/1988) lge 20+2/11gls, FLC 2+1/1gls, FAC 0+3, Others 2
Preston North End (loan in 21/1/1992) lge 1+2/1gls
Hartlepool (£50,000 signed in 28/2/1992) lge 59+7/11gls, FLC 5+1/4gls, FAC 5/1gls, Others 5
Bury (signed in 7/12/1993) lge 181+7/19gls, FLC 16+2/2gls, FAC 9/1gls, Others 9/1gls
Burnley (£225,000 signed in 12/2/1999) lge 46+26/4gls, FLC 2, FAC 1+2/1gls, Others 1
Bury (signed in 21/10/2002) lge 5+1, Others 2
Swansea City (signed in 25/1/2003) lge 36+4/3gls, FLC 1, FAC 3
Burnley (signed in 25/3/2004) lge 4+3

Honours: Second Division Champions–1997

Former Preston schoolboys player along with his brother Francis who started his career at Blackburn Rovers as a striker, making his league debut against Ipswich Town in the Second Division on the 11th April 1989, scoring Rovers's first goal. During his stay at Ewood Park he did not figure in either of the club's end of season Play Off matches, but in later years would gain promotion honours with both Bury and Burnley. After a couple of seasons with Hartlepool United in the Third Division, Lenny joined Bury in December 1993, and although he did not figure in the club's Third Division Play Off Final defeat by Chesterfield, made thirty-four league appearances the following season when the club gained promotion from the Third Division. Within twelve months, the 'Shakers' won the Second Division Championship, with Lenny missing just three league matches during the season. A regular inclusion in the 'Shakers' midfield over the next two seasons in the First Division, Lenny was then sold to Burnley in February 1999 for a fee of £225,000, and in his first full season at Turf Moor gained a Second Division Runners-Up Medal. Lenny returned to Gigg Lane for a second time in October 2002 on a three month contract, but when the club were unable to offer him an extension to his contract because of financial restraints at the club, he was released, and eventually signed for Brian Flynn at the Vetch

Field, initially on a non-contract basis. His strength and experience in midfield for the Swans was a critical factor in the club retaining it's League status, with Johnrose scoring one of the goals in the final game of the season against Hull City which secured Third Division football at least for another season at the Vetch Field. In July 2003 he signed a one year contract with the Swans, and opened the season in an unfamiliar central defensive role against his old club Bury. He struggled with a hamstring injury shortly after the start of the season, but after returning in his familiar midfield position, became his usual influential self during the club's exciting FA Cup run, even taking on the role of skipper in December, a decision well worthy of the experienced campaigner. With talk of his contract being renewed at the end of the season, following the sacking of manager Brian Flynn, Lenny had his contract paid up within a couple of days of Flynn leaving the Vetch Field, and within a week had rejoined his former club, Burnley. The 2004/05 season saw Lenny retire from the game, take on a coaching role at Leeds United, and also utilised as a summariser on matchdays by BBC Radio Lancashire.

16. JOHNSON, GEORGE Henry

Birthplace: Darnall, OND, 1903
Ht: 5ft-7ins, **Wt:** 10st-8lbs
Swans debut: v. Plymouth Argyle (a), 14/4/1923

Swansea Town Career Statistics	
Season	League
1922/23	1
Total	1

Career:
Darnall Old Boys
Swansea Town (trial in December, professional in 18/1/1923)
Southend United (signed in June 1923) lge 62/13gls, FAC 5/1gls
Newport County (signed in May 1926) lge 38/9gls
Coventry City (signed in August 1927) lge 14/2gls

Honours: West Wales Senior Cup Winner–1923

Initially joined the Swans in mid December on a trial basis, the outside right signed professional in mid-January 1923 from Sheffield junior football. He made just the one appearance for the Swans, on the right wing, as a replacement for Billy Hole in a 2-0 defeat at Plymouth Argyle in April 1923, with just three games to go before the end of the season. In May 1923 he was included in the Swans reserve side that beat Llanelly to win the West Wales Senior Cup. Released at the end of the season he joined Third Division South side Southend United, playing against the Swans over the next two seasons. Created a name for himself on the right wing with the 'Shrimpers' with his goal scoring, but prior to the start of the 1926/27 season returned to South Wales to sign for Newport County in the Third Division South League. Twelve months later he joined fellow Third Division South side Coventry City, finishing his league career with Torquay United.

17. JOHNSON, Jeffrey (JEFF) David

Birthplace: Cardiff, 26/11/1953
Ht: 5ft-8ins, **Wt:** 10st-0lbs
Swans debut: v. Scunthorpe United (a), 12/8/1972

Career:
Manchester City (from apprentice in December 1970) lge 4+2

Swansea City (loan signing in 19/7/1972)
Crystal Palace (£12,000 after initial loan in 13/12/1973)
   lge 82+5/4gls
Sheffield Wednesday (signed in July 1976) lge 175+5/6gls
Newport County (£60,000 signed in August 1981) lge 34/2gls
Gillingham (£8,000 signed in September 1982) lge 85+3/4gls
Port Vale (signed in July 1985) lge 10/1gls, FLC 4, FRT 2
Barrow (signed in close season 1986)

Swansea City Career Statistics		
Season	League	FLC
1972/73	37+1/5gls	2
Total	37+1/5gls	2

Honours: Wales Sch–5, Yth–6

Former Welsh international schoolboy player who joined Manchester City as an apprentice straight from school, had played for local junior side Clifton Athletic, turned professional in November 1970, and was signed by manager Roy Bentley on a season loan transfer along with City team mates Phil Henson and Keith Hanvey just prior to the start of the 1972/73 season. He made his First Division debut for City shortly after signing professional in December 1970 against Everton on the 3rd April 1971 as substitute for Tony Towers, making his first start three matches later at Newcastle United. An attacking right sided midfielder, with good skill, and turn of pace, he made his Swans debut in the first match of the 1972/73 season, and was consistently included in the Swans starting line-up, even after a change of management when Harry Gregg took over from Bentley in November 1972. He scored his first goal for the Swans at Shrewsbury in September 1972, and despite being offered a contract at the end of the season by the Swans, decided to return to Maine Road. Returning to Maine Road at the end of the season, he went on to become an influential midfielder during his career with Crystal Palace, Sheffield Wednesday (promotion from the Third Division at the end of the 1979/80 season), Newport County, Gillingham and Port Vale. He joined Palace on an initial loan in December 1973, making the transfer permanent just over a month later. Relegated to the Third Division at the end of his first season at Selhurst Park, he became a regular first team player over the next two seasons as the club finished in fifth place on both occasions, before being allowed to join fellow Third Division side Sheffield Wednesday on a free transfer in July 1976. His third season at Hillsborough saw him involved in the club's successful promotion, finishing in third place, and a return to the Second Division. Joining Newport County for a fee of £60,000 in August 1981, he remained only one season at Somerton Park, joining Third Division Gillingham just over twelve months later for a fee in the region of £8,000. After three seasons in the Third Division with Gillingham, with the club finishing the 1984/85 season in fourth place, he joined Fourth Division Port Vale, but after playing in the first ten league games, broke his foot in October 1985, failed to make another appearance for the club, and was released, joining Multipart League side Barrow in the 1986 close season. Vale were promoted from the Fourth Division in his only season at the club.

18. JOHNSON, Michael (MIKE) George

Birthplace: Swansea, 13/10/1941. **Died:** Newport, Gwent, October 1991
Ht: 5ft-10ins, **Wt:** 11st-4lbs
Swans debut: v. Scunthorpe United (h), 12/3/1960

Swansea Town Career Statistics					
Season	League	FLC	FAC	WC	ECWC
1959/60	7				
1960/61	6				
1961/62	24	2	1	2	2
1962/63	30	1	2	3	
1963/64	40	2	7	2	
1964/65	35/1gls	2/1gls	4	3	
1965/66	23	1	1	3	
Total	165/1gls	8/1gls	15	13	2

Career:
Swansea Town (signed in October 1958)
Worcester City (signed in August 1966)
South Wales Switchgear (signed in November 1966)
Pembroke Borough (signed in August 1968)
Haverfordwest County (signed in August 1973)

Honours: Wales Sch, Yth, U-23–2, Full–1, Welsh Cup Winner–1966, West Wales Senior Cup Winner–1960, 1961, 1965, Football Combination Second Division Champions–1961

Welsh Schoolboy and youth international defender, who was tipped at an early age to do well in the game. Brought up in the Sandfields area of Swansea, Mike attended St. Helens School and the Technical School prior to joining the groundstaff at the Vetch Field after leaving school. Skipper of the Swansea Schoolboys side, he signed professional forms in 1958 at the age of seventeen, making his league debut at the Vetch Field against Scunthorpe United in March 1960 at right half instead of Roy Saunders. In May 1960 he was included in the Swans side that won the West Wales Senior Cup Final, also in 1961 and in 1965. By the end of season 1960/61 he had made regular appearances in the Swans reserve side that won the Football Combination

Second Division Championship. The 1961/62 season saw him emerge as a regular in the Swans first team line-up, also being included in the first Welsh side to play in an European competition for club sides, the European Cup Winner's Cup, against East German side Motor Jena. He gained his first U-23 cap for Wales in 1963 against Scotland, winning his second cap the following season against England. Initially a reserve to Mel Nurse earlier in his career, he gained a regular place in the Swans side following Nurse's transfer to Middlesbrough shortly after the start of the 1962/63 season. The following season saw him skipper the side to the FA Cup semi-final, playing in all the cup ties leading up to the historic game against Preston North End. On the 11th April 1964 he gained his Full cap for Wales against Northern Ireland at the Vetch Field as a replacement for Terry Hennessey. The combination of Mike England and Hennessey at the heart of the Welsh defence was probably one of the reasons why Johnson did not feature on more than one occasion for his country. Included at right half in the 3-2 defeat, was Swans' inside forward Jimmy McLaughlin, and a certain George Best, who was making his international debut for Northern Ireland. Possessing a commanding presence in the centre of the defence, he also had the ability to turn defence into attack. Despite the euphoria over the club's run in the FA Cup in season 1963/64, the following season saw the club relegated to the Third Division, with Johnson scoring his one and only league goal for the Swans, in a 4-0 revenge win over Preston North End at the Vetch Field. His last season with the Swans saw him make an appearance in the 1966 Welsh Cup Final replay against Chester, before he was released in May 1966. Signing for non-league Worcester City in 1966, he failed to settle at the club, and after scoring one goal from seventeen appearances joined Welsh League side South Wales Switchgear. He returned to West Wales to sign for Pembroke Borough in August 1968, later joining rivals Haverfordwest. From 1974 to 1979, when he retired from playing, he was player manager of Haverfordwest. He then managed Welsh League Premier Division side Afan Lido for one season (1979-80) before his job as a Safety Officer with the Welsh Water Authority saw him relocated to Chepstow, and linking up with Caldicot Town in 1985. He spent five years as club football manager before giving up management in 1990. Under his guidance the club progressed from the Gwent County League into the National Division of the Abacus League, winning the Division Two Championship and being Division One Runners-Up. His professionalism, disciplined standards and personal commitment rubbed off on all those players with whom he was involved with at the club. He was still employed by the Water Authority until his death in October 1991.

19. JONES, ALAN Michael

Birthplace: Townhill, Swansea, 6/10/1945
Ht: 6ft-0ins, **Wt:** 12st-10lbs
Swans debut: v. Bolton Wanderers (h), 31/10/1964

Swansea Town Career Statistics					
Season	League	FLC	FAC	WC	ECWC
1964/65	6	2			
1965/66	26/3gls	1		2/1gls	
1966/67	23/3gls	2	2	1	2
1967/68	6				
Total	61/6gls	5	2	3/1gls	2

Career:
Swansea Town (amateur signed in December 1960, apprentice in October 1961, professional in 18/10/1963)
Hereford United (signed in January 1968) Total Apps 362+1/24gls (F/Lge 52+1/2gls)

Southport (signed in July 1974) lge 49/2gls
Los Angeles Aztecs (signed in April 1975)
Ammanford Town
Haverfordwest

Honours: Wales Sch, U-23–1, Welsh Cup Winner–1966, West Wales Senior Cup Winner–1965

Brought up in the Townhill district of Swansea, Alan attended Townhill Infants, Powys Avenue and Dynevor Grammar Schools, played for his school teams, Swansea Schoolboys, and was also capped at Schoolboy level for Wales. After playing junior football with Swansea Boys Club, St. Josephs and the Swans 'A' side, he arrived at the Vetch Field as an apprentice on leaving school, making his first team debut as a replacement for Mike Johnson against Bolton Wanderers in October 1964. The following season saw him start the season as centre half, and towards the end of the term played in the first leg of the Welsh Cup Final against Chester. In May 1965 he was included in the Swans side that beat Llanelli in the West Wales Senior Cup Final. A strong, rugged defender, with good aerial ability, he scored his first league goal for the Swans against Brentford during season 1965/66, scoring again two games later in a 7-2 win over York City. The following season saw him make appearances for the Swans in both European Cup Winners Cup ties against Slavia Sofia in central defence alongside Brian Purcell. In 1967 he gained international recognition with his selection for the Wales U-23 side that played England. With the side regularly scoring over eighty league goals during seasons 1965/66, and 1967/68, it was the defence that was to be the club's downfall at the end of the 1967/68 season, suffering relegation to the Fourth Division, conceding more goals than the team were able to score. He became one of manager John Charles' first signings for Hereford United, making his debut against Barnet in the Southern League on the 17th January 1968. The 1971/72 season saw the club not only gain election to the Football League, at the expense of Barrow, but also to win acclaim by beating Newcastle United in a replay at Edgar Street to reach the fourth round of the FA Cup competition, losing to First Division side West Ham United in a replay at Upton Park, and also win the Giant Killers Cup. Two years later the centre back scored the winning goal in a revenge Fourth Round replay success over the Hammers at Edgar Street. Also, the same season had seen the club draw with Barnet over two legs in the Southern League Cup Final, and finish in second place behind Chelmsford in the Southern Premier League. Alan played in Hereford's first Football League game and had two league seasons with the Bulls, playing a full-part in the promotion-winning side of 1972-3, and later having the 'distinction' of being the first Hereford player to be sent off in a Football League match, at Southport the club he joined after being released by Hereford in the summer of 1974. A regular inclusion in Southport's league side, he made further league appearances before he went on loan to Los Angeles Aztecs in April 1975 for four months. Released in October 1975 by Southport, he returned to the Swansea area, finishing his playing career with Welsh League sides Ammanford Town and then Haverfordwest.

Since leaving Southport, he has been employed as a van salesman, a process operator at BP Chemicals at Baglan Bay, a process operator with Sirte Oil Company in Libya, and is currently employed as a prison officer at HM Prison in Swansea.

20. JONES, BARRIE Spencer

Birthplace: Swansea, 10/10/1941
Ht: 5ft-7ins, **Wt:** 11st-2lbs
Swans debut: v. Portsmouth (a), 12/9/1959

Swansea Town Career Statistics					
Season	League	FLC	FAC	WC	ECWC
1959/60	15/3gls		3/1gls	1	
1960/61	27/5gls			5/2gls	
1961/62	40/5gls	2	1	2/2gls	2
1962/63	39/2gls	1/1gls	1	4/4gls	
1963/64	39/8gls	2	6	2	
1964/65	6				
Total	166/23gls	5/1gls	11/1gls	14/8gls	2

Career:
Swansea Town (joined groundstaff in 1957, professional in 25/4/1959)
Plymouth Argyle (£45,000 signed in 11/9/1964) lge 98+1/9gls
Cardiff City (£25,000 signed in March 1967) lge 107/18gls, ECWC 12+1/2gls
Yeovil Town (signed in October 1971)
Worcester City (signed in July 1972)
Merthyr Tydfil (signed in 1973)

Honours: Wales Sch, Yth–3, U-23–8, Full–15, Welsh Cup Winner–1961, 1967, 1968, 1969, West Wales Senior Cup Winner–1960, 1961, 1962

Swansea Schoolboy and Welsh international schoolboy winger who signed amateur forms along with Mike Johnson in the summer of 1957, signing as a professional two years later in April 1959, despite the efforts of a number of clubs to entice him away from the Vetch Field. During season 1958/59 he played in three Youth Internationals for Wales, and also appeared in one of the amateur trials for Wales. Initially on the groundstaff at the Vetch Field, he developed into a pacy winger, could play on either flank, and was capable of delivering accurate crosses from the flanks. At the end of his first season he played in the Swans side that beat Llanelly to win the West Wales Senior Cup, also playing in successful finals in 1961 and in 1962. Possessing good ball control, his £45,000 transfer to Plymouth Argyle in

September 1964 would prove to be a record transfer fee for any player leaving a Welsh club at the time. After making his league debut at Portsmouth, he scored his first league goal against Bristol City in a 2-2 away draw at Ashton Gate in March 1960, scoring a further two goals against Bristol City in the return league fixture in the last home game of the season. He gained his first Wales–23 cap in 1961 against England, going on to make a further seven international appearances for the U-23 side. Initially replacing the injured Lennie Allchurch during his first season in the game, he then alternated on the left flank for the second half of the season with Graham 'Flicka' Williams. Following Allchurch's transfer to Sheffield United in March 1961, he was regularly used by the Swans on the right wing. Being a member of the Swans side that beat Bangor City at the end of the 1960/61 season to win the Welsh Cup Final, the following season saw him play in both 'away' legs of the European Cup Winners Cup ties against the East German side Motor Jena. Scoring on a consistent basis from the flanks, in season 1962/63 he scored his first hat-trick for the Swans, in a Welsh Cup fifth round tie against Caerau. That same season saw him gain his first full international cap for Wales, playing against Scotland at Ninian Park on the 20th October 1962. Of his fifteen international appearances, seven were gained whilst with the Swans. Following his inclusion at U-23 level by Wales, his form was continually being monitored by clubs, and it came as no surprise when he moved to Plymouth Argyle in September 1964, despite a number of previous offers being rejected by the Swans Board of Directors. Staying at Home Park for less than three seasons, he returned to South Wales in March 1967, to join Cardiff City for £25,000. With the Bluebirds pushing hard for First Division status under manager Jimmy Scoular, the added bonus of playing in European competition on a regular basis, by virtue of winning the Welsh Cup on an annual basis, was also another attraction at the time to join the club. He won three consecutive Welsh Cup Final Winners medals with the 'Bluebirds' in 1967, 1968 and 1969, and within twelve months of arriving at Ninian Park, he played in the semi-finals of the European Cup Winners Cup competition, with only a goalkeeping error by the Bluebirds keeper, which resulted in a 2-3 defeat against Hamburg, preventing the club from reaching the final against AC Milan. In 1969 he suffered a double fracture of the leg, putting him out of action for eleven months, and following another setback in training, he decided to call it a day, and retire from first class football. Playing on the non-league circuit with Yeovil Town, Worcester City and then Merthyr Tydfil, he was also able to combine his playing with a coaching role with the Welsh FA, before moving away from football altogether to concentrate his efforts on running a squash centre in Swansea. Currently involved in coaching sport at school level, he still enjoys playing for his village pub side Newton in charity matches, and attempting to lower his golf handicap at Pennard Golf Club.

21. JONES, Brinley Roy (BRYN)

Birthplace: Swansea, 20/5/1931. **Died:** Camden, London, 5/10/1990.
Ht: 5ft-6ins, **Wt:** 11st-2lbs
Swans debut: v. Leeds United (a), 13th December 1952

Swansea Town Career Statistics

Season	League	FAC	WC
1952/53	11/2gls		1
1953/54	8	1	1
1954/55	2		
1955/56	38/1gls	1	3
1956/57	36	1	5
1957/58	26/1gls		1
Total	121/4gls	3	11

Career:
Swansea Town (signed in September 1951)
Newport County (£2,600 signed in 12/6/1958) lge 71/11gls
Bournemouth (signed in February 1960) lge 118/5gls
Northampton Town (£7,000 signed in October 1963) lge 7
Watford (player exchange signed in November 1963)
    lge 90+1/1gls, FLC 5, FAC 3
Chelmsford City (signed in October 1966)
Folkestone (player manager until December 1967)

Honours: Football Combination Second Division Champions–1955, West Wales Senior Cup Winner–1954, 1955, 1956, 1957

The older brother of Cliff Jones, Brin was the son of Ivor Jones, and nephew of Bryn Jones, and played all his football for the Swans at either inside forward, wing half, or at left full back. Making his name with the Swansea schoolboy side, he joined the Vetch Field staff as a professional in September 1951, making his Swans' debut as a replacement at inside right for Des Palmer at Bury in October 1952, and it was against the same club that he scored his first league goal, this time at the Vetch Field in March 1953. A tough, and accurate tackler, following the appointment of Ronnie Burgess as manager, he was given the opportunity to stake a regular claim in the Swans' first team line-up, usually in the left half position. A sound league professional who played his games with a neatness, which reflected a good football brain, something not unusual if you looked at his pedigree. He was a member of the Swans side that won the West Wales Senior Cup Finals in 1954, 1955, 1956 and 1957. Season 1954/55 saw him make regular appearances in the Swans' reserve side that won the Football Combination Second Division Championship. In February 1956 he played at Leeds United in a side that included three sets of brothers on the field for both clubs, the Len and Ivor Allchurch's, Cliff and Brin Jones, and Mel and John Charles. His last two seasons with the Swans saw him play in two consecutive Welsh Cup Final defeats against Cardiff City and Wrexham respectively. Playing at left full back in his last season at the Vetch Field, he was allowed to sign for Newport County in June 1958, and by the time he returned to the Vetch Field in a Watford shirt in January 1966 for a Third Division League game, was close to making 300 league appearances since leaving for Somerton Park. He made over one hundred league appearances for Bournemouth, joined Northampton Town for a £7,000 fee in October 1973, but within a month had signed for Watford, in a player, plus cash deal involving R.H. Brown. He later went on to captain Watford during his spell at Vicarage Road. Finishing his career in non-league with firstly Chelmsford City, and then as player manager at Folkestone, he retired in December 1967, and became a sports teacher at Holloway Boys Comprehensive School until illness forced his retirement and he died in October 1990.

22. JONES, Clifford (CLIFF) William

Birthplace: Swansea, 7/2/1935
Ht: 5ft-7ins, **Wt:** 10st-6lbs
Swans debut: v. Bury (h), 18/10/1952

Swansea Town Career Statistics			
Season	League	FAC	WC
1952/53	3/1gls		1
1953/54	24/4gls	3	1
1954/55	41/11gls	4/1gls	3
1955/56	41/11gls		4/1gls
1956/57	32/9gls	1	6/3gls
1957/58	27/12gls	1	1/1gls
Total	168/48gls	9/1gls	16/5gls

Career:
Swansea Town (signed in May 1952)
Tottenham Hotspur (£35,000 signed in February 1958)
  lge 314+4/135gls
Fulham (£5,000 signed in October 1968) lge 23+2/2gls, FLC 1
Kings Lynn (signed in July 1970)
Bedford Town (signed in January 1971)
Wealdstone (signed in July 1971, player coach in 1973)
Cambridge City
Wingate

Honours: Wales Sch, Yth, U-23–1, Full–59, Football League
Rep XI, First Division Champions–1961, FA Cup Winners–1961,
1962, 1967, ECWC Winners–1963, London FA XI, Army XI, Great
Britain Army Cadets, English Schools Shield Winner–1950,
West Wales Senior Cup Winner–1955, 1956, 1957

Son of Welsh international Ivor Jones, uncle to Bryn Jones, the
former Wolverhampton Wanderers, Arsenal and Wales
international, and brother to Bryn, who he played alongside for
a number of seasons with the Swans. Originally an inside
forward when he made his league debut for the Swans against
Bury in October 1952, he developed into a lightning quick
winger with an eye for goal. His pace and bravery made him
one of the most feared wingers of his time, and he was
recognised at his peak as the greatest left winger in world
football. Graduating from the Swansea schoolboys side, which
he captained in the 1949/50 season, beating Manchester Boys in
the Final of the English Schools Shield, he gained honours at
international level as a schoolboy, youth, U-23, and full levels
for his country. In season 1950/51 he represented the Great
Britain Army Cadet Force at Wembley, and for a time after
leaving school continued to work shiftwork as a sheet metal
worker, as well as playing league football. He gained his first
Full cap whilst on the staff at the Vetch Field with the Swans in

Vienna against Austria on the 9th May 1954, replacing Clarke on
the left wing, going on to make a further fifteen appearances for
Wales before joining Spurs. He scored his first goal for the
Swans against Leeds United in only his third league game.
Midway through his second season in the first team at the Vetch
Field he switched from an inside forward role to left wing,
replacing Harry Griffiths, and over the next four seasons would
return double figures for goals scored on three occasions, and
score his first league hat-trick, against Bristol Rovers in
December 1957 at the Vetch Field. In 1955, 1956 and 1957 he
played in consecutive West Wales Senior Cup Final successes.
In February 1958 he was transferred to Tottenham Hotspur for a
then record fee for a winger of £35,000, and within a couple of
weeks of his arriving at White Hart Lane he had been selected to
play for an Army XI against Scottish side Hibernians on the 10th
February, picked to play in an Army team against his French
counterparts for the Kentish Cup, and on the 5th March 1958
selected to play for a London XI in the first leg of the Inter Cities
Fairs Cup competition against Barcelona. It was at White Hart
Lane that he gained his only U-23 cap in April 1958 at Wrexham
against England. Cliff broke his leg soon after joining Spurs, but
came back in tremendous fashion in the great double winning
side of 1960/61, the FA Cup winning side twelve months later,
and also winning the European Cup Winners Cup in Rotterdam,
beating Atletico Madrid 5-1. On the 12th October 1960 he was
included in a Football League Representative side that played
an Irish league Representative side at Ewood Park, Blackburn.
The 1962/63 season also saw him win a First Division runners
up medal when Spurs finished the season behind Everton.
The 1967 FA Cup Final saw Cliff as a non-playing substitute, but
he still qualified for a winner's medal. By the time he left White
Hart Lane in October 1969 to join Fulham, Cliff had scored a
remarkable 135 league goals from 318 appearances for Spurs, a
strike rate of 2.3 per game. Leaving Craven Cottage to sign for
non-league side Kings Lyn in July 1970, in later years he played
for Bedford Town, Wealdstone, Cambridge City and Wingate as
player coach, retiring in 1977. After leaving football he ran a
butcher's shop, was a coach in a Sports Centre in North
London, later becoming involved with coaching in schools in
London.

23. JONES, DAVID

Birthplace: Swansea, 3/3/1935
Ht: 5ft-11½ins, **Wt:** 11st-1lbs
Swans debut: v. Sheffield United (a), 1/1/1957

Swansea Town Career Statistics			
Season	League	FAC	WC
1956/57	2	1	
1957/58	1		1
Total	3	1	1

Career:
Swansea Town (signed in December 1955)
Yeovil Town (signed in July 1958) Total apps 362+1/1gls

Honours: Southern League Premier Division Champions–1964,
Southern League Cup Winner–1961

A former corporal in the REME before signing for the Swans in
December 1955, the goalkeeper made three consecutive
appearances for the Swans when given his opportunity during
season 1956/57, during a season which saw the Swans also use
Ken Evans and Johnny King as goalkeepers. Making his debut
as a replacement for King who had suffered a knee injury, in the
2-2 draw at Bramall Lane against Sheffield United, he played at
Molineux against Wolverhampton Wanderers four days later,

conceding five goals in a 3-5 FA Cup defeat, and conceded a further five goals at the Vetch Field against Fulham seven days later in a 4-5 defeat for the Swans. Signed by non-league Yeovil Town manager Jimmy Baldwin after being released by the Swans in July 1958, he helped them win the Southern League Cup in season 1960/61, and reach the FA Cup third round in 1963/64, playing 362 games while at Huish before being released in May 1967. Against Romford on the 23rd April 1962, having suffered an injury earlier in the game, and been replaced in goal, he continued for the rest of the match in an outfield position, scoring a goal for Yeovil Town. During season 1963/64 he played fifty-six league and cup games in a season which saw the club win the Southern League Premier Division Championship. Nicknamed 'Milkbottle' at Yeovil because of his all white kit, he was forced to retire from the game at the end of the 1966/67 season through injury.

24. JONES, William ERNEST (ERNIE) Arthur

Birthplace: Swansea, 12/11/1920 **Died:** Bolton, November 2002
Ht: 5ft-11ins, **Wt:** 11st-10lbs
Swans debut: v. West Bromwich Albion (h), 31/8/1946

Swansea Town Career Statistics		
Season	*League*	*FAC*
1946/47	37/3gls	2/1gls
Total	37/3gls	2/1gls

Career:
Swansea Town (amateur signed in August 1937)
Bolton Wanderers (amateur signed in August 1938)
Swansea Town (signed in October 1943)
Tottenham Hotspur (£7,000 signed in 30/5/1947) lge 56/14gls
Southampton (signed in May 1949) lge 44/4gls
Bristol City (£4,875 signed as player coach in November 1951) lge 50/7gls
Rhyl (as manager in December 1954)

Honours: Wales Full–4

Swansea schoolboy player who joined Bolton Wanderers in 1938, and was nicknamed 'Alphabet' at Bolton because of the number of initials in his name. An old fashioned style right, or left sided winger, who possessed pace, and a lovely dip of the shoulder he progressed through Cwmbwrla Juniors and Manselton Schools football, and along with Jack Roberts, they were brought up in an area of Swansea, Alice Street, Cwmbwrla, which was also the birthplace of the Charles brothers, John and Mel. He led the Swansea Schoolboys forward line in consecutive English Schools Shield Finals in 1934 and 1935 against Manchester Boys, and after signing as an amateur for the Swans

in August 1937, was not retained twelve months later. He was immediately signed by Bolton Wanderer after a short trial, linking up with former schoolmate Roberts. During WW2 he played for the Swans in season 1944/45 in Regional Football, League West, and also played in 37 matches of the 'Victory' season, 1945/46. He also made guest appearances for Bury and Chester in season 1940/41. When the Football League was resumed in 1946, he started the season on the right wing for the Swans in the first match of the new season against West Bromwich Albion, and three games later scored his first league goal for the club in a 3-1 win over Nottingham Forest at the Vetch Field. On the 19th October 1946 he gained his first Welsh cap, in a 3-1 win over Scotland at Wrexham, retaining his place a month later at Maine Road, Manchester against England, losing 0-3. During the 1946/47 season he was 'kidnapped' by students of Swansea University during Rag Week, and held to ransom for £50. The Swans manager Haydn Green refused too pay the ransom, and eventually Jones was released in time for the next Swans game. With the Swans being relegated at the end of the season to the Third Division South, he was transferred in June 1947 to Second Division side Tottenham Hotspur for a fee of £7,000, gaining a further two international caps during his time at White Hart Lane. After two seasons at White Hart Lane with Spurs he joined Second Division side Southampton in May 1949 in an exchange deal which included full back Alf Ramsey, plus a small cash fee paid by Spurs to Southampton. Joining Bristol City in November 1951 as player coach, he later took over as manager of Rhyl in December 1954. Resigning his position as manager at Rhyl in August 1955, he remained at the club for a short while to oversee the installation of floodlights at the request of the club's directors, later joining Poole Town in January 1956 before taking up a coaching appointment at the Dell with Southampton. Working as an Engineer for Hawker Siddeley, he was also a member of the Innovators and Inventors Association, and after returning to the Bolton area, he later became chairman of Horwich RMI in 1961. As a schoolboy, Ernie was a prominent member of the Highbury Cricket Team in the Swansea Sunday League.

25. JONES, FRED

Birthplace: Pontypool, 26/8/1909. **Died:** Chelmsford, August 1934
Ht: 5ft-10ins, **Wt:** 10st-11lbs
Swans debut: v. Plymouth Argyle (a), 4/2/1933

Swansea Town Career Statistics		
Season	*League*	*WC*
1932/33	4	
1933/34		1
Total	4	1

Career:
Aberaman (signed in 1931)
Swansea Town (signed in 18/7/1932)
Notts. County (signed in July 1934) lge 1
Millwall (signed in December 1934)
Folkestone (signed in September 1936)
Ipswich Town (£150+£100 signed in February 1938)

Centre forward who was a regular member of the Swans Football Combination and Welsh League side, and who made his debut as a replacement for influenza victim Tudor Martin at Plymouth Argyle in February 1933. A prolific goalscorer, he was sought after by a number of clubs prior to his signing for the Swans. Primarily a centre forward, he also made appearances for the Swans when needed at inside forward and as a right winger during his first season at the Vetch Field. His second season with the Swans saw him make just the one appearance in a Welsh Cup defeat at Chester, and he was released at the end of the season joining Notts. County. Former Swans reserve team inside forward Maldwyn Jones followed him shortly after to County. Played rugby initially, then signed for the Swans from Aberaman, after making a name for himself with Pontnewydd. At the time of his signing for the Swans, Sheffield Wednesday, Bristol City and Birmingham were interested in his signature. Making just the one league appearance for County, after failing to make an appearance with Millwall he joined non-league Folkestone in September 1936, before linking up with then non-league side Ipswich Town in February 1938. Following the club's election to the Football League Third Division South in 1938, Jones scored the club's first ever league goal in a 4-2 win over Southend United in 27/8/1938, also scoring a second goal in the club's first Football League game. During WW2 he made guest appearances for Watford and Fulham in season 1944/45. Later in his career he became manager of non-league side Marconi FC.

26. JONES, GARY Roy

Birthplace: Birkenhead, 3/6/1977
Ht: 5ft-10ins, **Wt:** 12st-0lbs
Swans debut: v. Reading (a), CCC-1, 12/8/1997

Swansea City Career Statistics			
Season	League	FLC	FAWP
1997/98	3+5	0+1	5
Total	3+5	0+1	5

Career:
Caernarfon Town
Swansea City (signed in 11/7/1997)
Rochdale (loan in 15/1/1998, signed in 22/2/1998)
   lge 123+17/22gls, FLC 4+1, FAC 6+3, Others 7+2/3gls

Barnsley (£175,000 signed in 30/11/2001) lge 56+2, FLC 1
Rochdale (signed in 12/11/2003) lge 10/2gls, FAC 1
Rochdale (signed in 13/2/2004) lge 55/10gls, FLC 1, FAC 4,
   Others 1

Signed by Swans manager Jan Molby after impressing in a trial spell in July 1997 from League of Wales side Caernarfon Town. He made his first team debut as a substitute for trialist Dave Puttnam in a first round, Coca Cola Cup tie at Reading in August 1997. A non-stop runner in midfield, who also likes to get forward, he initially was a regular inclusion in the Swans first team squad, but after Molby was replaced by Micky Adams, and then Alan Cork, his opportunities became less and less, prompting a loan transfer to Rochdale in January 1998. After scoring his first league goal in his fourth game for Rochdale, his transfer was made permanent in 22/2/1998 on a free transfer. Becoming a regular under Rochdale boss Steve Parkin, in three seasons at Spotland he developed into an all action midfielder who possessed the ability to get forward in support, and also score vital goals from outside the penalty area. In late November 2001 he became one of Steve Parkin's first signings after taking over as manager at First Division Barnsley, joining him at Oakwell for a fee of £175,000, and, after making his First Division debut with a win over Sheffield Wednesday, by the end of the season his new club had been relegated to the Second Division, with Gary playing in twenty-five consecutive league games. Despite a season of struggle on and off the field at Oakwell, Gary made thirty-one league appearances during his second season for Barnsley, and after manager Parkin had been sacked, and re-instated as manager at his former club, Rochdale, rejoined the 'Dale' on an initial loan basis in November 2003, which was made permanent three months later.

27. JONES, IDWAL Gwyn

Birthplace: Rhondda, 3/8/1924. **Died:** Bridgend, July 1997
Swans debut: v. Manchester City (a), 19/10/1946

Swansea Town Career Statistics	
Season	League
1946/47	4
Total	4

Career:
Ton Pentre
Swansea Town (professional signed in 12/10/1946)
Ton Pentre (signed in close season 1947)
Caerau (by January 1950)

In what was his first season playing in the Welsh League for Ton Pentre, he had earlier in the season impressed when playing against the Swans' Welsh League side. Along with Ton Pentre team-mate O. Davies, and Gwynfi's E. Morris, Idwal gave a good account of himself during a trial period when played in the Swans' Combination team in late September 1946. Signing professional in October 1946, within a week he had made his debut as a replacement for Ernie Jones, who was playing for Wales against Scotland at Wrexham on the same day. Possessing good speed, an accurate crosser of the ball, he also had the ability to take his opponent on. He kept his place for the next two matches, but was then replaced by Jones on the right wing. Later in the season he made his last appearance for the Swans as a right half back at Birmingham City, before being released at the end of the season, returning to Ton Pentre. In what had been his first season in Welsh League football, the young right winger was working in the pits before his debut against Manchester City. In January 1950 the right winger played for Caerau against the Swans in a Welsh Cup tie.

28. JONES, IVOR

Birthplace: Merthyr, 31/7/1899. **Died:** Swansea, 24/11/1974
Ht: 5ft-6ins, **Wt:** 10st-10lbs
Swans debut: v. Southend United (a), 29/11/1919, Sth. Lge

Swansea Town Career Statistics			
Season	League	FAC	WC
1920/21	36/7gls	2	
1921/22	29/7gls	7/3gls	2/1gls
Total	65/14gls	9/3gls	2/1gls

Career:
Merthyr Town (signed in April 1915)
Armed Forces, serving in France
Caerphilly Town (signed in season 1918/19)
Swansea Town (£50 signed in 21/11/1919)
West Bromwich Albion (£2,500 signed in 25/3/1922) lge 63/9gls
Swansea Town (signed in May 1926)
Aberystwyth (signed as player-coach in August 1927)
Aldershot (signed in June 1928)
Thames Association (signed in 28/11/1928)
Eastside (signed in February 1930)
Aberavon Harlequins (signed in 22/3/1934)
Aberystwyth (signed as coach in September 1933

Honours: Wales Full–10, Southern League Representative XI, Welsh League Representative XI

Impressed the Swans management during a game for Caerphilly Town against the Swans reserves, which led to him signing for the Swans on the 21st November 1919 for a fee of £50, with the Swans a Southern League First Division side, playing his first game for the Swans a couple of days later against Porth. The father of Swans players Cliff and Brin, his wife had the surname Messer, a well known Swansea footballing family from the Southern League days. The former Merthyr Schoolboy had played for Merthyr Town at the age of sixteen, volunteered for the Army in 1917, returned to sign for Caerphilly Town prior to being signed by the Swans. Signed by manager Joe Bradshaw, he played as an inside forward, usually alongside Billy Hole, with the pair developing an understanding that was to see them both play in the Welsh international side together. In April 1920 he was included in a Southern League Welsh Clubs Representative side to play a Southern League English Clubs Representative side at the Vetch Field, and later in the month was invited to play for a 'Billy' Wedlake XI against the Players Union. His first league appearance for the Swans came in the club's first ever Football League match, against Portsmouth in August 1920. In the next game, the club's first ever Football League game at the Vetch Field, Jones scored one of the Swans goals in a 2-1 win over Watford. Although at times his team mates were frustrated at his tendency to take on too much

himself, he was a wonderful ball player who could use the ball well. Ivor gained his first Welsh international cap against Ireland on the 14th February 1920, before he had played a full season with the Swans, and in April 1921 at the Vetch Field partnered Billy Hole on the right side of the Welsh attack against Ireland. On the 15th January 1920 he was included in a Welsh League Representative XI that played a South Wales & Monmouthshire Representative XI at Mid-Rhondda in an Amateur International trial match, and in late September 1921 he made a second appearance for the Welsh League Representative side, this time against the Southern League XI at Aberdare. Capped on six occasions whilst at the Vetch Field with the Swans, Ivor gained a further four caps at the Hawthorns with Albion after his transfer. He was transferred to Albion in March 1922 for a fee of £2,500, which was a Swans record at the time. At the Hawthorns with First Division West Bromwich Albion, Ivor made a good impression in his four full seasons with the club, which included a runners up medal from the 1924/25 season. In January 1925, Ivor was the recipient of a specially designed Championship Gold Medal, a gift from the Football Association of Wales in recognition of playing for his country during the previous season when they won the International Championship, beating England, Scotland and Ireland. He returned to the Vetch Field in 1926, but after failing to make a first team appearance, went on to make non-league appearances firstly with Aberystwyth, and then played for Aldershot, Thames, before returning to the Swansea area to play for Eastside, later in March 1934 joining Aberavon Harlequins along with former Swans left winger Harry Thomas. He joined Aberystwyth as coach in September 1933, retiring from football in May 1935. Ivor Jones's son, Cliff, was the star-winger for Tottenham Hotspur and Wales during the 1960s. Ivor's brothers Bryn (Arsenal and Wolves), William (Merthyr Town), Emlyn (Merthyr, Everton and Southend United) and Bert (Southend and Wolves) were all talented footballers, Bryn especially who won 17 caps for Wales and was Britain's most expensive footballer when he joined the Gunners from Wolves for £14,000 in 1938.

29. JONES, JASON Andrew

Birthplace: Wrexham, 10/5/1979
Ht: 6ft-2ins, **Wt:** 12st-7lbs
Swans debut: v. Mansfield Town (a), 2/5/1998

Career:
Liverpool (trainee)
Swansea City (signed in November 1997)
Rhayader Town (loan in 13/1/1998)
Llanelli (signed in August 2002)

Honours: Wales Yth, U-21–3, West Wales Senior Cup Winner–2002

Swansea City Career Statistics

Season	League	FAWP
1997/98	1	
1998/99	3	2
1999/2000		6
2000/01	3	5
2001/02	3	
Total	10	13

Signed by manager Alan Cork on a six month trial after being released on completion of his YTS training at Liverpool, the North Wales born goalkeeper signed a two year contract at the Vetch Field at the end of the 1997/98 season, making his league debut in the last game of the season at Mansfield Town. Deputy to the legendary Roger Freestone at the Vetch Field, his first team opportunities were few and far between, and suffered as time went on because of no reserve team football at the club. Within a few weeks of arriving at the club, he was sent on loan to Rhayader Town to gain match experience. A back injury to Freestone saw Jason given his opportunity midway through the 1998/99 season, but after colliding with defender Steve Jones, he suffered concussion, and was sidelined himself for a number of matches, with the Swans having to bring in a goalkeeper on loan. The 2000/01 season saw Jason given his opportunity at Bury in a league fixture, but after being yellow carded early in the game, he unfortunately received a second yellow card, and was back in the dressing room shortly after the start of the second half. Capped at youth level by Wales, during his time at the Vetch Field he gained 2 caps at U-21 level in 2001, and one as a substitute the following season. His last away league game for the Swans saw him concede seven goals in what was one of the worst performances by a Swans side for years. In late April 2002 he was included in the Swans side that beat Hakin United to win the West Wales Senior Cup. He was released by the Swans in June 2002, joining Llanelli in the League of Wales, but after a couple of matches started a degree course in physiotherapy at Swansea University, retiring from the game with knee problems. During his time at Anfield with Liverpool he did his 'C' licence coaching badge, and after leaving the Vetch Field he completed his 'A' and 'B' coaching badges. In mid-November 2003 he left the United Kingdom to take up a two year coaching position in the Centre of Excellence Football Departments in New South Wales, Australia.

30. JONES, John (JACK) Lewis

Birthplace: Penrhiwceiber, OND, 1909
Ht: 5ft-10ins, **Wt:** 12st-0lbs
Swans debut: v. Burnley (a), 28/11/1931

Swansea Town Career Statistics

Season	League	WC
1931/32	14/3gls	3
1932/33	7	1
1933/34	17/2gls	
Total	38/5gls	4

Career:
Pentwyn Albion
Penrhiwceiber
Swansea Town (trial in August 1931, professional in August 1931)
Newport County
Torquay United (signed in May 1934) lge 157/8gls

Bournemouth & Boscombe (signed in June 1938) lge 11/1gls
Chester (signed in June 1939) lge 0

Honours: Welsh Cup Winner–1932

Impressed during Public Trial matches in August 1931, signing professional later in the same month. Played mainly at inside right for the Swans, but during his three seasons on the Vetch Field playing staff also played at right half back, and at centre half on occasions. Made his debut at inside right, replacing Boston in a 5-1 win at the Vetch Field over Burnley, scoring the fifth goal for the Swans, which saw Gunn score a hat-trick. Two matches later he scored his second goal, in a 4-1 win over Nottingham Forest. His second season with the Swans saw him a member of the side that beat Wrexham 2-0 to win the Welsh Cup Final. Released in April 1934 he joined Third Division South side Torquay United, going on to make 157 league appearances for the club before signing for Bournemouth & Boscombe, also in the same division. Joining Third Division North side Chester for the 1939/40 season, he failed to make any appearances, with the Football League being suspended following the onset of the Second World War. He made guest appearances for the Swans during WW2 in season 1942/43, and also for Aberaman.

31. JONES, LEE

Birthplace: Pontypridd, 9/8/1970
Ht: 6ft-3ins, **Wt:** 14st-4lbs
Swans debut: v. Torquay United (a), 18/10/1994

Swansea City Career Statistics

Season	League	AWS	FAWP
1994/95	2	1	
1995/96	1		
1996/97	1		
1997/98	2		4
Total	6	1	4

Career:
Swansea City (trainee in 1/8/1988)
AFC Porth
Swansea City (£7,500 signed in 24/3/1994)
Crewe Alexandra (loan in October 1995) lge 0
Bristol Rovers (loan in February 1998) lge 76, FLC 6, FAC 7, Others 4
Stockport County (£50,000 signed in 19/7/2000) lge 72+3, FLC 5, FAC 4
Blackpool (loan in 9/8/2003) lge 3, FLC 1
Blackpool (signed in 27/8/2003) lge 47, FLC 2, FAC 4, Others 5

Honours: Wales Yth, AutoGlass Trophy Winner–1994, West Wales Senior Cup Winner–1995, LDV Vans Trophy Winner–2004

Former trainee with the Swans who after being released returned to his native Rhondda and made a name for himself with Welsh League side AFC Porth. Signed on a full time professional contract after completing his training at the Vetch Field, after less than eighteen months as a professional he had his contract cancelled during the 1989/90 season, leaving the professional game. Swans manager Frank Burrows looking for cover in the number one jersey signed him on transfer deadline day March 1994, and within a month was named as the club's substitute goalkeeper in the AutoGlass Trophy Cup Final at Wembley against Huddersfield Town, having yet to make an appearance for the Swans. Like a number of goalkeepers at the Vetch Field through the 1990's, the reliable, consistent Roger Freestone gave very little opportunities for youngsters in the wings. Lee's opportunity came in an AWS cup tie at Torquay United in a match the Swans won 3-1, and he kept his place a few days later for the league game at Blackpool. Unfortunately for him, he was replaced by Freestone at the half time interval. In May 1995 he was included in the Swans side that beat Morriston Town to win the West Wales Senior Cup. The next two seasons his opportunities were few and far between, limited to games at the end of the season. He was loaned to Crewe Alexandra in October and November 1998, and although Crewe were interested in making the transfer permanent, their offer was turned down by the Swans. He joined Bristol Rovers in February 1998, and his form impressed the Rovers managerial staff to make the transfer permanent. A tall, commanding goalkeeper, he also possessed the ability to kick the ball a long way, and was very much an integral part of the Rovers side that lost the Division Two Play Off semi-finals to Northampton Town on aggregate. Prior to joining Stockport County for £50,000 in July 2000, he had been called up for the Wales 'B' squad as cover. His first season at Edgeley Park saw him play a prominent part in the club's successful escape from relegation from the First Division. Won a series of 'Man of the Match' performances during early part of season 2002/03, but a loss of form midway through the season saw him lose his place, and joined Blackpool initially on loan in August 2003, with the transfer being made permanent on the 27th August 2003. On the 21st March 2004 he was a member of the 'Tangerines' team that beat Southend United in the LDV Vans Trophy Final in the Millenium Stadium in Cardiff in April 2004.

32. JONES, Leslie (LES) Jenkin

Birthplace: Aberdare, 1/7/1911. **Died:** Llanfyrnach, Pembrokeshire, 11/1/1981
Ht: 5ft-7½ins, **Wt:** 11st-6lbs
Swans debut: v. Nottingham Forest (h), 9/9/1946

Swansea Town Career Statistics	
Season	League
1946/47	2
Total	2

Career:
Aberdare Athletic
Cardiff City (signed in August 1929) lge 139/31gls
Coventry City (signed in 20/1/1934) lge 138/70gls
Arsenal (£2,000 signed in 4/11/1937) lge 46/3gls
Swansea Town (signed in 24/5/1946)
Barry Town (signed in August 1947)
Brighton & Hove Albion (signed in August 1948) lge 3

Honours: Wales Full–11, War-Time International–5, Third Division South Champions–1936, First Division Champions–1938, F.A. Charity Shield Winner–1938, Mayor of Colchester Cup Winner–1939

An experienced Welsh international inside forward before arriving at the Vetch Field, who played just the two league matches for the Swans, before being released to join non-league Barry Town as player manager in 1947. He replaced Roy Paul for his debut at right half, and a couple of games later played his last game for the Swans at Burnley in the inside left position. He was signed by Swans manager Haydn Green as player coach, with a view to develop the club's younger players in the London Combination team. Les began as a youngster with his local club Aberdare Athletic while working in his father's butcher's shop. Cardiff City offered him professional terms in August 1929, and he began to make his name as a skilful schemer who could also score goals, gaining his first Welsh international cap whilst on the staff at Ninian Park against France on the 25th May 1933 at Cardiff. At the time, the Bluebirds were struggling in the Second Division, suffered relegation to the Third Division South, and his last season at Ninian Park saw the club finish bottom of the league. Towards the end of the 1929/30 season he played in the 'Bluebirds' side that drew 0-0 with Rhyl in the final of the Welsh Cup. He made a name for himself as a goal scoring wing half, inside forward with both Cardiff City and Coventry City, and at Highfield Road, after finishing second and third place in his first two seasons with the club, in 1936 the 'Sky Blues' won the Third Division South Championship, with Les scoring twenty goals. Attracting the attention of numerous scouts, he joined First Division Arsenal in November 1937 for a fee in the region of £2,000, plus Bobby Davidson moving in the opposite direction, and in his first full season at Highbury, the Gunners won the First Division Championship. One of several inside-forwards signed by Arsenal manager George Allison in the late 1930s in an effort to fill the gap left by the retirement of the great Alex James, Les Jones performed a difficult task well, scoring three goals in 28 matches in 1937–38 as the 'Gunners' clinched their fifth championship in eight years, also winning the Charity Shield. At Highbury with Arsenal he was also a member of the side that won the Mayor of Colchester Cup in 1939, and also losing in the final of the 1941 Football League War Cup competition against Preston North End. The Second World War effectively ended his career, seeing service in the RAF, with his skill levels unable to cope with Second Division football. After assisting a whole host of clubs in the emergency competitions* during the war, and adding five wartime caps to his collection, he returned to Wales to join the Swans in June 1946, and in August 1947 was appointed player-manager of Southern League Barry Town. Twelve months later he was recruited by Albion manager Don Welsh chiefly as a scout, but also on a part-time playing/coaching basis, training at the Vetch Field and travelling to matches from his Swansea home. At the age of 37, after just three league appearances for Albion, he was appointed manager of Scunthorpe United in June 1950 on their election to the Football League, a position he held until the following year. He subsequently held a coaching post with Stockport County, was secretary of the British Timken Company's Social Club in

Northampton, and had a second spell as manager of Barry Town. His brother in law was former Coventry City player Harry Boileau.

* The clubs for which he made guest appearances during the war were: Southampton (1939/40), Fulham (1939/40), Nottingham Forest (December 1940), Coventry City (1940/41), Leicester City (October 1941), Brighton (February 1941), Chelsea (April 1941), Lincoln City (1940/41), Manchester City (1941/42), Sheffield Wednesday (1941/42), West Ham United (March 1942), Notts County (1942/43), Mansfield Town (1944/45), Swansea Town (1944/45).

33. JONES, PETER Alfred

Birthplace: Ellesmere Port, 25/11/1949
Ht: 5ft-7ins, **Wt**: 10st-0lbs
Swans debut: v. Bradford City (a), 14/8/1971

Swansea City Career Statistics				
Season	League	FLC	FAC	WC
1971/72	36	1	6	1
1972/73	38+1/1gls		1	2
1973/74	6			
Total	80+1/1gls	1	7	3

Career:
Burnley (signed in May 1967) lge 2, FLC 2
Swansea City (signed in July 1971)
Great Harwood

Honours: England Sch–1, Yth–3, FA Youth Cup Winner–1968

Capped at schoolboy level for England, and was taken on as an apprentice by Burnley on leaving school, signing professional in 1967. He gained further international representation whilst at Turf Moor, winning youth caps for England, signing professional forms for Burnley in 1968, shortly after being involved in the Burnley youth side that won the FA Youth Cup beating Coventry City 3-2. An ever present that season in the Burnley youth side, he scored a spectacular goal in the home leg of the semi-final against Everton. Generally reckoned to be one of the brightest members of that youth side, he made his league debut at right full back at Everton early in the 1968/69 season. Making just one more league appearance the following season against Sheffield Wednesday, and two in the League Cup ties against Manchester United the same season, he was released in May 1971. Signed by Swans manager Roy Bentley on a free transfer in July 1971, he impressed at right full back for the Swans with his cool play, and tackling ability. Started the season at right back, but after suffering an injury in April missed the remainder of the season, and the start of the following season.

Following a change of management at the Vetch Field, with Harry Gregg taking over from Bentley, he was switched to a midfield role during the season, which saw the Swans not only beaten in the FA Cup by non-league Margate, but also suffered relegation to the Fourth Division. He scored his only goal for the Swans during the season however, in a 3-1 win over Welsh rivals Wrexham. His third season at the Vetch Field saw him play most of his games in midfield during the first half of the season, and in May 1974 was released on a free transfer. He returned to live in Burnley where he became a milkman and played for Great Harwood in the Northern Premier League and later for Burnley United.

34. JONES, RICHARD John

Birthplace: Usk, 26/4/1969
Ht: 5ft-11ins, **Wt:** 12st-0lbs
Swans debut: v. Huddersfield Town (h), 31/8/1993

Swansea City Career Statistics		
Season	League	WC
1993/94	6+1	1
Total	6+1	1

Career:
Newport County (signed from trainee in July 1987)
    lge 31+10/1gls
Hereford United (signed in August 1988) lge 142+6/9gls
Swansea City (trial in July 1993, professional in August 1993)
Barry Town (signed in June 1994)
Merthyr Tydfil (signed in close season 2001)
Haverfordwest County (signed in December 2001)

Honours: Wales Semi-Professional XI, League of Wales Champions–1996, 1997, 1998, 1999, 2001, Welsh Cup Winner–1997, 2001, Gilbert Cup Winner–1997, 1998, 1999, 2000, 2001, FAW Premier Cup Winner–1999

Richard made his league debut whilst still a trainee with Newport County, a couple of months short of his seventeenth birthday at Somerton Park against Bolton Wanderers in November 1986, and at the end of the season played in the Welsh Cup Final defeat by Merthyr Tydfil. Twelve months later however, County finished bottom of the Fourth Division and relegated to the Vauxhall Conference, with Richard signing for Hereford United. He became a regular member of United's league side in the five seasons prior to joining the Swans, and joined the Vetch Field playing squad after impressing in pre-season trial games, signing a one year contract for Frank Burrows. Richard's early career saw him attend Greenlawn Junior and West Mon Grammar School in Pontypool, play for New Inn U-10's and Coed Eva, Cwmbran U-12 to U-16's.

He also captained the Gwent Schoolboys Rugby team. He made his Swans' debut as a replacement for the injured Colin Pascoe in a 1-0 Vetch Field win over Huddersfield Town, making six consecutive league appearances before making way for the returning Pascoe. Basically a squad player at the Vetch Field, for the remainder of the season he was utilised as a replacement for injuries in the Swans' midfield. He was released at the end of the season, joining Konica League side Barry Town, becoming the club's first full time professional, and over the next seven seasons would become an integral, driving force in the club's success in the League of Wales, Welsh Cup and League Cup, as well as regularly participating in European Cup, and EUFA Cup matches, also gaining two Welsh Cup Winner's medals in 1997 and 2001, and beating Wrexham in the 1999 FAW Premier Cup Final. His last couple of seasons at Barry saw him take on a player/coaching role with manager Gary Barnett, and for a short time as player/manager of the club after Barnet's departure to Kidderminster Harriers as assistant to Jan Molby. Winning 'Player of the Year' Awards earlier in his career at both Newport County and at Hereford United, Richard has also been awarded the League of Wales 'Player of the Year' Award, and also captained the Wales Semi-Professional side. A hard working midfielder during his career who never shirked a challenge, but at the time of his arrival at the Vetch Field, the central midfield position at the club was very strong, and opportunities were few and far between. In the 2001 close season he joined Merthyr Tydfil as assistant to manager John Lewis, but after a poor run of form, both Lewis and Jones resigned their positions after a 3-0 defeat at Hednesford Town in November 2001. In early December 2001 he joined League of Wales side Haverfordwest County, but after just six games, in January 2002 he was forced to retire as a player through injury problems, although he retained an interest in the club for a short time afterwards through coaching. Since leaving full time football Richard has been a self-employed sales representative.

35. JONES, Stephen (STEVE)

Birthplace: Bristol, 25/12/1970
Ht: 5ft-10ins, **Wt:** 12st-2lbs
Swans debut: v. Crewe Alexandra (a), 17/11/1995

	Swansea City Career Statistics					
Season	League	FLC	FAC	AWS	P/Offs	FAWP
1995/96	16+1			1		
1996/97	46/1gls	2	2	2	2	
1997/98						
1998/99	31+1/2gls		5	1	2	3
1999/00	34+4	0+1	1	1		3/1gls
2000/01	13		1			3
Total	140+6/3gls	2+1	9	5	4	9/1gls

Career:
Forest Green Rovers
Cheltenham Town (signed in July 1993)
Swansea City (£25,000 in 14/11/1995)
Cheltenham Town (signed in 11/7/2001) lge 7+3
Forest Green Rovers (signed in July 2003)
Bath City (signed in June 2004) Total Apps 35+6/1gls

Honours: Third Division Champions–2000

A gutsy defender, capable of playing as an attacking right full back, or as a central defender, possessing good aerial skills. Steve started his senior career with Gloucestershire League side Wotton Rovers, progressed to Hellenic League team Fairford Town, prior to signing for Beazer Homes League Midland Division side Forest Green Rovers. Signed by Swans manager Bobby Smith for £25,000 from non-league Cheltenham Town, during his career at the Vetch Field he would show great commitment when playing for the club, despite suffering horrendous injuries which would have sidelined lesser players. In July 1993 he joined Beazer Homes League Premier Division side Cheltenham Town, making appearances in a team that would over the next two seasons finish runners up in the league in both seasons. A part-time professional prior to arriving at the Vetch Field, he had worked in his own electrical business in the South West. His first full season at the Vetch Field saw him play in every league game, also in the Third Division Play Off semi-final games against Chester, only to suffer a broken leg, making him miss the Final against Northampton Town at Wembley. During the season when he was an ever present, he scored his first league goal, in an away win at Ninian Park against rivals Cardiff City, and also be awarded the Player of the Year Award. Recovering from his broken leg, he returned to action for the 1998/99 season, scoring the goal of the season at the Vetch Field with a twenty-five yard drive against Brighton & Hove Albion, and also played a prominent part in the club reaching the Third Division Play Off semi-finals. The following season he featured strongly in the Swans' Third Division Championship success, the first Championship for the club since 1949. Despite starting as first choice in the Second Division side, he had to undergo groin and stomach operations during the season which prevented him from re-inforcing the defence, in what turned out to be a relegation season. Released in July 2001, he returned to Cheltenham Town, who by now had gained promotion to the Football League. Again, injury problems, which saw him break his leg twice, limited him to just five league appearances in the Town side that gained promotion at the end of the season via the Play Off. He was released in July 2003, joining Forest Green Rovers where he made eleven appearances before signing for Bath City in June 2004, returning also to his trade as an electrician.

36. JONES, STUART

Birthplace: Aberystwyth, 14/3/1984
Ht: 6ft-0ins, **Wt:** 11st-8lbs
Swans debut: v. Stevenage Borough (a), LDV-1, 22/10/2002

Swansea City Career Statistics

Season	League	FLC	FAC	LDV	FAWC
2002/03	5+1			1	
2003/04	16+8	1	1	1	1
2004/05	2+2				2
Total	23+11	1	1	2	3

Career:
Swansea City (from scholar in 28/7/2003)
Llanelli (signed in June 2005)

Honours: Wales Sch, Yth, U-21–1

Second year scholar who made his first team debut for the Swans in an LDV cup tie at non-league side Stevenage Borough. With the Swans unable to field their quota of substitutes because of injuries to members of the playing squad, he was thrust into first team action, and at the end of the game was awarded the Player of the Match Award. He retained his place four days later for the league game at Carlisle United, again showing great maturity in his defensive awareness at right full back.

Brought up in Aberystwyth, Stuart attended Ysgol Penglais School, Aberystwyth, and played in a Victory Shield game for Wales against England. Attached to Manchester United earlier in his school days, he played mostly in central defence in the Swans' U-19 side, and shortly before the end of season 2002/03 was offered a one year professional contract by Swans manager Brian Flynn. The first game of season 2003/04 Stuart started at right full back against Bury at the Vetch Field in 4-2 win, also featuring in the Carling Cup tie at Bristol City a couple of games later. A training ground injury however saw him sidelined for almost all of September, and after being included as substitute on a number of occasions, a hamstring injury during the last third of the season saw him sidelined once more. Included in the Wales U-21 squad in May, he was offered a new contract by manager Kenny Jackett at the end of the season. He gained representative honours for Wales at U-21 level in early September 2004 in Azerbaijan, but unfortunately received a red card in the second half. Despite starting in the opening league game of the 2004/05 season, the young defender featured in just one more league game plus a few appearances from the substitute's bench, and at the end of the season was released by Swans manager Kenny Jackett. In mid-June 2005 he signed a one year contract with Welsh Premier League side Llanelli.

K

1. KEAN, Stephen (STEVE)

Birthplace: Glasgow, 30/9/1967
Ht: 5ft-9ins, **Wt:** 74kg
Swans debut: v. Crewe Alexandra (h), 21/2/1987

Swansea City Career Statistics	
Season	*League*
1986/87	3+1
Total	3+1

Career:
Glasgow Celtic (signed in 1986)
Swansea City (loan in 4/2/1987)
Academica, Portugal (signed in 1988)
Naval FC, Portugal (signed in 2001)
Reading (signed in September 1993)

Honours: Scotland Sch, Glasgow Cup Winner

Signed on a month's loan by Swans manager Terry Yorath in February 1987, after being recommended by Celtic Chief Scout John Kellman, the nineteen-year-old midfielder made his debut as substitute for Keri Andrews against Crewe Alexandra, and started the next two league games at Aldershot and Wolverhampton Wanderers, with both matches ending 1-4, and 0-4 respectively. A young inexperienced midfielder, who had yet to make his first team appearance for Celtic, he played in one further league game against Torquay United at the Vetch, before returning to Parkhead. Born in Glasgow, he attended St. Helens and St. Maurices High School, played for Celtic Boys Club, gaining International recognition at Schoolboy level for Scotland. Joining Celtic as an apprentice after leaving school, despite not making a league appearance for Celtic he was involved in the team that won the Glasgow Cup during his time at Parkhead. He was released at the end of the 1987/88 season, went to play in Portugal for five years, with Academica for three years, and two years with Naval FC. He returned to the UK in September 1993 to link up with former Celtic playing colleague Mark McGhee, who at the time was manager of Reading, but after a couple of months suffered a broken leg which eventually forced him to retire from the professional game. After becoming Reading's Youth Team Manager, he later became Technical Director of the club's Academy, before joining Fulham in 2000 as Academy Director. Following the appointment of former Swans defender Chris Coleman as First Team Manager towards the end of season 2002/03, he was involved with Coleman in coaching the club's first team in a bid to preserve their Premiership status, which they achieved. At the end of the season when Coleman's appointment was made permanent, he was promoted to assistant manager with the club, still retaining his role as Academy Director.

2. KEANE, Thomas Roderick (RORY)

Birthplace: Limerick, 31/8/1922. **Died:** Swansea, 13/2/2004
Ht: 5ft-10ins, **Wt:** 12st-0lbs
Swans debut: v. Leyton Orient (h), 27/9/1947

Swansea Town Career Statistics			
Season	*League*	*FAC*	*WC*
1947/48	29	1	1
1948/49	36	2	4
1949/50	34	2	3
1950/51			
1951/52	17	2	1
1952/53	21		
1953/54	23		
1954/55	4	2	2
Total	164	9	11

Career:
Limerick
Swansea Town (£600 signed in 10/6/1947)
Llanelly (signed in August 1955)
Pembroke Borough (signed in September 1956)

Honours: Republic of Ireland–4, All Ireland–1, Third Division South Champions–1949, Welsh League First Division Champions–1951, Football Combination Second Division Champions–1955

Rory Keane joined Limerick initially as an inside forward before reverting to a centre half role prior to joining the Swans in June 1947. But after arriving at the Vetch Field he settled into a right, or left full back, working a good partnership with Irishman Jim Feeney in the other full back berth. Whilst Feeney was the more cultured full back, Keane became a solid, uncompromising full back, fearless, good timer of the sliding tackle, and extremely popular with the Vetch Field fans. One of a number of Irishmen signed by Swans manager Haydn Green, he made his league debut at left full back instead of 'Kitch' Fisher, but after playing a number of times on the other flank, made the left back position his own for the remainder of the season. Shortly after starting his second season at the Vetch Field he was capped for the 'All' Ireland International team in November 1948 at Hampden Park against Scotland, and the following season became one of an elite band of Irishmen who also gained international caps for the Republic of Ireland International side against Switzerland, Portugal, Sweden and Spain. His second season with the Swans also saw him make an appearance against Merthyr in the 1949 Welsh Cup Final, and twelve months later, after playing in the semi-final of the competition against Merthyr, injury prevented him from making a second successive appearance in the Final of the competition. He suffered a double fracture of the leg playing against Chesterfield in April 1949, an injury which saw him endure a lengthy stay in hospital, miss the whole of the next season, with many supporters feeling that it was the start of the end of his career as a professional footballer. The latter half of the 1950/51 season saw him make appearances in the Welsh League side that by the end of the season would win the First Division Championship. In late September 1954, former England international full back Arthur Willis was signed from Tottenham Hotspur, taking over the right full back shirt, and at the end of the season Keane was released from the playing staff at the Vetch Field, joining Southern League side Llanelly on a free transfer. His last twelve months at the Vetch Field saw him make several appearances in the reserve side that won the Football Combination Second Division Championship. In September 1956, following a dispute at Stebonheath Park he signed for Welsh League side Pembroke Borough, and after his retirement as a professional footballer, Rory worked for some years at the Aluminium Wire and Cable Company in Port Tennant. He died in Swansea in February 2004 after a long illness.

3. KEAVENY, (JOHN) Jonathan

Birthplace: Swansea, 24/5/1981
Ht: 5ft-9ins, **Wt:** 11st-2lbs
Swans debut: v. Bournemouth (h), 24/8/2002

Swansea City Career Statistics	
Season	League
2002/03	4+5
Total	4+5

Career:
Port Tennant Stars
Goytre United (signed in August 2001)

Pontardawe Town (signed in October 2001)
Carmarthen Town (signed in March 2002)
Swansea City (signed in 1/7/2002)
Carmarthen Town (signed in December 2002)
Haverfordwest County (signed in October 2004)
Skewen (signed in December 2004)
Pontypridd (signed in January 2005)
Neath Athletic (signed in close season 2005)

Talented, striker, who within twelve months of leaving the Swansea Senior League with Port Tennant Stars to join Welsh League side Goytre United, created a name for himself in front of goal with both Pontardawe Town and League of Wales side Carmarthen Town, to bring himself to the attention of Swans manager Nick Cusack. In early May 2002, along with a number of out of contract players, he had impressed the Swans coaching staff in a behind closed doors trial match at the Vetch Field, and within a couple of weeks had signed a one year professional contract with the Swans, and was preparing himself for the pre-season tour of Holland as a professional footballer, leaving behind his job as a postman in the city. During the trial match he had caught the eye with his willingness to run at defenders, and despite his lack of experience, was not afraid to try for goal. His goal scoring exploits during his first season in the Welsh League, firstly with Goytre United where he scored five goals in six games, and with Pontardawe Town, where he scored 22 goals in nineteen games had caught the eye of League of Wales side Carmarthen Town. Signing for the club in March 2002 he scored a further eleven goals in nine matches, prompting manager Cusack to invite him to the Vetch Field for the trial match. He made his Swans' debut at the Vetch Field against Bournemouth, as a second half substitute for Jamie Wood, making his first start in the next home game against York City. Unfortunately for him, despite his promise, the Swans' poor form during the early part of the season saw Cusack replaced by Brian Flynn, and in mid November 2002 he had agreed a settlement with the Swans to cancel his contract. In early December he made his first appearance for Carmarthen Town against Llanelli, scoring in the 2-1 over the Reds, and had returned to his job as a postman in the city, after the company had agreed to keep his job open for twelve months. In early October 2004 he was released by Carmarthen Town, joining Haverfordwest County, making his debut against Connah's Quay Nomads on 16/10/2004, but a week before Xmas 2004 signed for Welsh League Division One side Skewen. Without playing a game for Skewen, in mid-January 2005 he dropped down to the Second Division to sign for Pontypridd, scoring two goals in his debut against Aberaman. In the 2005 close season he linked up with Neath Athletic.

4. KEEGAN, MICHAEL Jerard

Birthplace: Wallasay, 12/5/1981
Ht: 5ft-10ins, **Wt:** 11st-0lbs
Swans debut: v. Rochdale (h), 22/10/1999

Swansea City Career Statistics					
Season	League	FLC	FAC	AWS/LDV	FAWP
1999/2000	3+1		1	2	6+1/1gls
2000/01	4	1+1	0+1	2	6+1/2gls
2001/02	0+2				
Total	7+3	1+1	1+1	4	12+2/3gls

Career:
Swansea City (from trainee in 5/7/1999)
Kidderminster Harriers (loan in 8/11/2001)
Marine
Rhyl (signed in June 2004)

Michael Keegan made his Swans' debut as substitute for Stuart Roberts at the Vetch Field against Rochdale in October 1999, and two games later made his first start in an FA Cup tie at the Vetch Field against Colchester United. Formerly a trainee at the Vetch Field, he had earlier in his career been included in an England U-18 training camp at Lilleshall, a considerable achievement for a player who was based in a Welsh Football League team at the time. Always capable of providing accurate crosses from the flanks, it was during his debut that he supplied the cross for the only goal of the game after coming on as substitute. Primarily a right sided, wide midfielder, he had few opportunities at the Vetch Field, especially during the relegation season of 2000, and the following season when the club was in financial difficulty. Like a number of players at the time with the Swans, one contributing factor which did not help his progress at the Vetch Field was a lack of competitive reserve team fixtures for players trying to make their way in the game. In early November 2001 he joined former Swans manager Jan Molby at Kidderminster Harriers on loan, and, a manager who had been instrumental in him signing as a trainee for the Swans. When the Swans were sold to Australian businessman Tony Petty in October 2001, seven days later, Keegan was one of 15 players who were either sacked, or offered reduced contracts at the Vetch Field. Following a local consortium taking over the club in the New Year, he had his contract paid up in mid-February, as he was about to start a month's loan with Merthyr Tydfil. After a brief trial spell at Kidderminster Harriers, he returned home to Merseyside where he linked up with non-league sides Southport and Marine. In late June 2004 he signed for League of Wales Champions Rhyl in time to be included in their squad for Champions League qualifying tie against Skonto Riga.

5. KELLOW, TONY

Birthplace: Falmouth, 1/5/1952
Ht: 5ft-10ins, **Wt:** 12st-7lbs
Swans debut: v. Newport County (a), 13/10/1984

Swansea City Career Statistics	
Season	League
1984/85	0+1
Total	0+1

Career:
Falmouth
Exeter City (signed in July 1976) lge 107/40gls, FLC 12/4gls, FAC 7/4gls
Blackpool (£105,000 signed in 15/11/1978) lge 57/23gls, FLC 4, FAC 3/1gls
Exeter City (£65,000 signed in 14/3/1980) lge 140+3/61gls, FLC 10/5gls, FAC 10/6gls, Other 2/1gls
Plymouth Argyle (signed in November 1983) lge 8+2/2gls,

Swansea City (signed non contract in October 1984)
Newport County (signed non contract in November 1984)
lge 17+3/8gls, Others 2+1
Exeter City (signed in July 1985) lge 51+31/28gls, FLC 3+4, FAC 1+1/1gls, Others 2+2

Prolific goalscorer for the 'Grecians' after joining the club from non-league Falmouth Town in July 1976, where he worked in the local dockyards. Had three separate spells at St. James Park with Exeter City, and by the time he retired from the game at the end of the 1987/88 season to take over as Commercial Manager of the Football Club had created an aggregate league goalscoring record for the club with 129 goals during 1976-78, 1980-83, and 1985-88. During his playing career for the 'Grecians' he also created a record in the transfer market when he was sold to Blackpool in November 1978 for £105,000, and in March 1980 when he returned to St. James Park for £65,000. Between 1976 and 1983 he returned double figures in the goalscoring stakes during each season, and during the 1980/81 season scored two hat-tricks in the league, and also three goals in an FA Cup replay against First Division Leicester City. His only honours came during his first season (1976/77) when the 'Grecians' ended the season as runners up in the Fourth Division, and season 1980/81 when the club equalled their best run in the FA Cup by reaching the sixth round. He arrived at the Vetch Field in October 1984 at a time when manager Colin Appleton had a transfer embargo on the club from the Football League, and was only able to bring in non-contract players. With trialists and non-contract players turning up almost every weekend, Kellow managed just the one appearance for the Swans, as substitute for David Hough at Somerton Park against Newport County in October 1984, which ended in a 2-0 defeat. In the previous game he had been a non-playing substitute in the win over Orient at the Vetch Field. The return game later in the season at the Vetch Field against County, saw him start the game for Newport County, only to be replaced by substitute, and former Swans striker David Gwyther. With no offer of a contract at the Vetch Field, he joined Newport County the next month, and by the end of the season had scored eight league goals. Returning to Exeter City in July 1985, he was top goalscorer for the club during the next two seasons, and was released at the end of the 1987/88 season. After a period in the club's Commercial Department, he also spent some time as steward in the St. James Park Social Club, and later ran the Eagle Tavern in Exeter.

6. KENDALL, MARK

Birthplace: Blackwood, 20/9/1958
Ht: 6ft-0ins, **Wt:** 12st-4lbs
Swans debut: v. Tranmere Rovers (a), 15/3/1991

Career:
Tottenham Hotspur (from apprentice in July 1976) lge 29

Chesterfield (loan in 20/11/1979) lge 9
Newport County (£45,000 signed in 23/9/1980) lge 272
Wolverhampton Wanderers (£25,000 signed in December 1986) lge 147
Swansea City (signed in 17/7/1990)
Burnley (loan in 26/12/1991) lge 2
Cwmbran Town

Swansea City Career Statistics			
Season	League	WC	ECWC
1990/91	11	3	
1991/92	1		2
Total	12	3	2

Honours: Wales Sch, Yth, U-21–1, Fourth Division Champions–1988, Third Division Champions–1989, Sherpa Van Trophy Winner–1988, Welsh Cup Winner–1991

Former Tredegar, Gwent, Welsh International Schoolboy goalkeeper, Mark Kendall made his league debut for Tottenham Hotspur in the First Division at Norwich in November 1978 as a replacement for Barry Daines. Going on to make 23 appearances in the league during that season, following a loan spell at Chesterfield 12 months later, and six more league matches for Spurs, he returned to South East Wales to join Newport County shortly after the start of the 1980/81 season. Capped for the Wales U-21 side in 1978 against Scotland, he became part of probably the most successful County sides of all times, under former Swans boss Colin Addison, almost earning themselves promotion from the Third Division, finishing fourth in 1983, and reaching the quarter finals of the European Cup Winners Cup competition in 1981, losing to Carl Zeiss Jena, one of the eventual finalists. By the time of his transfer to Wolverhampton in December 1986, the County were already having financial problems, and by the end of the 1987/88 season when they were relegated to the Conference, within twelve months they would cease to exist. Ironically, a young Roger Freestone who took over as County's goalkeeper after Kendall had left for Wolverhampton, joined the Swans on a permanent basis in September 1991, replacing Kendall, who had twelve months previously been signed by Swans manager Terry Yorath on a free transfer from Wolves. Despite Wolves struggling financially off the field, and in the Fourth Division for the first time in the club's history, fortunes on the field started to change, with Kendall becoming a major influence in the club winning consecutive Championships of the Fourth and the Third Divisions, and also beating Burnley 2-0 to win the Sherpa Van Trophy at Wembley. His return to Wales to sign for the Swans under Terry Yorath in August 1990 was seen as giving more competition and experience to young Lee Bracey, but it took Kendall almost eight months before he was to make his Swans debut, at Tranmere Rovers in March 1989. The following season, with Frank Burrows at the helm, he faired even worse as far as league appearances were concerned, making just one league appearance, before Burrows decided to sign former Newport County apprentice Roger Freestone. Despite not making many league appearances for the Swans, he did however play in the 1991 Welsh Cup Final win over Wrexham, and the following season made two European Cup Winners Cup appearances for the Swans against Monaco. He made two loan appearances for Burnley in December 1991, but at the end of the 1991/92 season he was released by the Swans, linking up with his local Welsh League side Cwmbran Town. He later became a policeman in the Gwent Police Force in 1992. His son Lee followed him into the professional ranks, starting as a trainee with Crystal Palace, and also gaining Welsh U-21 honours like his father previously, later joining Cardiff City and also played for Haverfordwest County.

7. KENNEDY, Malcolm (MAL) Stephen John

Birthplace: Swansea, 13/10/1939
Ht: 5ft-10ins, **Wt:** 11st-0lbs
Swans debut: v. Bristol Rovers (h), 25/12/1957

Swansea Town Career Statistics		
Season	League	FAC
1957/58	4	1
1958/59	8	1
1959/60	3	
1960/61	3	
Total	18	2

Career:
Swansea Town (from juniors in May 1957)
Carlisle United (signed in 1961)
Ammanford Town (signed in 1964)

Honours: Wales Sch–3, Yth, English Schools Trophy Winner–1955, Welsh Schools Shield Winner–1955, Football Combination Second Division Champions–1961

A product of Swansea Schools football, the former Waun Wen and Townhill Schoolboy was capped at schoolboy level for Wales whilst at Swansea Technical School. A member of the Swansea Schoolboys side that won the English Trophy and Welsh Shield during season 1954/55, he also made International appearances for Wales against England, Scotland and Ireland that season. In November 1957 he played for the West Wales Representative side at Monmouth against Monmouth County. After leaving school he became an apprentice fitter with Richard Thomas & Baldwins at Landore, later signing as a part-time professional at the Vetch Field after gaining his youth cap for Wales against Scotland during season 1956/57, signing full time professional in his last season with the Swans. A sound, competent wing half, he made his league debut at the Vetch Field against Bristol Rovers in December 1957, missed the return game with Rovers twenty-four hours later, then returned to play in three consecutive league matches, plus an FA Cup tie at Burnley. Brought into the side to replace Mel Nurse, he contested the wing half berth with Tom Brown, Roy Saunders and Dixie Hale during his time at the Vetch Field before he was released in May 1961. His last season at the Vetch Field saw him make regular appearances in the reserve side that won the Combination Second Division Championship. A period with Carlisle United after his release in 1961 saw him then return to South Wales to play in the Welsh League with Ammanford Town under former Swans player Roy Saunders, before finishing his playing career with Pembroke Borough and Port Talbot. Since returning to Swansea he has returned to his trade as a fitter and turner.

8. KENNEDY, Raymond (RAY)

Birthplace: Seaton Delaval, 28/7/1951
Ht: 5ft-11ins, **Wt:** 13st-4lbs
Swans debut: v. Manchester United (h), 30/1/1982

Swansea City Career Statistics				
Season	League	FLC	WC	ECWC
1981/82	18/2gls		4	
1982/83	21	3	4	4
1983/84	3			2
Total	42/2gls	3	8	6

Career:
Arsenal (apprentice in May 1968, professional in November 1968) lge 156+2/53gls
Liverpool (£180,000 signed in 20/7/1974) lge 272+3/51gls
Swansea City (£160,000 signed in 27/1/1982)
Hartlepool United (signed in November 1983) lge 18+5/3gls

Honours: England U-23–6, Full–17, First Division Champions–1971, 1976, 1977, 1979, 1980, 1982, F.A. Cup Winner–1971, Football League Cup Winner–1981, European Cup Winner–1977, 1978, 1981, EUFA Cup Winner–1976, Fairs Cup Winner–1970, European Super Cup Winner–1977, Charity Shield Winner–1976, 1977 (shared), 1979, 1980, Welsh Cup Winner–1982, 1983

Former South Northumberland Schoolboy who played for New Hartley Juniors and had a trial spell at Port Vale prior to signing as an apprentice with Arsenal in May 1968. One of the most decorated footballers in the professional game, Ray Kennedy made his league debut for Arsenal against Chelsea in 17 January 1969. A member of the Arsenal 'Double' team of 1970/71, he also made a substitute appearance for George Graham in the 1969/70 Fairs Cup Final, first leg against Anderlecht, scoring Arsenal's goal in a 3-1 away defeat. Making a significant contribution to Arsenal's league runners up side of 1972/73 before he joined Liverpool in July 1974 for £180,000, he gained his first International cap for England whilst with Liverpool, against Wales at Wrexham in March 1976. In 1972 whilst on the staff at Highbury he won the first of 6 U-23 caps for England, also against Wales. He started his playing career as a centre forward, but after switching to an attacking midfield role developed into a top class midfielder, having the ability to get forward to score goals, and also possess a good workrate in the defensive side of the game. Believed to have been the last piece of the jigsaw in Toshack's ambitious plan for establishing the Swans in the First Division and winning the First Division Championship, his £160,000 transfer, although initially a success, proved to be the one of the club's financial headaches during his second season at the Vetch Field, as acute financial problems off the field ultimately saw the club nosedive to the

lower divisions, with Liverpool eventually wiping the slate clean, despite a sizeable chunk of Kennedy's transfer fee still outstanding. His playing career honours included 6 First Division Championships, 3 First Division Runners-Up, 1 FA Cup Winner, 1 FA Cup Finalist, FA Cup Finalist in 1972 (substitute), 1 League Cup Winner, League Cup Finalist in 1978, 1 League Cup Finalist, 4 FA Charity Shield Winners, 3 European Cup Winners, 1 Fairs Cup Winner, 1 EUFA Cup Winner, 1 Super Cup Winner, 1 World Club Championship Runner-Up, and 2 Welsh Cup Winners medals. He collected his last First Division Winner's Medal the season he left Liverpool, as he had already played enough matches for Liverpool, entitling him to receive a medal. Despite a promising start to his second season at the Vetch Field, by November 1982 the club had announced a debt of nearly £2Million. Suspended by the Swans in January 1983 for two weeks, he was put on the transfer list in March 1983, with the club preparing for a clearout prior to the start of the new season. The highlight of his first two seasons with the Swans was finishing in the league in sixth place, and consecutive Welsh Cup Final wins over Cardiff City and Wrexham respectively. With the club back in the Second Division, by October the club's bankers had given the club just a couple of weeks to pay back some of the outstanding debt, and by November, Kennedy, one of the club's highest earners was given a free transfer, returning to his native north east to sign for Hartlepool United. He scored United's only goal on his debut at Reading in a 1-5 defeat, but at the end of the season he retired from the game, becoming a coach under manager Billy Horner for two seasons. In February 1987 he became a part-time coach at Sunderland, gaining promotion to first team coach in April 1987. During the last eighteen months of his career at the Vetch Field, there were many rumours regarding his supposed lack of fitness, and sluggishness, but within a few years it was made public that he had been diagnosed in the initial stages of Parkinson's disease, and it was this illness which would curtail his playing and coaching career in years to come.

9. KENNERLEY, KEVIN Robert

Birthplace: Chester, 26/4/1954
Ht: 5ft-10ins, **Wt:** 11st-8lbs
Swans debut: v. Newport County (h), 17/2/1978

Swansea City Career Statistics	
Season	League
1977/78	2
Total	2

Career:
Arsenal (from apprentice in 1970)
Burnley (signed in May 1972) lge 6/1gls
Port Vale (signed in 25/5/1976) lge 16+8/1gls, FLC 2, FAC 4/1gls, Debenhams Cup 0+1.
Swansea City (loan in 2/2/1978)
Stafford Rangers (signed in close season 1978)
Nantwich Town
Droylsden

Honours: FAYC Winner–1971

Previously an Ellesmere Port Schoolboy, the former apprentice at Highbury with Arsenal had been a member of the Gunners youth side that won the 1971 FA Youth Cup, scoring one of the goals that beat Cardiff City in the second leg of the final at Ninian Park 2-0. He joined First Division side Burnley in May 1972, but had to wait until December 1975 before he made his league debut, against Liverpool in December 1975 at Anfield, which resulted in a 0-0 draw. The following match he scored

Burnley's second goal in a 2-0 home win over West Ham United. Playing in six out of seven consecutive league games for Burnley, at the end of the season he was released, joining Third Division side Port Vale on a free transfer. He became Swans manager Harry Griffith's last signing in 2nd February 1978, with the aim of re-establishing the Swans claim for promotion, after a home defeat by Darlington had seen the Swans slip to fifth place in the league. A talented, central midfielder, he impressed on his debut in a 4-0 home win over Newport County, but after playing in a 2-2 draw at Aldershot, a few days later John Toshack arrived as player manager and he returned to Port Vale, where he was released at the end of the season on a free transfer. He helped Vale reach the fifth round of the F.A. Cup in season 1976/77, scoring in the giant killing win over Hull City. After being released by Vale he made non-league appearances for Stafford Rangers, Nantwich and Droylsden.

10. KILEY, Thomas (TOM) James

Birthplace: Swansea, 15/6/1924. **Died:** Swansea, 9/9/2000
Ht: 6ft-1ins, **Wt:** 13st-6lbs
Swans debut: v. Queens Park Rangers (a), 7/4/1950

Swansea Town Career Statistics

Season	League	FAC	WC
1949/50	3		1
1950/51	6	1	1
1951/52	6		
1952/53	27/1gls	1	2
1953/54	20	3/1gls	
1954/55	37/1gls	4	3
1955/56	22		3/1gls
1956/57	8		
Total	129/2gls	9/1gls	10/1gls

Career:
Swansea Town (signed in June 1946)

Honours: Welsh Cup Winner 1950, West Wales Senior Cup Winner–1949

Former Swansea schoolboy who signed for the Swans in June 1946 from local junior football, a member of the same Swansea Schoolboys side as Trevor Ford, and who would have played more games for the Swans but for the presence of Reg Weston, and his early retirement from the game because of injury. Brought up in the Greenhill, St.Josephs district of Swansea, he attended St. Josephs and Dynevor Grammar Schools, and after leaving school went to work in the Savings Bank in Swansea.

Joining the RAF, he served for four years, and with the intention of furthering his career in the RAF as an air crewman, with the end of WW2, and a surplus of servicemen, he left the RAF and signed for the Swans. He made his debut as a substitute for the injured Weston, playing two more matches, and also played in the Welsh Cup Final win over Cardiff City, his first Welsh Cup appearance for the Swans. Twelve months previously he had played in the Swans side that beat Llanelly to win the West Wales Senior Cup. The next two seasons saw his playing opportunities limited, and although predominantly a centre half, during the 1951/52 season played a number of matches at right full back. The 1952/53 season was to be his first season starting in the Swans line-up as centre half, and in November 1952 he scored his first goal for the Swans in a 1-1 draw at the Vetch Field against Leicester City. A commanding, classy defender, he used the ball well from defence, and played a large part in the Swans team that topped the Second Division for a long period during season 1955/56, looking certainties to win promotion to the First Division until his injury. During his absence the side won just four games out of the fifteen he missed, with the knee injury ultimately to force him to end his playing career. His last league game saw him come up against a young Brian Clough at the Vetch Field in October 1956 in a 2-2 draw. After his retirement from the game, he was for a time chief scout at the Vetch Field, and then became a Legal Executive/Office Manager, working for a series of Law Firms in Swansea for many years. He became a keen follower of Swansea RFC, took on the Treasurer's role with the Supporters Club, also taking a great interest in the League of Supporters Club in South Wales. Prior to the game going professional he became Office Manager at St. Helens, involving himself with all the tasks involved with the running of the club on a daily basis, also acting as Transport Manager for the All Whites Supporters Club. After the game had gone professional he was still actively involved with the Swansea Rugby & Cricket Club Committee up until his death in September 2000. In earlier years he had also been a keen batsman with Swansea CC in the summer months.

11. KING, DEREK Albert

Birthplace: Hackney, 15/8/1929. **Died:** Huntingdon, 16/6/2003
Ht: 5ft-11ins, **Wt:** 11st-11lbs
Swans debut: v. Blackburn Rovers (h), 18/8/1956

Swansea Town Career Statistics	
Season	League
1956/57	5
Total	5

Career:
Tottenham Hotspur (signed professional in August 1950) lge 19
Swansea Town (£2,000 signed in 2/8/1956)
Romford (signed in August 1959)

A £2,000 signing by Swans manager Ronnie Burgess from Tottenham Hotspur, having previous knowledge of the player when Burgess was a player with Spurs, prior to joining the Swans. Kept out of the Spurs side by Harry Clarke and John Ryden, Derek was a clever player who could also play at wing half. He made his Spurs debut in 1951 under the captaincy of Burgess, a year after signing professional forms for the club. Born in Hackney, he played for Hackney schoolboys and for the Albion Football Club in the Clapton & District League. He became a Spurs Junior, then went on to the groundstaff on leaving school, becoming a professional after he had completed his National Service in 1950. Spending the first year in the club's Eastern League side, he made occasional appearances in the London Combination side before making his first team debut.

Starting the 1956/57 season at right half, the Swans won the first three matches out of four he played in, and after missing one game returned to play against Fulham at centre half, with the game ending in a 7-3 win for the London side. He failed to make another appearance for the Swans, having been forced to retire from the game with a knee problem. In mid-December 1956 following a specialist's report, it was stated that he was unlikely to play professional football again. It was said at the time he joined the Swans that he signed without having a medical examination, and in later transfers, all potential signings at the Vetch Field had to undergo a stringent medical examination. Returning to the London area he signed for Romford in August 1959.

12. KING, JOHN

Birthplace: Blaenllechau, Ferndale, Rhondda, 29/11/1933.
Died: Australia, 1982
Ht: 6ft-0ins, **Wt:** 13st-10lbs
Swans debut: v. Birmingham City (a), 16/12/1950

Swansea Town Career Statistics				
Season	League	FLC	FAC	WC
1950/51	20			1
1951/52	42		3	1
1952/53	18			
1953/54	38		3	
1954/55	35		1	1
1955/56	41		1	4
1956/57	35			6
1957/58	28			1
1958/59	41		1	2
1959/60	39		3	2
1960/61	15	1	3	1
1961/62	10			1
1962/63	3			1
1963/64	5			1
Total	370	1	15	22

Career:
Blaenllechau Welfare
Swansea Town (signed groundstaff in close season 1949, professional in February 1950)
Bath City (signed in July 1964)

Honours: Wales Sch–6, Full–1, Welsh Lge Rep XI, British Army Representative XI, West Wales Senior Cup Winner–1955, 1956, 1957, Football Combination Second Division Champions–1961, Welsh League First Division Champions–1963, 1964

Former Wales schoolboy international who joined the groundstaff on leaving school, signing professional forms in February 1950. Captain of Ferndale Secondary Modern School, at an early age he possessed a safe pair of hands, and a keen sense of anticipation for a goalkeeper. At school he had also displayed a talent at swimming and cricket. Graduating from the Swans 'A' side, he made his league debut a week past his seventeenth birthday, played the next two matches, missed two, then returned to play in the remaining seventeen league games of the season, and was an ever present the following season. In season 1951/52 he played for the Welsh League Representative side against their Irish League counterparts. By the time he entered the forces for his National Service he had made forty-two league appearances for the club. In May 1952, Gunner John King was included in a British Army Representative XI that played two games in France later in the month. He gained his only Full international cap for Wales against England at Wembley in 10th November 1954, in a 2-3 defeat, but would have gained more caps but for the outstanding Jack Kelsey. A thickset goalkeeper, not flashy, he could hold his own with the big shoulder charging centre forwards of the day, and was very strong, and quick for his size. He often liked to play at centre forward in training, and he was given his opportunity to play at centre forward at Rotherham United in season 1956/57, following some injury problems to players at the time. Played in consecutive Welsh Cup Final defeats by Cardiff City and Wrexham respectively in 1956 and 1957, and also in consecutive West Wales Senior Cup Final successes in 1955, 1956 and 1957. Following the signing of Noel Dwyer, season 1960/61 saw King make a number of appearances in the Swans reserve side that won the Football Combination Second Division title, also in the reserve side that won consecutive Welsh League Championships. During his career with the Swans, he set a new goalkeeper appearances record, beating Alex Ferguson, and a record that stood until it was beaten by Roger Freestone in 1999. Released by the Swans at the end of the 1963/64 season, he had a spell in non-league football with Bath City, but then emigrated to Australia, played for Prague, Sydney, before finishing his playing career in South Australian football, until his death in 1982. Like Harry Griffiths, he was a staunch supporter of the Swans, as well as a stalwart player, and the Swans were the only team that mattered to him.

13. KING, Robert (ROB) David

Birthplace: Merthyr Tydfil, 2/9/1977
Ht: 5ft-8ins, **Wt:** 10st-6lbs
Swans debut: v. Cambridge United (a), 9/11/1996

Career:
Torquay United
Swansea City (signed in 1/7/1996)
Ebbw Vale (loan in 5/2/1998)
Merthyr Tydfil (signed in March 1998)

Swansea City Career Statistics				
Season	League	FAC	AWS	FAWC
1996/97	2	0+1	0+1	
1997/98				1
Total	2	0+1	0+1	1

Honours: Wales U-16, U-18–3, CC Sports Welsh League First Division Champions–2002, CC Sports Welsh League Second Division Champions–2003

Former pupil at Bishop Hadley RC School in Merthyr Tydfil, Rob played for Merthyr Schoolboys prior to signing for Torquay United as a YTS Trainee, and played for the Wales U-16 side that won the Milk Cup Tournament in 1992. During his YTS training he later played for the Wales U-18 side against the Faroe Islands, Lithuania and Iceland. He was released by Torquay after fifteen months with the Swans taking over his YTS contract, and during the 1996 Swans' pre-season tour of Denmark, impressed the club's coaching staff, and was offered a professional contract. He made his league debut as a replacement for player manager Jan Molby at Cambridge United, and during the same season made two substitute appearances against Bristol City in the FA Cup, and the AWS Cup competitions. During his second season at the Vetch Field, he struggled to break into the side, making just one appearance in the FAW Invitation Cup competition against Conwy, and in February 1998 he joined Ebbw Vale on loan. In late March he was given a free transfer, joining Merthyr Tydfil. After six months at Penydarren Park he joined League of Wales side Inter Cardiff, making an appearance in the second leg of the UEFA Cup tie against Gorica during season 1999/2000, which Inter won 1-0, but lost 2-1 on aggregate. Unfortunately financial problems saw the club cease to exist within a couple of months, with Rob signing for manager Gary Proctor at Rhayader. Over the next couple of months Rob made appearances for Llanelli, Merthyr Tydfil, and Haverfordwest County before being a member of the Ton Pentre side that won the CC Sports Welsh League First Division Championship in 2002. The following season after signing for Dinas Powis, the club won the CC Sports Welsh League Second Division Championship. Season 2003/04 has seen Rob join Grange Quins, and he is currently working in Sekisui in Merthyr Tydfil. After finishing runners up to Ton Pentre in the Motaquote Welsh First Division, in May 2005 the club was promoted to the Welsh Premier League.

14. KIRBY, GEORGE

Birthplace: Liverpool, 20/12/1933. **Died:** Elland, 24/3/2000
Ht: 6ft-0ins, **Wt:** 11st-10lbs
Swans debut: v. Portsmouth (a), 3/10/1964

Swansea Town Career Statistics				
Season	League	FLC	FAC	WC
1964/65	25/8gls	1	4/1gls	3
Total	25/8gls	1	4/1gls	3

Career:
Everton (from juniors in June 1952) lge 26/9gls
Sheffield Wednesday (signed in March 1959) lge 3
Plymouth Argyle (signed in January 1960) lge 93/38gls
Southampton (£17,000 signed in September 1962) lge 63/28gls
Coventry City (£12,000 signed in March 1964) lge 18/10gls
Swansea Town (£12,000 signed in October 1964)
Walsall (signed in May 1965) lge 74+1/25gls
New York Generals, USA (end of season 1966/67)
Brentford (signed in October 1968) lge 5/1gls, FAC 1+1
Worcester City (signed in March 1969)

The season after the Swans had reached the semi-final of the FA Cup competition, and were struggling to move away from the relegation places at the foot of the Second Division, manager Trevor Morris paid a fee in the region of £12,000 for George Kirby, an old fashioned style centre forward. Despite returning a respectable eight league goals, in which he scored in three consecutive home games, and reached the fifth round of the FA Cup, the club were unable to save themselves from relegation to the Third Division. In the fourth round of the FA Cup tie at the Vetch field against Huddersfield Town, he scored the only goal of the game, with a cheeky tap in with his hand, which, understandably was hotly contested by the visitors. Following relegation, along with a number of senior professionals he left the Vetch Field, joining Walsall. Making his debut for Walsall in a 1-0 win over Bournemouth on the 25th August 1965, in two seasons he was not only consistent in front of goal, but also helped considerably in the development of his striking partner Allan Clarke, who would go on to become a respected goalscorer at club and international level. A tall, brave, much travelled old fashioned type centre forward, who signed for Everton in June 1952 as an 18-year-old, after playing for Longwen Juniors, he gained a good reputation in league football, scoring consistently for all of his clubs, Everton, Sheffield Wednesday, Plymouth Argyle, Southampton and Coventry City up to his arrival at the Vetch Field. At Goodison Park with Everton, in his second season as a professional the club were runners up in the Second Division. Shortly after arriving at Hillsbrough, Sheffield Wednesday won the Second Division Championship, and after signing for Coventry City helped the club win the Third Division Championship at the end of season 1963/64. He became one of a number of professional footballers to be enticed to the USA in the late 1960's, signing for New York Generals from Walsall at the end of the 1966/67 season. Making 47 NASL appearances, and scoring 23 goals, he returned to the Football League in October 1968 to sign for Brentford, basically as cover for the suspended Pat Terry, later in 1969 signing for ambitious non-league side Worcester City on a match by match basis, where he scored two goals from nine games, retiring from the game in May 1969. Nicknamed 'Ripper' at Griffin Park, Terry and Kirby played together for Brentford on just two occasions, with Griffin Park being described at the time as a ground not suited for the faint hearted. He was appointed assistant trainer at Halifax Town in the summer of 1969 and stepped up to become manager a year later. He left the Shay in August 1971 to become manager of Watford and stayed in charge at Vicarage Road until May 1973. He then managed clubs in Kuwait and Iceland before returning as manager of Halifax Town in November 1978. During his second spell in charge he led the club to a famous victory over Manchester City and for a time he was a paid director and chief executive of the club. He left in June 1981 and later managed clubs in Kuwait, Akranes (Iceland), Indonesia and Saudi Arabia. He scouted for QPR until the end of the 1998/99 season, but fell ill and died after a long battle against cancer.

15. KNILL, ALAN Richard

Birthplace: Eton, 8/10/1964
Ht: 6ft-2ins, **Wt:** 10st-9lbs
Swans debut: v. Stockport County (a), 15/8/1987

Swansea City Career Statistics

Season	League	FLC	FAC	WC	FRT	P/Offs
1987/88	46/1gls	2	2	2/1gls	2	4
1988/89	43/2gls	2	3	7	1	
Total	89/3gls	4	5	9/1gls	3	4

Career:
Southampton (from apprentice in October 1982) lge 0
Halifax Town (signed in July 1984) lge 118/6gls
Swansea City (£10,000 signed in August 1987)
Bury (£95,000 signed in August 1989) lge 141+3/8gls
Cardiff City (loan in September 1993) lge 4
Scunthorpe United (signed in November 1993) lge 131/8gls
Rotherham United (signed in July 1997) 38/3gls

Honours: Wales Yth, Full–1, Fourth Division Play Off
Winner–1988, Welsh Cup Winner–1989

Tall, slightly built central defender who was a former apprentice with Southampton, and who was signed by manager Terry Yorath, from Halifax Town, for a tribunal set fee of £10,000 in August 1987. During the 1986/87 season his form for Halifax Town had impressed manager Yorath during a 2-0 defeat imposed on the Swans by Halifax at the Vetch Field. At the Dell with Southampton, he had gained representative honours at youth team level for Wales, by virtue of his Welsh ancestry, although born in Eton, but failed to make the first team grade with the Saints, moving to Halifax Town in July 1984 after he had been given a free transfer. A bargain signing for the Swans, he was an ever present during the Swans Play Off success against Torquay United at the end of season 1987/88, and missed just two league games the following season, which culminated in the Swans beating Kidderminster Harriers at the Vetch Field in the Welsh Cup Final. With Terry Yorath having resigned his post to join Bradford City, his replacement, Ian Evans failed to persuade him to sign a new contract, with the central defender opting to join Bury, for a fee, which was later set at a Football League Tribunal of £95,000. Despite his slight frame, he was a strong player in aerial challenges, both in his own, and the opposition penalty area, as well as having the ability to put a foot in at tackles. During Yorath's term as manager at the Vetch Field, he was also the Wales international manager, and for one World Cup qualifying match in September 1988, he had no hesitation in naming Knill as a replacement for Pat Van Den Hauwe in the Wales defence. In what turned out to be his only 'Full' cap, he came out of the game against Holland with credit, despite facing the world class skills of Marco van Basten, and Ruud Gullit. Despite the lure of European football after winning the Welsh Cup, he opted to join fellow Third Division side Bury in August 1989, stating at the time that his new club had more ambition than the Swans. His appearance for the Swans in the 1987/88 Play Off Final against Torquay United was to prove to be his only success in the end of season Play Off matches. For Bury he lost in the 1989/90 Second Division semi-final against Tranmere Rovers. He missed the following season's semi-final defeat by Bolton Wanderers through injury, but at the end of the 1992/93 season, were beaten by York City in the Third Division Play Off semi-final. After joining Rotherham United in July 1997, his last chance of Play Off glory came in the 1998/99 Third Division semi-final against Leyton Orient, but this time United lost out on penalties. At the end of the 1998/99 season he was released by the club after struggling to shake off a niggling back injury, and reverted to reserve and youth team coach at Millmoor. On the 31st January 2005 he was appointed caretaker manager at Millmoor until the end of the season replacing Ronnie Moore.

L

1. LACEY, DAMIEN James

Birthplace: Cefn Cribbwr, Bridgend, 3/8/1977
Ht: 5ft-9ins, **Wt:** 11st-3lbs:
Swans debut: v. Rochdale (h), 17/8/1996

Swansea City Career Statistics					
Season	League	FLC	FAC	AWS/LDV	FAWP
1996/97	9+1	1			
1997/98	16+6/1gls	1		1	2+2
1998/99	7+5		1	1	3
1999/2000	14+2	1	1+1		1
2000/01	17+1			3/1gls	1+1
2001/02	5+11		1		1
2002/03	7+3	0+1		1	
Total	75+29/1gls	3+1	3+1	6/1gls	8+3

Career:
Swansea City (from trainee in 1/7/1996)

Honours: Third Division Champions–2000

Impressed the coaching staff during the 1996 pre-season tour of Denmark, which resulted in him starting the 1996/97 season as first choice in midfield alongside player manager Jan Molby. Possessing high fitness levels, a kidney infection saw him sidelined in late October, and miss the rest of the season, returning as a non-playing substitute at Wembley against Northampton Town in the Third Division Play Off Final. Returning for the start of the 1997/98 season, alternating between a midfield, and a right wing back role, a stress fracture to his foot during the 1998/99, and a fractured heelbone was to be the start of the problems which would ultimately force his retirement in January 2003 at the age of 25, after taking medical advice. Struggling to combine the demands of full time training and playing, it became apparent that he was risking severe long term damage if he continued, and following discussions with a consultant, decided to retire from the professional game. Despite calling time on his full time playing career, he did not turn his back on the Vetch Field altogether, and started to climb the coaching ladder, with an involvement with the club's centre of excellence U-13 team, also undergoing a further operation in the summer of 2003 on his ankle. Looking to gain his coaching qualifications, he was also, on a part-time basis doing a Sports Science Degree in college. Midway through the 2003/04 season, after assisting physiotherapist Richard Evans at the Vetch Field on a part-time basis, he was taken on full time with the Swans as his assistant. Following a re-structuring of the backroom staff he was released in July 2005.

2. LAKE, Huw Gilwyn Taylor

Birthplace: Fforestfach, Swansea, 20/8/1963
Ht: 5ft-9ins, **Wt:** 10st-9lbs
Swans debut: v. Nottingham Forest (h), 14/5/1983

Swansea City Career Statistics				
Season	League	FLC	WC	ECWC
1982/83	0+1			
1983/84	14+4/2gls	1	1+1/2gls	1
Total	14+5/2gls	1	1+1/2gls	1

Career:
Swansea City (from apprentice in August 1981)
Llanelli (signed in close season 1984)
Perth Azzurri, Australia
Haverfordwest

Honours: Wales Sch–4, Boys Club of Wales

Former Gwyrosydd School, Penlan Schoolboy, and Swansea Schoolboy who earlier in his career as an apprentice at the Vetch Field, made his league debut as a substitute for Colin Pascoe at the Vetch Field against Nottingham Forest in the First Division. Prior to joining the Swans as an apprentice, he also played for Sketty Boys Club and Rockspur Juniors, gaining honours with the Welsh Boys Club of Wales side when he was selected to play against Scotland on the 18th March 1978. Skipper of Swansea Schoolboys, he also captained the Swansea Boys Club Group side to the semi-final stages of the Boys Club Competition. A midfielder with good fitness levels, he was also capable of scoring goals from outside the penalty area with his long range shooting ability. Following relegation, despite starting the new season in the Second Division, and scoring his first league goal against Brighton, he was unable to command a regular place in the starting line-up, and at the end of the season was released on a free transfer. With homesickness preventing him from extending his trial period with Blackpool after leaving the Vetch Field, he signed for Llanelli, later having a week's trial at the Racecourse with Wrexham, before returning to Stebonheath Park. He then had the opportunity via former Swans' players Roy Saunders and Reg Davies, to go to Australia to play for Perth Azzurri in 1985, and before too long was joined by former team-mates Colin Irwin and Tony Guard. After a two year spell in Australian football he returned to Swansea to sign for Haverfordwest, making further Welsh league appearances for Llanelli and Ammanford, before getting involved in a player coach role with Swansea Senior League sides Waunarlwydd and the Marquis Arms. Working in the family security business in Swansea (Lakeside Shutters) for a number of years, apart from his coaching involvement with Junior side West End, in November 2004 he was appointed chief scout at the Vetch Field. On the 23rd May 2005 he was appointed Youth Development Officer by Swans' manager Kenny Jackett, working alongside newly installed Head of Youth, David Moss.

3. LALLY, Patrick (PAT) Anthony

Birthplace: Paddington, 11/1/1952
Ht: 5ft-10ins, **Wt:** 10st-9lbs
Swans debut: v. Chester (h), 25/8/1973

Career:
Ockendon Town
Millwall (associate schoolboy in January 1967, apprentice in August 1968, professional in January 1970) lge 1
York City (signed in July 1971) lge 64+7/5gls
Swansea City (£8,000 signed in 3/8/1973)
Aldershot (loan in October 1975) lge 3
Doncaster Rovers (£19,500 in 7/9/1978) lge 118+4
Boston Town (signed in close season 1982)

Swansea City Career Statistics				
Season	League	FLC	FAC	WC
1973/74	45/4gls	2	1/1gls	1
1974/75	21+6/1gls	1	2/1gls	3
1975/76	9/1gls	1		3
1976/77	46	6	1	2
1977/78	31+2/4gls		5	1
1978/79	1	2		
Total	153+8/10gls	12	9/2gls	10

Honours: West Wales Senior Cup Winner–1975

An excellent signing for the Swans by manager Harry Gregg in August 1973, Pat was signed initially as a midfielder, but after the appointment of Harry Griffiths, was used also as a striker, and in central defence. He had earlier joined Millwall as a schoolboy from Ockendon Town, signing as an apprentice in August 1968, before signing as a professional. He made just one league start, lasting forty-five minutes, but later in his career he established himself as an attacking midfielder after his transfer to York City. Possessing excellent ball skills, and creative vision, he was a good competitor in midfield, and linked up well with the young and up and coming Swans players Curtis, James and Charles in a free scoring Swans outfit. In May 1975 he was included in the Swans side that beat Briton Ferry Athletic in the West Wales Senior Cup Final. During Harry Griffith's first full season as manager, he allowed Lally to go on loan to Aldershot to gain match fitness in October 1975, but the following season was an ever present when the club missed out on promotion. Pat continued to be an influential figure in the club's midfield, and was consistent in the Swans side under John Toshack that eventually gained promotion in May 1978. Shortly after the start of the 1978/79 season, despite starting in the first three matches in the Third Division, the signing of former Liverpool stars Tommy Smith and Ian Callaghan, was to be the decision for him to transfer to Doncaster Rovers. During his time at the Vetch Field he was on two occasions in a side that lost to non-league opposition in the FA Cup competition, losing to Kettering Town, and Minehead. His first season at Doncaster saw the club finish in the bottom four of the Fourth Division, and apply for re-election. By May 1981 they had moved themselves up the league and finished in third place, gaining promotion to the Third Division. Released in May 1982, he played for three seasons in non-league with Boston Town, later with Burton Albion. Following his retirement as a full time professional, Pat went to work for the Professional Footballers Association at their Manchester office. He has since graduated himself into becoming an Education Officer with the PFA, involving himself with the education scheme, which the PFA fund ex-professionals who undertake degree courses in Sports Science, Physiotherapy, Psychology. Pat had planned to become a teacher prior to becoming a professional footballer, and during his period with the Swans and Doncaster Rovers took an interest in the PFA, becoming a full time official when he retired.

4. LAMB, WALTER Charles

Birthplace: Tarleton, Lancs, 8/8/1897. **Died:** Huddersfield, JFM, 1973
Ht: 5ft-8½ins, **Wt:** 10st-9lbs
Swans debut: v. Exeter City, 22/3/1924

Swansea Town Career Statistics	
Season	League
1923/24	1
1924/25	2
Total	3

Career:
Liverpool
Fleetwood (signed in April 1920)
Sheffield Wednesday (signed in August 1921) lge 2
Swansea Town (trial in early August, signed professional in August 1923)
Southend United (signed in May 1925) lge 1
Rhyl (signed in June 1926)
Abergele (signed in November 1931)

Honours: West Wales Senior Cup Winner–1925

Former 'A' team player at Anfield with Liverpool, joined Fleetwood, then Sheffield Wednesday in July 1921 on an initial trial basis. He made his Wednesday debut on the 29th August 1921 against Derby County, also playing in the next game a few days later against Barnsley. Arriving at the Vetch Field in early August 1923 on an initial trial basis, he made his league debut for the Swans at the Vetch Field against Exeter City, and his other two appearances were in the following season, 1924/25, the Third Division South Championship winning season, playing in consecutive games as a replacement for the injured Milne. As with Wednesday he was primarily a reserve team left full back, whose appearances in the Swans first team were as a replacement for either Milne, or Morley. In January 1925 he was included in the Swans reserve side that beat Llanelly to win the West Wales Senior Cup. Released by the Swans in May 1925, he signed for Division Three (South) Southend United, making just the one league appearance at left full back during the 1925/26 season in a 1-3 away defeat at Brentford, before being released, and returning north to sign for Welsh non-league sides Rhyl and Abergele.

5. LAMIE, Robert (BOB)

Birthplace: Newarthill, 28/12/1928. **Died:** Northampton, JAS, 1981
Ht: 5ft-6½ins, **Wt:** 10st-10lbs
Swans debut: v. Nottingham Forest (a), 20/10/1951

Swansea Town Career Statistics	
Season	League
1951/52	2
Total	2

Career:
Stonehouse Violet
Cardiff City (signed in October 1949) lge 6/1gls
Swansea Town (signed in 3/3/1951)
Lincoln City

Outside Right, or outside left who made just the one other league appearance for the Swans, after his debut game in October 1951 against Nottingham Forest, on the 29th December at the Vetch against QPR. He replaced O'Driscoll in the first game, and for his second appearance, with O'Driscoll still injured, replaced Cyril Beech. He had earlier made his debut for the Swans in a friendly game at the Vetch Field against Dundee United, (which the Swans won 5-4). Following his transfer from Cardiff City in March 1951, the Swans entered into a dispute with the Bluebirds, regarding an injury, stating that he was unfit prior to his signing for the Swans, which Cardiff denied. Modern arrangements regarding transfers have been designed to obviate such difficulties. Failing to add to his first team appearances, he was placed on the open to transfer list in May 1952, later joining Lincoln City, where he played primarily for the reserve team. Earlier in his career he had joined Cardiff City from Scottish junior side Stonehouse Violet in October 1949.

6. LAMPARD, FRANK James

Birthplace: Romford, 20/6/1978
Ht: 5ft-10ins, **Wt:** 12st-4lbs
Swans debut: v. Bradford City (h), 7/10/1995

Swansea City Career Statistics		
Season	League	AWS
1995/96	8+1/1gls	1+1
Total	8+1/1gls	1+1

Career:
West Ham United (from trainee in 1/7/1995) lge 132+16/23gls, FLC 15+1/9gls, FAC 13/2gls, Others 10/4gls
Swansea City (loan in 6/10/1995)
Chelsea (£11M signed in 3/7/2001) Plge 147+4/34gls, FLC 11+4/2gls, FAC 16+3/3gls, Others 30+2/10gls

Honours: England Yth, U-21–19, 'B'–1, Full–23, FAYC–1996, Premiership Champions–2005, Football League Cup Winner–2005

Young inexperienced first year professional who had yet to make a league appearance for the 'Hammers', was signed by caretaker manager Bobby Smith a couple of days after Frank Burrows had resigned his position as manager for personal reasons. The son of former West Ham United legend, Frank (Junior) impressed all of the Swans supporters with his strong, attacking prowess in midfield, possessing a high workrate, and opened his goalscoring account, with a goal in the Swans first away win of the season at Brighton. Later in the season he skippered the 'Hammers' youth side, winning their Championship, and losing in the Final of the FA Youth Cup over two legs to Liverpool, with Lampard scoring the 'Hammers' goal in the second leg. He returned to Upton Park after his two month loan period, and on the 31st January 1996 made his debut in the Premiership against Coventry City, as a substitute for John Moncur. The last game of the season against Sheffield Wednesday saw Frank make his second appearance for the Hammers, again as substitute. The following season he started in the first team, making a total of 13 league appearances from midfield, and before he could establish himself he broke his leg, sidelining him for the remainder of the season. Capped at Youth, U-21 and at 'B' level, he gained his first Full cap on the 10th October 1999 at Sunderland against Belgium in a 2-1 win, with Frank scoring the second England goal. In July 2001 he joined Chelsea for a fee in the region of £11,000,000 and gradually built himself up to become one of the outstanding midfielders in the Premiership, adding also to his appearances for England. The 2003/04 season saw him help Chelsea to runners up spot in the Premiership, reach the semi-final of the Champions League, and also secure himself a place in the England squad for the European Championships in Portugal. In late February 2005 he was included in the Chelsea side that beat Liverpool at the Millenium Stadium, Cardiff to win the Carling Cup, and by the end of the season had been an influential figure in the Chelsea side that won the Premiership Championship, also playing in his second successive Champions League semi-final defeat. He was also voted the Football Writers Player of the Year for 2005.

7. LANG, CLIFFORD

Birthplace: Cardiff, 1/9/1908. **Died:** Cheltenham, 26/9/1978
Ht: 5ft-8ins, **Wt:** 11st-0lbs
Swans debut: v. Reading (a), 31/1/1931

Swansea Town Career Statistics	
Season	League
1930/31	1
Total	1

Career:
Ely United
Aston Villa (trial)
Swansea Town (signed in 29/7/1930)
Clapton Orient (signed in May 1931)
Clifton
Cheltenham Town

Honours: West Wales Senior Cup Winner–1930

Since joining the Swans prior to the start of the 1930/31 season, he had to be content with games in the reserve side at the Vetch Field, but had still given a good impression, playing many fine games for the reserves, and thoroughly deserved his first team opportunity when it came at Reading in the Second Division in January 1931 at right half back instead of Joe Sykes. Unfortunately for him that proved to be his only game for the Swans, and he was released at the end of the season. In October 1930 he was included in the Swans reserve side that beat Newport County in the West Wales Senior Cup Final. Earlier in his career he had played for Cardiff based side Ely United, had an unsuccessful trial with Aston Villa, and had been signed for the Swans by manager James Hunter Thomson. After signing for Cheltenham Town, for a number of years after retiring as a player in October 1948, he became a committee member.

8. LANG, Thomas (TOMMY)

Birthplace: Larkhall, Motherwell, 3/4/1905. **Died:** Cleland, 12/5/1988
Ht: 5ft-6½ins, **Wt:** 10st-7lbs
Swans debut: v. Blackburn Rovers (h), 28/8/1937

Swansea Town Career Statistics			
Season	League	FAC	WC
1937/38	33/1gls	1	2/1gls
Total	33/1gls	1	2/1gls

Career:
Larkhall Thistle
Newcastle United (£110 signed in October 1926) lge 215/53gls
Huddersfield Town (player exchange signed in December 1934) lge 24/5gls
Manchester United (signed in December 1935) lge 12/1gls
Swansea Town (£550 signed in 27/4/1937)
Queen of the South (signed in 17/8/1938)
Ipswich Town (signed in October 1946) lge 5/1gls

Honours: FA Cup Winner–1932

Outside Left who joined the Swans shortly after his 32nd birthday, and who earlier in his playing career had made almost 250 league appearances with Newcastle United and Huddersfield Town, mostly in the First Division, and had also played in a winning Wembley FA Cup Final in 1932 against Arsenal at outside left. Joining Newcastle United from Scottish junior side Larkhall Thistle, whilst still working on his father's fruit farm in Lanarkshire, his first season saw the club win the First Division Championship, and despite relegation to the Second Division in 1934, returned to the First Division with Huddersfield Town in December 1934. He made his United debut at Cardiff City on the 24th September 1927, and during United's 1932 FA Cup run was an ever present, scoring in the semi-final win over Chelsea. Joining Manchester United twelve months later, in exchange for Reg Chester, by the end of the season he had made appearances in United's Second Division Championship winning side. He arrived at the Vetch Field almost at the end of the 1936/37 season, making his Swans debut in the opening league match of the 1937/38 season at the Vetch against Blackburn Rovers, scoring the Swans third goal in a 3-2 home win. His only other goal for the Swans came in a Welsh Cup semi-final, 7-2 defeat over Rhyl later in the same season. During his period with the Swans he had great ability on the ball, but years of attention from the opposing full backs had taken it's toll. A neat player in tight situations, he also possessed a powerful shot. He left the Vetch Field in August 1938, returning North of the Border to sign for Queen of the South, and during his first season was a consistent goalscorer for the club in the First Division. After the Second World War he returned to the Football League, making five league appearances for Ipswich Town in the Third Division (South), retiring in June 1947 at the age of forty-one, to become the club's trainer. During the war years he made guest appearances for Burnbank Thistle. His brother James played for Halifax Town.

9. LANGFORD, Albert Edward (SAM)

Birthplace: Tipton, 16/10/1899. **Died:** Rowley Regis, Staffs, OND, 1965
Ht: 5ft-8ins, **Wt:** 10st-10lbs
Swans debut: v. Charlton Athletic (h), 1/12/1923

Swansea Town Career Statistics			
Season	League	FAC	WC
1923/24	22	4	3
1924/25	14		1
1925/26	34	7	3
1926/27	8	5	1
Total	78	16	8

Career:

Merthyr Town (signed in 1920) lge 106/1gls
Swansea Town (£750 signed in November 1923)
Worcester City (signed in November 1927)
Charlton Athletic (£250 signed in 16/8/1928) lge 135/1gls,
    FAC 12
Walsall (signed in June 1932) lge 24/1gls
Dudley Town (signed in August 1933)

Honours: Third Division South Champions–1925, 1929,
Welsh League Representative XI

Former Merthyr Town defender who had five seasons at
Penydarren Park, playing against the Swans in the Southern
league, and also when both clubs joined the Football League
Third Division in 1920. Signed for the Swans midway through
the 1923/24 season, making his debut at right full back instead
of Morley. He made most of his appearances in the right full
back position, but also made a couple on the opposite flank.
An experienced defender with Merthyr, he had joined the
Swans at half of Merthyr's transfer value of the player, owing to
Merthyr's financial position at the time. In March 1925 he was
included in a Welsh League Representative side that played the
Irish Free State in Dublin and Cork, also playing against the
same opposition in March 1928. A member of the Swans FA Cup
Semi-Final side during the 1925/26 season, Sam also played in
the Welsh Cup Final defeat by Ebbw Vale at the end of the
season. Losing his place to Ben Williams in season 1926/27, he
joined Worcester City on loan as player coach, but after making
twenty-three appearances returned to the Vetch Field after being
overlooked for the player manager's position that arose at the
time at Worcester, and in August 1928 was sold to Charlton
Athletic for £250. His first season at the Valley with Charlton
Athletic saw the club win the Third Division South
Championship, and over the next three seasons would play
regularly against the Swans in the Second Division. An ever
present during his first two seasons with Charlton, he finished
his league career with Third Division North side Walsall,
signing for them in August 1932. Making his debut for the
'Saddlers' in August 1932, after playing in the first twenty-six
league games of the season, and was by this time captaining his
side, he sustained an injury which saw him not only miss his
club's 2-0 F.A. Cup win over Arsenal in January 1933, but also
fail to make another appearance.

10. LATCHFORD, Robert (BOB) Dennis

Birthplace: Birmingham, 18/1/1951
Ht: 6ft-0ins, **Wt:** 12st-11lbs
Swans debut: v. Leeds United (h), 29/8/1981

Career:

Birmingham City (from apprentice in August 1968)
    lge 158+2/68gls

Everton (£350,000 signed in 14/2/1974) lge 235+1/106gls
Swansea City (£125,000 signed in July 1981)
NAC Breda, Holland (signed in 1/2/1984)
Coventry City (signed in July 1984) lge 11+1/2gls
Lincoln City (signed in August 1985) lge 14+1/2gls
Newport County (signed in 10/1/1986) lge 20/5gls
Merthyr Tydfil (signed in October 1986)

Swansea City Career Statistics					
Season	League	FLC	FAC	WC	ECWC
1981/82	31/12gls	2	1	5/3gls	2
1982/83	28/20gls	4/4gls	1	7/9gls	5/1gls
1983/84	18/3gls	1		2/1gls	2
Total	77/35gls	7/4gls	2	14/13gls	9/1gls

Honours: England Yth, U-23–6, Full–12, Football League
XI–1974, Welsh Cup Winner–1982, 1983, 1987

Prolific, experienced goalscorer who became the final piece in
John Toshack's jigsaw prior to the start of the Swans' first season
in the First Division. He justified his transfer fee, scoring a hat-
trick in the second half in just ten minutes against Leeds United
in an opening 5-1 home win for the Swans. Born in Kings Heath,
he played centre-forward for Brandwood Secondary School,
South Birmingham Boys and Warwickshire County Schools
before joining Blues as an apprentice in May 1967, signing
professional in August 1968, making his league debut against
Preston on the 22nd March 1969, and three months later played
for England in the International Youth Tournament in East
Germany. His progress at Birmingham City was rapid and he
established himself in the first eleven at St. Andrew's in season
1970-71 scoring 13 goals in 42 senior appearances. Part of a
formidable strikeforce, comprising himself, Trevor Francis and
Phil Summerhill and later Bob Hatton, Latchford was strong
and powerful, a sound header of the ball and could shoot with
either foot. In the 1971-72 season he hit 30 goals, including 23 in
the league, in 52 appearances as Blues won promotion to the
First Division and reached the semi-final of the FA Cup. He
followed up with another 20 goals in 49 outings in 1972-73 and
then got 18 goals in 36 games the following season before his
departure to Everton for a League record fee of £350,000, a deal
which saw Howard Kendall and Archie Styles switch from
Goodison Park to St. Andrew's. The youngest of three brothers
who made their way into professional football, Bob was also
capped at U-23 level prior to making his first Full appearance
for England against Italy at Wembley on the 16th November
1977. Latchford was top league scorer in each of his first four
seasons at Everton and in 1977-78 he was presented with a
cheque for £10,000 by a national newspaper for becoming the
first player to reach 30 goals in a season in the First Division for
six years. Apart from honours gained at international level, and
representing the Football League against the Scottish League in
March 1974 at Maine Road, his only club honours prior to
arriving at the Vetch Field came in a League Cup Final replay

defeat by Aston Villa in 1977, and an FA Cup semi-final replay defeat by West Ham United in 1980. Following his arrival in South Wales, he won the Welsh Cup with the Swans in 1982 and 1983, and, after linking up with non-league side Merthyr, won the Welsh Cup for a third time in 1987. Apart from the hat-trick in his debut match for the Swans against Leeds United in August 1981, the following season he scored two further hat-tricks, against Norwich City in the league, and against Bristol Rovers in the Milk Cup competition. During season 1982/83, he scored in every round of the Welsh Cup competition, scoring a total of nine goals that season in the competition.

Following relegation to the Second Division in 1983, and with pressing demands from the club's bankers, he was given a free transfer in late December 1983, and by the start of the following February had joined Dutch side N.A.C. Breda. Returning to the Football League for the start of the 1984/85 season with Coventry City, he joined Lincoln City twelve months later, and in January 1986 returned to South Wales to sign for Newport County. The following season he joined Merthyr, playing in the side that beat his former club, Newport County in the Welsh Cup Final, and helping the side to third place in the Beazer Homes League, Midland Division. Retaining a base in Swansea for a number of years after leaving the Vetch Field, with his wife owning a business in the city, Bob worked for The Brickyard, based in the Enterprise Zone. After leaving there he worked for Ladbrokes, and then went to work for the Community Department back at his old club Birmingham City. Prior to working for the Community Department at St. Andrews, Bob became a Director with non-league club Alvechurch. In February 2001 he was presented with the Dixie Dean Memorial Award at the Echo Sports Personality of the Year Awards in Liverpool. He resigned from his post in 2002 to start a new life in Germany.

11. LAWRENCE, David (DAI) William

Birthplace: Swansea, 18/1/1947
Ht: 5ft-8ins, **Wt:** 10st-12lbs
Swans debut: v. Workington (h), 14/10/1967

Swansea Town/City Career Statistics				
Season	League	FLC	FAC	WC
1967/68	17+2/1gls			
1968/69	42+1/1gls	4	4	7
1969/70	22+1	2	1	1
1970/71	12	1		1
Total	93+4/2gls	7	5	9

Career:
Swansea Town (signed in 16/5/1967)
Chelmsford (signed in August 1971)
Merthyr Tydfil (signed in season 1972/73)

Honours: Wales Amateur International–5, Southern League Premier Division Champions–1972, Welsh League Premier Division Champions–1977, 1978

Welsh Amateur international full back who followed his father (Syd), who earlier had captained the Swans, into the professional game at the Vetch Field. The former Oxford Street schoolboy played for his school and Swansea Schoolboys prior to starting an apprenticeship as a carpenter on leaving school, despite being offered an apprenticeship by the Swans at the Vetch Field. Signing as an amateur, he played for the YMCA team on a Saturday morning, and the Swans youth side in the afternoon. Making five appearances for the Wales Amateur International side, the first against Scotland in season 1965/66, Dai also became his country's youngest captain at this level. The 1966/67 season saw him make a further four appearances against Iceland, Republic of Ireland, England and Ireland. Prior to making his league debut for the Swans he had loan periods with both Bridgend Town and Merthyr Tydfil. He made his league debut at left full back instead of Vic Gomersall, but for the reminder of his career usually operated at right full back, and occasionally in central defence. A strong tackler with a good turn of pace, he scored his first league goal during his debut season, against Lincoln City at the Vetch Field in a 2-2 draw in March 1968. The 1968/69 season saw him have his best run in the Swans first team, missing just three league games, but following a change of management at the Vetch Field, after Roy Bentley had been appointed manager prior to the start of the 1969/70 season, he was unable to command a regular place at right full back. During the 1968/69 season he played in both Welsh Cup Final legs against Cardiff City, and through the season missed just the one cup game out of sixteen played. The following season, in which the club achieved promotion by finishing in third place behind Chesterfield and Wrexham, despite starting the season at right full back, he lost his place to Carl Slee, and from October on, played occasionally in either full back position. He was released by the Swans at the end of the 1970/71 season, and along with defender Vic Gomersall, joined Southern League side Chelmsford, helping them to win the Southern League Premier Division Championship in 1972. A part-time professional with Chelmsford, and working on ground maintenance during the week, after a season with the club he decided to return home to South Wales, signing for John Charles at Merthyr Tydfil. After two seasons at Penydarren Park, he later made appearances for Bridgend Town, Lewistown, and linked up with former Swans defender Carl Slee at Maesteg Park, before both players signed for Llanelli, winning the Welsh League Premier Division Championship in consecutive seasons. At the age of thirty-three Dai suffered a broken leg in a match with Llanelli which brought an end to his playing career. Since returning to South Wales, Dai has continued to work in the building industry in Swansea for various companies. Dai Lawrence is one of the few number of Swans players who have played for the club when it was known as Swansea Town, and Swansea City.

12. LAWRENCE, Sidney (SYD) Wilfred

Birthplace: Penrhiwceiber, 16/3/1909. **Died:** Swansea, 10/6/1949
Ht: 5ft-9ins, **Wt:** 12st-0lbs
Swans debut: v. Southampton (a), 28/2/1931

Career:
Penrhiwceiber Rangers
Swansea Town (amateur signed in July 1930, professional in August 1930)
Swindon Town (signed in 20/6/1939) lge 1
Haverfordwest (by season 1946/47)

Honours: Wales Full–8, Welsh Cup Winner–1932

Swansea Town Career Statistics

Season	League	FAC	WC
1930/31	12		2
1931/32	41	1	5
1932/33	39	1	2
1933/34	38	4	1
1934/35	37	2	2
1935/36	40/4gls	1	2
1936/37	39/3gls	4	1
1937/38	38/2gls	1	2
1938/39	28/2gls	1	2
Total	312/11gls	15	19

An incredibly consistent full back who, after signing for the Swans in late July 1930, made his league debut in February 1931, playing in the remaining 12 league matches of the season. By the time of the start of the 1938/39 season (his last at the Vetch Field) he missed just 22 league games in seven seasons. He gained his first international cap for Wales during his first full season, playing against Ireland in Belfast on the 5th December 1931, as a replacement for former Swans defender Ben Williams. Apart from playing in his next international against France in Paris in May 1933 (World Cup Qualifier), all his international appearances for Wales came in the Home International Championships. During his first full season he gained a Welsh Cup Winners Medal, when the Swans defeated Wrexham 2-0 in the final. He was to play in a second Welsh Cup Final, this time against Shrewsbury Town in September 1938, in a replay held over from the previous season, which the Swans lost 1-2. The scorer of eleven league goals for the Swans, all of his goals came from the penalty spot, from February 1936 onwards, opening his account at Charlton Athletic in a 1-4 defeat. During his last season, 1938/39 he scored two penalties in the same match against Bradford Park Avenue in a 2-2 home draw. In June 1939, he followed Swans manager John Harris to sign for Swindon Town, after the manager had left the previous month. However, he would only play the one league game for Swindon, following the onset of the Second World War. The 1946/47 season saw him skipper Haverfordwest in the Welsh League. Prior to his death in June 1949 at Swansea Hospital, Syd had been a licensee in a number of public houses in Swansea, one of which included the Ye Old Red Cow in High Street, Swansea.

13. LAWSON, NORMAN

Birthplace: Hetton-le-Hole, 6/4/1935
Ht: 5ft-9ins, **Wt:** 11st-2lbs
Swans debut: v. Sheffield Wednesday (a), 23/8/1958

Career:
Hednesford Town
Bury (signed in September 1955) lge 56/8gls
Swansea Town (£4,000 signed in 10/7/1958)
Watford (signed in July 1960) lge 0, FLC 1
Kettering Town (signed in July 1961)
Hereford United (signed during 1963/64 season) Slge apps 32
Merthyr Tydfil (signed in close season 1964)

Swansea Town Career Statistics

Season	League	WC
1958/59	23/3gls	2/1gls
1959/60	1	
Total	24/3gls	2/1gls

Former Second Division winger with Bury who made regular appearances against the Swans for Bury prior to arriving at the Vetch Field. During his school days he played for Houghton-le-Spring Grammar School, played for the County U-18 side, and was also selected for the England Grammar & Public School side that played the famous amateur side at the time, Pegasus. Stationed at RAF Hednesford during his National Service, his first taste of senior football came with the local club, Hednesford Town. After three seasons at Gigg Lane, Norman signed for the Swans as an outside left in July 1958, but also covered on five occasions at left full back during his first season at the Vetch Field. Making his debut in the opening match of the 1958/59 season at Hillsborough against Sheffield Wednesday, he scored in the Swans 2-1 defeat, and scored two further goals during the season, against Middlesbrough (home), and at Rotherham United. His only other goal that season came at Bangor City, in a Welsh Cup, sixth round defeat. Making just the one appearance the following season, he was released in May 1960 to join Watford for a four figure transfer fee. He failed to make a league appearance for the 'Hornets', playing just the one game in the club's first ever Football League Cup tie at left back against Derby County. He then signed for non-league Kettering Town in July 1961, but later returned to Swansea to study part-time in accountancy, business management and marketing. Over the three year period studying at Swansea Technical College, he was Branch Manager for BTD, selling Business Systems, and then joined Hereford United for season 1963/64, when they were managed by Ray Daniel. During a campaign which ended in relegation from the Southern League Premier Division, Norman played in thirty-two Southern League matches before being released by new boss Bob Dennison at the end of the campaign, linking up then with Harry Griffiths at Merthyr Tydfil in the 1964 close season. After Merthyr he was involved with Welsh League side Ton Pentre as player manager for a three year period, prior to his retirement from the game. By this time he had established his company, Lawson Computers in the city. A keen cricketer in the summer months, Norman continued playing cricket long after his retirement from football, captaining Sketty Quins, the Swansea Central League Representative side, and also the Wales Over 50's side.

14. LEAVY, Stephen (STEVE) Francis

Birthplace: Longford, 18/6/1925. **Died:** Swansea 26/1/1996
Ht: 5ft-10ins, **Wt:** 12st-7lbs
Swans debut: v. Birmingham City (h), 19/8/1950

Swansea Town Career Statistics		
Season	*League*	*WC*
1950/51	5	
1951/52		
1952/53	10	2
1953/54	5	1
1954/55	4	
1955/56	5	1
1956/57		
1957/58	8/1gls	2
Total	37/1gls	6

Career:
Sligo Rovers
Swansea Town (signed in 5/7/1950)

Honours: Republic of Ireland Amateur, League of Ireland
Representative XI, Welsh League First Division
Champions–1951, West Wales Senior Cup Winner–1954, 1955,
Football Combination Second Division Champions–1955

Represented the League of Ireland whilst with Sligo Rovers, he
joined the Swans in July 1950, one of a number of Irish players
brought to the Vetch Field by manager Billy McCandless.
A Republic of Ireland Junior International in season 1946/47
against Scotland, he also played left full back for the League of
Ireland Representative side against the English League at
Wolverhampton in season 1949/50. He had also played for the
League of Ireland at Dublin and in Belfast. As well as playing
for Sligo Rovers, he was a dental mechanic by trade. At the
Vetch Field he was mainly a reserve right, or left sided full back,
deputising for internationals like David Thomas and Arthur
Willis, but he did have first team opportunities at centre half,
and centre forward. His first season at the Vetch Field saw him
make appearances in the club's reserve team that won the Welsh
League First Division Championship. It was at centre forward
during the 1957/58 season, deputising for the injured Des
Palmer, that he scored his only goal for the Swans in a 4-1 home
defeat by Middlesbrough. Primarily a reserve team player, he
was considered to be too short for a defender at the time, but
was renowned as a classy player, who made up for lack of
height by his astute positioning play. He was a member of the
Swans side that beat Llanelly to win the West Wales Senior Cup
in May 1954, and in May 1955, and during season 1954/55 made
regular appearances in the reserve side that won the Football
Combination Second Division Championship. Injury
unfortunately ended his playing career in 1959, and he took on

the role of trainer of the Swans' Combination and Welsh League
side, taking them to the Championship for three consecutive
seasons, 1962/3 to 1964/65, and also the Combination Second
Division Championship in 1961. He left at the end of season
1964/65, soon after the resignation of manager Trevor Morris.
He was later to be involved as trainer with Port Talbot, Afan
Lido and Swansea Senior League side Oystermouth whilst
running a popular fish and chip shop in Swansea. He was a
season ticket holder at Swansea up to the time of his death.

15. LEGG, ANDREW

Birthplace: Briton Ferry, 28/7/1966
Ht: 5ft-8ins, **Wt:** 10st-8lbs
Swans debut: v. Bristol City (a), 1/10/1988

Swansea City Career Statistics							
Season	*League*	*FLC*	*FAC*	*WC*	*L/DAF AGT*	*ECWC*	*P/Offs*
1988/89	6			0+1			
1989/90	20+5/3gls	1+1	4		1+1	1	
1990/91	37+2/5gls	2	4/2gls	5+2	4+1/2gls		
1991/92	46/9gls	4	3	3	2/1gls	2/1gls	
1992/93	46/12gls	2	5/1gls	1	3/2gls		2
Total	155+7/29gls	9+1	16/3gls	9+3	10+2/5gls	3/1gls	2

Career:
Briton Ferry Athletic
Swansea City (signed in 12/8/1988)
Notts. County (£275,000 signed in 23/7/1993) lge 85+4/9gls,
    FLC 11, FAC 7+1/2gls, Others 13+2/6gls
Birmingham City (£250,000 signed in 29/2/1996)
    lge 31+14/5gls, FLC 3+1, FAC 2+1
Ipswich Town (loan in 3/11/1997) lge 6/1gls, FLC 1
Reading (£75,000 in 20/2/1998) lge 12, FLC 1
Peterborough United (loan in 15/10/1998) lge 5
Cardiff City (signed in 16/12/1998) lge 152+23/12gls, FLC 8+1,
    FAC 17+4, Others 4
Peterborough United (signed in 21/7/2003) lge 76+5/5gls,
    FLC 2, FAC 4+1, Others 1+2

Honours: Wales Full–6, Welsh Cup Winner–1989, 1991,
Anglo Italian Cup Winner–1995

Former Glanamman School and Afan Nedd schoolboy winger
before joining Welsh League side Briton Ferry, signing for the
Swans in August 1988. Had previously had trials with
Middlesbrough, but after being told by manager Bruce Rioch to
get his hair cut, or he would not get a contract, he refused to
sign for Boro, and after trials with the Swans, signed

professional forms at the Vetch Field. His first season with the Swans, saw him play in the Welsh Cup Final as substitute at the end of season against Kidderminster Harriers at the Vetch Field coming on for Brian Wade. In his last season for the Swans he finished joint top goalscorer with 12 league goals with Colin West. Left sided midfielder with the longest throw in the Football League at the time, he also played occasionally for the Swans at left full back, a position he was to revert to in later years. Possessing a remarkable standard of fitness, up to his last season with the Swans, he played 136 consecutive league and cup matches, from 19th March 1991 to end of season 1992/93, scoring many memorable goals with his left foot from outside the penalty area. One notable effort beating Stoke City keeper Bruce Grobbelaar in March 1993 at the Vetch Field in a 2-1 defeat for the Swans. He scored his first Swans goal during his second season, in a 1-0 home win over Mansfield Town. In season 1989/90 he played in the record cup defeat at Liverpool 0-8, and also against Greek side Panathinaikos in the European Cup Winners Cup tie. At the end of season 1990/91 he played in his second Welsh Cup Final, beating Wrexham 2-0. After the Swans had lost in the Second Division Play Offs semi-final to West Bromwich Albion, he left the Vetch Field to join Notts. County for a tribunal fixed fee of £275,000. On the 19th March he was a member of the County side that won the Anglo Italian Cup Final at Wembley, beating Ascoli, 2-1. He joined Birmingham City in February 1996, but after a loan period with Ipswich Town, joined Reading in February 1998 for £75,000. It was at St. Andrews with City that he was to gain his first International cap for Wales in a 2-0 defeat in Lugano against Switzerland on the 24th April 1996. Struggling to command a regular place in the 'Royals' starting line-up, following a loan period with Peterborough United in October 1998, he joined his former boss at Swansea, Frank Burrows, in a free transfer move to Cardiff City, two months later. He soon became a hugely influential figure with the 'Bluebirds', gaining promotion in his first season in the Third Division in third place. Relegated within twelve months back to the Third Division, within three seasons 'Leggie' had been one of the club's most consistent performers as the Bluebirds reached the First Division following a dramatic Play Off Final win over QPR in May 2003. At Ninian Park he had also regained his place in the Welsh International side. Playing in a mainly defensive left sided role for Cardiff, he was surprisingly offered a free transfer at the end of the 2002/03 season, after the 'Bluebirds' had gained promotion to the First Division, signing instead for Peterborough United. The *South Wales Evening Post* revealed in March 2005 that the former Swans' midfielder was facing a second operation to remove a tumour on his neck, after undergoing a similar operation four years previously. However, on the 28th April 2005 he was forced to retire from the game when his neck tumour was found to be cancerous.

16. LEITCH, Andrew (ANDY) Buchanan

Birthplace: Exeter, 27/3/1950
Ht: 6ft-5ins, **Wt:** 12st-7lbs
Swans debut: v. Torquay United (h), FLC 1-1, 9/8/1975

Swansea City Career Statistics				
Season	*League*	*FLC*	*FAC*	*WC*
1975/76	15+1/6gls	1+1/2gls	1	1/2gls
Total	15+1/6gls	1+1/2gls	1	1/2gls

Career:
Swansea City (trial in August 1970)
Paulton Rovers (signed in close season 1974)
Swansea City (signed in July 1975)
Minehead (signed in February 1976)
Weymouth (£2,000 signed in season 1978/79)
Bath City (signed in close season 1979/80)
Yeovil Town (signed in close season 1980/81)
Forest Green Rovers (signed in close season 1981/82)
Gloucester City
Dorchester Town

Honours: Southern League First Division South Champions–1976, F.A. Vase Winner–1982, Hellenic League Premier Division Champions–1982

Tall, gangling centre forward who made Football Combination appearances for the Swans on a trial basis in August 1970 under Roy Bentley, but returned to non-league football with no offer of a professional contract. In the close season of 1975, John Charles, reserve/youth team manager and Swans manager Harry Griffiths persuaded the prolific goalscorer at non-league level to sign a professional contract with the Swans. The former Monkspark Comprehensive schoolboy had been a late developer in the game, only playing boys club football up to the age of twenty-one, before he played in the Gloucester County League with Cadbury Heath, winning three consecutive championships with the club. Stepping into senior football with Bath City, after a couple of games, he then joined Western league side Paulton Rovers, and twelve months later entered the professional scene at the Vetch Field. Whilst with Bath City he played in an Anglo Italian competition with Bangor City, and Italian sides Udinese and Reggina. He made his Swans debut as substitute for Robbie James at the Vetch Field in the first round of the League Cup competition against Torquay United, losing 1-2, missed the next match, the opening league fixture of the season, but then made his full debut in the second league game at Rochdale, scoring the Swans goal in a 1-2 defeat. The next game, the second round of the League Cup at Plainmoor, he scored two goals in a 3-5 defeat for the Swans. As the season progressed he formed a useful partnership with striker Geoff Bray, scoring six league goals, and four in the cup, two in the League, and two in the Welsh Cup. He left the Vetch Field in February 1976, joining Southern League side Minehead, and in his first season the club won the Championship of the Southern League First Division South, with Leitch scoring 17 goals from 14 games. The following season, Minehead were runners up to Wimbledon in the Southern League Premier Division, who themselves were elected to the Football League in the close season. In November 1976 he returned to the Vetch Field to play for Minehead in the first round of the FA Cup competition, scoring the only goal of the game to take the club into the second round, where they lost 2-1 at Portsmouth. Despite being beaten by Portsmouth, Andy's goal was one of six consecutive F.A Cup matches he had scored in (over two years 1976-1978), which at the time equalled the record held by West Bromwich Albion's Jeff Astle. Relegated at the end of the season, he was then signed by Weymouth for £2,000, and in season 1979/80 was sold to Alliance League side Bath City. Following a season with Yeovil Town (1980/81), he then joined Hellenic Premier Division side Forest Green Rovers, winning the Championship at the end of season 1981/82, and also beating Rainworth MW in the F.A. Vase Cup Final at Wembley, with Andy scoring two goals. A cartilage problem saw him sidelined for a period, and after a couple of games in local football joined Southern league side Gloucester City. Andy finished his playing career with Dorchester Town, with a broken foot forcing him into retirement. Since leaving school and starting an apprenticeship in the printing industry, Andy has worked for the last fifteen years for Henry Long Printers, and nowadays is tending to improve his golf handicap, rather than watch football.

17. LENIHAN, Michael (MICKY) Martin

Birthplace: Swansea, 15/10/1946
Ht: 5ft-9ins, **Wt:** 10st-10lbs
Swans debut: v. Southend United (a), 25/8/1972

Swansea City Career Statistics		
Season	League	WC
1972/73	6+1	1
1973/74	3+2	1
Total	9+3	2

Career:
Swansea Boys Club
Swansea City (amateur in season 1971/72, signed part-time in 22/8/1972)
Merthyr Tydfil (signed in close season 1974)
Haverfordwest County (signed in 1979)

Honours: Welsh League First Division Champions–1979, Welsh League Premier Division Champions–1980

Prolific goalscorer in local Swansea Senior League with Star Athletic and Swansea Boys Club team, Micky played for the Swans reserve team in the Football Combination during second half of season 1971/72, signing as a part-time professional in August 1972 for Swans manager Roy Bentley, whilst working as a Post Office Sorter in Swansea. Brought up in the Mount Pleasant district of Swansea, the former St. Josephs and Dynevor Grammar schoolboy did not feature in the Swansea schoolboys line-up, making his mark after leaving school in the Swansea Senior League. A change of management saw Harry Gregg take over at the Vetch Field, and with a different approach to the game, Lenihan very rarely featured in the Swans first team line-up. He was released at the end of season 1973/74 joining Southern League side Merthyr Tydfil, where he proved to be a consistent goalscorer, top scorer in season 1975/76 in Southern League Division One North with 27 goals, and in 1977/78 season he scored 22, joint top scorer at Merthyr with Paul Cavell. After almost five seasons in the Southern League with Merthyr he signed for Haverfordwest County, as player manager, and in consecutive seasons won the Welsh League First Division and Premiership Championships. In charge at County for over ten seasons, in that time the club finished each season in a top six position in the league. After retiring from the game he assisted former County manager Ray Davies at Welsh

League side Briton Ferry, and also had a period with the Swans junior sides at the Vetch Field. Since leaving the professional game, Micky has been employed as a sales representative, worked for a financial company for twenty years, and is currently working for a courier company delivering legal documents.

18. LETHERAN, Glanville (GLAN)

Birthplace: Briton Ferry, 1/5/1956
Ht: 6ft-1½ins, **Wt:** 12st-4lbs
Swans debut: v. Notts. County (a), 22/9/1979

Swansea City Career Statistics			
Season	League	FAC	WC
1979/80	21	5	
1980/81			1
Total	21	5	1

Career:
Leeds United (from apprentice in May 1973) lge 1
Scunthorpe United (loan in 12/8/1976) lge 27
Chelsea (loan in 19/8/1977) lge 0
Notts County (loan in 11/11/1977) lge 0
Chesterfield (signed in 2/12/1977) lge 63
Swansea City (£50,000 signed in 19/9/1979)

Honours: Wales Yth, U-21–2, U-23–1

Former apprentice with Leeds United, had loan spells with Scunthorpe United, Chelsea and Notts. County prior to joining Chesterfield in December 1977 on a permanent transfer. Born in Briton Ferry but moved to Dafen, near Llanelli at the age of eight, going to Havard Road School and Stebonheath Secondary Modern. His last year in school saw him make appearances at the age of fifteen for Llanelli in the Welsh League, joining Leeds United as an apprentice on leaving school. He made his first team debut for United as substitute for keeper Shaw against Hibernian in the second round, first leg of the UEFA Cup competition in season 1973/74, keeping a clean sheet, and at the end of the following season he was on the bench in the European Cup Final defeat in Paris by Bayern Munich. Glan made just one league appearance for Leeds United, at Elland Road on the 19th April 1975 in a 2-1 win over Ipswich Town. He signed for Third Division Chesterfield after their keeper Steve Ogrizovic had joined Liverpool, making 23 consecutive appearances before making way for Phil Tingay to see out the season. He made 34 appearances the following season for Chesterfield, and started season 1979/80 as first choice for Chesterfield prior to his move to the Vetch Field. Took over from Geoff Crudgington in goal at the Vetch Field, played 21 consecutive league games, and five matches in the FA Cup before making way for Scottish international keeper, and former Elland Road team mate Dave Stewart. Making just the one Welsh Cup appearance during his second season with the Swans, against Caerleon, he had his contract cancelled on the

12th May 1981. He signed for Blackpool after leaving the Vetch Field, but failed to make a league appearance, drifting into non-league football at Oxford City, then joining Alliance League side Scarborough. Returning to Wales he signed for Bangor City, and played in the F.A Trophy Cup Final against Northwich Victoria at the end of season 1983/84, losing out in the replay at Maine Road. Glan returned to West Wales, finishing his career with Carmarthenshire League side Dafen, Llanelli and occasional games for Carmarthen Town in the Welsh League at the age of 38. Since then he has taken his coaching badges, become a UEFA 'A' licensed coach, currently doing his professional licence. Since the early 1990's, Glan was employed as a scout in South Wales for Leeds United and Manchester United, and besides being a goalkeeper coach at the Vetch Field and at Exeter City, has also been working for the FAW of Wales as a specialist goalkeeper coach, and has travelled to Australia, St. Kitts and Nevis, Haiti, and St. Vincent working for UEFA. Season 2004/05 saw Glan join Leicester City as a specialist goalkeeper coach, but he left the club in November 2004 following a change of management, and by January 2005 had linked up with Ian Rush at Chester on a part-time coaching role. In the summer of 2004 his son Kyle, also a goalkeeper, was taken on as a scholar at the Vetch Field with the Swans. For a number of years in the close season Glan has been an accomplished local cricketer in the South Wales League, mainly with his local club Dafen.

19. LEWIS, David Jenkin (JINKY)

Birthplace: Merthyr Tydfil, November 1912. **Died:** Llanharan, Bridgend, 4/8/1997
Ht: 5ft-7ins, **Wt:** 10st-4lbs
Swans debut: v. Burnley (a), 18/10/1930

Swansea Town Career Statistics			
Season	*League*	*FAC*	*WC*
1930/31	14		2/1gls
1931/32	39/1gls	1	7/1gls
1932/33	13/1gls		
1933/34	16/1gls		
1934/35	10/1gls		2/1gls
1935/36	20/1gls		1
Total	112/5gls	1	12/3gls

Career:
Gellifaelog Amateurs
Swansea Town (amateur in September 1930, professional in 25/10/1930)
Bury (signed in 2/5/1936) lge 8
Crystal Palace (signed in October 1937) lge 0

Bristol Rovers (signed in 1938) lge 0
Bath City (signed in season 1938/39)

Honours: Wales Full–2, Welsh Cup Winner–1932

Former Merthyr and Georgetown schoolboy, who signed for the Swans as a seventeen-year-old, but unfortunately the left winger was hampered with knee problems throughout his career at the Vetch Field. As a schoolboy he figured in an International trial match, also winning Championship Honours in consecutive seasons with his local side in the Merthyr & District League. Replacing Gordon Bell for his league debut at Burnley in October 1930, 'Jinky' played in the next two league matches, but had to wait until midway through the second half of the season to make further appearances. The following season he started on the left wing in the opening league fixture, and had his best season for the Swans, missing just three league games, also scoring his first league goal in a 1-0 win over Oldham Athletic. That season was to see 'Jinky' provide numerous opportunities for Cyril Pearce to score his record thirty-five league goals during the season. At the end of the season he also played in the Welsh Cup Final replay winning team that beat Wrexham 2-0. The original fixture had ended in a 1-1 draw, with Lewis scoring the Swans goal. The 1932/33 season saw 'Jinky' gain his first Welsh international cap, when he played in Edinburgh on the 26th October 1932 in a 5-2 win over Scotland. His other international appearance came in the next game against England, in a 0-0 draw at Wrexham. Missing all the second half of season 1932/33 through injury, 'Jinky' failed to make regular appearances for the Swans over the next three seasons, and in May 1936 he signed for Second Division Bury. Making just eight league appearances for Bury, one of those was against the Swans in November 1936, in a 2-0 win at Gigg Lane. The next two seasons saw Lewis sign for Crystal Palace and Bristol Rovers, but failed to make an appearance for either side, joining non-league side Bath City for the 1938/39 season. During WW2 he made guest appearances for Blyth Shipyard, Newcastle United, Bristol Rovers, Llanelly and Aberaman. He retired from playing in 1945, had a number of jobs, including a postman in Sketty, Swansea.

20. LEWIS, David (DAI) Sandbrook

Birthplace: Cardigan, 12/2/1936
Ht: 5ft-8ins, **Wt:** 10st-0lbs
Swans debut: v. Bristol City (h), 14/12/1957

Swansea Town Career Statistics			
Season	*League*	*FAC*	*WC*
1957/58	14/1gls	1/1gls	1/1gls
1958/59	5		
Total	19/1gls	1/1gls	1/1gls

Career:
Swansea Town (signed professional in 21/12/1957)
Torquay United (signed in July 1960) lge 16/2gls
Haverfordwest County (signed in 9/8/1961)
Llanelly (signed by September 1965)

Former Pentrepoeth Infants, Martin Street Boys School and Dynevor Secondary Modern Schoolboy who signed for the Swans from local league side St. Judes. After appearances in the club's Combination and Welsh League sides he made his league debut at the Vetch Field in December 1957, taking over from Woods at inside forward in a 5-1 win over Bristol City, signing professional forms for the Swans a week later. After leaving school he started training as an Engineer with Post Office Telephones, did his National Service in the RAF, and following the death of his father, took over the family Ironmonger's business in Morriston. Within a week of making his league debut he signed professional forms at the Vetch Field, but unbeknown to him he had been in line for international Honours at Amateur level for Wales prior to his turning professional. Over the next fifteen league games he missed just two matches, and also appeared for the Swans, scoring in both the FA Cup tie defeat at Burnley, and in the Welsh Cup win over Newport County at Somerton Park. On the 19th February 1958, along with Mel Nurse he was selected to play in a trial match at Somerton Park for the first Welsh U-23 side. He scored his only league goal for the Swans in a 1-2 home defeat by Leyton Orient in March 1958. His second season at the Vetch Field saw him make just five league appearances, and after being placed on the open to transfer list in April 1960, in July 1960 he signed for Third Division Torquay United. Despite having a good run in the Torquay United first team, he returned to West Wales in the 1961 close season joining former Swans player Arthur Willis at Haverfordwest County, playing against the Swans in the West Wales Senior Cup Final in September 1961. He remained at Bridge Meadow until the end of the 1964/65 season, before linking up with manager Doug Wallace at Llanelly, later playing under former Swans team mate Des Palmer twelve months later. Within a couple of months of his returning to the Swansea area from Torquay he started work in the Steel Company of Wales at Port Talbot, later worked for Robin Wayne Florists, before working fifteen years for the Health Authority at Singleton Hospital in the Sterile Supply Department up to his retirement.

21. LEWIS, DUDLEY Keith

Birthplace: Swansea, 17/11/1962
Ht: 5ft-10½ins, **Wt:** 10st-9lbs
Swans debut: v. Notts. County (a), 7/2/1981

Career:
Swansea City (from apprentice in July 1981)
Huddersfield Town (£50,000 signed in 11/7/1989) lge 32+2
Halifax Town (loan in 24/10/1991) lge 11

Wrexham (signed in March 1992) lge 8+1
Halifax Town (signed in August 1992) lge 10+3
Torquay United (signed in December 1992) lge 9
Weymouth (signed in February 1993)
Merthyr Tydfil (signed in August 1993) Conf apps 34
Carmarthen Town (signed in July 1994)
Llanelli (signed in November 1996)

Swansea City Career Statistics						
Season	League	FLC	FAC	WC	ECWC	FRT
1980/81	12			4		
1981/82	1	1				
1982/83	23/1gls	1	1	5	2+1	
1983/84	37	1	1	5	2	
1984/85	43/1gls	1	2	6	4	
1985/86	22+2	2	1	2		2
1986/87	32	4	5	1		3
1987/88	18		1	0+1		
1988/89	40		3	5+1		2
Total	228+2/2gls	10	14	28+2	8+1	7

Honours: Wales–1, Sch–2, Yth–5, U-21–9, Welsh Cup Winner–1981,1983, 1989, West Wales Senior Cup Winner–1987, 1988

Outstanding defender in schools football partnered regularly by team mate at the Vetch Field Gary Richards, played for both Waun Wen and Pentrehafod Schools, Swansea Schoolboys, before signing as an apprentice with the Swans along with Gary Richards. He made his debut as a replacement for Jeremy Charles at Notts. County in the beginning of February 1981, and after missing the next league game, he returned in place of the experienced Leighton Phillips to forge a youthful partnership in the heart of the Swans defence with Nigel Stevenson, that was to take the club to the First Division following a memorable victory at Preston in the last match of the season. Not particularly tall for a central defender, his asset being his pace across the park in covering, and the ability to read the game well, especially during his early years. His First Division debut came in the last game of the 1981/82 season at Villa Park, but during the club's second term in the top flight, he made regular appearances, especially when financial problems surfaced and experienced professionals were released. Already capped as a schoolboy, he captained Wales in season 1980/81 in West Germany in the finals of the European Youth Championship, and in October 1981 made his U-21 debut for Wales at Somerton Park against France, winning 2-0. His only Full international appearance came at Ninian Park against Brazil in June 1993. Following the Swans relegation to the Second Division, he became a regular in the club's rearguard, partnering Stevenson for many seasons, reverting to a right full back, before regaining his place in central defence under manager Terry Yorath alongside a young Andrew Melville. An alert defender, not always noted for his passing ability, and goal prowess, he was in particularly fine form during season 1986/87, when the Swans were doing well in the league, and after the Swans had beaten West Bromwich Albion in the third round of the F.A. Cup, lost at the Vetch Field to Hull City, which saw Dudley carried off on a stretcher after a late tackle by one of the opposing strikers. By the end of the season he had returned to first team duty, playing in the end of season West Wales Senior Cup Final against Briton Ferry Athletic. He also played in the final of the same competition twelve months later against Pembroke Borough. In July 1989 after failing to agree a new contract he joined Huddersfield Town, for a tribunal fixed fee of £50,000. His first game for the Terriers the next season was ironically at Leeds Road against the Swans. After a loan spell with Halifax Town, he left the Terriers in March 1992 to sign for Wrexham on non-contract terms until the end of the season. He started season 1992/93 with Halifax Town, but before Xmas had returned south to sign for Torquay

United, and in February 1993 joined Southern League side Weymouth. He started the 1993/94 season with Conference side Merthyr Tydfil, making 34 appearances, before signing for Welsh League side Carmarthen Town, and then signing for Llanelli as player manager in November 1996. He did not enjoy a particularly successful spell as player manager at Stebonheah Park, and was replaced by his former Swans team mate Robbie James in July 1997 as manager, and joined Pontardawe Athletic. He later had spells as a player with Welsh League clubs Bridgend Town, Port Talbot Athletic until the end of season 2000/01 to join Ammanford Town, then had a similar role at Morriston Town. On his return to his hometown he went to work for the Post Office, where he continues to work up to the present day. Besides his international honours with Wales, Dudley played in three Welsh Cup Final winning teams with the Swans, in 1981 (against Hereford United), 1983 (against Wrexham) and 1989 (against Kidderminster Harriers), and also in two Welsh Cup semi-finals in 1984 and 1985. His knee problem also prevented him from making appearances in the Swans successful Third Division Play Offs at the end of the 1987/88 season. Scoring just two league goals for the Swans during his career, the first was at Brighton in October 1982. A nephew of former Swans player Frankie Squires, his elder brother Paul was also an apprentice with Everton in the late 1970's.

22. LEWIS, Harold (HARRY) Howell

Birthplace: Merthyr, 25/10/1910
Ht: 5ft-10ins, **Wt:** 11st-10lbs
Swans debut: v. Bury (h), 20/3/1937

Swansea Town Career Statistics			
Season	League	FAC	WC
1936/37	9/3gls		
1937/38	23/8gls	1	1
1938/39	13/2gls		
Total	45/13gls	1	1

Career:
Dowlais United
Rochdale (amateur in July 1928, professional in August 1928) lge 62/16gls
Arsenal (signed in February 1931) lge 0
Southend United (signed in May 1932) lge 18/6gls, FAC 3
Notts. County (signed in June 1933) lge 32/7gls
West Ham United (signed in June 1935) lge 4/4gls
Swansea Town (signed in 11/3/1937)
Queen of the South (£400 signed in 12/6/1939)
Watford (signed in October 1940)

Honours: Wales Sch–1

Clever inside forward who made his league debut with Third Division North side Rochdale, scoring on his debut against Crewe Alexandra on 2/3/1929 after joining the club from Dowlais, initially as an amateur, before signing professional in August 1928, creating a name for himself at Rochdale as a goal scoring inside forward later to join First Division Arsenal. Brought up in the Twyn area of Merthyr, Harry attended Twynyrodyn School, Merthyr, played for Merthyr Scholboys, made one appearance for the Wales Schoolboys against Scotland at inside right on the 25th April 1925 at Ninian Park, Cardiff, and after leaving school worked at the local Packman's Office and at a Men's Outfitters, playing for Merthyr YMCA and Dowlais United, prior to joining Rochdale at the age of seventeen along with goalkeeper Jackie Mittell. Unable to make an appearance at Highbury for the Gunners, he then joined Third Division South side Southend United, later stepping up a division to join Notts. County, and continue with his ratio of goals from inside forward. After a short period with West Ham United he joined the Swans for a substantial fee, making his debut for the club in March 1937, scoring his first Swans goal in his second league game, against Nottingham Forest. The 1937/38 season saw him start at inside left, and by the end of the season was joint top goalscorer with Tommy Lang with eight league goals. Bad health forced him to miss almost all of the 1938/39 season, but in the last match of the season he scored the Swans goal in a 1-6 defeat at Chesterfield. In June 1939 he was transferred to Scottish side Queen of the South for £400. The high point of his career came on the 7th May 1938 when late in the match he beat a Bradford Park Avenue player and smashed the ball into the net. The two points the Swans earned from that away win was enough to save them from relegation that season. It was the Swans only away win of the season, against a Bradford side that finished the season in seventh place. Harry played in the Swans side that lost to Shrewsbury Town in a Welsh Cup Final replay in September 1938, held over from the previous season. Returning south, he made guest appearances for Reading and Southend United in season 1939/40, and signed for Watford in October 1940. During WW2 he worked in a factory in Watford making Instruments for Submarines, also a member of the Homeguard. Having no involvement in football when the Football League was resumed after WW2, Harry was employed in general factory work, and for a spell worked at Southend Airport up to his retirement.

23. LEWIS, IDRIS

Birthplace: Trealaw, 26/8/1915. **Died:** Swansea, March 1996
Ht: 5ft-6ins, **Wt:** 10st-0lbs
Swans debut: v. Sheffield United (a), 26/12/1935

Career:
Ton Boys Club
Gelli Colliery

Swansea Town (signed in May 1935)
Sheffield Wednesday (signed in 22/6/1938) lge 18/7gls,
FAC 5/1gls
Swansea Town (signed in 1939)
Bristol Rovers (signed in 31/7/1946) lge 13/2gls
Newport County (signed in October 1946) lge 27/4gls
Haverfordwest County (signed in 30/7/1948)
Pembroke Borough

Swansea Town Career Statistics			
Season	League	FAC	WC
1935/36	17	1	2
1936/37	26/2gls	4	
1937/38	23/2gls		4/2gls
Total	66/4gls	5	6/2gls

Another player on the Vetch Field playing staff who lost a large part of his playing career because of the Second World War. A traditional winger at outside right, he was a good crosser of the ball with right or left foot. Speedy and brave he was his 'own man'. Initially with Ton Boys Club, after signing for Gelli Colliery, Idris joined the Swans and made his league debut at Sheffield United in December 1935, retaining his place for almost the remainder of the season on the right wing. He scored his first goal for the Swans at the Vetch Field against Burnley, on the 11th February 1936 in a 3-0 win. Consistent appearances over the next two seasons with the Swans saw him included in the Welsh Cup Final side that played Shrewsbury Town in May 1938. He refused to accept the deal offered to him by the Swans in the 1938 close season, declined to play in a trial match, and was included in the transfer that brought Rhodes to the Vetch Field, with Lewis going to Second Division side Sheffield Wednesday, making a large impact in the side that ended the season in third place, one point behind runners-up, local rivals Sheffield United. In his first game for Wednesday he scored a hat-trick, and after two appearances in the 1939/40 season, following the suspension of the Football League because of the outbreak of WW2, returned to the Vetch Field, making occasional appearances in the South West Regional League before joining the Army. As well as representing the Army during WW2, he also played for the Welsh Serviceman against the Metropolitan Police in May 1942. When he came back from the Army, he then went to Bristol Rovers, then signed for Newport County halfway through the season. Remaining in South Wales in July 1948 he signed for Welsh League side Haverfordwest County. He later joined Pembroke Borough, making an appearance against the Swans in a Welsh Cup tie in February 1951.

24. LEWIS, JOHN

Birthplace: Tredegar, 15/10/1955
Ht: 5ft-9ins, **Wt:** 11st-3lbs
Swans debut: v. Bolton Wanderers (a), 31/10/1987

Swansea City Career Statistics				
Season	League	FAC	WC	P/Offs
1987/88	25/1gls	2	2	0+2
Total	25/1gls	2	2	0+2

Career:
Aberbargoed
Pontllanfraith
Cardiff City (signed in August 1978) lge 135+5/9gls
Newport County (signed in September 1983) lge 153/8gls

Swansea City (signed in 26/10/1987)
Abergavenny Thursday (signed in February 1989)

Honours: Wales U-21–1, Fourth Division Play Off Winner–1989, Abacus National Division Champions–1991, 1992, Welsh Intermediate Cup Winner–1991, West Wales Senior Cup Winner–1988

Experienced left side midfielder who was signed by Swans manager Terry Yorath in October 1987 from Newport County, and by the end of the season had helped the club win promotion via the Play Offs, the first season the Play Offs had been used for determining promotion in the Football League. On schoolboy forms with Bristol Rovers for three years earlier in his career, John played most of his early football for Gwent Senior League side Aberbargoed, and after just one game for Pontllanfraith was signed by Cardiff City, just prior to the start of the 1978/79 season. Within a couple of seasons he became an influential figure on the left side of the 'Bluebirds' midfield, making thirty-nine league appearances during season 1982/83 when they finished runners up in the Third Division to Portsmouth. In September 1982, as an over age player, he captained the Wales U-21 side that drew 0-0 at Ninian Park in a European Championship U-21 qualifying match against Norway. Making almost one hundred and fifty league appearances for the Bluebirds, he then joined Newport County in September 1983, and despite a couple of seasons when the club enjoyed mid-table success in the Third Division, found themselves relegated to the Fourth Division at the end of the 1986/87 season. County also lost in the final of the Welsh Cup at the end of the season to Merthyr Tydfil, with Lewis, now player manager, playing in the final, and the replay at Ninian Park. In October 1987 he completed the trio of South Wales league clubs by signing for the Swans, but by the end of the season, County had lost their league status, and relegated to the Conference. He developed back problems during his only season at the Vetch Field, which restricted his appearances for the Swans, and following the club's promotion to the Third Division he retired from the full time game altogether, joining Abergavenny in February 1989, initially as a player, but then as player coach. One of his last games for the Swans was the West Wales Senior Cup Final win over Pembroke Borough in May 1988. In four seasons the club won the Abacus National Division Championship in consecutive seasons, also winning the Welsh Intermediate Cup Final in 1991 against Mostyn. Returning to the newly formed Newport AFC as player and assistant manager, after a short period with Barry Town, he guided Ebbw Vale into qualifying for the Inter Toto Cup competition on two consecutive seasons in 1996/97 and 1997/98. Further managerial positions at Merthyr and Rhayader saw him become assistant to Roddy Collins at Irish side Bohemians, before returning to the League of Wales scene with Llanelli. A further spell at Merthyr as player coach, and four months as manager, saw him then travel to West Wales side Haverfordwest County as manager. Following a period of eighteen months out of the game, in which he became Glasgow Celtic's Chief Recruitment Officer for Wales, in November 2003 he took over as manager of Tredegar Town, working also as an NVQ Assessor for Sport and Recreation in local colleges.

25. LEWIS, Wilfred (WILF) Leslie

Birthplace: Swansea, 1/7/1903. **Died:** Swansea, November 1979
Ht: 5ft-10ins, **Wt**: 12st-0lbs
Swans debut: v. Colwyn Bay, WC-4, 24/2/1926

Swansea Town Career Statistics			
Season	League	FAC	WC
1925/26	8/3gls		3/3gls
1926/27	8/6gls	1	1
1927/28	39/25gls	1	2
1928/29	10/9gls		
Total	65/43gls	2	6/3gls

Career:
Baldwins Welfare
Swansea Amateurs
Swansea Town (signed in March 1924)
Huddersfield Town (£7,000 signed in November) lge 15/7gls
Derby County (signed in April 1931) lge 8/3gls
Yeovil & Petters United (signed in July 1932)
    Total apps 73/85gls
Bath City (signed in December 1933)
Altrincham (signed in July 1934)
Cardiff City (signed in August 1934) lge 34/6gls
Haverfordwest Athletic (signed in September 1936)

Honours: Wales Full–6, Wales Junior International, Welsh
League Representative XI, West Wales Senior Cup Winner–1925,
1926, 1927

Previously with local league sides Baldwins Welfare and
Swansea Amateurs, he initially had difficulty in establishing
himself in the Swans league side because of the form of Deacon,
Fowler and Thompson, despite having the ability to play in
either inside forward position, or at centre forward. Early in his
career with the Swans he played in three consecutive West
Wales Senior Cup Finals, beating Llanelly in January 1925,
Merthyr Town in April 1926, and twelve months later Bridgend
Town, when he scored a hat-trick in a 3-1 win. Wilf made his
Swans' first team debut in a Welsh Cup tie at Colwyn Bay,
scoring in a 1-1 draw, and in his first league start for the Swans
scored both goals in a 2-2 Vetch Field draw against Sheffield
Wednesday. A natural player with two good feet, and good in
the air, he had earlier in his career been coached by former
Swans player Jack Nicholas. His first season at the Vetch Field
saw him play in the Welsh Cup Final in April 1926, losing 3-2 to
Ebbw Vale. The following season, despite only making eight
league appearances, he scored his first hat-trick for the Swans,
in a 3-0 Vetch Field win over Oldham Athletic in December 1927.
Capped at Junior level for Wales against Ireland on the 20th
February 1926 at Holyhead, almost twelve months later, he

gained his first Welsh international cap, against England in
Wrexham scoring in a 3-3 draw. In February 1924, whilst with
Swansea Amateurs, during a trial game between North and
South for the Wales Amateur side, Wilf scored two goals for the
South team, and failed to gain selection for the Welsh team that
played England the following month at Llandudno. In April
1927 he scored for the Welsh League Representative side that
played the Irish Free State in Dublin. With Len Thompson
missing for the first half of the 1927/28 season, Lewis was given
the opportunity of starting the season at inside left, and for the
remainder of the season was a regular in the side, topping the
goal scoring charts with 25 league goals, also scoring two more
goals for Wales at international level, against England and
Ireland, and scoring his second league hat-trick for the Swans,
this time against South Shields at the Vetch Field in October
1927. Reputed to be a cool player under pressure, he was sold
for a Swans' record transfer fee of £7,000 in November 1928, but
in only his second game for the Yorkshire club suffered a broken
leg which virtually ended his league career, despite making
league appearances later for Derby County and Cardiff City.
An injury towards the end of the 1929/30 season would also see
him miss the FA Cup Final against Arsenal. Prior to joining
Cardiff City he enjoyed a successful spell with non-league side
Yeovil & Petters United and Bath City, and finished his career
with Haverfordwest Athletic, who were due to start their first
season in the Welsh League, Second Division (Western Section).
At Yeovil, during his first season at the club he scored sixty-
three goals, scoring five in one game. During the summer
months he was a prominent member of Swansea CC, and at one
stage it was thought he would be invited to join the Glamorgan
County Cricket Club's playing staff.

26. LEYLAND, PETER

Birthplace: Golebourne, Lancs, JAS, 1911
Ht: 5ft-10½ins, **Wt**: 11st-7lbs
Swans debut: v. Charlton Athletic (a), 29/2/1936

Swansea Town Career Statistics			
Season	League	FAC	WC
1935/36	11		
1936/37	7	2	
1937/38	5		3/4gls
1938/39	2		
Total	25	2	3/4gls

Career:
Atherton
Bolton Wanderers (amateur in May 1930)
Blackpool (amateur in November 1930)
Chorley (signed in May 1931)
Sheffield Wednesday (signed in 6/8/1932) lge 0
Swansea Town (£500 signed in 25/2/1936)
Runcorn (signed in June 1939)

Centre half signed in a part exchange deal for Swans centre half
Harry Hanford from Sheffield Wednesday in February 1936,
with Leyland at the time valued at £500. After his arrival he
missed just the one league match until the end of the season.
The following season, despite starting the new term at centre
half, he lost his place to Reuben Simons, and for the remainder
of his time at the Vetch Field was unable to command a regular
starting place in the Swans line-up, despite making the
occasional appearance at centre forward. In February 1938 he
scored four goals for the Swans in a Welsh Cup sixth round tie
against Llanelly at the Vetch Field. The same season he played in
the Welsh Cup Final against Shrewsbury Town, which ended in
a 2-2 draw, with the replay being held over until the start of the

next season. He was placed on the transfer list in May 1938, valued at £400, which was reduced to £300 in 1939. After starting his career with non-league Atherton, he signed amateur forms with First Division Bolton Wanderers in May 1930, failed to make an appearance, drifted back into non-league with Chorley, then joined Sheffield Wednesday in August 1932. He failed to make the staring line-up with Wednesday in the First Division, with his league debut being made with the Swans following his arrival at the Vetch Field. He was released by the Swans at the end of the 1938/39 season, and returned to the non-league scene with Runcorn.

27. LINDSAY, JOHN

Birthplace: Cardenden, Fife
Ht: 5ft-9ins, **Wt:** 11st-7lbs
Swans debut: v. Barnsley (h), 1/2/1930

Swansea Town Career Statistics			
Season	League	FAC	WC
1929/30	8/2gls		2
1930/31	8	1	1
Total	16/2gls	1	3

Career:
Clyde (signed in October 1924)
Partick Thistle (signed in close season 1924)
Rhyl Athletic (signed in June 1927)
Liverpool (signed in April 1928) lge 14/2gls
Swansea Town (signed in January 1930)
Rhyl (signed in June 1931)
Bangor City (signed in January 1933)
Lochgelly Amateurs

Joined the Swans as an inside forward from First Division side Liverpool at the end of January 1930 for a fee in the region of £550. He scored in his second league game for the Swans, the only goal of the match against Cardiff City at the Vetch Field, scoring his second league goal for the Swans two games later in a 3-3 draw at Bradford City. After his first season he struggled to command a regular place in the starting line-up, despite playing at outside right, and at the time was deemed as being not strong enough for the physical element of the game. Earlier in his career he had made a name for himself as a dashing winger who at times made good use of his pace, sprinting past his full back before firing over a cross, or cutting in to deliver a powerful shot. He was placed on the transfer list in May 1931 at £500, returned to North Wales to sign for Rhyl Athletic later played for Bangor City before returning north to join Lochgelly Amateurs. He started his senior career with Clyde in 1924, after previously playing for Inverkeithing and Bowhill Juniors.

Joining Partick Thistle prior to the start of season 1924/5, after making nineteen appearances, scoring three goals, spread over three seasons, he travelled south to sign for North Wales side Rhyl Athletic, then linking up with Liverpool almost a year later. Earlier in his career in Scotland he served a seven year apprenticeship as a plater with Babcock & Wilcox, later worked at Leyland Motors, then at the ROF at Euxton, a Fleetwood Engineering Company, and later in Preston docks. His wife was singer Dorothy Dix.

28. LLOYD, Clifford (BOCCO) John

Birthplace: Swansea, 30/9/1902. **Died:** Swansea, 3/10/1975
Ht: 5ft-9ins, **Wt:** 10st-6lbs
Swans debut: v. Port Vale (h), 4/2/1928

Swansea Town Career Statistics			
Season	League	FAC	WC
1927/28	6		1
1928/29	24	1	
1929/30	9		
Total	39	1	1

Career:
Swansea Town (signed during season 1925/26)
Lincoln City (trial in September 1930)
Nottingham Forest (£250 signed in November 1930) lge 4
Crystal Palace (trial in January to March 1931)
Waterford
Barrow (signed in November 1932)
Ammanford Corries (signed in season 1932/33)

Honours: West Wales Representative XI, West Wales Senior Cup Winner–1927

Joined the Swans from local football during season 1925/26, and on the 23rd January 1926 was selected to play for a West Wales Representative side in an Inter Association game in Mid-Rhondda against a South Wales & Monmouthshire team, whilst still playing for the Swans 'A' side. He was primarily a left half back, but who made his first two league appearances for the Swans at right half back. In April 1927 he was included in a Swans reserve side that beat Bridgend Town in the West Wales Senior Cup Final. Season 1928/29 proved to be his best season as far as appearances in the Swans first team was concerned, making 24 league appearances, but throughout his career at the Vetch Field had to contend with Lachlan McPherson as the main occupant of the left half shirt for the Swans. Placed on the open to transfer list in May 1930, after an extended trial with Lincoln City in September 1930 he signed for Nottingham Forest in November 1930 for £250, making four appearances for the club, drawing one, and losing in the remaining three in the Second Division. He later returned to the Swansea area, and following another trial period, this time with Crystal Palace, he later joined Irish side Waterford, before returning to the Football League to sign for Barrow. He later returned home to South Wales, joining Ammanford Corries.

29. LLOYD, Joseph (JOE) Millington

Birthplace: Shotton, 30/9/1912. **Died:** Shotton, 1/4/1996
Ht: 5ft-10ins, **Wt:** 11st-10lbs
Swans debut: v. Millwall (a), 28/8/1933

Swansea Town Career Statistics			
Season	League	FAC	WC
1933/34	39	4	
1934/35	42	2	3
1935/36	36	1	2
1936/37	39	3	
1937/38	23	1	3/1gls
1938/39	32/1gls	1	1
Total	211/1gls	12	9/1gls

Career:
Connah's Quay & Shotton
Everton (signed in February 1931) lge 0
Swansea Town (trial in August 1932, professional in August 1932)
Wrexham (signed in 10/7/1946) lge 20

Played schoolboy football for Shotton Council School, Flintshire schoolboys, and when playing for local side Connah's Quay & Shotton FC signed for Everton as an amateur in February 1931. Spent eighteen months at Goodison Park, playing in the club's reserve side, without making a first team appearance, before being invited to play in trial games with the Swans in August 1932. Signing professional shortly before the start of the season, he had to wait almost twelve months before he made his debut at Millwall. He had missed the first game of season 1933/34, but replaced Jimmy Miller at left half back, retaining his place for almost the remainder of the season, and for the remaining seasons up to the outbreak of the Second World War. Primarily a defensive left half back, renowned as a good tackler and header of the ball, it took him until March 1938 for him to score his first goal for the Swans, in a Welsh Cup quarter final tie at the Vetch Field against Worcester City, scoring the only goal of the game. The following season he scored his only league goal, in a 2-1 home win over Plymouth Argyle. The 1938/39 season also saw him play for the Swans in the Welsh Cup Final against Shrewsbury Town in May 1938, which resulted in a 2-2 draw.

The replay was held over until the following season, but unfortunately he played no part in the game. Placed on the transfer list at £1,000 at the end of the 1938/39 season, he was re-engaged by manager Green in July 1939, dispelling rumours at the time about the player's future. After serving in the RAF during the war, he returned to his native North Wales, joining Third Division North side Wrexham as a part-time professional, going on to make 20 league appearances. After his playing career ended, he worked as a joiner, settling in the Shotton area until his death in April 1996. A cousin to former Wrexham player Bill Tudor.

30. LOCKHART, NORMAN

Birthplace: Belfast, 4/3/1924
Ht: 5ft-6½ins, **Wt:** 10st-0lbs
Swans debut: v. Southampton, 3/10/1946

Swansea Town Career Statistics			
Season	League	FAC	WC
1946/47	34/11gls	2	1/1gls
1947/48	13/2gls		
Total	47/13gls	2	1/1gls

Career:
Distillery (signed in 15/10/1942)
Linfield (signed in 8/4/1944) 80/34gls
Swansea Town (signed in 28/9/1946)
Coventry City (signed in October 1947) lge 182/41gls
Aston Villa (signed in 20/9/1952) lge 74/10gls, FAC 11/2gls
Bury (£2,000 signed in November 1956) lge 41/6gls
Ards (signed in 1959)

Honours: Northern Ireland–8, Irish League Champions–1945, 1946, Irish Cup Winners–1945, 1946, Gold Cup Winner–1945

Capped at International level whilst with Linfield, the outside left was signed by Swans manager Haydn Green from Irish side Linfield, and in the short time he was at the Vetch Field he was sold to Coventry City for three times his original transfer fee, just prior to Billy McCandless taking over the managerial role at the club. In just over two seasons with Linfield, he was a member of the side that won the Irish League Championship and Irish Cup in 1945 and 1946, also Runners-Up in both competitions in 1944, Gold Cup Winner in 1945, and Runner-Up in 1946, and a County Antrim Shield Runner-Up in 1945. He made his international debut for Ireland on the 28th September 1946 against England at Windsor Park, Belfast, in the first official full Home International after WW2, with Lockhart scoring two goals in a 2-7 defeat, in front of a record crowd of 57,000 fans. He made further international appearances whilst with Coventry City and Aston Villa later in his career, also taking part in a tour of United States and Canada arranged by the Irish F.A. in 1953, appearing in seven of the ten games played. He scored on his league debut for the Swans against Southampton in a 4-2 win at the Vetch Field, and in his first nine league games, scored seven goals, finishing the season as top goalscorer with eleven league goals from the outside left position. Unfortunately for the Swans, they were unable to prevent themselves from relegation to the Third Division South, and within a couple of months of the start of the 1947/48 season he had been transferred to Second Division side Coventry City, where he continued to make an impact as a goalscoring front runner. During the 1949/50 season he scored one of the Sky Blues goals in a 2-1 Swans defeat at the Vetch Field, and in his last season at Highfield Road finished top goalscorer with fifteen goals. He continued his career in the Midlands with First Division side Aston Villa, scoring on his debut for Villa against

League Champions Manchester United, before signing for Bury in November 1956. He made three more appearances for his country whilst with Coventry City, and four whilst with Aston Villa. During season 1956/57 he played for Bury at the Vetch Field in a wing half role. He returned to Ireland to join Ards in 1959.

31. LOGIE, JAMES

Birthplace: Inverness, 1904
Ht: 5ft-8ins, **Wt:** 11st-9 lbs
Swans debut: v. Gillingham (h), 4/4/1925

Swansea Town Career Statistics		
Season	League	WC
1924/25	2/1gls	1
Total	2/1gls	1

Career:
Inverness Clachnacuddin
Aberdeen (trial in January 1924)
Swansea Town (signed in 28/7/1924)
Dunfermline Athletic (signed in July 1925) Slge 3

Signed in July 1924 from Inverness Clachnacuddin, George Logie made his league debut for the Swans at the Vetch Field against Gillingham, scoring the Swans second goal. He had replaced Len Thompson at inside left, played the next league match, but was then left out for the returning Thompson. That season the Swans won the Third Division South Championship. His only other first team appearance was in the Welsh Cup in a 3-1 semi final defeat in Wrexham. In July 1925 he returned to Scottish football signing for Dunfermline Athletic, but after playing in the opening match of the 1925/26 season on the 15th August against Nithsdale Wanderers (won 4-1), played four games later in September against Kings Park (lost 0-2), and his last game on the 3rd October against Arbroath (lost 0-5), all in the inside right position. That season saw Dunfermline break a number of club records and gain promotion to the First Division, but unfortunately, by the time of the end of season team photograph he had left the club.

32. LOVE, IAN James

Birthplace: Cardiff, 1/3/1958
Ht: 5ft-11ins, **Wt:** 11st-4lbs
Swans debut: v. Stockport County (h), 23/8/1986

Career:
Cardiff Corries
Barry Town (signed in August 1979)
Merthyr Tydfil (signed in August 1982)

Barry Town (signed in August 1984)
Eastern, Hong Kong (signed in close season 1985)
Swansea City (signed in August 1986)
Torquay United (loan in March 1989, £2,000 signed in 23/3/1989) lge 8+1
Cardiff City (non-contract signed in September 1989) lge 1+1
Barry Town (signed in August 1989)
Lisvane
Cardiff Corries (player manager in close season 1997)

Swansea City Career Statistics						
Season	League	FLC	FAC	WC	FRT	P/Offs
1986/87	15/3gls	4	2		2/1gls	
1987/88	11+1/5gls					1+2/1gls
1988/89	7+7	2		1	1+1	
Total	33+8/8gls	6	2	1	3+1/1gls	1+2/1gls

Honours: Wales Semi-Professional–2, Fourth Division Play Off Winners–1988

Following the Swans relegation to the Fourth Division, and former Welsh international midfielder Terry Yorath being appointed as manager of the Swans, Ian Love along with co-striker at Barry Town Phil Green attended pre-season training with the Swans, playing in a number of friendly matches. Both players had recently returned to the UK after a stint in Hong Kong with Eastern (Tung Fong). With finances at a premium at the Vetch Field, having just recovered from several High Court battles to avoid being wound up, Love was signed just prior to the start of the season, making his league debut in the opening game of the 1986/87 season, scoring against Stockport County. He created a good impression during the first half of the season as a central striker, with his strong running, hunger for work, and particularly good aerial ability, until he broke his leg in the Boxing Day match at Ninian Park against Cardiff City, forcing him to miss the remainder of the season. He returned for the 1987/88 season in time to make appearances in the end of season Play Offs, which saw the Swans gain promotion to the Third Division. Struggling to command a regular place in the Swans Third Division side, he joined Torquay United on an initial loan period in March 1989, with the transfer then being made permanent on 23rd March 1989 for £2,000. By September 1989 he had joined Cardiff City on a non-contract basis, making just two league appearances before he was released, joining Barry Town. Early in his career he had been a prolific goalscorer with both Barry Town and Merthyr Tydfil in the Southern League, and during season 1982/83 was joint top goalscorer with Derek Elliott at Merthyr with 16 goals. He made appearances for the Wales Semi-professional side in successive seasons whilst with Merthyr Tydfil and Barry Town. Brought up in the Heath area of Cardiff, Ian attended Birchgrove Junior and Llanishen High School, played for Cardiff Schoolboys, Heath Hornets and Cardiff Corinthians in the Cardiff & District Youth Leagues. Finishing his senior playing career at Barry Town, he then took over as manager of the club, later becoming manager of South Wales Senior League side Lisvane. He became manager of Cardiff Corinthians in 1997, played a few matches when needed, and retired from the game completely in 2001. Since leaving the professional game, Ian has worked in Insurance, and is currently involved in the claims department in the Insurance Industry.

33. LOVELL, Stephen (STEVE) John

Birthplace: Swansea, 16/7/1960
Ht: 5ft-9ins, **Wt:** 12st-3lbs
Swans debut: v. Burnley (h), 6/2/1987

Swansea City Career Statistics	
Season	*League*
1986/87	2/1gls
Total	2/1gls

Career:
Crystal Palace (from apprentice in 4/8/1977) lge 68+6/3gls
Memphis Rogues, USA (signed in May 1979)
Stockport County (loan in 3/10/1979) lge 12
Millwall (loan in February 1983, signed in 10/3/1983)
  lge 143+3/43gls
Swansea City (loan in 4/2/1987)
Gillingham (£20,000 signed in 19/2/1987) lge 222+11/94 gls
Bournemouth (signed in November 1992) lge 3

Honours: Wales Sch, Yth, Full–6, FA Youth Cup Winner–1977, 1978

Former Gowerton Grammar School, Swansea schoolboy, Gowerton Juniors and Welsh schoolboy international who joined Crystal Palace as an apprentice, made his First Division debut with the 'Eagles' against Wolverhampton Wanderers in August 1980. The previous season he had made 12 consecutive Fourth Division matches on loan for Stockport County. In 1977 and 1978 he played in consecutive FA Youth Cup Final victories over Everton and Aston Villa. His father Alan had earlier in his career had been a professional with the Swans, and after failing to make a league appearance, made his Football League debut with Stockport County in season 1960/61. Steve gained his first Wales Full international cap on the 18th November 1981 in Russia in a World Cup qualifying game, as a substitute for Jones whilst at Selhurst Park, and following his transfer to Millwall in March 1983 gained a further five Full caps for Wales. The 1984/85 season at Millwall saw Lovell finish top goalscorer with twenty league goals as the club finished runners up in the Third Division behind Champions Bradford City. The following season he again finished top goalscorer, this time with fourteen goals in the Second Division. He joined his hometown club, Swansea on a month loan in early February 1987, scoring on his Swans debut against Burnley at the Vetch Field in a 2-2 draw. Making one further appearance for the Swans he returned to Millwall before his loan had expired, only to sign for Gillingham for £20,000 on the 19th February 1987. There he would go on to prove himself to be a consistent goalscorer, finishing four successive seasons as top goalscorer in the league for the club, making over 200 league appearances, and almost scoring 100 league goals for the club, before joining Bournemouth in November 1992 on a non-contract basis. During seasons 1993/94 and 1994/95 he made non-league appearances with Braintree, Sittingbourne, St. Albans and Hastings, before returning to Sittingbourne in February 1995 as player manager. Winning the Beazer Homes League Southern Division at the end of season 1995/96, he then joined Gravesend & Northfleet in September 1996 as manager. He later made appearances for

Weymouth, Tonbridge Angels, Deal Town, Ashford Town (player coach) and Sittingbourne, before returning to Gillingham in April 2000 to become the Club's Football in the Community Officer. Between August 2003 and December 2004 he was manager of Ryman League Division One side Hastings United. By July 2005 he had returned to Sittingbourne as manager.

34. LOVERIDGE, James (JIMMY) Charles

Birthplace: Swansea, 19/10/1962
Ht: 5ft-8¼ins, **Wt:** 11st-1lbs
Swans debut: v. Chelsea (a), 15/12/1979

Swansea City Career Statistics					
Season	*League*	*FLC*	*FAC*	*WC*	*ECWC*
1979/80	1+1				
1980/81	0+1				
1981/82	1				
1982/83	16+1/1gls	1+1/1gls		3	2/2gls
1983/84	16+2/2gls	1	1	3	
1984/85	5+3/1gls	1	1	1	
Total	39+8/4gls	3+1/1gls	2	7	2/2gls

Career:
Swansea City (from apprentice in November 1979)
Charlton Athletic (signed in June 1985) lge 5+1, FLC 1

Honours: Wales Sch, Yth, U-21–3

Swansea schoolboy, and Welsh schoolboy international striker, who joined the Swans as an apprentice, making his league debut at Stamford Bridge against Chelsea as substitute for Nigel Stevenson, making his full league debut six days later at the Vetch Field against Orient. The former Hafod and Pentrehafod schoolboy played for Wales from the age of fifteen, up to twenty-one, gaining the first of his U-21 caps against Holland in 1982, playing a further two occasions the following year against Norway and Bulgaria. He became a regular in the Swans first team midway through the second season in the First Division when the club were offloading players to ease their wage bill, and it was during this season that he scored his first league goal, at Southampton in a 2-1 defeat. The same season saw him make appearances for the Swans in the ECWC, scoring twice against Sliema Wanderers in a record 12-0 Vetch Field win.
The following season in the Second Division he managed two league goals, one against Charlton Athletic at the Valley, and the second at the Vetch Field against Leeds United, in the last league game of the season, before the club was relegated for a second consecutive time. With the club's financial battle continuing, and after John Bond had replaced Colin Appleton as Swans'

manager, he was released in May 1985, and prior to the start of the 1985/86 season had joined Charlton Athletic. Making his debut for Charlton in the Milk Cup First Round, Second Leg tie at Crystal Palace, Jimmy made his league debut against the same opposition four days later on the 7th September 1985 in a 3-1 win. During his career at the Vetch Field, Jimmy had suffered with knee injuries, but in late 1986 he suffered a knee cruciate injury which ultimately forced him to retire from the professional game. Returning to Swansea, he attempted a comeback with Haverfordwest, but was only able to play one game before he called it a day. Since then Jimmy has established himself in the motor trade in the city with his own business, buying and selling cars, and at the start of season 2003/04 returned to the Vetch Field coaching staff, working as a part-time coach with the Swans' centre of excellence.

35. LOWRIE, GEORGE

Birthplace: Tonypandy, 19/12/1919. **Died:** Kingsmead, Bristol, 4/5/1989
Ht: 5ft-9ins, **Wt:** 11st-7lbs
Swans debut: v. Fulham (a), 6/2/1937

Swansea Town Career Statistics

Season	League	FAC	WC
1936/37	5/1gls	1	2/1gls
1937/38	14/2gls		
Total	19/3gls	1	2/1gls

Career:
Tonypandy (signed in 1933)
Swansea Town (amateur signed in August 1936, professional in January 1937)
Preston North End (signed in December 1937) lge 5
Coventry City (£1,750 signed in June 1939) lge 57/45gls
Northampton Town (signed for season 1941/42) 23/23gls
Newcastle United (£18,500 signed in 11/3/1948) lge 12/5gls
Bristol City (£10,000 signed in September 1949) lge 48/21gls
Coventry City (signed in February 1952) lge 27/12gls
Lovells Athletic (signed in July 1953 until 1956)

Honours: Wales Full–4, War Time International–9

Discovered by Swans' Chief Scout Glyn Evans, George Lowrie signed as an amateur from Tonypandy in 1936, signing professional in January 1937, making his Swans debut a month later in February 1937 against Fulham at outside left, replacing Joe Pears. He kept his place for three consecutive league games, returning to the reserves when Pears came back in to the Swans league side. Came back into the Swans league line-up for last two league games, scoring his first league goal in last league

game of the season against Chesterfield in 4-1 Vetch Field win. He also scored in a Welsh Cup away win at Bristol City in March 1937. The 1937/38 season saw him start the term in the outside right position, scoring in the 3-2 opening game win over Blackburn Rovers. It was said at the time that Arsenal, Huddersfield Town and Preston North End were taking notice of his form, and in December 1937 he joined Preston North End in a part exchange transfer which saw Joe Beresford arrive at the Vetch Field. He arrived at Deepdale after making just 19 league appearances, and at the time, had become the most talked about inside forward in the game. After just five First Division games for Preston, he joined Coventry City, creating a large impression as a goalscorer for the club, which saw him score four hat-tricks. Making his first appearance for Wales in a War-Time International in 1942 whilst a guest player with Northampton Town, it was at Coventry City that he made his Full International debut for Wales in the Home International Championships against England in 3-0 defeat at Cardiff, on the 18th October 1947. He also made international appearances against Scotland and Northern Ireland that season, scoring in both games. After joining Second Division Newcastle United in March 1948, helping the club to finish as runners up in the league, he made his last international appearance almost twelve months later against Portugal in a 3-2 defeat in Lisbon, in an end of season F.A.W. Touring party that also played international matches against Belgium and Switzerland. He joined the Tynesiders as the club's record signing and the third most expensive in the game at the time. Despite having a good start to his career at St. James Park, he was injured shortly after the start of the 1948/49 season, putting him out of action for six months, and when he returned to fitness his place had been taken by George Robledo and he was surplus to requirements. During WW2, he appeared in nine International War Time matches for Wales, and when playing for Northampton Town in season 1941/42, scored twenty-three goals from the same number of games. He also made war time appearances for Nottingham Forest and Bristol City in season 1940/41, and Lincoln City (1943/44). In his first season after the War, when the Football League resumed, he made appearances against the Swans for Coventry City, and in a league game at Highfield Road scored a hat-trick in 3-0 win on the 8th April 1947. Possessing good ball control, an excellent worker, on his day he was a magical player in the Jimmy Greaves mould. A consistent goalscorer with Coventry City, Newcastle United and Bristol City, he returned to Coventry City for a second spell in February 1952 at the age of 33, and finally finished his career with Lovells Athletic. He resided for a period in Suffolk, before settling in Bristol.

36. LOWRY, Sydney (SYD) Harold

Birthplace: Hay-on-Wye, 27/8/1912. **Died:** Melton Mowbray, OND, 1982
Ht: 5ft-11ins, **Wt:** 12st-0lbs
Swans debut: v. Preston North End (a), 22/4/1933

Swansea Town Career Statistics

Season	League	FAC	WC
1932/33	1		
1933/34	26/11gls	4	
1934/35	33/10gls	2/2gls	1
Total	60/21gls	6/2gls	1

Career:
South Wales Borderers
Hereford Town (signed in season 1930/31)
Merthyr Town (signed in 21/7/1932)
Swansea Town (signed in 17/3/1933)
Swindon Town (signed in June 1935) lge 30/14gls
Newport County (signed in June 1936) lge 14/2gls
Burton Town (signed in August 1937)
Wellington Town (signed in June 1939)

Honours: Regional League Cup Winner–1943

Stationed with the South Wales Borderers at Brecon, Lowry played five games in three spells for Hereford United, spread over nine years. He played in the last two Birmingham League games of the 1930-1 season, scoring on his debut with a well-taken goal, returned to play in the last two Birmingham League games of the 1931-2 season, and then scored on his re-appearances in a war-time Southern League defeat by Bath in December 1939. The outside left joined the Swans from Merthyr Town in mid-March 1933, making his Swans debut almost a month later at Preston North End, replacing Tommy Olsen, and during his career at the Vetch Field also played at inside left. His first full season at the Vetch Field (1933/34) saw him miss the opening league game, but when he was introduced for the second match, scored in the 2-1 defeat at Millwall. Following the next match he was sidelined with an injury until the first week in December, returning for most of the second half of the season, ending top goalscorer with 11 league goals. His second full season saw him finish as second top goalscorer, one behind Tudor Martin on 11 league goals, plus two goals in an FA Cup tie against Stoke City. Tall for a winger, but extremely lively, he was a useful performer who certainly knew his way to goal. At the end of the 1934/35 season he joined Swindon Town, scoring consistently, before moving to Newport County in 1936, before finishing joining non-league side Burton Town. In one FA Cup tie with Burton he scored ten goals, and finished season 1938/39 as top goalscorer at the club. Joining Wellington Town in June 1939, following the onset of WW2, during season 1941/42 he made guest appearances for the Swans. Towards the end of the 1942/43 season he played in a Regional League West Cup Final win over two legs against Lovells Athletic, scoring in the second leg at the Vetch Field.

37. LUCAS, William (BILLY) Henry

Birthplace: Newport, 15/1/1918. **Died:** Newport, 29/10/1998
Ht: 5ft-6ins, **Wt:** 11st-6lbs
Swans debut: v. Torquay United (h), 20/3/1948

Career:
Brookside Athletic
Treharris (signed in October 1935)
Wolverhampton Wanderers (amateur in 1935, professional in May 1936) lge 0
Swindon Town (£500 signed in May 1937) lge 144/32gls
Swansea Town (£11,000 signed in 16/3/1948)
Newport County (signed in December 1953) lge 93/6gls

Honours: Wales Full–7, War Time International–8, Third Division South Champions–1949, Welsh Cup Winner–1950, Welsh League Representative XI

Swansea Town Career Statistics

Season	League	FAC	WC
1947/48	4/2gls		
1948/49	36/6gls	2	4
1949/50	40/8gls	2	4/1gls
1950/51	35/6gls	1	1
1951/52	34/5gls	3	
1952/53	38/8gls		1/1gls
1953/54	18		
Total	205/35gls	8	10/2gls

Signed for a Swans' club record transfer fee of £11,000 from Swindon Town in March 1948, he went on to become club captain, lead the Swans to the Third Division South Championship in his first full season at the Vetch Field, and to take the club to two consecutive Welsh Cup Finals, in 1949, losing to Merthyr Town 2-0, and in 1950, beating Wrexham 4-1. He made his Swans' debut at inside left against Torquay United, replacing Sam McCrory, and the next game he scored his first Swans' goal, against Newport County in a 3-0 defeat at the Vetch Field. Capped by Wales on seven occasions, the first against Scotland at Cardiff, playing at inside right on the 23rd October 1948, losing 3-1. In the remaining internationals he played for Wales he also played at inside left, and in his last international at left half back against England in Sunderland in November 1950. In April 1949 he was included in an F.A.W. Touring party that played international matches against Portugal, Belgium and Switzerland at the end of the season. Signed by Wolverhampton Wanderers from Welsh League side Treharris initially as an amateur, signing professional in May 1936, the former Corporation Road Schoolboy failed to make any league appearances for the club, joining Swindon Town, twelve months later. After the onset of the Second World War he was capped in War Time internationals between 1942 and 1946 whilst with Swindon Town. During the period of WW2 he made guest appearances for Mansfield Town (January 1940), Hull City (September 1940), Chesterfield (1940/41), Chester (January 1942), Blackburn Rovers (October 1942), Aldershot (September 1943), Lovells Athletic (1944/45) and Newport County (1945/46). In May 1951 he played at the Vetch Field for a Welsh League Representative XI against their Irish league counterparts. A ball player of great skill, Billy could read the game, and make up for his lack of height by his timing. A beautiful passer of the ball, he became a key figure in the Swans promotion side, bringing out the best in his wingers and centre forward, and was sorely missed by the Swans after leaving to join Newport County in December 1953 as player manager, succeeding Fred Stansfield, also becoming licensee of the Black Horse public house near Somerton Park. He was also a more than useful cricketer in the summer months, one of the leading lights of the Newport club side. Originally an inside forward with Swindon Town, he successfully converted to a wing half role during his playing career at the Vetch Field, and for Wales.

At Somerton Park with County he was to be the club's manager on three separate occasions. In February 1967 he returned to the Vetch Field, during a time when the club had been relegated to the Third Division, and also when the club was struggling financially. During his first period as manager of County he gained a reputation for keeping the club on an even keel, in a mid-table position initially in the Third Division South, and then the Third Division after re-organization, until April 1961, when after only one win in County's last 13 games, after criticism from the fans he resigned. His successor, Bobby Evans fared worse, and by the time he had taken over as manager for a second time in March 1962, the club were virtually relegated to Division Four. In five seasons he kept County in the top half of the Fourth Division, before joining the Swans as Manager in February 1967. His success at operating on a shoestring budget at Somerton Park had prompted the Swans Board of Directors to entrust him with the responsibility of turning round the fortunes of the football club. However, he was unable to prevent the club being relegated to the Fourth Division despite losing just 2 out of the last 10 league games. As in his previous managerial position at Newport County, a lack of finances did not prevent him bringing stability to the football club, but he also had faith in the club's young players, giving many youngsters their debut in the club's first team. In March 1969 with the Swans in the top ten positions of the league, Lucas resigned his managerial post to take up a position as a publican in Newport, with Walter Robbins taking over until the end of the season in a caretaker capacity. Highlight of his period as manager at the Vetch Field was during the 1967/68 season when the club reached the Fourth Round of the F.A. Cup competition before, losing 1-0 to Arsenal at the Vetch Field before a record breaking attendance of 32,796. The following season the club also reached the Third Round of the League Cup before losing 3-0 at Liverpool. After County had made two successive re-election applications, by November 1970 they had picked up only two points and lost in the F.A. Cup to Barnet 6-1, and in dire straits they turned to Lucas again, and he rallied them to such an extent that they took 25 points from 22 games, and he was named manager of the month. He handed the reins over to former Everton and Cardiff City wing half Brian Harris in January 1974, and was General Manager for a time. His father George had played for County in the early days before the first World War, the Lucas connection to the club had been almost unbroken for 60 years. He retired to live in the village of Ponthir, Gwent, and was regularly to be found in the local parks spotting the starts of the future.

38. LYTTLE, Desmond (DES)

Birthplace: Wolverhampton, 24/9/1971
Ht: 5ft-9ins, **Wt:** 12st-13lbs
Swans debut: v. Burnley (a), 15/8/1992

Career:
Leicester City (from trainee in 1/9/1990) lge 0
Burton Albion (loan in 1990/91 season)
Worcester City (signed in March 1991)
Swansea City (£12,000 signed in 9/7/1992)
Nottingham Forest (£375,000 signed in 27/7/1993) Flge/PLge 177+8/3gls, FLC 19+1, FAC 16, Others 8
Port Vale (loan in 20/11/1998) lge 7
Watford (signed in 28/7/1999) Plge 11, FLC 1
West Bromwich Albion (signed in 21/3/2000) Plge/Flge 61+15/1gls, FLC 8, FAC 2+1, Others 2
Northampton Town (signed in 4/11/2003) lge 23+4, FAC 5, Others 3
Forest Green Rovers (signed in late August 2004) Conf 23
Worcester City (signed in July 2005)

Honours: First Division Champions–1998

Signed by Swans manager Frank Burrows from non-league Worcester City for a bargain fee of £12,000, the former Leicester

Swansea City Career Statistics						
Season	League	FLC	FAC	WC	AGT	P/Offs
1992/93	46/1gls	2	5	1	3	2
Total	46/1gls	2	5	1	3	2

City trainee was an ever present in the Swans Second Division line-up through season 1992/93, also playing in every cup tie, plus the two Play Offs against West Bromwich Albion. Scoring three goals from sixty four appearances for Worcester City, his transfer to Forest would net City a further £37,500, which became a record for Worcester City. Extremely quick for a defender, and also a solid tackler, he was also good in aerial challenges for a player under six foot tall. He made an instant impression with the Swans' fans, with his strong inclination for overlapping, and at the end of his first season at the Vetch Field was sold to Nottingham Forest for a record transfer fee of £375,000. His first season at the County Ground saw him make 37 league appearances in the club's First Division side that was to reach the Premiership as runners up, and he continued to make appearances for Forest's Premiership team, before the club was relegated at the end of season 1996/97. Following relegation to Division One in 1997, the club bounced back, winning the First Division Championship in 1997/98. After making appearances for Watford in the Premiership, he joined West Bromwich Albion, and was a member of the side that reached the 2002 First Division Play Off semi-finals. At the end of the 2001/02 season the club were promoted to the Premiership in runners up position, with Lyttle making 23 league appearances through the season. He was released by WBA at the end of the 2002/03 season, had a number of trials, but then signed for Third Division Northampton Town on an initial non-contract basis. He made his first league appearance for the 'Cobblers' against the Swans, having made two previous appearances in cup matches for the club. At the end of the season the 'Cobblers' reached the Third Division Play Offs, but were knocked out in the semi-final by Mansfield Town, with Des also being given a free transfer by the club. Shortly after the start of the 2004/05 season he signed for Conference side Forest Green Rovers. In July 2005 he rejoined Worcester City, over fourteen years after joining the club in March 1991.

M

1. MACKAY, William (BILL) Alexander

Birthplace: Togston, Northumberland, 19/3/1910.
Died: Northumberland Central, 2001
Ht: 5ft-8ins
Swans debut: v. Tottenham Hotspur (a), 2/11/1935

Swansea Town Career Statistics		
Season	*League*	*WC*
1935/36	8/1gls	
1936/37	11/2gls	2
Total	19/3gls	2

Career:
Sheffield Wednesday (signed in April 1932)
Tranmere Rovers (signed in May 1933)
Linfield (signed in 21/12/1933) Apps 65/18gls
Swansea Town (signed in 10/6/1935)
Hull City (signed in May 1937) lge 12
Ashington (signed in 1938)
Amble (signed in September 1938)

Honours: Irish League Champions–1934, 1945, Irish F.A. Cup Winner–1934, County Antrim Shield Winner–1934, Charity Cup Winner–1934

Born in Northumberland, William made appearances for junior sides Broomhill FC, Bedlington United, Ashington, Gateshead and Pegswood United (February 1932), prior to joining the professional ranks at Hillsbrough with Sheffield Wednesday in April 1932. Failing to make any league appearances with the 'Owls', and later Tranmere Rovers, he then joined Irish side Linfield in November 1933, enjoying success at the end of the season by winning the Irish League Championship, the Irish Cup, the County Antrim Shield, and the Charity Cup. By the end of the following season he was involved in a second successive Championship success. Shortly after the end of his second season with Linfield, in June 1935 he was signed by manager Neil Harris, making his Swans' debut at White Hart Lane against Tottenham Hotspur at Outside Left, replacing DJ Lewis. He scored his first goal for the Swans in his second league outing seven days later in a 2-1 home win over Manchester United. During his time with the Swans he also played at outside right. He joined Third Division North side Hull City in May 1937, making his debut at home to Wrexham on the 28th August 1937, as first choice on the 'Tigers' right wing, played in the first eleven league games, then lost his place to the returning Cliff Hubbard, making just one more appearance before being released at the end of the season. A useful sprinter, Mackay finished second in the Morpeth handicap on three occasions, with his pace serving him well in his role on the right-wing.

2. MADDY, PAUL Michael

Birthplace: Cwmcarn, 17/8/1962
Ht: 5ft-10ins, **Wt:** 9st-10½lbs
Swans debut: v. Derby County (a), 3/9/1983

Swansea City Career Statistics		
Season	*League*	*WC*
1983/84	18+2/3gls	3/1gls
Total	18+2/3gls	3/1gls

Career:
Cardiff City (from apprentice in August 1980) lge 35+8/3gls
Hereford United (loan in March 1983) lge 9/1gls
Swansea City (signed in August 1983)
Hereford United (signed in 22/3/1984) lge 75+2/16gls
Brentford (£8,000 in 8/7/1986) lge 29+2/5gls, FLC 2, FAC 2, Others 3/1gls

Chester City (£15,000 in 22/6/1987) lge 17+1/1gls
Hereford United (signed in 11/3/1988) lge 27+8/1gls

Honours: Wales Yth, U-21–2, Welsh Youth Cup Winner–1980

Signed on a free transfer from Cardiff City by manager John
Toshack, Paul arrived at the Vetch Field following relegation
from the First Division, at the start of what was to be a turbulent
time for everybody concerned with the football club. He made
his Swans debut at Derby County in the opening away fixture of
the 1983/84 season, going on as substitute for Ray Kennedy.
Predominantly a left sided midfielder, he went on to make a
further nineteen league appearances for the Swans, before he
was transferred to Hereford United for a small fee on the 22nd
March 1984. By this time the Swans had been forced to offload a
number of players, and first year professionals, and apprentices
were being given their league debuts in the Football League.
He scored three goals for the Swans, the first in a 2-1 home
defeat by Portsmouth in December 1983, also scoring in the
Welsh Cup 4-2 home win over Bangor City. Brought up in
Cwmcarn, Paul attended Cwmcarn Comprehensive School,
played for the school side as well as for Gwent Schoolboys and
Cwmcarn Athletic Junior side. Attached from the age of eleven
to Cardiff City he played in the Cardiff City Youth side that beat
Wrexham at the end of the 1979/80 season to win the Welsh
Youth Cup Final, and the following season made an appearance
for the Wales U-18 International side. He later made U-21
appearances for Wales, the first against Holland in 1982, and the
second as substitute against Norway a year later. An extremely
gifted, left sided midfielder, Paul had a reputation for scoring
spectacular goals with most of his clubs during his league
career. He joined Brentford under manager Frank McLintock,
but was sold to Chester by new manager Steve Perryman.
After a loan transfer to Hereford United during his period with
Cardiff City, he joined United on a permanent basis in March
1984 from the Swans, and was a star performer in the Hereford
side which missed promotion by just a place from Division Four
under John Newman at the end of the 1984/85 season.
After further league appearances for Brentford and Chester City
he returned to Edgar Street for a third time in March 1988 on a
free transfer, and was released from the playing staff at Edgar
Street at the end of the 1988/89 season. He returned to Ninian
Park on a month to month contract when Frank Burrows was in
charge, trying to overcome at the same time a snapped Achilles
tendon injury. When Len Ashurst replaced Burrows as manager,
Paul left Ninian Park, and after a short spell in Malta with
Hamrun Spartans, had a six month period in Australia, playing
occasionally in minor football in the Sydney area. After
returning, he linked up with Steve Williams at Ebbw Vale in the
Konica League, but after half a season retired from the game.
Paul is currently a team leader for Unilever Best foods in a
factory at Cross Penmaen, near Crumlin, Gwent, plays golf and
his only involvement in football is watching his young son
playing for the Cwmcarn Junior side.

3. MAHONEY, JOHN Francis

Birthplace: Cardiff, 20/9/1946
Ht: 5ft-8ins, **Wt:** 11st-4lbs
Swans debut: v. Bournemouth (h), FLC-1, 11/8/1979

Swansea City Career Statistics					
Season	League	FLC	FAC	WC	ECWC
1979/80	26	4/1gls	2	2	
1980/81	31+4	1	1	4	
1981/82	25	1	1	3	2
1982/83	24	3	0+1	2	3
Total	106+4	9/1gls	4+1	11	5

Career:
Ashton United
Crewe Alexandra (signed in March 1966) lge 16+2/5gls
Stoke City (£19,500 signed in March 1967) lge 270+12/25gls,
    UEFA Cup–4
Middlesbrough (£90,000 signed in 18/8/1977) lge 77/1gls
Swansea City (£100,000 signed in 25/7/1979)

Honours: Wales U-23–3, Full–51, League Cup Winner–1972,
Welsh Cup Winner–1981

An experienced Welsh International by the time he joined the
Swans staff in July 1979 for £110,000 from Middlesbrough,
acquired by his cousin, Swans manager John Toshack as the club
prepared for it's first season back in the Second Division. Born
in Cardiff, his family had moved north after his father had
joined the professional Rugby League code, with 'Josh' starting
his senior football career playing a couple of games for non-
league Ashton United, prior to joining Fourth Division side
Crewe Alexandra in March 1966, and within twelve months had
signed for Stoke City for £19,500. At Alexandra he had been
capped at U-23 level for Wales in 1967 against Northern Ireland,
gaining a further U-23 cap after joining Stoke City, and being
recognised for the Full Welsh International side on the 21st
October 1967 to play England at Ninian Park, Cardiff. During
his ten years at the Victoria Ground, he became an integral
member of the club's midfield, and made a substitute
appearance for Greenhoff in the 1972 League Cup Final defeat of
Chelsea at Wembley, which City won 2-1, and in 1972/73, and
1974/75 sampled European Club Football with City in the UEFA
Cup. Gaining 31 international caps at Stoke City, 13 whilst with
Middlesbrough, he gained a further 7 caps whilst on the books
of the Swans. He failed to score a league goal for the Swans, but
did score against his old club Stoke City in a League Cup, First
Round tie at the Victoria Ground in late August 1979, in a 1-1
draw, his only goal for the Swans. During his second season at
the Vetch Field, he not only helped the club to gain promotion to
the First Division, but also played in both legs of the Welsh Cup
Final against Hereford United. The following two seasons he
played in Europe for the Swans in the European Cup winners
Cup competition. On March 1st 1983, he suffered a broken ankle
at the Vetch Field in a game against Brighton & Hove Albion, an
injury that was to see him fail to make a full recovery, and
ultimately retire from the game. Following his retirement as a
player, he was employed in the Commercial Department at the
Vetch Field, before he took up his first post in management with
North Wales side Bangor City in September 1984 in the
Northern Premier League, where he was to remain until October
1987. At the end of the 1984/85 season he led the club to the
Welsh Cup Final, and the following season into European Cup
Winners Cup action against Fredrikstad, and Atletico Madrid.
The 1986/87 season saw Bangor finish runners up to
Macclesfield Town in the Multipart League, but he then moved
south to manage Newport County in August 1988, later
returning to Farrar Road in May 1991 for his second spell as
boss of Bangor City. Unfortunately, problems off the field with
the club divided over whether to stay in the NPL or join the

newly proposed League of Wales saw results on the field disappoint, with 'Josh' eventually leaving the club. He later had a spell as manager of Carmarthen Town, but more recently his involvement in football has seen him with Carmarthenshire League side Llangennech.

4. MAINWARING, CARL Andrew

Birthplace: Swansea, 15/3/1980
Ht: 5ft-11ins, **Wt:** 12st-7lbs
Swans debut: v. Peterborough United (h), FAC-1, 14/11/1997

Swansea City Career Statistics			
Season	League	FAC	FAWP
1997/98	2+1	0+1	0+2
Total	2+1	0+1	0+2

Career:
Swansea City (from trainee in July 1998)
Haverfordwest (signed in March 1999)

Young Swans striker, a prolific goalscorer in the club's youth side, made his first team appearances whilst still a second year trainee at the Vetch Field. He made a substitute appearance in the FAW Invitation Cup competition at Bangor City on 11th November, losing 1-0, and then three days later made a substitute's appearance, replacing Aidan Newhouse at the Vetch Field in the First Round of the F.A. Cup against Peterborough United, losing 4-1. Following injuries to Swans' regular strikers Watkin, and Newhouse, he was given his league debut twelve days later at Chester City, starting the match. He later made a substitute appearance in a 4-2 defeat at Hartlepool United, and the last game of the season, at Mansfield Town he started his second league game for the Swans. Given a professional contract before the end of the season, he failed to add to his first team appearances during season 1998/99, and in early March 1999, along with Mark Clode, and Karl Munroe he was released from his contract, signing for League of Wales side Haverfordwest. He later played League of Wales, and Welsh League football with Aberystwyth, Inter Cardiff, Llanelli, Pontardawe, and in season 2002/03 was playing for Skewen Athletic. During season 1999/2000 he played for Inter Cardiff in the UEFA Cup competition against Gorica, scoring the only goal of the game in the second leg, losing unfortunately 2-1 on aggregate. Carl worked for Alberto Culver in the Swansea Enterprise Zone for a time, but has recently started a Plumbing Training programme.

5. MARDENBOROUGH, Stephen (STEVE) Alexander

Birthplace: Birmingham, 11/9/1964
Ht: 5ft-8ins, **Wt:** 11st-0lbs
Swans debut: v. Millwall (a), 25/8/1984

Swansea City Career Statistics					
Season	League	FLC	FAC	WC	FRT
1984/85	32+4/7gls	2	2	6/4gls	3+1/1gls
1995/96	1				
Total	33+4/7gls	2	2	6/4gls	3+1/1gls

Career:
Coventry City (from apprentice in August 1982) lge 0
Wolverhampton Wanderers (signed in September 1983) lge 9/1gls
Cambridge United (loan in February 1984) lge 6
Swansea City (signed in July 1984)
Newport County (signed in July 1985) lge 50+14/11gls
Cardiff City (signed in March 1987) lge 18+14/1gls
Hereford United (signed in July 1988) lge 20+7
Cheltenham Town (signed in November 1989)
Darlington (signed in July 1990) lge 79+27/18gls
Lincoln City (signed in July 1993) lge 14+7/2gls
IK Ostersund, Norway
Scarborough (signed in February 1995) lge 0+1
Stafford Rangers
Colchester United (signed in August 1995) lge 4+8/2gls
Swansea City (non-contract in December 1995)
Newport AFC
Gloucester City

Honours: GM Vauxhall Conference Champions–1990

Steve Mardenborough started his playing career as an apprentice professional with Coventry City, but after failing to make a first team appearance joined Wolverhampton Wanderers in September 1983 on a professional contract. Playing mainly in the youth and reserve sides at Molyneaux, Steve's first glimpse of glory came early in the season when he made his first team debut against Preston North End in the first leg of the Milk Cup Second Round as a second half substitute for Mel Eves. By mid-December he had made his First Division debut, and had a run of seven consecutive games for the Wolves. Just prior to the away league game at Anfield against Liverpool on the 14th January, assistant manager Jim Barron had told him to prepare himself for the game as there was a possibility that because of injuries to a number of strikers, including Mel Eves, he would be playing. With his pre-match brief being to get himself in front of the defenders at the near post from crosses from the flanks, after just seven minutes he got in front of Mark Lawrenson and

Alan Hansen to flick a cross from Danny Crainie over the stranded Bruce Grobbelaar, and into the net. At the end of ninety minutes, after withstanding constant pressure from the Liverpool side, Wolves emerged 1-0 winners, and Steve Mardenborough was headline news the following day. One other first team appearance, plus a six game loan spell at Cambridge United summed up Steve's appearances for his debut season in the professional game. The win at Anfield was to prove to be the highlight of the season for the club, as by May they were stranded at the foot of the table and heading for the Second Division. A change of management at the club saw a number of players including Steve being released at the end of the season, and by July had been enticed by new manager at the Vetch Field, Colin Appleton to sign for the Swans. Despite the financial problems which were to surface at the club over the next twelve months, and changes in management personnel, Steve scored 7 league goals from 36 appearances. Despite scoring six goals during the first third of the season, a change in management which saw John Bond replace Appleton, Steve scored just the one more goal in the league for the Swans, against Bristol Rovers in December, and by the end of the season he had been mainly used as a substitute. Securing their place in the Third Division for another season, by virtue of a draw in the last game at the Vetch Field against Bristol City, Steve, along with nine other professionals were given free transfers. One player who was among the ten released was a certain Dean Saunders. Over the next eleven years Steve made league appearances for Newport County, Cardiff City, Hereford United, Cheltenham Town, Darlington (GM Vauxhall Conference Champions-1990), Lincoln City, Scarborough, Stafford Rangers and Colchester United. At the age of 31 he was given the opportunity of league football by Swans manager Bobby Smith, but after playing on a non-contract basis at Oxford United, he was surprisingly told that the club were unable to offer him a contract. From that period on, living in Cardiff, Steve has made appearances for Newport AFC, Gloucester City, Merthyr, and League of Wales sides Inter Cardiff, Aberystwyth, Haverfordwest, Rhayader, Port Talbot Town, Carmarthen Town (Sept 2002), Llanelli (Jan 2003) and Barry Town. Looking at getting involved in the coaching side of football, Steve has worked with former Cardiff and Swans player Derek Brazil in the Football in the Community scheme at Cardiff City.

6. MARLOW, OWEN

Birthplace: Bolton, JFM,1909 **Died**: Farnworth, 27/1/1969
Ht: 6ft-1½ins, **Wt:** 12st-0lbs
Swans debut: v. Oldham Athletic (h), 27/12/1926

Swansea Town Career Statistics	
Season	League
1926/27	2
Total	2

Career:
Arsenal
Swansea Town (signed amateur in season 1925/26, professional in 6/8/1926)
Mansfield Town (signed in June 1927)
Grantham Town

Honours: West Wales Representative XI, Midland Combination Cup Winner–1927, Mansfield Hospital Charity Cup Winner–1928

Failed to make any appearances for the 'Gunners' first, or reserve sides at Highbury, and was probably one of a number of promising amateurs each season in the 1920's and 1930's who were given trials and played in minor matches for Arsenal. He joined the Swans during season 1925/26, playing all his games in the Swans 'A' side, signing professional in August 1926. In January 1926 he was selected to play for a West Wales Representative side against a South Wales & Monmouthshire side in an Inter Association match in Mid-Rhondda on the 23rd January 1926. He nearly made his debut for the Swans in November 1926 when both Denoon and Hills had injury problems, with Marlow, just sixteen and a half at the time. If he had played he would have created a record in the Football League by being the youngest goalkeeper to make a league appearance. Fortunately Hills recovered to play in the league side, with Marlow having to wait until the end of December before making his debut. Later in the season Alex Ferguson became the fourth goalkeeper to be used by the Swans in the season, limiting Marlow's opportunities even more. He left the Vetch Field at the end of his only season with the Swans, with his job taking him to Nottingham, where he linked up with Mansfield Town, and was a virtual ever present during season 1927/28 for the club. Was a member of the Mansfield Town side that won the Midland Combination Cup in 1927, and the Mansfield Hospital Charity Cup Final in 1928. With his job taking more priority than his football career, he dropped out of the professional game, later linking up with non-league Grantham Town.

7. MARSH, IAN James

Birthplace: Swansea, 27/10/1969
Ht: 5ft-7ins, **Wt:** 9st-9lbs
Swans debut: v. Crewe Alexandra (h), 26/9/1987

Swansea City Career Statistics		
Season	League	FRT
1987/88	1	
1988/89		1
Total	1	1

Career:
Swansea City (signed from trainee in July 1988)
Bradford City (signed in July 1989) lge 0
Southall (signed in season 1990/91)

Honours: Macbar Cup Winner–1987

Brought up in the Waun Wen area of Swansea, Ian attended St. Josephs and Bishop Vaughan Schools, played for the school sides and Swansea Schoolboys, winning the Welsh U-15 Shield in 1985 against Deeside, who had a certain Gary Speed in their line-up. A left sided midfielder/defender, he made his league debut for the Swans under Terry Yorath as replacement for Chris

Coleman at the Vetch Field against Crewe Alexandra, whilst still a trainee at the Vetch Field. In May 1987 he was included in the Swans reserve side that beat Plymouth Argyle in the Macbar Cup Final at the Vetch Field. The following season, his first as a professional he made a further start in the Swans first team in a Freight Rover Trophy Cup tie, Preliminary round at Cardiff City in December 1988. When Yorath departed the Vetch Field in February 1989 to manage Bradford City, at the end of the season, Marsh linked up with Yorath for a second time, after being released by Swans manager Ian Evans. He suffered knee problems during his season at Valley Parade, failed to make an appearance for Bradford City, and was released by the club at the end of the 1989/90 season. After a period on trial with Exeter City, he joined Vauxhall League side Southall, before returning to Swansea, linking up with Haverfordwest, Maesteg Park, Briton Ferry Athletic, and finishing his playing career with Morriston Town. Looking to take his coaching badges and coach football in the USA, a change in career saw him take employment in the communications industry, and he has since become manager of a communications store in Gloucester.

8. MARSON, FRED

Birthplace: Moxley, West Midlands, 18/1/1900. **Died:** Lichfield, OND, 1976
Ht: 5ft-6½ins, **Wt:** 10st-11lbs
Swans debut: v. Blackpool (a), 3/9/1928

Swansea Town Career Statistics			
Season	League	FAC	WC
1928/29	14/4gls	1	1
Total	14/4gls	1	1

Career:
Darlaston
Wolverhampton Wanderers (signed in May 1923) lge 8/4gls
Sheffield Wednesday (signed in June 1925) lge 10
Swansea Town (£350 signed in 7/5/1928)
Darlaston (signed in close season 1932)
Wellington Town (signed in August 1931)
Shrewsbury Town (signed in May 1932)

Started his career in non-league football with Darlaston, before signing for Third Division North side Wolverhampton Wanderers the season they won the Division Championship, then joined First Division Sheffield Wednesday making his debut on the 23rd October 1926 at Highbury against Arsenal in the First Division. A fast and clever attacker who spent three seasons at Hillsborough, and who had impressed Wednesday officials in reserve team games for Wolves against Wednesday the season prior to his transfer. Primarily an inside left for

Wednesday, it was as a left winger that he played the majority of his matches for the club. Signed by Swans manager Thomson for £350 in May 1928, the outside left replaced Nicholas, scoring on his debut at Blackpool, and after a spell out of the Swans side, returned for his second game at the Vetch Field against West Bromwich Albion at the beginning of February to score his second goal in a 6-1 win. He scored two further goals for the Swans during the season, and in late April 1929 was de-registered by the Swans, and returned to non-league side Darlaston, later making appearances for Wellington and Shrewsbury Town.

9. MARTIN, Ted (TUDOR) James

Birthplace: Caerau, 20/4/1904. **Died:** Newport, 6/9/1979
Ht: 5ft-10ins, **Wt:** 11st-8lbs
Swans debut: v. West Ham United (h), 27/8/1932

Swansea Town Career Statistics			
Season	League	FAC	WC
1932/33	34/16gls	1/2gls	2/1gls
1933/34	32/7gls	4/1gls	
1934/35	25/11gls		2/3gls
1935/36	26/12gls		1
Total	117/46gls	5/3gls	5/4gls

Career:
Caerau Harlequins
Bridgend Town
West Bromwich Albion (signed in October 1926) lge 0
Newport County (signed in July 1929) lge 29/34gls
Wolverhampton Wanderers (£1,500 signed in May 1930) lge 15/9gls
Swansea Town (£750 signed in 19/7/1932)
West Ham United (£350 signed in 13/6/1936) lge 11/7gls
Southend United (signed in February 1937) lge 60/28gls

Honours: Wales Full–1, Central League Champions–1932, West Wales Senior Cup Winner–1934

Tudor Martin started his playing career with local side Caerau Harlequins before signing for Bridgend Town. After leaving his job in the coal mines, he was then signed by First Division side West Bromwich Albion in 1926, but after failing to make a league appearance, joined Third Division South side Newport County. He met with instant success at Somerton Park, and despite missing the first three months of the season through injury, went on to score a club record 37 league and cup goals, 34 in the league. He also gained his only Welsh international cap during his one season with County, being selected to play in Belfast against Northern Ireland on the 1st February 1930, in a

7-0 defeat. He signed for Second Division Wolverhampton Wanderers in May 1930, and scored against the Swans in both seasons he played for Wolves. Although he struggled to make an impression with Wolves, he did score 49 league and cup goals in season 1931/32 when the club won the Central League Championship. Making only 15 appearances for the Wolves in two seasons, he once more returned to South Wales, this time to join the Swans in July 1932 for £750, making an instant impression on his league debut by scoring in the opening league game of the 1932/33 season at the Vetch Field against West Ham United. The first season saw him end up as top goalscorer with 16 league goals, plus two in an FA Cup 3-2 defeat by Sheffield United. During that season he also scored his first hat-trick for the Swans, against Fulham at the Vetch Field in January 1933, in a 3-0 win. In October 1934 he scored the only goal in the West Wales Senior Cup Final defeat of Llanelly. The 1934/35 season saw him again finish as top goalscorer, also recording his second Swans' hat-trick, this time against West Ham United, in a 5-4 home win. The 1935/36 saw Martin score four goals in a game against Bury at the Vetch Field, but was runner-up this time to Joe Brain as top goalscorer. His goalscoring prowess must have impressed West Ham United, and in 13th June 1936 he was sold to the club for £350. Surprisingly they let him go to Southend United after seven goals from eleven matches. Martin remained with the Shrimpers until 1939 when war broke out, which finished his career in the Football League. A hard working centre forward, and a good leader of the line, he had a tough task in following the legendary Cyril Pearce at the Vetch Field, but during his career proved to be a fearless raider with a good turn of speed. After returning to live in the Newport area, he worked for Stewart & Lloyds for a number of years, and was Vice-President of Newport Defence Snooker League.

10. MARTINEZ, ROBERTO

Birthplace: Balaguer Lerida, Spain, 13/7/1973
Ht: 5ft-10ins, **Wt:** 12st-2lbs
Swans debut: v. Rushden & Diamonds (a), 1/2/2003

Swansea City Career Statistics					
Season	League	FLC	FAC	LDV	FAWC
2002/03	19/2gls				
2003/04	24+3	1	2		2
2004/05	34+3		3	2	2
Total	77+6/2gls	1	5	2	4

Career:
CFS Vipla Balageur
Real Zaragoza
Wigan Athletic (signed in 25/7/1995) lge 148+39/17gls,
 FLC 11+1/1gls, FAC 13+2/4gls, Others 7+5/2gls

Motherwell (signed in July 2001) SPL 8+9
Walsall (signed in 13/8/2002) lge 1+5
Swansea City (signed in 28/1/2003)

Honours: Third Division Champions–1997, FAW Cup Winner–2005

Signed in February 2003 on a contract until the end of the season from Walsall, Roberto impressed immediately in a central midfield role, scoring his first Swans' goal in only his third game at Macclesfield, with a shot from outside the penalty area. Starting his playing career with CFS Vipla Balaguer in Spain, he then had five seasons with top Spanish side Zaragoza, signing his first professional contract at the age of sixteen. A Catalan, Roberto has spent all of his playing career outside the Catalan area of Spain, and in July 1995, along with team mates Jesus Seba and Isidro Diaz he was persuaded to sign for Third Division Wigan Athletic. Dave Whelan, owner of JJB Sports was opening a store in Zaragoza and after watching a game in the city, was persuasive enough to bring all three players over to the UK. In his first season Roberto finished with nine league goals, one behind top scorer Diaz, and his second season saw the club win the Third Division Championship. His Football League debut at Gillingham on the 12th August 1995 saw Roberto score in a 2-1 defeat for Athletic. With the club reaching the Second Division Play Offs at the end of season 1998/99, Roberto failed to feature because of injury, but in the next two seasons played in the Play Off final defeat by Gillingham, and also as a substitute in the first leg semi-final defeat by Reading in 2001. Signing for Scottish Premiership side Motherwell on a three year contract in July 2001, Roberto found himself within a couple of weeks after the start of the season, of playing for a club that had been placed in administration, and ten months later returning to the Football league to sign for Walsall, only to join the Swans five months later. Following the Swans' successful fight to avoid relegation to the Conference at the end of the season, Roberto signed a two year contract in the 2003 close season, but in the second home game of the season suffered a serious knee ligament injury, which sidelined him for a couple of weeks. He returned to action in early October, but after a training ground injury was sidelined for a further period with knee problems, and despite playing most of the second half of the season, it took him a long time to regain his match fitness. For a number of years Roberto has been used by Sky Sports as one of their studio summarisers covering Spain's La Liga football programme. Besides his television work, Roberto has also qualified as a physiotherapist, and has done post graduate courses in Marketing at Manchester University. Season 2004/05 saw Roberto lose his place after the opening game of the season defeat by Northampton Town, but after regaining his place, showed a good level of consistency, possessing good vision and passing ability in midfield, and the composure required when the team was under pressure. A knee injury during the Xmas period saw him miss a number of games, but after clinching an automatic promotion place in the last match of the season at Bury, four days later he captained the side in their FAW Cup Final success over Wrexham.

11. MARUSTIK, (CHRIS) Christopher

Birthplace: Swansea, 10/8/1961
Ht: 5ft-8ins, **Wt:** 11st-11½lbs
Swans debut: v. Tottenham Hotspur (h), FLC-2, 29/8/1978

Career:
Swansea City (from apprentice in August 1978)
Cardiff City (signed in October 1985) lge 43/1gls
Barry Town (signed in August 1987)
Newport County (signed in June 1988) Conf 14/3gls

Honours: Wales Sch–5, Yth–5, U-21–7, Full–6, Welsh Cup Winner–1982, 1983

Swansea City Career Statistics

Season	League	FLC	FAC	WC	ECWC	FRT
1978/79	2+2	0+1	1			
1979/80	10+2	1	4	1		
1980/81	3	1		1		
1981/82	19+3/1gls	2	1	5		
1982/83	22+1/1gls	1	1	6	5	
1983/84	38+/4gls	2	1	6	2	
1984/85	41+1/5gls	1	1/1gls	5/1gls		4
1985/86	8	3/1gls				
Total	143+9/11gls	11+1/1gls	9/1gls	24/1gls	7	4

Brought up in the Sketty Park area of Swansea, Chris attended Parklands, Olchfa, and spent his last year in school at Bishop Gore School. Recognised at an early age with his school sides, Swansea Schoolboys, and at International level for Wales, the midfielder also made appearances for the Swans from either full back positions. He was taken on as an apprentice at the Vetch Field, making his debut as substitute for Kevin Moore, nineteen days after celebrating his 17th birthday, in the League Cup at the Vetch Field against Tottenham Hotspur, in a game which saw British Football have it's first glimpse of Argentinian footballers Ardiles and Villa. He continued to be a regular member of the Swans first team squad under John Toshack, despite the continued influx of experienced players, as the club moved it's way up the Football League divisions. His first goal for the Swans came in the First Division, against West Bromwich Albion, in a 3-1 win at the Vetch Field in April 1982. At the end of seasons 1981/82 and 1982/83 he had made appearances in successive Welsh Cup Finals, playing in the first leg against Cardiff City in 1982, and in the second leg against Wrexham the following year. He gained his first U-21 cap for Wales against France at Newport in October 1981, playing in the return in France two months later. With the Swans having a successful season in the top flight, he gained his first Full cap one month after making his second U-21 appearance, against Spain on the 24th March 1982, in Valencia in a Welsh side which also featured Dai Davies, Robbie James, David Giles (substitute), Ian Walsh and Alan Curtis. From the 1982/83 season on he became a regular fixture in the Swans' starting line-up, usually in midfield, where he was also to become a regular on the goalscoring sheet, despite financial problems at the Vetch Field, suffering two consecutive relegations, and avoiding a third by drawing the last game of the 1984/85 season. In October 1985 he was involved in a player exchange transfer to Cardiff City, with midfielder Roger Gibbins joining the Swans, and Chris going to Ninian Park. He remained at Ninian Park until two thirds through the 1986/87 season, his last appearance for the 'Bluebirds' coming in mid March against Colchester United, and then had just over a season with Barry Town in the Abacus Welsh League National Division, finishing runners up in season 1987/88 to Ebbw Vale, playing alongside former Swans players David Giles and Chris Sander. Joining Vauxhall Conference side

Newport County in June 1988, he remained at Somerton Park up to the period the club folded, and then went to live in Australia, with the initial intention of taking up residency. Chris had a period of five years living in Perth, Western Australia, playing and managing football sides, but then decided to return to Swansea, taking up employment with Welsh Brewers as a Drayman, where he worked for around ten years, later joining ALCOA at Waunarlwydd. Although he has no connections with football at present, he still involves himself in charity games.

12. MAXWELL, LAYTON Jonathan

Birthplace: Rhyl, 3/10/1979
Ht: 5ft-8ins, **Wt:** 11st-6lbs
Swans debut: v. Huddersfield Town (a), 27/3/2004

Swansea City Career Statistics	
Season	League
2003/04	1+2
Total	1+2

Career:
Liverpool (from trainee in 17/7/1997) FLC 1/1gls
Stockport County (loan in 17/7/2000) lge 8+12/2gls, FLC 1+1, FAC 0+1
Cardiff City (signed in 7/8/2001) lge 10+23/1gls, FLC 1+1, FAC 1+3, Others 3+1
Swansea City (signed in 25/3/2004)
Rhyl (signed in close season 2004)
Newport County (signed in October 2004)
Mansfield Town (trial in 6/12/2004)
Carmarthen Town (signed by March 2005)

Honours: Wales Yth, U-21–14

Started his career as an orthodox winger at Liverpool, product of the club's academy. Capable of beating players and having good crossing ability he made his Liverpool debut in September 1999 in a Worthington Cup game against Hull City, scoring with a brilliant right footed shot from outside the area. Capped at youth level for Wales, he gained his first U-21 cap as a substitute for Matthew Jones against Switzerland in October 1999, making his first start in the next game against Scotland. He started season 2000/01 on a long term loan with Stockport County, scoring on his debut against Gillingham in the opening game of the season. Capable of playing in a wide right sided role, or in a central midfield position, he joined Cardiff City on a free transfer, but struggled at first to break into the Bluebirds side featuring mainly from a substitute role, and was unable to break up the midfield partnership of Kavanagh and Boland. Offered a free transfer by City at the start of the 2003/04 season, but after being unable to work his way into the Bluebirds first team squad, had his contract paid up, and after numerous enquiries from clubs started a trial spell at the Vetch Field in January 2004. Unfortunately for him in his first session he injured his ankle, sidelining him for a number of weeks. After playing in a couple of reserve team games for the Swans, and for Barry Town in the League of Wales, he signed a contract until the end of the season with the Swans on the 25th March 2004, making his debut as substitute for Jonathan Coates at Huddersfield Town two days later. Just prior to the end of the season he was told by Swans manager Kenny Jackett that he was not being offered a contract, and was released from the Vetch Field playing staff. By the start of season 2004/05, Layton had returned to North Wales to sign for League of Wales side Rhyl, but in late October made his debut for Newport County in their F.A. Cup tie at Tiverton. A couple of weeks later however he was released by County, and on the 6th December 2004 started a trial period with Second Division side Mansfield Town before signing for League of Wales side Carmarthen Town.

13. MAY, Edwin (EDDIE) Charles

Birthplace: Epping, 19/5/1943
Ht: 6ft-1½ins, **Wt:** 13st-3½lbs
Swans debut: v. Newport County (h), FLC-1, 14/8/1976

Swansea City Career Statistics

Season	League	FLC	FAC	WC
1976/77	46/6gls	6		2/2gls
1977/78	44/2gls	2	5	2
Total	90/8gls	8	5	4/2gls

Career:
Dagenham
Southend United (signed in January 1965) lge 107/4gls
Wrexham (£5,000 signed in 1/6/1968) lge 330/4gls,
    FLC 19/5gls, FAC 24/2gls, WC 24/2gls, ECWC 9,
Chicago (loan in May 1975)
Swansea City (signed in 6/8/1976)

Honours: Welsh Cup Winner–1972

Played Primary and Secondary school football in his native West Ham, and on leaving school went to work in Smithfield Market, following in his father's footsteps handling large carcases of meat. Missing a number of seasons of playing football after leaving school, he then signed for Athenian League side Dagenham. His form caught the eye of Southend United manager Benny Fenton during a London Challenge Cup match, and he joined United in January 1965 as a full back. Two months later he made his league debut at Colchester, but after a spell on

the sidelines through injury, and a change of management saw him moved to centre half by new manager Alvan Williams. Williams moved to Wrexham as manager in April 1967, and one of his first signings was to take May to the Racecourse for a fee of £5,000. It did not take long for the towering defender to become a popular figure at the Racecourse, going on to spend eight seasons with the club, earning promotion from the Fourth Division in 1970, beating Cardiff City to win the Welsh Cup in 1972, and the following season competing in European competition. In 1971, the 'Bluebirds' had beaten Wrexham in the Welsh Cup Final. The club also reached the quarter final stages of the ECWC, and the F.A. Cup during his period at the Racecourse. With Harry Griffiths taking over as manager at the Vetch Field, May was one of the experienced players brought to the club, along with midfielder George Smith, that was to be the turning point in the fortunes of the Swans, transforming the club into a free scoring, attacking outfit, which would ultimately lead to the First Division. A tower of strength in central defence, he was also a threat at set piece situations for the opposition. Gaining promotion from the Fourth Division at the end of his second season at the Vetch Field, May moved into coaching at Leicester City, then linking up with Lennie Lawrence as assistant manager at Charlton Athletic, and after three years moving to Saudi Arabia as coach with AL Hahda. Following coaching spells in Kenya and Qatar, and a managerial position in Finland, he returned to Wales to take over Conference side Newport County on 7th July 1988, after the club had just been relegated from the Football League. However, financial problems at Somerton Park saw him resign after just a month of taking charge, and then joined Lincoln City as assistant manager, before going to Norway as coach with IFK Ravdeberg in 1989. Returning to the UK in July 1991, he took over at Cardiff City, winning both the Third Division Championship, and the Welsh Cup in 1993. May was then replaced by Terry Yorath at Ninian Park, who was leading a consortium to take over the club, but after the takeover had collapsed, May returned as manager on te 30th March 1995. In the meantime he had been in charge at Barry Town, but on his return to Ninian Park was unable to save the club from relegation, but he did lead the club to the Welsh Cup Final against his old club Wrexham, losing 2-1. With rumours of another consortium taking over at Ninian Park, he resigned his position due to the uncertainty of life at Ninian Park, returning to Barry Town in May 1995, following the announcement that the club were going to become the first League of Wales side to go full time professional. With the season only a couple of weeks old, he was surprisingly sacked by Barry Town, but he quickly found employment as manager of League side Torquay United. With another club in deep financial problems at the time, they finished the season bottom of the Football League, escaping relegation to the Conference by virtue of the Conference Champions, Stevenage Borough's ground being unsuitable. Resigning after the last league game of the season, he was appointed manager at Brentford, replacing Dave Webb. Another brief stay however at Griffin Park, and he was relieved of his position at the beginning of November 1997. Before the end of the season however, he returned to management, this time with League of Wales side Haverfordwest. Just prior to the start of the 1998/99 season he was allowed by Haverfordwest to answer an SOS call from Helsinki club FinPa, in August 1998, staying there until the end of the season. There then followed a brief spell as manager of Merthyr Tydfil on his return to the UK. In early August 2004 he was unveiled as the new manager of League of Wales side Llanelli, replacing Neil O'Brien. May had recently returned to the UK after a two year stint in Zimbabwe as head coach to Ama-Zulu and Highlanders. Following Llanelli's home defeat by Caersws, May stepped down as manager, having failed to register a victory.

14. MAYLETT, Bradley (BRAD)

Birthplace: Manchester, 24/12/1980
Ht: 5ft-8ins, **Wt:** 10st-10lbs
Swans debut: v. Carlisle United (h), 15/3/2003

Swansea City Career Statistics					
Season	League	FLC	FAC	LDV	FAWC
2002/03	6				
2003/04	26+7/5gls	1	3		2
2004/05	4+12	0+1	0+1	2	2/1gls
Total	36+19/5gls	1+1	3+1	2	4/1gls

Career:
Burnley (from trainee in 19/2/1999) lge 3+42, FLC 1+2.
   FAC 0+1, Others 1
Swansea City (loan in 14/3/2003)
Swansea City (signed in 18/6/2003)
Boston United (loan in 18/3/2005) lge 4
Boston United (signed in 7/4/2005) lge 3+1/3gls

Signed initially in March 2003 on a loan transfer to assist the Swans fight against relegation to the Conference, within days of having his loan extended until the end of the season, he had to return to Turf Moor because of an injury crisis at the First Division Club. When he made his league debut for the Swans he equalled the club's record for debutants in a season, becoming the club's 22nd player to make his debut during the 2002/03 season. An extremely quick winger, wide midfielder, and very direct, he initially made a good impression at the Vetch Field, despite his experience being limited to short appearances as a substitute with Burnley. Returning to Turf Moor, he continued his appearances with the club as substitute, and shortly after the end of the season, with Burnley giving him the opportunity of cancelling the one year left on his contract, Swans manager Brian Flynn offered him a one year contract, with the option of a further year. He took his first full season of 2003/04 by storm, scoring an opening day hat-trick at the Vetch Field against Bury, only to suffer the downside of life as a footballer by being given a red card a couple of days later at Ashton Gate against Bristol City in a Carling Cup tie. As a youngster he trained at Old Trafford with Manchester United for six years, but after being told that he was not being offered a YTS contract, joined Burnley, then under manager Chris Waddle as a trainee. His opening day hat-trick had been the first hat-trick scored by a Swans player since the opening fixture against Leeds United in the First Division, when Bob Latchford scored. With the club topping the Third Division for a number of weeks after the start of the 2003/04 season, a dead leg, and then a hamstring injury saw Brad's games affected with a couple of weeks on the sidelines. He took some time to return to fitness, but prior to the last league game of season was looking to extend his contract at the Vetch Field. Shortly after the start of the 2004/05 season he

had to undergo surgery for an hernia problem which sidelined him until the Xmas period. Struggling to make an impact in the Swans' side, in mid-March 2005 he joined Boston United on loan, and after four league appearances impressed sufficiently to sign a permanent contract at the club until the end of the 2006/7 season.

15. MAZZINA, Jorge NICOLAS

Birthplace: Buenos Aires, Argentina, 31/1/1979
Ht: 5ft-10ins, **Wt:** 11st-7lbs
Swans debut: v. Peterborough United (h), WC-1, 21/8/2001

Swansea City Career Statistics		
Season	League	FLC
2001/02	3	1
Total	3	1

Career:
AC Kimberley, Argentina
Swansea City (signed in 10/8/2001)
York City (signed in 2/9/2002) lge 0+3

Honours: Argentina U-18, 21

An attacking midfielder, Nicolas signed a one year contract with the Swans in August 2001 after impressing in pre-season trial games. Formerly with the Boca Juniors Youth Academy, Nicolas had been capped for Argentina at U-18 and U-21 level, and the previous twelve months had seen him play for Second Division side AC Kimberley, scoring 8 goals from 29 appearances. Prior to the start of the 2001/02 season, he was one of four Argentinian players who made trial appearances for the Swans in pre-season friendly matches. He was a non-playing substitute in the Swans' two opening league games, and he then made his debut in the Worthington Cup, First Round tie against Peterborough United at the Vetch Field, making his first league start at Lincoln City four days later. Following a knee injury in September, Nicolas struggled to regain his first team place, and by December had started trials with Walsall, then followed by trials with Scottish clubs Motherwell and Livingstone. In February he left the Vetch Field with his contract having been paid up, and at the start of the following season had signed a short term contract with Third Division side York City. He was released by the club in October after making just three appearances for the club, all as substitute, and went to play in the Spanish League.

16. MEDWIN, Terence (TERRY) Cameron

Birthplace: Swansea, 25/9/1932
Ht: 5ft-9ins, **Wt:** 11st-8lbs
Swans debut: v. Blackburn Rovers (a), 5/1/1952

Swansea Town Career Statistics			
Season	League	FAC	WC
1951/52	10/2gls		
1952/53	39/17gls	1	2/1gls
1953/54	29/8gls	2	1
1954/55	33/12gls	4/3gls	3/2gls
1955/56	36/18gls	1	3/1gls
Total	147/57gls	9/3gls	9/4gls

Career:
Swansea Town (signed in 25/10/1948)
Tottenham Hotspur (£18,000 signed in 2/5/1956) lge197/65gls

Honours: Wales Sch, Full–30, Division One Champions–1961, FA Cup Winner–1963, West Wales Senior Cup Winner–1950, 1955, 1956

Brought up in the Sandfields area of Swansea outside the Vetch Field, Terry's father was a prison warder in Swansea Prison, and Terry was born in one of 12 flats inside the prison. He went to St. Helens School, Oxford Street School, skippered the Swansea Schoolboys, playing alongside big John Charles. After leaving school, he worked for five years at Morsmith Motors, training to be a mechanic, playing part-time football between the ages of 17 and 20 years of age. He initially signed for the Swans as a part-time professional in 25/10/1948, signing full time in 25/11/1949. His normal working day whilst he worked for Morsmith Motors, was to train at 6.45 in the morning, go to work, and then go to the Vetch Field at 10.30 in the morning to train with the players. He also trained on Tuesday and Thursday nights, growing up with Len Allchurch and Cliff Jones. Playing initially in the Swans third team, he then graduated through to the reserves, before making his league debut at Blackburn Rovers in 5th January 1952. Next to Ivor Allchurch, he was the youngest player at the time to play for the club. Initially playing part-time for the Swans, following the signing of the experienced Ronnie Burgess, Terry enjoyed his football at the club, playing in any forward position, winger, inside, or at centre forward, anywhere the club wanted him to play. He gained his first representative honour whilst with the Swans, getting his first cap for Wales in Belfast on the 15th April 1953 in the Home International Championships, winning 3-2, gaining two further caps for Wales whilst on the playing staff at the Vetch Field. At the end of season 1952/53 he was included in the Welsh International Touring party that played games in France and Yugoslavia. Terry scored his first goal for the Swans five days after he had made his debut at Blackburn Rovers, scoring

in an FA Cup tie at Reading. His first league goal came in his third league game in a home defeat by Doncaster Rovers at the age of seventeen. During his playing career at the Vetch Field, Terry scored just the one hat-trick, but did score two goals in a game on ten occasions. A versatile player who had vision, pace, fine positional sense, plus the ability to score goals, his career was cut short through injury. Played in the 1950 West Wales Senior Cup Final success, and also in 1955 and 1956. He signed for Tottenham Hotspur on the 2nd May 1956 for £18,000, and at White Hart Lane, because of the quality of talent available, was able to concentrate on playing in just the one position, unlike his time with the Swans where he played wherever he was asked. It was also at International level for Wales that he played in almost all forward positions, a testament to the player's ability to adapt his style of play to suit his team mates. The 1958 World Cup in Sweden saw Terry play in four out of the five matches, scoring in the 2-1 defeat of Hungary in the Play Off, which took Wales forward to play Brazil in the quarter finals. Returning to play for Spurs, prior to the start of the 1960/61 season he caught influenza, which prevented him from taking part in most of the pre-season work, and it was only through an injury to Cliff Jones that he was able to get back into the side, that would win the First Division Championship, and receive a Championship medal, but, unfortunately did not make the FA Cup Final side that beat Leicester City. When Spurs returned to Wembley twelve months later, he was included in the side that beat Burnley 3-1. The following season he was again unlucky to be out of the game through injury, this time tackled during a game by his fellow Welsh International colleague Graham Williams, with the ankle injury keeping him out for almost two months, and forcing him to miss the European Cup Winners Cup Final in Rotterdam against Atletico Madrid. Injury struck again during the close season in Cape Town, South Africa when he broke his leg, and at the age of thirty had to eventually retire from the professional game, although he tried for two years to get back to full fitness. At this time he was assisting with the coaching of non-league side Cheshunt, and after leaving White Hart Lane worked for Jimmy Scoular at Cardiff. Between 1969 and 1976 he had coaching and scouting appointments at Fulham, achieving promotion in 1971 from the Third Division, and getting to the 1975 FA Cup Final, where they were beaten by West Ham United. In 1976 he worked alongside John Bond at Norwich City as reserve team coach, and in 1978 was persuaded by John Toshack to join him at the Vetch Field as assistant manager. In what was to be the start of the finest days in the club's history, unfortunately for Terry he later suffered from depression, and had to retire from the game through poor health.

17. MEEK, Joseph (JOE)

Birthplace: Hazlerigg, 31/5/1910. **Died:** Hazlerigg, 17/9/1976
Ht: 5ft-6ins, **Wt:** 11st-7lbs
Swans debut: v. West Ham United (h), 10/2/1939

Swansea Town Career Statistics	
Season	League
1938/39	16/5gls
Total	16/5gls

Career:
Bussadon FC
Newcastle Co-operative Society
Seaton Delaval (signed in close season 1926)
Bedlington United (signed in July 1927)
Liverpool (trial in March 1928)
Stockton
Middlesbrough (amateur signed in January 1931) lge 0
Gateshead (signed in February 1931) lge 135/50gls

Bradford Park Avenue (signed in October 1934) lge 31/11gls
Tottenham Hotspur (signed in March 1936) lge 45/15gls
Swansea Town (signed in February 1939)

Inside forward who joined the Swans in a part-exchange deal for John Harris, who went to White Hart Lane, in the opposite direction. He made his Swans debut at inside right, replacing Paton, at the Vetch Field against West Ham United in a 3-2, Division Two defeat. John Harris had played for most of the season prior to his moving to White Hart Lane at inside right. His first goal for the Swans came in his third league game, at Luton Town in a 3-6 defeat. An experienced inside forward, earlier in his playing career he had been on trial with Liverpool, but after being rejected returned to non-league football with Stockton, before signing for Middlesbrough as an amateur. He signed professional for Gateshead, and started to create a name for himself as a goalscoring inside forward, with Gateshead, Bradford Park Avenue, and Spurs prior to his arrival at the Vetch Field. In season 1936/37 and 1937/38 he scored against the Swans for Spurs in league games. He started his second season with the Swans, 1939/40, played in all three league games, before the Football League was suspended because of the outbreak of the Second World War. During WW2 he made guest appearances for Newcastle United (1939/40), Lincoln City (1940/41), Nottingham Forest (September 1941), Middlesbrough (1940/41), Southport (1940/41), Grimsby Town (1941/42), and Rochdale (1945/46). In May 1957 he was a committee member of Bussadon Welfare.

18. MELVILLE, Andrew (ANDY) Roger

Birthplace: Swansea, 29/11/1968
Ht: 6ft-1ins, **Wt:** 12st-6lbs
Swans debut: v. Leyton Wingate (h), FAC-1, 16/11/1985

Swansea City Career Statistics

Season	League	FLC	FAC	WC	FRT	P/Offs	ECWC
1985/86	2+3		1+1	0+1			
1986/87	42/3gls	4	4/1gls	1	3		
1987/88	31+6/5gls	2	2	2	2	4	
1988/89	44+1/10gls	2	3/2gls	5/2gls			
1989/90	46/5gls	2	4/2gls	1	2		2/2gls
Total	165+10/23gls	10	14+1/5gls	9+1/2gls	7	4	2/2gls

Career:
Swansea City (from trainee in 25/7/1986)
Oxford United (£275,000 signed in 23/7/1990) lge 135/13gls, FLC 12/1gls, FAC 14+1/5gls, Others 6/1gls
Sunderland (£750,000 signed in 9/8/1993) P/Lge 204/14gls, FLC 18+1, FAC 11, Others 2
Bradford City (loan in 13/2/1998) lge 6/1gls

Fulham (signed in 1/7/1999) P/Lge 150+3/4gls, FLC 12+1, FAC 13+2, Others 12
West Ham United (signed in 16/1/2004) lge 14+3, FLC 0+1, Others 3
Nottm. Forest (loan in 4/2/2005) lge 13, FAC 2

Honours: Wales U-21–2, 'B', Full–61, Fourth Division Play Off Winner–1988, Welsh Cup Winner–1989, First Division Champions–1996, 2001, West Wales Senior Cup Winner–1987

Andrew made his Swans debut as substitute for the injured Colin Pascoe at the Vetch Field against non-league side Leyton Wingate, just thirteen days short of his seventeenth birthday, and still a second year trainee with the club. Seven days later he made a second half entry in the Football League game at the Vetch Field against Bristol City, making his first league start two games later against York City, also playing in the next league game at Ninian Park against Cardiff City. From an early age, whether at centre half, or at centre forward, the former Cefn Hengoed schoolboy, and Lon Las Boys Club player showed signs he would have a long career in the professional game. A good reader of the game from central defence, he possessed a sharp footballing brain. Always dangerous at set pieces, it was only a matter of time before he was recognised at International level, making his U-21 debut against Poland on the 19th May 1989, and his full debut in a friendly game against the Republic of Ireland in Dublin on the 28th March 1990. He made two further appearances for Wales later in the season against Sweden and Costa Rica while on the Vetch Field playing staff. Making his Swans first team debut whilst still a trainee, his first professional season (1986/87) following the club's relegation to the Fourth Division saw Melville miss just four league games, scoring his first goal against Orient in September 1986. In May 1987 he was included in the Swans side that won the West Wales Senior Cup. From this season on he became a regular member of the Swans line-up, playing an important part in the club's Fourth Division Play Off success in 1988, and the following season a member of the Swans side that beat non-league side Kidderminster Harriers to win the Welsh Cup, also end the season as top goalscorer in the league with ten goals. By the end of season 1989/90, an ever present, he joined Oxford United for a £275,000 transfer fee, decided by a Football League tribunal, and also allowing the Swans a percentage of any future transfer. Missing just three league games over the next three seasons, he then signed for Sunderland in a £750,000 transfer, which netted the Swans another £237,000 from a sell on clause. Winning the First Division Championships with Sunderland in 1996, and then with Fulham in 2001, he continued to become not only an influential defender in the Premiership, but also at international level with Wales, being particularly unlucky to finish his career by just losing out on qualifying for the 1994 World Cup, and the 2004 European Championships in Portugal. In mid-January 2004 he signed for West Ham United on an initial loan basis, playing in their unsuccessful First Division Play Off Final in Cardiff against Crystal Palace. Unable to command a place in the 'Hammers' starting line-up the following season, he joined Championship strugglers Nottm. Forest in early February 2005 on loan.

19. MESSER, Brinley (BRYN) Charles

Birthplace: Swansea, 11/5/1895. **Died:** Swansea, 28/9/1969
Ht: 5ft-8ins, **Wt:** 10st-0lbs
Swans debut: v. Gillingham (a), 19/4/1920, Sth. Lge

Swansea Town Career Statistics

Season	League
1920/21	1
Total	1

Career:
Swansea Town (amateur in season 1919/20, professional in
  28/1/1920)
Bridgend Town (signed in October 1923)

Honours: South Wales & Monmouthshire Representative XI

Local product who signed for the Swans as an amateur in
season 1919/20, playing regularly for the club's Welsh League
side before signing professional along with Alex Houston in late
January 1920. In April 1920 he made an appearance at
Gillingham for the Swans in a Southern League fixture. Bryn's
family relations include former Swans' players Ivor and Cliff
Jones, Ray Powell and Keith Huntley. Brought up in the St.
Thomas district of Swansea, Bryn made his only league
appearance in the last league game of the season in a 0-0 draw at
Swindon Town, at wing half instead of George Gray.
During WW1 he saw service in France, sustaining severe
injuries to his shoulder. He was retained for the 1921/22 season,
but after failing to make any further first team appearances was
released in May 1922. His uncle, WT Messer at the time was a
Director of Swansea Town Football Club. On the 15th January
1920 he was selected to play for a South Wales &
Monmouthshire Representative side against a Welsh League
Representative side in an Amateur International trial match at
Mid-Rhondda. In late October 1923 he signed for Bridgend
Town, made his debut on 27th October 1923 against
Penrhiwceiber, alongside his cousin Willie. After leaving the
Vetch Field playing staff he worked in his father's Fish and Chip
Shop in Oxford Street, eventually taking over the business up to
his retirement in the mid-1950's, and during WW2 he worked in
the Docks. A member of the Conservative Club in Swansea, he
was also a keen bowls player with the Victoria Bowls Club, and
a former Swansea Champion in the Annual Swansea Festival at
Victoria Park.

20. MIDDLETON, JOHN

Birthplace: Mickley, 15/4/1910. **Died:** Darlington, 3/8/1971
Ht: 5ft-8ins, **Wt:** 10st-6lbs
Swans debut: v. Reading (a), 25/1/1930

Swansea Town Career Statistics		
Season	League	WC
1929/30	1	
1930/31		1
Total	1	1

Career:
Mickley
Swansea Town (trial in February, professional in 27/2/1929)
Mickley
Walker Celtic (signed in July 1932)
Waterford (signed in 1932)
Darlington (signed in 4/7/1933) lge 77/22gls, FAC 3/1gls, Div 3
  North Cup 6/2gls
Blackpool (signed in April) lge 6/3gls
Norwich City (signed in June 1937) lge 3
South Shields (signed in July 1938)

Honours: Third Division North Cup Winner–1935, West Wales
Senior Cup Winner–1930

Former Mickley schoolboy inside forward who made just the
one league appearance for the Swans at Reading shortly after
the arriving at the Vetch Field. Signed by Swans manager James
Thomson on an initial trial basis, he signed professional in late
February 1929, but was released in April 1931 to return to
Mickley, joining Walker Celtic in July 1932. He was included in

the Swans' reserve side that were beaten by Cardiff City at
Llanelly in the South Wales & Monmouthshire Cup Final in
early May 1929, and in October 1930 played in the Swans
reserve side that beat Newport County in the West Wales Senior
Cup Final. He returned to the Football League in 1933 with
Third Division North side Darlington, missing just one game
out of forty-eight league and cup appearances in his first season.
He was a member of the team that won the Third Division
North Cup Final at Old Trafford in May 1935, scoring in
Darlington's 4-3 victory over Stockport County. He joined
Blackpool shortly after the final, also making appearances for
Norwich City, making appearances for both sides against the
Swans in the Second Division between 1935 and 1938. During
WW2 he made guest appearances during the 1939/40 season for
Hartlepool United and Aldershot. His brother William played
for Darlington in 1938.

21. MILLER, James (JIMMY)

Birthplace: Percy Main, Northumberland, 10/5/1889
Ht: 5ft-7ins, **Wt:** 11st-8lbs
Swans debut: v. Swindon Town (h), 30/8/1924

Swansea Town Career Statistics			
Season	League	FAC	WC
1924/25	25/1gls	2	1
Total	25/1gls	2	1

Career:
South Shields Albion
Wallsend Park Villa
Newcastle United (£25 signed in May 1912) lge 0
Grimsby Town (£50 signed in April 1913) lge 6/1gls
Everton (signed in June 1919) lge 8/1gls
Coventry City (£1,500 signed in December 1919) lge 7
Preston North End (signed in January 1920) lge 15/1gls, FAC 2
Pontypridd (signed in close season 1920)
Chesterfield (signed in May 1922) lge 32/1gls, FAC 4
Bournemouth & Boscombe (signed in June 1923) lge 38
Swansea Town (signed in May 1924)
Luton Town (signed in May 1925) lge 10/3gls, FAC 1

Honours: Lancashire Regional Champions–1919, Third Division
South Champions–1925

Signed prior to the start of the 1924/25 season from
Bournemouth & Boscombe, the right winger had been included
in the Swans close season tour of Denmark in 1924, and had
played in both league games against the Swans for
Bournemouth & Boscombe in season 1923/24. He made his
Swans debut in the opening fixture of the new season, held his

place for the first twenty-four league games, and then made way for the returning Billy Hole, making just one more league appearance during a season which saw the Swans win the Third Division South Championship, ironically against his old club Bournemouth in April 1925. His only goal for the Swans came against Bournemouth at the Vetch Field in December 1925. An experienced winger who joined First Division Newcastle United from Wallsend Park Villa in 1912, it was only after signing for Second Division Grimsby Town that he was given his league debut, against Notts. County on the 6th September 1913. A noted amateur sprinter on Tyneside, his pace on the flank made him a much sought after player in the immediate inter-war period. Joining the forces at the beginning of the Great War he initially played as a guest player with Everton, signing in September 1918, making twenty-eight appearances, scoring seven goals during season 1918/19 when the club won the Lancashire Regional League Championship, prior to signing as a professional in May 1919. Joining Coventry City in December 1919, he had the distinction of scoring in the 'Sky Blues' first ever league victory, but within two months had signed for Preston North End. In the 1920 close season he travelled south to sign for Southern League side Pontypridd. Following a season with Chesterfield, he signed for Bournemouth in June 1923, making his debut at Swindon in the club's first ever Football League game. He left the Vetch Field after just one season, joining Third Division South side Luton Town, retiring after making his final league appearance, at the age of 37.

22. MILLER, James (JIM)

Birthplace: Glasgow, 29/1/1904
Ht: 5ft-9½ins, **Wt:** 12st-0lbs
Swans debut: v. Bury (h), 13/9/1930

Swansea Town Career Statistics			
Season	League	FAC	WC
1930/31	35	1	1
1931/32	42/1gls	1	7/2gls
1932/33	39/1gls		2
1933/34	19	4	1
Total	135/2gls	6	11/2gls

Career:
Raith Rovers (signed in February 1925) SL 21/7gls, SC 1, Others 8
Preston North End (trial in October 1925)
East Fife (signed in April 1927)
Dumbarton (signed in July 1927)
Swansea Town (signed in June 1930)
Millwall (£200 signed in June 1934) lge 33/3gls
Hibernian (signed in August 1935)
Dunfermline Athletic (signed in June 1938)

Honours: Scotland Junior International–1, Welsh Cup Winner–1932

Former Scotland Junior International wing half who had a trial with Preston North End in October 1925, but had started his senior career with Scottish side Raith Rovers in February 1925, signing from junior side Maryhill. Signed by Swans manager James Hunter Thomson prior to the start of the 1930/31 season after the player had returned to Scottish football with East Fife and Dumbarton, he made his league debut for the Swans shortly after the start of the 1930/31 season at left half back, and became a feature of the Swans line-up for the next three seasons at left half back, and also, in his last season at the Vetch Field at right half back. During season 1931/32 he was an ever present in the Swans league line-up, also playing in the Welsh Cup Final

victory over Wrexham in May 1932. His first goal for the Swans came against Manchester United at the Vetch Field in January 1932, in a 3-1 win. Signing for Millwall in July 1934, after just the one season at the Den, he was surprisingly released, returning to Scottish Football to play for Hibernian, and then Dunfermline Athletic.

23. MILLER, PAUL Richard

Birthplace: Stepney, 11/10/1959
Ht: 6ft-1ins, **Wt:** 12st-2lbs
Swans debut: v. Brentford (a), 26/1/1991

Swansea City Career Statistics		
Season	League	WC
1990/91	8+4	4
Total	8+4	4

Career:
Tottenham Hotspur (signed as schoolboy in January 1975, apprentice in April 1976, professional in May 1977)
lge 206+2/7gls
Skeid, Norway (loan in 1978)
Charlton Athletic (£130,000 signed in 26/2/1987) lge 40+2/2gls
Watford (£85,000 signed in 13/10/1988) lge 20/1gls
Bournemouth (£50,000 signed in 18/8/1989) lge 43+4/1gls
Brentford (loan in 22/11/1989) lge 3
Swansea City (signed in 24/1/1991)

Honours: FA Cup Winner–1981, 1982, UEFA Cup Winner–1984

Experienced defender who was signed by Swans manager Terry Yorath on a free transfer from Bournemouth in January 1991, to add experience to the Swans rearguard, but unfortunately for the former Spurs central defender, after making his Swans debut as substitute for Keith Walker at Brentford in late January 1991, he played in the next 8 league games, which all ended in defeat for the Swans, and after the Crewe Alexandra defeat, Yorath was sacked. His only appearance in a winning Swans team under Yorath was in a Welsh Cup defeat of Colwyn Bay, after a replay. Frank Burrows took over as manager, with Miller making just three more substitute appearances for the Swans, plus two starts in the Welsh Cup semi-finals legs against Barry Town. He was released at the end of the season, with a fitness problem through a knee injury. A couple of years ater it was revealed in the press that he had threatened to sue the Swans over conditions in his contract. Starting off as an apprentice at White Hart Lane with Spurs, he became a prominent member of the side that was to win two consecutive FA Cup Finals, against Manchester City and QPR respectively, and also be a member of a UEFA Cup Final side that beat Anderlecht on penalties in 1984.

The following season Spurs reached the quarter final stage of the competition. In 1982 he was a member of the side that lost in the semi-final stages of the ECWC to Real Madrid, and the following season lost to Bayern Munich in the second round. After over 200 league appearances for Spurs he joined Charlton Athletic in February 1987, then linking up with Watford in October 1988. The following season saw him start for Bournemouth, and after a loan spell with Brentford, he arrived at the Vetch Field in January 1991. After leaving the Vetch Field and retiring as a player, he was youth team coach at Wingate & Finchley, and has since worked for leading merchant bank Kleinwort Benson in the City and been a director of FIFA licensed agents PML.

24. MILLINGTON, JOHN

Birthplace: Bolton, 1916
Ht: 5ft-8½ins, **Wt:** 11st-0lbs
Swans debut: v. Luton Town (h),11/12/1937

Swansea Town Career Statistics

Season	League	FAC	WC
1937/38	13/2gls		2/1gls
1938/39	31/5gls	1	3
Total	44/7gls	1	5/1gls

Career:
Bolton Wanderers (signed amateur in May 1933, professional in August 1933) lge 0
Clapton Orient (signed in June 1934) lge 2
Notts. County (signed in May 1935) lge 15/2gls
Birmingham (signed in May 1936) lge 0
Swansea Town (£250 signed in December 1937)
Scunthorpe & Lindsay United (signed in June 1939)

Signed from Birmingham in early December 1937 for £250, the outside left made his debut against Luton Town at the Vetch Field in December 1937, playing in eleven consecutive league matches. He scored his first goal for the Swans at Blackburn Rovers in a 3-1 defeat, and his second goal came in a record 1-8 defeat at Craven Cottage against Fulham. At the end of the season he scored in the Welsh Cup Final against Shrewsbury Town in a 2-2 draw, and when the Final was replayed in September of the following season, he played in a losing Swans side. His second season at the Vetch Field saw him make a regular contribution on the Swans left wing, but in May 1939 he was released. He then signed for non-league side Scunthorpe & Lindsay United. At the start of his career he was unable to make a league appearance for Second Division side Bolton Wanderers, his league debut being made with Clapton Orient, at Coventry City in September 1934, making his second appearance shortly after at Watford, before making further league appearances for Notts. County and Birmingham.

25. MILLINGTON, Anthony (TONY) Horace

Birthplace: Hawarden, 5/6/1943
Ht: 5ft-11ins, **Wt:** 11st-10lbs
Swans debut: v. Chesterfield (h), 7/8/1969

Swansea Town/City Career Statistics

Season	League	FLC	FAC	WC
1969/70	43	1	3	4
1970/71	38	3	2	2
1971/72	35	1	6	1
1972/73	43	2	1	2
1973/74	19	2		
Total	178	9	12	9

Career:
West Bromwich Albion (from juniors in July 1960) lge 40
Crystal Palace (signed in October 1964) lge 16
Peterborough United (signed in March 1966) lge 118
Swansea Town City (signed in July 1969)
Glenavon (signed prior to start of season 1974/75)

Honours: Wales U-23–4, Full–21

Flamboyant goalkeeper who Brian Clough once described as a 'clown' after his antics in the Wales v. England Home International Championship match at Ninian Park, after he had repelled almost single handed the England attack, with the game finishing in a 1-1 draw. He joined the Swans along with veteran winger Len Allchurch in July 1969, at a time with the club having no manager, and a new influx of Directors to the Boardroom, headed by Malcolm Struel. Shortly before the start of the season Roy Bentley had been placed in charge of team affairs, and within nine months the club had ended the season in third position, and promotion to the Third Division. With the Home Internationals being played at the end of the season, Millington's form for the Swans had seen him earn himself a recall to the international stage. The former Hawarden & Mancot and Flintshire schoolboy keeper had started his career as a fifteen-year-old with West Bromwich Albion, gained four U-23 caps for Wales whilst at the Hawthorns, and also gained his first Full international cap, playing against Scotland in Cardiff on the 20th October 1962. Gaining two further caps whilst at the Hawthorns, he continued to gain international recognition after transfers to Crystal Palace and Peterborough United, vying initially with Dave Hollins after the legendary Jack Kelsey had retired, and then with the up and coming Gary Sprake of Leeds United. Joining the Swans for a small fee in July 1969 from Peterborough United, he established himself as one of the finest goalkeepers to have played for the club in post war football, making memorable appearances in cup competition against the likes of Liverpool, Tottenham Hotspur and Leeds United. On the down side he also made an appearance for the Swans when they were beaten by non-league Margate in the FA

Cup in November 1972. A fearless goalkeeper, and a model of consistency during his first couple of seasons with the Swans, despite a relegation season in 1972/73, he was released from the Vetch Field at the end of the 1973/74 season, to take over as a publican in Northern Ireland, and also signing part-time for Glenavon. His parting joke when leaving the Vetch Field was, 'what do you reckon I've been working for all these years in football? Goalkeeping has been my preparation for playing the fastest game in the world. Playing pass the parcel in an Irish pub!' During his time with the Swans, almost on every occasion the Swans scored, he would do hand stands in the penalty area. His younger brother Grenville, also had a career as a goalkeeper in league football, and on 2nd January 1971 they faced each other at the Vetch Field in an FA Cup clash between the Swans and North Wales side Rhyl, with the Swans winning 6-1, courtesy of a Dai Gwyther hat-trick. Sadly, he was involved in a road crash in early 1975, and confined to a wheelchair for the rest of his life. West Bromwich Albion played the Swans in a Testimonial game for him at the Vetch Field. Nowadays he involves himself with running a disabled supporters club at the Racecourse with Wrexham.

26. MILNE, Wilfred (WILFIE) Ellis

Birthplace: Hebburn-on-Tyne, 24/3/1899. **Died:** Swansea, 29/11/1977
Ht: 5ft-8½ins, **Wt:** 11st-10lbs
Swans debut: v. Northampton Town (a), 25/9/1920

Swansea Town Career Statistics			
Season	League	FAC	WC
1920/21	35	3	
1921/22	32	7	2
1922/23	29	2	3
1923/24	38	4	3
1924/25	29	2	3
1925/26	27	7	2
1926/27	38	5	1
1927/28	40	1	2
1928/29	37	2	1
1929/30	38	1	1
1930/31	42	1	2
1931/32	40	1	7
1932/33	41	1	2
1933/34	41/2gls	4	
1934/35	41/2gls	2	1
1935/36	35/3gls	1	
1936/37	3		
Total	586/7gls	44	30

Career:
Walker Celtic
Swansea Town (signed in 22/5/1920)
Milford United (player manager signed in 27/7/1937)

Honours: Third Division South Champions–1925, Welsh Cup Winner–1932, Northumberland Senior Cup Winner–1920, Welsh League Representative XI

The Northumberland Senior Cup medalist, signed for the Swans in May 1920 from junior club Walker Celtic, for the price of a fish tea, and a cup of tea (2/9d) in a Newcastle café, with Manchester United and West Ham United also interested at the time for his signature. Capable of playing in either right or left full back positions, his brother was former Stoke City captain A. J. Milne. Joining the Swans following the club's elevation to Football League status, he did not play in the club's first Football League match, but six games later he made his entry to League football at Northampton, at left full back in place of Ogley, and become a permanent member of the club's defence through to the end of the 1935/36 season. Captaining the side in September 1930, he gained honours in season 1924/25 winning the Third Division South Championship, the following season playing in the semi-final of the FA Cup against Bolton Wanderers, and also losing to Ebbw Vale the same season in the Final of the Welsh Cup. In season 1931/32 he was a member of the Swans side that won the Welsh Cup Final against Wrexham. The current record holder of league appearances by a Swans player, he also started two league games in goal for the Swans in an emergency. Travelling to two away games as reserve, regular custodian Stan Moore was taken injured, and Milne replaced him in goal, at Leicester City on 27th March 1937, drawing 0-0, and two days later at Nottingham Forest, losing 6-1. It took him until his 501st league game to score his first goal for the Swans, from the penalty spot, and in season 1933/34 he scored from two penalties in the same game against Brentford. The following season he scored his only goal, other than from a penalty, against Norwich City at the Vetch Field, also scoring in the same game from the penalty spot. A dour defender, and a thoughtful user of the ball, he was adept at the sliding tackle, but was handicapped in later years by a knee problem. During his career in the game he also played through times when the offside law changed. He left the Vetch Field on the 27th July 1937 to join Milford United as player manager, but in January 1938 he retired from football to become mine host at the Badminton Hotel in Swansea.

27. MOLBY, JAN

Birthplace: Kolding, Denmark 4/7/1963
Ht: 6ft-1ins, **Wt:** 14st-7lbs
Swans debut: v. York City (a), 24/2/1996

Swansea City Career Statistics				
Season	League	FLC	AWS	P/Offs
1995/96	12/2gls			
1996/97	26+2/1gls	1	1	1
1997/98	1			
Total	39+2/3gls	1	1	1

Career:
Kolding, Denmark
Ajax, Holland
Liverpool (£225,000 signed in August 1984) lge 195+23/44gls
Barnsley (loan in September 1995) lge 5
Norwich City (loan in December 1995) lge 3
Swansea City (player manager from 22/2/1996)

Honours: Denmark Full–33, First Division Champions–1986, 1988, 1990, FA Cup Winner–1986, 1992, Charity Shield Winner (shared)–1986

Following the departure of Frank Burrows, the club embarked on a scenario more resembling a Whitehall farce, as events off the field saw the club embarrassed in an on/off take over bid, plus a continuous stream of managers occupying the hot seat on a caretaker basis. Needless to say events off the field was not conducive to stability on the field as the club headed for relegation to the Fourth Division. On February 22nd 1996, after being given a free transfer by Liverpool Jan Molby was appointed the Swans player manager. His selection was seen as a breath of fresh air by the club's supporters as his presence and skill on the field transformed the side, previously shorn of confidence, to a side capable of beating most teams in the league. Despite being unable to avoid relegation, Molby's influence on and off the field, especially with the club's younger professionals almost saw the club regain promotion at the first time of asking, only to lose out in the last minute in the Play Off Final at Wembley. Along with his assistant Billy Ayre, despite a poor start to the 1996/97 season, they took the club to the Play Off Final, where they were unlucky to lose to a last minute goal against Northampton Town. Pacing himself through matches, his skill on the ball, was a beacon amidst the mediocrity of lower division fare, and at the end of the season he was selected for the PFA Third Division side of the season. Having to sell players prior to the start of the 1997/98 season, and a takeover of the club behind the scenes in the offing did not help his cause. After his only appearance in season 1997/98 at Peterborough United, he was sacked by the club's Board of Directors who felt that he should have played himself more, rather than rely on his younger players who had graduated from the club's youth side. Out of the game for a short spell, he was linked to the manager's job at Carlisle United, Norwich City and Welsh League side Rhayader, whilst keeping himself busy commentating on BBC Radio's 5 Live, and his own radio show with Manchester's Century 105 radio station. In May 1999 he was appointed Kidderminster Harriers manager, and within twelve months had led the side to the Conference Championship, and into the Football League. His success with Harriers prompted speculation linking him to other manager's positions, even suggestions at the time with the manager's job at FC Copenhagen. He resigned from his position at Harriers in April 2002 to take over at Hull City, however, despite signing a number of players in the close season, a poor start in the league saw him sacked in early October after just sixteen games in charge, with the club sitting in 18th position. Jan's name continued to crop up as a candidate for manager's positions, and after helping former Liverpool player Mike Marsh with coaching at Nuneaton Borough, as well as his media work, he returned to the Harriers two days after the club had played a goalless game at the Vetch Field on the 18th October 2003, to take over for a second time as the club's manager. In his early days the 'great Dane' was brought up in the renowned Ajax youth academy with Marco van Basten, Frank Rijkaard and

Jesper Olsen, heavily influenced by Dutch master Johann Cruyff. Signed by Liverpool manager Joe Fagan for £225,000 in August 1984, he became one of the most successful of English football's foreign imports, combining subtlety and power, with measured passing. He was also an expert penalty taker, and at Liverpool scored with 40 of his 42 spot kicks, and in November 1986 earned a niche in the record books with a penalty hat trick against Coventry in the League Cup. Molby made 52 appearances in Liverpool's League and FA Cup double season of 1985/86 before playing for Denmark in the World Cup Finals in Mexico. He won a second title medal in 1990 and another F A Cup medal in 1992. By the end of October 2004 a poor set of results at Aggborough, with Harriers bottom of the League saw Jan resign his position as manager.

28. MOLLOY, WILLIAM Henry B.

Birthplace: Barrow-in-Furness, JAS, 1904
Ht: 5ft-8ins, **Wt:** 11st-0lbs
Swans debut: v. West Ham United (h), 27/8/1932

Swansea Town Career Statistics			
Season	League	FAC	WC
1932/33	11/2gls	1	1
Total	11/2gls	1	1

Career:
Dumbarton Harp (signed in 1923)
Celtic (signed in October 1925)
Arthurlie (loan in November 1926)
Ayr United (loan in November 1927)
Arthurlie (loan in December 1927)
Dumbarton (signed in September 1928)
Yeovil & Petters United (signed in July 1931)
    Total apps 51/41gls
Swansea Town (signed in 9/7/1932)
Bristol City (£500 signed in 11/9/1933) lge 7/2gls
Falkirk (signed in August 1934)
Dumbarton (trial in Sept-October 1935)

William Molloy signed for the Swans at a time when the club did not have a manager, and was being run by the club's Board of Directors. Starting his career in the Scottish League with Dumbarton and Glasgow Celtic, making loan appearances for Arthurlie and Ayr United whilst with Celtic, he came south to sign for non-league side Yeovil & Petters United (later to be renamed Yeovil Town), prior to arriving at the Vetch Field in July 1932. After joining Yeovil he created a name for himself in non-league by scoring forty-one league and cup goals in his only season at Yeovil. He made his Swans debut against West Ham United in the opening fixture of the 1932/33 season, playing at inside left. He remained in the side for the next eight league games, before losing his place to Anstiss. In early September he scored his only goal for the Swans in a game at the Vetch Field against Chesterfield. Later in the season he made one appearance at outside left, and one at inside right. He made his last appearance for the Swans against Grimsby Town in early April, signing for Third Division South side Bristol City for £500 in early September 1933. He was released by Bristol City in the 1934 close season, returning to Scotland to sign for Falkirk, and the following season having a trial period at Dumbarton.

29. MONK, GARRY Alan

Birthplace: Bedford, 6/3/1979
Ht: 6ft-0ins, **Wt**: 12st-1lbs
Swans debut: v. Northampton Town (h), 7/8/2004

	Swansea City Career Statistics				
Season	League	FLC	FAC	LDV	FAWC
2004/05	34	1	4	2	1
Total	34	1	4	2	1

Career:
Torquay United (from trainee in 1/8/1995) lge 4+1
Southampton (from trainee in 23/5/1997) PL 9+2, FLC 1, FAC 0+1
Torquay United (loan in 25/9/1998) lge 6
Stockport County (loan in 9/9/1999) lge 2, FLC 2
Oxford United (loan in 12/1/2001) lge 5
Sheffield Wednesday (loan in 13/12/2002) lge 15
Barnsley (loan in 20/11/2003) lge 13+1, FAC 4/1gls
Barnsley (signed in 26/2/2004) lge 1+2
Swansea City (signed in 4/6/2004)

One of Swans' manager Kenny Jackett's first close season signings, he made his Swans debut in the opening fixture of season 2004/05 at the Vetch Field in a 2-0 defeat by Northampton Town. In the next game, three days later at Rochdale, he took over the captaincy from Martinez, but during the first half of his debut season with the Swans he received two red cards, at Yeovil in early September 2004, and at Shrewsbury in November, later suffering a ban which kept him out of the game for six matches. He received a third red card in February 2005 at Mansfield. Despite that, he proved to be an assured central defender, and a good reader of the game. Garry attended St. Marychurch Juniors and Audley Park Schools in Torquay, played for Torbay and Devon County Schoolboys, also having U-17 trials with England. Joining Torquay United as a YTS trainee from school, he made his Football League debut whilst still a trainee, replacing Ian Gore in central defence in a 4-1 away defeat at Chester on the 4th November 1995, and by the end of

the season had transferred his YTS traineeship to the Dell with Southampton. He had to wait until the 1998/99 season for his next senior appearance, returning to Plainmoor on a loan transfer, and after returning to the Dell, made his Premiership debut against Derby County on the 28th November 1998, making a further three appearances, also appearing as substitute for Claus Lundekvam in the FA Cup tie against Fulham. After making further loan appearances with Stockport County and Oxford United, and occasional Premiership appearances for the 'Saints', his loan move to Hillsborough with Sheffield Wednesday saw him have his best period in first team football, making fifteen league appearances over a three month period, before returning to the Dell. Joining Division Two side Barnsley on loan in November 2003 his impressive form earned him a permanent contract at Oakwell during the second half of the season, but after picking up an injury, he struggled to regain his first team place, and was unfortunate to be released at the end of the season. During his first season at the Vetch Field, despite accumulating three red cards, he possessed good defensive qualities and read the game well, had a good understanding with Iriekpen in the heart of the Swans defence, and played a significant part in the club achieving one of the automatic promotion places at the end of his first season at the Vetch Field.

30. MOORE, GARY

Birthplace: South Hetton, Co. Durham, 4/11/1945
Ht: 6ft-2ins, **Wt**: 12st-10lbs
Swans debut: v. Bradford City (a), 25/8/1976

	Swansea City Career Statistics			
Season	League	FLC	FAC	WC
1976/77	16+4/6gls	2	1	0+1
1977/78	14/3gls	2/1gls	3/1gls	1
Total	30+4/9gls	4/1gls	4/1gls	1+1

Career:
Sunderland (signed amateur in 1960, professional in November 1962) lge 13/2gls, FAC 1
Grimsby Town (£8,000 signed in February 1967) lge 52+1/15gls, FLC 6, FAC 1
Southend United (£8,000 signed in November 1968) lge 156+7/46gls, FLC 9/2gls, FAC 7+1/7gls
Colchester United (loan in 15/3/1974) lge 11/7gls
Chester City (£6,000 signed in 5/8/1974) lge 29+14/4gls, FLC 1+2/1gls, FAC 2/1gls, WC 1+1
Swansea City (signed in July 1976)

Signed by Swans manager Harry Griffiths prior to the start of the 1976/77 season, along with the experienced Eddie May, Les Chappell and Gil Reece as part of the plan to bring on the club's younger players. The idea at the time was to link the experienced front runner with youngsters Curtis and James, and also support the previous season's top goalscorer Geoff Bray. The former South Moor Technical School, and Sunderland & County Durham schoolboy player joined Sunderland initially as an amateur in 1960 before signing professional in November 1962, progressing through to the club's league side to make his debut against Wolverhampton Wanderers on the 20th April 1965. Following trials with the England youth team whilst at Roker Park, he joined Grimsby Town in February 1967 for a small fee, and started to create a name for himself in the lower leagues as a consistent goalscorer, firstly with the 'Mariners', Southend United, and in a loan spell with Colchester United in March 1974, scored 7 goals in eleven league games, helping the club to clinch promotion from the Third Division. Moving to Chester City in August 1974, he was again involved in a promotion winning side twelve months later when the club finished fourth, and clinched automatic promotion, and also when the club reached the semi-final stages of the League Cup the same season, losing to Aston Villa, with Moore scoring in the first leg 2-2 home draw. He made his Swans debut as a substitute for Danny Bartley in a 4-1 defeat at Bradford City, making his first start two days later in a 3-0 defeat at Stockport County. However, injury problems had started to take their toll by the time he arrived at the Vetch Field, limiting his availability for the Swans. He scored his first goal for the Swans in his second start at the Vetch Field against Barnsley. By the time of John Toshack's arrival at the Vetch Field during his second season with the Swans, Moore was sidelined with an injury, and did not feature in any of Toshack's sides through to the end of the season, with the pelvic injury forcing him to retire from the professional game in May 1978, just after the Swans had clinched promotion. Prior to announcing his retirement he had been involved with coaching Swansea Senior League side Velindre Sports, winning the West Wales Amateur Cup competition in 1977, and after leaving the Vetch Field, remained in the area for some time, devoting more time to his industrial cleaning business. He later returned home to his native Sunderland area where he was involved in coaching with Blyth Spartans in 1980, manager of Consett in 1982, manager of Crook Town in 1984, before being involved on a part-time basis under his former skipper at Grimsby, Graham Taylor, as North East area scout for Watford in 1986, Aston Villa in 1987, and England between 1996 and 2000, whilst working as a sales representative in the medical field prior to retiring on medical grounds in 1997.

31. MOORE, JOHN

Birthplace: Walton, Liverpool, 9/9/1945
Ht: 5ft-9½ins, **Wt:** 11st-4lbs
Swans debut: v. York City (h), 29/1/1973

Career:
Everton (apprentice in July 1960, professional in 1962)

Stoke City (signed in July 1963) lge 12+1
Shrewsbury Town (signed in August 1968) lge 144/1gls
Swansea City (£5,000 signed in January 1973)

Swansea City Career Statistics		
Season	League	FLC
1973/74	18	
1974/75	13	2
Total	31	2

A former Everton apprentice, who made his league debut with Stoke City, before establishing himself in defence with Shrewsbury Town under manager Harry Gregg. When Gregg joined the Swans as manager he returned to his old club to pay £5,000 for the central defender in January 1973. Capable of also operating in midfield, he was a strong tackler, but a cruciate knee ligament injury eventually saw him having to retire from the game in January 1975, less than eighteen months after arriving at the Vetch Field. Living in the Bishopston area of the Gower peninsular, he continued to play in the Swansea Senior League with Bishopston, and then Murton Rovers well into the 1990's, whilst working in the building industry in the area. At the time of his leaving the professional game, the recession in South Wales saw his job opportunities limited, with him eventually taking a bricklaying course in a Skill Centre in Port Talbot. Two years later he returned to the Skill Centre to do a Plastering Course, and since then, after working on numerous building sites has started his own building company from his Bishopston base. Brought up in the Walton district of Liverpool, he attended Gladys Street School, adjacent to Goodison Park, played for Liverpool and Lancashire Schoolboys, losing in the final of the English Schools Shield Final against Barnsley 2-1, over two legs. On leaving school, the year he started his apprenticeship was the first year of the scheme in the professional game, taking over from the time when youngsters went on the groundstaff.

32. MOORE, KEVIN John

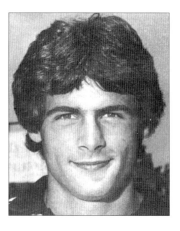

Birthplace: Blackpool, 30/1/1956
Ht: 5ft-9ins, **Wt:** 10st-9lbs
Swans debut: v. Swindon Town (h), FLC 1-1, 13/8/1977

Swansea City Career Statistics				
Season	League	FLC	FAC	WC
1977/78	37+3/5gls	2	3/1gls	2
1978/79	14+1/1gls	3	1	1
Total	51+4/6gls	5	4/1gls	3

Career:
Blackpool (from apprentice in October 1973) lge 33+5/3gls,
    FLC 2, FAC 2+1
Bury (loan in 24/12/1976) lge 4
Swansea City (signed in July 1977)
Newport County (£12,000 signed in 18/2/1979)
    lge 140+8/14gls, FLC 10/1gls, FAC 5+1, ECWC 6/2gls
Swindon Town (loan in March 1983) lge 1

Honours: Welsh Cup Winner–1980

Former Lancashire Schoolboy winger Kevin More was an exceptionally quick right winger who made his name as not only a provider of goal scoring opportunities for his team mates, but also as a goalscorer. Signed by manager Harry Griffiths in late July 1977, there had been doubts about the fitness of winger Micky Conway at the time, and manager Griffiths wanted a player to play in the same vein, fast, skilful, and capable of scoring goals. On the 20th August 1974 he made his Football League debut for Blackpool on the right wing in a 0-0 draw against Orient in the Second Division, having to wait a further thirteen months before he registered his first league goal, in a 4-1 win over Southampton. His first season at the Vetch Field saw him make forty league appearances, scoring five league goals, his first in a 4-0 away win at Hartlepool, in which he scored two goals, with Curtis scoring the other two. Following the arrival of John Toshack as manager, Moore played the last thirteen league matches of the season as the Swans gained promotion from the Fourth Division. Despite starting the 1978/79 season in the Swans line-up, with the arrival of new players adding to the squad, by late October he had lost his place, and in February 1979 he joined Newport County for £12,000. He maintained a regular place in County's side over the next four seasons, also participating in the side that won promotion to the Third Division at the end of the 1979/80 season, and playing in the sided that beat Shrewsbury Town over two legs to win the Welsh Cup Final. The following season he had his first taste of European Football, playing in the European Cup Winners Cup competition with Newport County, as they beat Crusaders and Haugar, before losing in the quarter final stages to Carl Zeiss Jena, one of the eventual finalists. After a month on loan with Swindon Town in March 1983, he returned to Somerton Park but was released on a free transfer at the end of the season, later having a trial in July 1983 with Burnley. His father, Len Moore was President of Blackpool Football Club from 1979 to 1982, and his daughter Louise is five times United Kingdom National Wakeboarding Champion. In later years, after he had retired from football Kevin owned a Nursing Home in Blackpool.

33. MOORE, MICHAEL

Birthplace: Birmingham, 7/10/1973
Ht: 5ft-10ins, **Wt:** 11st-0lbs
Swans debut: v. Reading (a), 25/3/1994

Swansea City Career Statistics	
Season	League
1993/94	0+1
Total	0+1

Career:
Derby County (from trainee in June 1992) lge 0
Swansea City (signed in August 1993)

Former Derby County trainee who arrived at the Vetch Field on a non-contract basis shortly after the start of the 1993/94 season on an initial trial, but struggled to break into the first team. After completing his training at the Baseball Ground he had been on

the 'Rams' playing staff as a non-contract player. He eventually signed a contract until the end of the season at the Vetch Field, but after suffering a back injury was given an extension to his contract by manager Frank Burrows in a bid to see if he could get over the injury. Unfortunately he had to concede that his back would not be able to withstand the rigours of full time training, forcing him in December 1994 to retire as a full time professional. His only first team appearance came as a substitute for John Cornforth at Reading in a tense end of season promotion tussle with the home side. A striker, who was quick, and impressed in reserve team matches, his back injury affected his first team opportunities at the Vetch Field. His only other inclusions in the first team came as non-playing substitutes against Plymouth in an AutoGlass Trophy game early in season 1993/94, and at Burnley in mid-April 1994. Dropping into non-league football he has since earned himself a fine reputation as a prolific goalscorer, finishing top goalscorer with almost all of the clubs he has played for. Since leaving the Vetch Field his clubs include, Cradley Town, Stafford Rangers, Moor Green, Telford United, Stourbridge, Rothwell Town, Redditch United, Stourbridge, Bromsgrove Rovers, Gresley Rovers, Stratford Town, Stourport Swifts, Hednesford Town (August 2003), Cradley Town. In May 2004 his worsening back problem saw him retire from the game completely. For a number of years Michael has held a full time football coaching position at North Birmingham College, coaches the Birmingham City Ladies team, as well as managing the U-9's.

34. MOORE, Stanley (STAN)

Birthplace: Worksop, 31/12/1909. **Died:** Leeds, 4/10/1982
Ht: 5ft-10ins, **Wt:** 12st-0lbs
Swans debut: v. Southampton (a), 31/8/1935

Swansea Town Career Statistics			
Season	League	FAC	WC
1935/36	40	1	2
1936/37	39	4	2
1937/38	25	1	
1938/39	19	2	
Total	123	8	4

Career:
Anston Athletic
Worksop Town
Bradford City (amateur in February 1931)
Leeds United (signed in August 1931) lge 78
Swansea Town (signed in 9/6/1935)

Signed by Leeds United manager Dick Ray from local club Worksop Town in August 1931, making 78 league appearances for United before breaking his leg in February 1935, and was released by the club in May 1935. Overcoming his injury, he joined the Swans in June 1935, taking over from the experienced Alex Ferguson to make his debut at Southampton at the start of the 1935/36 season in an exciting 4-3 defeat. His first two seasons at the Vetch Field saw him miss just 5 league games, and in season 1936/37, veteran defender Wilf Milne made two appearances in away games at Leicester City and Nottingham Forest after Moore was taken ill just prior to the game. During his period at the Vetch Field he became something of a hero with the younger Swans fans, with his spectacular saves in goal. He lost his place midway through the 1937/38 season to Roy John, but still managed 19 league appearances the following season. After playing in the first three league fixtures of the 1939/40 season, the Football League was cancelled following the onset of the Second World War. When friendly matches were organised in September 1939, he played in the first two with the Swans, but then joined the services. After the war he settled back in Leeds, working in the Engineering and Printing industries prior to his death in October 1982.

35. MOORE, THOMAS

Birthplace: Dudley Port, JAS, 1910
Ht: 5ft-8ins, **Wt:** 9st-6lbs
Swans debut: v. Coventry City (a), 31/8/1936

Swansea Town Career Statistics	
Season	*League*
1936/37	4
Total	4

Career:
Tipton All Souls
Stourbridge
Aston Villa (signed in February 1932) lge 1/1gls
Stourbridge
Bournemouth & Boscombe Athletic (signed in July 1934) lge 6/2gls
Stourbridge (signed in May 1935)
Birmingham (signed in November 1935) lge 0
Swansea Town (signed in 4/5/1936)
Stourbridge (signed in July 1937)
Dudley Town
Vono Sports Club (signed in March 1939)

Honours: England Junior International–1

Former English Junior International capped against Scotland in 1932 whilst with Aston Villa, who started his career with non-league Stourbridge, and who played for the club on three further occasions after being released by Football League clubs. Making his Football League debut at outside left with Aston Villa in the last match of the 1931/32 season, on the 7th May 1932 against Huddersfield Town, despite scoring on his debut, ended up on the losing side. He unfortunately broke his leg in a reserve team game in late December 1932, was out of the game for eight months, never recovered his Villa career and joined Bournemouth in July 1934. Making just six league games for Boscombe, after a spell in non-league with Stourbridge returned to the Football League with Birmingham, prior to arriving at the Vetch Field in May 1936. He made his debut for the Swans in the second match of the 1936/37 season, replacing Bussey at inside left, but had to wait until early December before he made his next appearances, this time at inside right against Newcastle United and Bradford Park Avenue. Making one further appearance four matches later at Chesterfield, he was transfer listed at the end of the season at £200, before being released, and

returning to Stourbridge. After his last stint with Stourbridge he continued to play non-league with Dudley Town and Vono Sports Club. Tom was the grandson of former Villa player Ike Moore.

36. MOREIRA, Joao (JOE) Manuel Silva

Birthplace: Angola, 30/6/1970
Ht: 6ft-2ins, **Wt:** 13st-0lbs
Swans debut: v. Gillingham (a), CCC 1-2, 3/9/1996

Swansea City Career Statistics						
Season	*League*	*FLC*	*FAC*	*AWS*	*P/Offs*	*FAW Inv*
1996/97	10	0+1	2	2	3	
1997/98	5	2				3
Total	15	2+1	2	2	3	3

Career:
Benfica (Portugal)
Nacional de Madeira (loan)
Swansea City (signed in 20/5/1996)

Signed for a reputed £56,000 transfer fee from top Portugal side Benfica, he had been spotted playing in a trial game for Birmingham City, and joined the Swans in May 1996. A tall, strong, attacking left full back, he missed the start of his first season at the Vetch Field after suffering a knee injury in pre-season training, eventually making his Swans' debut at Gillingham in a Coca Cola Cup, First Round, Second Leg game, and soon became a favourite with the North Bank supporters with his charging runs down the left flank, although his defensive skill needed a lot to be desired. His first league start came in mid-November 1996 as a replacement for the injured Keith Walker, against Brighton & Hove Albion at the Vetch Field. Despite not being a regular inclusion in the Swans starting line-up after making his league debut, he did play at left full back in the club's march to the 1997 Third Division Play Off Final at Wembley against Northampton Town, and also in the semi-final stages against Chester City. He failed to command a regular place in the Swans side during his second season at the Vetch Field, and he was made available for transfer in November 1997, and on 26th March 1998 he was released along with Linton Brown. At the end of the season he had a trial period with Leyton Orient

37. MORGAN, ARTHUR Robert

Birthplace: Llanharan, Glam, 13/9/1930. **Died:** Barry, 13/10/2000
Ht: 5ft-7ins, **Wt:** 11st-0lbs
Swans debut: v. Hull City (a), 26/8/1950

Swansea Town Career Statistics			
Season	League	FAC	WC
1950/51	2		
1951/52	1		
1952/53	9	1	1
Total	12	1	1

Career:
Swansea Town (amateur signed in December 1948, professional in August 1950)
Plymouth Argyle (signed in November 1953) lge 36/4gls
Barry Town (signed in August 1959)

Honours: Wales Army Cadets

Signed for the Swans in December 1948 from the Army Cadets, it was only after returning from his National Service in the Forces, and impressing in trial games at the Vetch Field in the 1950 close season, that he was given his league debut at Hull City shortly after the start of the 1950/51 season at right full back in place of Terry Elwell. Playing in the Swans' Welsh League and Combination sides prior to joining the Forces, many fans likened him to Wilf Milne for his fearless tackling, two footed kicking, and positional sense. He retained his place for the next game, but his next first team opportunity came in April 1952 against Southampton, instead of Iorrie Symmons. The 1952/53 season would see him make nine league appearances, and also an appearance in an FA Cup tie at Newcastle United, and a Welsh Cup tie against Kidderminster Harriers in January 1953. Capable of playing at either left, or right full back, he was sold to Second Division Plymouth Argyle in November 1953, and played just the once against the Swans, towards the end of season 1955/56. Capped for the Wales Army Cadets against England, he was a speedy, tough tackling full back.
Made regular appearances for Plymouth Argyle following his transfer in November 1953, then returned to South Wales to sign for Southern League side Barry Town, until his retirement in May 1964. Settling in Barry after his retirement from the game, he was killed in a gas explosion at his home in October 2000.

38. MORGAN, David BARI Rees

Birthplace: Carmarthen, 13/8/1980
Ht: 5ft-6ins, **Wt:** 10st-8lbs
Swans debut: v. Exeter City (a), AWS-2, 11/1/2000

Swansea City Career Statistics			
Season	League	AWS	FAWP
1999/2000		0+1	1+3
2000/01	0+5		3+2/1gls
Total	0+5	0+1	4+5/1gls

Career:
Swansea City (signed from trainee in 5/7/1999)
Aberystwyth (signed in July 2001)

Former West Wales schoolboy footballer who became a trainee at the Vetch Field on leaving school, signing professional in July 1999, and who made his first team debut in a flu ravaged Swans squad that played at Exeter City in a second round AWS Cup tie in January 2000, going on as substitute for Lee Jenkins. On the 26th October 1999 he had made a substitute appearance, replacing Gareth Phillips in a Welsh Premier Cup tie at the Vetch Field against Cwmbran Town, making his first start in a Swans shirt against the same opponents at Cwmbran in mid-December. Following the Swans Championship winning season of 1999/2000, he made his first league appearance for the Swans as a substitute for Walter Boyd at Millwall, making a further four substitute appearances for the Swans during the season. In the Welsh Premier Cup competition that season, he scored his only goal for the Swans, in a 3-2 defeat at Barry Town on the 7th November 2000. Capable of playing in either midfield, or as a striker, he suffered along with a number of young professionals on the fringe of the first team at that time at the Vetch Field, from the absence of regular reserve team football. With the Swans suffering relegation after just one season in a higher division, he was released on the 25th July 2001, joining League of Wales side Aberystwyth. He was still playing for Aberystwyth in season 2003/04 along with former Swans trainee Chris O'Sullivan. In June 2004 he captained 'Aber' against Latvian side FC Dinaburg in the first round of the Intertoto Cup competition. Bari currently works for a Logistics Computer Company in West Wales.

39. MORGAN, DENLEY James

Birthplace: Llanelli, 13/2/1951
Ht: 5ft-8ins, **Wt:** 10st-8lbs
Swans debut: v. Exeter City (h), 5/5/1969

Swansea Town/City Career Statistics	
Season	League
1968/69	1
1969/70	
1970/71	2
1971/72	11
Total	14

Career:
Llanelli (signed in close season 1966)
Llanelli Steel (signed in season 1966/67)
Swansea City (amateur signed in 1967, professional in July 1971)
Llanelli (signed in close season 1972)
Ammanford Town (signed in close season 1978)
Pembroke Borough (signed in close season 1979)
Llanelli (signed in close season 1980)

Honours: Welsh League Premier Division Champions–1977, 1978, Brains Cup Winners–1979, 1980

Signed for the Swans on an amateur basis at the age of sixteen, having played for Llanelli and Carmarthenshire League side Llanelli Steel as a fifteen-year-old. Brought up in the Tyisha, Penyfan area of Llanelli, Denley attended Llanelli Grammar School, playing for Llanelli Schoolboys during the first year of the schoolboys fielding a side. He left school to become an apprentice electrician with British Leyland in Felinfoel, and was a part-time professional at the Vetch Field for four years.
He made his league debut in the last game of the 1968/69 season at the Vetch Field in a 2-0 win over Exeter City, playing in a midfield role, three months after his eighteenth birthday, with the club being run by caretaker manager Walter Robbins. He had been due to make his league debut in the previous match at York City, but had developed tonsillitis on the way to the game. The following season Roy Bentley took over as manager, and with the club gaining promotion from the Fourth Division, Morgan failed to add to his starts for the Swans, playing only in the club's successful Football Combination side. Signed as a full time professional for the start of season 1971/72, it was only towards the end of the season that Denley featured regularly in the Swans first team line-up, making eleven league appearances. Unfortunately for him he was released at the end of the season, returning to Stebonheath Park with the Reds. Over the next six seasons, and when he returned to Stebonheath Park in 1980, Denley made over 500 appearances for the Reds, also skippering the side. Runners-Up in the Welsh League Premier Division in 1973, in 1977 and 1978 the Reds won consecutive Welsh League Premier Division Championships, and the following two seasons after joining Ammanford Town and Pembroke Borough, won the Brains Cup competition. Returning to Llanelli in 1980 he later became assistant to manager Wyndham Evans, renewing a friendship that started in the Grammar School side, going right through to his period at the Vetch Field. Denley later followed Wyndham to Carmarthen Town as his assistant during a period when the club won the Welsh League Premier Division Championship in 1996, gaining promotion to the League of Wales, and also successfully winning the Brains Cup Competition. Within weeks of the club's new season in the League of Wales, both Wyndham and Denley were controversially sacked from their positions, with Denley taking no further involvement in football. Since leaving the professional ranks at the Vetch Field, Denley returned to his trade as an electrician, and after working as an electrical contractor returned to British Leyland, followed by his move to the Ford Motor Factory in Swansea, now renamed Visteon, fifteen years ago.

40. MORGAN, HUW

Birthplace: Neath, 20/8/1964
Ht: 5ft-4ins, **Wt:** 9st-4lbs
Swans debut: v. Grimsby Town (h), 19/11/1983

Swansea City Career Statistics		
Season	League	WC
1983/84	5+2	1
Total	5+2	1

Career:
Swansea City (from apprentice in August 1982)
Port Talbot Town (signed in close season 1984)
Finn Harps (signed in season 1984/85)

Honours: Wales Yth–5, Boys Club of Wales

Former Afan Nedd schoolboy midfielder who joined the Swans as an apprentice straight from school. Huw attended Sandfields Junior school and Glanafan Comprehensive, played for Afan Lido, gaining Boys Club of Wales representation in 1979 against Scotland in Arbroath. During his apprenticeship at the Vetch Field he made five appearances for the Welsh youth side, four in the European Championship against Scotland and Northern Ireland, and one appearance in a friendly against the Republic of Ireland. Despite being on the short side, he was nevertheless a keen competitor in midfield, with all his first team appearances during the 1983/84 season when senior professionals at the Vetch Field were being offloaded to make savings on the monthly wage bill following pressure from the club's bankers. He made his Swans debut as a substitute following the injury to keeper Jimmy Rimmer, with defender Gary Chivers going in goal, and Morgan slotting into midfield. He had been a non-playing substitute in the previous game at Barnsley. His first start came five games later, at the Vetch Field against high flyers Portsmouth, in a 2-1 defeat. His next appearances came consecutively at Newcastle United in late March, and seven days later at the Vetch Field against Manchester City. Making one substitute appearance, and two starts towards the end of the season with the Swans already relegated to the Third Division, he also made a Welsh Cup appearance against Shrewsbury Town in the second leg of the semi-final at the Vetch Field, which the Swans won 1-0, his only winning appearance in a Swans shirt. He was released in May 1984, joined his hometown side Port Talbot Town, but after a couple of weeks went to Ireland to play for Finn Harps. Only in Ireland a couple of weeks, he returned to make appearances for Port Talbot Town, but played the second half of the season with Leighton Phillips's Llanelli. He later played a couple of seasons with Afan Lido, before finishing his playing career back at Port Talbot Town. Working initially in BSC Port Talbot as a contractor, he has since joined BSC as a production worker, and his only involvement in football nowadays is coaching the Port Talbot Town U-14 side.

41. MORGAN, Morton (MONTY) Meredith

Birthplace: Mountain Ash, 1/5/1910. **Died:** Mountain Ash, 15/8/1990
Ht: 5ft-9ins, **Wt:** 11st-2lbs
Swans debut: v. Hull City (h), 2/9/1933

Swansea Town Career Statistics	
Season	League
1933/34	3
Total	3

Career:
Manchester United (signed amateur in November 1930) lge 0
Penrhiwceiber
Swansea Town (amateur signed in 1931/32, professional in August 1932)
Torquay United (signed in June 1934) lge 121/22gls
Plymouth Argyle (signed in July 1937) lge 11/2gls
Bristol City (signed in July 1938) lge 2

Outside right who played for the reserve side at the Vetch Field during the second half of the 1931/32 season after being released as an amateur with Manchester United. It was initially thought he was to be released by the Swans in May 1932, but he was later offered professional terms at the Vetch Field. He failed to make a first team appearance during his first season as a professional, making his first appearance for the Swans at outside right in place of Hugh Blair against Hull City, played in the next game against Millwall, with his only other first team appearance coming in February 1934 at Southampton. He was released at the end of the season, joining Third Division South side Torquay United in July 1934, where he was to make a good impression, playing 121 league games, and scoring 22 goals. He later played for Second Division Plymouth Argyle and Third Division South side Bristol City. He was also a good golfer.

42. MORGAN, WENDELL

Birthplace: Gorseinon, 22/4/1935
Ht: 5ft-7ins, **Wt:** 10st-7lbs
Swans debut: v. Leyton Orient (h), 11/9/1958

Swansea Town Career Statistics	
Season	League
1958/59	7
Total	7

Career:
Grovesend Welfare
Cardiff City (from juniors in May 1952) lge 0
Brentford (signed amateur in June 1954, professional in 1955) lge 47/6gls, FAC 2
Gillingham (signed in September 1957) lge 34/3gls
Swansea Town (£5,000 signed in 10/7/1958)
Newport County (signed in June 1959) lge 26/3gls
Carlisle United (signed in June 1960) lge 35/2gls
Llanelly (signed in close season 1961)

Honours: Great Britain Boys Clubs–2, Wales Boys Clubs–4

Brought up in Garncoch Terrace, Gorseinon, the former Cardiff City junior, who also had the opportunity of joining Leeds United's groundstaff on leaving school, gained Boys Club of

Wales Honours for Wales, two appearances coming against England and Scotland in May 1952, and also represented Great Britain Boys Clubs against the Sea Cadets Corps earlier in the year, and against a Combined Army and Navy side at Wembley. Joining Cardiff City at the age of seventeen from Welsh League Second Division side Grovesend Welfare, he was unable to break into professional football whilst with the 'Bluebirds', but made a good impression after joining Third Division South Brentford in June 1954, scoring 6 goals from 47 league appearances. He joined Third Division South side Gillingham shortly after the start of the 1957/58 season, but by the start of the next season had refused terms and returned to his native South West Wales to sign for the Swans. He missed the start of the season at the Vetch Field, but after making his league debut in place of Norman Lawson, played six consecutive league matches before losing his place to new signing Colin Webster. He made just the one more appearance for the Swans in Division Two, and at the end of the season was released, joining Third Division side Newport County in June 1959.
Despite having a regular place in the County line-up he was on his travels once more after a season at Somerton Park, this time dropping down to the Fourth Division to sign for Carlisle United. Twelve months later he returned to South West Wales, joined Llanelly, also attending Gorseinon Technical College to study Accountancy. He retired from football after one season at Stebonheath Park, and was then involved in restarting the Garden Village side at U-16 level, taking the youngsters later into senior football in the Carmarthenshire League. He remained in accountancy up to his retirement in 1996.

43. MORGANS, Kenneth (KEN) Godfrey

Birthplace: Swansea, 16/3/1939
Ht: 5ft-8ins, **Wt:** 10st-8lbs
Swans debut: v. Leeds United (a), 8/4/1961

Swansea Town Career Statistics				
Season	League	FLC	FAC	WC
1960/61	2			
1961/62	15/1gls	1		1
1962/63	34/7gls	1	2	3
1963/64	3			
Total	54/8gls	2	2	4

Career:
Manchester United (juniors signed in January 1955, professional in April 1956) lge 17
Swansea Town (£5,000 signed in 15/3/1961)
Newport County (signed in June 1964) lge 125/43gls
Cwmbran Town (player manager signed in June 1967)

Honours: Wales U-23–2, F.A. Youth Cup Winner–1956, 1957, West Wales Senior Cup Winner–1961, 1962

Former Swansea schoolboy footballer who joined Manchester United from school, signed on the groundstaff at Old Trafford in January 1955, signing professional in August 1956. The outside right was a member of the United side that won the 1956 and 1957 FA Youth Cup, possessing at the time a great deal of confidence in his play. Sadly though, he was deeply affected by the Munich air crash from which he escaped serious injury, but never recovered his early promise. He made seventeen First Division appearances for United, but returned to his hometown in March 1961 to sign for the Swans on the same day that Len Allchurch left the Vetch Field to join Sheffield United. At Old Trafford he had made two appearances for the Welsh U-23 side against Scotland, in 1959, and in 1960. Replacing young Barrie Jones for his Swans' debut at Elland Road against Leeds United at outside right, his only other league appearance came in the last match of the season at Ipswich, which the Swans won 2-1. He featured mainly at outside left from his second season on at the Vetch Field, and scored his first goal for the Swans in April 1962 in a 5-0 win over Plymouth Argyle at the Vetch Field. He also played in the Welsh Cup semi-final that same season at Ninian Park, losing 3-2 to Wrexham. Included in the Swans side that beat Haverfordwest in the West Wales Senior Cup Final in 1961, he also played twelve months late when the Swans beat Llanelly. 1962/63 season saw him make a bigger impact for the Swans on the left wing, scoring seven goals, although during the last third of the season he reverted to an inside left role. The 1963/64 season was to be his last at the Vetch Field, failing to make the Swans FA Cup semi-final line-up, after losing his place shortly after the star of the season, firstly to Barrie Jones, and then to new signing from Welsh League football, Brian Evans. He was released by the Swans in June 1964, joining Fourth Division side Newport County, playing against the Swans in January 1965 in a Welsh Cup fifth round cup tie at Somerton Park, which the Swans won 3-2, with Morgans scoring the second goal for County. By the time the Swans had been relegated to the Fourth Division for the first time in August 1967, Morgans had joined Cwmbran Town as player manager, staying at the club for three years. After his retirement from football he became a publican in Pontypool, later a salesman.

44. MORLEY, Ernest (ERNIE) James

Birthplace: Sketty, Swansea, 11/9/1901. **Died:** Swansea, 26/1/1975
Ht: 5ft-7ins, **Wt:** 11st-0lbs
Swans debut: v. Mid-Rhondda (a), WC-4, 15/1/1921

Swansea Town Career Statistics			
Season	League	FAC	WC
1920/21			1
1921/22	11		1
1922/23	27	2	1
1923/24	22		
1924/25	36	2	
1925/26	11		2
1926/27	14		
1927/28	2		
Total	123	4	5

Career:
Sketty FC
Swansea Town (signed in 29/9/1920)
Clapton Orient (£500 signed in 12/6/1928) lge 71
Aberavon Harlequins (signed in 4/4/1933)

Honours: Wales Full–4, Third Division South Champions–1925, Welsh League Representative XI–1924, 1927

Signed from local football side Sketty, Ernie Morley was a tight, difficult to beat opponent, a good marker and tackler, who also used the ball well in his distribution. He learned his football at Sketty School, and in 1914 played for Swansea Schoolboys. Although he made his league debut at left full back instead of Milne, he was primarily a right full back, and had to compete firstly with Langford, and then with Ben Williams for a place in the Swans starting line-up. In January 1921 he made his first team debut for the Swans in a Welsh Cup tie at Mid-Rhondda in a side that was a reserve team as the date clashed with a league fixture the same day at Southend United. During the Third Division South Championship winning season of 1924/25, he missed just six league appearances. He gained his first cap for Wales during his first season as a professional, playing against England at the Vetch Field at right full back on the 28th February 1925, losing 2-1, becoming the second Swansea born player to be capped for Wales, the first being Billy Hole. The 1925/26 season saw him unable to feature in the club's FA Cup semi-final line-up, and for the next two seasons his first team appearances were limited because of the form of Williams and Milne at full back. In February 1924 he was selected to play for a Welsh League Representative side in Dublin against the Irish Free State, and three years later in 1927 made his second appearance for the League side against the Irish League. With the feeling at the time that he was too good for the reserve team, he was sold to Second Division rivals Clapton Orient for £500 on the 12th June 1928, making two appearances during the 1928/29 season, which unfortunately saw Orient finish bottom of the league and relegated to the Third Division South. He gained three more international caps for Wales whilst with Clapton Orient, playing against England, Scotland and Northern Ireland in the 1928/29 Home International Championships, with the England fixture being played at the Vetch Field. He captained Orient for one season, but after breaking his leg in 1931, although offered terms by the Swans to return to the Vetch Field retired from the game. In early April 1933 he came out of retirement to play for Aberavon Harlequins, linking up with former Swans players Ivor Jones and Harry Thomas.

45. MORRIS, ALAN

Birthplace: Swansea, 6/4/1941
Ht: 5ft-7ins, **Wt:** 10st-0lbs
Swans debut: v. Blackburn Rover (h), 28/9/1957

Swansea Town Career Statistics	
Season	League
1957/58	1
1958/59	
1959/60	
1960/61	2/1gls
1961/62	2
1962/63	7
Total	12/1gls

Career:
Swansea Town (signed from juniors in June 1958)
Reading (£4,500 signed in 13/8/1963) lge 12, FLC 2, FAC 2

Honours: Wales Yth, Football Combination Second Division Champions–1961, Welsh League First Division Champions–1962, 1963

Young, extremely quick outside right who graduated through the club's junior sides making his debut as a replacement for Len Allchurch against Blackburn Rovers at the Vetch Field, five months past his sixteenth birthday, and who had yet to sign professional forms. The former Townhill Schoolboy at the time was an apprentice fitter and turner at George Brothers in Swansea, and his appearances for the Swans had been limited to mainly Welsh League appearances. A few months later, in November, after making his first team debut he played in a Welsh Youth trial game against Monmouthshire County, but surprisingly failed to make the final trial. However, in April 1958 he was included in the Wales Youth side that beat Scotland Youth 4-3 at the Vetch Field. He was unfortunate throughout his career with the Swans that he was up against quality wingers on the playing staff in Allchurch, Barrie Jones, Graham Williams, and even Ken Morgans when he joined the Swans from Manchester United. After his debut, he had to wait until the 1960/61 season before making his second league appearance for the Swans, playing in two consecutive league games as a replacement this time for Brayley Reynolds, with Allchurch moving to inside forward. At the end of that season he had made regular appearances in the reserve side that won the Combination Second Division Championship, also winning the Welsh League First Division Championship in consecutive seasons. That season also saw Lennie Allchurch transferred to Sheffield United, but by then Barrie Jones had taken over as the regular outside right, He scored his only goal for the Swans during the same season, in a 3-2 Vetch Field win over Leeds United. The goal was scored after just 10 seconds, the quickest goal scored at the Vetch by a Swans player since the League was resumed after WW2. Playing two league games the following season, in his last season with the Swans, he made seven appearances, three on the left wing instead of Morgans, and two at outside right. He was released in August 1963 joining Third Division side Reading. Making all of his Reading appearances shortly after arriving at Elm Park, the second half of the season saw him restricted to reserve team outings, and it was in a reserve game in April 1964 that he sustained a knee injury which ended his playing career. Returning to Swansea he later took up employment at the IMI Works in Waunarlwyd.

46. MORRIS, David Hyman (ABE)

Birthplace: Spittalfields, London, 25/11/1897. **Died:** San Mateo, California, USA, 20/12/1985
Ht: 5ft-10ins, **Wt:** 12st-0lbs
Swans debut: v. Nottingham Forest (h), 17/10/1925

Swansea Town Career Statistics		
Season	League	WC
1925/26	9/5gls	5/5gls
Total	9/5gls	5/5gls

Career:
Vicar of Wakefield FC
Fulham (£250 signed in May 1920) lge 6/2gls, FAC 1
Brentford (signed in June 1921) lge 59/29gls, FAC 4/1gls
Millwall Athletic (£1,200 signed in February 1923) lge 74/30gls
Swansea Town (£400 signed in 26/5/1925)
Swindon Town (£300 signed in 17/6/1926) lge 260/215gls, FAC 6/10gls
Clapton Orient (signed in July 1933) lge 13/8gls
Cheltenham Town (signed in September 1934)

Of Jewish religion, born within the sound of Bow Bells, his early football career came at the Vicar of Wakefield FC, Jew's Free School, Middlesex Regiment, East London Sunday Football and Discharged Soldiers Football League. He was unlucky at the Vetch Field in that Fowler and Deacon prevented him from making a bigger impact with the Swans. Making his debut for the Swans at centre forward instead of Jack Fowler, his next appearance in the Swans line-up was in February 1926 against Derby County in which he scored two goals in a 2-0 home win, again as a replacement for Fowler. Through to the end of the season he made occasional appearances, usually as a

replacement for Fowler and Deacon, scoring three more goals, plus one goal in a Welsh Cup tie against Wrexham. Towards the end of April 1926 he played in the Swans side that lost 3-2 in the Welsh Cup Final defeat by Ebbw Vale. In the Fourth Round replay against Colwyn Bay at the Vetch Field he scored four of the Swans eight goals in the game. Prior to his departure from the Vetch Field it was thought that the Swans wanted him to accept a drop in wages, with the player declining. A good conscientious centre forward, he stayed just the one season after his arrival in May 1925 from Millwall for £400, and was then sold to Swindon Town in June 1926 for a fee of £300. During his career at the County Ground he went on to become a firm favourite making 260 league appearances, scoring 215 goals, before returning to the London area to sign for Clapton Orient at the age of thirty-six. A record breaking goalscorer with Swindon Town, he scored in six successive F.A. Cup ties for the club from 1927 over two seasons, and in season 1926/27 scored a record 47 goals. Losing his place in the Orient side to Halliday at Christmas time, he continued to score regularly for the reserve side, netting twenty-three goals in the remaining five months of the season. Making his Football League debut in the First Division with Fulham, after signing from non-league side Vicar of Wakefield for £250 in May 1919, it was only after dropping down a couple of divisions with Brentford that he started to establish himself in the starting line-up. Over the next four seasons, prior to his arrival at the Vetch Field, he averaged almost a goal every two league games for Brentford and Millwall in the Third Division South, scoring against the Swans in league games for either club. Apart from his last season at the County Ground (1932/33), most of the seasons he played for the club, the 'Robins' finished in either a top ten, or mid-table place in the Third Division South, and in 1933 he signed for Clapton Orient, before finishing his playing career at non-league Cheltenham Town, and then going to Sweden for a coaching role with Gothenburg. Morris had worked as a printer when he was young but after ending his playing career, worked for the British Embassy in Stockholm, Sweden and when he moved to the USA in 1955, Morris worked for the British Information Bureau in New York until his retirement in 1965.

47. MORRIS, Maldwyn (MAL) Jones Gravell

Birthplace: Neyland, 3/8/1932. **Died:** Neyland 2001
Ht: 5ft-8½ins, **Wt:** 11st-4lbs
Swans debut: v. Notts. County (a), 17/11/1956

Swansea Town Career Statistics		
Season	League	WC
1956/57	8/2gls	3
1957/58	7/3gls	2
Total	15/5gls	5

Career:
Pembroke Borough
Swansea Town (£500 signed in October 1956)
Gloucester City (signed in close season 1958)
Pembroke Borough (signed in 23/10/1959)

Honours: Welsh League First Division Champions–1954, Welsh League Challenge Cup Winner–1954, West Wales Senior Cup Winner–1957

Mal Morris was a relatively late starter to the professional game at the age of 24, signing from Welsh League side Pembroke Borough for £500 in October 1956. A prolific goalscorer in the Welsh League with Borough, in season 1953/54 he had been involved with the club winning the Welsh League First Division Championship, and also scoring one of the goals in the Final of the Welsh League Challenge Cup at Llanelly against Aberystwyth. He made his debut for the Swans at Notts. County, six weeks after leaving the Welsh League, scoring in a 4-1 away win, playing as a replacement for Dai Thomas, with Mel Charles moving into the defence. In the short time of his arrival at the Vetch Field, he had already scored six goals in Combination and Welsh League matches prior to his being given his league debut, possessing speed off the ball, a real power drive, and more than useful in the air. In his debut game for the Swans' Combination side against Bournemouth, both of his goals scored were from headers. Unfortunately for him, he suffered a broken bone in his toe during his leagaue debut which sidelined him for a number of weeks. Keen competition for places during his time at the Vetch Field limited his number of first team outings, with his second league goal being scored later in the season at Port Vale, in another away win for the Swans. In May 1957 he scored two goals in the final of the West Wales Senior Cup win over Haverfordwest. Despite scoring in his first game of the 1957/58 season, in a 4-4 Vetch Field draw with Fulham, Mal again found first team opportunities limited, usually being used as a replacement for Des Palmer, and when recalled to first team action against Blackburn Rovers in February 1958 scored two goals in a 2-2 draw, retaining his place for the next fixture against Ipswich Town. After being placed on the 'open to transfer list' in May 1958, he was released, joining Gloucester City in the 1958 close season. He proved to be a consistent goalscorer for Gloucester City, scoring twenty-six goals during season 1958/59. In late October 1959 he returned to West Wales to rejoin his former club Pembroke Borough, remaining at the club into the mid-1960's until his retirement from the game. An excellent cricketer in the summer months for Britannia CC of Pembroke Dock, Mal worked for a number of years for Hancocks Ship Builders in Pembroke Dock.

48. MORRIS, STEPHEN Granville

Birthplace: Swansea, 8/10/1958
Ht: 5ft-11ins, **Wt:** 11st-6lbs
Swans debut: v. Southport (h), 10/4/1976

Swans City Career Statistics				
Season	League	FLC	FAC	WC
1975/76	2+2			
1976/77				
1977/78	24+2/1gls		4	2
1978/79	7+2	1+2	1	1
Total	33+6/1gls	1+2	5	3

Career:
Swansea City (from apprentice in June 1976)
Plymouth Argyle (£10,000 signed in 9/1/1980)

Bridgend Town (signed in close season 1981)
Trebanos (signed in close season 1982)

Honours: Wales Sch–3, Yth, Welsh League First Division Champions–1976

Initially brought up in Clydach, Steve played rugby for Swansea Schoolboys at U-11 age group while at Clydach Comprehensive, and after moving to Morriston, and attending Llansamlet Comprehensive, started playing football at the age of thirteen, playing for Kilvey Colts. After switching to Cefn Hengoed Comprehensive, he played for the school, and Swansea Schoolboys alongside Nigel Stevenson, also gaining recognition at International level for Wales in the Home International Championship matches against England, Scotland and Northern Ireland. Signing schoolboys forms initially with the Swans, on leaving school he became an apprentice at the Vetch Field, also playing for the Welsh Youth side during his second season as an apprentice. He was still a young apprentice at the Vetch Field, along with fellow seventeen-year-old apprentice Nigel Stevenson when they made their league debuts for the Swans at the Vetch Field against Southport, in what was the youngest ever central defensive partnership ever put out by the Swans in a league fixture. Replacing Dave Bruton, he made a further two appearances from the substitute bench, before making his second first team start in the last game of the season at Darlington in a 1-1 draw. He signed professional in 1976, and with the experienced Eddie May being signed by manager Harry Griffiths, and paired with Bruton, Morris did not get any opportunities in the first team, and was limited to appearances in the club's reserve team, with the free scoring first team just missing out on promotion. During season 1977/78 he made his first start at Leatherhead in an FA Cup first round cup tie, replacing Wyndham Evans at right full back. He missed the replay at the Vetch Field, but after being included in the second round tie at Portsmouth, kept his place for the remainder of the season, in either a left full back, or central defensive role. Possessing a slight frame, he was a strong tackler, and excelled when placed in a man marking role during the club's promotion season of 1977/78. During season 1977/78 he scored his only goal for the Swans, in a 4-1 away win at Reading. Following the club's promotion to the Third Division, he was regularly included in the first half of the season, and played at the Vetch Field against Tottenham Hotspur in the League Cup first round, against recently signed Argentina World Cup stars, Ossie Ardiles and Ricky Villa. He did not play in the away leg win at White Hart Lane, but came on as substitute at QPR in the second round. A valuable squad member during the second successive promotion winning season, when the Swans returned to the Second Division, opportunities became few and far between, with manager John Toshack recruiting experienced professionals as the months went by. In early January 1980 he was sold to Plymouth Argyle for £10,000, but, surprisingly, failed to make a first team appearance for Argyle, and was released in May 1981 on a free transfer, despite being awarded 'Player of the Year' for the club's reserve side at Home Park. Returning to South Wales, he played one season for Bridgend Town in the Southern League, and the following season joined Neath League side Trebanos, playing in the side that lost to Garden Suburbs in the 1985 West Wales Amateur Cup Final. Since returning to the Swansea area, Steve worked for Sainsbury's for ten years, and since 1996 has been working for Bemis on the Enterprise Zone as a machine operator. For the last thirteen years he has also been a retained fireman, based in Morriston Fire Station.

49. MORRIS, William (BILLY) Henry

Birthplace: Swansea, 28/9/1920. **Died:** Swansea, March 1994
Ht: 5ft-9ins, **Wt:** 11st-12lbs
Swans debut: v. Ipswich Town (a), 3/1/1948

Career:
Swansea Town (signed in May 1946)
Brighton & Hove Albion (signed in September 1949) lge 28/4gls

Swansea Town Career Statistics			
Season	*League*	*FAC*	*WC*
1947/48	12/1gls	1	1
1948/49	4		1/4gls
Total	16/1gls	1	2/4gls

Honours: Wales Sch, London Combination Cup Winner–1947, West Wales Senior Cup Winner–1949

A relative latecomer to professional football, the former Welsh schoolboy international in 1935, began his Football League career somewhat late in life because of the war, signing for the Swans in May 1946 at the age of 25. His first season at the Vetch Field saw him fail to make an appearance in a side that was relegated along with Newport County, the first season the Football League had been restarted after the Second World War. In June 1947 he was a member of the Swans reserve side that beat Arsenal at White Hart Lane to win the London Combination Cup. A left winger, after making his debut in January 1948 at Ipswich Town, he had occasional games at inside left for the Swans, but always struggled to oust the reliable Frankie Scrine for a first team start at the Vetch Field. His third season with the Swans saw him make just four league appearances during the Third Division South Championship season, but in a Welsh Cup sixth round tie at the Vetch Field against South Liverpool, he scored four goals from the left wing position, in a 9-1 victory. Was a member of the Swans side that beat Llanelly in May 1949 to win the West Wales Senior Cup. In September 1949 he joined Brighton & Hove Albion for a substantial fee, sharing the number eleven shirt with Ken Davies, and impressing fans with his pace and control. However, he was forced to play a reserve role to Doug Keene the following term, although he did turn out at left-half for a five-match spell. In May 1951 he was released and moved into non-League football.

50. MORRISSEY, Patrick (PAT) Joseph

Birthplace: Enniscorthy, Co Wexford, Ireland, 23/2/1948.
Died: Northwood, late February 2005
Ht: 5ft-7ins, **Wt:** 10st-5lbs
Swans debut: v. York City (h), 15/10/1977

Career:
Coventry City (signed apprentice in April 1963, professional in July 1965) lge 6+4
Torquay United (signed in July 1968) lge 19+2

Crewe Alexandra (signed in July 1969) lge 95+1/28gls
Chester City (£3,500 signed in October 1971) lge 9/1gls
Watford (£8,000 signed in December 1971) lge 101+6/27gls, FLC 5/1gls, FAC 5/1gls
Aldershot (signed in 15/11/1974) lge 109/27gls
Swansea City (loan in 12/10/1977)
Dartford (signed in November 1977)

Swansea City Career Statistics	
Season	*League*
1977/78	3+1
Total	3+1

Honours: Republic of Ireland U-23–1

Experienced midfielder signed on loan by Swans manager Harry Griffiths in October 1977 to give his young side some experience in midfield. Having narrowly failed to get promotion the previous season, the Swans had been favourites for the 1977/78 season to get amongst the honours, but with a shortage of money available to recruit a higher quality player, manager Griffiths was having to bring in experienced players like Morrissey at the lower end of the market in an attempt to keep his side amongst the frontrunners of the Fourth Division. He made his first appearance for the Swans at the Vetch Field in a lacklustre 1-1 draw with York City, replacing Micky Conway midway through the game. He started the next three league games as a replacement for Les Chappell, but after his month loan had ended, returned to Aldershot. Within a couple of days of his returning, he had his contract cancelled with the club. Despite having an Irish birthplace, he lived in England from an early age, playing for Hackney Schools and Coventry Schools prior to signing as an apprentice for the 'Sky Blues' in April 1963. After making a handful of first team appearances at Highfield Road, Pat dropped down to the Third Division to secure a more regular place in the starting line-up with Torquay United in July 1968. Twelve months later he signed for Fourth Division Crewe Alexandra, and after making almost one hundred league appearances for the 'Railwaymen', signed for Chester, before returning to Second Division football with Watford two months later. By the end of the season however, the 'Hornets' found themselves bottom of the league, and back in the Third Division. Making over one hundred league appearances for Watford, he joined Fourth Division Aldershot in November 1974 in a player exchange deal with Roger Joslyn, with Pat being valued at £10,000 in the transfer, making a further 109 league appearances, and also scoring regularly from his midfield role. Within a few days of returning to the Recreation Ground at Aldershot following his loan spell with the Swans, he joined non-league side Dartford. Further non-league appearances were made with Hayes (by November 1977), Slough Town (by October 1980), Carshalton Athletic (close season 1981), Hendon, and Chesham United (1982), taking over as player manager in November 1982 until March

1985. Joining Dunstable Town in April 1985, he was later appointed manager at the club, before becoming manager of Buckingham Town in the 1988 close season. He later had managerial spells with Chesham United (October 1988), returned to a player manager position at Southall in the 1989 close season, up until February 1990, Hemel Hempstead (1993), Colney Heath Veterans (December 1994), and manager of Colney Heath (1995). In late February 2005 Pat died after a two and a half year battle with cancer.

51. MOSS, David (DAVE) Albert

Birthplace: Doncaster, 15/11/1968
Ht: 6ft-2ins, **Wt:** 13st-7lbs
Swans debut: v. AFC Bournemouth (h), 24/8/2002

Swansea City Career Statistics		
Season	League	FLC
2002/03	3+6/2gls	1
Total	3+6/2gls	1

Career:
Doncaster Rovers (apprentice in 1984)
Rotorua Suburbs (New Zealand)
Worksop
Boston United
Doncaster Rovers (signed in 10/3/1993) lge 18/5gls, FLC 2, Others 0+1
Chesterfield (signed in 8/10/1993) lge 59+12/16gls, FLC 2/1gls, FAC 2+1, Others 3
Scunthorpe United (signed in 1/7/1996) lge 4, FLC 1/1gls
Partick Thistle (signed in 10/9/1996) SL 31/11gls, SLC 1, SC 1
Falkirk (signed in 6/8/1997) SL 59+2/25gls, SLC 3/2gls, SC 8/6gls, Others 4
Dunfermline Athletic (£120,000 in 9/9/1999) SL 36+13/12gls, SLC 3/1gls, SC 3+1/1gls
Ayr United (loan in 1/11/2001) SL 5/1gls, SLC 1
Falkirk (signed in 22/3/2002) SL 3
Swansea City (signed in 9/8/2002)
Hednesford Town (signed in 1/4/2003)
Barry Town (signed in July 2003)
Carmarthen Town (signed in August 2003)

Honours: Scottish League Challenge Cup Winner–1998

Started his playing career initially with Doncaster Rovers as an apprentice, but after being released at the age of 18 had the opportunity to go and play for Rotorua Suburbs in New Zealand. After a two year spell, playing in the division below the Premier Division he returned to the UK and signed for non-league side Worksop Town, taking a job in the Insurance business. Linking up with another non-league side, Boston

United, a good goalscoring spell saw him sign a second time with his first club Doncaster Rovers, still maintaining his job with Lloyds of London Insurance Company. His growing reputation in the Insurance industry saw him given the opportunity with Kwik Fit Tyre and Exhaust Company who offered him a job in Scotland in a new branch they were setting up in Glasgow, as a Business Development Manager. Cancelling his contract with Scunthorpe United, and retiring from the game, within six months he quit the insurance business to go back to the game as a full time professional at the age of 29 with Partick Thistle. Top goalscorer in his first season with Thistle with eleven league goals, David joined Falkirk, where he took over as captain, finishing his first season at Brockville Park top goalscorer in the league with twelve goals, and also beating Queen of the South in the Scottish League Challenge Cup Final. His second season with the club saw them finish runners up in the First Division, and just prior to his 31st birthday he was transferred to Dunfermline Athletic for £120,000, a team that had just been relegated from the Scottish Premier League, and were looking for experienced players to take them back up. That gamble saw them get promotion at the first attempt, finishing the season as runners up to St. Mirren. After a spell of six years in Scotland, an offer out of the blue to join the Swans came from manager Nick Cusack, who had remembered him as a player earlier in his career. After talking to John Hughes, a former Swans' player with Falkirk who recommended the Swans as a friendly club, following some impressive performances on the club's pre-season tour of Holland, he signed a contract, and despite missing the first couple of matches through injury, made his debut as a substitute for Andrew Mumford at the Vetch Field against Bournemouth. He was substitute in his next match at Bristol Rovers, coming off the bench to score the Swans goal in a 3-1 defeat. The next match saw him start at the Vetch Field in a midfield role against York City, scoring again in a 2-1 home defeat. With the Swans struggling at the bottom of the Third Division, and two teams being relegated to the Conference for the first time, manager Cusack was replaced by former Wrexham manager Brian Flynn. He struggled to make an impression under the new manager, despite having a toe injury which kept him sidelined for a number of weeks, and on 28th January 2003 had his contract paid up by the Swans. Continuing to train with the first team squad at the Vetch Field, he linked up with Dr. Martens side Hednesford Town in April 2003, helping then to avoid relegation from the Premier Division. He started season 2003/04 with League of Wales side Barry Town, featuring as a non-playing substitute in their Champions League qualifying matches. However, financial problems at the club saw them offload almost all of their playing staff, with Moss joining Carmarthen Town in a playing coaching capacity, later signing for Afan Lido, working with the Football Association of Wales in a coaching capacity, as well as concentrating on his children's shoe shop in the Mumbles. Following his retirement as a player, the start of season 2004/05 saw him become assistant manager of Afan Lido. On the 23rd May 2005 he was appointed Head of Youth at Swansea City Football Club by manager Kenny Jackett, working alongside former chief scout Huw Lake.

52. MULLEN, ROGER Colin

Birthplace: Tonyrefail, 2/3/1966
Ht: 5ft-10½ins, **Wt:** 11st-12lbs
Swans debut: v. Barry Town (a), WC-5, 8/2/1984

Swansea City Career Statistics		
Season	League	WC
1983/84	0+1	2
1984/85	2	1
Total	2+1	3

Career:
Swansea City (from apprentice in March 1984)
Basingstoke Town (signed in close season 1985)
Merthyr Tydfil (signed in close season 1986) Conf 20+20/1gls
Abergavenny Thursday (signed in close season 1991)

Honours: Wales Sch, Yth, Welsh Cup Winner–1987, Sth Lge.
Midland Division Champions–1988, Beazer Homes Premier
Division Champions–1989, Abacus League Premier Division
Champions–1992

Former Tonyrefail schoolboy capped on eight occasions for the
Wales schoolboys side, also captaining the side, who joined the
Swans as an apprentice in 1982, after signing on schoolboy
forms the previous season. Educated at Tonyrefail
Comprehensive, his early football was played with St. George's,
and Llwynypia prior to arriving at the Vetch Field. He made his
Swans debut whilst still an apprentice, a month before his
eighteenth birthday in a Welsh Cup fifth round match at Barry
Town. Signing professional forms on his eighteenth birthday,
one month later he made his first start, at the Vetch Field against
Shrewsbury Town in a second leg of the Welsh Cup semi-final,
which the Swans won 1-0. In the first leg he had been a non-
playing substitute. His first league appearance for the Swans
came when he went on as substitute at Shrewsbury Town for
Ante Rajkovic. With the Swans being relegated to the Third
Division, and a new manager, Colin Appleton struggling to
come to terms with the ongoing financial problems behind the
scenes at the Vetch Field, Mullen's only start before December
came against Spencer Works in a Welsh Cup tie replay, after
being a non-playing substitute in the first game, with Appleton
being sacked just prior to the replay. The next two games, both
away at Burnley and Bristol Rovers saw Mullen start league
matches for the first time since turning professional.
Unfortunately, with John Bond being introduced as the Swans'
new manager, at the end of the season he was given a free
transfer, linking up with former Swans coach Les Chappell at
Southern League Premier Division side Basingstoke Town. At
this period Roger had also gone back to college, and started a
degree course in Business Studies at Swansea Institute. Within
twelve months he had returned to South Wales to sign for
Merthyr Tydfil, winning a Championship medal twelve months
later, and also a Welsh Cup Winners medal after beating
Newport County after a replay at Ninian Park, playing in both
cup ties. The following season saw him play in both European
Cup Winners Cup ties against Italian side Atalanta, losing
narrowly 3-2 on aggregate. That same season he played his part
in Merthyr winning the Southern League Midland Division
Championship, and within twelve months had been part of the
squad that had won the Beazer Homes Premier Division
Championship, and promotion to the Vauxhall Conference,
making Conference appearances through to the end of season
1990/91. In the 1991 close season he linked up with former
Swans midfielder John Lewis at Abergavenny Thursdays,
winning the Abacus League National Division Championship at
the end of the season. After a short time at Barry Town, he
linked up for the second time with John Lewis, this time at

Ebbw Vale, before signing for Rhondda based side AFC Porth.
Midway through the 2002/03 season he linked up with his
former Merthyr Tydfil manager Lyn Jones at newly promoted
Welsh League side Cwmamman, seeing the club through a
difficult transition period from the Neath League to Welsh
League. Since gaining his degree in college, Roger has worked
for TT Electronics, and is currently Finance Director with AB
Connectors.

53. MUMFORD, ANDREW Owen

Birthplace: Neath, 18/6/1981
Ht: 6ft-2ins, **Wt:** 13st-6lbs
Swans debut: v. Port Vale (a), 16/4/2001

Swansea City Career Statistics			
Season	League	FAC	FAWP
2000/01	2+4		1+1
2001/02	28+4/5gls		3
2002/03	17+7/1gls	1	1
Total	47+15/6gls	1	5+1

Career:
Llanelli
Swansea City (signed in 14/6/2000)
Haverfordwest (loan in 2000/01 season)
Port Talbot (loan in 2000/01 season)
Merthyr Tydfil (loan in 9/11/2001)
Newport County (loan in September 2003)
Aldershot (loan in December 2003)
Newport County (loan in January 2004)
Port Talbot Town (signed in August 2004)
Aberystwyth Town (signed in October 2004)

Honours: Wales Sch, Yth, U–21–4, West Wales Senior Cup
Winner–2002

Andrew Mumford rejected the opportunity of an apprenticeship
in the Nationwide League with Norwich City in favour of
furthering his education at Swansea College in a Sports Science
degree, and playing League of Wales football at the weekend for
Llanelli. At this time he was selected to play for the Welsh Youth
team, as well as representing the British Colleges side, and also
being invited to a trial with Grimsby Town. Despite being
offered a contract with Grimsby Town, once the Swans came in
for him, he signed a professional contract in June 2000, just after
the club had won the Third Division Championship.
However, his first season as a professional proved to be a
frustrating one, and after loan periods with League of Wales
clubs Haverfordwest and Port Talbot, he eventually made his
league debut at Port Vale on Easter Monday, with the Swans

already condemned to relegation. Signing a new one-year deal, following a change of management at the Vetch Field with Colin Addison and Peter Nicholas taking over from Hollins and Curtis, he found himself getting a longer run in the first team, and starting to show consistent form from a central defensive position, rather than in midfield. In late April 2002 he was included in the Swans side that beat Hakin United to win the West Wales Senior Cup. Gaining his first Wales U-21 against Finland on the 6th September 2002, by the end of the season he had made a further three U-21 appearances against Italy, and Azerbaijan (twice). A difficult player to knock off the ball, following a period on loan at Merthyr, he returned to the Vetch Field much sharper, scoring a number of goals, when pushing forward from defence into midfield with goals from outside the penalty area. He was offered a free transfer by Brian Flynn at the end of the 2002/03 season, despite 12 months to go on his contract, and within a month of the start of the 2003/04 season, despite offers from Oxford United and Scottish side Raith Rovers, joined Dr. Martens side Newport County on loan, linking up with former Swans coach Peter Nicholas, and former players Terry Evans, and Gareth Phillips. Midway through the season he started a loan spell with Conference side Aldershot, made his first appearance on Boxing Day, 26th December 2003, scoring in a 3-2 win at Dagenham. Before the end of the month loan, he had rejoined Newport County on loan, remaining with the club for the remainder of the season, and then being released from the Vetch Field shortly after the end of the season. In mid-July he played in pre-season friendly games with Grimsby Town and Aldershot, but on the 24th August 2004 signed for League of Wales side Port Talbot Town, but shortly after the start of October 2004 joined fellow League of Wales side Aberystwyth Town. In late March 2005 he signed dual registration forms with Welsh League side Garden Village.

54. MUNROE, KARL Augustus

Birthplace: Manchester, 23/9/1979
Ht: 6ft-0ins, **Wt:** 10st-11lbs
Swans debut: v. Mansfield Town (a), 2/5/1998

Swansea City Career Statistics	
Season	League
1997/98	0+1
Total	0+1

Career:
Swansea City (from trainee in 9/7/1998)
Aberystwyth (loan in 4/9/1998)
Macclesfield Town (signed in 14/10/1999) lge 94+25/1gls, FLC 5+2/1gls, FAC 7, Others 3
Halifax Town (signed in August 2004)
Northwich Victoria (signed in 4/3/2005) Conf 6+2
Altrincham (signed in July 2005)

Karl first signed associate schoolboy forms with Oldham Athletic and represented Manchester boys while still in school. Signed a one year YTS at the Vetch Field under Jan Molby and progressed to a one year professional contract, and was given his league debut by Swans manager Alan Cork in the last game of the 1997/98 season at Mansfield Town, as a second half substitute for Keith Walker. With a new manager, John Hollins taking over shortly before the start of the season, he failed to break into the first team squad, and had a loan period with League Wales side Aberystwyth before having his contract cancelled on 5th March 1999. Following his release he had a trial with Brighton & Hove Albion, but when there was no offer of a contract, he went back to his native Manchester, signing non-contract forms for Macclesfield Town in October 1999. Putting in some impressive performances in the club's Central League side, he earned himself a full time contract, and became a regular member of the Silkmen line-up, either in a central defensive role, or in midfield. A fiery competitor, the 2001/02 season saw him suspended for the last six matches. At the end of the 2003/04 season he was released on a free transfer by the Silkmen, joined Conference side Halifax Town, but in March 2005 after being released by Halifax Town joined Nationwide Conference strugglers Northwich Victoria. In July 2005 he signed for Conference side Altrincham.

55. MURPHY, BRIAN

Birthplace: Waterford, 7/5/1983
Ht: 6ft-0ins, **Wt:** 13st-1lbs
Swans debut: v. Bury (h), 9/8/2003

Swansea City Career Statistics				
Season	League	FLC	LDV	FAWC
2003/04	11	1	1	1
2004/05	2			2
Total	13	1	1	3

Career:
Manchester City (from trainee in 13/5/2000) lge 0
Peterborough United (loan in 2/5/2003) lge 1
Swansea City (signed in July 2003)

Honours: Republic of Ireland Yth, U-19, U-20, U-21, FAW Cup Winner–2005

Republic of Ireland Under 20 goalkeeper Brian Murphy turned down a new deal at Manchester City in the 2003 close season, signing a contract with the Swans, after a short trial period. Behind David Seaman, Nicky Weaver and Carlo Nash in the pecking order at Premiership side Manchester City, Murphy also had the opportunity to sign for Peterborough United, the club he made his league debut for the previous season on a loan transfer. Capped at Youth and U-19 level for the Republic of Ireland, in late November 2003 he joined the U-20 squad for the World U-20 Championships in the United Arab Emirates. A regular in the squad under Brian Kerr, he was preferred to Aston Villa goalkeeper Wayne Henderson for the European U-19 Championships qualification matches and finals in 2002 until a shoulder injury allowed Henderson to reclaim his place in the team. Murphy made a second half appearance for the Republic in the September friendly international against the Czech Republic. He was selected ahead of the experienced Roger Freestone for the opening league game of the 2003/04 season, and despite an encouraging first couple of games, the keeper was replaced after a particularly harrowing 3-0 defeat at Oxford United, in which all the goals came in the last couple of minutes. After regaining his first team place in early March, he received a red card at Southend United for handball outside the penalty area, and in the last away game of the season was carried off with a hip injury at Darlington. An excellent shot stopper, with good reflexes, he was prone to be a little suspect on crosses, but with no out and out central defender with good aerial strengths in front of him, he was always under a great deal of pressure whenever the ball was in the air. Making just two league appearances during his second season at the Vetch Field, he was still however a regular inclusion in the Republic's U-21 squad for international competition, and in May was a non-playing substitute for the Swans when they beat Wrexham to win the FAW Cup.

56. MURPHY, Matthew (MATT) Simon

Birthplace: Northampton, 20/8/1971
Ht: 6ft-0ins, **Wt:** 12st-2lbs
Swans debut: v. Rushden & Diamonds (h), 10/8/2002

Swansea City Career Statistics			
Season	League	FAC	AWS
2002/03	9+3/3gls	1/1gls	0+1
Total	9+3/3gls	1/1gls	0+1

Career:
Corby Town
Oxford United (£20,000 signed in 12/2/1993) lge 168+78/38gls, FLC 10+9/8gls, FAC 12+3/6gls, Others 6+3/3gls
Scunthorpe United (loan in 12/12/1997) lge 1+2, Others 1
Bury (signed in 9/8/2001) lge 5+4, Others 1
Swansea City (signed in 1/7/2002)
Kettering Town (signed in season 2003/04)

A late entry into the professional game, Matt started his playing career in non-league football with Long Buckby, Cogenhoe United and Irthlingborough Diamonds, whilst working for the Nationwide Building Society before joining Corby Town, becoming the Steelmen's record transfer when he was sold to

Oxford United in 1993. During one season for Corby in which he scored 29 goals from midfield, he started to catch the eye of a number of clubs, and had a two week trial with Coventry City, and then Port Vale. Oxford United then asked him to play in their reserves side and, and at the age of 22 signed his first professional contract. Making almost 300 appearances for United, and scoring on a consistent basis over an eight year period, off the field financial problems at United saw the club forced to trim it's playing staff, with Murphy joining Bury on a free transfer. Despite showing impressive form in the club's reserve side, he failed to establish himself at Gigg Lane, and after just one season he was given a free transfer. He was invited to play in a behind doors end of season trial match at the Vetch Field, and impressed new Swans manager Nick Cusack, a former team mate of his at the Manor Ground, sufficiently to be offered a one year contract on the 1st July 2002. His early games at the Vetch Field were interrupted through injury, and when he did return to the first team was used as a central striker, because of an injury crisis at the Vetch Field. Scoring a number of crucial goals for the Swans, his season was effectively over, following a cruciate ligament injury he sustained at Exeter in mid-December 2002. At the end of the season he was released by the Swans, and after regaining his fitness signed for non-league side Kettering Town for the 2003/04 season. In late September 2004 he walked out on the club after being left out of the side for a match, and after appearances for Kings Lynn signed for United Counties League side Ford Sports in October 2003. In September 2004 he joined Ryman Premier League side Slough Town, and after scoring 25 goals from 34 appearances linked up with former Oxford team mate Mike Ford at Brackley Town in late June 2005.

57. MURRAY, Donald (DON) James

Birthplace: Duffus, Elgin, 18/1/1946
Ht: 6ft-0ins, **Wt:** 13st-10lbs
Swans debut: v. Newport County (h), 15/10/1974

Swansea City Career Statistics	
Season	League
1974/75	5
Total	5

Career:
Cardiff City (from juniors in January 1963) lge 406/6gls
Swansea City (loan in 13/10/1974)
Hearts (£15,000 signed in December 1974) SL 37, SC 8, SLC 3
Newport County (signed in October 1976) lge 16+2
Barry Town (signed in January 1978)
Cardiff City (signed in August 1979)

Honours: Scotland Yth, U-23–1, Welsh Cup Winner–1964, 1965, 1967, 1968, 1969, 1970, 1971, 1973

Born in Duffus, near Elgin in Scotland, he first played junior football for Burghead Thistle before joining Cardiff City at the age of 15. He established himself as a commanding centre half, strong in the tackle, and in aerial challenges. Formerly captain of the Scottish Youth side, he was capped at U-23 level on the one occasion, in 1965 against England. An experienced defender, who had regularly played in European Cup Winners Cup games for the 'Bluebirds', gained Welsh Cup Winners medals in 1964, 1965, 1967, 1968, 1969, 1970, 1971, 1973, and was also a finalist in 1972. Played all his football for Cardiff City in the Second Division, and apart from season 1970/71 when they finished in third position, nearly all of the seasons he played for the 'Bluebirds', the club held a mid-lower position in the league table. A member of the 'Bluebirds' side that reached the League

Cup semi-finals in season 1965/66, Don was also a member of the side that lost narrowly to German side SV Hamburg in the 1967/68 ECWC Semi-Finals. He was signed by Swans manager Harry Gregg in October 1974 on a one month loan transfer, a couple of months short of his 28th birthday, replacing young John Tones who had returned to Arsenal, and arrived at the Vetch Field during a time when the club was struggling at the bottom of the Fourth Division, and later, in May 1975 would have to apply for re-election to the Football League. Returning to Ninian Park after his loan period, within a month he had travelled north to play for Hearts in the Scottish First Division, but in October 1976 returned to South Wales to join Newport County. All of his appearances for County came in season 1976/77, and in January 1978 he joined Barry Town. By the start of the 1979/80 season he had returned to Cardiff City, primarily to add experience to a youthful Welsh League side.

In September 1988 he was a coach with Welsh League side Ynysybwl. Since leaving the professional game he has held a senior management post at a Residential Special School.

58. MUTTON, Thomas (TOMMY) James

Birthplace: Huddersfield, 17/1/1978
Ht: 5ft-8ins, **Wt:** 10st-2lbs
Swans debut: v. Hull City (a), 18/9/1999

Swansea City Career Statistics

Season	League	FLC	AWS	FAWP
1999/2000	1+1	0+1	2/1gls	5/1gls
2000/01	3+2	0+2		1+2/1gls
Total	4+3	0+3	2/1gls	6+2/2gls

Career:
Burnley
Bangor City
Swansea City (£20,000 signed in 16/9/1999)
Merthyr Tydfil (loan in January 2001)
Rhyl (signed in March 2001)
Connah's Quay Nomads (signed in August 2001)
Rhyl (signed by 4/6/2005)

An impressive showing in a trial match for the Swans reserves against Plymouth Argyle, saw Swans manager John Hollins pay Bangor City £20,000 to secure the striker's services in September 1999. Exceptionally quick off the mark, he impressed on occasions, but after suffering a number of injuries did not have the consistency to make himself a regular in the Swans line-up. He started his career as an apprentice with Burnley, but after failing to make the grade, dropped into the non-league scene in North Wales, firstly with Denbigh, Rhyl, and then Bangor City. He made his first team debut as substitute at Hull City for striker Julian Alsop, and also making a substitute appearance in the following match against Derby County in the Worthington Cup tie. His first league start came two league games later at the Vetch Field against Mansfield Town, but after showing good form, was taken off with an injury, and did not appear again until the early December's AWS tie against Colchester United, scoring the Swans first goal. Despite a number of games being included as a non-playing substitute, his next first team opportunity came at Exeter City in the next round of the AWS cup competition. Following the club's successful promotion to the Second Division, he was a regular member of the Swans' first team squad for the early part of the 2000/01 season, but with a loss of form, and the club's struggle to compete in the division, his only goal came in a Welsh Premier Cup tie defeat at Barry Town in November 2000. Soon after he was released from the playing staff, and signed for Rhyl. Since returning to North Wales, he has become one of the most consistent goalscorers in the League of Wales, regularly topping the Connah's Quay Nomads goalscoring charts. In the 2005 close season he rejoined Rhyl.

Mc

1. McCALLUM, DONALD

Birthplace: Dunfermline
Ht: 5ft-9ins, **Wt:** 11st-7lbs
Swans debut: v. QPR (a), 30/10/1920

Swansea Town Career Statistics			
Season	*League*	*FAC*	*WC*
1920/21	17		
1921/22	38/1gls	2	1
1922/23	5/1gls		
Total	60/2gls	2	1

Career:
Mid-Rhondda (signed by September 1913)
Swansea Town (£250 signed in 9/10/1920)
Clackmannan (signed in August 1924)

Honours: Southern League Representative XI, West Wales Senior Cup Winner–1923

Signed for £250 from Mid-Rhondda in October 1920, with Grimsby Town also interested in signing the defender, he made his league debut for the Swans at QPR in October 1920, during the Swans first season in the Football League, playing in nine consecutive league matches. An experienced defender at Welsh League level, he had been noticed by the Swans as far back as September 1913 playing for Mid-Rhondda in Welsh League games against the Swans. Over the rest of the season he made occasional appearances in the Swans' first team line-up, but it was during the following season where he was to make a greater impact, starting the season at left half, making 38 league appearances, and scoring his first goal for the Swans at Exeter City in a 1-1 draw in October 1921. His third season at the Vetch Field saw him make just 9 appearances, scoring one goal at the Vetch Field against Reading before he returned to Scotland to sign for Clackmannan. In April 1920 he had played at the Vetch Field for a Southern League Welsh Clubs XI against a Southern League English Clubs XI, and in May 1923 was included in the Swans reserve side that beat Llanelly to win the West Wales Senior Cup.

2. McCARTHY, IAN

Birthplace: Porth, 4/9/1960
Swans debut: v. Stockport County (h), 17/3/1978

Career:
Coventry City (from apprentice in 1975)
Swansea City (non-contract in January 1978, professional in 22/3/1978)
Ton Pentre (signed in season 1978/79)
Ferndale (signed in season 1979/80)

Swansea City Career Statistics	
Season	*League*
1977/78	0+1
Total	0+1

Rhondda born, a former apprentice at Coventry City who arrived at the Vetch Field in January 1978 on a non-contract basis, signing professional shortly after making his league debut as a substitute against Stockport County at the Vetch Field. An old fashioned style right winger, with skill and pace, he failed to make the first team at Highfield Road with City, and with an ankle ligament problem, had failed to settle in the Midlands, returning home to Porth in the Rhondda. Despite City manager Gordon Milne pleading with him to return, Coventry City scout, former Swans player Cyril Beech recommended the player to Swans manager Harry Griffiths, who in turn invited him to the Vetch Field in January 1978 on an initial trial. Following the arrival of John Toshack as manager at the Vetch Field, Ian impressed the new Swans boss, and after giving a polished performance in a Welsh League reserve team fixture against Bridgend Town, scoring three goals, was given his first team opportunity, after just seven weeks in the reserve side. On signing professional for the Swans, he became Toshack's first signing since embarking as a manager. The following season, with the club promoted to the Third Division, and experienced players being brought into the Vetch Field, Ian failed to make any further appearances, and midway through the season was released from his contract at the Vetch Field.

Brought up in Porth, he attended Llwyncelyn and Porth County Comprehensive Schools, played for the Llwydcoed Athletic (Aberdare League) Junior team, Rhondda and Mid-Glamorgan Schoolboys, also attending trials for the Wales Schoolboys team. After being released from the Vetch Field playing staff he joined Welsh League side Ton Pentre, but after just one season signed for Ferndale, playing for the club for almost four seasons. Ian worked in the Mining Industry for eight years, working at Lewis Merthyr and Cwm Colliery in Beddau, before taking on factory work following the demise of the Mining Industry in South Wales. The last couple of years has seen Ian work in the London area on Railtrack and Sidings Maintenance for Murphys, a sub-contractor to the Rail Transport Service in London.

3. McCARTHY, SEAN Casey

Birthplace: Bridgend, 12/9/1967
Ht: 6ft-1ins, **Wt:** 12st-12lbs
Swans debut: v. Bury (h), 2/11/1985

Swansea City Career Statistics

Season	League	FLC	FAC	WC	FRT	P/Offs
1985/86	16+6/3gls			3/1gls	2/2gls	
1986/87	43+1/14gls	3/3gls	5/4gls	1	2+1	
1987/88	17+8/8gls	1+1	0+2	0+1/1gls	1	4/4gls
Total	76+15/25gls	4+1/3gls	5+2/4gls	4+1/2gls	5+1/2gls	4/4gls

Career:
Bridgend Town
Swansea City (signed in 22/10/1985)
Plymouth Argyle (£50,000 signed in 18/8/1988) lge 67+3/19gls, FLC 7/5gls, FAC 3/1gls, Others 0+1/1gls
Bradford City (£250,000 signed in 4/7/1990) lge 127+4/60gls, FLC 10+2/10gls, FAC 8/2gls, Others 8+1/7gls
Oldham Athletic (£500,000 signed in 3/12/1993) P/Lge 117+23/60gls, FLC 10/1gls, FAC 6+1/11gls, Others 4/1gls
Bristol City (loan in 26/3/1998) lge 7/1gls
Plymouth Argyle (signed in 7/8/1998) lge 66+16/19gls, FLC 3+2/3gls, FAC 8
Exeter City (signed in 3/7/2001) lge 18+8/6gls, FLC 1, FAC 1

Honours: Wales 'B'–1, Wales Boys Club–2, Fourth Division Play Off Winner–1988, West Wales Senior Cup Winner–1987

Worked in a shoe factory in the Bridgend area on leaving school, also playing in the Welsh League with Bridgend Town. A raw, old fashioned style centre forward during the early part of his career, and in the short time he was at the Vetch Field matured into a fearless front runner, with an eye for goal. That goal scoring ability was evident early in his career with the Swans, shortly after signing for the Swans in October 1985, scoring his first league goal against Bournemouth at the Vetch Field, in front of almost 7,000 supporters, and during a time when the club was struggling to overcome a High Court winding up order. In November 1985 he made his league debut for the Swans against Bury at the Vetch Field, coming on as substitute for defender Paul Price. He also endeared himself to the hearts of Swans supporters when he scored two goals at Ninian Park against rivals Cardiff City in a Freight Rover Trophy cup tie later in the season. Following the club's relegation to the Fourth Division, and survival off the field looking more promising, Terry Yorath was appointed manager at the Vetch Field in the close season, with the Swans immediately adopting an attacking style of play. The 1986/87 season saw Sean miss just two league matches, end the season as top goalscorer in the league with 14 goals, and also score two goals in an F.A. Cup tie against West Bromwich Albion, and in a League Cup tie against Hereford United. In league matches he also scored two goals in a game on three occasions. In May 1987 he was included in the Swans side that beat Briton Ferry Athletic in the West Wales Senior Cup Final. The 1987/88 season saw him miss a number of games through a knee injury, but came back to fitness during the latter part of the season to score goals in each round of the Play Offs, which saw the club gain promotion to the Third Division. It came as something of a shock to supporters shortly after the end of the season, when he was transferred to Plymouth Argyle for a miserly £50,000 transfer fee. Within two seasons he had moved for a six figure transfer fee to Bradford City, and a further three seasons later saw him join Premiership side Oldham Athletic for a half million pound transfer fee, increasing his reputation as a feared goalscorer season by season. Prior to re-joining Argyle in August 1988, Sean had averaged a goal every two and a half games. During season 1992/93 he made an appearance for the Wales 'B' international side, and two years later was on the short list to be included in the Republic of Ireland World Cup Final squad. Returning to Argyle in August 1988, he later linked up with former Swans midfielder John Cornforth at Exeter City in July 2001, in a player assistant manager/coaching role. When Cornforth was sacked during the early part of the 2002/03 season, he was listed as just a player on the club's staff following the arrival of new manager Neil McNab, but did not make any further appearances for the club. Sean has since been involved with coaching at Plymouth Argyle's Centre of Excellence department.

4. McCLEAN, CHRISTIAN Alphonso

Birthplace: Colchester, 17/10/1963
Ht: 6ft-4ins, **Wt** 14st-0lbs
Swans debut: v. Walsall (h), FLC 1-1, 20/8/1991

Career:
Colchester United (signed in 1982)

Zeebrugge (Belgium)
Chelmsford City (signed in 1984)
Clacton Town (signed in 1985)
Bristol Rovers (signed in 24/3/1988) lge 28+23/6gls
Swansea City (signed in July 1991)
Northampton Town (signed in 7/11/1991) lge 19/3gls,
    FAC 1/1gls, Others 1

Swansea City Career Statistics			
Season	League	FLC	ECWC
1991/92	4	2	1
Total	4	2	1

Honours: Third Division Champions–1990

Born at Colchester, educated at St. Helens Comprehensive
School where he started playing soccer, signing for Colchester at
the age of 17, and stayed with them for 3 years before joining
Zeebrugge in Belgium. After a year in Belgium he joined
Chelmsford City, then Clacton Town as a centre back, moving
after a year and a half to Bristol Rovers. Joining Rovers in March
1988, he failed to score in either of his six league appearances
during his first season with Rovers, but during the 1988/89
season he made twenty-eight league appearances during a
season which saw Rovers reach the Third Division Play Off
Final. Replacing Holloway in the home leg of the final, Christian
did not participate in second leg. The following season saw him
make 15 league appearances, scoring four league goals in
Rovers Third Division Championship success, and also come on
as substitute in the Leyland Daf Cup Final at Wembley against
Tranmere Rovers, again as substitute, this time for Purnell,
losing 1-2. He struggled to feature in Rovers Second Division
line-up, and was released at the end of the season, signing for
Frank Burrows at the Vetch Field on an initial trial basis.
Following his debut for the Swans against Walsall at the Vetch
Field, within a couple of weeks he had made appearances in the
Football League for the Swans, and also against Monaco at the
Vetch Field in the first round of the European Cup Winners Cup
competition, losing 1-2. However, before the second leg he had
been released from his trial period at the Vetch Field, joining
Northampton Town until the end of the season when he was
released along with nine other players and the management
team by the club's administrators. Not a prolific goalscorer but
he did manage two for the 'Cobblers' against Rochdale in his
last ever game for the club. He returned to Belgium to sign for
Zeebrugge, before returning to the UK to make appearances for
non-league sides Chelmsford City (close season 1992),
Wivenhoe Town (October 1992), Brightlingsea (March 1993),
Wivenhoe Town (April 1993), Braintree (4/8/1994),Wivenhoe
Town (29/10/1994), Sudbury (July 1995), Braintree Town (July
1998), Heybridge Swifts (July 1999), Cambridge Celtic (August
2000), Harwich & Parkeston (December 2000), and Cornard
United (July 2001).

5. McCRORY, Samuel (SAM) McKee

Birthplace: Belfast, 11/10/1924
Ht: 5ft-9ins, **Wt:** 11st-10lbs
Swans debut: v. Southampton (h), 3/10/1946

Swansea Town Career Statistics			
Season	League	FAC	WC
1946/47	21/5gls	2/1gls	1
1947/48	29/14gls	1	
1948/49	37/19gls		4/5gls
1949/50	17/9gls		1
Total	104/47gls	3/1gls	6/5gls

Career:
Linfield (signed in 8/4/1944) Apps 91/60gls
Swansea (signed in 28/9/1946)
Ipswich Town (signed in 3/5/1950) lge 97/39gls
Plymouth Argyle (signed in August 1952) lge 50/11gls
Southend United (signed in June 1955) lge 205/91gls,
    FAC 17/8gls
Cambridge United (signed in May 1960)

Honours: Northern Ireland 'B', Full–1, Irish League
Representative XI, Third Division South Champions–1949, Irish
League Winner–1945, 1946, Irish Cup Winner–1945, 1946, Gold
Cup Winner–1945

Swans manager Haydn Green, after an indifferent start to the
1946/47 season returned from a scouting trip from Ireland
having signed forwards Sam McCrory and Norman Lockhart,
with both players making goalscoring debuts in October 1946
against Southampton in a 4-2 victory. McCrory, an inside
forward was signed for an undisclosed fee from Linfield, and in
just over two seasons had been a member of the side that won
the Irish League Championship and Irish Cup in seasons 1945
and 1946, Irish League Runners-Up and Irish Cup Runners up
in 1944, Gold Cup Winner in 1945, Gold Cup Runner-Up in
1946, and County Antrim Shield Runner-Up in 1945. He had
also played in two Inter League matches in 1946, scoring one
goal. In the short time he had at the Vetch Field he was credited
by former Swans team mate Terry Medwin, as one of the best
inside forwards to play for the Swans. Not particularly fast, he
was a first rate craftsman, also a regular goalscorer from his
position. Possessing good looks, and a fine body swerve, he also
delighted the fans with his dribbling, and passing ability.
As early as his second season with the Swans he came to the
fore as a goalscorer, scoring two goals in a game on five
occasions, and during the 1948/49 Third Division South
Championship winning season, ended as top goalscorer with
19 goals, plus five in the Welsh Cup. That Championship season
saw him score his only hat-trick for the Swans, in a 6-1 win over
Torquay United at the Vetch Field in February 1949. At the end
of that season the Swans lost to Wrexham in the Welsh Cup
Final, 2-0, at Ninian Park, Cardiff. In March 1950, along with Jim
Feeney he was transferred to Ipswich Town, and ironically, in
the previous ten games he played, had scored eight goals, and
was top of the goalscoring charts for the Swans. Playing three
seasons for Ipswich Town in the Third Division South, it was
only when he signed for Plymouth Argyle that he faced the
Swans in the Second Division, scoring against the Swans in the
last game of the 1952/53 season at Home Park. Following a
transfer to Third Division South side Southend United in June
1955, Sam scored almost a hundred league goals for the
'Shrimpers' during his career at Roots Hall, finishing the
1957/58 season as top goalscorer with thirty league goals, three
cup goals, including three hat-tricks. Capped at 'B' level in 1957
whilst at Roots Hall, he later made his only Full International
appearance for Ireland, against England at Wembley, when he
replaced Simpson. The 3-2 victory saw McCrory score his team's
second goal, a month after his 32nd birthday, also going in the

record books as being the oldest player to make his debut for Ireland. On leaving the 'Shrimpers' in May 1960, at the age of thirty-five, he joined non-league Cambridge United, later returning to his native Northern Ireland to Donaghadee near Aabansagor, where he ran a bar called the 'Port of Call', where he remained mine host in his early 70's.

6. McDEVITT, William (BILLY)

Birthplace: Belfast, 5/1/1895. **Died:** Lisburn, OND, 1974
Ht: 5ft-11½ins, **Wt:** 11st-10lbs
Swans debut: v. Bristol Rovers (h), 15/4/1922

Swansea Town Career Statistics	
Season	League
1921/22	5
Total	5

Career:
Mount Cuba (signed in 26/8/1918)
Linfield Swifts
Belfast United (signed in 1/9/1919)
Swansea Town (£300 signed in 15/3/1921)
Belfast United (signed in 14/8/1922)
Liverpool (£150 signed in 20/5/1923) lge 4
Exeter City (£300 signed in May 1925) lge 125/9gls

A £300 signing from Belfast United in March 1921, making his Swans debut in a Western League reserve team game at Exeter City in which he scored the Swans goal in a 2-1 defeat in mid-March 1921. Billy had to wait until mid-April 1922 to make his Swans debut in a record breaking league victory of 8-1 over Bristol Rovers at the Vetch Field. He played in the remaining four league games, but following a dispute with the management over wages in the close season returned to Ireland to rejoin Belfast United before returning to the Football League to sign for Liverpool in June 1923 for £150, with the fee being shared between the Swans and Belfast because of the Swans retaining his League registration. The centre half struggled to hold down a place at Anfield, and later joined Exeter City, where he not only made over one hundred league appearances, but was also to become the club's player manager between April 1929 to 1931, and after retiring as a player was manager until September 1935. His early career saw him start with Mount Cuba, prior to joining Linfield Swifts (Linfield's reserve side), later linking up with Belfast United in September 1919. After returning to Ireland, he later became manager at both Belfast Celtic and Distillery.

7. McDONALD, COLIN

Birthplace: Musselburgh, 10/4/1974
Ht: 5ft-7ins, **Wt:** 11st-4lbs
Swans debut: v. Brentford (a), 23/3/1995

Swansea City Career Statistics	
Season	League
1995/96	3+5
1996/97	3+7
Total	6+12

Career:
Hibernian (signed in 14/5/1991) SL 0

Falkirk (signed in 8/7/1993) SL 35+21/10gls, SLC 2+2/1gls, SFC 1+1, Others 2+2/2gls
Swansea City (signed in 18/3/1996)
Ayr United (signed in July 1997) SLC 2+2, SLC 1
Clydebank (signed in November 1997) SL 45+8/22gls, SLC 2/1gls, SC 6
Falkirk (signed by August 1999) SL 26+5/6gls, SLC 1+1, SFC 1+2, Others 1+1
Airdrieonians (signed by August 2001) SL 0+4/1gls, SLC 0+1, Others 0+2
Berwick Rangers (signed by January 2002) SL 7+4
Montrose (signed by August 2002) SL 12+6/1gls, SLC 1/1gls, Others 1
Gala Fairydean
Whitehill Welfare (signed by August 2004)

Honours: Scotland Sch–5, Yth–8, U-21–5, Scottish Youth Cup Winner–1992, Scottish First Division Champions–1994

A strange signing by Swans manager Jan Molby in March 1996, with the former Scotland schoolboy, Youth and U-21 International arriving at the Vetch Field from Falkirk for a reported £40,000, which was made up of money owing to the Swans from Falkirk from a sell on clause following John Hughes's transfer to Glasgow Celtic, with Falkirk at the time in severe financial difficulties, being unable to pay the Swans their share of the sell on fee, and thus offering the young striker in exchange. The previous September to joining the Swans, the young frontrunner had made his Scotland U-21 debut as a substitute for Donnelly against Finland, made his first start in the next U-21 game against Russia, and in June 1996 came on as a substitute for Freedman in a 4-0 defeat by Brazil. Brought up in Musselburgh, Colin attended Mussleburgh Grammar School, played for the school team, East Lothian Schoolboys, also making five appearances at International level for Scotland. Joining Hibernian as an apprentice after leaving school, in 1992 he played in the club's Youth side that won the BP Scottish Youth Cup Final, but after failing to make a first team appearance signed for Falkirk in July 1993. He made his senior debut as substitute for Sloan in a Scottish League Cup tie at Stenhousemuir in early August 1993, making his Scottish League debut a few weeks later on the 21st August 1993 at home to Stirling Albion again as a substitute. By the end of his first season at Falkirk he had made sixteen league appearances in the side that won the Scottish First Division Championship. His debut league goal was scored against Brechin City in November 1993, also scoring two goals that season in the B&Q Cup competition. Colin arrived at the Vetch Field on the 18th March 1996, almost a month after new manager, Jan Molby had been appointed. Making his Swans debut five days later at Brentford, as a substitute for Mark Clode, he made a further three substitute appearances before he made his first start, at Bournemouth. Despite making regular substitute appearances at the start of the 1996/97 season, he struggled to find the net, and the second half of the season saw him failing to make an impression. He was released in June 1997, returned to Scotland to sign for First Division side Ayr United. By November, he had been transferred to Scottish First Division side Clydebank, and at the end of the season finished as top goalscorer for the club with 13 goals from 23 league appearances. His second season with Clydebank saw him score 9 goals from 30 league appearances before he returned to Falkirk. Joining Airdrieonians prior to the start of the 2001/02 season, after leaving midway through the term to join Berwick Rangers, at the end of the season Airdrieonians had gone out of business. After starting the 2002/03 season with Montrose, Colin later drifted into semi-professional football with Gala Fairydean, and in August 2004 signed for East of Scotland League side Whitehill Welfare. For the last couple of years Colin has been employed as a gym instructor in White Kirk, North Berwick.

8. McFARLANE, Andrew (ANDY) Antonie

Birthplace: Wolverhampton, 30/11/1966
Ht: 6ft-3ins, **Wt:** 13st-8lbs
Swans debut: v. Burnley (a), 15/8/1992

Swansea City Career Statistics

Season	League	FLC	FAC	WC	AGT	P/Offs
1992/93	17+7/5gls	2/1gls	0+2		1+2	2/1gls
1993/94	15+13/3gls	1	0+2	2+2/1gls	3+2/2gls	
1994/95	1+2		0+2	1/2gls	0+1	
Total	33+22/8gls	3/1gls	0+6	3+2/3gls	4+5/2gls	2/1gls

Career:
Cradley Town
Portsmouth (£20,000 signed in 20/11/1990) lge 0+2
Swansea City (£20,000 signed in 24/7/1992)
Scunthorpe United (£15,000 signed in 4/8/1995)
    lge 48+12/19gls, FLC 4/1gls, FAC 2+2/2gls, Others 3/2gls
Torquay United (£20,000 signed in 10/1/1997) lge 42+14/11gls,
    FLC 3+1/1gls, Others 3+1/1gls

Honours: AutoGlass Trophy Winner–1994, West Wales Senior Cup Winner–1994, 1995

Former non-league player with Cradley Town, playing alongside another ex-Swans favourite John Williams, combining to be prolific goalscorers on the non-league circuit. Frank Burrows signed Andy initially for Portsmouth in 1990, but after the Scotsman had taken over as manager at the Vetch Field, signed him a second time, for £20,000 in July 1992. He scored his first goal for the Swans in his third game, at the Vetch Field in the second leg of the Coca Cola Cup tie against Oxford United. During his time at the Vetch Field, a back injury restricted his appearances, but nevertheless, he always proved to be a handful for defenders with his style of play. In the 1992/93 Second Division Play Off semi-finals against West

Bromwich Albion, he scored for the Swans in the first leg at the Vetch Field in a 2-1 win, but unfortunately scored an own goal in the same game, with the Swans losing out in the second leg at the Hawthorns. His second season proved to be more successful, with the tall striker scoring the Swans goal in a 1-1 draw after 90 minutes, and extra time at Wembley in the Auto Glass Trophy Cup Final, which eventually went in the Swans favour on penalties. In May 1994 he was included in the Swans side that beat Ammanford Town in the West Wales Senior Cup Final, and twelve months later scored a hat-trick in the final of the same competition, this time against Morriston Town. A disappointing third season, saw him restricted through a back injury, and in the close season of 1994 joined Scunthorpe United for £15,000, moving on to Torquay United 18 months later for £20,000. At Scunthorpe, and at Torquay he continued to prove himself as a regular goalscorer, and a handful for the best of defenders, with his ability in the air, and awkwardness around the field. By the end of the 1998/99 season, injuries had restricted his appearances, forcing him to retire from the professional game.

9. McGIBBON, Patrick (PAT) Colm

Birthplace: Lurgan, 6/9/1973
Ht: 6ft-2ins, **Wt:** 13st-12lbs
Swans debut: v. Doncaster Rovers (a), 21/9/1996

Swansea City Career Statistics

Season	League
1996/97	1
Total	1

Career:
Portadown
Manchester United (£100,000 signed in 1/8/1992) FLC 1
Swansea City (loan in 20/9/1996)
Wigan Athletic (£250,000 signed in 3/3/1997) lge163+10/11gls,
    FLC 11+1, FAC 9+1, Others 18
Scunthorpe United (loan in 15/2/2002) lge 6
Tranmere Rovers (signed in 1/8/2002) lge 4
Portadown (signed in season 2003/04)
Glentoran (signed in summer 2004)

Honours: Northern Ireland Sch, U-21–1, 'B'–5, Full–7, Auto Windscreens Shield Winner–1999, Irish League Champions–2005, CIS Cup Winner–2005

Pat made his senior debut for Manchester United in a League Cup tie against York City in season 1995/96, which unfortunately for him saw him red carded for a foul, and the following month he made his fourth full Northern Ireland appearance. His first Full appearance for Northern Ireland had been in the Canada Cup in Edmonton on the 22nd May 1995 as a substitute for McDonald, losing 2-0. Pat was signed by Swans manager Jan Molby on a month loan, but after making his first appearance for the Swans at Doncaster Rovers in a 1-0 win, he was injured in training, and returned to Old Trafford without playing another game for the Swans. Later in the season he joined Wigan Athletic on an initial loan basis, and scored his first goal in a game against Colchester United which ensured promotion for Athletic. Dominant in aerial challenges, a strong tackler, he was also composed on the ball. Shortly after sealing promotion his transfer was made permanent for a fee in the region of £250,000. In five seasons with Wigan Athletic, Pat played in three consecutive end of season Second Division Play Offs, and was also a member of the Wigan side that beat Millwall 1-0 in April 1999 to win the Auto Windscreens Shield competition. In season 1998/99 lost 2-1 to Manchester City on aggregate in the semi-final stage, in season 1999/2000 beat Millwall in the semi-final, only to lose 3-2 to Gillingham in the final, and in season 2000/01 losing 2-1 on aggregate to Reading in the semi-final. By the time 'The Latics' had won the Second Division Championship at the end of the 2002/03 season, Pat had been re-united with his former Wigan manager Ray Mathias at Tranmere Rovers. Midway through the 2002/03 season Pat returned to Northern Ireland to rejoin Portadown, later joining Glentoran in the summer of 2005. A qualified physiotherapist, at Glentoran he was involved in their UEFA Cup games with Swedish side IF Elfsborg, and by the end of the season had made appearances in the side that won the CIS Cup Final against Linfield, and also the Irish League Championship.

10. McGUIGAN, JOHN Joseph

Birthplace: Motherwell, 29/10/1932
Ht: 5ft-8ins, **Wt:** 10st-4lbs
Swans debut: v. Middlesbrough (h), 20/3/1965

Swansea Town Career Statistics			
Season	League	FAC	WC
1964/65	10/1gls		
1965/66	18/3gls	1	1/1gls
Total	28/4gls	1	1/1gls

Career:
St. Mirren (signed in November 1953)
Southend United (signed in May 1955) lge 125/34gls, FAC 13/3gls
Newcastle United (£2,250 signed in June 1958) lge 50/15gls, FLC 2/1gls, FAC 3/1gls
Scunthorpe United (signed in January 1962) lge 57/17gls
Southampton (£10,000 signed in August 1963) lge 33/8gls
Swansea Town (£6,500 signed in March 1965)

Experienced inside forward, having created a good goalscoring reputation with his previous clubs since leaving Scottish football at St. Mirren, signed by Swans manager Trevor Morris for £5,000 from Southampton in March 1965, just prior to transfer deadline day, in a bid to save the club from relegation to the Third Division. He only scored one goal in his first season, against Derby County at the Vetch Field, with the Swans almost assured of relegation, and during the next season in the Third Division, returned three league goals, plus one in a Welsh Cup semi-final against Merthyr. Joining St. Mirren from junior sides Muirkirk and Bo'ness, he signed for Third Division South Southend United in May 1955, and was a virtual ever present on the left wing in his three seasons at Roots Hall, with the 'Shrimpers' consistently finishing in the top seven league placings each season, before he was transferred to First Division Newcastle

United in July 1958 for £2,250, plus Punton. Making just fifty league appearances in three and a half seasons at St. James' Park at either outside left, inside left, or at centre forward, he then joined Second Division Scunthorpe United, in an exchange deal with Barrie Thomas, scoring in a 2-0 win over the Swans in February 1962. A further transfer to Second Division Southampton in August 1963 saw John score two goals for the 'Saints' in a 4-0 home win over the Swans in September 1963, but in the return fixture at the Vetch Field, McGuigan played against a Swans side that scored an emphatic 6-0 win over the 'Saints'. He was released by the Swans at the end of the 1965/66 season, returned to the Southampton area where he became licensee of the Swan Hotel in Portsmouth Road, Woolston, returning three years later to Scotland where he worked in the tool room of Glasgow's Rolls-Royce plant in Hillington. John's father appeared for Motherwell in inter-war football.

11. McHALE, Raymond (RAY)

Birthplace: Sheffield, 12/8/1950
Ht: 5ft-8ins, **Wt:** 12st-6lbs
Swans debut: v. Bradford City (a), 26/1/1985

Swansea City Career Statistics					
Season	League	FLC	FAC	WC	FRT
1984/85	19			3	4
1985/86	26+2/1gls	3	2	2/3gls	1
Total	45+2/1gls	3	2	5/3gls	5

Career:
Hillsborough Boys Club
Huddersfield Town (amateur)
Chesterfield (signed in August 1970) lge 123+1/27gls
Halifax Town (£3,000 + p/exchange in 1/10/1974) lge 86/21gls
Swindon Town (signed in 9/9/1976) lge 171+2/32gls
Brighton & Hove Albion (£100,000 signed in 19/5/1980) lge 9+2
Barnsley (£60,000 signed in March 1981) lge 52+1/1gls
Sheffield United (£20,000 signed in August 1982) lge 66+1/2gls
Bury (loan in February 1983) lge 6
Swansea City (signed in 16/1/1985)
Rochdale (non-contract signed in August 1986) lge 6+1
Scarborough (non-contract signed in December 1986) lge 25/3gls
Goole Town (signed in February 1988)
Northwich Victoria (signed in 1988 close season)
Guiseley (player manager in October 1988)

Honours: GMVC Champions–1987

Formerly an amateur with Huddersfield Town and a junior league player with Sheffield based side Hillsborough Boys Club prior to signing as a professional with Chesterfield at the age of 20 as a winger. Ray played on the wing in the 1968/69 Chesterfield side that won the Northern Intermediate League Cup. By the time of his first-team debut he was converted to a midfielder and became respected for his persistent, tireless approach, his aggressive but skilful play and for his thunderbolt shot as well as his success rate at penalties. In October 1974 he was transferred to Halifax Town in exchange for Terry Shanahan, after a dispute over loyalty bonuses that embroiled several of Chesterfield's leading players. The deal was perceived as a poor one, given the success that Ray later achieved at Swindon, and given the money that changed hands as he was subsequently transferred. One of a number of experienced professionals Swans manager John Bond brought to the Vetch Field midway through the 1984/85 season in a bid to prevent a third consecutive relegation from the First, to the Fourth Division. 34 years of age when he signed for the Swans, he always gave 100% effort in matches, working tirelessly in midfield. His only league goal for the Swans came during his second season at Walsall in the second league match of season. In the Welsh Cup however, he scored a hat-trick at Haverfordwest, in a 6-2 victory for the Swans. Playing through particularly bleak times at the Vetch Field, with the club overcoming eventually a High Court winding up order, he was released in June 1986, after the club had been unable to prevent relegation to the Fourth Division. He joined Rochdale on non-contract terms for the 1986/87 season, but in December 1986 signed for GM Vauxhall side Scarborough, playing a large part in the club's Championship success, and elevation to Football League status at the end of the 1986/87 season. He later played non-league with Goole Town and Northwich Victoria before joining Guiseley as player manager in October 1988, guiding the team to success in the FA Vase and Northern Premier League. He returned to Scarborough as assistant manager in January 1989, served as manager between November 1989 to April 1993 before returning to Guisley, after a dispute with the Scarborough chairman. In December '94 he went back to Seamer Road as Manager but moved aside to the assistant's position in March, 1996. When Mick Wadsworth left for Colchester in January 1999, Ray assumed joint caretaker-managership with Kevin Ratcliffe, later taking over as youth team coach in September 2001. Between November 2001 and June 2002 Ray was chief scout at Oldham Athletic. Since starting his playing career at Chesterfield, Ray, apart from one season in the First Division with Brighton & Hove Albion in season 1980/81 had played all of his football in either the Second, or Third Divisions, prior to signing for the Swans. An integral member of the Swindon Town midfield that competed with the Swans for one of the promotion places during the 1978/79 season, Ray also had promotion success during his career with Barnsley, playing thirteen league games as they secured runners up position in the Third Division in season 1980/81, and with Sheffield United, as they secured third place behind Wimbledon and Oxford United at the end of season 1983/84.

12. McINTOSH, ALBERT

Birthplace: Dundee, 6/4/1930
Ht: 5ft-8ins, **Wt:** 11st-6lbs
Swans debut: v. Everton (h), 6/3/1954

Swansea Town Career Statistics		
Season	League	WC
1953/54	5/1gls	
1954/55	2	
1955/56		
1956/57	7/2gls	1
Total	14/3gls	1

Career:
Downfield Juniors, Dundee
Swansea Town (£200 signed in 22/2/1954)

Honours: Dundee Select XI, Football Combination Second Division Champions–1955, West Wales Senior Cup Winner–1956

Scottish born centre forward who joined the Swans from Dundee junior side Downfield for £200 in March 1954, after earlier representing a Select Dundee XI. He scored his first league goal in his second game for the Swans, against Derby County at the Vetch Field, but throughout his Swans career did not appear to have the pace for league football and a lack of height, despite being skilful on the ball. Season 1954/5 saw him make regular appearances in the Swans' reserve side that won the Football Combination Second Division Championship, and in April 1956 he was a member of the Swans side that beat Llanelly to win the West Wales Senior Cup. He started season 1956/57 at centre forward, scoring in his third game in a defeat against Barnsley. During season 1957/58 he had a cartilage operation, and after failing to make any appearances during the season was given a free transfer in May 1958, returning to Scotland.

13. McLAUGHLIN, James (JIMMY) Christopher

Birthplace: Derry, 22/12/1940
Ht: 5ft-9¼ins, **Wt:** 11st-0½lbs
Swans debut: v. Grimsby Town (h), 24/8/1963

Swansea Town/City Career Statistics					
Season	League	FLC	FAC	WC	ECWC
1963/64	26/8gls	1	7/5gls	2	
1964/65	38/9gls	3/1gls	4/1gls	3/2gls	
1965/66	40+2/20gls	1	1/1gls	8/5gls	
1966/67	17+1/7gls	3/2gls	3/5gls		2
1972/73	8+4				
1973/74	12+3/2gls	2			
Total	141+10/46gls	10/3gls	15/12gls	13/7gls	2

Career:
Derry City
Birmingham City (signed in June 1958)
Shrewsbury Town (signed in July 1960) lge 124/56gls
Swansea Town (signed in May 1963)
Peterborough United (signed in March 1967) lge 8/2gls
Shrewsbury Town (signed in September 1967) lge 159+14/21gls
Swansea City (signed in November 1972)

Honours: Northern Ireland U-23–2, Full-12, Welsh Cup Winner–1966

Northern Ireland International winger Jimmy McLaughlin was signed by Swans manager Trevor Morris from Shrewsbury Town in May 1963 for a club record £16,000. Capped at U-23 level whilst with Shrewsbury Town, he also gained his first Full cap for Northern Ireland on the 7th October 1961 in Belfast against Scotland in a 6-1 defeat, scoring his side's goal, and was capped on 7 occasions whilst on the Vetch Field playing staff. His international career saw him score two goals in a game on two occasions, against Greece in Belfast in October 1961, and against England in Belfast in October 1964. Joining Birmingham City from his local club Derry City in June 1958, Jimmy failed to make a first team appearance at St. Andrews with Birmingham, but after moving to Shrewsbury in July 1960 made 124 league appearances, scoring 56 league goals prior to joining the Swans. During his first season at the Vetch Field he scored 4 goals in the famous FA Cup run which saw the club knocked out with a freak 40 yard shot from the Preston centre half at a rain lashed Villa Park in the semi-finals. A clever ball playing winger, who could also play as an out and out striker, Jimmy had his best goalscoring return for the Swans in the 1965/66 season which saw him score 20 league goals, including 7 goals from 9 league games between October to December 1965. He scored two hat-tricks during his Swans career, against Bournemouth in November 1965, and in the FA Cup against Folkestone at the Vetch Field in November 1966. In March 1967 he was transferred to Peterborough United, but after making just 8 league appearances rejoined Shrewsbury Town in September 1967. Following a further 173 league appearances for Shrewsbury Town, he returned to the Vetch Field in mid-November 1972, a month short of his 32nd birthday to take up a player coach role alongside Harry Gregg, his former manager at Gay Meadow. With little or no money to spend on new players at the Vetch Field, Gregg had turned to the experienced McLaughlin to try and add some stability to a side that was facing relegation to the Fourth Division. By the time of his departure in mid November 1974, Jimmy had also taken on the role as secretary at the Vetch Field, with his last competitive game for the Swans being almost twelve months earlier. Returning to his native Northern Ireland, Jimmy was initially appointed player manager with Dundalk in 1974, and following a successful period which saw the club win the league and cup on three occasions, he joined Shamrock Rovers as manager in 1983, gaining a further 3 league championships, plus appearances in 3 Cup finals. He returned to his hometown Derry City in 1986, and by the time he left in 1991 the club had won the treble. Following further managerial roles at Shelbourne, Drogheda and Dundalk, Jimmy retired as a manger in 1996 to work for an oil distribution company in North Leinster. His success as a manager had given him the opportunity to test his ability as a manager in European competitions for nine consecutive seasons, playing against top sides like Tottenham Hotspur, Liverpool, Benfica, Oporto and Celtic.

14. McLEOD, KEVIN Andrew

Birthplace: Liverpool, 12/9/1980
Ht: 5ft-11ins, **Wt:** 11st-3lbs
Swans debut: v. Grimsby Town (h), 19/2/2005

Swansea City Career Statistics		
Season	*League*	*FAWC*
2004/05	7+4	0+1
Total	7+4	0+1

Career:
Everton (from trainee in 24/9/1998) Plge 0+5, FLC 1, FAC 0+1
QPR (loan in 21/3/2003) lge 8/2gls, Others 3
QPR (loan in 18/8/2004) lge 0+1
QPR (£250,000 signed in 20/8/2004) lge 30+28/4gls,
    FLC 3+1/1gls, FAC 2, Others 1/1gls
Swansea City (£60,000 signed in 16/2/2005)

Honours: FAYC–1998

Kevin McLeod was signed for an initial £60,000 signing fee, plus add ons if the Swans gained promotion at the end of season 2004/05, signing an eighteen month contract at the Vetch Field. A former Liverpool Schoolboys winger, he had been attached to Everton from the age of nine, and been included in the club's youth squad when they beat Blackburn Rovers in 1998 to win the FA Youth Cup. Growing up at Goodison Park with Wayne Rooney, Michael Ball and Francis Jeffers, he made his Premiership debut for Everton as a substitute for Niclas Alexandersson in a 3- home defeat by Ipswich Town on the 30th September 2000, making a further four substitute appearances in the season. A direct and pacy left sided winger who came up through the ranks at Goodison Park he also played left wing back for Everton in a Worthington Cup tie, and in January 2003 played in the Everton side that were beaten by Third Division Shrewsbury Town in an FA Cup tie. Joining Queens Park Rangers in March 2003 on an initial loan transfer, he played in the remaining eight league games, also featuring in the Second Division Play Off Final defeat against Cardiff City at the Millennium Stadium. Starting the 2003/04 season on a second loan spell at Loftus Road, after just one game his transfer was made permanent for £250,000, and by the end of the season he had made thirty-five league appearances in the Rangers side that finished Runners-Up to Plymouth Argyle in the Nationwide Second Division, gaining automatic promotion. The following season in the Coca Cola Championship he made regular appearances for Rangers, also playing against the Swans in an early season Coca Cola Cup First Round tie at Loftus Road. He struggled with fitness problems after arriving at the Vetch Field, but by the end of the season had made a significant impact in the Swans side that claimed one of the automatic promotion places from Division Two.

15. McMAHON, Steven (STEVE)

Birthplace: Glasgow, 22/4/1970
Ht: 6ft-4ins, **Wt:** 14st 0lbs
Swans debut: v. Chester City, 13/3/1993

Swansea City Career Statistics	
Season	League
1992/93	2
Total	2

Career:
Ferguslie United
Swansea City (signed in July 1991)
Carlisle United (signed in July 1993) lge 2
Foshan (China)
Partick Thistle (signed in season 1995/96) Slge 0+1
Darlington (signed in 15/1/1996) lge 6+4/1gls
Clydebank (signed in close season 1996) Slge 12+8/3gls

Attended Bella Houston Academy and played centre half for the school team and Glasgow schoolboys. On leaving school he joined Ferguslie United youth team before joining the Swans in July 1991 on a trial basis. He had a knee operation in August 1991 which took a long time to heal and after a few games in the reserves he suffered a further setback when he was laid low with a stress fracture. His only Swans appearances came during his second season at the Vetch Field, making his debut at home to Chester City, unfortunately receiving a red card, and playing in the next match at Plymouth Argyle. The combination of Mark Harris and Keith Walker in central defence prevented Steve from making further first team appearances for the Swans. He was released in July 1993 joining Third Division side Carlisle United, but struggled to make an impression at Brunton Park, before going to play in China with Foshan. Returning to the UK after two years in China, he made a substitute appearance whilst on a monthly contract with Partick Thistle in a 3-0 home defeat by Falkirk on the 9th January 1996, signing a six month contract at Darlington six days later. He failed to make the Darlington side that played at Wembley at the end of the season in the Third Division Play Off Final, and was released, starting the 1996/97 season back in Scottish football with Clydebank.

16. McMILLAN, WILLIAM H.

Swans debut: v. Everton (a), 6/9/1930

Swansea Town Career Statistics	
Season	League
1930/31	8
Total	8

Career:
Rothesay Royal Victoria
Swansea Town (trial in August, signed in September 1930)

An outside right signed by Swans manager James Hunter Thomson initially in August 1930, who made his Swans debut in the third game of the 1930/31 season as a replacement for Billy Hole, shortly after signing as a professional. He had earlier shown good form in the club's public trial games and reserve team matches. Retaining his place for the next game at Charlton Athletic, over the following couple of months he made a further six appearances as a replacement for either Armand, Thomas or Hole for the outside right position in the Swans side, failing to feature during the second half of the season. By the end of the season he had been released from the playing staff at the Vetch Field.

17. McMORRAN, James (JIMMY) Wilson

Birthplace: Muirkirk, Ayrshire, 29/10/1942
Ht: 5ft-7ins, **Wt:** 10st-12lbs
Swans debut: v. Bradford Park Avenue (a), 10/8/1968

Swansea Town Career Statistics		
Season	League	FLC
1968/69	14/1gls	4
Total	14/1gls	4

Career:
Aston Villa (groundstaff in July 1958, professional in October 1959) lge 11/1gls, FLC 1, FAC 2
Third Lanark (signed in February 1963)
Walsall (£6,000 signed in November 1964) lge 93+1/9gls
Swansea Town (£4,000 signed in June 1968)
Walsall (£6,000 signed in 31/10/1968) lge 9+1/1gls
Notts. County (signed in July 1969) lge 6
Halifax Town (signed in August 1970)
Worcester City (signed in February 1971 to July 1971)
Redditch United (signed in August 1974)

Honours: Scotland Sch.

A skilful inside left, the former East Ayrshire Schoolboy was capped at schoolboy level for Scotland, before joining the groundstaff at Villa Park in June 1958, signing professional in October 1959, and made his First Division debut against Bolton Wanderers on the 3rd April 1961. His only league goal for Villa was the winning goal that beat Blackpool at Bloomfield Road on the 10th February 1962. Unable to secure a regular place at Villa Park, he returned to Scotland, had a trial spell with Falkirk before signing for Third Lanark, prior to joining Third Division Walsall for £6,000 in 1964. He made his Walsall debut in a 2-1 home defeat by Oldham Athletic on the 7th November 1964, and went on to make almost one hundred league appearances in his first stint at Fellows Park prior to joining the Swans. Signed by Swans manager Billy Lucas in June 1968, he scored his first goal for the Swans in his home debut, from the penalty spot against Aldershot. Missing just one game from the first nineteen league and cup matches, he surprisingly returned to Fellows Park with Walsall in late October 1968 in a player exchange deal involving veteran centre forward Alfie Biggs. In November 1969 he was in outstanding form for Walsall in a 1-0 F.A. Cup defeat by Spurs. Released at the end of the season he then signed for Notts. County, joining Halifax Town in August 1970 for a brief period, then made subsequent appearances for non-league sides Worcester City, Hednesford Town, Blakenhall, and Redditch United. During a spell in Australia he played for Fitzroy Alexandra and Preston Macedonia. Returning to the U.K, he made appearances for Sutton Town, and Rushall Olympic, prior to re-uniting with Rhys Griffiths as Darlaston's player coach, and was their manager up until Christmas 2000. Now living in Willenhall, he worked in Kirkpatricks' Foundry in Walsall for over 22 years.

18. McPHERSON, Lachlan (LACKY)

Birthplace: Denniston, Glasgow, 11/7/1900
Ht: 5ft-9½ins, **Wt:** 12st-0lbs
Swans debut: v. Swindon Town (h), 30/8/1924

Swansea Town Career Statistics			
Season	League	FAC	WC
1924/25	28	2	3
1925/26	31	7	2
1926/27	41/5gls	5/1gls	1
1927/28	42/12gls	1	2
1928/29	36/6gls	2	
1929/30	21/5gls		
Total	199/28gls	17/1gls	8

Career:
Cambuslang Rangers
Notts. County (signed in May 1921) lge 32/5gls
Swansea Town (signed in June 1924)
Everton (£6,000 signed in 2/1/1930) lge 30/1gls
New Brighton (signed in 23/8/1933) lge 53/3gls
Hereford United (player coach signed in July 1935)
Milford United (player manager in season 1936/37)

Honours: Second Division Champions–1923, Third Division (South) Champions–1925, Second Division Champions–1931

Signed prior to the start of the 1924/25 season from Notts. County, after he had been spotted playing for County on Tour in Denmark at the same time as the Swans were touring the country. In his second season of league football with County, Lachlan made league appearances during the club's Second Division Championship success in season 1922/23. He made his Swans debut in the first game of the 1924/25 season at left half, and throughout his playing career at the Vetch Field alternated between left half, and inside left. His first season with the Swans saw the club win the Championship of the Third Division South, and the following year reached the FA Cup semi-finals before being beaten by Bolton Wanderers. That same season the Swans also lost in the Final of the Welsh Cup to Ebbw Vale. He scored his first goal for the Swans in December 1926 in a 7-1 defeat at Middlesbrough, but the following season from the inside left position scored two hat-tricks for the Swans in the space of twelve days, against Manchester City, and Wolverhampton Wanderers. After scoring from the penalty spot in a 2-0 win over Hull City in late December 1929 he was transferred to Everton for a fee of £6,000, a record at the time, and at the end of the

season gained a Second Division Championship medal, and twelve months later made appearances in the First Division Championship winning team. His transfer to Goodison Park came almost a month after Swans defender Ben Williams had joined the club. Born in Lanarkshire, he played his early football with junior sides Cambuslang Juniors, and Cambuslang Rangers, prior to joining Notts. County in 1921. He finished his playing career with Third Division North side New Brighton and then took on a player coach role at non-league side Hereford United. Injuries restricted his appearances for United, and after returning to Swansea to take over as landlord of the Gorse Inn, in season 1936/37 he was appointed player manager of Milford United.

19. McQUILLAN, Patrick (PAT) Gerard

Birthplace: Belfast, 27/6/1961
Ht: 6ft-0ins, **Wt:** 11st-4lbs
Swans debut: v. Derby County (h), 31/12/1983

Swansea City Career Statistics				
Season	League	FLC	FAC	WC
1983/84	19		1	
1984/85	6+1/1gls	2	1	2
Total	25+1/1gls	2	2	2

Career:
Pembroke Borough
Swansea City (signed in August 1979)
Pembroke Borough (start of season 1982/83
Swansea City (signed in December 1983)
Pembroke Borough (start of season 1985/86)

Pat joined the Swans as an apprentice after impressing in Pembrokeshire Schools and County football. Arriving in West Wales at the age of five, Pat attended St. Mary's Catholic School and Bush Comprehensive School prior to starting his apprenticeship at the Vetch Field. He failed to make an appearance for the Swans first team during his first spell at the club, and was released in May 1983, returning to West Wales to sign for Pembroke Borough. When John Toshack returned to the Vetch Field for his second managerial stint, with financial problems at the club limiting him in signing players, Pat was taken on for a second time with the Swans, making his league debut at the Vetch Field against Derby County a couple of days after signing. He had returned to the Vetch Field along with former defender Wyndham Evans, who at the time was also playing for Pembroke Borough, and had signed for the Swans in a player coach capacity. He made one FA Cup appearance for the Swans in season 1983/84, and the following season played in the Swans side that was beaten by Bognor Regis in an FA Cup, first round replay. At this stage Colin Appleton was manager of the Swans, but by the end of season 1984/85 with John Bond in charge, he was given a free transfer, returning to Pembroke Borough. He scored his only goal for the Swans at Burnley in a 1-1 draw in December 1984. After leaving the Vetch Field he went to college to learn carpentry, working for his father's building business in the town. A broken leg playing for Pembroke Borough saw him sidelined for two years, and on his return he played half a season for Monkton Swifts, before rejoining Borough. Unfortunately the club folded, with Pat returning to Monkton Swifts, and finally ending his playing career with Pennar Robins in the late 1990's.

N

1. NARDIELLO, Daniel (DANNY)

Birthplace: Coventry, 22/10/1982
Ht: 5ft-11ins, **Wt:** 11st-4lbs
Swans debut: v. Rochdale (a), 25/10/2003

Swansea City Career Statistics		
Season	*League*	*LDV*
2003/04	3+1	1/1gls
Total	3+1	1/1gls

Career
Manchester United (from scholar in 1/11/1999) FLC 1+2, Others 0+1
Swansea City (loan in 24/10/2003)
Barnsley (loan in 27/1/2004) lge 14+2/7gls
Barnsley (loan in 16/7/2004) lge 11+17/7gls, FLC 0+2, Others 1
Barnsley (signed in 25/6/2005)

Honours: England Sch, Yth

Exciting, young United front runner, capped at schoolboy and youth level for England, and who is also the son of former Welsh international winger Donato Nardiello. He arrived at the Vetch Field along with defender Alan Tate in late October 2004, making his league debut in the away win at Rochdale, in which he set up Wilson for the only goal of the game. A very quick, prolific goalscorer at reserve team level at Old Trafford, although he had been unable to make an appearance in United's Premiership side, had made first team appearances in the Worthington Cup against Arsenal and Leicester City, and also in the Champions League against Maccabi Haifa in Nicosia. Daniels' father, Donato, was capped at full level for Wales when playing for Coventry City in the late 1970's. Daniel scored his only goal for the Swans against Southend United in the LDV Vans Trophy cup tie in early November. He returned to Old Trafford at the end of his month loan, made one further appearance as substitute for Kleberson in the League Cup tie with West Bromwich Albion, and in late January started a loan spell with Second Division Barnsley. He made an immediate impact at Oakwell, scoring two goals on his debut against Blackpool, also scoring in the next home league game with Hartlepool United. By the end of his loan period, and his return to Old Trafford, Daniel had scored seven league goals, and finished the season joint second top goalscorer with Dean Gorre. In July 2004 he returned to Oakwell for a second loan period with Barnsley, and in June 2005 the transfer was made permanent.

2. NEWELL, EDGAR

Birthplace: Swansea, 17/4/1920
Ht: 5ft-11½ins, **Wt:** 11st-0lbs
Swans debut: v. Swindon Town (h), 25/10/1947

Swansea Town Career Statistics		
Season	*League*	*WC*
1947/48	5	1
1948/49	11	
1949/50	3	
1950/51	3	
Total	22	1

Career:
Hafod Athletic
Swansea Town (signed in 22/8/1946)
Milford United (signed start of season 1951/52)
Llanelly (signed start of season 1952/53)

Honours: Third Division South Champions 1949, London Combination Cup Winner–1947, West Wales Senior Cup Winner–1949, 1950, 1953

Edgar Newell was brought up in the Dyfatty area of Swansea, before going to live in Cwmbwrla and Townhill. He was called up to the Army during the war, played rugby and football for the Welsh Regiment, seeing action in Germany and France.

He started his playing career with Hafod Athletic and actually turned down a trial with Bolton Wanderers prior to joining the Swans in August 1946, while working in the ICI Landore works. At the time of his signing for the Swans, a number of young players had signed for Bolton Wanderers from Swansea, including Jackie Roberts and Ernie Jones, both of whom would go on to play international football for Wales, and also return to play for the Swans. A right full back when arriving at the Vetch Field, during his playing career he was unfortunate not to have played more league games for the Swans because of the high quality of defenders at the time on the club's playing staff, with his twenty-two league appearances being spread over four seasons. He made his debut deputising for Roy Paul against Swindon Town in October 1947 retaining his place for the next two matches, with all three games being unbeaten. Playing two further games towards the end of the season, one at left back, it was during the following season, a season in which the club won the Championship of the Third Division South, that he was to have a longer run in the first team, making eleven league starts. He occupied both full back positions as well as wing half and centre half during a season which saw the club clinch only its second championship, with a forward line that scored 87 league goals, and finish the season seven points ahead of their nearest rivals, Reading. During his first season at the Vetch Field he was also a member of the Swans reserve side that won the London Combination Cup for the first time, playing at right full back in the side that beat Arsenal in the final at White Hart Lane. In the semi-final the Swans had overcome the favourites Chelsea at the Vetch Field. He remained at the Vetch Field a further two seasons after the Championship winning season of 1948/489 struggling in both seasons to get a run of games in the first team. Gained three winning West Wales Senior Cup Winners Medals, in 1949 and 1950 playing for the Swans against Llanelly, and Haverfordwest, and three years later when he was in the Llanelly side that beat the Swans at Stebonheath Park. Released in May 1951 he joined Milford United in the Welsh League, before linking up with Llanelly, who at the time were playing in the Southern League. After leaving the Vetch Field he worked for thirty years as a gantry driver with Alcoa up until his retirement, living in the same house he bought off Swans player Jack O'Driscoll in the late 1940's. Primarily a reserve team player for the Swans his versatility allowed him to play in any defensive position, also playing one game late in his career for Llanelly in goal. By the time he retired at the end of season 1955/56, on only one occasion was he booked by the referee during his career, and that was at Stebonheath Park with Llanelly.

3. NEWHOUSE, AIDAN Robert

Birthplace: Wallasey, Cheshire, 23/5/1972
Ht: 6ft-2ins, **Wt:** 13st-10lbs
Swans debut: v. Cardiff City (a), 2/11/1997

Swansea City Career Statistics				
Season	League	FAC	AWS	FAWP
1997/98	3+5	1		
1998/99	5+1	1	0+1	3+2
Total	8+6	2	0+1	3+2

Career:
Chester City (associate schoolboy in October 1986, trainee in July 1988, signed professional in July 1989) lge 29+15/6gls, FLC 5+1, FAC 0+2, Others 2+3/1gls
Wimbledon (£100,000 signed in 22/2/1990) F/Plge 7+16/2gls, FLC 1+1, FAC 2, Others 0+1
Port Vale (loaned in 21/1/1994) lge 0+2, FAC 0+1
Portsmouth (loan in 2/12/1994) lge 6/1gls
Torquay United (loan in 7/12/1995) lge 4/2gls
Fulham (signed in 20/6/1997) lge 7+1/1gls, FLC 3+1/3gls
Swansea City (£30,000 signed in 31/10/1997)
Brighton & Hove Albion (signed in 2/8/1999) lge 1+11/2gls, FLC 1, FAC 0+1
Sutton United (signed in December 1999) Conf 17+1/3gls
Northwich Victoria (signed in December 2000) Conf 0+1

Honours: England Yth

Started his career at Chester City, gained youth recognition for England, and from where Wimbledon paid £100,000 for the youngster in February 1990. In May 1988 he became Chester's youngest ever league debutant, making his first team debut as substitute for Bennett at the age of fifteen years, and three hundred and fifty days old. The promise he had shown at Chester did not materialise during his time with Wimbledon, and after making loan appearances for Port Vale, Portsmouth and Torquay United, signed for Micky Adams at Fulham. Following Adams's short reign as manager at the Vetch Field, and after his assistant, Alan Cork had taken over as manager, he signed for the Swans for a fee in the region of £30,000, prior to the local derby with Cardiff City on the 31st October 1997 at Ninian Park, coming on as a substitute for Tony Bird. Throughout his time at the Vetch Field he struggled to overcome a succession of injury problems, and after failing to score any goals, had his contract paid up in April 1999. A couple of months later he signed for Micky Adams a second time, this time at Brighton & Hove Albion, where he scored two goals on his debut in a 6-0 home win over Mansfield Town. Midway through the season he was released at Brighton, signing for Conference side Sutton United in December 1999, scored on his debut against Kettering and in three of his first four league games, but after that his only goals came in the FA Trophy. In all he made 26 league and cup appearances with 6 goals, but left Sutton United shortly before the start of the following season, returning north to sign for Northwich Victoria in December 2000, making one substitute appearance for the club.

4. NICHOLAS, David (DAI) Sidney

Birthplace: Aberdare, 12/8/1897. **Died:** Aberdare, 7/4/1982
Ht: 5ft-9ins, **Wt:** 12st-0lbs
Swans debut: v. Bournemouth (h), 6/12/1924

Career:
Merthyr Town (signed in 1914 to 1916)
Royal Navy
Swansea Town (signed as amateur in 29/4/1919)
Merthyr Town (signed in 1920) lge 46/2gls
Stoke City (£1,000 signed in March 1922) lge 54/3gls
Aberdare Athletic (signed in October 1924)
Swansea Town (signed in 5/12/1924)

Swansea Town Career Statistics			
Season	*League*	*FAC*	*WC*
1924/25	19/2gls		
1925/26	25/4gls	7/2gls	2
1926/27	34/2gls	5	1/1gls
1927/28	37/2gls	1	
1928/29	31/2gls	2	
1929/30	5/2gls		
Total	151/14gls	15/2gls	3/1gls

Honours: Wales Sch, Wales Full–3, Third Division South Champions–1925, West Wales Senior Cup Winner–1925, Welsh League Representative XI

The former Aberdare Intermediate and Aberdare Grammar Schoolboy, who was capped at schoolboy level for Wales in 1912, made Southern League appearances for Merthyr Town between 1914 and 1916, joined the Royal Navy during WW1, and after the war was originally on the Swans books as an amateur. In late September 1921 he made an appearance for a Welsh League Representative side against a Southern League Representative side at Aberdare. After making appearances for the Swans in the Southern League, he re-joined Merthyr Town following the club's elevation to Football League status. Signing for Second Division Stoke City in October 1921, by the end of his first season he had made appearances in the 'Potters' side that finished runners up, and promotion to the First Division. He attended Teacher Training College in Carmarthen whilst making appearances for Stoke City, and in October 1924 he left Stoke City to take up a scholastic appointment in Aberdare, joining Aberdare Athletic in October 1924. When the Swans showed an interest in signing the player, Stoke City, who held his signature initially asked for a fee, but after a couple of weeks of negotiations between the two sets of Directors, he joined the Swans without a fee changing hands. A speedy left winger, and a good crosser of the ball, he made his Swans debut in early December 1924, during a season which saw the club win its first Championship, and the following season played his part in the Swans reaching the semi-final of the FA Cup, also playing in the Swans side that lost in the final of the Welsh Cup the same season against Ebbw Vale. In January 1925 he was included in the Swans side that beat Llanelly to win the West Wales Senior Cup. He scored his first goal for the Swans in his third game, against QPR in a 2-0 win at the Vetch Field. Capped for Wales during his career with Stoke City on the 17th March 1923 in Glasgow against Scotland, after signing for the Swans he gained a further two international games whilst at the Vetch Field, in February 1926 against England, and in April the same year against Northern Ireland. In April 1930, Nicholas, along with George Thomas and Joe Sykes received Benefits from the Swans, with friendly matches played later in the month against Motherwell and Cardiff City. He retired at the end of the 1929/30 season, returning full time to the teaching profession.

5. NUGENT, KEVIN Patrick

Birthplace: Wood Green, North London, 10/4/1969
Ht: 6ft-1ins, **Wt:** 12st-11lbs
Swans debut: v. York City (a), 18/1/2003

Swansea City Career Statistics					
Season	*League*	*FLC*	*FAC*	*LDV*	*FAWC*
2002/03	15/5gls				1
2003/04	31+8/8gls	0+1	2+2/2gls		1/1gls
2004/05	7+12/3gls	1	0+1	0+2/1gls	
Total	53+20/16gls	1+1	2+3/2gls	0+2/1gls	2/1gls

Career:
Leyton Orient (from trainee in 8/7/1987) lge 86+8/20gls,
    FLC 9+3/6gls, FAC 9/3gls, Others 9+1/1gls
Plymouth Argyle (£200,000 in 23/3/1992) lge 124+7/32gls,
    FLC 11/2gls, FAC 10/3gls, Others 5+3
Bristol City (player/exchange signed in 29/9/1995)
    lge 48+22/14gls, FLC 2+2, FAC 3+2/1gls, Others 2+1
Cardiff City (£65,000 in 4/8/1997) lge 94+5/29gls, FLC 2+2, FAC
    3+2/1gls, Others 2+1
Leyton Orient (signed in 31/1/2002) lge 17+11/4gls,
    FLC 1/1gls, FAC 2, Others 1
Swansea City (signed in 17/1/2003)

Honours: Rep of Ireland Yth

An experienced striker who initially arrived at the Vetch Field on loan from Leyton Orient, and after making his debut at York City in January 2003, scored on his home debut for the Swans against Lincoln City, his second game for the Swans. With uncertainty surrounding his permanent future with the Swans, at the end of his month loan, he finally put pen-to-paper at the Vetch two days after the Swans beat Cambridge United at the Vetch Field, to complete his free transfer from Leyton Orient. At the end of the season he was offered, and signed a one year contract extension with the Swans, with the former Cardiff City front runner winning over his critics on the Vetch Field North Bank. Born in Wood Green, North London, of Irish parents, he attended St. Ignatius school, playing for the school team, Middlesex County, London schoolboys, and also with Sunday League side Beaumont F.C. He had the opportunity for trials with both England and the Republic of Ireland, but after choosing the latter played at U-17's level. Kevin made his league debut for Leyton Orient with a goal against Scarborough in 1987. Missing out on the 1988/89 Fourth Division Play Off win over Wrexham, two seasons later he had become a regular in the Orient starting line-up, finishing the 1991/92 season as top goalscorer in the league with twelve goals. In March 1992 he was sold to Plymouth Argyle for £200,000, but was unable to help the club avoid relegation to the Third Division. Top goalscorer on two occasions at Home Park, in September 1995 he was involved in a transfer to Bristol City which saw City striker Ian Baird, plus £75,000 go in the opposite direction to Argyle. Managed by former Leeds United striker Joe Jordan, he learnt a lot during his time at Ashton Gate, and after qualifying for the Second Division Play Offs in 1997, was sold to Cardiff City in August 1997 for £65,000. Overcoming a bad injury, which saw him miss almost the whole of his first season at Ninian Park, he linked up with former Swans striker John Williams for season 1998/99, with both strikers sharing 40 goals, as the club secured promotion from the Third Division. Despite suffering relegation in the first season back in the Second Division, within twelve months, the 'Bluebirds' had finished runners up to Brighton & Hove Albion, with Kevin scoring four goals from fourteen appearances. In January 2002 he re-joined his first club Leyton Orient, at the time thinking it would be his last transfer, but with the club having financial problems, the doors opened for him to return to South Wales, and sign for the Swans. Making an important contribution during his first season, his second season with the Swans saw him carve out a good understanding with Lee Trundle, and despite carrying a hamstring injury for most of the season, missed just seven league games, scoring ten league and cup goals. Captaining the side on occasions, Kevin always gave 100% endeavour during ninety minutes, proving himself to be a good battler, and still dangerous in aerial challenges. Released at the end of the season by manager Kenny Jackett, within a couple of weeks of the season ending, Kevin had accepted the offer of reserve team manager with the Swans, with the club still retaining his player registration. The first half of the 2004/05 season saw Kevin used regularly by Kenny Jackett in the first team squad until a cartilage problem in January saw him sidelined.

6. NURSE, Melvyn (MEL) Tudor George

Birthplace: Swansea, 11/10/1937
Ht: 6ft-2ins, **Wt:** 13st-1lbs
Swans Debut: v. Leicester City (h), 24/3/1956

Swansea Town/City Career Statistics					
Season	League	FLC	FAC	WC	ECWC
1955/56	3				
1956/57					
1957/58	9			1	
1958/59	25/3gls		1	1/1gls	
1959/60	42/4gls		3/1gls	2	
1960/61	41/1gls	1	3	4	
1961/62	33/1gls	2	1	1	2/1gls
1962/63	6	1			
1968/69	39+1/2gls	4	3	5	
1969/70	36	2/1gls	3	4	
1970/71	22/1gls		4	3	
Total	256+1/12gls	10/1gls	18/1gls	21/1gls	2/1gls

Career
Swansea Town (signed from juniors in June 1955)
Middlesbrough (signed in October 1962) lge 113/8gls
Swindon Town (signed in September 1965) lge 122+1/10gls
Swansea Town (£4,000 signed in June 1968)
Pembroke Borough (signed in March 1971)
Merthyr Tydfil (signed in August 1972)

Honours: Wales Sch, Yth, U-23–2, Full–12, English Schools Trophy Winner–1953, Welsh Cup Winner–1961, West Wales Senior Cup Winner–1960

Superb footballer from the centre half position, where he had the ability to read the game, good ball distribution, a solid tackler, and excellent in the air. An overall commanding figure at the heart of the defence, and also a good talker during the game, Mel captained all of his school sides in Cwmbwrla from infants to seniors. Mel played for Swansea schoolboys winning the English Trophy against Chesterfield in 1953 and runners up in the Welsh Shield at the age of fourteen, also playing the following year for Swansea and Wales schoolboys. Despite having offers from a number of top clubs on leaving school, Mel had set his heart on joining the groundstaff at the Vetch Field, eventually signing for the Swans and graduating to a professional in June 1955. In November 1959 he captained the U-23 side at Wrexham against Scotland, making his debut at Full level for Wales on the 17th October 1959 at Ninian Park against England. Of his total of twelve caps for Wales, nine were obtained whilst on the Swans playing staff. He made his Swans debut at the Vetch Field on 24th March 1956 against Leicester City, playing in the next two league games covering for Tom Kiley. He had to wait until the 1958/59 season before he was to start the new season in the Swans side, during which he scored his first league goal, against Barnsley from the penalty spot. The following season saw him become an ever present in the league with 42 appearances. Played in the May 1960 West Wales Senior Cup Final win over Llanelly. In 1961 the Swans beat Bangor City to win the Welsh Cup Final, becoming the first Welsh side the following season to participate in the European Cup Winners Cup competition, with Mel making appearances in both legs of the European Cup Winners Cup tie against Motor Jena.
In September 1962 he was transferred to Second Division side Middlesbrough for £25,000, staying in the North East for three seasons before returning south to sign for Third Division side Swindon Town. In June 1968 he returned to the Vetch Field to sign for manager Billy Lucas for a small fee, a couple of months short of his 31st birthday. His first season back at the Vetch Field saw the Swans lose out in the Welsh Cup Final against Cardiff City, but following a change of management with Roy Bentley taking control, ended the 1969/70 season in third place, and promotion to the Third Division. In the close season of 1970/71, with Mel wanting to concentrate on his business interests in the City, and refusing to accept full time playing terms, he announced his retirement from the game. However, after some persuasion he rejoined the Swans shortly after the start of the 1970/71 season, but by the end of February 1971 quit the game for a second time, citing the need to concentrate on his hotel and property ventures in the city. Persuaded later to sign for Welsh League side Pembroke Borough, Mel played for a number of seasons for the West Wales club before linking up with John Charles at Merthyr Tydfil. Three seasons at Merthyr saw Mel produce consistent performances, eventually becoming player manager after Les Graham was sacked. For a brief period Mel joined the club's Board of Directors, becoming chairman in a short time before retiring from football. In the mid-nineteen eighties he became involved as a Director of the Swans, and after a number of years having no involvement with the club, apart from being a spectator, was an instrumental figure behind the scenes in the 2001/02 season leading a group of supporters in a takeover of the club from Australian businessman Tony Petty. In October 2004 he received a Special Professional Award from the Football Association of Wales for his service to the game on and off the field.

O

1. O'DRISCOLL, John (JACKIE) Francis

Birthplace: Cork, 20/9/1921. **Died:** Swansea, 11/3/1988
Ht: 5ft-8ins, **Wt:** 11st-7lbs
Swans debut: v. Bournemouth (a), 23/8/1947

Swansea Town Career Statistics			
Season	League	FAC	WC
1947/48	22/7gls		
1948/49	36/7gls	2/2gls	1/1gls
1949/50	28/5gls	2	2
1950/51	11/2gls	1	1
1951/52	21/3gls	1	
Total	118/24gls	6/2gls	4/1gls

Career:
Cork City (signed in 1939)
Waterford (signed in 1941)
Shelbourne (signed in 1942)
Cork United (signed in 1943)
Swansea Town (£3,000 signed in 4/6/1947)
Llanelly (signed in September 1952)

Honours: Ireland–3, Northern Ireland–3, Third Division South Champions–1949, FAI Cup Winner–1947, West Wales Senior Cup Winner–1953

A speedy winger with a cannonball shot during his career with the Swans, he was signed by manager Haydn Green at the end of July 1947 for a £3,000 transfer fee. Starting his senior career with Irish side Cork City, he was involved in Waterford's FAI Cup Runner-Up side in 1941, and after joining Cork United in 1943 from Shelbourne, was a member of the FAI Cup Runner-Up side the same year, also playing in the 1947 FAI Cup Winning team. He proved himself to be a great favourite with the Vetch Field supporters, who felt that after he had fractured his ankle in season 1950/51 was never the same player. At the Vetch Field with the Swans he gained international honours with both the All Ireland, and Ireland representative sides during the 1948/49 season, playing in the Home International Championship matches against England (9/10/1948), Scotland (17/11/1948), and against Wales (9/3/1949). His appearances for All Ireland were against Switzerland, Belgium and Sweden. During the Swans Championship winning season of 1948/49 Jack made twenty-eight league appearances, scoring five goals, but missed out at the end of the season Welsh Cup Final match against Wrexham. He scored his first goal for the Swans in his second game, in a 4-1 away win at Watford. Shortly after the start of the 1952/53 season he left the Vetch Field playing staff, signing for Southern League side Llanelly, later becoming a licensee on the Gower peninsular at the Greyhound Inn at Reynoldston. In four seasons at Stebonheath Park with the Reds he missed few games, scoring forty goals, and after a period on the sidelines through illness, announced his retirement from the game in late September 1956. In May 1953 he was included in the Llanelly side that beat the Swans at Stebonheath Park to win the West Wales Senior Cup Final.

2. OGLEY, William (BILL)

Birthplace: Rotherham, JFM, 1896
Ht: 5ft-10ins, **Wt:** 12st-0lbs
Swans debut: v. Luton Town (a), 30/8/1919, Sth. Lge

Swansea Town Career Statistics		
Season	League	WC
1920/21	6/3gls	1
Total	6/3gls	1

Career:
Army Football
Swansea Town (signed in 12/7/1919)

Porth (signed in 25/6/1921)
Newport County (signed in April 1922) lge 40/2gls
QPR (signed in July 1924) lge 36/2gls
Castleford Town (signed in August 1925)
Denaby United (signed in February 1926)
Denaby Welfare (signed in October 1933)

Played for the Footballers Battalion in the Army prior to signing for the Swans in July 1919, making thirty appearances for the Swans in the Southern League prior to the club's elevation to the Football League in the 1920 close season. A centre forward in Army football, he scored on his debut for the Swans at left full back, made six consecutive league appearances, scoring two goals in one game against Norwich City, which included a penalty, and was then replaced by Wilf Milne. He missed the Swans' first Football League match at Portsmouth, but played in the club's debut home game in the League against Watford on 2nd September 1920. In October 1920, along with Robson and Ogley, he was suspended for a month for an alleged serious breach of training discipline. In August 1921 he was given a free transfer, joining Porth, then had spells with Third Division South sides Newport County and QPR in the Football League, before finishing his career in Yorkshire with Castleford Town. With both County and QPR he made appearances against the Swans between 1923 and 1925, scoring for County in a 4-1 home win in April 1924.

3. O'GORMAN, David (DAVE) John

Birthplace: Chester, 20/6/1972
Ht: 5ft-8ins, **Wt:** 11st-10lbs
Swans debut: v. Brighton & Hove Albion (h), 9/8/1997

Swansea City Career Statistics				
Season	League	FLC	AWS	FAWP
1997/98	12+22/5gls	2	1	5+2/1gls
1998/99	2+3	1		0+1
Total	14+25/5gls	3	1	5+3/1gls

Career:
Wrexham (from YTS in July 1990) lge 8+9
Northwich Victoria (loan in 4/12/1990) lge 3/2gls
Northwich Victoria (signed in July 1991) lge 7/1gls
Hyde United (signed in close season 1992)
Connah's Quay Nomads (signed in October 1992) lge 78/2gls
Barry Town (signed in June 1995) lge 36/5gls, UEFA 2+1/2gls
Swansea City (£30,000 signed in 8/8/1997)
Connah's Quay Nomads (signed in 12/2/1999)
Hellenic (South Africa in June 1999)
Connah's Quay Nomads
Oswestry (signed in June 2003)

Honours: League of Wales Champions–1996, 1997, North Wales Coast Rep. XI

Former Wrexham junior who graduated to the first team at the Racecourse, sampled loan appearances with Northwich Victoria, before signing for the club on a full time basis after being released by manager Brian Flynn. Following a period with Hyde United and Connah's Quay Nomads, he was signed by manager Eddie May for Barry Town in June 1995, when the club became the first club in the League of Wales to go full time professional. Winning two consecutive League of Wales Championships, and a runners-up medal in the 1996 Welsh Cup Final when they lost on penalties to Llansantffraid, Dave also played in the EUFA Cup competition with Barry Town, scoring two goals. A fleet footed wide midfielder, who possessed a lethal shot, he signed for the Swans in a combined £60,000 package with team mate Tony Bird, on the 8th August 1997, the day before the start of the season. Both players had impressed Swans manager Jan Molby in pre-season friendlies with the Swans. Along with Bird, he made his league debut in a 1-0 home win over Brighton & Hove Albion. Finding the net fairly regularly in his first season back in the Football League, off the field saw the club announce a takeover, and by the start of his second season Dave would be playing under his fourth Swans' manager in John Hollins. His second season at the Vetch Field saw him unable to break into the first team squad, and in February 1999 he rejoined Connah's Quay Nomads on a regular basis. At the end of the season he took up an offer to play in South Africa with Hellenic, and after returning to the U.K. started season 2003/04 with Oswestry Town in the League of Wales, and has since made appearances for Flint, Cymru Alliance side Lex XI and Rhyl. Since returning to the UK from South Africa he has been involved in a Garden Services Company in the Chester area.

4. O'LEARY, Kristian (KRIS) Denis

Birthplace: Port Talbot, 30/8/1977
Ht: 6ft-0ins, **Wt:** 13st-4lbs
Swans debut: v. Bradford City (a), 30/3/1996

Swansea City Career Statistics					
Season	League	FLC	FAC	AWS/LDV	FAWC
1995/96	1				
1996/97	9+3/1gls	1	1+1		
1997/98	25+4		1	1	4
1998/99	17+2/2gls		1	1+1	6
1999/2000	9+11	3	1		3/1gls
2000/01	22+2/2gls	2		3	2+2/1gls
2001/02	30+1/2gls	1	1	1	3
2002/03	29+4	1		1	
2003/04	28+6	1	4+1		1
2004/05	32/1gls	1	3/1gls	2	2
Total	202+33/8gls	10	12+2/1gls	9+1	21+2/2gls

Career:
Swansea City (from trainee in 1/7/1996)

Honours: Wales Sch, U-18, Third Division Champions–2000, West Wales Senior Cup Winner–1995, FAW Cup Winner–2005

Port Talbot Schoolboy who represented Afan Nedd and Wales Schoolboys prior to signing for the Swans as a YTS trainee, making his first team debut whilst still a second year trainee at Bradford City in March 1996 under manager Jan Molby. He made a number of appearances in his first season as a professional in midfield, scoring his first league goal at the Vetch Field in November 1996 against Torquay United. In May 1995 he was included in the Swans reserve side that beat Morriston Town in the West Wales Senior Cup Final. He failed to make the end of season Third Division Play Off Final against Northampton Town at Wembley in May 1997, but a few years later made a substitute appearance in the second leg of the Third Division semi-final Play Off match at Scunthorpe United in May 1999. Eventually settling into a central defensive role, either as a central defender, or in a three-man central defence, he gained a Third Division Championship medal in May 2000. During Nick Cusack's elevation to a managerial role at the start of the 2002/03 season, he was appointed captain, but also suffered a number of red cards. A strong, resolute tackler, with good aerial ability, Kristian has always given 100% commitment when playing for the Swans in whatever role he is asked to play in. In 2001 and 2002 he played in consecutive Welsh Premier Cup Finals for the Swans against Wrexham and Cardiff City respectively. Despite starting season 2003/04 in the Swans defensive line-up, it was soon evident that he did not figure as an automatic selection under Brian Flynn, although he made numerous appearances from the substitute's bench. He continued to show his versatility by playing in any defensive position, and towards the end of the season reverted to a midfield role which saw him being offered a new contract at the end of the season by new manager Kenny Jackett. Continuing the 2004/05 season in a midfield role, despite missing almost three months with a knee injury, by the end of the season after the Swans had clinched one of the automatic promotion places, and played in the FAW Cup Final defeat of Wrexham, he was voted 'Player of the Year.'

5. OLI, DENNIS Chiedozie

Birthplace: Newham, 28/1/1984
Ht: 6ft-0ins, **Wt:** 12st-4lbs
Swans debut: v. Northampton Town (h), 7/8/2004

Swansea City Career Statistics	
Season	League
2004/05	0+1
Total	0+1

Career:
QPR (from juniors in 24/10/2001) lge 8+15, FLC 0+1, FAC 1+2, Others 2+1
Gravesend (loan in 20/11/2003) Conf 5
Farnborough (loan in 13/2/2004) Conf 4
Swansea City (trial in July 2004, signed in 6/8/2004)
Cambridge United (signed in 10/9/2004) lge 4/1gls, Others 1
Grays Athletic (signed in November 2004)

Honours: Conference South Champions–2005, FA Trophy Winner–2005, England National XI

Young QPR frontrunner who came through the ranks at Loftus Road, making his league debut as substitute for Leroy Griffiths against Wigan Athletic on the 26th February 2002, making a further substitute appearance against Peterborough United a few weeks later. The next season after being given his first start against Swindon Town in mid-September, he played in the next thirteen league games, either from the start, or from the substitute's bench. He was released in May 2004 following the club's successful promotion to the Coca Cola Championship, with his first team opportunities limited at Loftus Road by the likes of Jamie Cureton, Tony Thorpe and Paul Furlong. Possessing a lot of pace, and a strong runner, he initially arrived at the Vetch Field on a trial basis, but after impressing in pre-season friendly matches, scorer of two goals in one game against Worcester City, he signed a monthly contract just prior to the start of the season. Capable of playing wide on the right, or as a central striker, he made his only appearance for the Swans as a second half substitute for Adrian Forbes in the opening league game of the 2004/05 season at the Vetch Field against Northampton Town. By the end of the month however, with his opportunities limited, he was not offered a new contract and was released. In early September he had a trial with Cambridge United, scoring on his arrival as a second half substitute in a mid-week friendly at St. Albans, and after signing a monthly contract with the 'U's', scored his first league goal twenty-four hours later at the Abbey Stadium against Mansfield Town. In mid-October he walked out on Cambridge United after the club had failed to improve on his week to week contract, linking up later with Conference South side Grays Athletic. By the end of March 2005, Grays Athletic had already secured the Conference South Championship, with Dennis featuring regularly on the scoresheet with fourteen league and cup goals, and in May gained an FA Trophy Cup Winners medal when they beat Hucknall Town on penalties at Villa Park. The same month also saw him included in the England National XI squad that played in the Four Nations Championship in Ireland.

6. OLSEN, Thomas (TOMMY) Bernard

Birthplace: Tirphil, Glam, 13/1/1913. **Died:** Swansea, JAS, 1969
Ht: 5ft-9ins, **Wt:** 10st-4lbs
Swans debut: v. Preston North End (a), 21/11/1931

Swansea Town Career Statistics			
Season	*League*	*FAC*	*WC*
1931/32	3		2/1gls
1932/33	22/5gls		1
1933/34	31/9gls	4	
1934/35	23/7gls		
1935/36	36/10gls	1	1
1936/37	21/5gls		
1937/38	22/4gls		1
1938/39	30/10gls	1	3/1gls
Total	188/50gls	6	8/2gls

Career:
Aberaman Juniors
New Tredegar
Swansea Town (signed in 22/1/1930)
Bury (£1,000 signed in 5/6/1939) lge 3

Honours: Wales Sch, West Wales Senior Cup Winner–1930, 1934

Former junior with the Swans with a Danish background who gained a Welsh Schoolboy cap in 1927, and who joined the Swans in January 1930 from New Tredegar. A week after signing he scored after just four minutes on his debut for the Swans reserve side at the Vetch Field against Luton Town. In October 1930 he was included in the Swans reserve side that beat Newport County in the West Wales Senior Cup Final, and four years later was included in the Swans reserve side that beat Llanelly in the final of the same competition. He had to wait until November 1931 before he made his league debut, at outside left instead of Dai Lewis, but from the 1933/34 season on he was to make his mark from the inside left position. He scored his first Swans goal during his first season against Merthyr in a Welsh Cup replay at the Vetch Field, three months after making his league debut. Scoring his first league goal in a 3-1 home win against Preston North End in December 1932, he became a consistent goalscorer for the Swans, up until he was transferred to Bury for £1,000 on the 5th June 1939. Teetotal, and a non-smoker, he scored his only hat-trick for the Swans at the Vetch Field against Hull City in April 1936. Despite being of slight build he was a hard working inside forward, who always gave 100%, and who was outstanding in heavy conditions. He gained a South Wales and Monmouthsire, and West Wales Cup medals with the Swans, and also played in a carried over Welsh Cup Final replay against Shrewsbury Town, in September 1938. At the end of season 1938/39 he was transfer listed at his own request, and signed for Bury in June 1939. A keen fisherman, he became a shopkeeper in Swansea after retiring from playing.

7. O'SULLIVAN, JOHN

Birthplace: Cork, 30/5/1922
Ht: 5ft-6½ins, **Wt:** 10st-7lbs
Swans debut: v. Bristol City (h), 17/1/1948

Swansea Town Career Statistics	
Season	*League*
1947/48	2
Total	2

Career:
Cork
Waterford
Swansea Town (signed in 7/1/1948)
Lovells Athletic
Llanelly (signed in 15/4/1950)
Haverfordwest (signed in August 1950)
Aldershot (signed in November 1951) lge 0

Honours: Army XI, League of Ireland XI

Following the appointment of Billy McCandless as Swans' manager in December 1947, his first signing in early January 1948 was outside left John O'Sullivan from Irish side Waterford. Earlier in his career he had played for Cork on the left wing, with O'Driscoll on the right wing. Apart from making representative appearances for the League of Ireland he had also played for an Army XI against the RAF. A diminutive player, he made his debut on the Swans right wing at the Vetch Field against Bristol City in a 6-1 win instead of Frank Scrine, who moved to the opposite flank in preference to WH Morris, and who also played in the next match at Reading. He failed to make any further appearances for the Swans, and after a spell with Lovells Athletic, joined Llanelly at the start of the 1949/50 season, joined Haverfordwest in August 1950, before returning to the Football League to join Aldershot. He failed to make an appearance for the Third Division South club.

8. OWEN, Robert (BOBBY)

Birthplace: Farnworth, Bolton, 17/10/1947
Ht: 5ft-10ins, **Wt:** 10st-7lbs
Swans debut: v. Grimsby Town (h), 17/3/1970

Swansea City Career Statistics	
Season	*League*
1969/70	5+1/1gls
Total	5+1/1gls

Career:
Bury (from apprentice in August 1965) lge 81+2/38gls
Manchester City (£35,000 signed in July 1968) lge 18+4/3gls
Swansea City (loan in March 1970)
Carlisle United (£20,000 signed in June 1970) lge 185+19/51gls
Northampton Town (loan in 28/10/1976) lge 5
Workington (loan in 2/12/1976) lge 8/2gls
Bury (loan in 23/2/1977) lge 4/1gls
Doncaster Rovers (signed in July 1977) lge 74+3/22gls

Honours: Charity Shield Winner–1968

Striker signed on loan from Manchester City in March 1970 by manager Roy Bentley to re-inforce the Swans promotion push from the Fourth Division, and who scored just one goal during his end of season loan spell at the Vetch Field. A lively front runner with good skill, he had earlier in his career made a name for himself as a goalscorer with Bury, prior to his £35,000 transfer to Manchester City in July 1968. With the Swans unable to afford to make his transfer permanent, he returned to Maine Road with City, but within a couple of weeks of the end of the season had joined Carlisle United. Captain of Bolton Schoolboys earlier in his career, after joining Bury from school, he made his league debut at the age of seventeen and a half in April 1965, and became another example of the flourishing youth policy at Gigg Lane at the time. Despite a relegation season during his first full term as a professional, the following season Bury bounced back, with Bobby scoring twenty-five goals, and a summer transfer to Manchester City. Making his debut for City in a 6-1 demolition of West Bromwich Albion in the Charity Shield, he struggled to command a regular place in the City line-up, which resulted in him later joining Carlisle United after his loan period at the Vetch Field. At Brunton Park he gained a good reputation as a consistent goalscorer, missing just four league games during the season when United gained promotion to the First Division, scoring eleven league goals.

Despite relegation after just one season in the top flight, and later having loan spells with Northampton Town, Workington and Bury, he signed for Doncaster Rovers in July 1977. Reverting to a sweeper role at Belle Vue, he finished top scorer in his second season, and was twice voted 'Player of the Year'. He was released at the end of the 1978/79 season, going on to play non-league football with Gainsborough and two spells with Retford Town before retiring from the game. Now living in Radcliffe, after a period as a licensee and a bowling club manager, he is currently working as a fork lift truck driver at Associated Plastics in Bolton.

P

1. PALMER, Desmond (DES) Frederick

Birthplace: Swansea, 23/9/1931
Ht: 5ft-9ins, **Wt:** 11st-7lbs
Swans debut: v. Hull City (a), 13/9/1952

Swansea Town Career Statistics			
Season	League	FAC	WC
1952/53	6/1gls	1	
1953/54	11/2gls		1/1gls
1954/55	5/2gls		1
1955/56	4/2gls		1/1gls
1956/57	30/18gls	1/2gls	4/2gls
1957/58	11/4gls		
1958/59	17/9gls	1	
Total	84/38gls	3/2gls	7/4gls

Career:
Swansea Town (signed from juniors in April 1950)
Liverpool (£4,000 signed in 3/3/1959) lge 0
Johannesburg Ramblers, South Africa (signed in 1960)
Derby County (signed in June 1961) lge 18/6gls
Wellington Town (signed in July 1962)
Slavia Melbourne, Australia (signed in 1963)
Yugal, Sydney, Australia (signed in 1964)
Llanelly (signed in May 1966)

Honours: Wales Full–3, Craven 'A' Cup Winner 1964, West Wales Senior Cup Winner–1957, Football Combination Second Division Champions–1955

Joining the Swans from the ground staff in 1950, the front runner took some time to establish himself in the Swans first team line-up, despite being a consistent goalscorer in the club's reserve side. Born in Crymlyn Burrows, after leaving Jersey Marine school at the age of fourteen, and having played no schoolboy football apart from playing for Crymlyn Burrows Y.M.C.A, he made his league debut in September 1952 at inside right against Hull City, played in the next five league games, scoring his first goal in his fifth match against Everton, and played just the one more game in the FA Cup at Newcastle United that season. Season 1954/55 saw him make regular appearances in the Swans' reserve side that won the Football Combination Second Division Championship. The 1955/56 and 1956/57 season saw him play in two consecutive Welsh Cup Final defeats against Cardiff City and Wrexham respectively, scoring two goals in the Cardiff City final defeat. In May 1957 he played in the Swans side that beat Haverfordwest to win the West Wales Senior Cup Final. Not a big man, he had a great eye for goal, a good first touch and distribution. An opportunist, he was also very quick over a short distance, and possibly could have added his name to the Swansea 'Hall of Greats' if it had not been for the injury he sustained before he had made a first team appearance at Anfield with Liverpool, following his transfer in March 1959 for £4,000, plus wing half Roy Saunders. The 1956/57 season saw him joint top goalscorer with Harry Griffiths on 18 league goals, and on the 26th May 1957 he was selected to play his first international match for Wales in Prague against Czechoslovakia. His next international appearance saw him score a hat-trick in a 4-1 win over East Germany at Ninian Park in September of the same year. Unable to establish himself following his injury at Anfield, he then played for South African side Johannesburg Ramblers, managed by former Liverpool goalkeeper Doug Rudham, before returning to make league appearances for Derby County, and non-league Wellington Town, before playing in Australia with Slavia Melbourne and Yugal, Sydney. At the end of his first season with Slavia he scored a hat-trick in the 3-2 Craven 'A' Cup Final win over Polonia, and twelve months later, this time with Yugal, Sydney, played in a losing end of season Cup Final. He returned to South Wales in May 1966, taking over as player manager with Llanelly, but twelve months later resigned his position after refusing to take a drop in wages, and took up employment with the Co-operative Insurance Company. Having qualified as a coach earlier in his career, for four years he was also a staff coach with the Football Association of Wales, when Mike Smith was the manager. A keen cricketer, during the summer months he played cricket for Elba in the local Swansea League.

2. PARK, COLIN Sidney John

Birthplace: Swansea, 8/2/1945
Ht: 5ft-8½ins, **Wt:** 11st-4lbs
Swans debut: v. Scunthorpe United (a), 12/9/1963

Career:
Swansea Town (signed in 1960)
Ton Pentre (signed in close season 1965)

Lovells Athletic
Ammanford
Port Tennant Colts

Swansea Town Career Statistics	
Season	League
1963/64	1
Total	1

Honours: Wales Yth–4, Welsh League First Division Champions–1962

Former Danygraig Schoolboy, who joined the Swans groundstaff in 1960, stayed part-time with the Swans learning his trade as a carpenter, and who made his only first team appearance for the Swans at Scunthorpe United in September 1963 as a replacement for Irishman Noel Dwyer. At the time competition for the goalkeeper's jersey at the Vetch Field included Dwyer and the veteran Johnny King. During season 1961/62 he made appearances in the Swans' Welsh League side that won their respective Championship, for the first time in eleven years. Capped four times at youth level for Wales, he played against George Best during one international appearance. He left the Vetch Field playing staff in 1965, joining Welsh League side Ton Pentre, but then signed for Lovells Athletic, linking up with a number of former Swans' players who had played alongside him in the Swans' Welsh League side, Mal Gilligan, Alan Wilkins and Brayley Reynolds. Following the closure of the Lovells sweet factory, and the ground taken over, resulting in the folding of the football club, he joined Welsh League side Ammanford Town, managed by former Swans wing half Roy Saunders. By this time he had taken employment with the Post Office in Swansea, and following a couple of appearances for Swansea Senior League side Port Tennant Colts he retired as a player, although he did represent the Post Office side on occasions. They initially would not let an ex-professional play in the side, but then relented after the rules were changed.

3. PARLANE, DEREK James

Birthplace: Helensburgh, 5/5/1953
Ht: 6ft-0ins, **Wt:** 11st-10lbs
Swans debut: v. Bradford City (a), 26/1/1985

Swansea City Career Statistics			
Season	League	WC	FRT
1984/85	21/3gls	2	4
Total	21/3gls	2	4

Career:
Queens Park
Glasgow Rangers (£160,000 signed in 1/4/1970) SL 202/80gls
Leeds United (£160,000 signed in 6/3/1980) lge 45+5/10gls
Bulova, Hong Kong (signed in season 1982/83)
Manchester City (signed in August 1983) lge 47+1/20gls
Burnley
Swansea City (signed in 17/1/1985)
North Shore, Hong Kong
Racing Jet, Belgium
Rochdale (signed in December 1986) lge 42/10gls
Airdrie (signed in December 1987) lge 9/4gls
Macclesfield Town (signed start of 1987/88 season)
    Conf 9+19/2gls
Curzon Ashton

Honours: Scotland U-21–1, U-23–5, Full–12, Scottish First Division Champions–1975, 1976, 1978, Scottish F.A. Cup Winners–1973, 1979, Scottish League Cup Winners–1976, 1978, 1979, Scottish League Representative XI–2

Experienced Scottish international striker signed by Swans manager John Bond who arrived at the Vetch Field at the same time as Paul Price, Ray McHale and Gary Williams, with all players making their Swans debuts in the same game at Bradford City, with Parlane scoring on his debut in a 1-1 draw. Joining Glasgow Rangers from Queens Park, he won three Scottish First Division Championships (1975, 1976, 1978), two Scottish F.A. Cups (1973, 1979), a finalist in 1977, three Scottish League Cups (1976, 1978, 1979), played for the Scottish League Representative side on two occasions, and was top goalscorer in a season on four occasions prior to his transfer to Leeds United in March 1980. He also scored in the semi-final win over Bayern Munich in the 1971/72 European Cup Winners Cup competition, but did not play in the final which Rangers won. Following his move to Elland Road, despite scoring on his debut against Southampton on the 8th March 1980 in a 2-0 home win and two top ten finishes in the First Division, his third season with United saw the club relegated to the Second Division. The opening match of the 1981/82 season saw Leeds open the season at the Vetch Field, and despite Parlane opening the scoring, the rest is history as far as Swans supporters are concerned. An equaliser from Charles was followed by a Bob Latchford hat-trick, and an outstanding individual effort from Alan Curtis. Making just one substitute appearance the following season, Derek signed for Hong Kong side Bulova, returning to the Football League in August 1983 to join Manchester City. Top goalscorer with sixteen league goals during season 1983/84, with City just missing out on promotion, within a couple of months after the start of the following season he had joined Burnley, but after failing to make an appearance, signed for the Swans in January 1985. Missing just the one league game after making his debut for the Swans, although he scored just three goals, he was an effective front runner, and was a critical influence in the Swans avoiding relegation to the Fourth Division. He refused the offer of a contract with the Swans at the end of the season returning to Hong Kong, then had a spell in Belgium with Racing Jet, before returning to the Football League to sign for Rochdale. After a couple of months back in the Scottish League with Airdrie, linking up with former Leeds United team mate Gordon McQueen, who was manager of the club, he returned south of the border to play for Conference side Macclesfield Town prior to the start of the 1987/88 season, then finished his playing career with Curzon Ashton, and concentrating on his sportswear agency based in Wilmslow.

4. PARRY, Brinley John (JACK)

Birthplace: Pontardawe, 11/1/1924
Ht: 5ft-9ins, **Wt:** 12st-0lbs
Swans debut: v. West Bromwich Albion (h), 31/8/1946

Swansea Town Career Statistics			
Season	*League*	*FAC*	*WC*
1946/47	13		
1947/48	26		
1948/49	22	2	2
1949/50	19	2	1
1950/51	16	1	1
Total	96	5	4

Career:
Ynystawe United (signed in 1939)
Clydach United
Swansea Town (signed in 12/6/1946)
Ipswich Town (£750 signed in 15/8/1951) lge 138
Chelmsford City (signed in July 1955)
Marconi FC (signed in 1960)

Honours: Wales Full–1, Third Division South Champions–1949, 1954, London Combination Cup Winners–1947, 1950, West Wales Senior Cup Winner–1949, 1950, Welsh League First Division Champions–1951

A fearless goalkeeper who started his senior career initially with Ynystawe United in 1939 prior to joining Clydach United, and who, after joining the Swans, made a remarkable recovery after a serious injury against Notts. County during the 1947/48 season. He made a couple of appearances in Regional War Time football for the Swans, but signed for the Swans in June 1946, making his league debut at the start of season 1946/47, the first season after the war. An agile goalkeeper, who was a good 'angle' man, he made up for his lack of stature with good positioning sense, and bravery, going in where it hurt. He was also an intelligent player who worked hard on positioning and shot saving in training. He attended Clydach School, and with no football played in school, played rugby for Clydach Schools XV in the morning, and in the afternoon played for Clydach Boys Club. On leaving school he started an apprenticeship as a bricklayer, working for local construction company Thomas Howells, and after retiring as a professional footballer, returned to his trade and worked for over twenty years in the London area. At the Vetch Field he competed with Turner and Canning during the Third Division South Championship season of 1948/49, making twenty-two league appearances, all coming during the first half of the season. In June 1947, and in May 1950 he was a member of the Swans reserve side that beat both Arsenal and Southend United to win the London Combination Cup Finals. His last season at the Vetch Field saw him make regular appearances in the Swans side that won the Welsh League First Division Championship. Played in consecutive West Wales Senior Cup Final successes in 1949 and 1950. Following the emergence of young Johnny King, by the end of season 1950/51, with his first team opportunities limited, he was transferred to Ipswich Town for £750. He played his part in Ipswich Town's Third Division South Championship winning season of 1953/54, being one of five players who were ever present during the season, and the following season played against the Swans for Ipswich, along with Feeney, in a 6-1 defeat at the Vetch Field. His only international appearance for Wales

came on the 21st October 1950 at Ninian Park against Scotland in a 3-1 defeat. Joining Southern League side Chelmsford City in July 1955, he finished his playing career with Marconi FC, making a dozen appearances for the side managed by former Swans' and Ipswich Town player Fred Jones.

5. PASCOE, COLIN James

Birthplace: Port Talbot, 9/4/1965
Ht: 5ft-10ins, **Wt:** 12st-0lbs
Swans debut: v. Brighton & Hove Albion (h), 1/3/1983

Swansea City Career Statistics					
Season	*League*	*FLC*	*FAC*	*WC*	*FRT/AGT*
1982/83	4+3/1gls			3+1	
1983/84	29+3/2gls	2	1	4+1/2gls	
1984/85	41/9gls	2/1gls	2	5/4gls	2
1985/86	18+1/3gls	3/1gls	1		1
1986/87	41/11gls	2/1gls	3/1gls		2/1gls
1987/88	34/13gls	2	2/1gls	2/1gls	2
1992/93	15/4gls	2		1	
1993/94	31+2/5gls	4/1gls	2	5/1gls	7/2gls
1994/95	32+3/5gls	3+1/1gls		3	2/1gls
1995/96	9+4/1gls		1		1+1
Total	254+16/54gls	20+1/5gls	12/2gls	23+2/8gls	17+1/4gls

Career:
Swansea City (from apprentice in 12/4/1983)
Sunderland (£70,000 signed in 25/3/1988) lge 116+10/22gls, FLC 12/3gls, FAC 4+2, Others 5
Swansea City (loan in 24/7/1992)
Swansea City (£70,000 signed in 1/8/1993)
Blackpool (trial in 29/3/1996) lge 0+1
Golden FC, Hong Kong
Merthyr Tydfil (signed in September 1996)
Carmarthen Town

Honours: Wales Sch, Yth, U–21–4, Full–10, Welsh Cup Winner–1983, AutoGlass Trophy Winner–1994, West Wales Senior Cup Winner–1987

A product of the Afan Nedd schoolboy side who graduated as an apprentice at the Vetch Field to make his debut as substitute for the injured John Mahoney against Brighton in the First (Premiership) Division at the Vetch Field in March 1983. Ironically, he finished his career under Mahoney in a player coaching role at Carmarthen Town, prior to joining the youth set up at Cardiff City shortly after the start of the 1998/99 season. A talented left sided winger during his youth team years, he graduated to a front line striker, then to an effective central midfielder, who was capable of not only scoring goals, but also sharing in the graft in midfield. Seven days after his substitute appearance, he made his first start for the Swans in a Welsh Cup semi-final, first leg tie at Colwyn Bay. He also played in both legs of the Welsh Cup Final later in season against Wrexham. Prior to the start of the 1984/85 season he gained his first international cap for Wales, playing in Trondheim on the 6th June 1984 against Norway, followed by his second appearance on the 10th June 19184 in Tel Aviv against Israel. His other ten international appearances for Wales came during his career with Sunderland. The 1984/85 season saw him joint top goalscorer with Dean Saunders, but midway through the 1985/86 season he suffered his first major injury during his career, suffering a broken leg in a Vetch Field First Round of the FA Cup game against Leyton Wingate. In May 1987 he was included in the Swans side that beat Briton Ferry Athletic to win the West Wales Senior Cup. Forging a good understanding with Sean McCarthy, with the Swans contesting a Play Off place in March 1988, a £70,000 transfer was secured to Sunderland, with Pascoe scoring four goals in nine games as the club clinched the Third Division Championship. Despite a 1-0 defeat in the 1989 Second Division Play Off Final at Wembley against Swindon Town, financial irregularities at Swindon saw Sunderland claim their place in the First Division, and after a couple of seasons in top flight football, he rejoined the Swans on a three month loan transfer prior to the start of the 1992/93 season. Unfortunately, despite a successful loan spell, a transfer fee could not be agreed between the two clubs and he returned to Roker Park. However, by the start of the next season he had rejoined the Swans for a £70,000 fee, and in his first season back at the Vetch Field saw the club win its first major cup at Wembley, beating Huddersfield Town in the 1994 AutoGlass Trophy Final. A succession of ankle ligament problems during the 1995/96 season saw Colin have his contract cancelled in February 1996, joining Blackpool on a trial basis. With a change of management at Bloomfield Road, and no offer of a contract Colin returned to South Wales, going to Hong Kong for a short period to play for Golden FC, before returning to the UK in September 1996 to sign for Merthyr Tydfil, and working part-time in Bridgend Recreation Centre. After one season at Penydarren Park, he joined League of Wales side Carmarthen Town, managed by his former Swans team-mate John Mahoney. He was influential in defender Mark Delaney signing for Cardiff City from Carmarthen Town, and in August 1998 Colin was offered the position of youth coach at Ninian Park by manager Frank Burrows. At the end of season 2003/04, Colin left his post as Youth Team Manager at Ninian Park with Cardiff City, and in late July 2004 was appointed First Team Coach with League of Wales side Port Talbot. Colin returned to the Vetch Field in early September 2004 on a part-time basis, assisting manager Kenny Jackett on the training ground while physio Richie Evans was away working to become a chartered physiotherapist, and in late March 2005 he joined the Swans' coaching staff on a full time basis.

6. PASSMORE, Edward (ERNIE)

Birthplace: Moorsley, 28/4/1922. **Died:** Durham Central, 5/12/1988
Swans debut: v. Tottenham Hotspur (h), 21/9/1946

Swansea Town Career Statistics		
Season	League	WC
1946/47	6/2gls	1
Total	6/2gls	1

Career:
Portsmouth (amateur)
Swansea Town (signed in February 1944)
Gateshead (signed in April 1947) lge 41/26gls

Guildford City (signed in August 1950)
Kidderminster Harriers (signed in January 1952)

Centre forward, previously an amateur with Portsmouth who signed for the Swans in June 1946 after being demobilised from the Forces, making his league debut in September at the Vetch Field against Tottenham Hotspur, taking the place of Frank Squires, with Trevor Ford moving to the inside right position. Playing in the next league game, he then had to wait until mid-February before his next appearance, where he scored two goals against Newport County. A consistent goalscorer in the Swans reserve side, he was unable to command a regular place in the Swans starting line-up, and in April 1947 signed for Third Division North side Gateshead. He made his debut for Gateshead in a 1-0 defeat of Rochdale at the end of the 1946/47 season. His first full season saw him make occasional appearances through the season, scoring his only goal in a 3-2 win at Hull in March 1948. Starting the 1948/49 season as the number one choice at centre forward, he played in the first thirteen games, scoring seven goals, returning to action at the end of the season after a spell on the sidelines. The 1949/50 season saw him score sixteen goals from the first thirteen games, scoring in six consecutive matches, including four goals in a home 7-1 win over Halifax Town, three goals in a 3-0 away win at Chester, and five goals in a 5-3 win over Hartlepools United. He left the club after a home defeat by Mansfield Town, joining Southern League club Guildford. He later made non-league appearances for Kidderminster Harriers, Stafford Rangers and Shotton CW.

7. PATON, Thomas (TOMMY) Gracie

Birthplace: Saltcoats, Ayrshire, 22/12/1918. **Died:** Folkestone, 14/1/1991
Ht: 5ft-10ins, **Wt:** 11st-4lbs
Swans debut: v. Norwich City (a), 15/10/1938

Swansea Town Career Statistics	
Season	League
1938/39	6
Total	6

Career:
Ardeer Recreation (amateur signed in July 1936)
Wolverhampton Wanderers (signed professional in June 1937) lge 0
Portsmouth (signed in August 1937)
Swansea Town (signed in October 1938)
Bournemouth & Boscombe Athletic (signed in February 1939) lge 49/9gls
Watford (£1,000 signed in January 1948) lge 141/1gls, FAC 8
Folkestone (signed in August 1948)

Failed to make a first team appearance for Wolverhampton Wanderers after travelling south from Scottish junior side Ardeer Recreation, he joined the Swans in October 1938, making his debut as a replacement at inside right for Idris Lewis in mid-October 1938 against Norwich City. Playing in four consecutive games, he made just two more appearances before signing for Bournemouth in February 1939. A good passer of the ball who preferred the carpet pass, rather than lofting the ball, he had a body swerve reminiscent of McPherson. Playing for Bournemouth before and after the war, in the first match of the 1947/48 season he scored the only goal for Bournemouth in a 1-0 defeat of the Swans. Later joining Third Division South side Watford he made almost 150 league appearances for the club before signing for Folkestone, where he remained until the late 1950's. Joining Watford initially as an inside forward, he settled down at wing half, later taking over the captaincy. In the late 1950's he was also a scout for Sheffield Wednesday. During the war he made guest appearances for Tottenham Hotspur (October 1940), Queens Park Rangers (1941/42), Manchester City (1942/43) and Leeds United (September 1943), As a wartime officer in Bomber Command he was taken prisoner after being shot down near Heidelburg. He is the son of Tom, a former player with Derby County and Sheffield United, and his brother captained Motherwell in the 1951 Scottish F.A. Cup Final.

8. PATTIMORE, HERBERT Alfred

Birthplace: Bedwellty, JFM, 1908
Ht: 5ft-10½ins, **Wt:** 11st-6lbs
Swans debut: v. Colwyn Bay (a), WC–4, 24/2/1926

Swansea Town Career Statistics		
Season	League	WC
1925/26		2
1926/27		
1927/28		
1928/29	2	
Total	2	2

Career:
Blaenavon United
Swansea Town (trial in January 1926, signed in February 1926)
Llanelly (signed in season 1929/30)
Epsom Town (signed in October 1930)

Arrived at the Vetch Field on a trial basis in mid-January 1926 from Blaenavon United, scoring on his debut for the Swans in a Welsh League match at the Vetch Field against Pembroke Dock. The inside forward made his first team debut a month later, in what was predominately a reserve team line-up in a Welsh Cup tie at Colwyn Bay at the end of February, playing in the replay a couple of weeks later. He had to wait until the 1928/29 season before making his league debut, on the 6th October at Stoke City, this time at left full back instead of the experienced Wilf Milne. His only other league match for the Swans came in the next league game against Grimsby Town at the Vetch Field, again as a replacement for Milne. On the 8th February 1929 the *Daily Post* reported that he had undergone a knee and cartilage operation, and had been out of action for some time previously. Released by the Swans in May 1929, he made appearances for Llanelly during season 1929/30 before signing for non-league side Epsom Town.

9. PAUL, ROY

Birthplace: Ton Pentre, 18/4/1920. **Died:** Treorchy 21/5/2002
Ht: 5ft-10ins, **Wt:** 12st-0lbs
Swans debut: v. West Bromwich Albion (h), 31/8/1946

Swansea Town Career Statistics			
Season	League	FAC	WC
1946/47	40/3gls	2	
1947/48	39	1	1
1948/49	41/1gls	2	4
1949/50	39/7gls	2	4
Total	159/11gls	7	9

Career:
Ton Boys Club
Swansea Town (signed in October 1938)
Manchester City (£19,500 signed in 18/7/1950) lge 270/9gls
Worcester City (signed in June 1957)
Brecon Corinthians (signed in February 1960)
Garw Athletic (signed in August 1960)

Honours: Wales Full–33, F.A. Cup Winner–1956, Welsh Cup Winner–1950, Third Division South Champions–1949, Regional League Cup Winner–1943

As a young boy Roy Paul wasn't considered good enough for his school team despite having had trials, writing in his autobiography, "I had three trials in the playground at the little school of Bronllwyn in my native village of Gelli Pentre, and in each trial I failed." One of twelve children, he was destined for the pits, and in a way was rescued by the war, and by his football and athletic talents. Undoubtedly one of the stars of Welsh football in the 1950's, he won 33 caps between 1949 and 1956, captaining his country with distinction, a classy wing half, who played for the Swans in a number of positions, before settling into an international quality wing half. He made his first appearance for Wales against Scotland on the 23rd October 1948, playing a further eight times for Wales whilst on the staff at the Vetch Field. A good reader of the game, besides being a good passer of the ball, he was also an inspirational player during his career. He initially signed for the Swans in November 1938 from Ton Boys Club, his only senior club, played 84 games for the Swans in Regional Football following the outbreak of the Second World War, and made seven appearances in League South (The Victory League) following his return from India, where he had been a P.T. Instructor in the Royal Marines. Towards the end of the 1942/43 season he played in a Regional League West Cup Final win over two legs against Lovells Athletic, scoring in the second leg at the Vetch Field. Such was his skill and versatility earlier in his career with the Swans he played at left half, inside left, right half, centre half and centre forward. Making his Football League debut for the Swans in the opening game of the first season after the war against West Bromwich Albion, by the time he had joined Manchester City in July 1950 had missed just nine league matches in four seasons. During that period he had made 41 league appearances in the Swans Third Division South Championship season, played in the Welsh Cup Final win over Wrexham, and also gained his first international cap for Wales. In April 1949 he was included in an F.A.W. Touring party that played international matches against Portugal, Belgium and Switzerland, and in May 1949 he also played in the Welsh Cup Final defeat by Merthyr at Ninian Park. He scored his first league goal for the Swans at Bury in his debut season, also scoring in the next league fixture at the Vetch Field against Luton Town. In an effort to better the £12 maximum wage for footballers, Roy Paul, and several other UK players, went to Bogota, in Colombia, to play for FC Millionarios of Bogota, but he soon returned as quickly as he had departed, only to be admonished by the F.A. Just a few months previous to his going to Bogota, he had been in receipt of a £750 Benefit from the

Swans. On July 18, 1950, City bought him for the then considerable sum of £19,500, despite a late offer from Manchester United of £20,000. He played his first game for the Sky Blues at Maine Road in August 1950, helping City win promotion to the top division in his first season. His manager at Maine Road, Les McDowall said after his transfer, that he was the greatest bargain ever, the best deal he had ever done. He captained City at Wembley on two consecutive seasons, in 1955 when they lost to Newcastle United, and the following year (known as the Trautmann final), when they beat Birmingham City. He remained with City, as Captain, for seven years, leaving in 1957, after 293 League and Cup appearances, to sign for Worcester City, captaining the side that beat Liverpool in the F.A. Cup, Third Round in January 1959. Had a short spell as player manager from September to December 1958 before asking to revert to a player's contract. With City he scored three goals from one hundred and twenty-four appearances, and was released after requesting a transfer following an internal club dispute early in 1960, joining Brecon Corinthians and later Garw Athletic as player manager for the 1960/61 season. For a time he had a sports shop in Manchester and returned to oversee the City Social Club, but the 1960's found him short of money and driving a lorry, and, his last years were plagued with ill-health, including the cruel ravages of Alzheimers, prior to his death in May 2002. His nephew, Alan Curtis, carried on the family tradition at the Vetch Field during the seventies and eighties.

10. PAYNE, Donald (DONNY)

Birthplace: Swansea, 18/11/1950
Ht: 5ft-10ins, **Wt:** 10st-10lbs
Swans debut: v. Bolton Wanderers (h),12/2/1972

Swansea City Career Statistics	
Season	League
1971/72	11
Total	11

Career:
Swansea City (signed from juniors in 1967, professional in December 1970)
Torquay United (signed in June 1972) lge 0
Newport County (signed in August 1973) lge 32
Merthyr Tydfil (signed in close season 1975)
Haverfordwest (signed in close season 1981)
Merthyr Tydfil (signed in September 1981)
Haverfordwest (signed in close season 1983)

Honours: Wales Yth–2

Born in the Dyfatty area of Swansea, Donny attended Dyfatty, Hafod, Mayhill and Oxford Street Schools, played for Swansea Boys Club at U-15 level, and Ragged School at U-17 level, signing for the Swans as an amateur at the age of sixteen, and represented Swansea Schoolboys as a goalkeeper, as well as at left half back. After leaving school he worked for Hughes & Morgan Timber Yard, later at Viscose for six months, prior to signing as a professional for the Swans after consistent displays

in the club's Football Combination and Welsh League sides. Despite not being the tallest of goalkeepers, Donny proved to be an extremely brave, and agile goalkeeper. In 1968 he made two appearances for the Welsh Youth side against Northern Ireland and Scotland. Competing with the experienced Tony Millington and young Dai Davies, before his transfer to Everton, for the goalkeeper's jersey, Donny made all his Swans' appearances during season 1971/72 under manager Roy Bentley. Earlier in his career he had a trial with Cardiff City as a youngster and also had an offer to show his paces with Wolverhampton Wanderers, but he eventually chose the Swans. After suffering a nasty injury in the last Welsh League game of season 1971/72, he was released by the Swans, signing for Torquay United, but after failing to make an appearance during his one season at Plainmoor, joined Newport County, where he contested the goalkeeper's jersey with John Macey. He made just three league appearances in his first season, but had his best spell in season 1974/75 making 29 league appearances for County. After two seasons at Somerton Park, Donny had a six season association with Merthyr Tydfil, before joining Micky Lenihan at Haverfordwest. After just a couple of appearances he returned to Penydarren Park in September 1981, remaining with the club until the 1983 close season when he rejoined Haverfordwest. In 1986 he finished his playing career as an outfield player with Swansea Senior League side Kilvey Athletic. After his retirement as a player, Donny started a junior side (Under-8), Port Tennant Stars, remaining with the club as they progressed through each age group to the Swansea Senior League. He is currently manager of North End Stars, an amalgamation of North End and Port Tennant Stars. Since leaving the professional game he has worked in the building industry, currently working as a plasterer with Edmunds and Webster in Swansea. During the summer months he was a keen cricketer with the Post Office and North End in the Swansea Industrial and Centre Leagues.

11. PAYNE, Irving (JOE) Ernest Henry

Birthplace: Briton Ferry, 29/6/1921. **Died:** Daventry, 12/9/2001
Ht: 5ft-9ins, **Wt:** 10st-6lbs
Swans debut: v. Nottingham Forest (h), 9/9/1946

Swansea Town Career Statistics			
Season	League	FAC	WC
1946/47	23/5gls	2/1gls	1
1947/48	6		
1948/49	23/8gls		2
Total	52/13gls	2/1gls	3

Career:
Briton Ferry Athletic
Swansea Town (signed in July 1938)

Newport County (£5,000 signed in 13/10/1949) lge 12/1gls
Scunthorpe United (signed in July 1950) lge 40/2gls
Northampton Town (signed in August 1951) lge 32/6gls,
   FAC 1/1gls

Honours: Third Division South Champions–1949,
Western Command Representative XI

'Joe' first joined the Swans as a groundstaff boy at the age of 16 from local side Briton Ferry Athletic, and played for the Swans Junior side during season 1937/38, making occasional reserve team appearances prior to WW2 being declared. His last season with the Juniors saw him score twenty-one goals in a side that won the Gwalia and Bryn Trophies, and also finish runners-up in the Gwalia Senior League. Making a number of appearances for the Swans in Regional Football matches during the war, he also made guest appearances for Wrexham (1942/43), Chester (1941/42), York City (1945/46) and Lovells Athletic before signing up for active service, taking part in the D-Day landings in Normandy, and was 25 years of age when he returned to the field during the first season of Football League Football in 1946. He made his Football League debut at outside right against Nottingham Forest in September 1946, the first season after the war. A popular player with the Swans fans, he was capable of playing on either flank, as well as at centre forward. He scored his first Swans goal in his second league game, against Barnsley in October 1946. The Championship winning season of 1948/49 saw Joe figure in 23 league games, scoring eight league goals, play in the Welsh Cup Final defeat by Merthyr at the end of the season at Ninian Park, and also coming close to making an appearance for Wales at International level. He joined Third Division South side Newport County in October 1949 for a fee in the region of £5,000, but by the start of season 1950/51 had signed for Scunthorpe United. He appeared in Scunthorpe's first ever football league match against Shrewsbury Town in August 1950, joining Northampton Town twelve months later. The scorer of a nineteen minute hat-trick for the 'Cobblers' against one of his former clubs, Newport County, on retiring from the game he spent many years on the backroom staff at the County Ground as youth team coach, reserve team coach, and in 1964 as first team coach helping the club to reach the First Division. As the club fell back down the divisions, players and staff being released, Joe left his position as trainer with Northampton in May 1968 after serving the club on and off the field for seventeen years, later taking over as manager of non-league side Rushton Town in mid-January 1969. Later he also had a short spell as manager of Banbury Town. He died after a long illness in September 2001.

12. PEAKE, DUDLEY John

Birthplace: Swansea, 26/10/1934
Ht: 5ft-11ins, **Wt:** 12st-4lbs
Swans debut: v. Plymouth Argyle (h), 21/4/1956

Swansea Town Career Statistics			
Season	League	FAC	WC
1955/56	2		
1956/57	33/2gls	1	5
1957/58	22	1	1
Total	57/2gls	2	6

Career:
Townhill Community Centre FC
Swansea Town (amateur signed in February 1956, professional
   in 17/4/1956)
Newport County (£2,000 signed in 24/6/1958) lge 129
Romford (signed in close season 1963)
Merthyr Tydfil (signed in 1964)

Honours: West Wales Senior Cup Winner–1957

Signed from local Swansea Senior League side Townhill Community Centre initially as an amateur, his progress was such that after just four Welsh League games and half a dozen Combination appearances for the Swans he signed professional and made his league debut at the Vetch Field against Plymouth Argyle as a replacement for the injured Tom Kiley. Prior to signing professional he had been employed by an Electrical Goods Company in Swansea. He started season 1956/57 as first choice centre half, later playing in the last 28 league games of the season, also appearing in the end of season Welsh Cup Final defeat by Wrexham. In May 1957 he played in the Swans side that beat Haverfordwest to win the West Wales Senior Cup Final. That season also saw him score his first league goal at West Ham United in a 2-1 victory for the Swans. By March 1958 his first team appearances became limited at the Vetch Field following the signing of Swansea born Welsh international defender Ray Daniel, and in June 1958 he was transferred to Third Division side Newport County for £2,000. He made over one hundred league appearances for County before signing for Romford in the 1963 close season, but after failing to make an appearance returned to South Wales to join Merthyr Tydfil in 1964.

13. PEARCE, CYRIL

Birthplace: Shirebrook, 28/1/1908. **Died:** Mansfield, June 1990
Ht: 5ft-10½ins, **Wt:** 11st-0lbs
Swans debut: v. Leeds United (h), 29/8/1931

Swansea Town Career Statistics			
Season	League	FAC	WC
1931/32	40/35gls	1	7/5gls
1937/38	15/8gls		
Total	55/43gls	1	7/5gls

Career:
Shirebrook (signed in 1923)
Warsop Main Byron (signed in 1926)
Staveley Town (signed in 1927)
Shirebrook (signed in March 1928)
Wolverhampton Wanderers (signed in June 1929) lge 0
Newport County (signed in May 1930) lge 27/22gls
Swansea Town (£250 signed in 6/6/1931)
Charlton Athletic (£2,250 signed in 10/6/1932) lge 68/52gls,
   FAC 7
Swansea Town (£400 signed in 3/5/1937)
Frickley Colliery (signed in July 1938)
Shirebrook Welfare

Honours: Welsh Cup Winner–1932, Derbyshire Cup Medal

Learned his football as a right winger with Carter Lane Boys School in Shirebrook, winning Derbyshire County schoolboys honours, and was unlucky not to be selected for England Schoolboys. Making his Midland League debut for Shirebrook at the age of 15, he moved on to Staveley, and in 1929 joined Wolverhampton Wanderers. Failing to make an appearance for Wolves he joined Newport County on a free transfer in 1930, as part of the deal that took Tudor Martin to Wolves. However, by the end of his first season at Somerton Park, County had lost their League status, despite his consistent goalscoring from his new position of centre forward, and he was snapped up by the Swans for £250 in August 1931, shortly after manager Thomson had left the Vetch Field. Failing to score in his debut game for the Swans against Leeds United, in the next 8 league games he scored 16 goals, which included four in a 5-1 defeat of Notts. County, and two days later a hat-trick at Port Vale. Creating a new club record for his goalscoring exploits by the end of the season, he had scored two goals in a game on eight occasions, and at the end of the season also scored in the Welsh Cup Final defeat of Wrexham in May 1932. He was described in the local newspaper at the time as being, 'a rare find,' and that 'Pearce liked the ball along the ground, and before opponents could guess his intentions, the ball was in the net,' Pearce's success was achieved despite close marking and he all too often was left to plough a lone furrow, with many of his goals scored with solo bursts from the halfway line. At the end of his first season at the Vetch Field the players were asked to take a drop in wages to balance the books. Cyril, understandably refused to re-sign, and with interest from Plymouth Argyle and Wolves, Charlton Athletic signed him for the then considerable fee of £2,250. His first season at the Valley saw him score 23 from 29 games, and by the end of March in his second season had scored 26 from 32 games, finishing top goalscorer for the club in each season. Labelled by his manager Jimmy Seed, as the 'best two footed player' he'd ever seen, tragedy struck Pearce when he broke his leg in two places at the end of March 1934 against Norwich City. Sitting out the 1934/35 Third Division South Championship winning season, Cyril made just a couple of appearances the following season when Athletic secured their second consecutive promotion, this time to the First Division. Although he remained a prolific goalscorer with the Charlton reserve side, he was never the same player when he returned to first team action, and returned to the Vetch Field prior to the start of the 1937/38 season, signed by Swans' Manager Neil Harris. Despite scoring eight goals from fifteen appearances for the Swans, he was transfer listed at £500, but when Ipswich Town were unable to afford his fee, he returned to his old job at Frickley Colliery, playing for the works side, before ending his playing career where he began at Shirebrook Welfare, retiring to the small village of Church Warsop, near Mansfield, up to his death in June 1990. Gained a Derbyshire Cup Medal, and won numerous awards for professional running earlier in his career.

14. PEARS, JOHN (JACK)

Birthplace: Ormskirk, 23/2/1907
Ht: 5ft-9ins, **Wt:** 11st-8lbs
Swans debut: v. Nottingham Forest (a), 14/9/1935

Swansea Town Career Statistics			
Season	League	FAC	WC
1935/36	19/4gls	1	1
1936/37	31/6gls	3	1/1gls
Total	50/10gls	4	2/1gls

Career:
Westhead St. James (signed season 1925/26)

Skelmersdale United (signed in June 1926)
Burscough Rangers (signed in December 1926)
Liverpool (amateur signed in August 1927, professional in February 1928) lge 0
Rotherham United (signed in August 1928) lge 21/7gls
Accrington Stanley (signed in May 1929) lge 21/8gls
Oldham Athletic (signed in July 1930) lge 92/33gls
Preston North End (signed in 15/3/1934) lge 18/4gls
Sheffield United (£1,500 signed in November 1934) lge 13/3gls
Swansea Town (£350 signed in 31/8/1935)
Hull City (£100 signed in 11/6/1937) lge 30/8gls, FAC 3, Others 2
Rochdale (signed in June 1938) lge 0
Mossley (signed in September 1938)

Outside Left who joined the Swans from Sheffield United in August 1935 for £350, replacing D. J. Lewis when he made his league debut for the Swans at Nottingham Forest in September 1935. During his career at the Vetch Field he was said to be a player of 'moods', but the solidly built, pacey winger on his day had a kick like a 'mule' scoring a number of goals from outside the penalty area. Starting his playing career at St. Anne's School in Ormskirk, he started his senior career as an amateur with Westhead St. James, made further appearances as an amateur with Burscough and Skelmersdale, before signing for Liverpool as an amateur, prior to signing professional in February 1928. It was only after joining Rotherham United in August 1928 that he made his debut in the Football League at outside left. He gained further experience with Accrington Stanley and Oldham Athletic before he was to be part of the Preston North End side that finished runners-up to Grimsby Town at the end of season 1933/34 in the Second Division, also scoring at the Vetch Field for North End in a 2-1 away win in March 1934. It was with Oldham however that Pears' reputation as a fast winger with an eye for goals was cemented, finishing season 1932/33 as top goalscorer. With over a century of League and Cup games, Pears goals tally of 33 goals was outstanding for a winger in the traditional mould. He scored his first goal for the Swans in his fourth appearance, at Doncaster Rovers in a 1-1 draw in September 1935. Originally released in May 1936, he resigned for the Swans on the 22nd August 1936, making a greater impact during his second season at the Vetch Field. However, despite making 31 league appearances, and scoring six goals during his second season at the Vetch Field, he was originally placed on the transfer list at £350, joining Third Division North side Hull City on the 11th June 1937 for £100. Pears's goal tally was outstanding for a winger in the traditional mould, and by the time he had pulled on the black and amber striped shirt of the Tigers, he was therefore very experienced and although his age went against him, at 30 years old he was still capable of doing the job. He went on to demonstrate this being ever present in the Hull City team until February 1938 when injury brought a premature end to his season. In the midst of that run he scored a hat-trick in the 10-1 rout of Southport. His final game in the Tigers' colours – against Accrington – proved to be the last League game of his career for although he moved on to Rochdale in the subsequent close season, he never turned out for them and the outbreak of WW2 brought down the curtain on his career.

15. PEARSON, Donald (DON) James

Birthplace: Swansea, 14/3/1930
Ht: 5ft-9ins, **Wt:** 12st-6lbs
Swans debut: v. Notts. County (a), 1/11/1952

Career:
Swansea Town (signed in June 1950)
Aldershot (signed in July 1958) lge 31/2gls
Haverfordwest (signed in August 1959)

Swansea Town Career Statistics			
Season	League	FAC	WC
1952/53	4		
1953/54	14	1	
1954/55	16		1
1955/56	1		
1956/57	12/1gls		1
1957/58	5		1
Total	52/1gls	1	3

Honours: West Wales Senior Cup Winner–1957, Welsh League Challenge Cup Winner–1961

Signed professional in June 1950 from local side St. Jude's, a product of the Swansea Youth League. Brought up in the Mount Pleasant and St. Davids' area of Swansea, Don attended Terrace Road and St. Helens schools prior to taking employment with CEM Days Ltd on leaving school. Prior to playing for St. Jude's he also played for Terrace Road and St. Helen's Institute football teams. He had to wait a number of years before making his first team debut for the Swans, confined to regular appearances in either the Combination or Welsh League sides. After making his debut at Notts. County as a replacement for Billy Lucas he retained his place in the side for the next three matches, but overall, for the remainder of his career at the Vetch Field struggled to maintain a regular place in the Swans line-up, usually making league appearances following injuries, or suspensions to key players. His only league goal for the Swans came at the Vetch Field against Huddersfield Town in a 4-2 win, in December 1956. The same season he was a member of the Swans side that lost to Wrexham, 2-1 in the Final of the Welsh Cup at Ninian Park. At the end of the 1956/57 season he played in the Swans side that beat Haverfordwest to win the West Wales Senior Cup Final. In July 1958 he was released, joining Fourth Division Aldershot, where he remained until May 1959. He returned to Swansea, joining Welsh League side Haverfordwest in August 1959, finishing his first season as top goalscorer, remaining with the West Wales side until the end of the 1968/69 season, when he retired as a player. In May 1961 he was a member of the Haverfordwest side that beat Llanelly in the Welsh League Challenge Cup Final. After retiring as a player he was involved for a number of years as manager of both Haverfordwest and Morriston Town. During the 1977/78 season, he was invited by former team colleague Harry Griffiths, who was manager of the Swans at the time, to take charge of the club's Welsh League side on matchdays. Since returning to the Swansea area he was employed for a number of years at the Ford Motor Car Dealership, CEM Days Ltd as a Service Manager.

16. PENNEY, David (DAVE) Mark

Birthplace: Wakefield, 17/8/1964
Ht: 5ft-10ins, **Wt:** 12st-0lbs
Swans debut: v. Stoke City (h), 30/3/1991

Swansea City Career Statistics						
Season	League	FLC	FAC	WC	AGT/ AWS	P/Offs
1990/91	12/3gls			1/1gls		
1993/94	11/2gls					
1994/95	29+6/5gls	3+1/2gls	5/1gls	3	5	
1995/96	2+2	0+1	0+1			
1996/97	44/13gls	2	2		2	3
Total	98+8/23gls	5+2/2gls	7+1/1gls	4/1gls	7	3

Career:
Pontefract Colliery
Derby County (£1,500 signed in 26/9/1985) lge 6+13, FLC 2+3/1gls, FAC 1/1gls, Others 1+3/1gls
Oxford United (£175,000 signed in 23/6/1989) lge 76+34/15gls, FLC 10+1, FAC 2+2/1gls, Others 3+1
Swansea City (loan in 28/3/1991)
Swansea City (loan in 24/3/1994)
Swansea City (£20,000 signed in August 1994)
Cardiff City (£20,000 signed in 24/7/1997) lge 33+2/5gls, FLC 1+1, FAC 6
Doncaster Rovers (signed in 28/8/1998) Conf 83+11/15gls

Honours: Welsh Cup Winner–1991

David Penney had two separate loan spells at the Vetch Field before his transfer was made permanent for a £20,000 fee during the 1994/95 close season. A midfielder who was able to combine aggression in the tackle with explosive shooting ability, his versatility also saw him occupy the right full back role when needed. One instance came in the Play Off Final at Wembley against Northampton Town, when he was asked to forgo his midfield role to play at full back instead of the injured Steve Jones. That season, Penney had been top goalscorer for the Swans with 13 league goals, and no doubt over a disappointing 90 minutes, the Swans side suffered without his presence bursting from midfield. Despite the Play Off misery, his consistent form during the season, and a takeover imminent at the Vetch Field, a disappointing contract offer from the Swans saw David join neighbours Cardiff City for a £20,000 transfer fee. Being the skipper at the Vetch Field, top goalscorer during the season, a drop in wages, he felt that he had no alternative to accept the 'Bluebirds' offer of a two year deal. One of the surprising things about Penney's move to the Vetch Field to many supporters is why it took the club almost 3 years before his transfer was made permanent, as it was obvious to everybody at the time of his initial loan move in March 1991 that he was a player who would add a lot of talent to the side. A sure penalty taker, besides his explosive shooting ability from outside the penalty area, he added one penalty for the Swans in the Welsh Cup Final at the National Stadium against Wrexham at the end of his loan transfer. Staying just 14 months at Ninian Park, David had offers to remain in the Football League with Scarborough, but decided to step down to the Conference to join former league side Doncaster Rovers in September 1998 as player coach alongside manager Ian Snodin. Playing his last game for Rovers during season 2001/02, he has since his retirement as a player not only led the club back into the Football League following their Play Off success in May 2002 against Dagenham & Redbridge at Stoke City's Britannia Stadium, but also won the Third Division Championship twelve months later. The start of his professional career had seen David leave his job as a bricklayer, playing part-time for Pontefract Colliery to join newly promoted Third Division side Derby County, before a six figure transfer fee saw him join Oxford United in June 1989.

17. PERRETT, DARREN John

Birthplace: Cardiff, 29/12/1969
Ht: 5ft-8ins, **Wt:** 11st-6lbs
Swans debut: v. Plymouth Argyle (a), AGT-1, 28/9/1993

	Swansea City Career Statistics				
Season	League	FLC	FAC	WC	AGT
1993/94	8+3/1gls	1	1	2+1/3gls	3/1gls
1994/95	3+12	1	0+1	1+1/3gls	
1995/96	2+2	0+1	0+1		
Total	13+17/1gls	2+1	1+2	3+2/6gls	3/1gls

Career:
Bridgend Town
Cheltenham Town (signed in January 1992)
    Total Apps 15+10/4gls
Swansea City (trial in March 1993, professional in 9/7/1993)
Merthyr Tydfil (signed in mid-November 1995)
Cwmbran Town

Honours: West Wales Senior Cup Winner–1994, 1995

Signed on an initial trial basis from Beazer Homes League side Cheltenham Town in late March 1993 by manager Frank Burrows, he made his Swans' debut in a Football Combination Cup game against Bournemouth, and remained at the Vetch Field on a trial basis until the end of the season. The front

runner had earlier made a good impression for Bridgend Town in an FA Cup, First Qualifying Round game against Cheltenham, signing for the club shortly after in January 1992. Signing a professional contract with the Swans in the 1993 close season, he made his debut for the Swans at Plymouth Argyle in a first round AutoGlass Trophy cup tie, scoring the Swans third goal, and making his league debut as substitute for skipper John Cornforth against Reading at the Vetch Field four days later. Used as a left sided attacker, his electric pace, and good ball control set him out initially as an exciting prospect, but he failed to realise his potential, and in November 1995 his contract was cancelled at the Vetch Field. Scoring his only league goal in the last league game of the 1993/94 season against Fulham, he had already scored two goals against Rhyl in a Welsh Cup tie the same season, and the following term went one better when he scored the fastest hat-trick recorded in the history of the club against the same opponents at the Vetch Field in December 1994 (8 minutes, and 39 seconds), beating Bob Latchford's record by 34 seconds. In May 1994 he was included in the Swans side that beat Ammanford Town in the West Wales Senior Cup Final, also twelve months later when the Swans beat Morriston Town in the same final. Following the 7-0 FA Cup First Round defeat at Fulham on the 11th November 1995, in which he made an appearance as a substitute, within a couple of days his contract was cancelled at the Vetch Field. Joining Merthyr Tydfil shortly after, he then linked up with League of Wales side Cwmbran Town, later making appearances in the Welsh League for Cardiff Civil Service and Grange Quins.

18. PHELAN, Terence (TERRY)

Birthplace: Manchester, 16/3/1967
Ht: 5ft-8ins, **Wt:** 10st-6lbs
Swans debut: v. Stockport County (h), 23/8/1986

	Swansea City Career Statistics				
Season	League	FLC	FAC	WC	FRT
1986/87	45	4	5	1	3
Total	45	4	5	1	3

Career:
Leeds United (associate schoolboy in March 1982, trainee in August 1983, professional in August 1984) lge 12+2, FLC 3, Others 2
Swansea City (signed in 30/7/1986)
Wimbledon (£100,000 signed in 29/7/1987) lge 155+4/1gls, FLC 13+2, FAC 16/2gls, Others 8
Manchester City (£2,500,000 signed in 25/8/1992) lge 102+1/1gls, FLC 11, FAC 8/1gls
Chelsea (£900,000 signed in 15/11/1995) lge 13+2, FLC 0+1, FAC 8

Everton (£850,000 signed in 1/1/1997) lge 23+2, FLC 1+1, FAC 1
Crystal Palace (loan in 23/10/1999) lge 14
Fulham (signed in 3/2/2000) lge 18+1/2gls, FLC 1
Sheffield United (signed in 10/8/2001) lge 8, FLC 1
Charleston Battery, USA (signed in 2001/2 season)

Honours: F.A. Cup Winner–1988, Republic of Ireland Full–41, Yth, U-21–1, U-23–1, 'B'–1, West Wales Senior Cup Winner–1987

Former apprentice at Elland Road with Leeds United who was signed by manager Terry Yorath after he had been released at the end of the 1985/86 season. The young left full back linked up effectively with the veteran Swans midfielder Tommy Hutchison on the left flank, and it came as no surprise when he was sold to Wimbledon after just the one season at the Vetch Field. His last game for the Swans was against Briton Ferry Athletic in the West Wales Senior Cup Final. Twelve months later he had established himself in the 'Dons' First Division defence, and also gained an F.A. Cup Winners medal in a dramatic 2-1 victory over Liverpool at Wembley. An exciting, overlapping full back, he also possessed good defensive qualities. Capped at Yth, U-21, and U-23 level for the Republic of Ireland, he gained his first Full cap for the Republic in 11th September 1991 in a friendly in Gyor against Hungary, becoming a regular in the squad, and making three appearances in the 1994 World Cup Finals. Six years after leaving the Vetch Field, Terry was the subject of quarter of a million pound transfer back to his native Manchester, signing for City, after over 150 league appearances for the 'Dons.' Attended Cathedral School, played for Manchester and Salford Schoolboys prior to signing for Leeds United initially as an associate schoolboy, before joining the club as a trainee in August 1983. He made his league debut for Leeds United in a 3-1 win at Shrewsbury Town on the 7th September 1985 as a replacement at left full back for Gary Hamson, retaining his place for the next ten league games, also playing in League Cup and Full Members Cup games for United. Later in his career, after further transfers totalling almost £2M to Chelsea and Everton, and a loan spell in London with Crystal Palace, Terry joined First Division side Fulham, linking up a second time with former Swans' defender Andrew Melville. Following a free transfer to Sheffield United on a short term contract in August 2001, Terry joined US-A League side Charleston Battery. In May 2004 he was believed to be coaching a woman's football team in Washington DC in America.

19. PHILLIPS, Donald (DON)

Birthplace: Llanelli, 3/3/1933
Ht: 5ft-11½ins, **Wt:** 11st-8lbs
Swans debut: v. Huddersfield Town (a), 20/4/1957

Swansea Town Career Statistics	
Season	League
1956/57	2
1957/58	1
Total	3

Career:
Buckleys, Llanelly
Swansea Town (signed in December 1956)
Yeovil Town (signed in close season 1958/59)
  Total apps 78/30gls
Bath City (signed in close season 1961)

Joining the Swans in December 1956 from Carmarthenshire League side Buckleys, he had to wait four months before being given his league opportunity in the Easter Holiday fixtures at Huddersfield Town. Since arriving at the Vetch Field, the inside forward had shown consistent form in both the Swans'

Combination and Welsh League sides. Playing also in the next league game, against Port Vale at the Vetch Field, he made one more league appearance the following season, but was then released at the end of season 1957/58, joining Yeovil Town, then later Bath City. At Yeovil Town he made consistent appearances during his first two seasons at the club, but in his next two seasons, he played mainly in the club's reserve side, making just nine first team appearances before he was given a free transfer in May 1961.

20. PHILLIPS, GARETH Russell

Birthplace: Church Farm, Gwent, 19/8/1979
Ht: 5ft-7ins, **Wt:** 11st-0lbs
Swans debut: v. Cambridge United (a), 9/11/1996

Swansea City Career Statistics					
Season	League	FLC	FAC	AWS/LDV	FAWP
1996/97	0+1				
1997/98	0+6				
1998/99	0+1				
1999/2000	2+1	0+1		1	6+1
2000/01	9+6				5
2001/02	29+6/2gls	1	0+2	1	1+1
2002/03	19+8	1	1	1	
Total	59+29/2gls	2+1	1+2	3	12+2

Career:
Swansea City (from trainee in 9/7/1998)
Merthyr Tydfil (loan in season1998/99)
Carmarthen Town (loan in season 1998/99)
Newport County (signed in August 2003)
Port Talbot (signed in close season 2004)

Honours: Wales Sch, Yth, U-21–3, West Wales Senior Cup Winner–2002

Former youth team skipper who made his league debut under manager Jan Molby whilst still a first year trainee at Cambridge United in November 1996. Apart from loan spells with Merthyr Tydfil and Carmarthen Town in season 1998/99, and further substitute appearances over the next three seasons, he had to wait until January 2000 at Southend United before he made his first start in a Swans shirt, starting the following game at Cheltenham Town. Small in stature, Gareth competed well in midfield, occasionally deputising at right wing back when needed. In March 2001 he gained his first U-21 honour for Wales when going on as a substitute for Maxwell against Ukraine. A further substitute appearance against Armenia saw Gareth finally get his first international start, against Belarus in October

2001. The start of the 2001/02 season saw Gareth finally start a new season in the Swans line-up, also scoring his first league goal, in a 3-1 away win at Macclesfield Town. He scored one more goal that season, at the Vetch Field in a 2-2 draw with promotion challengers Scunthorpe United, also appearing at the end of season FAW Invitation Cup Final at Ninian Park against Cardiff City. In late April 2002 he was included in the Swans side that beat Hakin United to win the West Wales Senior Cup. Despite regular appearances during season 2002/03, he was released by manager Brian Flynn in May 2003, linking up with his former assistant manager at the Vetch Field Peter Nicholas at Newport County in the Dr. Martens Premier League. In May 2004 he was not offered a new contract by Newport County, despite being a virtual ever present during the previous twelve months with County, and in the 2004 close season signed for League of Wales side Port Talbot.

21. PHILLIPS, LEIGHTON

Birthplace: Briton Ferry, 26/9/1949
Ht: 5ft-10ins, **Wt:** 10st-11lbs
Swans debut: v. Bury (a), 11/11/1978

Swansea City Career Statistics				
Season	*League*	*FLC*	*FAC*	*WC*
1978/79	28		4	1
1979/80	40	4	4	4
1980/81	29	2		4
Total	97	6	8	9

Career:
Cardiff City (apprentice in June 1966, professional in April 1967)
  lge 169+11/11gls, ECWC 8+3/1gls
Aston Villa (£100,000 signed in 18/9/1974) lge 134+6/4gls
Swansea City (£70,000 signed in 8/11/1978)
Charlton Athletic (£25,000 signed in 15/7/1981) lge 45/1gls
Exeter City (non-contract signed in March 1983) lge 10
Llanelli (player manager signed in January 1984)

Honours: Wales Sch–1, U-21–2, U-23–4, Full–58, Football League Cup Winner–1977, Welsh Cup Winner–1971, 1973, 1974

Stylish, Welsh international central defender who was signed by manager John Toshack for a club record transfer fee of £70,000 in November 1978 to boost the Swans promotion challenge from the Third Division. Born in Briton Ferry, the former Brynhyfryd School, Cwrt Sart, Afan Nedd Schoolboy, and Neath Boys Club player had started his career as an apprentice with Cardiff City, gained valuable Second Division and European Cup Winners Cup experience with the Bluebirds prior to a £100,000 transfer to Aston Villa in September 1974. At Ninian Park Leighton had

gained Welsh Cup Winners Medals from seasons 1970/71, 1972/73, and 1973/74, also playing in the Welsh Cup Final defeat by Wrexham in season 1971/72. His first season at Villa Park saw him play in a side that ended the season as runners-up to Manchester United, and gain promotion to the First Division. Unfortunately for him, as he had played for Cardiff City in the first round of the League Cup prior to his transfer to Villa Park, he was unable to play in the Villa side that beat Norwich City at Wembley to win the League Cup later in the season. Making two appearances in the EUFA Cup the following season, he was also a member of the Villa side that won the League Cup in 1977, beating Everton in the second replay, and during the following season's matches in the EUFA Cup competition played in all the rounds up to the quarter final defeat by Barcelona. He made one appearance for Wales at schoolboy level against Northern Ireland prior to joining the Bluebirds, and also made five appearances for the Welsh U-23 side, four whilst at Ninian Park with City, making his first appearance at Full level at the Vetch Field whilst with Cardiff City, against Czechoslovakia on the 21st April 1971. After signing for the Swans he made a further eighteen appearances for Wales as a Swansea City player. Also during his time at the Vetch Field he was selected as an over age player for the Wales U-21 side that lost 1-0 to England at the Vetch Field in February 1979, gaining his second cap at that level after signing for Charlton Athletic, against Norway in September 1982. A good reader of the game, cool under pressure, and possessing a good range of passing, he made a significant impact with the Swans following his transfer, experiencing promotion from the Third Division in his first season, and helping the club to establish themselves in the Second Division, for the first time since being relegated in 1965. The 1980/81 season saw Leighton continue to marshal the Swans rearguard, but after 29 league appearances, and the club's promotion prospects appearing to falter, he was replaced by young Dudley Lewis, and failed to make any further appearances for the club prior to his transfer to Charlton Athletic for £25,000 in August 1981. An ever present in Athletic's Second Division side during the 1981/82 season, he was appointed player coach in June 1982, and after a period where he was sidelined through injury, in March 1983 he joined Third Division Exeter City on a non-contract basis, before being released in May. Returning to his native South West Wales, he became player manager of Llanelli in January 1984 for a two year spell, and for a number of years has worked as an Independent Financial Advisor.

22. PHILLIPS, STEWART Gavin

Birthplace: Halifax, 30/12/1961
Ht: 6ft-0ins, **Wt:** 12st-2lbs
Swans debut: v. Notts. County (h), 7/1/1989

Career:
Hereford United (from apprentice in November 1979)
  lge 285+8/83gls

West Bromwich Albion (£25,000 signed in 4/3/1988) lge 15/4gls
Swansea City (signed in 4/1/1989)
Hereford United (loan in 20/8/1990) lge 31+6/10gls
Wrexham (signed in August 1991) lge 1+1/1gls
Aldershot (signed in Oct 1991) lge 5
Sudbury Town (signed in December 1991)
Worcester City (signed in October 1992)
AFC Newport (signed in June 1993)

Swansea City Career Statistics				
Season	League	FLC	WC	ECWC
1988/89	4+2		1+1/1gls	
1989/90	6+7/1gls	2		1
Total	10+9/1gls	2	1+1/1gls	1

Honours: PFA Division Four XI–1984

Representing Herefordshire schoolboys at ages 14 and 16, Stewart served a two year apprenticeship at Edgar Street, prior to signing as a professional in November 1979. His debut against Swindon Town in April 1978 saw him become Hereford's youngest ever player to have played for the club in the Football League. His father at the time was a director of the club, and later chairman. Going on to become a prolific goalscorer for United, topping the goalscorer's charts in four consecutive seasons between 1981 and 1985, he joined West Bromwich Albion for £25,000 in March 1988. Successfully helping the club to avoid relegation, he was signed by Swans manager Terry Yorath in January 1989 for £25,000. At that time the Swans were playing their first season back in the Third Division, and although struggling to score regularly, were handily placed in the top ten positions of the league to mount a promotion challenge. Unfortunately for Phillips his period at the Vetch Field saw him suffer with injuries and illness, and in August 1990 he had returned to Edgar Street on an initial loan basis, which was made permanent for a £5,000 fee on the 11th October 1990, having scored just two goals for the Swans, one in the league (in a 6-1 home defeat by Reading), and one in a Welsh Cup win at the Racecourse over Wrexham. During his time with the Swans he made an appearance in the second leg of the European Cup Winners Cup game with Greek side Panathinaikos in a 3-3 draw at the Vetch Field. Despite scoring ten league goals for United, he was released at the end of the season, joining Wrexham on a non-contract basis, but despite being offered a contract to stay at the Racecourse, decided to play in Hong Kong, returning to the UK in October 1991 to sign for Aldershot, making five league appearances in their final season in the Football League before the club folded. Drifting into the non-league scene with Sudbury Town, then Worcester City (scored thirteen goals from thirty-six appearances), he then joined AFC Newport on a non-contract basis, also studying for his diploma in F.A. Management of Injuries, Fitness and Nutrition, Sports Therapy, and Sport Psychology, which has led him to open up his own Sports Injury Clinic in Hereford.

23. PINNER, Michael (MIKE) John

Swansea Town Career Statistics	
Season	League
1961/62	1
Total	1

Birthplace: Boston, Lincs, 16/2/1934
Ht: 6ft-0ins, **Wt:** 12st-0lbs
Swans debut: v. Liverpool (h), 4/5/1962

Career:
Wyberton Rangers
Notts. County (amateur signed in October 1948)
Cambridge University
Pegasus
Aston Villa (signed in May 1954) lge 4
Corinthian Casuals
Sheffield Wednesday (signed in December 1957) lge 7
Queens Park Rangers (signed in July 1959) lge 19
Manchester United (signed in February 1961) lge 4
Chelsea (signed in October 1961) lge 1
Swansea Town (signed in May 1962)
Hendon
Leyton Orient (amateur signed in October 1962, part-time professional in October 1963) lge 77
Belfast Distillery (signed in close season 1965 to 1967)

Honours: England Amateur International–52, British Olympic XI, RAF

Former England amateur international goalkeeper who made over fifty appearances for his country, and who, despite the transfer deadline was allowed to play for the Swans in the last game of the season against Liverpool, who had already won the Championship of the Second Division, and the result would have no bearing on the positions in the league for either side. Within a week of playing for the Swans, he played for the England Amateur International side against Italy.
After attending Boston Grammar School, he started his playing career with Boston side Wyberton Rangers, prior to a spell as an amateur with Notts County in 1948, and then studied at Cambridge University. He continued his playing career after university with leading amateur side at the time, Pegasus, made his league debut with Aston Villa on the 25th September 1954 at Bolton Wanderers at Burnden Park, before returning to the amateur scene with Corinthian Casuals. Retaining his amateur status, and his position as a solicitor, he continued to make league appearances for Sheffield Wednesday, QPR, Chelsea and Manchester United, prior to arriving at the Vetch Field. Pinner had been brought into the Swans side because of injuries initially to first choice Dwyer, but then to the veteran Johnny King. Shortly after returning to the non-league scene with Hendon and Middlesex Wanderers, Pinner returned to the Football League with Leyton Orient, signing professional twelve months after joining the club. He was a member of the F.A. Touring Party to Nigeria and Ghana in 1958, when he was an amateur with Pegasus. Mike made more than fifty Amateur International appearances for England, played in the Melbourne and Rome Olympic games, represented the R.A.F. during his time as an Officer and played in four Varsity matches against Oxford University. He also played for Belfast Distillery before retiring to concentrate on his work as a solicitor.

24. POPE, DAVID William

Birthplace: St. Pancras, 8/1/1963
Ht: 6ft-0ins, **Wt:** 13st-0lbs
Swans debut: v. Middlesbrough (h), 19/10/1957

Swansea Town Career Statistics		
Season	League	WC
1957/58	4	1
Total	4	1

Career:
Chelsea
Crystal Palace (signed in September 1953) lge 0
Swansea Town (signed in September 1956)
Sittingbourne (signed in 1958 close season)

A former apprentice at Stamford Bridge with Chelsea who joined Third Division South side Crystal Palace in September 1953. He failed to make any first team appearances for Palace in the three seasons he was at Selhurst Park and was signed by the Swans player manager Ronnie Burgess in September 1956, making his league debut in October 1957 at the Vetch Field against Middlesbrough as deputy for Tom Brown. His arrival at the Vetch Field at the start of pre-season training in early August saw him make an appearance in the Swans' first Public Trial game at the Vetch Field, along with another new signing, Derek King. He made a further three league appearances at right back instead of Arthur Willis, and was released at the end of the season, joining non-league Sittingbourne in the 1958 close season.

25. POTTER, Stephen (STEVE) Derek

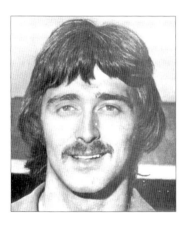

Birthplace: Belper, 1/10/1955
Ht: 6ft-1ins, **Wt:** 12st-2lbs
Swans debut: v. Doncaster Rovers (h), 7/9/1974

	Swansea City Career Statistics			
Season	League	FLC	FAC	WC
1974/75	27			4
1975/76	46	2	1	3
1976/77	41	6		2
1977/78	4	1		
Total	118	9	1	9

Career:
Manchester City (from apprentice in October 1973)
Swansea City (signed in 27/8/1974)
Bridgend Town (signed in July 1978)
Australia (1979)

Honours: West Wales Senior Cup Winner–1975

Former Manchester City apprentice goalkeeper, who despite being a professional at Maine Road for two seasons had yet to make his league debut prior to his signing for the Swans on an initial loan transfer on the 27th August 1974, with the transfer being made permanent for a fee of £1,250 on 11th February 1975. His first season at the Vetch Field saw the Swans having to apply for re-election to the League in May 1975, but after manager Harry Grififths had been able to bring in experienced players, the team became a more attacking, adventurous outfit, which at times provided little cover for goalkeeper Potter. In May 1975 he was included in the squad that beat Briton Ferry Athletic to win the West Wales Senior Cup. Despite being prone to the occasional mishap, he produced many memorable performances during his time at the Vetch Field. After narrowly missing promotion from the Fourth Division in 1977, and with

Keith Barber being brought in by Griffiths in the close season, Potter made few appearances during season 1977/78, especially after Toshack had been appointed Swans player manager towards the end of the season. In May 1978 he was released, joining Bridgend Town, and twelve months later emigrated to Australia.

26. POUND, John Henry Kenneth (KEN)

Birthplace: Portsmouth, 24/8/1944
Ht: 5ft-7½ins, **Wt:** 12st-1lbs
Swans debut: v. Rotherham United (a) FLC-3, 14/10/1964

	Swansea Town Career Statistics			
Season	League	FLC	FAC	WC
1964/65	14/3gls	1	2	3/1gls
1965/66	11ı1/1gls			3
Total	25+1/4gls	1	2	6/1gls

Career:
Portsmouth
Yeovil Town (signed in July 1963)
Swansea Town (£1,000 signed in July 1964)
Bournemouth (signed in August 1966) lge 102/24gls
Gillingham (signed in July 1969) lge 62+10/11gls
Weymouth (signed in July 1971)

Honours: Southern League Premier Champions–1964, Southern League Cup Winner–1973, Welsh Cup Winner–1966, West Wales Senior Cup Winner–1965

Initially an amateur with Portsmouth, he joined non-league Yeovil Town in July 1963, featuring in the club's 1963/64 Southern League title triumph, also scoring in Yeovil's FA Cup second round victory at home to Crystal Palace, before signing for Swans manager Trevor Morris in July 1964 for £1,000. An exceptionally quick left winger, he had to wait until a couple of months into the season before he made his debut for the Swans in a League Cup tie at Rotherham United, making his first league appearance a month later in a home win over Newcastle United. Despite a good run in the Swans league line-up, he was unable to produce the level of consistency required in the Football League, even when his old manager of Yeovil Town, Glyn Davies had been placed in charge at the Vetch Field in July 1965, after the Swans had been relegated to the Third Division. In May 1965 he was included in the Swans side that beat Llanelli to win the West Wales Senior Cup. He scored his first league goal for the Swans in the local derby at the Vetch Field against neighbours Cardiff City in an exciting 3-2 win for the Swans, followed two games later with his second goal in a 3-2 away win at Leyton Orient. His only other goal that season came in a Welsh Cup sixth round tie at Pwllheli. With just one more goal in his second season at the Vetch Field, his only other highlight during the season was playing in the first leg of the Welsh Cup Final at the Vetch Field against Chester in mid-April 1966. In August 1966 he was involved in a part exchange transfer with Bournemouth midfielder/striker Denis Coughlin, and three seasons later was involved in a second player exchange transfer, this time with Gillingham's John Meredith. Moving to Weymouth in July 1971, he was involved in the club's 1973 Southern League Cup success, and after becoming the club's reserve team coach, worked in the commercial department of Bath City, Maidstone United and Southampton, prior to rejoining Bournemouth as promotions officer. Following a spell with Brighton & Hove Albion as commercial manager he has since been working as a financial adviser for Britannic Assurance on the South Coast.

27. POWELL, BARRY Ivor

Birthplace: Kenilworth, 29/1/1954
Ht: 5ft-7½ins, **Wt:** 11st-0lbs
Swans debut: v. Cambridge United (h), 1/3/1985

Swansea City Career Statistics		
Season	League	WC
1984/85	8	1
Total	8	1

Career:
Wolverhampton Wanderers (from apprentice in January 1972) lge 58+6/7gls
Coventry City (signed in September 1975) lge 162+2/27gls
Derby County (signed in October 1979) lge 86/7gls
Bulova, Hong Kong
Burnley (signed in July 1984) lge 9+2
Swansea City (signed in 22/2/1985)
South China, Hong Kong
Wolverhampton Wanderers (signed in November 1986) lge 10+4

Honours: England U-23–4, Football League Cup Winner–1974

Experienced midfielder who was signed in February 1985 from Burnley, for a second time by John Bond during his spell as manager at the Vetch Field, after previously signing him when he was manager at Burnley. One of a number of experienced professionals who were brought in by Bond in what turned out to be a successful attempt to stave off relegation to the Fourth Division. Formerly an apprentice with Wolverhampton Wanderers, shortly after breaking into the Wolves first team, he made an appearance for Wolves in their F.A. Cup semi-final defeat by Leeds United during the 1972/73 season, and the following season made a substitute's appearance at Wembley,

replacing Wagstaffe, as Wolves beat Manchester City to win the League Cup Final. Capped on four occasions for the England U-23 side, his first appearance came on the 13th March 1974 against Scotland, followed by three more appearances during the 1974/75 season against Scotland, Czechoslovakia and Portugal. Joining Coventry City in September 1975, he was a regular member of the 'Sky Blues' First Division line-up, and at the end of season 1977/78 was runner-up in the goalscoring charts. Joining Derby County in October 1979, he was unable to prevent the club from losing its First Division status in 1980, and following a spell in Hong Kong with Bulova, signed for Burnley. At the Vetch Field he made just eight league appearances, and one appearance in a Welsh Cup semi-final, first leg against Shrewsbury Town, and was released in May 1985, returning to Hong Kong this time to play for South China. On his return to the UK, he re-joined Wolverhampton Wanderers in a player coach, and assistant manager capacity, working alongside Kenny Hibbitt, and played in the second leg of the 1987 Third Division Play Off Final against Aldershot. He did not make any further appearances for Wolves, and was reserve team coach during the period when the club won successive promotions. He continued as a coach until June 1991, then became Coventry City's community officer before assisting Kenny Hibbitt at Hednesford Town. In season 2001/02 he was manager of League of Wales side Aberystwyth Town, and led the club to fourth place in the League of Wales, and into the Intertoto Cup competition against Maltese side Floriana in 2002. In late March 2003 took over as manager of Hednesford Town, playing a big part in the club retaining its Dr. Martens Premier Division status, and in May 2004 led the club to a 3-2 F.A. Trophy Final win over Canvey Island. A couple of days later he was sensationally sacked from his manager's position with the club, with experienced player Chris Brindley taking over.

28. POWELL, Raymond (RAY)

Birthplace: Swansea, 5/8/1924
Ht: 5ft-9ins, **Wt:** 10st-10lbs
Swans debut: v. Walsall (h), 7/2/1948

Swansea Town Career Statistics			
Season	League	FAC	WC
1947/48	13/4gls		1
1948/49	2/1gls	1	3
1949/50	1		
1950/51	2		
Total	18/5gls	1	4

Career:
Haverfordwest
Swansea Town (signed in May 1947)
Scunthorpe United (£2,000 signed in 31/7/1951) lge 31/14gls
Kettering Town (signed in June 1952)

Honours: West Wales Senior Cup Winner–1949, 1950

The front runner started his senior career in the Swansea League initially with Morriston, before graduating to the Welsh League with Haverfordwest. Signed by manager Haydn Green, he went on to become a prolific goalscorer in the Combination or Welsh League sides, playing in a variety of forward positions for the Swans. His first season at the Vetch Field saw him produce some outstanding performances, and in the 1948 close season he spent some time farming in Scotland in a bid to improve his slender frame. Making his league debut at inside left, during his career with the Swans he also played outside right, inside right, and at centre forward. He scored the Swans goal in a 1-1 draw on his debut for the club against Walsall at the Vetch Field, scoring his second goal in his third game, again at the Vetch Field against Exeter City. Scored one of the goals that beat Llanelly 5-1 at Stebonheath Park in May 1949 to win the West Wales Senior Cup Final, and two goals twelve months later when the Swans beat Haverfordwest in the final of the same competition. For the next three seasons he struggled to command a regular place in the Swans starting line-up, and in July 1951 was transferred to Third Division North side Scunthorpe United for £2,000, their second season as a Football League club. Finishing top goalscorer in his first season with thirty-one goals at Scunthorpe United, he surprisingly left the club in June 1952 to take up a job offer with Northampton company British Timkin in their Planning Department, also signing for Southern League side Kettering Town, for whom former Swans and Arsenal player Les Jones had connections. At the same time, Wrexham had also made him an offer to stay in the Football League.

29. PRENTICE, JOHN Harkness

Birthplace: Glasgow, 19/10/1898
Ht: 5ft-8ins, **Wt:** 11st-7lbs
Swans debut: v. Luton Town (a), 11/9/1920

Swansea Town Career Statistics	
Season	League
1920/21	3
Total	3

Career:
Manchester United (signed in November 1919) lge 1
Swansea Town (signed in June 1920)
Tranmere Rovers (signed in December 1921) lge 23/3gls
Manchester North End
Hurst (signed in August 1928)
Chester (signed in August 1929)
Great Harwood (signed in September 1930)

Honours: Scotland Junior International

A Scotsman brought up in Manchester, John Prentice joined United in November 1919 after winning a Scottish Junior international cap at the age of 16, but made only one league appearance before refusing terms and signing for the Swans. Played initially as an amateur in Manchester League Football prior to joining United as an amateur, before signing professional in November 1919. His only league game for United came against Bradford Park Avenue at home in April 1920, deputising for Fred Hopkin in a 1-0 defeat. Arriving at the Vetch Field in June 1920, prior to the start of the club's first season in the Football League, he failed to settle in South Wales, returned north to his native Manchester. Made his Swans debut as a replacement at outside left for Spottiswoode, playing in three consecutive league games before the return of Spottiswoode. He was persuaded to sign for Rovers by Charlie Cunningham, and at Prenton Park he was noted for having an inward swerve when on the run that was very deceptive. He made his league debut for Rovers at inside left in Rovers' second ever league game at Crewe, scoring in a 1-1 draw. Early in February 1922 he lost his place to Billy Rainford, making just one more appearance before leaving at the end of the season to sign for Manchester North End, before joining Hurst in August 1928. He later signed for Chester in August 1929, before finishing his playing career at Great Harwood.

30. PRESSDEE, James (JIM) Stuart

Birthplace: Swansea, 19/6/1933
Ht: 5ft-11ins, **Wt:** 11st-6lbs
Swans debut: v. Everton (h), 6/3/1954

Swansea Town Career Statistics	
Season	League
1953/54	4
1954/55	3
1955/56	1
Total	8

Career:
Swansea Town (signed from juniors, professional in August 1951)
Brecon Corinthians (signed in close season 1956)
Llanelly (signed in August 1959)

Honours: Wales Sch, Yth–3

Signing professional for the Swans from the 'A' team in August 1951, the former Oystermouth and Swansea schoolboy footballer had already represented Wales as a schoolboy and played for the Wales Youth side against England and Scotland in season 1950/51. He had played for the Welsh Schoolboy side in 1947 and 1948, skippering the side in his second year with the Schoolboy's side. In April 1950 he played for a Swansea Youth League XI against a Scottish Juvenile XI at the Vetch Field. Brought up in Mumbles on the Gower Peninsula, Jim was born in Russell House, and attended Oystermouth Board School, captained Swansea Schoolboys prior to leaving school, worked in his family's Bakery before joining the groundstaff at the Vetch Field. Also on the Glamorgan County Cricket Club ground staff, he had played for the County's Second Eleven at the age of fifteen against the RAF, and in 1949 became the County's youngest player in post-war cricket by making his first-class debut for the county against Nottinghamshire at Cardiff Arms Park aged 16 years and 59 days. Despite failing to score with the bat, and taking no wickets for thirty-five runs off nineteen overs, in time he would make a tremendous contribution to not only Glamorgan County Cricket Club, but also as a coach in South Africa. However, cricket was his favourite game, and after doing his National Service in the RAF he opted to become a professional cricketer, despite making a number of league appearances for the Swans in a three season spell from 1953 to 1956. After making his league debut at centre half against Everton in March 1954, he played in the next league game, but had to wait until the last two league fixtures of the season for further appearances. Over the next two seasons he made just four more league appearances, before being released to concentrate on his cricketing career. He stayed in touch with football during the winter months by playing on a regular basis in the Welsh League for Brecon Corinthians and Llanelly. As a cricketer he subsequently developed into a clever left arm spinner and an aggressive batsman, who moved up the batting order as his run rate and confidence increased. Scoring a maiden century against India at Cardiff Arms Park, he continued to be a heavy run scorer in the 1960`s, hitting 1,892 runs in 1961, and a career best 1911 runs in 1962. But whilst his batting went from strength to strength, Pressdee lost confidence as a spinner, and only regained his self-belief after bowling in South Africa during the winter months, and in the summer of 1963 he returned an impressive 104 dismissals. In 1965 Pressdee claimed a career-best 9-43 against Yorkshire at Swansea, but this was a season when he had many run-ins with the county`s administrators, and by the end of the summer, he had had enough, and his career with the Welsh county came to an abrupt end as he decided to emigrate to South Africa. He continued to play in South Africa for North-East Transvaal until 1969/70, and apart from a short spell back in Mumbles following the death of his father and working in the family business, he returned to South Africa. He returned to the U.K. in the mid-1980's, captained the Glamorgan Colts side in the South Wales Cricket Association, but returned once more to South Africa, involving himself in a sports shop business, and also coaching in High Schools in Durban. Currently living in South Africa, his son in law is former Glamorgan cricketer Rodney Ontong.

31. PRICE, Thomas DUDLEY

Birthplace: Morriston, Swansea, 17/11/1931
Ht: 5ft-6ins, **Wt:** 10st-7lbs
Swans debut: v. Leicester City (a), 23/2/1954

Swansea Town Career Statistics

Season	League	FAC	WC
1953/54	4/1gls		
1954/55	6/3gls		
1955/56	3	1	
1956/57	13/3gls		2/2gls
1957/58	8/2gls		
Total	34/9gls	1	2/2gls

Career:
Bolton Wanderers (trial in May 1949)
Swansea Town (from juniors in April 1950)
Southend United (£3,000 signed in 6/1/1958) lge 91/41gls, FAC 3/1gls
Hull City (£2,500 signed in 7/9/1960) lge 76/26gls, FLC 6/1gls, FAC 8/3gls
Bradford City (signed in 1/7/1963) lge 62/21gls, FLC 6/3gls, FAC 2/1gls
Merthyr Tydfil (signed in June 1965)

Honours: Wales Army Cadets XI–2, Football Combination Second Division Champions–1955

A trialist with Bolton Wanderers in May 1949, the front runner made his debut for the Swans at inside right, but also played in all other forward positions during his time with the Swans at the Vetch Field, and during his early years represented the Welsh Army Cadets against Scotland, and also played at the Vetch Field for the side in an international against Northern Ireland in mid-January 1950. A product of youth soccer, he was attached to Morriston and Vicarage Road Youth clubs, and in one youth game for the Swans on Good Friday against Cardiff scored four goals. He was unfortunate to have been on the playing staff at the Vetch Field during an era when the Swans had an abundance of talent, Allchurch's, Griffiths, Jones, Medwin etc. Born in Morriston, Dudley played for his school team in Cwmrhydyceirw, and also the Swansea & District U-16 side before arriving at the Vetch Field, signing professional from the ground staff in April 1950, and making his league debut, replacing Brin Jones at Leicester City in February 1954. Playing in four consecutive league games, at inside right and at outside right, he scored his first goal for the Swans at Oldham Athletic in his second league game, four days after making his debut. Towards the end of the 1954/55 season he made four consecutive league appearances, scoring two goals in a 5-3 defeat in the first game against Stoke City, and scoring his third goal that season in his fourth game in a 3-0 win over Derby County. That same season he had made regular appearances in the Swans' reserve side that won the Football Combination Second Division Championship. The 1956/57 season saw Dudley start the season at outside right, playing in the first eight league matches, scoring three goals. In January 1958 he joined Third Division South side Southend United for a £3,000 fee, made his debut on the 11th January 1958 against Colchester United, and during his playing career at Roots Hall scored in almost every other game. The 1959/60 season saw Dudley score thirty-two goals, just four short of the club record held by former Swans centre forward Sam McCrory, and the second highest in the club's history. Further transfers saw him join Third Division Hull City and Fourth Division Bradford City, scoring consistently for both clubs. He made his debut for Hull City at Bournemouth on the 12th September 1960, scoring within two minutes of making his debut, and scoring his second in the 2-2 draw. He formed a useful partnership with a young and inexperienced Chris Chilton at Hull City, with the young Chilton gaining from playing alongside an experienced player such as Price, whilst Price benefited from the opportunities that 'Chillo' created. Making his league debut for City against Exeter City on the 24th August 1963, during his first season at Valley

Parade, the club was denied promotion by just two points, finishing in fifth place in 1964. He returned to South Wales to finish his playing career with Harry Griffiths at Merthyr Tydfil in June 1965, but an earlier injury at Bradford City, in which he tore ankle ligaments ultimately forced him to retire from the game, despite making appearances for Bridgend Town and Haverfordwest in later years. Working as a representative for an Office Equipment Company, he then went to work in the distribution department at the *South Wales Evening Post* before he was made redundant, taking early retirement.

32. PRICE, JASON Jeffrey

Birthplace: Pontypridd, 12/4/1977
Ht: 6ft-2ins, **Wt:** 11st-5lbs
Swans debut: v. Doncaster Rovers (h), 28/1/1997

Swansea City Career Statistics

Season	League	FLC	FAC	AWS	P/Offs	FAWP
1996/97	1+1					
1997/98	31+3/3gls	2	1			5/1gls
1998/99	25+3/4gls	2	2/1gls	2	0+1	3
1999/2000	35+4/6gls	4	1			1
2000/01	41+4gls	2		2/1gls		3+2
Total	133+11/17gls	10	4/1gls	4/1gls	0+1	12+2/1gls

Career:
Aberaman
Swansea City (signed in 17/7/1995)
Brentford (signed in 6/8/2001) lge 15/1gls, FLC 2, Others 1
Tranmere Rovers (signed in 8/11/2001) lge 34+15/11gls,
    FAC 5/4gls
Hull City (signed in 3/7/2003) lge 35+25/11gls, FLC 2,
    FAC 2+1/1gls, Others 2/1gls

Honours: Wales U-21–7, Third Division Champions–2000

Impressed the Swans management when playing in midfield for Aberaman youth side against the Swans in the McWhirter Youth League, resulting in him being offered a professional contract in July 1995 by manager Frank Burrows. He had to wait until January 1997 for manager Jan Molby to give him his league debut, at the Vetch Field as substitute for Linton Brown. From the start of the 1997/98 season he became a regular in the Swans line-up, either as an attacking right wing back, or in a wide right sided midfield position, where his long stride, and pace were able to get him to the by-line, or into goal scoring positions. In February 1998, the Swans paid Aberamman a fee in excess of £1,000, as part of the transfer that took him to the Vetch Field in July 1995. He gained the first of his seven U-21 appearances for Wales as a substitute for Williams against Italy on the 22nd April

1998, and in September 1998. Jason scored his first goal for the Swans in a 7-4 defeat at Hull City in August 1997, and by the time he left the Vetch Field at the end of the 2000/01 season on a Bosman transfer to Brentford, had gained a reputation as a midfielder with an eye for the spectacular goal, as many fans would testify. He initially arrived at Griffin Park on a three month trial with Brentford, but after his move to Tranmere Rovers later in the same season, scored seven goals in his first six games in a central striker role for the club. At Griffin Park JJ played right midfield as well as at right full back. His second season at Prenton Park was upset by injury problems, including a broken collarbone, and a broken wrist, and at the end of the season with him out of contract, signed for Third Division Hull City. With the 'Tigers' moving into a new stadium, and former England U-21 coach Peter Taylor in charge, by the end of his first twelve months at Hull, the club had gained promotion, finishing in runners-up spot in the Third Division, with Jason supplying nine league goals from his midfield role. Twelve months later for the second successive season the 'Tigers' claimed the runners-up position, this time gaining promotion to the Football League Championship.

33. PRICE, NEIL

Birthplace: Hemel Hempstead, 15/2/1964
Ht: 5ft-7ins, **Wt:** 11st-6lbs
Swans debut: v. Chesterfield (h), 5/11/1985

Swansea City Career Statistics

Season	League
1985/86	1+2
Total	1+2

Career:
Watford (schoolboy in August 1978, apprentice in July 1980, professional in February 1982) lge 7+1, FAC 2, UEFA 2
Plymouth Argyle (loan in February 1984) lge 1
Blackpool (loan in March 1985) lge 13
Swansea City (signed in July 1985)
Wycombe Wanderers (signed in February 1986)
    Conf apps, 9/1gls
Wealdstone (£5,000 signed in December 1989)
Staines Town (player manager in June 1991)

Honours: F.A. Youth Cup Winner–1982

Initially joined Watford as a schoolboy in August 1978, signing as an apprentice in July 1980, playing in the FA Youth Cup Final defeat of Manchester United at the end of the 1981/82 season. Despite struggling to make appearances in the 'Hornets' starting line-up, his brief spell as a professional at Vicarage Road saw him play in front of 60,000 Bulgarians, appear in an F.A. Cup semi final and Final, and receive a red card at Highbury. His brother Josh had also won a F.A. Youth Cup winners medal five years previously with Watford. Following a loan spell at Plymouth Argyle in February 1984, he was called into the Watford F.A. Cup line-up for the semi-final and the Final against Everton, replacing Wilf Rostron at left full back. The following season, after failing to make any further appearances for the 'Hornets' he joined Blackpool on a loan transfer, playing in the last thirteen out of fifteen matches of the season. Given a free transfer by Watford in May 1985, Swans manager John Bond persuaded him to sign for the Swans in July 1985, but after missing the start of the season through injury and illness, had to wait until early November before making his Swans' debut at the Vetch Field against Chesterfield. Making just two substitute appearances over the next couple of games, he had his contract cancelled by the Swans shortly before Christmas, and left the Vetch Field playing staff. He joined Wycombe in February 1986 and at left-back was a key figure in the 1986/87 side that won promotion to the Conference – scoring twice in 46 League games. In December 1989 he joined Wealdstone, before signing for Staines Town as player manager in June 1991. Taking over as manager of Walton & Hersham in the 1993 close season, until March 1995, he was then appointed Hendon manager in November 1995. At the start of season 1998/99 he was involved with Roy Butler at Hemel Hempstead F.C, turning the club around, narrowly missing out on promotion at the end of the season, and reaching the final of the South Midlands Floodlight Cup competition. Their first full season in charge ended with Hemel winning the Ryman Division Two Championship with 101 points, gaining the club's highest ever league finish in the process. However, Hemel were refused promotion after their Vauxhall Road ground was not granted the required grading for Division One.

34. PRICE, PAUL Terence

Birthplace: St. Albans, 23/3/1954
Ht: 5ft-11ins, **Wt:** 12st-0lbs
Swans debut: v. Bradford City (a), 26/1/1985

Swansea City Career Statistics

Season	League	FLC	FAC	WC	FRT
1984/85	21			3	4
1985/86	40/1gls	4	1	4/1gls	4
Total	61/1gls	4	1	7/1gls	8

Career:
Welwyn Gardens
Luton Town (signed from juniors in July 1971) lge 206+1/8gls
Tottenham Hotspur (£200,000 signed in June 1981) lge 35+4

Minnesota Strikers, USA (signed in July 1984)
Swansea City (signed in January 1985)
Peterborough United (signed in August 1986) lge 86
Wivenhoe Town (signed in 1988)
St. Albans (signed in close season 1991)

Honours: Wales U-21–1, U-23–4, Full–25, F.A. Cup Winner–1982, League Cup Winner–1982

Joining Luton Town from junior side Welwyn Garden, Paul had made a name for himself in schoolboy football with Welwyn and Middlesex Schoolboys before becoming a polished central defender at Kenilworth Road, making four International appearances for Wales, prior to joining Tottenham Hotspur in June 1981 for £200,000. Despite being born in St. Albans, his qualification for Wales came through his father's Welsh nationality, with his only U-21 appearance against Holland in September 1981, after previously gaining his Full cap against England, in a 4-1 victory on the 17th May 1980. His early period at Kenilworth Road saw him overcome two broken legs to command a regular place in a team that earned promotion honours at the end of the 1976/77 season, and also reach the fifth round of the League Cup, before losing 4-1 to Leeds United. During his first season at White Hart Lane, he was in competition with Paul Miller and Graham Roberts for a central defensive position, making just 21 league appearances, but, also playing in three Wembley Finals against Liverpool (League Cup Final), and QPR (FA Cup Final and Replay). Further competition from Gary Mabbutt, and John Lacy during the 1982/83 season, saw his league appearances reduced to just 16, and, at the end of the season after being given a free transfer, joined a number of players in sampling football in the USA with Minnesota Strikers. In January 1985, along with Derek Parlane, Ray McHale and Gary Williams he was one of a number of players signed by manager John Bond, in an attempt to escape from consecutive relegation seasons. Despite what appeared to be a lost cause, Paul was a tower of strength at the heart of the Swans defence as the club escaped relegation by virtue of drawing their last game of the season against Bristol City. The following season however, with financial problems escalating, the Swans were relegated to the Fourth Division, with the consolation being that the club was still in existence, despite numerous visits to the High Court. He scored his only league goal for the Swans at Ashton Gate against Bristol City in April 1986, with the Swans virtually assured of relegation to the Fourth Division. His only other goal for the Swans came in a 6-2 Welsh Cup, Third Round victory at Haverfordwest. At the end of the 1985/86 season, despite the offer of a new contract, he was unwilling to move his family from the Luton area, and signed for Peterborough United on a free transfer. After missing just six league games in two seasons and winning the Player of the Year Award in his first season at London Road, in 1988 he joined non-league Wivenhoe Town, made appearances for St. Albans City, and later linked up with former Spurs team mate Micky Hazard, becoming joint manager of Hitchin Town.

35. PRITCHARD, MARK

Birthplace: Tredegar, 23/11/1985
Ht: 5ft-9ins, **Wt:** 11st-0lbs
Swans debut: v. Cambridge United (h), 21/10/2003

Swansea City Career Statistics

Season	League	FAWC
2003/04	1+3	
2004/05		1/2gls
Total	1+3	1/2gls

Career:
Swansea City (scholar from July 2002)
Merthyr Tydfil (loan in 31/3/2005) Total Apps 5

Honours: Wales Sch, U-18, 19, Welsh Youth Cup Winner–2003, West Wales Senior Cup Winner–2003

Attached from the age of twelve to the Swans' Centre of Excellence sides, Mark was offered YTS at the age of thirteen, and arrived at the Vetch Field as a first year scholar in July 2002. He had earlier attended Georgetown Primary, and Tredegar Comprehensive School, gaining an U-15 cap for Wales, later playing at U-18 and U-19 level whilst with the Swans. Whilst in school, and prior to starting his scholarship at the Vetch Field, Mark played for Tredegar Town and Ashvale Colts. During the second year of his scholarship, the front runner took advantage of a lengthy injury list at the Vetch Field to make his league debut against Cambridge United at the Vetch Field on Tuesday 21st October 2003, after previously being involved on four occasions as a non-playing substitute earlier in the season. Despite playing in a side that lost 2-0, Mark displayed a good touch, going close with several opportunities. He made substitute appearances later in the season against Southend United, Torquay United and Rochdale, all at the Vetch Field. A prolific goalscorer at youth, and reserve team level for the Swans, Mark played in the Swans youth team that beat Llanelli to win the Welsh Youth Cup in May 2003, beat Carmarthen Town in the West Wales Senior Cup Final, and in May 2004 when they were beaten by Cardiff City in the final. Included in the Swans' pre-season tour of Holland in July 2004, shortly after the season started he received a setback, suffering a fractured cheekbone in a Football Combination game at the Vetch Field which kept him on the sidelines for a number of weeks. In late March 2005 he joined Merthyr Tydfil on a loan basis, and at the end of the season was offered professional terms by the Swans.

36. PUCKETT, DAVID Charles

Birthplace: Southampton, 29/10/1960
Ht: 5ft-7ins, **Wt:** 10st-5lbs
Swans debut: v. Blackpool (a), 26/11/1988

Swansea City Career Statistics				
Season	*League*	*FAC*	*WC*	*FRT*
1988/89	7+1/3gls	0+1	1	2
Total	7+1/3gls	0+1	1	2

Career:
Southampton (apprentice in March 1977, professional in October 1978) lge 51+43/14gls
Nottingham Forest (loan in October 1983)
Bournemouth (signed in July 1986) lge 29+6/14gls
Stoke City (loan in March 1988) lge 7
Swansea City (loan in November 1988)
Aldershot (signed in January 1989) lge 113/50gls
Bournemouth (signed in March 1992) lge 1+3
Woking (signed in August 1992) Conf apps, 50+9/14gls
Weymouth

Honours: Third Division Champions–1987, FA Trophy Winner–1994

A striker signed on loan by manager Terry Yorath from Bournemouth, who created a good impression in the two months he was at the Vetch Field, but the Swans were unwilling to pay the asking price to make the transfer permanent, and he returned to Dean Court, followed shortly by a transfer to Aldershot. The scorer of three goals during his period with the Swans, the first coming at Ninian Park against Cardiff City on Boxing Day 1988, his second in the next game at Bristol Rovers, and his third in what turned out to be his last game for the Swans, at the Vetch Field against Southend United. Attended Merry Oak School in Southampton earlier in his career, arriving at the Dell as an apprentice in March 1977, making his league debut alongside Kevin Keegan against Everton in March 1981, and helping the Saints to finish as First Division Runners-Up in season 1983/84, making 18 league appearances, eleven as substitute. Joining Bournemouth prior to the start of the 1986/87 season in a part exchange deal involving himself and Mark Whitlock, with Colin Clarke moving in the opposite direction, he scored ten goals as the 'Cherries' clinched the Third Division Championship. A knee injury on Boxing Day 1986 sidelined him for almost a season at Dean Court, and after loan spells with Stoke City and the Swans, he signed for Aldershot on a permanent transfer, and for the next four seasons, to the period when the club folded from the Football League, was top goalscorer on each occasion. Signing for Conference side Woking in August 1992, he enjoyed a substitute role at Wembley, replacing Hay in the 1994 F.A. Trophy Cup Final success over Runcorn. Since leaving Woking, he has made appearances for Weymouth, Newport (IOW), Salisbury City, Havant Town, Wokingham, Bashley, Eastleigh and BAT. During his time at the Dell with Southampton he became the club's first player to reach fifty substitute league and cup appearances for the club.

37. PURCELL, BRIAN Patrick John

Born: Swansea, 23/11/1938. **Died:** Bedwellty, 20/1/1969
Ht: 5ft-9¾ins, **Wt:** 10st-12¼lbs
Swans debut: v. Bristol City (h), 26/4/1960

Career:
Waun Wen
Swansea Town (signed in January 1958)
Hereford United (signed in July 1968)

Honours: Welsh Cup Winner–1966, Football Combination Second Division Champions–1961, Welsh League First Division Champions–1962

Swansea Town Career Statistics					
Season	League	FLC	FAC	WC	ECWC
1959/60	1				
1960/61				1	
1961/62	6			2	
1962/63	8				
1963/64	25		7	2	
1964/65	13		2		
1965/66	33+1	1		7	
1966/67	44	4	3	1	2
1967/68	34/1gls	1	4	2	
Total	164+1/1gls	6	16	15	2

Waun Wen born, and formerly with Swansea Senior League side Waun Wen, who after showing good form for the Swans' Football Combination and Welsh League sides, signed a professional contract in January 1958, and after completing his National Service, made his league debut in the last home match of the 1959/60 season against Bristol City, in a Swans side that had an average age of 21, setting a club record. During season 1960/61 he made regular appearances in the reserve side that won the Combination Second Division Championship, and the following season when they won the Welsh League First Division Championship. He had to wait until the 1961/62 season before he was given an extended run in the Swans line-up, making six consecutive league appearances for the injured Alan Sanders at right full back. The opening game of the 1962/63 season saw Purcell play at centre half, a position he was to go on to make a name for himself for the remainder of his career, with the 1963/64 season seeing the defender make a huge contribution as the Swans marched to the FA Cup semi-final at Villa Park, before losing out on a quagmire of a pitch by the odd goal in three. A member of the Welsh Cup winning side of 1965/66 over Chester, Purcell featured in the following season's European Cup Winners Cup games against Slavia Sofia, and by now had firmly established himself as the defensive pivot in the Swans line-up. The 1967/68 season was too be his last at the Vetch Field, but it also co-incided with the Vetch Field attracting a record attendance of 32,796 for the visit of Arsenal in the F.A Cup Fourth Round, and also for Purcell to score his only goal for the Swans, in a league game against Exeter City in February 1968. At the end of the season, along with experienced right full back Roy Evans, both players were given free transfers, joining Hereford United. Tragically, both players were killed in a car crash on a fog bound Heads of the Valleys road near Ebbw Vale, on their way to play for Hereford in a cup match at Nuneaton in January 1969. After leaving the Swans, Brian was also working part-time as a security guard, and at the end of the season he was due to tour the USA and Canada in a John Charles select team.

38. PURNELL, Philip (PHIL)

Birthplace: Bristol, 16/9/1964
Ht: 5ft-8ins, **Wt:** 10st-2lbs
Swans debut: v. Exeter City (h), 14/12/1991

Swansea City Career Statistics	
Season	League
1991/92	5/1gls
Total	5/1gls

Career:
Forest Green Rovers (signed in 1983)
Frome Town (signed in November 1983)
Mangotsfield United (signed in December 1983)
Bristol Rovers (signed in September 1985) lge 130+23/22gls
Swansea City (loan in 12/12/1991)

Honours: Third Division Champions–1990

Phil Purnell started his football career with Ridings High School, Winterbourne and Frampton Rangers before he signed as a junior with Rovers in 1975. After linking up with Parkway Juniors in 1978, he had a couple of years out of the game due to a back injury, resumed his career with Winterbourne United in 1982, then signed for Forest Green Rovers in 1983. He made further non-league appearances for Frome Town and Mangotsfield United before joining Bristol Rovers in September 1985, signing professional in July 1986. Scoring two league goals during his first season 1985/86, the last game of the 1986/87 season proved to be decisive for Purnell, as he scored the only goal of the game for Rovers at Somerton Park, a win which kept the 'Pirates' in the Third Division. The 1987/88 season proved to be the best as far as goal scoring during his time with the Rovers, returning eight league goals, and the following season when the 'Pirates' reached the Third Division Play Off Final at Wembley, Purnell scored seven league goals. Making twenty-two league appearances during the Rovers Third Division Championship winning season of 1989/90, he also played at Wembley against Port Vale in the Leyland Daf Final against Port Vale, losing 2-1. Signed by manager Frank Burrows on a month loan in December 1991, his only goal for the Swans came in his third appearance, against Stockport County at the Vetch Field. Returning to Rovers after his loan spell, he suffered a broken leg playing against Yeovil Town reserves in April 1992 which saw him retire from the game twelve months later, and take up employment in the Insurance business. A keen cricketer in the summer months, he has played representative cricket for the Bristol & District League XI, and has since had coaching/managerial links with Clevedon Town (youth team manager, January 1994), Bristol Rovers (schoolboy coach, July 1994), Yate Town (assistant manager, November 1994), and Winterbourne United (September 1998).

39. PUTTNAM, David (DAVE) Paul

Birthplace: Leicester, 3/2/1967
Ht: 5ft-10ins, **Wt:** 11st-12lbs
Swans debut: v. Brighton & Hove Albion (h), 9/8/1997

Swansea City Career Statistics		
Season	League	FLC
1997/98	4	2
Total	4	2

Career:
Leicester United (signed in 1986)
Leicester City (£8,000 signed in 9/2/1989) lge 4+3, FLC 4+3, FAC 0+1
Lincoln City (£40,000 signed in 21/1/1990) lge 160+17/21gls, FLC 13+1/1gls, FAC 4, Others 8+1

Gillingham (£50,000 signed in 6/10/1995) lge 15+25/2gls, FLC 1+5/1gls, FAC 0+5, Others 2
Yeovil Town (loan in April 1997)
Swansea City (signed in 7/8/1997)
Gresley Rovers (signed in 1997)

Former non-league player with Kirby Muxloe and Leicester United who signed for Leicester City in February 1989, before going on to make his league debut with City, and create a good impression as a left sided winger, wide midfielder, who could beat his opposing defender with pace and skill. Signed by City manager David Pleat after impressing in the club's Central League side, and given a professional contract with a view to take over from Peter Weir's return to Scottish football. However, he failed to consolidate his progress in his second season, and after rejecting a move to Carlisle United, joined Lincoln City initially on a loan transfer before making the move permanent. Player of the Year for 1993, he made over 200 league and cup appearances for Third Division side Lincoln City prior to signing for Gillingham in October 1995, making twenty-six league appearances in the club's promotion season, when they finished runners-up to Preston in the Third Division. Towards the end of his second season with Gillingham he had a loan spell with Yeovil Town, helping them to gain promotion to the Conference, before being released in May 1997, prior to arriving at the Vetch Field on an initial trial basis. Signed by manager Jan Molby, he made just four league appearances, and two in the League Cup competition, before being released after a defeat at Barnet in early September 1997. After leaving the Vetch Field he signed for Gresley Rovers, linking with Anstey Nomads later in December 1997. Returning to South Wales to make appearances for Barry Town in 1998, he returned to Gresley Rovers before signing for Kings Lynn where he was top goalscorer in the 1999/2000 season, and later made appearances for Barwell (July 2003) and Coalville.

R

1. RAJKOVIC, ANTE

Birthplace: Yugoslavia, 17/8/1952
Ht: 5ft-11ins, **Wt:** 12st-13lbs
Swans debut: v. Bristol City (h), 17/3/1981

Swansea City Career Statistics

Season	League	FLC	FAC	WC	ECWC
1980/81	2				
1981/82	40/1gls	1	1	7	2
1982/83	33/1gls	3	1	4	4/1gls
1983/84	3				
1984/85	1+1	2			
Total	79+1/2gls	6	2	11	6/1gls

Career:
Sarajevo
Swansea City (£100,000 signed in 6/2/1981)

Honours: Yugoslavia 'B'–10, Full–7, Welsh Cup Winner–1982, 1983

Ante became the Swans' second Yugoslavian player, following Dzemal Hadziabdic's addition to the Swans playing squad the previous September. Signing for the Swans for a £100,000 transfer fee from Yugoslavian side Sarajevo in February 1981, he made his first Swans appearance in front of 6,132 fans in a Vetch Field friendly against Red Star Belgrade, which the Swans won 7-1. He made his Swans debut five games later at the Vetch Field against Bristol City, suffered an injury which saw him miss five games, returning for the local derby against Cardiff City, only to miss out on the end of season promotion charge to the First Division. However, he was to make his mark in the top flight the following season, acclaimed by many pundits at the most accomplished sweeper in the First Division. An exceptionally

strong tackler, he also possessed excellent ball control, besides being a good reader of the game, taking numerous 'Man of the Match' performances through the club's first season in the First Division. He scored his first league goal for the Swans at Southampton in December 1981 in a 3-1 defeat, scoring his second goal the following season at the Vetch Field against Ipswich Town, also scoring in the Swans club record 12-0 European Cup Winners Cup tie at the Vetch Field against Sliema Wanderers. Later that season he played in the Welsh Cup Final against Cardiff City, playing also the following season in the first leg against Wrexham. Ante returned home at the end of season 1982/83, after the club had been relegated to the Second Division, but surprised supporters when he returned in April 1984 to play in three consecutive league games. With the club facing bankruptcy, and struggling to pay player's wages, he returned to Yugoslavia within a month after the start of the 1984/85 season, and within a couple of years was caught up in the civil war which broke up his homeland. Prior to signing for the Swans, Ante had gained ten 'B' caps for his country, and made his international debut for Yugoslavia against Brazil at Belo Horizonte on the 18th May 1978, the first of seven full caps.

2. RANDELL, COLIN William

Birthplace: Skewen, 12/12/1952
Ht: 5ft-7ins, **Wt:** 10st-13lbs
Swans debut: v. Blackpool (a), 31/8/1985

Swansea City Career Statistics

Season	League	FLC	FAC	WC	FRT
1985/86	18+1/1gls	3/3gls	1	1	1
1986/87	2+1	1			
Total	20+2/1gls	4/3gls	1	1	1

Career:
Coventry City (apprentice in November 1968, professional in
    12/12/1969) lge 0
Plymouth Argyle (signed in 5/9/1973) lge 137+2/9gls
Exeter City (£10,000 signed in 13/9/1977) lge 78/4gls
Plymouth Argyle (£60,000 signed in 31/7/1979) lge 110/8gls
Blackburn Rovers (£40,000 signed in August 1982) lge 72+1/7gls
Newport County (loan in March 1984) lge 15
Swansea City (signed in July 1985)
Preston North End (signed in September 1986)
Barry Town (signed in February 1987)
Briton Ferry (player manager in May 1987)

Honours: Wales Sch–5, Yth–14, U-23–2, FAW Touring XI–3,
Abacus Welsh League National Division Champions–1987,
South Wales Senior Cup Winner–1987

Former Coedffranc, Rhyd-Hir, Neath Boys Club and skipper of
Afan Nedd Schoolboys, who made five International Schoolboy
appearances for Wales against England (2), Scotland (2) and
Ireland prior to joining Coventry City after leaving school.
Although he failed to make a league appearance for the 'Sky
Blues', he was included in the squad that played Bayern Munich
in the Inter City Fairs Cup Competition in season 1970/71.
Skipper of the first Wales Professional Youth team in season
1969/70, over two seasons Colin made fourteen appearances for
Wales at Youth level, qualifying for the European Youth Cup in
each season in Scotland and Czechoslovakia. In 1971 he was a
member of an FAW Representative XI who toured New
Zealand, playing games against Auckland, Christchurch and
Wellington. Signing for Plymouth Argyle in September 1973, his
first season at Home Park saw the club reach the semi-final of
the League Cup, before losing 3-1 on aggregate to Manchester
City, with Colin playing in both semi-final legs. The following
season he was a regular in the Argyle midfield that were
runners-up to Blackburn Rovers in the Third Division, gaining
promotion, and also receiving his U-23 cap for Wales against
England at Wrexham on 21st January 1975, later playing against
Scotland. A strong tackler, and a hard worker in midfield, he
made over 400 league and cup appearances in the Second and
Third Divisions for Argyle, Exeter City, and Blackburn Rovers,
as well as a short loan spell at Somerton Park with Newport
County, prior to signing for Swans' manager John Bond in July
1985 on a free transfer. He missed the first three league games of
the season, making his debut instead of Keri Andrews in a 2-0
defeat at Blackpool. The scorer of two goals in the League Cup
win over Cardiff City, he scored his only league goal for the
Swans in a 5-1 away win at Wolverhampton Wanderers in
September 1985. His arrival at the Vetch Field was during the
most critical in the club's history, with a High Court winding up
order issued in December, with the club having an ongoing
battle for survival off the field, as well as having to come to
terms with a battle against relegation. With manager John Bond
being sacked by the Official Receiver, and the veteran Tommy
Hutchison taking over until the end of the season, former Wales
international Terry Yorath was appointed manager in July 1986,
and within a couple of weeks of the start of his second season at
the Vetch Field, Colin was released from his contract. After a
short period with Preston North End, he signed for Barry Town
in January 1987 as player manager, winning the Abacus Welsh
League National Division Championship and the South Wales
Senior Cup, and at the end of the season was installed as player
manager at Welsh League side Briton Ferry. He resigned as
player manager of Briton Ferry Athletic in March 1990, joining
the Police Force as a Physical Education Officer, and since then
has been based at Bridgend Headquarters and has achieved the
position of Head of Physical Education and Personal Safety.
During Brian Flynn's reign as manager at the Vetch Field, Colin
did scouting work for the football club.

3. RANSON, John George (JACK)

Birthplace: Norwich, 1/4/1909 **Died:** Goole, 2/9/1992
Ht: 5ft-10ins, **Wt:** 12st-0lbs
Swans debut: v. Cardiff City (a) WC-6, 2/4/1930

Swansea Town Career Statistics		
Season	League	WC
1929/30		1
1930/31	2	
Total	2	1

Career:
Norwich City (trial in October 1927, amateur in August 1928,
    professional in September 1928) lge 0
Swansea Town (signed in 17/6/1929)
Chester (signed in July 1931) lge 8/1gls
Colwyn Bay (signed in October 1931)
Gateshead (signed in June 1932) lge 32/21gls
Millwall (signed in May 1933) lge 14/3gls
Carlisle United (signed in November 1934) lge 15/9gls
Lincoln City (signed in June 1935) lge 5/1gls
Blyth Spartans (signed in June 1936)
Spennymoor United (signed in September 1936)
Durham City (signed in October 1936)
Horden C.W. (signed in March 1938 to September 1939)

Honours: West Wales Senior Cup Winner–1930

Inside forward who arrived at the Vetch Field from Norwich
City in 1930, played for the Swans whilst a B.A. student reading
English at Swansea University, and earlier in his career had
played Minor Counties cricket for Norfolk. He made his first
team debut in a sixth round Welsh Cup tie at Ninian Park,
which the Swans lost 4-0, and had to wait until the end of
January 1931 before making his league debut at inside left at
Reading. He made just one more league appearance for the
Swans, at Preston later in the season. In October 1930 he was
included in the Swans reserve side that beat Newport County to
win the West Wales Senior Cup Final. The former City of
Norwich Secondary Schoolboy signed for newly elected
Football League side Chester in the summer of 1931, and was
included in the club's first ever League game, on the 2nd
September 1931 at Wrexham, but after making just eight league
appearances joined non-league Colwyn Bay. Returning to
Football League action with Gateshead prior to the start of the
1932/33 season, John had probably his best campaign, scoring
twenty-one goals from thirty-two league appearances, with his
form attracting the attention of Second Division side Millwall.
Despite scoring a hat-trick in a 3-2 win over Southampton, he
found life difficult in London, returning north to sign for
Carlisle United in November 1934. Unfortunately for John, his
arrival at Carlisle United co-incided with what was probably the
club's most unsuccessful period, going a club record fourteen
games without a win early in 1935, despite the fact that John
finished the season as the club's second top goalscorer. Finishing
his League career with Lincoln City, where he was top scorer for
the club's reserve team in season 1935/36, John continued his
playing career on the non-league circuit with Blyth Spartans,
Spennymoor United, Durham City and Horden Colliery
Welfare. Concentrating on his career after leaving the
professional game, he initially worked as a teacher, but then
proceeded to build up a flourishing hotel and catering business
in Durham City. After selling his business, John moved to live
on a farm owned by his son near Goole, up to his death in
September 1992. His son, John junior, made seven international
appearances on the wing for England at Rugby Union, all
coming during the 1963/64 season.

4. RAWCLIFFE, FRANK

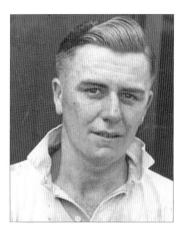

Birthplace: Blackburn, 10/12/1921. **Died:** Blackburn, 21/12/1986
Swans debut: v. Bournemouth (a), 23/8/1947

Swansea Town Career Statistics		
Season	League	FAC
1947/48	25/17gls	1
Total	25/17gls	1

Career:
Tranmere Rovers (signed in 1936)
Wolverhampton Wanderers (signed in January 1939) lge 0
Colchester United
Notts. County (signed in February 1943) lge 0
Newport County (signed in June 1946) lge 37/14gls
Swansea Town (£3,500 signed in 28/6/1947)
Aldershot (signed in July 1948) lge 35/14gls
Allessandria, Italy (signed in September 1949)
South Liverpool
Allessandria, Italy (signed in January 1951)

Signed on the 28th June 1947 for £3,500 from Newport County, Frank had just the one season at the Vetch Field, finishing top goalscorer with 17 league goals. The previous season had seen him score 14 league goals for County, with both the Swans and County being relegated to the Third Division South at the end of the season. During his only season at the Vetch Field, he opened his goalscoring account in only his second match for the Swans, in a 3-0 home win over Watford. Between the middle of November and the middle of January he scored eleven league goals from eight games, including a hat-trick at the Vetch Field against Norwich City. With the signing of Stan Richards for season 1948/49, Frank was transferred to Aldershot, scoring against the Swans at the Recreation Ground in a 2-1 away win for the Swans during season 1948/49. The start of his playing career saw him as an amateur with Tranmere Rovers, but after signing for Wolverhampton Wanderers, Colchester United and Notts. County, he had to wait until his arrival at Somerton Park with County to make his Football League debut. During WW2 he made guest appearances for Southport (1939/40), New Brighton (1939/40), Chester (1942/43), Crewe Alexandra (1942/43), Stockport County (1943/44) and Liverpool (1944/45). After one season with Aldershot in the Third Division South, and being placed on the 'open to offers' list in June 1949, went to play in Italy with Allessandria in September 1949, returning to play for non-league South Liverpool, but after a couple of months returned to play for Italian side Allessandria in January 1951.

5. RAYBOULD, Philip (PHIL) Edward

Birthplace: Caerphilly, 26/5/1948
Ht: 5ft-9¼ins, **Wt:** 11st-8½lbs
Swans debut: v. Aldershot (h), 13/4/1968

Swansea Town Career Statistics		
Season	League	FLC
1967/68	5/2gls	
1968/69	5+1/2gls	2
Total	10+1/4gls	2

Career:
Cardiff Corries (signed in 1963)
Bridgend Town (signed by October 1964)
Barry Town (signed in 1965)
Bridgend Town (signed in 1966)
Swansea Town (signed in July 1967)
Newport County (trial in August, signed in September 1969)
 lge 5+1/1gls
Barry Town (signed in August 1970)
Everwarm (signed in August 1976)

Honours: Wales Sch, Amateur–7

Former captain of the Wales Schoolboy side in May 1963 against Scotland, Phil also represented his country at Amateur level whilst with Bridgend Town, making his first appearance during season 1966/67 against Republic of Ireland, later against Scotland, England and Ireland. Early in his career he had caught the eye at Cardiff Corries and Bridgend Town prior to sampling Southern League football with Barry Town. After returning to Bridgend Town the hard working, attacking midfielder with an eye for goal was signed by manager Billy Lucas in July 1947 whilst still a student in Swansea University, but had to wait until almost the end of the season before he made his Swans debut. He scored his first goal in only his second league game in a 2-1 away win at Rochdale, scoring his second goal in a 1-0 defeat of Chester at the Vetch Field shortly before the end of the season. A part-time professional at the Vetch Field, despite starting the 1968/69 season at left half, he had been sidelined since mid-September 1968 with a knee injury, picked up in the match against Newport County, returning to fitness the following March. That injury prevented him from making a bigger impact, and at the end of the season was released, joining Newport County in September 1969 after an initial trial spell. He later played for Barry Town and Everwarm (Bridgend Town) before emigrating to Australia.

6. RAYNOR, PAUL James

Birthplace: Nottingham, 29/4/1966
Ht: 6ft-0ins, **Wt:** 12st-11lbs
Swans debut: v. Halifax Town (h), 29/3/1987

Career:
Nottingham Forest (from apprentice in April 1984) lge 3, FLC 1
Bristol Rovers (loan in March 1985) lge 7+1
Huddersfield Town (£30,000 in 15/8/1985) lge 38+12/9gls,
 FLC 3, FAC 2+1, Others 1
Swansea City (signed in 26/3/1987)
Wrexham (loan in 17/10/1988) lge 6
Cambridge United (signed in 10/3/1992) lge 46+3/2gls, FLC 5,
 FAC 1, Others 2+1/1gls
Preston North End (£36,000 signed in 23//7/1993)
 lge 72+8/9gls, FLC 4+1, FAC 7/1gls, Others 10/2gls

Cambridge United (signed in 12/9/1995) lge 78+1/7gls, FLC 1+1, FAC 2, Others 1
Guang Deong Wen Yuan, China (£20,000 signed in June 1997)
Leyton Orient (signed in 26/2/1998) lge 6+9, FLC 1+1
Stevenage Borough (signed in August 1998)
Kettering Town (signed in September 1998)

Honours: Welsh Cup Winner–1989, 1991, Fourth Division Play Off Winner–1988, West Wales Senior Cup Winner–1987

Swansea City Career Statistics							
Season	League	FLC	FAC	WC	FRT/ AGT	ECWC	P/Offs
1986/87	12/1gls						
1987/88	43+1/7gls	2/2gls	2	2/1gls	2		4/1gls
1988/89	23+3/5gls	2		4+1/4gls			
1989/90	38+2/6gls	2/1gls	2/1gls		1/1gls	2/1gls	
1990/91	36+7/5gls	2	4	5/1gls	4+1		
1991/92	18+8/2gls	3+1	0+1	1+1	1	1	
Total	170+21/ 26gls	11+1/ 3gls	8+1/ 1gls	12+2/ 6gls	8+1/ 1gls	3/1gls	4/1gls

Paul Raynor made almost 200 league appearances for the Swans in five years following his transfer from Huddersfield Town in March 1987, gaining a lot of respect from the home supporters for his hard work, and unselfish attitude to the game, whether in a striker, midfield, or as an occasional right full back. Starting his career as an apprentice with Nottingham Forest, following a short loan spell with Bristol Rovers, he signed for Second (First) Division side Huddersfield Town in August 1985, prior to being signed by manager Terry Yorath on transfer deadline day in March 1987 as a front line striker, scoring his first goal for the Swans in his fifth league game, at Exeter City in a 2-2 draw. At the time a £20,000 transfer fee was publicised, but later it turned out that he had joined the Swans on a free transfer. In May 1987 he was included in the Swans side that beat Briton Ferry Athletic in the West Wales Senior Cup Final. The following season he played his part in the club's Fourth Division Play Off success, scoring in the second leg of the final, and in both of the Welsh Cup Finals in 1989 and 1991. Enjoying every moment of his time at the Vetch Field, scoring a hat-trick in a Welsh Cup semi-final, second leg at the Vetch Field against Barry Town, twice Welsh Cup Final Winner, against Kidderminster Harriers and Wrexham, and also playing in the European Cup Winners Cup competition, against Panathinaikos, and Monaco, who were at the time managed by Arsenal boss Arsene Wenger. Following a short loan spell at the Racecourse with Wrexham in October 1988, he was allowed by manager Frank Burrows to join Cambridge United's promotion drive in March 1992. His playing career also saw him for twelve months play in China for Guang Deong Wen Yuan in a player coaching capacity, where games in Beijing and Shanghai regularly drew attendances of 50,000. He was given the opportunity to go to China in his

wedding reception by his manager Tommy Taylor, who had been approached by an agent who was looking for British players, or coaches who wanted the opportunity to go to China. Regarding the short period in China, Paul thought it was an ideal opportunity to increase his coaching experience, as he was looking to move into this field when he retired from full time football. Paul rejoined Leyton Orient for a short time after returning from China, but after moving into non-league football with Kettering in the Conference, also played for Ilkeston, Boston United, King's Lynn, Hednesford (brief spell as manager) and Ossett Albion. Fortunately for Paul, apart from the daily knocks picked up during his career, the only serious injury he has encountered was at Forest, as a youngster when he broke his leg. As well as playing for Kings Lynn during season 2003/04, he was also able to combine his coaching duties with the Sheffield United academy sides, and also help his father in his security business. In February 2004 he returned to Boston United as first team coach, later upgraded to assistant manager. During season 1999/2000 he played a number of games for Boston United when they won the Dr. Martens Premier Division Championship.

7. REECE, Gilbert (GIL) Ivor

Birthplace: Cardiff, 2/7/1942. **Died:** Cardiff, 20/12/2003
Ht: 5ft-7ins, **Wt:** 9st-9lbs
Swans debut: v. Doncaster Rovers (h), 18/9/1976

Swansea City Career Statistics	
Season	League
1976/77	0+2
Total	0+2

Career:
Ton Pentre (signed by January 1961)
Cardiff City (from juniors in May 1961) lge 0
Pembroke Borough (signed in 1962)
Newport County (signed in June 1963) lge 32/9gls
Sheffield United (£8,000 signed in April 1965) lge 197+13/58gls
Cardiff City (£25,000 + player exchange, signed in 22/9/1972) lge 94+6/23gls, ECWC 1+1
Swansea City (signed in July 1976)

Honours: Wales Sch, Full–29, Welsh Cup Winner–1973, 1974, 1976

Former Cardiff City skipper Gil Reece was Wales' outstanding left winger of his time, and from his early days as a part-timer with Cardiff City, where he doubled as a plumber, he was recognised as a brilliant prospect. After graduating from junior football with St. Patrick's FC, he initially caught the eye in Welsh

League football with Ton Pentre during the 1960/61 season, and by May 1961 had joined the playing staff at Ninian Park. He failed to break into the league side with the 'Bluebirds', and after returning to the Welsh League, this time with Pembroke Borough, was given his second opportunity of league football by Newport County manager Billy Lucas in June 1963. Although slightly built, he was a speedy flank man, strong in aerial challenges, and who gave many a defender a torrid time, and, in his schooldays represented Wales at Boxing. Attracting a number of scouts to Somerton Park with his skilful wing play on the left flank, before the end of the 1964/65 season he was sold to First Division side Sheffield United for £8,000, after scoring nine league goals for County. His seven full seasons at Bramall Lane saw him gain international honours with Wales, following his debut appearance on the international stage at Ninian Park against England on the 2nd October 1965, and become a valued member of the 'Blades' First Division squad. A colourful character, Reece was memorably forced to stay at the airport for a World Cup qualifier against East Germany in Dresden in 1969 because the Welsh FA had not booked enough plane seats. He had actually taken his seat on the plane when it was discovered the FAW discovered they were a seat short, and it was decided that the player last named alphabetically should get off and board a later flight – and that was Reece. Despite relegation to the Second Division in 1968, he played a major part in the club's promotion season of 1970/71, pipping his hometown side in the final run in for promotion back to the top flight of football, finishing runners-up to Leicester City. In October 1972 he found himself back at Ninian Park playing for Cardiff City, along with fellow United player Dave Powell in a deal that saw £25,000 and Alan Warboys head to Bramall Lane, scored in three consecutive Welsh Cup Finals (including a hat-trick against Bangor City in the 1972/73 Final), which the Bluebirds won twice, appointed club captain, and after suffering relegation in 1975 (finishing as top goalscorer with nine league goals), bounced back the following season from the Third Division as runners-up to Hereford United. He played in four consecutive Welsh Cup Finals for the 'Bluebirds', winning in 1973, 1974 and 1976, and losing to Wrexham in the 1975 final. Signed by manager Harry Griffiths to add some experience to a relatively youthful Swans' line-up, at the age of 34 he made just one more substitute appearance for the Swans after making his Swans' debut, at the Vetch Field against Doncaster Rovers in September 1976, as substitute for Jeremy Charles. Released after one season at the Vetch Field he finished his playing career with Irish side Athlone Town, and Barry Town, and continued in the plumbing and central heating business he had set up with his brother Les, before becoming a hotelier, running the Clare Court Hotel in Grangetown, Cardiff with his wife Carol. He suffered with poor health in later years, and in April 2000 had his right leg amputated after cysts kept appearing behind the knee, prior to his death in December 2003.

8. REED, William (BILLY) George

Birthplace: Ynyshir, Rhondda, 25/1/1928. **Died:** Swansea, January 2003
Ht: 5ft-8ins, **Wt:** 10st-3lbs
Swans debut: v. Middlesbrough (a), 1/3/1958

Swansea Town Career Statistics	
Season	League
1957/58	8
Total	8

Career:
Rhondda Transport
Cardiff City (signed in July 1947) lge 0
Brighton & Hove Albion (signed in August 1948) lge 129/36gls
Ipswich Town (£1,750 in July 1953) lge 155/43gls

Swansea Town (£3,000 in 27/2/1958)
Worcester City (signed in July 1959)

Honours: Wales Sch, Wales Amateur–2, Full–2, Third Division South Champions–1954, 1957

A Welsh schoolboy international, Billy played for WattsTown F.C. from the age of fourteen, and also represented the South Wales Federation of Boys' Clubs. In season 1946/47 he won two caps against England at amateur level while playing for Rhondda Transport, before joining Cardiff City as a nineteen-year-old professional in July of that year. After playing for the reserve team at Ninian Park, the young Welshman joined the Albion in August 1948 and contributed to the great improvement under manager Don Welsh. Billy Reed was one of the few players to gain international status after leaving the Goldstone. A fast-raiding winger, he proved a great success in his five seasons in Hove after an initial settling-in period, and developed an excellent understanding with Johnny McNichol down the right flank. For a winger his scoring rate was tremendous, and he was joint top goalscorer on nineteen goals in 1951–52 when he played in every match. Billy's time at the Goldstone Ground was not all plain-sailing, though, and after requesting a move on several occasions, his wish was fulfilled when he was transferred to Ipswich Town for £1,750 in July 1953. In just over 4 seasons at Portman Road, Billy made a further 155 league appearances, scoring 43 goals, and gained his two Welsh International caps whilst on the playing staff at Portman Road, his first against Yugoslavia at Ninian Park on the 22nd September 1954, and his second, on the 16th October at the same ground against Scotland, with both games resulting in defeats. His first season at Portman Road saw the club win the Third Division South Championship, with Billy scoring thirteen goals from forty-one league games. Despite suffering relegation in the first season in the Second Division, within two seasons the club had won the Third Division South Championship for a second time, this time Billy scoring ten goals from thirty-seven league appearances. A 'wily' winger, who also played in either inside forward positions, he had deceptive pace, and the ability to cross and shoot well. Signing for the Swans for a fee of £3,000 in February 1958 from Ipswich Town, he made his Swans' debut at inside right instead of D Lewis, playing the remainder of his appearances that season, at either outside right, inside left, or at outside left before being forced into retirement at the end of the season. Joining Worcester City in July 1959, he scored five goals from fourteen matches, but after failing to overcome a long standing injury problem, he failed to regain full fitness, and stepped down to the Welsh League to sign for Abergavenny Thursdays. He subsequently played in minor football with Kaer Athletic, and worked as a local government officer in Swansea, coached local youngsters and did some scouting work for Dave Bowen, manager of the Welsh national side up to his retirement.

9. REES, Evan Glasnant (GUS)

Birthplace: Loughor, 29/10/1903. **Died:** Swansea, July 1991
Ht: 5ft-9ins, **Wt:** 11st-8lbs
Swans debut: v. Bury (h), 13/9/1930

Swansea Town Career Statistics		
Season	League	WC
1930/31	5	1
1931/32	2	2
1932/33	2	1
Total	9	4

Career:
Loughor Juniors

Swansea Town (signed in season 1927/28)
Loughor Stars
Swansea Town (trial in August 1930, professional in 30/8/1930)
Torquay United (signed in June 1933) lge 46/2gls
Altrincham (signed in August 1935)

Former Loughor Juniors inside forward who joined the Swans in season 1927/28, and after failing to impress the club's management, returned to play senior football with Loughor Stars. In August 1930 he was invited back to the Vetch Field for a pre-season trial, along with Loughor Stars team mate, Iorwerth Jones, a former Llanelly and Wales International Rugby player. 'Gus' had previously been on the Swans staff as an inside forward, but after switching to half back had been invited back to the Vetch Field for the pre-season trial by manager Thomson. Possessing a small frame during his first period with the Swans, over three years he had developed into a right half back who could more than hold his own in the game. Signing professional shortly after impressing in the trial, during his career at the Vetch Field he made league appearances at half back, full back, and at outside left. He made his league debut as a replacement for Deacon, making five consecutive league appearances during season 1930/31. His appearances over the next two seasons came as replacements for either Milne, or Lawrence at full back, or in one match for Tommy Olsen at outside left. He also made three Welsh Cup appearances during the last two seasons with the Swans. He was released by the Swans in March 1933, joining Third Division South side Torquay United, and two seasons later signed for non-league side Altrincham.

10. REES, David IOAN

Birthplace: Cross Hands, 21/9/1943
Ht: 5ft-8ins, **Wt:** 10st-0lbs
Swans debut: v. Swindon Town (h) FLC-1, 23/9/1964

Swansea Town Career Statistics		
Season	*League*	*FLC*
1964/65	1	1/1gls
1968/69	0+1	
Total	1+1	1/1gls

Career:
Ammanford Town
Swansea Town (signed in December 1961)
Ammanford Town (signed prior to start of season 1965/66)
Swansea Town (signed in August 1968)
Haverfordwest County (signed in season 1968/69)
Ammanford Town (signed in close season 1970)

Honours: Welsh League Champions–1962, 1963, 1964, 1965

Attended Gorslas Junior School, then Cross Hands Secondary Modern, played for Carmel Stars in Ammanford & District League, and played Welsh League for Ammanford Town when he was 14 years of age, leaving school to be an apprentice mechanic. Signed for Ammanford Town, and was getting £2 a week in the garage, and £3 playing for Ammanford Town on a Saturday. Signed initially for the Swans by Trevor Morris in 1961, he made his first team debut at the Vetch Field against Swindon Town in late September 1964 in the Football Legaue Cup, winning 3-1, scoring the third goal, and then played against Manchester City three days later, winning 3-0, with Keith Todd scoring a hat-trick. Top goalscorer for the Swans in every season for the Welsh League side (no Combination Team in those days), and also won the Welsh League Championship in four consecutive seasons. He was released in May 1965, the year the club was relegated to the Third Division, and signed for Ammanford, managed by former Swans player Roy Saunders. In two and a half years at Rice Road, they finished runners-up twice to Cardiff City in the Welsh League, then following the appointment of Billy Lucas as manager at the Vetch Field had his second spell with the Swans, shortly after the start of the 1968/69 season, making his debut as a substitute against Southend United in a 2-2 draw. A week later he played in the 3-0 win over Notts. County, and four days later was a non-playing substitute at Anfield against Liverpool in a League Cup tie, which the Swans lost 2-0. Midway through the season he linked up with Ivor Allchurch and Mel Charles at Haverfordwest County, also finishing each season at Bridge Meadow in runners-up position. He had an offer to go play in Holland, but declined, remaining at home and rejoining Ammanford Town. Later in his career he made appearances for an Ammanford based factory side called Pullmans, who played in the Carmarthenshire League. During his career he appeared in trial games for the Wales Amateur side, but was never selected, and played up to the age of 49 for his hometown side, ending up at full back. During his time in the game he was probably the most prolific goalscorer in the Welsh League scene at the time. Went to work in open cast mining after leaving full time football, and then followed his wife, who was a nurse in Amman Valley Hospital, to work as a porter. During his early career under Trevor Morris he felt that when things went wrong on the field he felt he was always the first player to be dropped, although when he was on the field he never played in a losing side! His son Anthony for a short period was involved with the Swans, but did not make a first team appearance.

11. REES, MATTHEW

Birthplace: Swansea, 2/9/1982
Ht: 6ft-3ins, **Wt:** 13st-2lbs
Swans debut: v. Lincoln City (a), 10/4/2004

Swansea City Career Statistics	
Season	League
2003/04	3/1gls
Total	3/1gls

Career:
Millwall (from scholar in 1999)
Swansea City (loan in 25/3/2004)
Crawley Town (signed in August 2004)
Newport County (signed in November 2004)
Port Talbot (signed in December 2004)

Honours: Wales U-21–2

Former Pentrehafod Comprehensive schoolboy, and Swansea schoolboy defender who joined Millwall as a trainee on leaving school. A regular in the Millwall reserve team during the past couple of seasons, he has also had loan spells with non-league sides Aldershot and Dagenham & Redbridge, prior to joining the Swans on loan on transfer deadline day in March 2004. Despite his lack of first team experience, he impressed with his aerial ability, and overall play, scoring on his league debut at Lincoln City. He made two further starts for the Swans against Hull City and at Bristol Rovers before returning to Millwall, where he was released at the end of the season on a free transfer. On the 6th September 2002 he made his first appearance for the Wales U-21 side as a substitute for Rhys Day in Finland, making his first start for the U-21 side in March 2003 against Azerbaijan. In mid-August 2004 he signed non-contract with Nationwide Conference side Crawley Town, but in mid-October he had his contract at the club cancelled. On the 2nd November 2004 he made his debut for Newport County in a Carthium cup tie at Weymouth, but within a couple of weeks had signed for League of Wales side Port Talbot.

12. REES, Ronald (RONNIE) Raymond

Birthplace: Ystradgynlais, 4/4/1944
Ht: 5ft-8ins, **Wt:** 10st-8lbs
Swans debut: v. Rotherham United (h), 22/1/1972

Career:
Coventry City (apprentice in July 1960, professional in May 1962) lge 230/42gls

West Bromwich Albion (£65,000 signed in March 1968)
   lge 34+1/9gls
Nottingham Forest (£60,000 signed in February 1969)
   lge 76+9/12gls
Swansea City (£26,000 in January 1972)
Haverfordwest (signed in August 1975)

Swansea City Career Statistics				
Season	League	FLC	FAC	WC
1971/72	21		1	
1972/73	34+1/2gls	2	1	2
1973/74	24/3gls		1	1
1974/75	9	1		2
Total	88+1/5gls	3	3	5

Honours: Wales U-23–7, Full–39, Third Division Champions–1964, Second Division Champions–1967, West Wales Senior Cup Winner–1975

Former Coventry City apprentice who had gained 39 international caps for Wales by the time he arrived at the Vetch Field for a club record transfer fee of £26,000. At the time it was felt that he would be the player that would give the Swans side that touch more quality, to enable them to push themselves for a more realistic promotion challenge. However, such was his treatment in his debut game at the Vetch Field from the opposition, it proved to have the opposite effect. Born in Ystradgynlais, but brought up in Merthyr, Ronnie attended Queens Road School and represented Merthyr Schoolboys prior to arriving at Highfield Road as an apprentice in July 1960, turning professional at the age of 18, becoming part of the Coventry City 'Sky Blue' revolution that swept from the Third to the First Division in the 1960's, winning Championship honours in both the Third and Second Divisions. He gained his first Wales U-23 honour whilst at Highfield Road, in 1963 against Scotland, gaining his first Full international cap on the 30th October 1964 at Ninian Park in a 3-2 win over Scotland. Following further transfers to First Division sides West Bromwich Albion and Nottingham Forest, he was signed by manager Roy Bentley, during the club's second season back in the Third Division. However, the left, or right sided winger was unable to produce any consistent performances in a tough tackling division. Possessing an electric turn of pace, and good ball skills, Ronnie had to wait until October 1972 before he scored his first goal for the Swans, in a 6-2 Vetch Field victory over Grimsby Town. A change of management at the Vetch Field with Harry Gregg taking over from Bentley in November 1972 also brought a change in playing style for the Swans, which didn't complement the potential skill on the ball provided by Rees, but a more workmanlike performance from the team as a whole. In May 1975 he was included in the Swans side that beat Briton Ferry Athletic to win the West Wales Senior Cup. He was released by the Swans at the end of the 1974/75 season, signing for Welsh League side Haverfordwest, and working in the Ford factory in Swansea, then transferring to their new factory at Bridgend. He finished his playing career with Swansea Senior League side Bishopston, where his sons first entered senior football, and in later years was forced to take early retirement through illness.

13. REES, William (BILLY)

Birthplace: Swansea, 31/9/1937
Ht: 5ft-8ins, **Wt:** 10st-8lbs
Swans debut: v. Rotherham United (h), 6/11/1954

Swansea Town Career Statistics		
Season	League	WC
1954/55	1	
1955/56		
1956/57		
1957/58	5	2
Total	6	2

Career:
Swansea Town (from juniors in October 1954)
Peterborough United (signed in 3/7/1958)
Crystal Palace (signed in 20/5/1959) lge 17/1gls
Hastings United (signed in July 1960)

Honours: Wales Sch, West Wales Senior Cup Winner–1954, Football Combination Second Division Champions–1955

Former junior at the Vetch Field who made his league debut for the Swans six weeks past his seventeenth birthday at outside left instead of Cliff Jones. In May 1954 he had been a member of the Swans side that beat Llanelly to win the West Wales Senior Cup, and the following season had been regularly included in the Swans' reserve side that won the Football Combination Second Division Championship. The former Pentrepoeth schoolboy had earlier played at Wembley for the Wales Schoolboys side against England. He started his National Service in early March 1956 in the R.E.M.E, based in the West Country, and had to be content with reserve team appearances for the Swans until the 1957/58 season, when in mid-February 1958 he played against Ipswich Town at the Vetch Field, again as a replacement for Jones. He played in the next two league matches, making his fourth appearance of the season a few weeks later at Derby County. He was released at the end of the season joining non-league side Peterborough United along with Swans reserve defender Jeff Rees in July 1958, but after failing to make an appearance, signed for Fourth Division side Crystal Palace. Making his Palace debut at Darlington on the 24th October 1959, he made a further sixteen league appearances before being released at the end of the season. In July 1960 he signed for non-league Hastings United.

14. REEVES, PETER Philip

Birthplace: Swansea, 20/1/1959
Ht: 5ft-6½ins, **Wt:** 10st-2lbs
Swans debut: v. Newport County (h), FLC 1–2, 15/8/1978

Swansea City Career Statistics		
Season	League	FLC
1978/79	2+2	1
Total	2+2	1

Career:
Coventry City (from apprentice in December 1976) lge 0
Swansea City (signed in July 1978)
Barry Town (signed in season 1979/80)

Honours: Wales Sch–1

Former Swansea schoolboy who joined Coventry City from school as an apprentice, signing professional in December 1976. Originally from Cwmbwrla, the Bishop Gore schoolboy played for Swansea schoolboys at the same time as Nigel Stevenson and Stephen Morris, and made one appearance for the Welsh schoolboys side at Goodison Park against England. He failed to make an appearance in the 'Sky Blues' first team during his two seasons as a professional at Highfield Road, although he did get close in his second year to a first team opportunity. After being released from the 'Sky Blues', he joined the Swans prior to the start of the 1978/79 season, making his debut in the second leg of the League Cup tie at the Vetch Field against Newport County, with his league debut four days later in a 2-2 draw at Colchester United. He struggled to command a place in the Swans midfield through the season, making a further start in a 1-0 win at Bury, plus two appearances as substitute. Shortly after the start of the 1979/80 season his contract with the Swans was cancelled, and he joined Southern League side Barry Town. During his second season at Jenner Park he suffered a broken leg which sidelined him for a year, and on his return made appearances for Haverfordwest County, Ton Pentre, before having a three year spell with Bridgend Town. Making further Welsh League appearances for Maesteg Park and Port Talbot, Peter finished his career with Swansea Senior League side Mumbles Rangers, where he became involved in training and coaching at the club. Going to work for former Swans defender Doug Rosser at Abbey Life after leaving the professional game, Peter remained in financial services with Sun Alliance, and is currently working as an IFA in his own company.

15. REID, Ernest (ERNIE) James

Birthplace: Pentrebach, 25/3/1914
Ht: 5ft-7ins, **Wt:** 11st-0lbs
Swans debut: v. Cardiff City (a), WC-6 Rep, 15/3/1933

Swansea Town Career Statistics		
Season	League	WC
1932/33	1	1
1933/34		1
Total	1	2

Career:
Troedyrhiw
Plymouth United

Swansea Town (trial in late season 1931/32, signed professional in July 1932)
Chelsea (amateur signed in October 1937, professional in May 1940) lge 1
Norwich City (signed in June 1945) lge 5
Bedford Town (signed in October 1947)

Inside right who made his Swans debut at Ninian Park against Cardiff City in the sixth round replay of the Welsh Cup, making his league debut three days later at the Vetch Field against Stoke City. He made just one more first team appearance for the Swans, in a Welsh Cup, sixth round defeat at Chester in February 1934. Earlier in his career he had non-league experience with Rhondda sides Troedyrhiw, and Plymouth United prior to arriving at the Vetch Field midway through the 1931/32 season, playing on trial in reserve team matches. He later signed for First Division Chelsea in September 1937, and in his two seasons at Stamford Bridge, spent mainly in the reserve team, made just one league appearance, in a 2-1 defeat at Grimsby Town on the 5th November 1938. During WW2 he made guest appearances for Bournemouth (1940/41), Millwall (February 1941), Brighton & Hove Albion (September 1942) and Norwich City (May 1943). When the league was resumed after the war he signed for Third Division South side Norwich City, later played for Bedford Town. He is the younger brother of Sydney Reid who played for Luton Town.

16. REID, PAUL Robert

Birthplace: Oldbury, 19/1/1968
Ht: 5ft-9ins, **Wt:** 11st-8lbs
Swans debut: v. Rushden & Diamonds (h), 10/8/2002

Career:
Leicester City (from apprentice in 9/1/1986) lge 140+22/21gls, FLC 13/4gls, FAC 5+1, Others 6+2
Bradford City (loan in 19/3/1992) lge 7

Bradford City (£25,000 signed in 27/7/1992) lge 80+2/15gls, FLC 3/2gls, FAC 3, Others 5/1gls
Huddersfield Town (£70,000 signed in 20/5/1994) lge 70+7/6gls, FLC 9/1gls, FAC 5+1, Others 1
Oldham Athletic (£100,000 signed in 27/3/1997) lge 93/6gls, FLC 4/1gls, FAC 8, Others 1
Bury (signed in 2/7/1999) lge 102+8/9gls, FLC 5/1gls, FAC 5+1, Others 5
Swansea City (signed in 1/7/2002)
Carmarthen Town (signed in 27/3/2003)

Swansea City Career Statistics				
Season	League	FLC	LDV	FAWP
2002/03	18+2/1gls	1	1	1
Total	18+2/1gls	1	1	1

Experienced midfielder who by the time he was signed by manager Nick Cusack had made over 600 league and cup appearances, mostly in the Second Division, after starting his career as an apprentice with Leicester City, signing professional in January 1986. A competitive midfielder, during the early part of his career, he was a consistent goalscorer, regularly on the goalsheet for his clubs. His only successful period as a player was during a spell with Huddersfield Town during season 1994/95, which saw him make 42 league appearances, but was ruled out of the Second Division Play Off Final success against Bristol Rovers. One of Cusack's first signings during the close season of 2002, he made an immediate impact on the field during his debut game for the Swans against Rushden & Diamonds, putting the Swans ahead in the first half with a tremendous shot from outside the penalty area. However, with the early season form slowly deteriorating, and a change of management at the club, he struggled to make an impact under manager Flynn, and in March 2003 he signed non-contract terms for JT Hughes Mitsubishi Welsh Premiership side Carmarthen Town, and also taking up a position with the Royal Mail as a postman in the city. The 35 year-old midfielder had his contract terminated by mutual consent after falling out of favour with Brian Flynn, and at the time of his release he admitted that he would like to sign for a local club. Reid joined a sizable ex-Swans contingent at Richmond Park that included David Barnhouse, Shaun Chapple, Jonathan Keaveny, Leigh De-Vulgt and Nigel Stevenson (assistant manager). In late July 2004 he signed for League of Wales side Afan Lido.

17. REID, Robert (BOBBY) Bell Alexander

Birthplace: Dundee 18/11/1936. **Died:** Kirkcaldy 29/7/2000
Ht: 5ft-9ins, **Wt:** 10st-4lbs
Swans debut: v. Barnsley (a), 7/9/1957

Swansea Town Career Statistics		
Season	League	FAC
1957/58	13	1
1958/59	1	
1959/60	3	
Total	17	1

Career:
Lochee Harp
Swansea Town (signed in September 1957)
Arbroath (signed in 1/9/1960)
Raith Rovers (£1,000 signed in 31/5/1963) SL 239, SLC 49, SFC 8, Others 30+1

Bobby attended Morgan Academy in Dundee, and then Pitlochry High School, playing for Monifieth in Tayside Juvenile football at the age of sixteen, and two years later joining Lochee Harp. Despite a number of scouts from professional clubs watching his progress, it was the Swans who signed him in September 1957, giving him his first opportunity of a professional contract, taking over from keeper Dai Jones for his debut against Barnsley, with Johnny King injured. Bobby made ten consecutive league appearances before King was re-instated as first choice, but by the end of the season, Reid had made a further three more starts for the Swans. He also made an appearance in the FA Cup third round tie at Burnley, which the Swans lost 4-2. Over the next two seasons he was unable to oust King from the first team apart from four league games, and in September 1960 returned north to sign for recently relegated from the First Division side, Arbroath. Three years later he joined Raith Rovers for £1,000, making his debut on the opening day of the 1963/64 season in a 1-1 draw against East Fife in the League Cup. One of his team mates in that game was Frank Burrows, a defender who would not only make a name for himself as a player, but also as one of the most astute manager's around the lower leagues in later years. Two seasons later another player who would later make a large contribution to the Swans fortunes in later years, Tommy Hutchison, would also play in the same Raith Rovers side as Bobby. When Bobby returned to Scotland after leaving the Vetch Field he remained a part-time professional, with his full time career being with Ross Electrical, a job which saw him work away from home on many occasions. During the club's promotion season of 1966/67, when they came runners-up to Morton and returned to the First Division, Bobby played in forty-nine matches. Another member of the Raith side that season that also had connections with South West Wales was Gordon Wallace, who's father Doug, was at one time manager of Llanelly in the Southern League. An agile keeper, despite his lack of inches, Bobby was also a good shot stopper, possessed good timing and athleticism, as well as being no push over when it came to physical challenges in the penalty area. Basically a reserve team player in his latter years at Raith Rovers, Bobby retired in February 1974, but having reached the position of Managing Director at Ross Electrical, he was invited onto the Board of Directors at Stark Park where his business acumen was put to the club's benefit. He resigned from the Board in August 1982, becoming purely a spectator at the club's home matches. A guitarist in a popular ceilidh band for many years, after retiring from the electrical business, he and his family ran a pub and restaurant in Dysart before the early signs of ill health forced him to retire for good, prior to his passing away in July 2000. Bobby's last match for Raith came a good three years after he had officially retired, when after an outbreak of flu had decimated the Rovers squad, on the 14th February 1976, and with no reserve team and no back up goalkeeper available, Bobby played his last game, in a 2-1 defeat by Montrose, at the age of 39 years and 3 months old.

18. REWBURY, JAMIE

Birthplace: Wattstown, Rhondda, 15/2/1986
Ht: 6ft-2ins, **Wt:** 12st-01lbs
Swans debut: v. Lincoln City (a), 10/4/2004

Swansea City Career Statistics		
Season	League	FAWC
2003/04	1+1	0+1
Total	1+1	0+1

Career:
Swansea City (signed as scholar in July 2002)
Cardiff City (trial in December 2004)

Honours: Wales Sch, U-17, 19, 20, Welsh Youth Cup Winner–2003, West Wales Senior Cup Winner–2003

Second year scholar who made his league debut as substitute for Stuart Jones at right full back at Lincoln City in April 2004. Two days later against Hull City at the Vetch Field he made his first start, in central defence alongside inexperienced loan signing Matthew Rees. An extremely talented player, capable of playing in either a defensive, or attacking role, within a couple of weeks of starting his scholarship at the Vetch Field after leaving school, he had been included in pre-season matches with the Swans under manager Nick Cusack, playing in a pre-season friendly at Hednesford Town in August 2002. Jamie attended Aberllechau Junior, and Porth County Comprehensive School prior to arriving at the Vetch Field as a first year scholar in July 2002. At the age of eleven he had been attached to the Swans Centre of Excellence sides, and gained his Welsh Schoolboy cap at the age of fifteen in the Victory Shield. He has since been capped at U-17, 19, and 20 age groups for Wales. Whilst in school Jamie played for Ynyshir & Wattstown Boys Club, and then Trebanog Rangers. At the end of season 2002/03 he was a member of the Swans Youth side that beat Llanelli to win the Welsh Youth Cup, also a member of the Swans side that beat Carmarthen Town in the West Wales Senior Cup Final, and twelve months later, was also in the youth side that were beaten by Cardiff City in the Welsh Youth Cup Final. He was included in the Swans 2004 pre-season squad that played friendly games in Holland. Finding first team opportunities limited in central defence, on the 17th November 2004, after discussions with manager Kenny Jackett, the third year scholar left the Vetch Field playing staff and began a search for a new club. By the beginning of December he started training at Ninian Park with Cardiff City, later signed a contract at the club playing against the Swans at the Vetch Field in a Combination game in early March 2005. In May he was released by the Bluebirds from the playing squad at Ninian Park, and in mid-July lined up for Merthyr Tydfil in a pre-season friendly against the Swans.

19. REYNOLDS, Arthur BRAYLEY

Birthplace: Blackwood, 30/5/1935
Ht: 5ft-9ins, **Wt:** 11st-6lbs
Swans debut: v. Lincoln City (h), 22/8/1959

Swansea Town Career Statistics					
Season	League	FLC	FAC	WC	ECWC
1959/60	37/16gls		3	2/2gls	
1960/61	29/8gls		3/3gls	5/6gls	
1961/62	33/18gls	1/1gls	1	3/4gls	2/2gls
1962/63	15/3gls		2/1gls	1	
1963/64	29/12gls	2/1gls		1	
1964/65	7/1gls				
Total	150/58gls	3/2gls	9/4gls	12/12gls	2/2gls

Career:
Fleur-de-Lys
Lovells Athletic
Cardiff City (£2,500 signed in May 1956) lge 54/15gls
Swansea Town (£6,000 signed in 16/5/1959)
Lovells Athletic (signed in close season 1965)
Merthyr Tydfil (signed in close season 1967)
Worcester City (signed in September 1968)
Merthyr Tydfil (signed in May 1969)

Honours: Welsh Cup Winner–1961, West Wales Senior Cup Winner–1961, 1962, South Wales Senior Cup Winner–1970

Frontrunner who had an exceptional goalscoring record with the Swans following his £6,000 transfer from Cardiff City in May 1959. Signed by manager Trevor Morris, he had initially played under Morris during his period as manager at Ninian Park, when Morris had signed him from Lovells Athletic for £2,500. Brought up in Fleur-de-Lys in the Rhymney Valley, Brayley attended Fairview Council and New Tredegar Technical Schools, won the Blackwood & District League Championship with Fairview School, but at the Technical School played only rugby. After leaving school he worked at the Lovells sweet factory for a short time, and then entered the mining industry, where he would return to after leaving the professional game. Starting his senior career with Fleur-de-Lys in the South Wales Amateur League, he then signed for Lovells Athletic, prior to Cardiff City. A miner, and part-time professional at Ninian Park, he finished top goalscorer for the Swans in season 1961/62 and 1963/64, but was unfortunate to miss out on the club's 1963/64 FA Cup semi-final run. In the 1961 West Wales Senior Cup Final against Haverfordwest he scored four goals in a 7-6 win, and twelve months later scored a hat-trick in a 4-0 win in the same final, this time over Llanelly. Runner up to Colin Webster during his first season at the Vetch Field with sixteen league goals, having to wait until his fifth game before he opened his account for the season, which included two goals in a game on three occasions. His second season at the Vetch Field saw him score in the Welsh Cup Final against Bangor City, also scoring the following season in both legs of the European Cup Winners Cup tie against East German side Motor Jena. A whole hearted player, Brayley was an opportunist in the penalty area, as his 78 goals from 176 league and cup appearances testify, and who was able to keep his forward line moving. Scored two hat-tricks for the Swans during season 1963/64, against Plymouth Argyle at the Vetch Field, and against Haverfordwest in a Welsh Cup, Fifth Round tie. Returning to Lovells Athletic as player coach after leaving the Vetch Field, he later had two spells with Merthyr Tydfil and also played for Worcester City (scoring eight goals from forty appearances). With recurring ankle problems eventually forcing him into retirement, his second spell with Merthyr saw him win the South Wales Senior Cup in 1970, beating Cardiff City in the final. After his retirement as a player Brayley became involved with coaching U-12's and U-14's at Pengam for a number of years. He worked for Girlings at Cwmbran for nine years, and after returning to the mining industry was the last man out of Penallta Colliery, Hengoed when the pit shut down, retiring in October 1991.

20. RHODES, Richard (DICKIE) A.

Birthplace: Wolverhampton, 18/2//1908.
Died: Wolverhampton, 21/1/1993
Ht: 5ft-10ins, **Wt:** 12st-0lbs
Swans debut: v. Manchester City (a), 27/8/1938

Swansea Town Career Statistics			
Season	League	FAC	WC
1938/39	25/1gls	1	3
Total	25/1gls	1	3

Career:
Redditch United
Wolverhampton Wanderers (signed in May 1926) lge 149/7gls
Sheffield Wednesday (signed in October 1935) lge 57
Swansea Town (£400 signed in 22/6/1938)
Rochdale (£150 signed in 29/7/1939) lge 3

Honours: England Junior International–1924/25, Second Division Champions–1932

Former Wolverhampton schoolboy player who played at centre forward with his first senior club, Redditch United, but was converted to right half back at Wolverhampton Wanderers, where he went on to make almost 150 league appearances, before transferring to Sheffield Wednesday in 1935. Was a member of the Wolverhampton Wanderers side that won the Second Division Championship at the end of season 1931/32, playing in both league games against the Swans, also gaining Junior International honours for England against Scotland in season 1924/25. Played two seasons for Sheffield Wednesday in the First Division, and after the 'Owls' had been relegated at the end of the 1936/37 season, played twice against the Swans the following season in the Second Division. Signed by manager Neil Harris in June 1938 for £400 from Sheffield Wednesday, with Idris Lewis joining Wednesday at the same time, he played just the one season at the Vetch Field before being sold to Rochdale for £150 on the 29th July 1939. He scored his only goal for the Swans in his second league game, at Bradford Park Avenue in a 1-1. Playing mainly at right half back, throughout the season he contested the position with Bill Imrie and John Harris. He was also a member of the Swans side that were beaten by Shrewsbury Town in a Welsh Cup Final replay carried over from the previous season. At Rochdale he played in their first game of season 1939/40 at Doncaster Rovers. The League was abandoned after just three matches due to the war. History book lists him as having played 4 'other' games for Rochdale.

21. RICHARDS, GARY Vivian

Birthplace: Swansea, 2/8/1963
Ht: 5ft-8½ins, **Wt:** 11st-2lbs
Swans debut: v. Aston Villa (a), 21/5/1982

Swansea City Career Statistics				
Season	*League*	*FLC*	*FAC*	*WC*
1981/82	1			
1982/83	15		1	4
1983/84	32+2/1gls	2	1	6/1gls
1984/85	15+1		2/1gls	2
Total	63+3/1gls	2	4/1gls	12/1gls

Career:
Swansea City (from apprentice in August 1981)
Jankoping, Sweden
Lincoln City (non-contract signed in November 1985) lge 2+5
Cambridge United (non-contract signed in March 1986) lge 8
Torquay United (signed in July 1986) lge 24+1/1gls
Newport County (signed in season 1988/89) Conf apps 14/2gls
Llanelli (signed in season 1988/89)
Saltash United (signed in season 1989/90)

Honours: Wales Yth–7, Welsh Cup Winner–1983

Joined the Swans along with Dudley Lewis as apprentices at the Vetch Field, the former Townhill, Powys Avenue and Bishop Gore Schoolboy played together in the same Swansea schoolboys team, and continued through to the Swans youth, reserve and first team after turning professional. Capable of playing in any defensive position, Gary also played many games in a midfield role, a position from where he scored at the Vetch Field against the Swans for Torquay United after just fifteen seconds. Making his league debut in the Swans final game of the 1981/82 season in the First Division at Villa Park, he made fifteen league appearances the following season when the Swans were relegated from the First Division, also playing in both legs of the Welsh Cup Final win over Wrexham, and also being a non-playing substitute in Paris against Paris St. Germain in the European Cup Winners Cup Second Round tie. Financial cutbacks at the Vetch Field, which saw a number of experienced players being released gave Gary the opportunity during season 1983/84 to make thirty-four league appearances, also scoring his only league goal for the club at Cambridge United in a 1-1 draw. The same season he also scored the only goal of the game in a second leg Welsh Cup semi-final success over Shrewsbury Town at the Vetch Field. With the Swans continuing to slide down the divisions following a second consecutive relegation, he was released by manage John Bond in May 1985, linking up with Swedish Second Division side Jankoping. Returning to the UK he linked up with Lincoln City, and after a short spell with Cambridge United, signed for Torquay United in July 1986,

managed by former Swansea schoolboy Stuart Morgan, and former Swans player and coach Les Chappell. He initially shared digs in Torquay with a young, and up and coming star, Lee Sharpe, who was to go on to make a name for himself with Manchester United, and gain honours for England. The downside of scoring a goal against his former team at the Vetch Field for the 'Gulls' was that shortly after, he was taken from the field with a knee injury, which would ultimately force his retirement from the full time game. After a period in plaster, his first game back saw him suffer snapped knee ligaments leaving him sidelined for a further thirteen months. It was during this period when he was regaining fitness that he was offered the youth team manager role at Plainmoor, but turned down the job in favour of resuming his career at Vauxhall Conference club Newport County. Unfortunately, after playing fourteen matches, along with the rest of the playing staff he was made redundant when the club folded before the end of the season. He completed the season with Llanelli, then joined Saltash United, managed at the time by former Swans' defender Chris Harrison. After further non-league appearances with Stroud and Barry Town he was forced to retire from the game after suffering further knee problems whilst playing for Haverfordwest. Since retiring he has taken up a position with the Royal Mail in the city, and has been involved with the Swansea Schoolboys side, Swansea Bravehearts, and coaching with the Swans' Centre of Excellence sides.

22. RICHARDS, MARC John

Born: Wolverhampton, 8/7/1982
Ht: 6ft-0ins, **Wt:** 12st-7lbs
Swans debut: v. Scunthorpe United (a), 23/11/2002

Swansea City Career Statistics	
Season	*League*
2002/03	14+3/7gls
Total	14+3/7gls

Career:
Hednesford Town
Blackburn Rovers (from trainee on 12/7/1999) FLC 1+1
Crewe Alexandra (loan in 10/8/2001) lge 1+3, FLC 0+1/1gls
Oldham Athletic (loan in 12/10/2001) lge 3+2, Others 1/1gls
Halifax Town (loan in 12/2/2002) lge 5
Swansea City (loan in 18/11/2002)
Northampton Town (signed in 14/6/2003) lge 35+19/10gls, FLC 3, FAC 0+4/2gls, Others 4+1/1gls
Rochdale (loan in 24/3/2005) lge 4+1/2gls

Honours: England U-18, U-20

Born in Wolverhampton in July 1982, Richards was a highly rated young striker who graduated through the Blackburn Rovers Youth Academy, becoming a regular in the reserve side at Ewood Park, making his first team debut in a Worthington Cup tie, and early in season 2002/03 he scored the deciding penalty to beat Walsall in his second Worthington Cup appearance for Rovers. He previously had loan experience with Crewe Alexandra, Oldham Athletic and Halifax Town prior to signing for Brian Flynn on loan in November 2002. Remained at the Vetch Field on an extended loan until the end of the season, playing a major role with his seven league goals, alongside former Rovers team mate James Thomas, earning the Swans a last game reprieve from relegation to the Conference following a win over Hull City. Released by Stoke City as a teenager, he started playing in the local leagues and then at the age of 15 joined Hednesford Town, playing for the reserves. His goal scoring exploits caught the eye of a few clubs, and after leaving school at the age of sixteen, and starting a course at a local college, was offered a trial at Blackburn Rovers which eventually led to him being offered a three year scholarship at Ewood Park. Despite struggling to make the first team at Rovers, he did catch the eye of the England U-20 selectors, playing against Italy and Poland. One of the players offered a contract by manager Brian Flynn in May 2003 after being released by Rovers, he signed for Northampton Town in June 2003, with the club being closer to his hometown. Despite a slow start to the 2003/04 season, and a change of management at Sixfields Stadium, Marc eventually finished with nine league goals, playing also in the semi-finals of the Third Division Play Off defeat by Mansfield Town, which they lost on penalties. Just prior to the 2005 transfer deadline day he joined Rochdale on loan, but after returning to Sixfields Stadium, made a substitute appearance for the Cobblers in the end of season Play Off semi-final defeat by Southend United.

23. RICHARDS, Stanley (STAN) Verdon

Birthplace: Cardiff, 21/1/1917. **Died:** South Glamorgan, 19/4/1987
Ht: 5ft-10ins, **Wt:** 11st-0lbs
Swans debut: v. Watford (h), 21/8/1948

Swansea Town Career Statistics			
Season	League	FAC	WC
1948/49	32/26gls	1	1
1949/50	21/4gls		1/1gls
1950/51	9/5gls		1
Total	62/35gls	1	3/1gls

Career:
Cardiff Corinthians
Tufnell Park FC
Cardiff Corinthians
Cardiff City (signed in January 1946) lge 57/40gls
Swansea City (£6,000 signed in 11/6/1948)
Barry Town (signed in August 1951)
Haverfordwest (signed in October 1955)

Honours: Wales Full–1, Third Division South Champions–1947, 1949, London Combination Cup Winner–1950

A late comer to the professional game, signing for Cardiff City in January 1946 from Cardiff Corinthians after previously playing for Tufnell Park, London, whilst stationed there during WW2 on anti-aircraft duty. He attended Grange Council School earlier in his career, represented the school football side and Cardiff schoolboys, and went to work in Cardiff Docks after leaving school, starting his senior football career with Cardiff Corinthians. Making a big impact during the 'Bluebirds' Third Division South Championship winning season of 1946/47 scoring 30 goals, a record which stood until 2003 when Robert Earnshaw scored 31 goals, it was during his time at Ninian Park that he received his only international cap for Wales, when he was selected to replace Trevor Ford for the match at Maine Road against England on the 13th November 1946, losing 3-0. Signed by his former manager at Ninian Park, Billy McCandless, his first season saw him not only receive his second Third Division South Championship medal, but also return the highest goals during a season since Cyril Pearce scored 35 league goals during the 1931/32 season. A tremendous opportunist in front of goal he developed a wonderful positional sense which led to him being in the right place at the right time, with most of his goals being scored from a distance of less than ten feet from goal. His first season at the Vetch Field saw him open his account in his debut against Watford, score four goals in a 4-0 home win over Swindon Town in September 1948, and score two goals in a game on five occasions during the season. In May 1950 he was a member of the Swans reserve side that won at Southend United to win the London Combination Cup Final. Knee problems during his Swans' career saw him for most of the time being unable to train properly, ultimately forcing him to retire from the professional game, but he did continue for four seasons with Barry Town in the Southern League, ending his playing career after signing for Welsh League side Haverfordwest in October 1955. After leaving the professional game he entered the Building Industry becoming a Master Builder, but his knee problems forced him to take on a less physically demanding employment, and up to his retirement he worked at the fruit and vegetable market in Bessemer Road, Cardiff. Tragically, he collapsed and died whilst out one day walking his dog in April 1987.

24. RICHARDSON, ERNEST WILLIAM

Birthplace: Bishop Burton, York, 8/3/1916. **Died:** Birmingham, 2/3/1977
Ht: 5ft-7ins, **Wt:** 10st-0lbs
Swans debut: v. Chesterfield (h), 9/9/1938

Swansea Town Career Statistics		
Season	League	WC
1938/39	18/2gls	1
Total	18/2gls	1

Career:
Leven FC
Birmingham (amateur signed in November 1935, professional in
    January 1936) lge 3
Swansea Town (£250 signed in 3/6/1938)
Aldershot (signed in June 1939)

Outside Right who started his career with non-league side
Leven F.C., made three league appearances for Birmingham,
before signing for the Swans for a fee of £250 on the 3rd June
1938. He replaced Chedzoy on the right wing for his debut game
against Chesterfield at the Vetch Field, played in the next
thirteen league games, scoring the first of his two goals in his
fifth outing at West Ham United in a 5-2 defeat. Shortly after
making his league debut he played against Shrewsbury Town in
a carried over Welsh Cup replay from the previous season.
Returning to the Swans' first team for the last three league
games of the season, he scored his second goal in a 2-1 away
win at Newcastle United in mid-April 1939. In June 1939 he was
released by the Swans joining Aldershot. During WW2 he made
guest appearances for Hull City in season 1939/40.

25. RICHARDSON, PAUL

Birthplace: Selston (Notts), 25/10/1949
Ht: 5ft-11ins, **Wt:** 12st-0lbs
Swans debut: v. Bristol City (a), 8/9/1984

Swansea City Career Statistics		
Season	League	WC
1984/85	12	1
Total	12	1

Career:
Nottingham Forest (from apprentice in August 1967)
    lge 199+24/18gls, FLC 9+1/2gls, FAC 16/1gls
Chester City (signed in 2/10/1976) lge 28/2gls
Stoke City (signed in 17/6/1977) lge 124+3/10gls
Sheffield United (signed in August 1981) lge 35+1/2gls
Blackpool (loan in January 1983) lge 4
Swindon Town (signed in July 1983) lge 7
Swansea City (non-contract signed in 6/9/1984)
Witney Town (signed in December 1984)
Gloucester City

Honours: England Yth, Fourth Division Champions–1982

Experienced midfielder who was signed by manager Colin
Appleton on a non-contract basis, at a time when, because of a
transfer embargo by the Football League, a number of trialists
and non-contract players were utilised in the Swans first team.
Joining Forest as an apprentice in August 1966, signing
professional two years later, he made 111 First Division
appearances for Forest prior to their relegation to the Second
Division in 1972, and had made a total of over 200 league
appearances, and gained international youth honours for
England, before he signed for Chester City in October 1976.
His debut for Forest saw them lose 6-1 against Liverpool.
Following a transfer to Stoke City in June 1977, he made 40
appearances in the side that gained promotion in Third place
from the Second Division, making a further 54 league
appearances for the club in the First Division. Joining Sheffield

United in August 1981 he made 20 appearances for the 'Blades'
during the season they won the Fourth Division Championship.
He made further appearances on loan for Blackpool, and a short
spell at Swindon Town prior to joining the Swans in September
1984, making his debut two days later at Ashton Gate against
Bristol City. His last game for the Swans was in a 1-1 draw
against Welsh League side Spencer Works in the Third Round of
the Welsh Cup at the Vetch Field, later joining non-league side
Witney Town. During his period with the Swans he undertook
an Insurance course, and declined the offer of a contract until
the end of the season at the Vetch Field. In one of his last league
games for the Swans he received a red card at Somerton Park
against Newport County. He later had a spell as Gloucester
City's player manager before managing Fairford and taking
employment with British Telecom.

26. RICKETTS, Samuel (SAM)

Birthplace: Aylesbury, 11/10/1981
Ht: 6ft-0ins, **Wt:** 11st-12lbs
Swans debut: v. Northampton Town (h), 7/8/2004

Swansea City Career Statistics				
Season	League	FLC	FAC	LDV
2004/05	42	1	5	2/1gls
Total	42	1	5	2/1gls

Career:
Oxford United (signed from trainee in 20/4/2000)
    lge 32+13/1gls, FLC 1, Others 2
Nuneaton Borough (loan in season 2002/03) Conf 11/1gls
Telford United (signed in August 2003) Conf 39+1/4gls,
    FAC 5/1gls
Swansea City (signed in 27/5/2004)

Honours: Wales–3, England National Game XI–4, PFA XI

Signed from Conference side Telford United in May 2004, Sam
made his Swans' debut in the opening fixture of the season at
the Vetch Field in the 2-0 defeat by Northampton Town, playing
at left full back. Despite a successful season on the field, cash
problems behind the scenes had seen Telford United go into
administration, offload all of their players, with Sam arriving at
the Vetch Field on a free transfer. The son of former World Show
Jumping Champion in 1978 Derek Ricketts, Sam attended
Sutherland School in Leighton Buzzard, Audney House, Akeley
Wood, playing for the Mid-Oxon and Oxfordshire Schoolboys
teams, and had been attached to Oxford United from the age of
ten. Joining Oxford United on leaving school as a trainee he
made his Football League debut at Swindon Town on the 8th
October 2000 at right full back, retained his place for the next

game, and was recalled to the side during the latter part of the season as the club faced relegation alongside the Swans to the Third Division. The 2001/02 season saw him appear as substitute in the opening fixture against the Swans, score his first league goal in a 2-0 win over Southend United in September 2001, and become a regular inclusion in the first team under manager Mark Wright. The following season he failed to continue his progress, had a loan spell at Conference side Nuneaton Borough, and after returning to Oxford broke his collarbone in a reserve team game. Despite a further year left on his contract with United, he took up the option of regular football with Conference side Telford United, playing regularly through the season, reaching the Fourth Round of the FA Cup, before being beaten by finalist's Millwall. He was included in the England National Game XI in November 2003 that played Belgium in Darlington, scoring the first goal in a 2-2 draw, and later in the season, in May 2003 played in the Four Nations Tournament in Scotland against the Republic of Ireland, Wales and Scotland. A versatile player, as well as being capable of playing in either right, or left full back positions, Sam has also operated in midfield, as well as at centre back during his career. His consistent form for the Swans attracted the attention of John Toshack, newly appointed manager of the Wales National side, and with a qualification to play for Wales via his grandmother, he made his first International appearance in the friendly at the Millenium Stadium, Cardiff, against Hungary on the 9th February 2005, and in late March 2005 played in both World Cup Qualifying matches against Austria. In late April 2005 he was selected by his fellow PFA members for the PFA Second Division side of season 2004/05, missing just four league matches during the club's successful automatic promotion from Coca Cola League Two

27. RIGSBY, Herbert (BERT)

Birthplace: Aintree, 22/7/1894. **Died:** Anfield, 8/12/1972
Ht: 5ft-8ins, **Wt:** 11st-6lbs
Swans debut: v. Portsmouth (a), 28/8/1920

Swansea Town Career Statistics		
Season	League	WC
1920/21	10	1
Total	10	1

Career:
Inglewood
Everton (signed in May 1919) lge 14/5gls
Swansea Town (signed in 13/5/1920)
Southport (signed in June 1921) lge 49/10gls
Burscough Rangers (signed in 1923)
Marine
Hartleys (signed in August 1927)

Signed from Everton in May 1920, capable of playing in either inside forward position, at the time of his signing he was considered to be one of the most important signings the club had made. Bert played in the first Swans' Football League game at the start of the 1920/21 season at Portsmouth at inside left. Retaining his place for the next three league games, after missing a game, he returned to first team duty for the next five games. In April he played his last match for the Swans before being released to join newly elected Third Division North side Southport on the 12th June 1921. Prior to joining the Swans his league experience with First Division Everton was limited to 14 games, in which he scored 5 goals. The former Longmoor Lane, Aintree schoolboy started playing football for Hartleys Jam and Inglewood until being called to the colours in the RHA, but returned home after being injured in France, later making occasional wartime appearances for Southport Central during

the war while on Everton's books. Selected to play in Southport's first League game, he played mainly in the inside forward position and after a spell in non-league football with Burscough Rangers, Marine and Hartley's, he retired and had a newsagents shop in Liverpool. He was one of the first people locally to have a personalised number plate with HR4 on his Morris 1000.

28. RIMMER, John James (JIMMY)

Birthplace: Southport, 10/2/1948
Ht: 5ft-11ins, **Wt:** 11st-12lbs
Swans debut: v. Doncaster Rovers (a), 3/11/1973

Swansea City Career Statistics						
Season	League	FLC	FAC	WC	ECWC	FRT
1973/74	17			1		
1983/84	14	2			2	
1984/85	33	2	2	3		2
1985/86	19	3	1			1
Total	83	7	3	4	2	3

Career:
Manchester United (amateur signed in May 1963, apprentice in
    September 1963, professional in May 1965) lge 34
Swansea City (loan in 31/10/1973)
Arsenal (£40,000 signed in 2/4/1974) lge 124
Aston Villa (£70,000 signed in 13/8/1977) lge 229
Swansea City (£40,000 signed in 27/7/1983)
Hamrun Spartans, Malta (signed in August 1986)

Honours: England: Full–1, First Division Champions–1981,
European Cup Winner–1982

Brought in by manager Harry Gregg in late October 1973, during a season in which the Swans used four goalkeepers, with three of them, Rimmer, Bala'c and Dai Davies coming on loan to the Vetch Field, replacing the experienced Tony Millington during the season. The former Southport and Merseyside Schoolboy keeper had struggled to make any appearances at Old Trafford owing to the consistency of Alex Stepney, and despite the Swans losing the first game with Rimmer in the side, he produced such consistent form during his three month's loan transfer, that the club had placed themselves in an outside promotion position by the time he had headed back to United. With the Swans unable to afford his £40,000 transfer fee, he was on his way to Highbury on an initial loan transfer, six days after playing his last game for the Swans, with the move being made permanent at the beginning of April 1974. From the start of the 1974/75 season to the end of season 1981/82, Rimmer was a model of consistency, missing just four league games from eight seasons in the top flight of football with either the 'Gunners', or with Aston Villa. During his period with Aston Villa, he was an ever present when Villa won the First Division Championship, and started the game against Bayern Munich in the European Cup Final, only to be replaced shortly after the kick off by Nigel Spink. He was unfortunate to be playing at a time when England had Ray Clemence and Peter Shilton vying for the England number one jersey, which limited Rimmer to just the one appearance, against Italy in New York, on the 28th May 1976. After the Swans had been relegated to the Second Division, he rejoined the club in July 1983, for a fee in the region of £40,000, with what was reported later that the keeper had paid half the transfer fee himself, such was his desire to return to the Vetch Field. Injury problems prevented him from making a greater impact at the Vetch Field during a time of financial problems off the field, and at the end of the 1985/86 season, after being unable to prevent the club from slipping into the Fourth Division, left the Vetch Field to join Maltese club Hamrun Spartans following a dispute over his contract. Retaining his roots in the city after he had retired from the game, he was actively involved in a golf shop business, and in the local Swansea Senior League with Southgate Football Club, prior to his returning to the Vetch Field for a third time by the start of the 1995/96 season as youth team manager. In late December 1995, following the resignation of manager Bobby Smith, Rimmer was given the caretaker manager's role, bringing to the Vetch Field his former Villa team mater Ken McNaught to assist him with coaching. He left the Vetch Field in 1996 to coach in China with the National team, and has since been goalkeeper coach, and assistant manager with Chinese National League side Dalian.

29. ROBERTS, ALBERT

Birthplace: Barnsley, 27/1/1907. **Died:** Elsecar, Nr. Barnsley, 27/1/1957
Ht: 5ft-9ins, **Wt:** 12st-0lbs
Swans debut: v. Sheffield Wednesday (a), 24/9/1938

Swansea Town Career Statistics			
Season	League	FAC	WC
1938/39	16	1	1
Total	16	1	1

Career:
Goldthorpe United
Ardsley Athletic
Southampton (signed in August 1929) lge 156
Swansea Town (£500 signed in 16/8/1938)
York City (signed in July 1946) lge 1

An experienced defender who joined the Swans from Second Division side Southampton for £500 in mid-August 1938, after

making 156 league appearances for the 'Saints'. The former Wanfield Schoolboy had joined Goldthorpe United, then Ardsley Athletic prior to arriving at the Dell in August 1929 as an understudy to Mike Keeping. It was not until the transfer of Keeping to Fulham in March 1933 that Roberts began to establish himself in the 'Saints' side. His 'Saints' debut ironically came against the Swans on the 28th February 1931. After refusing terms offered to him by Southampton, he was placed on the transfer list, later signing for the Swans. He made his Swans' debut at right full back instead of Lawrence, but his remaining matches for the club were played at left full back, and at the end of the season he was released. After the war years he joined York City in July 1946, made his debut for the club in the opening fixture of the 1946/47 season in a 4-4 home draw with Chester in the Third Division North. At the time he was York's oldest player (39) to appear for the club. He died on his 50th birthday, a fate also suffered by his father.

30. ROBERTS, David (DAVE)

Birthplace: Erdington, Birmingham, 21/ ?/1946
Ht: 6ft-0ins, **Wt:** 11st-0lbs
Swans debut: v. Darlington (a), 17/8/19. 4

Swansea City Career Statistics				
Season	League	FLC	FAC	WC
1974/75	31+5/1gls	1	2	2
Total	31+5/1gls	1	2	2

Career:
Aston Villa (from juniors in December 1963) lge 15+1/1gls, FLC 2, FAC 1
Shrewsbury Town (£5,000 signed in March 1968) lge 224+6/21gls
Swansea City (signed in May 1974)
Worcester City (signed in July 1975)

Experienced right winger who was re-united with manager Harry Gregg in May 1974 at the Vetch Field, after previously playing for the Swans boss during his period as manager of Shrewsbury Town. Formerly with Aston Villa, he made his senior debut with Villa in the Second Round of the Football League Cup at Kenilworth Road on 23rd September 1964, playing also in the next Round at Elland Road when Villa beat Leeds United 3-2, making his league debut on the 20th November 1965 at Turf Moor in a 3-1 defeat by Burnley. In his only F.A. Cup appearance for Villa he scored the only goal of the game at Deepdale in the Third Round on 28th January 1967. He was transferred to Shrewsbury Town in March 1968 for a reported fee of £5,000, became a consistent figure during his six seasons at Gay Meadow, making over two hundred league appearances. However, his period with the Swans saw the club have to apply for re-election at the end of his twelve months at the Vetch Field, and with a change in management, he was released from the playing staff in July 1975, joining non-league side Worcester City. The son-in-law of Nobby Clark, manager of Worcester City at the time, he combined playing for City with a job as the club's commercial manager. After scoring twenty-two goals from one hundred and fifty-two games, he retired due to a back injury, continued as commercial manager until the Spring of 1983, before moving to Redditch United to take up a similar position.

31. ROBERTS, JOHN Griffith

Birthplace: Abercynon, 11/9/1946
Ht: 5ft-11¼ins, **Wt:** 12st-9¼lbs
Swans debut: v. Rotherham United (a), FLC-3, 14/10/1964

Swansea Town Career Statistics			
Season	League	FLC	WC
1964/65		2	
1965/66	4		
1966/67	20/13gls		1
1967/68	12+1/3gls	1	
Total	36+1/16gls	3	1

Career:
Abercynon Athletic
Swansea Town (signed in 29/7/1964)
Northampton Town (£12,000 signed in 24/11/1967) lge 62/11gls
Arsenal (£45,000 signed in 1/5/1969) lge 56+3/4gls
Birmingham City (£140,000 signed in 13/10/1972) lge 61+5/1gls
Wrexham (£30,000 signed in 5/8/1976) lge 145/5gls
Hull City (£17,500 signed in 6/8/1980) lge 26/1gls
Oswestry Town (signed in July 1982)

Honours: Wales U-21–1 U-23–5, Full–22, First Division Champions–1971, Third Division Champions–1978, Welsh Cup Winner–1978, Football Combination Champions–1970, London FA Challenge Cup Winner–1970, West Wales Senior Cup Winner–1966

A former fireman on steam trains before arriving at the Vetch Field, initially as an amateur before signing as a full time professional in late July 1964. He attended Abertaff Primary School as a youngster, captained the school side, later going on to play for the senior school in Abercynon, and also play for the Mountain Ash District team. After leaving school he went to work for the Great Western Railways as a fireman, playing for Welsh League side Abercynon Athletic as a centre forward, and also Pontycynon in the Pontypridd League. Spotted by a Rhondda based Swans' scout, after a trial period at the Vetch

Field playing for the Swans youth team, he was invited to join the club in a youth tournament in Holland, and, on his return was asked to sign amateur forms with the Swans. He initially played for the youth side in the Swansea Senior League towards the end of season 1963/64, and played in a successful Swansea Senior Cup Final winning side. But shortly after the start of the 1964/65 season he was given his first team opportunity, making his debut in the League Cup Third Round tie at Rotherham United on the 14th October 1964, playing also in the replay at the Vetch Field. Making significant strides in the club's youth and reserve sides, John made his league debut the following season, in a 1-0 home win over Grimsby Town. Making a further three league appearances that season, it was during the 1966/67 season that he opened his goalscoring account, in a 3-2 away win at Oxford United on the 31st December 1966. In August 1966 he was included in Swans reserve side that beat Llanelly to win the West Wales Senior Cup. By the end of the season he finished top goalscorer for the Swans with 13 league goals, and had also gained his first of five Wales U-23 caps against Northern Ireland in Belfast. The 1967/68 season saw John start as first choice in the Swans' line-up, but with financial problems at the club following relegation to the Fourth Division, he was sold to Northampton Town for £12,000. At the time the 'Cobblers' were managed by Wales international boss Dave Bowen, and within eighteen months, Roberts had been converted to a central defender by the astute Bowen, and transferred to First Division Arsenal for £45,000. He had a difficult time breaking into the 'Gunners' line-up, but made his debut in a League Cup tie against Southampton in September 1969, winning 1-1, but had to wait a further 3 months for his next first team game. Making 10 appearances during his first season at Highbury, he won a Combination medal and a London F.A. Challenge Cup Winners Medal with the club's reserve side. The 1970/71 campaign was notable in the club's history as they became only the third team to do the double, with Roberts making eighteen league appearances to qualify for a League Championship Medal. On the 15th May 1971 he gained his first Full international cap for Wales, playing at Ninian Park against Scotland in a 0-0 draw. Despite having an extended run in the Gunners first team at the start of the 1972/73 season, in October 1972 he signed for Birmingham City for £140,000, following the arrival of experienced centre half Jeff Blockley to Highbury. Playing in a struggling 'Blues' side, the highlight of his time at St. Andrews was in reaching the semi-final stages of the FA Cup competition, and he returned to Wales in August 1976 to sign for Wrexham, with the club's veteran defender Eddie May having just signed for the Swans. Quickly winning over the home supporters despite missing out on promotion during his first season at the Racecourse, the following term the club swept everything before them, winning the Third Division Championship, the Welsh Cup, and reaching the quarter finals of the FA Cup, before being beaten narrowly by Arsenal at the Racecourse. The following season he played in the first leg of the Welsh Cup Final against Shrewsbury Town, losing out on aggregate. After establishing the club in the Second Division, he was invited by former Wales manager Mike Smith during the summer of 1980 to sign for Hull City. His spell on Humberside was dogged with knee injuries, and two years and 26 games later he was forced to retire from the game. He had a brief spell with Oswestry Town, and then began working as a salesman for a stationary company before leaving to start his own driving school. He then decided with his wife to set up a shop selling ladies and men's clothing, establishing themselves in 1995 with 3 branches in the Chester area.

32. ROBERTS, Hopkin John (JACKIE)

Birthplace: Swansea 30/6/1918. **Died:** Fforestfach, Swansea, 12/6/2001
Ht: 5ft-11ins, **Wt:** 12st-3lbs
Swans debut: v. Barnsley (h), 30/9/1950

Swansea Town Career Statistics			
Season	League	FAC	WC
1950/51	16/1gls	1	1
Total	16/1gls	1	1

Career:
Cwmbwrla
Bolton Wanderers (signed in April 1936) lge 162/19gls
Swansea Town (£5,000 signed in September 1950)
Llanelly (signed in August 1951)

Honours: Wales Full–1, West Wales Senior Cup Winner–1952, 1953

Former Swansea schoolboy player who joined Bolton Wanderers along with Ernie Jones before his eighteenth birthday, after making an impression with local junior sides Highbury AFC and Cwmbwrla. Initially signed for Wanderers as an inside right, where he made his First Division debut against Sunderland in February 1958 at Burnden Park in April 1936, making regular appearances the following season in that position, scoring a hat-trick in one game against Everton. He was converted to full back after the war, playing with such success, that he skippered the Wanderers side, gaining his only international cap in that position in Liege against Belgium on the 23rd May 1949, in an end of season F.A.W. Touring party that also played international matches against Portugal and Switzerland. Making all his appearances for Wanderers in the First Division, in September 1950 he returned to Swansea to sign for his hometown club for a £5,000 transfer fee. During the war years he guested for a number of teams including Bolton Wanderers, Norwich City, Reading, as well as his hometown club, Swansea. He made his debut for the Swans at the Vetch Field against Barnsley, making sixteen consecutive league appearances, scoring his only goal, in what was to be his last game for the Swans, at the Vetch Field against Brentford in mid-January 1951. Plagued by knee trouble during his time with the Swans, in 1951 he moved to Llanelly, then in the Southern League, where he formed a formidable defensive partnership with Jock Stein. During the 1952 close season, he was offered the post of player/manager, but was unable to agree terms with the club, but remained as a player, before retiring from the game in 1954, and working in a steelworks in Swansea. In May 1952 and in 1953 he was a member of the Llanelly side that beat the Swans at Stebonheath Park to win the West Wales Senior Cup Final in consecutive seasons. As a schoolboy, he was a prominent member of the Highbury Cricket Team in the Swansea Sunday League.

33. ROBERTS, OWEN John

Birthplace: Maerdy, 16/2/1919. **Died:** Pontygwaith, 29/5/2000
Ht: 5ft-10ins, **Wt:** 11st-7lbs
Swans debut: v. Fulham (h), 9/11/1946

Swansea Town Career Statistics			
Season	League	FAC	WC
1946/47	20	2	1
1947/48	4	1	1
Total	24	3	2

Career:
Maerdy
Plymouth Argyle (signed in February 1938) lge 0
Newry Town
Aberaman
Swansea Town (signed in 20/10/1945)
Newport County (signed in August 1948) lge 7

Nicknamed 'Tiger' after the famous Moscow Dynamo goalkeeper, Khomich, Owen Roberts joined the Swans in October 1945 from Welsh League side Aberaman, playing in the majority of matches during the 1945/46 'Victory League' season. On the resumption of the Football League in 1946, he competed with Jack Parry for the goalkeeper jersey, finally making his debut at the Vetch Field against Fulham in early November 1946. Playing in consecutive league matches he lost his place to Percy Hooper, but regained his position for the last four league matches of the season. His second season with the Swans saw him unable to wrestle the number one jersey from Parry, and after making just four league appearances, plus one in the FA Cup competition, he was released in August 1948, joining Newport County. His contract at Somerton Park with County was cancelled in December 1948. Brought up in Maerdy, 'Tiger' attended Maerdy and Ferndale Grammar Schools, playing in the Ferndale & District Schools League. Having four brothers, all five Roberts' brothers played in one match for Maerdy against N.O.R. of Skewen before the War. All four brothers went on to play football at senior level, with Noel having five seasons at Plymouth Argyle. Joining Plymouth Argyle after leaving school, it was during a spell in Northern Ireland playing for Newry Town, when WW2 broke out, returned home and enlisted in the RAF. Taking up the position as a PT Instructor he was based in Blackpool, and played a number of matches during the war alongside the legendary Stanley Mathews. After he left the professional game he worked underground at Maerdy Colliery for a number of years, before an accident to his foot saw him transferred to the surface and take up the position as a Colliery Weigher. For a number of seasons during the early to mid-1960's he was the South Wales scout for Plymouth Argyle.

34. ROBERTS, STUART Ian

Birthplace: Carmarthen, 22/7/1980
Ht: 5ft-7ins, **Wt:** 9st-8lbs
Swans debut: v. Norwich City (h), CC Cup 1-1, 11/8/1998

Career:
Swansea City (from trainee in 9/7/1998)
Wycombe Wanderers (£102,500 signed in 19/10/2001)
   lge 37+33/4gls, FLC 2+1, FAC 4+1, Others 2+2

Swansea City Career Statistics

Season	League	FLC	FAC	AWS	FAWP	P/Offs
1998/99	15+17/3gls	0+2	3	1+1	5/1gls	2
1999/2000	9+2/1gls	3		1+1	3	
2000/01	21+15/5gls	1+1	1	3	3/2gls	
2001/02	13/5gls					
2003/04	8+4/1gls				1	
Total	66+38/15gls	4+3	4	5+2	12/3gls	2

Swansea City (loan in 23/2/2004)
Kidderminster Harriers (non-contract signed in 20/8/2004)
  lge 4+1/1gls, FLC 1
Forest Green Rovers (signed in 16/9/2004) Conf 16+1
Aberystwyth (signed in July 2005)

Honours: Wales U-21–13, Third Division Champions–2000

Given a professional contract at the start of the 1998/99 season by manager John Hollins, the former Vetch Field trainee made an immediate impact, impressing in his debut against Norwich City in the First leg of the Coca Cola Cup competition. He remained in contention throughout the season, making a name for himself as a pacy, tricky ball player, with a lot of heart, who was a good crosser of the ball. On the 9th February 1999 he was a non-playing substitute for the Wales 'B' side that beat Northern Ireland 1-0, and by the end of March 1999 he had been awarded his first U-21 cap for Wales, against Switzerland, making two further appearances that season, against Italy and Denmark. His debut season in the Football League also saw him score his first league goal, in a 1-1 home draw with Carlisle United in February 1999. His second season as a professional saw Stuart laid low with a virus, in what was later diagnosed as having insufficient rest during the close season, and as a result, made only a handful of appearances in the club's Third Division Championship success. During the season, when not available for selection, he impressed a number of supporters with his unbiased viewpoint when used as a summariser on a local radio station covering the Swans matches. In 2000/2001 he returned to first team duty, linking up effectively on a number of occasions in a central striking role alongside Giovanni Savarese, as well as his customary flank role, winning a further five U-21 caps for Wales. His last season at the Vetch Field saw him produce his best form in front of goal, scoring many goals from around the penalty area, a fact which did not go un-noticed by a number of clubs, with the result of him signing for Wycombe Wanderers in October 2001 for a fee of just over £100,000. Continuing his form at Adams Park, he immediately excited the 'Chairboys' fans with forceful wing play, and accurate distribution from the flanks. Highlight of the 2002/03 season was his hat-trick at Northampton Town, after coming on the field as a late first half substitute. Otherwise his season was disrupted with two lengthy lay offs through ankle ligament damage, and a twisted ankle. With former Arsenal legend Tony Adams taking over at Adams Park, 'Robbo's' opportunities through the 2003/04 season were few and far between, and in late February 2004, Swans manager Brian Flynn signed him on an initial loan transfer to enable him to take his place on the substitute's bench against Leyton Orient at the Vetch Field, with the Swans taking over his contract until the end of the season two days later. The next home game against the Division's top side, Doncaster Rovers, saw 'Robbo' open the scoring with a blistering drive from outside the area. Unfortunately, that proved to be the high spot of his return to the Vetch Field, and with a change of management on the playing side at the Vetch Field, he was not offered a contract by manager Kenny Jackett, and was released in May 2004. In late June 2004 he signed for newly promoted Chester City on a non-contract basis, but after the manager Mark Wright had sensationally walked out on the club, just days before the start of season 2004/05, Stuart left the club, signed a non-contract agreement with Kidderminster Harriers, scoring in the first minute of his debut match for the club. A month later, with no offer of a contract with Harriers he joined Conference side Forest Green Rovers. Released at the end of the season, in late July 2005 he signed for Aberystwyth.

35. ROBINSON, (ANDY) Andrew Mark

Birthplace: Birkenhead, 3/11/1979
Ht: 5ft-8ins, **Wt:** 11st-4lbs
Swans debut: v. Cheltenham Town (a), 16/8/2003

Swansea City Career Statistics

Season	League	FLC	FAC	LDV	FAWC
2003/04	34+3/8gls		5/2gls		0+1/1gls
2004/05	29+8/8gls	1	3+1	1	1+2/1gls
Total	63+11/16gls	1	8+1/2gls	1	1+3/2gls

Career:
Cammell Laird
Tranmere Rovers (signed in 11/11/2002) Others 0+1
Swansea City (trial in July 2003, signed in 14/8/2003)

Honours: FAW Cup Winner–2005

Joined the Swans in pre-season training in July 2003 on an initial trial basis, signing a month to month contract, prior to it being updated to a more permanent contract. Manager Brian Flynn offered the Liverpool born forward a deal after he had impressed during pre-season, where he scored three goals in six friendly matches. Robinson only came into the professional game in December 2002, when he was offered a 6-month contract at Second Division Tranmere Rovers, after he had impressed on trial from Cammell Laird. Attached to Everton from an early age until being released at the age of sixteen, also playing in junior football with Ashville, he became a regular goalscorer with West Cheshire League side Cammell Laird, attracted the attention of Wrexham, played in their reserve team in October 2002 on trial, but in November 2002 signed for Tranmere Rovers until the end of season. His only first team appearance came in the LDV Vans Trophy cup tie against Bury, and he was released at the end of the season. Despite making a good impression in Rovers' reserve team, consistently scoring goals, due to a fine run by the first team strikers at the time, he was unable to make a league appearance at Prenton Park. Released by the Prenton Park outfit when his contract was up at the end of June, he was then invited by Brian Flynn to come on trial to South West Wales. Impressing during his trial period as a striker, it was as a left sided midfielder that he earned rave reviews, scoring on his home debut against Boston United, and making a name for himself as an assured free kick taker from outside the penalty area, scoring notable goals against Mansfield Town and Preston North End in the FA Cup competition. By the end of the season he had gone into double figures in league and cup games for goals scored, and has since commanded a regular place in the midfield engine room, where his tackling ability, and eye for goal has seen him score many spectacular goals from outside the penalty area, and from free kicks outside the area. Unanimously voted Player of the Year by the club's supporters at the end of his first full season as a professional. Despite scoring eight league goals during his second season at the Vetch Field, he struggled to recapture the previous season's form, and was also hampered with disciplinary problems on and off the field. After receiving his second red card of the season at Bristol Rovers, he was suspended for the last two league games, missing his team claim one of the automatic promotion places. However, he was able to score the last ever goal at the Vetch Field in the Swans 2-1 win over Wrexham in the FAW Cup Final.

36. ROBINSON, NEIL

Birthplace: Walton, Liverpool, 20/4/1957
Ht: 5ft-7ins, **Wt:** 9st-11lbs
Swans debut: v. QPR (a), 2/2/1980

Swansea City Career Statistics					
Season	League	FLC	FAC	WC	ECWC
1979/80	14+2		2	3	
1980/81	33+3/6gls	1	1	4/2gls	
1981/82	27+2/1gls	2		4	2
1982/83	17+1	1		1	
1983/84	18+1	1		3	2
1984/85	5	1			
Total	114+9/7gls	6	3	15/2gls	4

Career:
Everton (from apprentice May 1974) lge 13+3/1gls, FLC 3+1, FAC 1, UEFA 0+1
Swansea City (£70,000 signed in 13/10/1979)
Grimsby Town (£20,000 in September 1984) lge 109/6gls, FLC 4, FAC 6, FMC 0+1, FRT 3
Darlington (signed in July 1988) lge 36+2/1gls, Vaux Conf 8, FLC 4, FAC 1, SVT 3/1gls

Honours: Welsh Cup Winner–1981, 1982, Vauxhall Conference Champions–1990

One of John Toshack's main attributes during his reign as manager at the Vetch Field was his ability to not only recognise deficiencies in his side, but bring in players who would improve the quality of the playing standard of the squad at the Vetch Field. Unlike his previous captures from Merseyside, Tommy Smith and Ian Callaghan, Neil Robinson was a relatively unknown commodity to the vast majority of Swans' supporters when he was signed for a £70,000 transfer fee in October 1979. The majority of supporters who did not venture to see his debut in the reserve team against Bristol Rovers would have to wait another couple of months for his Swans' debut in the Football League, because during that game he suffered a knee injury, which would later involve two cartilage operations on his knee during his time with the club at the Vetch Field. The former Holt

High School (Childwall) player, joined Everton as an apprentice after completing his examinations at school, making his league debut against Burnley in January 1976, and before he had added to his appearances, had been selected to play in the 1976/77 League Cup Final second replay against Aston Villa. Having played relatively little football during his childhood, Neil was taken on as an apprentice with Everton, after trials with Liverpool, on the strength of his performances playing in the local Sunday league with his three brothers. After just 16 league appearances for the 'Toffees', he was enlisted by Toshack to continue the march upward to the First Division. Following his knee injury against Rovers, he had to wait until early February before he was given his first team opportunity when he was called into action as a substitute at QPR, replacing Ian Callaghan. An exciting, overlapping defender, as well as possessing sound defensive strengths, Neil would also show his qualities when pushed forward from midfield where his close control enabled him to link with his strikers and set up goal scoring opportunities. Thoroughly enjoying his five years at the Vetch Field, living initially in Pennard, before settling in Three Crosses, Neil enjoyed his best season with the Swans' during the club's promotion year to the First (Premiership) Division, playing a total of 36 league appearances, returning six goals, from a right sided midfield role. Neil played in both legs of the 1981 Welsh Cup Final defeat of Hereford United, but only played in the second leg twelve months later in the Final against Cardiff City. One interesting fact about Neil, is that for most of his playing career he was a Vegan, and that he had a preference for his football boots to be made out of synthetic fibres, rather than out of the normal leather product. Once the bubble had burst at the Vetch Field, and there were more pressing demands from the club's bankers, Neil became one of the playing squad who, unfortunately had to seek contracts with another club, in his case, Grimsby Town. Signed by manager Dave Booth in September 1984, he scored an own goal in his debut match, and after just four games had to undergo a hernia operation which sidelined him for four months. At the end of his second season however, he was voted Player of the Year at Blundell Park. Making over 100 league appearances for Grimsby Town, he was re-united with his former boss, Dave Booth in July 1988, signing for Darlington. Unfortunately for Neil, despite making 38 league appearances during his first season at Feethams, the club finished the 1988/89 season bottom of the Fourth Division, and relegated to the Conference. The following season, the club bounced back at the first attempt, and regained their place in the Football League, with Neil making just eight Conference appearances, because of an ankle injury, and having to undergo an operation on his stomach. With his contract not being renewed, he moved back to Widnes, and following some pre-season training with Runcorn, decided he did not have the same enthusiasm to continue playing, and retired from the game. In fact the only other game he has played in since then was to come back to Swansea to play in Dzemal Hadziabdic's Mostar Relief Fund Charity game at the Vetch Field in September 1992, a game between the Swans First Division team, and a side selected from the 1992 playing squad. Since retiring from the game, Neil was involved in running a Fitness Centre in Widnes, but has since been working for his brother in the computer business, processing data, and report making.

37. ROBSON, Edward (ED) Riddell

Birthplace: Hexham, 21/8/1890. **Died:** Hexham, Northumberland, JFM, 1977
Ht: 6ft-0ins, **Wt:** 12st-0lbs
Swans debut: v. Swindon Town (h), 30/8/1924

Career:
Gateshead
Watford (signed in June 1914)
Portsmouth (signed in July 1919) lge 75
Sunderland (£250 signed in 29/5/1922) lge 38

Swansea Town (£250 signed in 17/5/1924)
Wrexham (signed in 12/6/1926) lge 69
Grimsby Town (signed in July 1928) lge 0
Rochdale (signed in March 1928) lge 12

Swansea Town Career Statistics		
Season	League	WC
1924/25	14	
1925/26	15	5
Total	29	5

Honours: Third Division South Champions–1925,
Southern League Champions–1920, West Wales Senior Cup
Winner–1925

Played in goal for Gateshead before moving south to join
Watford, playing a couple of games in the club's 1920 Southern
League Championship winning team. Resuming his playing
career after the First World War with Portsmouth, he played
against the Swans in the first game of season 1920/21, the
Swans' first ever league match, also playing in the return at the
Vetch Field. Leaving Fratton Park to sign for Sunderland, he was
signed by Swans' manager Joe Bradshaw in May 1924 for £250,
having earlier been included as a guest on the Swans' summer
tour of Denmark. He opened season 1924/25 as first choice
keeper, lost his place after 7 games to Jock Denoon, reclaiming
his jersey towards the end of the season, during a season which
saw the Swans' win the Third Division South Championship. In
January 1925 he played in the Swans reserve side that beat
Llanelly to win the West Wales Senior Cup. The following
season saw Robson again start the season as first choice, but lost
out again to Denoon, who was the club's custodian when the
Swans reached the FA Cup semi-final. However, Robson did
play in the Welsh Cup Final defeat against Ebbw Vale in April
1926. Joining Third Division North side Wrexham in June 1926,
he was a regular at the Racecourse for two seasons, opened a
business in the town, and after a transfer to Grimsby Town in
July 1928, in which he failed to make any first team
appearances, returned north to sign for Third Division North
side Rochdale, replacing the injured Jackie Mittell, who had
broken his nose in the previous game. Making a total of 12
league games in season 1928/29 for Rochdale, he returned to his
native Hexham after retiring as a player, was involved with
Hexham as trainer, prior to his death in 1977. During WW1 he
made guest appearances for Sunderland.

38. ROBSON, Frederick (FRED) E.

Birthplace: Sunderland, 3/5/1892
Ht: 5ft-9ins, **Wt:** 11st-6lbs
Swans debut: v. Luton Town (a), 30/8/1919, Sth. Lge

Swansea Town Career Statistics			
Season	League	FAC	WC
1920/21	35	2	1
1921/22	41	6	1
Total	76	8	2

Career:
Ryhope Villa
Southend United (signed in June 1913)
Swansea Town (£200 signed in July 1919)
Easington Colliery (signed in close season 1922)
Durham City (signed in August 1923) lge 77/5gls
Hartlepools United (signed in July 1925) lge 12
Durham City (signed in August 1927) lge 0

Honours: Southern League Representative XI

Right Full Back signed by manager Joe Bradshaw in July 1919
for £200 from Southend United who went on to skipper the
Swans, and play in the club's first game in the Football League
in August 1920. In April 1920 he played at the Vetch Field for a
Southern League Welsh Clubs XI against a Southern League
English Clubs XI. Missing few matches during the club's first
two seasons in the Football League. In October 1920, along with
Robson and Ogley, he was suspended for a month for an alleged
serious breach of training discipline. He was transfer listed in
May 1922, with the club asking £500 for him, but it was later
reduced to £100, which saw him return to his native north east
to join Easington Colliery, before returning to play in the Third
Division North with firstly, Durham City, and then with
Hartlepools United. He returned to Durham City in August 1927
remaining at the club until 1928.

39. ROMO, DAVID

Birthplace: Nimes, France, 7/8/1978
Ht: 5ft-11ins, **Wt:** 12st-6lbs
Swans debut: v. Stoke City (h), 14/10/2000

Swansea City Career Statistics					
Season	League	FLC	FAC	LDAF	FAWP
2000/01	28+5		1	3	1
2001/02	3+7/1gls	1	0+1	0+1	
Total	31+12/1gls	1	1+1	3+1	1

Career:
Guingamp (signed in 1998)
Swansea City (signed in 13/10/2000)
Spain
Cherbourg (signed for season 2003/04)

Honours: France Yth

Surprise double signing with Giovanni Savarese, making a
winning debut at the Vetch Field against Stoke City in the
Second Division. An elegant, ball playing midfielder, who was
capable of delivering accurate service from either a dead ball
situation, or from open play, he struggled to come to terms with
the rugged style of lower division football, which resulted in
him losing his confidence, as well as playing in a side that was
struggling to avoid relegation. In May 2001 he played in the
Swans side that lost 2-0 at the Vetch Field to Wrexham in the
FAW Premier Cup Final. Prior to the start of his second season
at the Vetch Field he was included in a French Olympic squad
training camp in Lebanon, but within a month of the start of the
season had asked to be placed on the transfer list, after failing to

secure a place in the starting line-up. His only goal for the Swans came in mid-March 2002 against Mansfield Town at the Vetch Field after coming on as substitute, scoring a 25 yard scorcher with only his second touch of the ball. Earlier in the season, in January 2002 he took part in an organised football camp, nine day trial at the Marpafut SL International Elite Football Centre in Marbella. In May 2002 he left the Swans eight weeks before the end of his contract, returning to France, and was looking at offers from teams in Spain. Prior to the start of the 2003/04 season he had returned to French Football, joining French National Division side Cherbourg, making twenty-eight appearances during his first season at the club, scoring one goal. He remained at the club for season 2004/05.

40. ROSSER, Douglas (DOUG) Richard

Birthplace: Swansea, 8/9/1948
Ht: 5ft-10ins, **Wt:** 11st-4lbs
Swans debut: v. Peterborough United (a), 10/3/1969

Swansea Town/City Career Statistics		
Season	League	FLC
1968/69	7	
1969/70	8+1	
1970/71	13/1gls	1
Total	28+1/1gls	1

Career:
Swansea Town (from juniors in 13/5/1967)
Crewe Alexandra (signed in August 1971) lge 28+1, FAC 1
Merthyr Tydfil (signed in close season 1972)
Haverfordwest (signed in close season 1982)

Originally from the St. Mary's Church, Rutland Street area of Swansea, Doug moved to Llansamlet at a young age, and prior to leaving Llansamlet School had already signed for the Swans, graduating through the club's Colts sides, and reserve teams prior to making his league debut in 1969. A defender with Swansea Schoolboys, Doug played part-time for the Swans while doing his apprenticeship in British Steel as a Fabricator/Welder prior to turning professional. Signing as a professional in May 1967, he made his league debut the following season at Peterborough United, making a further six league appearances before the end of the season as deputy for the veteran Mel Nurse, and Brian Hughes. Making nine league appearances the following season when the Swans gained promotion from the Fourth Division, he had to wait until playing against Reading at the Vetch Field to score his first goal for the Swans in late March 1971. Season 1970/71 also saw him make an appearance for the Swans in a 3-0 League Cup defeat at White Hart Lane against Tottenham Hotspur. Released by

manager Roy Bentley at the end of the season he joined Crewe Alexandra in August 1971, missed the first couple of games of the 1971/72 season, but after making his Alexandra debut at Gillingham, played in the next twenty-four league games, also in the FA Cup First Round home defeat by non-league side Blyth Spartans, before returning to league duty for the last four league matches of the season. In May 1972, after being released by Alexandra, he returned to Swansea, returned to his trade, working for a time on the BP Chemicals expansion at Baglan Bay, and signed for John Charles at Merthyr Tydfil. Captaining Merthyr during the whole of his playing career at Penydarren Park, the last four and a half years of his ten years with Merthyr saw Doug take over as manager, taking the club to the Welsh Cup semi-finals on two occasions in 1977 and 1980. Doug played one season for Haverfordwest County in 1982, and later played a couple of games for North End in the Swansea Senior League. For the last twenty years he has been working in the Financial Services Sector, and is currently an Independent Financial Advisor based in Mumbles.

41. ROULSON, Joseph (JOE)

Birthplace: Sheffield, 7/10/1891. **Died:** Sheffield, 7/12/1952
Ht: 5ft-9ins, **Wt:** 12st-0lbs
Swans debut: v. Merthyr Town (h), 26/8/1922

Swansea Town Career Statistics			
Season	League	FAC	WC
1922/23	36/1gls	2	3
1923/24	13/1gls	4	2
Total	49/2gls	6	5

Career:
Cammel Laird (signed in 1910)
Birmingham (signed in August 1912) lge 116/4gls
Swansea Town (£500 signed in August 1922)
Clapton Orient (signed in August 1924) lge 16

Honours: Second Division Champions–1921, West Wales Senior Cup Winner–1923

Half back who joined the Swans for £500 in August 1922 after a lengthy career with Birmingham, who during his period with the club won the Second Division Championship in 1921. Made his Swans debut in the first match of the 1922/23 season against Merthyr Town, missing just six league games, and also playing in the semi-final of the Welsh Cup against Cardiff City. He scored his first goal for the Swans at the Vetch Field against Bristol City in a 4-1 win, scoring his only other goal the following season in a 1-0 home win over Exeter City. Regarded as a good tactician during his period at the Vetch

Field, he was a classy, and constructive half back. He failed to oust new signing Bellamy from the right half berth for the start of the 1923/24 season, making his first start of the season on the 25th December against Watford. In November 1923 he was included in the Swans reserve side that beat Pembroke Dock to win the West Wales Senior Cup. He was sold to Second Division side Clapton Orient for £250 in August 1924 at the age of 32, but after making sixteen league appearances, retired from the game at the end of the season. During WW1 he made guest appearances for Leicester Fosse in December 1916. A keen cricketer, during his period with the Swans, in the summer of 1924 he played for Temple Cricket Club in Swansea, and scored the first century at Morriston's New Park Ground. During that summer he scored a further two centuries. Also included in the Temple side that summer was Len Thompson, who also played for Swansea Cricket Club.

42. ROUSE, Valentine Alfred (VIC)

Birthplace: Hoddesdon, near Harlow, 14/2/1897
Ht: 5ft-9ins, **Wt:** 10st-10lbs
Swans debut: v. Nottingham Forest (a), 27/2/1926

Swansea Town Career Statistics		
Season	League	WC
1925/26	4	1/1gls
Total	4	1/1gls

Career:
Llanelly
Pontypridd (signed in July 1920)
Wolverhampton Wanderers (signed in May 1921) lge 5
Stoke City (£1,000 signed in June 1922) lge 92/2gls
Swansea Town (signed in 11/5/1925)
Port Vale (signed in June 1926) lge 95, FAC 7
Crewe Alexandra (signed in May 1929) lge 83/1gls
Connah's Quay (signed in August 1931)

Honours: West Wales Senior Cup Winner–1926

Played war time football for Llanelly and the Swans prior to signing for Pontypridd as a professional for season 1920/21. Later transferred to Second Division side Wolverhampton Wanderers in May 1921, along with team mate Edward Watson, he made just five league appearances before joining Stoke City shortly after the side had been relegated to the Second Division. At Stoke he captained the side, and also played alongside former Swans players Nicholas and Brookes. Over the three seasons he had with Stoke City, it was said that he was the cleverest half back in the Potteries, with his reputation built around his attacking ability. He was released by Stoke just prior to making his debut for the Swans at Nottingham Forest on the 27th February 1926. Replacing Collins at right half back, his next two matches were at left half back instead of McPherson, playing his fourth, and last game for the Swans at right half back. In April 1926 he was included in the Swans reserve side that beat Merthyr Town to win the West Wales Senior Cup. Joining Port Vale prior to the start of the 1926/27 season, over the next three season he made regular appearances for Vale at half back before being released in May 1929. Joining Third Division North side Crewe Alexandra, he became one of only seven players who have made appearances for the three local teams, Vale, Stoke and Crewe. He finished his playing career with Connah's Quay, then after returning to the Swansea area became player manager at the Elba Tin Works side. He was the father of Welsh International keeper Vic Rouse, who played league football for Millwall, Crystal Palace, Oxford United and Leyton Orient.

43. ROWDEN, Leonard (LEN) Albert

Birthplace: Swansea, 31/5/1927
Ht: 5ft-10ins, **Wt:** 11st-0lbs
Swans debut: v. Leicester City (h), 3/10/1953

Swansea Town Career Statistics	
Season	League
1953/54	1
Total	1

Career:
Plasmarl
Clydach United
Swansea Town (signed in October 1953)
Llanelly (signed in 9/8/1955)

Honours: West Wales Senior Cup Winner–1954, Welsh League Challenge Cup Winner–1961

Len Rowden was signed a couple of days before making his league debut for the Swans, going from the Welsh League straight into the Second Division in early October 1953. Tottenham Hotspur had also been interested in signing the front runner, but came down to offer him professional terms the day he made his debut for the Swans! He made his debut at the Vetch Field against Leicester City at centre forward, with Beech taking over on the left wing from Harry Griffiths, in what was to be his only appearance in the first team for the Swans, and at the end of season was released. Joining Southern League side Llanelly in August 1955 he had been a member of the Swans side that beat Llanelly to win the West Wales Senior Cup in the previous season. Brought up in the Plasmarl area of Swansea, after leaving Plasmarl School he initially played for Plasmarl in the Swansea League, prior to joining Welsh League side Clydach United, where he played for nearly four years. After just one season at Stebonheath Park with the 'Reds', Len went to Bangor College, also making appearances for Bangor City. Spending three years in Cardiff College doing a Physical Education Degree, Len played one season with Aberystwyth, and during his last year in college signed for Haverfordwest County, where he finished his career in 1966. In April 1961 he was a member of the Haverfordwest side that beat Llanelly in the Welsh League Challenge Cup Final. He also had a spell teaching in Walsall, and played for one season for Burton Albion. Prior to his retirement Len had been a Physical Education Teacher in Townhill, Cefn Hengoed and Olchfa Comprehensive Schools.

44. RUSH, MATTHEW James

Birthplace: Dalston, Hackney, London, 6/8/1971
Ht: 5ft-11ins, **Wt:** 12st-10lbs
Swans debut: v. Port Vale (h), AGT Q/F, 11/1/1994

Swansea City Career Statistics			
Season	League	AGT	WC
1993/94	13	4	1
Total	13	4	1

Career:
West Ham United (associate schoolboy in 1984, trainee in July 1988, professional in March 1990) lge, 29+19/5gls
Cambridge United (loan in 12/3/1993) lge 4+6
Swansea City (loan in 2/1/1994)

Norwich City (£330,000 signed in 18/8/1995) lge 0+3
Northampton Town (loan in 28/10/1996) lge 6/2gls
Northampton Town (loan in 19/12/1996) lge 8/1gls,
   Others 1/1gls
Oldham Athletic (£165,000 signed in 27/3/1997) lge 17+7/3gls,
   FAC 0+3, Others 0+1

Honours: Republic of Ireland U-21–4

Rated probably the best player to have played for the Swans on a loan basis, for a player so inexperienced his inspirational play during the early rounds of the 1993/94 AutoGlass Trophy competition saw the Swans reach Wembley for the first time ever, although Rush had to miss the final because his three month loan spell had ended, and the Swans were in no position to make the transfer permanent. Signed by manager Frank Burrows from West Ham United on an initial one month loan transfer on the 2nd January 1994, he created such an impression with the Swans fans, his loan was extended to the maximum permitted. Making his debut in the AutoGlass Trophy Quarter Final at the Vetch Field against Port Vale, his league debut three days later against Rotherham United saw him play in thirteen consecutive league appearances, during which the Swans lost just two games. After playing against Wycombe Wanderers in the Southern Area Final, he returned to Upton Park, regained his first team place, and in August 1995 was sold to Norwich City for £330,000. A wide midfielder, who possessed an abundance of pace, he also had an extremely high workrate. Playing for Vista FC and London County Football side as a schoolboy, he joined the 'Hammers' as a trainee, made his first team debut for the club at Upton Park on the 6th October 1990 against Hull City, replacing Jimmy Quinn as substitute. By the time he had signed for the Swans he had also made loan appearances for Cambridge United, and his arrival at the Vetch Field was intended initially to get him back to fitness after being out of action for some time. Such was his form after returning to Upton Park, that he was given a new three year contract by the club, and at one time Kevin Keegan, then manager at Newcastle United tried to sign him. He gained the first of four U-21 appearances for the Republic of Ireland against Poland in October 1991. His transfer to First Division side Norwich City in August 1995 was unfortunately to be the start of a period when he suffered a series of knee problems, which would ultimately force him to retire from the professional game in September 1998, after making a total of just 41 league appearances since leaving Upton Park for Carrow Road, including 14 on two separate loan spells with Northampton Town during the 1996/97 season. Throughout his professional career Mathew has had ten knee operations, and for almost three years did not play a game. After leaving Oldham Athletic he played a couple of games for Dagenham & Redbridge before moving to Cheshire, and doing a teacher training course. Since qualifying as a P.E. teacher, Matthew has played for Droylsden and Ashton United, and completed a University course in Applied Sports Science.

45. RUSHBURY, David (DAVE) Garreth

Birthplace: Wolverhampton, 20/2/1956
Ht: 5ft-10ins, **Wt:** 11st-4lbs
Swans debut: v. Bournemouth (h), FLC 1-1, 11/8/1979

Swansea City Career Statistics				
Season	*League*	*FLC*	*FAC*	*WC*
1979/80	40	4	5	3
1980/81	11+1	2	1	3/1gls
Total	51+1	6	6	6/1gls

Career:
West Bromwich Albion (signed as apprentice in 1972,
   professional in February 1974) lge 28
Sheffield Wednesday (signed in November 1976) lge 111+1/7gls
Swansea City (£60,000 signed in 16/5/1979)
Carlisle United (£40,000 signed in 24/8/1981) lge 120+9/1gls
Gillingham (£15,000 signed in 21/3/1985) lge 12
Doncaster Rovers (£10,000 signed in 8/7/1985) lge 66/2gls
Cambridge United (loan in 21/2/1987) lge 1
Bristol Rovers (signed in February 1987) lge 14+2
Goole Town (signed in close season 1987)

Educated in St. Chads College in Wolverhampton, he represented, and captained the school team at all levels, right up to U-17, and U-18, also played for Staffordshire County Football. Signed by West Bromwich Albion, after completing a three month apprenticeship, at the age of 17 signed his first professional contract. Despite attending England training camps he failed to get any international honours as a youth player, and was given his first team debut by manager Don Howe at the age of 18 at Millwall on the 26th October 1974. After gaining promotion to the First Division with WBA, he struggled to make regular appearances in the 'Baggies' first team, and then had an initial loan spell with Sheffield Wednesday in November 1976, before the transfer was made permanent three months later. Switched to a left full back role, instead of his usual central defensive position by manager Jack Charlton, he played against the Swans in the old Third Division, and by the start of the 1979/80 season had arrived at the Vetch Field, in what proved to be the first transfer to be undertaken by a Football League Tribunal, with the Swans paying £60,000, and Wednesday wanting £110,000. During exciting times for the Swans, he was converted by Toshack into a left wing back position, besides playing occasionally as a left sided central defender, believing that the Swans manager had added a new dimension to his overall play which involved passing, moving and awareness. Missing just two league games during his first season at the Vetch Field, his second term with the Swans saw him fail to make the same impact, and in August 1981 he was sold to Carlisle United for £40,000. Further moves as a player saw him make league appearances for Gillingham, Doncaster Rovers and Cambridge United, before he signed for Bristol Rovers manager Bobby Gould. However, within a couple of games after arriving at Rovers, the manager had left to join Wimbledon, and despite the offer of a contract from new boss Gerry Francis, Rushbury decided to return north, and after turning down an offer from non-league side Goole Town, decided to utilise his physiotherapy and coaching qualifications, obtained when he was a player at Carlisle United, and stay in the game, eventually joining Chesterfield as physiotherapist in January 1989, where he was to remain for almost fourteen years. After a couple of promotion seasons at Chesterfield, he resigned as manager of the club in 2002, and later became Director of Football of Unibond Premier side Alfreton Town, overseeing all the football aspects of a very ambitious non-league club. After completing a degree course in sports and exercise science, he has also combined his college work with lecturing. Having had both hips replaced, he has been able to return to playing squash, and still keeps in touch with former players in the Swansea area, playing regularly for the Newton Inn Charity side.

S

1. SALAKO, JOHN Akin

Birthplace: Ibadari, Nigeria, 11/2/1969
Ht: 5ft-11ins, **Wt:** 12st-8lbs
Swans debut: v. Huddersfield Town (a), 19/8/1989

Swansea City Career Statistics		
Season	*League*	*ECWC*
1989/90	13/3gls	2/1gls
Total	13/3gls	2/1gls

Career:
Crystal Palace (associate schoolboy in May 1984, apprentice in
    July 1985, professional in 3/11/1986) lge 172+43/22gls,
    FLC 19+5/5gls, FAC 20/4gls, Others 11+3/2gls
Swansea City (loan in 14/8/1989)
Coventry City (£1,500,000 signed in 7/8/1995) lge 68+4/4gls,
    FLC 9/3gls, FAC 4/1gls
Bolton Wanderers (signed in 26/3/1998) lge 0+7
Fulham (signed in 22/7/1998) lge 7+3/1gls, FLC 2/1gls,
    FAC 2+2, Others 1
Charlton Athletic (loan in August 1999, £150,000 signed in
    September 1999) lge 10+37/2gls, FLC 1+2, FAC 3+4/1gls
Reading (loan in 3/11/2001) lge 15/4gls, Others 1
Reading (£75,000 signed in 28/1/2002) lge 81+15/9gls,
    FLC 4+1/1gls, FAC 0+4
Brentford (signed in 20/7/2004) lge 30+5/4gls, FAC 8+1/1gls,
    Others 0+1

Honours: England Full–5, FMC 1991, Division One
Champions–1994, 2000, Second Division Champions–1999

Swans' manager Ian Evans returned to his former club, Crystal
Palace in mid-August 1989 to recruit John Salako on a three
month loan transfer. A talented winger who had progressed
through the ranks at Selhurst Park, his form for the Swans

impressed a large number of supporters, but the £100,000
transfer fee to make his move permanent was way beyond the
money available at the time at the Vetch Field. Possessing pace,
good close skills, and the ability to cross the ball accurately to
his strikers, he returned to Selhurst Park with a lot more
confidence, and within a couple of weeks had regained his first
team place, and by the end of the season was one of the stars of
the side that beat Liverpool in the FA Cup semi-final, only to
lose out to Manchester United in a replay in the FA Cup Final.
His first goal for the Swans came in Athens against
Panathinaikos, in the first round, first leg of the European Cup
Winners Cup tie, with the Swans recovering from a three goal
deficit, to finish at 3-2, and set up an exciting second leg in the
return at the Vetch Field. In the league he scored two goals for
the Swans in a 3-1 away win against Bristol City at Ashton Gate,
scoring his other Swans' goal in the next match at Bury.
Such was his consistency, he was rewarded with his first
international cap for England on the 1st June 1991 against
Australia, also playing in the following tour matches against
New Zealand and Malaya. The following season he was a
member of the Palace side that beat Everton in the Zenith Data
Systems Final at Wembley, scoring one of the four goals for his
side. In 1991 he suffered a cruciate ligament injury, which kept
him out for most of the season, but by the end of season 1993/94
he had regained his fitness, making thirty-eight league
appearances in the Palace side that won the First Division
Championship. A £1.5m signing for Coventry, he only lasted
two seasons in the Midlands before he was loaned out to Bolton
and finally released on a free to Fulham. The 1998/99 season
saw Fulham win the Second Division Championship, with John
making ten league appearances, mostly during the first half of
the season. In 1999 he joined Charlton on loan and impressed
enough for the newly-promoted club to sign him for £150,000,
and make twenty-seven appearances in the league, as the club
won the First Division Championship. After transferring to
Reading in November 2001, he became an integral part of
Reading's successful promotion campaign, when the club
finished the season as runners-up in the Second Division.
The end of season 2003/04 saw Reading fail by three points to
reach the end of season First Division Play Offs. Off the field,
with a view to when he retires from the professional game, John
has started his broadcasting career commentating on the African
Nations Cup for Channel Four, and has since then also worked
on the 1998 World Cup in France, Euro 2000, and also worked
for the BBC on the 2004 African Nations Cup. During the 2004
close season he appeared in pre-season friendly games with
Brentford, signing a contract prior to the start of the season.

2. SAMPY, William (BILL) Albert

Birthplace: Backworth, 21/1/1901. **Died:** Coventry, JFM, 1973
Ht: 5ft-8ins, **Wt:** 12st-0lbs
Swans debut: v. Fulham (h), 18/4/1927

Swansea Town Career Statistics			
Season	*League*	*FAC*	*WC*
1926/27	4		
1927/28	3		1
1928/29	27		1
1929/30	7	1	
Total	41	1	2

Career:
Chopwell Colliery Institute
Sheffield United (£250 signed in 26/4/1921) lge 34
Swansea Town (£500 signed in February 1927)
Waterford Celtic (signed in August 1930)
Nelson (signed in October 1933)

Honours: West Wales Senior Cup Winner–1927

Joined Sheffield United from Chopwell Colliery Institute for £250 with James Waugh as part of the transfer deal, following his brother Tom Sampy who had earlier signed for United. After appearing in a friendly game for United, he made his league debut on the 4th October 1924 against Bury, but only played in one further game for United that season. Making regular appearances the following season, after struggling to make inroads into the United First Division starting line-up for the 1926/27 season, joined the Swans in February 1927. During his period at the Vetch Field he was not only capable of playing in either full back position, but also occasionally at centre half. Within a few weeks of signing for the Swans he played for the reserve team in the West Wales Senior Cup Final defeat of Bridgend Town. He made his debut as a replacement for Milne at the Vetch Field against Fulham towards the end of the 1926/27 season, making a further three league appearances out of the last four games of the season. The 1927/28 season saw him make two appearances as a replacement for Hanford at centre half, but over the next two seasons he competed with Ben Williams for the right back position. In May 1929 he was included in the Swans reserve side that were beaten 4-2 by Cardiff City at Llanelly in the Final of the South Wales & Monmouthshire Cup Final. Captain of the Swans reserves on occasions when not included in the first team, his agreement with the Swans was terminated by mutual consent midway through the 1929/30 season. In August 1930 he joined Irish side Waterford Celtic, taking over as player manager in season 1931/32. In October 1933 he joined Nelson.

3. SANDER, Christopher (CHRIS) Andrew

Birthplace: Swansea, 11/11/1962
Ht: 6ft-0ins, **Wt:** 11st-5lbs
Swans debut: v. Pontllanfraith, WC-4, 22/1/1980

Swansea City Career Statistics			
Season	*League*	*WC*	*ECWC*
1979/80		2	
1980/81			
1981/82	1	1	
1982/83	12	4	1
1983/84	7	1	
1984/85			
Total	20	8	1

Career:
Swansea City (from apprentice in November 1979)
Wrexham (loan in 21/9/1984) lge 5
Cardiff City (signed non-contract in August 1985) lge 8
Haverfordwest County (signed in December 1985)
Cardiff City (signed non-contract in March 1986) lge 5
Barry Town (signed in August 1986)
Aberystwyth (signed in October 1989)

Honours: Wales Sch–6, Yth–2, Welsh Cup Winner–1983, Welsh League National Division Champions–1989

Graduating from the same Swansea schoolboys side as Dudley Lewis and Gary Richards, goalkeeper Chris Sander, prior to joining the Swans as an apprentice, represented Wales at Athletics, as well as in Gymnastics. The former Gowerton Comprehensive schoolboy gained goalkeeping honours with the Wales Schoolboys, as well as at youth level. Making his first team debut for the Swans in a Welsh Cup fourth round tie at the Vetch Field against Pontllanfraith on the 22nd January 1980, but had to wait until the final league game of the 1981/82 season at Villa Park against Aston Villa before making his first league start. The following season, as finances dictated a clear out of senior players at the club, he replaced Dai Davies for the last twelve league appearances of the season. The same season he also made an appearance in the second leg of the European Cup Winners Cup tie in Malta against Sliema Wanderers, and also played in both legs of the Welsh Cup Final against Wrexham. With the experienced Jimmy Rimmer returning to the Vetch Field for the start of the 1983/84 season, his first team opportunities were limited to seven starts, with young Michael Hughes also pressing for a first team place. In September 1984 he had a five game loan spell with North Wales side Wrexham, but shortly after being named a substitute against Sully in the Welsh Cup tie at the Vetch Field, he had his contract cancelled at the Vetch Field. Signing for Cardiff City in August 1985, he was released after making eight league appearances, joining Welsh League side Haverfordwest County. An injury crisis to the club's goalkeepers at Ninian Park in March 1986 saw Chris return to make a further five league appearances for the Bluebirds, before being released. Joining Barry Town at the start of the 1986/87 season he played a large part in the club winning the Championship of the National Division of the Welsh League, and after overcoming a knee injury made appearances for Aberystwyth Town in the League of Wales, before finishing his career in the Swansea Senior League with Dunvant & Three Crosses. Currently vice-chairman and treasurer of Dunvant & Three Crosses FC, he has since leaving the professional game been involved in IT, but is at present a company director with the family firm.

4. SANDERS, ALAN

Birthplace: Salford, 31/1/1934
Ht: 5ft-11ins, **Wt:** 13st-0lbs
Swans debut: v. Cardiff City (a), 7/11/1959

Career:
Manchester City (signed in August 1955)

Swansea Town Career Statistics					
Season	*League*	*FLC*	*FAC*	*WC*	*ECWC*
1959/60	21		3	2	
1960/61	31	1	3	5	
1961/62	36	2	1	1	2
1962/63	4				
Total	92	3	7	8	2

Everton (signed in July 1956) lge 56
Swansea Town (£5,000 signed in 5/11/1959)
Brighton & Hove Albion (£7,000 signed in January 1963) lge 80

Honours: Welsh Cup Winner–1961, West Wales Senior Cup
Winner–1961

A well built full back, quick, with an ability to read the game
well, Alan Sanders also possessed good ball distribution, and
was a polished player in his position. Initially with Manchester
City, all of his league appearances for Everton came in the First
Division, developing his game steadily at Goodison Park over
three years before he lost his place at right-back when Scottish
international Alex Parker was signed from Falkirk. Signed by
Swans manager Trevor Morris for a fee of £6,000 in November
1959, he replaced Dai Thomas at right full back for his Swans'
debut in November 1959 at Ninian Park against Cardiff City,
remaining in the Swans side for most of the season.
The following season saw him establish himself at right back,
also playing in the Welsh Cup triumph against North Wales side
Bangor City, and the West Wales Senior Cup Final against
Haverfordwest. Missing just six league matches during the
1961/62 season, he also played in both legs of the European Cup
Winners Cup tie against East German side Motor Jena.
Struggling to oust Brian Hughes at right back, after just four
league appearances during season 1962/63, and with the
emergence of young prospect Roy Evans, he was sold to
Brighton & Hove Albion in January 1963 for £7,000. A strong
and polished full-back, Alan used his experience to good effect
at the Goldstone Ground, helping to steady the ship following
the departure of the manager two weeks after Alan had signed
for the club, and suffering relegation to the Fourth Division for
the first time at the end of his first season. His debut for the
Albion was a 2–1 defeat of Arsenal in a friendly match at Hove,
and he remained first-choice right-back for almost two years
until the arrival of Mel Hopkins from Spurs effectively ended
his career at the Goldstone. At the end of the 1964–65 season,
he followed the popular trail of ex-league footballers to South
Africa, joining Cape Town City as player/assistant manager,
later coaching in the Western Province. On returning to the U.K.
he had a somewhat stormy season as manager of Worthing in
1968–69 before leaving the club the following October.

5. SAUNDERS, DEAN Nicholas

Birthplace: Swansea, 21/6/1964
Ht: 5ft-8ins, **Wt:** 10st-6lbs
Swans debut: v. Charlton Athletic (a), 22/10/1983

Swansea City Career Statistics					
Season	*League*	*FLC*	*FAC*	*WC*	*FRT*
1983/84	14+5/3gls	0+1		3/1gls	
1984/85	28+2/9gls	2	1	3/2gls	1+1/1gls
Total	42+7/12gls	2+1	1	6/3gls	1+1/1gls

Career:
Swansea City (from apprentice in 24/6/1982)
Cardiff City (loan in 29/3/1985) lge 3+1
Brighton & Hove Albion (signed in 7/8/1985) lge 66+6/21gls,
  FLC 4, FAC 7/5gls, Others 3
Oxford United (£60,000 signed in 12/3/1987) lge 57+2/22gls,
  FLC 9+1/8gls, FAC 2/2gls, Others 2/1gls
Derby County (£1M signed in 28/10/1989) lge 106/42gls,
  FLC 9+1/8gls, FAC 6, Others 7/5gls
Liverpool (£2.9M signed in 19/7/1991) lge 42/11gls,
  FLC 5/2gls, FAC 8/2gls, Others 6/10gls
Aston Villa (£2.3M signed in 10/9/1992) lge 111+1/37gls,
  FLC 15/7gls, FAC 9/4gls, Others 8/1gls
Galatasaray, Turkey (£2.35M signed in 1/7/1995)
Nottingham Forest (£1.5M signed in 16/7/1996) lge 39+4/5gls,
  FLC 5+1/2gls, FAC 2/2gls
Sheffield United (signed in 5/12/1997) lge 42+1/17gls,
  FLC 4/3gls, FAC 6/2gls, Others 2
Benfica, Portugal (£500,000 signed in 10/12/1998)
Bradford City (signed in 6/8/1999) lge 32+12/3gls,
  FLC 1+2/1gls, FAC 2+1/2gls, Others 3

Honours: Wales Full–75, F.A. Cup Winner–1992, Football
League Cup Winner–1994

Former Gwyrosydd, Penlan, and Swansea schoolboy who joined
the Swans as an apprentice, following his father Roy, who had
earlier played for the Swans after joining the club from
Liverpool. Unlike his father who played at half back, Dean
proved to be a prolific goalscorer during his career in the
Football League, and also in Portugal and Turkey. Given his
league debut by manager John Toshack at Charlton Athletic in
October 1983 as substitute for Colin Pascoe, he scored his first
goal for the Swans in a 3-3 draw at Oldham Athletic in March
1984, scoring two goals three weeks later at the Vetch Field in a
3-2 win over Cardiff City. Following relegation to the Third
Division, he finished the 1984/85 season as joint top goalscorer
with nine league goals with Colin Pascoe, despite missing the
last eleven league matches, and also having a loan spell with
Cardiff City. Surprisingly released by manager John Bond at the

end of season 1984/85, and joining Brighton & Hove Albion on an initial trial basis, during his career Dean has ended up top goalscorer for his club on eight occasions. After re-establishing himself at the Goldstone Ground with Brighton, Dean's value in the transfer market has seen almost £13M changed hands from the period he left Brighton for Oxford United in March 1987, to his arrival at Bradford City in August 1999. He gained his first international cap against the Republic of Ireland on the 26th March 1986 as substitute for Davies, and on the 24th March 2001 created a Welsh record for an outfield player, when he received his 74th international cap in Armenia. Club honours has seen Dean win the FA Cup in 1992 whilst with Liverpool, and in March 1994 he scored two goals for Aston Villa when they beat Manchester United to win the Coca Cola Cup at Wembley. The end of the 2000/01 season saw him out of contract at Bradford City, and begin a coaching career under Graeme Souness at Blackburn Rovers, leading to a position as first team coach during season 2003/04. Early September 2004 saw Dean follow Graeme Souness to Newcastle United as a member of his coaching team.

6. SAUNDERS, ROY

Birthplace: Salford, 4/9/1930
Ht: 5ft-7¼ins, **Wt:** 12st-0lbs
Swans debut: v. Cardiff City (a), 7/3/1959

Swansea Town Career Statistics			
Season	League	FAC	WC
1958/59	12		
1959/60	19/1gls	1	2
1960/61	26/1gls	3	3/1gls
1961/62	8/1gls		
1962/63	29	2	3/1gls
Total	94/3gls	6	8/2gls

Career:
Hull City (amateur)
Liverpool (signed in May 1948) lge 132/1gls
Swansea Town (signed in 7/3/1959)
Ammanford Town (signed as player manager in close season 1964)

Honours: England Yth, Welsh Cup Winner–1961, Great Britain XI

Strong, tenacious tackler, hardworking wing half, who always gave 100% during the full ninety minutes of a match. Attended St. Ambrose's School in Salford, played for the school team and Bar Hill junior club before signing on the groundstaff at Hull City. Gained honours for the England youth side whilst at

Boothferry Park, was the only ever present during one season, and was persuaded to sign for Liverpool at the age of seventeen. The manager of the England Youth team at the time was also on the coaching staff with Liverpool. During his time at Anfield, he came on as a second half substitute for Stanley Matthews for a Great Britain XI against the Rest of the World, and played against the Swans on a regular basis after the 'Reds' had lost their First Division status, signing for the Swans in a part exchange transfer which saw Des Palmer go in the opposite direction to Anfield, with Roy's valuation in the transfer being £4,000. After making his Swans debut at left half at Ninian Park against Cardiff City in March 1959, he retained his place for the remainder of the season, and was a consistent performer until the end of the 1962/63 season when he was released from the Vetch Field playing staff. A member of the Swans side that beat Bangor City to win the Welsh Cup Final in 1961, the following season injury problems prevented him from playing in the first Welsh side to play European Football, in the European Cup Winners Cup competition. Knee cartilage problems forced his retirement from the professional game, and in the 1964 close season he took over as player manager of Welsh League side Ammanford Town, moulding a side that won several Welsh League titles. During his playing career with the Swans he forged a great friendship with Harry Griffiths at the Vetch Field, and after Harry had been appointed manager of the Swans in the mid-1970's, Roy was involved in either a coaching, or reserve team manager role at the Vetch Field for a number of seasons. During one season when the 'Gentle Giant' John Charles was youth team manager of the Swans, Roy, a former ISBA Lightweight Boxing Champion, and 'Charlo', a former Army Heavyweight Boxing Champion fought each other during a training session organised for the Swans players. Since his retirement as a player, along with his wife, Roy has been involved in the Hairdressing business in the city.

7. SAVARESE, GIOVANNI

Birthplace: Caracas, Venezuela, 14/7/1971
Ht: 6ft-0ins, **Wt:** 13st-2lbs
Swans debut: v. Stoke City (h), 14/10/2000

Swansea City Career Statistics				
Season	League	FAC	LDV	FAWP
2000/01	28+3/12gls	0+1	3/2gls	2+1
Total	28+3/12gls	0+1	3/2gls	2+1

Career:
Caracas FC
Deportivo Tachira
Deportivo Italchacao
Long Island Rough Riders (signed for season 1994/95)

New York Metro Stars (signed for season 1996/97)
   lge apps 55/27gls
Miami Fusion (signed in 1998) lge apps 30/14gls
New England Revolution, USA (signed in 1999)
   lge apps 27/10gls
San Jose Earthquakes, USA (signed in 2000) lge apps 4
Swansea City (signed in 13/10/2000)
Millwall (signed in 8/8/2001) lge 0+1
Deportivo Italchacao, Venezuela
Sassari Torres, Italy (signed for season 2003/04)
Long Island Rough Riders (signed in 2004)

Honours: Venezuela Full–23, National Champions–1995

A surprise signing by manager John Hollins prior to the match at the Vetch Field against Stoke City in October 2000, in which the Venezuelan international striker scored the Swans' two goals on his debut for the club. In his first nine league games for the Swans, the former MLS striker scored seven goals, also scoring a hat-trick at Luton Town in February 2001 in a 5-3 defeat. Prior to joining the Swans he had made a huge impact in the USA with New England Revolution, and was all time leading goalscorer for Metro Stars with thirty goals. He started his playing career in Venezuala with Caracas FC, Deportivo Tachira and Deportivo Italchacao before going to college in Long Island, and joining the Rough Riders. In 1995 he played in the Rough Riders side that won the National Championship. One of the bright spots in a relegation season at the Vetch Field, he added to his international caps whilst with the Swans, by playing against Colombia in a World Cup qualifying game, and during his international career scored ten goals for his country. With the Swans relegated after just one season in the Second Division, his only black mark of an impressive season at the Vetch Field came when he was sent off against Wrexham in the FAW Premier Cup Final at the end of the season. Returning to the USA after declining the option of a second season at the Vetch Field, he returned to the Football League in August 2001 to sign for Millwall on a three month contract. However, after making just one substitute appearance, he returned to Venezuela to sign for Deportivo Italchacao, had a spell in Italian football with Sassari Torres, before returning to the USA to sign for USL Professional Select League side Long Island Rough Riders, and was still attached to the club for season 2004/05.

8. SCHRODER, Nicolaas (NICO)

Birthplace: Holland, 19/11/1947. **Died:** Swansea, October 2004
Ht: 6ft-1ins, **Wt:** 11st-0lbs
Swans debut: v. Stockport County (a), 27/8/1976

Career:
Alkmaar 54, Holland (signed in 1966)
Everwarm (Bridgend Town) (signed in 1975)
Swansea City (signed in July 1976)

Telstar, Holland (signed in 1977)
AFC 34, Holland
Slotenvaart, Amsterdam (signed in 1980)

Swansea City Career Statistics	
Season	*League*
1976/77	1
Total	1

Big, tall goalkeeper, with a large pair of hands who signed for the Swans in July 1976, creating a place in history by becoming the first foreign born footballer to sign for a Football League side since Great Britain entered the Common Market. Playing for Everwarm (Bridgend Town), the Swans had earlier noticed his potential, and for three months had been discussing his transfer with the Football League. Under the Treaty of Rome, and the freedom of movement of labour within the nine countries, no Football League club had taken advantage of the fact, until the Swans stepped in. He impressed manager Harry Griffiths in a pre-season friendly at Bridgend prior to the start of the 1976/77 season, which resulted in the goalkeeper signing for the Swans as back up to Steve Potter. Nico became an amateur non-contract player at the Vetch Field, impressing everybody with his enthusiasm in training as well as holding down a full time job as a contractor in BSC Port Talbot. A door factory worker in Holland, his early playing career saw him make his senior debut with Alkmaar 54, who later became known as AZ 34 before coming to the UK and signing for Everwarm. He made his only league appearance for the Swans in a 3-0 defeat at Stockport County in August 1976, and after being released by the Swans returned to Holland, joining First Division side Telstar in 1977. He later played for AFC 34, Amsterdam amateur side Slotenvaart, before finishing his playing career in indoor football with Bloemensteege. He returned to the UK in December 1984, became a self-employed flower and plant salesman at the ASDA store in Trallwn, Swansea, before becoming an ASDA employee when the store was relocated to Llansamlet, working for the company up to his death in October 2004.

9. SCOTT, Henry (HARRY)

Birthplace: Newburn, Northumberland 4/8/1898
Ht: 6ft-0ins, **Wt:** 13st-0lbs
Swans debut: v. West Ham United (h), 27/8/1932

Swansea Town Career Statistics			
Season	*League*	*FAC*	*WC*
1932/33	40/7gls	1	1
Total	40/7gls	1	1

Career:
Bankhead Albion
Newburn Grange
Sunderland (signed in January 1924) lge 2
Wolverhampton Wanderers (signed in June 1925) lge 35/6gls
Hull City (signed in November 1926) lge 29/8gls, FAC 5/2gls
Bradford Park Avenue (player exchange signed in June 1928)
 lge 69/20gls
Swansea Town (signed in July 1932)
Watford (signed in June 1933) lge 1
Nuneaton Town (signed in July 1934)
Vauxhall Motors, Luton (signed on permit in September 1935)

Reputed to be one of the tallest inside forward's to have played
for the Swans, he made his Swans' debut in the first game of the
1932/33 season at the Vetch Field against West Ham United.
Missing just the two league matches through the season, he
started at inside right, but played mostly at inside left. He had
earlier in his career made his Football League debut with
Sunderland in the First Division, signing from junior sides
Bankhead Albion and Newburn Grange in 1924, and had played
on numerous occasions against the Swans for Wolverhampton
Wanderers, Hull City and Bradford Park Avenue, prior to
arriving at the Vetch Field. Built along the right lines for a
centre-forward, with Hull City he was never tried in this
position, playing for the 'Tigers' mainly at inside-right, where
his foraging link play was better utilised. He scored his first goal
for the Swans against Millwall at the Vetch Field in a 1-0 win on
October 1932. He left the Swans after just the one season,
signing for Third Division South side Watford, but after playing
in the opening league game of the season, failed to make
another appearance for the club, joining non-league side
Nuneaton Town at the end of the season, and finishing his
playing career with Vauxhall Motors in Luton.

10. SCREEN, Anthony (TONY) Lewis

Birthplace: Swansea, 9/5/1952
Ht: 5ft-10ins, **Wt:** 10st-2lbs
Swans debut: v. York City (a), 2/5/1969

Swansea Town/City Career Statistics				
Season	League	FLC	FAC	WC
1968/69	2			
1969/70				
1970/71	26	3	4	1
1971/72	26	1	6	1
1972/73	23	2	1	2
1973/74	29/7gls	2/1gls	1	1/1gls
1974/75	19+3/2gls		1	2
Total	125+3/9gls	8/1gls	13	7/1gls

Career:
Swansea Town (from apprentice in May 1970)
Ammanford Town (signed in close season 1975)

Honours: Wales Yth–6, U-23–1, West Wales Senior Cup
Winner–1980

Signed as an apprentice on the 10th August 1967, the young
Swans' defender made his league debut a couple of days prior
to his seventeenth birthday at York City, retaining his place for
the next match, the last game of the 1968/69 season. A former
Swansea schoolboy player whilst at Bishop Vaughan school, he
made remarkable progress after joining the Swans' as an
apprentice, and was awarded six Welsh Youth caps, and was a
member of the Wales side that beat England to qualify for the
24th UEFA Youth Tournament. As a schoolboy he was a reserve
for the Wales Schoolboys side. Given his league debut by
caretaker manager Walter Robbins, he failed to make an
appearance during the Fourth Division promotion season under
Roy Bentley, but the following season in the Third Division,
after missing the opening match, made a number of
appearances at centre half, then reverting to a left, or right back
role for the most part of the season. A quick, capable defender,
who had good aerial strength, he gained his only appearance for
the Welsh U-23 side, when going on as a substitute against
Scotland in 1971 in the last couple of minutes at the Vetch Field.
With occasional appearances in midfield, it was in the last match
of the1972/73 season that he was given a opportunity at centre
forward by manager Harry Gregg, which was continued
throughout the following season, resulting in Tony finishing as
top goalscorer with seven league goals, plus two more in cup
matches. His first league goal of his career came in the first
match of the 1973/74 season, in a 2-0 away win at Chester,
during a season which saw the Swans struggle to come to terms
with life back in the Fourth Division. A change of management
midway through the 1974/75 season saw Tony alternate
between defence and attack as Harry Griffiths struggled in vain
to prevent the Swans from having to apply for re-election to the
Football League. Released at the end of the season, Tony joined
Welsh League side Ammanford Town, and took up employment
as a postman initially, but then worked at Cwmfelin Press for a
number of years. He was joined by his brother Willie at
Ammanford twelve months later, playing in the same side as his
brother for a number of seasons. During season 1979/80
Ammanford Town beat the Swans in the final of the West Wales
Senior Cup at Stebonheath Park, Llanelli. Tony later worked in
the reception area of the Guildhall for a number of years before
becoming a steward at Glynhir Golf Club in Llandeilo. For the
last couple of years he has been licensee of the Red Lion Public
House in Llandybie.

11. SCREEN, William (WILLIE) Robert

Birthplace: Swansea, 8/11/1948
Ht: 5ft-7ins, **Wt:** 8st-12lbs
Swans debut: v. Aldershot (a), 7/10/1967

Swansea Town/City Career Statistics

Season	League	FLC	FAC	WC
1967/68	27/2gls		4	2/1gls
1968/69	34+1/7gls	4	2/1gls	4/1gls
1969/70	25	1	2	4/1gls
1970/71	21+6/2gls	3	0+1	
1971/72	26+2		1+2	
Total	133+9/11gls	8	9+3/1gls	10/3gls

Career:
Swansea Town (signed from juniors, professional in March 1967)
Newport County (signed in June 1972) lge 137+5/7gls
Ammanford Town (signed in close season 1976)

Honours: Wales U-23–2

Brought up in the Waun Wen area of Swansea, Willie attended St. Josephs School prior to joining the Swans. The diminutive midfielder's potential was noted when he played for Swansea Schoolboys and he was subsequently invited to attend the Swans groundstaff at the age of 15 years on leaving school, signing professional on the 7th March 1967 by manager Billy Lucas, making his league debut in October 1967 at Aldershot. His stature and physique belied his physical strength and determination, a tenacious tackler who could be relied on to fight for every ball throughout the ninety minutes. Making twenty-seven league appearances during his first season in the first team line-up, he scored his first league goal in a 2-1 home defeat of Halifax Town shortly after making his league debut, and also figure prominently in the narrow home defeat by Arsenal in the FA Cup. The 1968/69 season which saw the Swans lose at Liverpool in the third round of the League Cup, and lose over two legs to Cardiff City in the Welsh Cup Final saw Willie return seven league goals from midfield. By now his inspirational qualities, and hard work in midfield had been recognised by the Wales U-23 side, with Willie making appearances in 1968 against Northern Ireland, and the following year against England. Despite a change of management for the 1969/70 season, which saw Roy Bentley take over the helm, success continued for both Willie and the Swans, with promotion from the Fourth Division being secured by the club. After two seasons of mid table security in the Third Division, with Willie making occasional appearances at full back, he was released by the Swans, linking up for a second time with Billy Lucas at Newport County, and in his first season at Somerton Park, the club were denied promotion from the Fourth Division by virtue of goal average. In 1976 he left County, linking up with Ammanford Town, initially as a player, but then took over from Evan Powell as player manager. Taking employment in Cwmfelin Steelworks in Llangyfelach Road, he also made appearances for the works side in the mid-week section of the Swansea Senior League. When the steelworks closed down, he was then employed by Swansea Council at the Guildhall up to the age when he retired in 1997.

12. SCRINE, Francis (FRANKIE) Henry

Birthplace: Swansea, 9/1/1925. **Died:** Swansea, 5/10/2001
Ht: 5ft-9ins, **Wt:** 11st-7lbs
Swans debut: v. Exeter City (a), 4/10/1947

Career:
Swansea Town (amateur signed in March 1943, professional in April 1947)
Oldham Athletic (£3,700 signed in October 1953) lge 78/21gls
Llanelly (loan in 14/9/1955)
Llanelly (signed in August 1956)
Milford United (signed in January 1957)

Haverfordwest County (signed by October 1958)
Bettws (signed by December 1959)

Swansea Town Career Statistics

Season	League	FAC	WC
1947/48	22/4gls	1	1
1948/49	38/18gls	2	4/8gls
1949/50	32/5gls	2/2gls	4/7gls
1950/51	2		
1951/52	30/10gls	2	1/1gls
1952/53	15/6gls		2/1gls
1953/54	5/2gls		
Total	144/45gls	7/2gls	12/17gls

Honours: Wales Full–2, Third Division Champions–1949, Welsh Cup Winner–1950, London Combination Cup Winner–1950

A former Dyfatty, and Swansea schoolboy player who was an amateur at the Vetch Field during the war, played in the local Swansea League for Baldwins, initially signing in 1943, called up to the Navy in 1944, signing professional in April 1947. The grandson of former All Whites, and Welsh international, Fred Scrine, he commenced playing rugby, but with rugby not being played during the last war, reverted to soccer. Jock Weir, a Swansea scout and a former member of the Swans' Southern League side, persuaded Frank to appear in a Swansea trial and in 1946 he became a member of the Swans, making his league debut at Exeter City in October 1947. Capable of playing at either inside forward, outside left, or at centre forward, he was a dangerous goalscorer, who possessed a wonderful body swerve, dipping his shoulder and sending his opponents the wrong way. Scoring his first goal in his eighth league game for the Swans, he scored three hat-tricks during the successful 1948/49 Third Division South Championship winning season, against Bristol Rovers in the league, and against Barry Town and South Liverpool in Welsh Cup ties. A member of the Swans side that were beaten by Merthyr in the 1949 Welsh Cup Final, twelve months later he scored a hat-trick in the Welsh Cup Final when the Swans beat Wrexham at Ninian Park 4-1. On the 15th October 1949 he was awarded his first international cap for Wales at Cardiff in a 4-1 defeat by England, receiving his second cap on the 8th March 1950 at Wrexham against Northern Ireland. He was stationed in Plymouth during WW2, made guest appearances for the Royal Navy in Plymouth, and for Plymouth Argyle. In May 1950 he scored two goals for the Swans reserve side that won at Southend United to win the London Combination Cup Final. During season 1950/51 he suffered an unfortunate knee injury which limited him to just two league appearances. After joining Second Division side Oldham Athletic for £3,700 in October 1953, he returned to South Wales to sign for Southern League side Llanelly in mid-September 1955, but returned to Boundary Park after playing just a couple of games for the 'Reds'. Playing a further twenty-league games for Oldham, at the end of the season he was at one stage about to take over as player manager of Pembroke Borough, but after negotiations had broken down with Oldham Athletic, he was released, and in late August 1956 signed for Llanelly. In early January 1957 he asked to be released from his contract at Stebonheath Park, and within a couple of weeks had signed for Welsh League side Milford United. After joining Haverfordwest County shortly after the start of the 1958/59 season, he finished his playing career with Bettws before retiring from the game due to knee trouble. He worked as foreman in AWCO in Swansea, and later as a caretaker in the St. David's Centre, retiring at 70, prior to his death in Swansea in October 2001.

13. SHARP, NEIL Anthony

Birthplace: Hemel Hempstead, 19/1/1978
Ht: 6ft-1ins, **Wt:** 12st-10lbs
Swans debut: v. Luton Town (a), 27/10/2001

Swansea City Career Statistics		
Season	League	FAWP
2001/02	22+3/1gls	1
2002/03	4+3	
Total	26+6/1gls	1

Career:
Hayes
Borehamwood Town
Barry Town
Merthyr Tydfil
Swansea City (signed in 25/10/2001)
Woking (signed in May 2003) Conf 24+1
Havant & Waterlooville (signed in July 2004)
    Conf Sth 36+1/5gls, FAC 0+1, FAT 4

Honours: West Wales Senior Cup Winner–2002

Signed from non-league Merthyr in October 2001 after impressing against the Swans in a friendly for Merthyr Tydfil at Penydarren Park, and who had earlier spent a couple of weeks training at the Vetch Field. He had earlier played for the Swans assistant manager Peter Nicholas, the previous season at Barry Town, and prior to that for Borehamwood Town, Hayes, and Queen's Park Rangers. Spending some time in the USA, he had also made appearances for Columbus Crew in the MLS while studying on an exercise physiology course in college. A rugged central defender, with good aerial ability, Neil took some time to adjust to the demands of the Third Division, but as the season progressed became a regular inclusion in the Swans' starting line-up. Dangerous at set pieces, on a number of

occasions he struck the woodwork before eventually scoring his first league goal, at the Vetch Field against Kidderminster Harriers. In late April 2002 he was included in the Swans side that beat Hakin United to win the West Wales Senior Cup. His second season with the Swans' saw him miss the opening matches, and then suffered ankle ligament damage at the Vetch Field against Hartlepool United which sidelined him for a number of months. His only matches in the second half of the season were in friendly games, and in May 2003 he was released by manager Flynn. Returning to his native Hertfordshire, he signed for Conference side Woking in May 2003 as a full time professional, making twenty-five league appearances in the Nationwide Conference prior to being released in mid-April 2004. He appeared as a trialist in the Yeovil Town reserve side that played the Swans reserves at the Vetch Field a week later. In mid-July he signed a contract with Conference South side Havant & Waterlooville, having been set a few weeks earlier for a return to the Vetch Field, with the move breaking down purely on a financial basis, with Swans manager Kenny Jackett's budget dictating he add a goalkeeper to the playing squad rather than another defender. Prior to the 2002 World Cup, Neil played in two warm up friendly games for the Cayman Islands after the Cayman Island F.A. had interpreted a FIFA rule allowing any UK citizen not committed to one of the home international sides to play for a British Colony. When FIFA insisted on proof of residency, his short international career came to an abrupt end.

14. SHARPE, JOHN William Henry

Birthplace: Portsmouth, 9/10/1957
Ht: 5ft-11ins, **Wt:** 11st-5lbs
Swans debut: v. Brentford (a), 5/10/1985

Swansea City Career Statistics		
Season	League	FLC
1985/86	5	1
Total	5	1

Career:
Southampton (apprentice in October 1974, professional in October 1975) lge 21
Gillingham (signed on 7/9/1978) lge 192+2/2gls
Southampton (signed non-contract in March 1985)
Swansea City (signed non-contract in September 1985)

Former Portsmouth Schoolboy captain, recommended to the 'Saints' by former player and scout Stan Cribb. He made his Football League debut as a replacement for Welsh international Peter Rodrigues at Bristol Rovers in April 1977, playing in the remaining matches of the season. The following season when the 'Saints' clinched promotion to the First Division as Runners-Up to Bolton Wanderers he made ten league appearances. His first team opportunities were further limited following the signing of Ivan Golac, and in early September 1978 he joined Third Division Gillingham on an initial loan transfer, making thirty-seven league appearances in the 'Gills' side that lost out by one point to the Swans for promotion to the Second Division at the end of the season. A consistent performer at right, or left full back for Gillingham, making almost two hundred league appearances, he rejoined the 'Saints' in March 1985 on a non-contract basis, but failed to make any first team appearances. In September 1985, Swans' manager John Bond signed him on non-contract, making his first team debut at Brentford on the 5th October 1985 replacing Dudley Lewis at right full back, and playing in the second leg of the second round of the Milk Cup tie against West Ham United three days later. After a further four league appearances he left the Vetch Field playing staff.

15. SIDIBE, MAMADY

Birthplace: Mali, 18/12/1979
Ht: 6ft-4ins, **Wt:** 12st-4lbs
Swans debut: v. Macclesfield Town (a), 11/8/2001

Swansea City Career Statistics					
Season	League	FLC	FAC	LDV	FAWP
2001/02	26+5/7gls	0+1	2/1gls	1	1
Total	26+5/7gls	0+1	2/1gls	1	1

Career:
Racing Club, Paris
CA Paris, France
Swansea City (signed 25/7/2001)
Gillingham (signed in 9/8/2002) lge 80+26/10gls,
    FLC 4+1/1gls, FAC 3+1/2gls
Stoke City (signed in 23/6/2005)

Honours: Mali–7

The tall, 6 feet 4 inch striker impressed during a trial period in the close season build up, signing a one year contract with John Hollins at the Vetch Field. Formerly with French Second Division side CA Paris, he possessed pace, good control, and the ability to win the ball in aerial challenges. Despite being sidelined on a number of occasions during the season with hamstring, ankle ligament, and also having 12 stitches in a cut just above the ankle suffered at Plymouth, 'Mama' impressed the Swans supporters with his skill on the ball. Following his performance in the televised FA Cup tie against QPR, he was the subject of a reported £200,000 offer from Barnsley in mid December, which was not taken any further. At the end of a season full of uncertainty, 'Mama' finished second top goalscorer for the Swans with eight league and cup goals. During the close season with former player Nick Cusack having taken over as manager at the Vetch Field, a doubt over an old injury on his knee saw him decline the option of proving his fitness with a view to securing a new contract, and leave the Vetch Field playing staff. His impressive form against QPR in the previous season's FA Cup tie saw him play a number of pre-season friendlies for the West London side, including scoring a goal against Chelsea in one friendly, but was then surprisingly not offered a contract at Loftus Road, instead signed for First Division side Gillingham, again on an initial trial basis, which eventually led to a full contract at Priestfield Stadium. Knee injuries affected his first season with the 'Gills', but after returning to action after a knee ligament injury, produced probably his best form for the club, scoring in games against Watford and Ipswich Town, and also scoring the all important equalizer in the televised FA Cup tie against Premiership side Leeds United. In October 2002 he scored for Mali against the Seychelles in his international debut in an African Nations Cup qualifier, featuring regularly in the national squad thereafter, also playing for Mali in the 2004 African Nations Cup

Competition Finals. In June 2005 he signed for Championship side Stoke City.

16. SIMMONDS, Robert LYNDON

Birthplace: Pontypool, 11/11/1966
Ht: 5ft-4ins, **Wt** 9st-10lbs
Swans debut: v. Wolverhampton Wanderers (h), 18/10/1986

Swansea City Career Statistics			
Season	League	WC	FRT
1986/87	7+1/1gls	1	1
Total	7+1/1gls	1	1

Career:
Leeds United (from apprentice in November 1984) lge 6+3/3gls
Swansea City (loan in 16/10/1986)
Rochdale (loan in 20/2/1987) lge 22/10gls
Rochdale (£4,000 signed in 3/6/1987) lge 43/12gls, FLC 4/1gls,
    FAC 1, Others 3/2gls

Honours: Wales Sch–11, Yth–5

A former apprentice at Elland Road with Leeds United who was signed by manager Terry Yorath on a month's loan in October 1986. The former Blackwood Comprehensive, Gwent, South Wales and Wales schoolboy striker gained further honours at youth level whilst at Elland Road, and made his Second Division debut for the club as a substitute for George McCluskey against Blackburn Rovers on the 6th April 1985. On the 2nd November 1985 he made his first start for United, scoring two goals, one from a penalty, in a 2-1 win over Portsmouth. Despite his short stature he was a willing worker, had good pace and an eye for goal. He scored only one goal for the Swans, against Rochdale at the Vetch Field in a 1-0 win, but after returning to Elland Road, joined Rochdale on a loan transfer in February 1987, scoring against the Swans later in the season in the return league fixture at Spotland. At Spotland he linked up with former Swans' and Leeds United striker Derek Parlane, and by the end of the season, Lyndon was top goalscorer in the league with ten goals. On the 3rd June 1987 his transfer to Rochdale was made permanent, and besides finishing for the second time as top goalscorer, this time with 12 league goals, also scored three goals against the Swans, two in a match at the Vetch Field which saw Rochdale win 3-0. In August 1988 a pelvic injury forced him to retire from the game, returning to live in Blackwood, where he became manager at RF Brookes food manufacturers.

17. SIMMS, JOHN

Birthplace: Burslem, AMJ, 1903
Ht: 5t-8ins, **Wt**: 11st-0lbs
Swans debut: v. Barnsley (a), 12/9/1931

Swansea Town Career Statistics	
Season	*League*
1931/32	4/2gls
Total	4/2gls

Career:
Whitfield Colliery
Stoke City (amateur signed in March 1924)
Leek Alexandra
Port Vale (amateur signed in June 1926, professional in October 1926) lge 81/25gls, FAC 3
Swansea Town (£250 signed in 19/5/1931)
Winsford Town (signed in August 1932)
Macclesfield
Northwich Victoria (signed in June 1934)

Experienced outside left who joined the Swans from Port Vale in May 1931 for £250, after he had been a prominent member of the Vale side in the Second Division, but made only made three league appearances during the club's 1929/30 Third Division North Championship success, in their first season after being relegated. The 1928/29 season saw him score twelve goals from thirty-one league appearances. Earlier in his career he had played for Burslem Juniors, Whitfield Colliery, Stoke and Leek Alexandra before joining Vale as an amateur in June 1926, turning professional in October the same year. Making his Swans' debut instead of D. J. Lewis at outside left, he scored the Swans' first goal after just 80 seconds at Barnsley in a 3-2 victory, also scoring in the next match, at the Vetch Field against Notts. County, in which Cyril Pearce scored four goals. Unable to oust Lewis from the outside left berth, his only other appearances that season came at outside right, and at wing half. He was transfer listed at £250 in May 1932, which was later reduced to £100, and before the start of the 1932/33 season had joined Cheshire non-league side Winsford United. He later made non-league appearances for Macclesfield and Northwich Victoria.

18. SIMONS, REUBEN Rhys

Birthplace: Swansea, 16/10/1908. **Died:** Swansea, February 1991
Ht: 5ft-10ins, **Wt**: 11st-3lbs
Swans debut: v. Hull City (h), 2/9/1933

Career:
Swansea Town (amateur signed in August 1931, professional in 1/10/1931)

Northampton Town (£400 signed in 25/5/1939) lge 3
Swansea Town (signed in 1942/43 season)
Llanelly (signed by May 1948)

Swansea Town Career Statistics			
Season	*League*	*FAC*	*WC*
1933/34	3		1
1934/35			2/1gls
1935/36	7		2
1936/37	35	3	1
1937/38	42	1	1
1938/39	20	1	1
Total	107	5	8/1gls

Honours: South Wales Police XI, West Wales Senior Cup Winner–1934, 1948

Centre half who initially joined the Swans as an amateur from Gorseinon side Beaufort FC, signing professional in August 1931, but had to wait until September 1933 before he made his first team debut as a replacement for Joe Sykes. He had previously only made occasional appearances during his first five seasons with the Swans, but from the 1936/37 season he became a regular inclusion in the Swans starting line-up. In October 1934 he was included in the Swans side that beat Llanelly to win the West Wales Senior Cup. He scored his only goal for the Swans in a Welsh Cup, fifth round tie against Milford United, failing to score in any of his league appearances. His last season with the Swans saw him play in a carried over Welsh Cup Final replay in September 1938 against Shrewsbury Town. During a period in the club's history when players were being sold, he emerged as one of the few stable elements in the Swans line-up. He was transferred to Northampton Town for £400 in late May 1939, and made 3 league apps with the 'Cobblers' in the disrupted 1939/40 season (the season that included their 'expunged' 10-0 defeat by Bournemouth). He returned to Swansea to make a further 41 war time league apps between 1942 and 1944 before leaving the full time game to become a policeman. Serving for 28 years in the force until his retirement, he retained close links with the club, with his son in law Brian Purcell a regular inclusion in the Swans starting line-up through the 1960's. He linked up with Llanelly after WW2, playing in the May 1948 West Wales Senior Cup success over Briton Ferry Athletic. In March 1950 he captained a South Wales Police XI at the Vetch Field against a West Wales Transport XI, captained by former Swans player Tom Emmanuel.

19. SLATER, John (JACKIE) Albert

Birthplace: Sheffield, JFM, 1899. **Died:** Sheffield, JAS, 1961
Ht: 5ft-7½ins, **Wt:** 10st-6lbs
Swans debut: v. Southampton (h), 16/10/1920

Swansea Town Career Statistics		
Season	*League*	*WC*
1920/21	2	1
1921/22	8/3gls	1
Total	10/3gls	2

Career:
Swansea Town (trial in September 1920, professional in 12/10/1920)
Southend United (signed in July 1922) lge 92/15gls, FAC 7/3gls
Grays Thurrock (signed in July 1925)

Inside forward who arrived at the Vetch Field in late September 1920 on a trial basis from junior football in Sheffield, played two trial games for the Swans' reserve side, scoring two goals in a Western League game against Mid-Rhondda. His form in the trial matches convinced the club's manager Joe Bradshaw that he was a player with youth on his side and after signing professional forms, made his league debut four days later as a replacement for WY Brown, in what was the club's first season in the Football League. After his debut at the Vetch Field against Southampton, he played in the following game, but had to wait until September 1921 before playing his next game, at the Vetch Field against Southend United. In his third match of the 1921/22 season he scored a brace of goals in the club's 3-2 victory over Newport County at Somerton Park, scoring a third goal for the Swans later in the season against Norwich City at the Vetch Field. His matches for the Swans were played mostly at inside left, and in May 1922 he was released, joining Southend United. Swans' goalkeeper Jennings was also released at the same time and also signed for Southend United, with both players playing in back to back league games against the Swans shortly after the start of the 1922/23 season. The inside forward became a consistent member of the 'Shrimper's league side, making almost a hundred league appearances before he was released at the end of the 1924/25 season, joining non-league side Grays Thurrock.

20. SLATTERY, James CLIVE

Birthplace: Swansea, 21/7/1946
Ht: 5ft-7ins, **Wt:** 10st-0lbs
Swans debut: v. Peterborough United (a), 10/3/ 1969

Swansea Town/City Career Statistics				
Season	*League*	*FLC*	*FAC*	*WC*
1968/69	6+1/2gls			1
1969/70	23+1/3gls		2	1
1970/71	19/2gls	1	1	
1971/72	17+3/3gls	1	2	
Total	65+5/10gls	2	5	2

Career:
Winch Wen (signed in close season 1962)
Swansea Town (signed in October 1968)
Hereford United (signed in July 1972) lge 3+5
Yeovil Town (signed in July 1973) Total apps 25/5gls
Merthyr Tydfil (signed in July 1974)
Haverfordwest
Morriston Town

Joining the Swans in October 1968, Clive was given his first team debut by manager Billy Lucas at Peterborough United in March 1969, going on the field as substitute for Brian Grey, in a game which saw the Swans drew 2-2, with Clive scoring the Swans second goal. Brought up in St. Thomas, he attended St. Thomas Juniors and Llansamlet Senior School, played for Swansea Schoolboys in football and captained the cricket team. On leaving school he started an apprenticeship as a fitter and turner in Swansea Vale, joined local Swansea Senior League side Winch Wen, also playing occasionally for the Swans Youth side during the six years he spent with the Senior League club. An attack minded winger, or midfielder, he had gained a good reputation with the Swans Combination side, regularly featuring on the goalscoring sheet. Possessing good pace and acceleration, he was unlucky at the Vetch Field in having Brian Evans and the veteran Len Allchurch ahead of him in the first team, as far as opportunities on the flanks were concerned. Two days after his substitute appearance he made his first start for the Swans, against Hereford United in a Welsh Cup semi-final tie. Missing the next league game, he started his first league game at the Vetch Field against York City, also scoring his second goal in a 2-1 win. The 1969/70 season saw him have a fourteen game run in the league for the Swans, returning three league goals, and also seeing the side gain promotion from the Fourth Division, besides playing in two FA Cup ties against Kettering Town and Oxford City. After two further seasons of being included in the Swans first team squad, he was released in July 1972, signing for Colin Addison's newly elected Fourth Division side Hereford United. He played in Hereford's first ever league match and their first win, the following weekend but then lost his place and started only one more league match before being released at the end of the season. Joining Yeovil Town in July 1973, after returning to South Wales twelve months later to sign for Merthyr Tydfil, returning to his trade as a fitter and turner, he later made appearances for Haverfordwest, before finishing his career as player manager of Welsh League side Morriston Town.

21. SLEE, David CARL

Birthplace: Swansea, 30/11/1947
Ht: 6ft-0ins, **Wt:** 10st-10lbs
Swans debut: v. Rochdale (a), 15/4/1968

Career:
Swansea Town (signed from juniors in 1/1/1966)
Merthyr Tydfil (signed in close season 1972)
Everwarm (signed in close season 1975)
Llanelli (signed in close season 1977)

Honours: Welsh League Premier Division Champions–1978, West Wales Senior Cup Winner–1966

Swansea Town/City Career Statistics				
Season	League	FLC	FAC	WC
1967/68	8			
1968/69	30+2	4	4	6
1969/70	33+2		3	4
1970/71	44	3	2	1
Total	115+4	7	9	11

Former St. Davids Schoolboy and Swansea schoolboy, brought up in the Sandfields area of Swansea, who initially signed for the Swans on a part-time basis prior to signing as a professional at the age of eighteen. A hard tackling defender during his career with the Swans, his grandfather was Billy Hole, while three of his uncles, Barrie, Alan and Colin all made appearances for the Swans during their careers. Carl played alongside Barrie during his last season at the Vetch Field. He was included in a Swans reserve side that beat Llanelly in August 1966 to win the West Wales Senior Cup. Given his first team opportunity by manager Billy Lucas in April 1968 at Rochdale at centre half instead of Joe Davis, Carl retained his place for the remaining seven league games afterwards. He started the 1968/69 season alongside the experienced Mel Nurse in central defence, playing in both legs of the Welsh Cup Final at the end of the season against Cardiff City. Missing the start of the 1969/70 season, he rejoined the first team, replacing Dai Lawrence at right full back, a position he was to remain in until he retired from the professional game in July 1971. The 1969/70 Fourth Division promotion season saw Carl make 35 league appearances, play in a tight FA Cup tie at Elland Road against Leeds United, and also in both Welsh Cup semi-final legs against Cardiff City. Missing just two league games during the 1970/71 season, he had also been included in the Welsh U-23 squad on two occasions, and it came as a shock to all supporters when it was announced that he had retired from the professional game to concentrate on his business interests in the city after being unable to agree a new contract with the football club. Taking a year's break from the game because of a contract dispute with the Swans, Carl returned to action with Merthyr Tydfil, played a couple of seasons before joining Welsh League side Everwarm. In season 1977/78, they lost by the odd goal to Cardiff City in the Welsh Cup semi-final. With the club looking to move into the Southern League, Carl decided against all the travelling involved, and instead signed for Llanelli, winning the Premier Division Championship in his first season. After a spell with Maesteg Park, a second spell at Stebonheath Park with Llanelli, Carl finished his Welsh League career with Ammanford Town. Following a number years away from the game he was persuaded to play for his son's team, Murton Rovers of the Swansea Senior League, and to date is still playing an active role in the club, on and off the park, as well as working in his newsagents business in the Sandfields area of the city.

22. SMITH, DAVID

Birthplace: Stonehouse, Glos, 29/3/1968
Ht: 5ft-8ins, **Wt:** 10st-7lbs
Swans debut: v. Rushden & Diamonds (h), 10/8/2002

Swansea City Career Statistics	
Season	League
2002/03	3+1/1gls
Total	3+1/1gls

Career:
Coventry City (from apprentice in 7/7/1986) lge 144+10/19gls, FLC 17, FAC 6, Others 4+1
Bournemouth (loan in 8/1/1993) lge 1
Birmingham City (signed in 12/3/1993) lge 35+3/3gls, FLC 4, FAC 0+1, Others 1
West Bromwich Albion (£90,000 signed in 31/1/1994) lge 87+20/2gls, FLC 4+2, FAC 1+3, Others 4+1
Grimsby Town (£200,000 signed in 16/1/1998) lge 101+11/9gls, FLC 9+3/1gls, FAC 2+1, Others 7/1gls
Swansea City (signed in 8/7/2002)

Honours: England U-21–10, AMC–1998, Second Division Play Off Winner–1998

Experienced left sided full back/midfielder was signed by manager Nick Cusack in the 2002 close season on a free transfer from Grimsby Town. He opened his goal scoring account in his first away game for the Swans, in a 2-2 draw at Darlington, but unfortunately suffered a groin injury, and then a calf problem, which sidelined him for a number of weeks. A change of management at the Vetch Field saw him have his contract paid up by Christmas 2002, leaving the club after just four league appearances. The former Maidenhill Comprehensive School (Stonehouse), and Stroud Boys player, played initially for Ebley FC, King Stanley (both Stroud sides), Frampton Rangers, and Frampton Cotterill in Bristol before having trials with Arsenal, Nottingham Forest, Wolverhampton Wanderers, Luton Town, Swindon Town and Bristol Rovers before signing for Coventry City as a YTS trainee in June 1984, making his league debut as substitute for Welsh midfielder David Phillips at Old Trafford against Manchester United on the 6th February 1988, missing just the one league game for the remainder of the season with the 'Sky Blues'. Shortly after the season had finished he gained the first of ten U-21 caps for England when he was selected to play against USSR in the Toulon tournament. Also included in the England side were Paul Gascoigne, David Platt and Nigel Clough. Dropping down to play in the First Division, firstly with Birmingham City, and then West Bromwich Albion, he joined Second Division side Grimsby Town in January 1998 for £200,000, and towards the end of the season, in the space of one month had played at Wembley for the club in two competitions.

Firstly, beating Bournemouth with a sudden death goal to win the Auto Windscreens Shield Final, and secondly, beating Northampton Town to gain promotion via the Second Division Play Off Final. With injury problems forcing him to retire from the playing side of football, he was involved in car sales after attending a course with Grimsby Town's sponsors Dixon's at Thorne in South Yorkshire, working for BMW in Coventry and at Swansea, Audi for a short period at Grimsby, before returning to Blundell Park as assistant commercial manager in December 2003.

23. SMITH, FRANK

Birthplace: Darnall, Sheffield, 22/11/1889. **Died:** Grimsby, September, 1982
Ht: 5ft-8ins, **Wt:** 11st-7lbs
Swans debut: v. Portsmouth (a), 28/8/1920

Swansea Town Career Statistics		
Season	League	WC
1920/21	1	1
Total	1	1

Career:
Sheffield FC
Barnsley (signed in May 1914) lge 4
Swansea Town (£90 signed in July 1920)
Grimsby Town (signed in 25/6/1921) lge 4

Frank left school at the age of 14 and played for the famous Sheffield club prior to joining Barnsley. Spending time in the newly established Royal Air Force towards the end of the Great War, he returned to become a regular with Barnsley during seasons 1918/19 and 1919/20. During the war he made thirty-seven appearances, scoring three goals, and also made twenty-two post war appearances for Barnsley. Although a right half, he was also tried at inside forward. His appearances for Grimsby Town were all at left half. His only first team appearance for the Swans was in the club's first ever Football League fixture, at Portsmouth. He was unable to make any further appearances, and joined Grimsby Town in June 1921. The former Sheffield Boys player ended his playing career in the Grimsby League with Charlton's and Haycroft Rovers, and finally with Lincolnshire League side Louth Town in season 1925/26. Employed as a plater's assistant at Charlton's Yard, he then became a docker with the Railway Company in Grimsby for many years.

24. SMITH, GEORGE

Birthplace: Newcastle, 7/10/1945
Ht: 5ft-7ins, **Wt:** 10st-8lbs
Swans debut: v. Torquay United (h), FLC 1-1, 9/8/1975

Swansea City Career Statistics				
Season	League	FLC	FAC	WC
1975/76	43	2	1	2
1976/77	35+2/8gls	4+1	1	2
1977/78	8	2		
Total	86+2/8gls	8+1	2	4

Career:
Newcastle United (from apprentice in September 1963) lge 0
Barrow (signed in March 1965) lge 91+1/11gls
Portsmouth (signed in May 1967) lge 64/3gls
Middlesbrough (signed in January 1969) lge 74
Birmingham City (signed in March 1971) lge 36+3
Cardiff City (£50,000 signed in June 1973) lge 43+2/1gls, ECWC 2
Swansea City (signed in May 1975)
Hartlepool United (signed in 27/10/1977) lge 81+4/2gls

Honours: Welsh Cup Winner–1974

Shortly before 5 p.m. on Saturday 1st April 1978, the Swans recorded a record league victory with an 8-0 demolition of Hartlepool United at the Vetch Field. Unfortunately, for one player in the opposition team that day, his team's performance left him so devastated he travelled home to the North East on his own by train! For George Smith it had been the first opportunity to play at the Vetch Field since he had joined Hartlepool United towards the end of October 1977 on a player coach, assistant manager capacity. An influential midfielder who had made over 300 league appearances for Barrow, Portsmouth, Middlesbrough, Birmingham City and Cardiff City during his playing career, George was targeted by Swans boss Harry Griffiths and Chairman Malcolm Struel as the one player, a leader who could turn the club's fortunes around, and influence the development of promising youngsters, Robbie James, Alan Curtis and Jeremy Charles. Failing to make an appearance for Newcastle United, George made his league debut for Barrow, became an integral part in the club's Fourth Division line-up of season 1966/67, before transferring to Portsmouth, and establishing himself as an attacking, goalscoring midfielder in the Second Division. Season 1971/72 saw him gain further promotion honours with Birmingham City as they finished runners-up in the Second Division, and eventually give him the opportunity of sampling First Division football. A regular member of the 'Bluebirds' side after transferring for £50,000 in June 1973, he played in the 1973/74 Welsh Cup Final, first leg against Stourbridge, and also sampled European Cup Winners Cup football in two seasons whilst on the staff at Ninian Park. By the end of the 1974/75 season, George was still only 29 years of age, and initially was reluctant to make the move from Second Division football with the Bluebirds, to a club which had just been re-elected to the Football League. However, a series of circumstances in his last season at Ninian Park, which included the birth of his second child, plus the selling powers of the Swans management team persuaded him to accept the challenge ahead of him at the Vetch Field. Within two seasons of his introduction, the Swans had been transformed from a struggling side at the bottom of the division, to a free scoring outfit that should have clinched promotion in May 1977. One typical example of the attacking approach play adopted by the side during this period came in March 1977 against Stockport County at the Vetch Field. Going in at half time after conceding four goals and a mountain to climb, the Swans came out for the second half, scored four goals to draw the game 4-4. A marvellous advertisement for football, but not so good if you were a defender. The 1976/77 season had seen the Swans score 92 league goals, scoring three or more goals on eleven occasions in home league matches. The Swans by now had been recognised as one of the finest football teams outside the Second Division by leading managers at the time, a tribute to manager Harry Griffiths who recognised his player's abilities, did not stifle them, and also believing in entertaining the public. An old team mate of his at Middlesbrough, Billy Horner, gave George the opportunity shortly after the start of the 1977/78 season to go into coaching, and assist him at Hartlepool, and, after a lot of thought, decided to return home to the North East to take up the challenge, Despite seven lean years, with little or no money to spend on players, a good spirit prevailed at the club, and the occasional cup success along the way highlighted the season. After leaving Pool in 1983 George became an FA Staff Coach in the North East for five years, with the responsibility in qualifying and assessing coaches in the area. Friendly with Trevor Francis from his Birmingham City days, he was offered the opportunity to work with him at QPR as youth team manager. However, after just eighteen months, a change in management saw him leave Loftus Road along with Francis. Still living in the London area, George was then appointed Chief Scout by Sheffield Wednesday, responsible for the South, and South West area. Since moving back to the North East seven years ago, he has set up his own football academy at Middlesbrough, and for the last couple of years has been Chief Scout for Wolverhampton Wanderers in the North East.

25. SMITH, JASON Leslie

Born: Bromsgrove, 6/9/1974
Ht: 6ft-3ins, **Wt:** 13st-7lbs
Swans debut: v. Exeter City (h), 8/8/1998

Swansea City Career Statistics						
Season	League	FLC	FAC	AWS/LDV	FAWP	P/Offs
1998/99	42/4gls	2	4/1gls	2/1gls	3	2
1999/2000	43/1gls	4	2	2	3	
2000/01	22	1	1	3	2	
2001/02	7+1		1		1	
2002/03	27/3gls		1		1	
Total	141+1/8gls	7	9/1gls	7/1gls	10	2

Career:
Coventry City
Tiverton Town (signed in 15/7/1995)
Swansea City (£10,000 signed in 26/6/1998)

Honours: England Sch, FA Vase Winner–1998, Third Division Champions–2000, West Wales Senior Cup Winner–2002

Signed by manager Alan Cork for a £10,000 transfer fee in July 1998, after he had played at Wembley the previous week for Tiverton Town in the FA Vase Final, beating Tow Law Town.

Unfortunately, four days after signing for the Swans, Cork was sacked from his position at the Vetch Field. The signing of Smith from Tiverton Town had been on the advice of Swans' Promotions Manager, Phil Chant who had relations, connections in the Tiverton area. Earlier in his career he had gained representative honours at schoolboy level for England, joined Coventry City as a trainee on leaving school, but then drifted into non-league football with Tiverton Town. His first two seasons at the Vetch Field saw the imposing central defender strike up a formidable partnership with Matthew Bound, with Smith missing just seven league matches, and also reaching the Third Division Play Off semi-finals in his first season, score a goal at Upton Park to bring Premiership side West Ham United back to the Vetch Field for an FA Cup replay, and in 2000 win the Third Division Championships. A disappointing season in the Second Division following promotion saw him injure his ankle in an LDV Vans Trophy tie with Brentford on Valentine's Day 2001, with the real damage done when he was stretchered off during the 2-1 win at Stoke three weeks later. Making a number of comebacks, including playing against Hakin United in the April 2002 West Wales Senior Cup Final, and against Cardiff City a month later in the FAW Premier Cup Final, since that injury, the range of movement in his ankle has not been the same, and it got to a stage where he had to come to terms to the fact that he could not perform as a professional anymore, despite all the operations he had to endure, and in late October 2003 had to call it a day as a professional. Deciding to stay in Swansea, Jason started his UEFA 'B' Coaching badge, and enrolled in a financial planning course at Cardiff University after leaving the professional game, and on the 23rd May 2004 rejoined Tiverton Town. Unfortunately for Jason, during pre-season training with Tiverton he felt that his ankle would not be strong enough to stand up to the rigours of football, and rather than let it deteriorate further decided to call it a day, and concentrate on a career as a financial consultant.

26. SMITH, Jonathan William (JACK)

Birthplace: Burton-on-Trent, AMJ, 1891
Ht: 5ft-9ins, **Wt:** 11st-0lbs
Swans debut: v. Merthyr Town (h), 26/8/1922

Swansea Town Career Statistics			
Season	League	FAC	WC
1922/23	37/21gls	2	3/5gls
1923/24	29/12gls	4/2gls	1
Total	66/33gls	6/2gls	4/5gls

Career:
Burton United
Manchester City (signed in November 1909)
Chesterfield (signed in close season 1912)
Third Lanark
QPR (signed in April 1919) lge 75/28gls
Swansea Town (£250 signed in May 1922)
Brighton & Hove Albion (£150 signed in August 1924)
  lge 14/4gls
Burton Town
Burton Wanderers (signed in September 1932)

Joining Second Division side Manchester City from Burton United in November 1909, after failing to make a league appearance, he joined Chesterfield a few years later, but then moved north of the border to sign for Scottish side Third Lanark. Making guest appearances for Chesterfield Town in April 1916 to the 1917 close season, he also guested extensively for Queen's Park Rangers in the last two wartime seasons, netting 21 goals in 37 London Combination appearances.

In April 1919 he was officially transferred to Rangers and became a great favourite at Loftus Road for three seasons. An ever-present in the Southern League side during 1919–20, Jack also played in every match the following season when, with eighteen goals, he led the Q.P.R. scorers in their initial campaign as a Football League club. After scoring 45 goals in 122 League and Cup matches, he was transferred to Swansea Town in May 1922 for £250 where he continued to find the net on a regular basis. In his first season at the Vetch Field he created a new goalscoring record for the Swans in the Football League with 21 league goals. Scoring on his Swans' debut against Merthyr Town, he scored two hat-tricks, the first at Portsmouth in the league, and the second against Newport County in the quarter final of the Welsh Cup at the Vetch Field in March 1923. During his first season he also scored two goals in a league game on four occasions. His second season with the Swans also saw him record another hat-trick in the league, this time against Merthyr in November 1923. In August 1924 he was transferred to Third Division South side Brighton & Hove Albion for £150. Whilst with both Q.P.R. and Swansea he had made a habit of scoring against the Albion – in December 1920 he hit a hat-trick into the Brighton net at Loftus Road – but, despite notching a brace on his debut, he met with less success at the Goldstone. With his time in Hove dogged by injuries, Jack was unable to win a regular place and was released in May 1925 when he left the first-class game, joining firstly Burton Town, and then Burton Wanderers in September 1932.

27. SMITH, Thomas (TOMMY) M.B.E.

Birthplace: Liverpool, 5/4/1945
Ht: 5ft-10½ins, **Wt:** 13st-5lbs
Swans debut: v. Lincoln City (h), 22/8/1978

Swansea City Career Statistics				
Season	*League*	*FLC*	*FAC*	*WC*
1978/79	34+2/2gls	3	4	2
Total	34+2/2gls	3	4	2

Career:
Liverpool (signed groundstaff in May 1960, professional in April 1962) lge 467/36gls
Los Angeles Aztecs, USA
Swansea City (signed in 18/8/1978, player coach from August to October 1979)

Honours: England Yth, U-23–10, Full–1, First Division Champions–1966, 1973, 1976, 1977, FA Cup Winner–1965, 1974, European Cup Winner–1977, UEFA Cup Winner–1973, 1976, Charity Shield–1965, 1966, 1974, European Super Cup Winner–1977, Football League Representative XI

A vastly experienced defender, a legend during his career in top flight football with Liverpool who joined the Swans after a short spell in the USA with Los Angeles Aztecs, after being released by Liverpool at the end of the 1977/78 season. The former Liverpool and England Schoolboy international joined the groundstaff at Anfield in May 1960 after leaving school, and made his first U-23 appearance for England against Czechoslovakia in 1965, making his only Full international appearance at Wembley against Wales in May 1971. Tommy was a member of the England team that won the Junior World Cup in 1963, playing alongside illustrious names such as Ron 'Chopper' Harris, Len Badger, Jon Sammels, John Sissons and Lew Chatterly. A totally committed player during his career, his competitiveness even at the age of 33 on arriving at the Vetch Field was noticeable to the Swans fans when Tottenham Hotspur arrived at the Vetch Field in a League Cup tie. Within the first couple of minutes, Spurs's recent acquisition from Argentina, World Cup winner, Osvaldo Ardiles had been tackled by the LEGEND, and had to leave the field, never to return. Given a free transfer by 'Pool, in recognition of his good service to the club, he was signed by manager John Toshack, and within weeks re-united with his former Liverpool playing colleague Ian Callaghan, with both players making telling contributions through the season as the club gained a second consecutive promotion. Appointed club captain at the Vetch Field shortly after his arrival, he struggled at times through the season with knee problems, and eventually had to retire shortly before the start of his second season with the Swans. The scorer of two goals for the Swans during the season, with both goals arriving in the same match at the Vetch Field against Hull City. His club honours obtained with Liverpool include winning the First Division Championship in 1966, 1973, 1976 and 1977, FA Cup Winner in 1965 and 1974, Finalist in 1971 and 1977, Football League Cup Finalist in 1978, European Cup Winner in 1977 (headed the second goal against Borussia Moenchengladbach in Rome in what was his 600th appearance for Liverpool), European Cup Winners Cup Finalist in 1966, UEFA Cup in 1973, 1976, Charity Shield Winner in 1965, 1966, 1974, and the European Super Cup in 1977. In 1977 he was awarded the MBE for his services to football. After leaving the Vetch Field shortly after announcing his retirement as a player, he had a short spell as manager of Caernarfon Town, returned to Anfield where he was employed for a period on the coaching staff, and despite suffering with arthritis has since been involved in media work and after dinner speaking.

28. SNEDDON William (BILLY) Cleland

Birthplace: Wishaw, 1/4/1914. **Died:** Bangor, 1/4/1995
Ht: 5ft-8ins, **Wt:** 11st-4lbs
Swans debut: v. Bradford Park Avenue (h), 14/9/1946

Swansea Town Career Statistics	
Season	*League*
1946/47	2
Total	2

Career:
Rutherglen Glencairn
Falkirk (signed in December 1935)
Brentford (£3,500 signed in June 1937) lge 66/2gls, FAC 4
Swansea Town (£2,000 signed in 11/7/1939)
Newport County (signed in November 1946) lge 18
Milford United (signed as player coach in June 1947)

Honours: London War Cup Winner–1942

Experienced left sided wing half who had made regular appearances in Brentford's First Division line-up following his travelling south from Scottish Football with Rutherglen Glencairn and Falkirk in 1937. Originally signed by manager Haydn Green from Brentford in July 1939 for £2,000, along with team-mate Sam Briddon. He played in the opening three league matches of the 1939/40 season until the Football League was suspended following the outbreak of WW2. He continued playing for the Swans for a number of months in the South West Regional Competition before leaving the Vetch Field, also making guest appearances for Brentford and Fulham in season 1941/42, and Cardiff City in season 1942/43. He was a member of the Brentford side that beat Portsmouth in the London War Cup Final in 1942 in front of 72,000 spectators. When the League resumed after the war he returned to the Vetch Field, making his first league appearance against Bradford Park Avenue in early September 1946 at left half, marking Len Shackleton in a 6-1 defeat. He played in the next game against Tottenham Hotspur, but was then transferred to Newport County in October 1946. Captain of Newport County on occasions, in May 1947 he was placed on the transfer list. A chunky, combative type of player, in June 1947 he joined Welsh League side Milford United as player coach, and after five season with the club joined Staffordshire League club Burton Albion as manager in late July 1952. He was unfortunate to lose five seasons of football because of the war.

29. SPOTTISWOOD, Joseph (JOE) Dominic

Birthplace: Carlisle, AMJ, 1893. **Died:** Paddington, AMJ, 1960
Ht: 5ft-9ins, **Wt:** 11st-0lbs
Swans debut: v. Watford (a), 24/1/1920, Sth. Lge

Swansea Town Career Statistics			
Season	League	FAC	WC
1920/21	34/4gls	3	
1921/22	40/2gls	7/1gls	2
1922/23	32/2gls	2	3
1923/24	27	1	3
1924/25	26/1gls	2	2
Total	159/9gls	15/1gls	10

Career:
Carlisle United (amateur signed in September 1912)
Manchester City (amateur signed in August 1913, professional in August 1913) lge 6
Bury (signed in May 1914) lge 6
Chelsea (signed in October 1919) lge 1
Swansea Town (£500 signed in 19/1/1920)
QPR (£400 signed in 24/6/1925) lge 22/2gls

Honours: Third Division South Champions–1925, Southern League Representative XI

Signed by manager Joe Bradshaw in January 1920 for a Swans record fee of £500 from First Division Chelsea, the outside left, from a footballing family had great speed on the flank, also possessing a great drive. His elder brother Robert made appearances for Clapton Orient and Crystal Palace. Joining non-league Carlisle United from the local Catholic Youngmen's Society side in September 1912, he made his Football League debut with First Division side Manchester City, making further league appearances for Bury and Chelsea prior to arriving at the Vetch Field. His only appearance for Chelsea came in a 2-0 win at Manchester United on the 3rd January 1920, and before the end of the month had joined the Swans. In April 1920 he played for a Southern League Welsh Clubs XI at the Vetch Field against a Southern League English Clubs XI. He was a member of the first Swans' side to play a Football League game, at Portsmouth in August 1920, and made consistent first team appearances

over the first five seasons the club competed in the Football League. His first league goal for the Swans came in a 2-1 away win at Brentford in February 1921, and in season 1921/22 he scored the only goal in the second replay of the FA Cup tie against West Ham United. Along with Billy Hole on the right flank, he provided a plentiful supply to the Swans' strikers, and in his last season at the Vetch Field (1924/25) made twenty-six league appearances during a season which saw the club win the Third Division South Championship. He was transferred to Third Division South side QPR on the 24th June 1925 for £400. After retiring as a player he became trainer to Italian side A.C. Milan.

30. SQUIRES, Frank (FRANKIE)

Birthplace: Swansea, 8/3/1921. **Died:** Swansea, 1/3/1988
Ht: 5ft-10ins, **Wt:** 11st-10lbs
Swans debut: v. West Bromwich Albion (h), 31/8/1946

Swansea Town Career Statistics		
Season	League	FAC
1946/47	28/3gls	2/1gls
1947/48	8/2gls	
Total	36/5gls	2/1gls

Career:
Swansea Town (signed in 23/6/1938)
Plymouth Argyle (£7,500 signed in October 1947) lge 86/13gls, FAC 3
Grimsby Town (£9,000 signed in July 1950) lge 36/2gls, FAC 2/1gls
Merthyr Town (signed in September 1951)
Barry Town (signed as player coach in July 1955)
Brecon Corries (signed as player manager in January 1957)

Honours: Wales Sch, Full–2, War-Time International–2

Former Danygraig and Swansea schoolboy player who was a prominent member of the Swansea Schoolboys English Shield winning side, and was selected for the Welsh schoolboys side that played England at Dover in 1935, He originally signed for the Swans from the Juniors side on the 23rd June 1938, played in South West Regional Football for the Swans from 1939 to 1941, the 'Victory' season of 1945/46, and was a member of the Swans' side that resumed League football after the war. His last season with the Swans' Juniors saw him score thirteen goals in a side that won the Gwalia and Bryn Trophies, and finish runners-up in the Gwalia Senior League. A 'Desert Rat', the key part of his footballing career was lost because of the Second World War, but he was also a member of Stan Cullis's footballing side that entertained the troops in Italy during the war. In season 1941/42 he played in a war-time international against England, and during the 1945/46 'Victory' season was a regular member of the Swans side, also making an appearance for Wales against Scotland at Hampden Park, forming a right sided partnership with Swans' outside right Ernie Jones. With the resumption of the Football League after the war, he was included in the Swans' first league game at the Vetch Field against West Bromwich Albion. Ironically, his first league goal came against the same opponents at the Hawthorns in the return league fixture, a 2-1 defeat in December 1946. Frankie was a creative inside forward, possessing good control and passing ability, and just prior to Bill McCandless's appointment as manager at the Vetch Field, was sold to Plymouth Argyle for £7,500 in late October 1947. During season 1949/50 he played in both league games against the Swans, scoring in the 2-2 draw at the Vetch Field, playing in an Argyle side that suffered relegation to the Third Division South. Joining Grimsby Town in July 1950, he suffered a second consecutive relegation from the Second Division, also playing in both league games against the Swans. He returned to South Wales in September 1951 to sign for Merthyr Town, joined Barry Town as player coach in July 1955, and finished his career with Welsh League side Brecon Corries in January 1957 as player manager, up to June 1959 when his contract was not renewed. An uncle to Swans defender Dudley Lewis, Frankie died in March 1988.

31. STANLEY, GARY Ernest

Birthplace: Burton, 4/3/1954
Ht: 5ft-10ins, **Wt:** 12st-2lbs
Swans debut: v. Barnsley (a), FLC 2-1, 6/10/1981

	Swansea City Career Statistics					
Season	League	FLC	FAC	WC	ECWC
1981/82	22+7/3gls	2	1	6/2gls	
1982/83	24+4	3		5	4
1983/84	14+1/1gls		1	2	2
Total	60+12/4gls	5	2	13/2gls	6

Career:
Chelsea (from apprentice in March 1971) lge 105+4/15gls
Fort Lauderdale Strikers (signed in 1979)
Everton (£300,000 signed in 25/8/1979) lge 52/1gls
Swansea City (£150,000 signed in 28/9/1981)
Portsmouth (signed in 11/1/1984) lge 43+4/1gls
Wichita (USA)
Bristol City (signed in August 1988) lge 8+2

Honours: Welsh Cup Winner–1982, 1983, Football League Representative XI

A former apprentice at Stamford Bridge with Chelsea who made his league debut for Chelsea in the Second Division at Roker Park against Sunderland in the opening league fixture of the 1975/76 season. He was recommended to Chelsea by former player Frank Upton after some impressive displays in Derbyshire Schools football. Continuing to become a regular member of the Chelsea first team he made 33 league appearances during season 1976/77, scoring six goals as the club gained promotion as runners-up to Wolverhampton Wanderers in the Second Division. On the 17th May 1977 he played for a Football League Representative XI at Hampden Park against a Glasgow Select XI in a game for the Jubilee Appeal Fund. Financial problems at the Bridge saw him join Everton in August 1979 for £300,000, but he failed to command a regular place in the Goodison Park starting line-up, and in late September 1981 he joined the Swans for a £150,000 transfer fee, making his Swans' debut in a League Cup, Second Round tie at Barnsley a couple of days later. An attacking midfielder earlier in his career, he was also utilised by John Toshack in a right sided attacking full back role. He scored his first goal for the Swans at Stoke City after replacing Leighton James as substitute, but his most memorable goal for Swans' supporters was his angled, swerving 30 yard effort at the Vetch Field, which left Williams in the Manchester City goal clutching at fresh air. He made the starting line-up for the second leg of the Welsh Cup final against Cardiff City towards the end of his first season with the Swans, and twelve months later played in both legs of the Welsh Cup Final defeat of Wrexham. With financial problems surfacing following the club's relegation to the Second Division, he was a number of players who were allowed to leave the club's pay roll, joining Portsmouth in January 1984, twenty-four hours after playing his last game for the Swans in a Welsh Cup tie against Bangor City. His first full season at Fratton Park with Portsmouth saw the club fail to gain promotion to the First Division on goal difference, with Stanley making twenty-nine league appearances through the season. He was released at the end of the 1985/86 season, joining a number of players from the Football League who went to the USA, signing for Wichita. He returned to the UK to sign for Third Division Bristol City in August 1988, but made just a handful of appearances before being released at the end of the season. Since returning to live in the Portsmouth area, Gary has regularly appeared in Charity games and has been employed by the NTI Communications Company.

32. STAPLETON, WILLIAM

Birthplace: Sheffield. **Died:** Sheffield 15/6/1929
Ht: 5ft-9½ins, **Wt:** 12st-6lbs
Swans debut: v. Southampton (a), 9/10/1920

	Swansea Town Career Statistics	
Season	League	FAC
1920/21	7	
1921/22		1
Total	7	1

Career:
Silverwood Colliery
Mexborough Town (signed in close season 1914)
Sheffield Wednesday (signed in May 1919) lge 19
Swansea Town (signed in 14/6/1920)

Former non-league player with Silverwood Colliery and Mexborough Town before signing for Sheffield Wednesday and making his Football League debut for the club in the First Division against Middlesbrough on the 30th August 1919. That season the club used a record forty-one players in a season that saw then finish bottom of the First Division. An attack minded full back, despite always looking pale and somewhat frail he proved a more than capable defender and was often found in the opposition half of the field. He started the first season of post war football as the club's first choice right back and competed with veteran Tom Brittleton for the role later in the season before being part of the close season cull as new manager Bob Brown cleared the decks. During WW1 he made 73 appearances, scoring one goal for Wednesday at Grimsby Town in December 1918. Prior to him joining the Swans he was involved in a freak mishap on his way to work, when walking he somehow managed to trip over a piece of wood and crash into a plate glass window, resulting in a cut forearm and severed artery but he thankfully recovered to start the new season with the Swans! He joined the Swans in June 1920, shortly before the start of the club's first season in the Football League and made his debut at Left Full Back at Southampton in early October 1920, playing his next four games at right full back, with Milne reverting to the left sided position. Making two more appearances later in the season, his only other first team appearance for the Swans came in the 1921/22 season, in an FA Cup tie against Bournemouth. He was released from the Vetch Field playing staff later in the season.

33. STEAD, Michael (MIKE) John

Birthplace: West Ham, 28/2/1957
Ht: 5ft-9ins, **Wt:** 11st-8lbs
Swans debut: v. Doncaster Rovers (a), 26/2/1977

Swansea City Career Statistics	
Season	League
1976/77	5
Total	5

Career:
Tottenham Hotspur (from apprentice in July 1973, professional in November 1974) lge 14+1
Swansea City (loan signed in 18/2/1977)
Southend United (signed in 7/9/1978) lge 296+1/5gls
Doncaster Rovers (player coach signed in 29/11/1985) lge 83+2
Fisher Athletic (signed in close season 1988) Conf 71+3
Heybridge Swifts (signed in close season 1990)
Stambridge (signed in close season 1990)
Chelmsford City

Honours: Fourth Division Champions–1981

Former Newham Schoolboy defender who joined Tottenham Hotspur as an apprentice at White Hart Lane, and who made his league debut for Spurs in September 1976 against Norwich City at left full back, playing in the next game at West Bromwich

Albion. He had earlier attended Prince Regent Lane and Shipman Road Schools, and also played for Rippleways Boys Club prior to arriving at White Hart Lane. He was signed by manager Harry Griffiths on a loan transfer in mid-February 1977, made five league appearances for the Swans at either left or right full back position, before returning to White Hart Lane where he played in the last six games of the season for Spurs. At the time Spurs were unwilling to extend the loan transfer owing to injuries at White Hart Lane. Shortly after the start of the 1978/79 season he signed for Southend United on an initial loan transfer with the move being made permanent two months later in November 1978. Making over 300 league and cup appearances for the 'Shrimpers', he made 35 appearances during season 1980/81 when the club won the Fourth Division Championship. He joined Doncaster Rovers as player coach in November 1985, linking up with former Southend United team-mate Dave Cusack. Prior to the start of the 1988/89 season he returned to the London area to sign for Vauxhall Conference side Fisher Athletic, and during his second season with Fisher was involved as a player coach. After two seasons in the Vauxhall Conference he made further non-league appearances for Vauxhall League First Division side Heybridge Swifts, Essex Senior League side Stambridge, finishing his playing career at Beazer Homes Premier Division side Chelmsford City.
He linked up with Dave Cusack at Dagenham & Redbridge in the Vauxhall Conference as coach in 1993, before returning to a coaching position at Fisher London for a period of four years. After leaving Doncaster Rovers, Micky worked in a Bank for fourteen years before he was made redundant, has obtained his London Cab licence, and for the last twelve months has been working as a cab driver in London.

34. STEELE, Alexander (ALEX)

Birthplace: Belfast, 19/3/1899. **Died:** Rayleigh, Essex, 25/5/1980
Ht: 5ft-10ins, **Wt:** 10st-7lbs
Swans debut: v. Wolverhampton Wanderers (h), 22/1/1927

Swansea Town Career Statistics	
Season	League
1926/27	2
Total	2

Career:
Glenavon (signed in June 1920)
Charlton Athletic (signed in September 1921) lge 132/4gls, FAC 14
Swansea Town (signed in July 1926)
Fulham (£450 signed in June 1927) lge 49, FAC 4
Distillery (signed in 17/4/1931)

Honours: Ireland Full–4, Ireland Amateur–2, City Cup Winner–1920, London Challenge Cup Winner–1923

Signed for Third Division South side Charlton Athletic after starting his career in Northern Ireland with Glenavon, he was regularly included in Athletic's first team line-up for five seasons, skippered the side on occasions, and during the club's debut season in the Football League (1921/22), made thirteen league appearances, although he failed to make the starting line-up in the club's first ever Football League match. During the 1922/23 season he was a member of the Athletic side that beat Crystal Palace in the London Challenge Cup Final at the Den. That season would see him finish as top goalscorer with thirteen goals from thirty-one league appearances. He also became the first Athletic player to play for his country when he was capped for Ireland in Belfast against Wales on the 13th February 1926 at left half, making his second international appearance later in the month against Scotland at Ibrox in February 1926. A member of the Glenavon side that won the City Cup in 1920, Alex had previously played for junior sides Barnville (Belfast) and Dunmurry, and also played two matches for his country's amateur international side, against England on the 13th November 1920, losing 4-0 at Cliftonville, and when the Irish beat France 2-1, at the Parc de Princes Stadium, Paris in February 1921. He was signed by Swans manager Joe Bradshaw in July 1926, but had to wait until halfway through the season before he made his debut, replacing Lachlan McPherson. He made just the one more appearance in the season before being re-united with Bradshaw at Fulham in the close season for a transfer fee of £450. At Craven Cottage with Fulham he made a further two appearances for Ireland in February 1929 against Wales and Scotland. He retired in May 1930, returned to Whitehead, near Belfast Lock to run a newsagent, but in mid-April 1931 had joined Distillery, as well as being a scout for Blackpool. By 1956 Steele had returned to England and was working as an audit clerk in the City of London and living in Rayleigh in Essex, where he died in May 1980, at the age of 81.

35. STEVENSON, NIGEL Charles Ashley

Birthplace: Swansea, 2/11/1958
Ht: 6ft-2ins, **Wt:** 11st-0lbs
Swans debut: v. Southport (h), 10/4/1976

Career:
Swansea City (signed from apprentice in November 1976)
Cardiff City (loan in October 1985) lge 14
Reading (loan in March 1986) lge 3
Cardiff City (signed in August 1987) lge 66+2/2gls
Merthyr Tydfil (signed in close season 1989)
Yeovil Town (£5,000 signed in December 1990)

Honours: Wales Yth–2, U-21–2, Full–4, Welsh Cup Winner–1982, 1983, 1988, Macbar Cup Winner–1987, Welsh League First Division Champions–1976, West Wales Senior Cup Winner–1987

	Swansea City Career Statistics					
Season	League	FLC	FAC	WC	ECWC	FRT
1975/76	2					
1976/77						
1977/78						
1978/79	36+3/2gls	3	2	2		
1979/80	31+1/3gls		3	2		
1980/81	39+1/5gls	2	1	5		
1981/82	20	0+1	1	7	2	
1982/83	24+2/1gls	2		4+1/1gls	4/1gls	
1983/84	37/3gls	2	1	5	2	
1984/85	34/1gls	2	2	5/2gls		4
1985/86	12	3+1				
1986/87	12+3	1	1	1		0+1
Total	247+10/15gls	15+2	11	31+1/3gls	8/1gls	4+1

Central defender Nigel Stevenson's claim to fame, apart from his international honours for Wales, and over 250 league appearances for the Swans, is that he is the only player to have played for the club from the Fourth to the First Division, and back down to the Fourth Division. Making his league debut at the Vetch Field against Southport in April 1976, alongside an equally in-experienced defender Steve Morris, who would have realised that in five seasons, partnering another in-experienced defender, this time Dudley Lewis he would be a central figure in the club's promotion to the First Division. Whilst a youth player he had make regular appearances in the reserve side that won the Welsh League First Division Championship in 1976. During a period in the club's history when finances were in extremely short supply, he was given his debut by Harry Griffiths, a manager, who had complete faith in his ability, despite his slender frame to cope with the rigorous demands of the Fourth Division. For the remainder of his playing career he did not fill out as far as his weight was concerned, gaining just over a stone and a half by the time he joined Cardiff City in 1987, but nevertheless his strong heading ability, and speed (hence the nickname SPEEDY) around the field compensated for the occasional buffeting he took over ninety minutes. Growing up in the East side of the City, the Danygraig schoolboy started his playing career with Danygraig Junior School, before going to Cefn Hengoed, playing as a schoolboy with Swansea schoolboys and Swansea Senior League side Kilvey Athletic. Although he had trials for the Welsh schoolboy squad, his first international honours came representing Wales Youth against Holland and England, and then for the Wales U-21 side against France and Holland, after he had already made his league debut for the Swans. After making his league debut whilst still an apprentice against Southport he made a further appearance a few weeks later against Rochdale, but had to be content with appearances in the club's Welsh League side, before he would go on to make his mark in the Swans side under John Toshack shortly after the start of the 1978/79 season. With experienced professionals continually being linked to the Vetch Field at this stage, 'Speedy' continued to be included in Toshack's starting line-up on matchdays, despite the presence of experienced professionals like Leighton Phillips, Dave Rushbury, Ante Rajkovic, Colin Irwin, Max Thompson, and even Toshack and Jeremy Charles on occasions playing in central defence. His partnership in central defence with apprentice Dudley Lewis was probably one of the most unexpected during his career with the Swans, because by the time they had been paired together in defence three quarters through the 1980/81 season, 'Speedy' was only in his third season as a professional, while Lewis had just started his first year as a professional at the Vetch Field. Memories from the start of that partnership would see the Swans re-inforce themselves into a promotion challenge, and Stevenson score a decisive goal against promotion contenders Blackburn Rovers at the Vetch Field, many a continental footballer would be proud of. Capped at full level for Wales on the 27th April 1982 against

England at Ninian Park, in a side which featured five other Swans players, he gained two further caps against Scotland and Northern Ireland in that season's Home International Championship, gaining his last cap at the Vetch Field in a Euro Championship Qualifier against Norway. With relatively little serious injury problems through his playing career, he made two appearances in consecutive Welsh Cup Finals for the Swans in 1982 and 1983, also gaining European Cup Winners Cup football experience on three occasions, also scoring in the Swans 12-0 record cup victory over Maltese side Sliema Wanderers in September 1982. With never a dull moment at the Vetch Field during the club's remarkable rise up the divisions, 'Speedy' also experienced the downside of life at the club when financial problems rose to the surface, forcing the club to offload players either for token transfer fees, and to lighten the load of the monthly salaries. Still on the playing staff in December 1985 he also experienced the time when the club was would up by the Official Receiver in December 1985, and when the club were successful in continuing to put a side in the Football League, he was given the opportunity, firstly to play for Cardiff City, then Reading on monthly loan deals. At the end of Terry Yorath's first season in charge at the Vetch Field he was released on a free transfer, linking up at Cardiff City with Frank Burrows, no mean judge of a central defender in his day. His last games for the Swans came in a reserve team Macbar Cup Final win over Plymouth Argyle in May 1987, and in the West Wales Senior Cup Final defeat of Briton Ferry Athletic. With two seasons at Ninian Park, he gained a Fourth Division Runners up medal in 1988, plus a third Welsh Cup Winners Medal, when the 'Bluebirds' beat Wrexham 2-0 at the Vetch Field in a Cardiff side that featured Swans' legend Alan Curtis. Released from the 'Bluebirds' playing staff at the end of the 1988/89 season, he stayed in full time football in the Vauxhall Conference, firstly with Merthyr, and then with Yeovil Town, had a season with Barry Town, then played for Carmarthen Town and Llanelli. 'Speedy' worked in the Post Office in 1993, but after studying on a part-time basis to be a physiotherapist, gained his diploma, and has for the last couple of years been working for the Health Authority at Cefn Coed Hospital. Before gaining his diploma, he gained practical experience at the Vetch Field for six months, combining his role as assistant manager to Tommy Morgan at Carmarthen Town and later, a physiotherapist's position at Llanelli. Season 2002/03 saw him link up with Steve Thomas as co-managers at Neath FC, but in early March 2005 he resigned his position at the club.

36. STIENS, CRAIG

Birthplace: Swansea, 31/7/1984
Ht: 5ft-8ins, **Wt:** 12st-6lbs
Swans debut: v. Exeter City (a), 14/12/2002

Career:
Leeds United (from trainee in 2/8/2001)
Swansea City (loan in 2/12/2003)
Merthyr Tydfil (signed on 23/1/2004) Total Apps 69/30gls

Swansea City Career Statistics		
Season	League	FAWP
2002/03	0+3	0+1
Total	0+3	0+1

Honours: Wales Yth, U-19, Wales Semi-Professional International

Former Swansea schoolboy front runner Craig Stiens returned to the Vetch Field on a loan transfer from Leeds United some four years after he last wore the white shirt of the Swans with the club's U-14 side. Hoping to make the loan transfer extended until the end of the season, he was unable to impress manager Brian Flynn, and after making three league appearances, all as substitute, returned to Elland Road before the end of the season. He had previously made a number of reserve team appearances for United prior to signing for the Swans, but his league debut came as a substitute for Jamie Wood as a right sided, wide striker at Exeter City. Both of his other substitute league appearances came at the Vetch Field against Leyton Orient and Bristol Rovers. He did make one other substitute appearance for the Swans, in a FAW Premier Cup defeat at Newport County, replacing Lee Jenkins. During his loan period with the Swans he played for the Wales U-19 side. Capable of also playing in midfield, he possessed good pace and an eye for openings. He started season 2003/04 making a number of reserve team appearances with Leeds United, but after his contract was cancelled at Elland Road joined Merthyr Tydfil on a contract until the end of the season. He opened his goal scoring account in his debut for the 'Martyrs' in a 3-0 away win at Welling United, following up with a second goal on his home debut against Stafford Rangers. In May 2004 he was named in the Wales Semi-Professional squad that won the Four Nations end of season competition in Scotland, and by the end of season 2004/05 Craig finished top goalscorer with twenty-two goals for the Martyrs, also reaching the semi-finals of the Southern Premier Play Offs.

37. STEWART, DAVID Steel

Birthplace: Glasgow, 11/3/1947
Ht: 6ft-1½ins, **Wt:** 13st-0lbs
Swans debut: v. Leicester City (a), 20/2/1980

Swansea City Career Statistics				
Season	League	FLC	FAC	WC
1979/80	15			2
1980/81	42	2	1	6
Total	57	2	1	8

Career:
Kilsyth Rangers
Ayr United (signed in 1/6/1967)
Leeds United (£30,000 signed in 3/10/1973) lge 55
West Bromwich Albion (£70,000 signed in 1/11/1978) lge 0
Swansea City (£55,000 signed in 18/2/1980)
Ryoden, Hong Kong (signed in July 1982)

Honours: Scotland U-23–2, Full–1, Welsh Cup Winner–1981

Experienced Scottish international goalkeeper who was signed by manager John Toshack from West Bromwich Albion in mid-February 1980 for £55,000. After making his Swans' debut at Leicester City, he became the third keeper used by the Swans that season, following Letheran and Crudgington. Ironically, it was at Leicester City in season 1973/74 that he had made his Leeds United debut following his £30,000 transfer from Scottish side Ayr United. Capped at U-23 level on two occasions, both against Wales, in season 1974/75 he replaced the injured Harvey in the Leeds United goal for the European Cup semi-final legs against Barcelona, and in the Final when they were defeated by Bayern Munich. Despite starting season 1977/78 as first choice keeper, he failed to command a regular place, and in November 1978 joined West Bromwich Albion. It was at Elland Road with United that he made his only Full international appearance for Scotland, in East Berlin against East Germany, replacing Alan Rough. Failing to oust Tony Godden from the number one jersey, he signed for the Swans, playing in 57 consecutive league appearances, which saw the club claim a place in the First Division, and also defeat Hereford United in the Welsh Cup Final. It came as a surprise to supporters prior to the start of the club's first season in the top flight when manager Toshack signed Welsh International keeper Dai Davies, a transfer which saw Stewart fail to make another first team appearance for the Swans, and ultimately leave the Vetch Field to play for Hong Kong side Ryoden. Following his return to the UK, he retired from football, retained his home in the Swansea area, and has since worked as a goldsmith in Swansea, and become a keen golfer at Pennard Golf Club on the Gower Peninsula.

38. SULLIVAN, ALAN

Birthplace: Aberdare, 12/11/1953
Ht: 6ft-1½ins, **Wt:** 12-7lbs
Swans debut: v. Shrewsbury Town (a), 28/4/1971

Swansea City Career Statistics		
Season	League	FAC
1970/71	3	
1971/72	4+1/1gls	3
Total	7+1/1gls	3

Career:
Reading
Swansea City (from apprentice in August 1971)
Merthyr Tydfil (signed in close season 1974)
Barry Town (signed in August 1981)
Merthyr Tydfil (signed in August 1982)
Barry Town (signed in November 1982)
Ebbw Vale (signed in May 1987)

Honours: Wales Sch, Yth, Wales Semi-Professional International

Former Wales schoolboy player who after being released by Reading was taken on as a second year apprentice at the Vetch Field, and although a star performer in the club's Football Combination side, his lack of genuine pace prevented him from making a bigger impact in the Football League. Possessing an abundance of skill, he was also a consistent goalscorer at reserve team level. Alan attended Maerdy House, and Church School in Aberdare, was capped by Wales at schoolboy level, and also played for Cwmbach prior to signing for Reading on leaving school. He made his Swans debut at Shrewsbury Town as a replacement on the left wing for Alan Beer, retaining his place for the next two games. His only goal for the Swans came in a 2-1 away win at Chesterfield the following season, after going on the field as substitute for Brian Evans. Despite being regularly included in the first team squad that season he was surprisingly released by manager Roy Bentley at the end of season 1971/72, signing for non-league side Merthyr Tydfil, later playing for Barry Town, and finishing his career as player manager at Ebbw Vale. Involved with coaching and on the managerial side at Ebbw Vale after retiring as a player, he has also been involved with coaching amateur side Cwmaman FC. Alan also gained honours with Wales at youth level whilst with the Swans, and also played for the Wales Semi- Professional side after leaving the Vetch Field. After retiring from the professional game Alan initially worked as a Foreman in a Furniture Factory, but for the last couple of years he has been a Prison Officer in HMP Cardiff.

39. SULLIVAN, COLIN John

Birthplace: Saltash, 24/6/1951
Ht: 5ft-7ins, **Wt:** 11st-3lbs
Swans debut: v. Millwall (h), 26/3/1985

Swansea City Career Statistics					
Season	League	FLC	FAC	WC	FRT
1984/85	12				2
1985/86	41	4	1	4	3
Total	53	4	1	4	5

Career:
Plymouth Argyle (from apprentice in July 1968) lge 225+5/7gls
Norwich City (£70,000 signed in 19/6/1974) lge 154+3/3gls

Cardiff City (£60,000 signed in 1/2/1979) lge 61+2/1gls
Hereford United (signed in December 1981) lge 8
Portsmouth (signed in March 1982) lge 94
Swansea City (signed in 22/3/1985)
Locksheath (player/trainer signed in July 1986)

Honours: England Yth, U-23–2, Third Division Champions–1983

Vastly experienced left full back who was signed by Swans' manager John Bond on a free transfer from Portsmouth, and who had previously played under the manager at Norwich City. Earlier in his career he had represented Plymouth Argyle Schoolboys and Cornwall Schoolboys, and had joined Argyle as an apprentice from Saltash United. Since turning professional in 1968, he has gained two U-23 caps for England, the first at Home Park against Poland in 16th October 1973, the second a month later at Portsmouth against Denmark. After playing in the Argyle side that was beaten by Manchester City in the semi-finals of the 1973/74 League Cup competition, he was transferred to Norwich City for £70,000 in June 1974, and in his first season at Carrow Road, where he made 36 league appearances, saw his club gain promotion to the First Division, and also play in the League Cup Final at Wembley against Aston Villa. A regular inclusion in City's First Division line-up, in February 1979 he joined Cardiff City in the Second Division for £60,000, again featuring prominently at left full back in his first two seasons, before a short term at Hereford United saw him join Third Division side Portsmouth. His first full season at Fratton Park saw the club win the Third Division Championship at the end of season 1982/83, during which he was an ever present. One of a number of players signed by manager John Bond in the second half of the 1984/85 season, despite lacking some of the pace he once possessed on the left side of defence, his defensive experience saw him miss just five league games before he was released in May 1986 following the club's relegation to the Fourth Division. He returned to his native Cornwall, signing for non-league side Locksheath, later becoming trainer with Warsash U-15's and U-16's sides.

40. SYKES, W. Joseph (JOE)

Birthplace: Sheffield, 8/1/1898. **Died:** Swansea, 4/9/1974
Ht: 5ft-9ins, **Wt:** 11st-7lbs
Swans debut: v. Merthyr Town (h), 13/9/1924

Career:
Army Football
Sheffield Wednesday (signed in June 1919) lge 29/1gls
Swansea Town (signed in 4/7/1924)

Honours: Third Division South Champions–1925, Welsh League Representative XI

Swansea Town Career Statistics			
Season	*League*	*FAC*	*WC*
1924/25	32	2	3
1925/26	35	7	3
1926/27	39	5	1
1927/28	24		1
1928/29	37	2	
1929/30	42/1gls	1	
1930/31	34/1gls	1	1
1931/32	27/4gls	1	1
1932/33	36	1	1
1933/34	2		
1934/35	4/1gls	2	
Total	312/7gls	22	11

Joined the Swans as a right half back, but also played at centre half, and at left half back. As a schoolboy he played for Carlisle Street, and subsequently became associated with All Saints BC, members of the Sheffield Bible Class League. Remaining with All Saints until WW1 broke out, Joe eventually enlisted in the Sportsmen's Battalion of the Middlesex Regiment, 17th Service Battalion in the Great War. He went to Salonika in 1916, and from there was transferred to India, coming in contact with Dicky Downs, the old Barnsley and Everton stalwart. Members of the same regiment team, Downs recommended him to Barnsley when League Football was resumed, but Sheffield Wednesday were the first club to offer him professional terms. Spending five full seasons at Hillsborough, Joe was understudy to England half back George Wilson for over four seasons, limiting him to just twenty-nine league starts. Joe made his league debut at Liverpool in March 1920, with his best period in the Wednesday first team coming in season 1922/23, when he made fourteen league appearances. During his time at Hillsbrough, Wednesday had refused to sell him to Liverpool, despite being offered £3,000 for his transfer. Signed by manager Joe Bradshaw shortly after the start of the 1924/25 season, Joe would go on to become a legendary figure at the Vetch Field, on and off the field long after he had retired as a player. His first season at the Vetch Field saw him skipper the side to its first Championship, the Third Division South, and also lose out in the Welsh Cup semi-final against Wrexham. His second saw the club reach the Final of the Welsh Cup, only to lose out to Ebbw Vale, and also reach the FA Cup semi-finals for the first time, losing to Bolton Wanderers. Starting at centre half, he reverted to wing half following the emergence of a young Harry Hanford, nurturing the player through matches as he gained experience. A natural leader, unpretentious, good in attack, or in defence, and the doyen of the carpet pass, he was highly respected by his fellow professionals, admired by all for his fair play. In April 1930, Sykes, along with George Thomas and Dai Nicholas received Benefits from the Swans, with friendly matches played later in the month against Motherwell and Cardiff City. In May 1931 he played for a Welsh League Representative side against the Irish Free State. Not a natural goalscorer, it took him six seasons to register his first league goal for the Swans, at Reading in January 1930 in a 3-1 defeat, but he did score four league goals during season 1931/32 from either centre half, or from left half back. At the end of season 1934/35 he was de-registered by the Swans, moved back to Sheffield to open a business, but eventually returned to Swansea in the summer of 1947, taking up the position of assistant trainer. His off the field activities as trainer saw him installed as trainer to the Wales Amateur side that played the Indian Olympic team at the Vetch Field in August 1948, and also to the Full Wales International team that played England at Wembley on the 10th November 1954. Managerial appointments at the Vetch Field saw him become assistant to Trevor Morris in July 1960, caretaker manager in January 1966, and in June 1968 he resigned as assistant to manager Billy Lucas. In early September 1974 he died at Morriston Hospital, Swansea.

41. SYMMONS, Iorwerth (IORIE)

Birthplace: Swansea, 3/2/1930. **Died:** Swansea, 24/3/2004
Ht: 5ft-9ins, **Wt:** 11st-7lbs
Swans debut: v. Newport County (a), WC–6, 1/3/1951

Swansea Town Career Statistics

Season	League	FAC
1950/51	10	1
1951/52	6	
Total	16	1

Career:
Sketty Church F.C.
Swansea Town (signed in May 1948)

Signed from local Swansea League side Sketty Church FC in May 1948 Iorie had to wait until 1st March 1951 before he made his first team debut, in a Welsh Cup sixth round tie at Newport County, replacing Gilbert Beech at left full back. Blotting out County's tricky winger Birch, what Symmons lacked in height, he more than made up in speed, deadly tackling and intelligent passing. He retained his place in the side for the next league game, against QPR at the Vetch Field, this time he was played in his customary right full back position replacing Terry Elwell, maintaining his place at right full back, missing just two more league games. The following season he struggled to hold down a regular place in the Swans starting line-up following the return from injury of Rory Keane, and in May 1954 was released by the Swans. Brought up in the Pentrechwyth district of Swansea, Iorie had earlier attended Pentrechwyth, Cwm, and Llansamlet Schools. A bad accident on the football pitch in which he received a serious muscle tear saw Iorrie forced to retire from the game at a professional level, but for many seasons after leaving the Vetch Field he remained active in local league football with Bonymaen Athletic and Hillside, working as a Fettler at the RTB Works in Landore until the late 1970's, and on two occasions as Steward of the Bonymaen Sports & Social Club. Known as 'Shimmy', during the summer months he was also a keen cricketer with the Sketty Baptist XI.

T

1. TABRAM, PHIL

Birthplace: Swansea, 11/11/1917. **Died:** Swansea, 17/10/1989
Ht: 6ft-2ins, **Wt:** 14st-6lbs
Swans debut: v. Cardiff City (a), WC-6, 8/2/1939

Swansea Town Career Statistics		
Season	League	WC
1938/39	11/1gls	2
Total	11/1gls	2

Career:
Cwm Mission
Swansea Town (signed in May 1937)
Merthyr Tydfil (signed in close season 1946)

Honours: Southern League Champions–1948, Welsh Cup
Winner–1949, West Wales Senior Cup Winner–1946

Like his elder brothers Billy and Bryn, Phil was brought up in
Cwm Road, Hafod, and attended Hafod School, played for
Swansea Schoolboys and later Cwm Mission prior to signing for
the Swans at the age of seventeen. He made his Swans first team
debut in a Welsh Cup, sixth round tie at Ninian Park against
Cardiff City, making his league debut two days later against
West Ham United at the Vetch Field. Replacing Reuben Simons
at centre half in the Swans side, by the end of the season he had
added to his first team starts, also playing at left half back.
He played in the first three league matches of the 1939/40
season, but when the Football League was suspended because
of the outbreak of WW2, he played in friendly games, and
Regional South West League Football, also making guest
appearances for Hartlepool United and Stockport County in
season 1943/44, prior to seeing active service with the Marines.
A well built footballer, sound in attack and defence, he was
likened at the time to former Swans stalwart Lachlan

McPherson. One of his last games for the Swans was with the
reserve side, beating Llanelly in the West Wales Senior Cup
Final. In 1947 he joined Merthyr Tydfil, and skippered the side
to the Championship of the Southern League at the end of
season 1947/48, and in May 1949 played in the Merthyr side
that beat the Swans at Ninian Park to win the Welsh Cup. He
failed to make an appearance two years later when Merthyr beat
Cardiff City to win the Welsh Cup at the Vetch Field. Released
by Merthyr in May 1952, he later assisted Swansea League side
Hafod Brotherhood, and worked for local construction company
Rees & Kirby prior to his retirement. In February 1953 he made
a guest appearance for Ralph Avery's Representative side.

2. TABRAM, William (BILLY) David

Birthplace: Swansea, 19/1/1909. **Died:** Swansea, 15/4/1992
Ht: 5ft-10ins, **Wt:** 10st-10lbs
Swans debut: v. Bradford City (a), 19/2/1930

Swansea Town Career Statistics			
Season	League	FAC	WC
1929/30	4		1
1930/31	4		
1931/32	10		3
1932/33	2	1	
Total	20	1	4

Career:
Cwm Mission
Cwm Athletic
Swansea Town (signed in 5/5/1928)
Port Vale (signed in May 1933) lge 35/1gls, FAC 1
Hull City (signed in May 1934) lge 106/5gls
South Shields (signed in June 1937)

Honours: Wales Sch, Wales Junior International, West Wales Senior Cup Winner–1930

Brought up in Cwm Road, Hafod, Billy attended Hafod School, played for Swansea schoolboys and played for Wales in a Junior International against Ireland in season 1928/29. He made a name for himself in the local Swansea League with Cwm Mission and Cwm Athletic, and after a trial with Preston North End signed for the Swans in May 1928, making his debut at Bradford City in February 1930, replacing Freeman at centre half. In October 1930 he was included in the Swans reserve side that beat Newport County in the West Wales Senior Cup Final. Along with Les Wilkins from Red Triangle, the both players had impressed on trial in reserve team games for the Swans, with both signing professional forms after playing Reading reserves on the 5th May 1928. His remaining games that season were played at right and left half back. His best season for the Swans as far as first team appearances are concerned came during 1931/32 season when he made ten league starts, and three in the Welsh Cup. He made his last Swans appearance on the 7th January 1933 against Fulham, and seven days later joined Port Vale, along with Ken Gunn, for a fee of £400, with both players playing in the two league games between the sides during season 1933/34. Despite being a regular in the Vale line-up, he was transferred to Second Division side Hull City prior to the start of the 1934/35 season, in what was at the time their third highest transfer fee. His brother Bryn also joined him at Hull City, but did not make any appearances for the club. Following the club's relegation to the Third Division North, he was transferred to non-league side South Shields in June 1937. During the war he was based in Whitley Bay with the RAF, made guest appearances for Hartlepool United in season 1945/46, and after returning home to Swansea, Billy finished his playing career with Welsh League side Haverfordwest, working in the Elba Tinworks, and the Smelter Plant in Llansamlet prior to his retirement.

3. TATE, ALAN

Birthplace: Easington, 2/9/1982
Ht: 6ft-1ins, **Wt:** 11st-10lbs
Swans debut: v. Scunthorpe United (a), 23/11/2003

Swansea City Career Statistics

Season	League	FLC	FAC	LDV	FAWC
2002/03	27				1
2003/04	25+1/1gls		1	1	1
2004/05	17+6	1	2+1	1	2
Total	69+7/1gls	1	3+1	2	4

Career:
Manchester United (from trainee in 18/7/2000)
Royal Antwerp (loan in January 2002)
Swansea City (loan in 22/11/2002)
Swansea City (loan in 24/10/2003)
Swansea City (signed in 6/2/2004)

Honours: FAW Cup Winner–2005

Signed along with Blackburn Rovers striker Marc Richards on a loan transfer in November 2002, he remained at the Vetch Field for the remainder of the season, making a good impression at the heart of the Swans defence with his cool, assured play. United manager Sir Alex Ferguson had told Tate at the time he was sending him to the Vetch Field to toughen him up! Alan's move to the Vetch was funded by the club's Supporters Trust, who launched the very successful 'Stop Moaning & Get A Loan In' scheme back in early November 2002, receiving over £20,000 in donations from fans, enabling the Club to pay his wages for the season. Brought up in Murton, County Durham, Alan attended Murton Primary and Easington Comprehensive Schools, played for East Durham and Durham Schoolboys, winning the County Cup on three occasions, and had been involved with Manchester United for half his life, signing for the Old Trafford Centre of Excellence as a 10 year-old. However, his career might have turned out very differently had his father allowed sentiment to cloud his judgement. He had initially started off at Sunderland, training with their Centre of Excellence, whilst playing for Kennick Roker, a local team in the North East on a Sunday, but following an approach from a United scout he made a decision to join United based on what he thought would give him the best opportunity. With the Sunday League side he had won numerous league and league cup finals from the U-11 side through to the U-16 teams. Signing scholarship forms upon leaving school, Alan joined United full-time in 1999, just after their incredible season that culminated in a last minute Champions League success. A trialist for the England U-16 squad, in 1999 he played in the Milk Cup Final against Crewe Alexandra, winning the 'Man of the Match Award'. He captained the United reserve team on many occasions, most notably in the Manchester Senior Cup Final in 2001 when they were beaten by rivals Manchester City. Playing in a European Tournament in Dusseldorf in 2001 with Manchester United he was voted 'Best Defender of the Tournament'. Alan signed his first professional contract at just 17 years of age, and in January 2002 he was told he would be joining Belgium side Royal Antwerp on loan along with Neil Wood. Playing a dozen games for the club over a four month period, he then returned to United, and despite not making an appearance in the United first team was signed by manager Brian Flynn for his first loan stint at the Vetch Field. After returning to Old Trafford at the end of the season, he was unable to make any inroads into the United first team squad at the start of the 2003/04 season, and in late October 2003 returned to the Vetch Field for a two month loan period. Within a couple of weeks of his returning to Old Trafford, following overtures from manger Flynn, he was released from his contract by United, and despite offers from First Division clubs, joined the Swans on a free transfer on the 6th February 2004, signing a two and a half year's contract. A composed defender, good striker of the ball, he scored his first goal for the Swans at the Vetch Field against Leyton Orient, in what turned out to be the winning goal of the game. A change in management at the Vetch Field towards the end of the season saw Alan struggle to command a first team place during the 2004/05 season, struggling at times to make the substitute's bench when the side eventually claimed one of the automatic promotion places from Coca Cola League Two. However, he did play in the FAW Cup Final victory over Wrexham.

4. TERRY, Patrick (PAT) Arthur

Birthplace: Brixton, London 2/10/1933
Ht: 5ft-11ins, **Wt:** 12st-0lbs
Swans debut: v. Huddersfield Town (h), 22/2/1958

Swansea Town Career Statistics	
Season	*League*
1957/58	12/5gls
1958/59	5/4gls
Total	17/9gls

Career:
Eastbourne United
Charlton Athletic (signed in 8/3/1954) lge 4/1gls
Newport County (signed in May 1956) lge 55/30gls
Swansea Town (£5,000 signed in February 1958)
Gillingham (£4,000 signed in October 1958) lge 109/62gls
Northampton Town (signed in July 1961) lge 24/10gls
Millwall (signed in February 1962) lge 97/41gls
Reading (£1,800 signed in 21/8/1964) lge 99/41gls
Swindon Town (£5,300 signed in 28/2/1967) lge 60+1/23gls
Brentford (signed in 29/6/1968) lge 29/12gls, FLC 2/1gls
Hillingdon Borough (signed in July 1969)
Folkestone (signed in May 1970)
Stevenage Borough (signed in August 1972)

Honours: Fourth Division Champions–1962

Apart from making his First Division debut with his first league club Charlton Athletic, centre forward Pat Terry's career was based mainly in the Third and Fourth Divisions, bar a brief spell at the Vetch Field with the Swans in the Second Division. After dropping down to join Newport County in the Third Division South in May 1956, Pat was a consistent goalscorer for all of his professional clubs. Averaging almost a goal every two games for County he was signed by manager Ronnie Burgess for £5,000 in February 1958, and after making his league debut at the Vetch Field against Huddersfield Town, scored his first goal for the Swans in the next game at Middlesbrough. At the time of his transfer it was thought that Gilbert Beech would also go as part of the transfer package. Finishing the season with five goals in the league, the start of the 1958/59 saw him score three goals from the first four league games. A spell on the sidelines with injury saw him return for one game, score in a 4-2 home win over Ipswich Town, and was then transferred to Gillingham for £4,000. He had to wait a number of seasons before playing against the Swans, and in his first game back at the Vetch Field, this time for Reading in April 1966, scored two goals in a 5-4 defeat by the Swans. His last season playing in the league saw him score in both league games for Brentford against the Swans during the 1968/69 season. A real football nomad, Pat never stayed long with any of his clubs, and yet he is well remembered at all of them. An old fashioned style centre forward who used his physical strength to the full, suffering many suspensions in his career, he was one of the best headers of the ball in the game, with almost two thirds of his goals scored with his head. He only enjoyed one promotion in his league career when he joined Millwall with three months of the season to go in their 1961/62 Fourth Division title win. Joining non-league side Hillingdon Borough in July 1969,

he made further non-league appearances for Folkestone, Stevenage Borough and Greenwich Borough, playing until he was almost forty years of age, working as a London cab driver.

5. THEOBALD, DAVID John

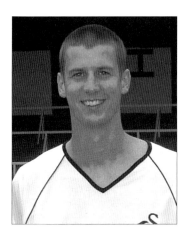

Birthplace: Cambridge, 15/12/1978
Ht: 6ft-3ins, **Wt**: 12st-0lbs
Swans debut: v. Bournemouth (h), 24/8/2002

Swansea City Career Statistics			
Season	*League*	*FAC*	*LDV*
2002/03	9+1	1	1
Total	9+1	1	1

Career:
Ipswich Town (from trainee in 2/6/1997)
Brentford (signed in 8/7/1999) lge 26+5, Others 6
Swansea City (signed in 26/7/2002)
Cambridge United (signed in 7/2/2003) lge 1+3
Canvey Island (signed in August 2003) Conf 8+1
Bishop's Stortford (loan in 19/10/2004)

Honours: Ryman Premier League Champions–2004

Tall, central defender who impressed during a pre-season trial at the Vetch Field after being released by Brentford in the 2002 close season. Possessing the ability to deliver accurate balls from defence, he missed the start of season 2002/03, making his debut in the second home game of the season against Bournemouth in a 2-0 win. He was regularly included in Nick Cusack's squad, but following a change of management at the Vetch Field, did not feature in Brian Flynn's sides very often, and he had his contract paid up on 27th January 2003 along with fellow squad member David Moss. With no reserve team at the Vetch Field, his options for impressing in matches were limited. He returned to his Cambridge home after his release and trained with his hometown club at the start of February as a means of keeping fit. With injuries to regular defenders Andy Duncan and Stevland Angus, he was added to the United playing squad as cover on a non-contract basis. He had earlier been on the books of Cambridge as a youngster, but joined Ipswich Town at the age of 14. After failing to make an appearance at Ipswich, he joined Brentford in 1999. His first season at Griffin Park saw him play mostly at right back, but the following season saw him play in the LDV Vans Trophy Final for Brentford at the Millenium Stadium in Cardiff, losing 2-1 to Port Vale. In May 2002 he was a non-playing substitute at the Millenium Stadium when Brentford lost to Stoke City in the Second Division Play Off Final. Within a couple of weeks of his being released by the Swans, and after he had signed on a non-contract basis for United, he was included as a non-playing substitute for United at the Vetch Field. After a couple of appearances for United, mostly as substitute, he was released shortly before the start of the season, and made a number of appearances for Dr. Martens side Cambridge City. Shortly after the start of the 2003/04 season he signed for Ryman League side Canvey Island, playing in the side that narrowly lost in a replay to Third Division side Southend United 2-3 in a first round replay of the F.A. Cup in mid-November 2003, and at the end of the season won the Ryman Premier League Championship, and promotion to the Conference. David was also a non-playing substitute in the 2004 FA Trophy final against Hednesford Town. In October 2004 he joined Conference South side Bishop's Stortford on a month's loan.

6. THOMAS, BARRIE

Birthplace: Merthyr Tydfil, 27/8/1954
Ht: 6ft-0ins, **Wt:** 13st-7lbs
Swans debut: v. Blackburn Rovers (h), 4/4/1972

Swansea City Career Statistics	
Season	League
1971/72	2
Total	2

Career:
Swansea City (signed in August 1971)
Merthyr Tydfil (signed in close season 1972)
Bournemouth (signed in August 1979) lge 3

Honours: Wales Sch, Yth, Oxford University XI

One of a number of players who arrived at the Vetch Field from the Rhondda Valley area in the late 1960's, and early 1970's, and who made his league debut after impressing in the club's Football Combination side whilst still in school. Merthyr born, Barrie attended Penywaun and Aberdare Grammar Schools, played for Aberdare schoolboys prior to arriving at the Vetch Field as an amateur, and played in the club's Football Combination side, whilst studying for his 'A' levels. He made his league debut for the Swans at centre half replacing the veteran Alan Williams, also playing in the next home league match with Plymouth Argyle. Deciding to take up the offer of a place at Oxford University to study for a History Degree, instead of a professional career in football, Barrie played a number of games for hometown side Merthyr Tydfil, managed by John Charles prior to going to college. Whilst at Oxford, Barrie captained the University Football Team during season 1974, gaining his Blue against Cambridge University.
After leaving University, he went to coach Football and PE in Jamaica for a number of years, and on returning to the UK gained his Full Coaching Badges with Fred Davies at Bournemouth. Returning to the Football League at the start of the 1979/80 season, he played for the 'Cherries' against the Swans in a League Cup First Round tie, but after breaking his leg, had his contract cancelled in October 1979, joining non-league side Dorchester Town, managed by former Spurs centre forward Martin Chivers, before finishing his career with Poole Town. Working with Lloyds Bank between 1990-2000, Barrie is currently HR Director with Logica CMG, and occasionally involves himself with playing and coaching in local football.

7. THOMAS, BRIAN Hugh

Birthplace: Glanamman, 28/6/1944
Ht: 6ft-0ins, **Wt:** 11st-7lbs
Swans debut: v. Swindon Town (h), FLC-2, 23/9/1964

Swansea Town Career Statistics		
Season	League	FLC
1964/65	4	2
Total	4	2

Career:
Swansea Town (from juniors in June 1962)
Lovells Athletic (signed in close season 1965)
Pembroke Borough (signed in season 1966/67)

Honours: Welsh League First Division Champions–1963, 1964, 1965, 1966

Local product who signed as a professional in June 1962, but had to wait until shortly after the start of the 1964/65 season before making his first team debut at the Vetch Field against Swindon Town in the second round of the League Cup competition. His family had been evacuated to Llandeilo during the war from their house in Northhill Road, with Brian being born in Glanamman. Returning to the family home in Swansea after the war, Brian went to Dyfatty Juniors, and then Hafod Schools, playing for the school teams as well as Swansea Schoolboys, at either centre half, or at centre forward. Leaving school at the age of fourteen, he went to work in his uncle's scrap business, playing football firstly for the YMCA, and then with Swansea Boys Club, where after one cup final at the Vetch Field against the Swans, he was offered professional terms. His first league start came against at the Vetch Field against Coventry City on the 29th September 1964. Missing the next league fixture, Brian then made his second league start at Preston North End in a 2-2 draw. Making his earlier appearances at left half back, later in the season he made a further two league appearances at inside left. He also made a second League Cup appearance, in the Fourth Round defeat at Stamford Bridge against Chelsea, where the Swans lost to two late headed goals from George Graham. At the end of the season a change of management and relegation to the Third Division saw the playing staff trimmed, with Brian given a free transfer. In three consecutive seasons playing for the Swans' Welsh League side, they won the Welsh League First Division Championships, and after leaving the Vetch Field, following a six week trial period with First Division Nottingham Forest joined Lovells Athletic, winning his fourth Welsh League Championship by the end of the season. His second season at Lovells saw the club suffer financial difficulties, with Brian linking up with a number of ex-Swans players at Pembroke Borough, finishing runners-up in the Welsh League First Division in his first season behind Bridgend Town. Since then

Brian has made appearances for Haverfordwest and Llanelli, returned to Pembroke Borough where he had a spell as player manager, finishing his Welsh League career with Ammanford Town. Returning to the Swansea Senior League to play for North End, after being employed by the Water Board, Brian started his own building company, and after going into the scrap business, initially in Gorseinon, relocated to his present position in Morriston as Trinity Metals. Maintaining a keen involvement in local football with North End, Brian played well into his forties for the club, and has been chairman of the league for ten years, also running the Swansea Senior League and Junior League Representative XI in games against South and West Wales League Representative sides.

8. THOMAS, David (DAI)

Birthplace: Abercregan, Port Talbot, 1/8/1926
Ht: 5ft-7ins, **Wt:** 11st-6lbs
Swans debut: v. Brentford (a), 15/10/1949

Swansea Town Career Statistics			
Season	League	FLC	FAC
1949/50	1		
1950/51	29/8gls	1	1
1951/52	11/1gls		
1952/53	37/1gls	1	3
1953/54	35	3/1gls	1
1954/55	41/1gls	3	1
1955/56	36/2gls	1	3
1956/57	39	1	6/1gls
1957/58	24		
1958/59	22	1	
1959/60	21/1gls		
Total	296/14gls	11/1gls	15/1gls

Career:
Abercregan YMCA
Swansea Town (amateur signed in 1947, professional in August 1948)
Newport County (signed in July 1961) lge 58/1gls
Hereford United (signed in July 1963) Total Apps 39/1gls
Port Talbot (signed in close season 1965)

Honours: Wales Full–2, London Combination Cup Winner–1950, Welsh League Representative XI, West Wales Senior Cup Winner–1949, 1950, 1956, 1957

Originally an inside forward who was converted to full back after a couple of seasons, capable of playing in either right, or left full back position. Born in Abercregan, Dai attended Cymmer Secondary School, played rugby in school, only playing football after leaving school at the age of fourteen, working in the pits until he was nineteen, and playing for Abercregan Y.M.C.A. Called up for his National Service, he was stationed at Weighbourne, near Sheringham, and he came to the attention of Cyril Spiers, at the time Norwich City manager, signing amateur forms for the club, with his only appearances being made in the club's third team. A great club servant who had good ball distribution, he was reserve to the Welsh Senior team that toured France and Yugoslavia in 1953, finally gaining international recognition, playing in two consecutive Welsh Internationals, against Czechoslovakia in Prague on the 26th May 1957, and in Cardiff against East Germany on the 25th September the same year. After making his league debut for the Swans at inside left, his first full season saw him finish runner-up as goalscorer in the league with eight goals in season 1950/51. The following season saw him start the new term in the starting line-up at left half back, later reverting to left full back. That season he played in his first Welsh Cup semi-final, against Rhyl, and in seasons 1955/56 and 1956/57 played in consecutive Welsh Cup Finals defeats against Cardiff City and Wrexham respectively. Making an appearance in the Swans successful West Wales Senior Cup winning side of 1949 and 1950, he also played in the 1956 and 1957 successful sides. The 1956/57 season saw Dai revert to right full back, a position he continued to play in effectively until his free transfer to Newport County in July 1961. Prior to making his league debut, Dai had been a member of the Swans reserve team that won the London Combination Cup Final in 1950 when they beat Southend United, and also making an appearance for the Welsh League Representative side. Dropping into the Third Division to sign for Newport County in July 1961, he suffered relegation to the Fourth Division in his first season, and midway through his second season at Somerton Park joined Hereford United, managed at the time by Ray Daniel. After two seasons at Edgar Street, and a new manager in Bob Dennison who wanted the playing staff to go full time, Dai declined the offer, returning to Port Talbot, playing for two seasons for the club in the Welsh League before retiring. His last game for United at Deal saw him score his only goal for the club. After dropping out of the Football League, for a number of years Dai had been a self employed carpenter after taking a training course, but for a number of years up to his retirement he worked as a rent collector for Neath/Port Talbot Council.

9. THOMAS, David (DAI) John

Birthplace: Caerphilly, 26/9/1975
Ht: 5ft-10ins, **Wt:** 12st-7lbs
Swans debut: v. Taffs Well (h), WC-3, 26/10/1994

Career:
Swansea City (from trainee in 25/7/1994)
Watford (£100,000 signed in 17/7/1997) lge 8+8/3gls, FAC 1+3

Cardiff City (£50,000 signed in 20/8/1998) lge 21+10/gls,
    FLC 0+1, FAC 0+3, Others 1
Merthyr Tydfil

Swansea City Career Statistics					
Season	League	FLC	WC	AWS	P/Offs
1994/95	2+2		0+3/1gls		
1995/96	3+13/1gls				
1996/97	31+5/9gls	2		1/1gls	0+1/1gls
Total	36+20/10gls	2	0+3/1gls	1/1gls	0+1/1gls

Honours: Wales U-21–2, Second Division Champions–1998,
West Wales Senior Cup Winner–1995

Former St. Llan Junior Schoolboy, Caerphilly, who joined the
Swans as a trainee, and who made his first team debut as a
substitute for winger John Hodge in a Welsh Cup tie against
Taffs Well, making his first Football League start also from the
substitute bench in April 1995 at Plymouth Argyle. The next
league fixture he made his first start, against Bournemouth at
the Vetch Field in a 1-0 win. He made a further substitute
appearance in the Welsh Cup, this time against Porthmadog,
scoring his first senior goal for the Swans. In May 1995 he was
included in a Swans reserve side that beat Morriston Town in
the West Wales Senior Cup Final. The following season saw the
club struggle on and off the field, with his opportunities limited
with various changes in management, and the club suffering
relegation. Appearing to be on the verge of a free transfer, he
worked hard under the encouragement from manager Molby
and his assistant Billy Ayre, and during the pre-season tour of
Denmark gave some encouraging displays. The 1996/97 season
saw him make the starting line-up under the management of Jan
Molby and make a name for himself as a robust front runner,
with good close skills, and finishing the season as runner-up in
the goalscoring stakes with nine league goals, and helping the
club to the Third Division Play Off Final at Wembley, where he
was unfortunate not to make the starting line-up. In the close
season that followed, with uncertainty off the field with a
proposed takeover of the football club, Dai opted to sign for
Second Division side Watford for a £100,000 transfer fee. In his
third game for the 'Hornets' he scored his first goal for the club,
but in a season which saw them win the Championship, he
managed to make just sixteen league appearances, scoring three
goals. In August 1997 he gained his first U-21 cap for Wales
when he was selected to play against Turkey, making his second
appearance in October against Belgium. Shortly after the start of
the 1998/99 he returned to South Wales to sign for Cardiff City
for £50,000, scoring on his debut at Shrewsbury Town. With the
'Bluebirds' gaining promotion after finishing in third place, he
struggled to make an impact the following season in the Second
Division, and in May 2000 he was offered a free transfer, despite
having two years left on his contract. In the summer of 2000 he
had some much publicised off the field problems after he was
deported by Belgian police following his arrest during
violence which marred England's 1-0 victory over Germany in
Euro 2000. Making just the one first team appearance, as
substitute in a Worthington Cup tie against Crystal Palace early
in season 2000/01, he had a spell with Dr. Martens League club
Merthyr Tydfil, before finishing the season with South Wales
Amateur League side Bryntirion. A *South Wales Evening Post*
article in February 2002 mentioned that the former Swans and
Cardiff City striker had been jailed for 60 days and banned from
all grounds in England and Wales for six years by Cardiff
Magistrates, following the part he played in the violence that
marred Cardiff City's defeat of Leeds United in the Third
Round of the F.A. Cup in January 2002. Thomas was captured
on camera throwing a hoarding towards Leeds United
supporters during a pitch invasion at Ninian Park on January
6th.

10. THOMAS, Edward (EDDIE)

Birthplace: Newton-le-Willows, 23/10/1933. **Died:** Derby,
12/11/2003
Ht: 5ft-9ins, **Wt:** 10st-9lbs
Swans debut: v. Charlton Athletic (a), 18/8/1962

Swansea Town Career Statistics				
Season	League	FLC	FAC	WC
1962/63	40/15gls	1	2/1gls	3/1gls
1963/64	27/6gls	1	5/4gls	1/1gls
1964/65	1			
Total	68/21gls	2	7/5gls	4/2gls

Career:
Everton (from juniors in October 1951) lge 86/39gls
Blackburn Rovers (signed in February 1960) lge 37/9gls
Swansea Town (£10,000 signed in July 1962)
Derby County (£3,500 signed in August 1964) lge 102+3/43gls,
    FLC 6/6gls, FAC 2
Leyton Orient (£5,000 signed in September 1967) lge 11/2gls
Nuneaton Borough (loan in February 1968)
Heanor Town (signed in August 1968)

Eddie Thomas started his professional career at Goodison Park
with Everton, signing professional in October 1951, and after the
club had gained promotion to the First Division in 1954 spent
most of his career prior to joining the Swans playing in the First
Division with Everton, and then with Blackburn Rovers.
His transfer to Rovers in February 1960 saw him included in a
£27,000 deal which saw Welsh international Roy Vernon move to
Everton in exchange. Signed by manager Trevor Morris for a
£10,000 transfer fee in July 1962 he made an immediate impact
finishing top goalscorer with fifteen league goals in his first
season, scoring two goals in his second league game for the
Swans. His second season at the Vetch Field saw him included
in the side that almost reached the FA Cup Final, only to lose in
the semi-final stage against Preston North End on a muddy Villa
Park surface, and also scoring one of the Swans goals in the
historic quarter final defeat of Liverpool at Anfield. After just
one league appearance in his third season with the Swans he
was transferred to Derby County for £6,000. His move to
County saw him create a record of scoring in his first six
appearances after signing for the club. After over a century of
appearances for County he joined Leyton Orient in September
1967, and after a loan spell with non-league Nuneaton Borough
in February 1968, signed for Heanor Town in August 1968.
Thomas is one of several co-holders of the Derby record, scoring
in six consecutive league games. His first season at the Baseball
Ground saw him finish as joint top goalscorer with Alan Durban
with twenty-four league and cup goals, and the following
season again finishing top goalscorer with Durban with
seventeen league and cup goals. Manager Tim Ward was quoted
as saying after his sacking at Derby: "Perhaps the worst thing I
ever did was to sign Eddie Thomas for £3,5000, because he
proved a marvellous bargain, and after that I was expected to
sign other players as cheaply." He died in Derby on the
12th November 2003.

11. THOMAS, Geoffrey (GEOFF)

Birthplace: Swansea, 18/2/1948
Ht: 5ft-8ins, **Wt:** 11st-4lbs
Swans debut: v. Workington (a), 4/10/1965

Swansea Town/City Career Statistics				
Season	League	FLC	FAC	WC
1965/66	24			6/2gls
1966/67	24+1	2		
1967/68	18+3/3gls	1	1	
1968/69	28+1/2gls	1	3+1/2gls	5/2gls
1969/70	44/11gls	2/1gls	2	4/5gls
1970/71	39/6gls	2	4/2gls	2/1gls
1971/72	43/7gls	1	6/1gls	1
1972/73	45+1/9gls	2/1gls	1	2
1973/74	11+4/2gls			0+1
1974/75	38+2/8gls	1	1	3
1975/76	31/4gls	1	1	2
Total	345+12/52gls	13/2gls	19+1/5gls	25+1/10gls

Career:
Swansea Town (signed from apprentice in February 1966)
Manchester United (loan in 20/12/1973) lge 0

Honours: Wales Sch–4, Yth, U-23–3, West Wales Senior Cup
Winner–1975, Welsh Cup Winner–1966

Former captain of the Swansea schoolboys side who became one
of the first apprentices at the Vetch Field after leaving school.
The former Hafod schoolboy was one of three Swansea
Schoolboy players selected to play against England at the Vetch
Field in April 1963. Gaining Youth honours for Wales, he also
made three appearances at U-23 level later in his career for his
country. Possessing an abundance of ability, he was an
extremely talented midfielder with a blistering shot, terrific
passer of the ball, a good competitor in the midfield engine
room, and in later years showed he was a good reader of the
game when playing as a sweeper. Making his league debut at
Workington on the 4th October 1965, he went on to make
regular appearances during his first season in the Swans first
team, also scoring his first goals for the club with two in the
Welsh Cup, Sixth Round replay at the Vetch Field in February
1965 against Porthmadog. His awareness in front of goal, and
the ability to score regularly from the penalty spot became
evident as he gained experience in the Swans first team,
finishing consistently high in the goalscoring charts season after
season. He scored two hat-tricks in the Football League, against
Grimsby Town in October 1972, and against Doncaster Rovers in
September 1974, and also scored four goals in one Welsh Cup tie
at the Vetch Field against Oswestry Town in January 1970. He
made his first appearance for the Welsh U-23 side against
England in 1968, with two other appearances against England

and Scotland coming in 1971, and would have played in other
U-23 internationals but for games being cancelled through bad
weather. He made an appearance in the first leg of the 1966
Welsh Cup Final against Chester, failed to make any
appearances in the following season's European Cup Winners
Cup games against Bulgarian side Slavia Sofia, also playing in a
losing Welsh Cup Final against Cardiff City in 1969 over two
legs. The 1969/70 season, under Roy Bentley saw Thomas score
eleven goals during a season which saw the Swans gain
promotion in third place from the Fourth Division. Following
the appointment of Harry Gregg as manager at the Vetch Field,
in December 1973 he had a month on loan at Old Trafford with
Manchester United, failing to make a first team appearance.
In May 1975 he was one of the goalscorers in the West Wales
Senior Cup Final win over Briton Ferry Athletic. At the end of
the 1975/76 season he was released by manager Harry Griffiths,
joining Welsh League side Milford United, and ended his
playing career in the Swansea Senior League with North End.
A talented all round sportsman, in the close season he was a
more than competent cricketer, playing in the Swansea Central
and Industrial Leagues.

12. THOMAS, GEORGE

Birthplace: Wrexham
Ht: 5ft-7ins, **Wt:** 10st-6lbs
Swans debut: v. Preston North End (h), 16/1/1926

Swansea Town Career Statistics			
Season	League	FAC	WC
1925/26	6		2
1926/27	2		
1927/28	5/1gls		2
1928/29	13/1gls		1
1929/30	26/6gls	1	1/1gls
1930/31	12/2gls		
Total	64/10gls	1	6/1gls

Career:
Chirk
Druids
Swansea Town (trial in October 1924, signed in November 1924)

Honours: West Wales Senior Cup Winner–1926, 1927,
Welsh League Representative XI

Signed in November 1924 by manager Joe Bradshaw from North
Wales side Chirk after an initial trial, making his league debut
on the 16th January 1926 at outside right. During most of his
career at the Vetch Field had difficulty in ousting Billy Hole
from the right flank, and had to wait until the 1929/30 season
before he was to make more of an impact, following the

retirement of Hole. In April 1926 and in 1927 he was included in the Swans reserve side that beat Merthyr Town and Bridgend Town in consecutive West Wales Senior Cup Finals. His first goal for the Swans came at Barnsley in September 1927, and the first season he started the season in the first match of the season came during his last season at the Vetch Field, season 1920/31. In April 1930, Thomas, along with Joe Sykes and Dai Nicholas received Benefits from the Swans, with friendly matches played later in the month against Motherwell and Cardiff City. He was released in May 1931, after being originally transfer listed at £250.

13. THOMAS, JAMES Alan

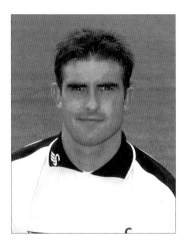

Born: Swansea, 16/1/1979
Ht: 6ft-0ins, **Wt:** 13st-0lbs
Swans debut: v. Rushden & Diamonds (h), 10/8/2002

Swansea City Career Statistics					
Season	League	FLC	FAC	LDV	FAWP
2002/03	34+5/13gls	1/1gls	1	1/1gls	1
2003/04	8+8/3gls	0+1	1+3	1	1
2004/05	0+2				
Total	42+15/16gls	1+1/1gls	2+3	2/1gls	2

Career:
Blackburn Rovers (signed from trainee in 2/7/1996)
  lge 1+3/1gls, FLC 1/2gls
West Bromwich Albion (loan in 29/8/1997) lge 1+2
Blackpool (loan in 21/3/2000) lge 9/2gls
Sheffield United (loan in 24/11/2000) lge 3+7/1gls, FAC 0+1
Bristol Rovers (loan in 22/3/2002) lge 7/1gls
Swansea City (signed in 9/7/2002)

Honours: Wales Sch, U-21–21

Former Glyncollen Primary School, Morriston Comprehensive schoolboy who gained international recognition playing at schoolboy level in the Victory Shield at U-15 level for Wales, prior to joining Blackburn Rovers as a trainee straight from school. He gained his first U-21 honour with Wales against San Marino in 1996, before going on to make a record twenty-one appearances at this level for his country. He made his league debut during a loan spell early in his career for West Bromwich Albion, replacing Bob Taylor as substitute at Stoke City in September 1997. A second loan transfer, this time with Blackpool saw James score his first league goal in his fifth match for the 'Seasiders', scoring his second goal three matches later. He finally made his first appearance for Rovers as substitute for Diawara at Sheffield United, starting the next league game at

Ewood Park against Bolton Wanderers, and scoring the only goal of the game. Four days later he scored two goals in the Worthington Cup Second Round, First leg tie against Portsmouth. Following further loan transfers to Sheffield United and Bristol Rovers he was given a free transfer by Rovers at the end of season 2001/02, signing for manager Nick Cusack at the Vetch Field on a one year contract. His debut for his hometown club saw James score in the opening league fixture of the 2002/03 season at the Vetch Field against Rushden & Diamonds, and end the term top goalscorer with thirteen league goals, including a hat-trick in the last game of the season against Hull City, which saw the Swans escape relegation to the Conference. A pacy, left sided front runner, he also showed his skill from deadball situations, scoring against Wolverhampton Wanderers in a Worthington Cup tie direct from a free kick outside the penalty area. Capable of also playing as a central striker, he was called up to the Full Welsh international squad for a Euro 2004 qualifying game in Azerbaijan, but was not called on from the substitute bench. In June 2003 he signed a two year contract with the Swans, but despite starting the new season in the first team line-up struggled to make an impact in the Swans first team, being unable to break up the Nugent/Trundle starting option. Season 2004/05 saw him feature during the early part of the season from the substitute bench, but with knee problems seeing him undergo a number of operations, as well as a period at the Lilleshall Sports Centre, he failed to make another appearance for the Swans. With his contract up for renewal at the end of the season, in April he was invited by Swans manager Kenny Jackett to attend pre-season training in July in a bid to earn himself a new contract.

14. THOMAS, MARTIN Russell

Birthplace: Lymington, 12/9/1973
Ht: 5ft-8ins, **Wt:** 12st-6lbs
Swans debut: v. Exeter City (h), 8/8/1998

Swansea City Career Statistics						
Season	League	FLC	FAC	AWS	FAWP	P/Offs
1998/99	26+4/3gls	2	4/2gls		1/1gls	2
1999/2000	32+8/4gls	4		2/1gls	2	
2000/01	12+9/1gls	2	1		3+2	
Total	70+21/8gls	8	5/2gls	2/1gls	6+2/1gls	2

Career:
Southampton (from trainee in August 1990, professional in
  19/6/1992) lge 0
Leyton Orient (loan in 24/3/1994) lge 5/2gls
Fulham (signed in 21/7/1994) lge 59+31/8gls, FLC 6+1,
  FAC 4/1gls, Others 7+1/2gls
Swansea City (signed in 24/6/1998)

Brighton & Hove Albion (signed in 22/3/2001) lge 1+7
Oxford United (signed in August 2001) lge 13+1/2gls, FLC 1
Exeter City (signed in May 2002) lge 22+4/3gls, FLC 1, FAC 2,
    Others 0+1, Conf 5+6
Eastleigh FC (signed in mid-July 2004) Total Apps 40/5gls

Honours: Third Division Champions–2000, Ryman Premier Play
Off Winners–2005

Competitive midfielder who became manager Alan Cork's third
signing from Fulham in late June 1998 for the Swans, but
unfortunately, Cork was sacked six days later as manager at the
Vetch Field. A wholehearted player, who always gave 100% over
ninety minutes for whichever team he played for, he will always
be remembered by Swans fans for the goal he scored that
knocked out Premiership side West Ham United in an F.A. Cup
replay at the Vetch Field. Unfortunately for Thomas, he suffered
an injury during the game which sidelined him for two months,
returning for the build up to the Play Offs at the end of the
season. Scoring in his debut game for the Swans at the start of
the season against Exeter City, he made a huge contribution
during his second season at the Vetch Field as the club won the
Third Division Championship, with Thomas making forty
league appearances. A new season in the Second Division saw
the Swans struggle, and after being placed on the transfer list
midway through the season after failing to agree terms over a
new contract, and, after he had overcome an ankle injury, he
linked up with his former boss at Fulham, Micky Adams at
Brighton & Hove Albion on a contract until the end of the
season. Starting his career as a trainee with Southampton it was
during a loan stint with Leyton Orient that he made his league
debut, scoring on his debut against Fulham, joining Fulham on a
permanent basis at the end of the season. During the club's
Third Division Runners-Up success of season 1996/97, Thomas
made 26 league appearances, twenty from the substitute bench.
During season 1995/96, along with Nick Cusack, both players
played for Fulham against the Swans in a 7-0 F.A. Cup victory at
Craven Cottage, with both players also scoring. After a season
with Oxford United, Thomas linked up with Exeter City for the
start of the 2002/03 season, but after a change of management,
despite being a consistent member of the first team for the first
two thirds of the season, was not included in the squad for the
last two months of the season as the 'Grecians' competed
unsuccessfully to maintain their league status. He remained
with the 'Grecians' for their first season in the Nationwide
Conference, but in mid-July 2004 joined non-league side
Eastleigh F.C. In May 2005 the club won the Ryman Premier
Play Off Final, beating Leyton to go into the Conference South.

15. THOMAS, Steven (STEVE)

Birthplace: Batley, 29/1/1957
Ht: 5ft-10ins, **Wt:** 12st-6lbs
Swans debut: v. Mansfield Town (h), 12/1/1974

Swansea City Career Statistics		
Season	League	FLC
1973/74	7	
1974/75	3	1
Total	10	1

Career:
Swansea City (signed from juniors in August 1973)
Afan Lido (signed in close season 1975)

Honours: West Wales Senior Cup Winner–1975

Steve Thomas was brought up in the Blaenymaes area, later
moving to Caerethin, and went to Penlan Comprehensive,
playing for Swansea schoolboys U-15 at the age of fourteen.
At one time it was thought that he would be taken on as an
apprentice at Stamford Bridge with Chelsea, but he later
decided to start an electrical apprenticeship with BSC at Port
Talbot, and sign for the Swans as an amateur. He was given his
first team debut by manager Harry Gregg after showing
promise in the club's reserve team at the Vetch Field against
Mansfield Town, a couple of weeks short of his seventeeth
birthday, replacing the suspended Mick Evans at left full back.
Later in the season he made a further six league appearances as
cover for either Micky Evans at left back, and for Wyndham
Evans at right back. A tough tackling full back, in the opening
game of the 1974/75 season at Darlington he was unlucky to be
sent off in a 3-2 defeat for the Swans, and going in the record
books as the youngest ever player to be sent off playing for the
club in a competitive fixture. In May 1975 he was included in
the Swans side that beat Briton Ferry Athletic to win the West
Wales Senior Cup. Following a change in management, he was
released by manager Harry Griffiths, signed for Welsh League
side Afan Lido and concentrated on his apprenticeship. His first
season with the Lido saw the club gain promotion to the
Premier Division of the Welsh League, but he then suffered an
injury in a car accident which forced him to retire from the
game. He continued to work at BCS Port Talbot for a number of
years, and after a five year period in the Middle East returned to
South Wales. Since his return he has been involved in Further
Education and is currently a Lecturer in the Engineering
Department at Tycoch College.

16. THOMPSON, ALBERT

Birthplace: Llanbradach, 1912
Ht: 5ft-10ins, **Wt:** 11st-7lbs
Swans debut: v. West Ham United (h), 6/9/1937

Career:
2nd Battalion South Wales Borderers
Barry Town

Bradford Park Avenue (signed in February 1935) lge 11/2gls
York City (signed in October 1936) lge 24/24gls
Swansea Town (£350 signed in 14/5/1937)
Wellington Town (signed in 17/8/1938)

Swansea Town Career Statistics	
Season	League
1937/38	4
Total	4

A member of the 2nd Battalion of the South Wales Borderers, who made a good impression with Barry Town earlier in his career, and who made his Football League debut for Second Division side Bradford Park Avenue in 1934. It was at Third Division North side York City that he caught the eye of Swans manager Neil Harris, giving an impressive performance in two FA Cup ties against the Swans. Signing for York City in October 1936, by the end of the season he had scored 28 goals in 29 League and Cup games that season, helping City reach the 4th round of the F.A. Cup for the first time in their history, losing at that stage to the Swans after a replay. Within a couple of weeks of the end of the season he had arrived at the Vetch Field for a £350 transfer fee, and made his Swans debut against West Ham United at the Vetch Field, shortly after the start of the season, as a replacement for Cyril Pearce, playing also in the next three league matches. He struggled to replace either Pearce, Williams or Vernon during the season, and after being listed at £250 in May 1938, joined non-league side Wellington Town.

17. THOMPSON, Leonard (LEN)

Birthplace: Wortley, Sheffield, 18/2/1901
Ht: 5ft-9ins, **Wt:** 11st-6lbs
Swans debut: v. Gillingham (a), 30/9/1922

Swansea Town Career Statistics			
Season	League	FAC	WC
1922/23	34/10gls	2	3/2gls
1923/24	39/13gls	4	1
1924/25	34/16gls	2/2gls	1/2gls
1925/26	39/19gls	7/4gls	2/2gls
1926/27	35/26gls	4/4gls	
1927/28	7/5gls	1	1
Total	188/89gls	20/10gls	8/6gls

Career:
Shire Green Primitive Methodist FC
Hallam

Barnsley (amateur signed in 1917) lge 2
Hallam
Birmingham (signed in 1918) lge 3
Swansea Town (£100 signed in June 1922)
Arsenal (£4,000 signed in 16/3/1928) lge 26/6gls, FAC 1
Crystal Palace (signed in June 1933) lge 2

Honours: England Sch, Third Division South Champions–1925, London Combination Champions–1929, 1930, 1931, London FA Challenge Cup Winners–1931

Born in Sheffield, the former Sheffield Schoolboy player gained International Schoolboy recognition in season 1914/15 with England, also skippering the England schoolboy team, then played in local football for Shire Green Primitive Methodist FC, Kiveton Park Colliery, Norfolk Amateurs and Hallam for about one and a half years before signing as an amateur for Barnsley in 1917 in war time football. In one game for Shire Green he scored ten goals in one game. After half a season as an inside left for Barnsley he returned to junior football in the Sheffield area with Hallam, switched to a centre forward role, and was employed at the same time by John Brown as a steelworker. In season 1918/19 he signed professional for First Division side Birmingham where he stayed until 1922, playing several first team matches, but playing mostly in the reserve team, and when called into first team action covered for Scottish International Crosbie. Len was then signed by Swans manager Joe Bradshaw for a £100 transfer fee in June 1922, scoring on his debut for the club at Gillingham. His inspirational play, and goal scoring ability soon became evident as he finished his first season at the Vetch Field in double figures for goals scored. In five seasons with the Swans he would consistently be vying with Deacon and Fowler for top goal scorer for the club, a feat he achieved in season 1926/27 with twenty-six league goals. Apart from being a key member of the 1925 Third Division South Championship winning team, and F.A Cup semi-finalist the following season, he also played in three losing Welsh Cup semi-finals. His goal scoring prowess saw him score four goals against Brentford in November 1924, three against Blackpool in February 1926, three against Bury in an F.A. Cup tie in January 1927, and during season 1926/27 scored two goals in a game on eight occasions. His play against Arsenal in the quarter final of the 1925/26 FA Cup competition, where he outshone Charlie Buchan was eventually to lead him to Highbury when the 'Gunners' manager Herbert Chapman paid £4,000 for his signature on the 16th March 1928, after he had missed seven months of the 1927/28 season through a cartilage injury in his left knee. He did well during his early days with Arsenal, became the club's penalty taker, but after the arrival of Alex James struggled to command a regular place in the 'Gunners' starting line-up. During Arsenal's Championship success in 1931, Len made just two league appearances, the following season making one appearance when the 'Gunners' finished the term as runners-up to Everton. Despite failing to make the first team regularly, in three consecutive seasons he was a member of the reserve side that won the London Combination Championship from 1929 to 1931, and also in 1931 when they won the London FA Challenge Cup. His last season at Highbury saw him fail to make any league appearances, with the 'Gunners' winning the First Division Championship once again. During his period at Highbury Len made 160 reserve team appearances, scoring 86 goals, and in the London FA Challenge Cup competition scored four goals from ten appearances. He joined Crystal Palace in May 1933, remaining as a player for one season, making just two league appearances. He then retired from the game, but later applied for, and got his re-instatement as an amateur, joining Islington Corinthians in February 1935. He toured with them to Holland, and renewed an old friendship in Gerry Keizer, a one time amateur keeper with Arsenal. Later assisting Tottenham Hotspur as reserve team manager in February 1936, as well as running his own business interests, he also managed some scouting work for Arsenal on Saturdays when the necessity arose. A keen cricketer during the summer months with Swansea CC, and with Swansea based side Temple CC in season

1924, in May 1926 he had an offer from Clydach to be their cricket professional for the summer season.

18. THOMPSON, Maxwell (MAX) Stewart

Birthplace: Liverpool, 31/12/1956
Ht: 6ft-2½ins, **Wt:** 14st-0lbs
Swans debut: v. Notts. County (h), 12/9/1981

Season	League	FLC	FAC	WC	ECWC
1981/82	22+1/1gls	1	0+1	4	
1982/83	3/1gls	1			1+1
Total	25+1/2gls	2	0+1	4	1+1

Swansea City Career Statistics

Career:
Liverpool (from apprentice in January 1974) lge 1
Blackpool (loan in 31/12/1977)
Blackpool (£80,000 signed in 9/3/1978) lge 92+7/6gls
Swansea City (£20,000 signed in 27/8/1981)
Bournemouth (signed in August 1983) lge 9
Port Vale (loan in November 1983) lge 2
Baltimore Blast, USA (signed in February 1984)

Honours: Welsh Cup Winner–1982

During a season of spectacular results, let alone goals scored by Swans' players, season 1981/82 will be remembered not only for the club failing to leave the top six places of the First (Premiership) Division, but also for goals scored which were featured on BBC's television programme Match Of The Day throughout the year, and candidates for Goal of the Month. One such goal was Max Thompson's at the Vetch Field against Arsenal in early October 1981. Signed for £20,000 prior to the start of the season, Max was re-united with a number of his former Anfield colleagues at the Vetch Field four seasons after leaving Liverpool in search of first team football for Blackpool in a £80,000 transfer deal. Brought up in Liverpool he attended Highfield Comprehensive, and played for Liverpool schoolboys prior to signing as an apprentice with the 'Reds' at the age of fifteen and half years old. Playing mostly in the club's reserve team, he made his first team debut at the age of seventeen at White Hart Lane in the last game of the 1973/74 season, drawing 1-1. He failed to make any further appearances in the Liverpool first team, and was offered the opportunity to sign for Second (First) Division Blackpool on an initial loan basis, which was made permanent two and half months later for £80,000. For the next three seasons he made regular appearances in the Blackpool rearguard, either at full back, or in central defence, scoring his first league goal at Chester during the 1978/79 season. That season also saw him make appearances for Blackpool at the Vetch Field, and in the return league game at Bloomfield Road. The 1980/81 season saw him score five league

goals, but despite his success in front of goal, the club were relegated to the Fourth Division. A couple of months later, Toshack paid Blackpool just £20,000 to add Max to his first team squad, as the club geared up for their first season in top flight football, and also returning to European action for the first time since the mid-1960's. Commanding a regular place in the Swans' starting line-up throughout his first season at the Vetch Field, expectations were high going into the 1982/83 season, especially after the convincing results the Swans had achieved against the top clubs, not only at the Vetch Field, but also on their away travels. Also, at the end of the season, the club had retained the Welsh Cup, and booked their place in European football for another season, with Max making an appearance in the first leg of the final against Cardiff City. However, disappointing attendances were given as the main reason for the start of the club's financial problems, and shortly after mid way through their second term in the First Division, the club had not only resigned themselves to relegation, but were also offloading as many players as they could in order to satisfy the club's bankers. At the time of Max Thompson's transfer from Blackpool in August 1981, an agreement was reached between the two clubs that after 30 appearances for the Swans, Blackpool would receive a further £20,000 payment. The Swans were in no way able to pay the extra sell on clause, and after making 26 league, 2 FLC and 1 FAC appearances, were unable to include Max in their starting line-up on matchdays. Welsh Cup and European matches were obviously not included in the agreement as Max had already made six appearances in both competitions. With the Swans relegated to the Second Division, Max was released on a free transfer to Bournemouth in August 1983, and despite starting the new season in the first team, following a loan spell at Port Vale in November 1983, had his contract cancelled in February 1984, giving him the opportunity to take up a playing role in the USA with the Baltimore Blast NSL side. Spending two years in the USA, he had spells in Portugal and Sweden before returning to the UK, making Conference appearances for Newport County during the 1988/89 season before they folded, and then had a spell with North Wales side Caernarfon Town, who were managed at the time by his former Liverpool and Swans team mate Tommy Smith. Following a spell as a player with Southport, he went to Lilleshall on a Football Association injuries course, qualifying him to be a physiotherapist, and took up appointments at non-league Knowsley, and returning to Anfield for two years with the Reds. Joining Southport as Physio, he almost had the opportunity of returning to the Vetch Field when Jan Molby was player manager of the Swans, getting down to the short list of two for the appointment. During his days at Southport, he also acted as assistant manager for a short time, at a time when Swans player Lee Trundle was making his way up the non-league ladder. Leaving Southport, Max severed all connections with football, and is currently working as an ambulance driver.

19. THORNBER, Stephen (STEVE) John

Birthplace: Dewsbury, 11/10/1965
Ht: 5ft-9½ins, **Wt:** 11st-2lbs:
Swans debut: v. Gillingham (a), 27/8/1988

Swansea City Career Statistics

Season	League	FLC	FAC	WC	FRT/AGT	ECWC
1988/89	27+4	2/1gls	3	4/1gls	2	
1989/90	34/1gls		4	1	2	
1990/91	11+8	2	1+2/1gls	4/1gls	1+3	
1991/92	27+6/4gls	4/2gls	1	1+1	1	2
Total	99+18/5gls	8/3gls	9+2/1gls	10+1/2gls	6+3	2

Career:
Halifax Town (from juniors in January 1983) lge 94+10/4gls
Swansea City (£5,000 signed in 23/8/1988)
Blackpool (signed in August 1992) lge 21+3
Scunthorpe United (signed in July 1993) lge 71+6/7gls
Halifax Town (signed in February 1996) Conf 1
Bradford Park Avenue

Honours: Welsh Cup Winner–1989

Tireless midfielder Steve Thornber was a determined, and competitive player for the Swans, also impressing at left full back during his last season at the Vetch Field. Signed by manager Terry Yorath from Halifax Town for what was to be a tribunal fixed fee of £5,000, plus further money linked to appearances, the left sided midfielder possessed an enormous appetite for work, in defence, or in support of his strikers. Not noted for his goalscoring exploits, he did however score a league hat-trick in 10 minutes at the Hawthorns against WBA in January 1992, after coming on the field as substitute with the Swans 2-1 behind. His first season after leaving the Shay Ground saw Steve score at Ninian Park against Cardiff City in the First Leg, First Round of the Littlewoods Cup competition, and also in the Final of the Welsh Cup at the Vetch Field later in the season against non-league Kidderminster Harriers. Earlier in his career, Steve had been a junior with Halifax Town, making his league debut in February 1983 against Chester. At the end of the 1991/92 season he was given a free transfer by manager Frank Burrows, linking up with his former Halifax Town player manager Billy Ayre at Blackpool. After just the one season at Bloomfield Road, Steve joined Scunthorpe United in July 1993, but, following a series of back problems, was released at the end of the 1994/95 season after making 77 league appearances for the 'Iron'. Returning to the Shay to sign for Halifax Town, now in the Conference, he then signed for Bradford Park Avenue, also continuing his position as Youth Team coach with Halifax Town.

20. THORPE, LEE Anthony

Birthplace: Wolverhampton, 14/12/1975
Ht: 6ft-0ins, **Wt:** 11st-6lbs
Swans debut: v. Mansfield Town (a), 8/2/2005

Career:
Blackpool (from trainee in 18/7/1994) lge 2+10, FLC 0+1, FAC 1, Others 1
Lincoln City (signed in 4/8/1997) lge 183+/58gls, FLC 5+1/1gls, FAC 14/1gls, Others 9+1/7gls
Leyton Orient (signed in 3/5/2002) lge 42+13/12gls, FLC 2/1gls, FAC 1, Others 1+1
Grimsby Town (loan in 6/2/2004) lge 5+1
Bristol Rovers (signed in 12/3/2004) lge 25+10/4gls, FLC 1/1gls, FAC 0+1, Others 4/1gls
Swansea City (loan in 8/2/2005, signed in 9/2/2005)

Swansea City Career Statistics		
Season	League	FAWC
2004/05	9+6/3gls	1+1
Total	9+6/3gls	1+1

Honours: FAW Cup Winner–2005

Former trainee with Blackpool who made his league debut while still a trainee in the last game of the 1993/94 season as substitute for Dave Bamber in a 4-1 win over Leyton Orient at Bloomfield Road. Three seasons as a professional with Blackpool saw him make just two starts, and fail to get his name on the goalsheet, but after dropping down a division to join Lincoln City in August 1997, he not only finished the season as top goalscorer with fourteen league goals, but also gained promotion to the Second Division by finishing in third position. Despite relegation twelve months later, in three out of the next four seasons with Lincoln City he finished top goalscorer. A strong, pacy, aggressive frontrunner, in May 2002 he signed for Leyton Orient on a free transfer, again finishing top goalscorer at the end of his first season at Brisbane Road. Injury problems during his second season with Orient saw him have a loan spell with Grimsby Town, but within a couple of days of his returning to Brisbane Road he signed on a free transfer for Bristol Rovers shortly before transfer deadline day. He opened his goalscoring account for Rovers in the last home game of the season against his old club Lincoln City, but during the 2004/05 campaign saw his opportunities limited, with most of his appearances from the substitute bench. In early February 2005 he joined the Swans on a loan transfer to enable him to play the same night at Mansfield Town, later signing an 18 month contract at the Vetch Field. He scored his first goal for the Swans in his second game at Leyton Orient, and by the end of the season had played a significant part in the Swans' claiming one of the automatic promotion places from Coca Cola League Two. Lee also made an appearance as a substitute in the FAW Cup Final win over Wrexham.

21. TODD, Christopher (CHRIS)

Birthplace: Swansea, 22/8/1981
Ht: 6ft-0ins, **Wt:** 11st-4lbs
Swans debut: v. Northampton Town (a), 27/2/2001

Career:
Swansea City (from trainee in 6/7/2000)
Drogheda United (signed in August 2002)
Exeter City (signed in 31/1/2003) lge 12, Conf 53+1/2gls

Honours: Wales Semi-Professional International, Devon St. Luke's Bowl Winner–2005

Swansea City Career Statistics

Season	League	FLC	FAC	AWS	FAWP
1999/2000					1+2
2000/01	11/1gls				8
2001/02	28+4/3gls	1	1	1	2
Total	39+4/4gls	1	1	1	11+2

Swansea Town Career Statistics

Season	League	FLC	FAC	WC	ECWC
1960/61	6/4gls				
1961/62	2				
1962/63	26/12gls		2	3/2gls	
1963/64	25/7gls	1/1gls	4/3gls	1	
1964/65	34/20gls	4/3gls	4	3/1gls	
1965/66	42/16gls	1/1gls	1/1gls	8/3gls	
1966/67	29+1/9gls	3/1gls	3	1	2/1gls
1967/68	32+1/10gls		4/1gls	2/2gls	
Total	196+2/78gls	9/6gls	18/5gls	18/8gls	2/1gls

Former Swansea schoolboy defender who joined the Swans as a trainee from school, made his debut in the first team in the invitation Welsh Premier Cup competition at the Vetch Field against Inter Cardiff, as a substitute for Jason Smith, making his league debut in February 2001 at Northampton Town in the Second Division. Possessing a lot of pace, he was capable of playing in any defensive position, and during the club's brief flirtation in the Second Division was the only bright spot in a gloomy season. Season 2000/01 saw him gain numerous 'Man of the Match' awards, also netting his first league goal against Brentford at the Vetch Field. During the 2001 close season he spent some time in a coaching camp in the USA, and from the start of the 2001/02 season became a regular inclusion in the Swans first team. Despite managerial changes, and off the field problems at the club, Chris continued to gain experience in the hustle and bustle of lower order football, creating a name for himself at set pieces, scoring three goals from two games during one spell in the season. Surprisingly released by new manager Nick Cusack at the end of the season, despite trials with other league clubs he joined Irish side Drogheda United, and in the January transfer 'window' returned to the Football League to sign for Third Division Exeter City, although there was a possibility that he would rejoin the Swans, keeping himself fit by training at the Vetch Field. During the remainder of the season he became a popular figure in the 'Grecians' rearguard, especially in the relegation end of season battle at the Vetch Field against his former club. Season 2003/04 saw Chris play a major part in the club's battle to get promotion from the Conference at the first attempt, failing to make the Play Offs in the last week of the season. In late May 2004 he was included in the Wales Semi-Professional squad that won the Four Nations Trophy in Scotland, and in the last game against Ireland scored Wales's second goal, playing in an unfamiliar midfield position. Twelve months later he was again included in the Welsh squad that defended their title in Ireland. In May 2005 he skippered the Exeter City side that defeated Plymouth Argyle 2-0 to win the Devon St. Luke's Bowl, also scoring one of the goals.

22. TODD, KEITH Harris

Birthplace: Clydach, Swansea, 2/3/1941
Ht: 5ft-7ins, **Wt:** 11st-3½lbs
Swans debut: v. Derby County (h), 8/10/1960

Career:
Clydach United
Swansea Town (signed in 2/9/1959)
Pembroke Borough (signed in August 1968)

Honours: Wales U-23-1, Welsh Cup Winner–1966, Football Combination Second Division Champions–1961, Welsh League First Division Champions–1962, West Wales Senior Cup Winner–1965

Local product who combined his football with Welsh League side Clydach United and being a fitter and turner apprentice at INCO prior to signing for the Swans in early September 1959. The former Clydach Junior school and Ystalyfera Grammar schoolboy initially started his playing career with Clydach Boys Club prior to being elevated to the Welsh League with his local club, and was initially limited to training in the evenings after signing for the Swans. He signed full time professional after the completion of his apprenticeship, developed rapidly, and soon made his mark as a prolific goalscorer in the club's reserve side, and then in the Football League. By the end of season 1960/61 he had made regular appearances in the reserve side that won the Combination Second Division Championship, and twelve months later played regularly for the reserve side that won the Welsh League First Division Championship. Replacing Brayley Reynolds, he scored on his league debut for the Swans at the Vetch Field against Derby County in the Second Division, scoring a second goal in his next league game, and a further two goals at the end of the season. The 1962/63 season saw Keith score his first league hat-trick, against Walsall in November 1962, finishing the season second top goalscorer in the league with twelve goals, three behind Eddie Thomas. He would go on to score two more hat-tricks for the Swans, against Swindon Town in December 1963, and against Manchester City in September 1964. Capped at U-23 level for Wales against Northern Ireland at the Vetch Field, and was also a reserve for the Full Welsh team for an international in Russia during his career. Despite his small stature, his sharpness, pace and fearless play in the penalty area became a feature of his game. A member of the Swans side that lost in the semi-final of the 1963/64 FA Cup competition against Preston North End, he also played in the 1966 Welsh Cup Final replay victory over Chester, which was to see the club play the following season in the European Cup Winners Cup against Slavia Sofia, with 'Toddy' scoring for the Swans. In May 1965 he was included in the Swans side that beat Llanelli to win the West Wales Senior Cup. Released in May 1968, despite offers to stay in the League with Luton Town, 'Toddy' signed for Welsh League side Pembroke Borough, remaining at the West Wales club for seven seasons before retiring. He returned to his trade after leaving the Vetch Field, gaining promotion to a Draughtsman, and finally an Engineer prior to his retirement.

23. TONES, John DAVID

Birthplace: Silkworth, Sunderland, 3/12/1950
Ht: 6ft-2ins, **Wt:** 13st-0lbs
Swans debut: v. Workington (a), 18/9/1974

Swansea City Career Statistics	
Season	League
1974/75	7
Total	7

Career:
Sunderland (from apprentice, professional in May 1968) lge 2+4, FAC 2, Others 1+1/1gls
Arsenal (signed in 22/5/1973) lge 0
Swansea City (loan in 17/9/1974)
Mansfield Town (loan in 18/10/1974) lge 3
Gateshead (signed in season 1974/75)

Former Sunderland Schoolboy defender who became an apprentice at Roker Park, and who was signed by manager Harry Gregg on a month loan from Arsenal in mid-September 1974. Replacing the experienced Herbie Williams at centre half, he made seven consecutive league appearances before returning to Highbury. His last league game for the Swans came against Mansfield Town, and within twenty-four hours of his returning to London, he joined the 'Stags' on a month loan. He made his first team debut for Sunderland in an Anglo Italian Cup tie against Lazio on the 17th May 1970, scoring on his debut. In the first league game of the 1972/73 season he made his league debut for Sunderland in the Second Division as substitute for Jim Hamilton at Middlesbrough. Following three consecutive substitute appearances, he finally made his first start for Sunderland at Roker Park against Preston North End. Making one further start for Sunderland, at the end of the season he was released, joining Arsenal. Following his three loan appearances for Mansfield Town, he returned to Highbury, having his contract cancelled in December 1974 returning back to his native north east to join non-league side Gateshead. A regular in the 'Gunners' Football Combination side, making thirty-three appearances, scoring one goal, and in the London FA Challenge Cup Combination made two appearances, scoring one goal.

24. TORPEY, Stephen (STEVE)

Birthplace: Islington, 8/1/1970
Ht: 6ft-3ins, **Wt:** 14st-10lbs
Swans debut: v. York City (a), 14/8/1993

Career:
Millwall (from trainee in 14/2/1989) lge 3+4, FLC 0+1
Bradford City (£80,000 signed in 21/11/1990) lge 86+10/22gls, FLC 6, FAC 2+1, Others 8/6gls
Swansea City (£80,000 signed in 6/8/1993)

Bristol City (£400,000 signed in 8/8/1997) lge 53+17/13gls, FLC 4+1/1gls, FAC 3, Others 3+1
Notts. County (loan in 7/8/1998) lge 4+2/1gls, FLC 1+1/1gls
Scunthorpe United (£175,000 signed in 3/2/2000) lge 193+6/59gls, FLC 5/2gls, FAC 18/7gls, Others 9+2/5gls

Swansea City Career Statistics						
Season	League	FLC	FAC	AGT/AWS	WC	P/Offs
1993/94	36+4/9gls	3+1/1gls	2/2gls	6+1/1gls	4+1	
1994/95	37+4/11gls	3	5/2gls	2+1/2gls	3/1gls	
1995/96	41+1/15gls	2/1gls	1	3/1gls		
1996/97	37+2/9gls	1+1	2/1gls	2		3/1gls
Total	151+11/44gls	9+2/2gls	10/5gls	13+2/4gls	7+1/1gls	3/1gls

Honours: AutoGlass Trophy Winner–1994

Vastly under rated striker during his days with the Swans, excellent target man, strong in aerial challenges, capable of holding the ball up well, and a constant threat to opposing defenders in the danger zone. The former Clopasco U-10's and Bedford Park Schoolboy joined Millwall as a trainee, making his First Division debut as a substitute for Steve Anthrobus at Wimbledon on the 29th August 1989. Later in the season he made his first start for Millwall against Aston Villa, playing in the next two league games. Joining Bradford City in November 1990, he scored his first league goal in his 4th game for the club against Shrewsbury Town. The 1991/92 season saw him finish as the club's second highest goalscorer, behind former Swans target man Sean McCarthy. Signed by manager Frank Burrows in August 1993 for £80,000, he provided the perfect foil during his first season for Jason Bowen and Colin Pascoe, also going on as a substitute at Wembley when the Swans beat Huddersfield Town on penalties to win the AutoGlass Trophy in April 1994. His next two seasons at the Vetch Field saw him finish as top goalscorer on each occasion, despite enduring a relegation season of 1995/96 which saw the club lose its Second Division status. Despite the brave promptings of Jan Molby's side in reaching the Third Division Play Off Final, and a takeover of the club imminent off the field, Steve joined Bristol City the day before the new season of 1997/98 started, for a club record £400,000 transfer fee. Finishing his first season at Ashton Gate with eight league goals, and the club finishing as runners-up in the Second Division to Watford, following a loan a spell at Notts. County, in February 2000 he joined Scunthorpe United for a club record fee of £200,000. Since arriving at Glanford Park, Steve has consistently been in double figures for goals scored, and played a major part in the club's attempt to gain promotion from the 2003 Third Division Play Offs. During season 2004/05 he scored against the Swans after just one minute, the only goal of the game, and by May 2005 the 'Iron' had finished the season in runners-up place on goal difference ahead of the Swans.

25. TOSHACK, JOHN Benjamin M.B.E.

Birthplace: Cardiff, 22/3/1949
Ht: 6ft-0ins, **Wt:** 11st-7lbs
Swans debut: v. Watford (h), 3/3/1978

Swansea City Career Statistics					
Season	League	FLC	FAC	WC	ECWC
1977/78	13/6gls				
1978/79	24+4/13gls	4/1gls	3/1gls		
1979/80	15+1/5gls	3/1gls	5/4gls	2/3gls	
1980/81	3	1+1		1/1gls	
1981/82					
1982/83					0+1/1gls
1983/84	3/1gls		1	2/1gls	
Total	58+5/25gls	8+1/2gls	9/5gls	5/5gls	0+1/1gls

Career:
Cardiff City (apprentice in June 1965, professional in March
   1966) lge 159+3/75gls, ECWC 20/11gls
Liverpool (£110,000 signed in November 1970) lge 169+3/74gls
Swansea City (signed in 27/2/1978)

Honours: Wales Sch, Yth, U-23–3, Full–40, Welsh Cup
Winner–1968, 1969, UEFA Cup Winner–1973, 1976, First Division
Champions–1973, 1976, 1977, FA Cup Winner–1974

A former Cardiff and Wales schoolboy international who
became the club's youngest player to make an appearance in the
Football League when he made his debut against Leyton Orient
in November 1965 at the age of 16 years and 236 days.
He attended Radyr Junior School and Canton High School,
played rugby for his High School side, as well as football for
junior side Pegasus in Cardiff prior to joining the 'Bluebirds' as
an apprentice in June 1965. His goalscoring prowess from an
early age with the 'Bluebirds' gave many of their supporters the
hope at the time that the club would regain their place in the
First Division, but following his £110,000 transfer to Liverpool in
November 1970, their promotion hopes disappeared. Gaining
his first U-23 cap for Wales at Ninian Park with the 'Bluebirds',
'Tosh' also made his first senior appearance for Wales whilst still
a player with the 'Bluebirds', against West Germany in March
1969 at Ninian Park. In the next international against West
Germany he scored his first goal at this level for Wales. With the
'Bluebirds' a strong Second Division outfit during this period,
he also played in two successful Welsh Cup Finals for the club
in 1968 and 1969, gaining European experience from matches
played in the resultant qualification for the European Cup
Winners Cup with City, also playing in the 'Bluebirds' side that
lost to Hamburg in the 1967/68 European Cup Winners Cup
semi-final. Following his transfer to Anfield, he took some time
to establish himself at Liverpool, the tall striker eventually
forging a tremendous understanding with Kevin Keegan, a
double act that would outclass the legendary Hunt and St. John
partnership earlier at Anfield. The 'Little and Large' strike force
soon blossomed with an uncanny telepathic understanding,
scoring and creating goals for each other. Toshack was unlucky
with injuries during his time at Anfield, not serious enough to
keep him sidelines for long periods, but usually niggling ones
which prevented him from playing on a more regular basis.
After near-misses in 1971 & 1972 in the F.A. Cup and First
Division Championship, 'Tosh' ended season 1973 as top
goalscorer with thirteen league goals, with the club winning the
First Division Championship, and the UEFA Cup. Winning the
FA Cup the following season, beating Newcastle United in the
Final at Wembley, season 1974/75 saw the club runners-up in
the league for the second successive season. However the
1975/76 season saw 'Tosh' again top the goalscorers charts with
sixteen league goals, a second First Championship medal, plus a
second UEFA Cup winning medal. That season was Toshack's
most productive, and injury-free season on Merseyside. He only
missed 7 League matches, played in 50 competitive matches for
the club in four different competitions. He passed 20 goals in a
season for the only time as a Liverpool player, including a hat-
trick of headers against Hibernian in the UEFA cup and also the
goal which brought a famous win in Spain against Barcelona in
the first leg of the semi-final. Injury prevented him from making
a greater impact in season 1976/77, only able to watch his side
win the European Cup. However, after just four appearances for
Liverpool early in the 1977/78 season, he was given the
opportunity to go into management at the Vetch Field, and after
watching a particularly poor performance by the Swans in a 2-1
defeat at Rochdale in late February 1978, took up the challenge
of managing the Swans, putting almost 10,000 fans on the gate
for his debut game at the Vetch Field on the 3rd March 1978
against Watford, scoring on his debut in an exciting 3-3 draw.
Scoring six goals for the Swans, promotion was secured at the
end of the season, and following the recruitment of former
team-mates Tommy Smith and Ian Callaghan in the close
season, a second successive promotion was obtained by the
Swans, reaching the Second Division for the first time since
1965. Beginning to create a name for himself as an astute, and
deep thinking tactician on and off the field, his playing career
once the Swans had reached the Second Division lessened,
despite taking the opportunity on numerous occasions as a
sweeper, in the Swans rearguard. However, his finest hour as a
manager came at Deepdale on the 2nd May 1981, following
goals from Leighton James, Tommy Craig and Jeremy Charles,
the Swans gained promotion to the top flight of football, the
First Division. 1981 would also see him claim the first of three
consecutive Welsh Cup Final winning sides, this time though as
a manager. A remarkably successful debut in the First Division
in which the Swans failed to drop out of the top six positions all
season, even leading the table on a number of occasions saw
'Tosh' then confronted with financial problems off the field
which would ultimately see the club drop through the leagues
almost as quickly as the club had risen from the Fourth Division.
Resigning his position as manager of the Swans on the 29th
October 1983, he later returned to his position on the 22nd
December 1983, scoring in his first game back with the Swans in
a 3-2 defeat at Ninian Park against Cardiff City. However, off the
field financial problems continued to mount, and on the field,
with a transfer embargo placed on the club, limiting the signing
of players, relegation to the Third Division became more and
more of a reality. 'Tosh' was sacked by chairman Doug Sharpe
on the 5th March 1984 over reputedly bad results, and despite
the overtures of vice chairman Malcolm Struel, 'Tosh' walked
away from the Vetch Field for the last time, bringing a close to a
truly historic period in the club's history, which is unlikely to
happen again. His remarkable period as player manager of the
Swans was too see him receive no shortage of offers after
leaving the Vetch Field, and within months he had taken over as
coach with Sporting Lisbon (May 1984 to 1985), and the
following year started the first of three periods with Spanish
side Real Sociedad, where he won the Spanish Cup in 1987, and
runners-up in the Spanish League the year after. Appointed

coach at Real Madrid in May 1989, winning the league championship in his first season, in January 1994 he was appointed the Welsh National Coach, but resigned after just the one game, a 3-1 defeat by Norway. Joining Spanish side Deportivo Coruna in March 1995, he was then involved with Turkish side Besiktas before returning to Real Madrid for a second time as coach in 1999. Further coaching appointments with French side St. Etienne, saw him then take on the manager position with Italian Serie B side Catania, only to resign his post in late January 2004. On the 12th November 2004 he was appointed manager of the Wales International side. In May 2005 he joined the Welsh Sports Hall of Fame Elite Roll of Honour.

26. TREVITT, SIMON

Birthplace: Dewsbury, 20/12/1967
Ht: 5ft-11ins, **Wt:** 12st-9lbs
Swans debut: v. Rochdale (a), 13/12/1997

Swansea City Career Statistics	
Season	League
1997/98	1
Total	1

Career:
Huddersfield Town (from trainee in June 1986) lge 216+13/3gls
Hull City (signed in 24/11/1995) lge 50+1/1gls
Swansea City (loan in 8/12/1997)
Guiseley (signed in July 1998)
Ossett Albion (loan in November 1999)

Honours: Second Division Play Off Winner–1995

A former YTS trainee with Huddersfield Town, he made his league debut at Leeds Road against Derby County on the 4th October 1986 at right full back as a replacement for Malcolm Brown. Playing in the next four league games, he had to wait almost until the end of the season before increasing his tally of first team appearances for the club, and despite relegation at the end of season 1987/88, Simon had consolidated his position at right full back for the 'Terriers'. The next four seasons would see him feature consistently in the Town first team at full back, also playing in a losing Second Division Play Off semi-final against Peterborough United. He missed the Wembley AutoGlass Trophy Final in 1994 through injury, but the following season played in the Town side that beat Bristol Rovers at Wembley to gain promotion via the Play Off Final. He was allowed to join Hull City during his benefit season on an initial loan basis on the 24th November 1995, and by the end of December he had made his transfer permanent with no fee involved. At the end of the season however, along with the Swans, both clubs suffered relegation to the Third Division. In early December 1997 he was signed by manager Alan Cork on a loan transfer, making his Swans debut at Rochdale, replacing Jason Price at right full back. Unfortunately for him he returned to Hull City on the 18th December after suffering a freak training injury which saw him twist his ankle after stepping into a pothole training on sand dunes, and also pulling a hamstring at Morfa Stadium two days later. He did not feature for the 'Tigers' after returning to Boothferry Park, and at the end of the season was released, joining non-league side Guiseley, where he combined playing with helping manager Bobby Davison. He failed to make any appearances in the 2003/04 season after undergoing an operation, but during the summer of 2004 was playing local cricket with his day job as a postman.

27. TRICK, Desmond (DES)

Birthplace: Swansea, 7/11/1969
Ht: 6ft-0ins, **Wt:** 12st-7lbs
Swans debut: v. Torquay United (h), FRT Prelim, 29/11/1988

Swansea City Career Statistics						
Season	League	FLC	FAC	WC	FRT/LDAF	ECWC
1988/89				0+1	1	
1989/90	11+3	0+1	3		2/1gls	
1990/91	14+1	1		2	2	
1991/92						0+1
Total	25+4	1+1	3	2+1	5/1gls	0+1

Career:
Swansea City (signed from trainee in July 1988)
Merthyr Tydfil (signed in July 1992) Conf 24+2
Haverfordwest (signed in close season 1993)

Honours: Welsh Cup Winner–1991, Macbar Cup Winner–1987, West Wales Senior Cup Winner–1988, 1990

Former Cefn Hengoed schoolboy who graduated through the Swansea schoolboys sides and signed for the Swans as a YTS on leaving school. In May 1987, whilst still a trainee, he was included in the Swans reserve side that beat Plymouth Argyle to win the Macbar Cup at the Vetch Field. Given his first team debut by manager Terry Yorath in a Freight Rover Preliminary game at the Vetch Field against Torquay United, he made a substitute appearance in a Welsh Cup tie later in the season against Caersws, making his league debut on the 23rd September 1989 as substitute for Andrew Melville in a 6-1 Vetch Field defeat by Reading. Season 1989/90 saw him play in both FA Cup ties against Liverpool, although the replay saw the Swans concede eight goals at Anfield. Des was to feature in another eight goal hammering two seasons later in Monaco. He was included in the Swans side that beat Pembroke Borough in May 1988 to win the West Wales Senior Cup Final, and also two years later when the Swans beat Llanelli in the final of the same competition. In mid-May 1991 he made the Swans line-up for the Welsh Cup Final defeat of Wrexham at the National Stadium in Cardiff. Struggling to get a consistent run of games in the Swans first team line-up, despite some impressive performances at reserve team level, being strong in aerial challenges, he did appear to lack that yard of pace for league football. Season 1991/92 saw him suffer cartilage and hamstring problems which saw him struggle to make an impact in the Swans first team, with his only first team appearance coming in a European Cup Winners Cup tie in Monaco, when he came on as substitute to replace Mark Harris. Released at the end of the season he signed for Conference side Merthyr Tydfil, staying one season at Penydarren Park, before joining League of Wales side Haverfordwest. During this period he joined the Police Force and is currently a Detective Constable in the CAT team based at Cockett Police Station, Swansea.

28. TRUNDLE, LEE

Birthplace: Liverpool, 10/10/1976
Ht: 6ft-0ins, **Wt:** 13st-3lbs
Swans debut: v. Bury (h), 9/8/2003

Swansea City Career Statistics

Season	League	FLC	FAC	LDV	FAWC
2003/04	29+2/16gls	1	5/5gls	0+1	1
2004/05	41+1/22gls	1	5/1gls	1	1
Total	70+3/38gls	2	10/6gls	1+1	2

Career:
Burscough (signed in September 1995)
Chorley (£7,000 signed in October 1995)
Stalybridge Celtic (signed in 1/8/1997)
Southport (signed in 26/12/1998)
Bamber Bridge (loan)
Rhyl (£10,000 signed in 19/7/2001)
Wrexham (£60,000 signed in 16/2/2001) lge 73+21/27gls, FLC 0+2, FAC 1, Others 4+1/3gls
Swansea City (signed in 8/7/2003)
Honours: FAW Cup Winner–2005, PFA XI–2004, 2005

Exciting front runner signed on a free from Wrexham in early July 2003, who did not take long to charm the Swans fans with his skill on the ball, and goalscoring ability. Within two months of his arrival at the Vetch Field, he had signed an extension to his contract with the Swans, sitting proudly on top of the goalscoring charts in the Third Division. Despite scoring eleven league goals the previous season in Wrexham's promotion from the Third Division, he had declined the offer a new contract at the Racecourse, preferring to sign for Brian Flynn, the manager who had plucked him from non-league football with Rhyl in February 2001. Possessing the ability to take on the opposition, despite accusations of 'showboating' by one or two managers in the game, he also possesses a good strike rate, and the ability to play his team mates into goalscoring positions. Scoring on his Swans debut at the Vetch Field against Bury in the opening fixture of the 2003/04 season, he then scored a hat-trick in the following league game at Cheltenham Town, scoring another goal in the next league game at the Vetch Field against Boston United. Lee received numerous Third Division Awards in the first half of the season, including the in-augral Umbro Isotonic award for his performances in the month of August, with his performances later in the season bringing him to the attention of the public nationwide following the Swans exciting FA Cup run which took them to the fifth round. He joined his first professional side, Burscough, of the Unibond League, in September 1995 from Liverpool amateur side St Dominics, who sold him six weeks later to Chorley for £7,000. From there he moved on to Stalybridge Celtic and Southport with a short loan spell at Bamber Bridge, before signing for Rhyl. Beginning the 2000/01 season with Rhyl in the League of Wales, following a hat-trick scored against Wrexham in a New Year friendly game, he was signed by Flynn for £60,000 in February 2001, becoming an overnight sensation, netting with a spectacular overhead kick at Walsall, and then hitting a hat-trick in a 5-3 over Oxford United, totalling eight goals in his first eleven games for Wrexham. During his first season at the Vetch Field he missed a number of matches through a knee ligament injury, a cheek fracture, and from suspension after receiving a red card at York, and from bookings incurred through the season. In April 2004, and in 2005 he was voted by his fellow professionals into the PFA Third Division and Second Division Team of the season. He continued his exciting, goalscoring form during his second season at the Vetch Field, again picking up numerous monthly awards, and became the first Swans' player since Bob Latchford in the 1982/83 season to score twenty league goals in a season, also playing in the FAW Cup Final win over his former team, Wrexham. In May 2005 a supporters poll for Powerade voted him Player of the Year for Coca Cola League Two.

29. TURNBULL, Ronald (RON) William

Birthplace: Newbiggin, 18/7/1922. **Died:** Sunderland, 17/11/1966
Ht: 5ft-11ins, **Wt:** 12st-0lbs
Swans debut: v. Doncaster Rovers (a), 27/1/1951

Swansea Town Career Statistics

Season	League	FAC	WC
1950/51	15/9gls		1/1gls
1951/52	40/22gls	3	1
1952/53	12/6gls	1	2
Total	67/37gls	4	4/1gls

Career:
RAF Football
Dundee (signed in 1944)
Sunderland (£10,000 signed in November 1947) lge 40/16gls
Manchester City (signed in September 1949) lge 30/5gls
Swansea Town (£7,500 signed in 25/1/1951)
Dundee (£1,500 signed in 16/3/1953)
Ashington (signed in August 1954)

Honours: Scottish League Division 'B' Champions–1947, Welsh League Representative XI

Signed by manager Billy McCandless in January 1951 for £7,500 from Second Division side Manchester City, he scored his first goal for the Swans in his second league game, and by the end of the season, after making just fifteen league appearances had topped the Swans goalscoring chart for the season with nine league goals. His goalscoring ability was noticed whilst playing in the RAF, and after making guest appearances for Dundee during WW2, and appearances in junior football, he started his professional career with the Scottish club, and by the end of the 1946/47 season, Dundee had scored over one hundred goals to win the Scottish League 'B' Division Championship.

In November 1947 he signed for First Division side Sunderland, joining fellow First Division outfit Manchester City almost two years later. During his first season at Maine Road the club suffered relegation to the Second Division, and shortly after signing for the Swans, scored two goals in a game in consecutive matches, including two against his old club Manchester City. In his first full season at the Vetch Field Turnbull finished top goalscorer for the season, with twenty-two league goals, including hat-tricks against Blackburn Rovers in September 1951, and against Rotherham United in December 1951. In May 1951 he played for a Welsh League Representative side at the Vetch Field against their Irish League counterparts. Missing a number of games during season 1952/3, and with the emergence of Terry Medwin, who was utilised at centre forward on many occasions, in March 1953 he returned to Scotland to join Dundee for £1,500, the club he started his professional career. Joining non-league side Ashington in August 1954, in November 1966 he died of a heart attack in Sunderland.

30. TURNER, Charles (CHARLIE) John

Birthplace: Newport, 1/7/1919. **Died:** Griffithstown, 15/4/1999
Ht: 6ft-0ins, **Wt:** 12st-0lbs
Swans debut: v. Reading (a), 25/12/1948

Swansea Town Career Statistics	
Season	League
1948/49	2
Total	2

Career:
Dewstonians
Ebbw Junction
Newport County (amateur signed in May 1938) lge 37
Swansea Town (signed in August 1948)
Yeovil Town (signed in season 1949/50) Total apps 38

Signed by manager Billy McCandless in August 1948 for the second time, after previously being signed by McCandless in May 1939 whilst he was in charge at Newport County.
He impressed when playing in the public trial matches at the Vetch Field in August 1948, and his earlier playing career had been with Dewstonians and Ebbw Junction. During County's Third Division South Championship winning season of 1938/39 Charlie made just the one league appearance, making most of his County appearances when the Football League was resumed following the end of the war in the Second Division, and in the Third Division South. In 1940 he had been captured at Boulogne, and was four years a P.O.W. Competing with Jack Parry for the goalkeeper's jersey at the start of the 1948/49 season at the Vetch Field, Turner made just one more appearance after making his league debut for the Swans at Reading, playing in the return game against the same opponents two days later at the Vetch Field. Within a couple of weeks however, Danny Canning was signed from Cardiff City, and became the Swans first choice keeper for the remainder of the season. Charlie was released at the end of the season joining non-league Yeovil. He struggled to make an impression in his first season, making just three appearances, but during the 1950/51 season made thirty-five league and cup appearances for Yeovil.

31. TURNER, ROBIN David

Birthplace: Carlisle, 10/9/1955
Ht: 5ft-10ins, **Wt:** 11st-2lbs
Swans debut: v. Preston North End (h), 30/3/1985

Swansea City Career Statistics			
Season	League	FLC	FRT
1984/85	11/5gls		2
1985/86	9/3gls	3	
Total	20/8gls	3	2

Career:
Ipswich Town (from apprentice in April 1973) lge 22+26/2gls
Beerschot, Belgium
Swansea City (signed in 28/3/1985)
Colchester United (signed in November 1985) lge 6+5

Honours: England Yth, EUFA Cup–1981

Former apprentice at Portman Road with Ipswich Town who was one of a number of experienced professionals recruited by manager John Bond two thirds the way through the 1984/85 season in a bid to steer the club away from the Third Division relegation zone. Earlier in his career, the former Harraby Secondary Schoolboy also made appearances for junior side Christus Rex prior to arriving at Portman Road after leaving school. He made his debut for Ipswich Town as substitute for Roger Osborne at Derby in October 1975, making his first start in September 1976 at Portman Road against Leicester City. Making regular appearances for Ipswich Town, he had to wait until September 1983 before he scored his first goal for the club, against Everton. However, his first goals for Town came during the club's successful FA Cup run during season 1977/78, when he scored two goals in a 2-2 draw with Bristol Rovers. He failed to make the line-up for the final at Wembley, but did play from the fourth round up to the semi-final against West Bromwich Albion. He was also a member of the Ipswich Town squad that beat AZ67 Alkmaar in 1981 to win the EUFA Cup competition over two legs, although he was not called from the substitute's bench. After he was released by Ipswich Town, he spent a couple of months in Belgium with Beerschot prior to arriving at the Vetch Field in late March 1985. Scoring two goals on his debut for the Swans, in a 4-1 home win over Preston North End, he scored a further three goals for the Swans as they successfully escaped from the relegation zone, but the following season, after a return of three league goals, which included two at Wolverhampton Wanderers in September 1985, he had his contract cancelled at the Vetch Field after failing to settle in the city, joining Fourth Division side Colchester United, initially on loan in early November 1985. Making all his appearances for Colchester United during season 1985/86, the following season he had his contract cancelled, and drifted out of the game.

Since leaving football, he has been involved with teaching sport in a Secondary School on the West Coast of Ireland.

32. TYNAN, Thomas (TOMMY) Edward

Birthplace: Liverpool, 17/11/1955
Ht: 5ft-8ins, **Wt:** 10st-7lbs
Swans debut: v. Doncaster Rovers (a), 18/10/1975

Swansea City Career Statistics	
Season	League
1975/76	6/2gls
Total	6/2gls

Career:
Liverpool (apprentice in 1971, professional in 1/11/1972) lge 0
Swansea City (loan in 17/10/1975)
Dallas Tornado (signed in close season 1976)
Sheffield Wednesday (£10,000 signed in 10/9/1976) lge 89+2/31gls
Lincoln City (£33,000 signed in 6/10/1978) lge 9/1gls
Newport Count (£25,000 signed in 23/2/1979) lge 168+15/66gls, ECWC 5/4gls
Plymouth Argyle (£55,000 signed in 8/8/1983) lge 80/43gls
Rotherham United (£30,000 signed in 31/7/1985) lge 32/13gls
Plymouth Argyle (loan in 1/4/1986) lge 9/10gls
Plymouth Argyle (£25,000 signed in 5/9/1986) lge 172+1/73gls
Torquay United (signed in 30/5/1990) lge 34+1/13gls
Doncaster Rovers (signed in 4/7/1991) lge 5+6/1gls
Goole Town (player manager in season 1991/92)

Honours: Welsh Cup Winner–1980

Loan signing from Liverpool by manager Harry Griffiths, scoring on his debut for the Swans at Doncaster Rovers twenty-four hours later. Born in Scotland Road, Liverpol, Tommy attended St. Margaret Mary's School in Dovecote, Liverpool earlier in his career, played for all the school sides from the age of nine to fifteen, but did not make any appearances for Liverpool Schoolboys. Spotted playing in a five a side competition organised by the local newspaper, after leaving school Tommy did a one year apprenticeship at Anfield, became a consistent goalscorer in the Liverpool reserve team, signed as a professional on his seventeenth birthday, but had yet to make his league debut for the club prior to joining the Swans. In the previous season to joining the Swans he had scored 40 league and cup goals for the Central League or 'A' teams at Anfield. Replacing Andy Leitch for his Swans debut, Tynan, in his six league games for the Swans, scored his second goal two games later, at the Vetch Field in a 3-1 win over Bradford City. He returned to Anfield after his loan transfer, with the Swans

not in a position to afford to make the transfer permanent. Shortly after the start of the 1976/77 season, Tynan signed for Third Division side Sheffield Wednesday, embarking on a career in the professional game which would see him become one of the most feared goalscorers in the lower leagues. Throughout his playing career he would end each season as one of his club's top goalscorers, and when he returned to South Wales to sign for Newport County in February 1979, also featured in European action for the club, following their Welsh Cup Final success the previous season. During season 1979/80 he forged a formidable goalscoring partnership at Somerton Park with John Aldridge, with the club gaining promotion, and also beating Shrewsbury Town in the Welsh Cup Final. Qualifying for the European Cup Winners Cup competition, County narrowly lost out to Carl Zeiss Jena in the quarter final, with Tynan scoring four goals in the competition. After failing by four points to gain promotion to the Second Division with County in 1983, and scoring twenty-five league goals, Tynan was transferred to Plymouth Argyle in August 1983 for £55,000, and in his first season ended up top goalscorer, and also played in the side that narrowly lost out to Watford in the semi-final of the FA Cup competition, losing 1-0 at Villa Park. Top goalscorer during each of his next seven seasons, which included a spell at Millmor with Rotherham United before returning to Home Park with Argyle, Tynan signed for Torquay United in May 1990, but missed out on the end of season Play Off success against Blackpool. Finishing his league career at Doncaster Rovers, midway through the 1991/92 season he left to take over at Goole Town as player manager. After making a handful of appearances for the non-league outfit, he left the club to go into Pub Management in the Sheffield area. Returning to Devon after a couple of years, he has since managed his own public houses in Plymouth, and is currently working for Ocean View Spanish Apartments, who have hospitality Boxes at Home Park, with Tommy involved on matchdays as one of the company's representatives.

33. TYSON, NATHAN

Birthplace: Reading, 4/5/1982
Ht: 5ft-10ins, **Wt:** 11st-12lbs
Swans debut: v. Exeter City (h), 8/9/2001

Swansea City Career Statistics	
Season	League
2001/02	7+4/1gls
Total	7+4/1gls

Career:
Reading (from trainee in 18/3/2000) lge 9+24/1gls, FLC 0+2, FAC 2+1, Others 0+2
Maidenhead (loan in 12/3/2001)

Swansea City (loan in 30/8/2001)
Cheltenham Town (loan in 22/3/2002) lge 1+7/1gls
Wycombe Wanderers (loan in 2/1/2004) lge 10/3gls
Wycombe Wanderers (signed in 12/3/2004) lge 51+2/28gls,
    FLC 1, FAC 2, Others 0+2

Honours: England Yth, U-20

Loan signing by manager John Hollins, who after making his Swans debut against Exeter City at the Vetch Field, within a couple of days was confronted with a new manager in Colin Addison at the Vetch Field. He was unfortunate to suffer a knee injury in his second game for the Swans at Plymouth Argyle, sidelining him for a couple of games, and after he had returned to action was red carded in his second substitute appearance for a late challenge on the Kidderminster Harriers goalkeeper. An extremely pacy frontrunner, his pace on the flank impressed a number of supporters during his two month loan period at the Vetch Field, in which his only goal was scored in a 2-0 home win over Darlington. The start of the 2001/02 season had seen him make a brief appearance for the 'Royals' in a Worthington Cup tie against Luton Town. Shortly before his eighteenth birthday he had made his league debut for Reading as substitute for

Henderson in an end of season game at Bury in April 2000. After returning to the Madejski Stadium, he made further appearances for Reading before joining Cheltenham Town on another loan transfer. Scoring the winning goal in the local derby game with Kidderminster Harriers, he featuring mainly from the substitute bench as the club gained promotion via the end of season Play Offs. The 2002/03 season saw the pacy frontrunner score two goals for the England U-20 side that beat Germany in front of his home town supporters, also displaying a number of exciting displays from the left wing position for Reading in the Nationwide League, which was enough to give him a two year extension to his contract. Struggling to make an impression in the 'Royals' 2003/04 first team line-up, he was given the opportunity of another loan transfer, this time to Second Division side Wycombe Wanderers in early January 2004, a move which was made permanent for a nominal transfer fee on the 12th March. By the end of the season, despite the club failing to escape from the relegation zone, he finished top goalscorer for Wanderers with nine league goals. He continued to show good form in front of goal during season 2004/05 as his club mounted a late charge for a Play Off position in the Coca Cola League Two.

V

1. VERNON, Leslie (LES) Joseph

Birthplace: Sheffield,
27/12/1905. **Died:** Bury, OND,
1979
Ht: 5ft-8½ins, **Wt:** 10st-6lbs
Swans debut: v. Southampton
(a), 25/12/1937

Career:
Netherton United
Worksop Town
Bury (£250 signed in February
    1926) lge 127/50gls
Preston North End (signed in
    October 1934) lge 14/2gls
Swansea Town (£500 signed in December 1937)
Lancaster Town (signed in July 1938)

Swansea Town Career Statistics			
Season	League	FAC	WC
1937/38	7	1	4/1gls
Total	7	1	4/1gls

Signed by manager Neil Harris from Preston North End along with Joe Beresford, which also saw George Lowrie go in the opposite direction to Deepdale as part of the transfer, with Vernon valued at £500. An experienced front runner since leaving non-league sides Netherton United and Worksop Town for Bury in 1927, making over a hundred league appearances for the 'Shakers', and scoring fifty league goals in the First and Second Divisions. Between 1929 and 1934 he regularly played against the Swans for the 'Shakers', scoring in a 4-1 victory in the opening game of season 1933/34. Failing to make the same impact with Preston, following his transfer to the Vetch Field, he made his Swans league debut as a replacement for Cyril Pearce at centre forward at Southampton in December 1937, making a further six league appearances by the end of the season at either centre forward, or at inside forward. His only goal for the Swans came in an 8-0 Welsh Cup triumph over Llanelli, playing also in the Final at the end of the season against Shrewsbury Town, which was drawn 2-2. The Final was held over to the following season. He was transfer listed on the 5th May 1938 at £200 by the Swans. Whilst with Preston North End, an entry in the *Lancashire Daily Post Yearbook* noted the player as: "an inside forward who was a useful, experienced player with a neat style, a good sense of opportunism and of the progressive style. Had excellent season with the reserves and several good games with the first eleven." In July 1938 he returned north to sign for Lancaster Town.

2. VERSCHAVE, MATTHIAS

Birthplace: Lille, France,
24/12/1977
Ht: 5ft-9ins, **Wt:** 11st-5lbs
Swans debut: v. Millwall (h),
12/2/2001

Career:
Paris St. Germain (signed in
    1996)
Swansea City (loan in 6/2/2001)
Clermont (signed for season
    2001/02) Total apps 52/16gls
Rheims (signed in season
    2002/03) Total apps 12/1gls
Nimes (signed for season
    2003/04)

Swansea City Career Statistics			
Season	League	LDV	FAWP
2000/01	12/3gls	1	4+1/3gls
Total	12/3gls	1	4+1/3gls

Honours: France Universities XI

One of two players who signed for the Swans on loan until the end of the season from French side Paris St. Germain. A hard running striker, extremely quick, with a good first touch he took some time to settle into the British game, and had to wait until almost the end of the season before scoring his first goal for the Swans in the league, scoring two goals in a 6-0 win over Brentford, followed by another goal in the last home game of the season against Cambridge United. However, he did open his account in his first game for the Swans, in the Invitation FAW Premier Cup competition, at Stebonheath Park, Llanelli, against Connah's Quay Nomads, four days before he made the starting line-up for the Millwall match. In later rounds of the competition, he scored the winner against Carmarthen Town at the Vetch Field, and against Merthyr Tydfil in the semi-final second leg victory. He also played in the 2-0 defeat by Wrexham in the Final of the competition at the Vetch Field. A professional since 1996 with Paris St. Germain, Matthias had been the club's top goalscorer in their reserve team prior to joining the Swans. During his period at the Vetch Field he was selected to play for the French Universities team against Libya. Returning to Paris St. Germain at the end of the season, he then joined National Division side Clermont for the 2001/02 season, returning fourteen goals from thirty-five appearances, and in season 2002/03 linked up with Second Division side Rheims. He returned to the National Division for season 2003/04 joining Nimes, and was still attached to the club for season 2004/05.

W

1. WADDLE, ALAN Robert

Birthplace: Wallsend, 9/6/1954
Ht: 6ft-3ins, **Wt:** 13st-0lbs
Swans debut: v. Newport County (a), FLC 1-1, 12/8/1978

	Swansea City Career Statistics				
Season	*League*	*FLC*	*FAC*	*WC*	*FRT*
1978/79	40/19gls	5/1gls	4/1gls	2	
1979/80	30+4/7gls	4/3gls	4/2gls	3/1gls	
1980/81	13+1/7gls				
1984/85	12/5gls			1	
1985/86	27/5gls	3/1gls	2/1gls	2	1+1
Total	122+5/43gls	12/5gls	10/4gls	8/1gls	1+1

Career:
Halifax Town (from juniors in November 1971) lge 33+6/4gls
Liverpool (£40,000 in June 1973) lge 11+5/1gls
Leicester City (£45,000 signed in September 1977) lge 11/1gls
Swansea City (£24,000 signed in 22/5/1978)
Newport County (£80,000 signed in 31/12/1980) lge 19+8/7gls
Mansfield Town (signed in August 1982) lge 14/4gls
Seeb, Hong Kong
Hartlepool United (signed in August 1983) lge 12/2gls
Peterborough United (£6,000 signed in October 1983)
   lge 35+1/12gls
Hartlepool United (non-contract signed in January 1985) lge 4
Swansea City (signed in March 1985)
Barry Town (signed in August 1986)
Llanelli (signed in July 1987)

Alan Waddle became John Toshack's first cash transfer at £24,000 when he arrived at the Vetch Field on the 22nd May 1978 from Leicester City. By the end of his first season at the Vetch Field he had become a huge favourite with the supporters, ended the season as top goalscorer with nineteen league goals,

playing a major part in the club's promotion from the Third Division. Starting his career at Halifax Town, the former Wallsend Boys Club front runner, and cousin of Chris Waddle, had during season 1971/72 played twice against the Swans, prior to signing his first professional contract. Joining Liverpool for a Halifax Town club record transfer fee of £40,000 in June 1973, he made his First Division debut against West Ham United in December 1973, and in the next game scored the only goal of the match in the local derby with Everton, during a season which saw Liverpool finish runners-up in the First Division. Struggling to make regular contributions in the Liverpool first team, he signed for Leicester City, but after just twelve months his former team mate at Anfield, John Toshack, paid £24,000 for his transfer to the Vetch Field. His first season with the Swans saw him score a hat-trick against Southend United, and in the opening fixture of the 1979/80 season, against Bournemouth in the League Cup, First Round, First leg, he scored his second hat-trick for the Swans. A tremendous leader of the forward line, with strong aerial ability, by the time the Swans had started their second season in the Second Division, his place in the side had become uncertain, and in December 1980, Newport County paid a club record fee of £80,000 to take him to Somerton Park. Scoring on his league debut for County in a 4-0 win over Sheffield United, he struggled to find the net as consistently as he had done with the Swans, and by March 1985 had returned to the Vetch Field on a non-contract basis after seeing service with Mansfield Town, Seeb in Hong Kong, Hartlepool United (two occasions) and Peterborough United. Although not as mobile during his second spell with the Swans, his presence in the penalty area in aerial challenges unsettled the majority of defenders he was up against. With the Swans battling against financial problems off the field, and eventually suffering relegation to the Fourth Division, Alan was given a free transfer in May 1986, joining Barry Town, subsequently playing Welsh League football with Llanelli, Port Talbot, Maesteg Park, Bridgend Town (November 1989), and Llanelli (December 1989). After joining Barry Town, midway through the season he joined Wakrah Sports Club in Qatar, returning to Jenner Park a month later. After leaving the professional game he worked for some time at the Vetch Field as Commercial Manager, then went to Swansea Institute to study computer programming, going on to work with the Siema Corporation on Merseyside.

2. WADE, BRYAN Alexander

Birthplace: Bath, 25/6/1963
Ht: 5ft-8ins, **Wt:** 11st-5lbs
Swans debut: v. Gillingham (a), 27/8/1988

Career:
Bath City
Trowbridge Town
Swindon Town (£500 signed in May 1985) lge 48+12/18gls

Swansea City (£10,000 signed in 24/8/1988)
Haverfordwest County (signed in close season 1990)
Brighton & Hove Albion (signed in September 1990)
  lge 12+6/9gls
Frome Town (signed in season 1992/93)
Trowbridge Town (signed in season 1993/94)

Swansea City Career Statistics					
Season	League	FLC	FAC	WC	FRT
1988/89	17+8/4gls	1	3/2gls	4+2/3gls	1+1/1gls
1989/90	2+9/1gls			1	
Total	19+17/5gls	1	3/2gls	5+2/3gls	1+1/1gls

Honours: Fourth Division Champions–1986,
Welsh Cup Winner–1989

Having started out with his home-town club, Bath City in the Alliance Premier League, he joined nearby Trowbridge Town in the Southern League, and entered the Football League ranks in May 1985 with Lou Macari's Swindon Town for a £500 transfer fee. Within twelve months he had not only scored ten league goals, but his club had also won the Fourth Division Championship. He made his Football League debut at Peterborough United as a substitute for Tony Evans in September 1985, scoring his first league goal in his first start for the club a couple of matches later. The following season he returned eight league goals in the Third Division from twenty-three league appearances, but failed to make the squad for the end of season Play Off matches, which saw Swindon reach the Second Division after beating Gillingham in the Final after a replay. After making just three substitute appearances for Swindon in the Second Division he was signed by manager Yorath on the 24th August 1988 for an initial fee of £10,000, with a further £5,000 to be paid after 30 games. He was unfortunate to suffer an injury shortly after his debut for the Swans at Gillingham in the opening game of the 1989/90 season, and it took him a further eight appearances for the Swans before he registered his first goal for the club, at Mansfield Town in November 1989. Possessing exceptional pace, he was a brave striker for his size, but, following a change in management at the Vetch Field in February 1989, he struggled to make manager Ian Evans's starting line-up. He did however play in the end of season Welsh Cup Final at the Vetch Field against non-league side Kidderminster Harriers, with Wade scoring in the 5-0 victory for the Swans. Injury problems disrupted the start of his second season at the Vetch Field, missing matches in the European Cup Winners Cup, and even after the return of Terry Yorath as manager in March 1990, his only appearances came from the substitute bench. Released by the Swans in May 1990, he remained in the Swansea area, signing for Welsh League side Haverfordwest County, before he was offered the opportunity of a trial with Second Division side Brighton & Hove Albion in September 1990. Albion manager Barry Lloyd offered the 27-year-old a trial and he responded with a hat-trick in his first

match for the reserves, a 5–0 win over Southampton. Offered a contract the following month, he suffered a hamstring injury which kept him on the sideline for several weeks, but, after his debut against Middlesbrough in October 1990, he scored on his full debut at Wolverhampton in January 1991, and entered the record books in the next game with his four-goal haul, the first by an Albion player since Peter Ward over fourteen years earlier. Quick and willing, Bryan maintained a good scoring rate in the few opportunities that came his way, but his role was mainly that of a reserve – he hit three hat-tricks for the second XI – until his release following Albion's relegation to the new Second Division in May 1992. Forced to quit the full-time game because of a knee injury, he continued to play for Frome Town in the Western League in season 1992–93, and returned to Southern League side Trowbridge Town the following season, returning to live in his home town of Bath and working in the building industry.

3. WALKER, KEITH Cameron

Birthplace: Edinburgh, 17/4/1966
Ht: 6ft-0ins, **Wt:** 12st-8lbs
Swans debut: v. Cardiff City (h), 26/12/1989

Swansea City Career Statistics							
Season	League	FLC	FAC	WC	AGT/ LDAF/AWS	P/Offs	FAWP
1989/90	11+2		2		1		
1990/91	21+3	2	4	3	2		
1991/92	30+2/ 1gls		3/ 1gls	2			
1992/93	42/2gls		5	1	3	2	
1993/94	27/2gls	4	2	3	4		
1994/95	28		4	4	2		
1995/96	32+1	2			3		
1996/97	31/1gls				2	3	
1997/98	39/3gls	2	1				5
1998/99	1						
Total	262+8/ 9gls	10	21/ 1gls	13	17	5	5

Career:
ICI Juveniles
Stirling Albion (signed in 1984) SL 82+9/17gls, SLC 5/3gls, SC 5/2gls
St. Mirren (£50,000 signed in 1987 close season) SL 41+2/6gls, SLC 3, SC 1, ECWC 3
Swansea City (£80,000 signed in 23/11/1989)
Merthyr Tydfil (loan in 10/9/1999)
Merthyr Tydfil (player manager in January 2000)

Brought up in the Granton district of Edinburgh, Keith Walker graduated from his school team to play for Leith District County team, and from the age of played for Inch Boys Club, where he was coached by Hearts player Eamon Bannon. After his family had moved home to Bo'ness, he joined Bo'ness Hearts at U-13 level, and at U-16 level was asked to join Rangers in a tournament in Belgium. Joining ICI Juveniles at U-18 level he played for Rangers in another tournament, this time in France, and on his return had trials with Hearts, Falkirk and Hibs. Winning a number of competitions with the U-18 side, at the end of the season he was offered terms by Falkirk on a part-time basis, also an offer to play for Stirling Albion in the Scottish Second Division. Under the management of Alex Smith, 'Sky' trained on Tuesday and Thursday nights, combining his day job as an apprentice fitter in the local Iron Foundry. Playing in the Albion first team at the age of eighteen, he was then transferred on a full time professional contract to St. Mirren for a £50,000 transfer fee. At the end of the season St. Mirren won the Scottish Cup, with Walker unable to play because of him being cup tied from playing in a previous round with Stirling Albion. Despite struggling in the league, 'Sky' experienced European football for the first time with games against Tromso and Mechelen, and in the opening match of the season made his debut for the club, scoring in a 2-0 victory. His second season at Love Street saw him suffer with shin splints in pre-season training, limiting his first team outings to just four appearances. Starting season 1989/90 in the first team with St. Mirren, and scoring the only goal of the game against Celtic, it came as a surprise when he was told that the club had agreed a transfer fee with the Swans, and he was on his way to South Wales in a triple transfer with Paul Chalmers and John Hughes. Making his debut for the Swans in a defeat at the Vetch Field against Cardiff City, in November 1997 he would gain revenge over the 'Bluebirds' by scoring the only goal of the game at Ninian Park against City. Originally a midfielder, following the appointment of Frank Burrows to the managerial hot seat at the Vetch Field in March 1991, from the 1991/92 season on, he played in central defence, forging a great understanding with Mark Harris, which almost took the club into the First Division, and also exciting the fans with some memorable cup conquests, and, after overcoming microsurgery to a back problem. An inspirational figure in defence, 'Sky' was also dogged by groin and hernia problems during his Vetch Field career, forcing him on one occasion to miss the AutoGlass Trophy Final at Wembley in 1994. His best season as far as his number of appearances are concerned came during season 1992/93 when he missed just four league games, and see the club fail to beat West Bromwich Albion in the Second Division Play Off semi-final. Following relegation to the Third Division in 1996, despite turning down a new contract, and offers from other clubs, following the off the field drama of the takeover of the club by the Silver Shield Consortium, he was finally persuaded to sign a new contract, and appointed captain for the 1996/97 season. By the end of the season he led the club to Wembley for the Third Division Play Off Final against Northampton Town, only to be devastated by an injury time winner for the 'Cobblers'. The 1998/99 season saw 'Sky' miss the start because of a pre-season training injury, and after making just the one appearance, saw his season come to an end through a stress fracture to his leg, and a broken bone in his ankle. In September 1999 'Sky' started a loan transfer with Dr. Martens side Merthyr Tydfil, and in late January 2000 announced his retirement through a persistent ankle injury from the full time professional game, taking over as player manager at Penydarren Park with Merthyr. He resigned as manager with Merthyr Tydfil after twelve months in charge, returned to his native Scotland, joined the police force, and after completing his probationary period with the force, is now based in Strathclyde.

4. WALLACE, Raymond (RAY) George

Birthplace: Lewisham, 2/10/1969
Ht: 5ft-7ins, **Wt:** 11st-4lbs
Swans debut: v. Bradford City (h), 28/3/1992

Swansea City Career Statistics	
Season	*League*
1991/92	2
Total	2

Career:
Southampton (trainee in July 1986, professional in 21/4/1988) lge 33+2, FLC 8, FAC 2, Others 2
Leeds United (£100,000 signed in 8/7/1991) lge 5+2
Swansea City (loan in 20/3/1992)
Reading (loan in 11/3/1994) lge 3
Stoke City (signed in 11/8/1994) lge 152+27/15gls, FLC 13+1, FAC 5+1, Others 12/1gls
Hull City (loan in 16/12/1994) lge 7
Airdrie (loan in September 1999) SL 0+1
Altrincham (loan in October 1999) Conf 1

Honours: England U-21–4

Twin brother of Rod Wallace, and younger brother of Danny Wallace, he joined the Swans on transfer deadline day on loan from Leeds United, making his Swans debut at the Vetch Field against Bradford City, replacing Stephen Jenkins at right full back. Three days later he made his second appearance at Preston North End in a 1-1 draw. Within a couple of days however, the Football League announced that his registration had not been faxed properly to the League, and after an enquiry, the Swans escaped with a fine, instead of the points being deducted. Unfortunately, he was unable to play anymore games for the Swans, and returned to Elland Road. Formerly a trainee at the Dell along with his brothers, Ray made his First Division debut in October 1988 against Sheffield Wednesday replacing Gerry Forrest at right full back. Retaining his place for a further ten league appearances, after a spell out of the side returned to First Division duty for the remaining twelve matches of the season. He gained his first U-21 cap for England in the Toulon Tournament in June 1988 when he was selected to play against Bulgaria, gaining further caps against Senegal (twice) and the Republic of Ireland. He followed his twin brother Rod to Leeds United in July 1991, and after loan transfers to the Swans and Reading, joined Stoke City on a free transfer in August 1994. A hard tackling no-nonsense type of defender, he also gained a good reputation for his competitive style of play in a midfield role, making him a favourite amongst fans, if not always with his manager. He was released by Stoke City in May 1999, joining Scottish side Aidrieonians, had a short period with Conference side Altrincham, before playing in Irish football. He returned to the Football League in August 2000, joining Exeter City, but after failing to make any appearances, signed for Witton Albion in March 2001.

5. WALSH, IAN Patrick

Birthplace: St. Davids, Pembs, 4/9/1958
Ht: 5ft-9½ins, **Wt:** 11st-6lbs
Swans debut: v. Arsenal (a), 27/2/1982

Swansea City Career Statistics				
Season	*League*	*FAC*	*WC*	*ECWC*
1981/82	3+2/2gls			
1982/83	7+1/3gls		1	0+4/3gls
1983/84	22+2/6gls	0+1	3/1gls	1+1/1gls
Total	32+5/11gls	0+1	4/1gls	1+5/4gls

Career:
Crystal Palace (from apprentice, professional in October 1975)
   lge 101+16/23gls
Swansea City (signed in 24/2/1982)
Barnsley (signed in July 1984) lge 45+4/15gls
Grimsby Town (signed in August 1986) lge 36+5/13gls
Cardiff City (signed in January 1988) lge 5+12/4gls
Cheltenham Town (loan in December 1988) Conf 3, FAT 1

Honours: Wales Sch, Yth–6, U-21–2, Full–18, FAYC–1977, Second Division Champions–1979

An international at schoolboy, youth, U-21, and at Full level for Wales during his playing career, Ian Walsh has become a respected figure at the BBC with his unbiased football commentaries in the Principality, whether on the radio, or on television over the last decade. Following a chance conversation with a BBC Wales employee at a Welsh language night school class an opportunity arose to work at Radio Wales as a second 'voice' and he has not looked back since, progressing to covering all the Welsh Internationals on radio and on television, as well as covering the domestic football scene in Wales. Since leaving professional football in 1989 at the age of 31, Ian joined the Insurance Industry, and has since become an Independent Financial Advisor, in his own company, specialising in mortgages. An accumulation of back and ankle problems ultimately forced his retirement from the game whilst at Ninian Park with Cardiff City, injuries he feels he suffered earlier in his career at Crystal Palace, and which he has struggled to overcome. The former Welsh Schoolboy International from St. Davids in Pembrokeshire had made a big impact earlier in his career, making regular appearances in Palace's First (Premier) Division line-up, and also gaining 13 international caps whilst on the playing staff at Selhurst Park. By the time he joined the 'Bluebirds', managed then by Frank Burrows, Ian's level of fitness was preventing him from making a bigger impact at the club, despite a loan transfer to Conference side Cheltenham Town in December 1988 to boost his fitness after recovering from injury. He made his league debut for Palace in September 1976 in a 2-1 defeat by Chester, and in his next league outing, against Notts. County, scored his first league

goal for Palace in a 2-0 victory. The 1976/77 season had seen him become a member of the Palace Youth side that won the FAYC competition, beating Everton in the final 1-0. Making 33 league appearances, and scoring eight league goals during Palace's Second Division Championship success of season 1978/79, he made regular appearances in Palace's First Division line-up the following season, also playing against the Swans in the twice replayed FA Cup tie, scoring in the 2-2 draw at the Vetch Field. He gained his first U-21 cap whilst at Palace, against England in February 1979 at the Vetch Field. Seven months later he would also gain his first Full cap for Wales, again at the Vetch Field, this time against the Republic of Ireland in a game which Ian scored the first goal, with Alan Curtis netting the second. Following relegation to the Second Division in 1981, he joined the Swans on the 24th February 1982 in a part exchange deal, which involved David Giles moving to Crystal Palace. After making his Swans debut as substitute for Leighton James at Highbury in February 1982, his first start came at Molineux, against Wolverhampton Wanderers, in which he scored the only goal of the game, and put the Swans on top of the First Division. Positioning himself at the far post, he managed to get on the end of a cross from Alan Curtis, and just beat the goalkeeper with a header in the top corner. His second season at the Vetch Field saw Ian score a hat-trick in a record 12-0 victory over Maltese side Sliema Wanderers in a European Cup Winners Cup tie at the Vetch Field. Despite relegation to the Second Division in 1983, Ian finished his last season at the Vetch Field as top goalscorer in the league with six goals, also scoring against Magdeburg in the European Cup Winners Cup. Within a couple of months of relegation to the Second Division, financial problems off the field forced the club to offload players to reduce overheads, with Ian joining Barnsley in July 1984 as one example. He failed to find the net during his first season at Oakwell, but his second season saw him top the goalscorers charts with fifteen league goals, topping also the Grimsby Town goalcharts during his first season at Blundell Park following his transfer in August 1986.

6. WALTON, Joseph (JOE) William

Birthplace: Bishop Auckland, 25/4/1907. **Died:** Kidderminster, AMJ 1940
Ht: 5ft-11ins, **Wt:** 10st-7lbs
Swans debut: v. Cardiff City (h),WC-6, 9/3/1933

Swansea Town Career Statistics			
Season	*League*	*FAC*	*WC*
1932/33	8		2
1933/34	26	4	
1934/35	30	2	3
Total	64	6	5

Career:
Hartlepool United (signed in February 1926)
Bishop Auckland

Huddersfield Town (signed in March 1928) lge 0
Swansea Town (signed in 5/5/1931)
Preston North End (signed in July 1935) lge 0
Kidderminster Harriers (signed in July 1936)

Honours: Central League Champions–1931,
Birmingham League Winner–1938, 1939

Former Close House Friends FC goalkeeper who joined
Hartlepool United in 1926, failed to make an appearance,
returned to non-league with Bishop Auckland, but then
returned to the Football League in March 1928 with
Huddersfield Town. He failed to make an appearance for the
'Terriers', although he did play in the club's reserve side that
won the Central League Championship in 1931. Joining the
Swans in May 1931, he had to wait until March 1933 before he
was to make his first class debut, against Cardiff City in the
sixth round of the Welsh Cup, also playing in the replay.
He made his league debut for the Swans on the 25th March 1933
at Bradford Park Avenue in a 1-0 defeat, but retained his place
for the remainder of the season, fighting off the challenge from
the experienced Ferguson. Over the next two seasons both
keepers would vie for the keeper's jersey in the Swans first
team. In March 1935 he was transfer listed, later joining Preston
North End, before joining non-league side Kidderminster
Harriers in 1936, after failing to make an appearance for Preston.
He was a member of the Harriers side that won the Birmingham
League in consecutive seasons in 1938 and 1939. The landlord of
the Shakespeare Inn in Kidderminster, he was taken ill during a
game in 1940, and died a few weeks later.

7. WARD, David (DAI) Alan

Birthplace: Crewe, 8/3/1941
Ht: 5ft-8lbs, **Wt:** 9st-10lbs
Swans debut: v. Leeds United (a), 8/4/1961

Swansea Town Career Statistics				
Season	League	FLC	FAC	WC
1960/61	2			
1961/62	1			
1962/63				
1963/64	6			
1964/65	25	4	4	3
1965/66	10	1		3
Total	44	5	4	6

Career:
Taunton Town
Swansea Town (trial in January 1959, professional in 10/1/1959)
Yeovil Town (signed in June 1966)
Pembroke Borough (signed in 8/7/1967)

Honours: Football Combination Second Division Champions–
1961, Welsh League First Division Champions–1962, 1963

Young 17-year-old left winger who was initially signed for the
Swans in early January 1959 by manager Trevor Morris, making
his debut at left full back in April 1961 at Leeds United,
replacing Brian Hughes, and retaining his place for the next
league game at the Vetch Field against Middlesbrough. By May
1961 he had made regular appearances in the Swans reserve side
that won the Football Combination Second Division title, and
twelve months later played regularly in the Welsh League side
that won the First Division Championship in consecutive
seasons. Impressing in a trial match at the Vetch Field in early
January 1959, manager Morris was so keen to sign the young
outside left, that he arranged to meet him, his father, and
Taunton's manager Price, at Bristol's Stapleton Road Railway
Station, with Ward putting his signature to a form inside a
railway compartment, while the Swans were en-route to play a
league game at Portsmouth. Plymouth Argyle had also been
monitoring the winger, and had made Taunton Town a higher
offer than the Swans. A consistent performer in the Swans
reserve team, possessing good tackling ability and aerial
strength, he struggled to oust the experienced Harry Griffiths
initially, and then Brian Hughes for a regular place in the Swans
starting line-up at left full back. He had his best run in the first
team in season 1964/65, playing in twenty-five league games
following an injury to Roy Evans, with Hughes switching to the
opposite flank. The 1965/66 season saw him play in both legs of
the Welsh Cup Final against Chester, but he did not feature in
the replay, which the Swans won. At the end of the season he
was given a free transfer, joining non-league Bath City in June
1966, remaining at the club for twelve months before he had a
job offer back in Swansea, refused offers from other Southern
League clubs, signing instead for Welsh League side Pembroke
Borough in early July 1967, remaining at the club into the 1970's.
At the time, Mike Johnson was player coach at Borough, along
with former Swans team mate Brian Thomas and Vetch Field
juniors Willie Abramson and Gary Owen.

8. WARD, JOSEPH

Birthplace: Sion Mills, County Tyrone
Ht: 5ft-9ins, **Wt:** 11st-6lbs
Swans debut: v. Merthyr Town (h), 26/8/1922

Swansea Town Career Statistics	
Season	League
1922/23	1
Total	1

Career:
St. Johnstone
Chelsea (signed in May 1920) lge 14, FAC 2
Swansea Town (signed in 1/7/1922)

One of a number of new players recruited by manager Joe
Bradshaw in the 1922 close season, signing for the Swans within
days of the club's AGM when manager Bradshaw realised that
there would be no transfer fee required to sign him. Joe made
his only Swans first team appearance in the opening game of the
1922/23 season at left half back, but after suffering a serious
knee injury did not make another appearance for the Swans.
In January 1923 he went into hospital to undergo an operation
to find out the problem with his knee injury, after an x-ray had
failed to detect the problem. He received a compensation
payment of forty-two weeks salary worth seventy-three pounds
and fifteen shillings, with a final payment of one hundred and
fifty-one pounds paid to him on the 7th March 1924. Playing his
early football in Ireland with Sion Mills Juniors, Rock Rangers

and Newton Stewart, his professional career started in Scottish football with St. Johnstone, travelling south to sign for Chelsea in May 1920, making his debut at home to Tottenham Hotspur in a 4-0 defeat on the 16th October 1920. Making a further eleven First Division appearances that season for Chelsea, during his second season at the Bridge he made just two appearances, before signing for the Swans. He initially signed for Chelsea as a centre half, but played all of his games for the club at wing half. Injury prevented him making an appearance for Ireland against Wales in April 1921, and on two other occasions he rejected the opportunity to make an appearance for his country.

9. WARNER, John (JACK)

Birthplace: Tonyrefail, 21/9/1911. **Died:** Tonypandy, 4/10/1980
Ht: 5ft-7ins, **Wt:** 11st-2lbs
Swans debut: v. Southampton (a), 5/2/1934

Swansea Town Career Statistics			
Season	League	FAC	WC
1933/34	2		
1934/35	32	2	
1935/36	26/1gls	1	2
1936/37	33/4gls	4	
1937/38	42/4gls	1	
Total	135/9gls	8	2

Career:
Treorchy Athletic (signed in 1930)
Aberaman Athletic (signed in 1932)
Swansea Town (signed in 13/1/1934)
Manchester United (signed in 7/5/1938) lge 105/1gls
Oldham Athletic (signed in June 1951) lge 34/2gls
Rochdale (player manager signed in July 1952) lge 21

Honours: Wales Full–2, War-Time International–1

Signed in January 1934 along with team mate George James from Aberaman, the former Treorchy Juniors, Trealaw Juniors and Trealaw Rangers player did not take long to establish himself in the Swans first team after making his league debut at Southampton in February 1934. Playing nearly all of his games for the Swans at right half back, he scored his first goal in February 1936 at the Vetch Field against Doncaster Rovers, and from the 1936/37 season, he started as first choice for the Swans, with the following season becoming an ever present. He signed for First Division side Manchester United in May 1938, continuing his service at Old Trafford after the war, when the Football League was resumed, being a regular member of the team that was runners-up in the First Division in three consecutive seasons, from 1946/47 to 1948/49, and the following season when the side finished in fourth place.

A player who prided himself on his physical fitness, he was a smart tackler, a fine passer, always appearing to have plenty of time on the ball. He was capped on two occasions for Wales, his first during the time he was with the Swans against England at Ninian Park on the 17th October 1936, and after joining Manchester United played against France on the 20th May 1939, also playing in one war-time international. His last season at Old Trafford saw him captain the club's reserve side, before joining Oldham Athletic as player coach in 1951, signed by former England international full back George Hardwick. His last first team game for United was against Newcastle United on the 22nd April 1950, at the age of 38 (the second oldest for United since the Second World War), and at the age of 42 he played his final league game for Rochdale. In July 1952 he had joined Rochdale as player manager, remaining at Spotland until May 1953. For a number of years after his retirement from football he ran a betting shop a couple of miles from Old Trafford.

10. WASSALL, KIM

Birthplace: Wolverhampton, 9/6/1957
Ht: 5ft-8ins, **Wt:** 11st-8lbs
Swans debut: v. Reading (h), 10/11/1984

Swansea City Career Statistics			
Season	League	FAC	WC
1984/85	1+1	1+1	1
Total	1+1	1+1	1

Career:
West Bromwich Albion (from apprentice in June 1975) lge 0
Northampton Town (signed in September 1977) lge 13+7/1gls, FLC 2, FAC 1
Worcester City (signed in 1977/78 season)
Aldershot (signed in November 1979)
Sydney, Australia (June 1980)
Hull City (non-contract signed in August 1983) lge 1
Bradford City (non-contract signed in September 1983)
Swansea City (non-contract signed in September 1984)
Wolverhampton Wanderers (non-contract signed in October 1985) lge 2
Gresley Rovers (loan in November 1985)
Finland (May 1986)
Shrewsbury Town (signed in November 1989) lge 0+2
Worcester City (signed in season 1989/90)

Utility player capable of playing at full back, or in midfield who was a number of non-contract players signed by manager Colin Appleton in the first half of season 1984/85. Failing to make an appearance after completing his apprenticeship with West Bromwich Albion, he joined Northampton Town in September

1977, making his league debut as substitute for Tucker at Crewe Alexandra in October 1977, coming on as substitute also in the next game against Bournemouth. He made his first league start at Aldershot in April 1978, playing regularly towards the end of the season. At the end of the 1978/79 season he was released by Northampton Town, and after a period with Aldershot, played minor football in Australia, returning to the Football League to sign for Hull City manager Colin Appleton on a non-contract basis, making his league debut for the 'Tigers' in the opening game of the 1983/84 season against Burnley. Failing to make another appearance for the 'Tigers' he joined Bradford City, but after failing to make an appearance for the club, was signed for the second time by Appleton in September 1984, this time during his period as manager at the Vetch Field. Replacing Gary Richards from the substitute bench against Reading in November 1984, he played in both FA Cup ties against non-league side Bognor Regis, made his first league start for the Swans in a 4-1 defeat at Doncaster Rovers, also playing against Sully in a Welsh Cup tie. A predominately left sided player, he was released after a couple of months, but surfaced again in the Football League with Wolverhampton Wanderers, making two starts for the 'Wolves' in October 1985 at Reading, and at Bristol City. Following a spell in Finland, he returned to the Football League to sign for Shrewsbury Town, making his debut for the club in November 1989 as substitute for Gorman at Rotherham United, with his second appearance coming in December at Notts. County. He made two appearances for Worcester City during season 1989/90, his second stint at the club, failing to make an appearance during a short period during the 1977/78 season. In May 2002 he headlined the national press after his appearance in court in Cheltenham where he was accused of battering his ex-lover to death with a cricket bat. In 1999 whilst working as a freight handler for Federal Express at Stanstead Airport, he had rekindled a romance with his former girlfriend Julia Foster, but during his court appearance was found not guilty and released.

11. WATKIN, Stephen (STEVE)

Swansea City Career Statistics						
Season	League	FLC	FAC	AWS	P/Offs	FAWP
1997/98	24+8/3gls		1			
1998/99	40+3/17gls	2	4	1	1	3/3gls
1999/00	36+3/7gls	3/1gls	1+1/1gls	0+1/1gls		0+1/1gls
2000/01	27+8/7gls	2	1	0+1		4/2gls
2001/02	25+6/8gls	1	0+1/1gls			3/2gls
2002/03	15+11/2gls		0+1			0+1
Total	167+39/ 44gls	8/1gls	7+3/2gls	1+2/1gls	1	10+2/ 8gls

Birthplace: Wrexham, 16/6/1971
Ht: 5ft-10ins, **Wt:** 11st-10lbs
Swans debut: v. Leyton Orient (h), 27/9/1997

Career:
Wrexham (from trainee in 24/7/1989) lge 167+33/55gls, FLC 11+3/3gls, FAC 16+6/12gls, Others 17+5/4gls
Ngongotaya, NZ (loan in July 1990)
Swansea City (£105,000 signed in 29/9/1997)
Caernarfon Town (signed in December 2003)

Honours: Wales 'B'–1, Welsh Cup Winner–1995, Third Division Champions–2000, West Wales Senior Cup Winner–2002

Joined Wrexham at the age of fifteen as a schoolboy, and had earlier gained selection for Wrexham and District Schools, Clwyd Schools, North Wales Schoolboys and a call up to the Wales Schoolboys team, but was only included as a non-playing substitute. He turned down the offer of a YTS contract at the Racecourse in favour of staying on at school, but after his examinations eventually signed a one year professional contract with Wrexham in July 1989. In July 1990 he took up the invitation of gaining experience by joining New Zealand Second Division side, Ngongotaya. Returning to Wrexham he signed a short term contract, also making his debut in October 1990 at Torquay United. The following season he ended as joint top goalscorer with Karl Connolly, but also made a name for himself by scoring the club's second goal at the Racecourse to defeat Arsenal in the FA Cup. In March 1992 he was selected to play for the Wales 'B' side against Canada, with the following season seeing him start for the first time in the opening game of the season for Wrexham. By the end of the season he had topped the goalscoring charts with eighteen league goals, with Gary Bennett on sixteen goals, and created a tremendous understanding between each other in the opposition penalty area. The 1992/93 season would see Wrexham finish as Runners-Up to Cardiff City, and gain promotion from the Third Division. Firmly established in the Wrexham frontline, Steve had the ability to hold the ball up well for his team mates, possessing good ball control. In May 1995 he played in the Wrexham side that beat Cardiff City to win the Welsh Cup at the National Stadium in Cardiff. Starting the 1996/97 season as substitute at the Racecourse, he was signed by manager Jan Molby for a £105,000 transfer fee in late September 1997. Making his debut at the Vetch Field against Leyton Orient, he unfortunately picked up an injury early in his days with the Swans, and struggled to make an impression, taking him three months to score his first goal for the Swans in a 1-1 draw at the Vetch Field with Cambridge United. The following season with John Hollins at the helm, Steve finished as top goalscorer with seventeen league goals, including four in the last two matches of the season to secure the Swans a place in the Third Division Play Offs. That season also saw him feature well with the Swans in the FA Cup defeat of West Ham United in the Third Round. The Swans went one better the following season by securing the Third Division Championship with Steve, Walter Boyd and Nick Cusack joint top goalcorers with seven league goals apiece. Despite relegation, and missing a number of games through an ankle injury, he still proved on his day that given the right support he was capable of consistently adding his name to the goalscoring charts. In late April 2002 he was included in the Swans side that beat Hakin United in the West Wales Senior Cup Final. Given a free transfer by Brian Flynn in May 2003, he returned to North Wales to recuperate after a knee operation which sidelined him for the start of the 2003/04 season. After spending some time training with League of Wales side Caernarfon Town, and attracting interest from Bangor City, TNS, Bath City and Forest Green, he signed for Caernarfon, scoring a hat-trick against Bangor City on Boxing Day 2003. In the 2004 close season he was joined at Caernarfon by former Wrexham team-mates Martin Chalk, Lee Jones and Wayne Phillips.

12. WATSON, Andrew (ANDY) Anthony

Birthplace: Leeds, 1/4/1967
Ht: 5ft-9ins, **Wt:** 12st-6lbs
Swans debut: v. Leyton Orient (a), 25/8/1990

Swansea City Career Statistics				
Season	League	FLC	LDC	WC
1990/91	9+5/1gls	0+1	1+1	1+1
1991/92				1/1gls
Total	9+5/1gls	0+1	1+1	2+1/1gls

Career:
Harrogate Town
Halifax Town (signed in 23/8/1988) lge 75+8/15gls,
    FLC 5+1/2gls, FAC 6/1gls, Others 7/1gls
Swansea City (£40,000 signing in 31/7/1990)
Carlisle United (£25,000 signed in 31/7/1990) lge 55+1/22gls,
    FLC 4/5gls, FAC 3, Others 1/1gls
Blackpool (£55,000 signed in 5/2/1993) lge 88+27/43gls,
    FLC 6/5gls, FAC 3+2, Others 7+1/1gls
Walsall (£60,000 signed in 5/9/1996) lge 57+27/15gls,
    FLC 6+1/4gls, FAC 4+5/3gls, Others 7/2gls

Honours: Welsh Cup Winner–1991, West Wales Senior Cup
Winner–1991

One of a number of close season signings by Swans manager
Terry Yorath in 1990 who unfortunately failed to live up to
expectations during his period with the Swans, although he was
unlucky with a number of injury problems during his time at
the Vetch Field. Extremely quick, he would prove in later
seasons after leaving the Vetch Field, that he possessed the
knack of being in the right place at the right time as far as
scoring goals was concerned. After making his name on the non-
league circuit with Harrogate Town, he joined Halifax Town in
August 1998, making his Football League debut at the Shay
Ground against Burnley in September 1988, scoring his first
league goal in a 4-1 away win at Doncaster Rovers in October
the same year. His second season saw him finish second top
goalscorer for Halifax Town with ten league goals, prompting
manage Yorath to secure his transfer to the Vetch Field in late
July 1990 for a £40,000 fee. Despite making his Swans debut as
substitute in the opening game of the 1990/91 season at Leyton
Orient, it took him ten league games before he scored his first
Swans goal, in a 2-1 midweek win at Shrewsbury Town.
Throughout his first season at the Vetch Field he struggled to
command a regular place in a Swans side struggling at the
lower end of the Third Division League table, but in May 1991
he played in the side that beat Wrexham at the National
Stadium, Cardiff, to win the Welsh Cup. The same month he
was also included in the Swans side that beat Llanelli to win the
West Wales Senior Cup Final. By this time Frank Burrows had
taken over from Yorath, and after making just the one start in his

second season, at Merthyr Tydfil in a Welsh Cup tie, he was
given the opportunity to go on loan to Fourth Division side
Carlisle United in November 1991 until the end of the season.
Scoring two goals on his debut at Northampton Town, by the
end of the season he had finished top goalscorer at Brunton Park
with fourteen league goals, scoring eight from ten games during
the second half of the season. With his transfer being made
permanent at the end of the season for a transfer fee in the
region of £25,000, plus a percentage of any future transfer fee
involving the player, Andy continued his goalscoring exploits at
Brunton Park, and before too long had attracted the attention of
Blackpool who eventually signed him in February 1993 for
£55,000. His first full season at Bloomfield Road saw him finish
as top goalscorer with twenty league goals, which included his
first league hat-trick, against Wrexham in February 1994, and his
second season saw him strike up a good partnership with Tony
Ellis, with Watson scoring fifteen league goals. His third full
season at Bloomfield Road saw Andy score just seven goals
from twenty-seven league appearances, also playing in the side
that lost out in the semi-final stages of the Play Offs to Bradford
City. In September 1996 he joined Second Division side Walsall
for £60,000, and in season 1997/98 was runner-up to Roger Boli
with seven league goals, plus three in the FA Cup competition
for the 'Saddlers'. In May 1999 he was released from the playing
staff at Walsall.

13. WEBBER, ANDREW Jeffrey

Birthplace: Port Talbot, 15/3/1963
Ht: 6ft-0ins, **Wt:** 12st-4lbs
Swans debut: v. Plymouth Argyle (h), 1/12/1984

Swansea City Career Statistics	
Season	League
1984/85	0+1
Total	0+1

Career:
Afan Lido
Swansea City (non-contract signed in November 1984)
Exeter City (non-contract signed in September 1985) lge 1
Afan Lido (signed in season 1985/86)

Honours: Boys Club of Wales–2, Konica League Cup
Winner–1993, 1994

Port Talbot born striker who was given his league opportunity
by manager Colin Appleton against Plymouth Argyle at the
Vetch Field, as a second half substitute for Chris Marustik.
Unfortunately, within five days Appleton had lost his job as
manager of the football club, and Webber saw out the remainder
of the season with the Swans playing in the club's Football

Combination side. Prior to making his league debut he had impressed in a reserve team 3-0 defeat of West Ham United, and had signed non-contract forms, allowing him to keep his job at BSC Port Talbot as a fitter. The former Sandfields Comprehensive schoolboy had started his playing career with Newton Wanderers, and after playing for the Afan Lido U-16 side had made two appearances for the Boys Club of Wales side, both against Scotland. He initially started his senior career with Port Talbot, but after one season he joined Afan Lido. Rejoining the Lido after being released by manager John Bond, within a couple of weeks of the new season, Colin Appleton, now in charge at Exeter City offered him a trial, with Andrew making his debut for the club at Mansfield Town in mid-October 1985 on a non-contract basis. After playing in a couple of reserve team matches, with no offer a full professional contract he returned to Afan Lido, declining also the offer of a two week trial with Charlton Athletic. Playing for the Lido on many occasions throughout his career, he won honours with the club as Champions and Runners-Up in the Welsh League First Division, and also played in the second leg in Latvia in the EUFA Cup competition against RAF Yergava in season 1995/96. Andrew also played in the Konica League Cup of Wales Final in the first two seasons of the competition, winning on penalties against Caersws in 1993, and twelve months later scoring the only goal of the game to beat Bangor City. Throughout his Welsh League and League of Wales playing career, Andrew also played for Llanelli, under manager Wyndham Evans, Maesteg Park, Barry Town, and Goytre United. He is currently playing for South Wales Amateur League side Corus Steel, and working as a production operator at Visteon, on Fabian Way in Swansea.

14. WEBSTER, COLIN

Birthplace: Cardiff 17/7/1932. **Died:** Swansea, 2/3/2001
Ht: 5ft-9ins, **Wt:** 11st-0lbs
Swans debut: v. Bristol City (a), 11/10/1958

Swansea Town Career Statistics					
Season	League	FLC	FAC	WC	ECWC
1958/59	23/9gls		1	1	
1959/60	37/22gls		3	2/1gls	
1960/61	39/19gls	1	3	5/4gls	
1961/62	36/14gls	1	1	2/1gls	1
1962/63	22/2gls	1/1gls			
Total	157/66gls	3/1gls	8	10/6gls	1

Career:
Cardiff City (from juniors in May 1950) lge 0
Manchester United (signed in May 1952) lge 65/26gls, FAC 9/4gls, EC 5/1gls
Swansea Town (£7,500 signed in October 1958)

Newport County (£3,500 signed in March 1963) lge 31/3gls
Worcester City (signed in July 1964)
Merthyr Tydfil (signed in January 1965)
Portmadoc (signed in 1965)

Honours: Wales Full–4, First Division Champions–1956, Welsh Cup Winner–1961, West Wales Senior Cup Winner–1960, 1961

Colin Webster was on the playing staff at Old Trafford with Manchester United at the time of the Munich air disaster, but missed the trip due to influenza. A product of Windsor Clive & Ely Schools, Avenue Villa FC (Cardiff), prior to joining Cardiff Nomads, and signing as an amateur with Cardiff City in 1949, and as a professional in the summer of 1950. During National Service he had played for the Northern Command side with United player Denis Viollet, his potential was spotted by Jimmy Murphy, assistant manager at United, and he moved to Old Trafford in May 1952 whilst he was still on National Service. A versatile forward, strong and aggressive, although not particularly big, he was at home in any of the forward positions, or at wing half. He unfortunately gained a reputation as a dirty player throughout his career, but he was more of a hard player, rather than dirty, and who was always prepared to go in where it hurt. His opportunities were limited at United due to the wealth of talent available at the club, but he made his debut in November 1953 in a 1-1 First Division match away at Portsmouth. Over the next two seasons he played fairly regularly in consecutive First Division Championship winning seasons of 1956 and 1957 (five appearances in season), and was an ideal squad player at Old Trafford, capable of playing in a number of positions. He struggled to make regular appearances prior to the Munich air crash, but afterwards was called up to help rebuild the stricken club. He had been due to fly with the squad to Munich, but was confined to bed with a bout of influenza. In previous rounds of the competition he had scored twice against Shamrock Rovers in the Preliminary round of the European Cup, and scored once against Dukla Prague in the First Round. Like all the other 'survivors' the loss of so many colleagues had a profound effect upon him for the remainder of his life. Colin's fighting spirit played a leading role in the revitalisation of the early post-Munich clan, playing in the club's first match after the air crash, a 3-0 win in the FA Cup against Sheffield Wednesday, and also in the European Cup semi-final, and also in that season's FA Cup Final which United lost 0-2 to Bolton. He received his first call up to the Wales National team for a World Cup qualifying match at Ninian Park against Czechoslovakia in May 1957, also making three appearances in the World Cup Final stages in Sweden, against Hungary, Mexico and Brazil. Despite starting season 1958/59 with 5 goals in 7 matches for United, he was signed by Swans manager Trevor Morris in September 1958 for a transfer fee of £7,500. Replacing Pat Terry in the Swans forward line for his league debut at Bristol City in October 1958, in his next match, at Huddersfield Town, he scored two goals in a 3-2 defeat for the Swans. The next two seasons at the Vetch Field saw him finish as top goalscorer on each occasion, scoring two hat-tricks against Plymouth Argyle and Charlton Athletic in season 1959/60, and hat-tricks against Holyhead Town in a Welsh Cup tie in February 1961, and a second hat-trick that season against Norwich City. In May 1960 he scored one of the Swans goals that beat Llanelly in the West Wales Senior Cup Final. The 1960/61 season also saw Colin play in a winning Welsh Cup Final with the Swans, beating Bangor City 3-1, sampling European Football the following season against East German side Motor Jena. During his period at the Vetch Field he proved himself to be a player of high quality, tactically aware, a good distributor of the ball, as well as being a dangerous marksman in the penalty area. In March 1963 he joined Newport County, playing just the one season before he joined non-league side Worcester City (three goals from nineteen appearances), then playing for Merthyr Tydfil, before linking up with former Swans team-mate Mel Charles at Portmadoc. After retiring as a full time footballer he worked as a scaffolder, then a Park Ranger, remaining in Swansea until his death in March 2001.

15. WELLINGS, BARRY

Birthplace: Liverpool, 10/6/1958
Ht: 5ft-7ins, **Wt:** 11st-0lbs
Swans debut: v. Brentford (a), 22/9/1984

Swansea City Career Statistics	
Season	League
1984/85	5/3gls
Total	5/3gls

Career:
Everton (from apprentice in June 1976) lge 0
York City (signed in 1/6/1978) lge 40+7/9gls
Rochdale (signed in July 1980) lge 111+5/30gls
Tranmere Rovers (signed in February 1983) lge 16/3gls
Northwich Victoria
Tranmere Rovers (non-contract signed in December 1983) lge 9
Oswestry Town
Swansea City (non-contract signed in 19/9/1984)

Striker signed on a non-contract basis by Swans manager Colin Appleton in mid-September 1984, at a time when the Vetch Field playing staff consisted of a number of trialists and non-contract players. Formerly an apprentice at Goodison Park with Everton, after failing to make a first team appearance, he joined York City in June 1978, making his league debut as a substitute for Peter Stronach at Barnsley in September 1978. His first league start came at Doncaster Rovers in November 1978 where he scored two goals in a 2-1 away victory. A successful transfer to Rochdale in July 1980 saw the striker play in every league game for two seasons, finish top goalscorer with fourteen league goals in his first season, and runners-up with eleven league goals in his second season. He joined Tranmere Rovers in February 1983, but at the end of the season was released, joining Alliance Premier League side Northwich Victoria. Halfway through the 1983/84 season however he returned to Prenton Park to sign on a non-contract basis for Rovers, being released at the end of the season, failing to score in his nine league games for the club.
He joined the Swans from Northern Premier League side Oswestry Town in September 1984, and despite failing to score in his first two league appearances, scored his first goal for the club in an away league win at Bournemouth, the first away victory for the Swans in over two seasons. He followed that goal by scoring two goals at the Vetch Field in a victory over Orient. Impressing a number of supporters with his ability to convert half chances, he was unable to agree a financial package with the Swans, deciding to return to non-league football.
He subsequently played for Southport, Runcorn and Droylsden, settling back on his native Merseyside.

16. WEST, COLIN

Birthplace: Wallsend, 13/11/1962
Ht: 6ft-1ins, **Wt:** 13st-11lbs
Swans debut: v. Oxford United (h), CCC 1-2, 25/8/1992

Swansea City Career Statistics						
Season	League	FLC	FAC	WC	AGT	P/Offs
1992/93	29+4/12gls	0+1	5/1gls	1	3/1gls	2
Total	29+4/12gls	0+1	5/1gls	1	3/1gls	2

Career:
Sunderland (schoolboy in January 1979, apprentice in July 1979, professional in 9/7/1980) lge 88+14/21gls, FLC 13+4/5gls, FAC 3+1/2gls
Watford (£115,000 signed in 28/3/1985) lge 45/20gls, FLC 2+1, FAC 8/3gls
Glasgow Rangers (£180,000 signed in 23/5/1986) SL 44+1/2gls, SLC 2/1gls, SC 0+1, Others 0+2
Sheffield Wednesday (£150,000 signed in 7/9/1987) lge 40+5/8gls, FLC 6/3gls, FAC 6/1gls, Others 3/1gls
West Bromwich Albion (signed in 24/2/1989) lge 64+9/22gls, FLC 2, FAC 4/1gls, Others 2/1gls
Port Vale (loan in 1/11/1991) lge 5/1gls
Swansea City (signed in 5/8/1992)
Leyton Orient (signed in 26/7/1993) lge 132+10/42gls, FLC 6/2gls, FAC 7+1/2gls, Others 9/4gls
Northampton Town (loan in 19/9/1997) lge 1+1
Rushden & Diamonds (loan in December 1997, then signed in 4/2/1998) Conf 26+6/10gls
Northwich Victoria (signed in season 1999/2000) Conf 2
Hartlepool United (signed in 2/10/1999) lge 0+1, Others 0+1

Honours: Scottish First Division Champions–1987

Experienced striker who was signed by manager Frank Burrows after an initial trial spell at the Vetch Field after he had been released by West Bromwich Albion at the end of the 1991/92 season. He made his Swans' debut as substitute for Andy McFarlane in a first round, second leg Coca Cola Cup tie at the Vetch Field against Oxford United, making his league debut four days later at Wigan Athletic, where he again replaced McFarlane from the substitute's bench. His first goals for the Swans came at the Vetch Field, where he scored twice against Port Vale, against a team that he had played on loan for the previous season, and also who were interested in signing the player. Within days of the Vale game, West signed a permanent contract to stay at the Vetch Field. During a season in which the Swans reached the fourth round of the FA Cup, the AutoGlass Trophy area semi-finals, and the Second Division Play Off semi-finals, West finished the season as joint top goalscorer with Andrew Legg with twelve league goals. With the Swans taking a one goal lead to the Hawthorns for the second leg of the Play Off semi-final, West received a red card within minutes of entering the field as substitute, and shortly after a West Bromwich Albion player had received a red card. With the Swans failing to reach the Play Off Final, Colin was released from his contract, signing for Leyton Orient. A former Wallsend and County Durham Schoolboy striker, after leaving school he joined Sunderland as an apprentice at Roker Park, making his First Division debut as substitute for Whitworth against Tottenham Hotspur in October 1981. Making a few more appearances from the bench, he played in the last eleven league games of the season, and after scoring his first senior goal against Ipswich Town in April 19782, scored a further five goals up to the end of the season. Top goalscorer for Sunderland in season 1983/84 with nine league goals, plus four in the FA Cup competition, he joined Watford for a six figure transfer fee in March 1985, scoring seven league goals for the club up to the end of the season. His first full season for Watford saw Colin finish top goalscorer with thirteen league goals, plus three FA Cup goals as the club reached the quarter final stage. He was lured to Scottish giants Glasgow Rangers in May 1986 for another six figure transfer fee, and despite scoring just two goals in the league, was an ever present as the club won the League Championship, with Ally McCoist, his striking partner notching up 33 league goals. Shortly after he had started his second season in Scottish Football, he returned to the Football League, again for a six figure transfer fee. Making regular appearances in Wednesday's First Division line-up in his first two seasons at Hillsbrough, he then joined Second Division side West Bromwich Albion in February 1989, staying at the Hawthorns until the end of season 1991/92. His first three seasons at Brisbane Road with Leyton Orient saw Colin top the goalscoring charts in each season, and remarkably, in February 1996 he scored his first league hat-trick, against Cardiff City. After a short loan spell with Northampton Town, Colin then dropped down to the Conference to sign for Rushden & Diamonds, and then finishing his playing career with Northwich Victoria. Appointed assistant manager to Chris Turner at Hartlepool United in October 1999, he was registered as a player in case of emergencies, only to be called into action as substitute in a league game against Brighton & Hove Albion, and against Carlisle United in the AWS competition that season. In November 2002, along with United manager Chris Turner, Colin returned to Hillsbrough as assistant manager of Sheffield Wednesday, after a period with Hartlepool which saw the club lose out in three consecutive Third Division Play Off semi-finals, but had firmly cemented in place an automatic promotion place for the club in May 2003. By the end of the season however, the 'Owls' suffered relegation to the Second Division, and after a mid-table placing in season 2003/04, following a poor start to the 2004/05 season, West and manager Turner were dismissed from their roles at the club.

17. WEST, COLIN William

Birthplace: Middlesbrough, 19/9/1967
Ht: 5ft-7ins, **Wt:** 11st-0lbs
Swans debut: v. Gillingham (h), 19/3/1989

Swansea City Career Statistics		
Season	League	WC
1988/89	14/3gls	2/1gls
Total	14/3gls	2/1gls

Career:
Chelsea (from apprentice in September 1985) lge 8+8/4gls
Partick Thistle (loan in 19/9/1986) SL 24/10gls, SC 1
Swansea City (loan in 17/3/1989)
Dundee (£105,000 signed in 3/8/1990) SL 25+10/6gls, SLC 1, SC 3/1gls
Hartlepool United (signed in August 1993) lge 29+7/5gls
Bishop Auckland (signed for season 1994/95)

Honours: England U-18–4

Despite his small frame, Colin was a very busy frontrunner, a handful in the opposition penalty area, with a deceptive turn of speed. The first signing made by Swans manager Ian Evans, on loan from Chelsea in mid-March 1989 until the end of the season, Colin scored on his debut for the Swans at the Vetch Field against Gillingham. Playing in a mid-table Second Division side, Colin scored in the first leg of the semi-final of the Welsh Cup at Barry Town, setting the club up for the end of season Cup Final, which unfortunately he missed, as he had already returned to Stamford Bridge. Earlier in his career Colin attended Coulby Newham School in Middlesbrough, played for Junior side Nunthorpe Athletic between the age of fourteen to sixteen, also for the Middlesbrough Schoolboys when they shared the English Schools Trophy in 1983 after drawing 4-4 over two legs with Sunderland Schoolboys. Reaching the last thirty-two in the England U-15 trials, Colin later in his career gained honours for England at U-18 level, playing on four occasions in the 1985 Cannes Tournament in France. Formerly an apprentice with Chelsea after leaving school, he made his senior debut on loan to Scottish First Division side Partick Thistle in September 1988, and by the time he had returned to Chelsea, was top goalscorer for the season with Thistle with ten league goals. Within days of his return to the Bridge, he made his league debut for Chelsea in the local derby with Arsenal, scoring the only goal of the game after just five minutes. He continued to be on the fringe of a first team place at Chelsea, and in season 1987/88 made a further nine league appearances, scoring three goals. After his return to Stamford Bridge from the Vetch Field, he failed to make a further league appearance for Chelsea, and in August 1990 joined Scottish First Division side Dundee for £105,000. Making regular appearances in his first season for Dundee, his next two seasons at Dens Park saw Colin struggle to make an impression, and in August 1993 he returned to the Football League to sign for Hartlepool United. Returning just five goals from thirty-six league games, he was released at the end of the season on a free transfer. Having undergone ankle and knee operations prior to joining Hartlepool United, it was on the advice of his surgeon that he retired from top class football, despite offers from Holland and Scotland, and signed for non-league side Bishop Auckland. However, six months later he retired from the game completely, and for the last four years Colin has been manager of a Homeless Hostel in Middlesbrough.

18. WESTON, Reginald (REG) Harold

Birthplace: Greenhithe, London, 16/1/1918. **Died:** Burton-on-Trent, 17/2/1998
Ht: 6ft-0ins, **Wt:** 12st-6lbs
Swans debut: v. West Bromwich Albion (h), 31/8/1946

Career:
Northfleet
Swansea Town (signed in 14/5/1946)
Derby County (signed in 30/10/1952) lge 0
Burton Albion (signed as player/manager in August 1953)

Swansea Town Career Statistics			
Season	League	FAC	WC
1946/47	30	2	1
1947/48	42	1	
1948/49	41	2	4
1949/50	38	2	3
1950/51	37/1gls	1	1
1951/52	41	3	1
Total	229/1gls	11	10

Honours: Third Division South Champions–1949, Welsh League Representative XI

A commanding centre half, he was at the heart of that fabled Swans' half back trio, which included Paul and Burns. A Londoner, who played his early football with Northfleet, he was spotted by manager Haydn Green playing for a Naval side in Pembrokeshire, and joined the Swans in mid-May 1946 on leaving the Mine Sweeping Service, before moving to Derby County as a player coach on the 30th October 1952, after refusing to renew his contract at the Vetch Field because of a dispute with the club's Board of Directors over a housing problem. A commanding figure in between Paul and Burns, he was cool, and methodical, rarely crossed the half way line, also possessing good distribution of the ball. Making his debut for the Swans in the opening game of the 1946/47 season, he rarely missed a game from his second season on at the Vetch Field, captaining the side that won the Third Division South Championship in 1949. That same season he also played in the Welsh Cup Final defeat by Merthyr, but in the following season, despite playing in the semi-final, missed the Welsh Cup Final win over Wrexham. In May 1951 he played for a Welsh League Representative XI at the Vetch Field against their Irish League counterparts. He joined Derby County in October 1952, apparently in a player coach capacity under Harry Storer, but he left the Rams a year later without having played for the first team. He then saw out his playing career as player manager of Birmingham League side, Burton Albion, a position he held until the 1957 close season. On retiring from football, he and his wife Olive ran a Post Office in the town for some twenty-seven years before retiring in 1983. He died at a nursing home in Burton on Trent on 18th February 1998.

19. WHITEHEAD, WILLIAM Thomas

Birthplace: Saffron Walden, 11/9/1897. **Died:** Swansea, 30/4/1986
Ht: 5ft-9½ins, **Wt:** 11st-0lbs
Swans debut: v. Bournemouth (a), 19/1/1924

Swansea Town Career Statistics		
Season	League	WC
1923/24	1	2
1924/25	3/1gls	2/2gls
Total	4/1gls	4/2gls

Career:
March G.E. United
Boston Town
Swansea Town (£420 signed in 24/2/1923)
QPR (signed in October 1925) lge 24/5gls
Preston North End (signed in June 1926) lge 3/1gls
Manchester City (signed in March 1927) lge 0
Boston Town (signed in June 1928)
Yeovil & Petters United (signed in September 1929)
   Total apps 62/31gls
Taunton Town
Westland United, Somerset (signed in September 1936)

Honours: Welsh League Representative XI, West Wales Senior Cup Winner–1923, 1925

Prolific goalscorer in the Swans' reserve teams following his signing by manager Joe Bradshaw in February 1923 for £420 from Midland League side Boston Town. Top goalscorer in the Midland League during the 1922/23 season, he had already scored three hat-tricks during the season, the last one against Barnsley Reserves two weeks before he signed, watched by Swans manager Joe Bradshaw. At the time of his signing the local newspaper remarked that his style of play was reminiscent of Bert Freeman, the demon goal getter. At the end of his first season at the Vetch Field he was included in the Swans reserve side that beat Llanelly to win the West Wales Senior Cup, and also in January 1925. Struggling to make league appearances because of the consistency of Smith, Fowler and Deacon, he made his league debut at Bournemouth in January 1924, also making two appearances in the Welsh Cup competition the same season. The 1924/25 season saw him score 40 goals for the Swans reserve teams as they won the Southern League and Welsh League titles, as well as scoring his only league goal for the Swans, at Bournemouth in April 1925. However, he did score two goals during the same season in a Welsh Cup tie against Cardiff City. In March 1925 he was included in a Welsh League Representative side that played against the Irish Free State in Dublin and in Cork, scoring the winning goal in Dublin in a 2-1 victory. The same season also saw Whitehead play for the Welsh League against the Irish Free State side. He was transferred to Third Division South side Queens Park Rangers in October 1925, after being originally listed at £350. After just the one season with Rangers, he joined Second Division side Preston North End, before signing for Manchester City. After a period with Boston Town, he had two seasons with Yeovil & Petters, starting in the 1929/30 season, finishing his first season with twenty-four league and cup goals, before joining Taunton Town, and then finishing his career with Westland United.

20. WHITEHOUSE, JOHN Frederick

Birthplace: Stafford, 14/6/1910 **Died**: Stafford, 26/11/1982
Ht: 5ft-9ins, **Wt:** 10st-6lbs
Swans debut: v. Wolverhampton Wanderers (a), 17/11/1928

Swansea Town Career Statistics	
Season	*League*
1928/29	2
Total	2

Career:
Sunbeam Motors (signed in close season 1926)
Wellington St. George's (signed in August 1927)
Stafford Rangers (signed in close season 1928)
Swansea Town (£250 signed in 7/11/1928)
Stourbridge
Manchester Central (signed in May 1930)
Burton Town
Stafford Rangers (signed in March 1932)

Centre forward who initially made a name for himself in non-league football with Birmingham League side Sunbeam Motors FC, where he was captain in two succesive seasons, scored one hundred and fourteen goals for the club, and then joined Wellington St. George's. Joining Stafford Rangers for the 1928/29 season, after scoring in eleven out of the twelve games he had played for the club, he was signed by Swans manager John Hunter Thomson for a fee in the region of £250 in November 1928, making his league debut as a replacement for Jack Fowler at Wolverhampton Wanderers on the 17th November 1928. Missing the next league game, he returned for the next league game against Millwall, again as replacement for Fowler. Following the signing of centre forward John Cheetham, he failed to make any further league appearances in the Swans first team, and was listed in May 1929 at £50. Joining Stourbridge, he then signed for Manchester Central in May 1930, returned to Burton Town, and then linked up with Stafford Rangers in March 1932.

21. WILKIE, CHARLES Henry

Birthplace: Cardiff, 19/7/1909. **Died:** Cardiff, April 2002
Swans debut: v. Lincoln City (a), 29/8/1932

Swansea Town Career Statistics	
Season	*League*
1932/33	5
Total	5

Career:
Merthyr Town
Swansea Town (trial in August 1932, professional in August 1932)
Burton Albion (signed in August 1933)
Hednesford Town (signed in 1934)
Worcester City (signed in May 1935)
Evesham Town (signed in August 1936)
Hednesford Town (signed in August 1937)
Stafford Rangers (signed in March 1938)
Worcester City

Invited to a month's trial at the Vetch Field in August 1932, after impressing in both public trial games he was signed as a professional at the end of the month. He made his Swans debut in the second league game of the season, at Lincoln City at

outside left, as a replacement for DJ Lewis. Making a total of five consecutive league appearances, he was then replaced by the returning Lewis, failing to make any further first team appearances for the Swans. After being released by the Swans, he joined non-league Burton Albion in August 1933, and remained in non-league football with Hednesford Town, Worcester City, Evesham Town, Hednesford Town (second spell), Stafford Rangers and Worcester City (second spell) up to the start of WW2. In November 1941 he made guest appearances for Walsall. His first spell at Worcester City saw him score one goal from thirty-nine appearances.

22. WILKINS, ALAN James

Birthplace: Treherbert, 3/10/1944
Ht: 5ft-5ins, **Wt:** 11st-5lbs
Swans debut: v. Leyton Orient (h), 7/9/1963

Swansea Town Career Statistics	
Season	*League*
1963/64	1
1964/65	4
Total	5

Career:
Swansea Town (signed in May 1963)
Lovells Athletic (signed in close season 1965)
Merthyr Tydfil (signed in close season 1969)
Caerleon (signed in 1970)

Honours: Welsh League First Division Champions–1963, 1964, 1965, 1966

Consistent goalscorer from midfield in the Swans reserve team in the Welsh League, Alan made his league debut at the Vetch Field as a replacement for Brayley Reynolds against Leyton Orient on the 7th September 1963. Failing to make any further appearances that season, his next first team start came in the next season when he made two consecutive league appearances against Swindon Town and Charlton Athletic in September 1964, again as replacement for Reynolds. Making a further two league appearances in the same season, in May 1965 he was released by the Swans, joining Welsh League side Lovells Athletic. Brought up in Treherbert, Alan attended Perengely school, and played for Treherbert and Treorchy Boys Clubs prior to arriving at the Vetch Field, spending a short time on the groundstaff before signing as a professional in May 1963. With the Swans reserve team playing in the Welsh League First Division, in three consecutive season they won the League Championship, and his first season with Lovells Athletic, saw him win a fourth consecutive League Championship.

Following the disbanding of the football club in 1969, Alan continued to work at Lovells for a short time, signed for Southern League side Barry Town, and after a season and a half, joined Merthyr Tydfil. After two seasons at Penydarren Park he joined Welsh League side Caerleon. Working for some time in civil engineering as a pipe layer, for the last twenty-four years Alan has been steward of the Coronation Club in Newport.

23. WILLER-JENSEN, THOMAS

Birthplace: Copenhagen, 19/9/1968
Ht: 6ft-4ins, **Wt:** 13st-4lbs
Swans debut: v. Barnet (a), 15/3/1997

Swansea City Career Statistics	
Season	League
1996/97	7
Total	7

Career:
GVI Helsinger
HIK Copenhagen
Swansea City (signed in 12/3/1997)

Danish central defender who impressed in trial games with the Swans Combination side in October 1996, warranting him being signed by manager Jan Molby on a short term contract in mid-March 1997, as cover for Keith Walker, with the Swans challenging for a Play Off position in the Third Division. Playing alongside Christian Edwards in central defence, he partnered the returning Walker in his last match for the Swans. Despite a persistent ankle injury, Thomas missed just two of the last nine league games of the season as the Swans secured their Play Off place. Strong in aerial challenges, he possessed good ball skills, and was a composed defender in the continental mould. Returned to Denmark just prior to the Swans reaching the Play Off Final at Wembley.

24. WILLIAMS, ALAN

Birthplace: Bristol, 3/6/1938
Ht: 6ft-0ins, **Wt:** 12st-2lbs
Swans debut: v. Scunthorpe United (a), 1/11/1968

Career:
Bristol City (amateur in June 1955, professional in September 1955) lge 135/2gls, FLC 3, FAC 7, Others 4
Oldham Athletic (£10,000 signed in June 1961) lge 172/9gls
Watford (£5,000 signed in July 1965) lge 43/4gls, FLC 2, FAC 2

Swansea Town/City Career Statistics				
Season	League	FLC	FAC	WC
1968/69	31/3gls		4	8
1969/70	45	2	2	4
1970/71	42/4gls	2	4	2
1971/72	23+2/3gls		6/1gls	1
Total	141+2/10gls	4	16/1gls	15

Newport County (£3,000 signed in November 1966) lge 64/3gls
Swansea City (signed in 22/10/1968)
Cheltenham Town (signed in July 1972) SLge 13
Gloucester City (signed in June 1973)

Honours: R.A.F. XI

Experienced wing half back, who after being signed by manager Billy Lucas in late October 1968 from Newport County, missed just five league games in his first three seasons playing for the Swans. An extremely reliable half back, he linked well with the experienced Mel Nurse at centre half, playing a large part in the club's 1969/70 promotion success from the Fourth Division, and FA Cup runs which saw the club reach the fourth round on two occasions. Signed for the second time by manager Billy Lucas, initially for Newport County in November 1966, the former Bristol City junior had made over 100 league appearances for City in the Second Division, prior to signing for Fourth Division side Oldham Athletic in July 1961. He was robbed of an England U-23 cap when the match against Scotland in 1959 was cancelled because of bad weather. Featuring strongly in the club's 1962/63 promotion from the Fourth Division, after two further seasons in the Third Division with Athletic he joined fellow Third Division side Watford before arriving at Somerton Park. He played for both Bristol and Gloucester Schoolboys prior to signing as an amateur for Bristol City in June 1955, before signing professional three months later. Captained the RAF during his National Service days, and was also skipper of Oldham Athletic in their record 11-0 win over Southport during their promotion season. He made his Swans debut at Scunthorpe United as a replacement for Geoff Thomas, scoring his first goal for the Swans ironically against Scunthorpe United in the return league fixture at the Vetch Field in January 1969. At the end of his first season with the Swans he played in both legs of the Welsh Cup Final defeat by Cardiff City, and within twelve months had celebrated a second promotion success from the Fourth Division, also reaching the semi-final stages of the Welsh Cup, this time under a new manager, Roy Bentley. The next couple of seasons saw the Swans reach the fourth round of the FA Cup competition, and following the retirement of Mel Nurse, Williams was appointed captain of the side. He was given a free transfer in June 1972, joining Southern League side Cheltenham Town, moved to Gloucester City twelve months later, before managing Keynsham Town and Almondsbury Greenway. He has since been landlord of the White Horse in Bedminster, and the Horse & Groom pub in Bristol, helped by his son Gary, who also made league appearances for the Swans.

25. WILLIAMS, AUSTIN

Birthplace: Aberdare, 13/3/1913. **Died:** Aberdare, 22/9/1984
Swans debut: v. West Ham United (a), 28/11/1936

Swansea Town Career Statistics		
Season	League	WC
1936/37	2	
1937/38	1	
1938/39	9	1
Total	12	1

Career:
Porth
Swansea Town (amateur signed in 13/10/1936, professional in 25/11/1936)
Chester (signed in August 1939)

Young outside right who joined the Swans as an amateur from Porth in mid-October 1936, making his Swans debut at West Ham United, as a replacement at outside right for Mackay in November 1936, and had signed as a professional for the Swans only a couple of days prior to making his league debut.
He played in the next league game at the Vetch Field against Norwich City, but his next first team start for the Swans came the following season against Manchester United, this time at outside left as a replacement for Tommy Lang. The 1938/39 season proved to be his most productive as far as a first team appearances were concerned, making nine appearances as well as an appearance in a Welsh Cup replay against Cardiff City.
All the appearances came during the last third of the season as a replacement for Sidney Chedgzoy on the right wing. He was released in May 1939, joining Chester shortly before the start of the new season, failed to make an appearance in the three league games of the 1939/30 season prior to the league being suspended, but did remain at the club for the remainder of the season, making regular war-time appearances.

26. WILLIAMS, Benjamin (BEN) David

Birthplace: Penrhiwceiber, 29/10/1900. **Died:** Bridgend, January, 1968
Ht: 5ft-11ins, **Wt:** 13st-0lbs
Swans debut: v. Colwyn Bay (a), WC-4, 24/2/1926

Career:
Penrhiwceiber
Swansea Town (£25 signed in March 1925)
Everton (£7,500 signed in 27/12/1929) lge 131
Newport County (signed in June 1936) lge 18

Honours: Wales Full–10, Second Division Champions–1931, First Division Champions–1932, Welsh League Representative XI, West Wales Senior Cup Winner–1926, 1927

Swansea Town Career Statistics			
Season	League	FAC	WC
1925/26	5		3
1926/27	20		1
1927/28	41	1	1
1928/29	15	2	
1929/30	20		
Total	101	3	5

Full Back signed by manager Joe Bradshaw during the 1925 close season from Welsh League side Penrhiwceiber. He was given his first team opportunity in a Welsh Cup tie at Colwyn Bay at left back instead of Milne, and later made his league debut against Bradford City at right back instead of Langford, consolidating his place in the Swans first team, before signing for Everton on Boxing Day 1929 for £7,500. Prior to joining Everton, Williams had already gained his first international cap for Wales, playing against England at Burnley on the 28th November 1927, making three more appearances for Wales before continuing his international experience at Goodison Park with Everton. In April 1926 and in 1927 he was included in a Swans reserve side that beat Bridgend Town and Merthyr Town in consecutive West Wales Senior Cup Finals. A classy player, although big for his size, he was a precise tackler, and had the ability to force his opponent away from the danger zone.
He was included in a Welsh League Representative side in April 1927, playing the Irish Free State in Dublin. The start of the 1926/27 season saw Williams become an automatic selection for the Swans at right full back, up to his transfer to Everton in December 1929. His first season at Goodison Park, in which he made nine league appearances saw the club relegated to the Second Division, but after winning the Second Division Championship twelve months later, with Williams skippering the side, the First Division Championship was obtained in the club's first season back in the top division, with Williams making over thirty league appearances during each season. Gaining six further international caps for Wales whilst at Goodison Park, he joined Newport County in August 1936, making eighteen league appearances during his only season at Somerton Park, prior to retiring in 1938 through knee problems, and becoming trainer at Somerton Park.

27. WILLIAMS, Darwel (DAVO)

Birthplace: Llanelli, 4/11/1926. **Died:** Swansea, 13/10/2001
Ht: 5ft-9ins, **Wt:** 11st-8lbs
Swans debut: v. Sheffield United (a), 28/8/1950

Career:
Loughor Rovers
Swansea Town (signed in 6/5/1946)

Llanelly (signed in 9/8/1955)
Milford United (signed in season 1956/57)

Swansea Town Career Statistics			
Season	League	FAC	WC
1950/51	30	1	1
1951/52	41/2gls	3/1gls	1
1952/53	22	1	3
1953/54	36/2gls	2	1/1gls
1954/55	1		
Total	130/4gls	7/1gls	6/1gls

Honours: London Combination Cup Winner–1947, 1950,
Football Combination Second Division Champions–1955,
West Wales Senior Cup Winner–1946, 1950

A wing half who joined the Swans from Carmarthenshire
League side Loughor Rovers in May 1946, before being released
shortly after the start of the 1954/55 season. After a period of
amateur service with the Swans, playing in the Welsh League,
and Combination teams, which included being a member of the
Swans side that won the London Combination Cup in 1947 and
in 1950, and when they won the West Wales Senior Cup in 1946
and 1950, Darwel made his league debut for the Swans at
Sheffield United in August 1950 at left back in place of Steve
Leavy. For almost all of his career with the Swans he played at
either right half back, or left half back. He attended Upper
Loughor School when he was younger, and after leaving school
worked in the Gorseinon Sheet Metal Works, and played senior
football with Loughor Rovers, before joining the Swans.
Following his league debut he missed the next nine league
games, but returned to first team duty, playing the remaining
twenty-nine league games at left half instead of Frank Burns.
The following season proved to be his best as far as appearances
were concerned, with 'Davo' missing just one league game,
scoring his first league goals for the Swans, and making 4 F.A.
Cup and Welsh Cup appearances. His first league goal was
against Sheffield United in a 3-1 win for the Swans in February
1952. The last match of that season saw him score his second
goal for the Swans in a 3-1 away win at Rotherham United.
The following season saw 'Davo' play for the Swans in a losing
Welsh Cup semi-final tie against Rhyl. His last twelve months at
the Vetch Field saw him make regular appearances in the
reserve side that won the Football Combination Second Division
Championship, but only one appearance in the Football League.
After being placed on the open to offers list in May 1955, he left
the Vetch Field and joined Southern League side Llanelly, and
taking employment initially with the Electricity Board and then
at the 3M's factory in Gorseinon. A true servant to the Swans, he
was promised a benefit by the club but it did not materialise,
with the excuse being because of financial problems at the club,
although Tom Kiley had had his benefit some period before.
During the 1956/57 season he joined Welsh League side Milford
United, remaining at the West Wales club for a couple of seasons
before retiring from the game. Davo retired through bad health
from 3M's, before his death in October 2001.

28. WILLIAMS, GARY Alan

Birthplace: Bristol, 8/6/1963
Ht: 5ft-8ins, **Wt:** 10st-11lbs
Swans debut: v. Bristol Rovers (h), FRT 1-1, 22/1/1985

Career:
Bristol City (apprentice signed in June 1979, professional in
    August 1980) lge 98+2/1gls
Portsmouth
Swansea City (signed non-contract in January 1985)

Bristol Rovers (signed non-contract in March 1985)
Oldham Athletic (signed in August 1985) lge 45+16/12gls
Heart of Midlothian (signed in July 1991)

Swansea City Career Statistics			
Season	League	FRT	WC
1984/85	6	1	1
Total	6	1	1

Former apprentice at Ashton Gate with Bristol City, following
his father Alan, who had started his career with the club.
He made his league debut at left full back against Oldham
Athletic in the last game of the 1980/81 season, with the club
already doomed to relegation. Despite being a regular inclusion
in the second half of season 1981/82, the club suffered a second
consecutive relegation, this time to the Fourth Division. He also
scored his first league goal during that season, in a 2-0 home
win over Gillingham in May 1982. Following a permanent
switch to a midfield role in season 1982/83, despite making
thirty league appearances, and the club gaining promotion by
finishing in fourth place, he was released on a free transfer.
Initially signing for Portsmouth on a non-contract basis, after
failing to make a first team appearance, was signed by Swans
manager John Bond, again on a non-contract basis. Making his
first team debut for the Swans in a Freight Rover Trophy cup tie
against Bristol Rovers at the Vetch Field, he made his league
debut four days later at Bradford City. Despite being regularly
included over the next couple of league matches, he was unable
to agree terms with the Swans, and left to join Bristol Rovers on
a non-contract basis in late March 1985. An attacking left sided
midfielder during his period with the Swans, he possessed a lot
of skill on the ball during his two month stay at the Vetch Field.
He failed to make an appearance for Bristol Rovers, and joined
Second Division side Oldham Athletic in August 1985, playing
in both legs of the 1986/87 Second Division Play Off semi-final
defeat by Leeds United, which saw Gary score in the second leg.
The next four seasons saw him have limited opportunities in the
'Latics' first team, missing out on the club's Littlewoods Cup
Final appearance in 1990, and after gaining promotion to the
First Division the following year, was released on a free transfer.
After a spell in Scottish football with Heart of Midlothian he
returned south to sign for non-league Bath City in season
1993/94. He later linked up with his father to work in the
licence trade in Bristol.

29. WILLIAMS, George GRAHAM

Birthplace: Wrexham, 31/12/1936
Ht: 5ft-5ins, **Wt:** 10st-4lbs
Swans debut: v. Stoke City (h), 7/2/1959

Career:
Oswestry Town

Bradford City (signed in August 1955) lge 8/2gls
Everton (£5,000 signed in 9/3/1956) lge 31/6gls
Swansea Town (£5,000 signed in 5/2/1959)
Wrexham (signed in 2/7/1964) lge 24/6gls
Glentoran (loan in January 1965)
Wellington Town (signed in 1965)
Tranmere Rovers (signed in August 1966) lge 73+1/12gls
Port Vale (signed in July 1968) lge 21+2/1gls
Runcorn (signed in 1969)
Oswestry Town (signed in 26/2/1970)

Swansea Town Career Statistics					
Season	League	FLC	FAC	WC	ECWC
1958/59	15/1gls				
1959/60	18/3gls			2/1gls	
1960/61	33/9gls	1	3	5	
1961/62	25/5gls	1	1	2	1
Total	91/18gls	2	4	9/1gls	1

Honours: Wales Sch, U-23–1, Full–5, Welsh Cup Winner–1961

An excellent prospect as a schoolboy with school sides Brynteg and Wrexham Technical College, from where he represented Wrexham & District schoolboys, reaching the semi-finals of the English School Shield, and winning the Welsh Schools Shield. Gaining three caps at schoolboy level for Wales, he initially signed for Tottenham Hotspur, but after trials with Wolves, where he was told he was too small by Stan Cullis, he was offered a groundstaff position with Blackpool. Unfortunately, they would not let him complete his apprenticeship as a joiner, so he signed amateur forms with Wrexham, but played his senior football with Oswestry Town. In August 1955 he followed former Wrexham manager Peter Jackson to Bradford City after failing to make an appearance at the Racecourse, making his league debut against rivals Bradford Park Avenue in August 1955. Less than eight months later, after just nine league appearances for Bradford City he joined First Division side Everton for £5,000. His football development at Goodison Park was interrupted when he had to complete his National Service with the Royal Engineers at Stratford-on-Avon, but it did give him the opportunity to play for the British Army XI. In February 1959 he was signed by Swans manager Trevor Morris for a fee of £5,000, immediately becoming a firm favourite with the fans with his tricky, elusive skills on the left wing. Admired for his bravery and willingness to take on defenders, he knew when to play the simple ball, and also had the ability to cross the ball well from the tightest of angles. He gained international honours at U-23 level whilst with the Swans in 1960 against Scotland, and in April 1961 gained the first of five senior caps when he was selected to play for Wales in Belfast against Northern Ireland. His last international appearance saw Graham score his only goal for Wales, in a 1-1 draw with England at Ninian Park. Making his debut for the Swans at outside left as a replacement for Norman Lawson against Stoke City in February

1959, his first goal was scored against Brighton & Hove Albion later in the season in April. His most prolific season as far as goals scoring was concerned with the Swans came during season 1960/61 when the returned nine league goals, also playing in the Welsh Cup Final defeat of Bangor City in April. The following season he made an appearance for the Swans in the first leg of the European Cup Winners Cup tie against Motor Jena. Unfortunately for Graham, later in the season at Middlesbrough he sustained a fractured leg which ultimately proved to be his last game for the Swans, before returning to Wrexham in July 1964. He re-established himself back in the game after his long spell out through injury at Fourth Division with Wrexham, including a two month loan spell with Glentoran, picking up a runners-up medal in the Welsh Cup Final defeat by Cardiff City in 1965. After just a twelve month spell at the Racecourse he received a good offer from Cheshire County League side Wellington Town, spending a season there before he was tempted back into the Football League to sign for Tranmere Rovers in August 1966, helping the club to win promotion in his first season, and also reach the fifth round of the FA Cup competition, losing 2-1 to his former club Everton. After signing for Port Vale in July 1968, he then drifted into the non-league scene, making appearances for Runcorn, and later Oswestry Town, where he eventually retired as a player. He returned to his job as a carpenter, later becoming an accomplished golfer on the North Wales golfing circuit. His son also made a career in the professional game after serving an apprenticeship at Arsenal, making league appearances for Crewe Alexandra, Wigan Athletic and Chester.

30. WILLIAMS, Herbert (HERBIE) John

Birthplace: Swansea, 6/10/1940
Ht: 6ft-0ins, **Wt:** 11st-12lbs
Swans debut: v. Sunderland (h), 13/9/1958

Career:
Swansea Town (from juniors in 15/5/1958)
Woollongong, Australia (player coach signed in January 1975)

Honours: Wales Sch–4, U-23–5, Full–3, Welsh Cup Winner–1966, Football Combination Second Division Champions–1961, English Schools Trophy Winner–1955, Welsh Schoolboy Shield Winner–1955, 1956

Former Danygraig Schoolboy footballer, who was rated highly at schoolboy level, gained four schoolboy caps for Wales, and by the time he had graduated to the Swans first team was rated a better prospect than Ivor Allchurch at the same age. In 1955, despite being underage he played in the Swansea Schoolboys side that won both the English Schools Trophy and the Welsh Shield, and the following year captained the schoolboys side that won the Welsh Shield. He joined the groundstaff at the Vetch Field at the age of fifteen, and during a time when he felt

Swansea Town/City Career Statistics					
Season	League	FLC	FAC	WC	ECWC
1958/59	10/3gls			2/1gls	
1959/60	23/3gls		1/2gls	2	
1960/61	15/6gls	1/1gls		1	
1961/62	36/4gls	1	1	3/2gls	2
1962/63	22/7gls	1			
1963/64	41/7gls	2	7/1gls	1	
1964/65	32/3gls	4/2gls	2	3	
1965/66	35+2/8gls	1		5/1gls	
1966/67	36+2/7gls	3	1		1
1967/68	39/10gls	1	3/1gls	2	
1968/69	44+1/10gls	4/3gls	4	8/2gls	
1969/70	42/15gls	2	3/2gls	4/2gls	
1970/71	22/6gls	1	3/1gls	1	
1971/72	22/1gls	1	3	1	
1972/73	40/8gls	2	1	2	
1973/74	15+12/1gls	2	0+1		
1974/75	17+2/3gls	0+1	2	1/3gls	
Total	491+19/102gls	26+1/6gls	31+1/7gls	36/11gls	3

he would not make the grade as a professional, started an apprenticeship as a fitter and turner at Palmers Dry Dock in Swansea's Prince of Wales Dock. Graduating through the club's reserve sides, he eventually made his mark initially at inside forward, and then wing half, where his long range shooting ability brought him many goals, also a danger to the opposition from free kicks around the penalty area. He later played at centre forward and towards the end of his career at centre half. Tall, and particularly strong in the tackle, his long range passing was also a delight, particularly as he became one of the first players in the game to wear contact lenses. A great clubman who served the Swans since leaving school, he made his first team debut against Sunderland at the Vetch Field in September 1958, and two months later scored his first goal for the Swans against Middlesbrough. The start of the 1960/61 season saw the formation of the League Cup competition, with Herbie scoring the first Swans goal in a defeat by Blackburn Rovers. Later that season he had a run of five goals from five games in the Swans Second Division side. By the end of the 1960/61 season he had made regular appearances in the Swans reserve side that won the Combination Second Division Championship. In 1961 he gained the first of his five U-23 caps for Wales, playing against England. Unlucky at Full level not to have made more appearances than the three caps he gained against Greece (twice), in December 1964 and May 1965, and against Rumania in November 1971. His international recognition against Greece had come at a time when the Swans had started to slip down the divisions, and his last cap against Rumania had recognised the part he had played in leading the Swans out of the Fourth Division in 1970, and established the side in the Third. Following the Swans victory in the 1961 Welsh Cup Final, Herbie sampled European football the following season, playing in both games against East German side Motor Jena. From the start of the 1961/62 season he had become a regular in the first team line-up with the Swans, featuring consistently in the goalscoring charts, and also playing a significant role in the club's FA Cup semi-final run in 1964. The 1963/64 season saw Herbie score his first league hat-trick, against Southampton at the Vetch Field in March 1964. In later seasons his consistency in front of goal would see him score four goals against York City in March 1966, a hat-trick against Bradford Park Avenue in March 1970, and a hat-trick in the Welsh Cup competition against Kidderminster Harriers in January 1975, and reach double figures in the league on three occasions. Towards the end of the 1968/69 season he played in both legs of the Welsh Cup Final defeat by Cardiff City. The Fourth Division promotion season of 1969/70 saw Herbie form a strong partnership in attack with

David Gwyther, with both players returning fifteen league goals during the season. Herbie sampled European football for a second time in 1967 against Slavia Sofia, after playing in the Welsh Cup Final success the previous season against Chester. Plainly mainly at centre half at the latter end of his career, in January 1975 he emigrated to Australia to take up a player coaching role in New South Wales with Woollongong. After his second season with the club he returned to Swansea and since November 1976 has worked locally as a postman, still residing in the East side of the city.

31. WILLIAMS, JOHN Nelson

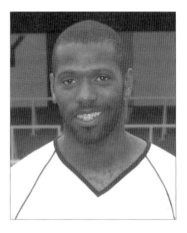

Birthplace: Birmingham, 11/5/1968
Ht: 6ft-1ins, **Wt:** 13st-12lbs
Swans debut: v. Bolton Wanderers (h), 24/8/1991

Swansea City Career Statistics						
Season	League	FLC	FAC	WC	AGT/LDV	FAWP
1991/92	36+3/11gls	2+1	3	2/1gls	1	
1994/95	6+1/2gls					
2001/02	26+14/4gls	1	2/1gls		1	2+1/2gls
2002/03	11+16/1gls	0+1	0+1			0+1
Total	79+34/18gls	3+2	5+1/1gls	2/1gls	2	2+2/2gls

Career:
Cradley Town
Swansea City (£5,000 signed in 19/8/1991)
Coventry City (£250,000 signed in 1/7/1992) PL 66+14/11gls,
 FLC 4, FAC 2
Notts. County (loan in 7/10/1994) lge 3+2/2gls
Stoke City (loan in 23/12/1994) lge 1+3
Swansea City (loan in 3/2/1995)
Wycombe Wanderers (£150,000 signed in 15/9/1995)
 lge 34+14/9gls, FLC 4+1/2gls, FAC 5/4gls, Others 2
Hereford United (signed in 14/2/1997) lge 8+3/3gls
Walsall (signed in 21/7/1997) lge 0+1
Exeter City (signed in 29/8/1997) lge 16+20/4gls
Cardiff City (signed in 3/8/1998) lge 25+18/12gls, FLC 2/1gls,
 FAC 5/3gls, Others 1
York City (£20,000 signed in 12/8/1999) lge 29+13/3gls, FLC 2,
 FAC 0+1, Others 1
Darlington (signed in 21/12/2000) lge 23+1/5gls, Others 1
Swansea City (signed in 17/7/2001)
Kidderminster Harriers (signed in 5/8/2003) lge 28+16/4gls,
 FLC 1, FAC 2+2/1gls, Others 1
Bath City (signed in June 2004) Total Apps 43+1/19gls
Redditch United (signed by 20/5/2005)

Honours: West Wales Senior Cup Winner–2002

Former postman who was signed from non-league football with Cradley Town by Swans manager Frank Burrows, in a £10,000 double transfer including midfielder John Ford. At Cradley, 'Willo' had formed a formidable goalscoring partnership with Andy McFarlane, a tall striker who Burrows had earlier signed for Portsmouth, and who would later join Burrows at the Vetch Field. His schoolboy football was played at the George Dixon School in Birmingham, also playing for Newton Albion. Possessing explosive pace, although raw during his debut season in the Football League, he finished top goalscorer with the Swans with eleven league goals, which included his first league hat-trick at Bradford City in November 1991, and at the end of the season won the Rumbelows Sprint Challenge Trophy for professional footballers at Wembley. From then on he was nicknamed the 'Flying Postman'. After just twelve months in the professional game, he was transferred to Premiership side Coventry City for a £250,000 transfer fee, making his mark immediately with a goal on his debut against Middlesbrough, and scoring two in his second game at Tottenham Hotspur. During the 1994/95 season he had loan spells with Notts. County and Stoke City prior to returning to the Vetch Field on a month's loan. Shortly after the start of the 1995/96 season he joined Second Division side Wycombe Wanderers in a club record transfer fee of £150,000. Midway through his first season at Adams Park, 'Willo' scored his second league hat-trick, against Stockport County in February 1996. Throughout his playing career, 'Willo' could be frustrating one minute, but the next, brilliant, with some of his goals scored from unbelievable angles, in, and outside the penalty area. He was released on a free transfer in February 1997, joining Third Division strugglers Hereford United, who unfortunately lost their league status in the last game of the season, when they were unable to beat Brighton at Edgar Street, with 'Willo' in the starting line-up for United. Following a short spell at Walsall, he was re-united with Frank Burrows at Cardiff City, finding his mark immediately to form a successful, goal scoring partnership with Kevin Nugent as the Bluebirds gained promotion from the Third Division, with 'Willo' scoring twelve league goals. He was on his travels again shortly before the start of season 1999/2000, joining York City, later joining Darlington, from where he eventually returned to the Vetch Field, when he was signed by manager John Hollins in July 2001. During the latter part of his career, 'Willo' proved to be a more effective player down the centre of the field, where he was quite strong in aerial situations as well as being able to utilise his pace. He was least effective however, when used by a number of clubs as an out and out right sided winger. His return to the Vetch Field saw him disappoint in front of goal, but with a lot of off the field problems at the Vetch Field, it was not surprising that the side were unable to concentrate on football. Although he had lost some of his electric pace, he still possessed the ability to go past his marker and set up goalscoring opportunities. Under manager Colin Addison he was utilised to the greatest effect when coming on as a second half substitute to make up a three man attack. In late April 2002 he scored a hat-trick in the West Wales Senior Cup Final win over Hakin United. Under Brian Flynn however he struggled to make an impact, and was released at the end of the 2002/03 season, and, following an initial trial period, signed a contract until the end of the season with Kidderminster Harriers. Released by manager Jan Molby in May 2004, a month later he signed a one year contract, with an option for another year with non-league side Bath City, but after finishing the season as top goalscorer, in May 2005 he signed for Conference North side Redditch United along with former Swans team-mate Lee Jenkins.

32. WILLIAMS, (JACK) John Lewis James

Birthplace: Rhayader, 15/1/1890. **Died:** Mold, 22/10/1969
Ht: 5ft-9ins, **Wt:** 11st-0lbs
Swans debut: v. Barry (h), 13/9/1913, Sth. Lge

Swansea Town Career Statistics			
Season	*League*	*FAC*	*WC*
1920/21	17	2	
1921/22	31/2gls	7	1
1922/23	37/2gls	2	3
Total	85/4gls	11	4

Career:
Builth Wells
Nottingham Forest (signed in March 1912) lge 4/1gls
Tottenham Hotspur (signed in close season 1912)
Swansea Town (signed in 8/9/1913)
Army Football
Swansea Town (signed in 10/12/1919)
Mold Town (signed in June 1925)

Honours: Southern League Representative XI, West Wales Senior Cup Winner–1923

Previously with Nottingham Forest and Tottenham Hotspur, he originally signed for the Swans in early September 1913, playing in ten Southern League games in the 1913/14 season, and seventeen during season 1919/20 after demobilisation. In February 1914 he was selected as a reserve for the Wales International game against Scotland in Glasgow. He initially played for the Swans in a forward position, playing in all three inside positions, and it was not until he returned after five years service with the colours, mostly in the Far East, that the discovery was made that his best position was at half back. In April 1920 he played at the Vetch Field for a Southern League Welsh Clubs XI against a Southern League English Clubs XI. He played in the first ever Swans Football League game at Portsmouth in August 1920 at left half back, and throughout his second period at the Vetch Field alternated between right half, and left half. His first goal for the Swans came during the club's second season in the Football League, against Merthyr Town in December 1921. The proceeds from the home game with Northampton Town on the 2nd October 1920 were set aside for his benefit. In November 1923 he was included in the Swans reserve side that beat Pembroke Dock to win the West Wales Senior Cup. He was released by the Swans on the 2nd May 1924, and in June 1925 he joined Mold Town. Known as a methodical half back, and a popular member of the playing staff at the time at the Vetch Field, he later became a businessman in Mold.

33. WILLIAMS, Leonard (LEN) Horace

Birthplace: Dalton Brook, Yorks, 17/5/1898. **Died:** Rotherham, 29/6/1932
Ht: 5ft-6ins, **Wt:** 10st-5lbs
Swans debut: v. Cardiff City (h), 8/2/1930

Swansea Town Career Statistics			
Season	*League*	*FAC*	*WC*
1929/30	15		2
1930/31	27	1	
Total	42	1	2

Career:
Wath Athletic (signed in close season 1921)
Sheffield Wednesday (signed in May 1923) lge 9
Stockport County (signed in June 1926) lge 39
Wolverhampton Wanderers (signed in June 1927) lge 49
Swansea Town (£350 signed in February 1930)
Wellington Town (signed in 22/9/1931)
Oswestry Town

Honours: Welsh League Representative XI

Full back recruited from non-league side Wath Athletic by Sheffield Wednesday in 1923 who made his Football League debut for Wednesday in the Second Division. Attended Thyburgh Council School, also played for Silverwood Colliery, Parkgate Christ Church prior to joining Wath Athletic. The former Rotherham Schoolboy footballer had earlier won the Rotherham Charity Cup and Mexborough Montague Cup whilst with Parkgate. Following transfers to Third Division North side Stockport County and Second Division side Wolverhampton Wanderers, he signed for the Swans in February1930, making his debut at the Vetch Field against Cardiff City a few days later, replacing Sampy at right full back, and retaining his place until the end of the season. In May 1930 he was one of eight Swans players selected to play for a Welsh League Representative side at the Vetch Field against the Irish Free State. Starting the following season in the Swans line-up he lost his place after twenty-seven league games to Syd Lawrence, and before the end of the season had been taken ill, forcing him to spend nearly all of the summer months in hospital. Released by the Swans, he joined non-league Wellington Town in September 1931, later playing for Oswestry Town.

34. WILLIAMS, PAUL Leslie

Birthplace: Liverpool, 25/9/1970
Ht: 6ft-0ins, **Wt:** 12st-2lbs
Swans debut: v. Stoke City (h), 30/3/1991

Swansea City Career Statistics		
Season	League	WC
1990/91	12	1
Total	12	1

Career:
Sunderland (YTS in July 1987, professional in July 1989) lge 6+4, FAC 1, Others 2
Swansea City (loan in 29/3/1991) lge 12
Doncaster Rovers (signed in July 1993) lge 6+2

Honours: Welsh Cup Winner–1991

Born in Liverpool, but after his family moved to Newcastle he played for his school team, and Sunderland schoolboys prior to joining Sunderland as a YTS trainee. He made his league debut whilst still a trainee as substitute for Brian Atkinson against Plymouth Argyle on the 4th April 1989. Signing as a professional in 1989, he made just two league appearances in the next two seasons, and after a particularly harrowing display at Old Trafford against Lee Sharpe, being substituted at half-time, he was then signed by Swans manager Frank Burrows on

transfer deadline day on the 29th March 1991, along with David Penney from Oxford United to bolster a Swans side in danger of relegation to the Fourth Division. Replacing Simon Davey at right full back, he made his league debut in the Vetch Field victory over Stoke City, retaining his place for the remainder of the season, as the Swans successfully avoided relegation. In May 1991 he was included in the Swans side that beat Wrexham in the Welsh Cup Final at the National Stadium in Cardiff. Returning to Roker Park at the end of the season, he played in the first three league games for Sunderland at the start of the 1991/92 season, before losing his place to John Kay at right full back. In May 1993 he was released by Sunderland, joining Doncaster Rovers on a free transfer. Unfortunately, at Rovers he developed an eye problem which kept him out of the game initially for eighteen months, returning to action in the second half of the 1994/95 season, before having to retire from playing football.

35. WILLIAMS, Philip (PHIL) Dean

Birthplace: Morriston, 24/11/1966
Ht: 5ft-10ins, **Wt:** 10st-12lbs
Swans debut: v. Portsmouth (a), 12/5/1984

	Swansea City Career Statistics				
Season	League	FLC	FAC	WC	FRT
1983/84	0+1				
1984/85	6+5	1		1	1
1985/86	11+1/3gls		1/1gls	1+1	1
1986/87	12+4/1gls	0+1	5/2gls	1	2
1987/88	13+5/1gls	2		2	0+1
Total	42+16/5gls	3+1	6/3gls	5+1	4+1

Career:
Swansea City (from apprentice in October 1984)
Newport County (signed in close season 1988) Conf 22/2gls
Cheltenham Town (signed in April 1989) Conf 65+6/3gls
Newport AFC (signed in close season 1991)
Inter Cardiff (signed in close season 1993)
Barry Town (signed in season 1993/94)
Carmarthen Town (signed in close season 1996)
Inter Cardiff (signed in season 1996/97)
Bridgend Town

Honours: Wales Sch, Yth, Wales Semi-Pro International–4, Welsh Cup Winner–1994, Welsh League First Division Champions–1994, Macbar Cup Winner–1987, West Wales Senior Cup Winner–1987, 1988

Brought up in the rugby stronghold of Llanelli, Phil attended Felinfoel Primary and Bryngwyn Schools, played for Llanelli

Schoolboys, made appearances for the Wales Schoolboys side, arriving at the Vetch Field as an apprentice after leaving school. He made his league debut as substitute for Jimmy Loveridge whilst still an apprentice at Portsmouth, in the club's last league game of the 1983/84 season. An attacking, left sided midfielder, and occasional left full back, he was given his first start for the Swans by manager Colin Appleton early in the next season, just prior to signing professional forms for the Swans. A committed player in the tackle, he also possessed long range shooting ability. Capped at youth level for Wales, he scored his first league goal against Gillingham in March 1986, also scoring in the next game at Bury. The following season he scored in both FA Cup ties against non-league side Wealdstone. During his period at the Vetch Field he had numerous opportunities to stake a regular claim in the starting line-up, but failed to convince the club's coaching staff of his ability, and was released at the end of the 1987/88 season. In May 1987 he played in the Swans reserve side that beat Plymouth Argyle to win the Macbar Cup Final, and was also included in the squad that defeated Briton Ferry Athletic in the West Wales Senior Cup Final. Twelve months later he scored the only goal in the final of the same competition, this time against Pembroke Borough. He signed for Conference side Newport County for the 1988/89 season, making twenty-two league appearances, before the club folded under severe financial problems, remaining in the Conference, signing for Cheltenham Town. He returned to South Wales prior to the start of the 1991/92 season to sign for Beazer Homes Midland Division side Newport AFC, and after two seasons joined Konica League of Wales side Inter Cardiff, signing for Barry Town a couple of months later. By the end of the season he had helped the club win the Welsh League First Division Championship, and also played in the Welsh Cup Final side that beat Cardiff City at the National Stadium in Cardiff. In August 1995 he played in the first leg of Barry Town's European Cup Winners Cup tie against Lithuanian side Zalgiris Vilnius. Following Barry Town's decision to go full time professional, Phil stayed as a part-timer with the club, later had spells with Carmarthen Town and Inter Cardiff, finishing the 1996/97 season as runners-up to Barry Town in the League of Wales, before a cruciate ligament injury suffered during a charity game saw him forced to retire as a player whilst with Bridgend Town. Whilst with Cheltenham Town and Newport Phil played for the Wales Semi-professional side against England on four occasions. Since the early 1990's Phil has worked at the Camford Factory in Llanelli.

36. WILLIAMS, Ronald (RON)

Birthplace: Llansamlet, 23/1/1907. **Died:** Swansea, 30/3/1987
Ht: 5ft-8ins, **Wt:** 10s-10lbs
Swans debut: v. Notts. County (h), 25/12/1929

Swansea Town Career Statistics			
Season	*League*	*FAC*	*WC*
1929/30	16/12gls	1	2/1gls
1930/31	39/17gls	1	1/1gls
1931/32	40/7gls	1	7/1gls
1932/33	28/8gls	1	
1933/34	14/2gls		
1936/37	31/3gls	4/2gls	1
1937/38	8/2gls		1/2gls
Total	176/51gls	8/2gls	12/5gls

Career:
Bethel Juniors
Swansea Amateurs

Llanelly (loan in season 1927/28)
Swansea Town (signed in 10/5/1929)
Newcastle United (£1,500 signed in 18/11/1933) lge 35/14gls, FAC 1
Chester (£800 signed in April 1935) lge 24/15gls
Swansea Town (signed in May 1936)
Lovells Athletic (signed in August 1938)
Llanelly (signed in 6/1/1939)
Milford United (signed in late February 1939)
Haverfordwest Athletic (signed in November 1946)

Honours: Wales Full–2, Welsh Cup Winner–1932, Welsh League Representative XI, Welsh League Challenge Cup Winner–1939

A former Loughor and Llansamlet Schoolboy who played rugby at school, and started his football career with the National Oil Refineries side in Skewen, and Swansea Sunday League side Bethel Juniors, prior to signing for Swansea Amateurs. Played a few games for Llanelly during season 1927/28, and in May 1929 signed as a professional for the Swans after playing most of the previous season for the Swans 'A' team. Limited to playing Welsh League and the occasional Combination matches, just a couple of days prior to making his league debut he had impressed against Watford at the Vetch Field scoring two goals in a Combination game. With the Swans at the time having a crisis with regards goalscoring, he was given his league debut against Notts. County on Christmas Day 1929, scoring a hat-trick in a 3-0 victory, and by the end of the season had finished top goalscorer with twelve league goals. In May 1930 he was one of eight Swans players who were selected to play for a Welsh League Representative side at the Vetch Field against the Irish Free State. His first full season saw Ronnie finish as joint top goalscorer with Easton, also scoring his second league hat-trick, against Nottingham Forest in November 1930. After the arrival of Cyril Pearce in 1931, he switched to a right wing role, but was still consistently amongst the goalscorers, and played in the Welsh Cup Final victory in May 1932 against Wrexham. Exceptionally quick off the mark, it was thought at the time that he could have become the greatest player to have led the Swans forward line if he had been able to curb his impetuosity, and eliminated the unnecessary vigour in his game. On many occasions his value to the side was not fully appreciated until he was injured, and sidelined. He was transferred for a fee of £1,500 to First Division side Newcastle United in November 1933, scoring thirteen league goals in what turned out to be a relegation season for United, but by the time he had signed for Chester in 1935 had made two international appearances for Wales. His first, on the 29th September 1934 at Cardiff against England, and his second on the 21st November 1934 against Scotland in Aberdeen. The 1935/36 season saw Chester gain promotion from the Third Division North in runners-up position with Ronnie scoring fifteen league goals, but in May 1936 he rejoined the Swans for a second spell. His first season back at the Vetch Field saw Ronnie included on a regular basis in the Swans starting line-up, but for the next two seasons he played mainly in the club's reserve teams. Released in May 1938 he joined Lovells Athletic, later, in early January 1939 he signed for Llanelly, making his debut for the 'Reds' at Milford Haven on the 14th January 1939. However, towards the end of February he joined Milford United, playing in the side that beat Aberaman to win the Welsh League Challenge Cup Final, also scoring a goal in the final. Season 1942/43 saw him make appearances in Regional Football for Aberaman, and in April 1943 he made a surprise guest appearance for Bristol City in a West Regional Cup tie against the Swans at the Vetch Field, scoring in a 1-1 draw. When organised football was resumed after WW2, he remained in Welsh League football with Haverfordwest Athletic, living in Swansea up to his death in March 1987. A fine cricketer with Swansea Cricket Club, during the Second World War he served as a policeman, later, during his employment in the Swansea Council Housing Department, was also a Bowls player of some note, playing for Wales in 1976.

37. WILLIAMS, Ronald (RONNIE) Arthur

Birthplace: Swansea, 12/9/1949
Ht: 5ft-4¼ins, **Wt:** 9st-10lbs
Swans debut: v. Chester (h), 27/4/1968

Swansea Town Career Statistics			
Season	League	FAC	WC
1967/68	1		
1968/69	7+1/1gls	1	2
Total	8+1/1gls	1	2

Career:
Swansea Town (signed from juniors, professional in September 1968)
Yeovil Town (signed in close season 1969) Total apps 7
Pembroke Borough (signed in close season 1970/71)

Honours: Wales Yth

Brought up in the Greenhill area of Swansea, Ronnie attended Hafod, Cadle and Penlan Schools, played for his school sides, Swansea Schoolboys and Caerethin Colts, prior to joining the groundstaff at the Vetch Field on leaving school. Despite his small stature, he was a consistent goalscorer in the Swans' Football Combination and Welsh League sides, prior to being given a professional contract in September 1968. Ronnie made his Swans debut as a replacement for Brian Evans at outside left against Chester in April 1968, after being selected a couple of days previously for the Wales Youth squad to play Scotland. The following season he made further appearances in the Swans side, scoring his only goal in a 2-1 defeat at Brentford in December 1968. Released at the end of the season, he joined non-league side Yeovil Town as a full time professional, but after just three months returned to Swansea, where he made occasional appearances in the Swansea Senior League for Hafod Brotherhood. Missing the next twelve months he joined Welsh league side Pembroke Borough in the 1970/1 close season, but after a handful of appearances, retired from the game at the age of twenty-two. Since returning to Swansea, Ronnie worked in a Timber Yard, and for the last fifteen years has worked for Alcoa in Waunarlwydd.

38. WILLIAMS, STEPHEN Michael

Birthplace: Swansea, 5/11/1954
Ht: 5ft-10ins, **Wt:** 9st-7lbs
Swans debut: v. Lincoln City (h), 9/3/1976

Swansea City Career Statistics	
Season	League
1975/766	7+1/1gls
Total	7+1/1gls

Career:
Arsenal (from apprentice in December 1971)
Bristol City (signed in close season 1973)
Swansea City (signed in March 1976)
Haverfordwest County (signed in close season 1976)

Honours: Wales Sch–2, FAYC–1972, South East Counties League Champions–1972

Former Swansea schoolboy who spent over two and a half years at Highbury with Arsenal, failed to make a first team appearance, and after spending a season with Bristol City as a semi-professional played for Haverfordwest County, Ammanford Town and Barry Town in the Southern League before drifting into Swansea Senior League football with Waun Wen. Brought up in the Brynmelyn area of Swansea, Stephen attended St. Josephs and Bishop Vaughan Schools, made two international appearances for Wales in 1969 against England and Scotland prior to signing apprentice forms for the 'Gunners'. A trialist with Arsenal at the age of eleven, Stephen played in the semi-final of the FA Youth Cup in season 1971/72, the same side as Liam Brady, and was included in the squad that beat Cardiff City in the final. He also appeared regularly that season in the side that won the Football Combination Cup and South East Counties League. Signed by manager Harry Grifiths on non-contract terms, he made his league debut as substitute for Micky Conway at the Vetch Field against Lincoln City. A left sided player who was capable of playing in attack, or in midfield, he scored his only goal for the Swans in his second game, his first start for the Swans, at the Vetch Field against Stockport County. He was surprisingly released at the end of the season, despite giving some impressive performances. Linking up with Welsh League side Haverfordwest County, after a number of seasons he finished his playing career in the Swansea Senior League with Waun Wen, working for a number of years on road resurfacing and construction.

39. WILLIAMS, WAYNE

Birthplace: Lower Cwmtwrch, Swansea 2/7/1945
Ht: 5ft-9ins, **Wt:** 10st-10lbs
Swans debut: v. Bradford City (a), 4/3/1969

Swansea Town Career Statistics	
Season	*League*
1968/69	0+1
Total	0+1

Career
Cwmtwrch Wanderers (signed in 1960)
Pontardawe Athletic (signed in close season 1961/62)
Ebbw Vale (signed in close season 1963/64)
Ammanford Town (signed in close season 1966/67)
Swansea Town (signed in close season 1967/68)
Ammanford Town (signed in season 1969/70)
Clydach United (signed in close season 1972/73)

Honours: Wales Amateur–3

A Welsh Amateur international inside forward who after some impressive performances in the Swans Football Combination and Welsh League sides during season 1968/69, was given his opportunity as a substitute for Willie Screen, thirteen minutes from the end of the game at Bradford City in early March 1969. He failed to make any further appearances for the Swans, and after refusing the terms offered to him to go full-time, left the Vetch Field at the end of the season, returning to Ammanford Town. During the 1968/69 season he made appearances for the Wales Amateur side against England at Vicarage Road, Watford, also against Ireland and Scotland. Brought up in Lower Cwmtwrch in the Swansea Valley, Wayne attended Troglen Juniors and Maes-yr-Dderwen Schools, and with only rugby played at school, played junior football with Gurnos Rebels. His first senior club was Neath League side Cwmtwrch Wanderers, before being elevated to the Welsh League with Pontardawe Athletic at the age of sixteen. Two seasons with Athletic saw him then have three seasons with Ebbw Vale, before returning to West Wales to sign for Roy Saunders at Ammanford Town. After only one season at Rice Road he was signed by Swans manager Billy Lucas shortly before the start of the 1967/68 season. After leaving school, Wayne worked initially as a timekeeper with Abercrave based factory Penny Chain, manufacturers of back pedalling brakes. After three years he went to work in the Open Cast Mining Industry, before he became self-employed as a Bread/Confectionery salesman. At this time he declined the opportunity of employment at the BP Llandarcy Refinery and playing for the club's football side. After returning to Ammanford Town, he played in a couple of friendly games for Carmarthenshire League side Pullmans, scoring four goals in one match, before taking over as player manager at Welsh League side Clydach United in the 1972 close season. After two seasons with Clydach, an achilles tendon problem saw him have to retire as a player, and later his position as manager.

40. WILLIS, ARTHUR

Birthplace: Denaby, 2/2/1920. **Died:** Haverfordwest, 7/11/1987
Ht: 5ft-7ins, **Wt:** 11st-5lbs
Swans debut: v. Liverpool (h), 25/9/1954

Career:
Tottenham Hotspur (amateur signed in 1938, professional in January 1944) lge 144/1gls

Northfleet (loan)
Finchley (loan during WW2)
Swansea Town (£3,000 signed in 22/9/1954)
Haverfordwest County (player manager signed in 8/10/1960)

Swansea Town Career Statistics			
Season	*League*	*FAC*	*WC*
1954/55	32	3	2
1955/56	41	1	3
1956/57	16		
1957/58	7	1	
Total	96	5	5

Honours: England Full–1, Second Division Champions–1950, First Division Champions–1951, West Wales Senior Cup Winner–1955, Welsh League First Division Champions–1961, Welsh League Challenge Cup Winner–1961

After playing at junior level near his home in Denaby Main, Yorkshire, he signed amateur forms for Spurs shortly before the outbreak of war, and joined the professional staff at White Hart Lane in 1945. In the early post war seasons he made regular first team appearances for the Londoners before losing his place after the arrival of Alf Ramsey, and was a member of the Spurs side that won the Second and First Division Championships in consecutive seasons. In October 1951 he made his only international appearance for England at left full back, replacing Eckersley at Highbury against France, with his Spurs team mate Alf Ramsey in the other full back position. A stylish full back who was signed by manager Billy McCandless for £3,000 in late September 1954, he followed his former Spurs team mate Ronnie Burgess to the Vetch Field. In May 1955 he was included in the Swans side that beat Llanelly in the West Wales Senior Cup Final. Missing few games during his first two seasons at the Vetch Field, playing in either full back position, he played in the 1956 Welsh Cup Final defeat by Cardiff City, and when the players reported back for pre-season training in August 1956 he assisted Joe Sykes in his new role as player/assistant coach. In October 1960 he became player manager at Welsh League side Haverfordwest County, the first time the club had made a full time appointment, and by the end of his first season in charge had led the club to the Welsh League First Division Championship, also beating Llanelly in the Welsh League Challenge Cup Final. However, within a couple of days of Haverfordwest winning the League Championship he had been taken into Withybush Hospital with internal problems. Retiring as a player in 1963, he remained at Bridge Meadow for a further three years as Steward, also running the club's Pembrokeshire League side, and later becoming a Driving Instructor in the town. For a number of years he was also a scout for his old club Tottenham Hotspur in West Wales, and remained in Haverfordwest up to his death in November 1987.

41. WILMOT, RHYS James

Birthplace: Rogiet, Gwent, 21/2/1962
Ht: 6ft-1ins, **Wt:** 12st-0lbs
Swans debut: v. Gillingham (a), 27/8/1988

Swansea City Career Statistics	
Season	League
1988/89	16
Total	16

Career:
Arsenal (apprentice in 1978, professional in 8/2/1980) lge 8, FLC 1
Hereford United (loan in 18/3/1983) lge 9
Leyton Orient (loan in 27/5/1984) lge 46, FLC 4, FAC 4
Swansea City (loan in 26/8/1988)
Plymouth Argyle (loan in 23/2/1989, £100,000 signed in March 1989) lge 133, FLC 8, FAC 2, Others 4
Grimsby Town (£87,500 signed in 1/7/1992) lge 33, FLC 4, FAC 4, Others 2
Crystal Palace (£80,000 signed in 9/8/1994) PL 5+1, FAC 1
Torquay United (signed in 16/8/1996) lge 34, FLC 1, Others 1
Aylesbury United (signed in August 1997)

Honours: Wales Sch, Yth, U-21–6

Former apprentice goalkeeper at Highbury with Arsenal who was signed by Swans manager Terry Yorath on a three month loan transfer prior to the start of the 1988/89 season. The Swans had gained promotion a few months earlier, and had yet to replace Michael Hughes, who had been forced to retire on medical advice. The only other goalkeeper on the playing staff at the Vetch Field was another recent recruit prior to the season, Lee Bracey. Capped at schoolboy, and youth level for Wales, the Newport born stopper was initially third choice at Highbury, behind Pat Jennings and George Wood, and then had to contend with the emerging John Lukic, with first team opportunities extremely limited. The former Chepstow High School, Newport Schoolboys and Rogiet Juniors keeper initially joined Arsenal on associate schoolboy forms in 1977, signing as an apprentice in July 1978. After gaining youth caps for Wales, he made his Wales U-21 debut against France during season 1981/82, making a further two appearances for the U-21's before he eventually made his league debut with Hereford United on loan in March 1983, becoming the sixth goalkeeper used by the club through the season. Following a season long loan transfer to Leyton Orient during 1984/85, where he was an ever present, in January 1986 he finally made his debut for the 'Gunners', in a Milk Cup, Fourth Round tie at Aston Villa. His next first team appearance for Arsenal, his league debut for the club, came against the same opponents at Villa Park later in the season in March. He impressed many observers during his loan period at the Vetch Field, with his consistent performances one of the

reasons the club had started the season successfully. With the £100,000 transfer fee proving to be a stumbling block in making his transfer permanent, within weeks of his returning to Highbury, he had agreed to join Second Division side Plymouth Argyle on an initial loan which was eventually made permanent. Over the next four seasons he made regular appearances for Argyle, and following the club's relegation in 1992, remained in the Second Division, signing for Grimsby Town. After a handful of appearances for Crystal Palace in the Premiership, as back up to Nigel Martyn, he finished his professional career in Devon with Torquay United. Shortly after drifting into the non-league scene with Ryman League side Aylesbury United in August 1997, a month later he retired through injury. He became the licensee of the Batemans Arms in the Herefordshire village of Shobdon until December 2000, and then joined the Devon & Cornwall Police Force in January 2001.

42. WILSON, AMBROSE Maxwell

Birthplace: Lurgan, Northern Ireland, 10/10/1924
Swans debut: v. Blackburn Rovers (h), 16/9/1950

Swansea Town Career Statistics		
Season	League	WC
1950/51	1	1
Total	1	1

Career:
Belfast Celtic (signed in 9/12/1944)
Glenavon (signed in 26/8/1946)
Belfast Celtic (signed in 28/9/1946)
Glenavon (signed in 28/1/1949)
Swansea Town (signed in 25/7/1950)

One of a number of Irish players introduced to the Vetch Field by managers Haydn Green and Billy McCandless in the late 1940's and early 1950's. Signed from Glenavon, Ambrose made just the one league appearance for the Swans, against Blackburn Rovers at the Vetch Field in September 1950, at right half back, with Billy Lucas reverting to inside forward to accommodate him. He joined the Swans within days of Roy Paul moving to Manchester City, and it was thought at the time that he would be a successor to the Welsh International in the Swans line-up. He also played in a Welsh Cup tie in March 1951 at Newport County. In May 1952 he was placed on the open to transfer list by the Swans and left the Vetch Field playing staff, returning to Ireland.

43. WILSON, MARK Anthony

Birthplace: Scunthorpe, 9/2/1979
Ht: 5ft-11ins, **Wt:** 13st-0lbs
Swans debut: v. Scunthorpe United (a), 13/9/2003

Swansea City Career Statistics		
Season	League	LDV
2003/04	12/2gls	1
Total	12/2gls	1

Career:
Manchester United (from trainee in 16/2/1996) PL 1+2, FLC 2, Others 3+2
Wrexham (loan in 23/2/1998) lge 12+1/4gls
Middlesbrough (£1,500,000 signed in 9/8/2001) PL 6+10, FLC 5/2gls, FAC 2+1

Stoke City (loan in 14/3/2003) lge 4
Swansea City (loan in 12/9/2003)
Sheffield Wednesday (loan in 21/1/2004) lge 3
Doncaster Rovers (loan in 3/9/2004) lge 1+2, LDV 1
Livingston (loan in 25/1/2005) Slge 4+1, SC 1

Honours: England Sch, Yth, U-21–6, FAW Inv Cup Winner–1998

Former trainee at Old Trafford with Manchester United who was signed by Wrexham manager Brian Flynn on loan in February 1998, making his league debut as substitute at Burnley on the 24th February 1998, making his first league start two games later at Northampton. Returning to Old Trafford, his debut for the first team came in the Worthington Cup competition against Bury on the 28th October 1998, also playing in the next round against Nottingham Forest. He had to wait until October 1999 before he made his Premiership debut, at Chelsea as substitute for David Beckham. Capped at schoolboy and youth level, he gained his first U-21 cap for England against Spain in February 2000. Along with team mate Jonathan Greening, he followed former United coach Steve McClaren to Middlesbrough for a fee in the region of £1,500,000 in August 2001, but unfortunately some early season injury problems restricted his effectiveness for his new club. Following a loan transfer to Stoke City in March 2003, and struggling to make an impact at the Riverside stadium in season 2003/04, he was signed for a second time by Brian Flynn, this time for the Swans. During his loan period at the Racecourse with Wrexham, he was a member of their side that beat Cardiff City in the Final of the FAW Invitation Cup. Making his debut at his hometown club, Scunthorpe United, Mark impressed during his two month loan transfer, which sadly saw him return to the Riverside with a hamstring injury picked up in his last appearance. A cultured midfielder, with a good range of ball skills, and passing ability, he scored two valuable goals for the Swans during his loan transfer at the Vetch Field. In the second half of season 2003/04 he joined Second Division Sheffield Wednesday on a month's loan transfer, and in early September 2004 he had a loan spell at Doncaster Rovers, followed by a loan spell in Scotland with Livingstone.

44. WIMBLETON, PAUL Philip

Birthplace: Havant, 13/11/1964
Ht: 5ft-8ins, **Wt:** 10st-12lbs
Swans debut: v. Exeter City (a), FAC-2, 5/12/1992

Swansea City Career Statistics			
Season	League	FAC	AGT
1992/93	10+4/1gls	4+1/1gls	1
Total	10+4/1gls	4+1/1gls	1

Career:
Portsmouth (from apprentice in 23/2/1982) lge 5+5
Cardiff City (signed in 15/8/1986) lge 118+1/17gls
Bristol City (£60,000 signed in 26/5/1989) lge 10+6/2gls
Shrewsbury Town (£60,000 signed in 18/1/1990) lge 25+9/1gls
Maidstone United (loan in 17/1/1991) lge 2/1gls
Exeter City (signed in 6/9/1991) lge 35+1/4gls
Swansea City (signed in August 1992)
Barry Town (signed in season 1993/94)

Honours: England Sch, Welsh League First Division Champions–1994, Welsh Cup Winner–1994

Former Havant and England schoolboy international who after starting his career as an apprentice at Fratton Park with Portsmouth, made his league debut against Fulham in March 1982. He was signed by Cardiff City manager Frank Burrows in August 1986, ending his first season at Ninian Park as top goalscorer with eight league goals. The following season the Bluebirds finished runners-up in the Fourth Division, with Paul scoring nine league goals, but missed out on an appearance in the Welsh Cup Final against Wrexham at the Vetch Field. Following two £60,000 transfers to Bristol City and Shrewsbury Town, and a loan period with Maidstone United, Paul joined Exeter City in September 1991, and after being released in May 1992 agreed to join Frank Burrows at the Vetch Field on an initial trial basis. He had to wait until almost half way through the season before he made his debut for the Swans, in an FA Cup, Second Round tie at Exeter City, which saw Paul score in a 5-2 win. His league debut came nearly two weeks later at Rotherham United. He was released at the end of the season joining Barry Town, winning the Welsh League First Division Championship, and also beating Cardiff City in the Welsh Cup Final at the National Stadium, Cardiff in his first season at the club.

45. WOOD, JAMIE

Birthplace: Salford, 21/9/1978
Ht: 5ft-10ins, **Wt:** 13st-0lbs
Swans debut: v. Rushden & Diamond (h), 10/8/2002

Swansea City Career Statistics					
Season	League	FLC	FAC	LDV	FAWP
2002/03	13+4/2gls	1/1gls	1	1	1/1gls
Total	13+4/2gls	1/1gls	1	1	1/1gls

Career:
Manchester United (from trainee in 10/7/1997)
Royal Antwerp, Belgium (loan in 1997/98 season)
Hull City (signed in 21/7/1999) lge 15+32/6gls, FLC 2+3,
    FAC 3+2/1gls, Others 2+1

Halifax Town (signed in 10/8/2001) lge 10+6, FLC 1,
    FAC 1/1gls, Others 0+1
Swansea City (signed in 26/7/2002)
Total Network Solutions (signed in close season 2003)

Honours: Cayman Islands–2, Welsh Premier Champions–2005,
Welsh Cup Winner–2005

Arrived on trial at the Vetch Field during the first week of pre-
season training and impressed Swans manager Nick Cusack
enough to be offered a one year deal, starting the new season
along side James Thomas, scoring two goals in his first four
games. Such was his form on the right side of attack that he
soon became a firm favourite with the supporters with his all
action style. Earlier in his career he had joined Manchester
United's centre of excellence at the age of nine, after being
picked up playing in the Sunday League in Salford. Graduating
to the United youth team he played alongside Mark Wilson,
John Curtis and Wes Brown, winning the Lancashire Youth Cup,
beating Blackburn Rovers in the Final, and Jamie scoring the
winning goal. Towards the end of his first year as a professional
he went to United feeder club Royal Antwerp in Belgium on
loan along with Ronnie Wallwork and Danny Higginbotham.
Failing to make a first team appearance at Old Trafford, he was
persuaded by former United school of excellence coach Warren
Joyce to join him at Hull City. Making his league debut at Exeter
City in the opening match of the 1999/2000 season as substitute
for Harris, his first league goal came, ironically against the
Swans a couple of days later. He finished his first full season in
the league with six league goals, two behind the 'Tigers' top
goalscorer Eyres. His first season at Boothferry Park also saw
Jamie join the international ranks, becoming the 'Tigers' third
current international on the playing staff, when in February 2000
he appeared for the Cayman Islands against Jamaica, who
included team mates Theodore Whitmore and Ian Goodison.
The link up with Cayman came when the Cayman Island
(a British Dependant Territory) took advantage of what they
perceived a loophole enabling them to select any British
passport holder for their team. Although this was later outlawed
by FIFA. The following season with a change of management at
Boothferry Park, and an ankle injury preventing him making a
bigger impact he was released, joining Paul Bracewell at Halifax
Town on an initial trial. Financial problems inside the club
however, saw the club tumble from one crisis to another, and
eventually relegation to the Conference at the end of the season,
with all the playing staff being made redundant. Despite a good
start with the Swans at the Vetch Field, his season was disrupted
through suspensions and a broken metatarsal in his foot, and
then a training ground injury further aggravated his foot
sidelining him for the large part of the second half of the season.
He was released at the end of the season, signing initial non-
contract forms for Total Network Solutions of the League of
Wales, scoring three goals in pre-season matches. At the start of
the season he played in the club's UEFA Cup tie at Manchester
against City losing 5-0, having ten minutes of the game as
substitute, in the new City of Manchester Stadium. The second
leg saw Jamie start the game. Signing a contract for the

remainder of the season with TNS, he led the goalscorers chart
as the club battled it out with Rhyl for the League of Wales
Championship, eventually finishing runners-up, and also
playing in the Welsh Cup Final defeat by Rhyl. At the end of the
season Jamie had scored twenty-six league and cup goals for
TNS. The 2004/05 season saw Jamie make appearances in TNS's
UEFA Cup matches against Swedish side Osters IF Vaxjo, and
by May 2005 the club had won the Welsh Premier
Championship, and also beaten Carmarthen Town in the Final
of the Welsh Cup at Llanelli. In July 2005 he played against
Liverpool in the qualifying round of the Champions League.

46. WOODS, ALAN Edward

Birthplace: Doncaster, 15/2/1937
Ht: 5ft-9ins, **Wt:** 11st-6lbs
Swans debut: v. Notts. County (h), 19/9/1957

Swansea Town Career Statistics		
Season	League	WC
1957/58	13	
1958/59	17	1
1959/60		1
Total	30	2

Career:
Tottenham, Hotspur (from juniors in February 1954) lge 54/6gls
Swansea Town (signed in December 1956)
York City (£2,000 signed in July 1960) lge 227+1/4gls
Boston United

Honours: England Sch, Yth

Former England schoolboy international who also gained
honours at youth team level for England prior to making his
league debut for Tottenham Hotspur. Signed by Swans manager
Ronnie Burgess, he made his debut against Notts. County at left
half back, replacing Tom Brown, and throughout his Swans
career also played at right half back, and at inside forward.
He started season 1958/59 as first choice at right half back,
contesting the position through the season with Tom Brown.
A strong tackler, he also used the ball well, but was placed on
the open to transfer list in April 1960. A couple of months later
he was transferred to York City for £2,000, scored on his debut
for the club in the opening fixture of the 1960/61 campaign in a
3-2 win over Millwall. He made over 200 league appearances for
the club, and played at the Vetch Field against the Swans in the
Third Division during season 1965/66, and helped the club win
promotion from the Fourth Division in season 1964/65. After
leaving York City, he played non-league football with Boston
United, Gainsborough Trinity and Bridlington, and settled in
York as a dairyman, with his son Neil also playing for York City.

47. WOODWARD, THOMAS George

Birthplace: Troedyrhiw, 13/11/1900. **Died:** Troedyrhiw,
    23/10/1981
Ht: 5ft-9ins, **Wt:** 11st-4lbs
Swans debut: v. Grimsby Town (a), 30/8/1926

Career:
Troedyrhiw Stars
Merthyr Thursdays
Merthyr Town (signed in 1921) lge 0
Chesterfield (signed in August 1922) lge 4

Bridgend (signed in August 1923)
Llanelly (signed in 1924)
Preston North End (trial in December 1924, signed in January
    1925) lge 24/7gls, FAC 1
Swansea Town (signed in May 1926)
Merthyr Town (signed in 23/5/1929) lge 35/2gls
Llanelly (signed in August 1930)
Taunton Town (signed in September 1931)
Troedyrhiw (signed in season 1931/32 season)

Swansea Town Career Statistics			
Season	League	FAC	WC
1926/27	20		
1927/28	34	1	2
1928/29	5		1
Total	59	1	3

Starting his professional career with Merthyr Town, having
previously played for local sides Troedyrhiw Stars and Merthyr
Thursdays, Thomas failed to make his Football League debut
with Merthyr Town, having to wait until he had signed for
Third Division North side Chesterfield in August 1922. His first
game for Merthyr was against Cardiff City in the Welsh League
on the 24th September 1921, remaining in the club's reserve side
on a regular basis throughout the season. Returning to South
Wales to play firstly for Bridgend and then for Llanelly, he later
signed for First Division side Preston North End after an initial
trial spell, making fifteen league appearances during season
1924/25 when they were relegated to the Second Division.
After making nine league appearances the following season he
joined the Swans in August 1926. Making his Swans debut at
Grimsby Town at right half back in the second league game of
the season, as a replacement for Jimmy Collins, he made
nineteen consecutive appearances, before the returning Collins
regained his place in the Swans line-up. His second season saw
Thomas play in either half back position. Captain of the reserve
side at the Vetch Field for season 1928/29, one of his last
matches for the Swans was when they were beaten by Cardiff
City at Llanelly in the Final of the South Wales &
Monmouthshire Cup Final in early May 1929. Released later in
the month, he returned to Penydarren Park to play in Merthyr's
last season in the Football League, making thirty-seven league
appearances, and also captaining the side. His first game for the
'Martyrs' was against Coventry City in the opening game of the
season. In August 1930 he returned to Stebonheath Park with
Llanelly, later joining non-league side Taunton Town, before
returning to play for Troedyrhiw during the 1931/32 season.
His nephew Vivian made league appearances for Fulham,
Millwall, Brentford and Aldershot, while his other nephew
Laurence made league appearances for Walsall and
Bournemouth. In the summer months he was a keen cricketer
with Troedyrhiw.

48. WOOKEY, Kenneth (KEN) William

Birthplace: Newport, 23/2/1922. **Died:** Newport, Gwent
    11/1/2003
Ht: 5ft-7ins, **Wt:** 11st-7lbs
Swans debut: v. Aldershot (a), 20/11/1948

Career:
Newport County (amateur signed in close season 1938,
    professional in February 1939) lge 14/2gls
Bristol Rovers (signed in 27/12/1946) lge 54/9gls
Swansea Town (£1,000 signed in 3/11/1948)
Hereford United (signed in August 1950) Slge 1/1gls
Ipswich Town (signed in October 1950) lge 15/1gls

Swansea Town Career Statistics			
Season	League	FAC	WC
1948/49	2	2	
1949/50	10		1
Total	12	2	1

Honours: Wales Sch, Welsh Cup Winner–1950, London
Combination Cup Winner–1950

A former Welsh schoolboy right winger in 1936 who, whilst
working at Newport Docks, and playing in the Newport &
District Amateur League, joined County as an amateur in the
close season of 1938 at the age of sixteen, signing professional in
February 1939, the season the club won the Third Division
South Championship. He later rejoined the club when the
Football League was resumed after the war, later transferring to
Bristol Rovers in December 1946. A couple of months prior to
signing for Rovers, Ken played in the County side that were
beaten 0-13 by Newcastle United in October 1946, equalling the
highest score in the Football League at the time. He joined
Rovers in a player exchange transfer involving Wilf Smith.
During wartime he saw service for a number of years in the
RAF. Joining the Swans for a £1,000 transfer fee in November
1948 he made his debut as a replacement for Jack O'Driscoll at
outside right, but was only able to make one further league
appearance in the Swans Third Division South Championship
winning side. He also made two appearances for the Swans in
the FA Cup competition, against Southend United, and Bristol
City. The following season, again as a replacement for
O'Driscoll, he made ten league appearances, also appearing in
the Welsh Cup Final defeat of Wrexham. In May 1950 he was a
member of the Swans reserve side that won at Southend United
to win the London Combination Cup Final. Released by the
Swans at the end of the season, he drifted into non-league
football to sign for Hereford United, but by October he had
returned to the Football League to sign for Third Division South
team Ipswich Town, retiring in May 1951. A one-game wonder
at Hereford, he appeared in just one Southern League game,
against Headington in September 1950, scoring the third goal in
a 3-1 win. He had impressed in a couple of pre-season trial
games but spent most of his time at Edgar Street in the reserves
before returning to the Football League with Ipswich. His son
Ken junior played for Newport County, Port Vale and
Workington, whilst grandson Gary played for Dorset
Combination side Shaftesbury.

49. WRIGHT, James (JIM)

Birthplace: Okehampton, 11/9/1910. **Died:** Grimsby, OND,
    1978
Ht: 5ft-7ins, **Wt:** 10st-12lbs
Swans debut: v. Manchester United (a), 4/12/1937

Swansea Town Career Statistics		
Season	*League*	*WC*
1937/38	4	2
Total	4	2

Career:
Okehampton FC
Exeter City (amateur)
Torquay United (signed in April 1930) lge 28/1gls, FAC 4
Grimsby Town (signed in June 1932) lge 27, FAC 3
Sheffield Wednesday (signed in March 1935) lge 3, FAC 1
Guildford City (signed in May 1936)
Swansea Town (£100 signed in June 1937)
Hartlepool United (signed in 29/7/1938) lge 37

Honours: Midland League Champions–1933, 1934

Signed by manager Neil Harris in June 1937 from Guildford City, Jim made his Swans debut at right full back, replacing Syd Lawrence at Manchester United in December 1937. Playing in the next two league fixtures, he made his last league appearance for the Swans in April 1938 against Luton Town also playing in the Welsh Cup Final drawn game with Shrewsbury Town in May 1938. Starting his playing carer in junior football in Devon, and playing for the Exeter District League side at the age of fifteen, he joined Okehampton FC, and after playing as an amateur for Exeter City, joined Torquay United, making his league debut in a 4-0 defeat at Walsall on the 27th September 1930. Signed by Torquay United manager Frank Womack to replace himself at right full back, he became Womack's first signing when the manager was appointed boss of Grimsby Town two years later, despite struggling to hold down a regular place in the 'Gulls' starting line-up. After a successful first season at Blundell Park, his only appearances in the 'Mariners' starting line-up during his second term was at left full back, but he did make regular appearances in the club's successful reserve side that won the Midland League Championship in 1933 and 1934. In March 1935 he signed for First Division side Sheffield Wednesday, utilised basically in the club's reserve side at Hillsborough, before drifting into non-league football with Southern League side Guildford City in June 1936. His transfer fee of £100 following his signing for the Swans went to Sheffield Wednesday, who had retained his Football League registration. Joining Hartlepool United in the 1938 close season, he was appointed captain, and probably enjoyed his most successful spell in league football immediately prior to the outbreak of the Second World War, making thirty-seven league appearances. He left the club after the outbreak of WW2 and although he was a Joiner by trade, his family were involved in farming.

Y

YORATH, Terence (TERRY) Charles

Birthplace: Cardiff, 27/3/1950
Ht: 5ft-10ins, **Wt:** 11st-10lbs
Swans debut: v. Wolverhampton Wanderers (a), 14/3/1987

Swansea City Career Statistics	
Season	League
1986/87	1
Total	1

Career:
Leeds United (apprentice in 1965, professional in April 1967)
    lge 120+21/10gls
Coventry City (£135,000 signed in August 1976) lge 99/3gls
Tottenham Hotspur (£300,000 signed in August 1979)
    lge 44+4/1gls
Vancouver, Canada (£140,000 in 1981)
Bradford City (signed in December 1982) lge 22+5
Swansea City (signed in 17/7/1986)

Honours: Wales Sch, Yth, U-23–7, Full–59, First Division Champions–1969, 1974

Former Gabalfa Primary, Cathays High School, and Cardiff Schoolboy footballer who joined Leeds United as an apprentice in 1965, and spent the most part of his career with the club as a substitute, or as cover in midfield during a period in the game when United possessed the finest midfield in the First Division. A combative, defensive midfielder, with good organization skills, he gained his first international cap in 1970 against Italy, after previously playing for Wales at Schoolboy, Youth, and at U-23 level, and by the time he had played his last game against Russia in May 1981, had captained his country in 42 out of 59 internationals played. His nine year period as a professional with Leeds United saw him make appearances during seasons 1968/69 and 1973/74 when the club won the First Division Championship, and in seasons 1969/70 and 1970/71 when the club were runners-up in the league. He also played in three losing major Cup Finals, the 1973 FA Cup Final against

Sunderland, the 1975 European Cup Final against Bayern Munich, and the 1973 European Cup Winners Cup Final against AC Milan. Leaving Elland Road in 1976, he remained in the top flight with Coventry City and Tottenham Hotspur, before crossing the Atlantic in 1981 to turn out for Vancouver Whitecaps. On his return to the UK, at the veteran stage of his career, Yorath joined Bradford City as player/assistant coach, before being persuaded by Swans chairman Doug Sharpe to become the Swans manager in July 1986. Shortly after chairman Doug Sharpe had won his High Court case, he offered the managerial position to Yorath, a position which was primarily a player managerial role, with a view to playing only in emergencies. Taking over a side recently relegated from the Third Division, Yorath inherited a very young side, and had the experienced Chris Harrison, Tommy Hutchison, Nigel Stevenson and Dudley Lewis to call on.
A tremendous start to his first season in charge saw the Swans occupy a top three placing for the first half of the season, reach the fourth round of the FA Cup competition, only for injuries in a small squad to take its toll. In March 1987 Yorath was forced to include himself in the side that played at Molineux against Wolverhampton Wanderers, with defenders Melville, Lewis and Williams all sidelined. Nevertheless, the following season the Swans achieved promotion albeit from the Play Offs, and his enthusiastic approach to management had alerted the Football Association of Wales, who offered him the role of manager of the Welsh National side for three matches in April 1988, replacing David Williams. A position which was later made into a permanent post, combined with his managerial duties with the Swans. In February 1989 he left the Vetch Field to take over as manager at Bradford City, only to return to the Vetch Field as manager in March 1990, replacing Ian Evans. Yorath lasted only twelve months in his second period as manager at the Vetch Field, with chairman Doug Sharpe sacking him in March 1991, with relegation to the Fourth Division looming. During his five year reign as manager of Wales, the national side recorded impressive victories over Germany, Italy and Brazil, and came within one game of becoming the only home nation to qualify for the 1994 World Cup Finals. His international pedigree was further enhanced between 1995 and 1997 when, as boss of the Lebanon national team, he helped them rise some 60 places in the FIFA World Rankings table. Since returning to the UK, Terry has been involved in coaching roles at Huddersfield Town and Bradford City, before joining Sheffield Wednesday, initially as First Team Coach, before the start of the 2000/01 campaign, later becoming manager. In November 2001, Terry was named as the new manager of Sheffield Wednesday, having taken on the job as caretaker when Peter Shreeves left. After an initial promising start, he lasted less than a year, and at the end of October 2002 following a poor run of results, with the club also struggling financially off the field he was released from his position as manager. He was made assistant to Peter Jackson at Huddersfield Town prior to the start of the 2003/04 season, and enjoyed instant success, as the club bounced back from being relegated, by winning the Third Division Play Off Final at the Millenium Stadium in Cardiff against Mansfield Town, winning 4-1 on penalties.

Other Players

The following players played at the start of season 1939/40 when the Football League was suspended because of the start of the Second World War.

COULTER, John (JACKIE)

Birthplace: Whiteabbey, County Antrim, Ireland, 1/12/1912.
Died: Belfast, 11/1/1981
Ht: 5ft-7½ins, **Wt:** 10st-5lbs
Swans debut: v. West Bromwich Albion (h), 26/8/1939

Swansea Town Career Statistics	
Season	League
1939/40	3
Total	3

Career:
Brantwood (signed in close season 1931)
Belfast Celtic (professional in April 1932)
Everton (£4,000 signed in February 1934) lge 50/16gls,
    FAC 8/8gls
Grimsby Town (signed in October 1937) lge 25/11gls, FAC 2
Chelmsford City (signed in June 1938)
Chester (signed in March 1939) lge 4
Swansea Town (signed in 8/7/1939)

Honours: Northern Ireland–11, Irish League XI–2, Carrick Summer League Cup Winner

Irish wing wizard Jackie Coulter, after starting his football career at Whiteabbey P.E.S. in 1924, made appearances for amateur sides North End FC, Carrickfergus, Brantwood, Dunmurry and Distillery 'A', returned to Brantwood for a second spell in the 1931 close season, prior to signing for Belfast Celtic almost twelve months later. He represented the Irish League and made his international debut against Scotland in Glasgow on the 16th September 1933, gaining three caps before signing for Everton. Just prior to signing for Everton, playing in an Irish Cup match against Ballymena he was sent off, but Everton were not to be deterred, having already opened talks to sign the winger. Serving his apprenticeship as a motor engineer in Ireland, he quit his trade to try his luck as a footballer in England, and in his early days on Merseyside was reported to be of the unorthodox type and adventurous for a wing man of the thirties. He made his league debut in the First Division for Everton in a 1-1 draw against Portsmouth on the 21st April 1934. After a successful first year at Goodison Park, Jackie unfortunately broke his leg playing for Ireland against Wales on the 27th March 1935 in Wrexham, in a collision with Everton

team mate Ben Williams, and sadly was never the same player again. Joining First Division side Grimsby Town in October 1937, Jackie had a good spell in the 'Mariners' first team line-up, also playing in two further internationals during the 1937/38 season whilst on Town's books against Scotland and Wales. All of his games for the Mariners were successive until he was carried off with a leg injury in his final game at Brentford where he was injured early in the game, and failed to make another appearance for the 'Mariners'. In November 1937, Grimsby Town were fined Four Guineas by the League for playing Coulter before the registration of the player had been completed. After drifting into the Southern League with Chelmsford City, he returned to league action with Chester, following his transfer in March 1939. Jackie was signed by Swans manager Haydn Green in July 1939, along with Sam Briddon and Billy Sneddon. He played in all three Football League matches prior to the league being suspended, plus the Football League Jubilee game, made no appearances for the Swans when Regional Football was established, returning to Ireland. In July 1946 he was appointed manager of Ards, and as late as the seventies, he was known to be scouting for his old club Everton. In his youth Jackie was also a Northern Ireland roller skating champion.

GALLON, John (JACKIE) William

Birthplace: Burradon, Newcastle 12/2/1914. **Died:** NW Surrey, July 1993
Ht: 5ft-8ins, **Wt:** 11st-7lbs
Swans debut: v. West Bromwich Albion (h), 26/8/1939

Swansea Town Career Statistics	
Season	League
1939/40	3
Total	3

Career:
Burradon Welfare
Blyth Spartans (signed in September 1931)
Bedlington United (signed in 1933)
Carlisle United (signed in March 1936)
Birmingham FC (trial in 1936)
Bradford City (signed in April 1936) lge 20/5gls, FAC 1/1gls
Bradford Park Avenue (signed in 15/2/1938) lge 31/4gls,
    FAC 1/1gls
Swansea Town (signed in June 1939)
Gateshead (signed in March 1946) lge 20/2gls, FAC 1
North Shields Athletic (signed in April 1947)

Honours: South Northumberland County FA XI, Northumberland County FA XI

Former Burradon Council Schoolboy inside forward who made his name playing for non-league Burradon Welfare, North Eastern League sides Blyth Spartans and Bedlington United before signing for Second Division side Bradford City in April 1936, making his Football League debut against West Ham United on the 5th December 1936 in the Second Division. His first senior goal came in an FA Cup tie against York City in January 1937. He also scored two goals on his debut in a Third Division North Challenge Cup tie against Darlington in September 1937. Following relegation to the Third Division North at the end of season 1936/37, in February 1938 he returned to Second Division football, signing for rivals Bradford Park Avenue in a player exchange transfer involving Jimmy Robertson, a transfer which was the first between the two clubs regarding a player exchange. Signed by Swans manager Haydn Green in June 1939, after playing in the Football League Jubilee game, he played in all three League matches before the League was suspended following the start of WW2. During WW2 he made guest appearances for Hartlepool United and Bristol City (1939/40), Bolton Wanderers and Bradford City (1940/41), Stockport County (September 1943), Manchester United, Burnley and Rochdale (1943/44), Walsall (September 1944), Port Vale (1944/45). When the Football League was resumed he returned north to sign for Gateshead, making his league debut for the club on the 31st August 1946 against Crewe Alexandra in the Third Division North. Joining North Shields Athletic in April 1947 he later joined Ashington FC in November 1948, and after retiring as a player was a scout for Leicester City for a number of years.

ROGERS, Ehud (TIM)

Birthplace: Chirk, 15/10/1909. **Died:** Chirk, 25/1/1996
Ht: 5ft-7ins, **Wt:** 10st-6lbs
Swans debut: v. West Bromwich Albion (h), 26/8/1939

Swansea Town Career Statistics	
Season	League
1939/40	3
Total	3

Career:
Oswestry Town (signed in 1933)
Wrexham (signed in May 1934) lge 11/2gls
Arsenal (£2,600 signed in January 1935) lge 16/5gls
Newcastle United (£2,500 signed in June 1936) lge 56/10gls, FAC 2
Swansea Town (£700 signed in 5/5/1939)
Wrexham (signed in April 1945) lge 1
Oswestry Town (signed in February 1947)

Honours: Wales Amateur–1, War-Time International–2, Welsh Lge XI, Wales & Ireland Combined XI–1935, London F.A. Challenge Cup Winner–1936, Regional League Cup Winner–1943

A Welsh Amateur International before he caught the eye of Arsenal in 1935. Light, fast and described as 'plucky', he possessed more than a touch of finesse on the ball. He started his amateur career with Weston Rhyn, Llanerch Celts and Chirk, before signing for Oswestry Town in 1933. Joining Wrexham in May 1934, he made his debut at York City in a 0-0 draw on the 27th October 1934, and midway through the season signed for the 'Gunners' for £2,600. In May 1935 he was included in a Wales/Ireland Combined Representative XI that lost 10-4 to an England/Scotland Combined Representative XI at Goodison Park in a King George Jubilee Game. At Highbury he was largely a reserve team player, but did make five appearances in the club's 1935 title winning season, also playing in the Arsenal side which saw Ted Drake score a record seven goals in a 7-1 win over Aston Villa on the 14th December 1935. The following season he was a member of the club's reserve side that won the London F.A. Challenge Cup. Whenever he did get the opportunity, he played well, and it was this form that persuaded Newcastle United to sign him in June 1936 for £2,500. He was known as 'Tim' because his colleagues apparently were unable to pronounce his biblical Christian name. Joining the 'Magpies' Second Division attack, he was lively and dangerous for two seasons, fading just before the outbreak of the Second World War, when he was replaced by another former Highbury reserve, Ralph Birkett. In the season prior to joining the Swans he scored the only goal of the game at the Vetch Field for Newcastle United. Often treating his colleague to a Welsh song in the dressing room before games, he was signed by Swans manager Neil Harris for £700 in early May 1939, but by the start of the season, Harris had tended his resignation to join Swindon Town, with Haydn Green becoming Swans manager in June 1939. He played in all three Football League matches prior to the League being suspended because of the start of the Second World War. Towards the end of the 1942/43 season he played in the second leg of the Regional League West Cup Final against Lovells Athletic at the Vetch Field. He failed to make any other appearances for the Swans when Regional Football was organised, but he did make wartime guest appearances for Wrexham in October 1939, Everton in April 1944, Lovells Athletic, and Aberaman. Rogers served with the RAF in Egypt for a time during the fighting, while he also appeared for his country at full level during the hostilities. He rejoined Wrexham in December 1945, later played for Oswestry Town in 1947, and in 1962 became coach at Chirk, residing in the town, and running a newsagency. His brother Joe, appeared for Manchester City, Chester and Shrewsbury Town.

Swansea Town
Southern League Players

ALLMAN, ARTHUR

Birthplace: Milton, Staffs, 24/12/1890.
Died: Milton, 22/12/1956
Ht: 5ft-11ins, **Wt:** 12st-7lbs

Career:
Smallthorne
Shrewsbury Town
Wolverhampton Wanderers (signed in May 1912)
Swansea Town (signed in 4/10/1913)
Manchester United (£175 in 1/5/1914) lge 12
Millwall (signed in December 1919) lge 6
Port Vale (trial in 1921)
Aberaman Athletic (signed in August 1921)
Crewe Alexandra (signed in August 1922) lge 22
Aberaman Athletic (signed in June 1924)

Consistent, robust right full back, a fearless tackler with an accurate kick who missed few matches during his only season at the Vetch Field. Former Sneyd Green Schoolboy who started his senior playing career with Smallthorne and Shrewsbury Town prior to signing for Wolverhampton Wanderers in May 1912. Along with Cubberley, both players were transferred at the same time from the Swans to Manchester United in May 1914. Allman had been a free transfer signing from Wolverhampton Wanderers, and in later years became captain of Aberaman Athletic.

ANDERSON, DAVID

Birthplace: Shettleston/Bonnyrigg 1881
Ht: 5ft-9ins, **Wt:** 11st-7lbs

Career:
Heart of Midlothian
Bonnyrigg Rose
Preston North End (1910-1911) lge 9/3gls
QPR (signed in July 1912)
Swansea Town (signed in 22/3/1913)
Halifax Town (signed in 1921) lge 10/2gls

Honours: Welsh Cup Winner–1913

The inside forward made a goal scoring debut at Treharris for the Swans in March 1913, and at the end of his first full season (1913/14) was top goalscorer with fourteen league goals which included a hat-trick against Caerphilly in February 1914. As well as playing in the Swans side that beat Pontypridd to win the Welsh Cup in March 1913, he also played in the Swans side that beat First Division side Blackburn Rovers in an FA Cup tie at the Vetch Field in January 1915, and also when the Swans were beaten by Wrexham in the 1915 Welsh Cup Final. He did not feature in the Swans' Southern League side of 1919/20, but later signed for Halifax Town in 1921. During WW1 he was employed in government works.

BALL, BILLY

Career:
Swansea Town (signed in September 1912)
Porth (signed in 17/12/1920)

Honours: Welsh League Representative XI

The scorer of the Swans' first ever competitive goal, against Cardiff City in the opening Southern League fixture in September 1912, he also became the first Swans' player to score a hat-trick, against Aberdare in January 1913, with another hat-trick being scored at Ninian Park against Cardiff City in the semi-final of the Welsh Cup almost a month later. His first season saw him finish as joint top goalscorer with Grierson, and during his four seasons with the Swans in the Southern League proved to be a consistent player, and played in the shock 1-0 win over First Division side Blackburn Rovers in the FA Cup competition. He also became the first Swans' player to be sent off when he received his marching orders in the game against Mid-Rhondda on the 8th March 1913. In April 1920, along with Denoon and Collins, he was selected to play for the Welsh League XI against the Champions of the Welsh League, Mid-Rhondda. Failing to break into the Swans' Football League side, he joined Porth in mid-December 1920, and in September 1921 scored a hat-trick for Porth against Rhymney. After he retired from playing he was involved off the field with Aberavon Quins, and in March 1933 said in the *Daily Post* that he regarded the area as the finest in South Wales with an abundance of talent. During WW1 he was employed in government works.

BASSETT, SPENCER Thomas

Birthplace: Blackheath, JAS, 1986. **Died**: Pozieres, Somme 11/4/1917

Career:
Woolwich Arsenal (amateur in 1906)
Maidstone United
Woolwich Arsenal (signed professional in 3/5/1907) lge 1
Exeter City (signed in 1910)
Swansea Town (signed in 6/9/1913)
Southend United (signed in 31/7/1914)

A former team mate of player manager Whittaker at Exeter City, who earlier in his career made his Football League debut with Woolwich Arsenal. After making his Swans' debut in the opening fixture of the 1913/14 season at Caerphilly, the centre half missed few matches during his only season at the Vetch Field, also playing in the Welsh Cup semi-final defeat by Llanelly. After transferring to Southend United prior to the start of the 1914/15 season, after enlisting for WW1, was killed in action at the Somme while acting as a Bombardier in the 140th Siege Battery, Royal Garrison Artillery.

BATTEN

Career:
Milford
Swansea Town (trial in February 1914)

Along with centre forward Attivel from Ystalyfera, both played on a trial basis in a friendly game at the Vetch Field against Walsall on the 19th February 1914. The goalkeeper made his only first team appearance for the Swans in the last game of the season at Stoke City in late April 1914 as a replacement for Storey

BIRCH, F. A.

Birthplace: Plymouth
Ht: 5ft-9ins, **Wt**: 11st-10lbs

Career:
Plymouth Argyle
Swansea Town (signed in 14/7/1919)

Honours: Royal Navy XI

A prolific goalscorer with Plymouth Argyle, after arriving at the Vetch Field he made just four Southern League appearances all at the start of the season. At the time of his signing for the Swans he was one of the best, if not the best centre forward in Southern League football, and during the few years preceding the war was always to the front with the goal averages. In season 1914/15 he was top goalscorer in the Southern League. During the war he served in the Navy, and supporters of the Swans who can recall the match with the Naval Division at the Vetch Field during the 1918/19 season would surely remember him, for he scored the winning goal, and was a shining light throughout the game.

BOWEN

Career:
Swansea Town (trial in March 1914)

Honours: Wales Amateur

Welsh Amateur International goalkeeper who played for Wales in the 9-1 defeat by England at Plymouth on the 7th February 1914. He had been invited for trial games with the Swans' Welsh League side prior to the international, and on the 21st March 1914 he made his Southern League debut at Aberdare Athletic replacing Storey.

BRAZELL, THOMAS

Career:
Hickleton Main
Swansea Town (12/10/1912)
Swansea Albion (signed by 8/10/1919)

A right winger who made just one Southern League appearance for the Swans, as a replacement for Messer against Pontypridd in November 1912, and who was mainly confined to Welsh League appearances for the club.

BROWN, IVOR Erwin Ronald John

Birthplace: Shardlow, 1/4/1888. **Died**: Swansea, 1966
Ht: 5ft-7ins, **Wt**: 11st-4lbs

Career:
Ripley Town
Tottenham Hotspur (trial in October 1909, professional in November 1909) lge 12
Coventry City (signed in July 1911)
Reading (signed in May 1913)
Swansea Town (signed in 26/2/1914)
Porth (signed by 19/9/1921)

Described in the *Daily Post* at the time of his signing for the Swans as the 'brainbox' of the Reading side. A very speedy and resourceful player, and the fee the Swans paid was almost a record for South Wales football. Earlier in his career he had made his Football League debut with Tottenham Hotspur. His first full season at the Vetch Field (1914/15) saw him finish joint top goalscorer on eight league goals with Lloyd and Breynon, including scoring a hat-trick in an 8-0 win over Brentford in April 1915. Earlier in the season he had been included in the Swans' side that beat First Division Blackburn Rovers in the FA Cup competition, and also in the same season, in May 1915 lose out to Wrexham in the Final of the Welsh Cup He failed to make an appearance in the Swans' Football League line-up, prior to joining Porth in September 1921.

BUCK, Frederick (FRED) Richard

Birthplace: Newcastle-under-Lyme, OND 1880. **Died:** 1952
Ht: 5ft-6½ins, **Wt:** 10st-5lbs

Career:
Stafford Wesleyans
Stafford Rangers
West Bromwich Albion (signed in November 1900) lge 22/6gls
Liverpool (signed in May 1903) lge 13/1gls
Plymouth Argyle (signed in early 1904)
West Bromwich Albion (signed in April 1906) lge 265/84gls
Swansea Town (signed in May 1914)

Honours: Division Two Champions–1911

An experienced centre half by the time he arrived at the Vetch Field in the 1914 close season, the former Newcastle-under-Lyme schoolboy made almost three hundred league appearances for West Bromwich Albion in two spells, including winning the Second Division Championship in 1911, selected to play for a Football League Representative XI, and also playing in the 1912 FA Cup Final defeat by Barnsley.
A misunderstanding over his transfer fee by the Swans, saw the Football League tell the Swans to pay £50 to WBA by the 7th April 1915, with the balance to be mutually agreed between the two clubs. During his only season at the Vetch Field he made just seven Southern League appearances.

BULCOCK, Joseph (JOE)

Birthplace: Burnley 1884
Ht: 5ft-10ins, **Wt:** 11st-6lbs

Career:
Bryn Central

Colne
Bury (signed in 4/5/1906) lge 5
Exeter City (signed in 18/5/1908)
Crystal Palace (signed in close season 1909)
Swansea Town (signed in 3/3/1914)

Honours: England FA Representative XI

A relatively in-experienced left full back at Football League level who had earlier in his career toured with an England Football Association team to South America. Known as one of the finest defenders in the Southern League, he had been with Crystal Palace for four and a half seasons, captained Colne earlier in his career, and played in the last twelve matches for the Swans during season 1913/14. The following season saw him miss few games for the Swans, also play in the shock FA Cup defeat of First Division side Blackburn Rovers, as well as in the Welsh Cup Final defeat by Wrexham.

CARTWRIGHT, William (BILL)

Birthplace: Burton-on-Trent, 24/6/1884. **Died:** Repton, 1971
Ht: 5ft-10ins, **Wt:** 12st-9lbs

Career:
Trent Rovers
Gainsborough Trinity (signed in 31/8/1906) lge 59/4gls
Chelsea (signed in May 1908) lge 44
Tottenham Hotspur (signed in May 1913) lge 13
Swansea Town (signed in close season 1919)
Gillingham

Formerly with Trent Royals earlier in his career, where he gained Junior Boston League Champions Honours on two occasions, and a Uttoxeter Challenge Cup Winner.
An experienced left full back prior to his arriving at the Vetch Field in the 1919 close season, his only Southern League outings for the Swans both came as replacement for Hewitt early in the 1919/20 season against Gillingham and Southampton.
After leaving the Vetch Field in May 1920 he had a spell with Gillingham prior to joining the Southend United coaching staff following his retirement as a player.

CLEVERLEY, ARTHUR

Birthplace: Erith, Kent. **Died:** Killed in action in Thiepual, Somme, France, 4/8/1916
Ht: 5ft-8ins, **Wt:**12st-0lbs

Career:
Brentford (signed in close season 1908)
Swansea Town (signed in 7/9/1912)
Newport County (signed in close season 1914)

Included at right full back for the Swans in the club's opening first class fixture in the Southern League against Cardiff City in September 1912. Missing few matches during his first season with the Swans, the former Brentford defender contested the full back position with Allman during his second season, playing in the semi-final defeat in the Welsh Cup by Llanelly. He joined Newport County for the 1914/15 season, but after enlisting for WW1, he was killed in action while serving as a Private in The King's Liverpool Regiment at Thiepual on the Somme, France, in 4/8/1916.

COLEMAN, JOE

Birthplace: Hastings
Ht: 5ft-8ins, **Wt:** 11st-10lbs

Career:
Hastings & St. Leonards
Brighton & Hove Albion (signed in close season 1909)
Swansea Town (signed in close season 1912)

Inside forward who played in the Swans' first Southern League fixture against Cardiff City at the Vetch Field in September 1912. Midway through the season he became only the second Swans player to record a hat-trick in league football, scoring three against Luton Town in February 1913. His second season at the Vetch Field saw him make nearly all of his appearances in the second half of the season.

CUBBERLEY, STAN (Stanley)

Birthplace: Edmonton, London, JAS, 1883. **Died:** Patricroft, Eccles, 15/6/1933

Career:
Cheshunt
Leeds City (signed in May 1906) lge 181/6gls
Swansea Town (signed in close season 1913)
Manchester United (signed in 1/5/1914) lge 0

Experienced Leeds City left half back who joined the Swans in the 1913 close season, missing few matches during his only season at the Vetch Field. The *Daily Post*, dated 1/5/1914, said that Allman and Cubberley were transferred to Manchester United at the same time, with Cubberley's free transfer to United being an agreement the player had from the Swans following his free transfer signing earlier from Leeds City. One of his last matches for the Swans came in March 1914 when he played in the Welsh Cup semi-final defeat by Llanelly. During WW1 he enlisted with the M.T. section of the R.A.S.C. and in August 1919 was based at Grove Park.

DUFFY, JOHN

Birthplace: Cleator Moor 1886
Ht: 5ft-9ins, **Wt:** 11st-7lbs

Career:
Workington
Bradford City (signed in close season 1909) lge 1
Exeter City (signed in May 1910)
Swansea Town (signed in 5/9/1912)

Honours: Welsh Cup Winner–1913

John Duffy was another player on the Vetch Field playing staff who had played with manager Whittaker at Exeter City, and who also played in the Swans' first Southern League fixture against Cardiff City in September 1912. An ever present that season, in the next two seasons he would miss few matches at right half back. A member of the Welsh Cup winning team of 1913, he also played in the Welsh Cup Final defeat by Wrexham in 1915, and also played earlier in the season in the Swans's side that beat First Division Blackburn Rovers in the Welsh Cup. Later in his career, after WW2 he was on the coaching staff of North Eastern League side Workington.

EAST

Career:
Swansea Town (signed in season 1914/15)

Centre half who made just the one Southern League appearance for the Swans as a replacement for Lock in the 1-0 defeat at Newport County on the 16th January 1915.

EVANS, D. J. (Tich)

Birthplace: Pontypridd. **Died:** Swansea, 18/12/1919
Ht: 5ft-7ins, **Wt:** 10st-0lbs

Career:
Barry
Swansea Town (signed in 30/8/1919)

The left winger's body was discovered by Jack Nicholas one afternoon underneath the grandstand with his head almost severed, and a razor in his hand. He had been depressed ever since the death of his wife Fanny three weeks previously. A native of Cadoxton, Barry he played for Hannah Street School, later with Cadoxton Old Boys, and after coming to the attention of the Barry Directors, played for almost five seasons on the left wing for the club. Employed in Barry as a Boilermaker at the Barry Graving Docks he played against the Swans on many occasions, and at the time of his signing for the Swans, he turned down an offer from Tottenham Hotspur. A promising left winger, he became very much an idol with the Swans supporters, and his death cast a great gloom over the football club, such was his popularity among the players, staff and supporters. He made his Swans' debut in the opening fixture of the 1919/20 season against Luton Town, and prior to his death missed just three league games.

FISHER, ERNIE

Career:
Swansea Eastside FC (signed by close season 1907)
Swansea Town (signed in 4/1/1913)
Swansea Albion (signed in 8/10/1919)

Honours: Welsh Cup Winner–1913

Took over from manager Whittaker in the Swans' goalkeeper jersey, playing for the remaining sixteen matches of the 1912/13 season, also playing in the Welsh Cup Final win over Pontypridd. Despite starting his second season at the Vetch Field in the number one jersey, by late October 1913 he had lost his place to Storey and only made occasional appearances for the Swans up to his last appearance in April 1915 at Ton Pentre. Enlisting in the Army during WW1, after demobilization he joined Swansea Albion.

FYFE, GEORGE

Birthplace: Govan, Lanark
Ht: 5ft-8ins, **Wt:** 11st-7lbs

Career:
Neilston Victoria
Hibernians (signed in May 1904)
Watford (signed in August 1905)
Dundee Hibs (signed in August 1910)
Dumbarton (signed in August 1911)
Dundee Hibs (signed in December 1911)
Halifax Town (signed in January 1912)
Swansea Town (signed in March 1913)

Scottish inside left who made his debut for the Swans at outside left, replacing Swarbrick in March 1913 at the Vetch Field against Croydon Common. His remaining six Southern league appearances that season came at inside left instead of Grierson. Making just two appearances during the 1913/14 season, he scored his only goal for the Swans in a 3-0 home win over Newport County in October 1913. During WW1 he made guest appearances for Abercorn (in season 1916/17) and with Watford.

GILBOY, BERT

Birthplace: Islington
Ht: 5ft-9ins, **Wt:** 11st-7lbs

Career:
Tottenham Hotspur
Preston North End (signed in close season 1913)
Swansea Town (signed in 13/3/1914)

Starting his career with Tottenham Hotspur, Bert Gilboy was primarily an 'A' team player with Preston North End, and after signing for the Swans made his debut at outside right instead of Messer at Barry in late March 1914, making another five appearances up until the end of the season. His only appearance during season 1914/15 came at inside left in mid-January 1915 at Newport County.

GREER, ROBERT

Ht: 5ft-8ins, **Wt:** 11st-7lbs

Career:
Paisley Abercorn
Clyde (signed in close season 1909)
Reading (signed in February 1912)
Swansea Town (signed in 1/8/1913)

The outside left started his career in Scotland with Paisley Abercorn and Clyde, arriving at the Vetch Field from Reading in August 1913. He made his Swans' debut in the opening Southern League fixture of the 1913/14 season, at outside left, making a total of twenty three league appearances during the season, scoring four goals. Three of those goals came in the second league fixture of the season in a 5-0 home win over Barry. He scored the Swans goal in the 2-1 FA Cup Second

Round defeat by Queens Park Rangers, but failed to make the semi-final line-up of the Welsh Cup tie against Llanelly.

GRIERSON, ROBERT

Ht: 5ft-8ins **Wt:** 12st-0lbs

Career:
Scotswood (signed in 28/10/1907)
Newcastle United (signed in 15/4/1908)
Bradford Park Avenue (1908) lge 4/1gls
Rochdale (signed in close season 1910)
Hartlepools United (signed in close season 1911)
Swansea Town (signed in close season 1912/13)
Rochdale (signed in close season 1913)

Honours: Welsh Cup Winner–1913

Inside left who arrived at the Vetch Field prior to the start of the 1912/13 season, playing in the Swans' first Southern League fixture against Cardiff City. By the end of the season he had missed few matches, and finished joint top goalscorer with Ball on eight league goals. He also played in the Welsh Cup Final win over Pontypridd in March 1913, scoring the only goal of the game in the replay. He was released at the end of the season joining Rochdale.

HAMILTON, John (JOCK)

Birthplace: Edinburgh
Ht: 5ft-10ins, **Wt:** 12st-7lbs

Career:
Leith Athletic
Brentford (signed in 26/7/1907)
Leeds City (signed in 25/6/1908) lge 21
Brentford (signed in May 1909)
Swansea Town (signed in August 1912)
Barry AFC (signed in 24/8/1914)

Honours: Welsh Cup Winner–1913

Centre half who prior to arriving at the Vetch Field had made his Football League debut with Leeds City, and who was included in the Swans' opening Southern League fixture against Cardiff City. Missing just four league games during his only season with the Swans, he also played in the Welsh Cup Final win over Pontypridd in March 1913. His second season with the Swans saw him lose his centre half position to Bassett, and after making just six league appearances left the Vetch Field playing staff at the end of the season, joining Barry. One of his last games for the Swans' came in the Welsh Cup semi-final defeat by Llanelly.

HARRIS, Frederick (FRED) McKenzie

Birthplace: Rothwell, Northants, JFM 1884
Ht: 5ft-9ins, **Wt:** 11st-0lbs

Career:
Northampton Town (signed in close season 1911)
Kettering Town (signed in 1912)
Nottingham Forest (signed amateur in February 1914)
    lge 47/12gls
Swansea Town (signed in 12/7/1919)

Kettering Town
South Shields (signed in 1919)
Southend United (signed in July 1921) lge 20/2gls
Kettering Town (signed in season 1922/23)
Rushden Town
Rothwell Town (signed in close season 1925)

An experienced outside right, also capable of playing at centre forward who earlier in his career had extensive experience on the non-league circuit with Rothwell Congs, Burton Swifts, Desborough Town and Kettering Town prior to joining Nottingham Forest as an amateur, graduating to the club's Football League side. During his playing career, Kettering Town appeared to be his base club, having several periods with the club as a player. Arriving at the Vetch Field in July 1919, he started his career with the Swans at outside right in the opening fixture of the 1919/20 season at Luton Town, making a further fourteen league appearances during the first half of the season before losing his place to a young Billy Hole. Prior to serving in the RAF during WW1 he had also played for the English Wanderers in 1914. A classy player, he possessed pace, determination, and was a keen opportunist. He returned to Football League action in season 1921/22 with Southend United before returning to Kettering Town and finishing his career in non-league football with Rushden Town and Rothwell Town in 1925.

HEATH, CLEM

Career:
Swansea Town (signed in season 1914/15)

Right half back who made his Swans' debut in December 1914 at Merthyr Town as a replacement for Duffy, making a further eight league appearances. He failed to make the starting line-up in the FA Cup defeat of Blackburn Rovers, but did feature in the FA Cup Second Round games against Newcastle United, and in the Welsh Cup Final defeat by Wrexham. Employed in Government work in WW1, he rejoined the Swans after the war, and during season 1919/20 made just the one Southern League appearance, in a 2-1 home win over Cardiff City in late September 1919.

HEWITT, Thomas JOHN

Birthplace: Connahs Quay, 26/4/1889.
Died: Cardiff 12/12/1980
Ht: 5ft-9ins, **Wt:** 11st-10lbs

Career:
Sandycroft (signed in season 1906/07)
Connahs Quay (signed in season 1907/08)
Saltney (signed in July 1908)
Wrexham (signed in 1910)
Chelsea (£350 signed in March 1911) lge 8
South Liverpool (signed in May 1913)
Swansea Town (signed in May 1914)

Honours: Wales–8, Chester & District League Champions–1907

An experienced full back in non-league football in North Wales, winning the Chester & District League Championship in 1907 with Sandycroft prior to playing for Connahs Quay, Saltney and then Wrexham. At Wrexham he made the first of three international appearances for Wales in Belfast against Ireland on the 28th January 1911 also playing against England and Scotland two months later. Joining Second Division Chelsea in March 1911, he made a further three international appearances in

season 1912/13, also making his Football League debut with the club. Returning to the North West to sign for South Liverpool, he made a further two appearances for Wales in season 1913/14 before signing for the Swans in May 1914. Missing just one Southern League fixture during his first season at the Vetch Field, he also captained the side that beat First Division Blackburn Rovers in the FA Cup competition, also playing in the Welsh Cup Final defeat by his old club Wrexham. Despite playing in the first fixture of the 1919/20 season at Luton Town, he failed to feature in the Swans line-up after November 1919. By June 1920 he had taken over as player manager of Aberaman Athletic, and was also an engineer with Messrs. Fitt Bros and Davies (Swansea & Cardiff) . The *Daily Post* mentioned on the 23rd January 1921 that along with a Director of the company they had travelled from Cardiff to Newport to execute urgent repairs on the Union Castle Steamer, 'War Soldier', and whilst leaving the boat in the darkness he slipped and fell into the dock. Unconscious for two days, the injuries he received would prevent him from playing football again, later winning damages of £750 against the Union Castle Mail Steamship Company. Later in the mid-1920's he became the Wales and South West representative for mineral water manufacturer Schweppes, working for the company for thirty years. His brother Charles Hewitt was manager of Millwall from 1948 to 1956.

HEYWARD

Career:
Swansea Town (signed in season 1919/20)

Right full back who made just the one Southern League appearance for the Swans as a replacement for Hewitt at the Vetch Field against Brighton & Hove Albion on the 25th October 1919.

HOUSTON, ALEX

Birthplace: Lochie
Ht: 5ft-9ins, **Wt:** 11st-8lbs

Career:
Dundee
Mid-Rhondda
Swansea Town (signed in season 1919/20)
Mid-Rhondda (signed in 22/6/1920)
Porth (signed by 20/9/1921)

Inside forward who joined the Swans from Dundee early in season 1919/20 season, made just the one Southern League appearance, at Millwall in October 1919, before joining Mid-Rhondda in June 1920. Early in season 1919/20 he assisted Dundee Fussel. During WW1 he had been in the Black Watch, a sergeant major in the Pioneer Corps. After retiring as a player he worked for a period as a representative with Fords in London, later settling in Manchester and working in a storeroom of a department store in the city. A keen Bowls player, he captained Lancashire against Yorkshire.

HURST, BEN

Career:
Abertillery
Swansea Town (signed in close season 1914)

Joined the Swans from Welsh League side Abertillery prior to the start of the 1914/15 season, making his Southern League debut at the Vetch Field against Ton Pentre. Missing just two games during the season, he also played in the historic FA Cup success over First Division Blackburn Rovers, also in the Welsh Cup Final defeat by Wrexham.

JEPP, Samuel (SAM) Richard

Birthplace: Northtown, Aldershot 22/2/1887.
Died: Aldershot AMJ 1968
Ht: 5ft-10ins, **Wt**: 12st-0lbs

Career:
Aldershot Athletic
R.A.M.C.
Aldershot Athletic
Southampton (signed amateur in October 1906, professional in April 1907)
South Farnborough (signed in close season 1911)
Swansea Town (signed in close season 1912)
Aberdare (signed in 21/11/1913)

Honours: Welsh Cup Winner–1913

Left half back who played in the Swans' opening Southern League fixture against Cardiff City, also playing in the Welsh Cup win over Pontypridd in March 1913. His second season at the Vetch Field saw him lose his place to Cubberley, playing in only one game, a Welsh Cup tie against Caerleon in October 1913. A jack of all trades, master of none, he later played for Wellington Works, Aldershot in 1919, Surrey Wanderers (1911/1912) and Representative football for the Aldershot F.A. in season 1911/12, Wellington Works in September 1922, and Aldershot Institute Albion in May 1924. During WW1 he served in the Royal Irish Guards, Hussars, and the Royal Warwickshire Regiment.

JOHNSON, B.

Birthplace: Swansea
Ht: 5ft-10ins, **Wt**: 11st-7lbs

Career:
Swansea Town (signed in season 1918/19)
Llanelly (signed in August 1920)

Local product who made his Southern League debut for the Swans in a 0-0 home draw with Portsmouth in November 1919, playing in the next three league matches as deputy for Jock Denoon. The previous season the goalkeeper had played with considerable success, earning himself a call up to the Swans' Southern League line-up. Making one further league appearance during the season, he also played in all three FA Cup ties against Gillingham. Released by the Swans at the end of the 1919/20 season, in August 1920 he signed for Llanelly.

JONES, EVAN

Birthplace: Trehafod, 20/10/1888. **Died**: Bedwellty, 20/10/1972
Ht: 5ft-8ins, **Wt**: 11st-10lbs

Career:
Trehafod
Treharris
Aberdare Athletic

Mardy
Chelsea (signed in May 1909) lge 21/4gls
Oldham Athletic (signed in February 1911) lge 50/25gls
Bolton Wanderers (£750 signed in May 1912) lge 90/24gls
Swansea Town (signed in July 1919)
Pontypridd (signed in July 1920)
Llanbradach (signed in close season 1921)
Porth (signed in August 1921)

Honours: Wales–7

An experienced forward by the time he signed for the Swans in July 1919, having made seven international appearances for Wales, scoring one goal. His first International appearance came at Kilmarnock against Scotland on the 5th March 1910 whilst with Chelsea, the last at Wrexham against Ireland on the 19th January 1914 where he scored a penalty in a 2-1 defeat. Appointed captain of the Swans in August 1919 after the trial matches, at the age of eighteen he had signed for Chelsea after playing in the Rhondda with Mardy, Aberdare Athletic, Treharris and Trehafod. During WW1 he made appearances for Cardiff City, Newport County and Pontypridd, and during his time with Bolton Wanderers was the club's top goalscorer. Making his Swans' debut in the opening game at Luton Town, he missed few league games, and at the end of the season was second top goalscorer with eight league goals, which included scoring in both opening matches of the season. He was released by the Swans at the end of the season, signed for Pontypridd, later made appearances for Llanbradach and Porth. In later years he was a cyclist of some note, and ended his working life with the Western Welsh Bus Company.

JONES, PERCY

Career:
Swansea Town (signed in season 1912/13)

Made only the one Southern League appearance for the Swans, replacing Sutherland at right full back in the last game of the 1912/13 season at the Vetch Field against Treharris.

KING

Career:
Swansea Town (signed in season 1919/20)

Right half back who made just the one Southern League appearance for the Swans at Queens Park Rangers on the 4th October 1919, replacing Clem Heath.

LLOYD, John AMOS

Birthplace: Pelsall, 1/5/1889. **Died**: 1943
Ht: 5ft-6½ins, **Wt**: 10st-10lbs

Career:
Nuneaton Town
Hednesford Town
West Bromwich Albion (signed in close season 1910) lge 45/8gls
Swansea Town (signed in 21/5/1914)

Outside left who joined the Swans prior to the start of the 1914/15 season, finishing the season as joint top goalscorer in the league with eight goals with Beynon and Ball. He struggled to make the same impact during his second season at the Vetch

Field, making just eleven league appearances. Prior to the Swans he had played non-league football in the Midlands with Nuneaton Town and Hednesford Town before signing for West Bromwich Albion where he went on to make his Football League debut. During the 1914/15 season he played in the FA Cup defeat of First Division side Blackburn Rovers, also playing in the Welsh Cup Final defeat by Wrexham in May 1915. Remaining in Swansea after leaving the Vetch Field playing staff, he continued to play in the local leagues and in May 1924 the *Daily Post* reported him as playing for Eastside against LM & SR in the Swansea Challenge Cup Final at the Vetch Field.

LOCK, CHARLES

Career:
Swansea Town (signed in close season 1914/15)

Centre half who deputised for the injured Buck shortly after the start of the season, making his debut against Ebbw Vale in October 1914 playing in the next seven league matches before Buck returned to fitness. His only other first team appearances came in a Welsh Cup tie against Newport County, and in three FA Cup ties against Port Vale, Leicester Fosse, and in the defeat of First Division side Blackburn Rovers.

MAYO, FRANK

Ht: 5ft-7ins, **Wt:** 11st-0lbs

Career:
Hartlepools United
Swansea Town (signed in close season 1913/14)
Newport County (signed in 21/5/1914)

Outside right who contested the right wing position with Messer during the 1913/14 season, and who made six consecutive appearances early in the season after making his debut for the Swans in mid-September 1913 against Barry. His only other appearances during the season came in the FA Cup defeat by Queens Park Rangers, and in Welsh Cup ties, including the semi-final defeat by Llanelly. In May 1914 he signed for Newport County.

MESSER, WILLIE

Birthplace: Swansea
Ht: 5ft-7ins, **Wt:** 11st-0lbs

Career:
Swansea United

Swansea Town (signed professional in 9/9/1912)
Newport County
Caerphilly (signed by 12/9/1921)
Bridgend Town (signed by October 1923)

Honours: Welsh Cup Winner–1913

Promising young amateur winger at the Vetch Field who was given a professional contract on the 9th September 1912 after playing in both of the club's opening Southern League matches. He was included in the first Southern League fixture undertaken by the Swans, at the Vetch Field against Cardiff City, missing few games during the club's first season in first class football. His progress since joining the Swans from local side Swansea United saw him attract interest from Liverpool later in the season. Selected to play for the Stripes team in the trial match for the Welsh International team at Taff Vale Park, Pontypridd on the 8th January 1914, he was later named as reserve for the International against Scotland on the 28th February 1914 at Glasgow. He was unable to make any league appearances after the Swans' had gained Football League status, managing only an appearance in a Welsh Cup tie at Mid-Rhondda in mid-January 1921. By October 1923 he was playing alongside his cousin Bryn for Bridgend Town in the Welsh League.

MITCHELL, Edward (TED)

Birthplace: South Bank. **Died:** Killed in action 15/1/1916
Ht: 5ft-5½ins, **Wt:** 11st-6lbs

Career:
Royal Field Artillery
Reading (signed in close season 1912)
Swansea Town (signed in 1/8/1913)

Inside forward made his Swans debut in the second game of the 1913/14 season at the Vetch Field against Barry. He struggled to make an impact through the season, making just eight more league appearances. He did play however in the FA Cup defeat by Queens Park Rangers, and also in the Welsh Cup semi-final defeat by Llanelly. Previously in the Royal Field Artillery, he was killed in action during WW1.

MORRIS, Llewellyn (LLEW)

Career:
Chester
Swansea Town (signed in late January 1914)

Honours: Wales Amateur

Llewellyn Morris signed for the Swans within a couple of weeks of playing for Chester in a Welsh Cup tie against the Swans. Capped previously for the Wales Amateur team, on the 7th February 1914 he was selected to play for the Wales Amateur side against England at Plymouth. He made his Swans debut as a replacement for Cleverley at left full back in a 6-0 defeat of Caerphilly, with his only other first team appearance being against Mid-Rhondda three games later.

MORTIMER, Frederick (FRED) Ernest

Career:
Grenadier Guards
Crystal Palace

Mansfield Town
Leicester Fosse (signed in May 1913) lge 22/8gls
Swansea Town (signed in 25/9/1914)
Rugby Town

Former Grenadier Guardsman who made Football League appearances for Leicester Fosse prior to joining the Swans in late September 1914 along with Hindmarsh, an inside forward from Wellington. He made his Swans debut at centre forward at the Vetch Field against Stalybridge Celtic, and in his third game a few weeks later scored a hat-trick in a 6-1 win over Abertillery. His only other first team appearance for the Swans came against Newport County in an FA Cup Qualifying match in late November 1914.

NICHOLAS, William Joseph (JACK)

Birthplace: Staines, JFM 1885
Ht: 5ft-10ins, **Wt**: 12st-7lbs

Career:
Staines
Derby County (signed in 1905-1910) lge 130
Swansea Town (signed in 5/9/1912)
Llanelly (signed in August 1920)

Honours: Southern League Representative XI, Welsh Cup Winner–1913

Included in the first competitive Swans' fixture when he lined up at the Vetch Field against Cardiff City in the club's opening Southern League fixture in September 1912. On the 18th September 1912 he played in a Southern League Welsh Clubs Representative side against a Southern League English Clubs Representative side at Ninian Park, Cardiff. A member of the Swans' team that beat Pontypridd to win the Welsh Cup in 1913, he made league appearances for the Swans in all four seasons prior to the club gaining elevation to the Football League. His only league goal for the Swans came in a Southern League defeat at Stoke City in November 1913, the previous month having opened his account in the 8-2 Welsh Cup defeat of Caerleon. He failed to make the starting line-up for the FA Cup tie against Blackburn Rovers, but after an injury to Lock, played in the next two FA Cup ties against Newcastle United. The first ever Swans captain, his son later skippered Derby County, and was a Wales schoolboy international. In late August 1920 he was named in the Llanelly side to play Bargoed on Saturday 28th August 1920. Later, when working as a supervisor in Baldwins his wish was that his son would play for the Swans, but he only played for the reserve team. The 1901 census gave him as a general labourer in a brewery.

PINCH, Charles (CHARLIE) Edwin

Birthplace: Cardiff, JFM 1890
Ht: 5ft-10ins, **Wt**: 11st-5lbs

Career:
Preston North End (signed in 1913) lge 3
Scunthorpe & Lindsey United
Swansea Town (signed in close season 1919)

Wing half who arrived at the Vetch Field shortly before the start of the 1919/20 season, making his debut at left half back against Southampton at the Vetch Field in the third match of the season as a replacement for Jimmy Collins. He failed to make an impression, making just two more appearances through the season.

PRIDEAUX

Career:
Swansea United
Swansea Town (signed in close season 1912)

Signed from local side Swansea United in the 1912 close season he made his Swans' debut at half back as a replacement for Hamilton in early November 1912, making a further five league appearances through the season. He was released at the end of the season.

READ, William Henry

Birthplace: Blackpool, 1885
Ht: 5ft-6ins, **Wt**: 11st-7lbs

Career:
Blackpool (signed in 8/5/1907) lge 32/3gls
Colne (signed in close season 1909)
Sunderland (signed in April 1910) lge 4/2gls
Chelsea (signed in May 1911) lge 3
Dundee (signed in March 1913)
Swansea Town (signed in close season 1914)

A right winger who played junior football prior to making his Football League debut with Blackpool, also making League appearances for Sunderland and Chelsea prior to joining the Swans in the 1915 close season. During his only season at the Vetch Field he was an ever present at outside right in Southern League games, and also played in all the FA Cup and Welsh Cup ties, including the win over Blackburn Rovers, and the Welsh Cup Final defeat by Wrexham.

SHELDON, Frederick (FRED)

Birthplace: West Bromwich, 10/12/1891.
Died: East Glamorgan, JFM 1973
Ht: 5ft-7ins, **Wt**: 10st-6lbs

Career:
Barry
Swansea Town (signed in September 1919)
Aberdare Athletic (signed in 28/5/1920) lge 178/11gls
Barry
Chester (trial in August 1927)

Inside forward who joined the Swans from Barry in September 1919, making his Southern League debut for the Swans' as a replacement for Evan Jones at inside right at the Vetch Field against Watford. He made a further eleven league matches through the season, and was released in May 1920 to join Aberdare Athletic. At Barry he played alongside his brother Frank in season 1913/14 in the Southern League. Earlier in his playing career he made appearances for Barry West End, Army Football, and was a guest player in a charity game for Tottenham Hotspur.

SOADY

Career:
Swansea Town (signed in season 1912/13)

Reserve team player at outside right who made his Southern League debut for the Swans as a replacement for Messer at Aberdare Athletic in late January 1913. He made just one more appearance towards the end of the season at the Vetch Field against Ton Pentre.

STOREY, Ernest (ERNIE)

Birthplace: Birtley, 1888

Career:
Hull City (signed in October 1908) lge 3
Spennymoor United (signed in July 1910)
Bradford City (signed in December 1911) lge 3
Blyth Spartans (signed in July 1912)
Swansea Town (£5 signed in 1/8/1913)
Belfast Distillery (signed in 13/5/1914)

Goalkeeper who played junior football in the North East prior to signing for Hull City in October 1908. The £5 the Swans paid for the goalkeeper for his signature was a standard fee paid in those days. After making his Football League debut with Hull City, he had also made league appearances for Bradford City prior to arriving at the Vetch Field from Blyth Spartans in August 1913. Replacing Fisher in the Swans' goal for his debut in late October 1913 at the Vetch Field against Newport County, he missed few league games in his only season with the Swans. He played in the FA Cup defeat by QPR, but failed to feature in the semi-final Welsh Cup defeat by Llanelly.

SUTHERLAND, ALBERT

Birthplace: Millwall, 24/8/1884. **Died:** Millwall, 30/6/1930
Ht: 5ft-8ins, **Wt:** 11st-8lbs

Career:
Millwall Athletic (signed in 24/11/1902)
Woolwich Arsenal (signed in May 1905)
Millwall Athletic (signed in May 1907)
New Brompton (signed in August 1909)
Swansea Town (signed in July 1912)
Croydon Common (signed in close season 1914)
Swansea Albion (signed in 8/10/1919)

Honours: Welsh Cup Winner–1913, London League XI, Western League Champions–1908, Southern Professional Charity Cup Winner–1904

Initially attended Glengall Road Board School, played for Millwall United, Millwall St. John's prior to signing for Millwall Athletic in November 1902, gained representative honours in 1905 playing for a London League XI against a Parisien League XI. At Millwall he won the Southern Professional Charity Cup in 1904, and in 1908 won the Western League Championship. Known as 'Sunny', he was a bit on the light side but kicked strongly. After arriving at the Vetch Field in October 1912, he made his Swans' debut in late December against Aberdare Athletic at right full back as a replacement for Cleverley, also making appearances at left full back during the season. In March 1913 he played at right full back in the Swans' Welsh Cup Final success over Pontypridd. His second season saw him make just two league appearances, failing to oust Allman, Nicholas or Bulcock from either full back positions, but he did make appearances in the FA Cup defeat by QPR, and in the Welsh Cup semi-final defeat by Llanelly. He joined Croydon Common for the 1914/15 season, later returned to the Swansea area to play for Swansea Albion.

SWARBRICK, James (JIMMY)

Birthplace: Lytham St. Annes 1881
Ht: 5ft-8ins, **Wt**: 11st-0lbs

Career:
Blackpool Red Star
Marton Combination
Blackpool Etrurians
Blackburn Rovers (signed in November 1901) lge 15
Accrington Stanley (loan in April 1903)
Brentford (signed in close season 1903)
Grimsby Town (signed in July 1905) lge 67/12gls
Oldham Athletic (signed in May 1907) lge 4/2gls
Southport Central (signed in November 1909)
Stoke (signed in May 1910)
Port Vale (signed in August 1911)
Swansea Town (signed in 5/9/1912)
Swansea Albion (signed by 8/10/1919)

Honours: Welsh Cup Winner–1913

A dextrous dribbler with plenty of speed, the left winger was included in the Swans' side that played it's first Southern League fixture against Cardiff City in September 1912. Missing just two league games during the club's first season in the Southern League, he played in the Welsh Cup Final win over Pontypridd in March 1913, but made few appearances during season 1913/14, including the Welsh Cup semi-final defeat by Llanelly, and just reserve team appearances during season 1914/15. Joining Blackburn Rovers in November 1901 the outside left made his Football League debut with the club, later made further league appearances for Grimsby Town and Oldham Athletic prior to joining the Swans. After his retirement from football with Swansea Albion he proved to be a good Bowls player, and in 7/9/1925 he won the Gibson-Watt Cup at the Llandrindod Wells Bowls Festival, and played for Morriston United Bowls Club.

THOMAS, Henry (HARRY)

Birthplace: Swansea, 28/2/1901
Ht: 5ft-6ins, **Wt**: 10st-7lbs

Career:
Swansea Town (signed by December 1919)
Porth (signed by 1920)
Manchester United (signed in April 1922) lge 128/12gls
Waterford (signed in 19/9/1930)
Merthyr Town (signed in October 1930 to March 1931)
Abercarn (signed in April 1932)
Aberavon Harlequins (March 1934)

Honours: Wales–1, Welsh League Champions–1922

A diminutive, clever, fleet footed left winger who earlier in his career struggled to hold down a regular place in the Swans' side, but in later years made over one hundred league appearances for Manchester United, and was capped by Wales in 1927 against England whilst at Old Trafford. With the Swans looking to experience in their first season in the Southern League, he had few opportunities, but after signing for Porth for the 1920/21 season, he became a prominent member of the side that won the Welsh League Championship in 1922, leading to a transfer to Manchester United who were on the verge of relegation to the Second Division. After a short period in Irish football with Waterford he returned to South Wales to sign for Merthyr Town, later making appearances for Abercarn and Aberavon Harlequins. His cousin Ronnie Thomas of Aberavon Quins signed for Charlton Athletic at the age of sixteen, and had played for the Welsh Schoolboys side.

WALTON, Joseph (JOE)

Birthplace: North Shields JFM 1884. **Died:** February 1922
Ht: 5ft-9ins, **Wt**: 12st-4lbs

Career:
Wallsend Park Villa (signed by 26/8/1902)
New Brompton (signed by 15/8/1904)
Chelsea (signed in August 1906 to May 1911) lge 53
Barry Town
Swansea Town (signed by November 1919)
Bridgend
Pembroke Dock

Honours: Northern Alliance Champions–1904

A full back who played for Barry prior to joining the Swans, and who earlier in his career had been a member of the Wallsend Park Villa side that won the Northern Alliance Championship Winner in 1904. A calm, reliable, unruffled defender, respected as a strong tackler, he was a Coppersmith by trade, and after joining Chelsea in August 1906, made over fifty Football League appearances for the club. He made his debut for the Swans' in mid-November 1919 as a replacement at left full back for Hewitt, making a further six league appearances during the season. His only other first team appearances were in the three FA Cup ties against Gillingham. He joined Bridgend after leaving the Vetch Field, later signing for Pembroke Dock,

and during a game against Pontypridd on the 25/2/1922 he sustained an injury during the game, later died from the injury.

WEIR, John (JOCK)

Birthplace: Glasgow, 1881
Ht: 5ft-8ins, **Wt**: 11st-7lbs

Career:
Bellshill Athletic
Fulham (signed in close season 1912) lge 1
Swansea Town (signed by March 1913)
Reading (signed in season 1919/20)
Pembroke Dock (signed in 5/3/1921)
Clydebank
Cowdenbeath (signed in close season 1925)

Honours: Southern League Representative XI, Welsh Cup Winner–1913

A centre forward who joined Fulham from Glasgow junior club Bellshill Athletic in the summer of 1912 at the age of 21, and made only one appearance for the club in a home match with Grimsby Town on the 4th January 1913. He did not impress in this game and was released by Fulham, joining the Swans in March 1913, making his Swans' debut on the 22nd March 1913 against Treharris. Two days later he was included in the Swans' side that beat Pontypridd in the Welsh Cup Final. His first two full seasons at the Vetch Field would see him make regular appearances for the Swans, scoring eleven league goals in the 1913/14 season, including a hat-trick against Aberdare Athletic in April 1914, also playing in the Swans side that lost in the Welsh Cup Final to Wrexham in 1915. He scored six goals when the Swans beat Leyton in September 1914, but when Leyton withdrew from the league, his goalscoring feat was removed from the record books. On the 31st October 1914 he was selected to represent a Southern League XI against the Irish League at the Vetch Field, scoring in a 1-1 draw. Returning to the Vetch Field joining the Swans after WW1, Jock made six appearances for the Swans during the early part of the 1919/20 season before joining Reading. The *Daily Post*, dated 15/9/1919, said that Weir had been loaned to the Swans. Reading had thought they had signed him, but when the split happened between the Football League and the Southern League both teams kept him on their retained lists, despite Weir initially signing for Reading. Before a League investigation could be conducted, he changed his mind and signed for the Swans. Joining Reading later in the season he scored two goals in 14 games, and although not making the Reading team for the Good Friday fixture against the Swans, played in the return match at the Vetch Field. After signing for Pembroke Dock in March 1921, he later played for Scottish sides Clydebank and Cowdenbeath. After returning to Swansea, he became trainer of the Swans' Junior side, and in season 1937/38 they won the Gwalia and Bryn Trophies, also finishing runners up in the Gwalia Senior League.

WHITTAKER, WALTER

Birthplace: Manchester, 20/9/1878. **Died:** Swansea, 2/6/1917
Ht: 6ft-2ins, **Wt**: 14st-7lbs

Career:
Molyneaux
Buxton
Newton Heath (signed in February 1895) lge 3

Fairfield (signed in June 1896)
Grimsby Town (£60 signed in May 1897) lge 28
Reading (signed in May 1898)
Blackburn Rovers (signed in February 1900) lge 52
Grimsby Town (£150 signed in December 1901) lge 47
Derby County (signed in April 1903) lge 12
Brentford (signed in May 1904)
Reading (signed in May 1906)
Clapton Orient (signed in May 1907) lge 90
Exeter City (signed in 1910)
Swansea Town (player manager signed in 5/9/1912)

An experienced goalkeeper prior to arriving at the Vetch Field from Exeter City, having previously made League appearances for Newton Heath, Grimsby Town, Blackburn Rovers, Derby County and Clapton Orient. Known in the dressing room as 'Big Walt', he lost his place at Exeter City to a young Ernie Pym prior to arriving at the Vetch Field as player manager of the Swans for the 1912/13 season. Not the most consistent of goalkeepers but did show touches of brilliance at times, and included himself in the Swans' opening first class fixture in the Southern League against Cardiff City in September 1912 playing a further six Southern League matches before relinquishing his place to Ernie Fisher. On the 29/4/1913, the *Daily Post* said that he was to be Manager of the Swans for the new season, but on the 20/4/1914 an announcement from the Swans Directors stated that they have decided not to retain the services of Whittaker as manager, causing much discussion in the Town. Whittaker felt at the time that he had been made the scapegoat for the club's failure to obtain promotion, but the official reason for not offering Whittaker a contract was that they intended to adopt a new method of management. In the 1914 close season he was appointed manager of Llanelly, remaining at Halfway Park until November 1914.